# WHAT'S MICHAEL?

## FATCAT COLLECTION VOLUME 1

PUBLISHER **MIKE RICHARDSON**
FATCAT COLLECTION EDITOR **PHILIP R. SIMON**
FATCAT COLLECTION ASSISTANT EDITOR **JOSHUA ENGLEDOW**
DESIGNER **SARAH TERRY**   DIGITAL ART TECHNICIAN **ANN GRAY**

DEDICATED TO TOREN SMITH.

This omnibus collects *What's Michael?* Volumes 1 to 6 (*Michael's Album*, *Living Together*, *Off the Deep End*, *Michael's Mambo*, *Michael's Favorite Spot*, and *A Hard Day's Life*) previously published by Dark Horse Comics in 1997, 1998, and 2002, and edited by David Land, Mike Hansen, and Toren Smith.

## WHAT'S MICHAEL? FATCAT COLLECTION VOLUME 1

Dark Horse Manga, a division of Dark Horse Comics LLC.
10956 SE Main Street | Milwaukie, OR 97222 | DarkHorse.com
First edition: February 2020 | ISBN 978-1-50671-414-1

1 3 5 7 9 10 8 6 4 2
Printed in China
To find a comics shop in your area, visit comicshoplocator.com

Library of Congress Cataloging-in-Publication Data

Names: Kobayashi, Makoto, 1958- artist, author. | Davisson, Zack, writer of
    introduction. | Gleason, Alan, translator. | Kotobuki, Hisashi,
    translator. | Buhalis, Lois, letterer. | Cisneros, Amador, letterer.
Title: What's Michael? : Fatcat collection / art and story, Makoto
    Kobayashi ; translation and adaptation, Alan Gleason, Hisashi Kotobuki
    [and others] ; lettering and retouch, L. Lois Buhalis, Amador Cisneros
    [and others].
Description: First edition. | Milwaukie, OR : Dark Horse Manga, 2020- | v.
    1: "This omnibus collects What's Michael? Volumes 1 to 6 (Michael's
    Album, Living Together, Off the Deep End, Michael's Mambo, Michael's
    Favorite Spot, and A Hard Day's Life) previously published by Dark Horse
    Comics in 1997, 1998, and 2002, and edited by David Land, Mike Hansen,
    and Toren Smith." | Summary: "True-to-life daily cat scenarios and
    off-the-walls-outlandish feline fantasies combine in this epic manga
    collection! Makoto Kobayashi's hilarious series returns in a set of
    oversized volumes, starting with our first Fatcat Collection.
    Introduction by award winning translator and scholar Zack Davisson.
    Feline fun and turmoil, as Michael wreaks havoc on his humans' lives!"--
    Provided by publisher.
Identifiers: LCCN 2019043944 | ISBN 9781506714141 (v. 1 ; trade paperback)
Subjects: LCSH: Comic books, strips, etc.
Classification: LCC PN6790.J33 K63813 2020 | DDC 741.5/952--dc23
LC record available at https://lccn.loc.gov/2019043944

# WHAT'S MICHAEL?

## FATCAT COLLECTION VOLUME 1

ART AND STORY
### MAKOTO KOBAYASHI

TRANSLATION AND ADAPTATION
**ALAN GLEASON**
**HISASHI KOTOBUKI**
**DANA LEWIS**
**JEANNE SATHER**
**LEA SEIDMAN**
**TOREN SMITH**
**ELIN WINKLER**

LETTERING AND RETOUCH
**L. LOIS BUHALIS**
**AMADOR CISNEROS**
**PAT DUKE & RADIO COMIX**
**TOM ORZECHOWSKI**
**AMY STELLA**

**DARK HORSE MANGA**

# INTRODUCTION

**C**ATS. SERIOUSLY, CATS. CATS RULE. And *What's Michael?* is all about cats. It's the agony and ecstasy of sharing your life with these hand-fed tigers, as they were known during Heian period Japan. The comic spins a reality/fantasy of what we know cats get up to when they are around the house—and what we suspect they are up to when they are not.

*What's Michael?* had an odd beginning. He first appeared not as a character, but as a cat illustration in artist Makoto Kobayashi's 1982 series *How to Draw Manga.* Kobayashi had recently finished *The Old One-Two Sanshiro* and had not yet started his follow-up series *Judo Club Monogatari.* As an artist, Kobayashi was best known for these kinds of martial arts-based sports series that appealed to young boys. He filled his comics with rugby, judo, and pro wrestling stunts. The *How to Draw Manga* series was essentially a side project between gigs. But then he drew that cat.

Japan, as you may have noticed, has a particular love affair with cats. Over the centuries they have played roles as varied from pampered palace pets to working mousers to folklore monsters to urban street rovers to train station masters to

enshrined deities. Although the details are hazy, it is thought the first ones appeared in Japan around 880 CE, a gift from the Emperor of Korea to the Emperor of Japan. In 889 CE, seventeen-year-old Emperor Uda inherited this cat when the old emperor died. He wrote in his diary:

When it lies down, it curls in a circle like a coin. You cannot see its feet, as if it were circular bi disk. When it stands, its cry expresses profound loneliness, like a black dragon floating above the clouds. Its color allows it to disappear at night. I am convinced it is superior to all other cats.

Over the years, cats moved from the palace to peasant homes, until by the 1600s they were everywhere. Along the way they had acquired a reputation for supernatural powers. Myths of transformed cats called bakeneko said they stood on their hind legs and performed strange dances in the night. (Hint: Keep this in mind when reading What's Michael? His dancing pose is something seen throughout centuries of Japanese art, the dance of the bakeneko.)

In 1842, Japanese cats got their biggest upgrade. The shogun's councilor Mizuno Tadakuni decided the country was being too naughty and issued the Tenpō Reforms, banning artists from producing works featuring geisha and kabuki actors. These were, of course, artists' bestselling works. Staring down ruin, they hit upon a world-changing idea—if they made the same pictures they did before, but replaced all the human heads with cat faces, well, then they were obeying the law. Thus, was born an entire secret world of cats. Artists drew cats having wild parties, dressing in elegant fashions while having illicit affairs, and generally being up to no good. When the Tenpō Reforms were repealed in 1845, artists found that their customers preferred the cat artwork to the human ones they had made prior. So, they kept drawing cats.

Kobayashi's editor knew a good thing when he saw it. When he saw that cat, he knew it was something special. There was magic there he needed to capture. He told Kobayashi to take that cat and create an entire series about it. And thus, What's Michael? was born.

**—Zack Davisson, September 2019**

*[Continues in our next volume:* What's Michael? Fatcat Collection *Volume 2.]*

*Zack Davisson is a writer and translator. He wrote* Kaibyo: The Supernatural Cats of Japan, *and he is currently translating* H. P. Lovecraft's At the Mountains of Madness *and* Star Blazers 2199 *for* Dark Horse Manga.

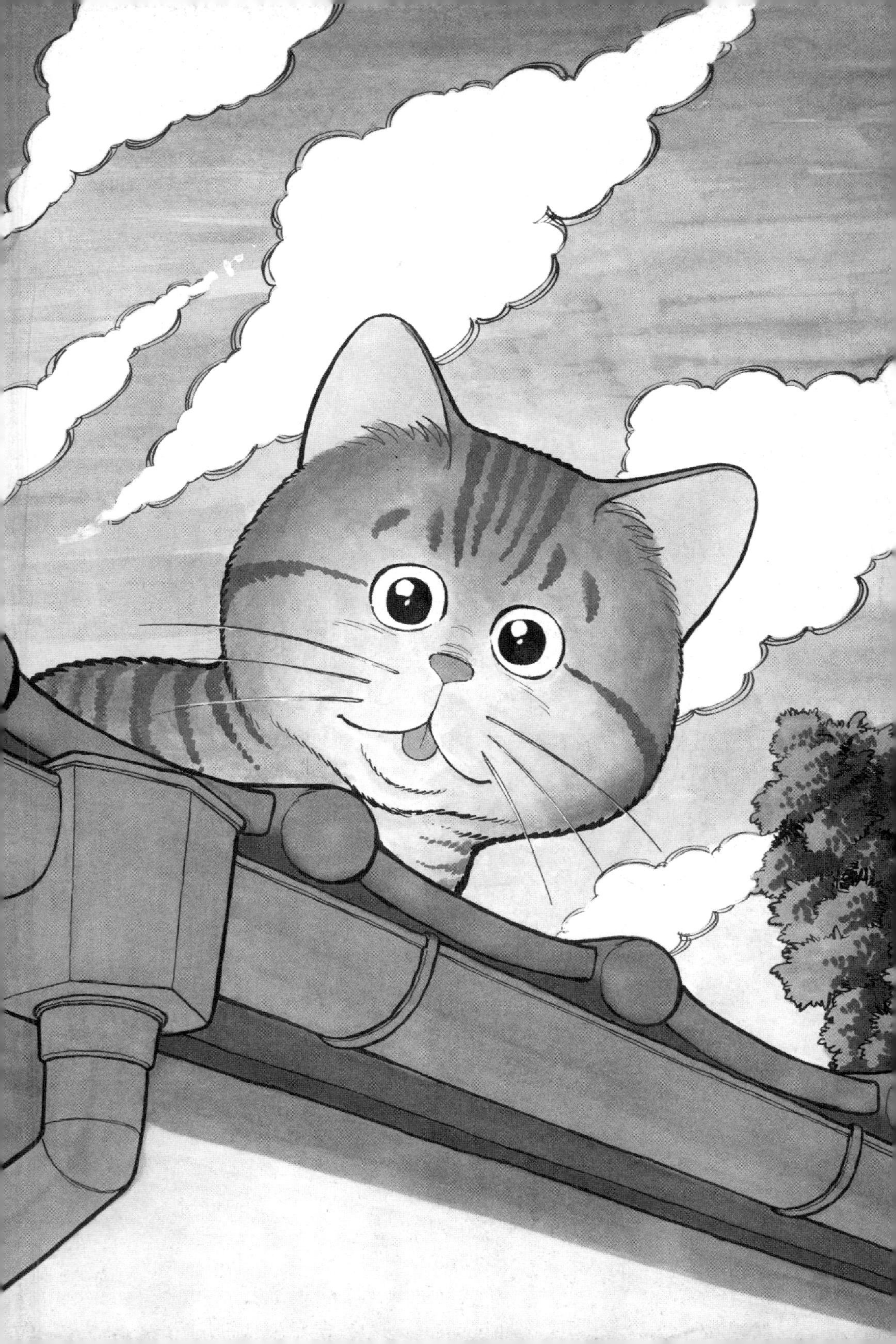

# WHAT'S MICHAEL?

## VOLUME 1: MICHAEL'S ALBUM

*This section was translated by Dana Lewis and Toren Smith and lettered by L. Lois Buhalis.*

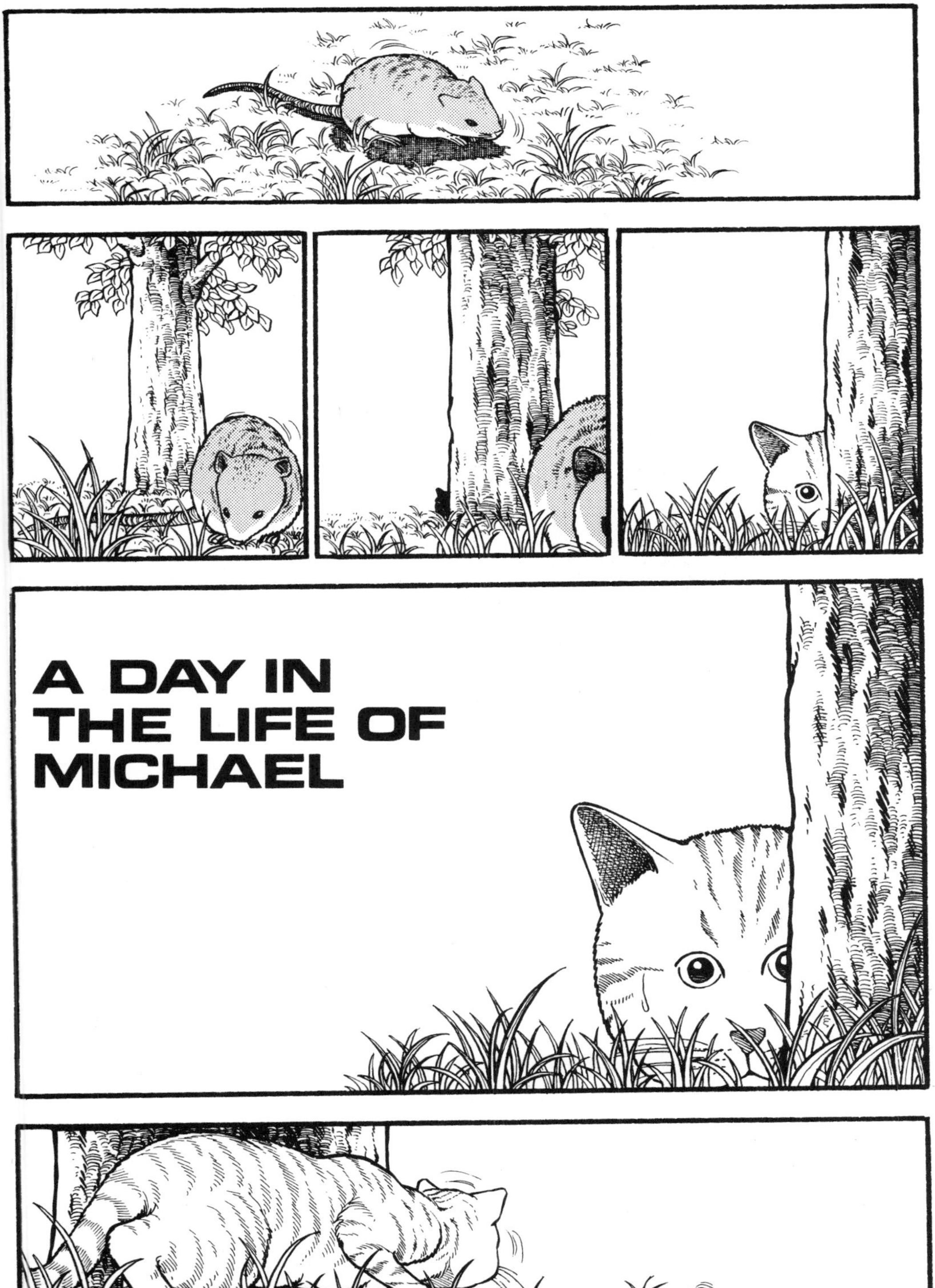
A DAY IN THE LIFE OF MICHAEL

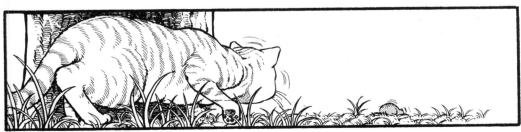

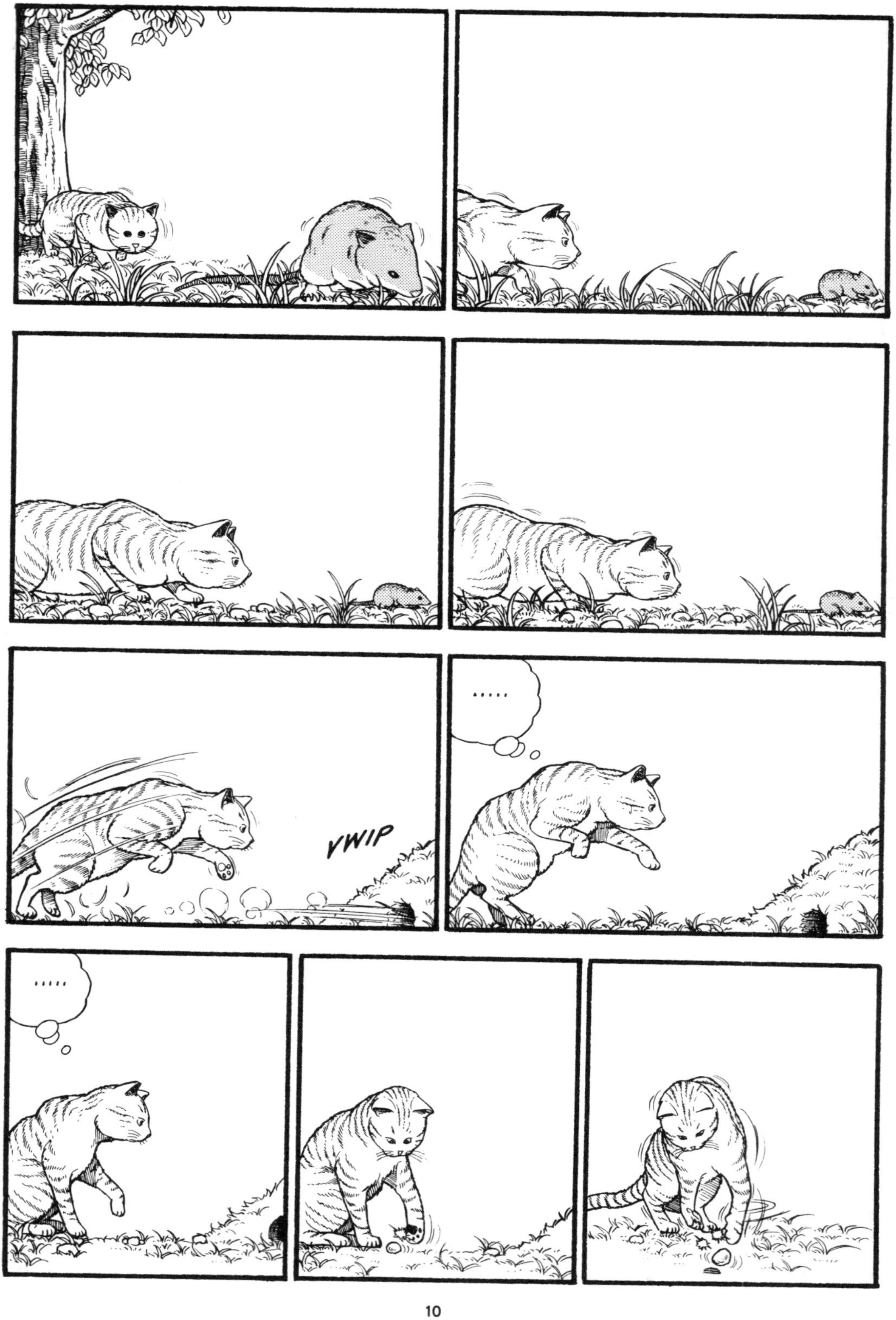
VWIP
.....
.....

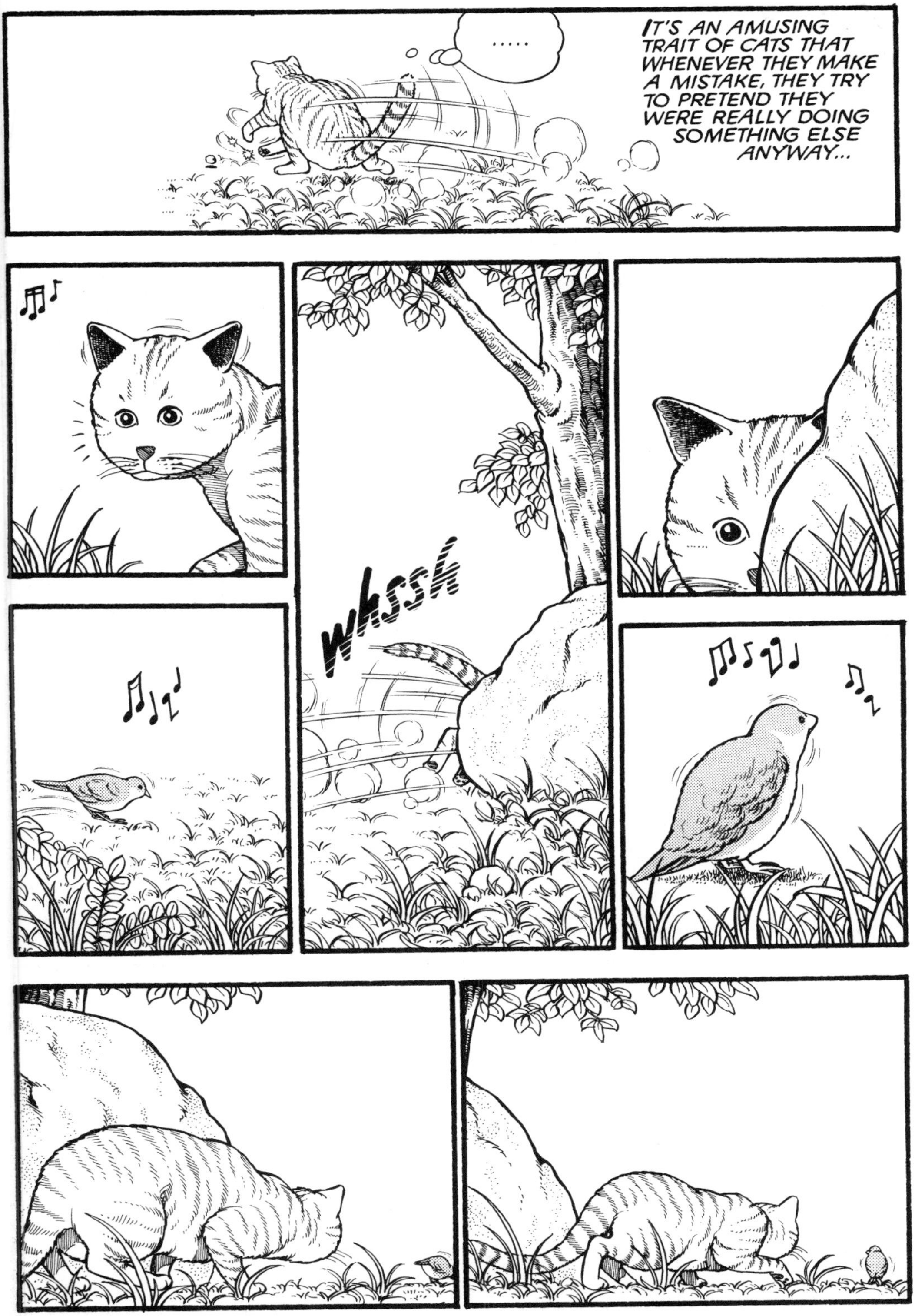
.....
IT'S AN AMUSING TRAIT OF CATS THAT WHENEVER THEY MAKE A MISTAKE, THEY TRY TO PRETEND THEY WERE REALLY DOING SOMETHING ELSE ANYWAY...
whssh

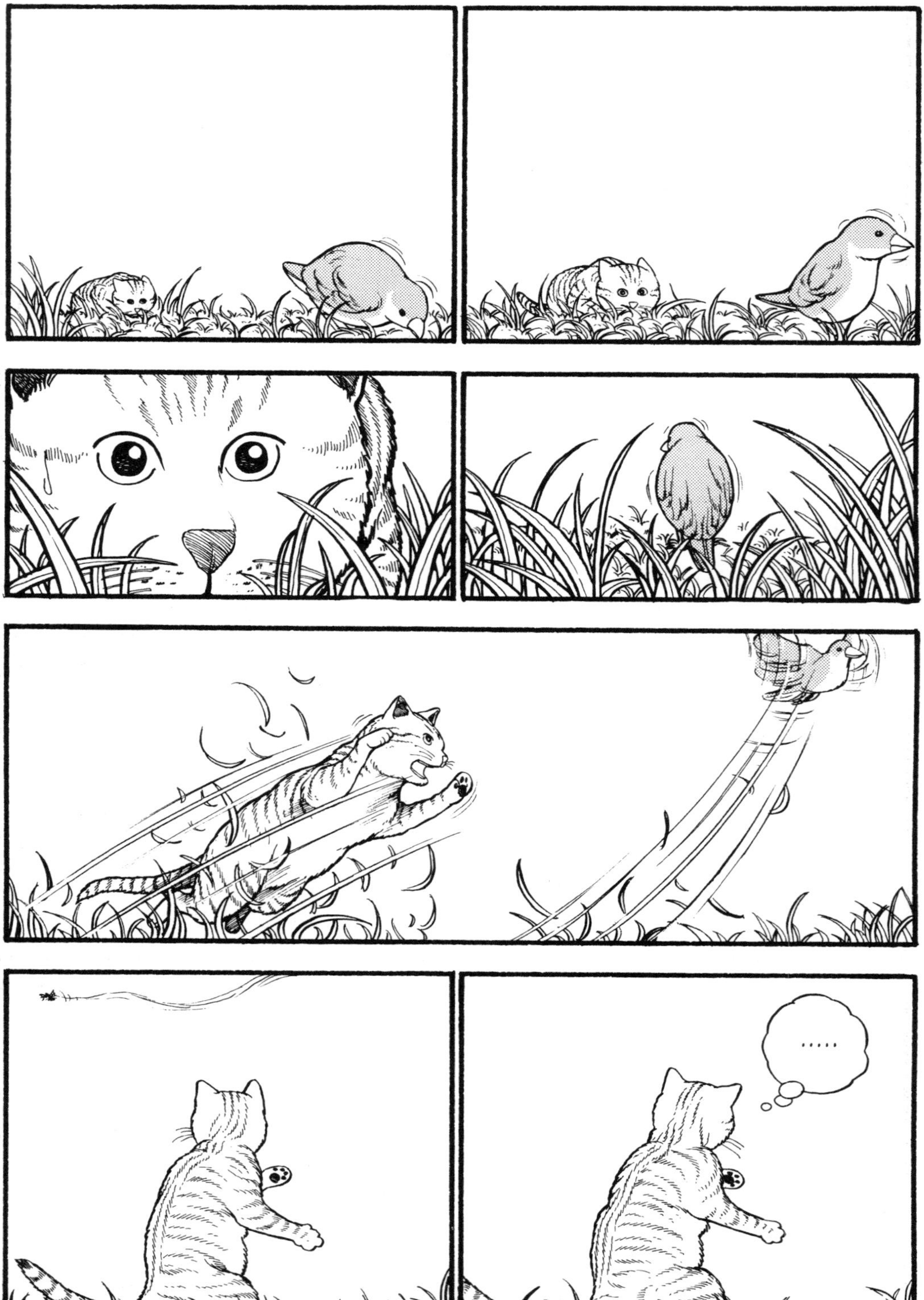
.....

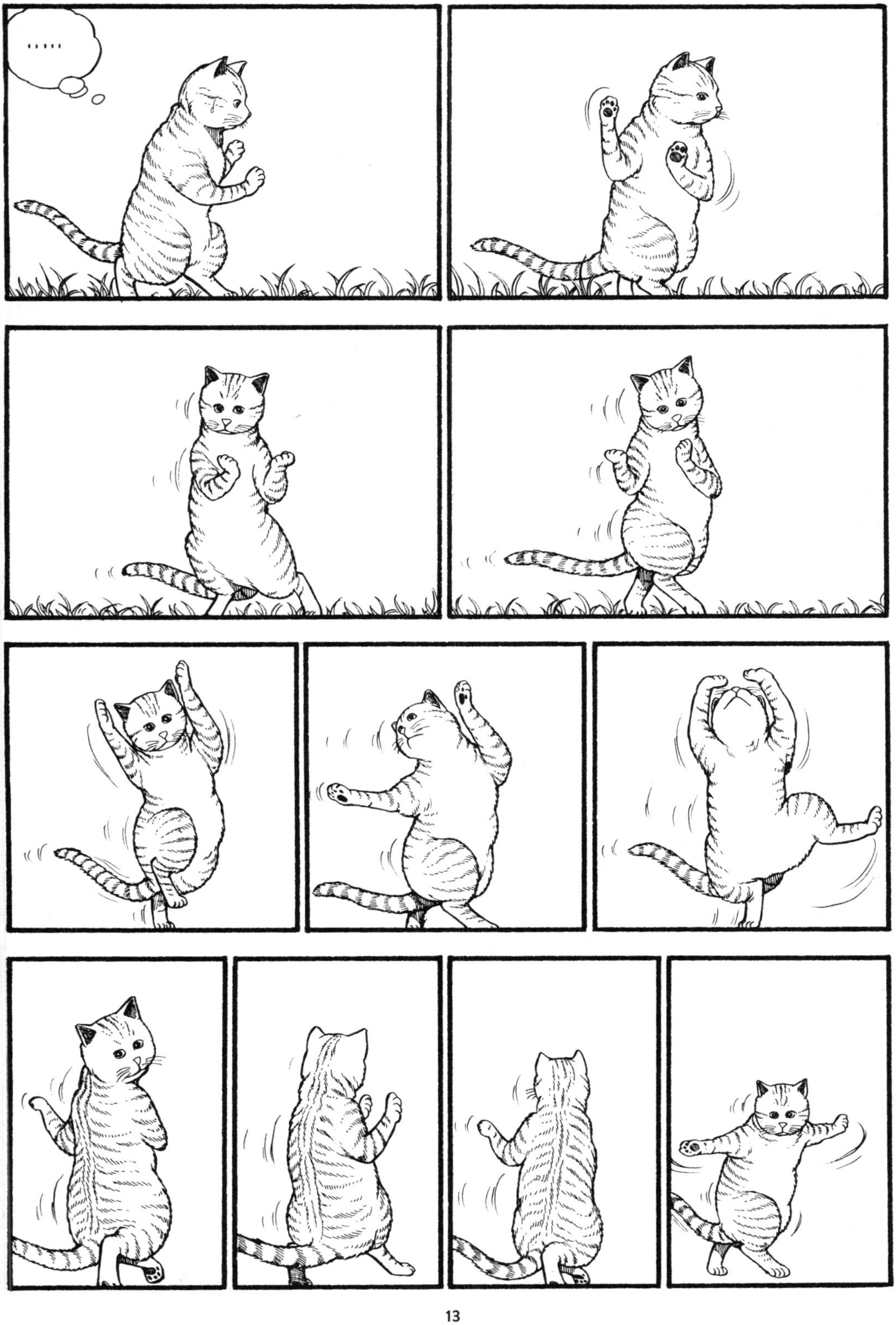
......

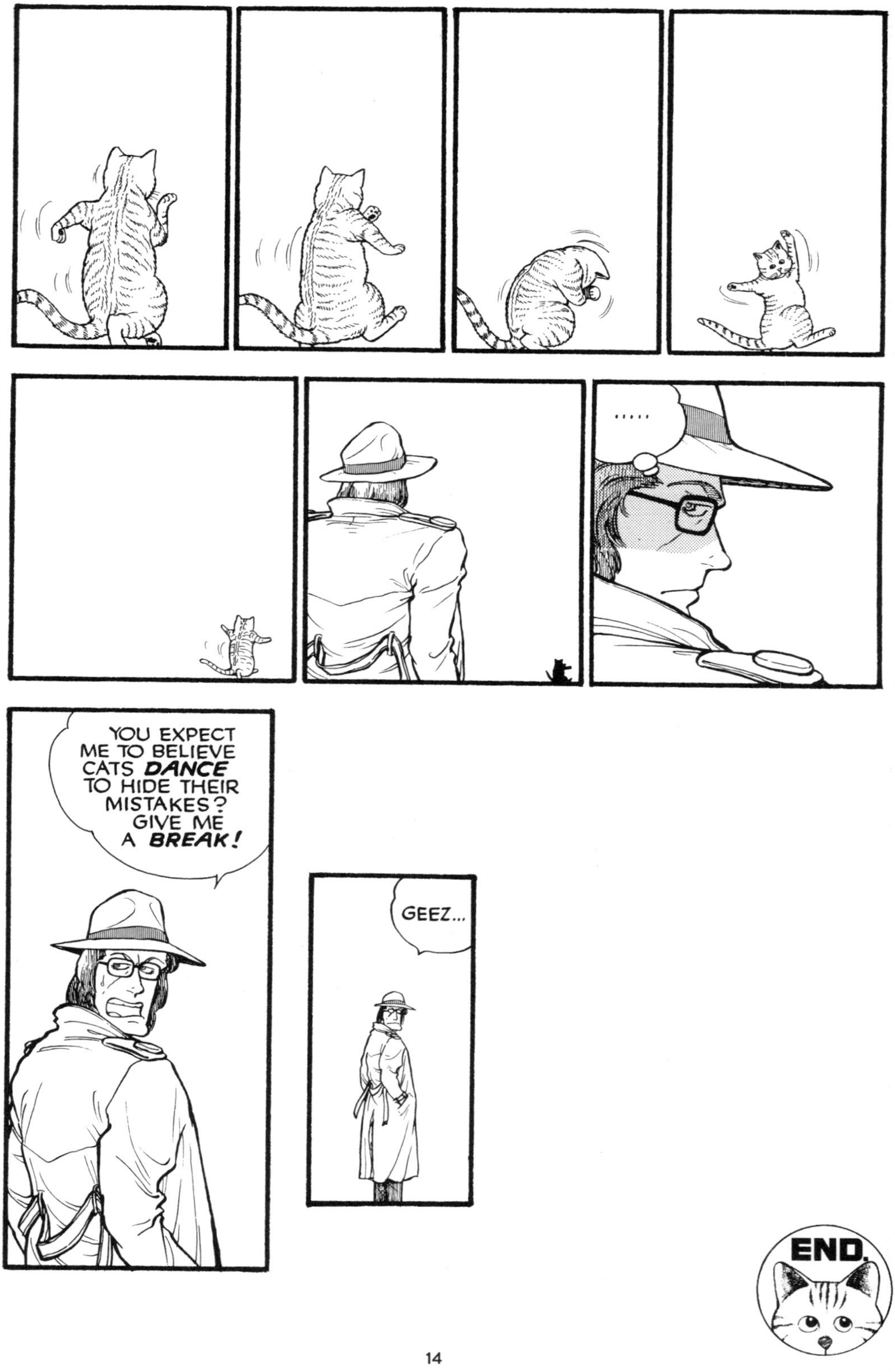
.....
YOU EXPECT ME TO BELIEVE CATS DANCE TO HIDE THEIR MISTAKES? GIVE ME A BREAK!
GEEZ...
END.

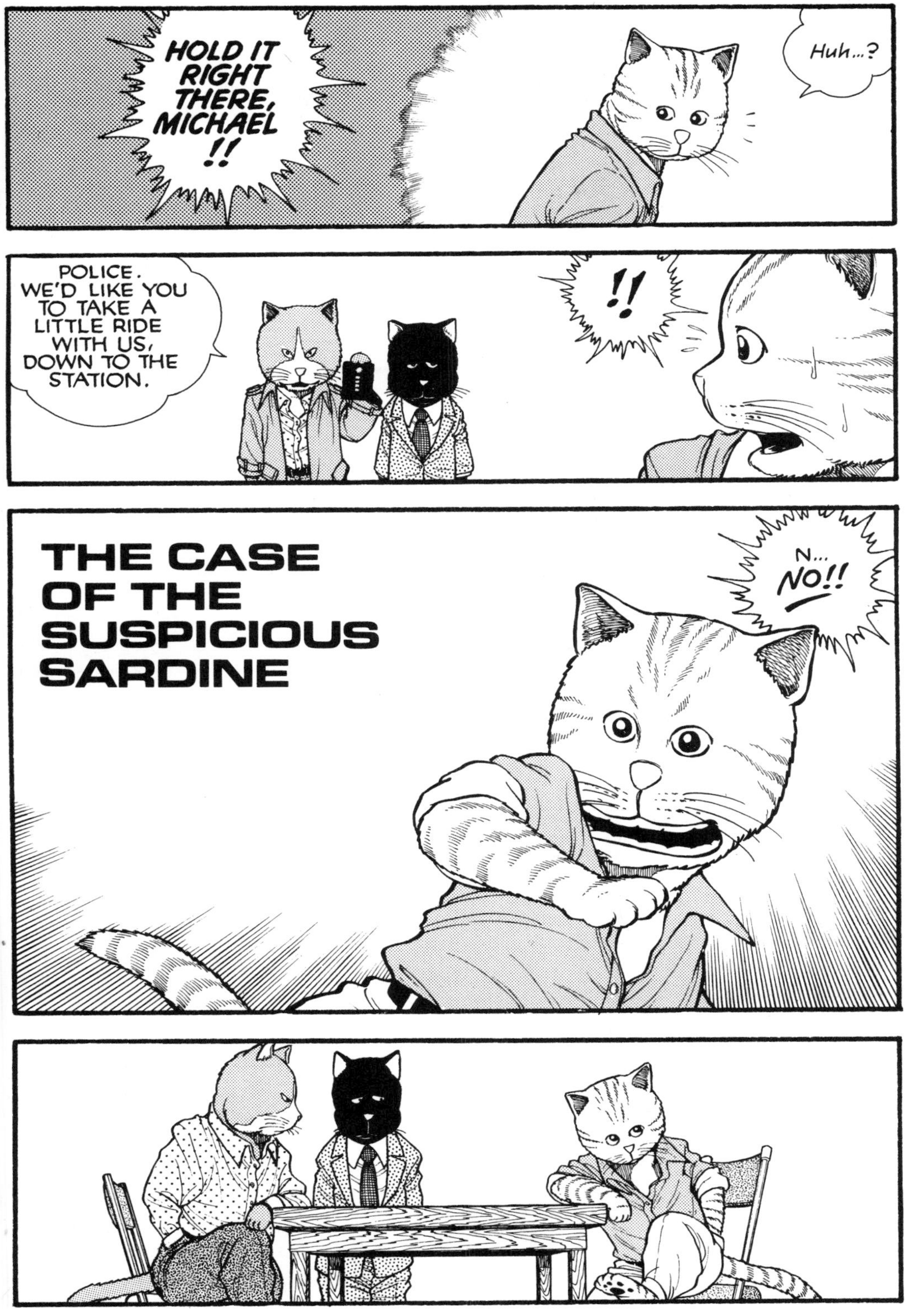
HOLD IT RIGHT THERE, MICHAEL !!
Huh...?
POLICE. WE'D LIKE YOU TO TAKE A LITTLE RIDE WITH US, DOWN TO THE STATION.
!!
THE CASE OF THE SUSPICIOUS SARDINE
N... NO!!

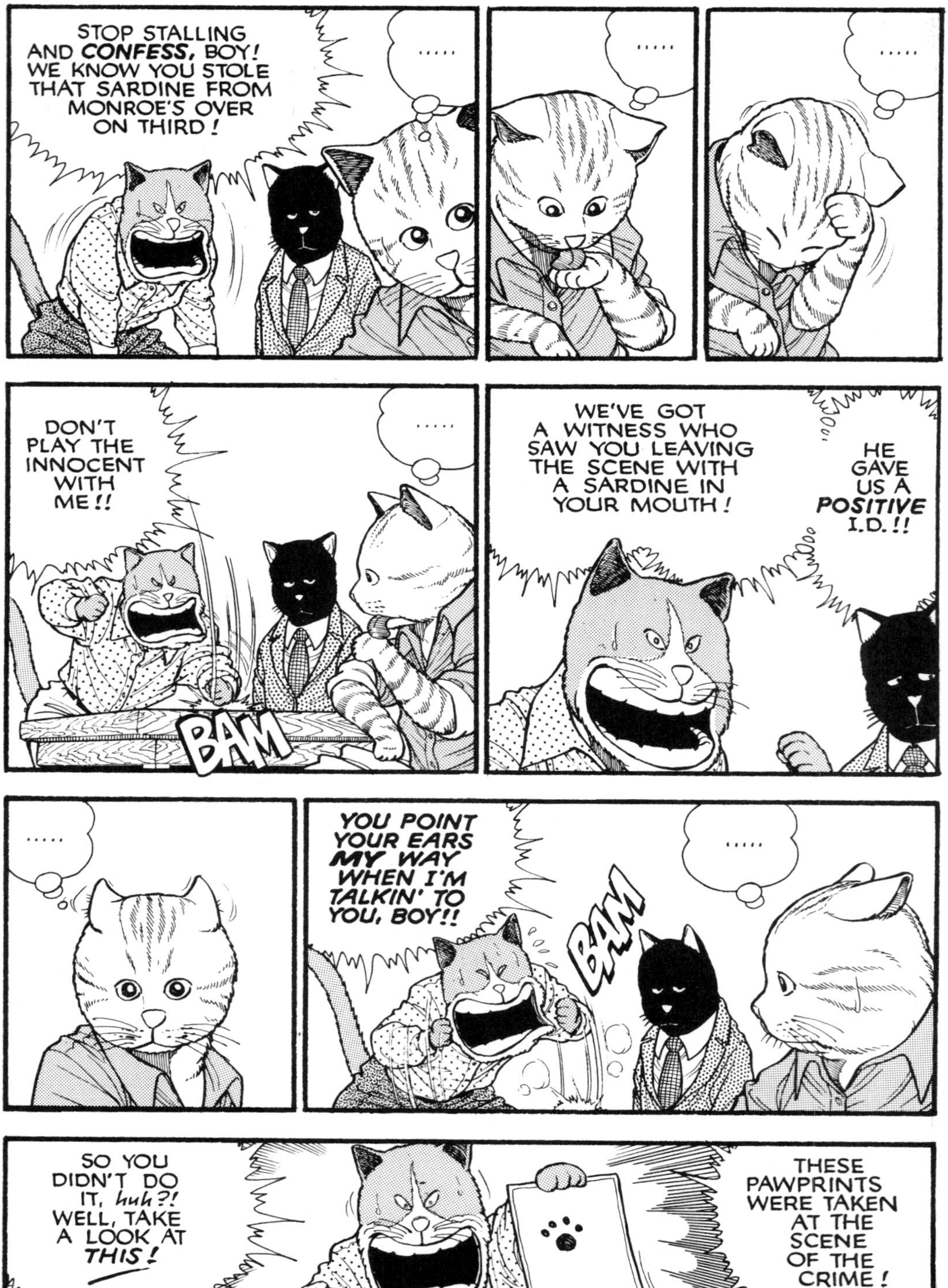
STOP STALLING AND CONFESS, BOY! WE KNOW YOU STOLE THAT SARDINE FROM MONROE'S OVER ON THIRD!
.....
.....
.....
DON'T PLAY THE INNOCENT WITH ME!!
.....
BAM
WE'VE GOT A WITNESS WHO SAW YOU LEAVING THE SCENE WITH A SARDINE IN YOUR MOUTH!
HE GAVE US A POSITIVE I.D.!!
.....
YOU POINT YOUR EARS MY WAY WHEN I'M TALKIN' TO YOU, BOY!!
BAM
.....
SO YOU DIDN'T DO IT, huh?! WELL, TAKE A LOOK AT THIS!
THESE PAWPRINTS WERE TAKEN AT THE SCENE OF THE CRIME!

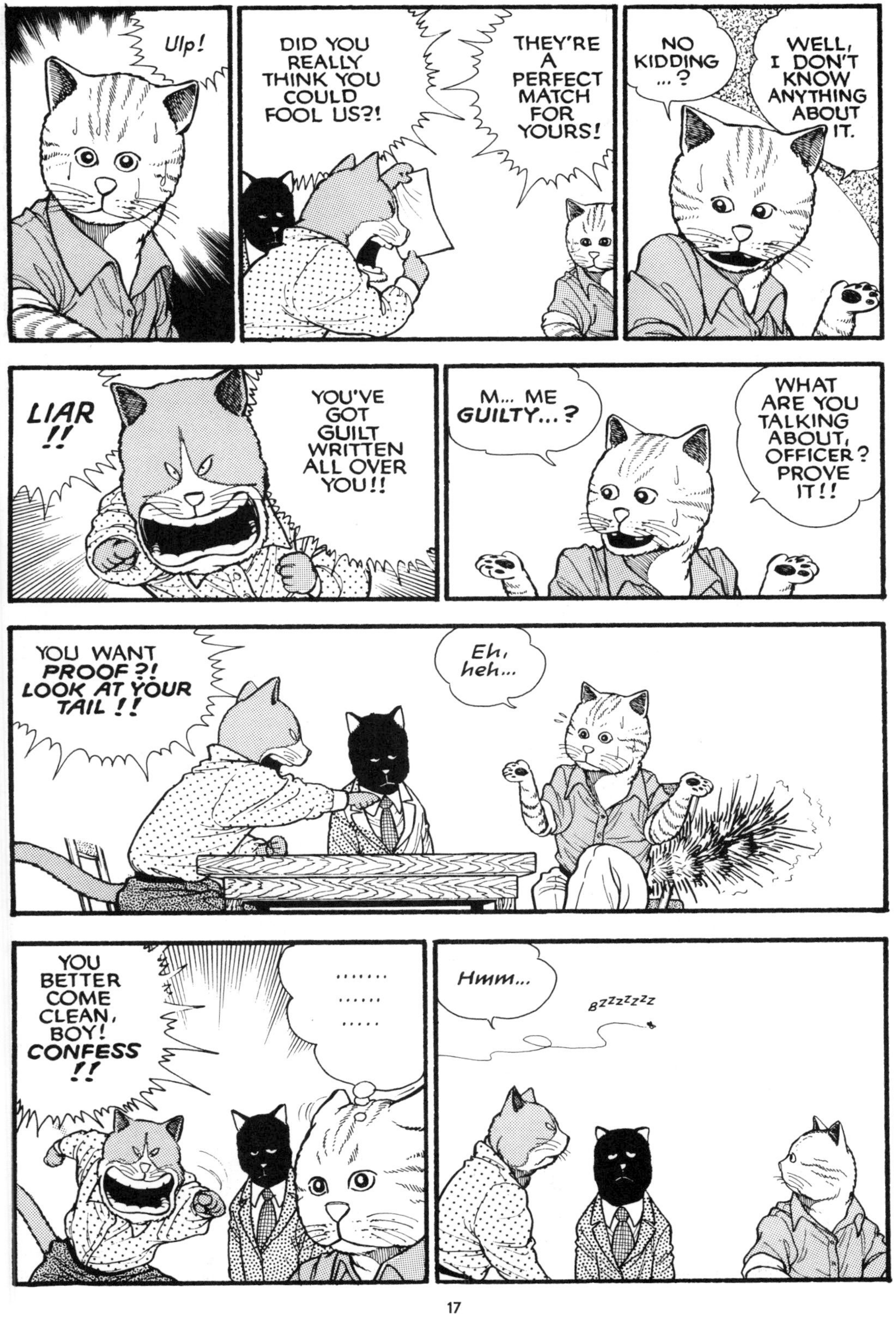

Ulp!
DID YOU REALLY THINK YOU COULD FOOL US?!
THEY'RE A PERFECT MATCH FOR YOURS!
NO KIDDING ...?
WELL, I DON'T KNOW ANYTHING ABOUT IT.
LIAR!!
YOU'VE GOT GUILT WRITTEN ALL OVER YOU!!
M... ME GUILTY...?
WHAT ARE YOU TALKING ABOUT, OFFICER? PROVE IT!!
YOU WANT PROOF?! LOOK AT YOUR TAIL!!
Eh, heh...
YOU BETTER COME CLEAN, BOY! CONFESS!!
.......
......
.....
Hmm...
BZZZZZZZ

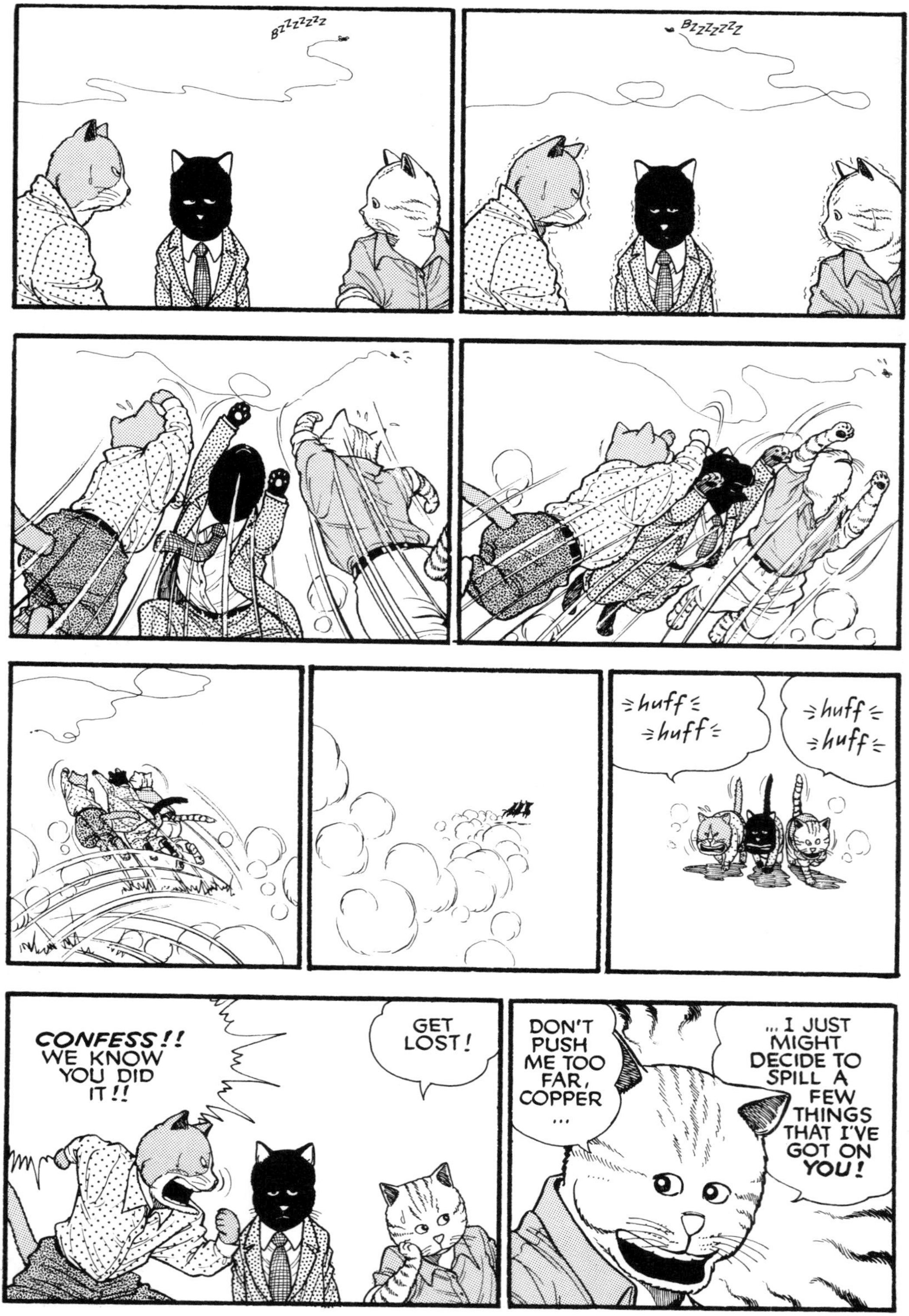
BZZZZZZZ
BZZZZZZZ
huff huff
huff huff
CONFESS!! WE KNOW YOU DID IT!!
GET LOST!
DON'T PUSH ME TOO FAR, COPPER ...
... I JUST MIGHT DECIDE TO SPILL A FEW THINGS THAT I'VE GOT ON YOU!

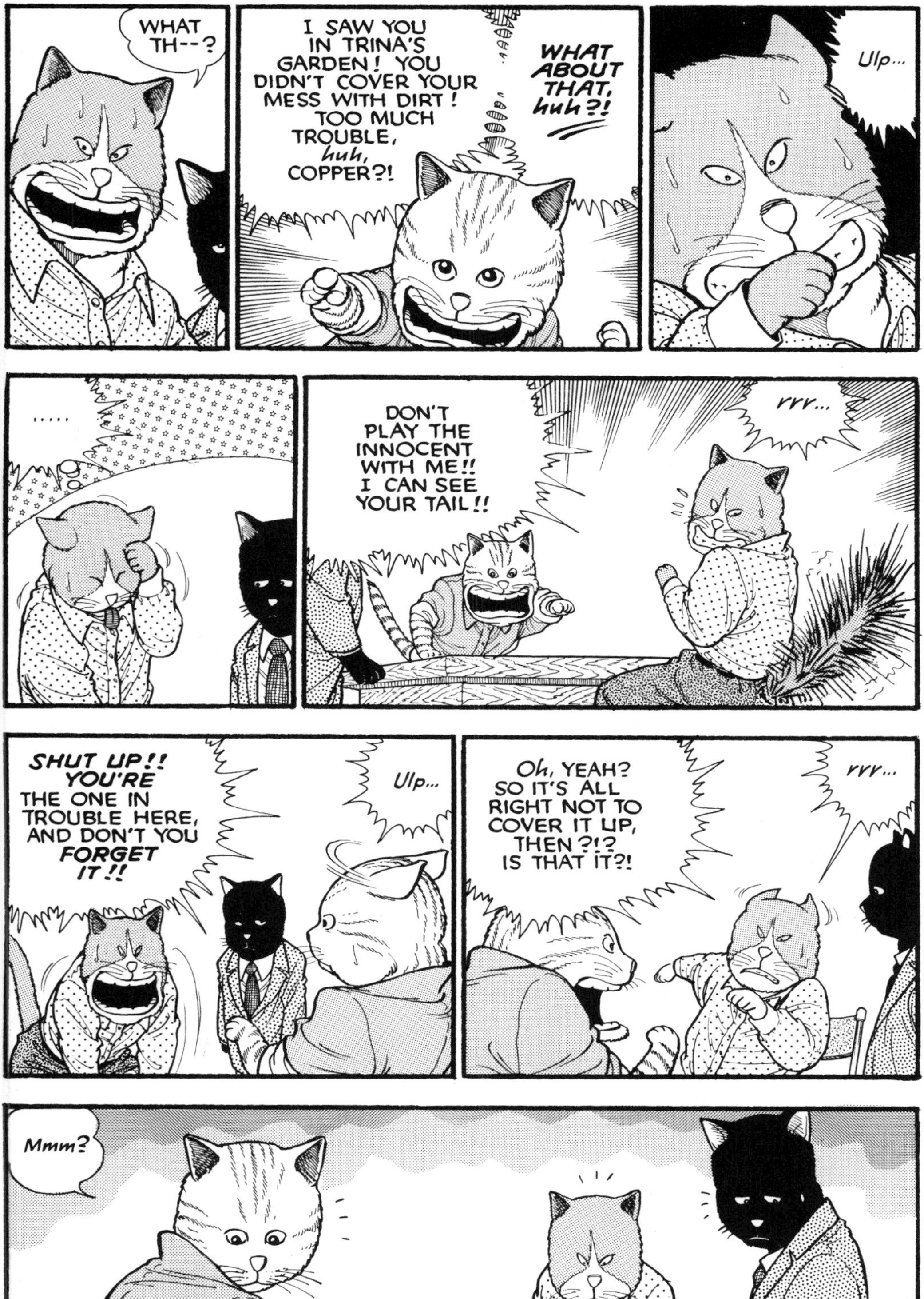
WHAT TH--?
I SAW YOU IN TRINA'S GARDEN! YOU DIDN'T COVER YOUR MESS WITH DIRT! TOO MUCH TROUBLE, huh, COPPER?!
WHAT ABOUT THAT, huh?!
Ulp...
.....
DON'T PLAY THE INNOCENT WITH ME!! I CAN SEE YOUR TAIL!!
rrr...
SHUT UP!! YOU'RE THE ONE IN TROUBLE HERE, AND DON'T YOU FORGET IT!!
Ulp...
Oh, YEAH? SO IT'S ALL RIGHT NOT TO COVER IT UP, THEN?!? IS THAT IT?!
rrr...
Mmm?

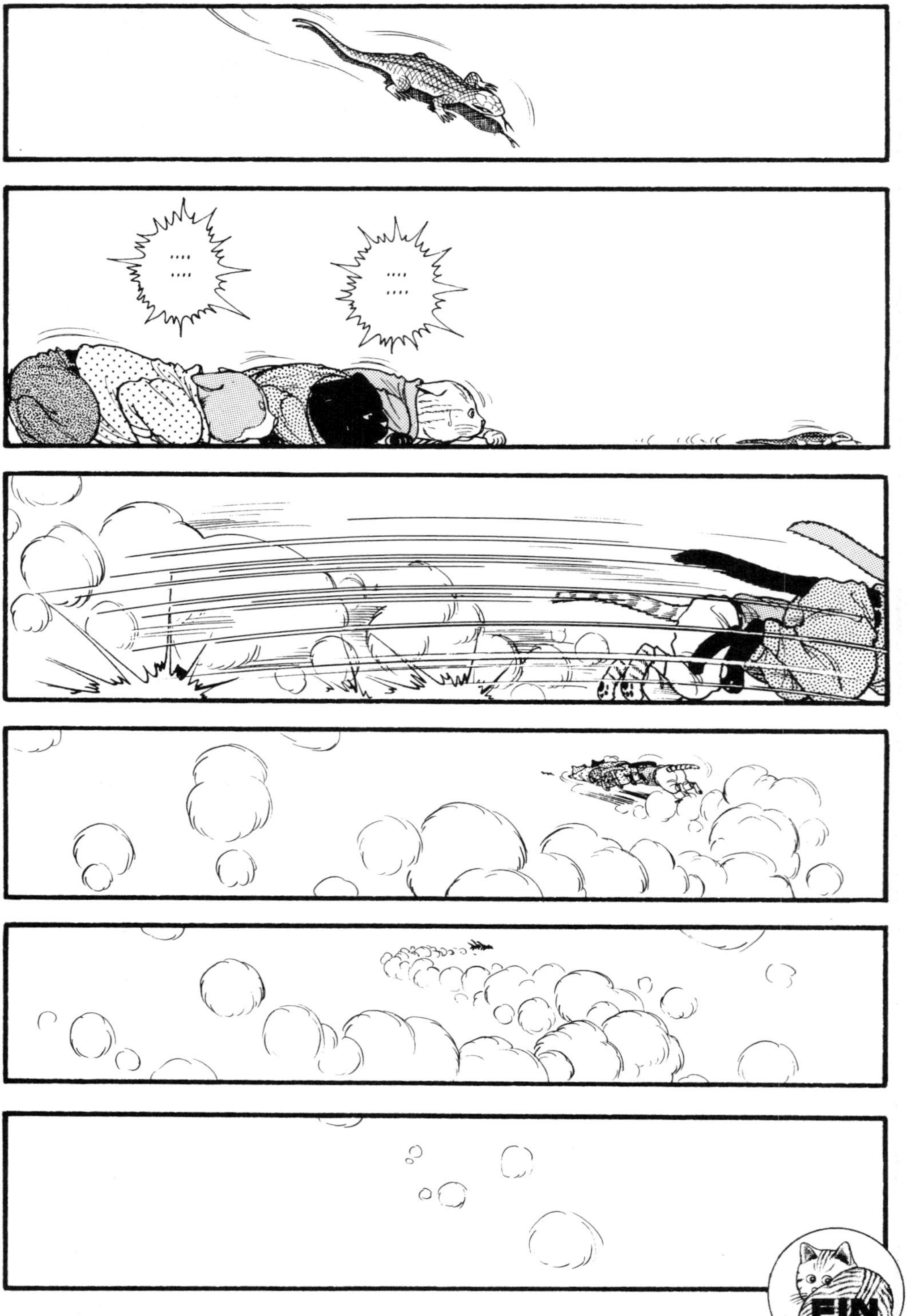
....
....
....
....
FIN.

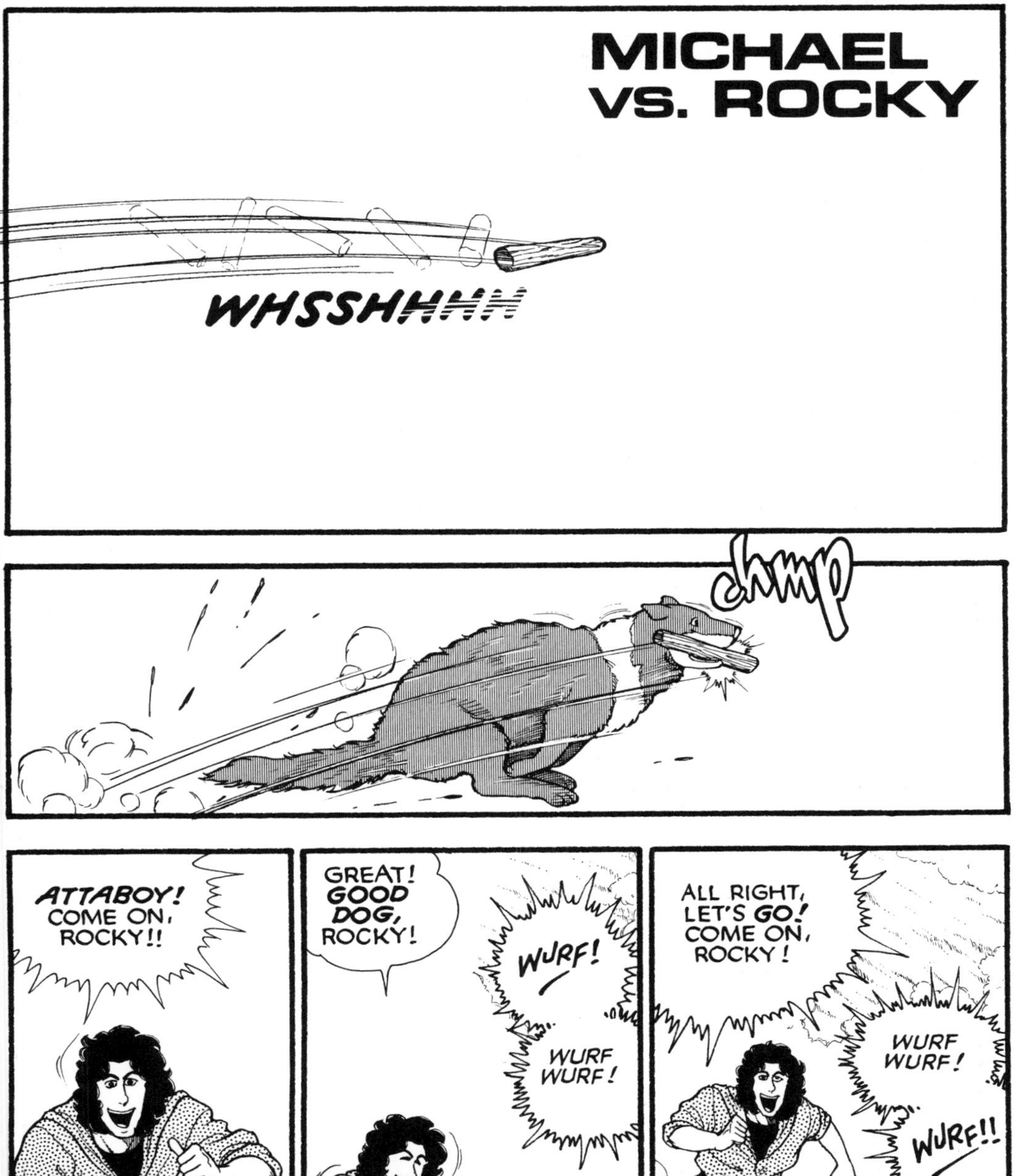
MICHAEL vs. ROCKY
WHSSHHHH
chmp
ATTABOY! COME ON, ROCKY!!
GREAT! GOOD DOG, ROCKY!
WURF!
WURF WURF!
ALL RIGHT, LET'S GO! COME ON, ROCKY!
WURF WURF!
WURF!!

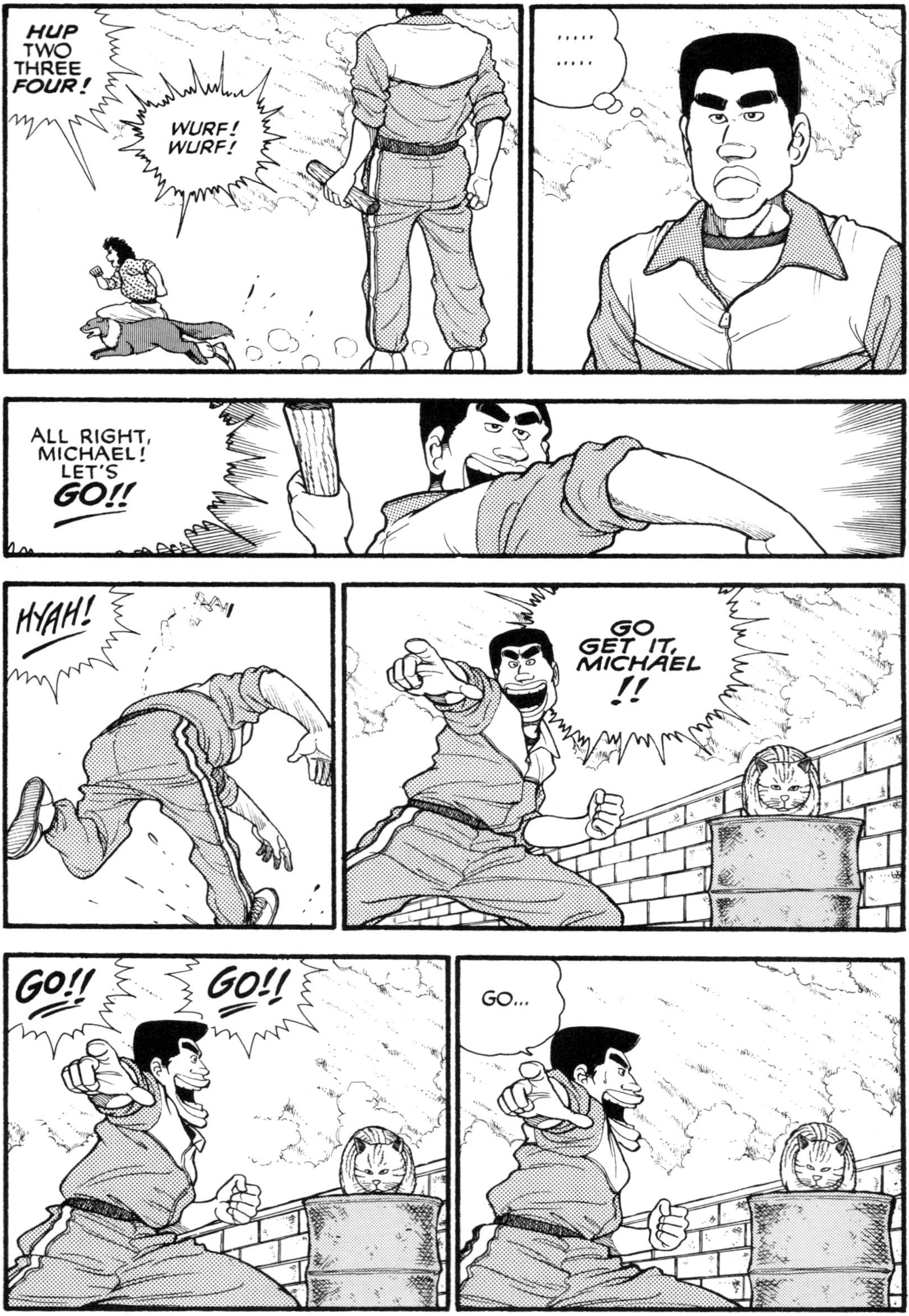
HUP TWO THREE FOUR!
WURF! WURF!
.....
.....
ALL RIGHT, MICHAEL! LET'S GO!!
HYAH!
GO GET IT, MICHAEL !!
GO!!
GO!!
GO...

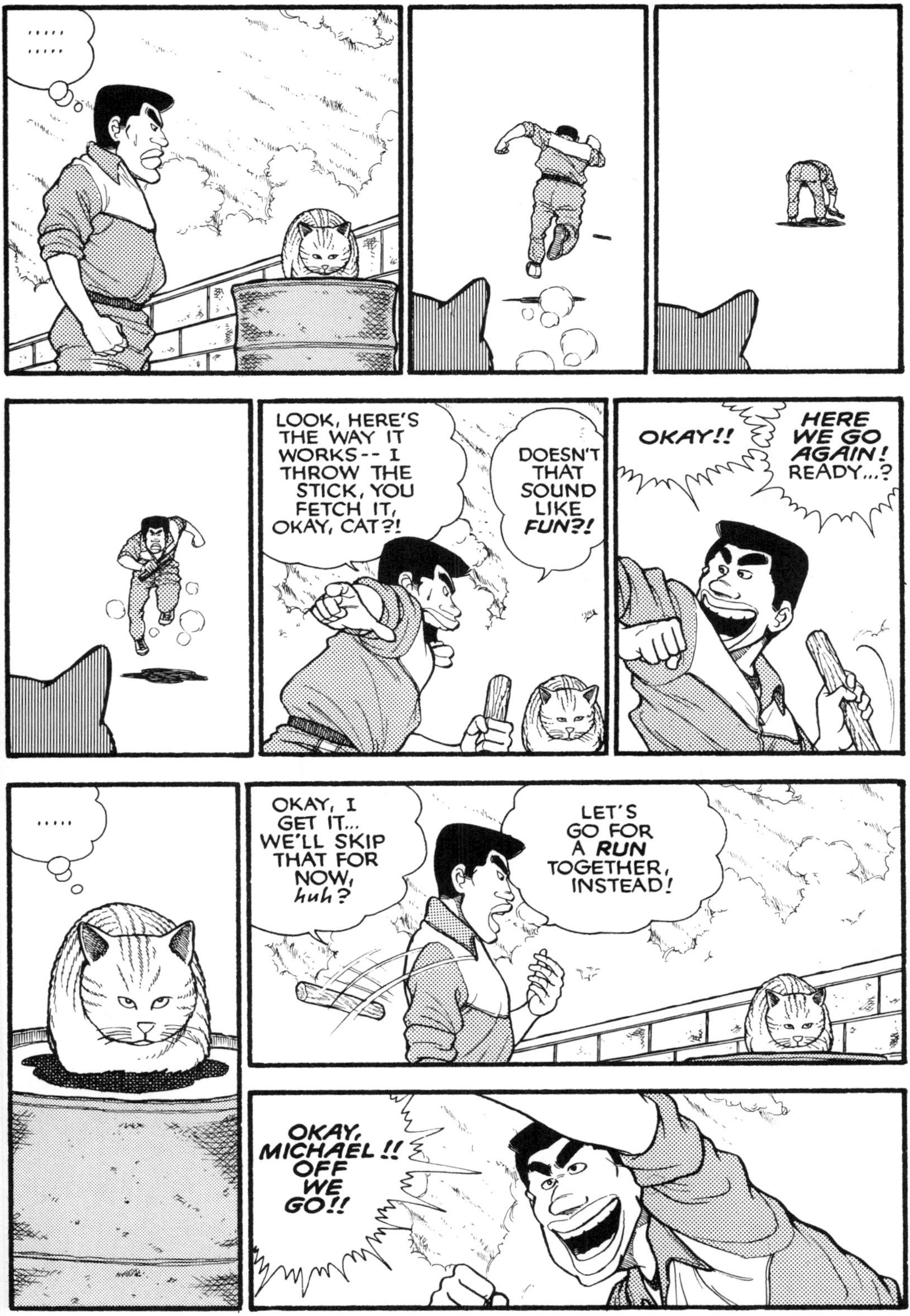
.....
.....
LOOK, HERE'S THE WAY IT WORKS-- I THROW THE STICK, YOU FETCH IT, OKAY, CAT?!
DOESN'T THAT SOUND LIKE *FUN?!*
*OKAY!!*
*HERE WE GO AGAIN!* READY...?
.....
OKAY, I GET IT... WE'LL SKIP THAT FOR NOW, *huh?*
LET'S GO FOR A *RUN* TOGETHER, INSTEAD!
*OKAY, MICHAEL!! OFF WE GO!!*

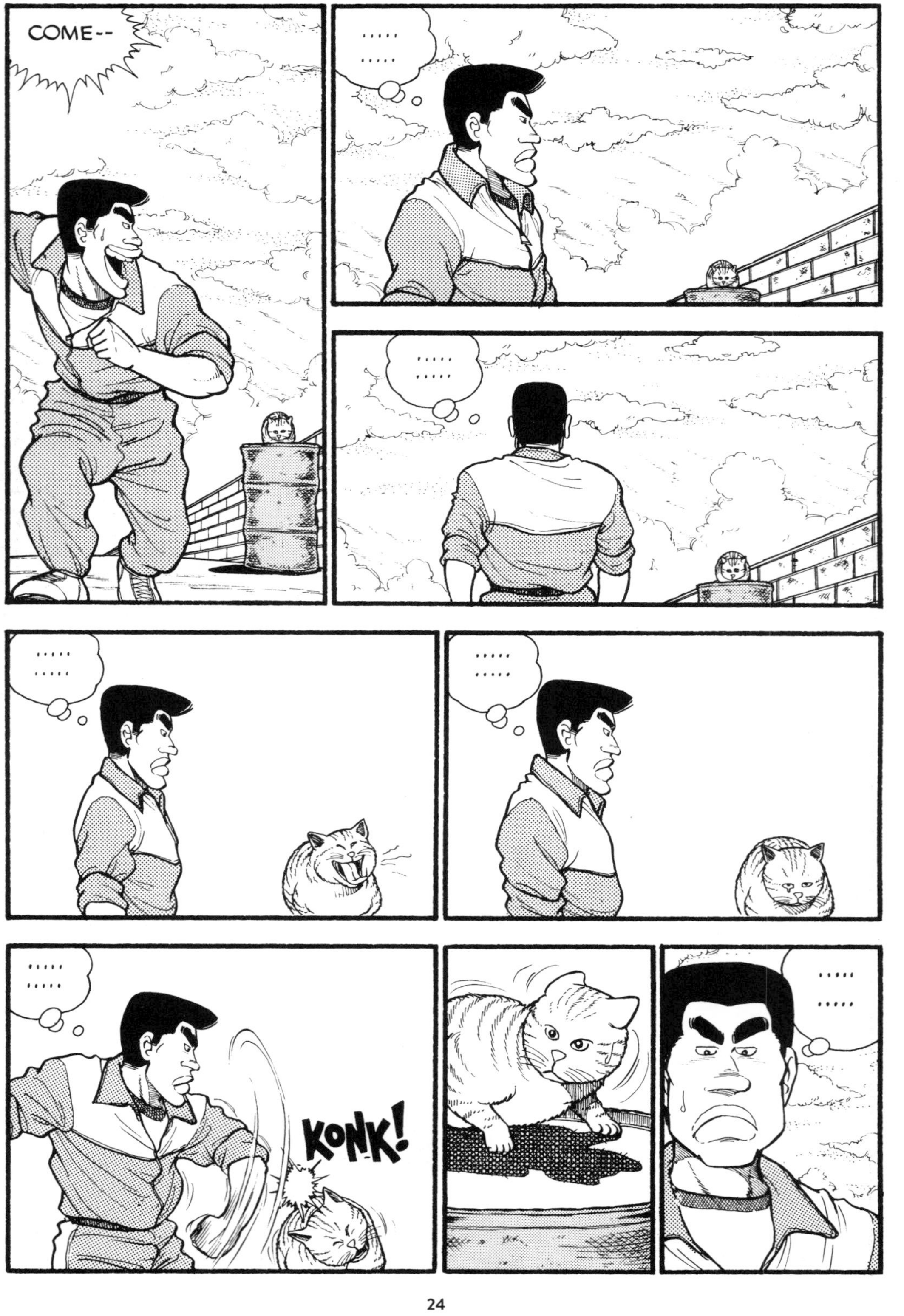
COME--
.....
.....
.....
.....
.....
.....
.....
.....
.....
.....
KONK!
.....
.....

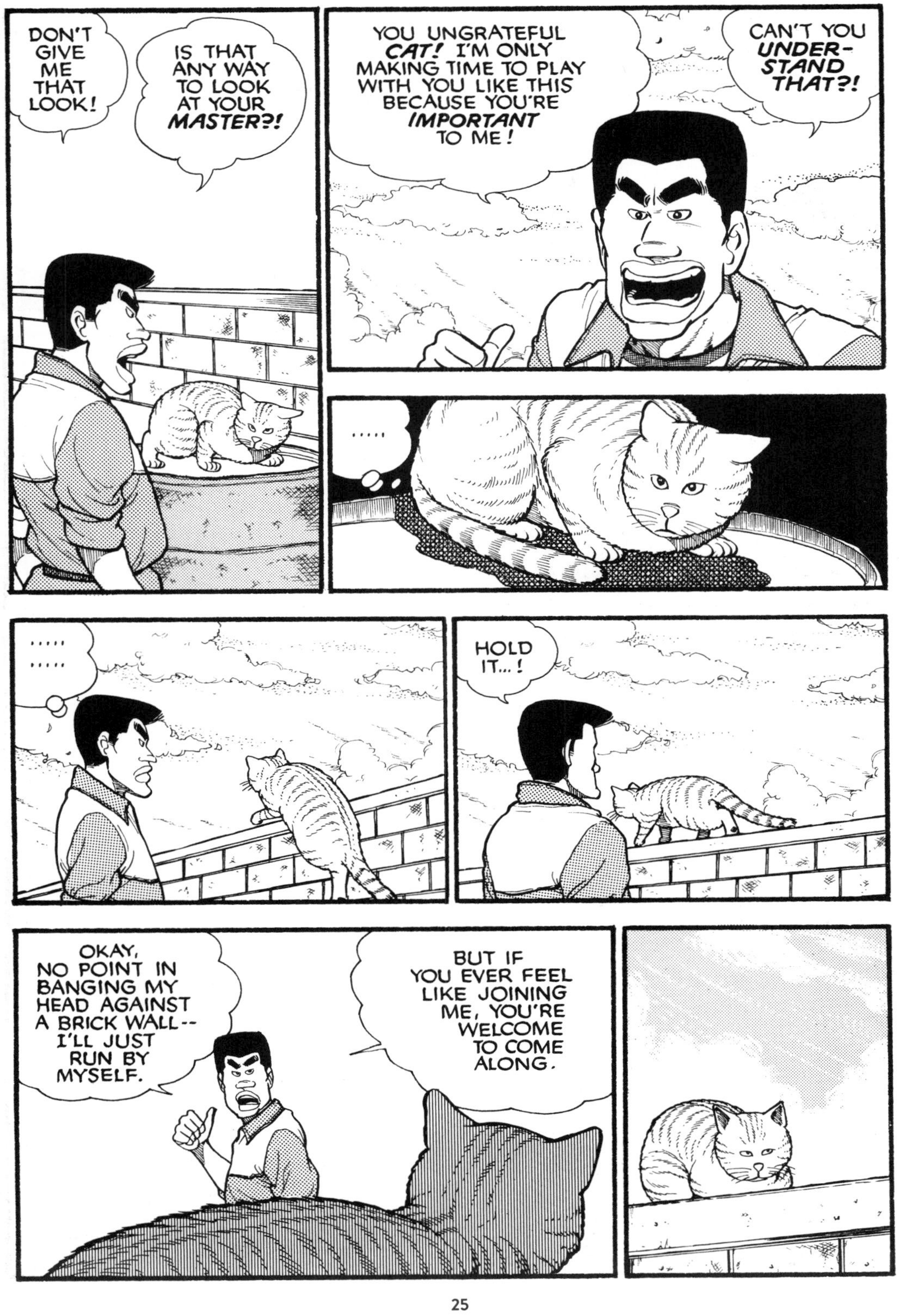
DON'T GIVE ME THAT LOOK!
IS THAT ANY WAY TO LOOK AT YOUR *MASTER?!*
YOU UNGRATEFUL *CAT!* I'M ONLY MAKING TIME TO PLAY WITH YOU LIKE THIS BECAUSE YOU'RE *IMPORTANT* TO ME!
CAN'T YOU *UNDERSTAND THAT?!*
.....
..... .....
HOLD IT...!
OKAY, NO POINT IN BANGING MY HEAD AGAINST A BRICK WALL-- I'LL JUST RUN BY MYSELF.
BUT IF YOU EVER FEEL LIKE JOINING ME, YOU'RE WELCOME TO COME ALONG.

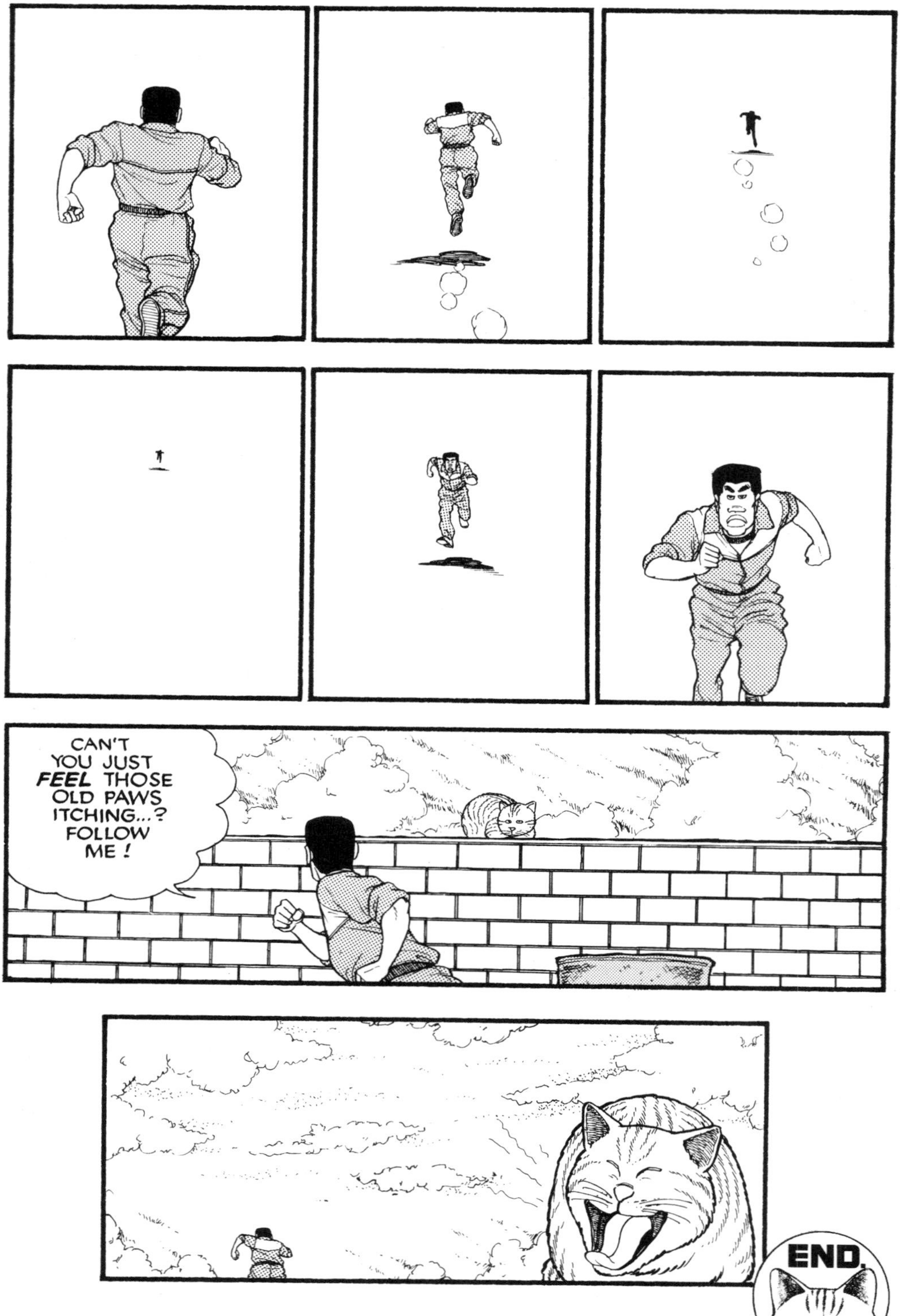
CAN'T YOU JUST FEEL THOSE OLD PAWS ITCHING...? FOLLOW ME!
END.

# MICHAEL'S ALBUM

Michael joins our family, just two months old.

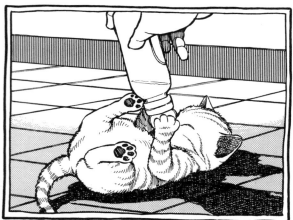

Michael and his bottle --
he's gonna be a big one!

Cat for breakfast???

Michael playing with
his favorite toy.

He loves to cuddle!

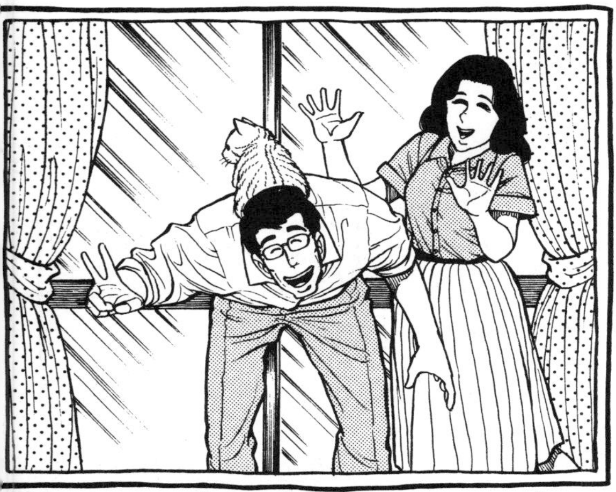

Six months old and growing fast--you're really a part of the family now, Michael!

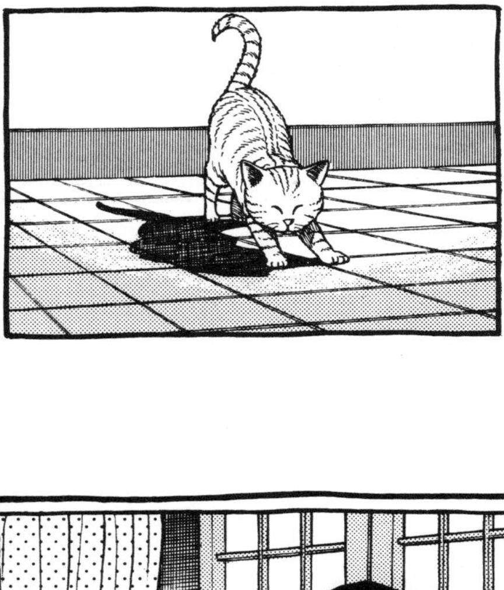

What are you looking at?

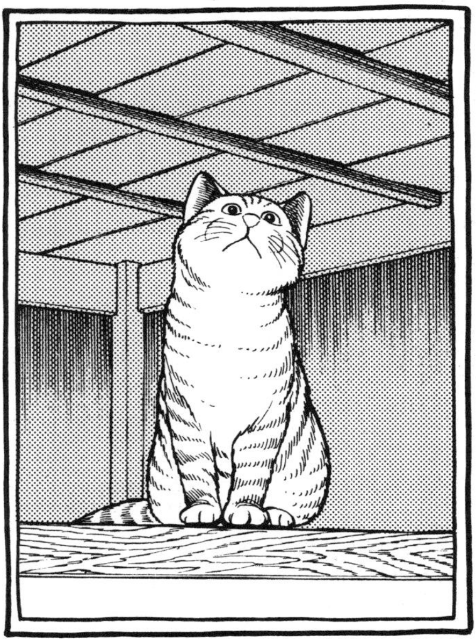

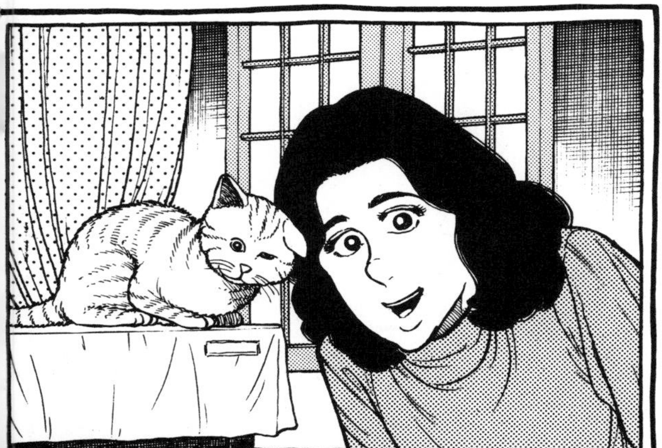

Which one is happiest? Impossible to tell!!

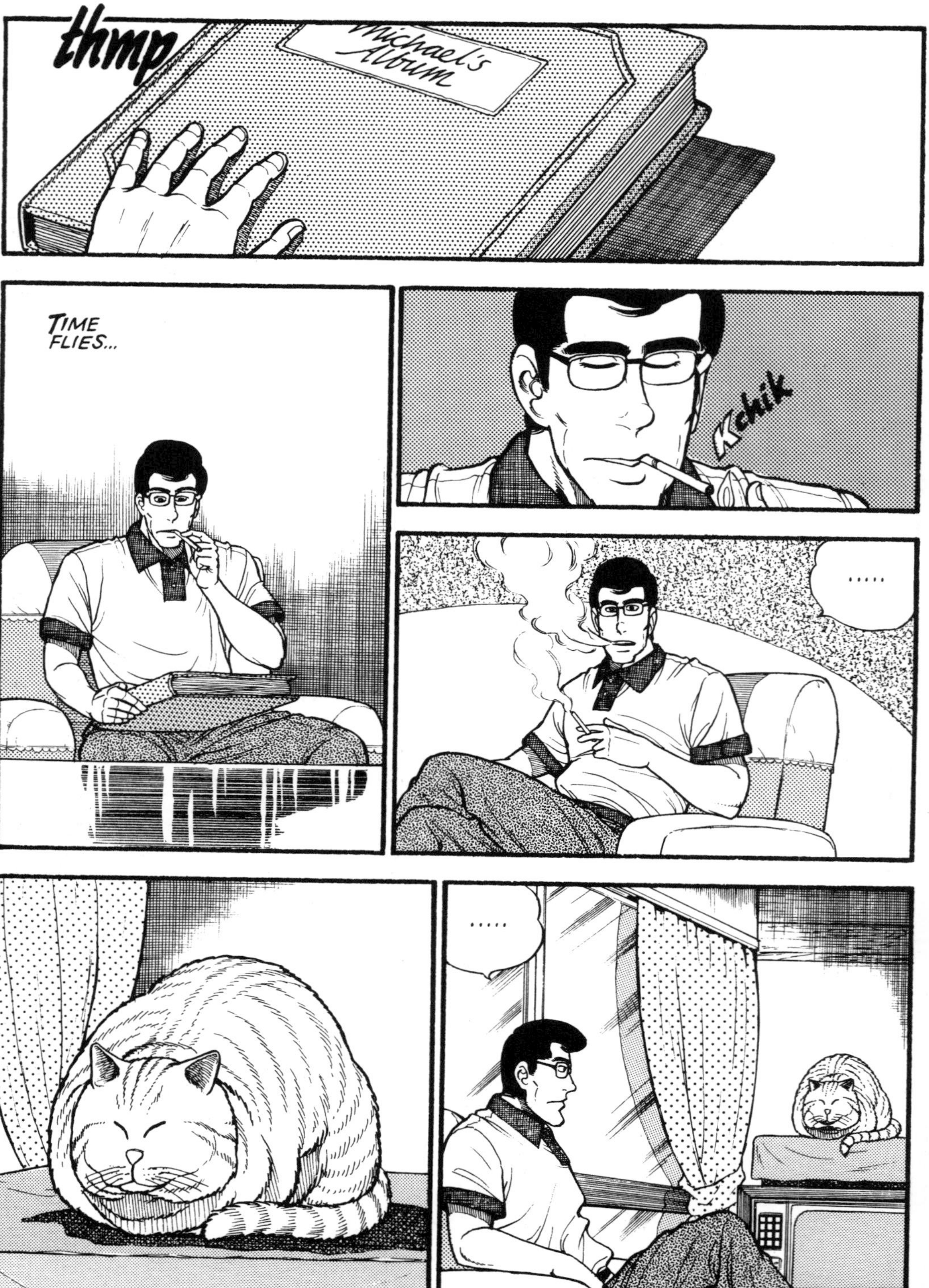
thmp
Michael's Album
TIME FLIES...
K-chik
.....
.....

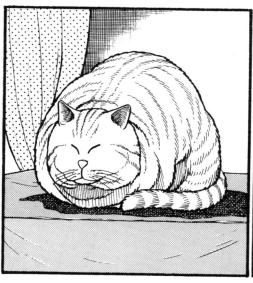

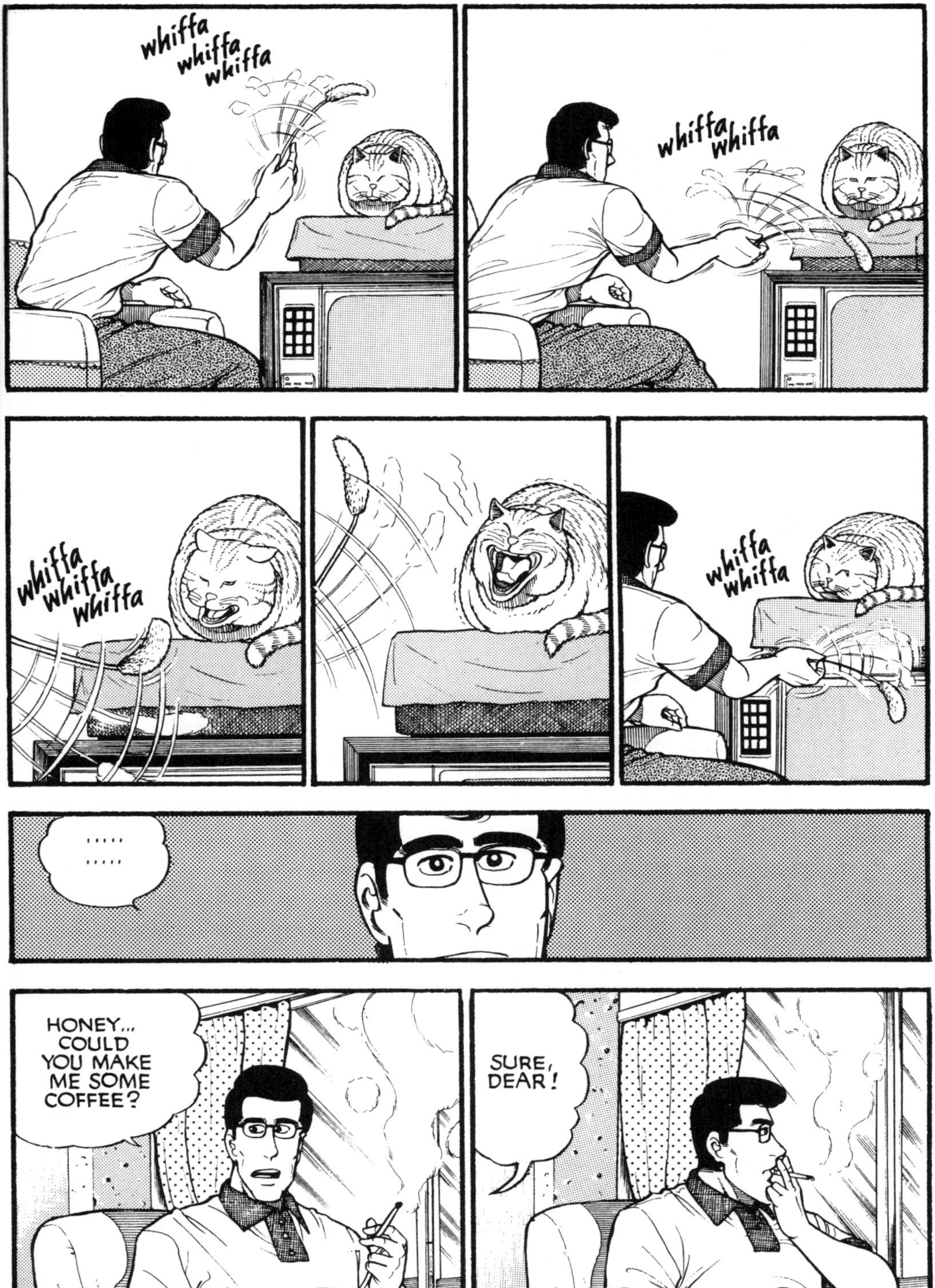
whiffa whiffa whiffa
whiffa whiffa
whiffa whiffa whiffa
whiffa whiffa
.....
.....
HONEY... COULD YOU MAKE ME SOME COFFEE?
SURE, DEAR!

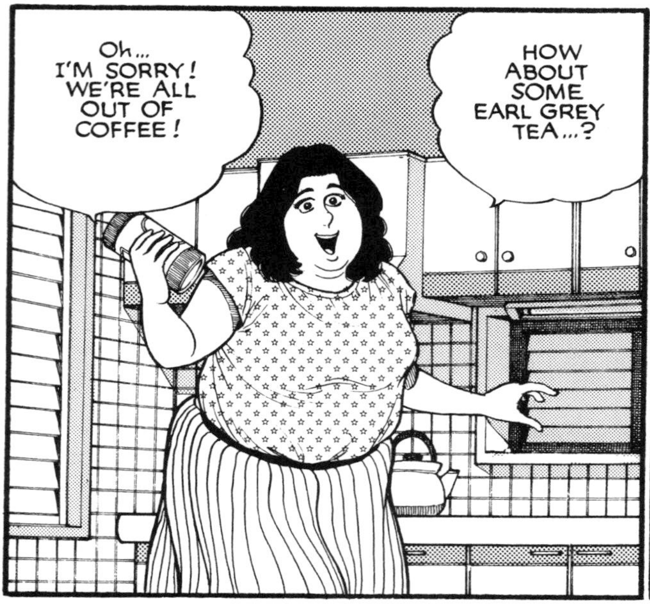
Oh... I'M SORRY! WE'RE ALL OUT OF COFFEE!
HOW ABOUT SOME EARL GREY TEA...?

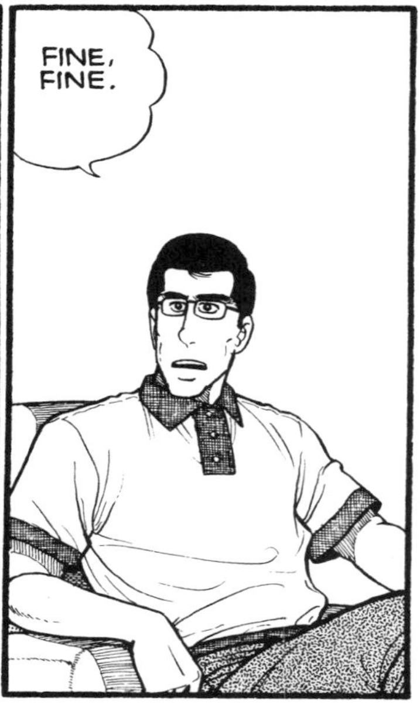
FINE, FINE.

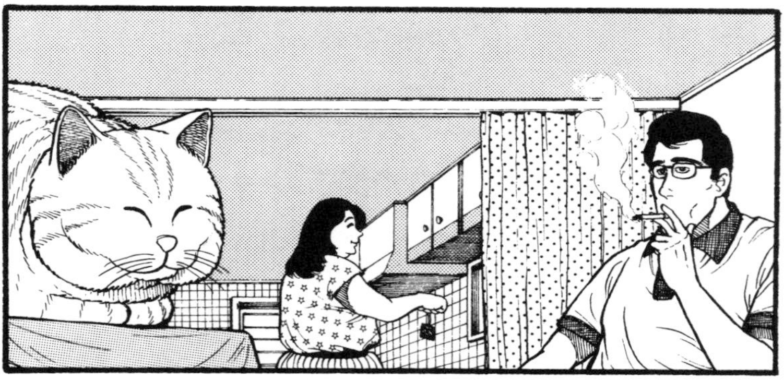

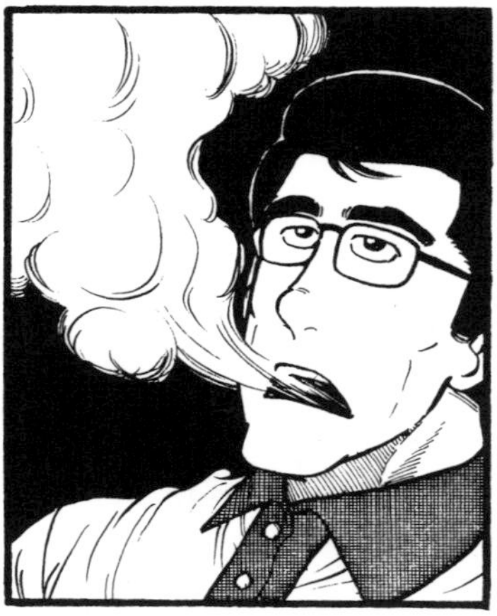

*THIS LIFE, THE LIFE OF AN AVERAGE JOE... IT'S SIMPLE, BUT IT'S GOOD.*

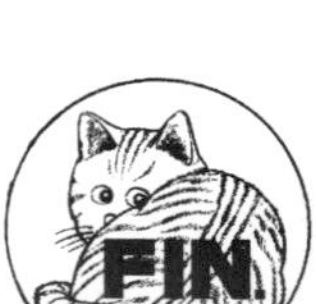
FIN

# THE YAKUZA
## (JAPANESE MAFIA)

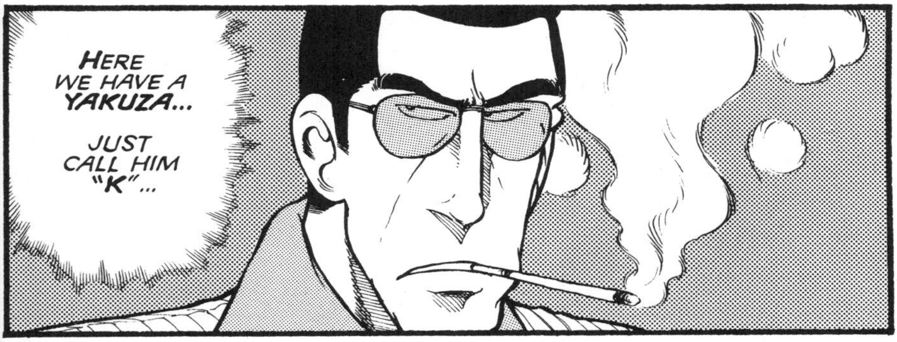
HERE WE HAVE A YAKUZA...
JUST CALL HIM "K"...

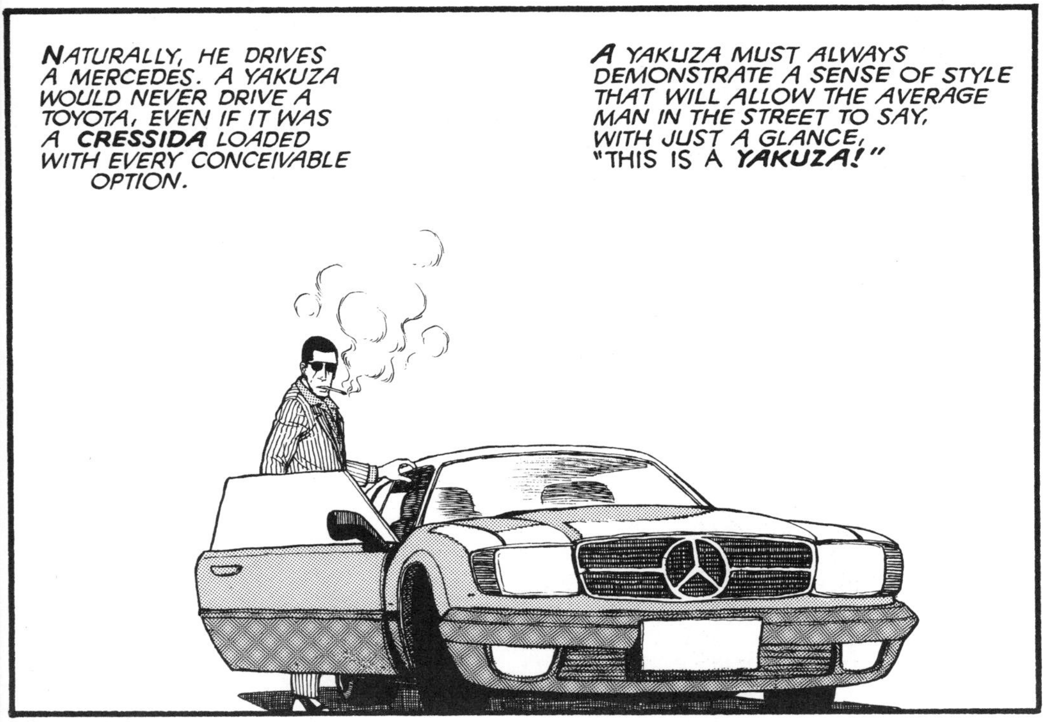
NATURALLY, HE DRIVES A MERCEDES. A YAKUZA WOULD NEVER DRIVE A TOYOTA, EVEN IF IT WAS A CRESSIDA LOADED WITH EVERY CONCEIVABLE OPTION.
A YAKUZA MUST ALWAYS DEMONSTRATE A SENSE OF STYLE THAT WILL ALLOW THE AVERAGE MAN IN THE STREET TO SAY, WITH JUST A GLANCE, "THIS IS A YAKUZA!"

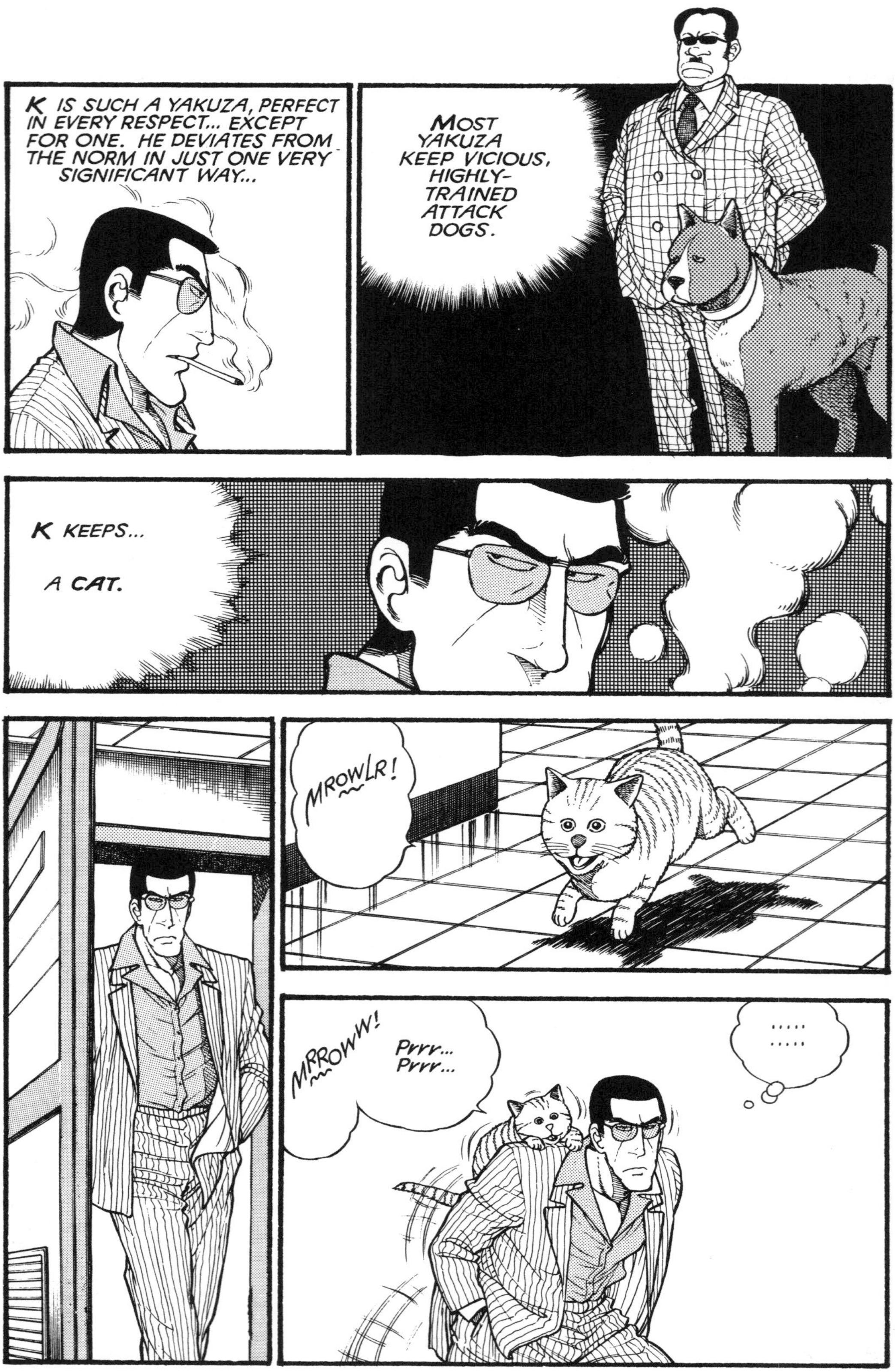
K IS SUCH A YAKUZA, PERFECT IN EVERY RESPECT... EXCEPT FOR ONE. HE DEVIATES FROM THE NORM IN JUST ONE VERY SIGNIFICANT WAY...
MOST YAKUZA KEEP VICIOUS, HIGHLY-TRAINED ATTACK DOGS.
K KEEPS...
A CAT.
MROWLR!
MRROWW!
Prrr... Prrr...
.....
.....

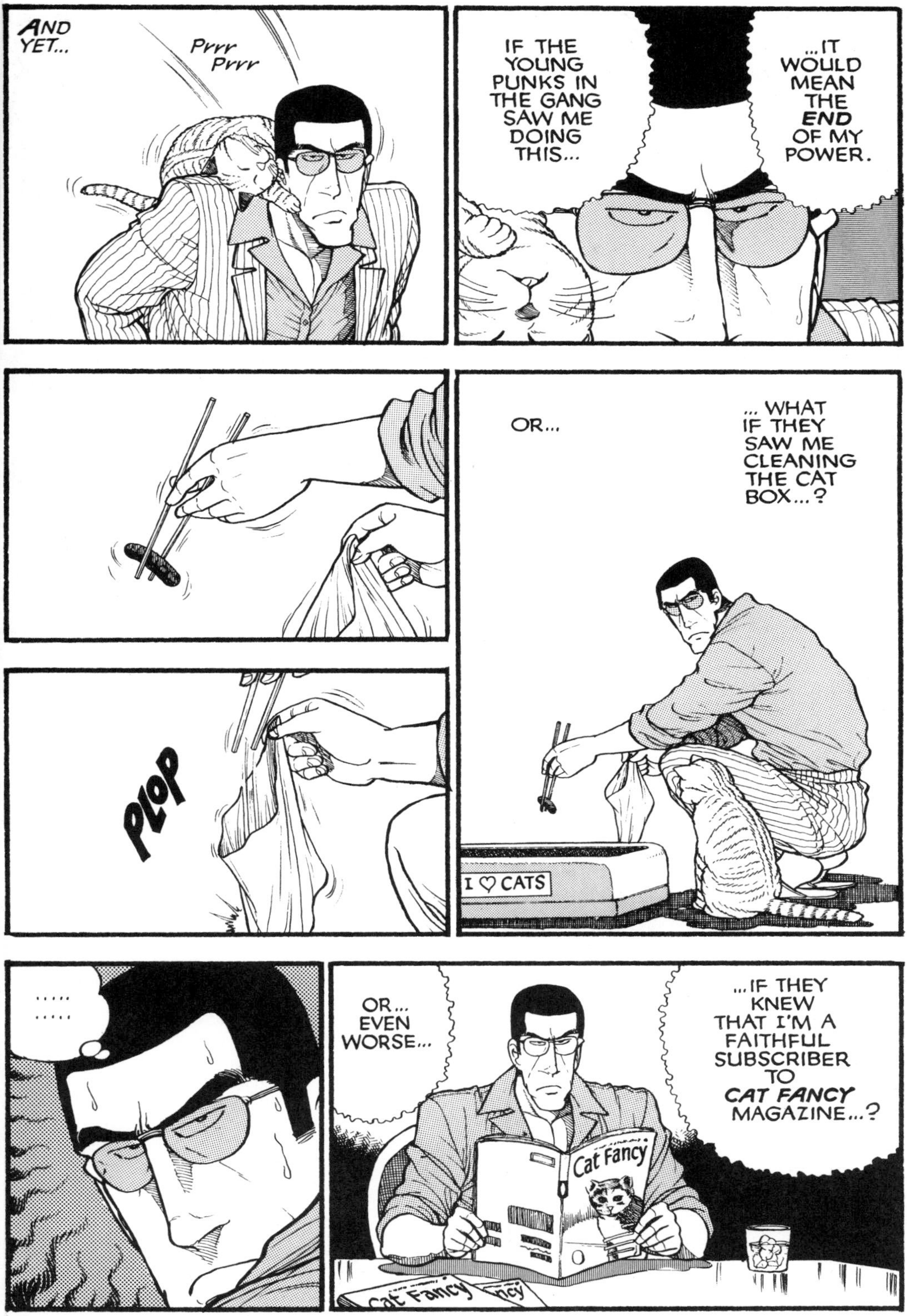
AND YET...
Prrr Prrr
IF THE YOUNG PUNKS IN THE GANG SAW ME DOING THIS...
...IT WOULD MEAN THE *END* OF MY POWER.
PLOP
OR...
... WHAT IF THEY SAW ME CLEANING THE CAT BOX...?
I ♡ CATS
.....
.....
OR... EVEN WORSE...
...IF THEY KNEW THAT I'M A FAITHFUL SUBSCRIBER TO *CAT FANCY* MAGAZINE...?
Cat Fancy

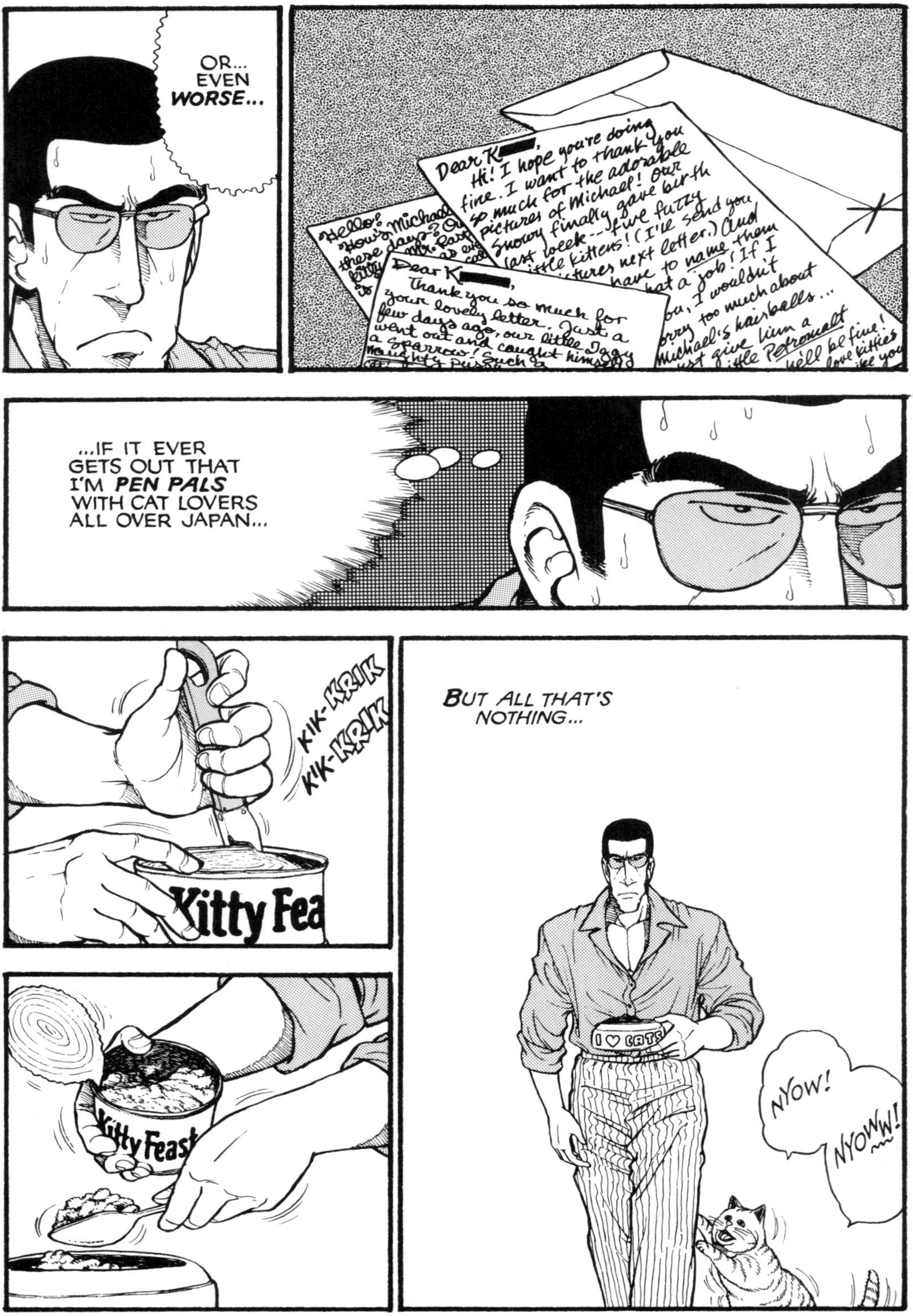
OR...
EVEN
WORSE...
Dear K[redacted],
Hi! I hope you're doing
fine. I want to thank you
so much for the adorable
pictures of Michael! Our
Snowy finally gave birth
last week--five fuzzy
little kittens! (I'll send you
he'll be fine!
Hello!
How's Michael
these days?
Dear K[redacted],
Thank you so much for
your lovely letter. Just a
few days ago, our little Iggy
went out and caught himself
a sparrow!
...IF IT EVER
GETS OUT THAT
I'M PEN PALS
WITH CAT LOVERS
ALL OVER JAPAN...
K'IK-KRIK
K'IK-KRIK
Kitty Fea
Kitty Feast
BUT ALL THAT'S
NOTHING...
I ♡ CATS
NYOW!
NYOWW!

...WHAT IF THOSE SCUM FROM THE **KODANSHA GANG** BREAK INTO MY APARTMENT SOME NIGHT? I CAN JUST IMAGINE...

K!! KRASH!

TIME TO **DIE!!**

!!

WHSST

CAT CAT LOVE CAT LOVE CAT CAT LOVE LOVE CAT LOVE CAT LOVE CAT CAT LOVE CAT LOVE CAT

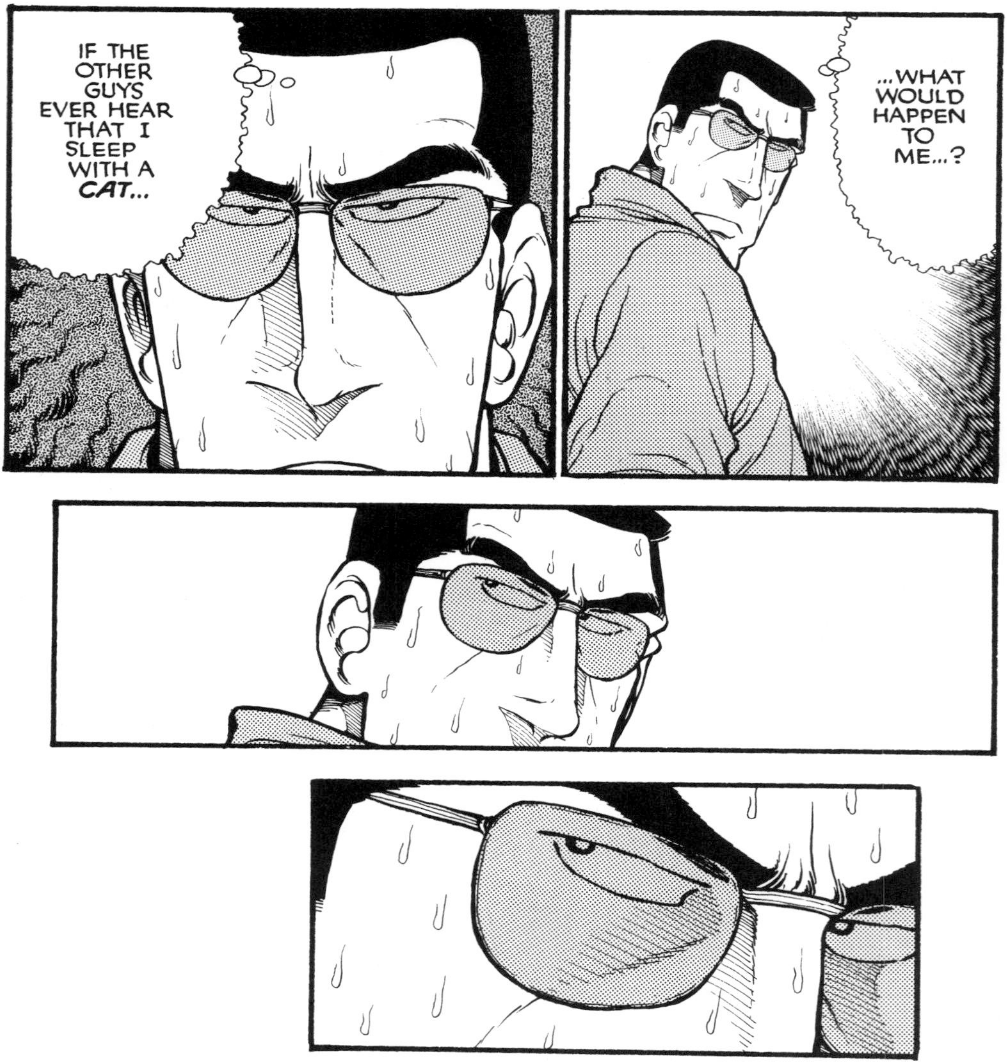
IF THE OTHER GUYS EVER HEAR THAT I SLEEP WITH A *CAT*...
...WHAT WOULD HAPPEN TO ME...?

**TO BE CONTINUED**

(Or so he says)

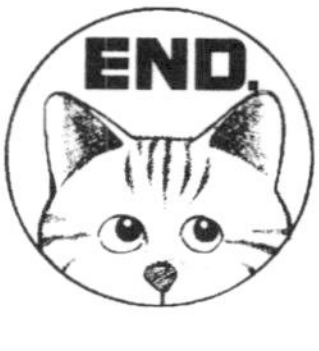
END.

# THE CAT CRIES AT MIDNIGHT

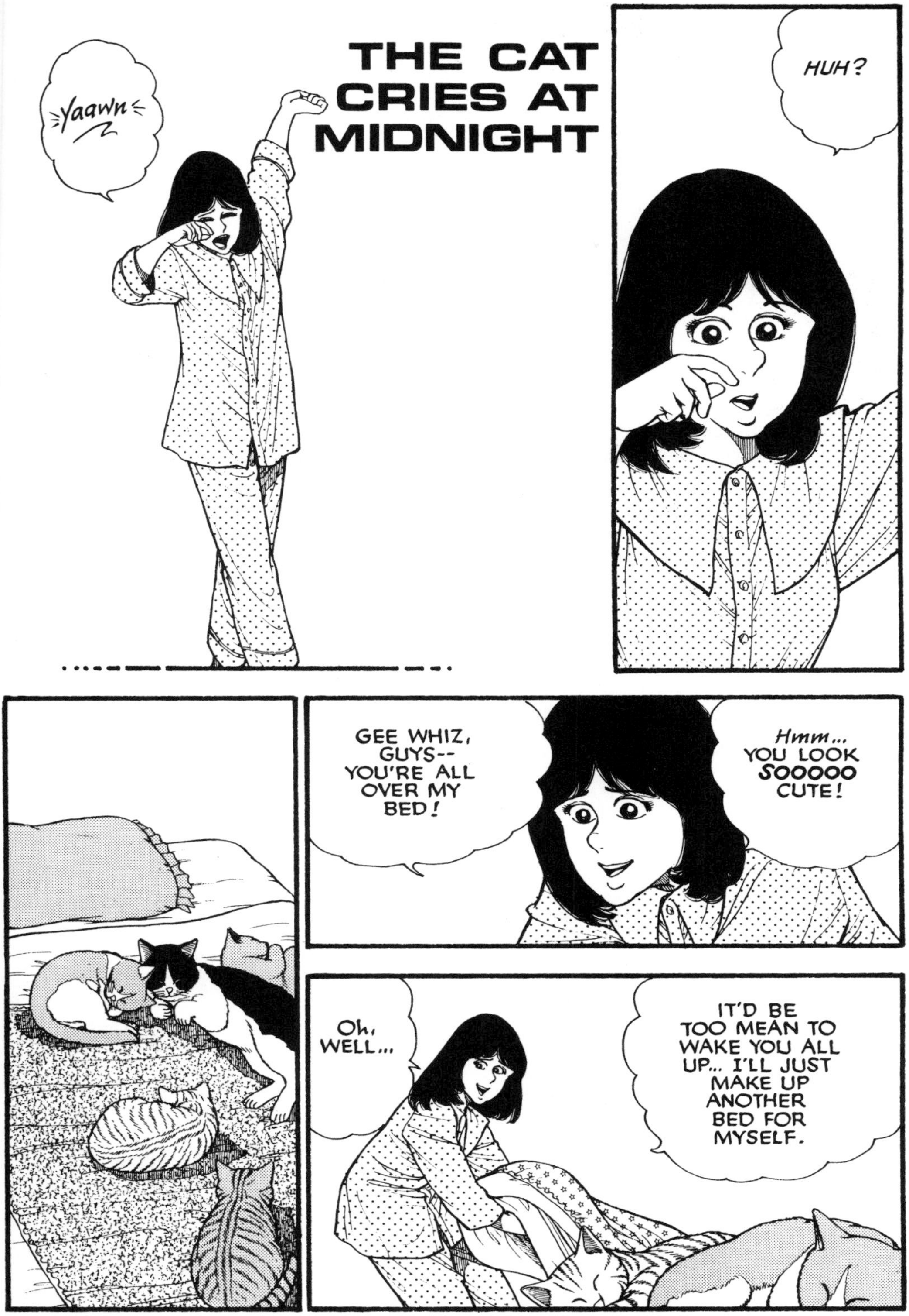

Yaawn
HUH?
GEE WHIZ, GUYS-- YOU'RE ALL OVER MY BED!
Hmm... YOU LOOK SOOOOO CUTE!
Oh, WELL...
IT'D BE TOO MEAN TO WAKE YOU ALL UP... I'LL JUST MAKE UP ANOTHER BED FOR MYSELF.

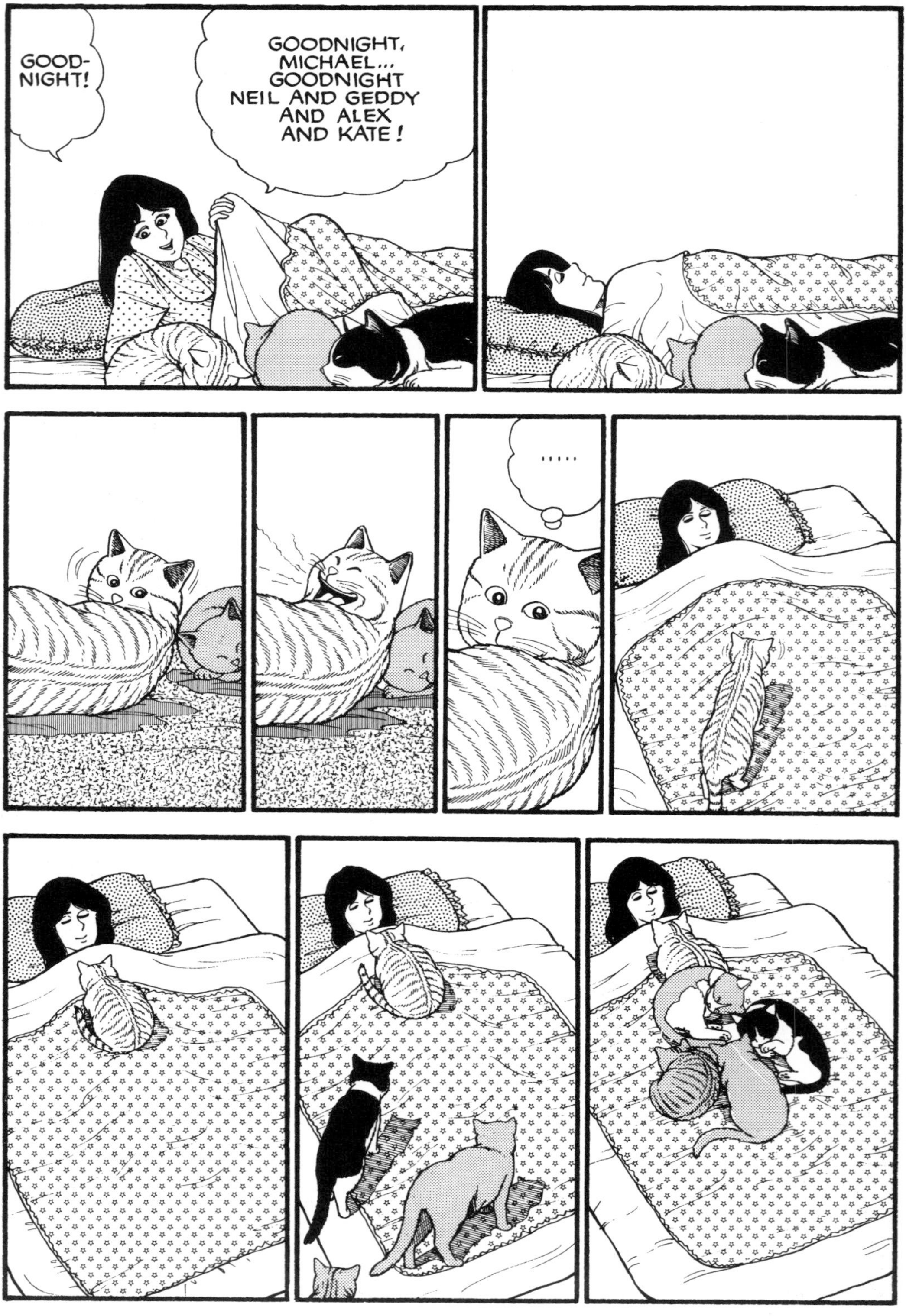
GOOD-NIGHT!
GOODNIGHT, MICHAEL... GOODNIGHT NEIL AND GEDDY AND ALEX AND KATE!
.....

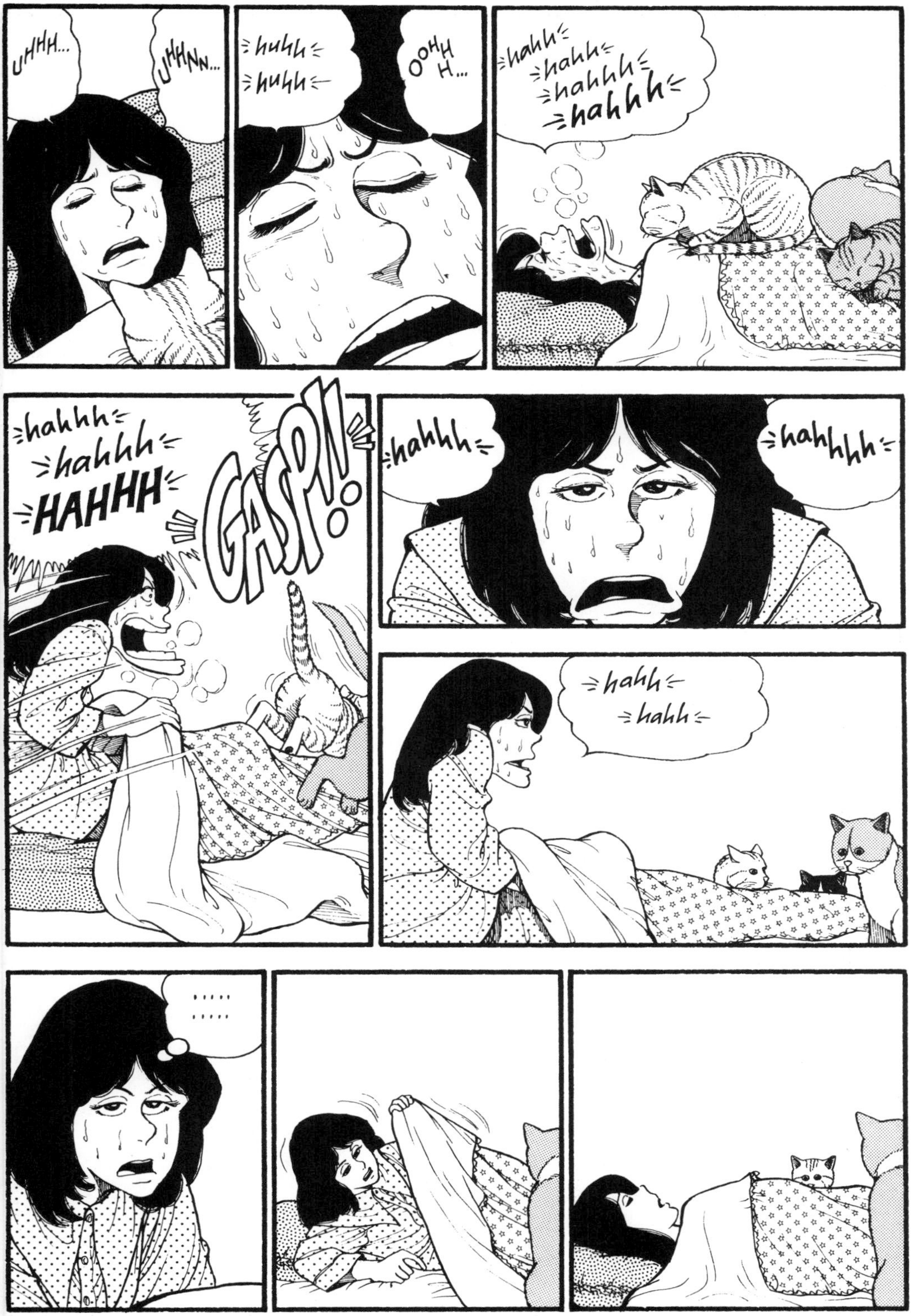
UHHH...
UHHNN...
huhh
huhh
OOHH H...
hahh
hahh
hahhh
hahhh
hahhh
hahhh
HAHHH
GASP!!
hahhh
hahhhh
hahh
hahh
.....
.....

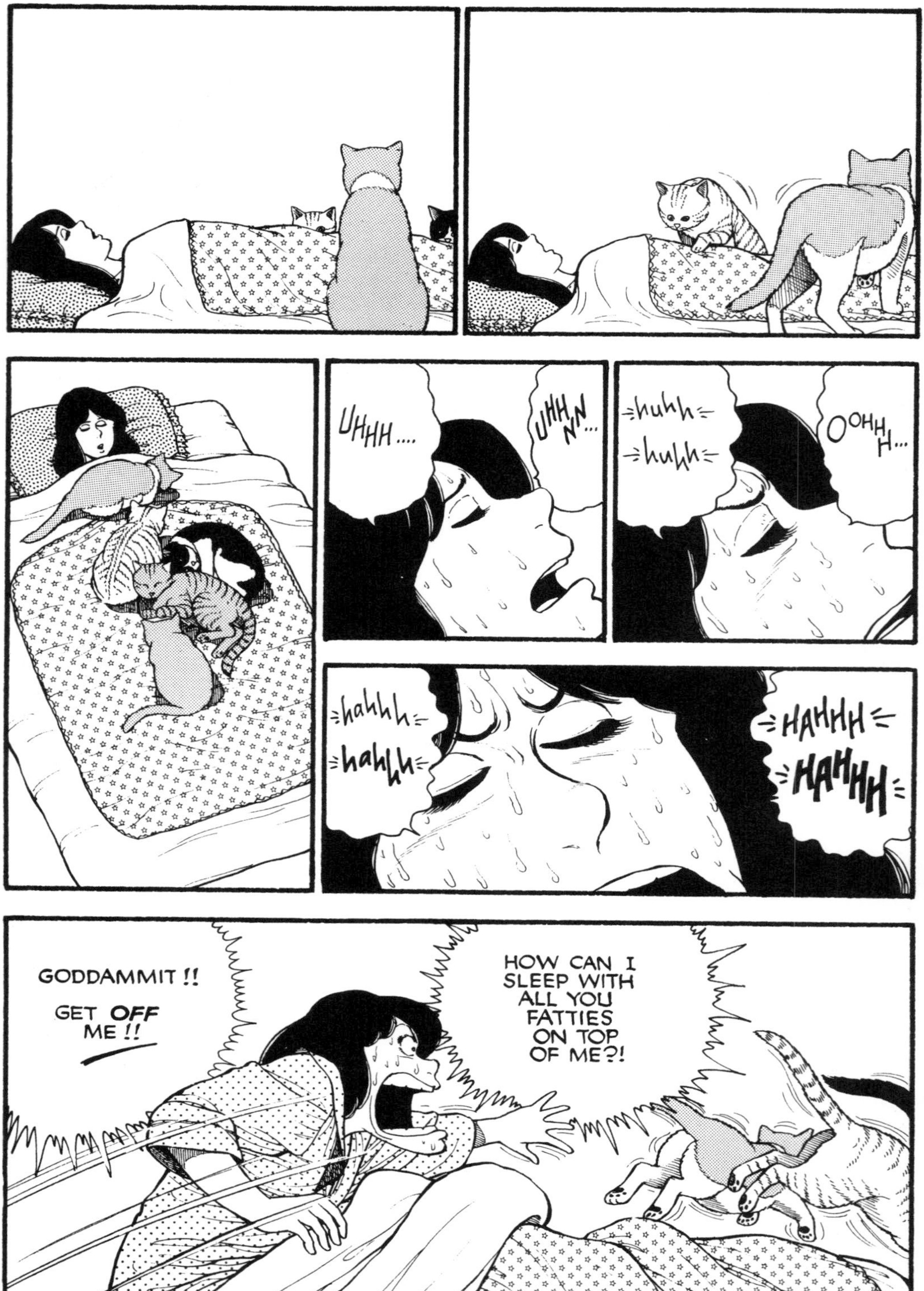

UHHH....
UHHNN...
huhh
huhh
OOHHH...
hahhh
hahhh
HAHHH
HAHHH
GODDAMMIT !!
GET OFF ME !!
HOW CAN I SLEEP WITH ALL YOU FATTIES ON TOP OF ME?!

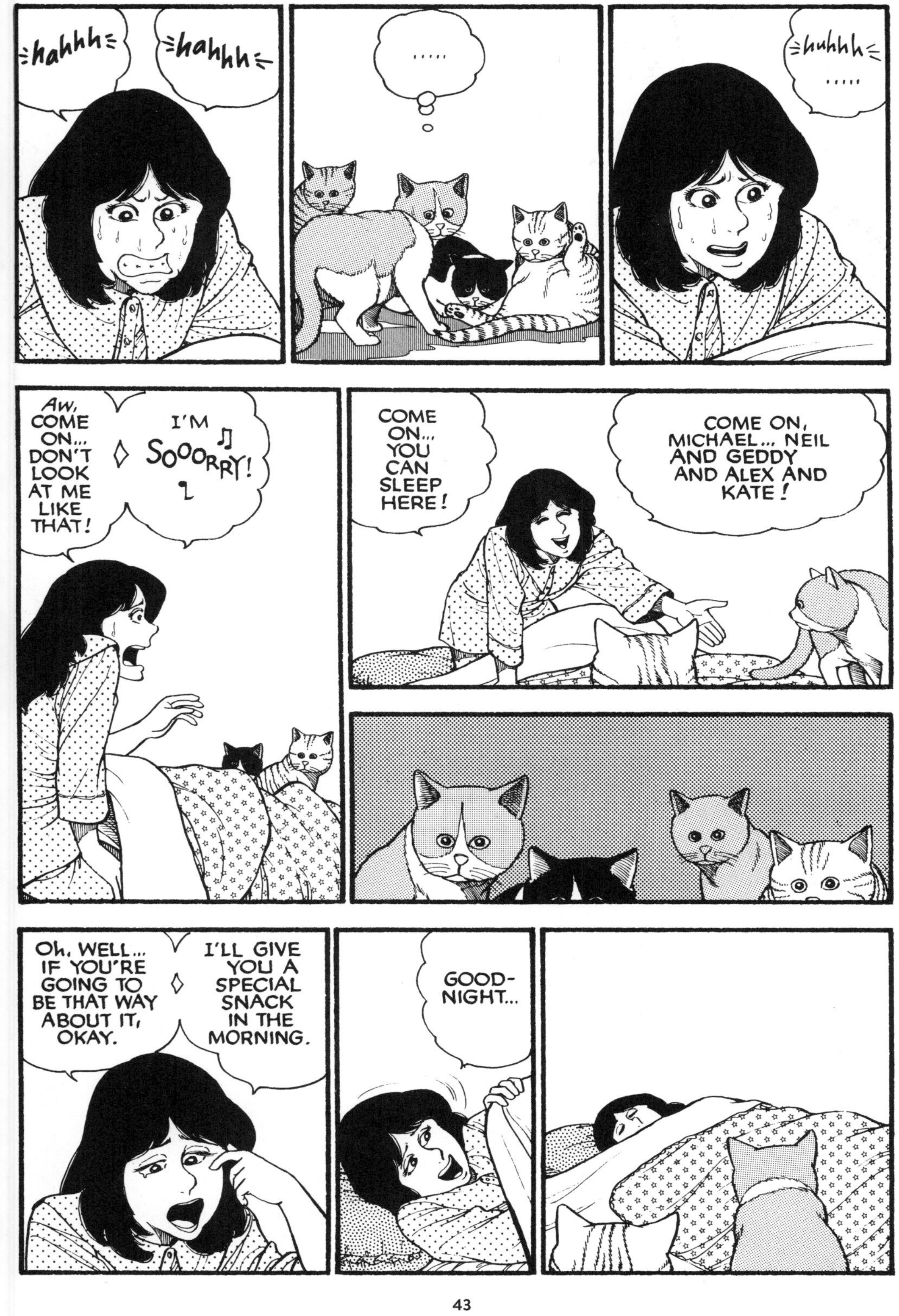
hahhh
hahhh
.....
huhhh
.....
Aw, COME ON... DON'T LOOK AT ME LIKE THAT!
I'M SOOORRY!
COME ON... YOU CAN SLEEP HERE!
COME ON, MICHAEL... NEIL AND GEDDY AND ALEX AND KATE!
Oh, WELL... IF YOU'RE GOING TO BE THAT WAY ABOUT IT, OKAY.
I'LL GIVE YOU A SPECIAL SNACK IN THE MORNING.
GOOD-NIGHT...

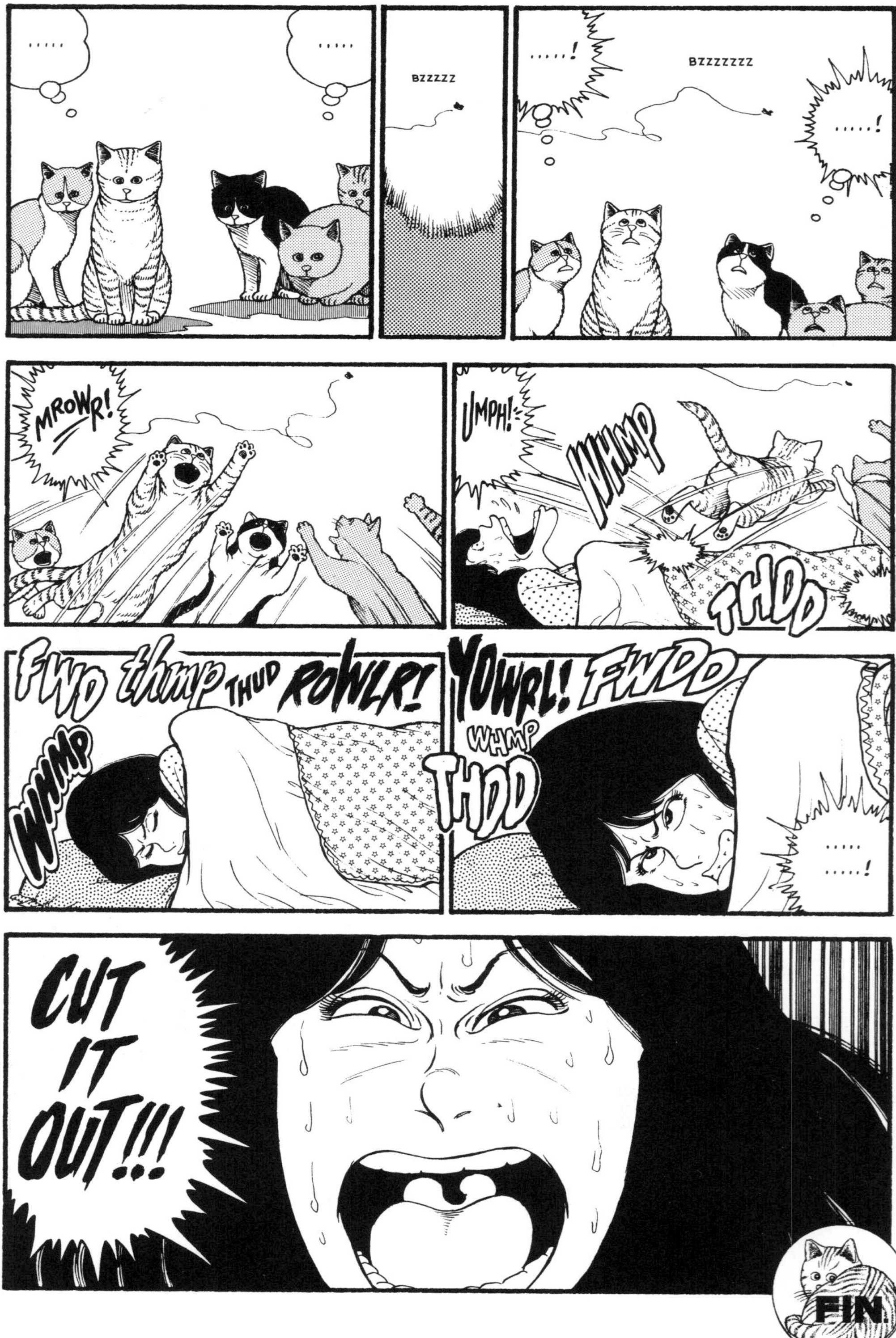

.....
.....
BZZZZZ
.....!
BZZZZZZZ
.....!
MROWR!
UMPH!
WHMP
THDD
FWD thmp THUD ROWLR!
WHMP
YOWRL! FWDD
WHMP
THDD
.....
.....!
CUT IT OUT!!!
FIN.

# MICHAEL'S SECRET

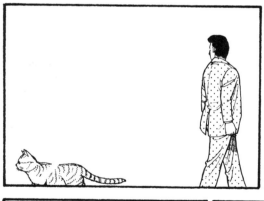

tch
tch
tch
tch...

WHEN YOU MAKE THE "tch tch tch" NOISE AT A CAT...

...HE'LL TURN AROUND AND CHECK IT OUT.

AND IF YOU SHOW HIM YOUR FINGER...

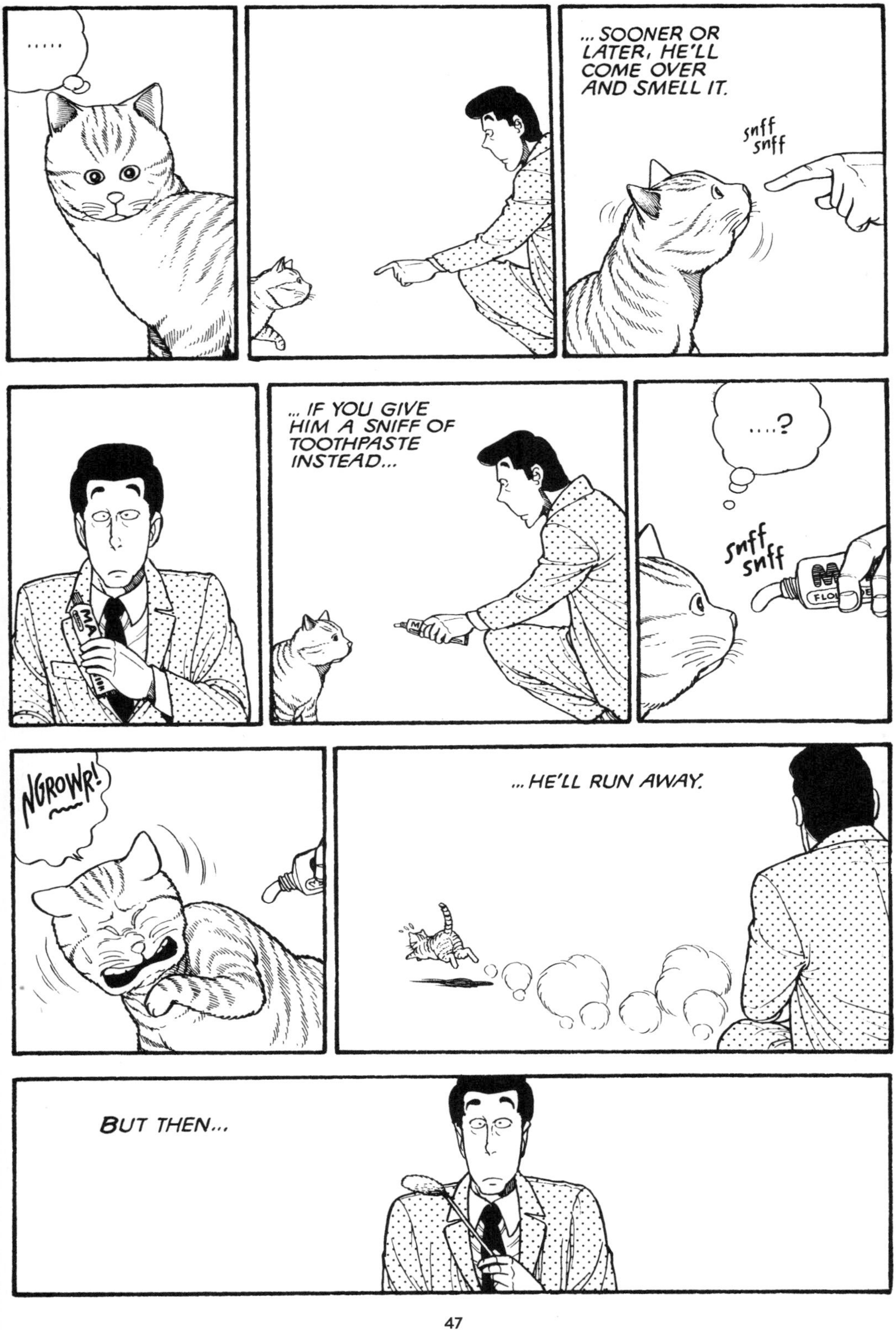
.....
...SOONER OR LATER, HE'LL COME OVER AND SMELL IT.
snff snff
...IF YOU GIVE HIM A SNIFF OF TOOTHPASTE INSTEAD...
....?
snff snff
NGROWR!
...HE'LL RUN AWAY.
BUT THEN...

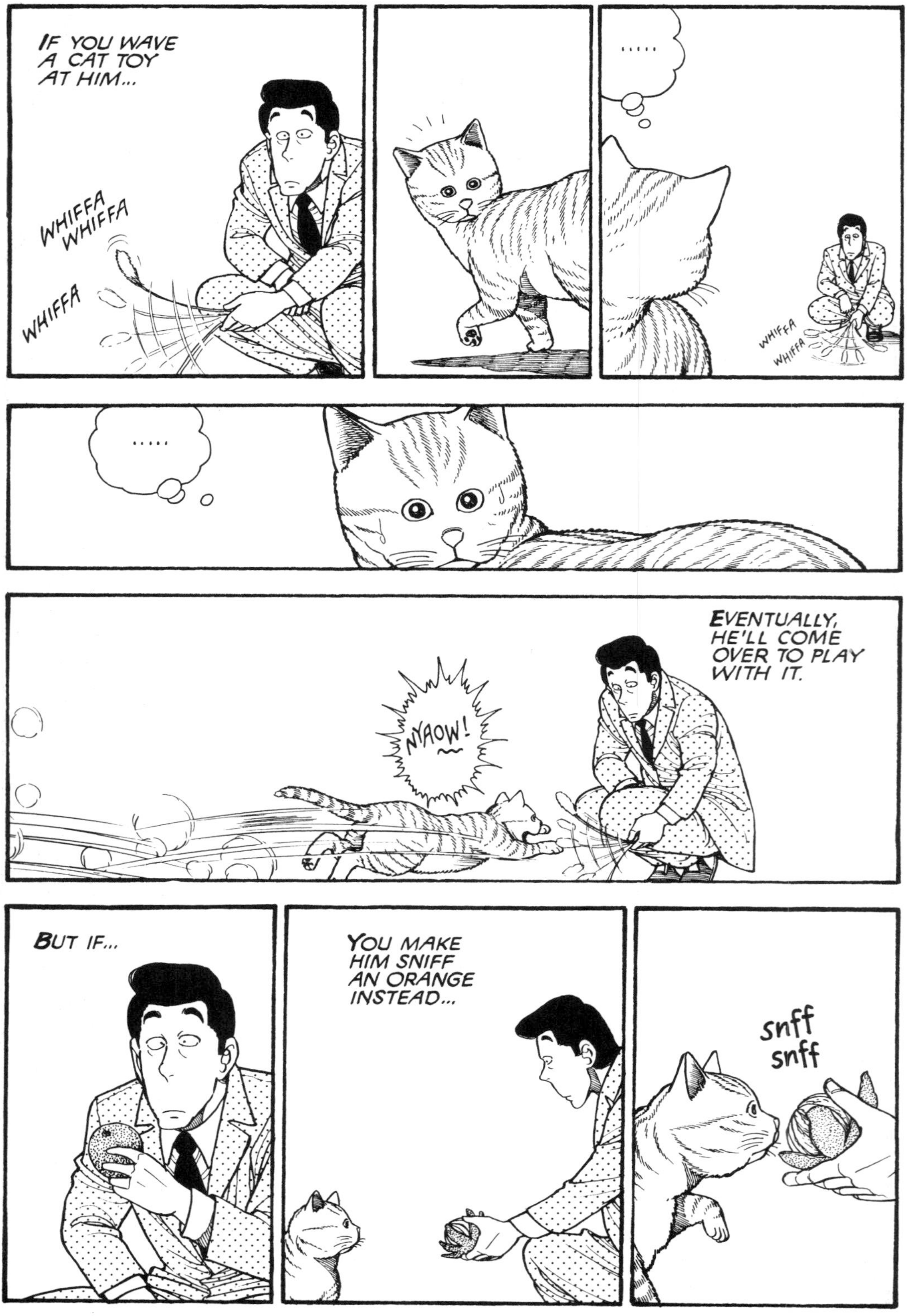
IF YOU WAVE A CAT TOY AT HIM...
WHIFFA WHIFFA
WHIFFA
.....
WHIFFA
WHIFFA
.....
EVENTUALLY, HE'LL COME OVER TO PLAY WITH IT.
NYAOW!
BUT IF...
YOU MAKE HIM SNIFF AN ORANGE INSTEAD...
snff snff

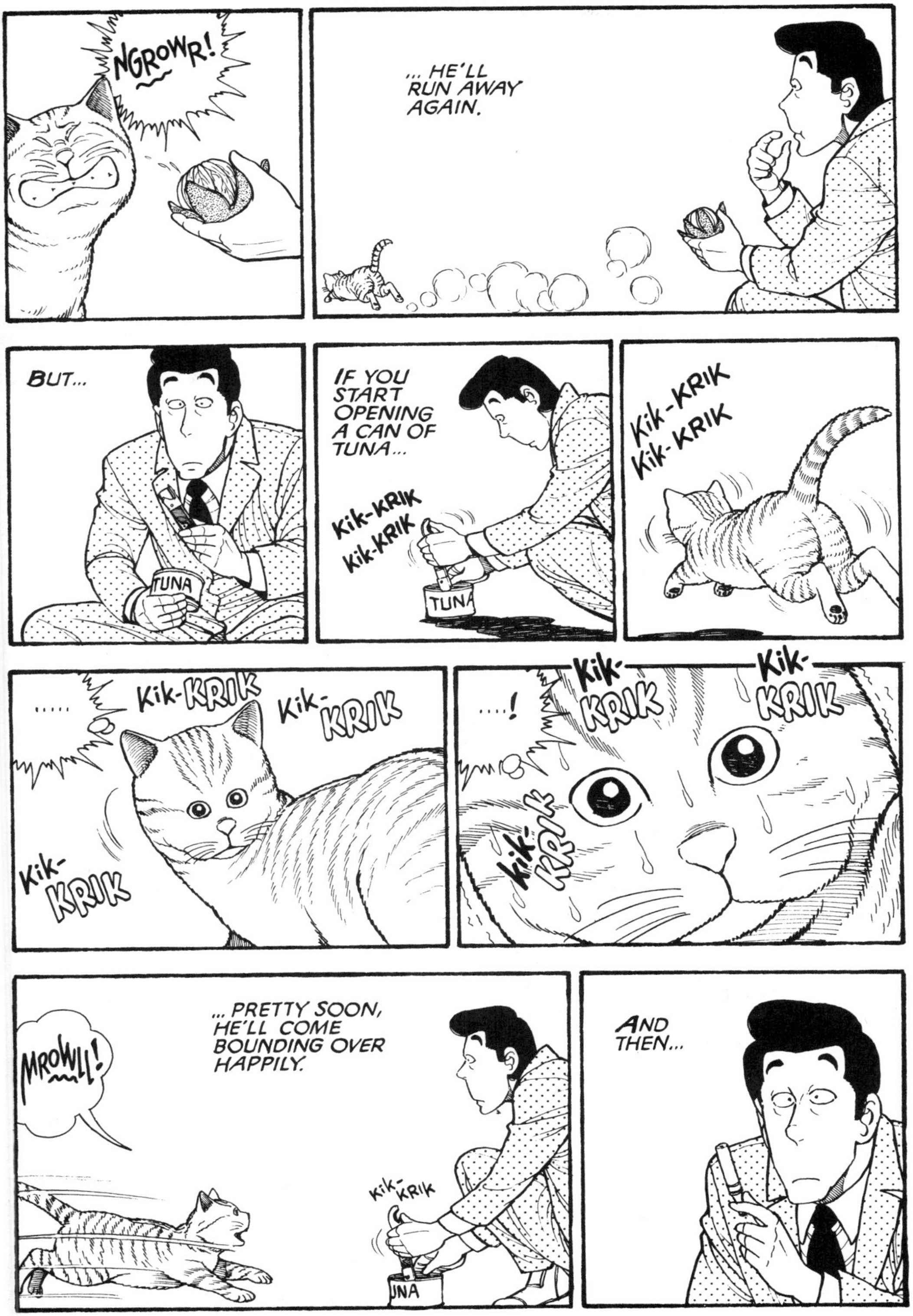
NGROWR!
... HE'LL RUN AWAY AGAIN.
BUT...
TUNA
IF YOU START OPENING A CAN OF TUNA...
Kik-KRIK Kik-KRIK
TUNA
Kik-KRIK Kik-KRIK
.....
Kik-KRIK
Kik-KRIK
Kik-KRIK
....!
Kik-KRIK
Kik-KRIK
Kik-KRIK
MROWLL!
... PRETTY SOON, HE'LL COME BOUNDING OVER HAPPILY.
Kik-KRIK
UNA
AND THEN...

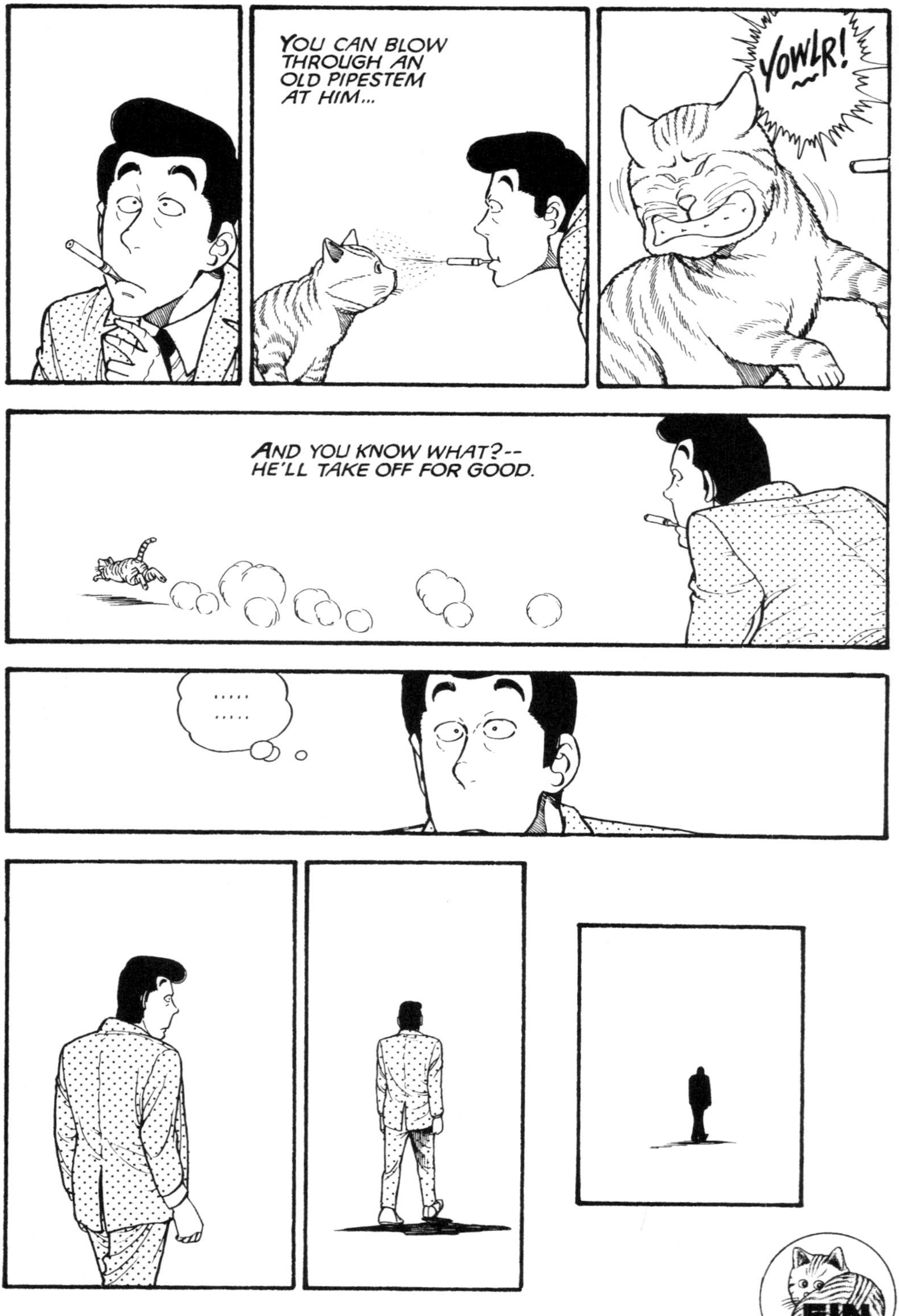
YOU CAN BLOW THROUGH AN OLD PIPESTEM AT HIM...
YOWLR!
AND YOU KNOW WHAT?-- HE'LL TAKE OFF FOR GOOD.
.....
.....
FIN

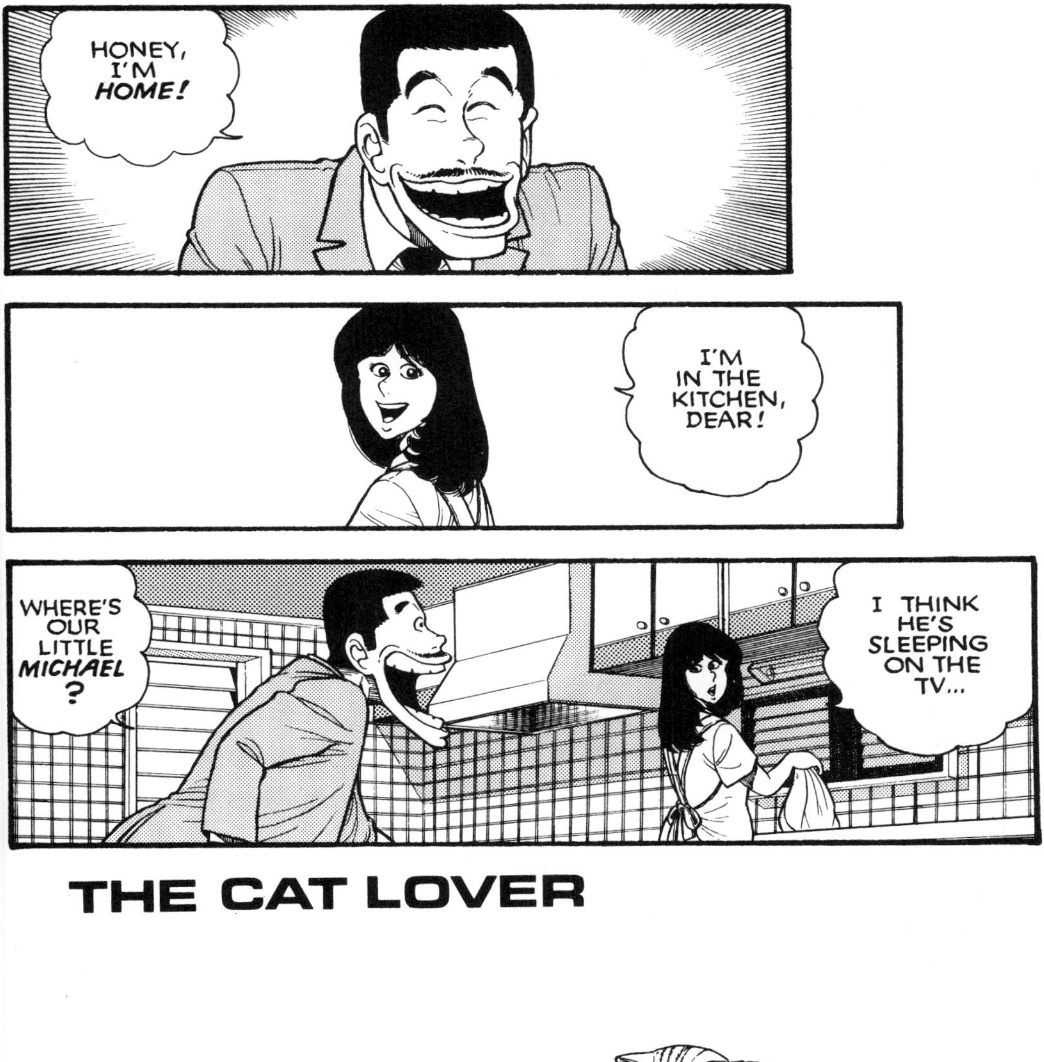
HONEY, I'M HOME!
I'M IN THE KITCHEN, DEAR!
WHERE'S OUR LITTLE MICHAEL?
I THINK HE'S SLEEPING ON THE TV...

# THE CAT LOVER

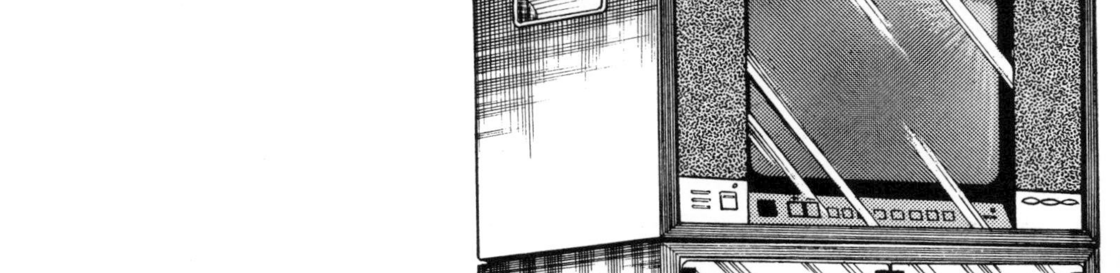

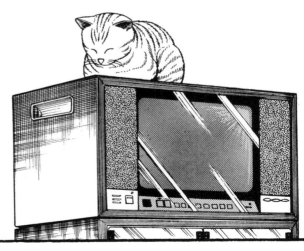

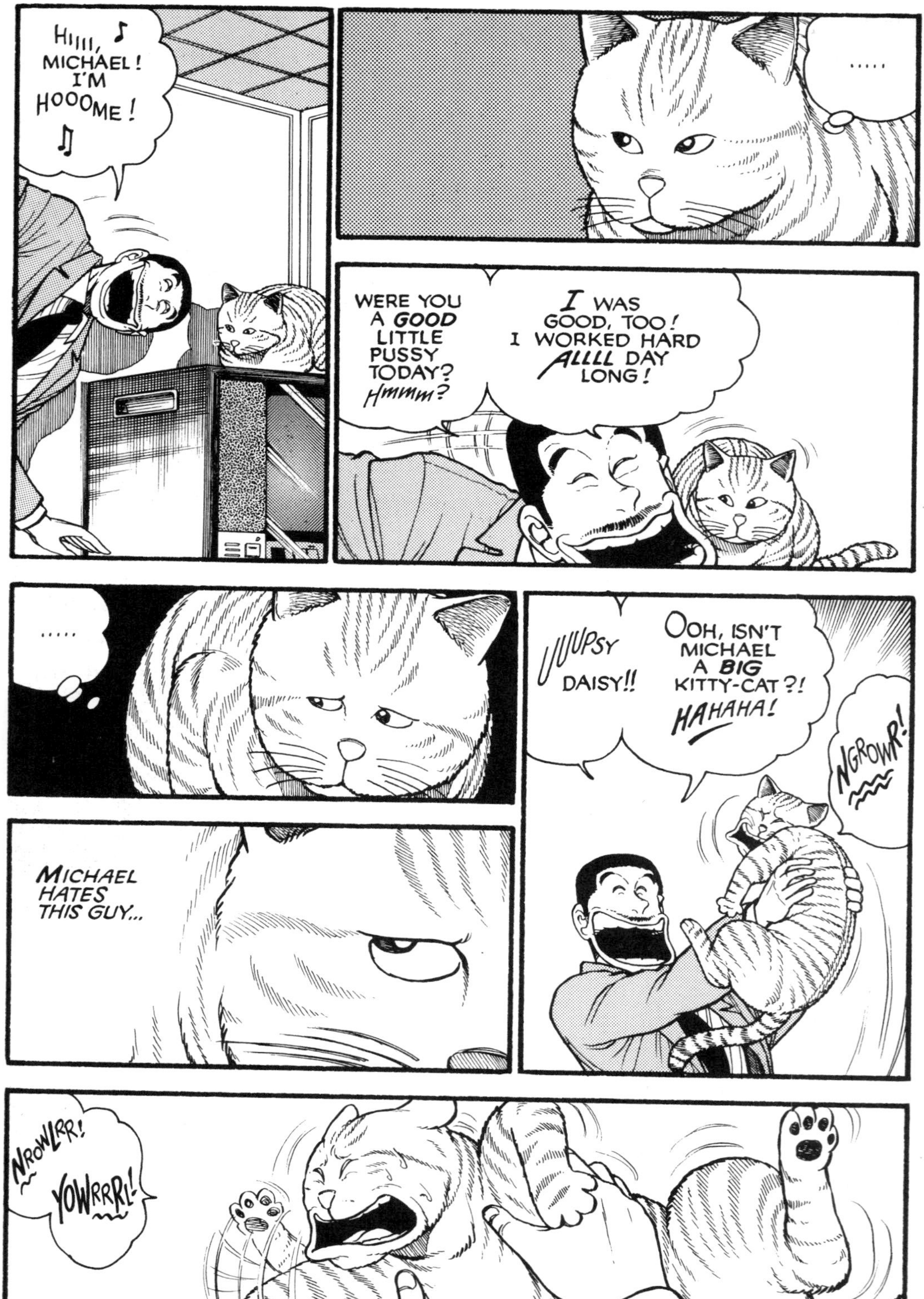

HIIII, ♪ MICHAEL! I'M HOOOME! ♫
.....
WERE YOU A GOOD LITTLE PUSSY TODAY? HMMM?
I WAS GOOD, TOO! I WORKED HARD ALLLL DAY LONG!
.....
MICHAEL HATES THIS GUY...
UUUPSY DAISY!!
OOH, ISN'T MICHAEL A BIG KITTY-CAT?! HAHAHA!
NGROWR!
NROWLRR! YOWRRRL!

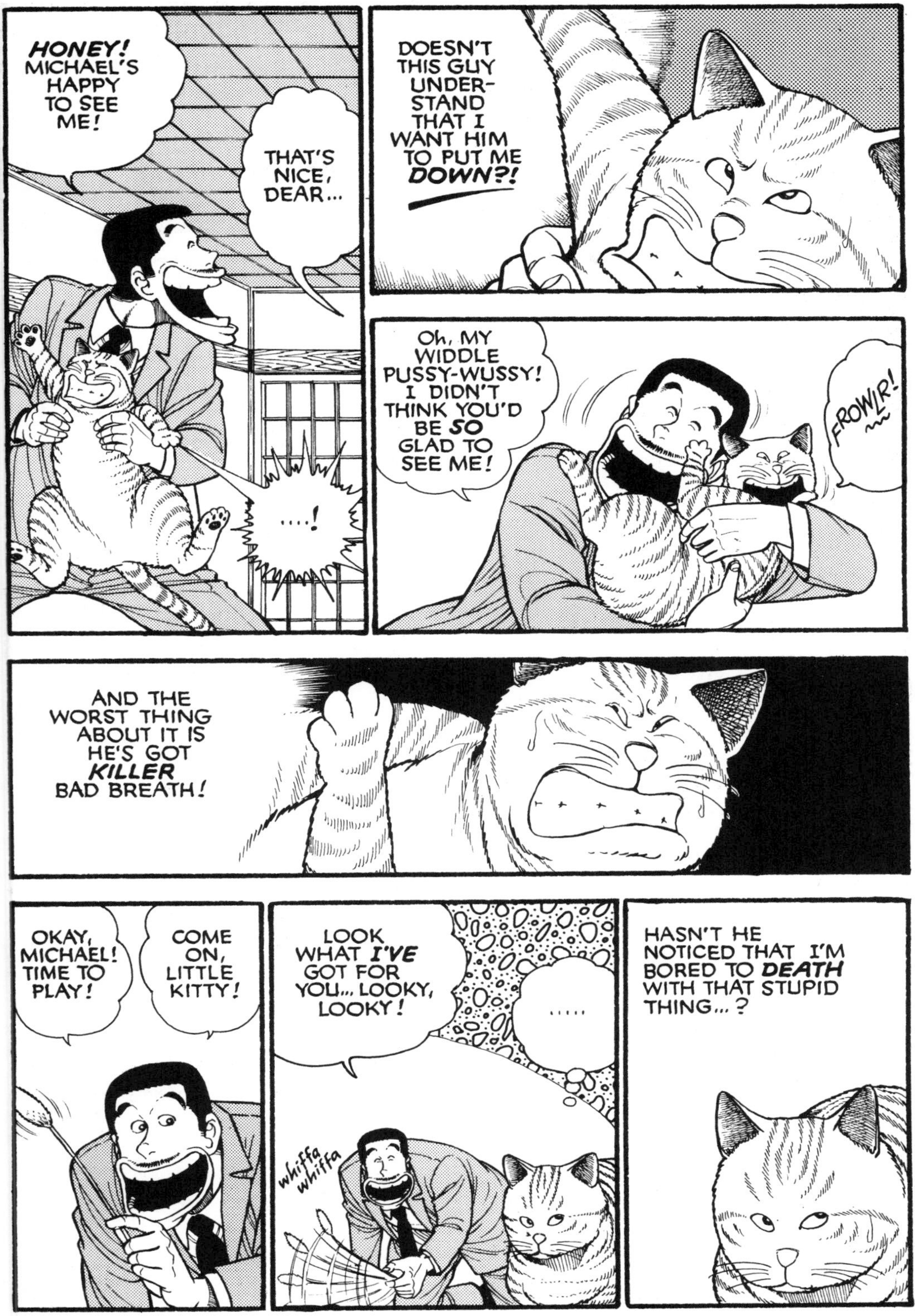
HONEY! MICHAEL'S HAPPY TO SEE ME!
THAT'S NICE, DEAR...
....!
DOESN'T THIS GUY UNDER-STAND THAT I WANT HIM TO PUT ME DOWN?!
Oh, MY WIDDLE PUSSY-WUSSY! I DIDN'T THINK YOU'D BE SO GLAD TO SEE ME!
FROWLR!
AND THE WORST THING ABOUT IT IS HE'S GOT KILLER BAD BREATH!
OKAY, MICHAEL! TIME TO PLAY!
COME ON, LITTLE KITTY!
LOOK WHAT I'VE GOT FOR YOU... LOOKY, LOOKY!
whiffa whiffa
.....
HASN'T HE NOTICED THAT I'M BORED TO DEATH WITH THAT STUPID THING...?

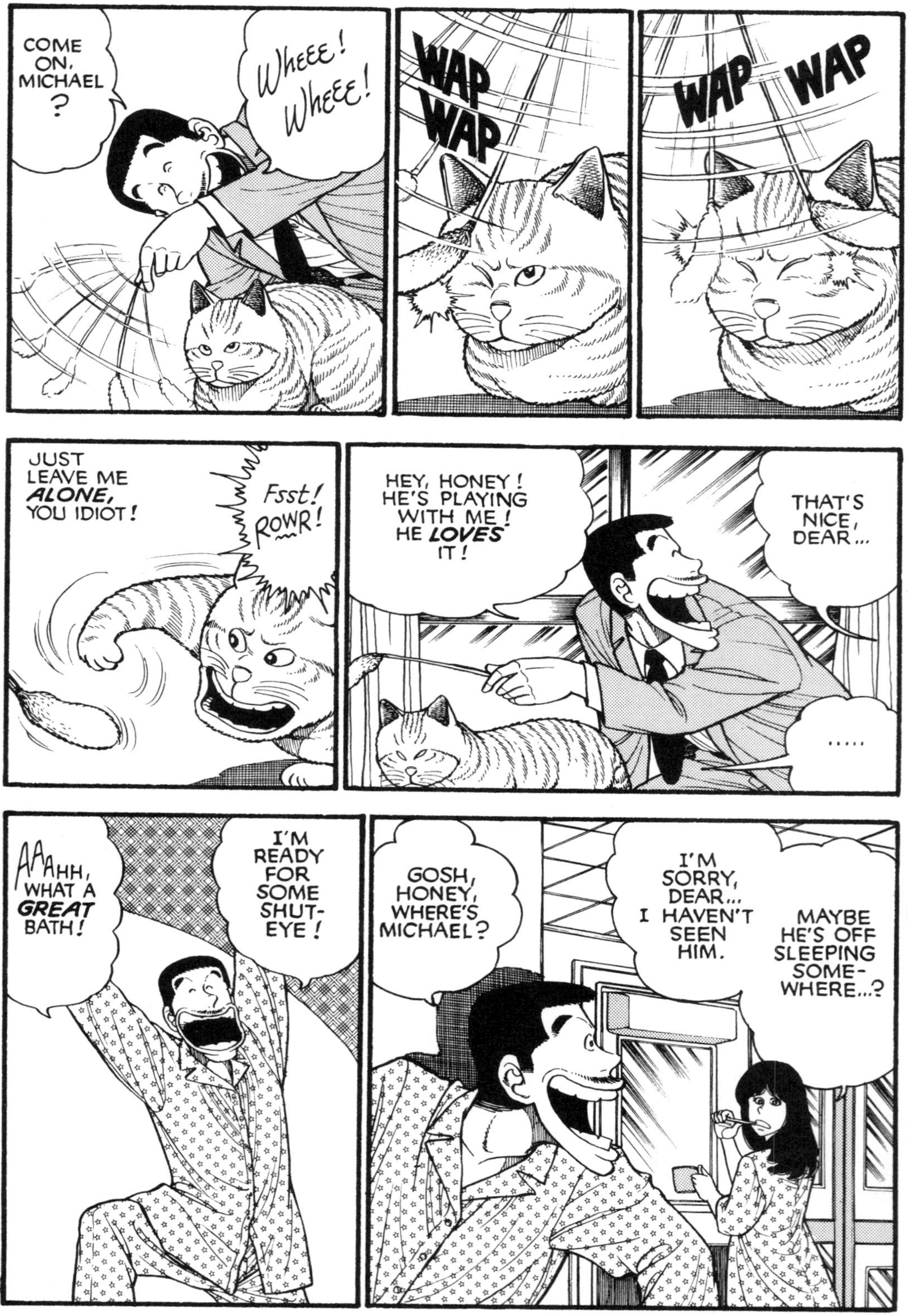
COME ON, MICHAEL ?
WhEEE! WhEEE!
WAP WAP
WAP WAP
JUST LEAVE ME ALONE, YOU IDIOT!
Fsst! ROWR!
HEY, HONEY! HE'S PLAYING WITH ME! HE LOVES IT!
THAT'S NICE, DEAR...
.....
AAAHH, WHAT A GREAT BATH!
I'M READY FOR SOME SHUT-EYE!
GOSH, HONEY, WHERE'S MICHAEL?
I'M SORRY, DEAR... I HAVEN'T SEEN HIM.
MAYBE HE'S OFF SLEEPING SOME-WHERE...?

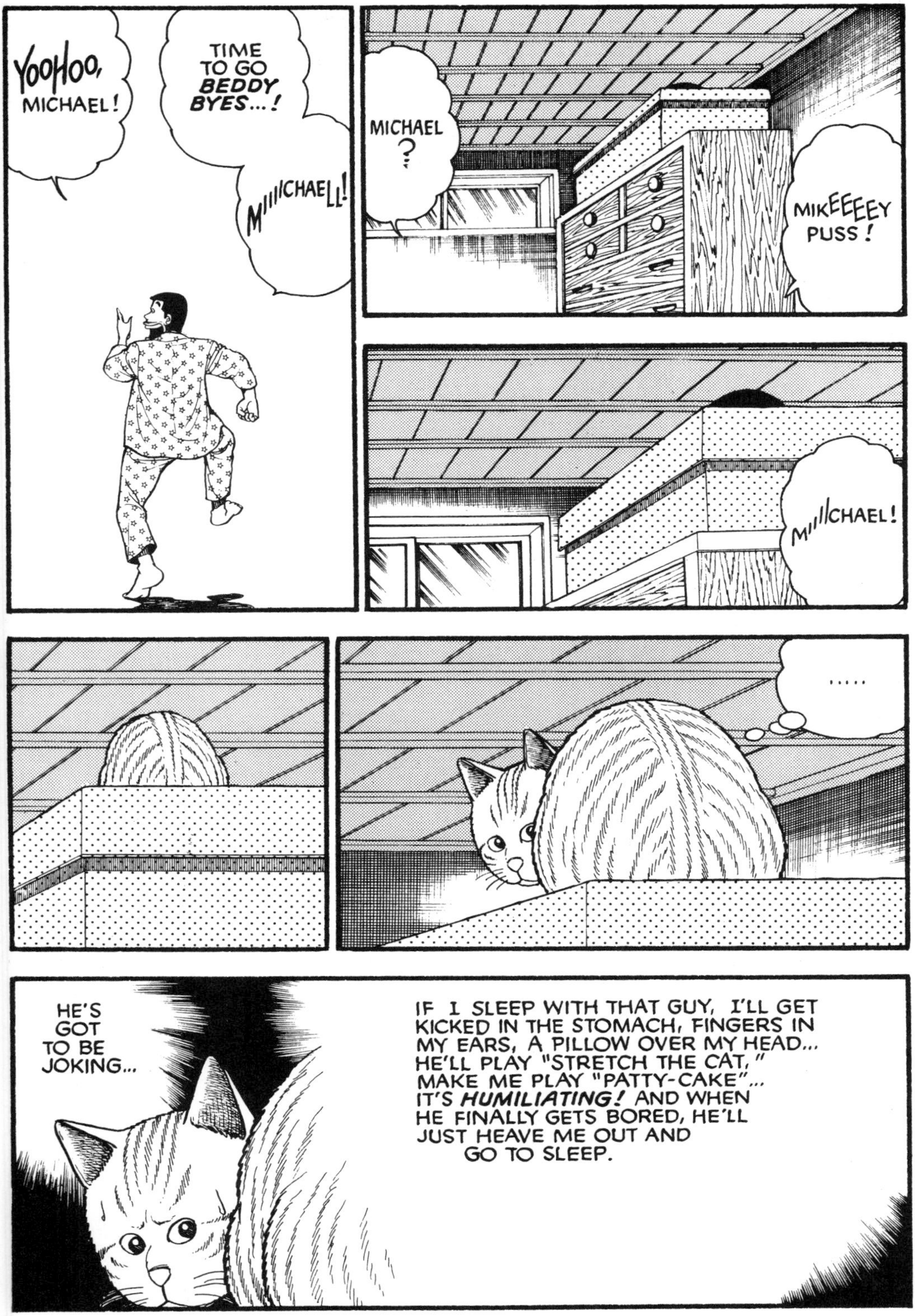
YOOHOO, MICHAEL!
TIME TO GO *BEDDY BYES*...!
MIIIICHAELL!
MICHAEL ?
MIKEEEEEY PUSS!
MIIICHAEL!
.....
HE'S GOT TO BE JOKING...
IF I SLEEP WITH THAT GUY, I'LL GET KICKED IN THE STOMACH, FINGERS IN MY EARS, A PILLOW OVER MY HEAD... HE'LL PLAY "STRETCH THE CAT," MAKE ME PLAY "PATTY-CAKE"... IT'S *HUMILIATING!* AND WHEN HE FINALLY GETS BORED, HE'LL JUST HEAVE ME OUT AND GO TO SLEEP.

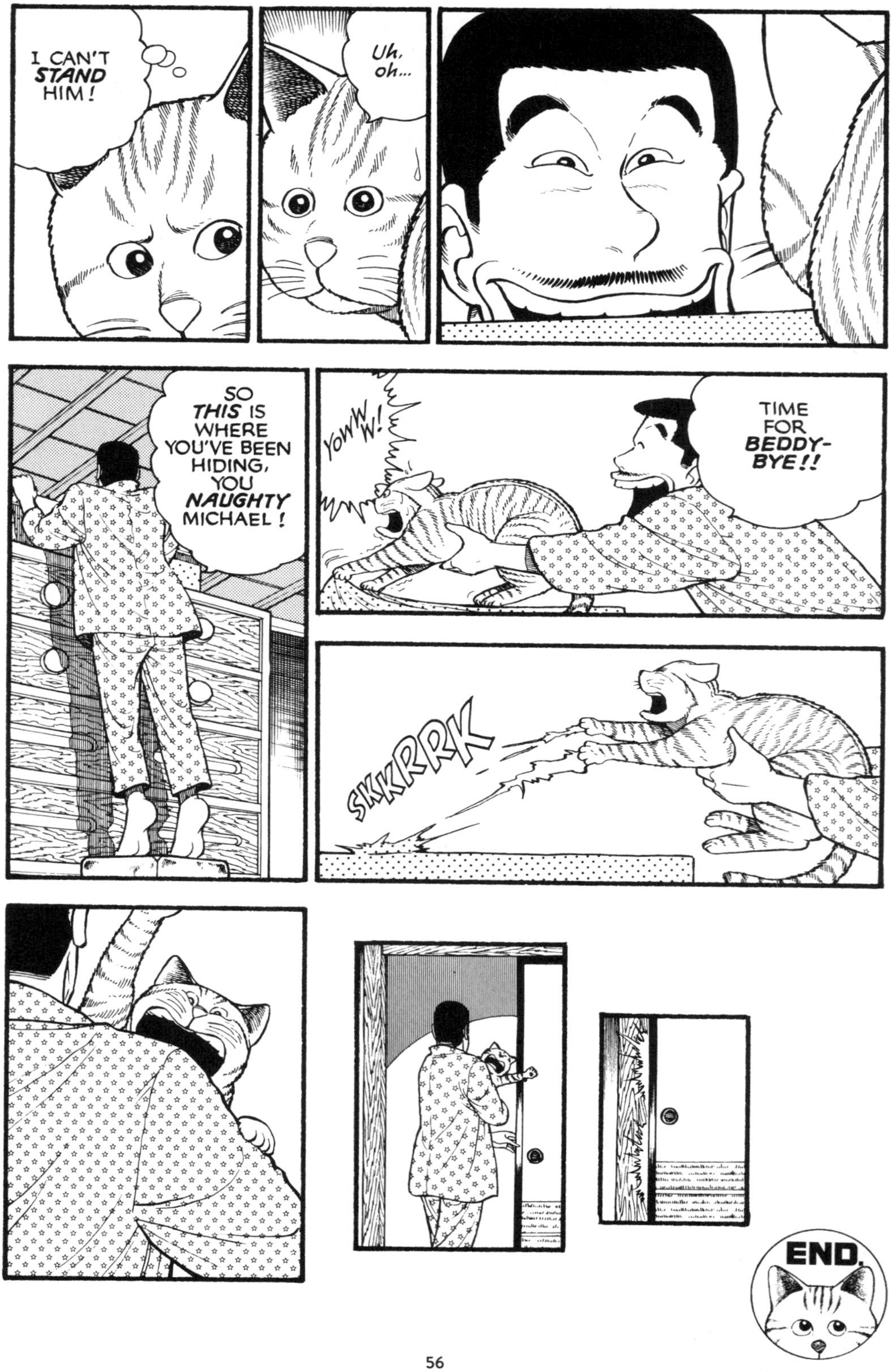
I CAN'T STAND HIM!
Uh, oh...
SO THIS IS WHERE YOU'VE BEEN HIDING, YOU NAUGHTY MICHAEL!
YOWWW!
TIME FOR BEDDY-BYE!!
SKKRRK
END.

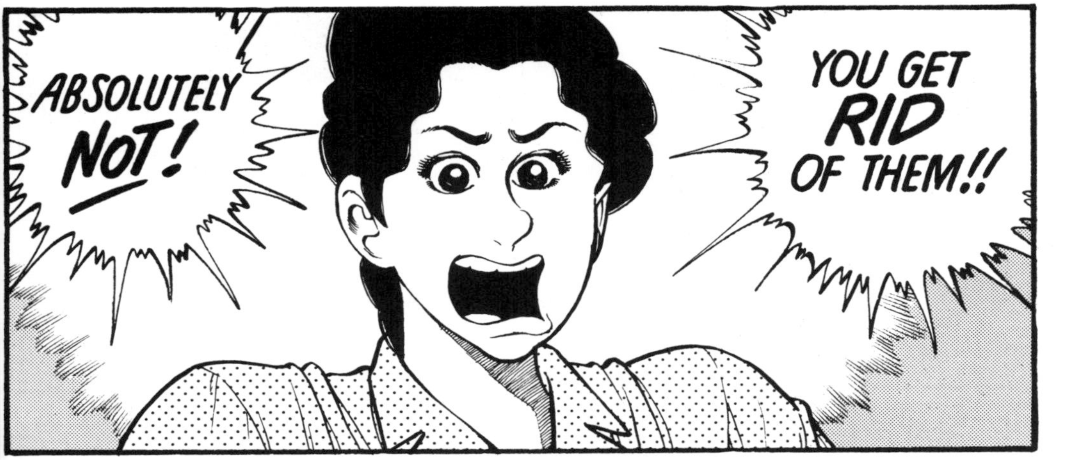
ABSOLUTELY NOT!
YOU GET RID OF THEM!!

# CURSE OF THE CAT'S PAW

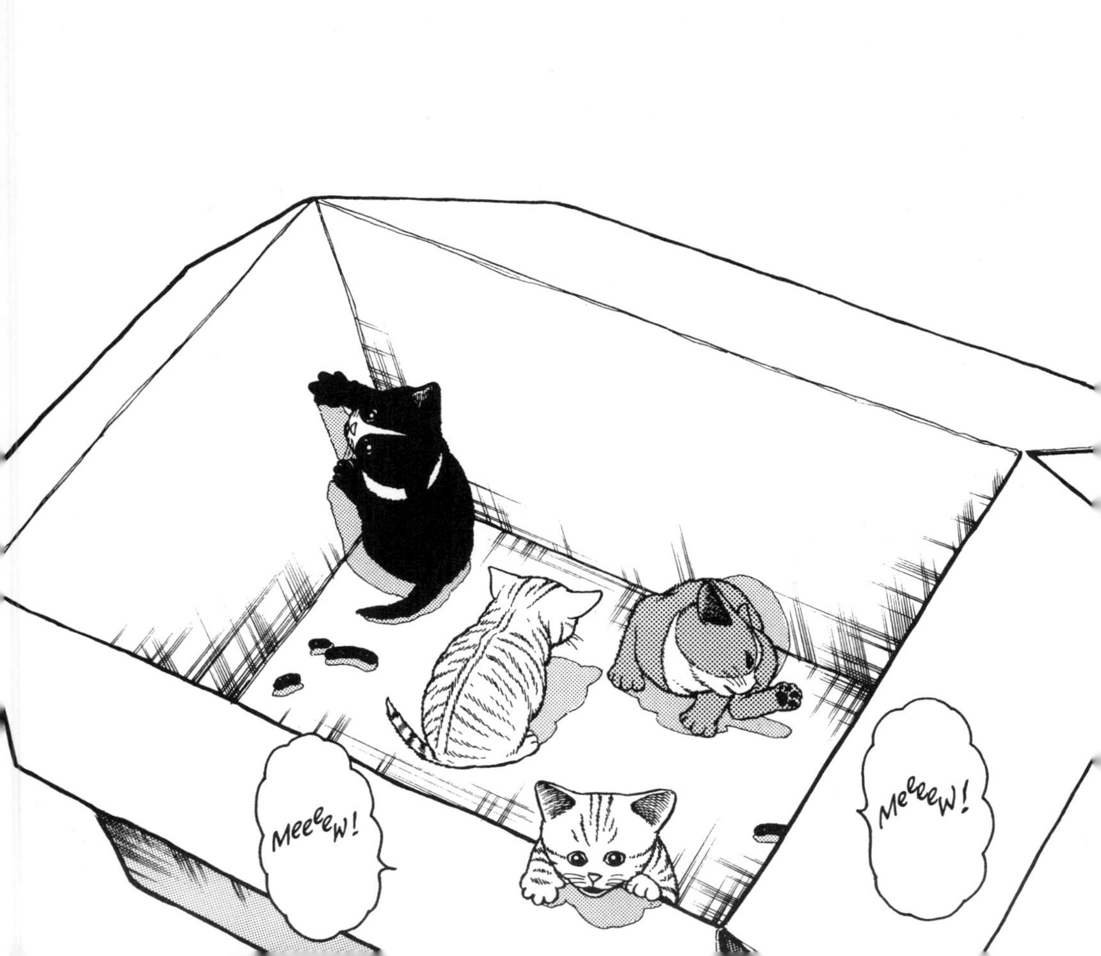
MeeeeW!
MeeeeW!

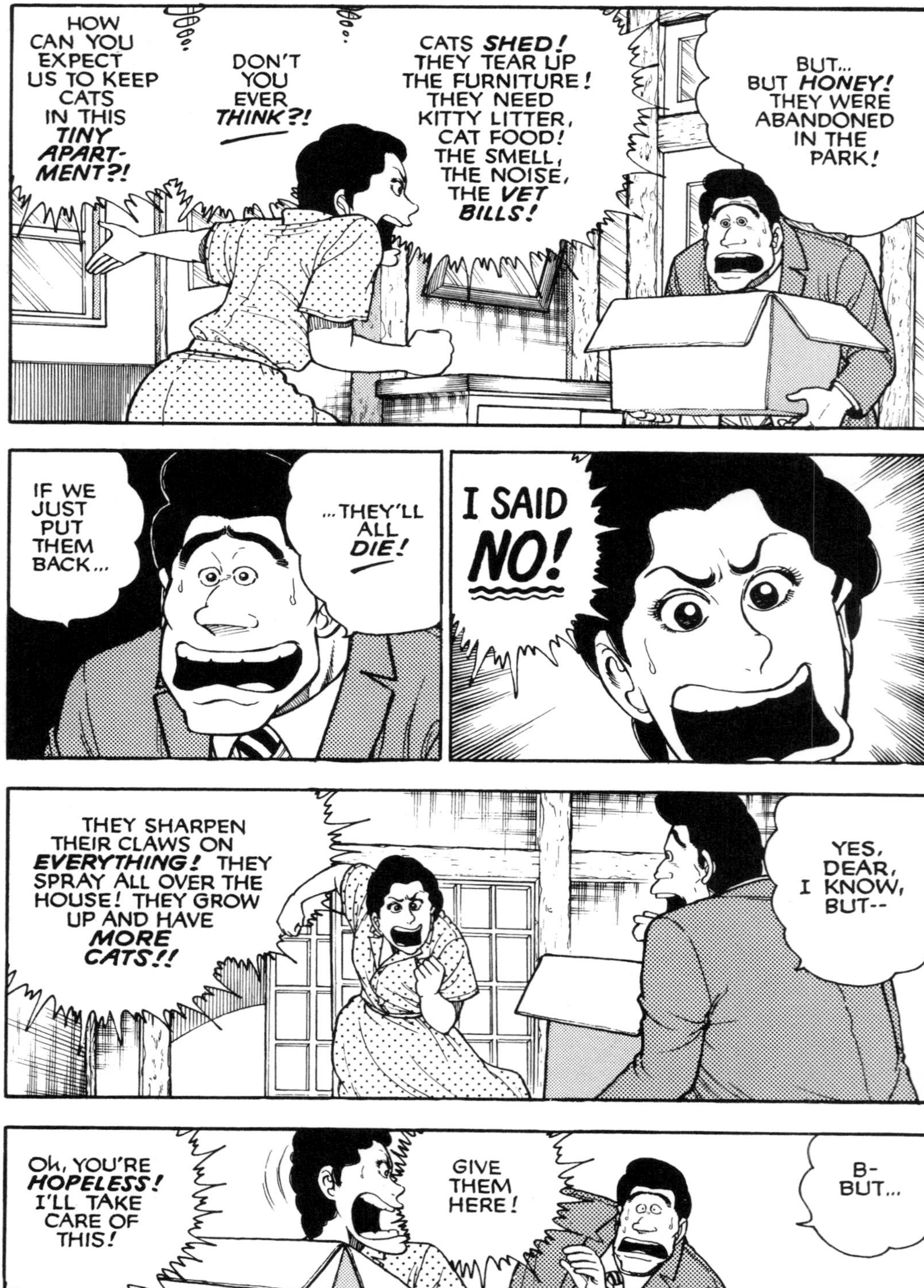
HOW CAN YOU EXPECT US TO KEEP CATS IN THIS TINY APARTMENT?!
DON'T YOU EVER THINK?!
CATS SHED! THEY TEAR UP THE FURNITURE! THEY NEED KITTY LITTER, CAT FOOD! THE SMELL, THE NOISE, THE VET BILLS!
BUT... BUT HONEY! THEY WERE ABANDONED IN THE PARK!
IF WE JUST PUT THEM BACK...
...THEY'LL ALL DIE!
I SAID NO!
THEY SHARPEN THEIR CLAWS ON EVERYTHING! THEY SPRAY ALL OVER THE HOUSE! THEY GROW UP AND HAVE MORE CATS!!
YES, DEAR, I KNOW, BUT--
OH, YOU'RE HOPELESS! I'LL TAKE CARE OF THIS!
GIVE THEM HERE!
B-BUT...

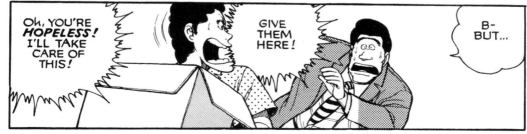

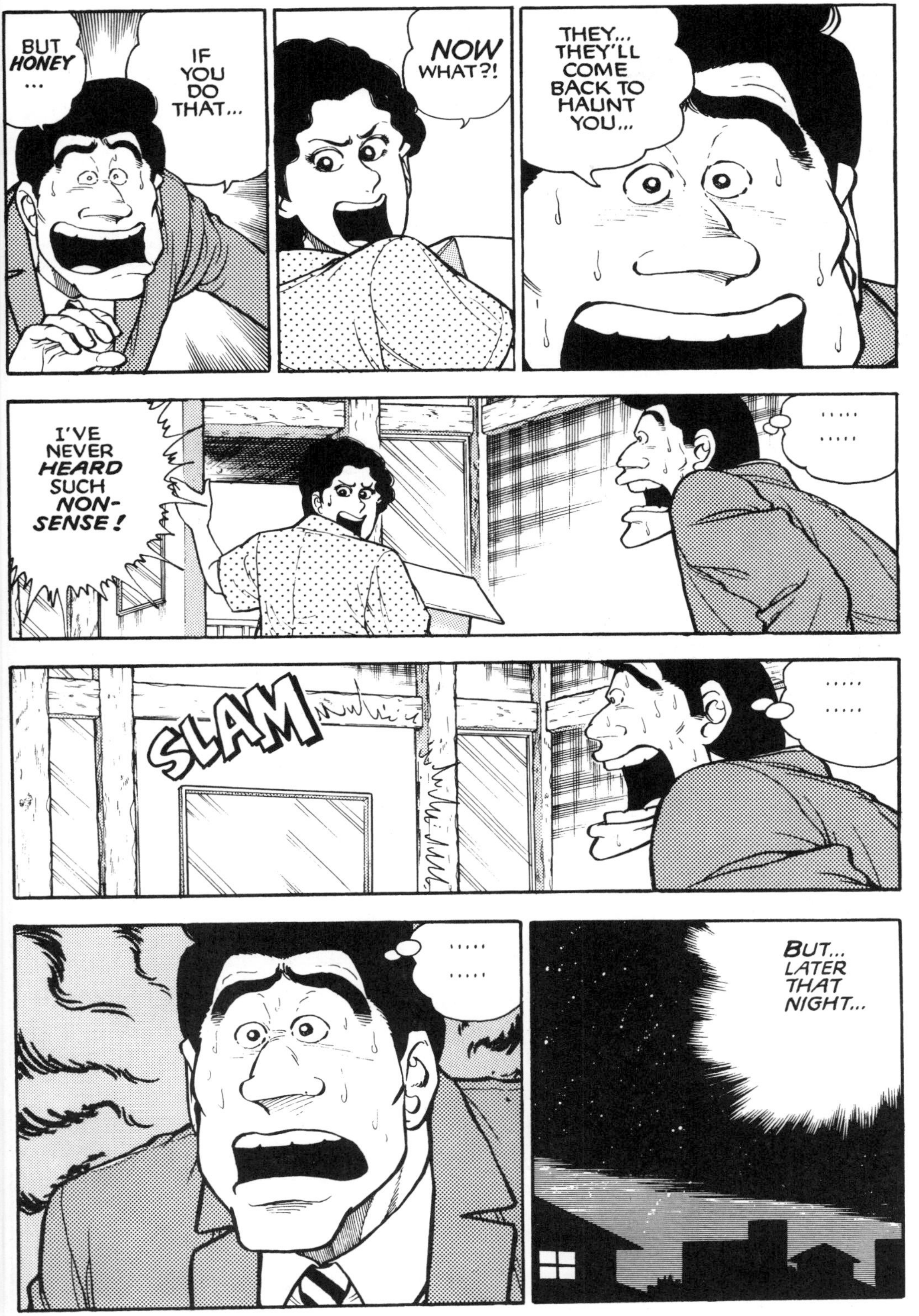
BUT HONEY ...
IF YOU DO THAT...
NOW WHAT?!
THEY... THEY'LL COME BACK TO HAUNT YOU...
I'VE NEVER HEARD SUCH NON-SENSE!
.....
.....
SLAM
.....
.....
.....
.....
BUT... LATER THAT NIGHT...

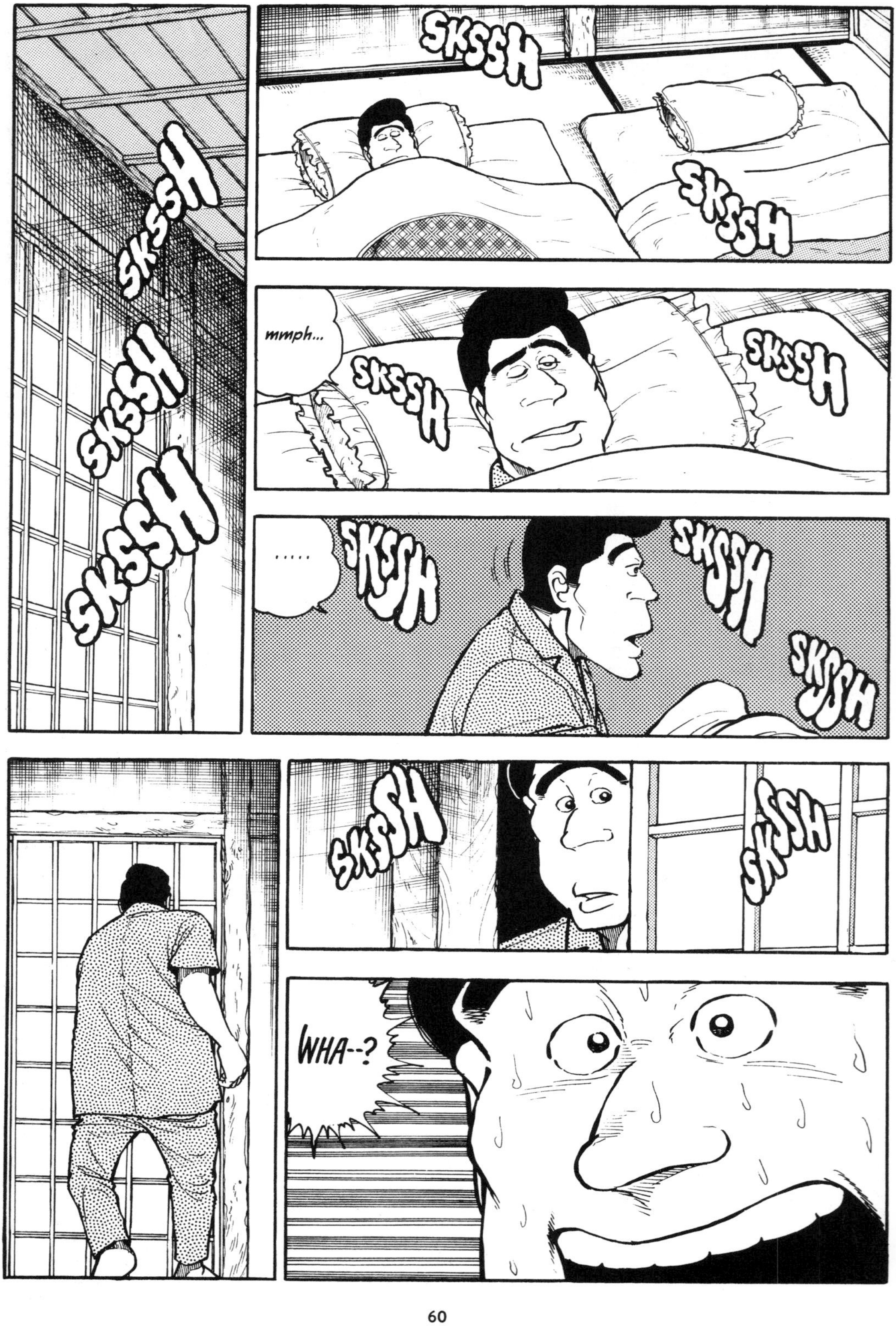
SKSSH
SKSSH
SKSSH
SKSSH
SKSSH
mmph...
SKSSH
SKSSH
.....
SKSSH
SKSSH
SKSSH
SKSSH
SKSSH
WHA--?

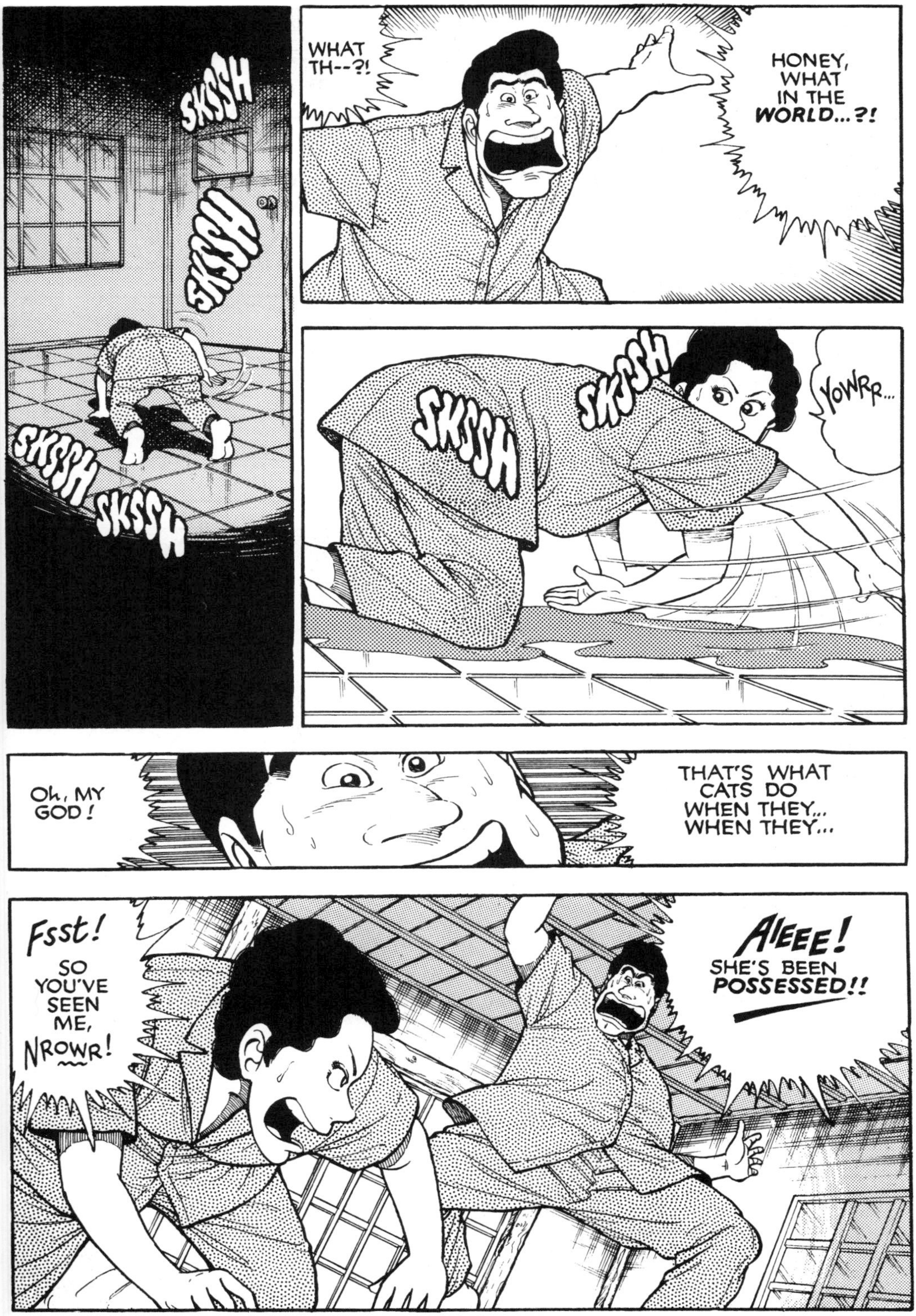
SKSSH
SKSSH
SKSSH
SKSSH
WHAT TH--?!
HONEY, WHAT IN THE ***WORLD...?!***
SKSSH
SKSSH
YOWRR...
OH, MY GOD!
THAT'S WHAT CATS DO WHEN THEY... WHEN THEY...
Fsst!
SO YOU'VE SEEN ME, NROWR!
AIEEE!
SHE'S BEEN **POSSESSED!!**

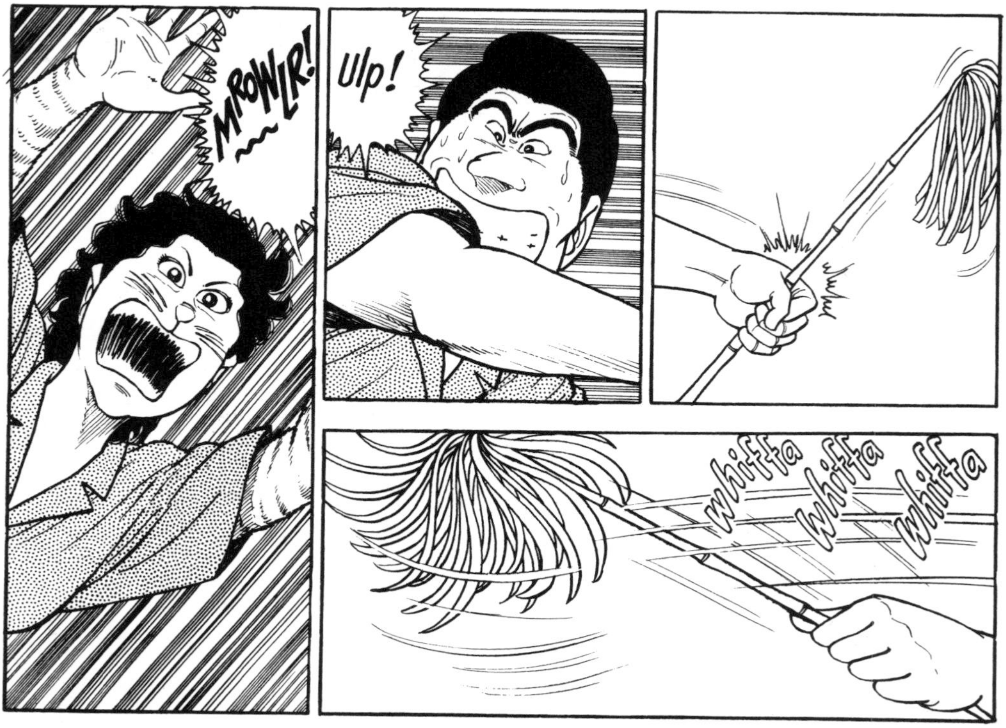
MROWLR!
Ulp!
whiffa whiffa whiffa

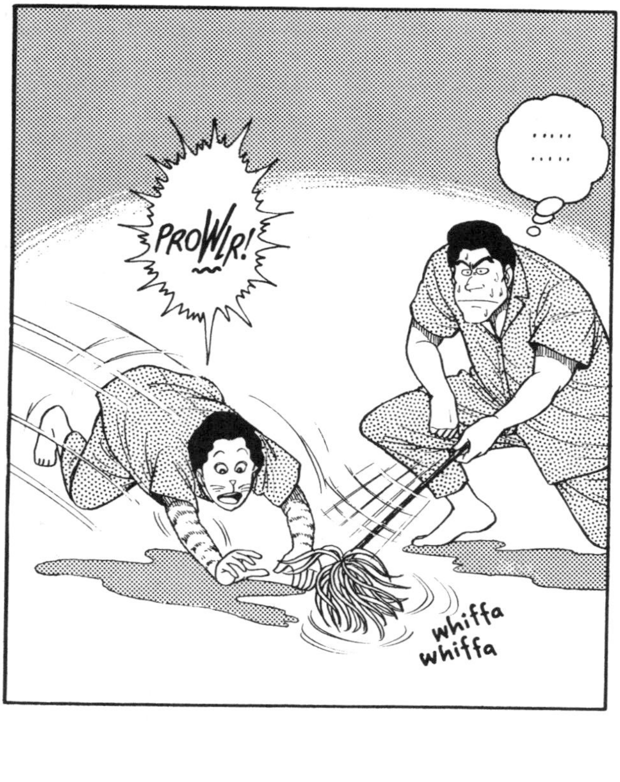
PROWLR!
.....
.....
whiffa
whiffa

SO LET THIS BE A LESSON TO THEE! BEWARE YE THE **CURSE OF THE CATS...** IF THERE BE AMONGST THEE ONE WHO DOETH THAT WHICH ONLY A CAT MAY DO, STAND THEE FOREWARNED! THAT PERSON HATH BEEN **POSSESSED** BY THE SPIRITS OF **ABANDONED CATS!**

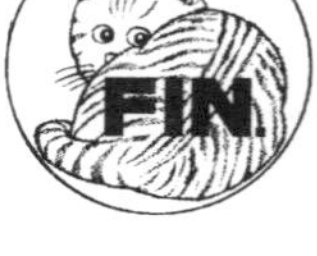
FIN

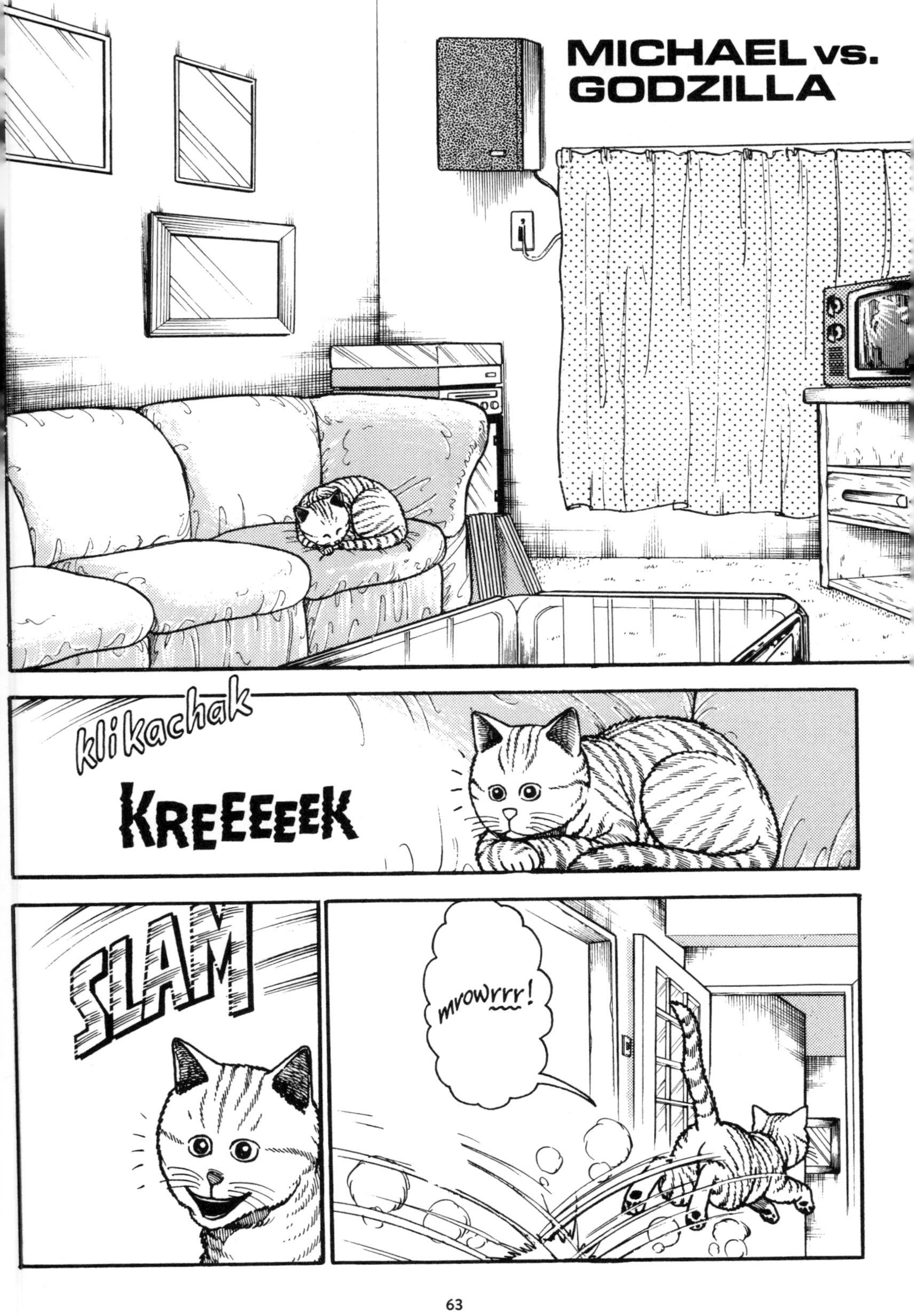
MICHAEL vs.
GODZILLA
klikachak
KREEEEEK
SLAM
mrowrrr!

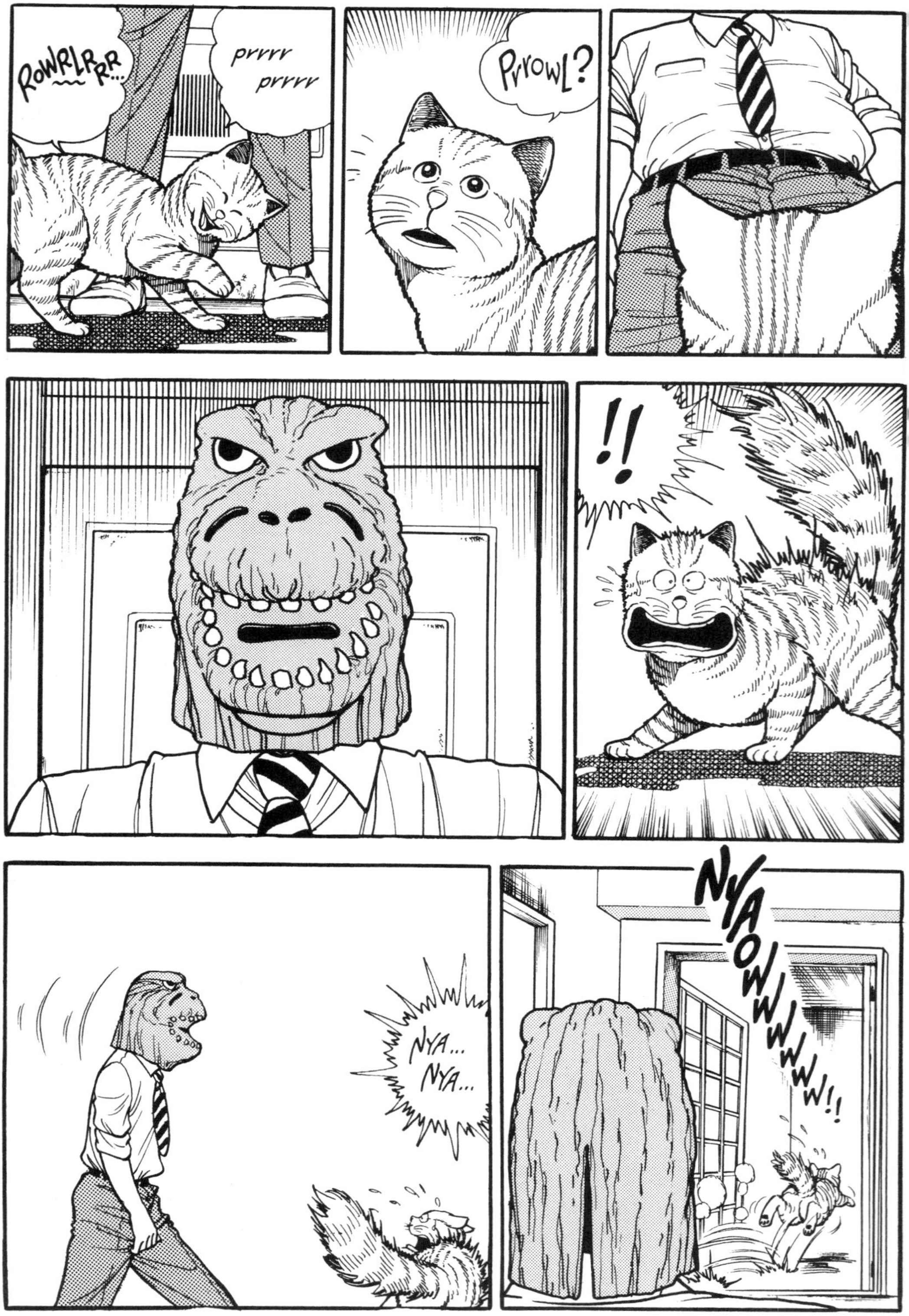
ROWRLRRR...
prrrr prrrr
PRROWL?
!!
NYA... NYA...
NYAOWWWWW!!

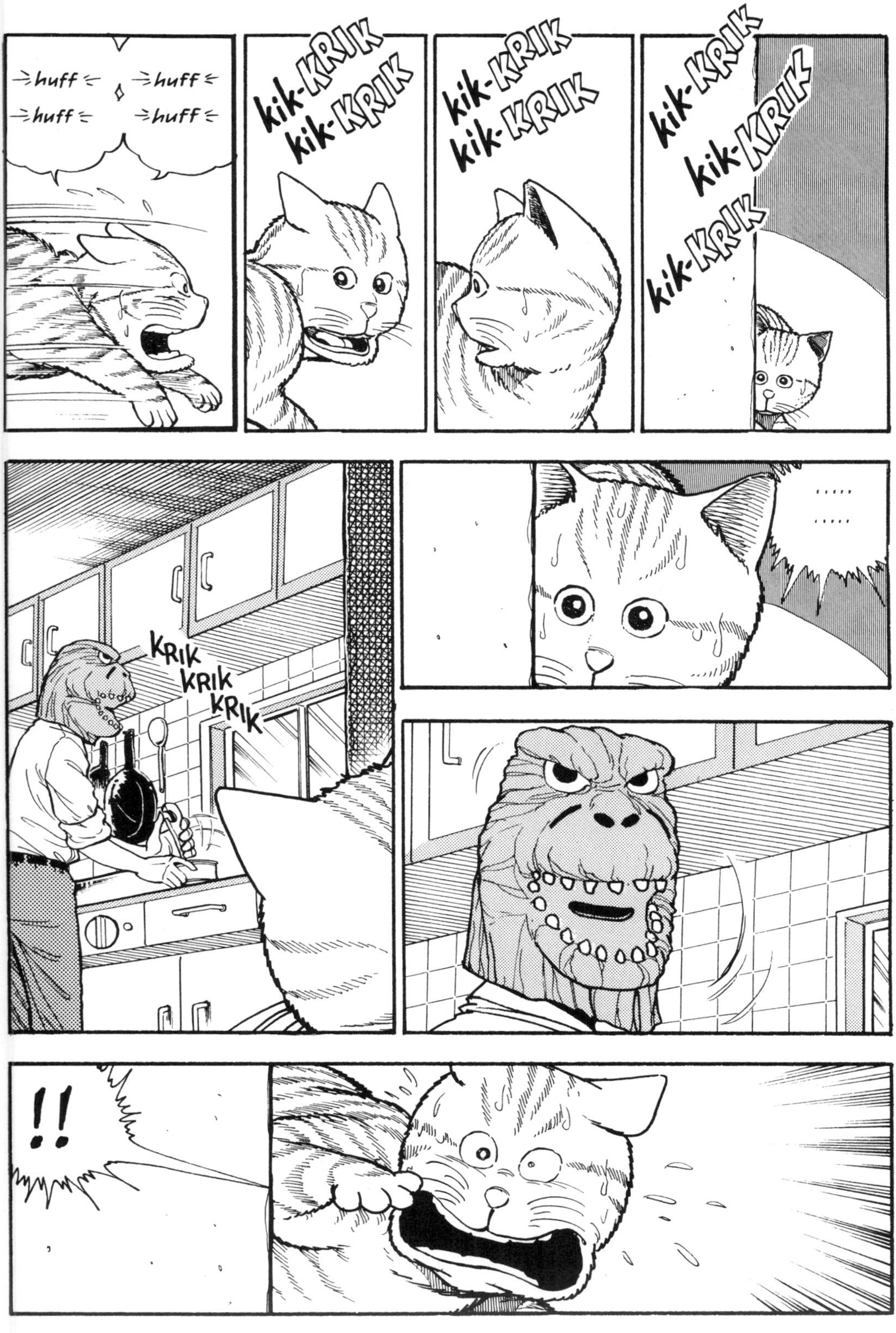
huff huff
huff huff
kik-KRIK
kik-KRIK
kik-KRIK
kik-KRIK
kik-KRIK
kik-KRIK
kik-KRIK
KRIK
KRIK
KRIK
.....
.....
!!

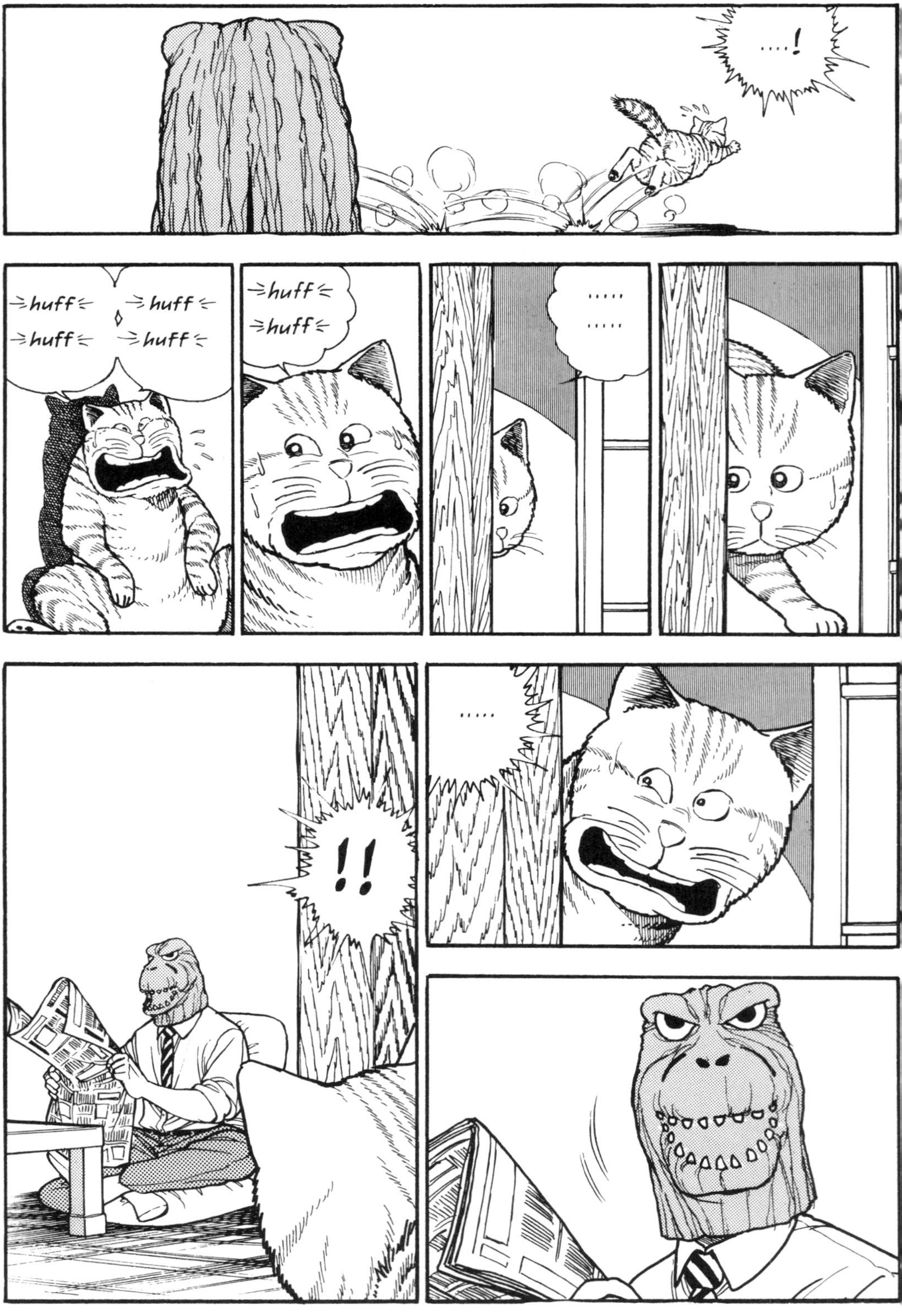

....!
huff huff huff huff
huff huff
.....
.....
!!
.....

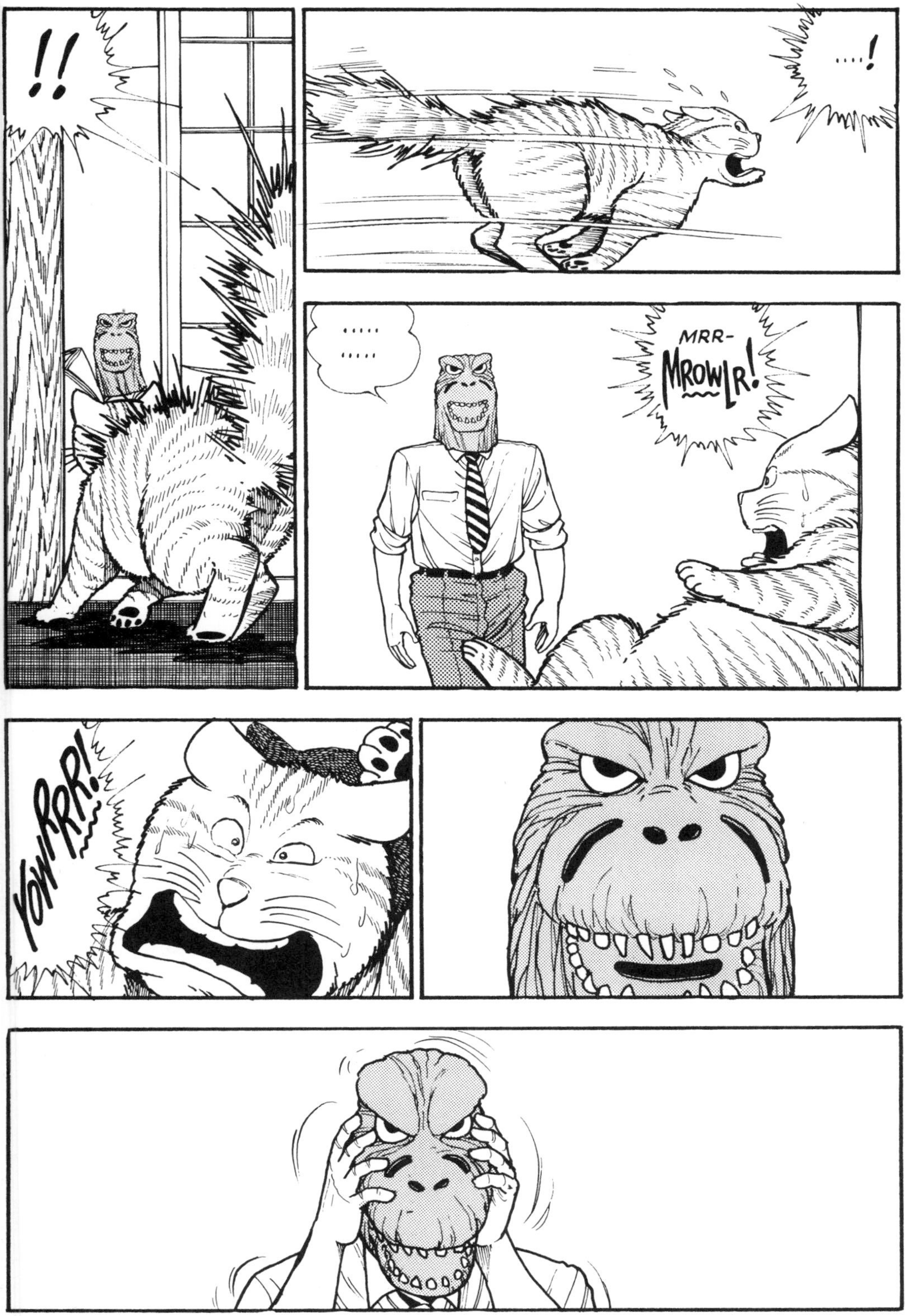
!!
....!
.....
.....
MRR-
MROWLR!
YOWRRR!

BOO!
MROW...
.....
YOWR!!
RROWL
NYOWR
MROW!
AW, COME ON, MICHAEL! IT'S NOTHING TO CRY ABOUT... COME ON!
END.

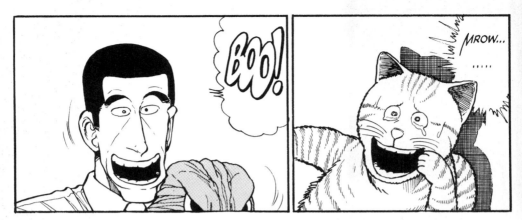

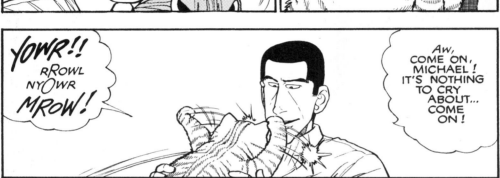

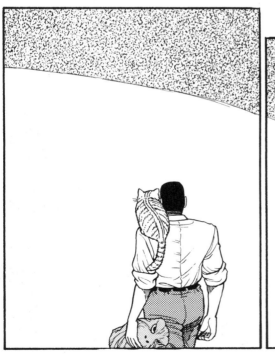

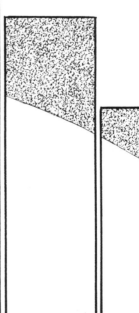

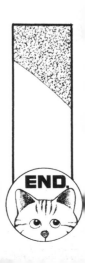

# MICHAEL
# AND THE FLY

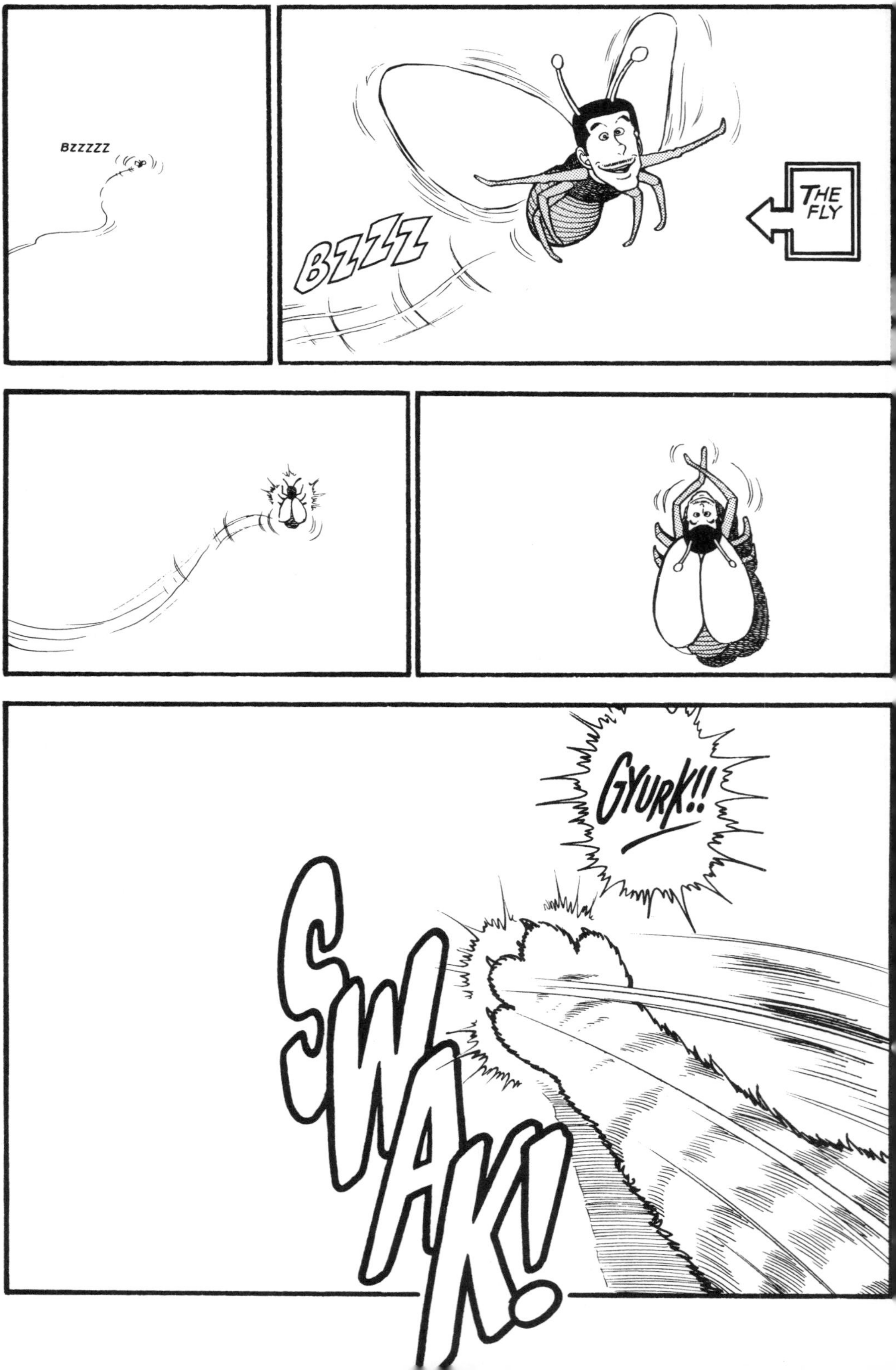
BZZZZZ
BZZZ
THE FLY
GYURK!!
SWAK!

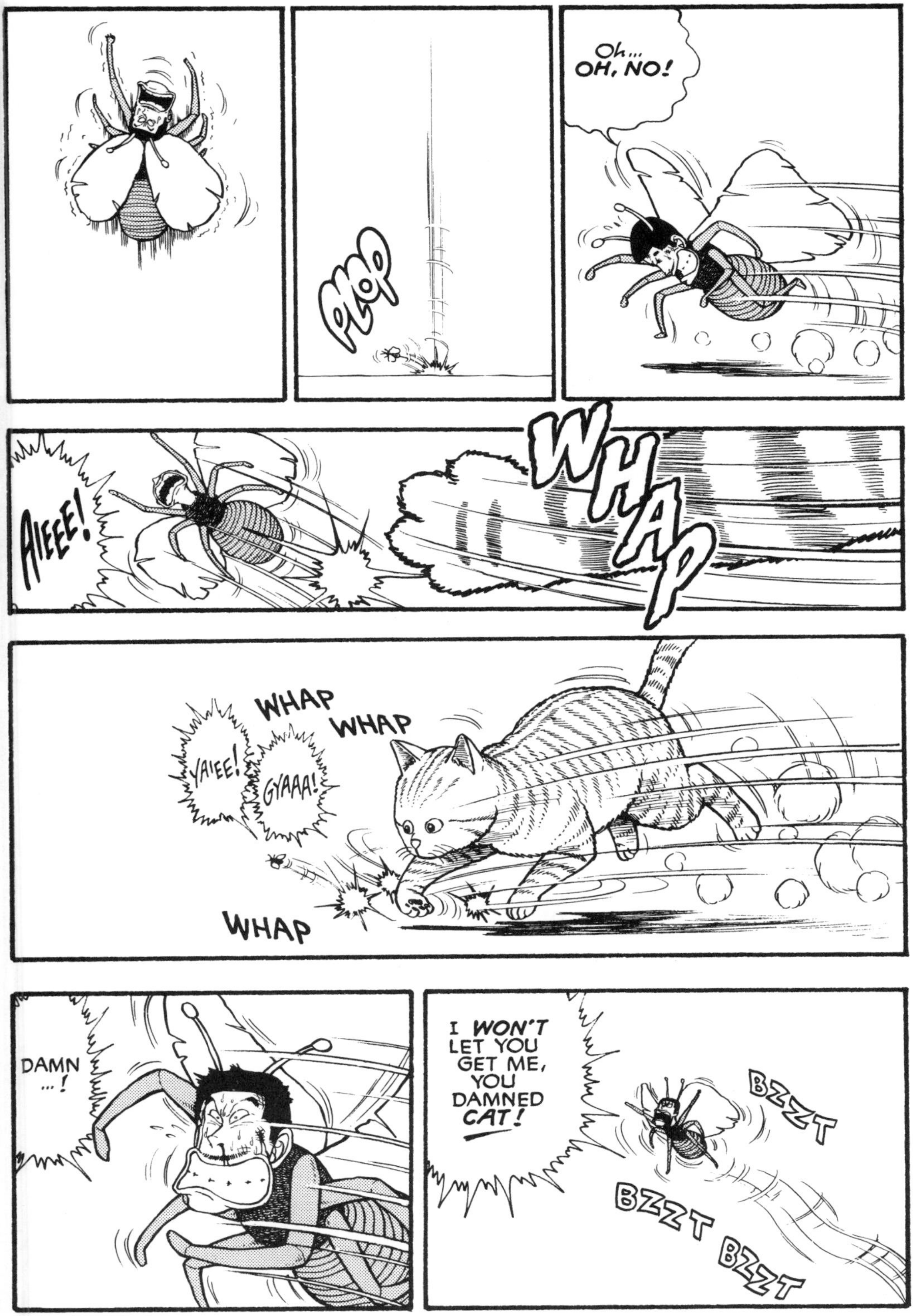

PLOP
Oh...
OH, NO!
AIEEE!
WHAP
WHAP
WHAP
YAIEE!
GYAAA!
WHAP
DAMN ...!
I WON'T LET YOU GET ME, YOU DAMNED CAT!
BZZT
BZZT BZZT

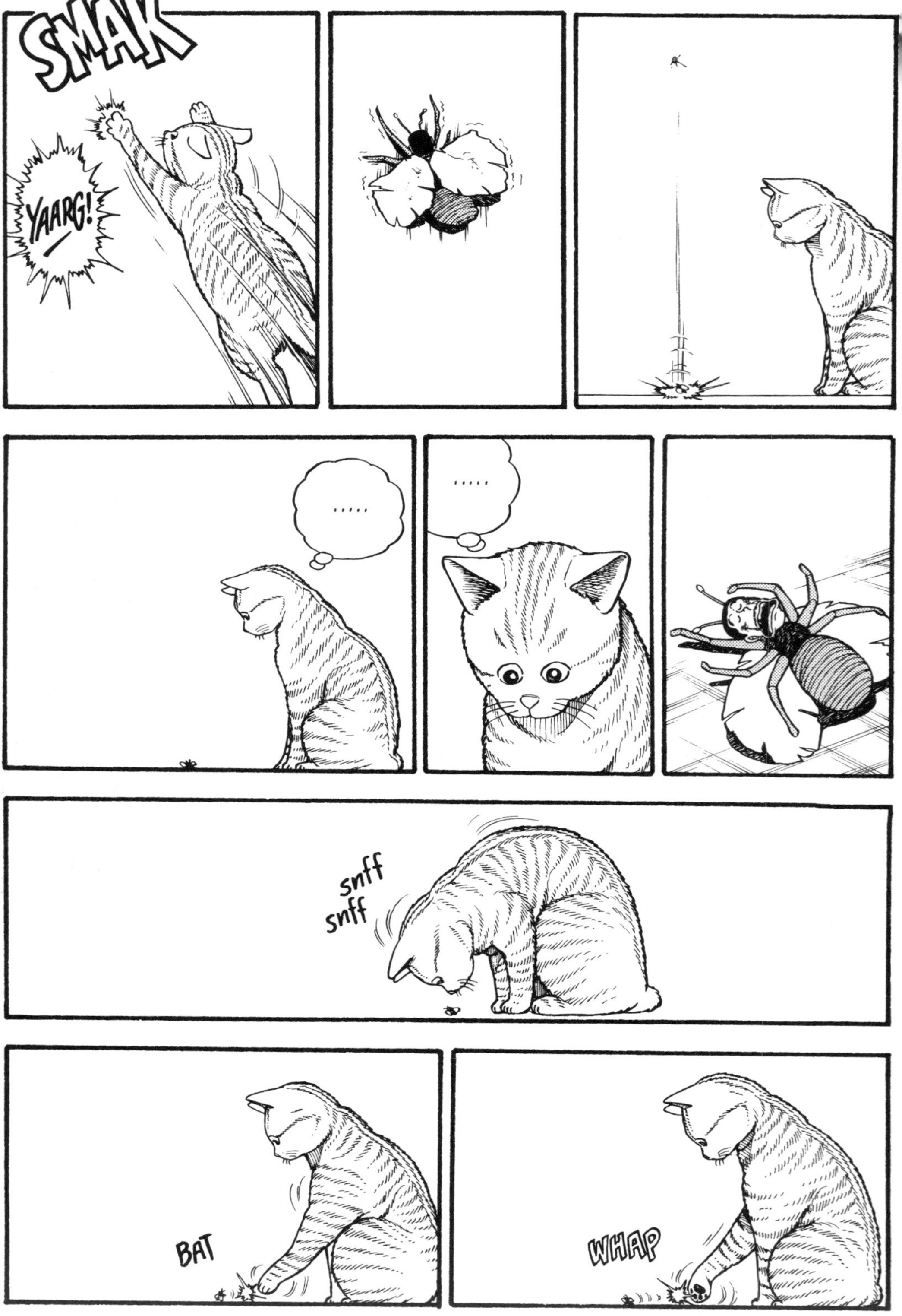
SMAK
YAARG!
.....
.....
snff
snff
BAT
WHAP

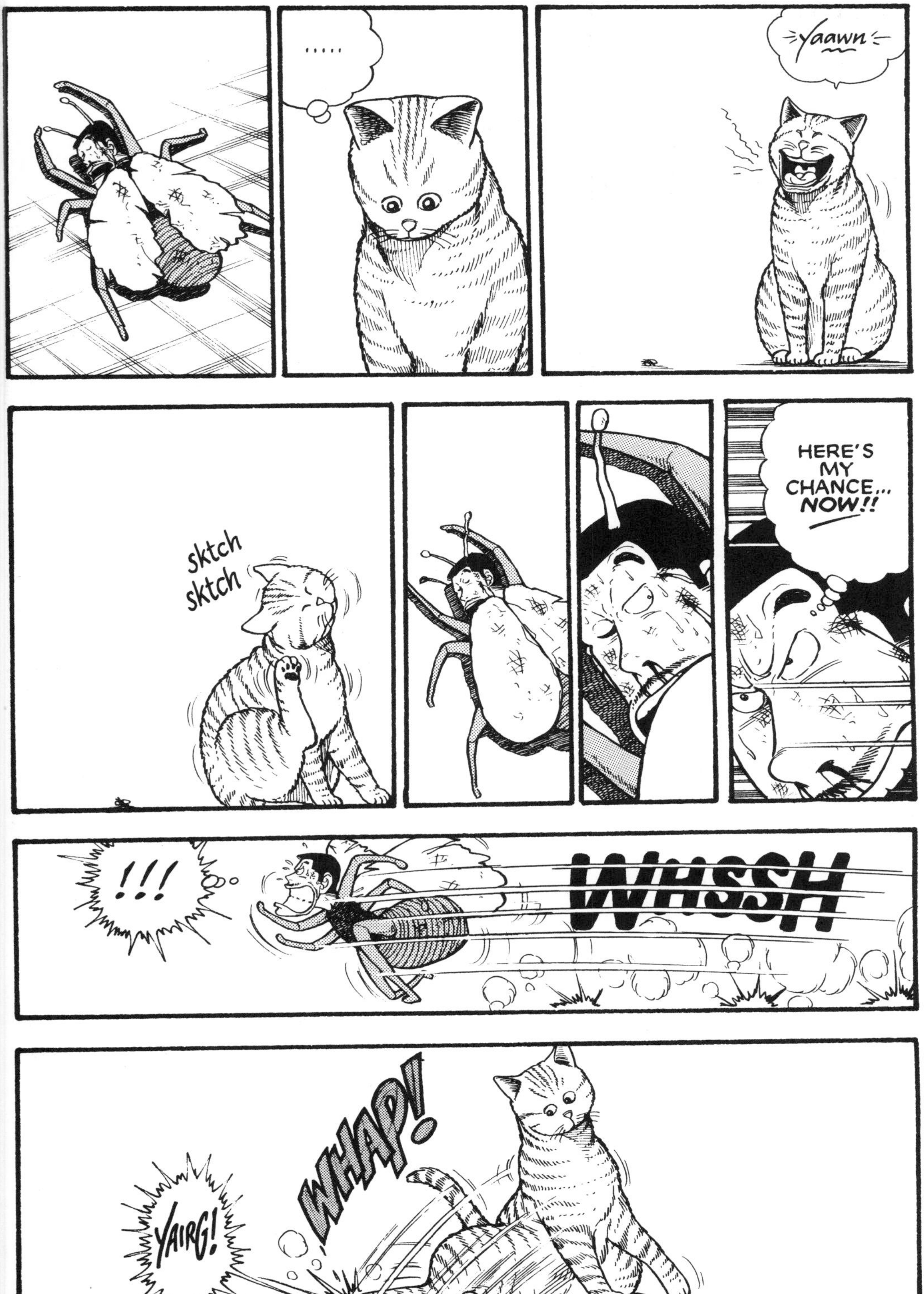
.....
Yaawn
sktch sktch
HERE'S MY CHANCE... NOW!!
!!!
WHSSH
YAIRG!
WHAP!

HRNNG...
!!!
WHSSSH
GNNARK!
SMAK
WHSSSH
WHAP
DAMMIT, CAT, IF YOU'RE GOING TO KILL ME, KILL ME!!
.....
FIN

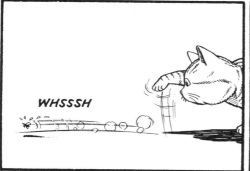

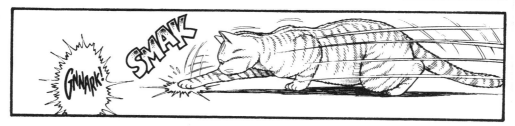

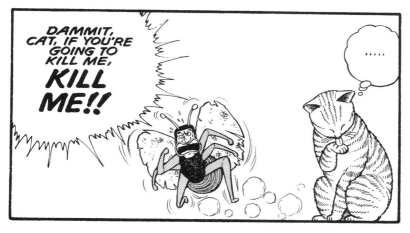

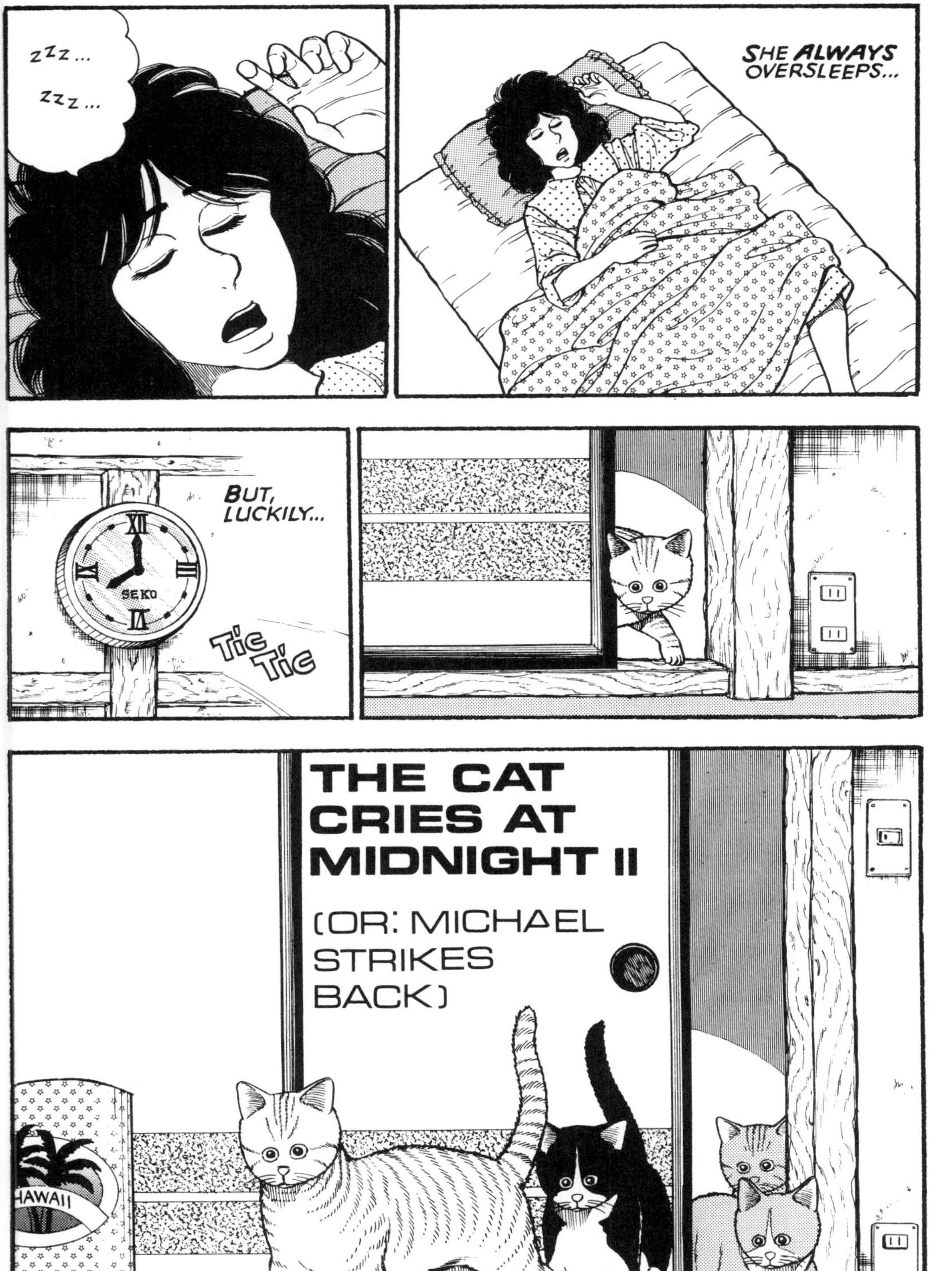

ZZZ...
ZZZ...
SHE ALWAYS OVERSLEEPS...
BUT, LUCKILY...
SEKO
TIC TIC
THE CAT CRIES AT MIDNIGHT II
(OR: MICHAEL STRIKES BACK)
HAWAII

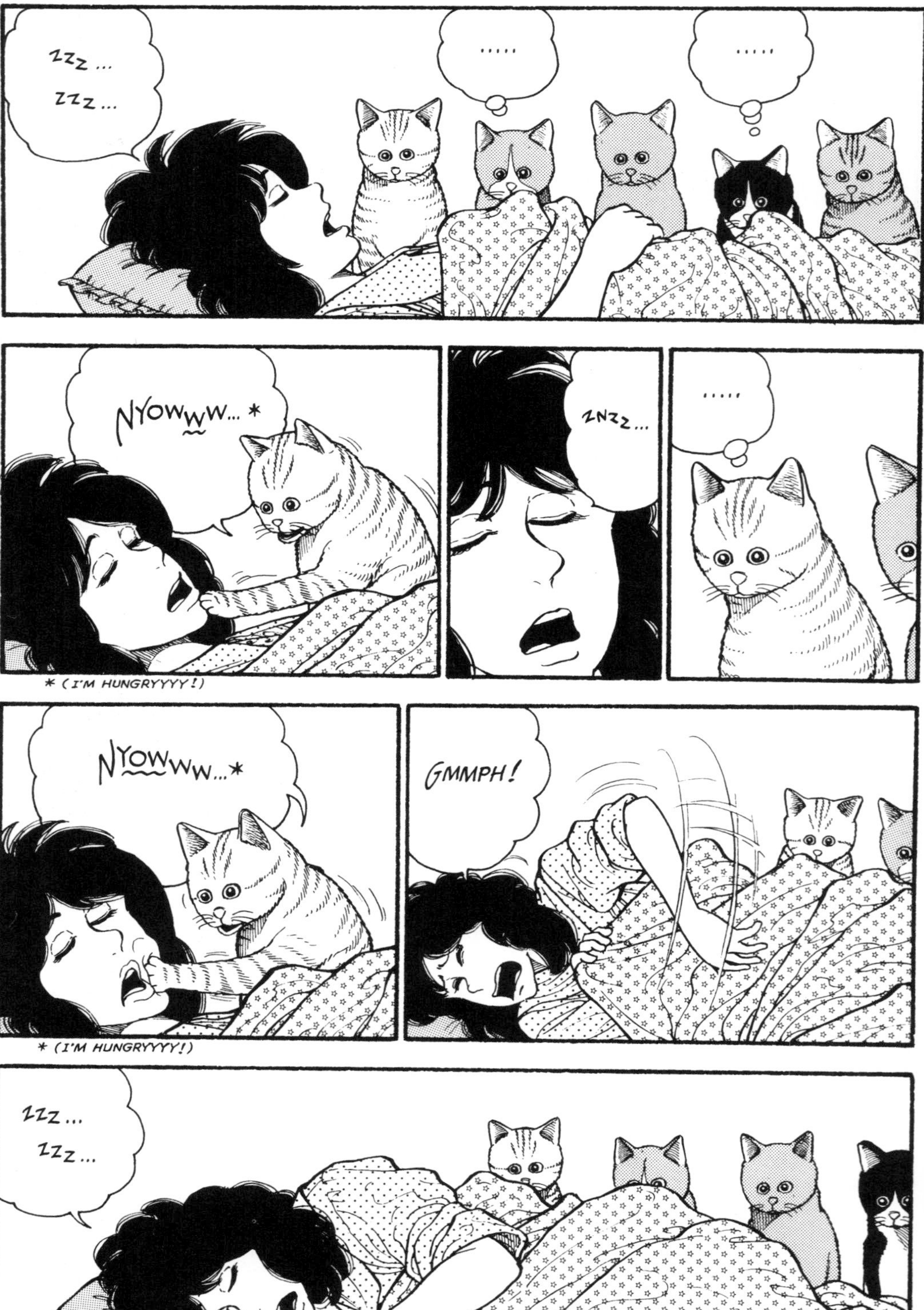
ZZZ... ZZZ...
.....
.....
NYOWWW...*
* (I'M HUNGRYYYY!)
ZNZZ...
.....
NYOWWW...*
* (I'M HUNGRYYYY!)
GMMPH!
ZZZ... ZZZ...

NYOWWW...
NYOWWW...
NYOWW...
NYOWWW...
Mmph... geddout...!

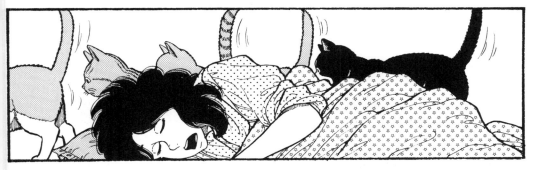

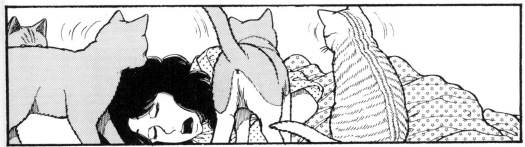

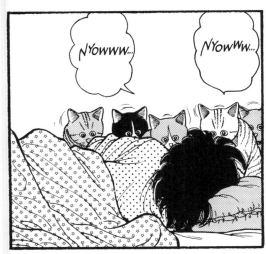

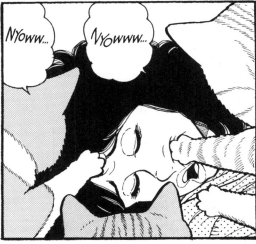

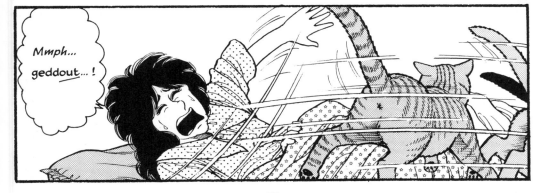

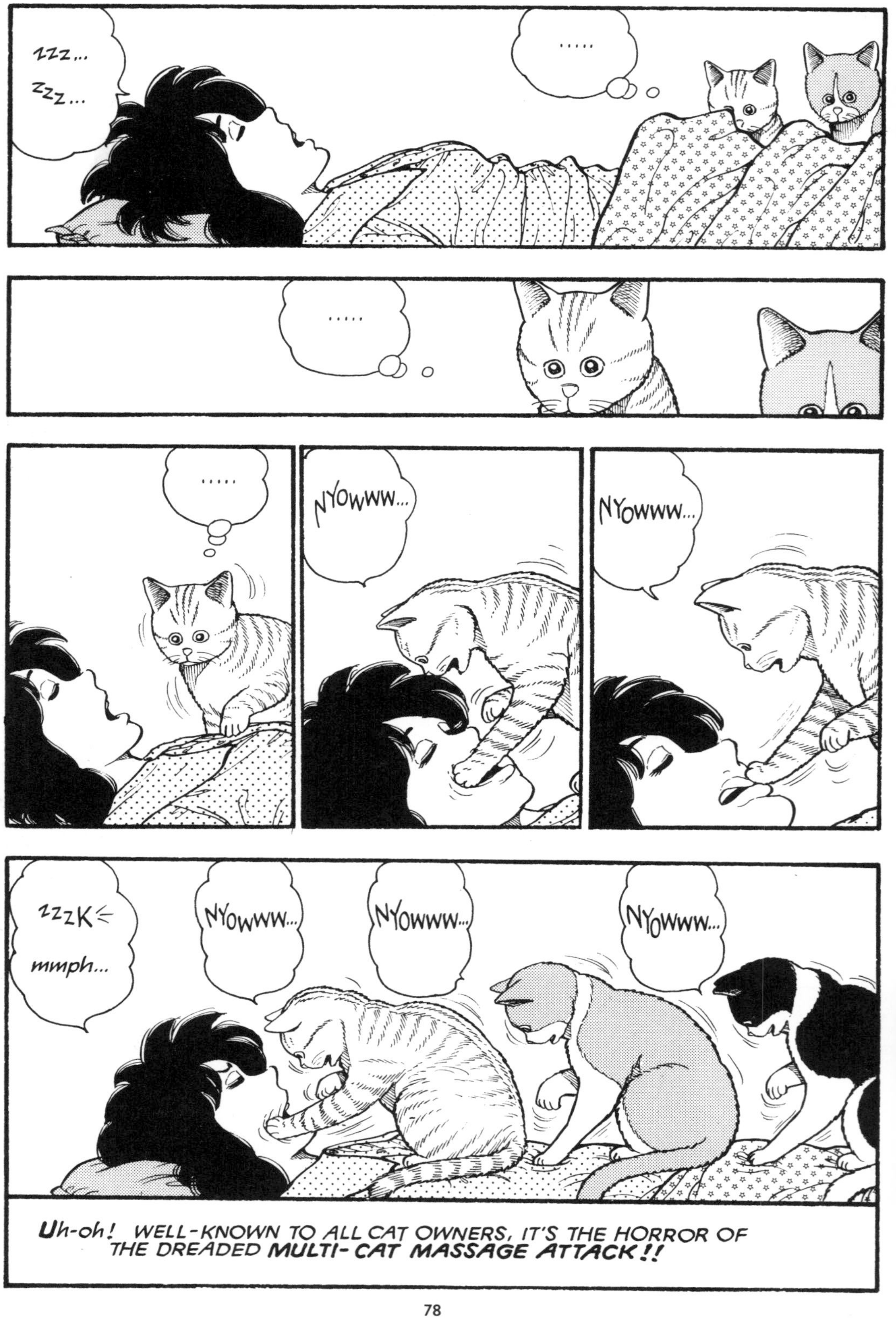

zzz... zzz...
.....
.....
.....
NYOWWW...
NYOWWW...
zzzK mmph...
NYOWWW...
NYOWWW...
NYOWWW...
Uh-oh! WELL-KNOWN TO ALL CAT OWNERS, IT'S THE HORROR OF THE DREADED MULTI-CAT MASSAGE ATTACK!!

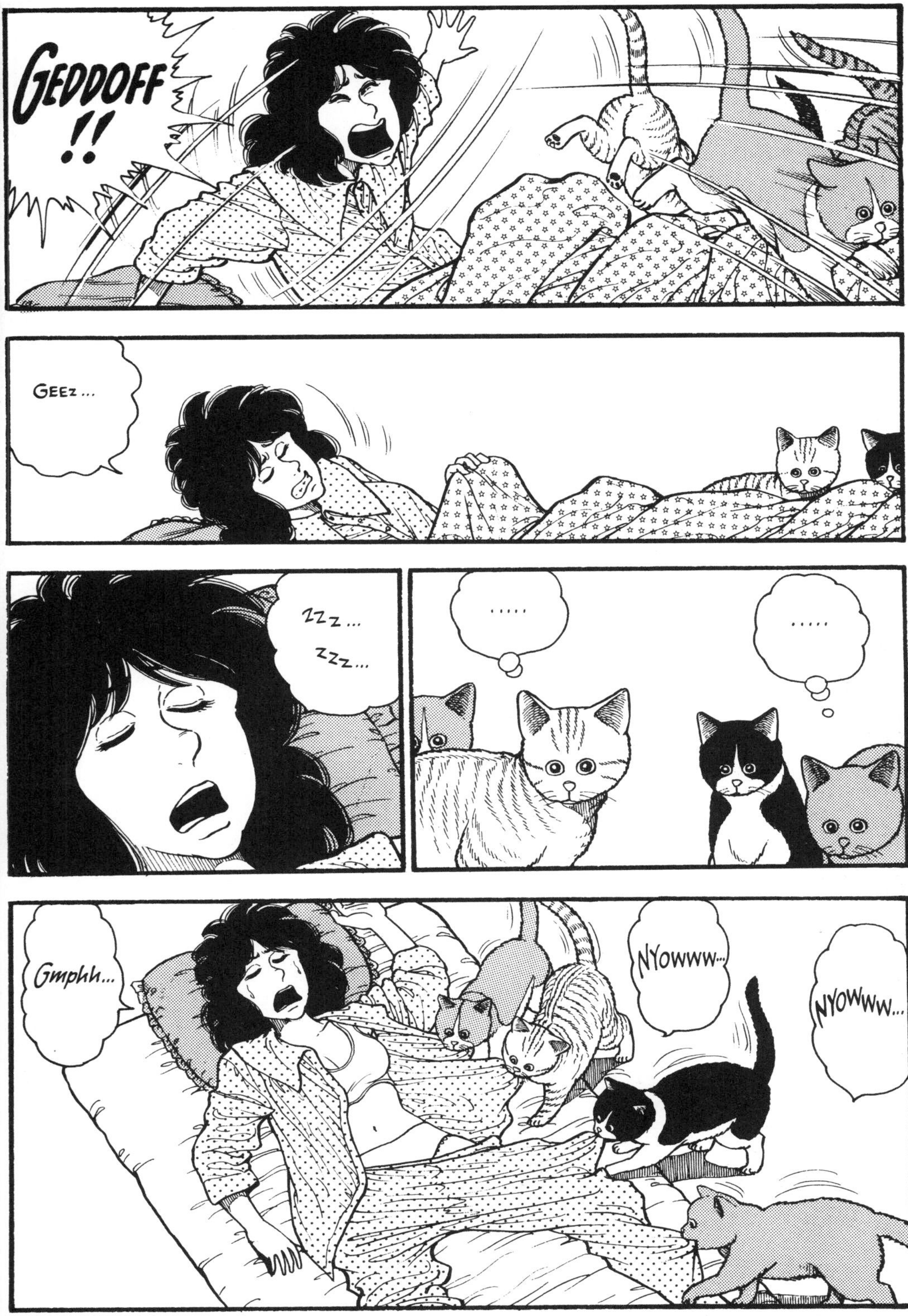
GEDDOFF !!
GEEZ...
ZZZ... ZZZ...
.....
.....
Gmphh...
NYOWWW...
NYOWWW...

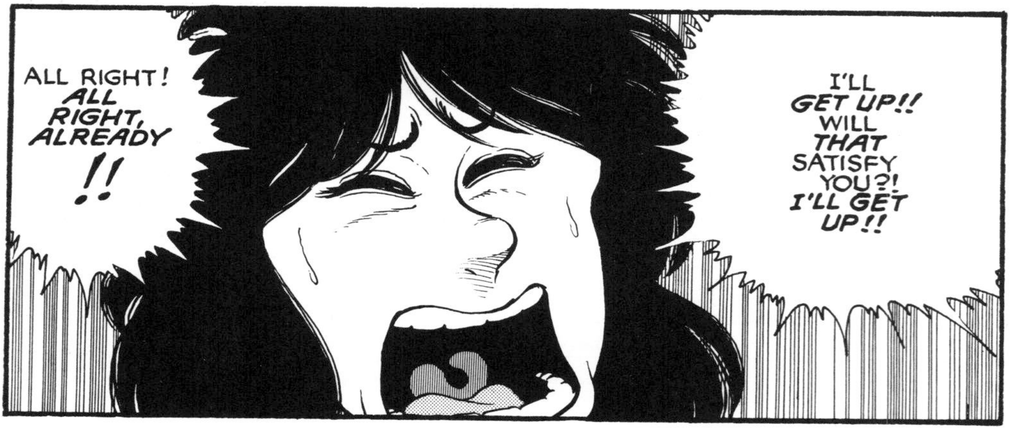
ALL RIGHT! ALL RIGHT, ALREADY!!
I'LL GET UP!! WILL THAT SATISFY YOU?! I'LL GET UP!!

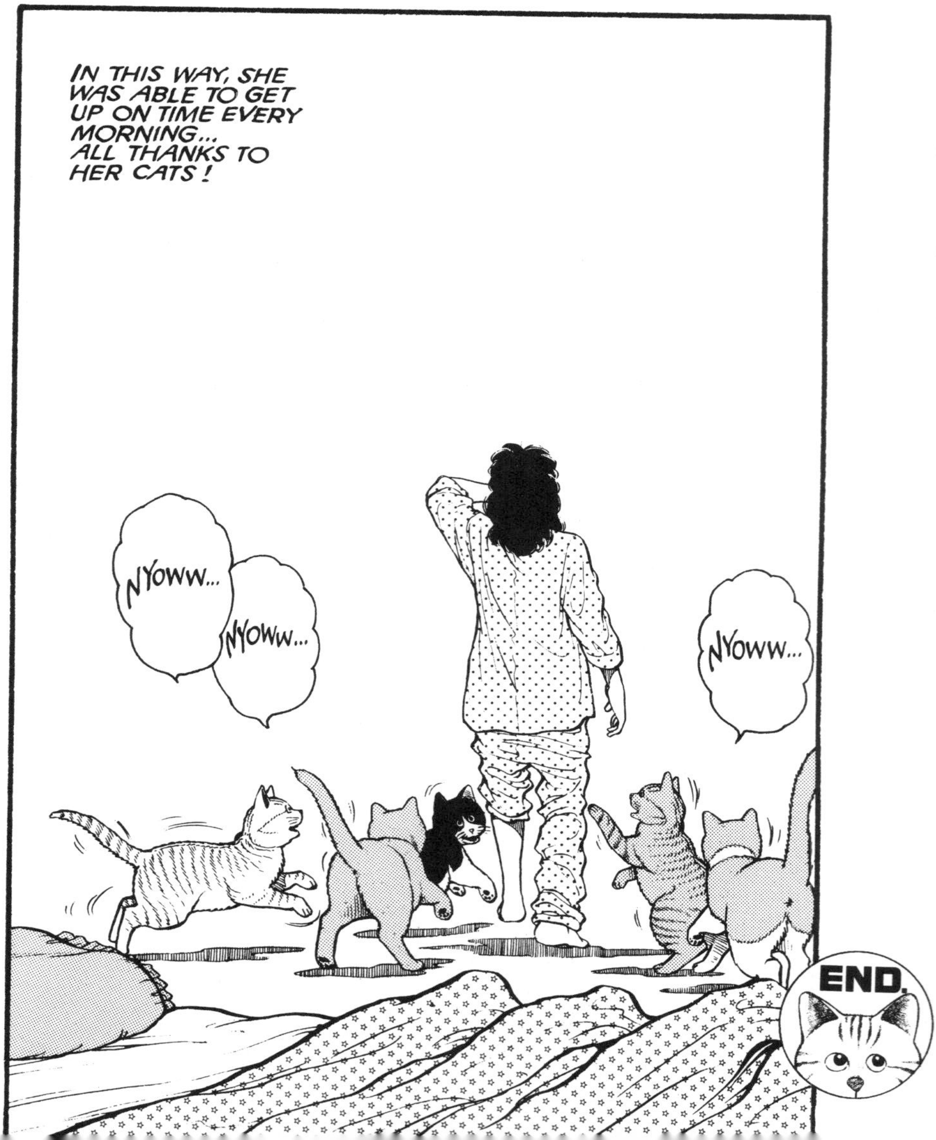
IN THIS WAY, SHE WAS ABLE TO GET UP ON TIME EVERY MORNING... ALL THANKS TO HER CATS!
NYOWW...
NYOWW...
NYOWW...
END.

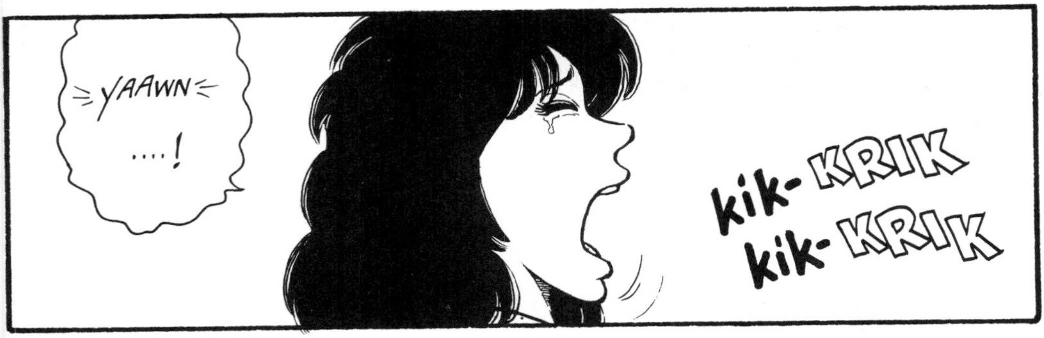
YAAWN
....!
kik-KRIK
kik-KRIK

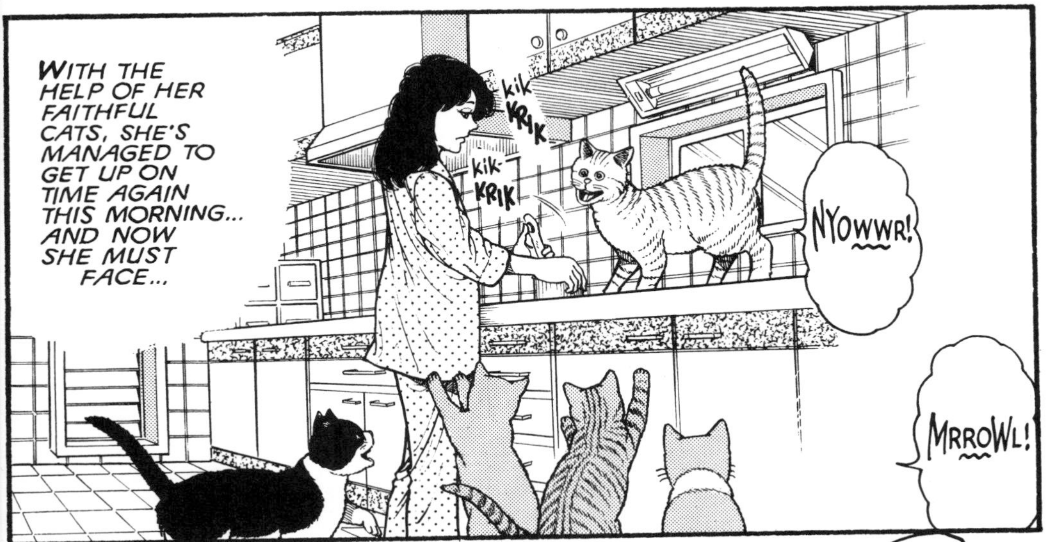
WITH THE HELP OF HER FAITHFUL CATS, SHE'S MANAGED TO GET UP ON TIME AGAIN THIS MORNING... AND NOW SHE MUST FACE...
kik KRIK
kik-KRIK
NYOWWR!
MRROWL!

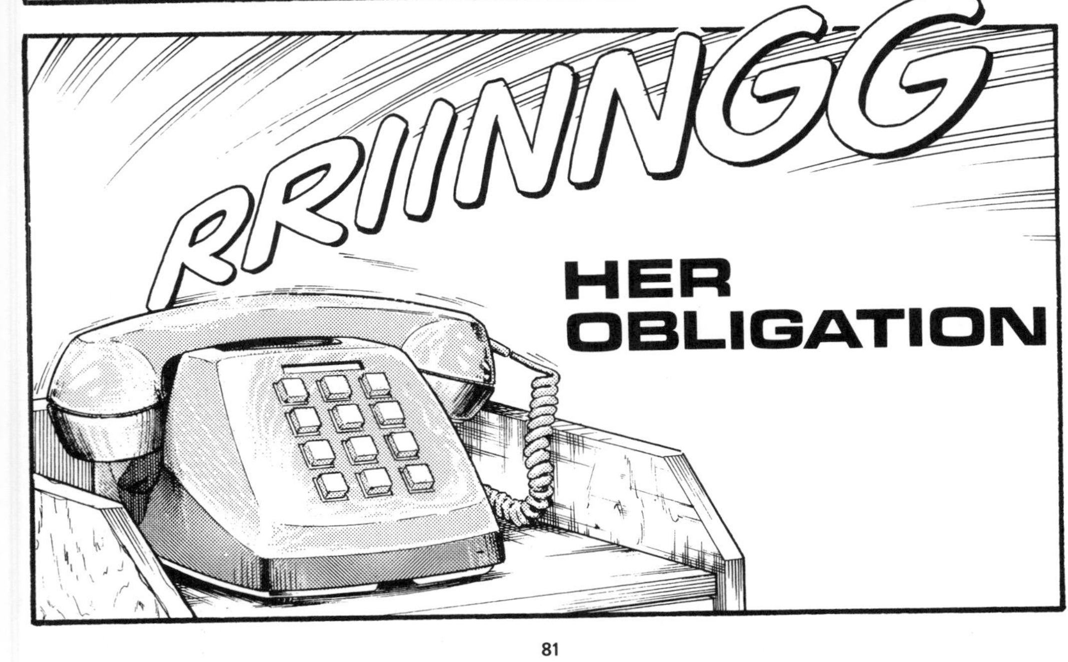
RRIINNGG
HER OBLIGATION

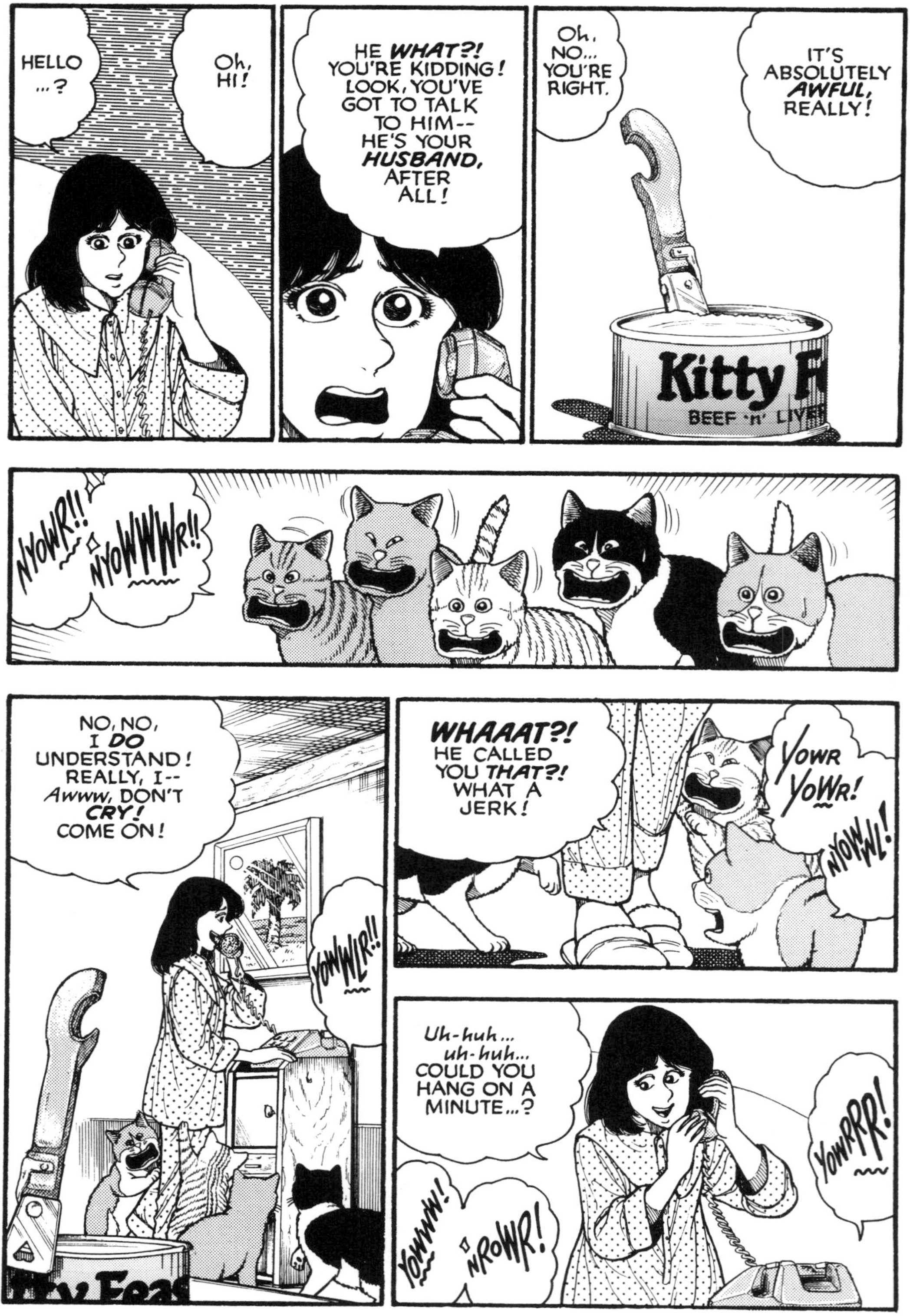
HELLO ...?
Oh, HI!
HE WHAT?! YOU'RE KIDDING! LOOK, YOU'VE GOT TO TALK TO HIM-- HE'S YOUR HUSBAND, AFTER ALL!
Oh, NO... YOU'RE RIGHT.
IT'S ABSOLUTELY AWFUL, REALLY!
Kitty F
BEEF 'n' LIVE
NYOWR!!
NYOWWWR!!
NO, NO, I DO UNDERSTAND! REALLY, I-- Awww, DON'T CRY! COME ON!
YOWWLR!!
WHAAAT?! HE CALLED YOU THAT?! WHAT A JERK!
YOWR YOWR!
NYOWWL!
Uh-huh... uh-huh... COULD YOU HANG ON A MINUTE...?
YOWRRR!
YOWWW!
NROWR!

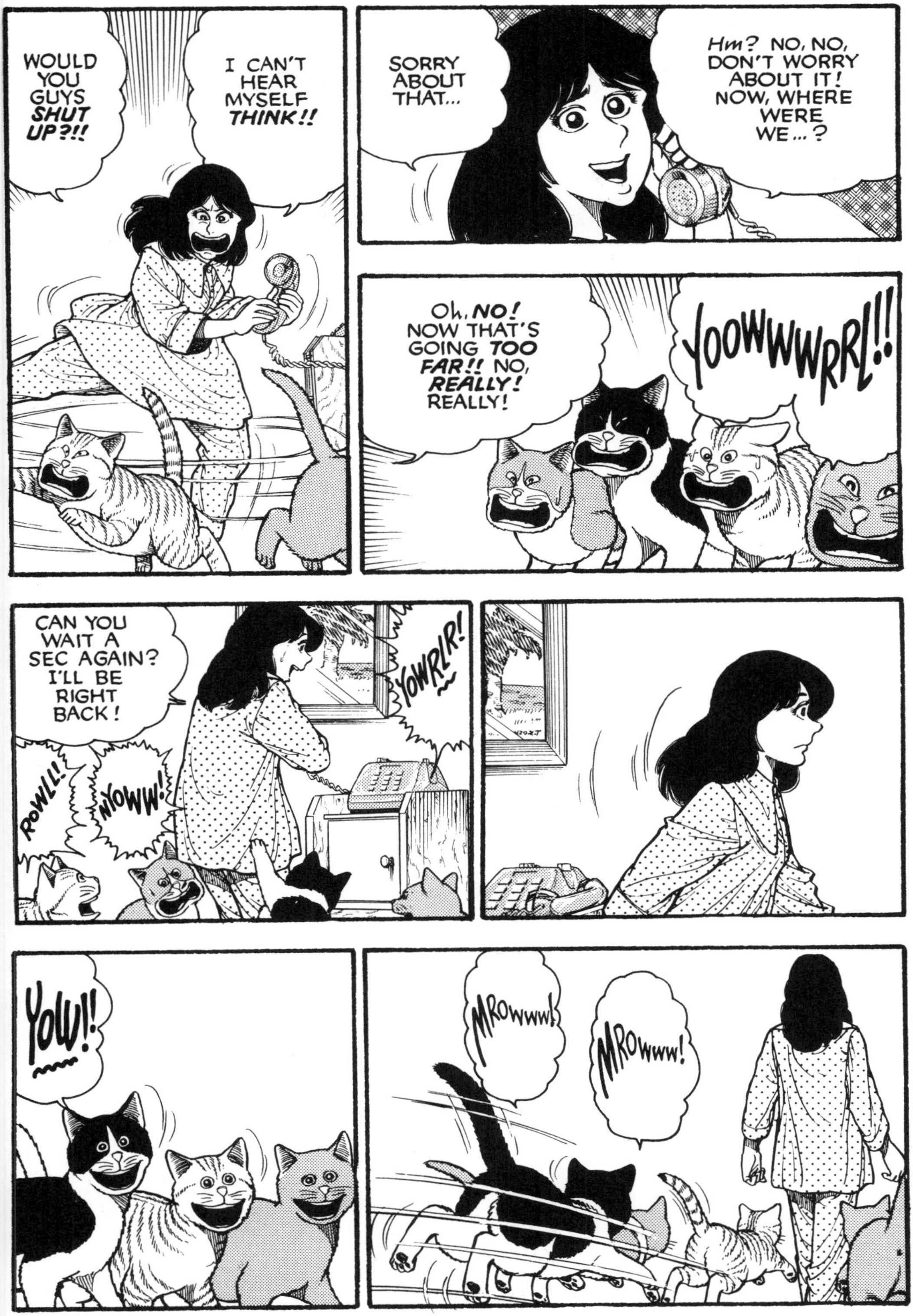
WOULD YOU GUYS ***SHUT UP?!!***
I CAN'T HEAR MYSELF ***THINK!!***
SORRY ABOUT THAT...
Hm? NO, NO, DON'T WORRY ABOUT IT! NOW, WHERE WERE WE...?
Oh, ***NO!*** NOW THAT'S GOING ***TOO FAR!!*** NO, ***REALLY!*** REALLY!
YOOWWWRRL!!
CAN YOU WAIT A SEC AGAIN? I'LL BE RIGHT BACK!
YOWRLR!
ROWLL!!
NYOWW!
YOW!!
MROWWW!
MROWWW!

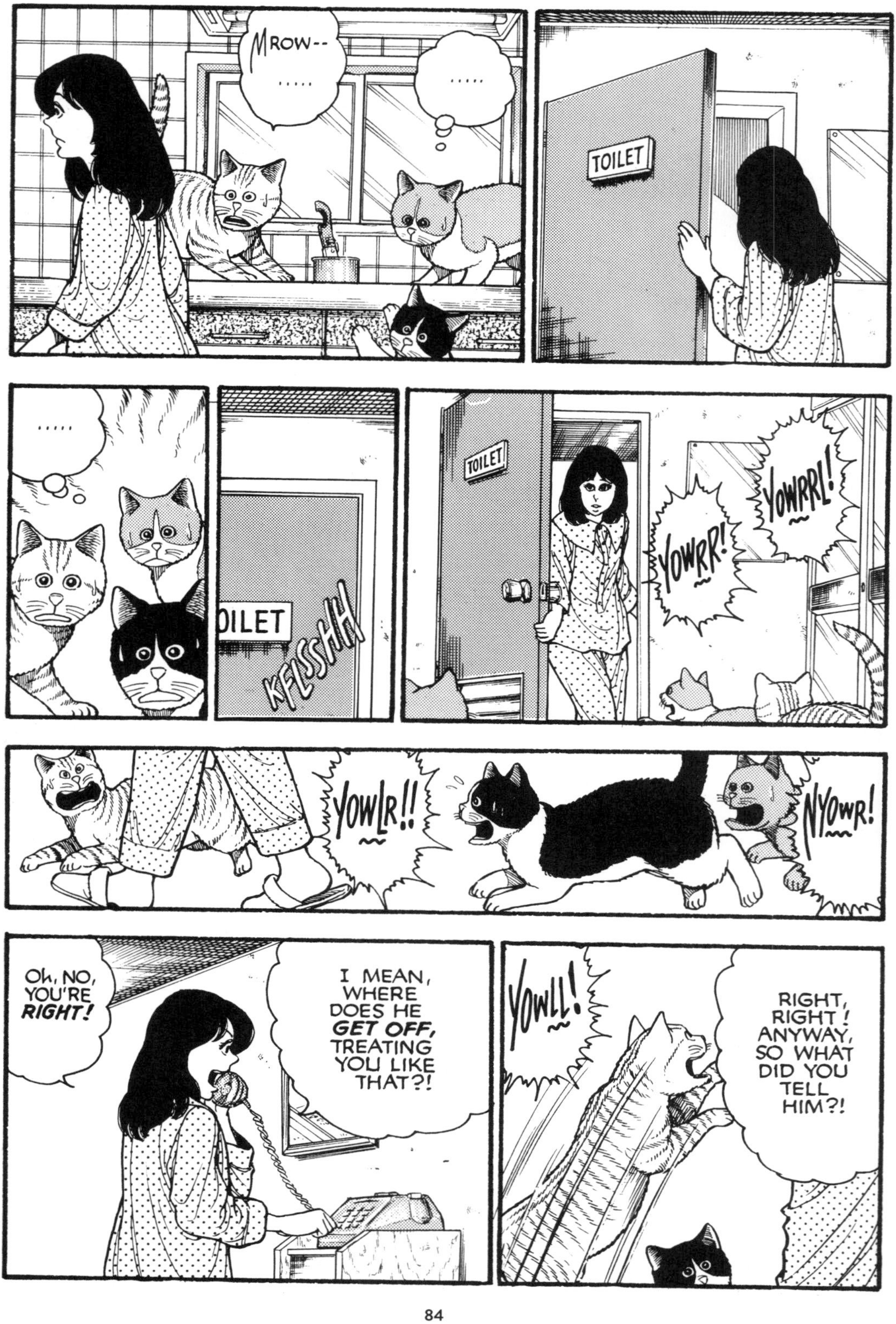

MROW-- .....
.....
TOILET
.....
OILET
KFLSSHH
TOILET
YOWRR!
YOWRRL!
YOWLR!!
NYOWR!
Oh, NO, YOU'RE **RIGHT**!
I MEAN, WHERE DOES HE **GET OFF,** TREATING YOU LIKE THAT?!
YOWLL!
RIGHT, RIGHT! ANYWAY, SO WHAT DID YOU TELL HIM?!

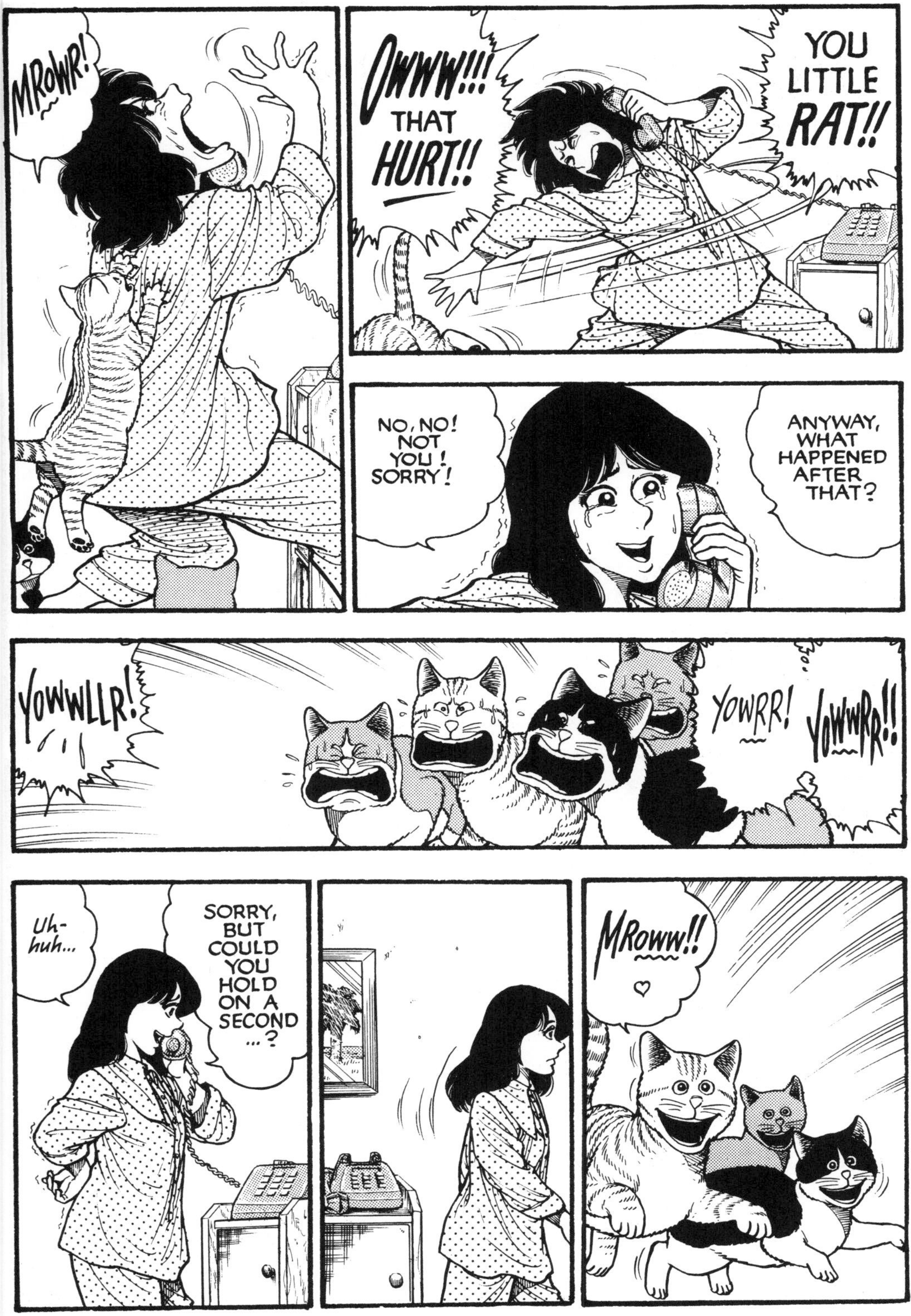
MROWR!
OWWW!!! THAT HURT!!
YOU LITTLE RAT!!
NO, NO! NOT YOU! SORRY!
ANYWAY, WHAT HAPPENED AFTER THAT?
YOWWLLR!
YOWRR!
YOWWRR!!
Uh-huh...
SORRY, BUT COULD YOU HOLD ON A SECOND ...?
MRoww!!

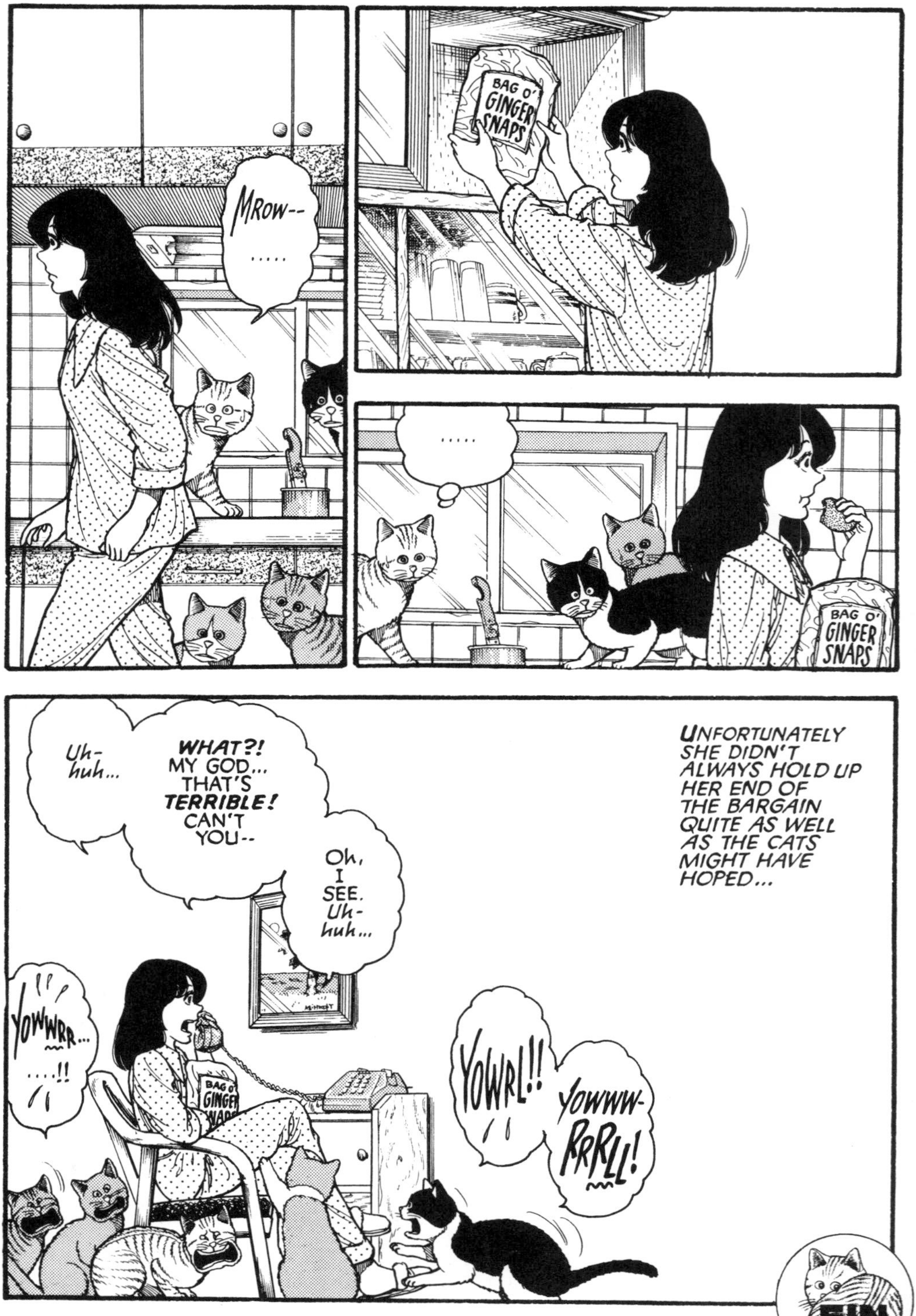
MROW--
.....
BAG O' GINGER SNAPS
.....
BAG O' GINGER SNAPS
Uh-huh...
WHAT?! MY GOD... THAT'S TERRIBLE! CAN'T YOU--
Oh, I SEE. Uh-huh...
UNFORTUNATELY SHE DIDN'T ALWAYS HOLD UP HER END OF THE BARGAIN QUITE AS WELL AS THE CATS MIGHT HAVE HOPED...
YOWWRR... ....!!
YOWRL!!
YOWWW-RRRLL!
FIN

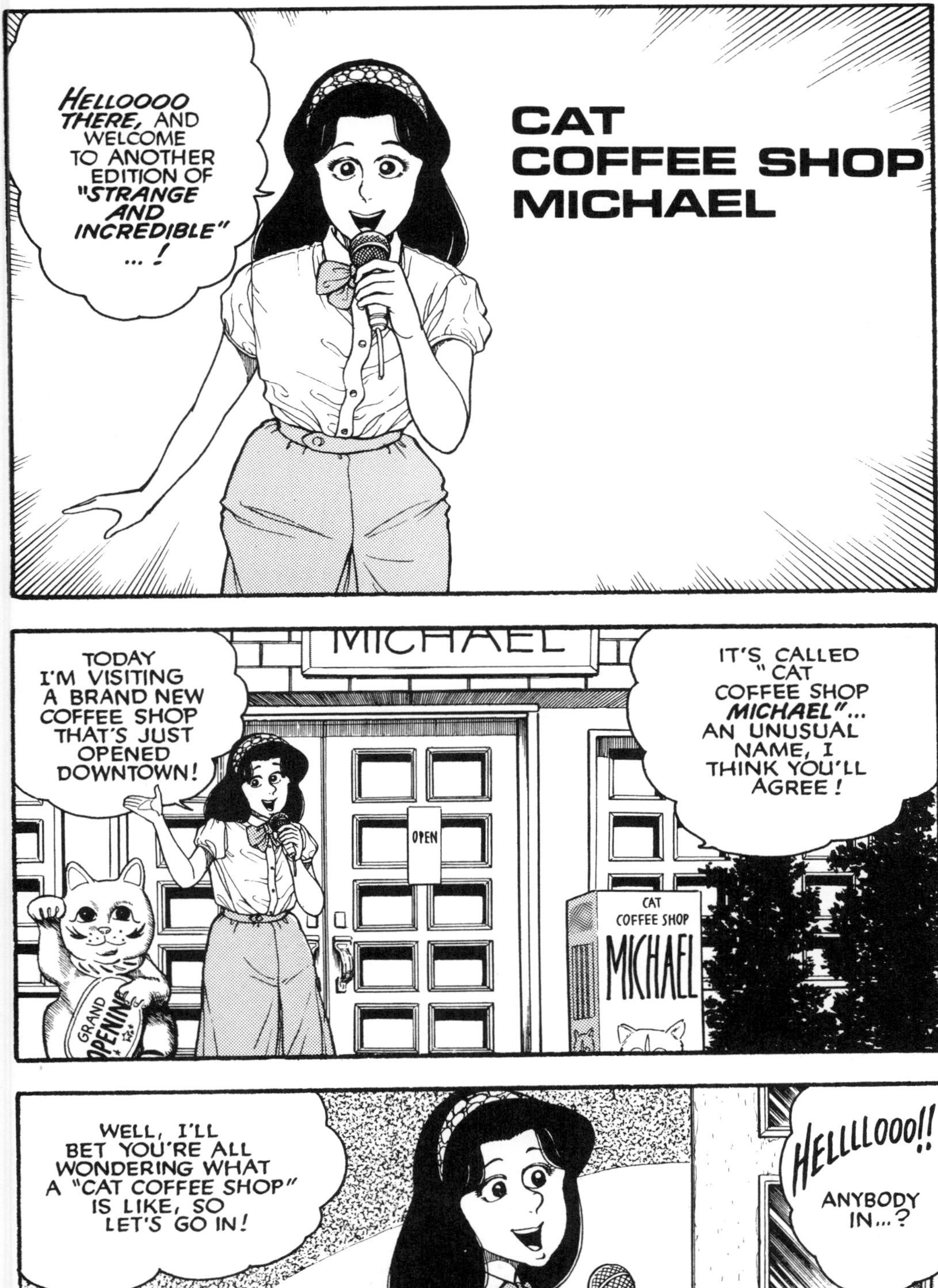
HELLOOOO THERE, AND WELCOME TO ANOTHER EDITION OF "STRANGE AND INCREDIBLE" ...!
CAT COFFEE SHOP MICHAEL
MICHAEL
TODAY I'M VISITING A BRAND NEW COFFEE SHOP THAT'S JUST OPENED DOWNTOWN!
OPEN
GRAND OPENING
CAT COFFEE SHOP MICHAEL
IT'S CALLED "CAT COFFEE SHOP MICHAEL"... AN UNUSUAL NAME, I THINK YOU'LL AGREE!
WELL, I'LL BET YOU'RE ALL WONDERING WHAT A "CAT COFFEE SHOP" IS LIKE, SO LET'S GO IN!
HELLLLOOO!!
ANYBODY IN...?

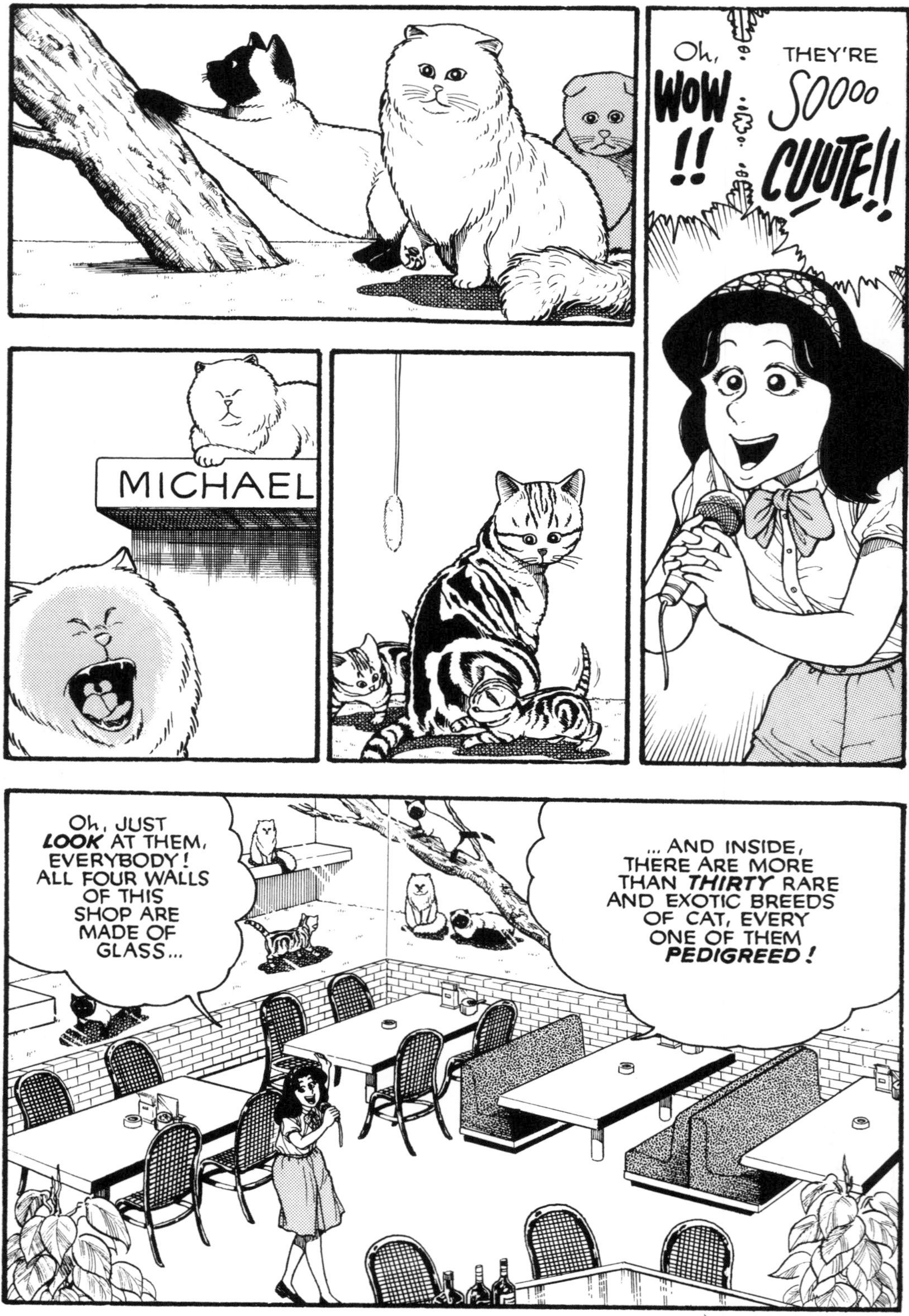

Oh, WOW!!
THEY'RE SOOOo CUUTE!!
MICHAEL
Oh, JUST LOOK AT THEM, EVERYBODY! ALL FOUR WALLS OF THIS SHOP ARE MADE OF GLASS...
... AND INSIDE, THERE ARE MORE THAN THIRTY RARE AND EXOTIC BREEDS OF CAT, EVERY ONE OF THEM PEDIGREED!

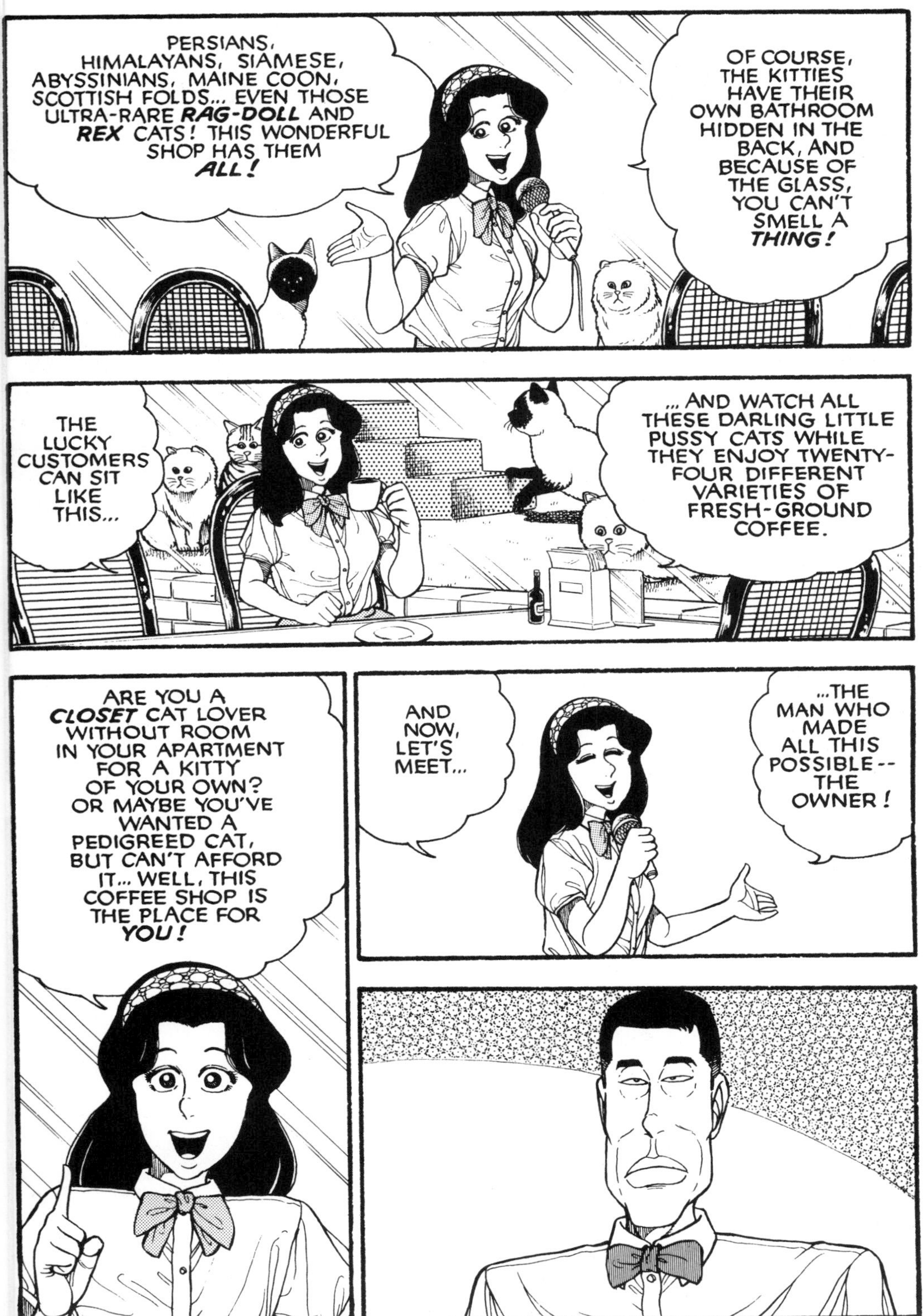
PERSIANS, HIMALAYANS, SIAMESE, ABYSSINIANS, MAINE COON, SCOTTISH FOLDS... EVEN THOSE ULTRA-RARE RAG-DOLL AND REX CATS! THIS WONDERFUL SHOP HAS THEM ALL!
OF COURSE, THE KITTIES HAVE THEIR OWN BATHROOM HIDDEN IN THE BACK, AND BECAUSE OF THE GLASS, YOU CAN'T SMELL A THING!
THE LUCKY CUSTOMERS CAN SIT LIKE THIS...
... AND WATCH ALL THESE DARLING LITTLE PUSSY CATS WHILE THEY ENJOY TWENTY-FOUR DIFFERENT VARIETIES OF FRESH-GROUND COFFEE.
ARE YOU A CLOSET CAT LOVER WITHOUT ROOM IN YOUR APARTMENT FOR A KITTY OF YOUR OWN? OR MAYBE YOU'VE WANTED A PEDIGREED CAT, BUT CAN'T AFFORD IT... WELL, THIS COFFEE SHOP IS THE PLACE FOR YOU!
AND NOW, LET'S MEET...
...THE MAN WHO MADE ALL THIS POSSIBLE-- THE OWNER!

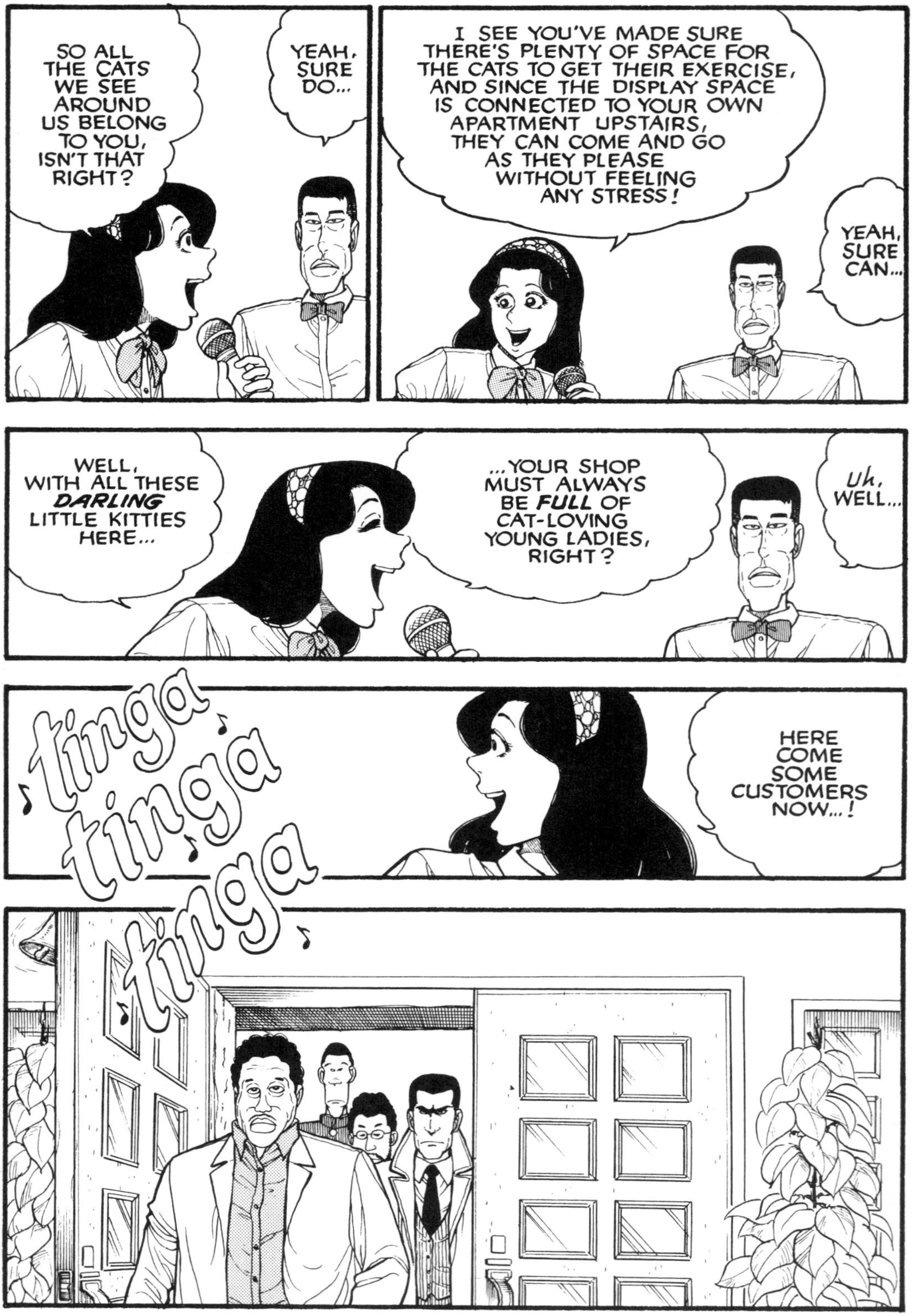

SO ALL THE CATS WE SEE AROUND US BELONG TO YOU, ISN'T THAT RIGHT?
YEAH, SURE DO...
I SEE YOU'VE MADE SURE THERE'S PLENTY OF SPACE FOR THE CATS TO GET THEIR EXERCISE, AND SINCE THE DISPLAY SPACE IS CONNECTED TO YOUR OWN APARTMENT UPSTAIRS, THEY CAN COME AND GO AS THEY PLEASE WITHOUT FEELING ANY STRESS!
YEAH, SURE CAN...
WELL, WITH ALL THESE *DARLING* LITTLE KITTIES HERE...
...YOUR SHOP MUST ALWAYS BE *FULL* OF CAT-LOVING YOUNG LADIES, RIGHT?
*Uh,* WELL...
tinga tinga tinga
HERE COME SOME CUSTOMERS NOW...!
tinga

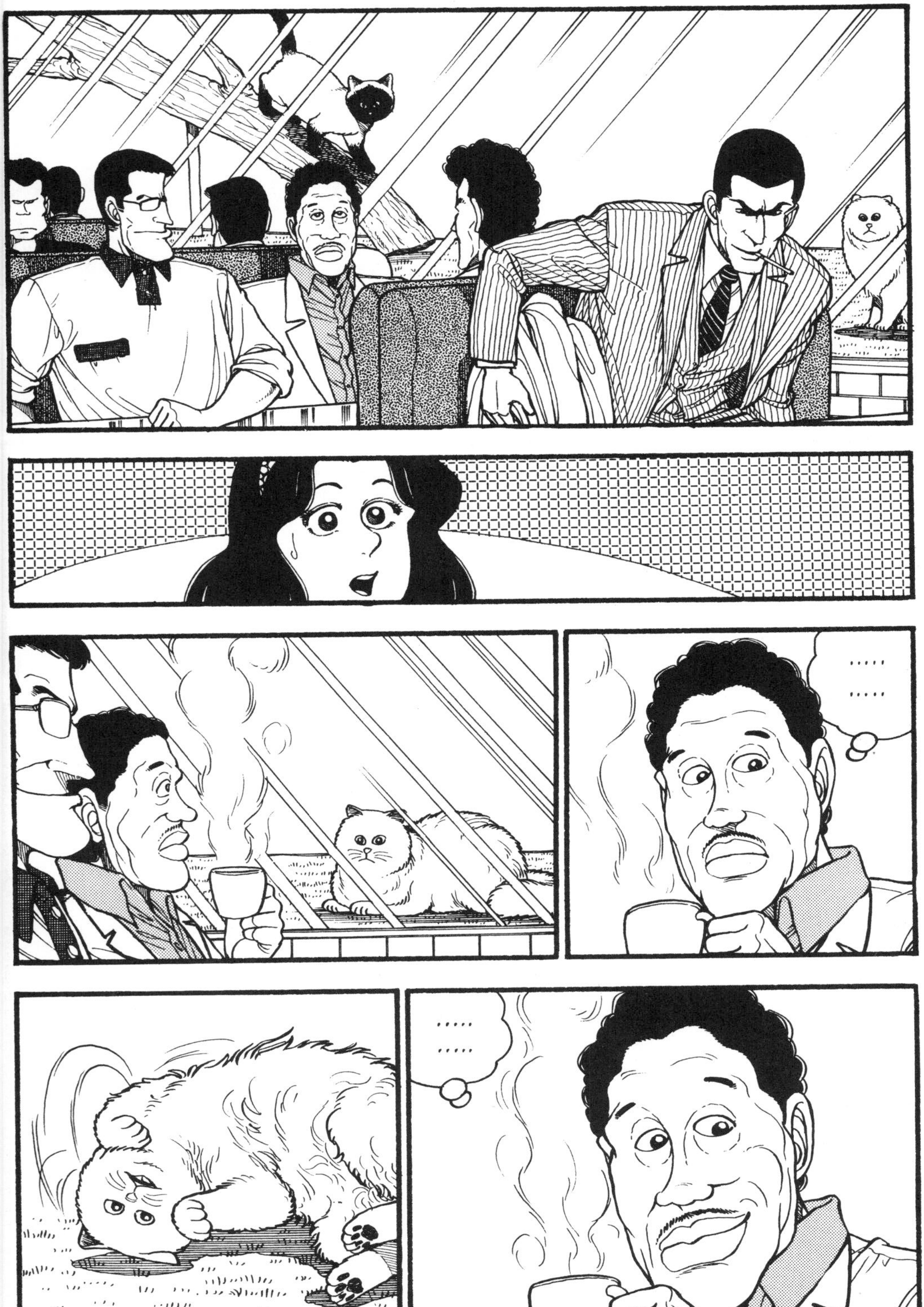
.....
.....
.....
.....

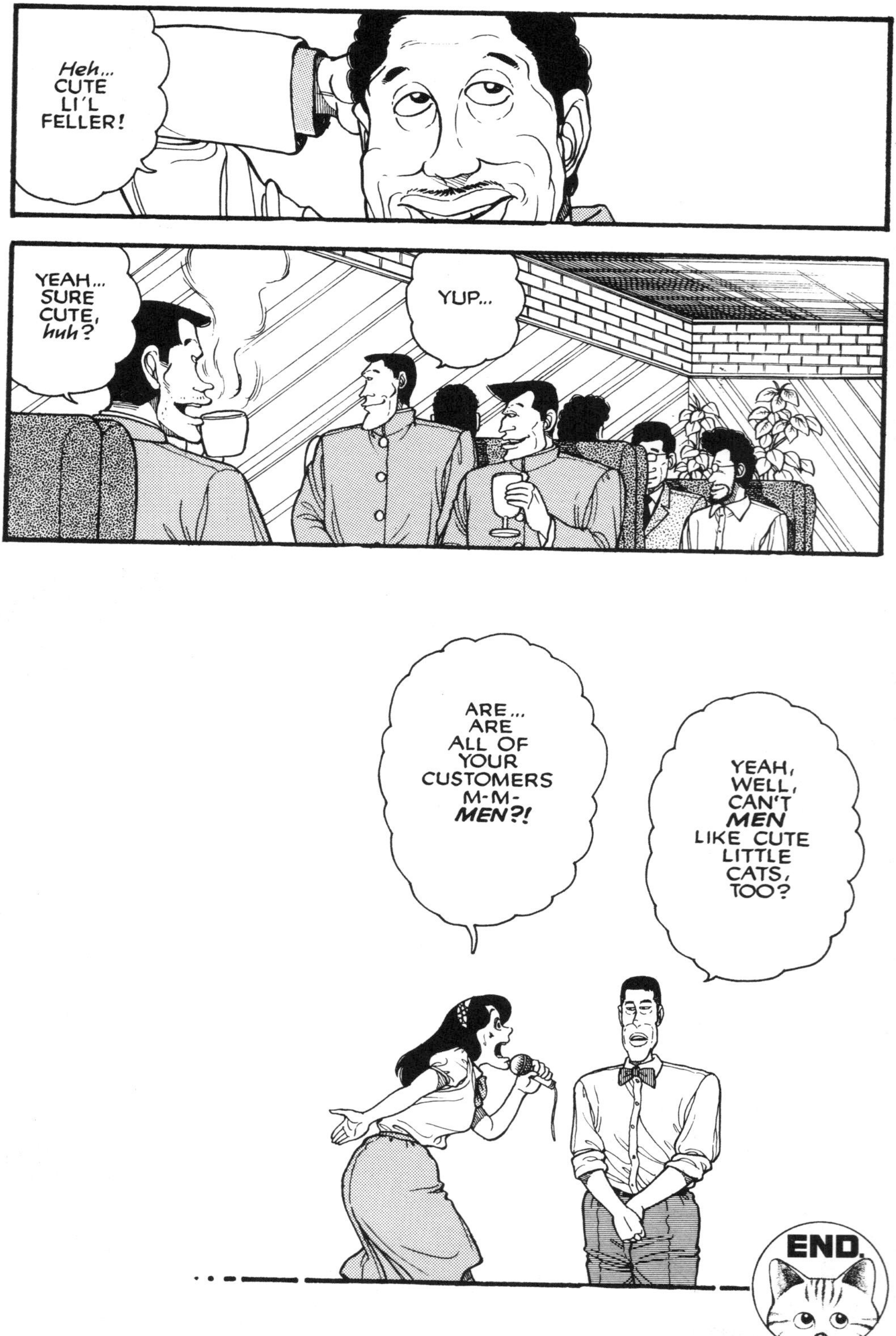
Heh... CUTE LI'L FELLER!
YEAH... SURE CUTE, huh?
YUP...
ARE... ARE ALL OF YOUR CUSTOMERS M-M-MEN?!
YEAH, WELL, CAN'T MEN LIKE CUTE LITTLE CATS, TOO?
END.

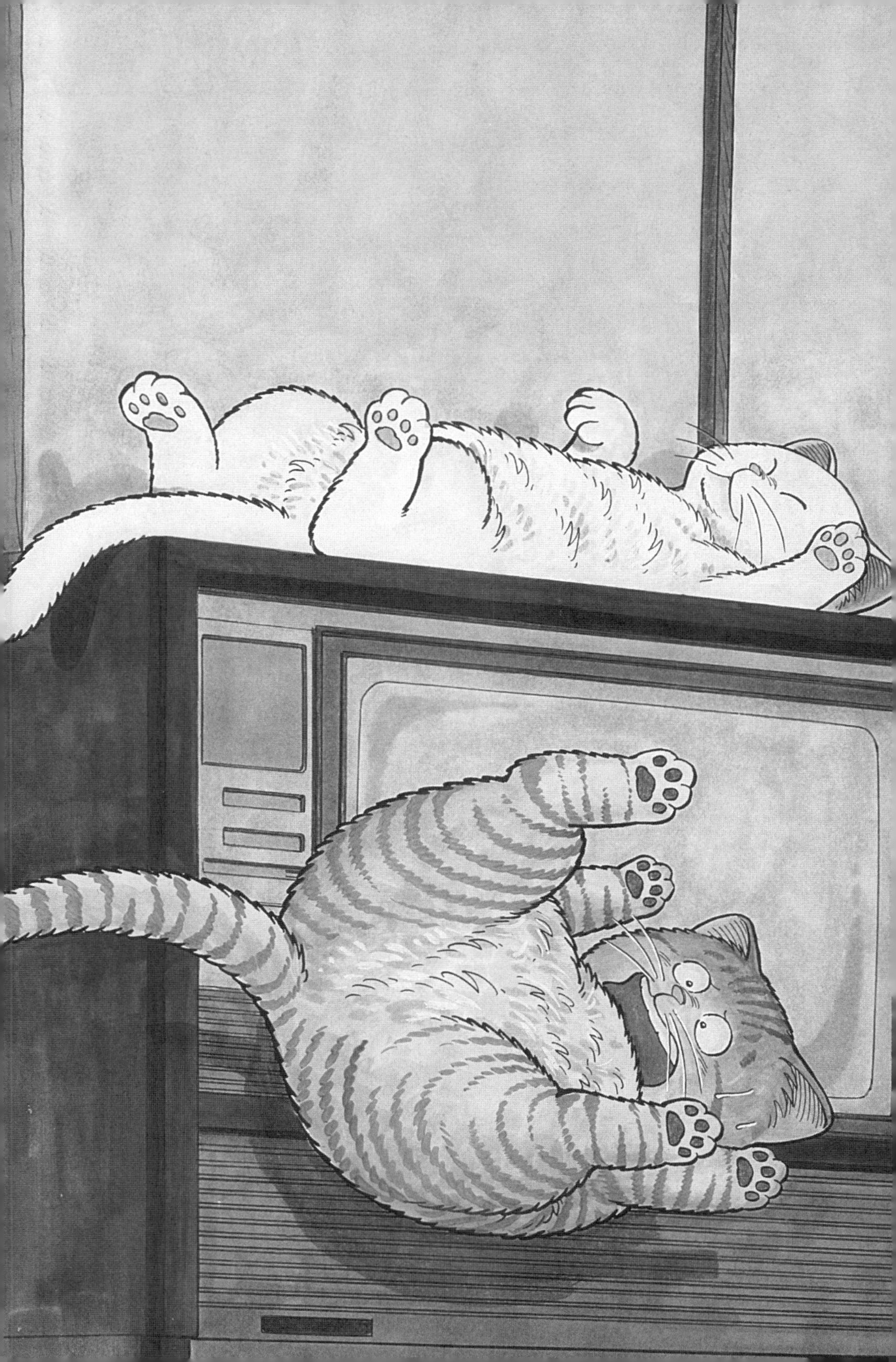

# WHAT'S MICHAEL?

## VOLUME 2: LIVING TOGETHER

*This section was translated by Dana Lewis and Toren Smith and lettered by L. Lois Buhalis.*

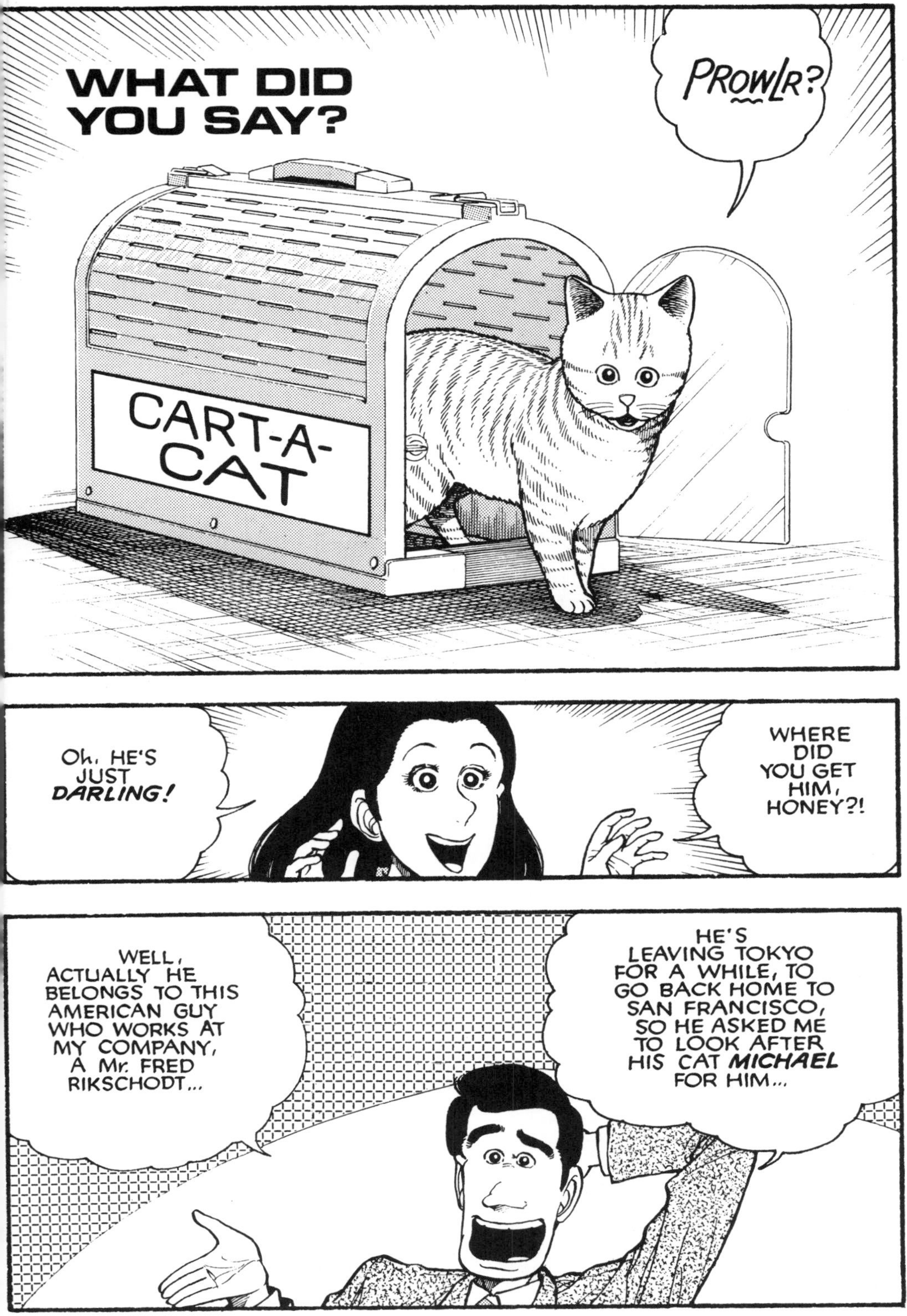
WHAT DID YOU SAY?
PROWLR?
CART-A-CAT
Oh, HE'S JUST DARLING!
WHERE DID YOU GET HIM, HONEY?!
WELL, ACTUALLY HE BELONGS TO THIS AMERICAN GUY WHO WORKS AT MY COMPANY, A Mr. FRED RIKSCHODT...
HE'S LEAVING TOKYO FOR A WHILE, TO GO BACK HOME TO SAN FRANCISCO, SO HE ASKED ME TO LOOK AFTER HIS CAT MICHAEL FOR HIM...

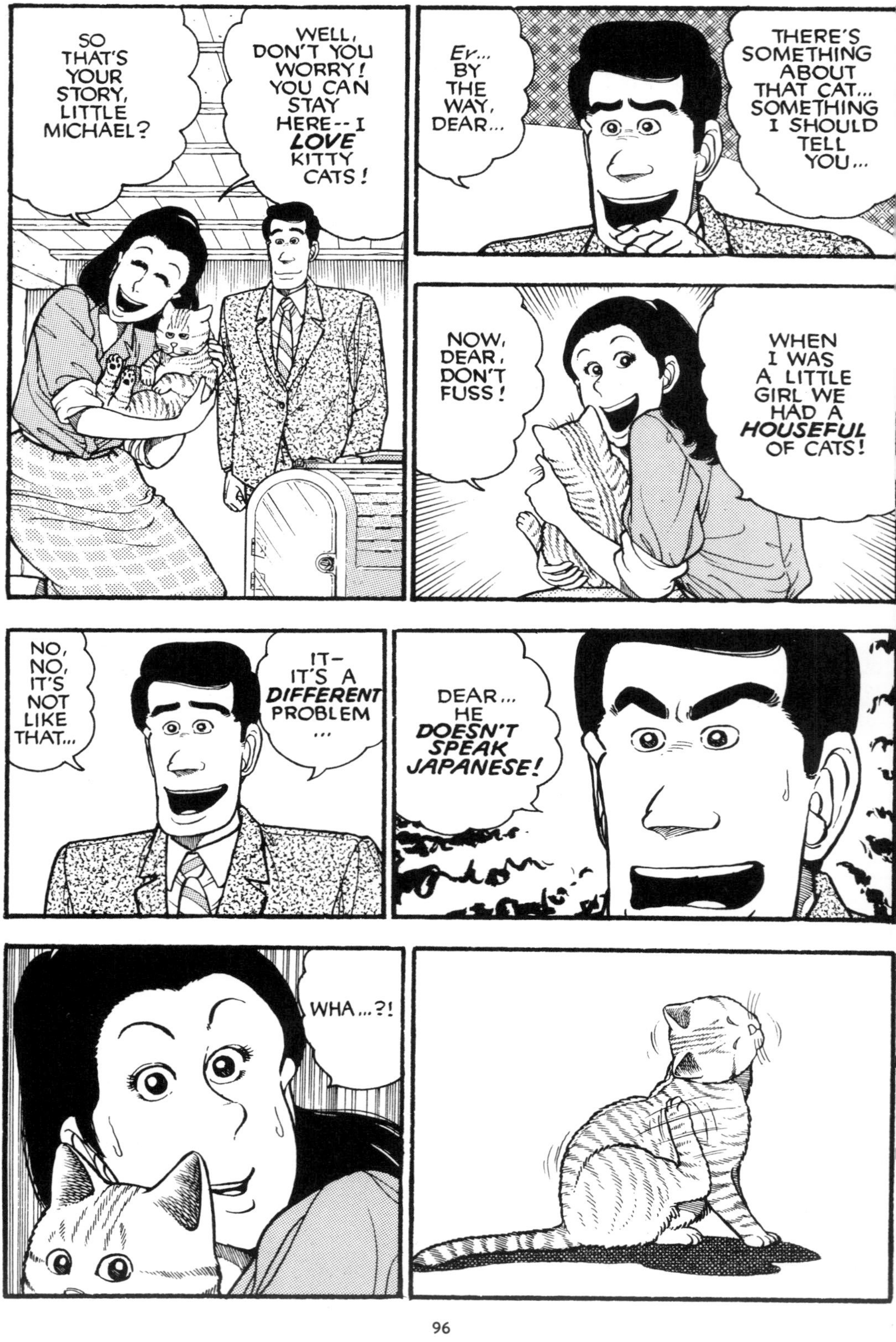

SO THAT'S YOUR STORY, LITTLE MICHAEL?
WELL, DON'T YOU WORRY! YOU CAN STAY HERE-- I LOVE KITTY CATS!
Er... BY THE WAY, DEAR...
THERE'S SOMETHING ABOUT THAT CAT... SOMETHING I SHOULD TELL YOU...
NOW, DEAR, DON'T FUSS!
WHEN I WAS A LITTLE GIRL WE HAD A HOUSEFUL OF CATS!
NO, NO, IT'S NOT LIKE THAT...
IT-IT'S A DIFFERENT PROBLEM...
DEAR... HE DOESN'T SPEAK JAPANESE!
WHA...?!

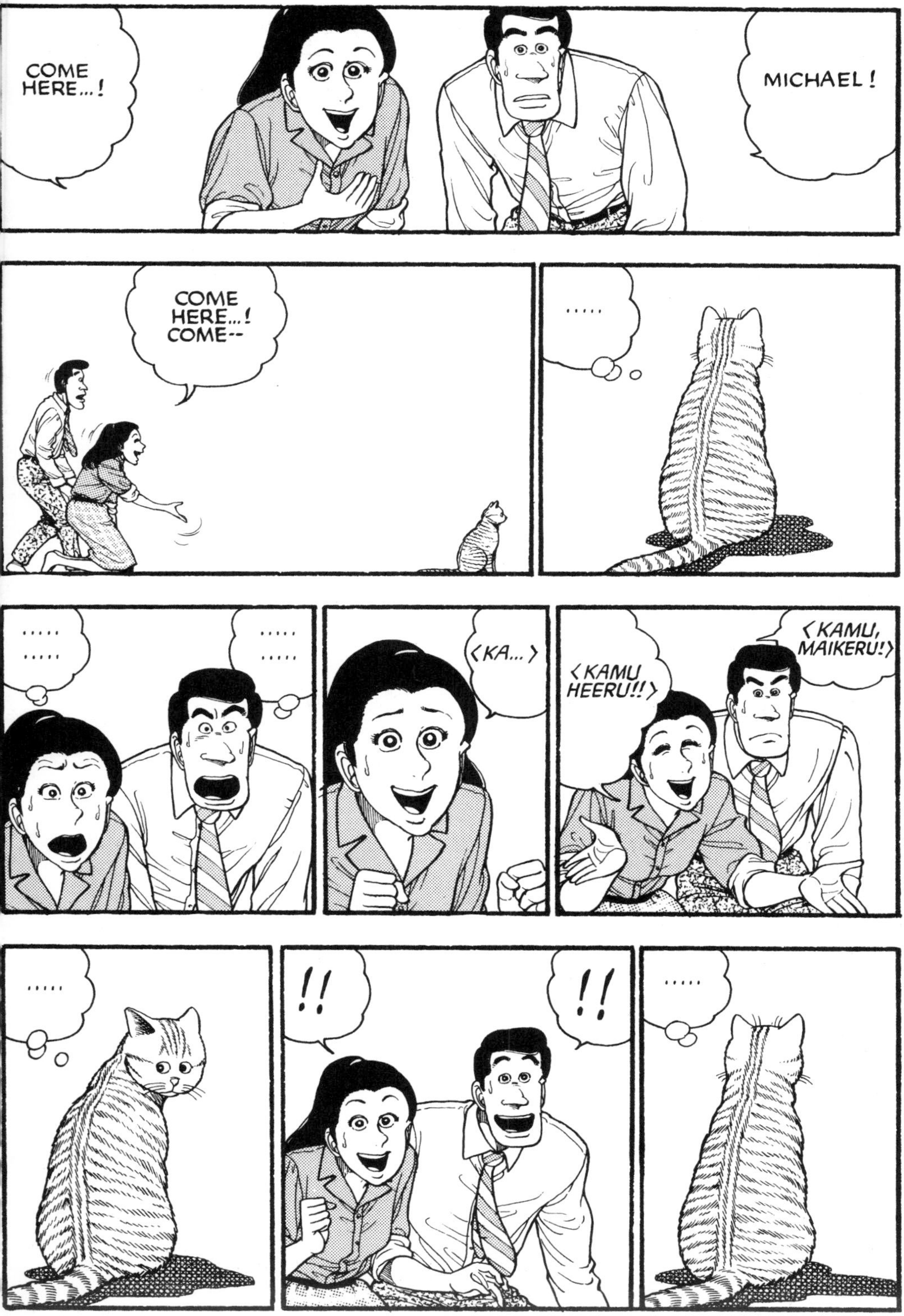

COME HERE...!
MICHAEL!
COME HERE...! COME--
.....
..... .....
..... .....
<KA...>
<KAMU HEERU!!>
<KAMU, MAIKERU!>
.....
!!
!!
.....

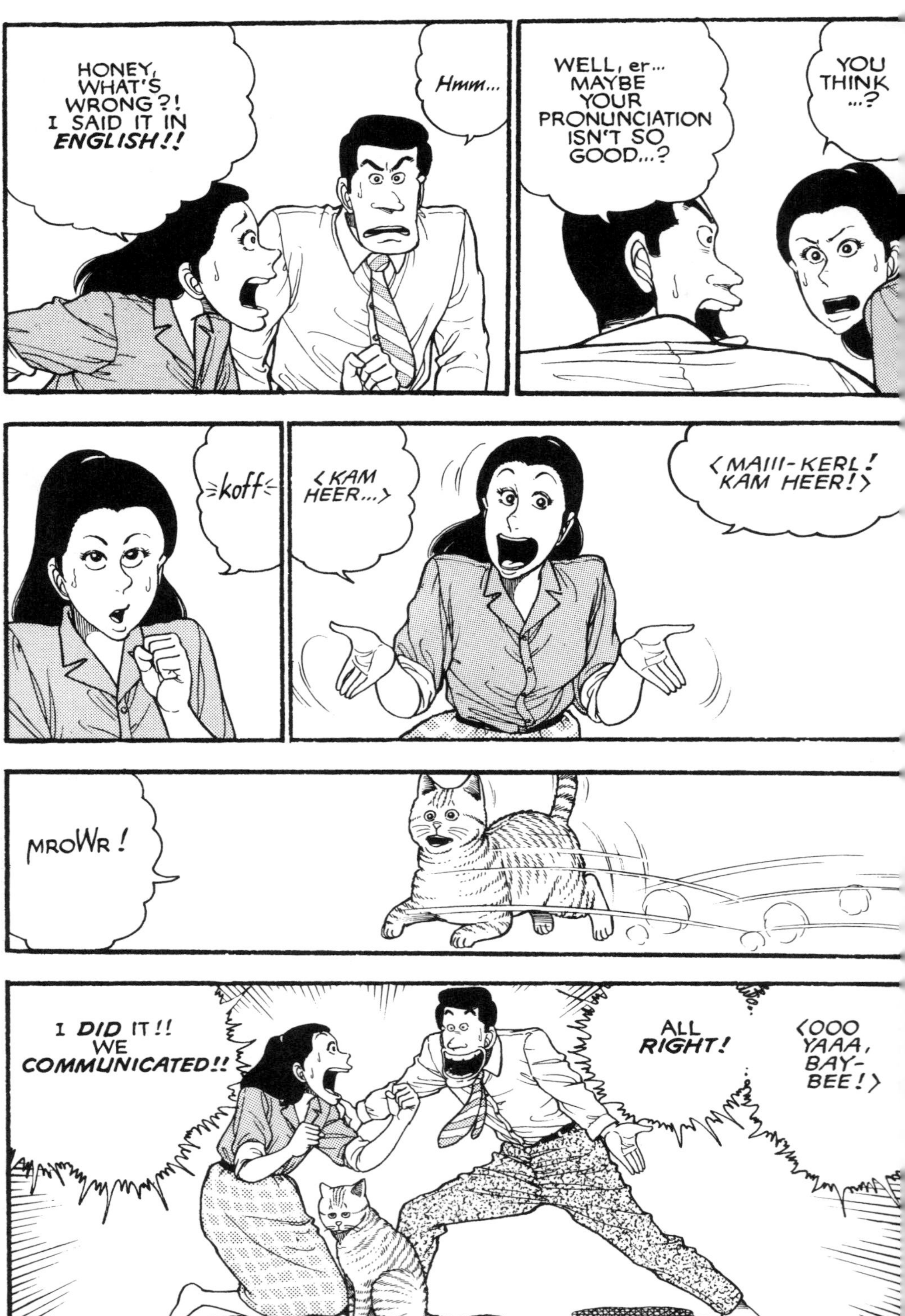
HONEY, WHAT'S WRONG?! I SAID IT IN ENGLISH!!
Hmm...
WELL, er... MAYBE YOUR PRONUNCIATION ISN'T SO GOOD...?
YOU THINK ...?
koff
<KAM HEER...>
<MAIII-KERL! KAM HEER!>
MROWR!
I DID IT!! WE COMMUNICATED!!
ALL RIGHT!
<OOO YAAA, BAY-BEE!>

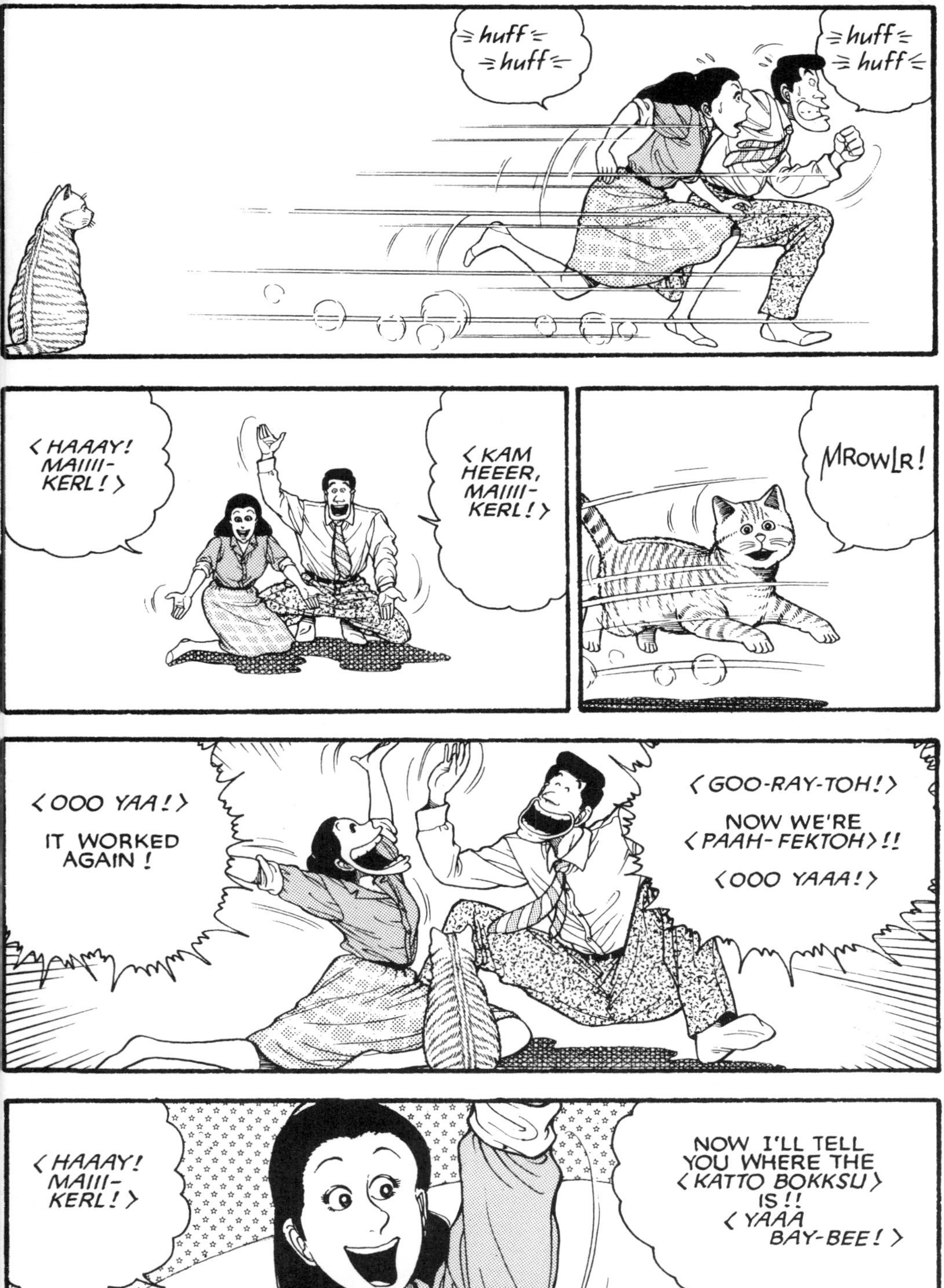
huff huff
huff huff
< HAAAY! MAIIII-KERL! >
< KAM HEEER, MAIIII-KERL! >
MROWLR!
< OOO YAA! >
IT WORKED AGAIN!
< GOO-RAY-TOH! >
NOW WE'RE < PAAH-FEKTOH >!!
< OOO YAAA! >
< HAAAY! MAIII-KERL! >
NOW I'LL TELL YOU WHERE THE < KATTO BOKKSU > IS!!
< YAAA BAY-BEE! >

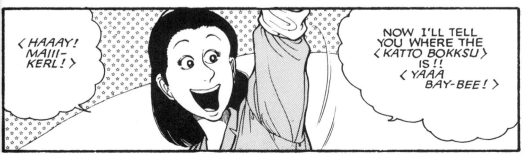

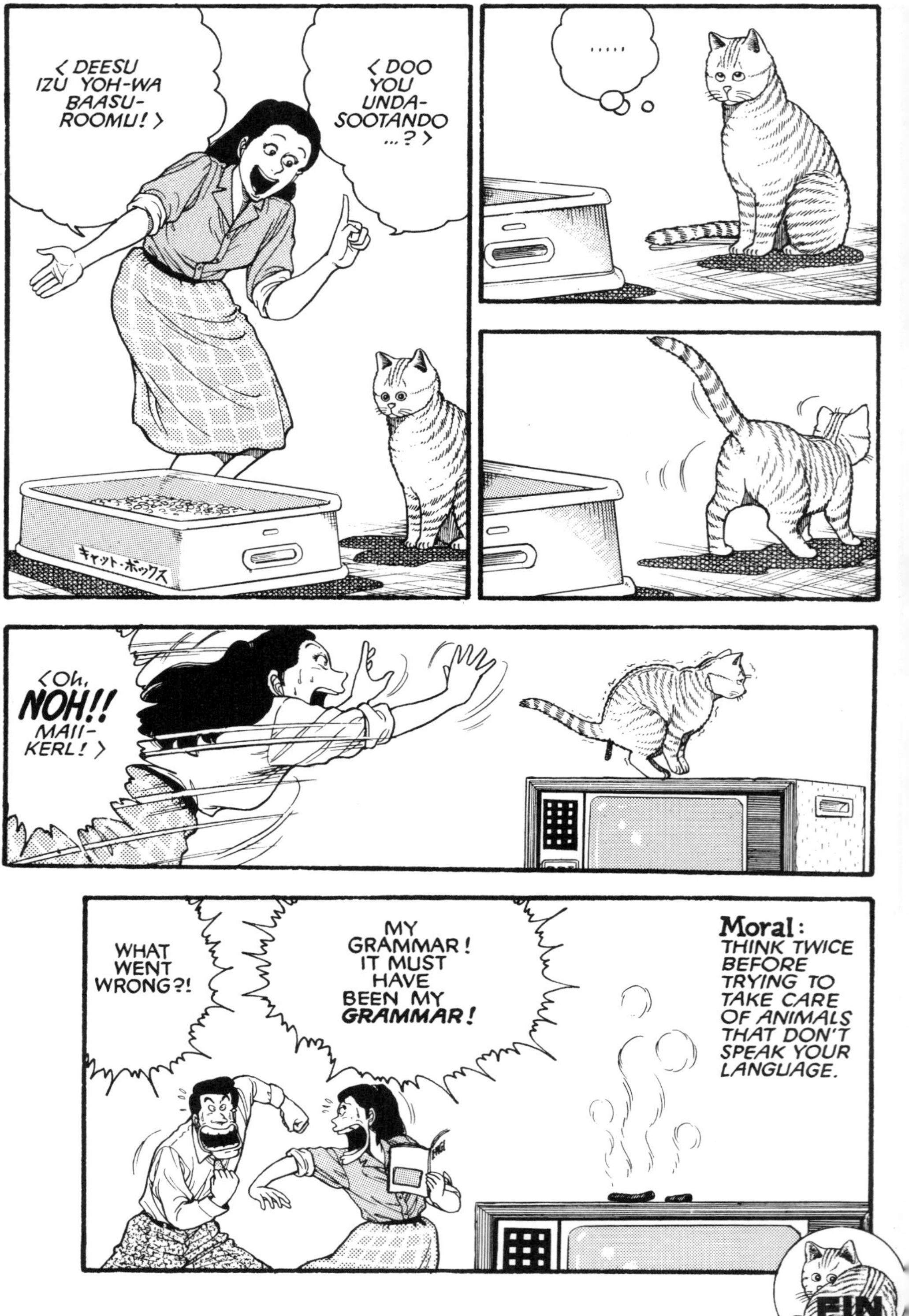
< DEESU IZU YOH-WA BAASU-ROOMU! >
< DOO YOU UNDA-SOOTANDO ...? >
キャット・ボックス
.....
<Oh, NOH!! MAII-KERL! >
WHAT WENT WRONG?!
MY GRAMMAR! IT MUST HAVE BEEN MY GRAMMAR!
Moral: THINK TWICE BEFORE TRYING TO TAKE CARE OF ANIMALS THAT DON'T SPEAK YOUR LANGUAGE.
FIN

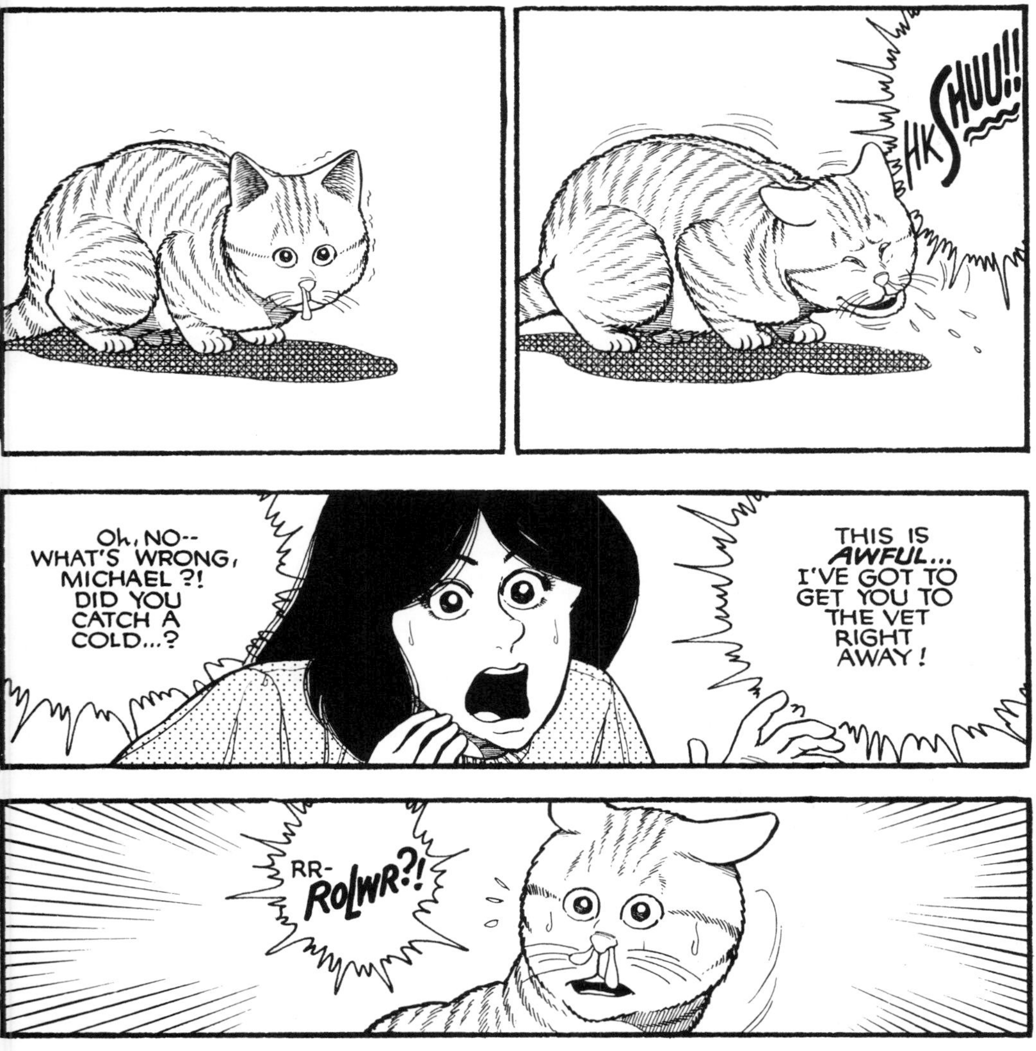
HKSHUU!!
Oh, NO-- WHAT'S WRONG, MICHAEL ?! DID YOU CATCH A COLD...?
THIS IS AWFUL... I'VE GOT TO GET YOU TO THE VET RIGHT AWAY !
RR-ROLWR?!

# SICK!
## HANG IN THERE, MICHAEL!

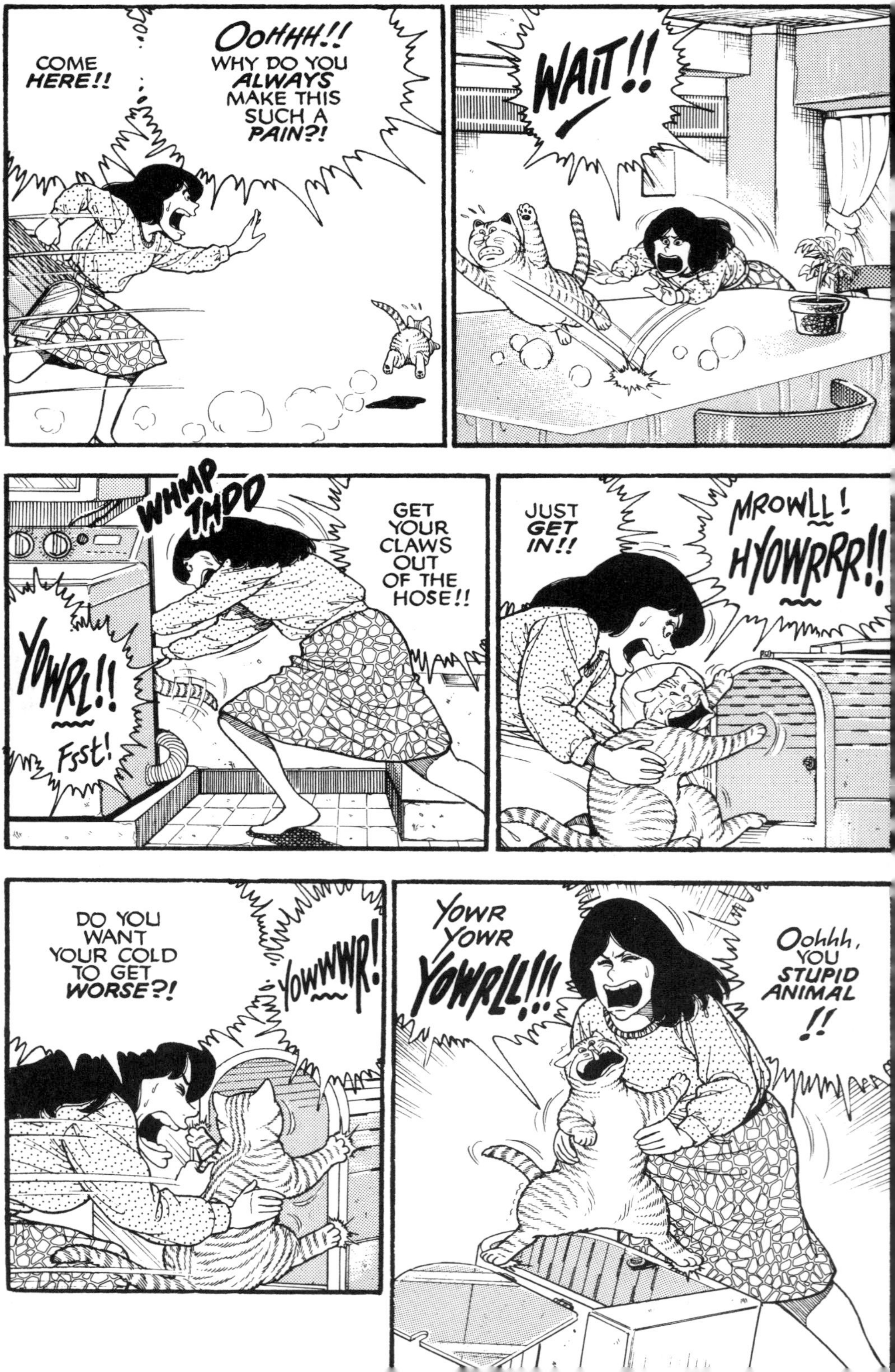
COME HERE!!
OOHHH!! WHY DO YOU ALWAYS MAKE THIS SUCH A PAIN?!
WAIT!!
WHMP THDD
GET YOUR CLAWS OUT OF THE HOSE!!
YOWRL!!
Fsst!
JUST GET IN!!
MROWLL!
HYOWRRR!!
DO YOU WANT YOUR COLD TO GET WORSE?!
YOWWWR!
YOWR YOWR YOWRLL!!!
Oohhh, YOU STUPID ANIMAL!!

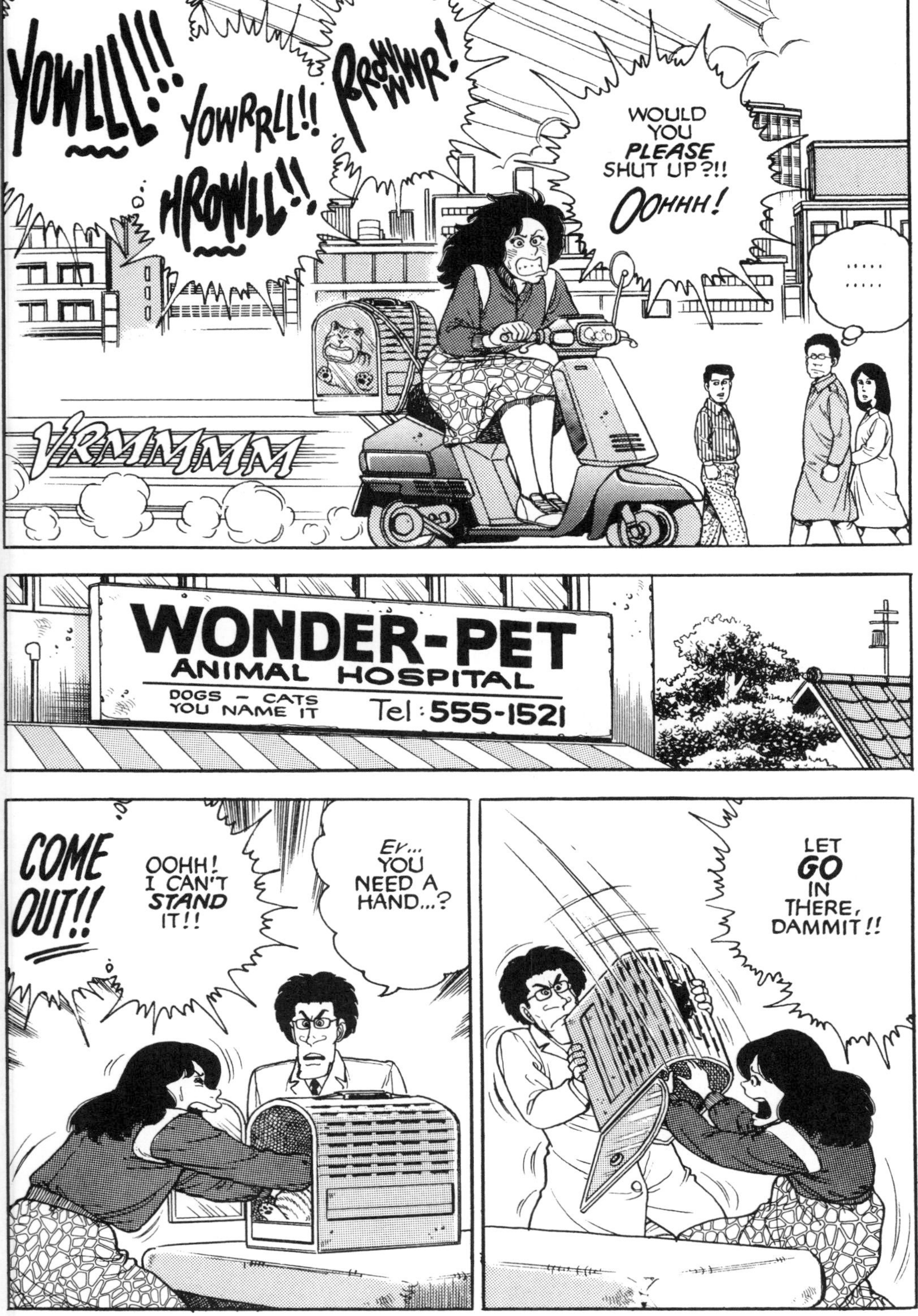
YOWLLL!!!
YOWRRLL!!
BROWWWR!
HROWLL!!
WOULD YOU PLEASE SHUT UP?!!
OOHHH!
.....
.....
VRMMMMM
WONDER-PET
ANIMAL HOSPITAL
DOGS – CATS
YOU NAME IT
Tel: 555-1521
COME OUT!!
OOHH! I CAN'T STAND IT!!
Er... YOU NEED A HAND...?
LET GO IN THERE, DAMMIT!!

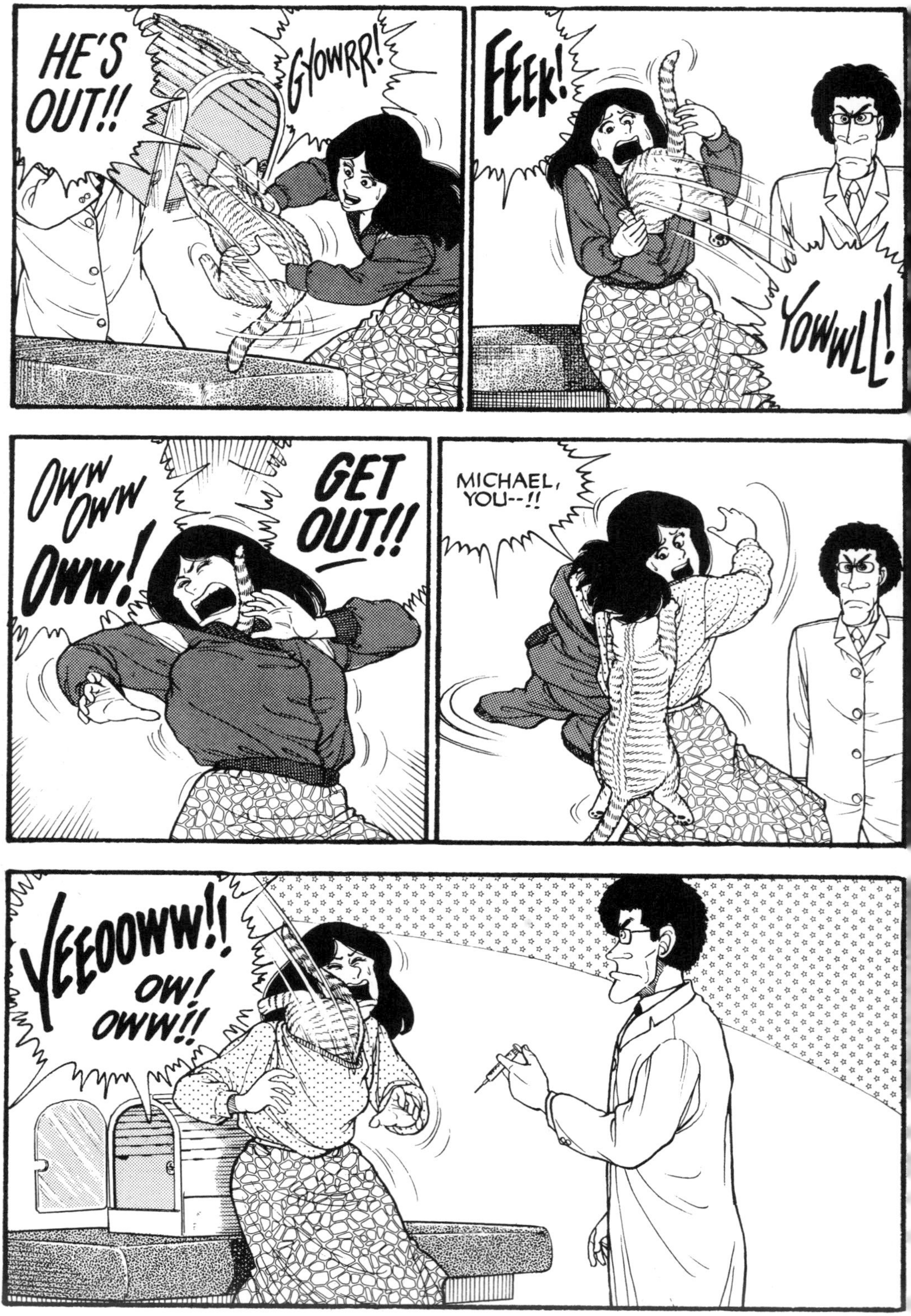
HE'S OUT!!
GYOWRR!
EEEK!
YOWWLL!
OWW OWW OWW!
GET OUT!!
MICHAEL, YOU--!!
YEEOOWW!!
OW! OWW!!

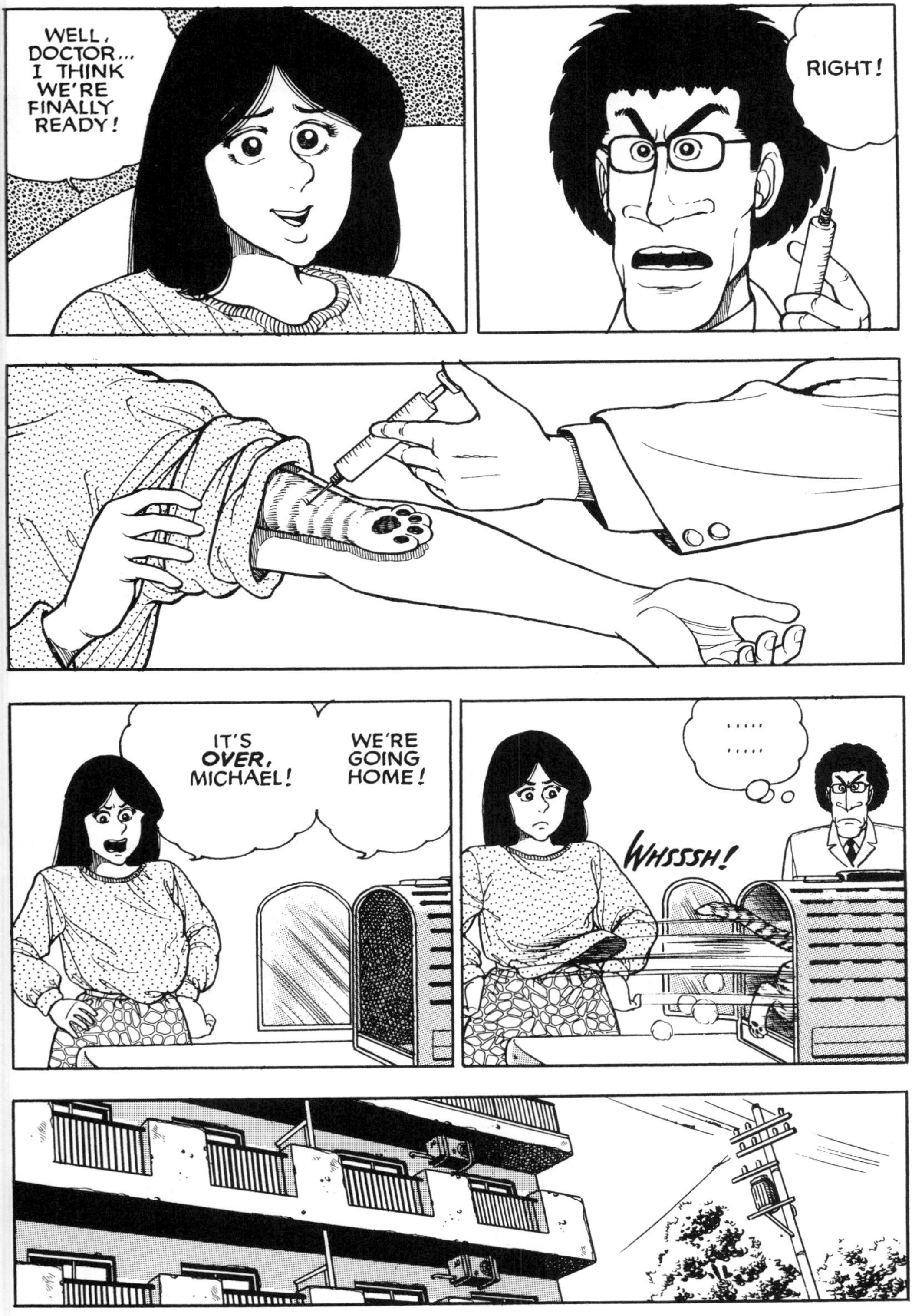
WELL, DOCTOR... I THINK WE'RE FINALLY READY!
RIGHT!
IT'S OVER, MICHAEL!
WE'RE GOING HOME!
.....
.....
WHSSSH!

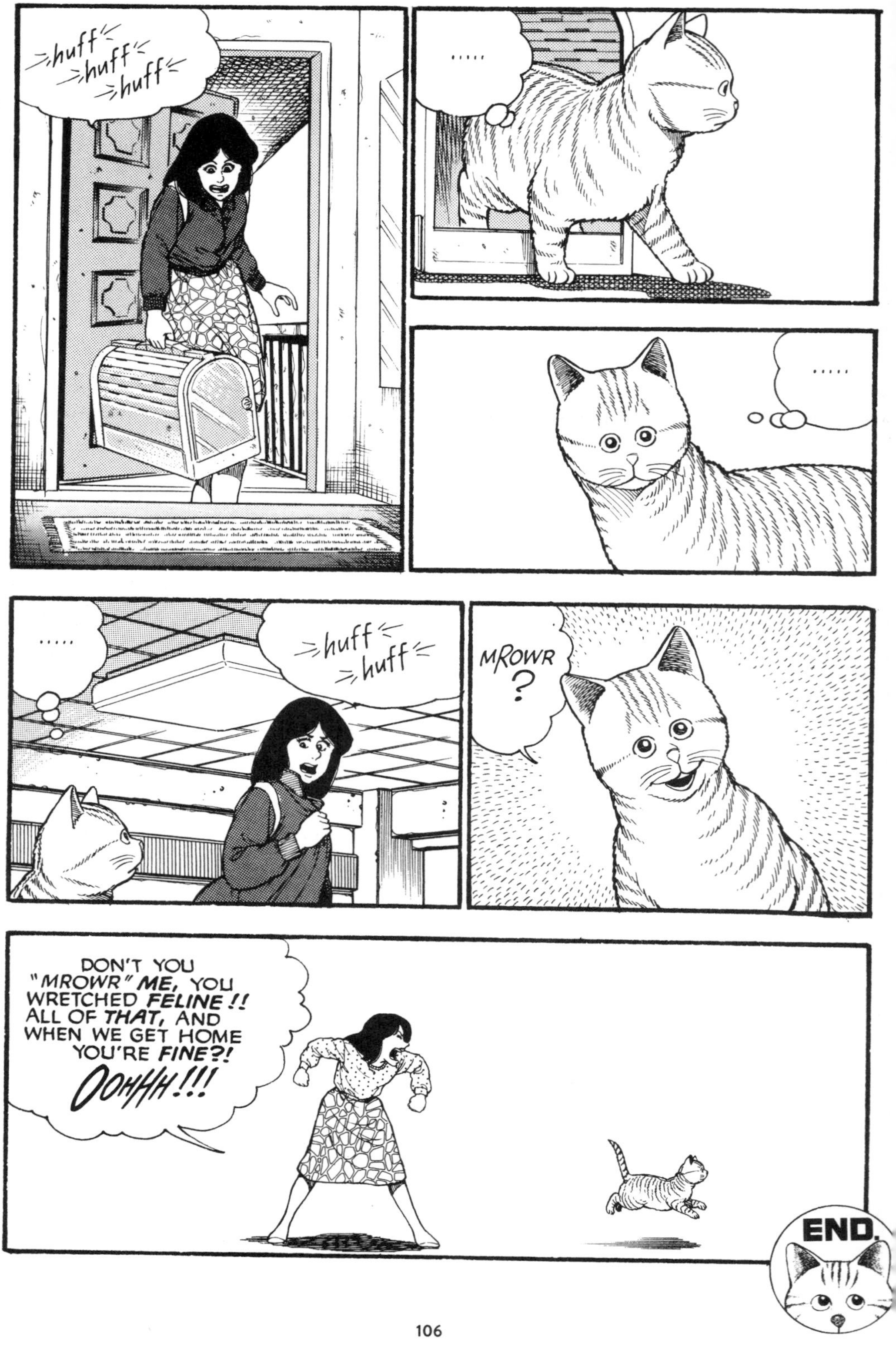
huff huff huff
.....
.....
.....
huff huff
MROWR ?
DON'T YOU "MROWR" ME, YOU WRETCHED FELINE!! ALL OF THAT, AND WHEN WE GET HOME YOU'RE FINE?! OOHHH!!!
END.

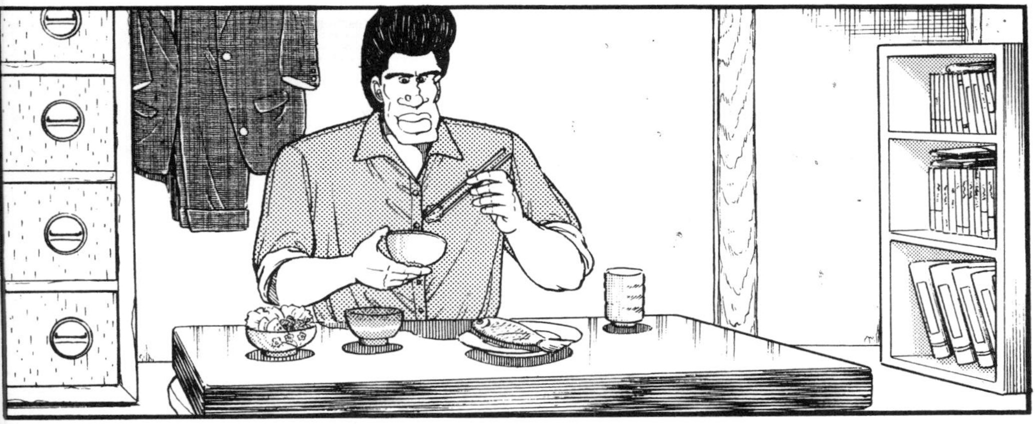

# SUDDENLY, ONE EVENING...

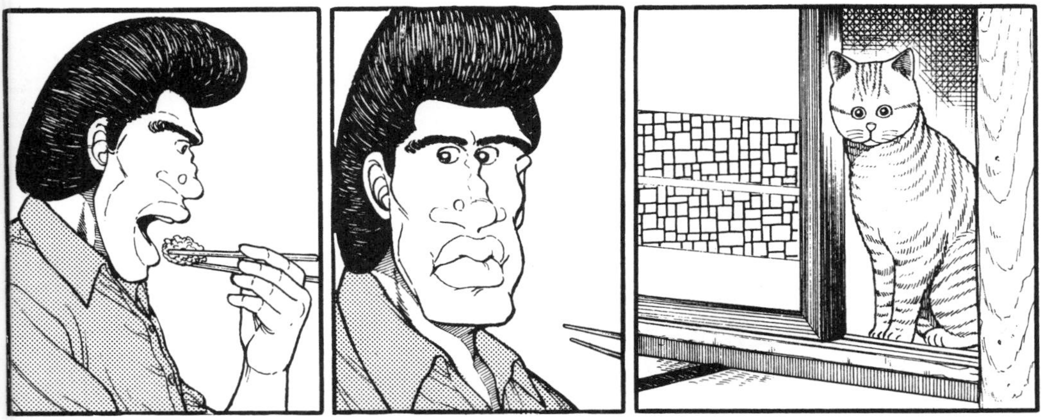

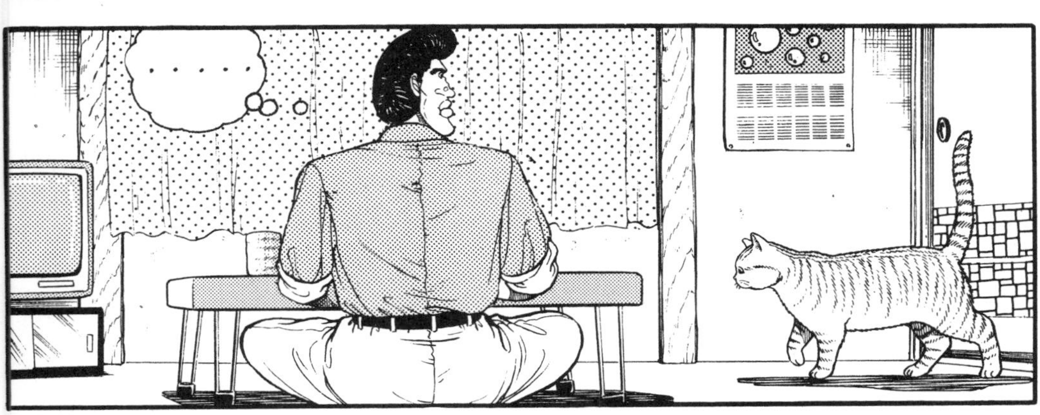
. . . . . .

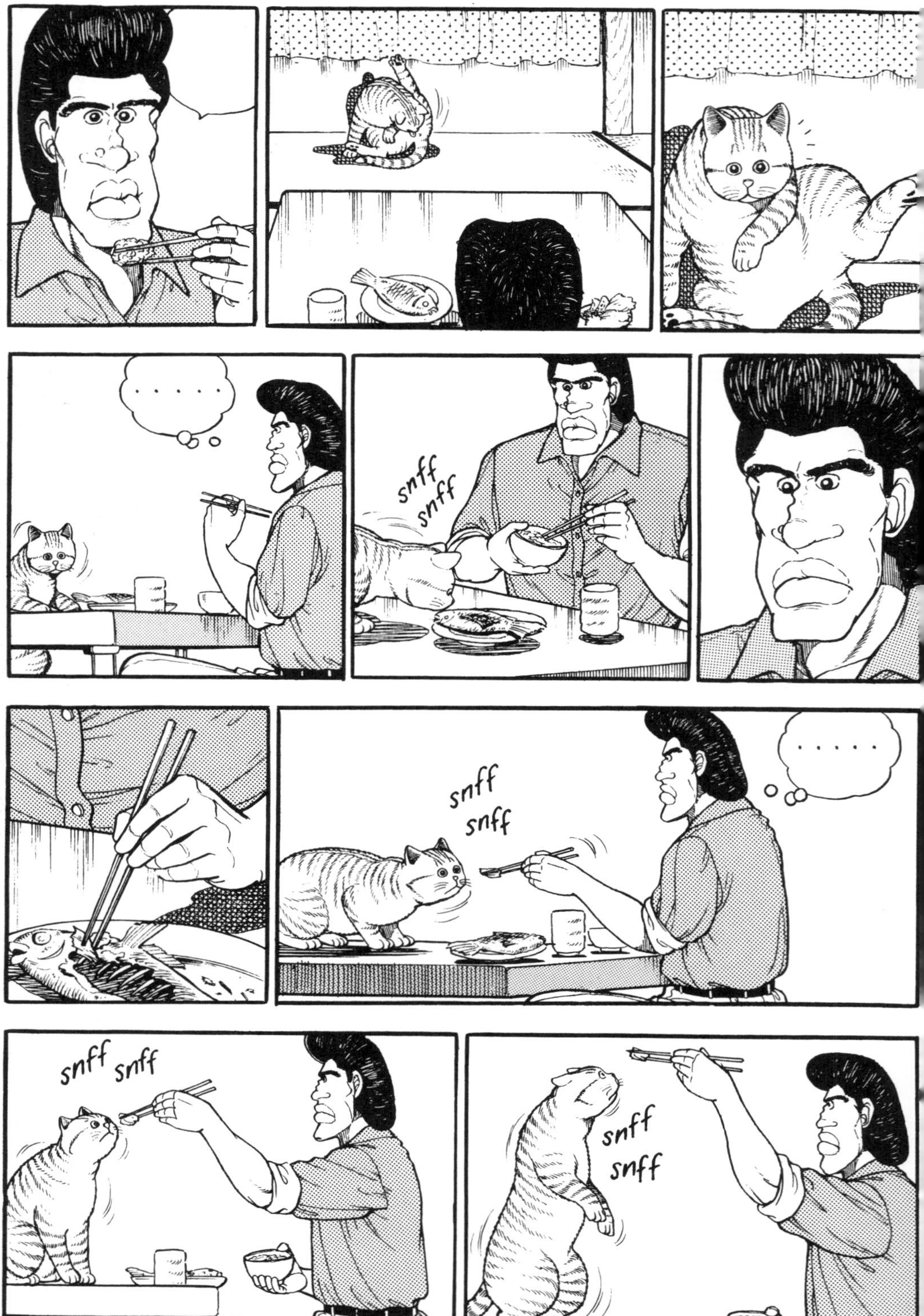
......
snff
snff
snff
snff
......
snff snff
snff
snff

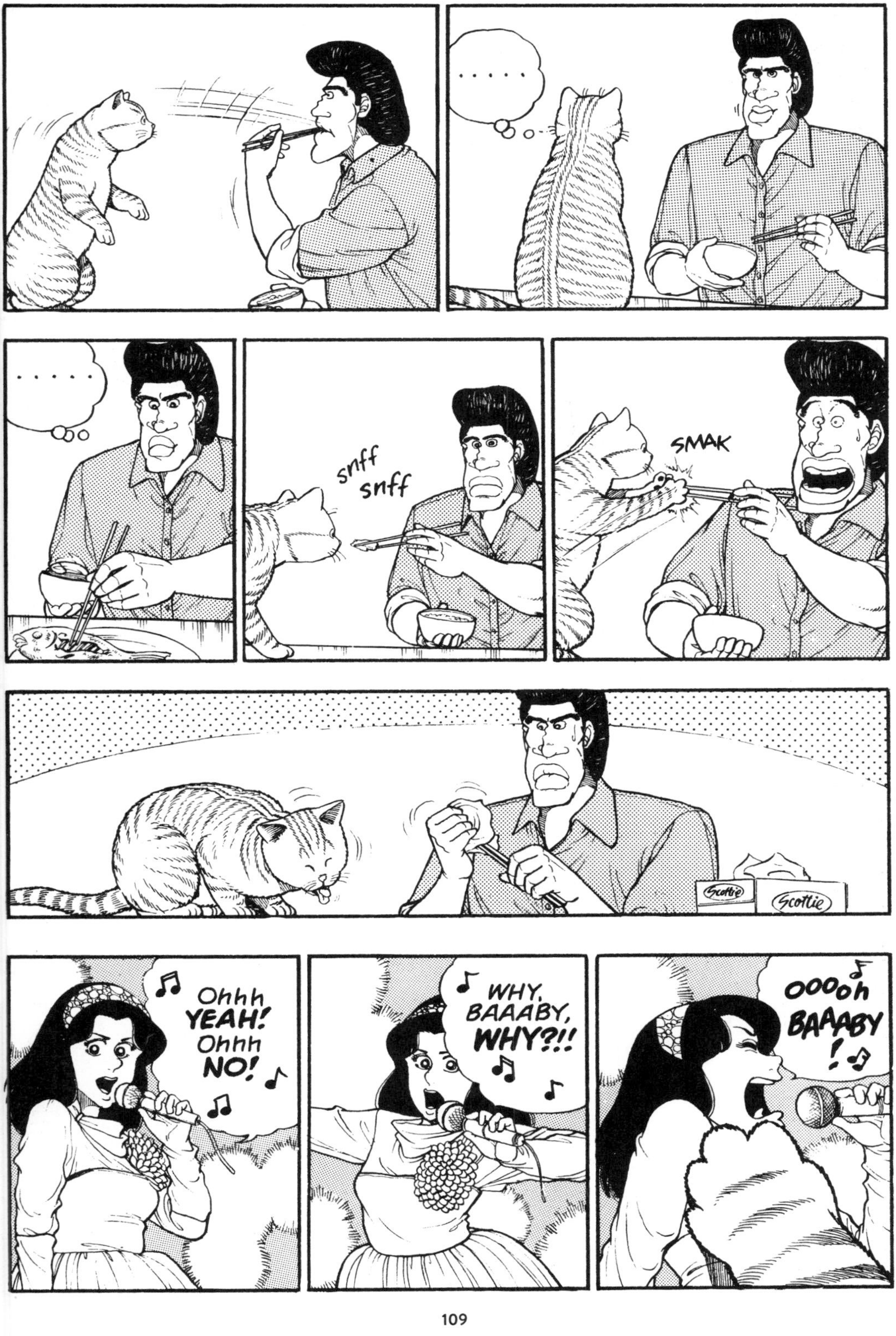
. . . . . .
. . . . . .
snff
snff
SMAK
Scottie
Scottie
Ohhh YEAH! Ohhh NO!
WHY, BAAABY, WHY?!!
OOOoh BAAABY!

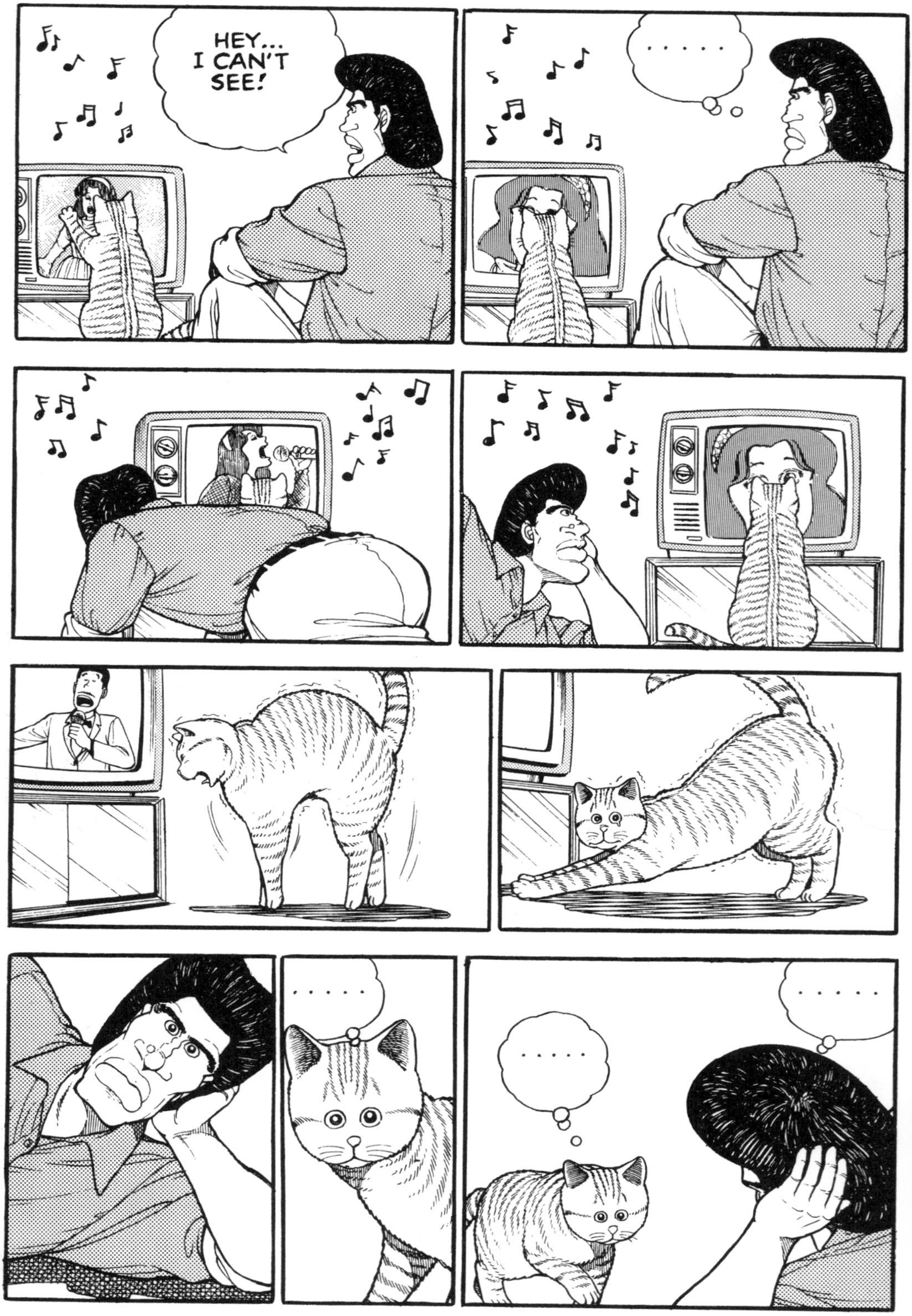
HEY... I CAN'T SEE!
. . . . .
. . . . .
. . . . .
. . . . .

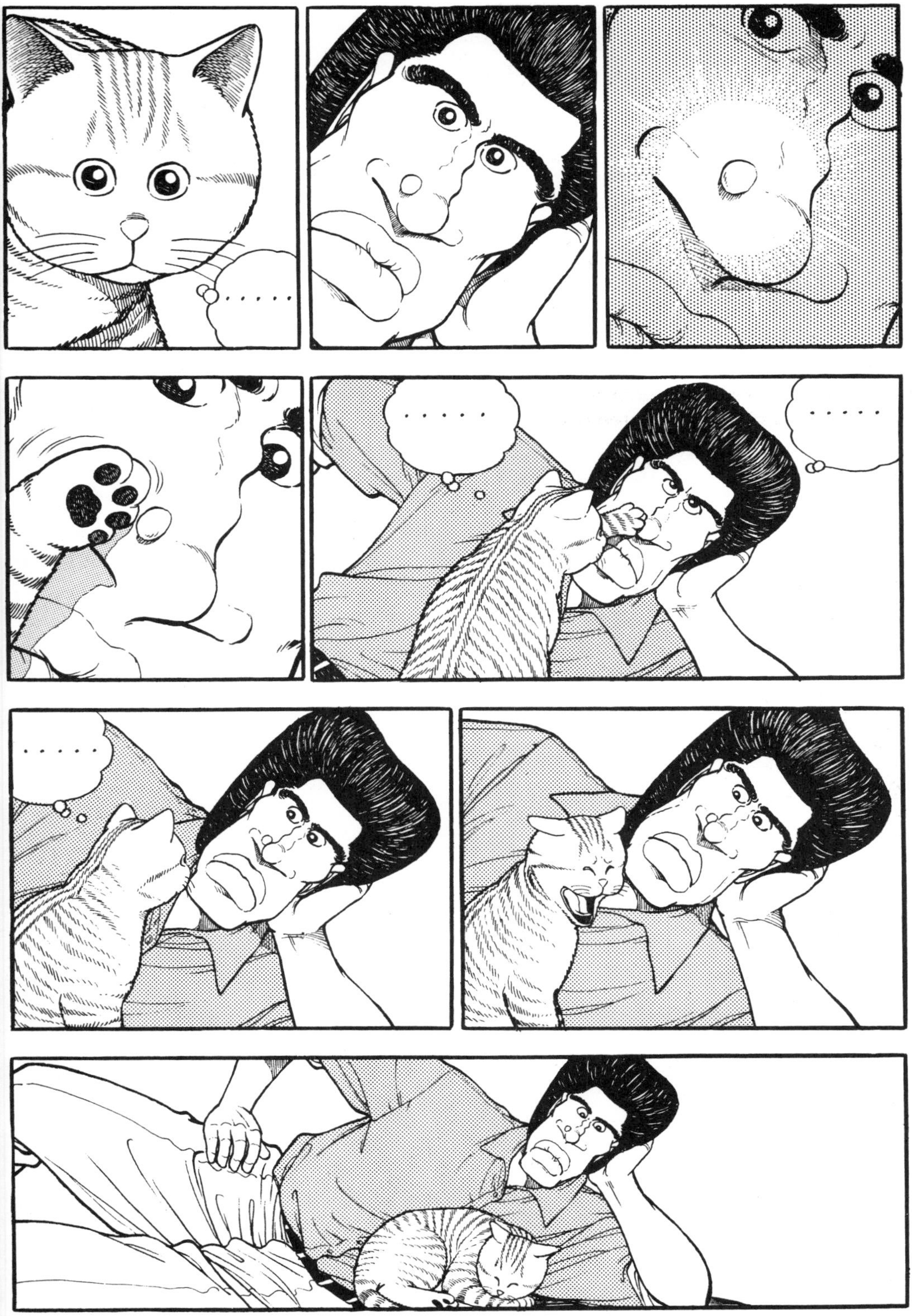
......
......
......
......

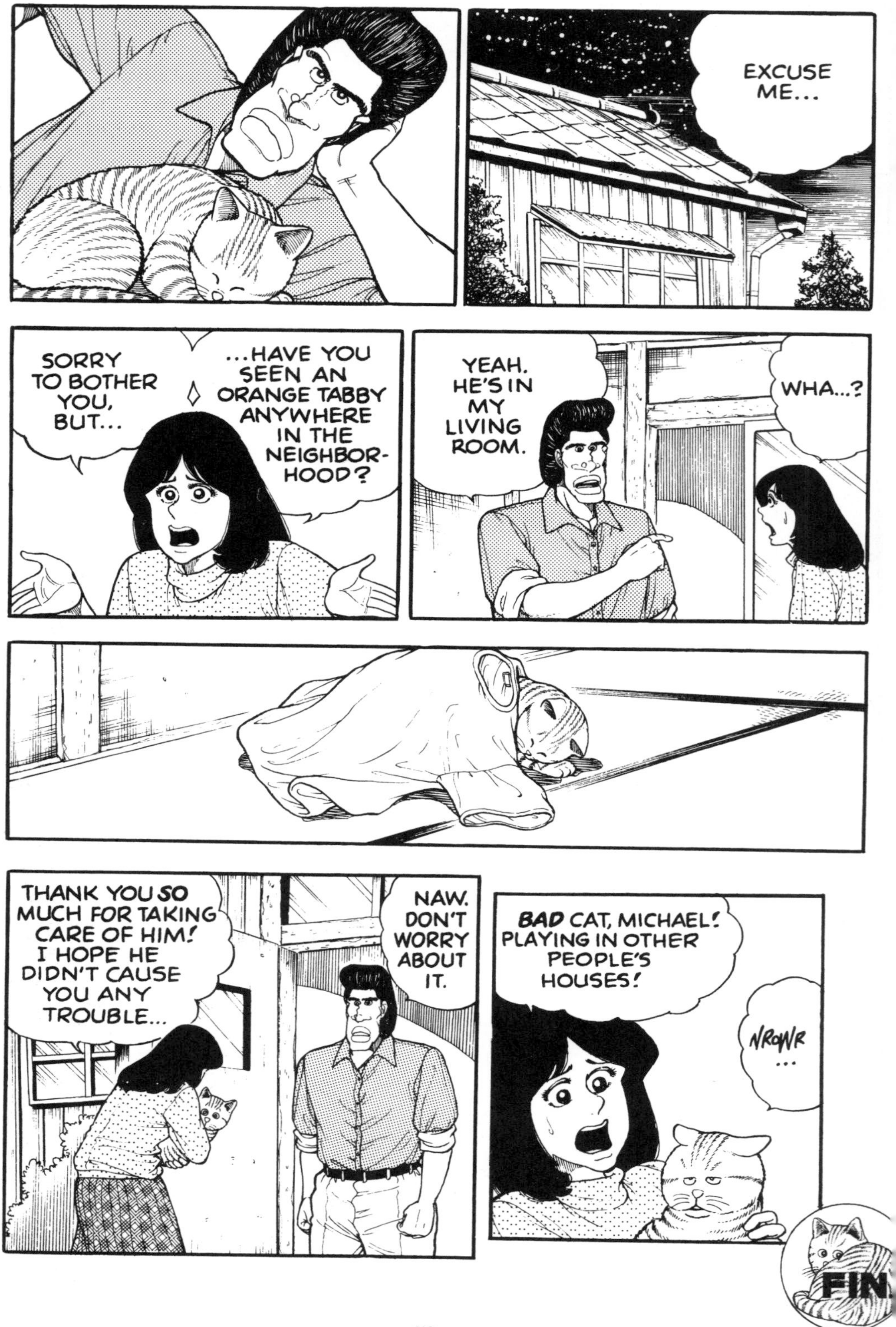
EXCUSE ME...
SORRY TO BOTHER YOU, BUT...
...HAVE YOU SEEN AN ORANGE TABBY ANYWHERE IN THE NEIGHBORHOOD?
YEAH. HE'S IN MY LIVING ROOM.
WHA...?
THANK YOU **SO** MUCH FOR TAKING CARE OF HIM! I HOPE HE DIDN'T CAUSE YOU ANY TROUBLE...
NAW. DON'T WORRY ABOUT IT.
**BAD** CAT, MICHAEL! PLAYING IN OTHER PEOPLE'S HOUSES!
NROWR...
FIN

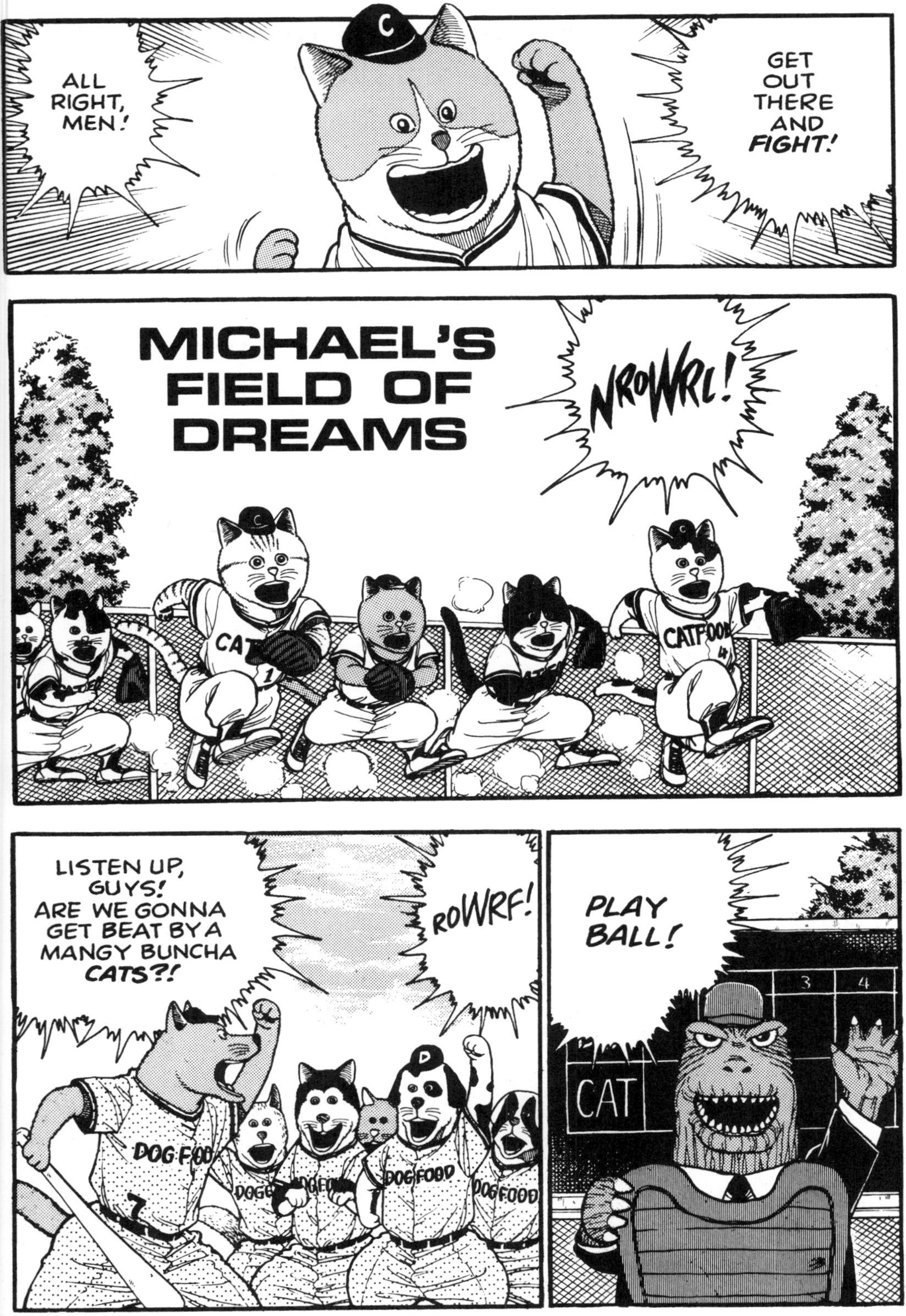
ALL RIGHT, MEN!
GET OUT THERE AND FIGHT!
MICHAEL'S FIELD OF DREAMS
NROWRL!
CAT
CATFOOD
LISTEN UP, GUYS! ARE WE GONNA GET BEAT BY A MANGY BUNCHA CATS?!
ROWRF!
DOG FOOD
PLAY BALL!
3
4
CAT

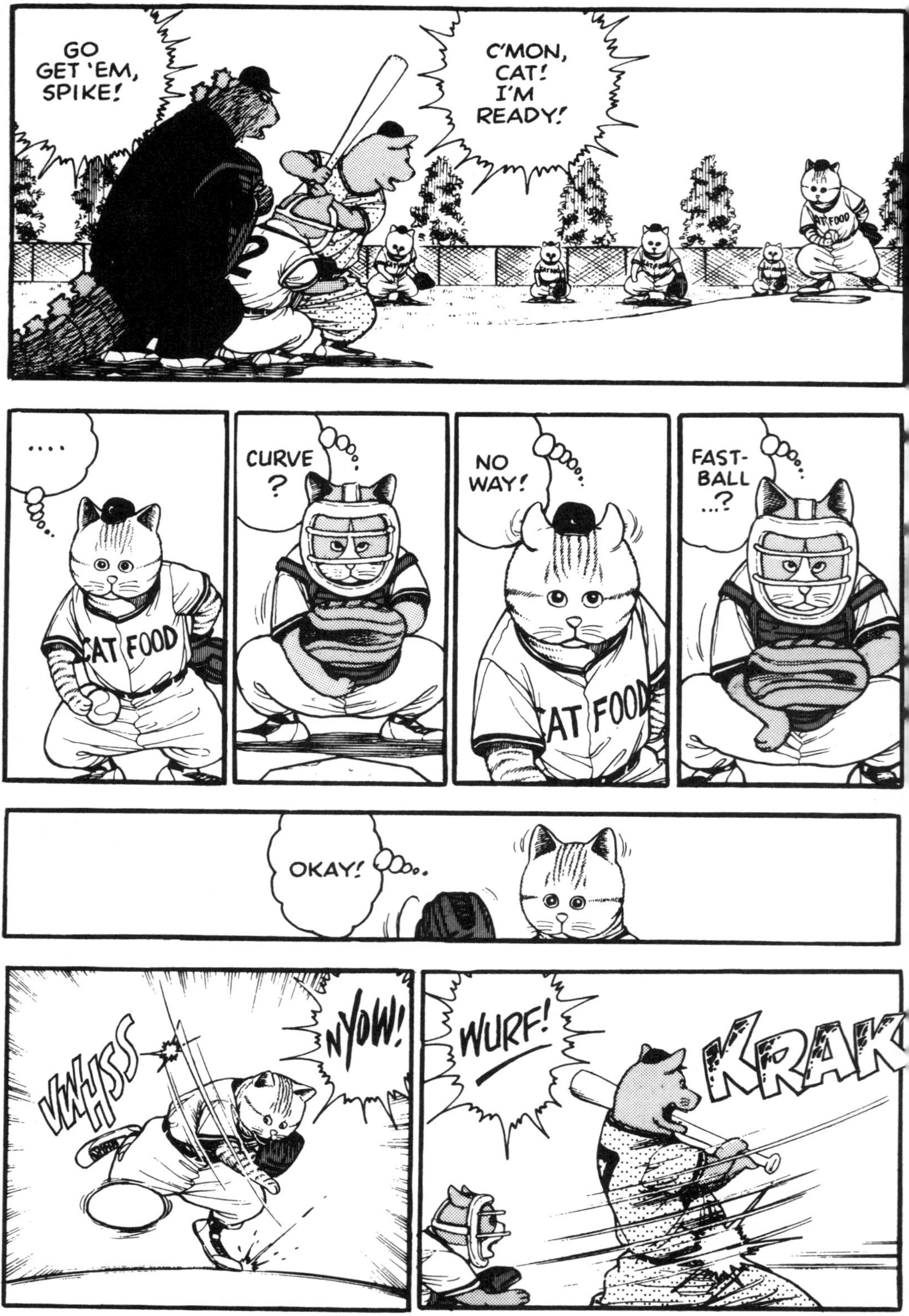
GO GET 'EM, SPIKE!
C'MON, CAT! I'M READY!
CAT FOOD
....
CAT FOOD
CURVE ?
NO WAY!
CAT FOOD
FAST-BALL ...?
OKAY!
VWHSS
NYOW!
WURF!
KRAK

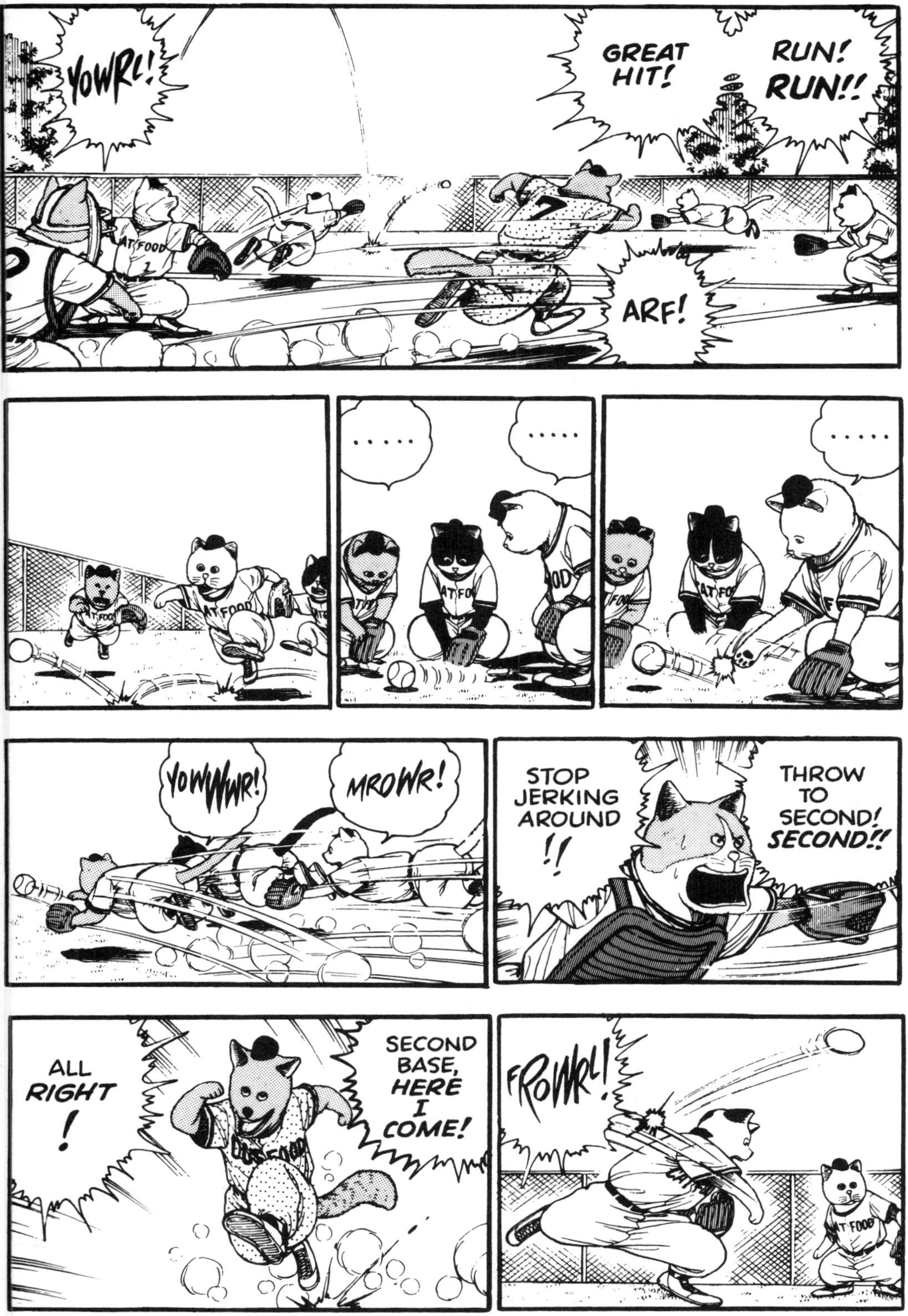
YOWRL!
GREAT HIT!
RUN! RUN!!
ARF!
.....
.....
.....
YOWWWR!
MROWR!
STOP JERKING AROUND !!
THROW TO SECOND! SECOND!!
ALL RIGHT !
SECOND BASE, HERE I COME!
FROWRL!

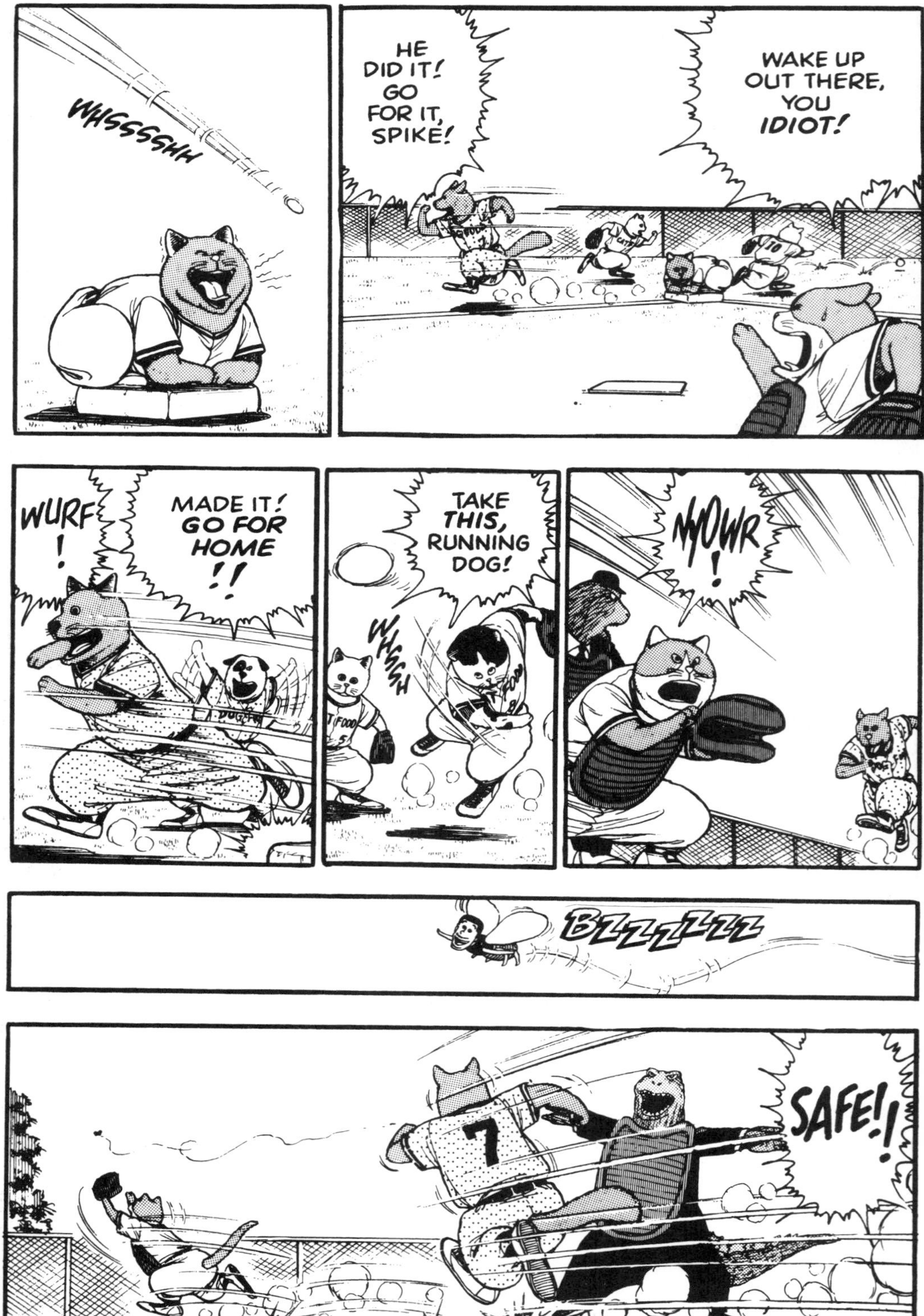

WHSSSSHH
HE DID IT! GO FOR IT, SPIKE!
WAKE UP OUT THERE, YOU IDIOT!
WURF!
MADE IT! GO FOR HOME!!
TAKE THIS, RUNNING DOG!
NYOWR!
SAFE!!

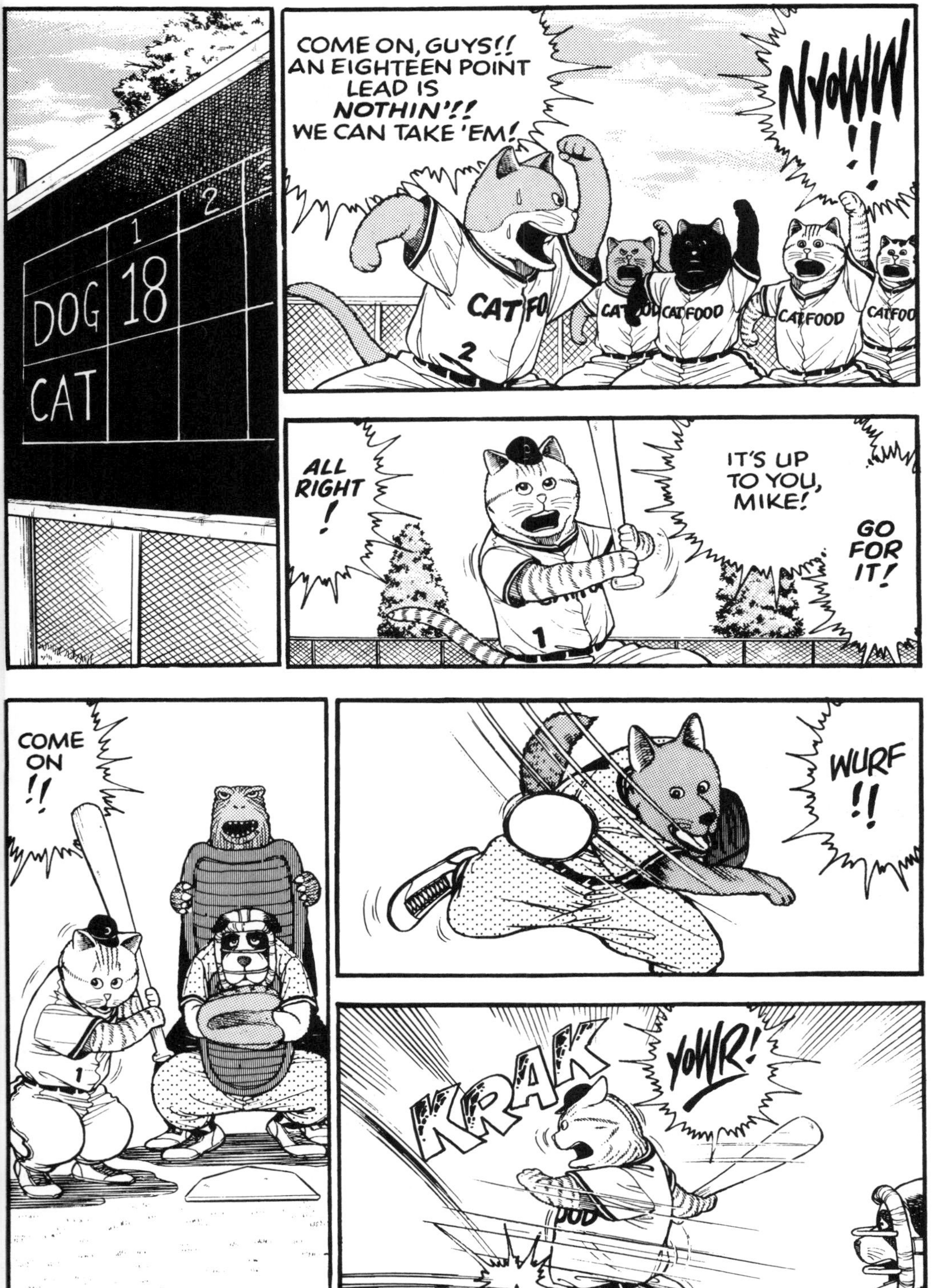
1
2
DOG
18
CAT
COME ON, GUYS!! AN EIGHTEEN POINT LEAD IS NOTHIN'!! WE CAN TAKE 'EM!
NYOWW!!
CATFOOD
ALL RIGHT!
IT'S UP TO YOU, MIKE!
GO FOR IT!
COME ON!!
WURF!!
KRAK
YOWR!

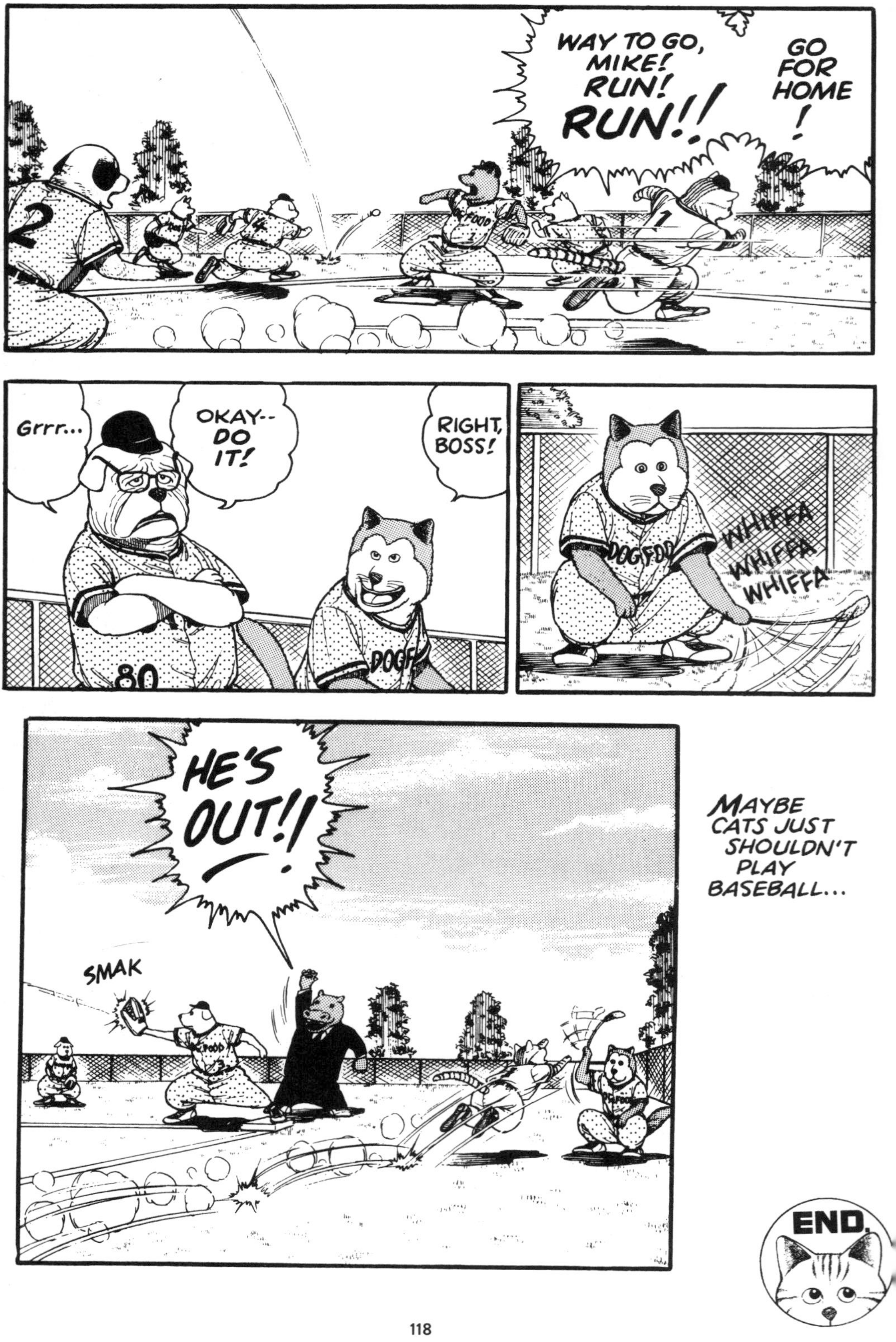

WAY TO GO, MIKE! RUN! RUN!!
GO FOR HOME!
Grrr...
OKAY-- DO IT!
RIGHT, BOSS!
WHIFFA WHIFFA WHIFFA
HE'S OUT!!
SMAK
MAYBE CATS JUST SHOULDN'T PLAY BASEBALL...
END.

# BEST OF FRIENDS

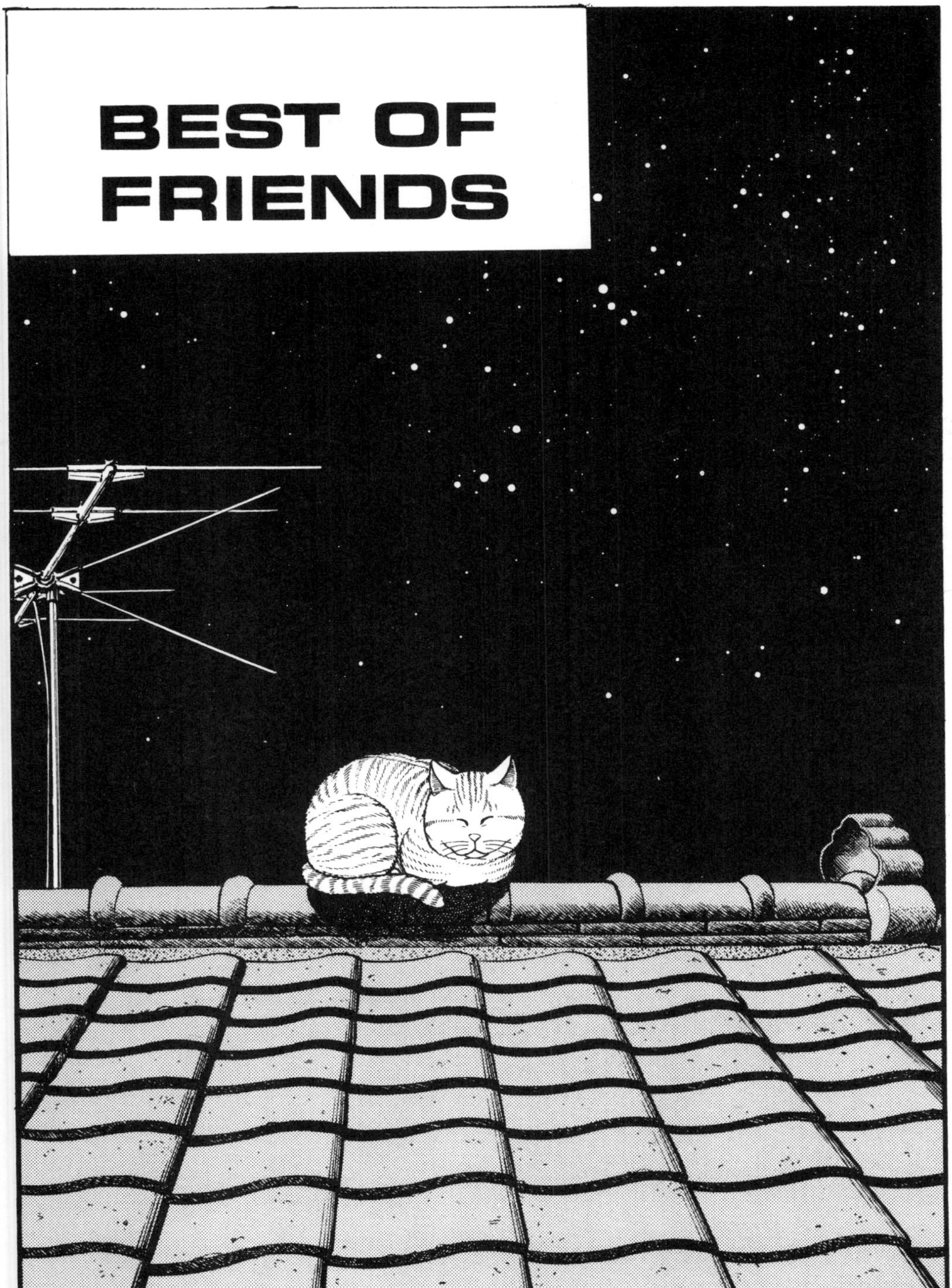

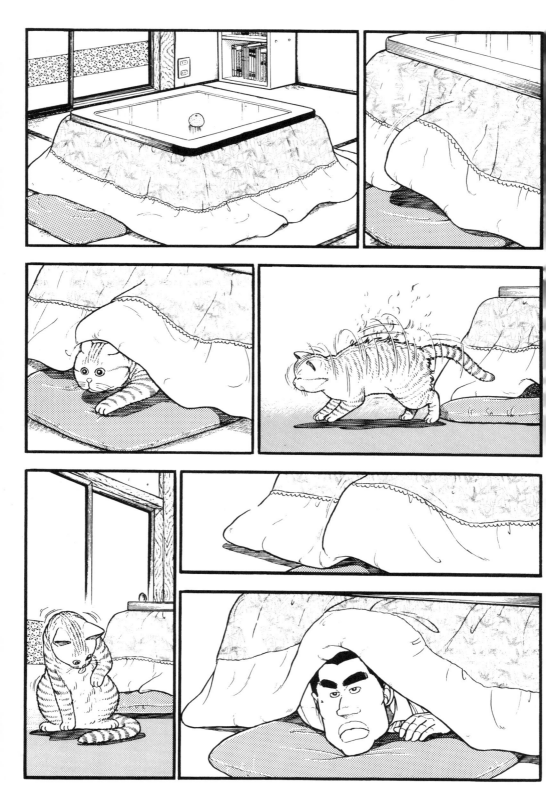

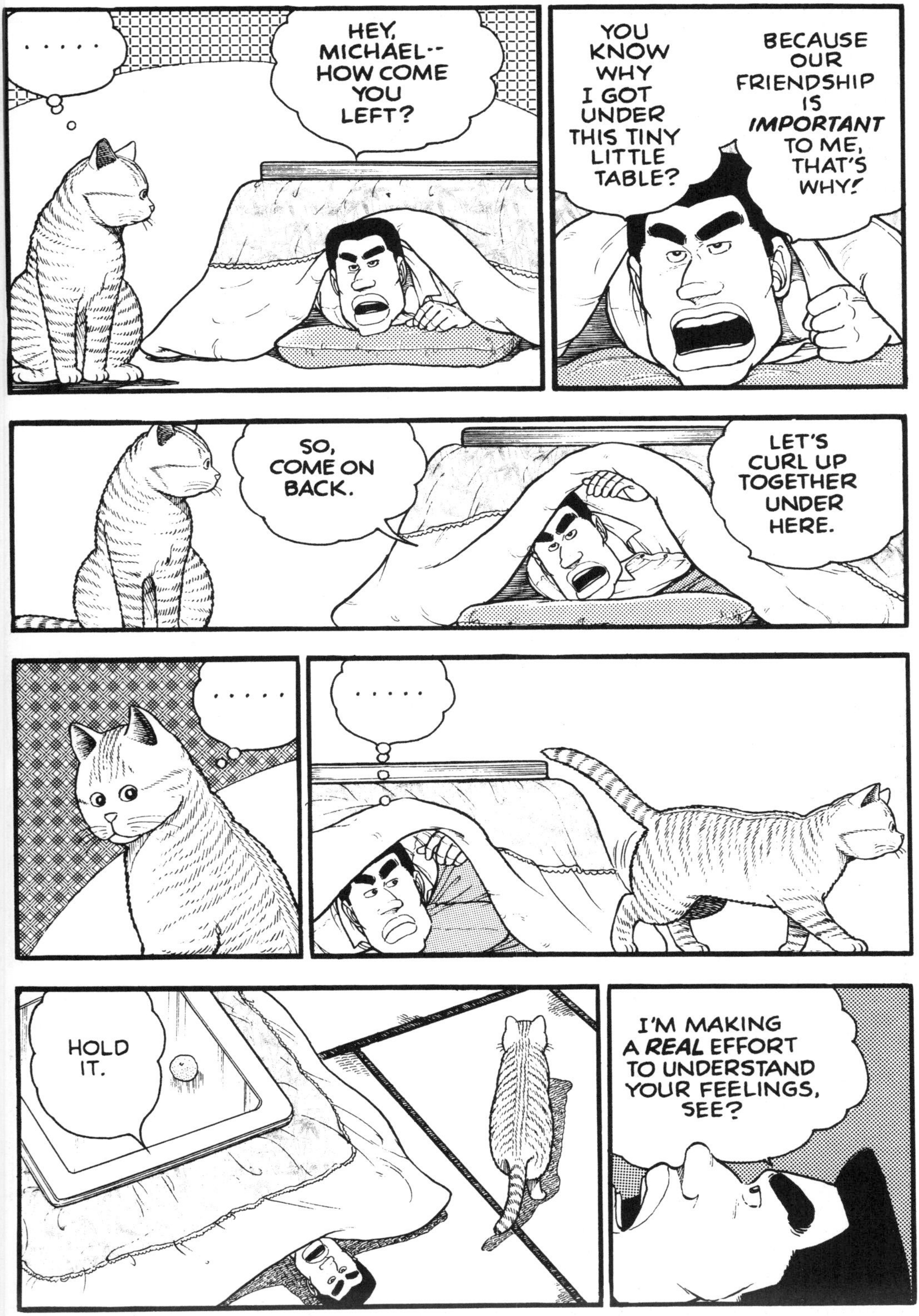
. . . . .
HEY, MICHAEL-- HOW COME YOU LEFT?
YOU KNOW WHY I GOT UNDER THIS TINY LITTLE TABLE?
BECAUSE OUR FRIENDSHIP IS *IMPORTANT* TO ME, THAT'S WHY!
SO, COME ON BACK.
LET'S CURL UP TOGETHER UNDER HERE.
. . . . .
. . . . .
HOLD IT.
I'M MAKING A ***REAL*** EFFORT TO UNDERSTAND YOUR FEELINGS, SEE?

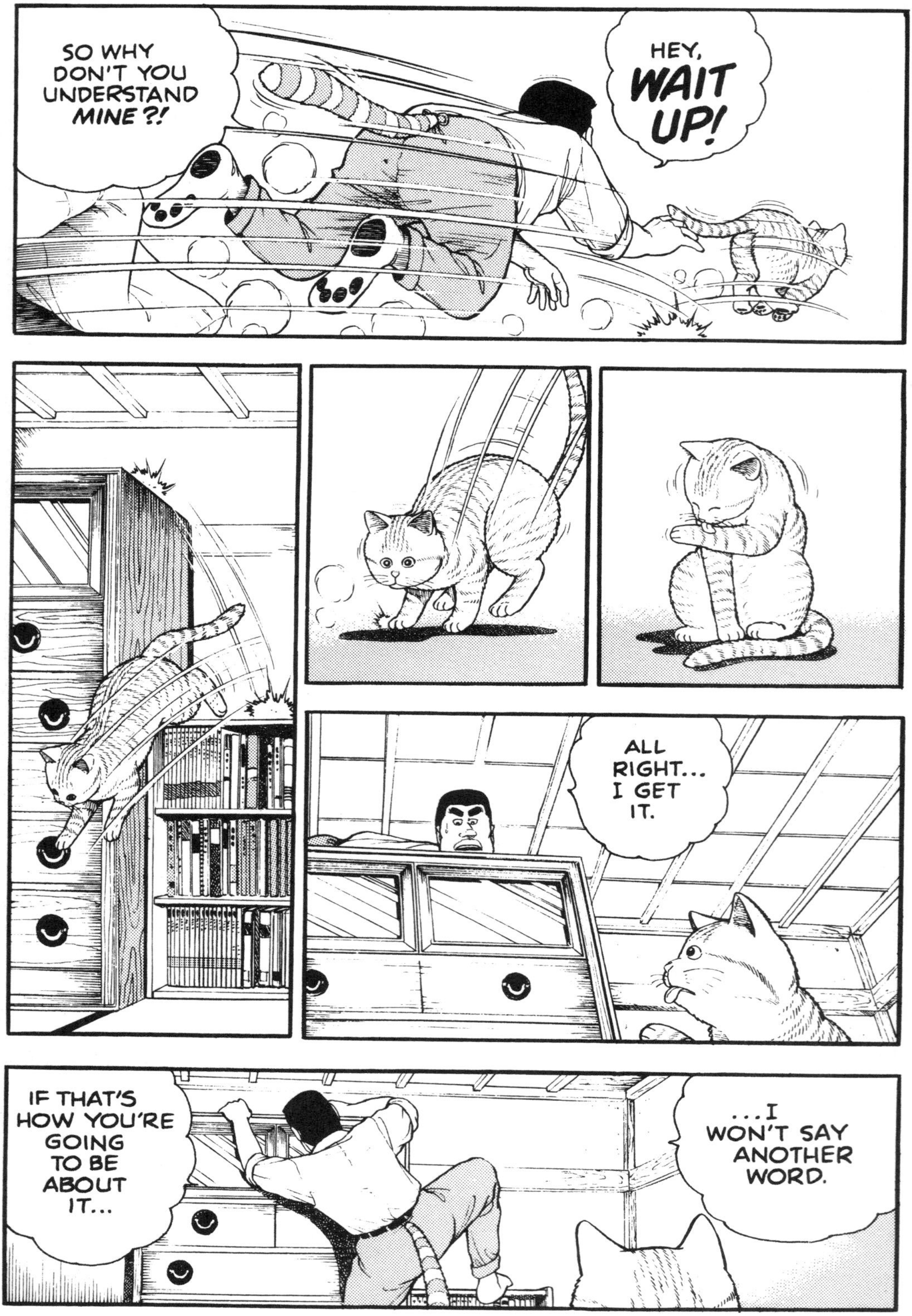
SO WHY DON'T YOU UNDERSTAND *MINE*?!
HEY, **WAIT UP!**
ALL RIGHT... I GET IT.
IF THAT'S HOW YOU'RE GOING TO BE ABOUT IT...
...I WON'T SAY ANOTHER WORD.

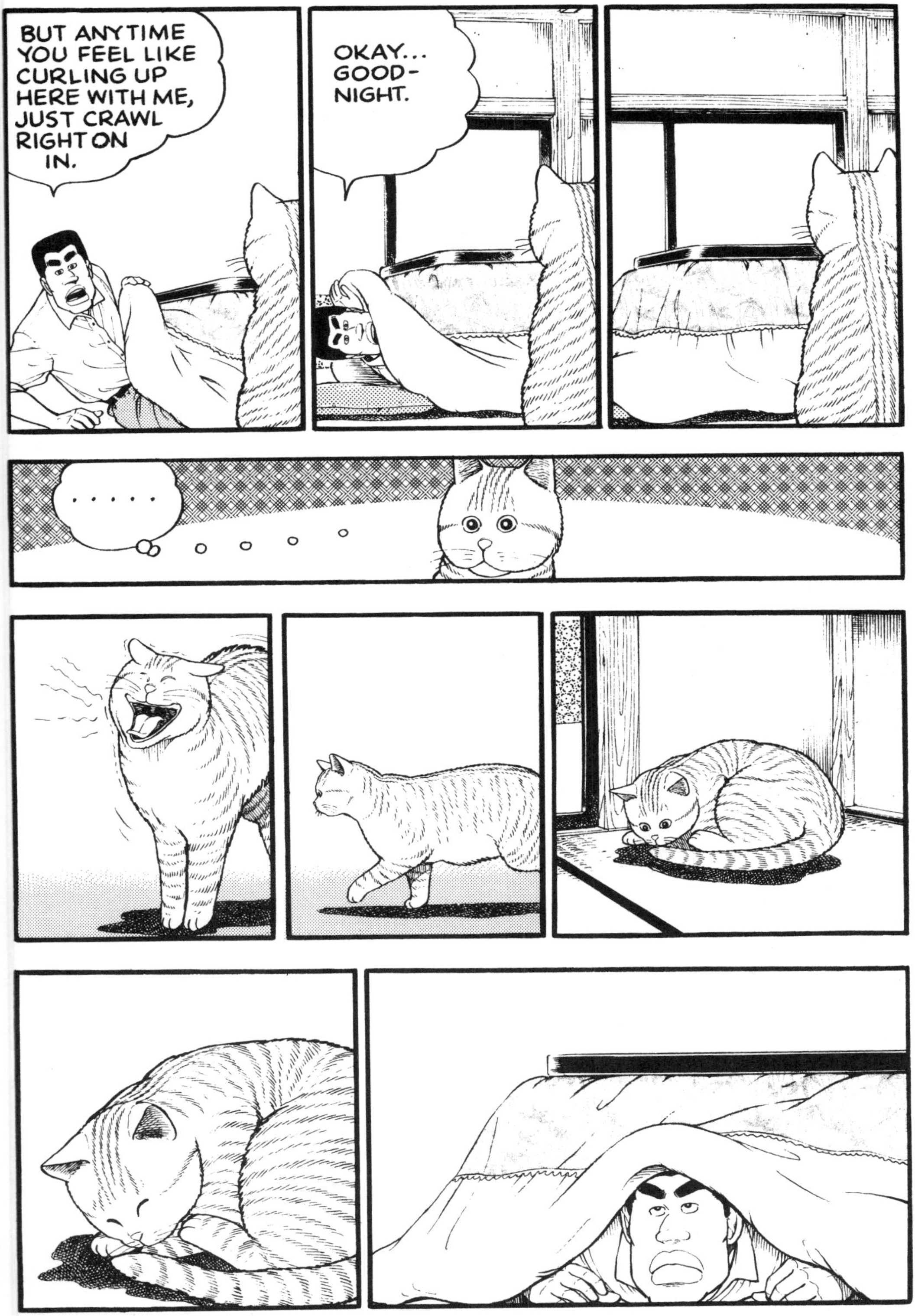
BUT ANYTIME YOU FEEL LIKE CURLING UP HERE WITH ME, JUST CRAWL RIGHT ON IN.
OKAY... GOOD-NIGHT.
.....

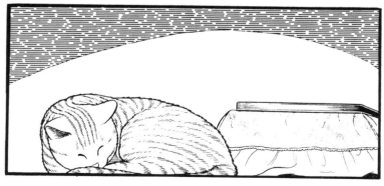

FROWR
!!

. . . . .

. . . . .

FIN

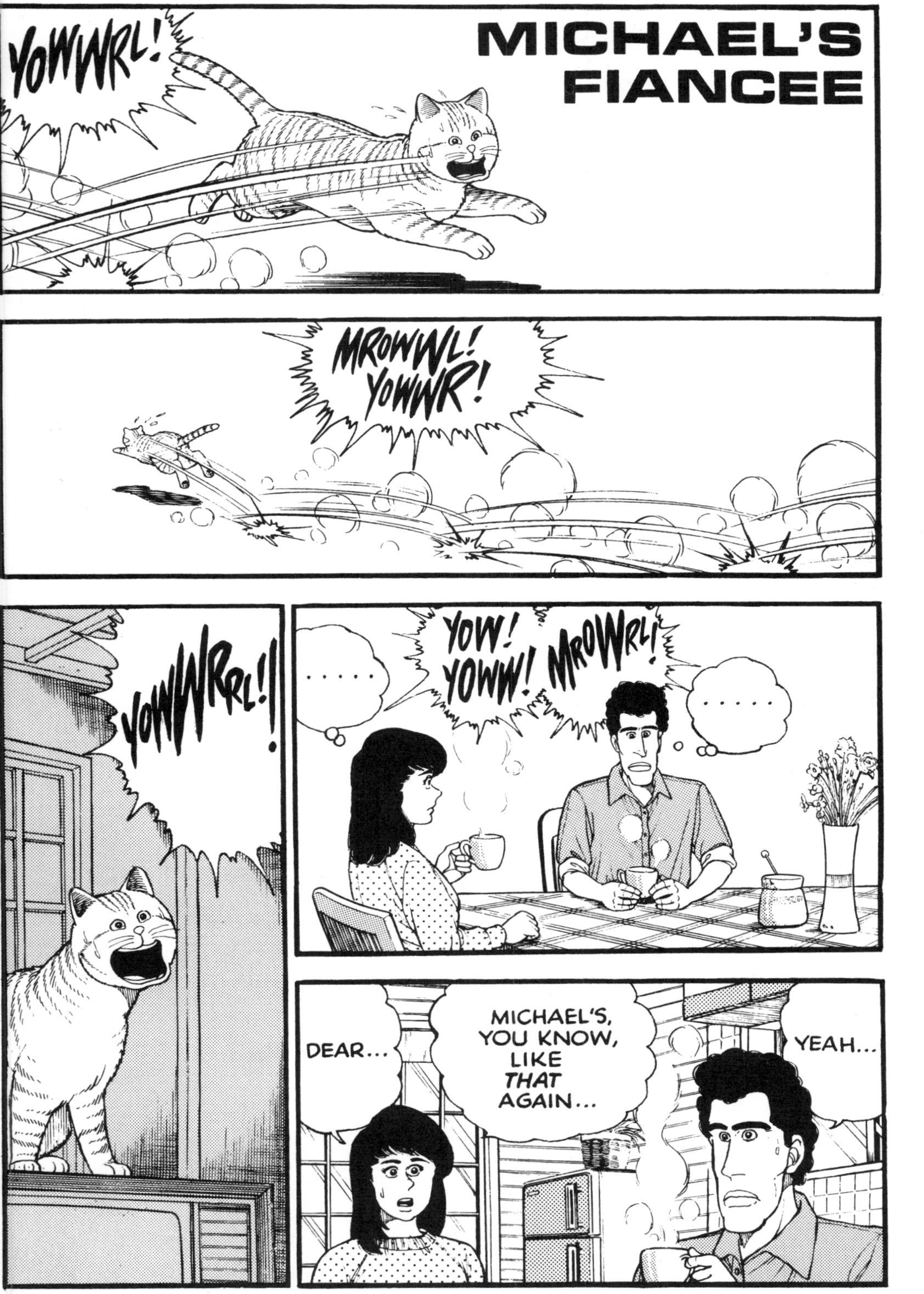
YOWWRL!
MICHAEL'S FIANCEE
MROWWL! YOWWR!
YOWWRRL!!
.....
YOW! YOWW!
MROWRL!
.....
DEAR...
MICHAEL'S, YOU KNOW, LIKE *THAT* AGAIN...
YEAH...

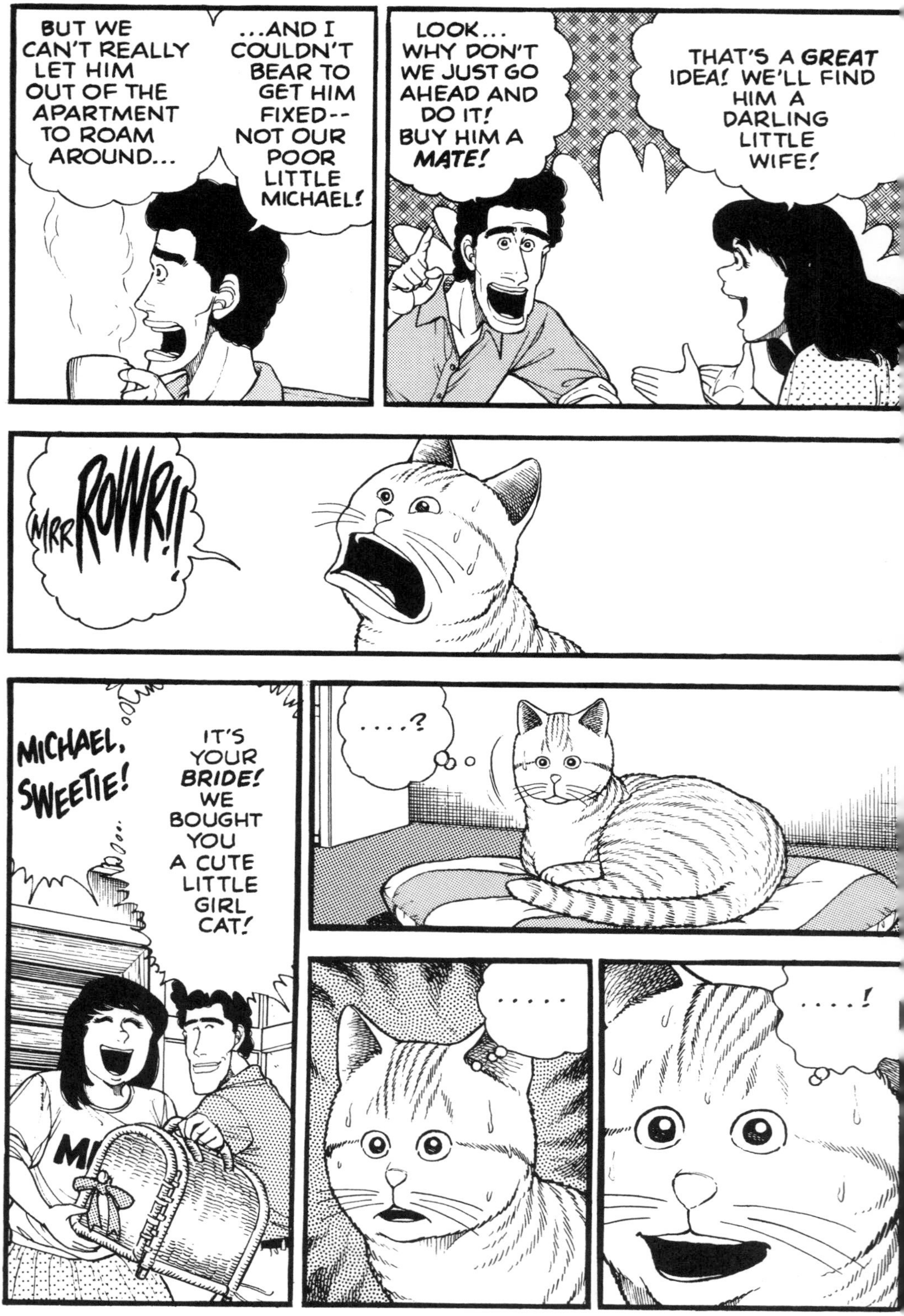

BUT WE CAN'T REALLY LET HIM OUT OF THE APARTMENT TO ROAM AROUND...
...AND I COULDN'T BEAR TO GET HIM FIXED--NOT OUR POOR LITTLE MICHAEL!
LOOK... WHY DON'T WE JUST GO AHEAD AND DO IT! BUY HIM A MATE!
THAT'S A GREAT IDEA! WE'LL FIND HIM A DARLING LITTLE WIFE!
MRRROWR!!
MICHAEL, SWEETIE!
IT'S YOUR BRIDE! WE BOUGHT YOU A CUTE LITTLE GIRL CAT!
....?
.....
....!

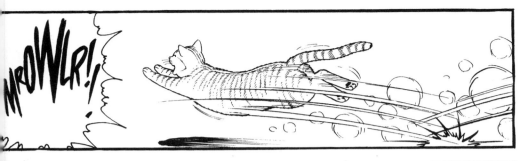

MROWLR!

meeww...

meeew...

MICHAEL, THIS IS *POPO*... SHE'S GOING TO BE YOUR WIFE-- *SOMEDAY!*

meww...

....!

.....

miiii...

mewuw...

ISN'T SHE JUST *DARLING*?!

NOW YOU TWO GET ALONG NICELY, OKAY?

.....

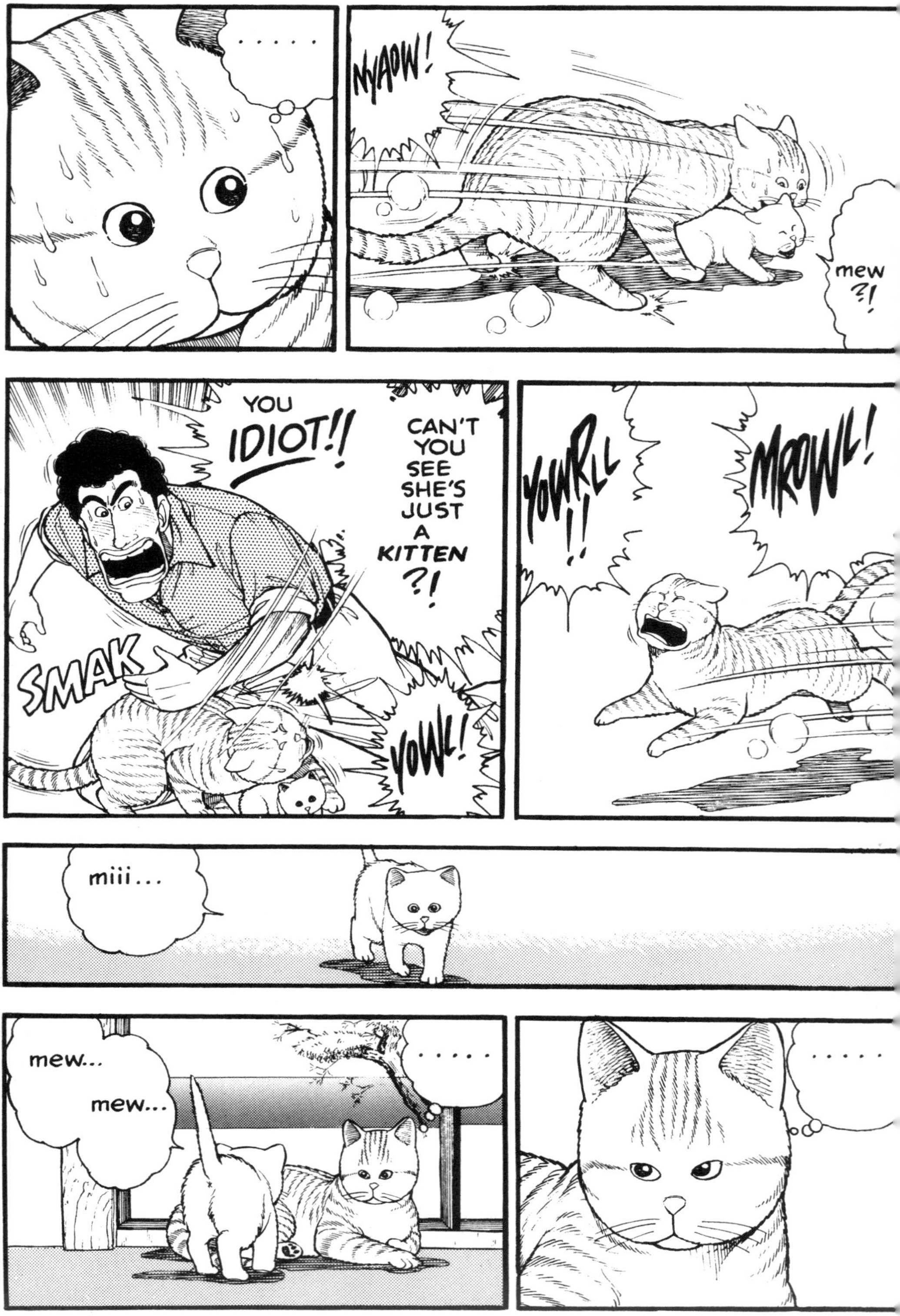
......
NYAOW!
mew ?!
YOU IDIOT!!
CAN'T YOU SEE SHE'S JUST A KITTEN ?!
SMAK
YOWL!
YOWRLL !!
MROWL!
miii...
mew...
mew...
.....
......

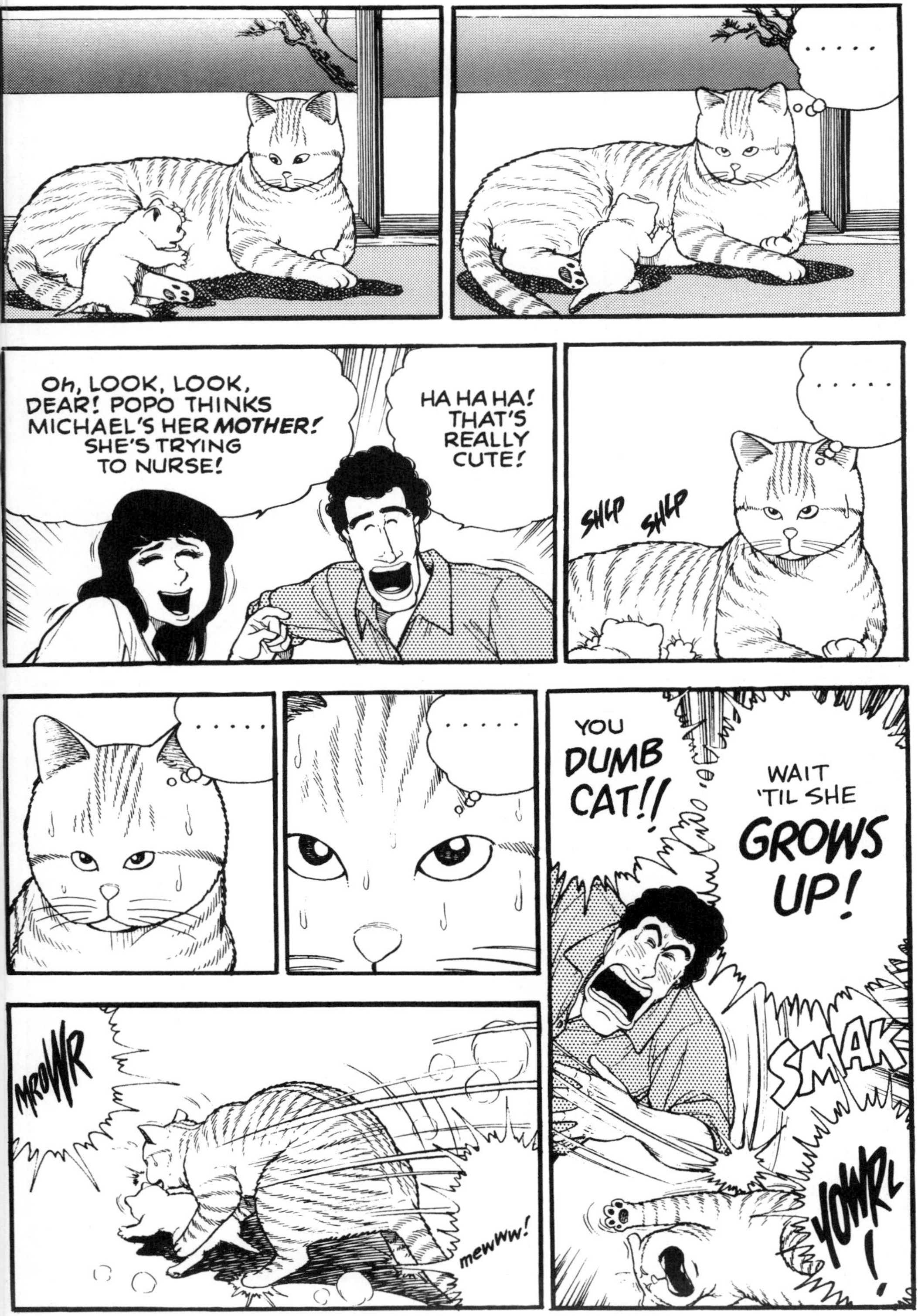
......
Oh, LOOK, LOOK, DEAR! POPO THINKS MICHAEL'S HER MOTHER! SHE'S TRYING TO NURSE!
HA HA HA! THAT'S REALLY CUTE!
......
SHLP SHLP
......
......
MROWR
mewww!
YOU DUMB CAT!!
WAIT 'TIL SHE GROWS UP!
SMAK
YOWRL!

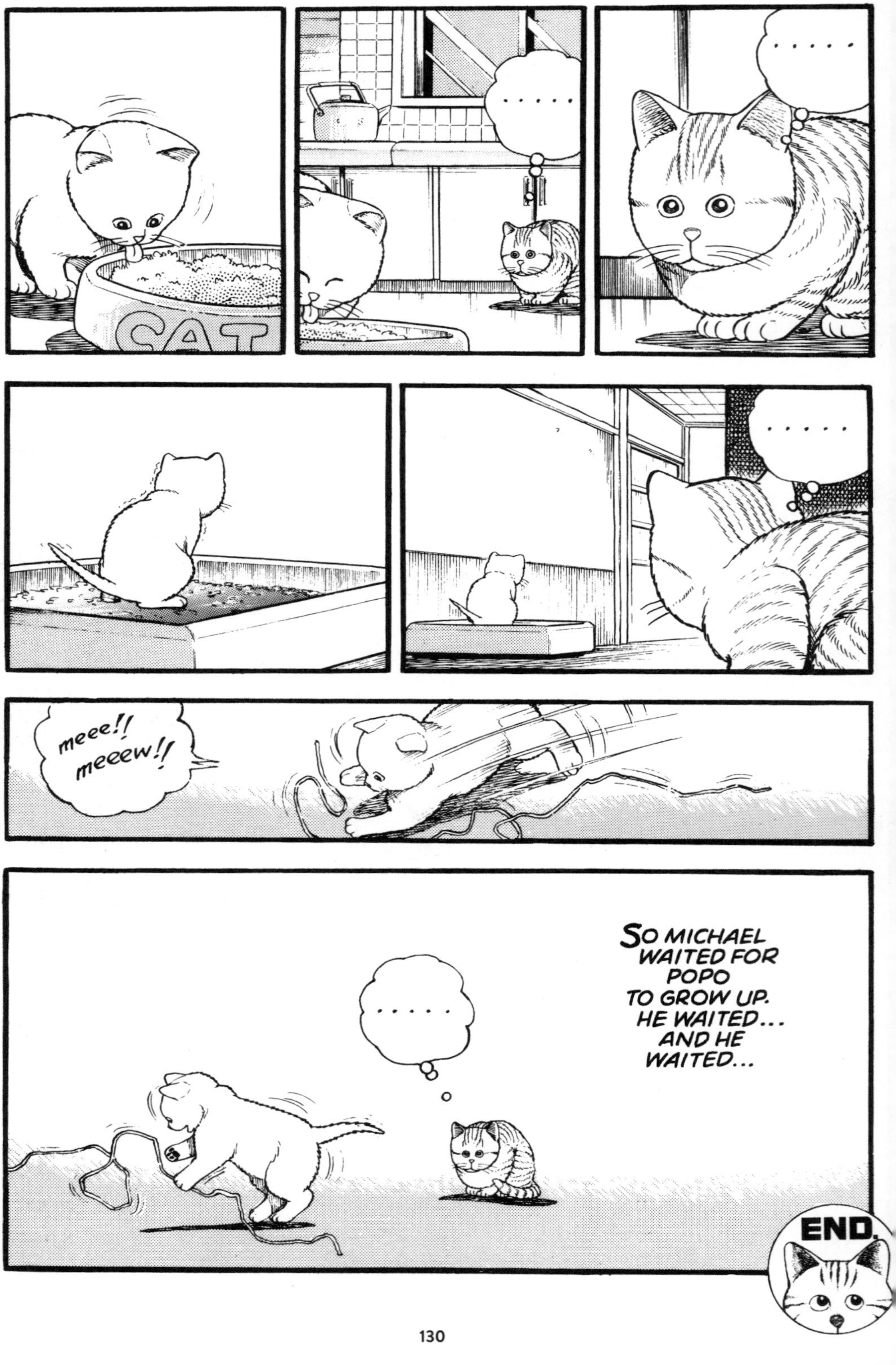
CAT
......
......
......
meee!! meeew!!
......
SO MICHAEL WAITED FOR POPO TO GROW UP. HE WAITED... AND HE WAITED...
END.

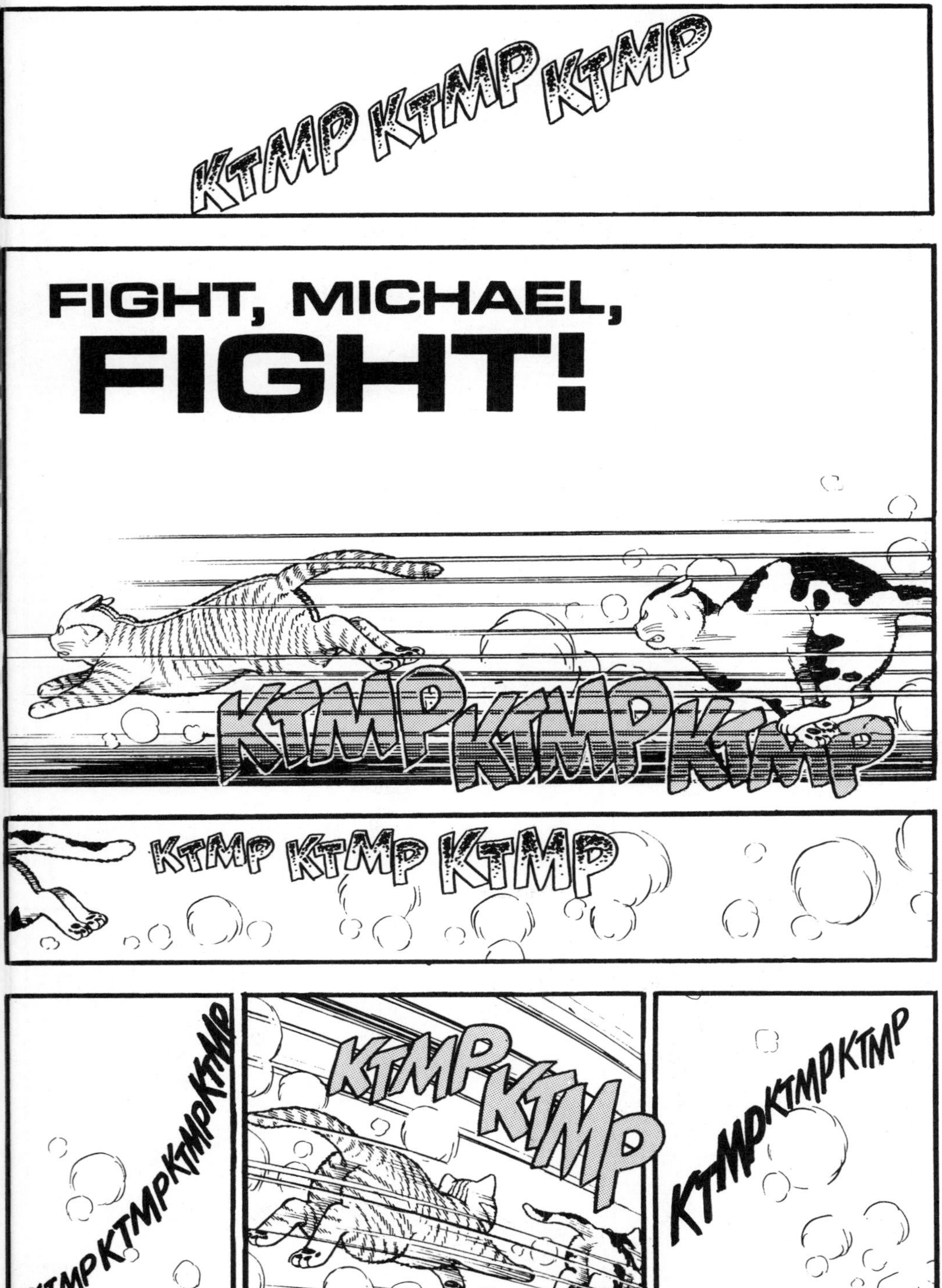
KTMP KTMP KTMP
FIGHT, MICHAEL,
FIGHT!
KTMP KTMP KTMP
KTMP KTMP KTMP
KTMP KTMP KTMP KTMP
KTMP KTMP
KTMP KTMP KTMP

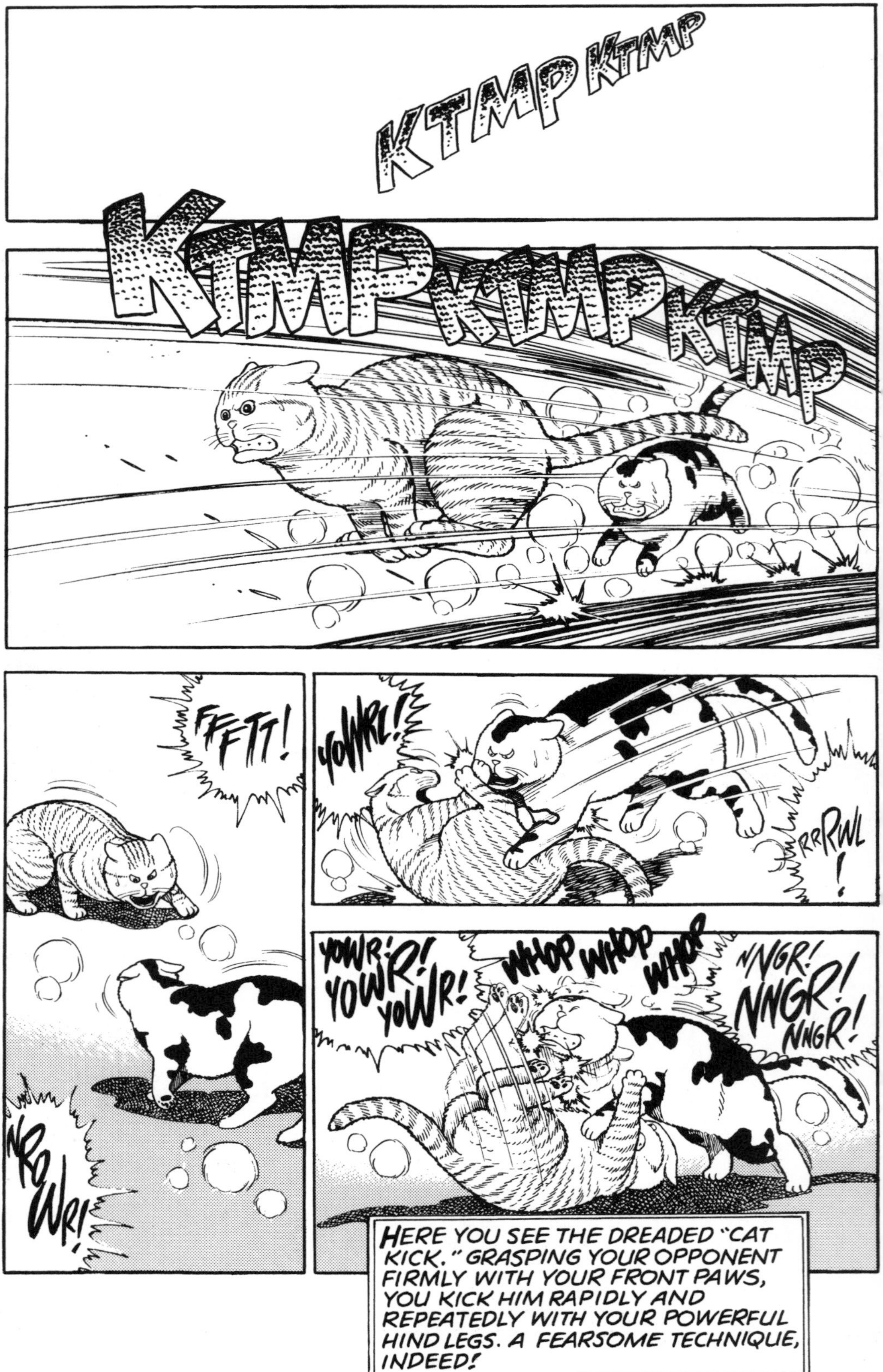
KTMP KTMP
KTMP KTMP KTMP KTMP
FFFTT!
NROWR!
YOWRL!
RRRWL!
YOWR! YOWR! YOWR!
WHOP WHOP WHOP
NNGR! NNGR! NNGR!
HERE YOU SEE THE DREADED "CAT KICK." GRASPING YOUR OPPONENT FIRMLY WITH YOUR FRONT PAWS, YOU KICK HIM RAPIDLY AND REPEATEDLY WITH YOUR POWERFUL HIND LEGS. A FEARSOME TECHNIQUE, INDEED!

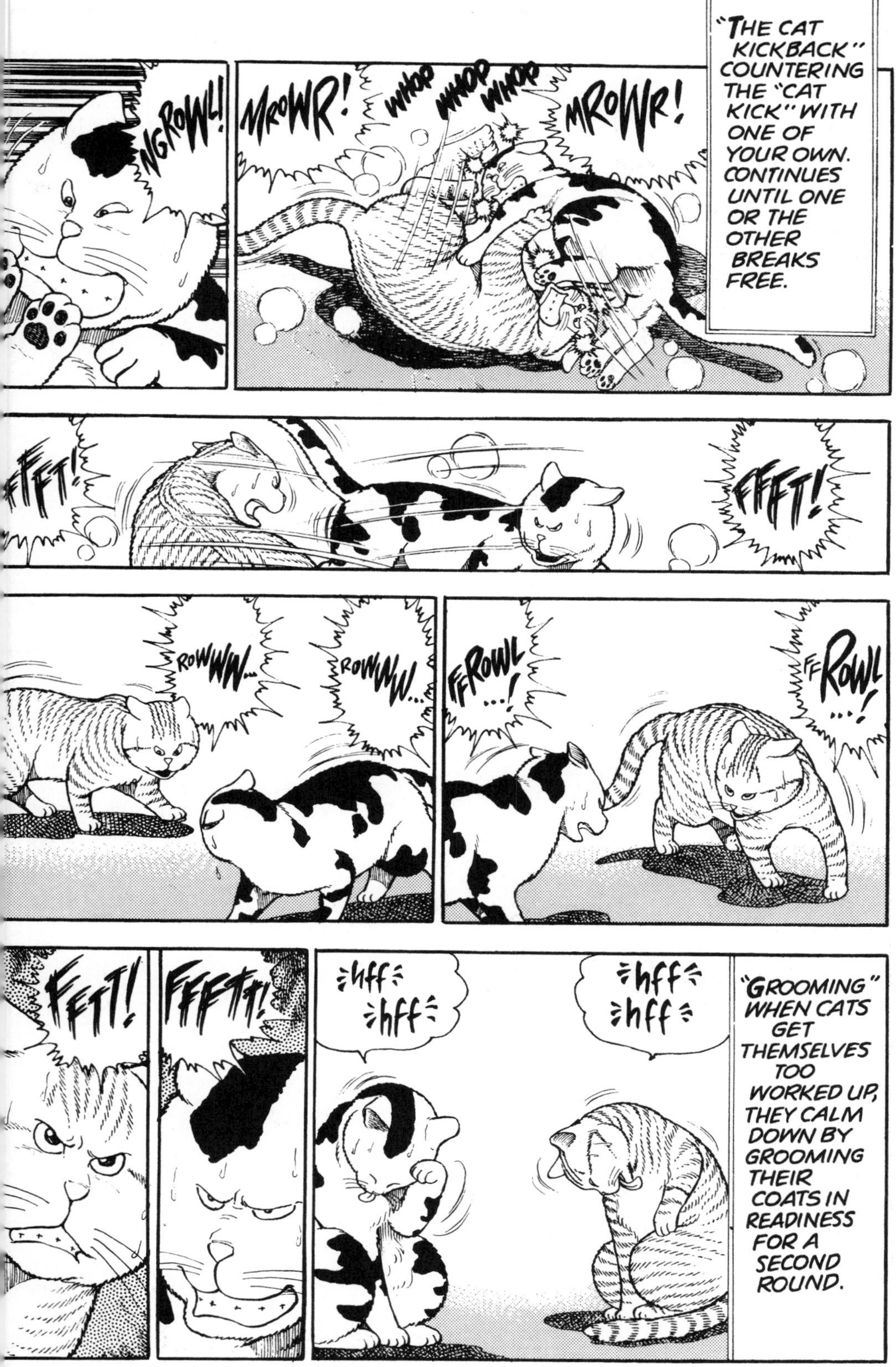
"THE CAT KICKBACK" COUNTERING THE "CAT KICK" WITH ONE OF YOUR OWN. CONTINUES UNTIL ONE OR THE OTHER BREAKS FREE.
NGROWL!!
MROWR!
WHOP
WHOP
WHOP
MROWR!
FFFT!
FFFT!
ROWWW...
ROWWW...
FFROWL...!
FFROWL...!
FFTT!
FFFFTTT!
hff hff
hff hff
"GROOMING" WHEN CATS GET THEMSELVES TOO WORKED UP, THEY CALM DOWN BY GROOMING THEIR COATS IN READINESS FOR A SECOND ROUND.

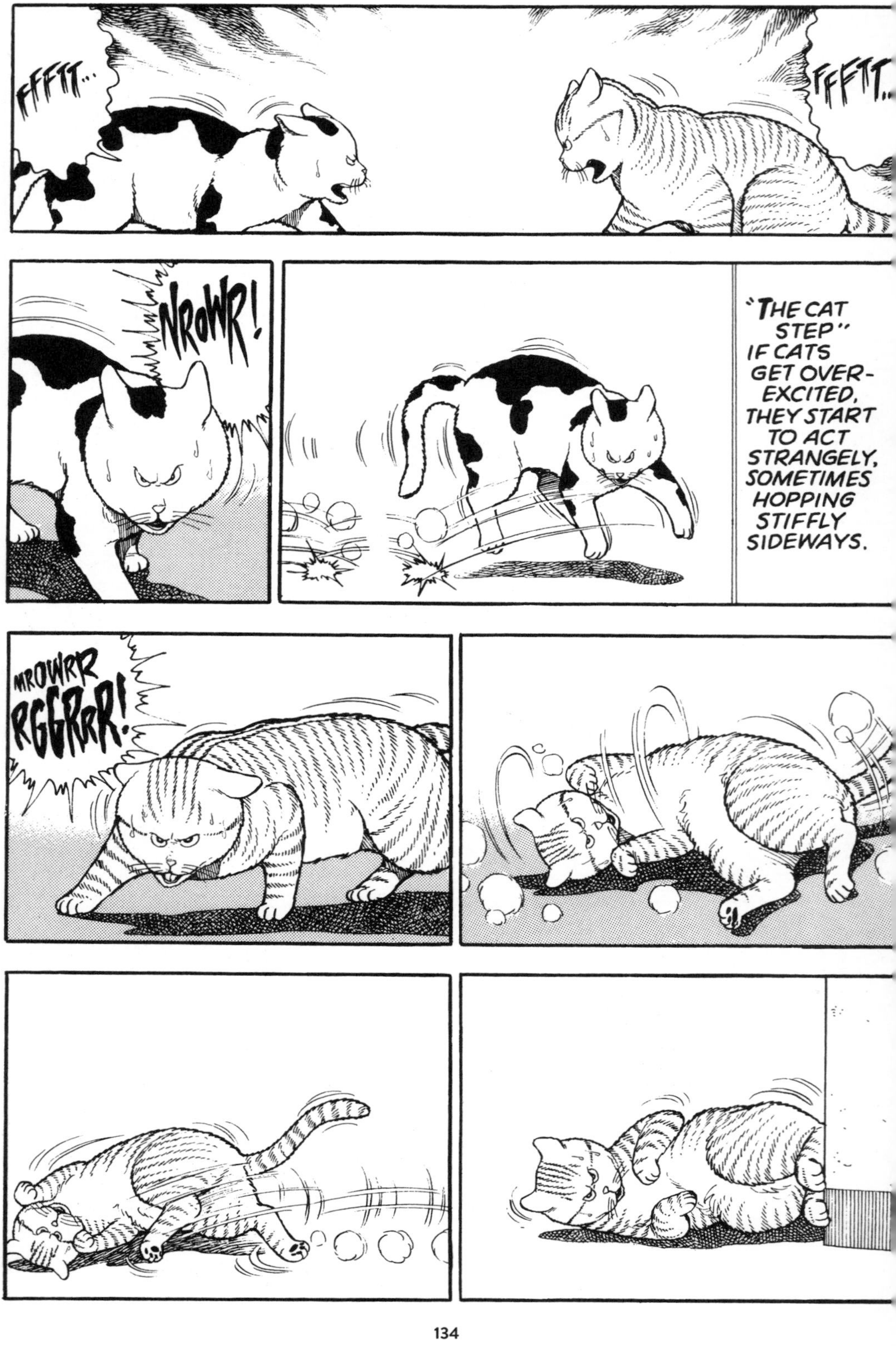
FFFTT...
FFFTT...
NROWR!
"THE CAT STEP" IF CATS GET OVER-EXCITED, THEY START TO ACT STRANGELY, SOMETIMES HOPPING STIFFLY SIDEWAYS.
MROWRR RGGRRR!

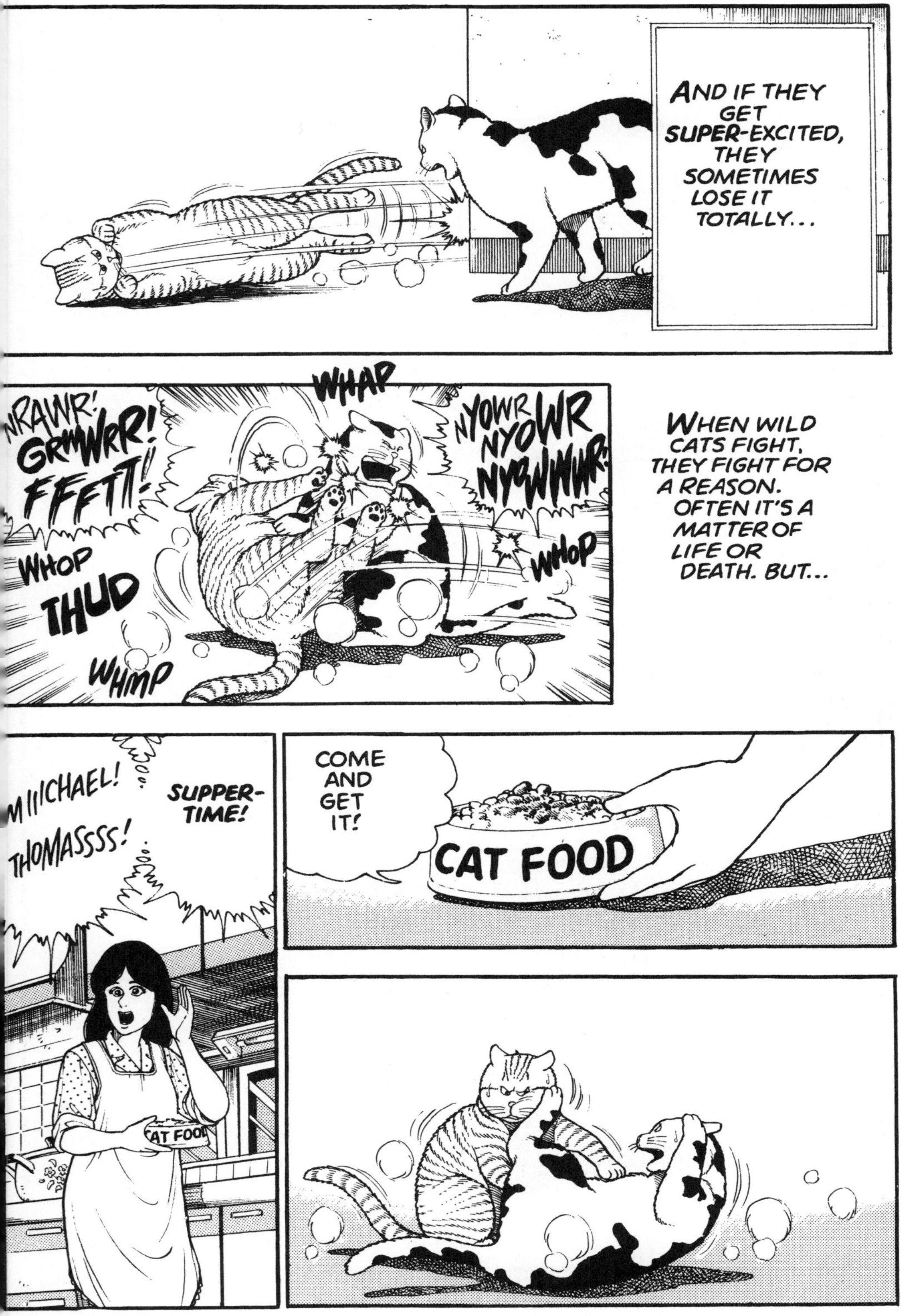

AND IF THEY GET SUPER-EXCITED, THEY SOMETIMES LOSE IT TOTALLY...
NRAWR!
GRMWRR!
FFFTT!
WHAP
WHOP
THUD
WHMP
NYOWR NYOWR
NYOWHWR!
WHOP
WHEN WILD CATS FIGHT, THEY FIGHT FOR A REASON. OFTEN IT'S A MATTER OF LIFE OR DEATH. BUT...
MIIICHAEL!
THOMASSSS!
SUPPER-TIME!
CAT FOOD
COME AND GET IT!
CAT FOOD

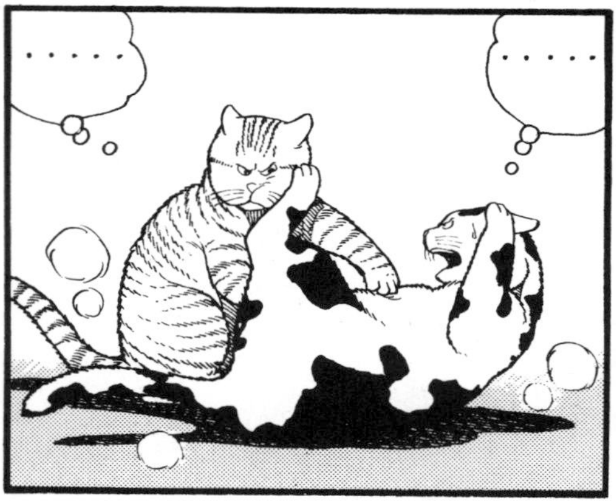
. . . . .
. . . . .

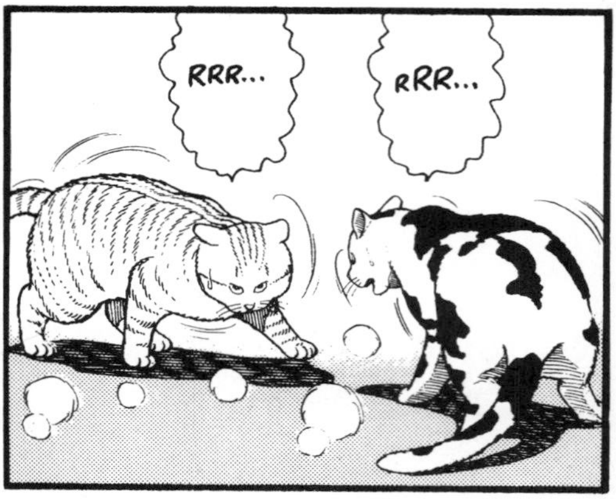
RRR...
rRR...

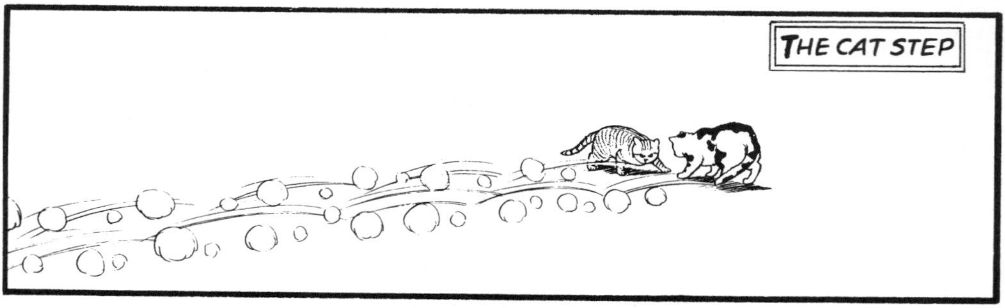
THE CAT STEP

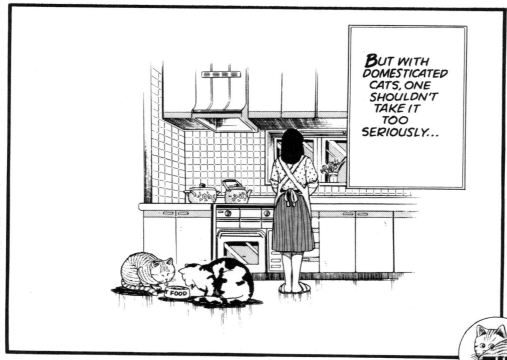

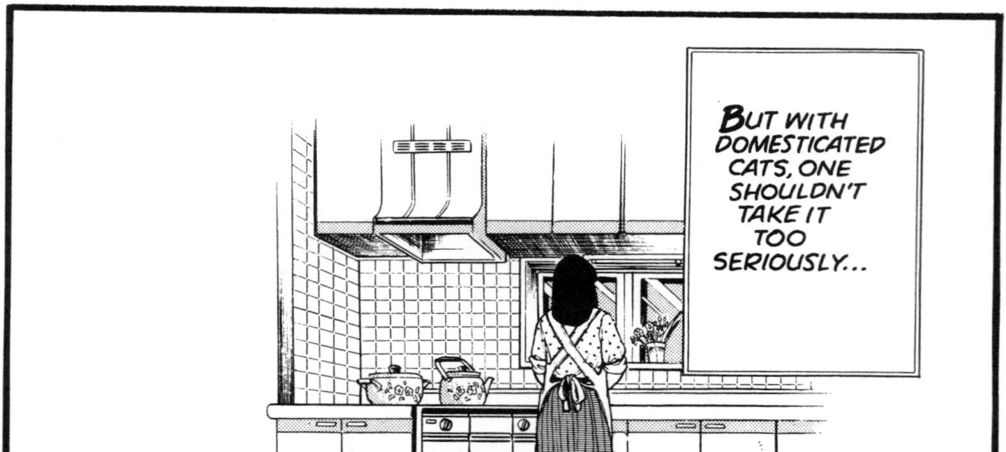
BUT WITH DOMESTICATED CATS, ONE SHOULDN'T TAKE IT TOO SERIOUSLY...
T FOOD

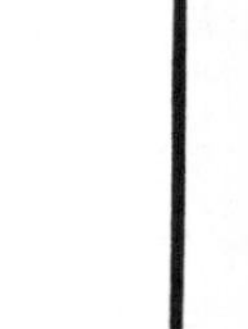
FIN

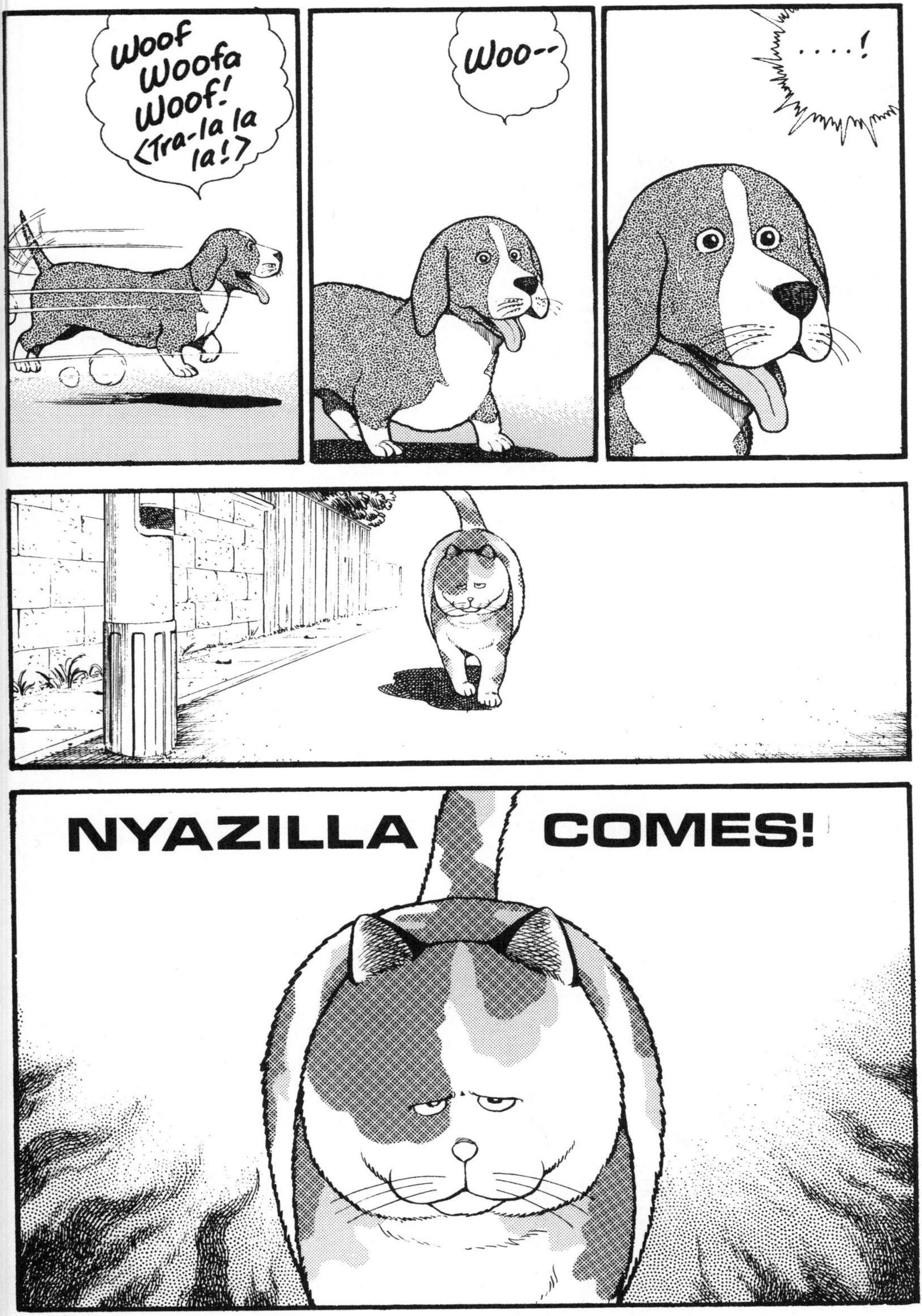
Woof Woofa Woof! <Tra-la la la!>
Woo--
....!
NYAZILLA COMES!

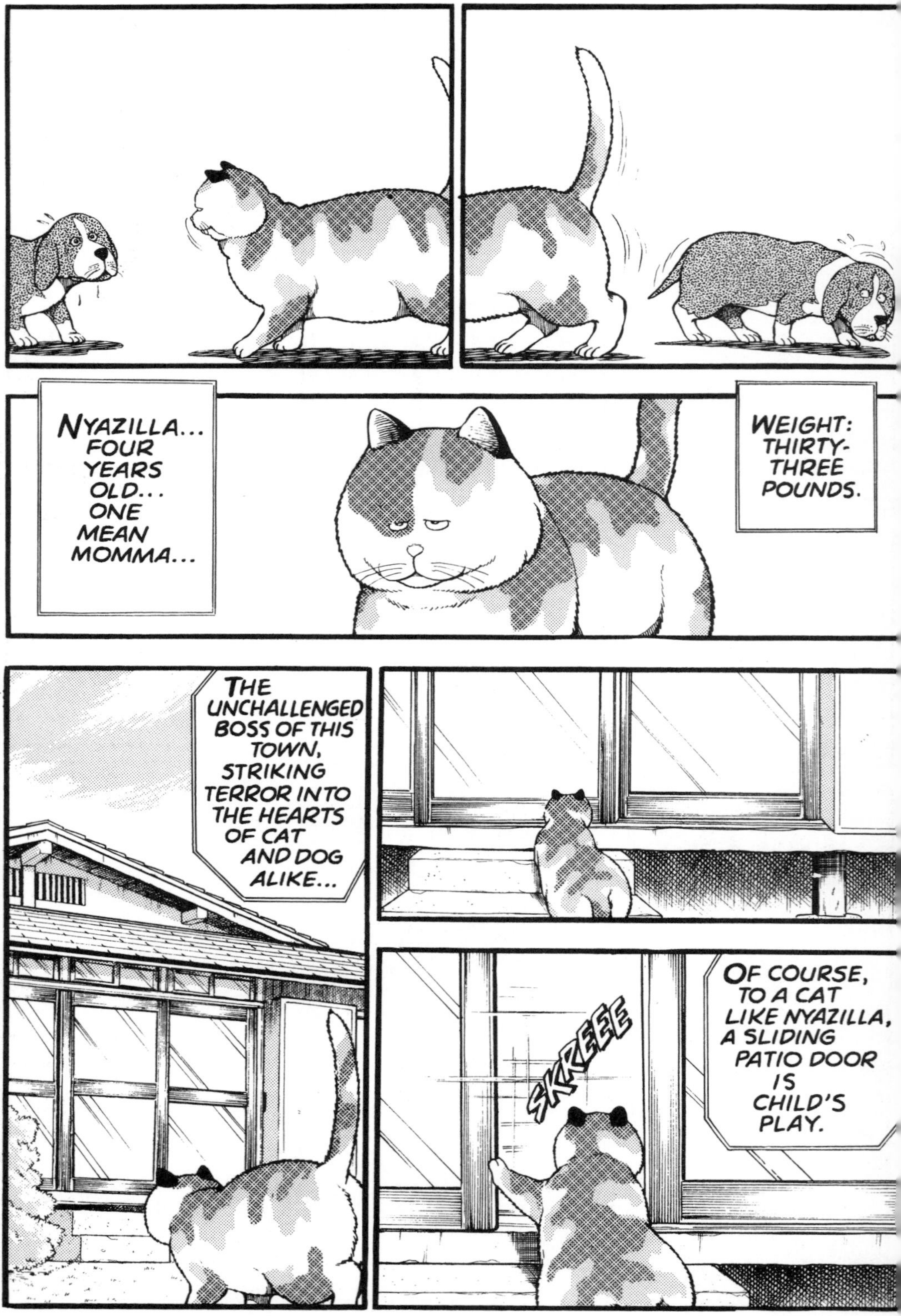

NYAZILLA... FOUR YEARS OLD... ONE MEAN MOMMA...
WEIGHT: THIRTY-THREE POUNDS.
THE UNCHALLENGED BOSS OF THIS TOWN, STRIKING TERROR INTO THE HEARTS OF CAT AND DOG ALIKE...
SKREEE
OF COURSE, TO A CAT LIKE NYAZILLA, A SLIDING PATIO DOOR IS CHILD'S PLAY.

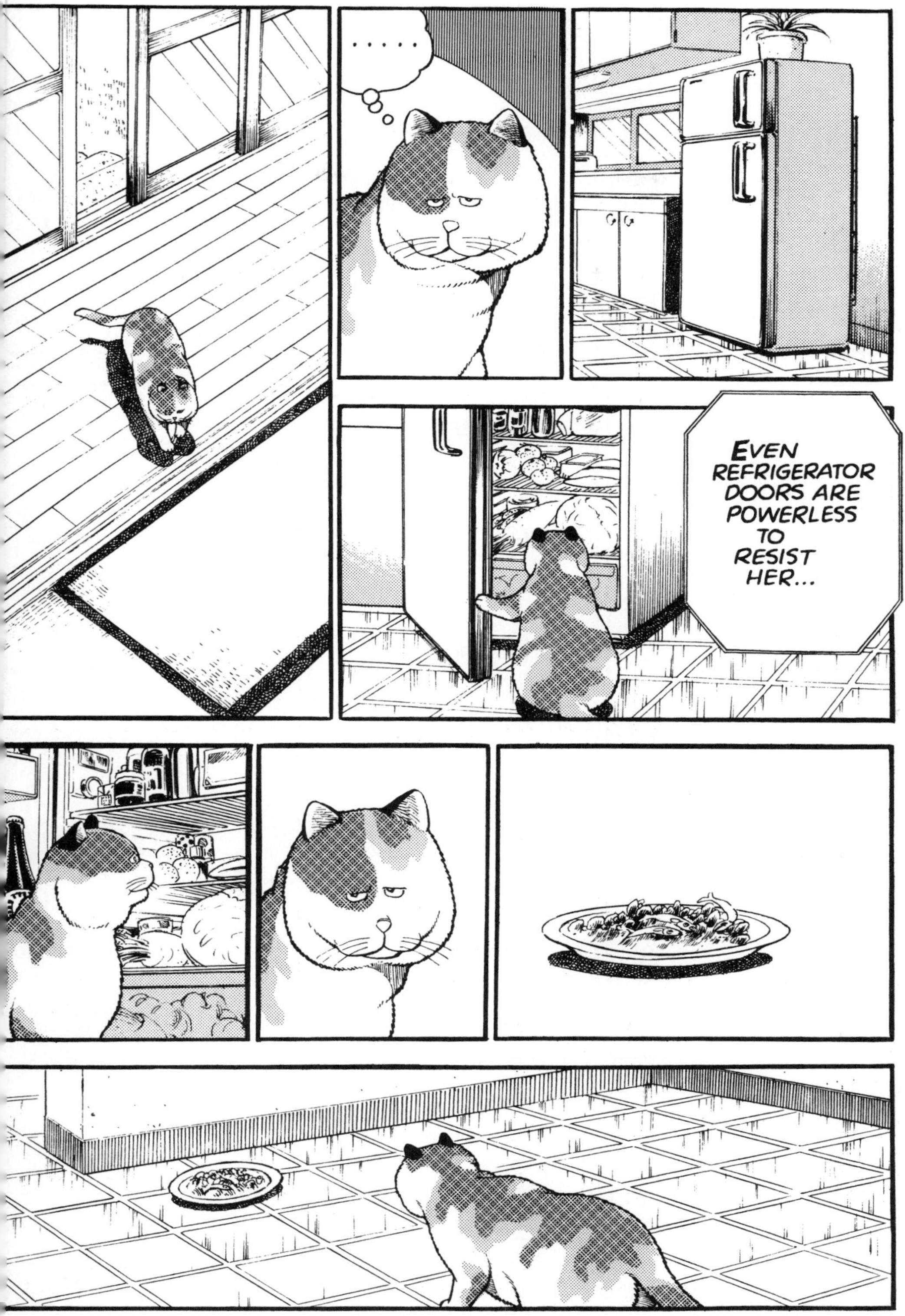
......
EVEN REFRIGERATOR DOORS ARE POWERLESS TO RESIST HER...

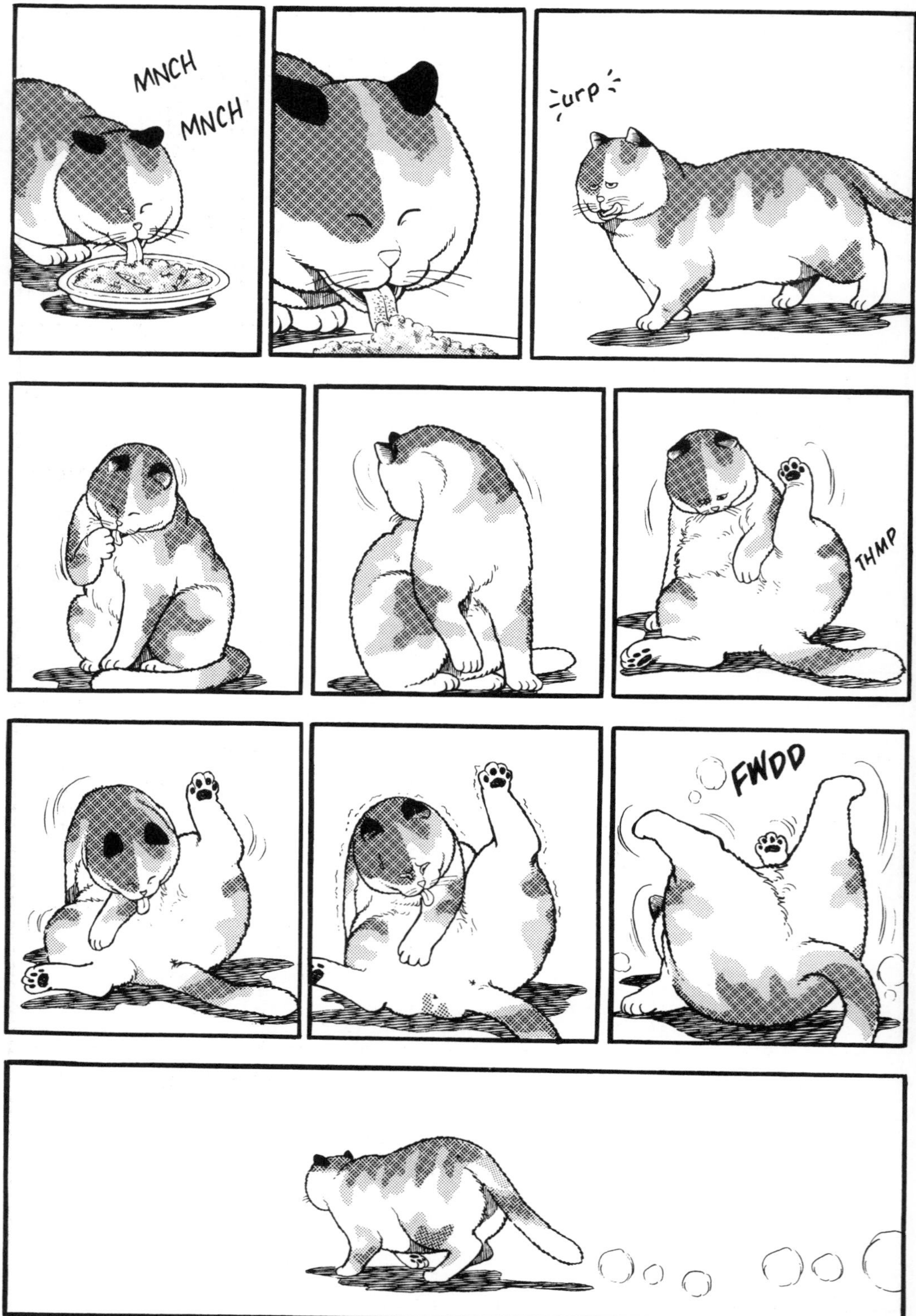
MNCH
MNCH
urp
THMP
FWDD

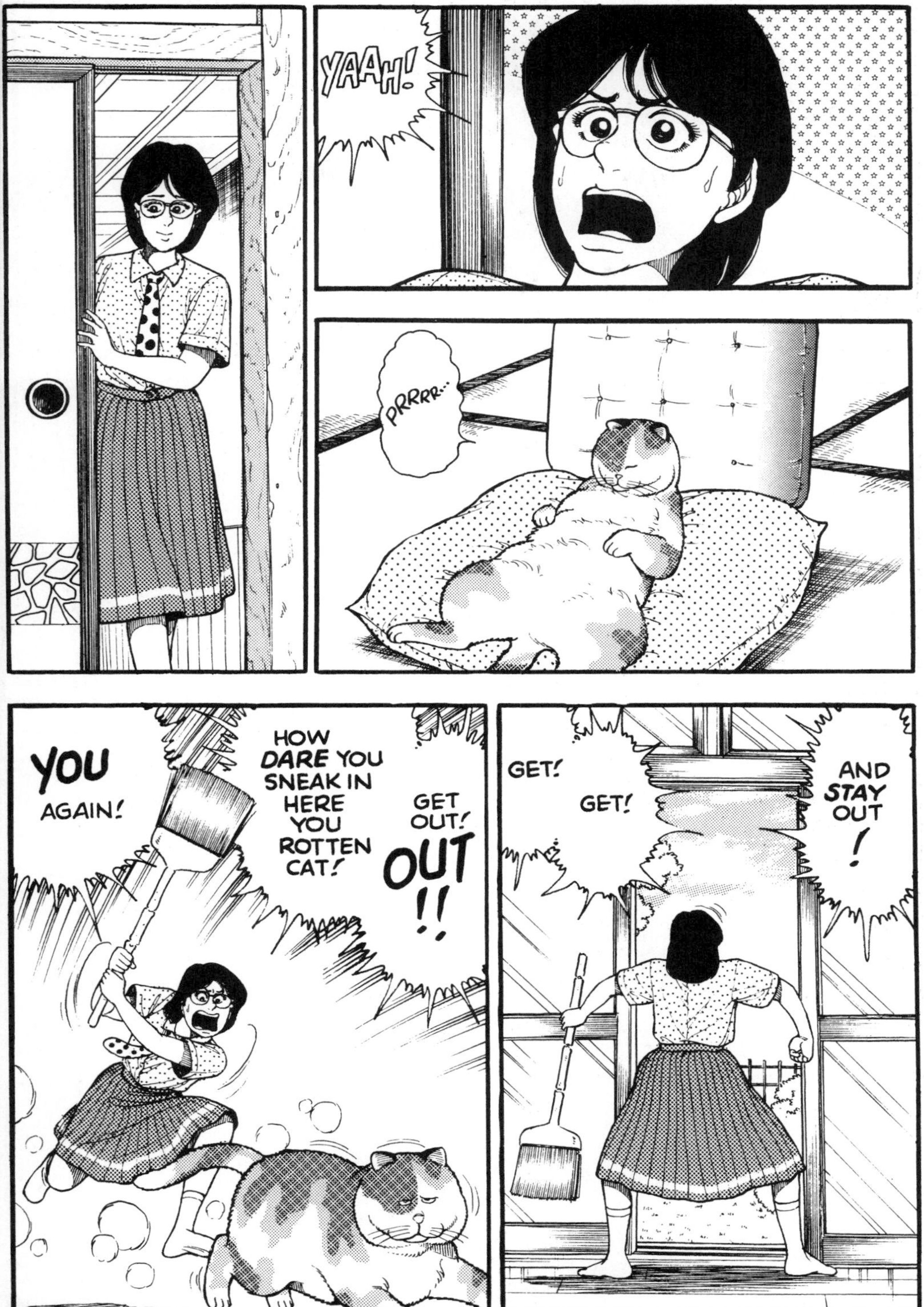
YAAH!
PRRRR...
YOU AGAIN!
HOW DARE YOU SNEAK IN HERE YOU ROTTEN CAT!
GET OUT! OUT!!
GET!
GET!
AND STAY OUT!

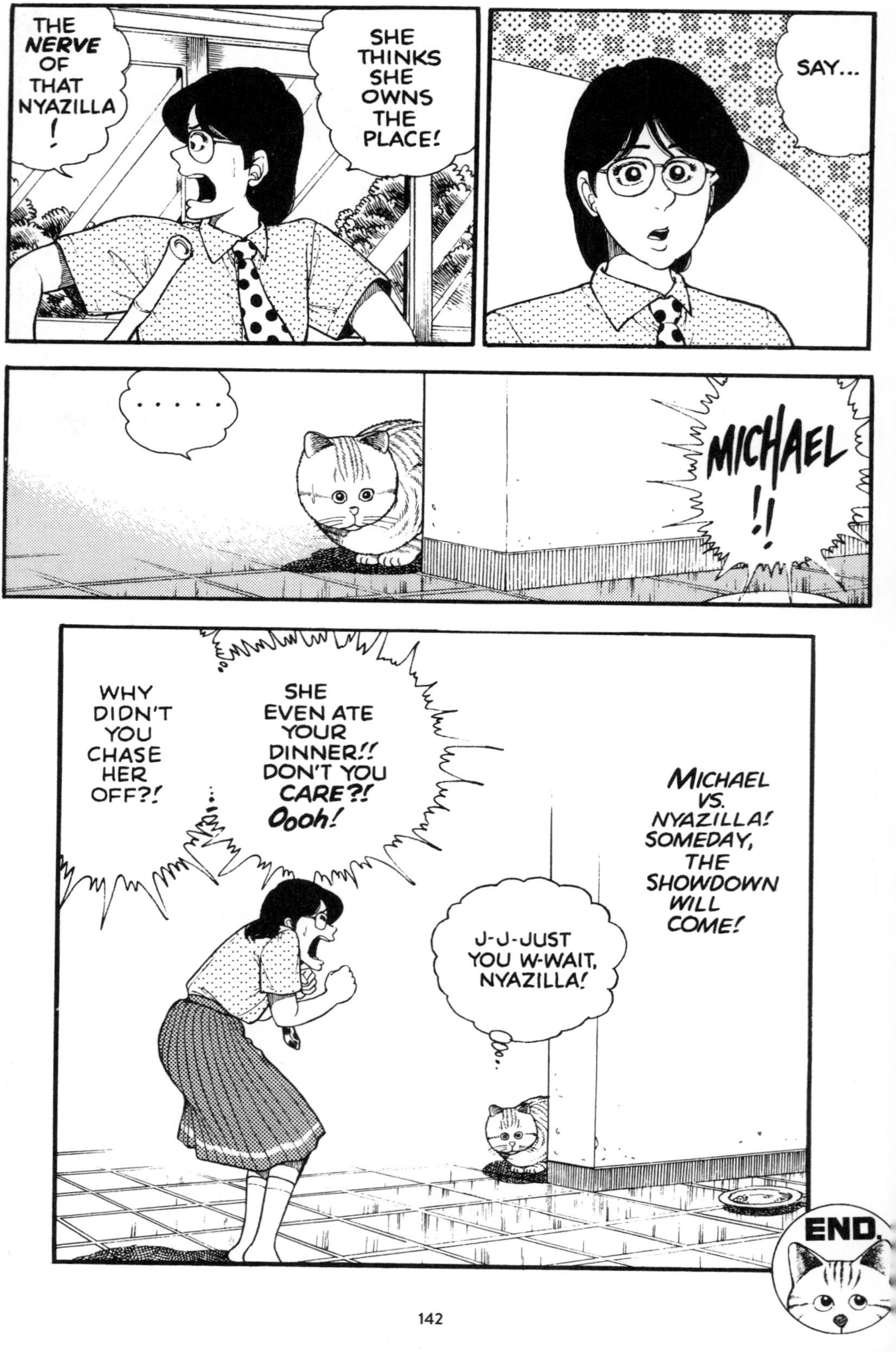
THE NERVE OF THAT NYAZILLA!
SHE THINKS SHE OWNS THE PLACE!
SAY...
. . . . . .
MICHAEL!!
WHY DIDN'T YOU CHASE HER OFF?!
SHE EVEN ATE YOUR DINNER!! DON'T YOU CARE?! Oooh!
J-J-JUST YOU W-WAIT, NYAZILLA!
MICHAEL VS. NYAZILLA! SOMEDAY, THE SHOWDOWN WILL COME!
END.

FOR SEVEN YEARS, THE TIRELESS DETECTIVE YAMAMURA HAS CEASE-LESSLY TRACKED THE HENIOUS TERRORIST GROUP *Z-28*. FINALLY, AT LAST, HE HAS LOCATED THEIR SECRET LAIR.

RIGHT NOW, THERE IS NO ONE THERE EXCEPT THEIR MINION MATSUMOTO-- A HOPELESS IDIOT.

BUT IF HE STAKES OUT THE APARTMENT, SOONER OR LATER THE BIG BOSS, *KIKUCHI* HIMSELF, WILL CERTAINLY FALL INTO HIS HANDS!

# DETECTIVE YAMAMURA in:

# "THE STAKEOUT"

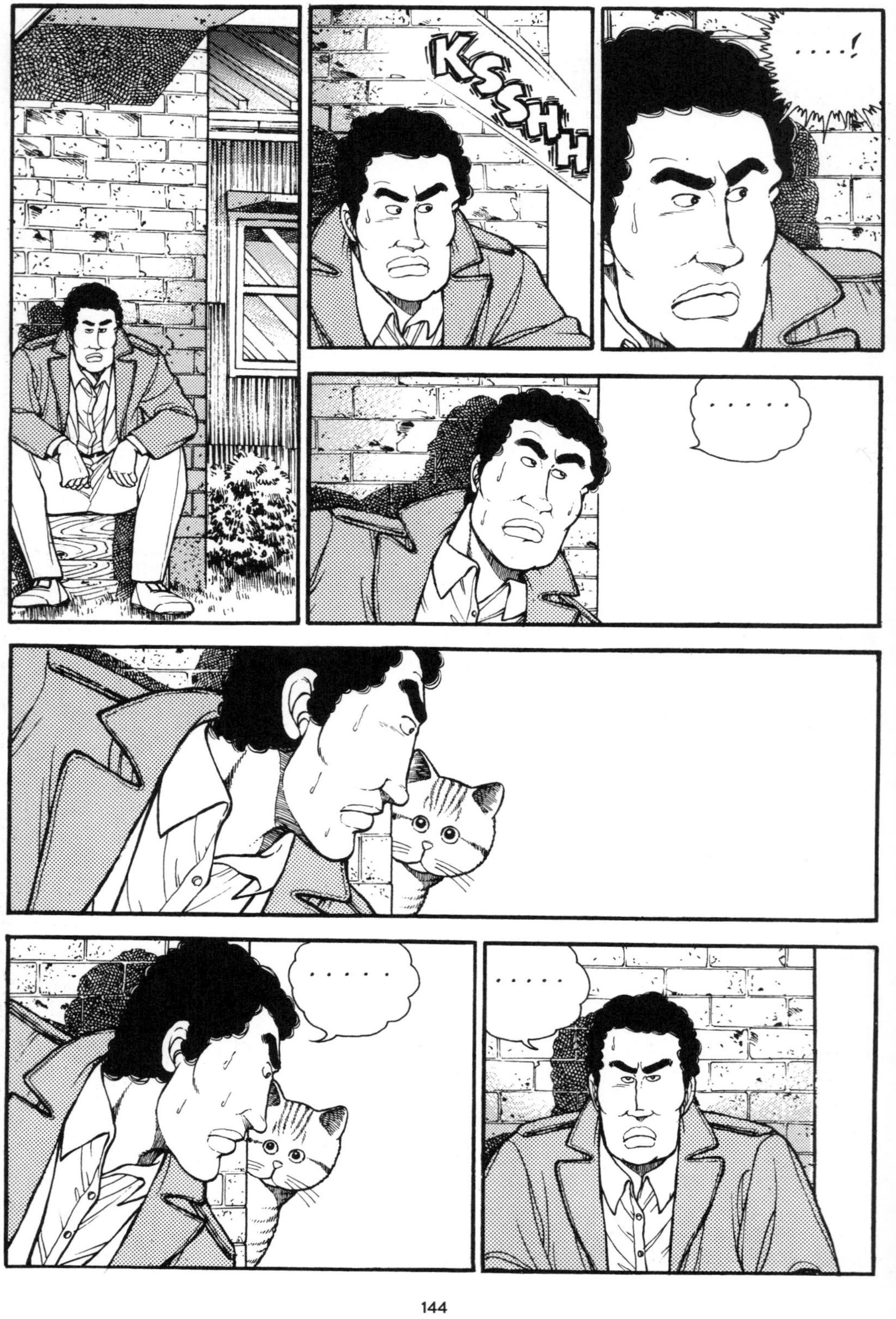
KSSHH
....!
.....
.....
.....

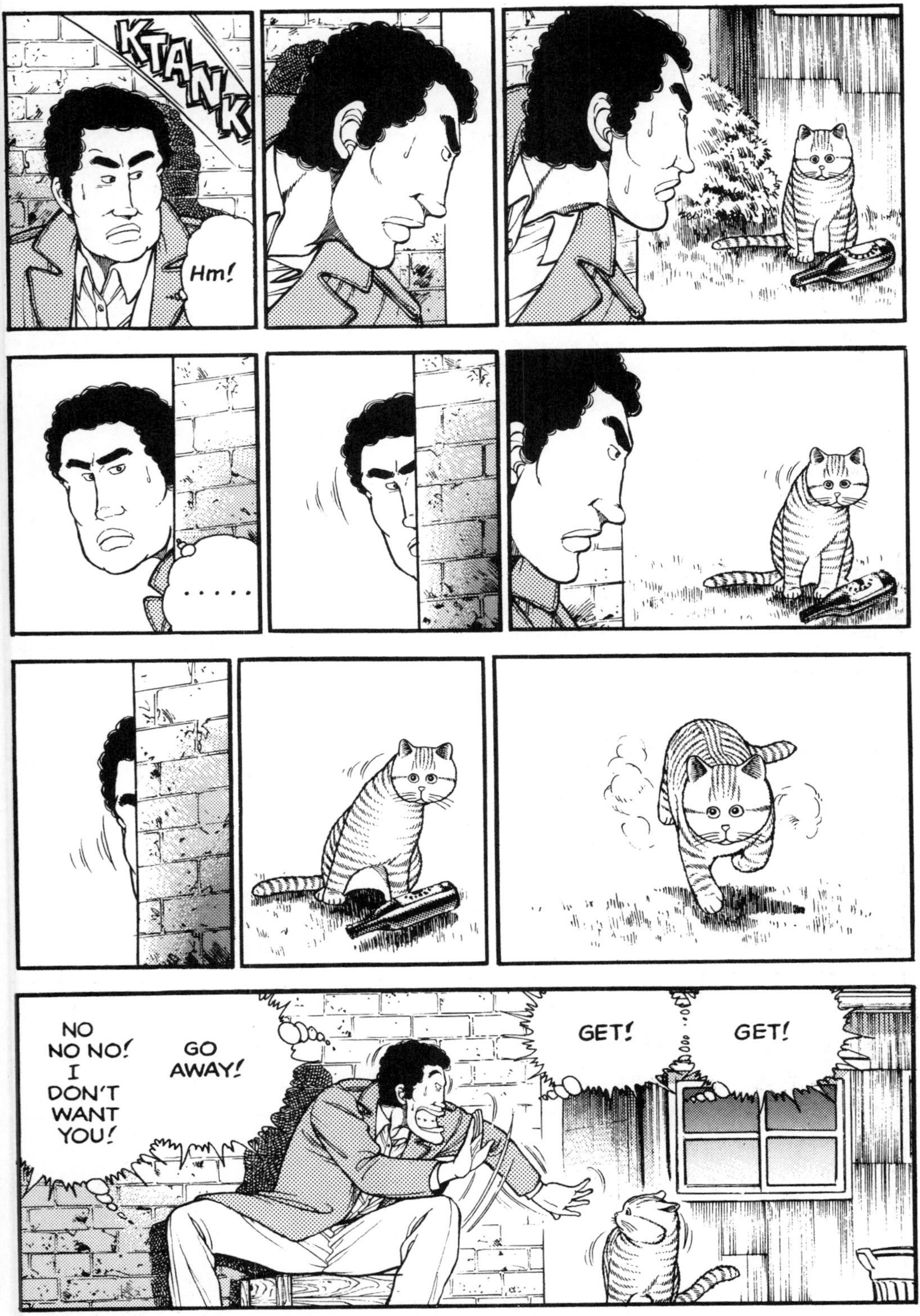
KTANK
Hm!
......
NO NO NO! I DON'T WANT YOU!
GO AWAY!
GET!
GET!

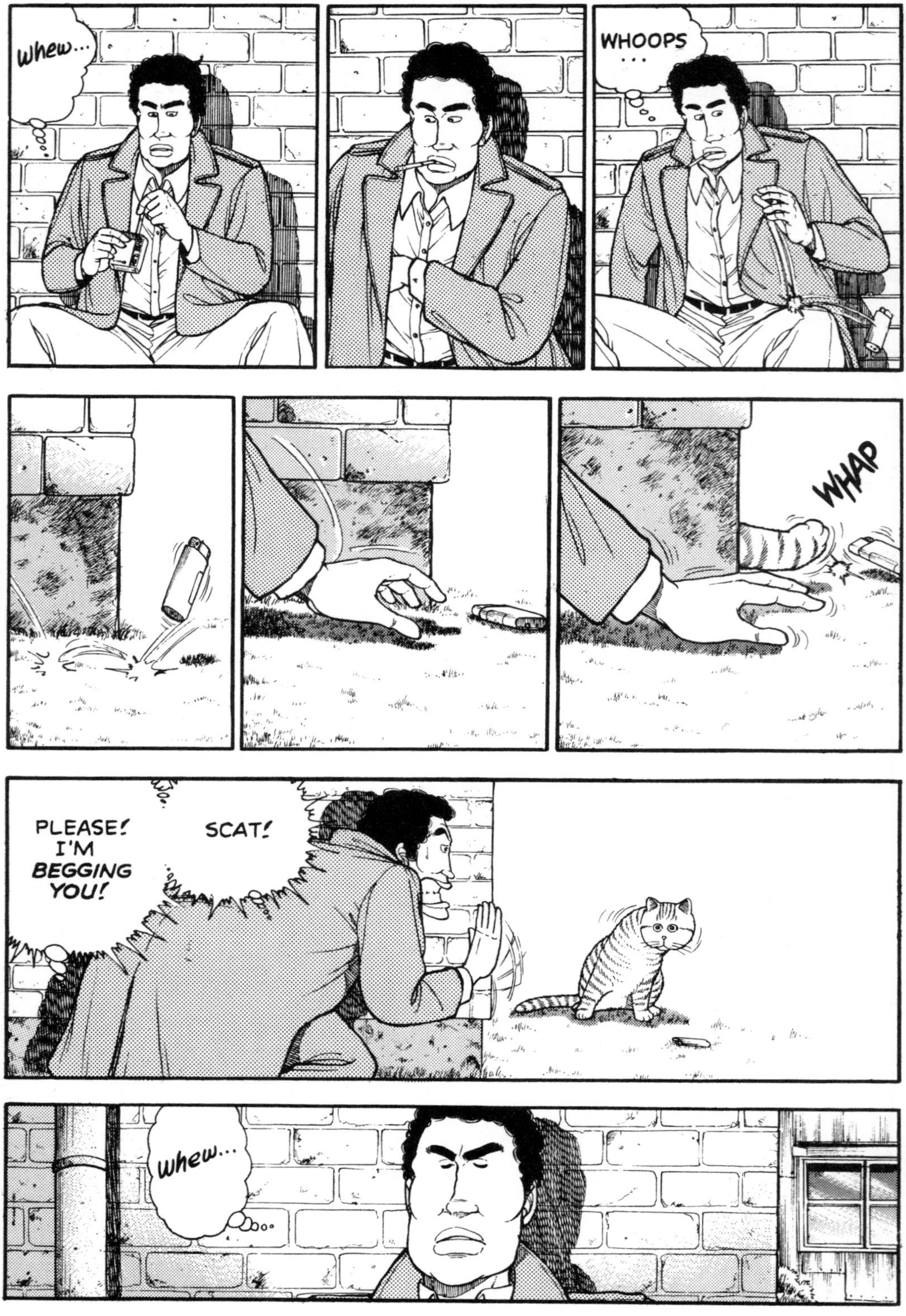
whew...
WHOOPS ...
WHAP
PLEASE! I'M BEGGING YOU!
SCAT!
whew...

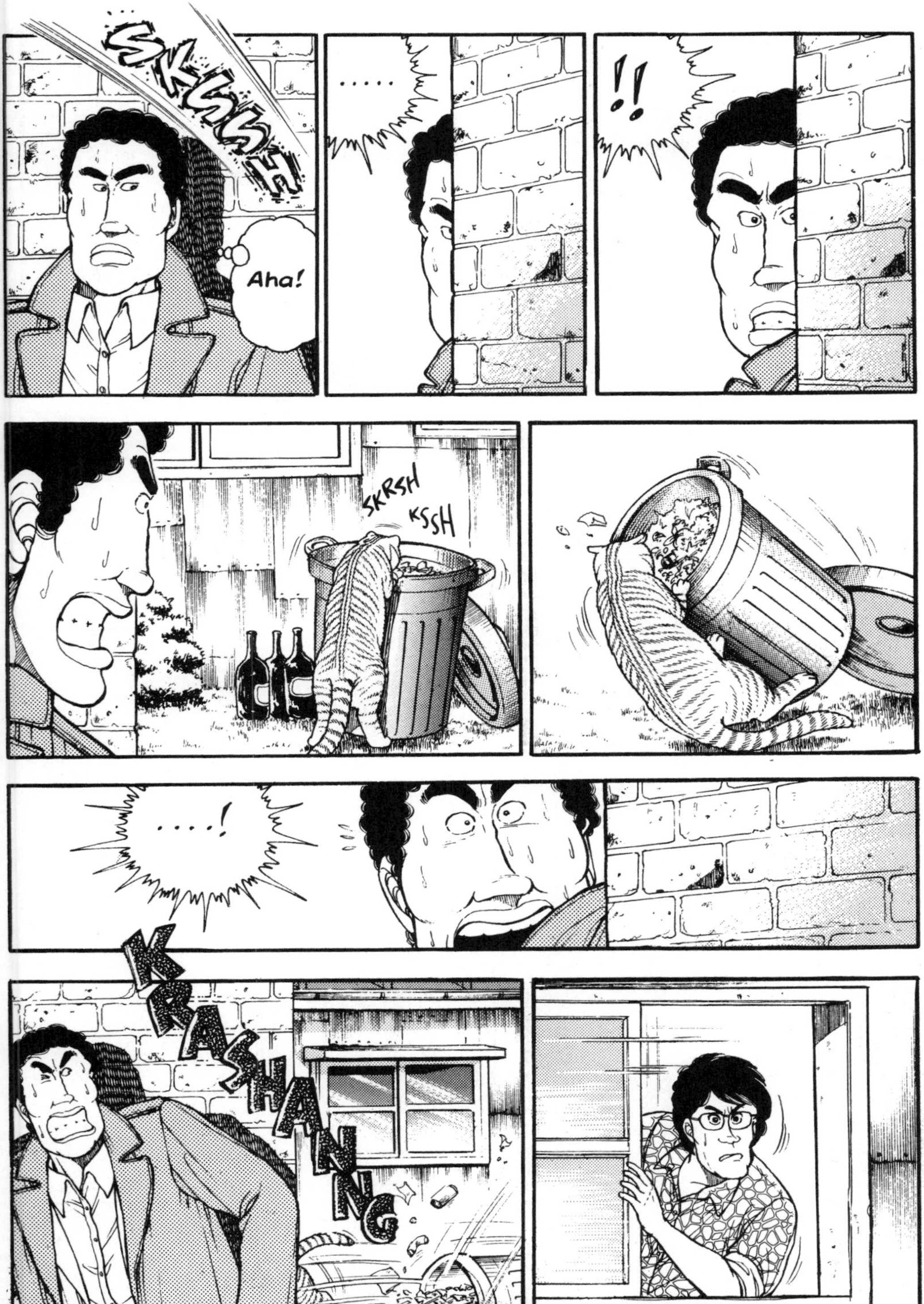
SKSSH
Aha!
......
!!
SKRSH
KSSH
.....!
KRASHANG

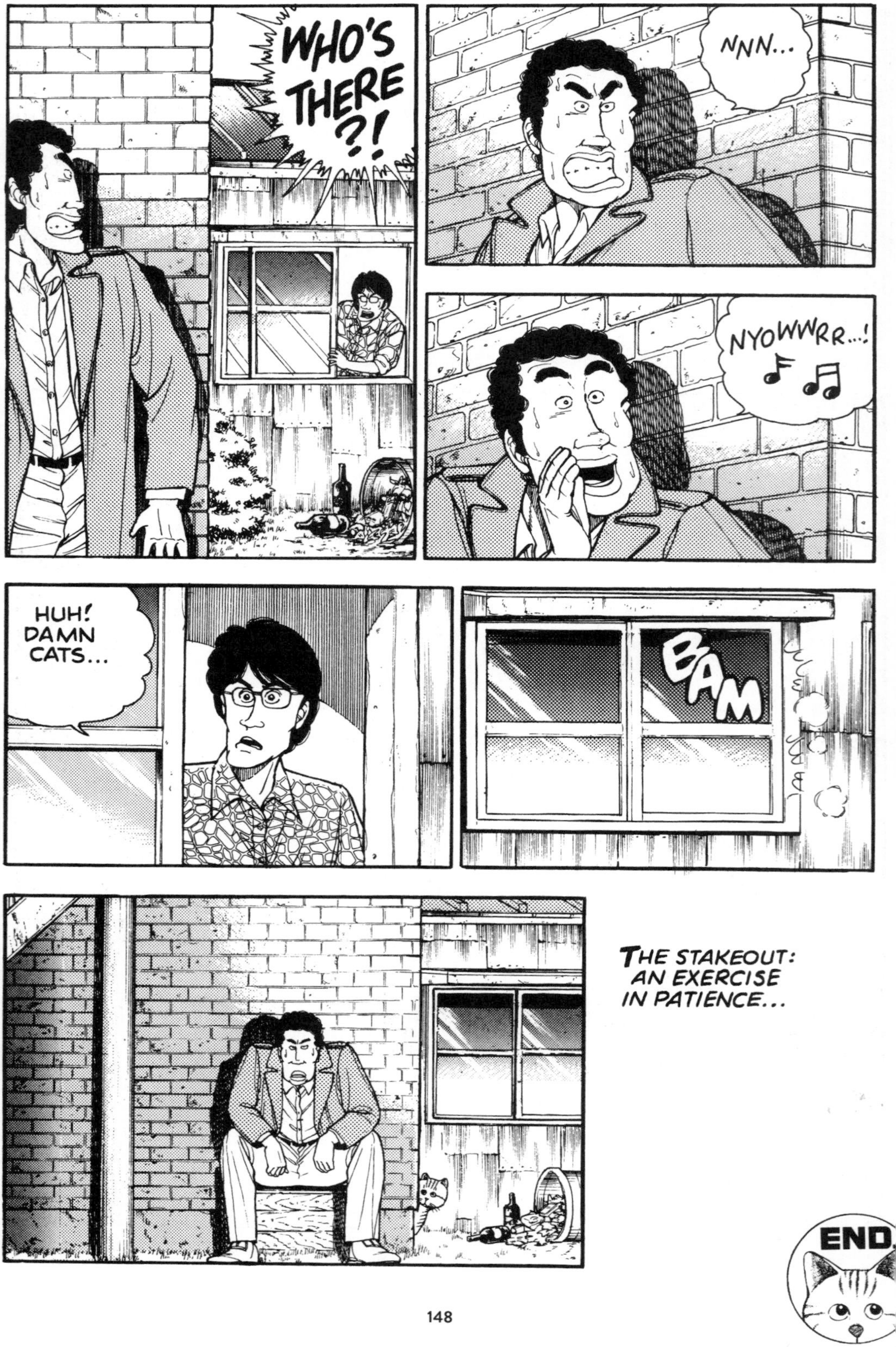
WHO'S THERE?!
NNN...
NYOWWRR...!
HUH! DAMN CATS...
BAM
THE STAKEOUT: AN EXERCISE IN PATIENCE...
END.

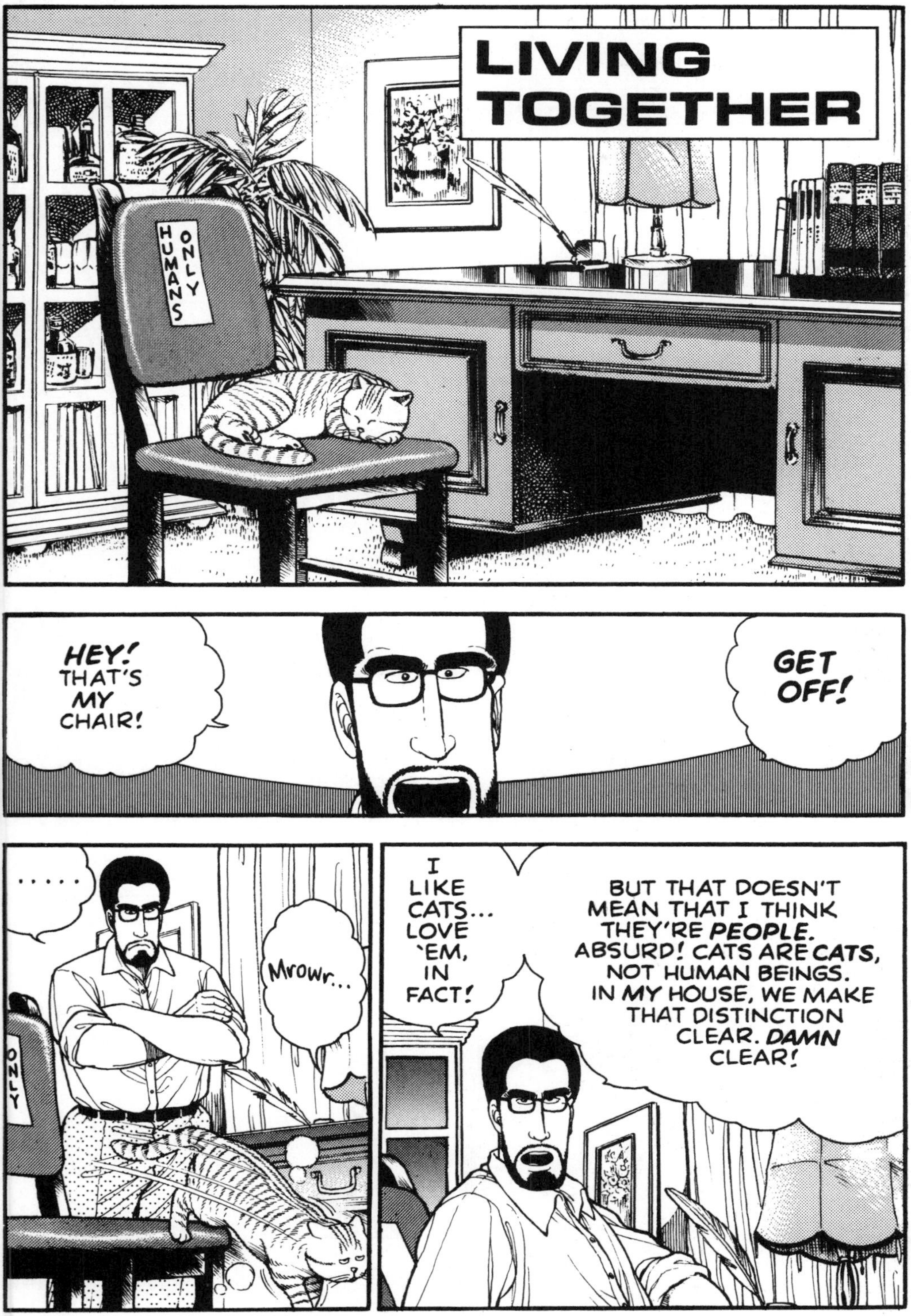
LIVING TOGETHER
HUMANS ONLY
HEY! THAT'S MY CHAIR!
GET OFF!
.....
ONLY
Mrowr...
I LIKE CATS... LOVE 'EM, IN FACT!
BUT THAT DOESN'T MEAN THAT I THINK THEY'RE PEOPLE. ABSURD! CATS ARE CATS, NOT HUMAN BEINGS. IN MY HOUSE, WE MAKE THAT DISTINCTION CLEAR. DAMN CLEAR!

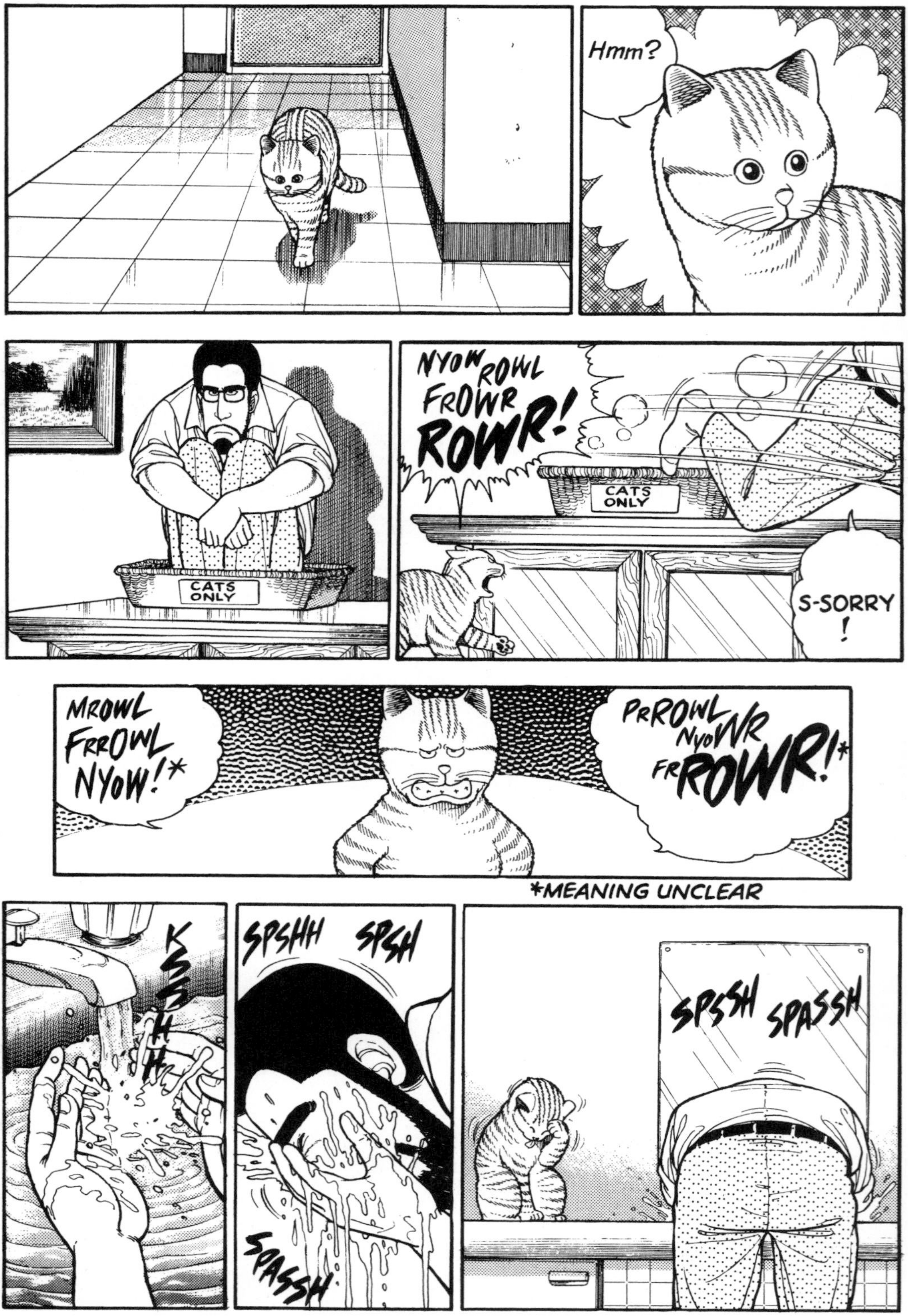
Hmm?
CATS ONLY
NYOW ROWL FROWR ROWR!
CATS ONLY
S-SORRY!
MROWL FRROWL NYOW!*
PRROWL NYOWR FRROWR!*
*MEANING UNCLEAR
KSSHHH
SPSHH SPSH
SPASSH
SPSSH SPASSH

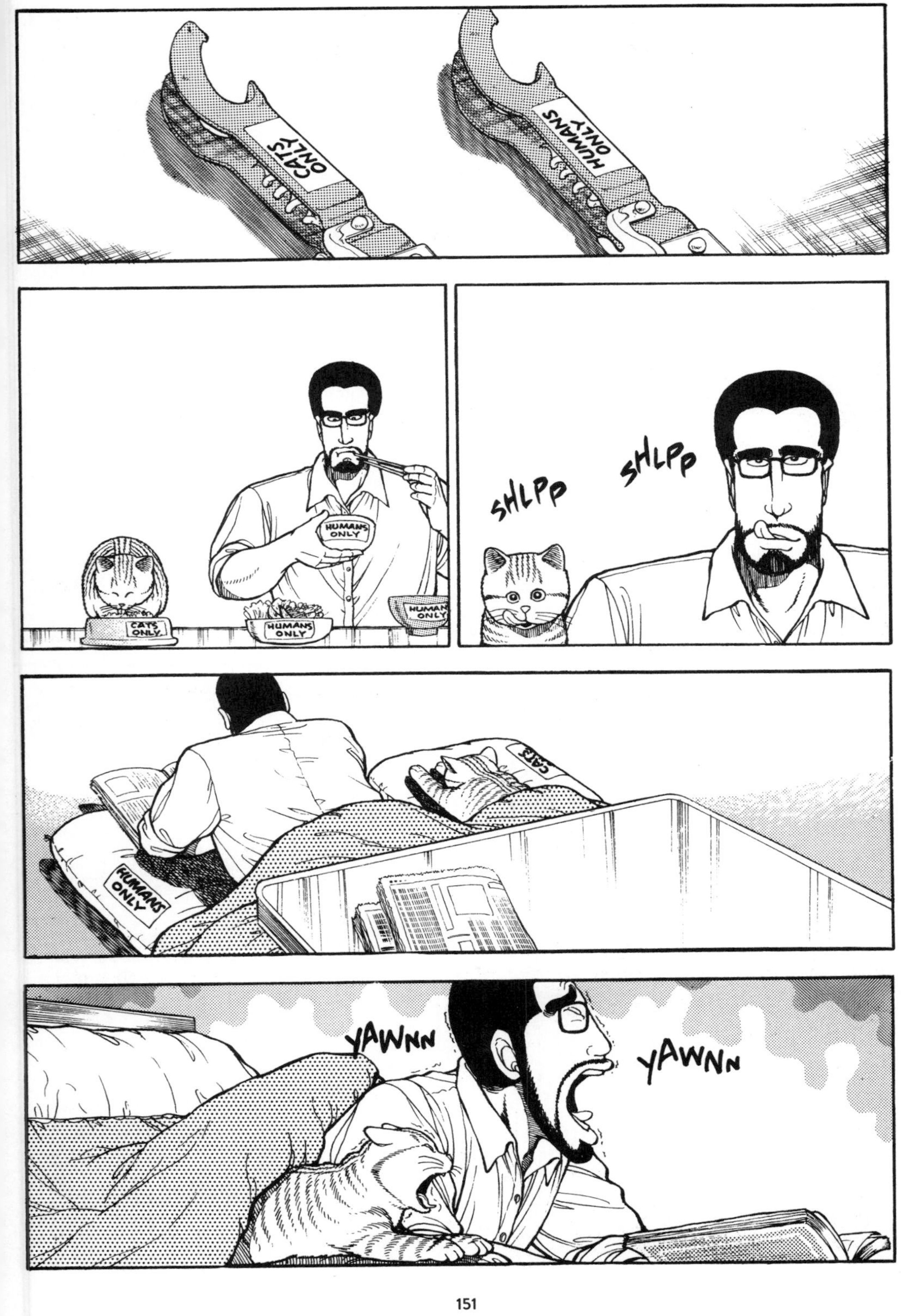
CATS ONLY
HUMANS ONLY
HUMANS ONLY
HUMANS ONLY
CATS ONLY
HUMANS ONLY
SHLPP
SHLPP
CATS
HUMANS ONLY
YAWNN
YAWNN

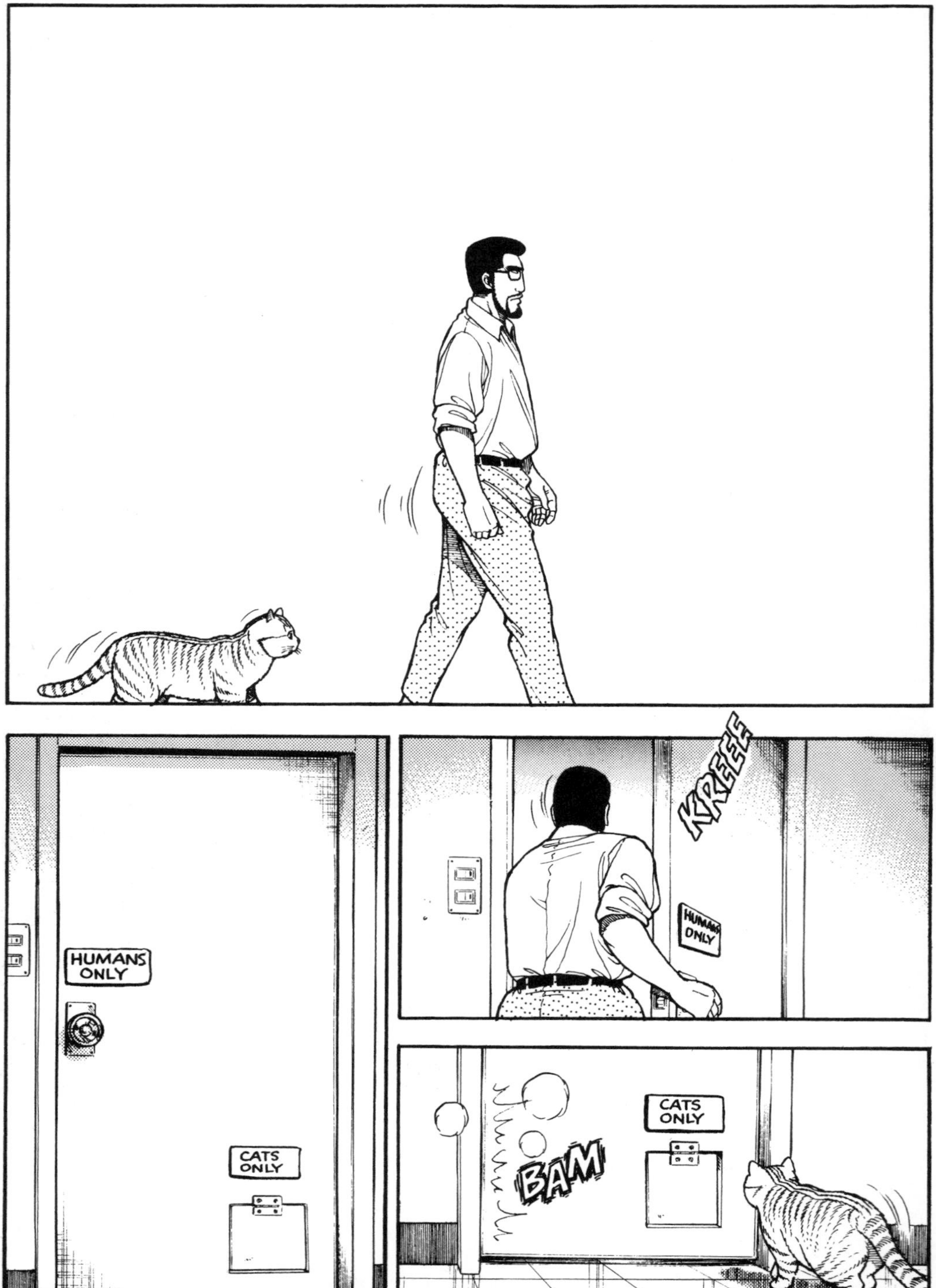
HUMANS ONLY
CATS ONLY
KREEE
HUMANS ONLY
CATS ONLY
BAM

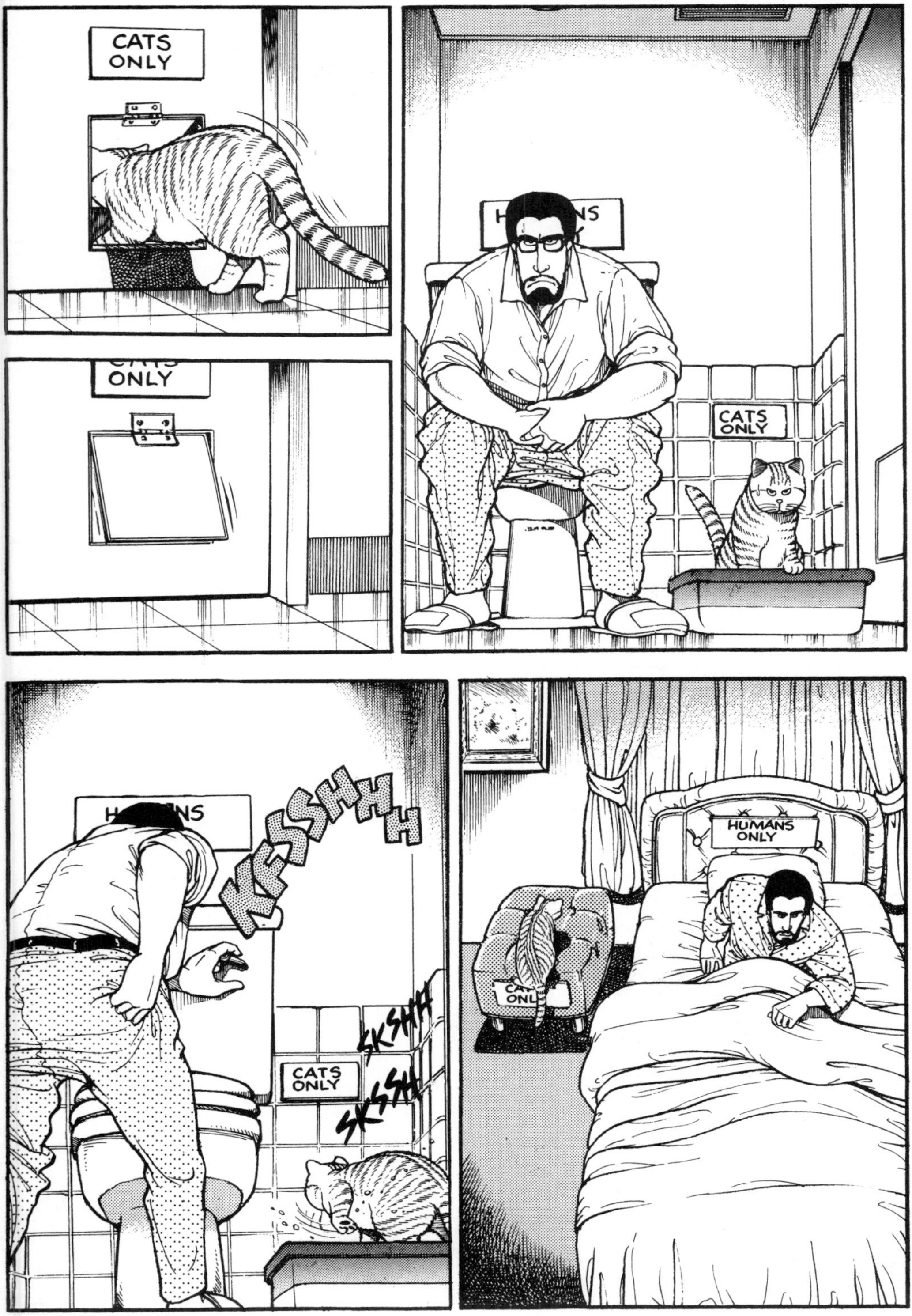
CATS ONLY
ONLY
CATS ONLY
KESSHHHH
SKSHH
CATS ONLY
SKSSH
HUMANS ONLY

ZZZZ

HUMANS
ONLY

CATS
ONLY

ZZZZ ZZZZ

Gmnph...

HUMANS
ONLY

CATS
ONLY

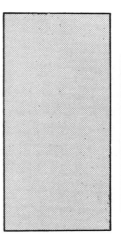

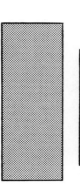

FIN

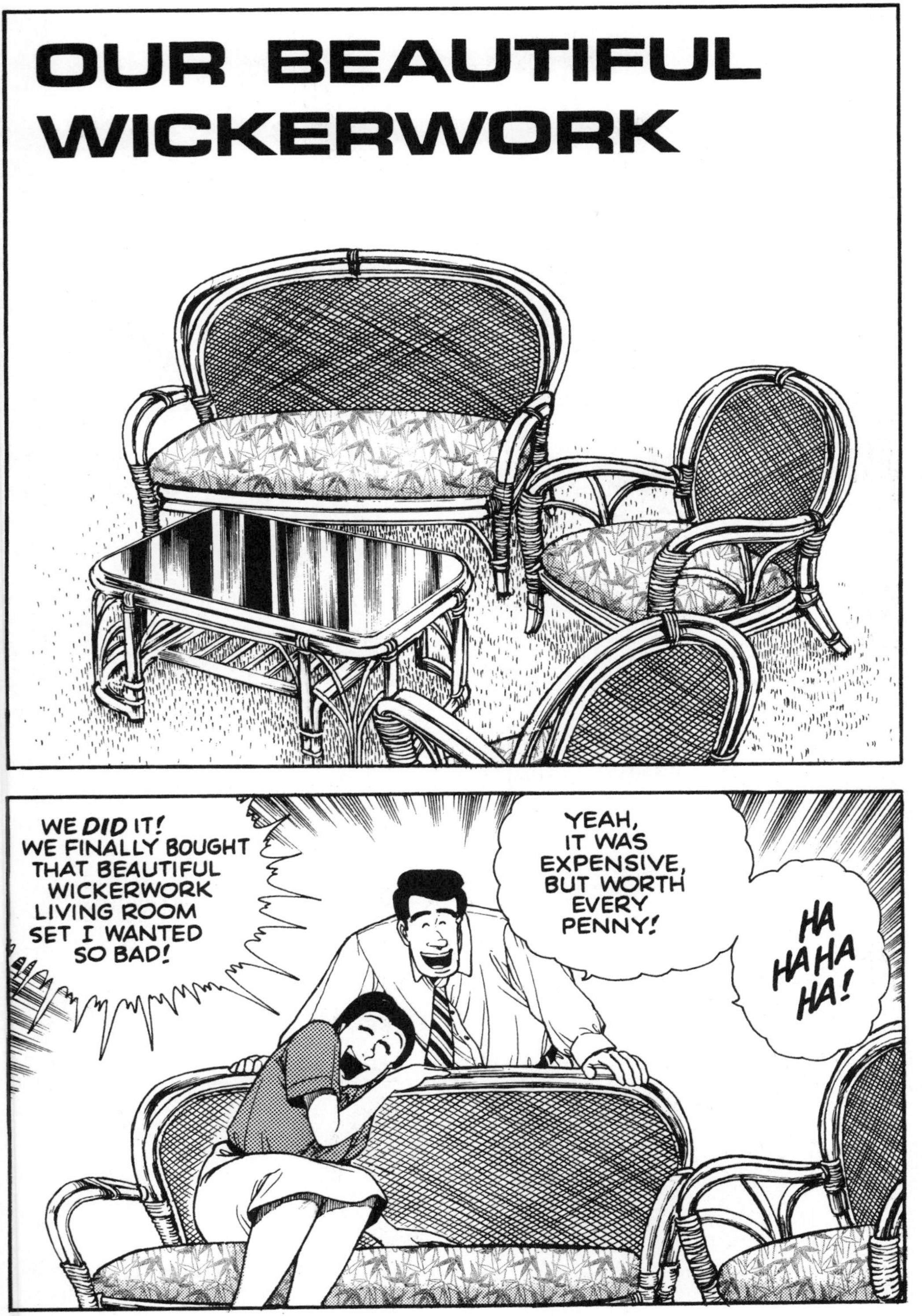
OUR BEAUTIFUL WICKERWORK
WE DID IT! WE FINALLY BOUGHT THAT BEAUTIFUL WICKERWORK LIVING ROOM SET I WANTED SO BAD!
YEAH, IT WAS EXPENSIVE, BUT WORTH EVERY PENNY!
HA HAHA HA!

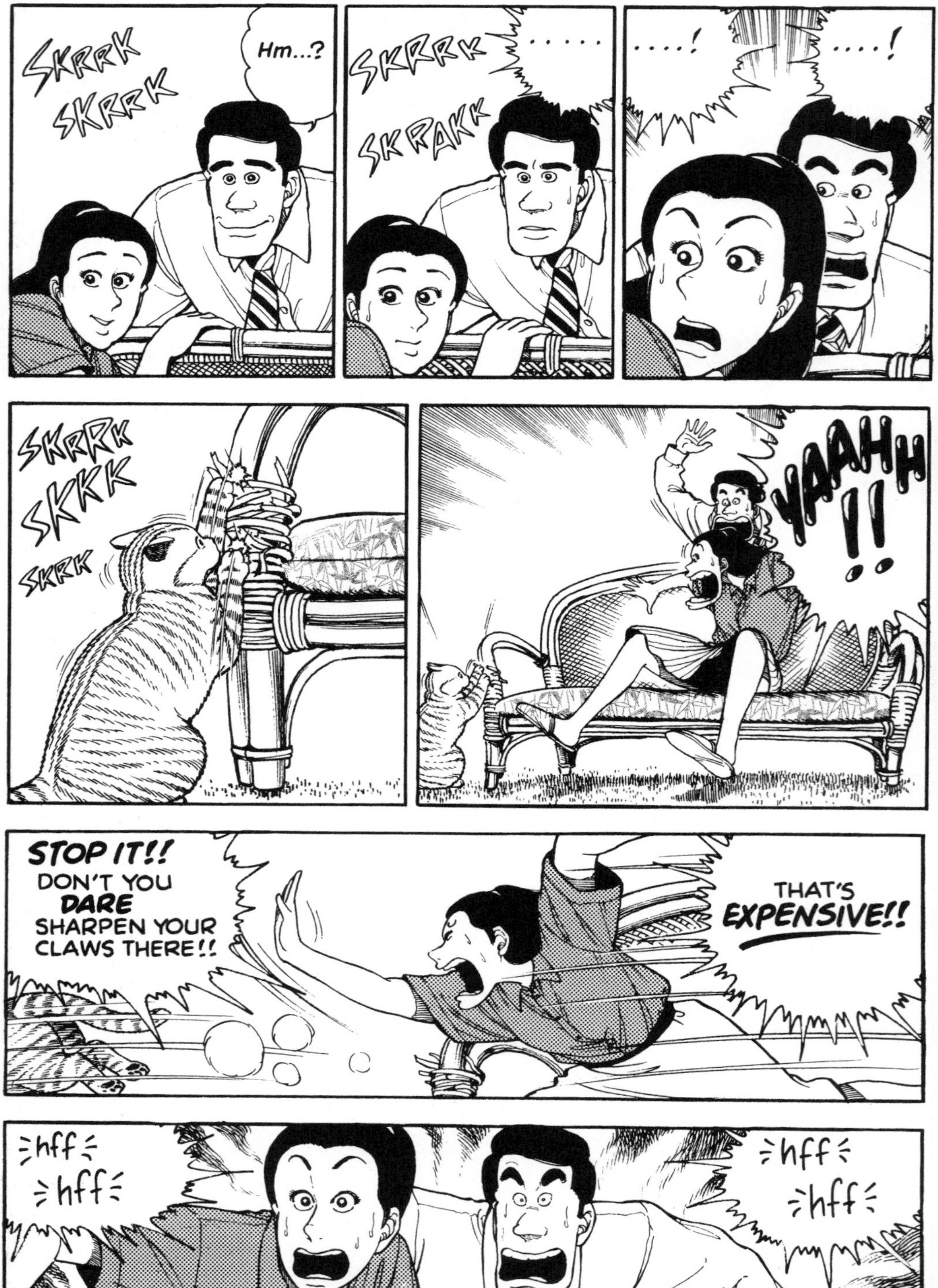
SKRRK
SKRRK
Hm...?
SKRRK
SKRAKK
......
....!
....!
SKRRK
SKKK
SKRK
YAAHH!!
STOP IT!! DON'T YOU DARE SHARPEN YOUR CLAWS THERE!!
THAT'S EXPENSIVE!!
hff
hff
hff
hff

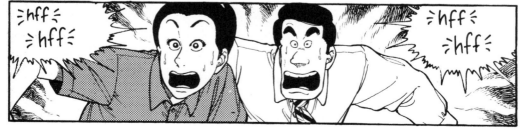

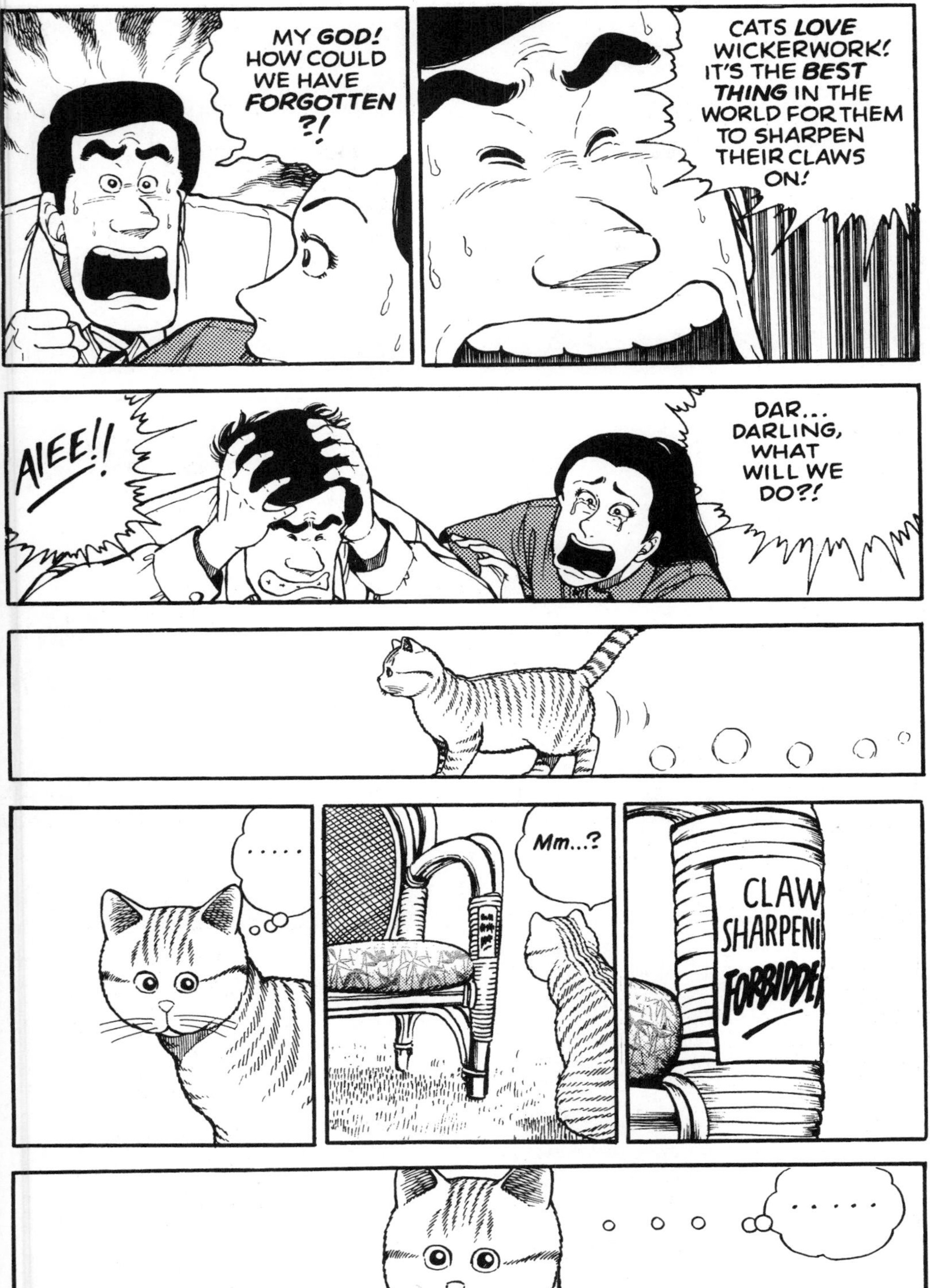
MY GOD! HOW COULD WE HAVE FORGOTTEN ?!
CATS LOVE WICKERWORK! IT'S THE BEST THING IN THE WORLD FOR THEM TO SHARPEN THEIR CLAWS ON!
AIEE!!
DAR... DARLING, WHAT WILL WE DO?!
.....
Mm...?
CLAW
SHARPENI
FORBIDDE
.....

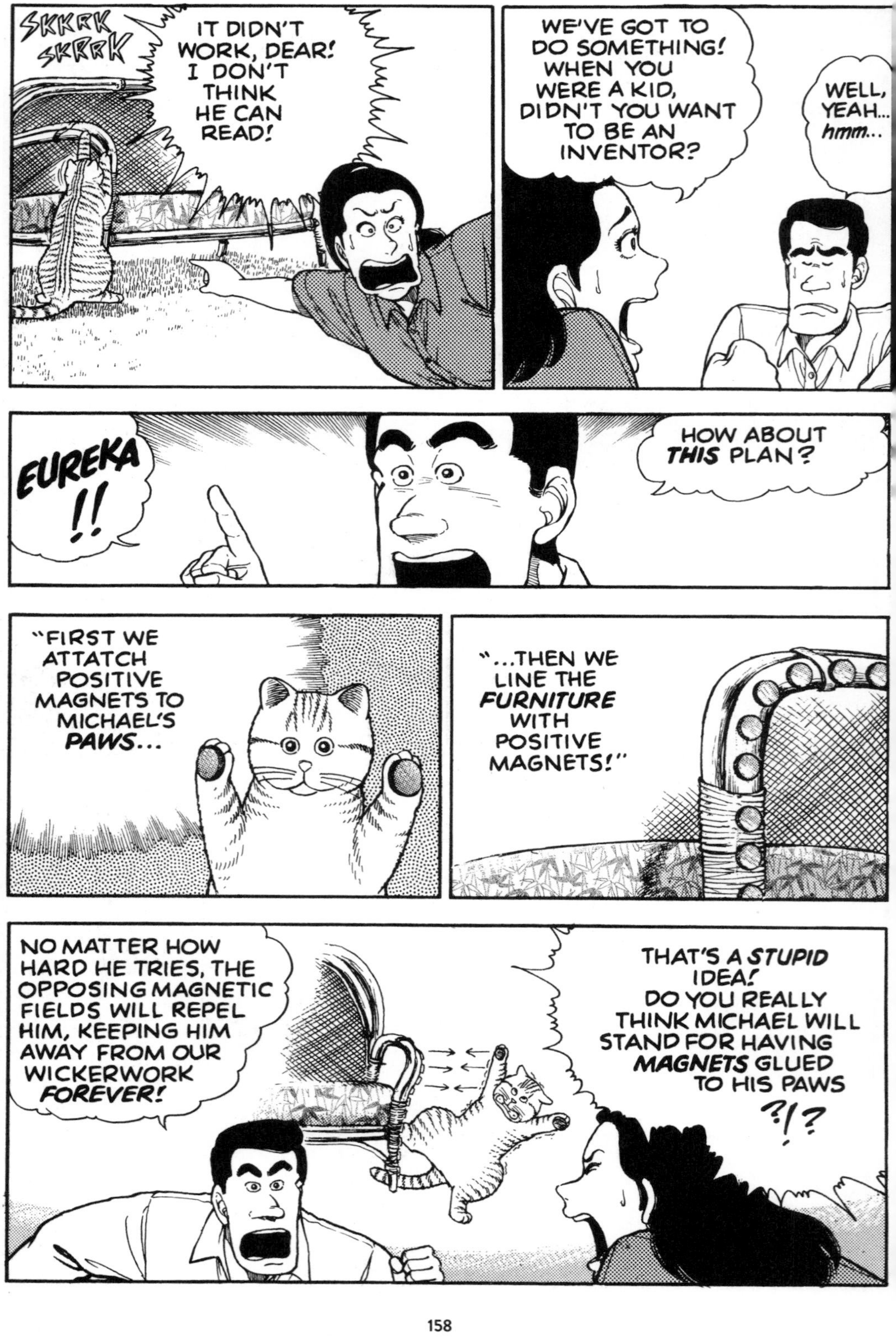
SKKRK SKRRK
IT DIDN'T WORK, DEAR! I DON'T THINK HE CAN READ!
WE'VE GOT TO DO SOMETHING! WHEN YOU WERE A KID, DIDN'T YOU WANT TO BE AN INVENTOR?
WELL, YEAH... *hmm...*
EUREKA !!
HOW ABOUT ***THIS*** PLAN?
"FIRST WE ATTATCH POSITIVE MAGNETS TO MICHAEL'S ***PAWS***...
"...THEN WE LINE THE ***FURNITURE*** WITH POSITIVE MAGNETS!"
NO MATTER HOW HARD HE TRIES, THE OPPOSING MAGNETIC FIELDS WILL REPEL HIM, KEEPING HIM AWAY FROM OUR WICKERWORK ***FOREVER!***
THAT'S A ***STUPID*** IDEA! DO YOU REALLY THINK MICHAEL WILL STAND FOR HAVING ***MAGNETS*** GLUED TO HIS PAWS ?!?

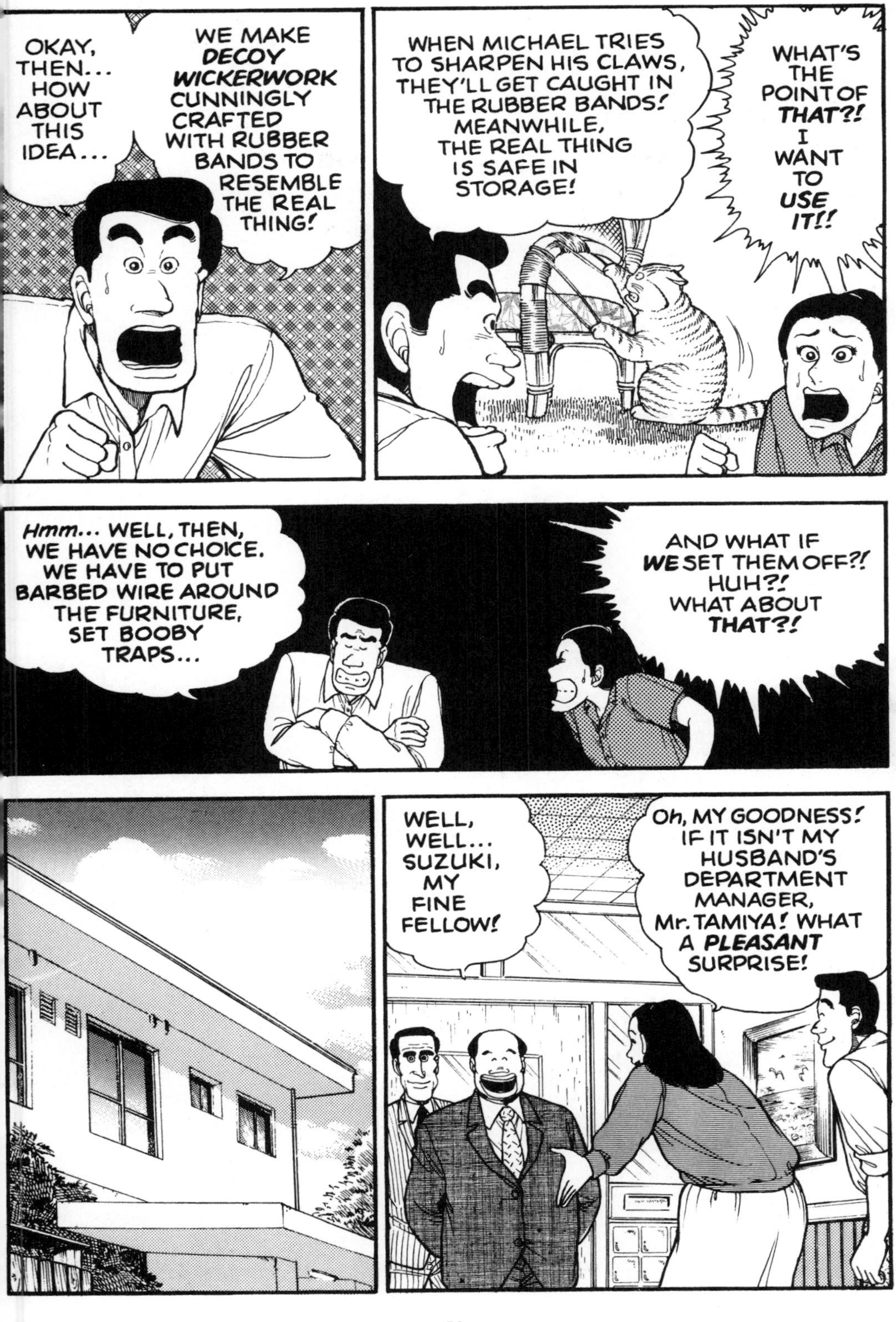
OKAY, THEN... HOW ABOUT THIS IDEA...
WE MAKE DECOY WICKERWORK CUNNINGLY CRAFTED WITH RUBBER BANDS TO RESEMBLE THE REAL THING!
WHEN MICHAEL TRIES TO SHARPEN HIS CLAWS, THEY'LL GET CAUGHT IN THE RUBBER BANDS! MEANWHILE, THE REAL THING IS SAFE IN STORAGE!
WHAT'S THE POINT OF THAT?! I WANT TO USE IT!!
Hmm... WELL, THEN, WE HAVE NO CHOICE. WE HAVE TO PUT BARBED WIRE AROUND THE FURNITURE, SET BOOBY TRAPS...
AND WHAT IF WE SET THEM OFF?! HUH?! WHAT ABOUT THAT?!
WELL, WELL... SUZUKI, MY FINE FELLOW!
Oh, MY GOODNESS! IF IT ISN'T MY HUSBAND'S DEPARTMENT MANAGER, Mr. TAMIYA! WHAT A PLEASANT SURPRISE!

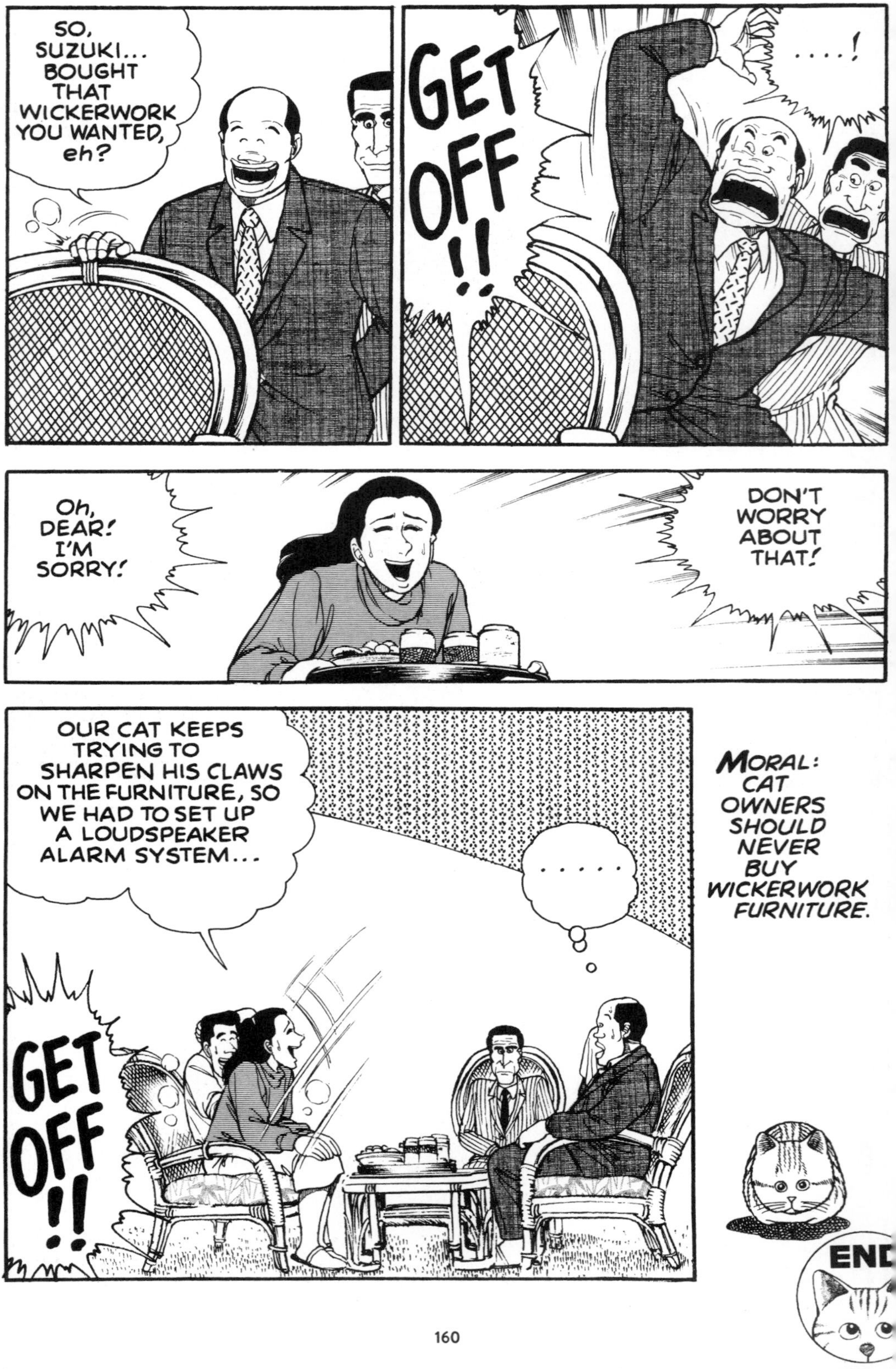
SO, SUZUKI... BOUGHT THAT WICKERWORK YOU WANTED, eh?
GET OFF !!
....!
Oh, DEAR! I'M SORRY!
DON'T WORRY ABOUT THAT!
OUR CAT KEEPS TRYING TO SHARPEN HIS CLAWS ON THE FURNITURE, SO WE HAD TO SET UP A LOUDSPEAKER ALARM SYSTEM...
.....
GET OFF !!
MORAL: CAT OWNERS SHOULD NEVER BUY WICKERWORK FURNITURE.
END

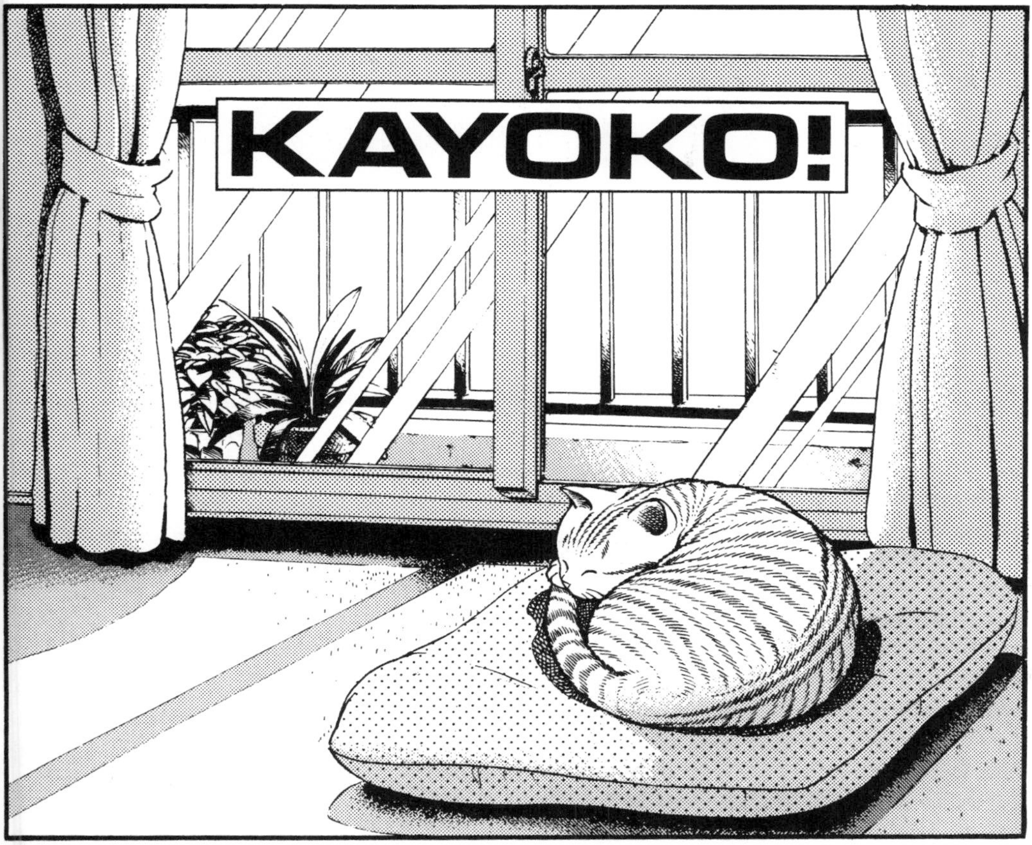
KAYOKO!

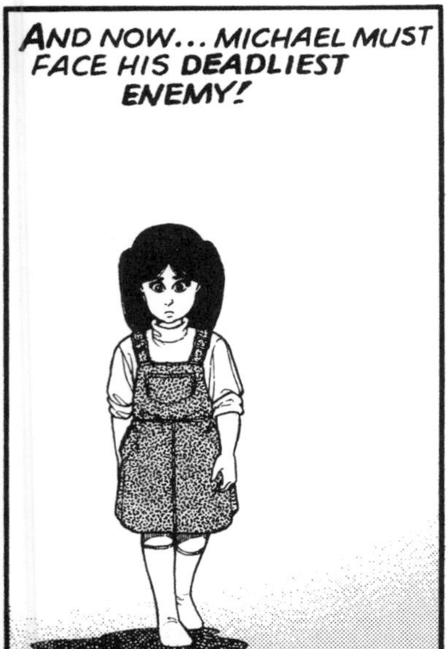
AND NOW... MICHAEL MUST FACE HIS DEADLIEST ENEMY!

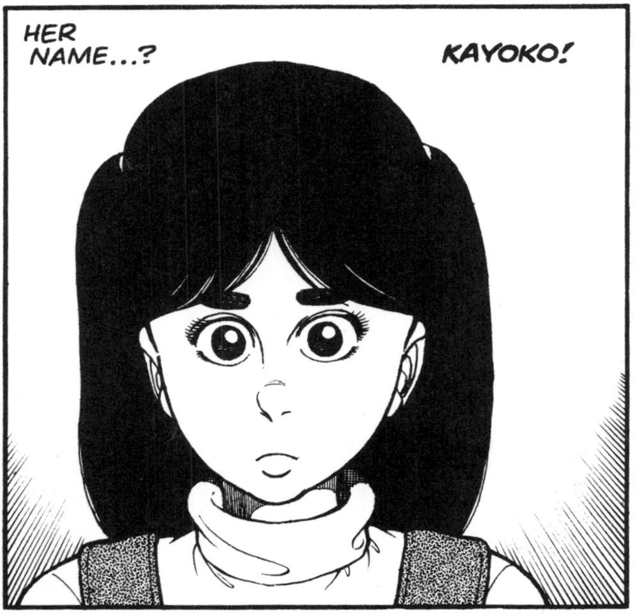
HER NAME...?
KAYOKO!

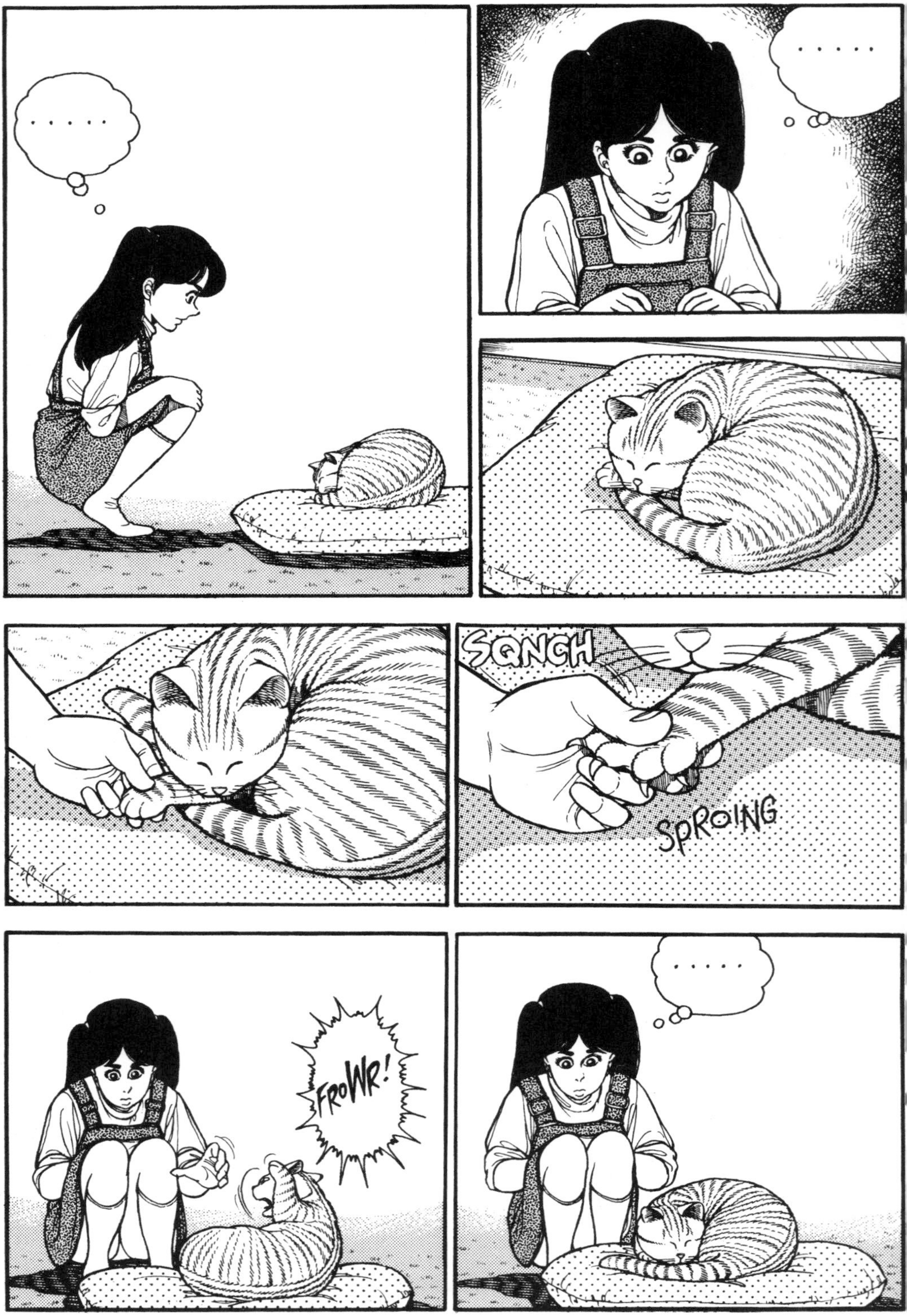
......
.....
SQNCH
SPROING
FROWR!
.....

......
SQNCH
FFROWR!
......
ZZZZ
ZZ--
SQNCH
......
nng...
GHAAH!

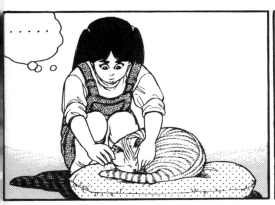

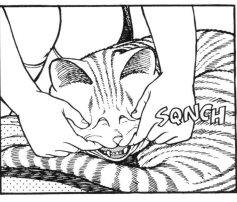

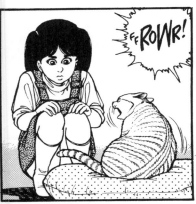

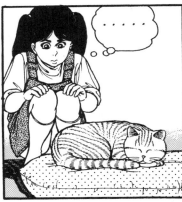

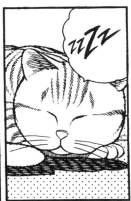

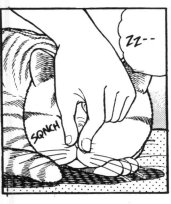

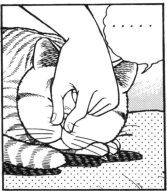

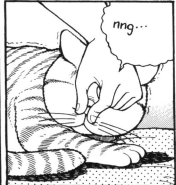

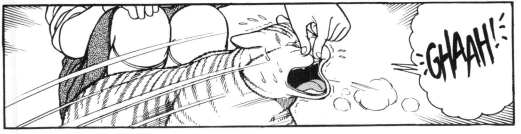

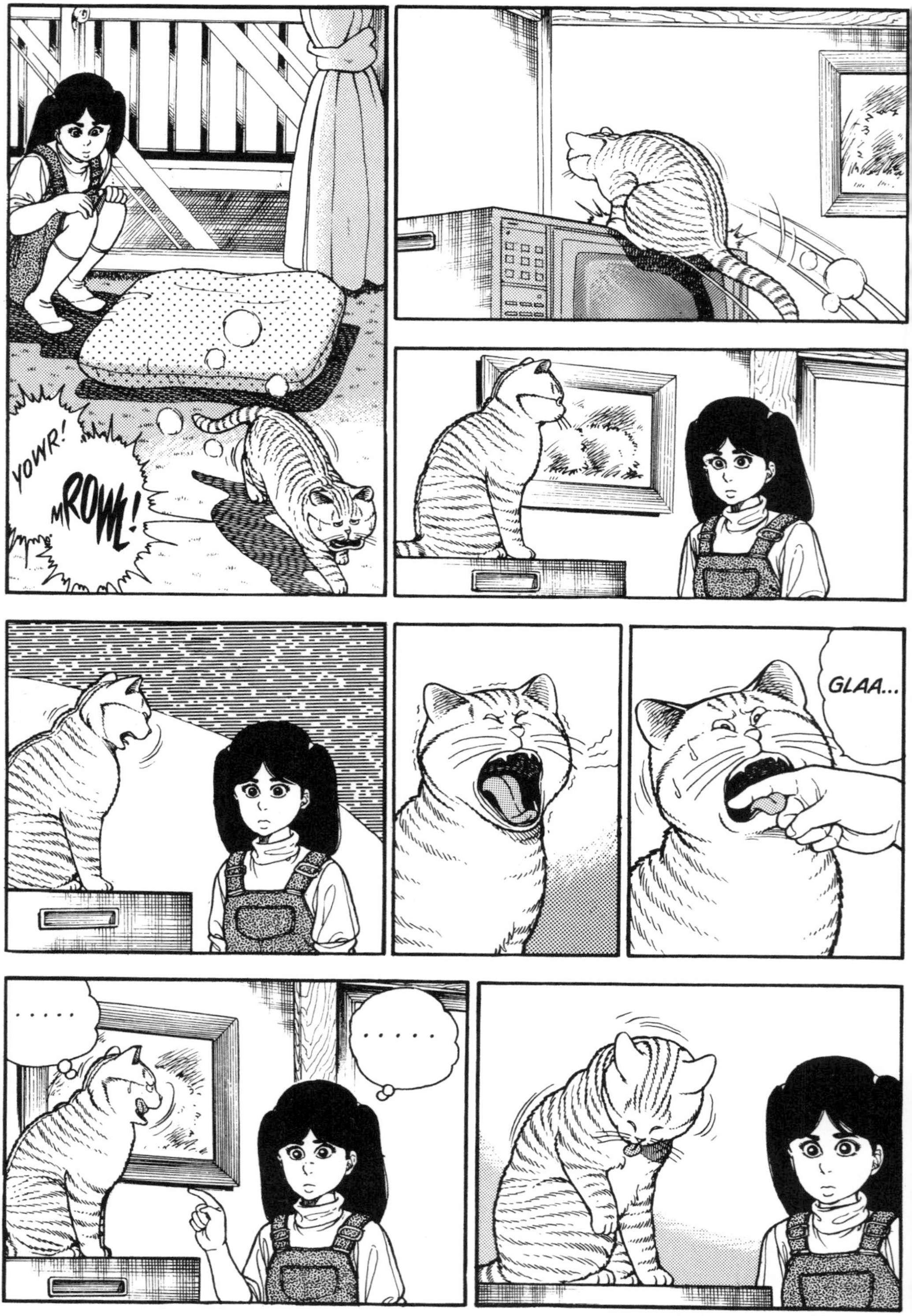
YOWR!
MROWL!
GLAA...
.....
.....

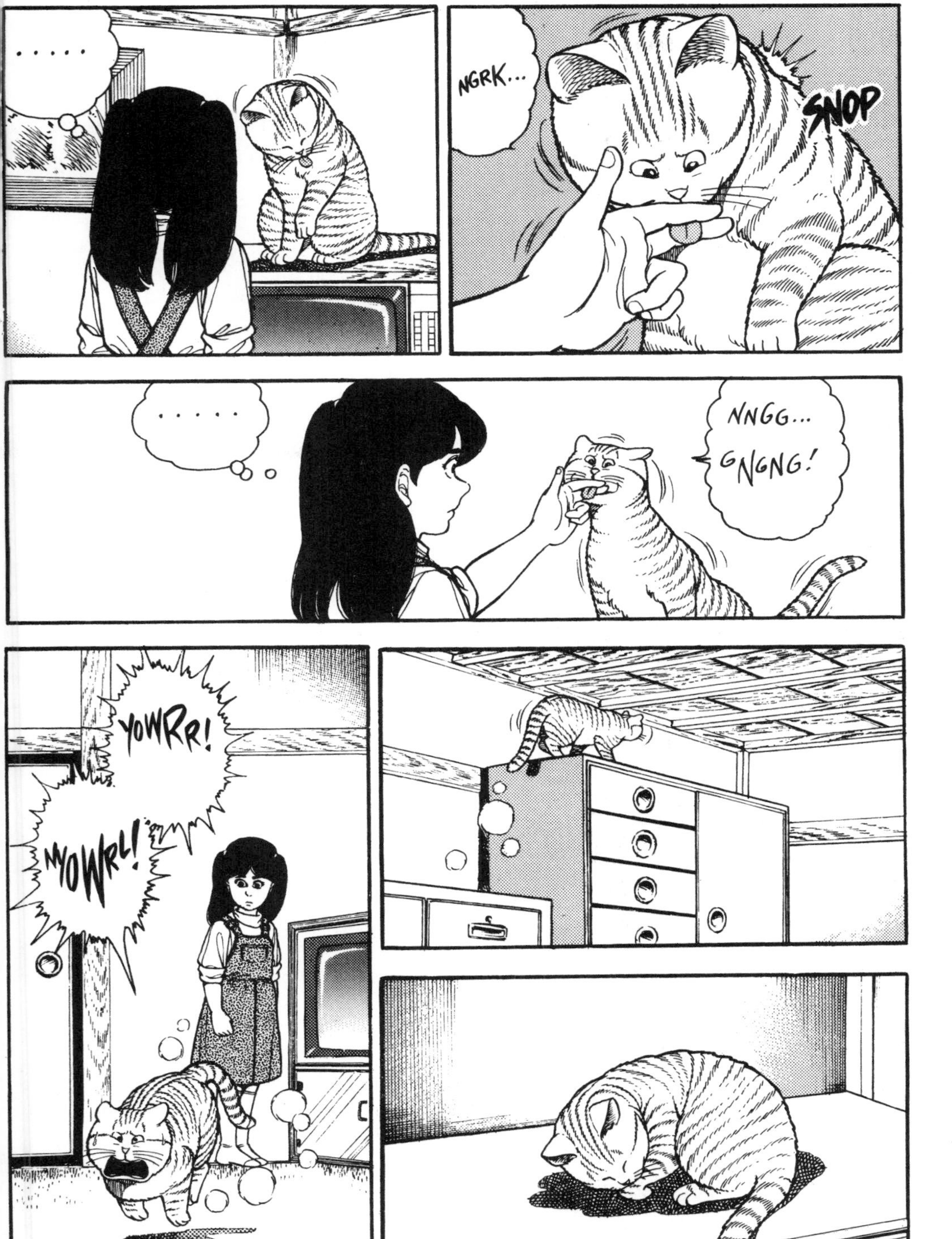

......
NGRK...
SNOP
......
NNGG...
GNGNG!
YOWRR!
NYOWRL!

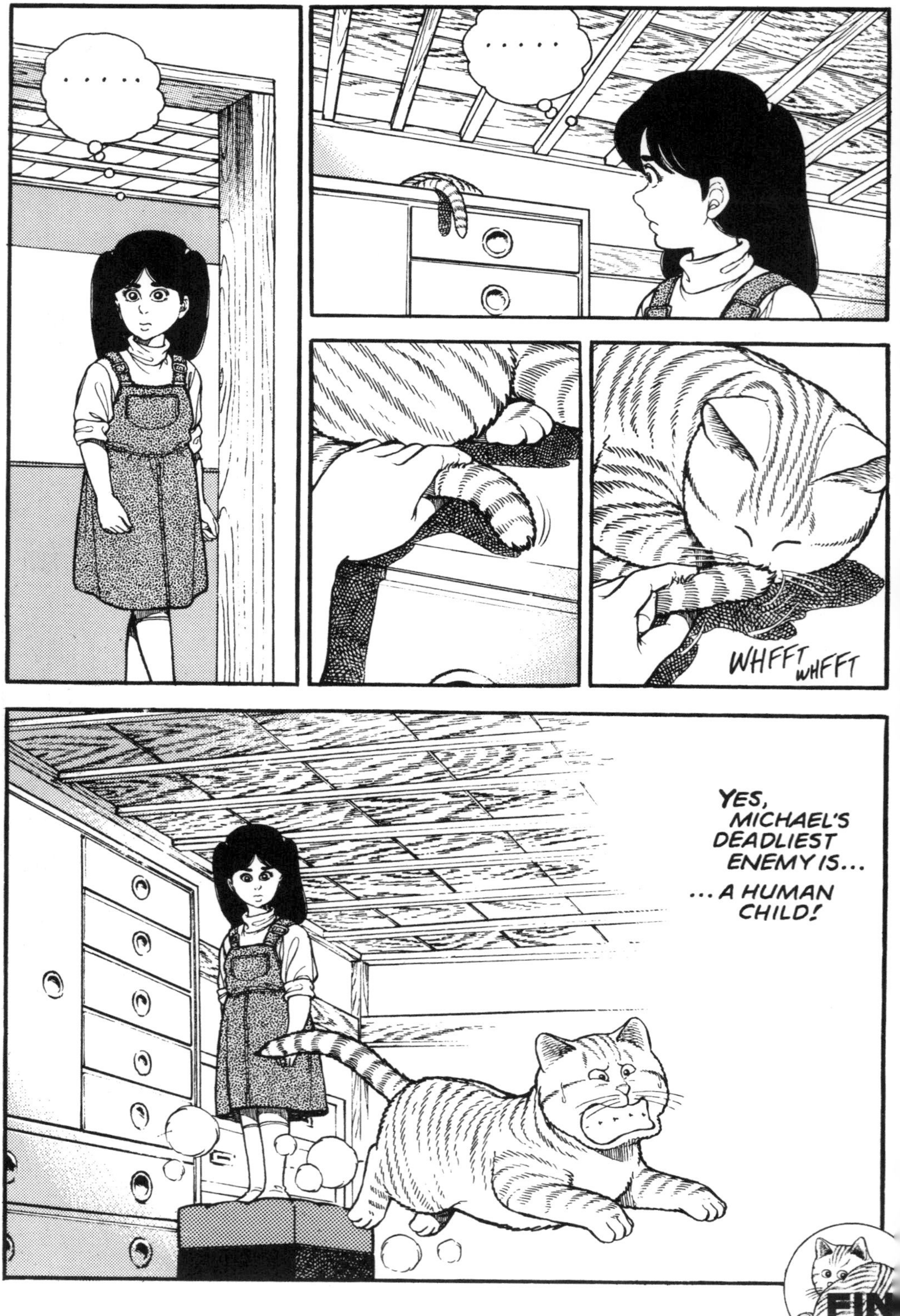

. . . . . .
. . . . . .
WHFFT WHFFT
YES, MICHAEL'S DEADLIEST ENEMY IS...
...A HUMAN CHILD!
FIN

# THE YAKUZA*, PART TWO:

# "K'S" OPULENT LIFESTYLE

*The Japanese Mafia

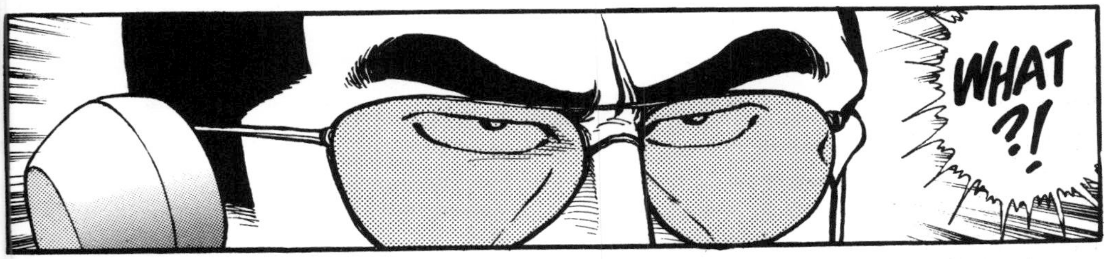
WHAT ?!

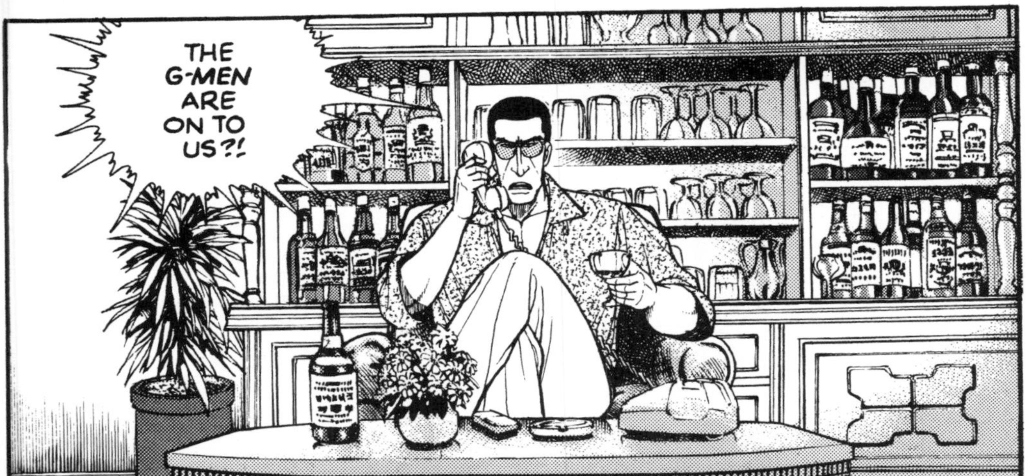
THE G-MEN ARE ON TO US?!

Ah -- I SEE.

THEN WE'RE OKAY SO FAR.

*Bzzzzz*

YOU'RE *DAMN* SURE YOU COVERED YOUR TRACKS?

*Bzzt*

WHAT?! FIFTY GRAND?

*Bzzz*

THAT'S A HELL OF A LOT.

*Bzzzzz*

YOU *SURE* IT'S TOP-GRADE STUFF?

*Bzzt*

THEY TRY TO UNLOAD SOME CHEAP JUNK ON US, AND WE'LL TEACH THEM WHO THEY'RE DEALING WITH.

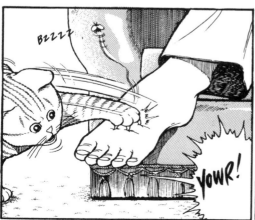

*Bzzzz*

YOWR!

. . . . !

S-SAY... HOW ABOUT THE KODANSHA GANG? I HEAR THEY'RE TRYING TO MUSCLE IN ON OUR TERRITORY...

*BZZZzz*

DAMN IT ALL...

*MROW!*

I DON'T LIKE THIS...

*WHAP*

HERE'S WHAT YOU DO... *OOF...*

*WHDD*

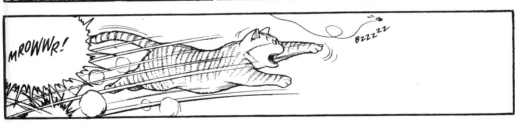

*MROWWR!*

*BZZZZ*

GRR...

*BZZT*

*YOW!*

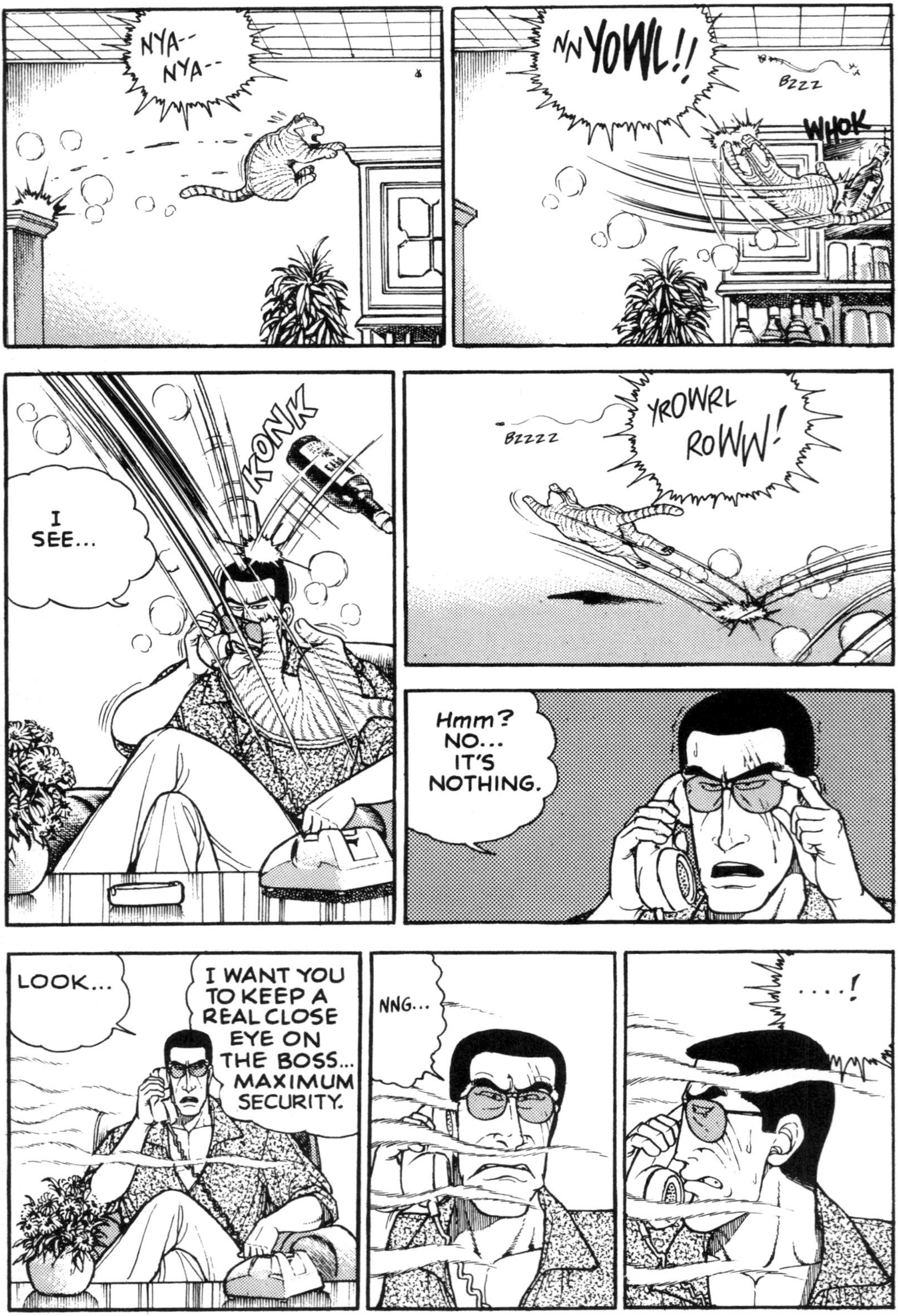
NYA-- NYA--
NN YOWL!!
Bzzz
WHOK
I SEE...
KONK
Bzzzz
YROWRL ROWW!
Hmm? NO... IT'S NOTHING.
LOOK...
I WANT YOU TO KEEP A REAL CLOSE EYE ON THE BOSS... MAXIMUM SECURITY.
NNG...
....!

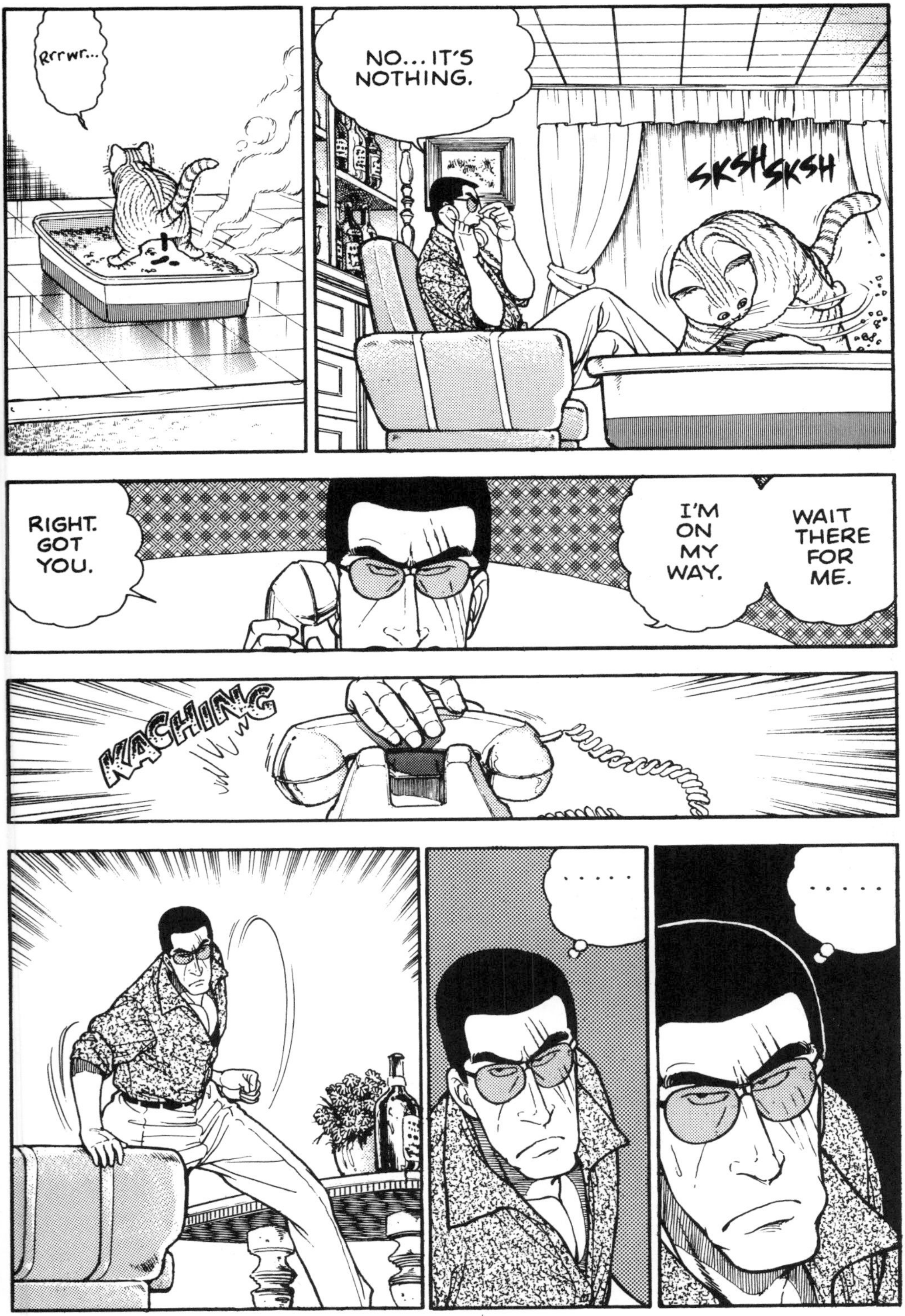
Rrrwr...
NO... IT'S NOTHING.
SKSH SKSH
RIGHT. GOT YOU.
I'M ON MY WAY.
WAIT THERE FOR ME.
KACHING
.....
.....

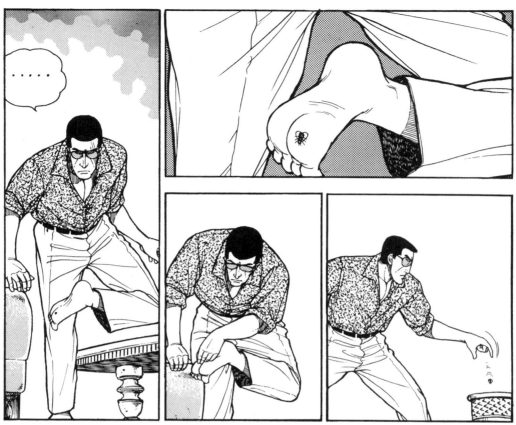

AS WE'VE SAID BEFORE... YAKUZA SHOULDN'T KEEP CATS.

END

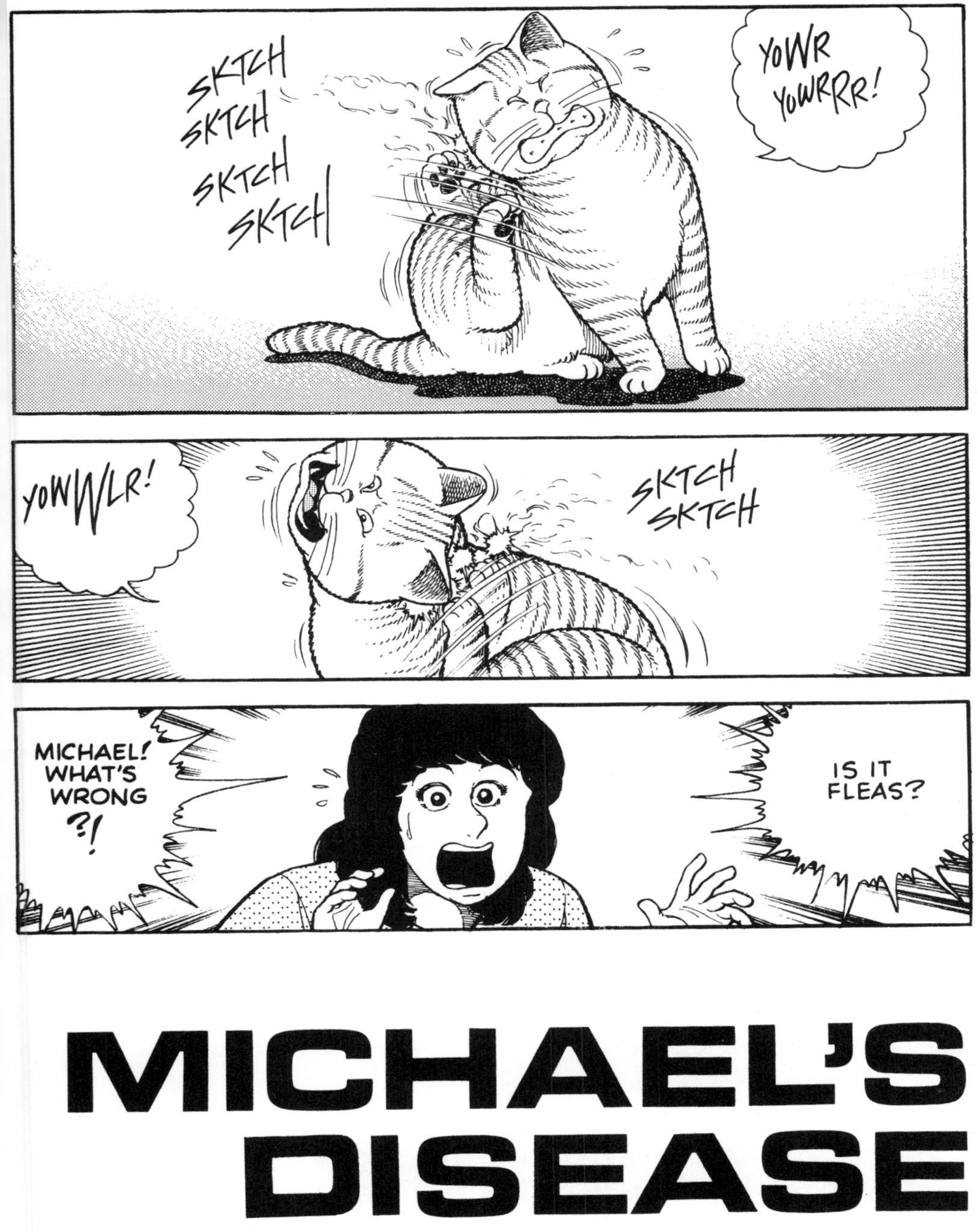
SKTCH
SKTCH
SKTCH
SKTCH
YOWR YOWRRR!
YOWWLR!
SKTCH
SKTCH
MICHAEL! WHAT'S WRONG ?!
IS IT FLEAS?

# MICHAEL'S DISEASE

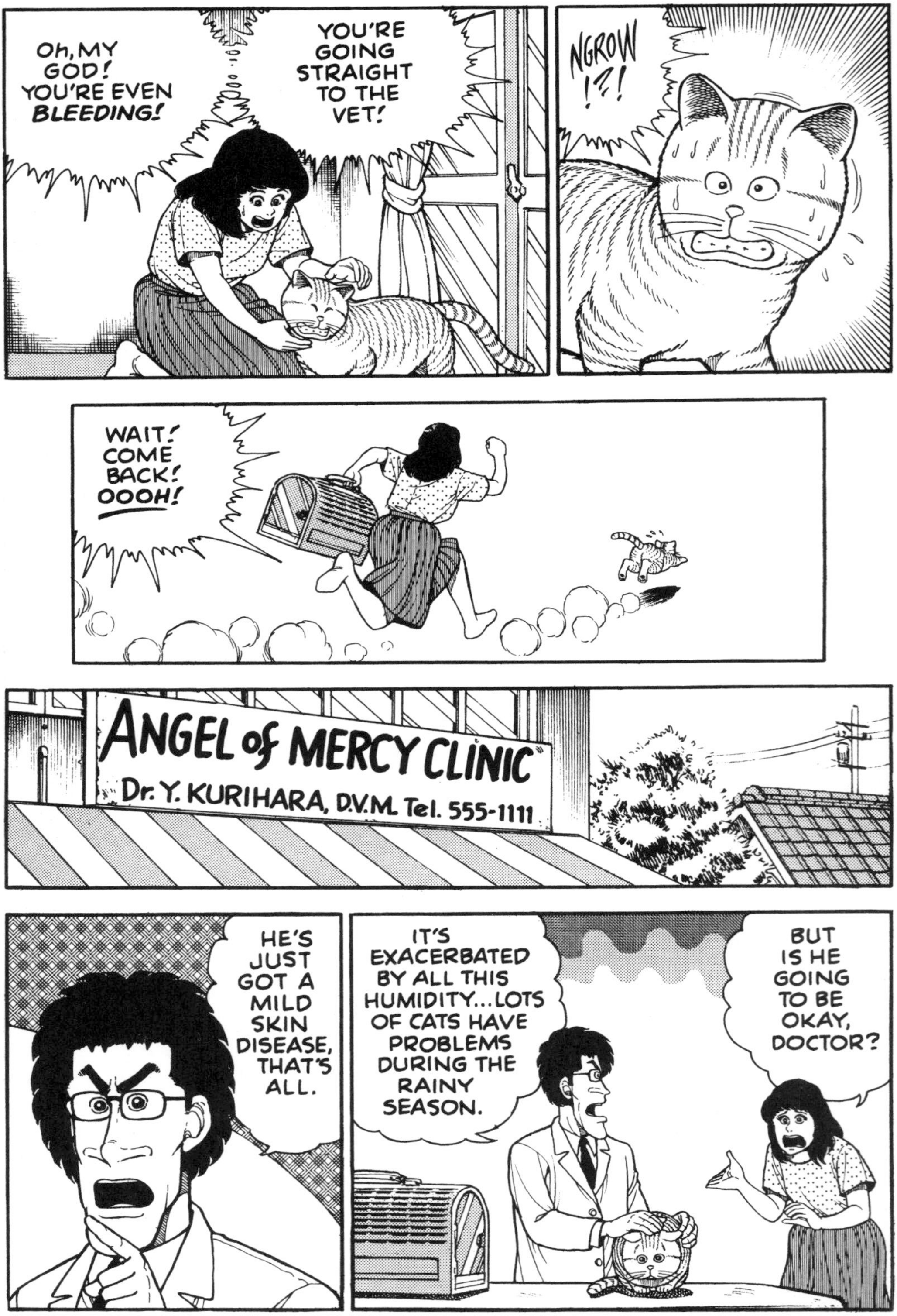
Oh, MY GOD! YOU'RE EVEN BLEEDING!
YOU'RE GOING STRAIGHT TO THE VET!
NGROW !?!
WAIT! COME BACK! OOOH!
ANGEL of MERCY CLINIC
Dr. Y. KURIHARA, D.V.M. Tel. 555-1111
HE'S JUST GOT A MILD SKIN DISEASE, THAT'S ALL.
IT'S EXACERBATED BY ALL THIS HUMIDITY... LOTS OF CATS HAVE PROBLEMS DURING THE RAINY SEASON.
BUT IS HE GOING TO BE OKAY, DOCTOR?

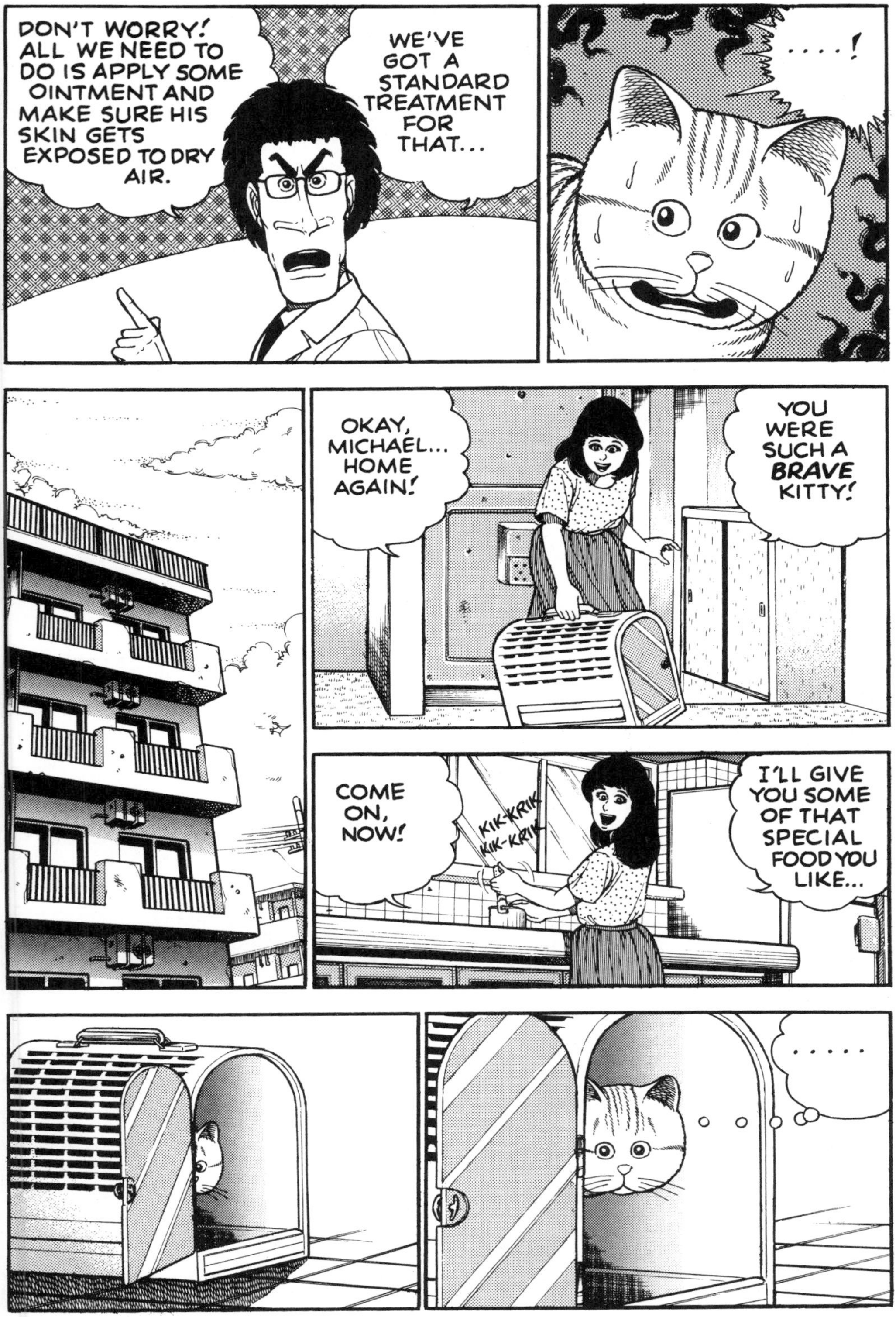
DON'T WORRY! ALL WE NEED TO DO IS APPLY SOME OINTMENT AND MAKE SURE HIS SKIN GETS EXPOSED TO DRY AIR.
WE'VE GOT A STANDARD TREATMENT FOR THAT...
....!
OKAY, MICHAEL... HOME AGAIN!
YOU WERE SUCH A BRAVE KITTY!
COME ON, NOW!
KIK-KRIK KIK-KRIK
I'LL GIVE YOU SOME OF THAT SPECIAL FOOD YOU LIKE...
.....

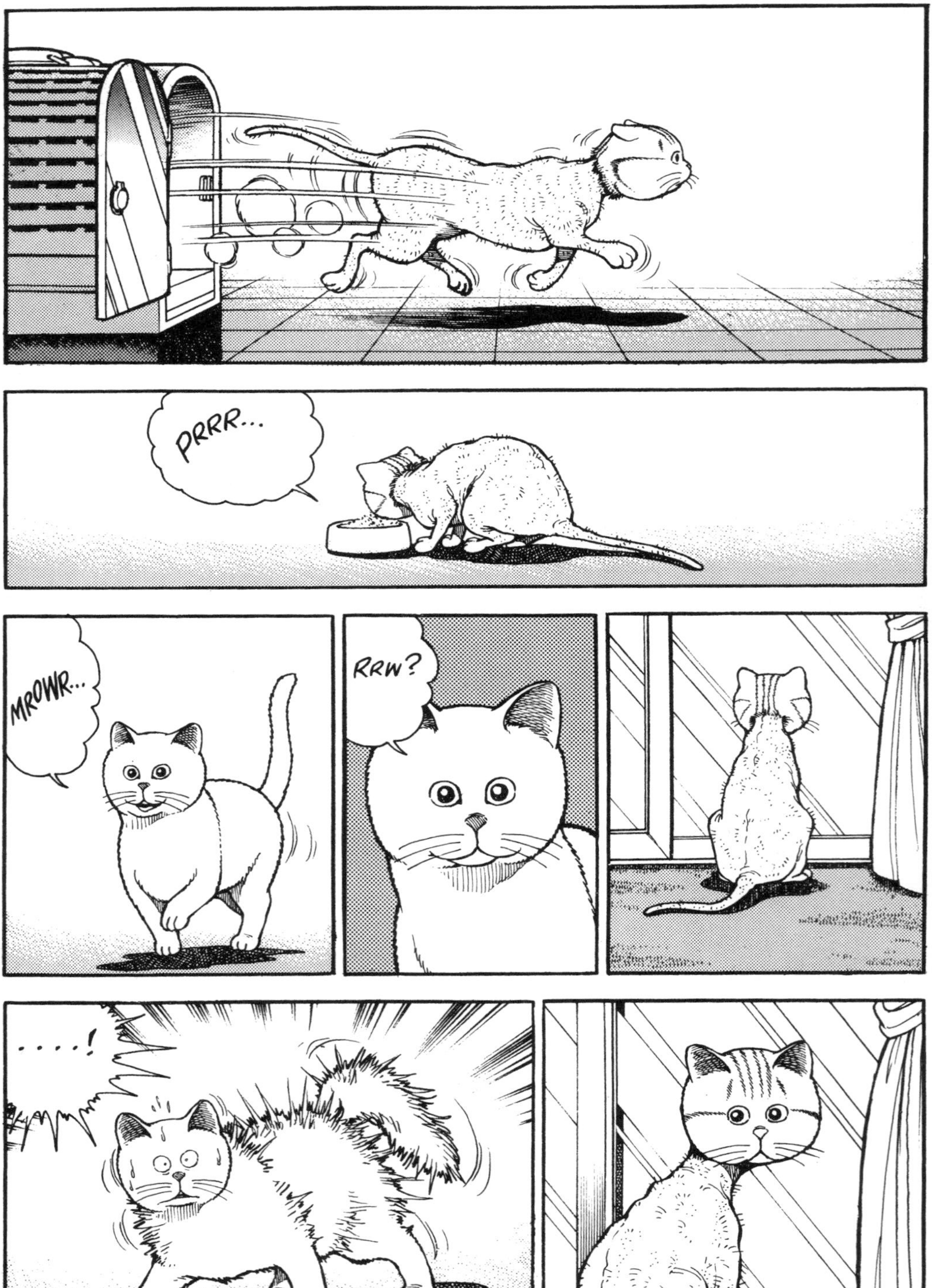
PRRR...
MROWR...
RRW?
....!

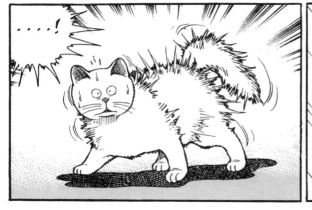

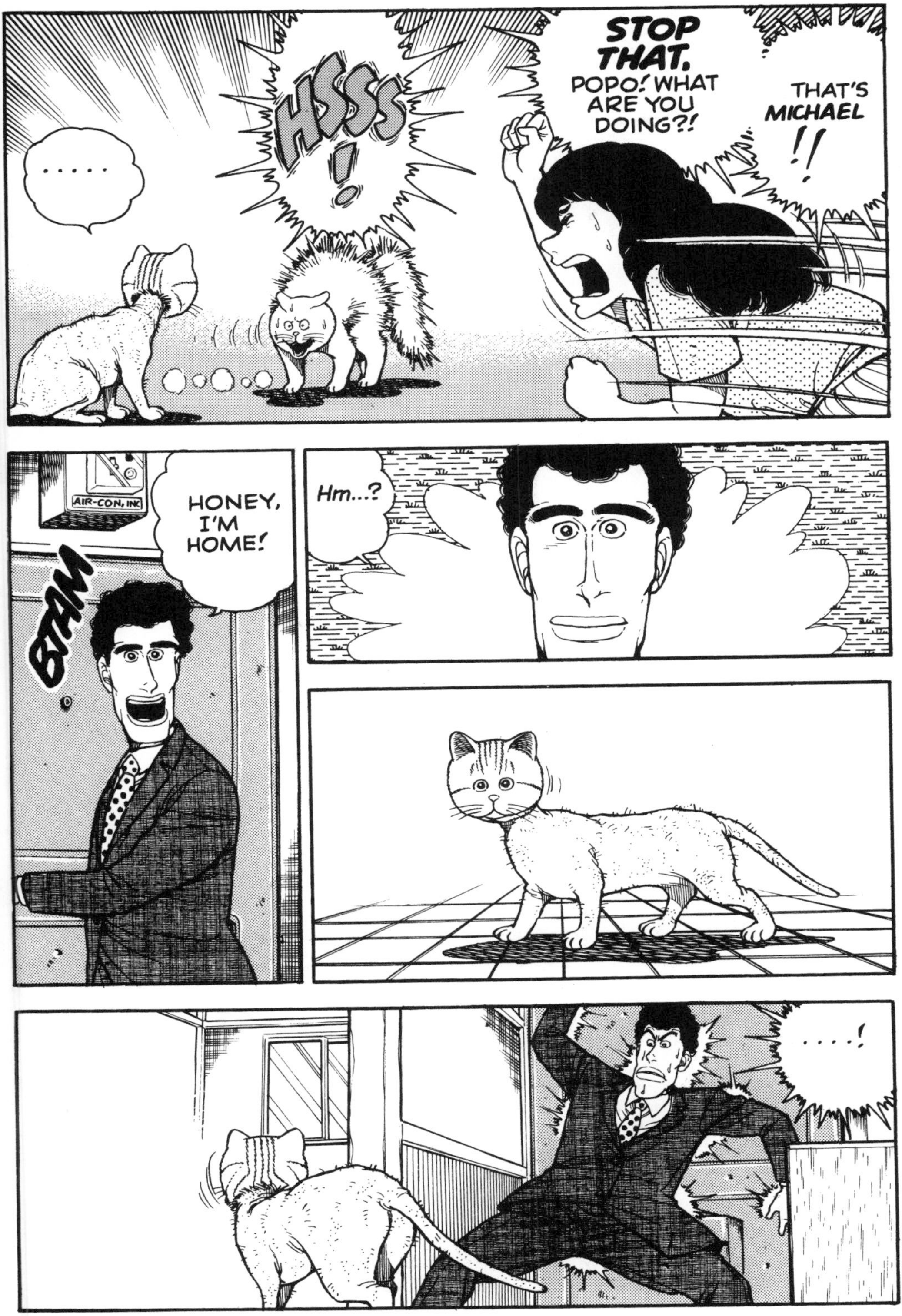

.....
HSSS!
STOP THAT. POPO! WHAT ARE YOU DOING?!
THAT'S MICHAEL!!
AIR-CON, INK
BTAM
HONEY, I'M HOME!
Hm...?
....!

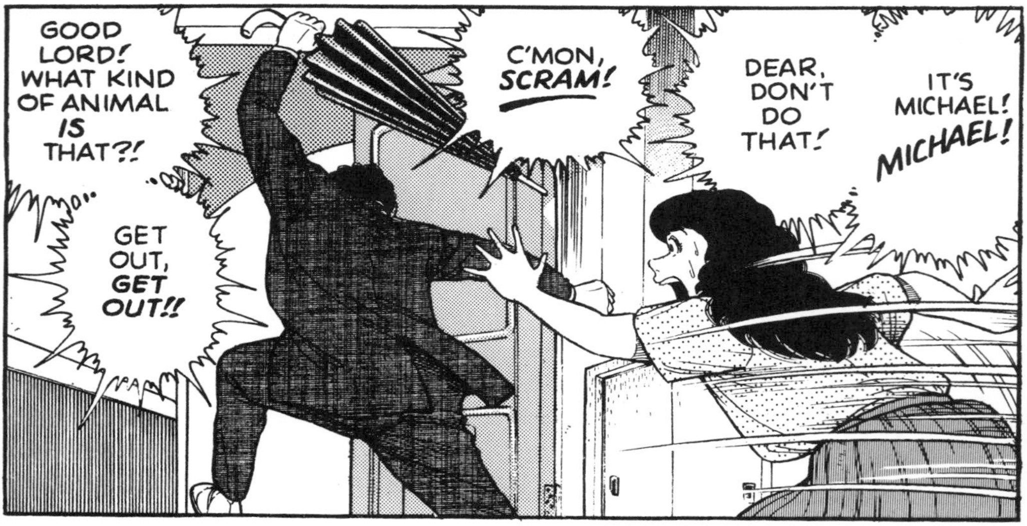
GOOD LORD! WHAT KIND OF ANIMAL IS THAT?!
GET OUT, GET OUT!!
C'MON, SCRAM!
DEAR, DON'T DO THAT!
IT'S MICHAEL! MICHAEL!

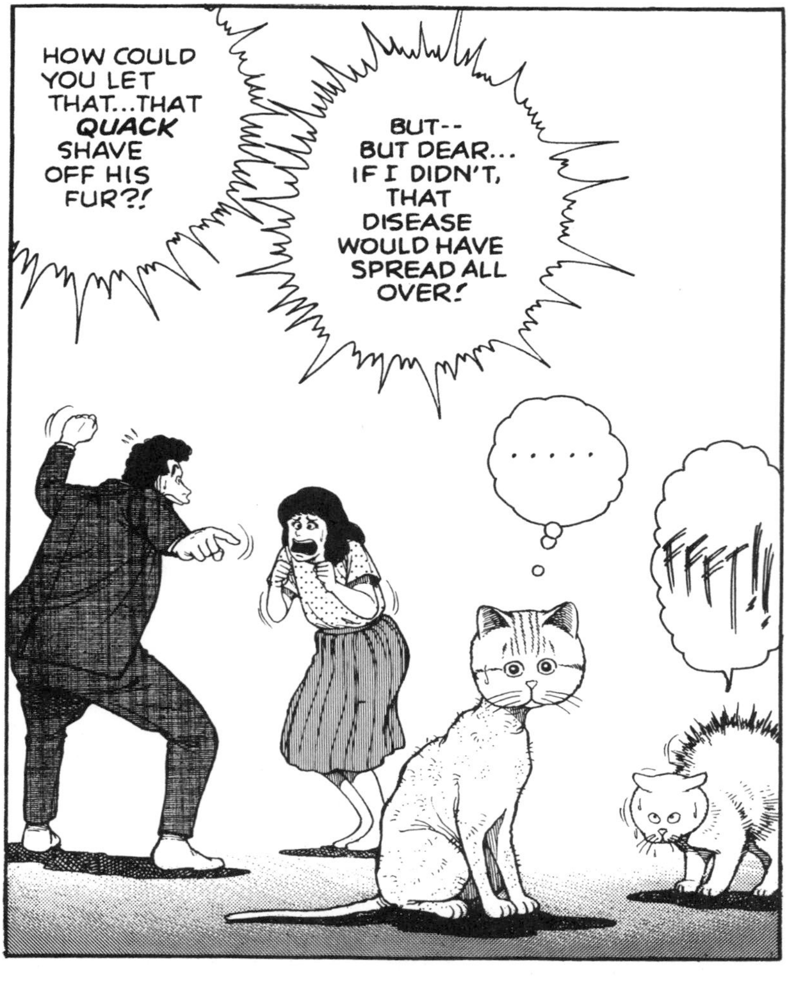
HOW COULD YOU LET THAT...THAT QUACK SHAVE OFF HIS FUR?!
BUT-- BUT DEAR... IF I DIDN'T, THAT DISEASE WOULD HAVE SPREAD ALL OVER!
. . . . .
FFFT!!

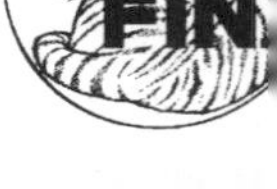
FIN

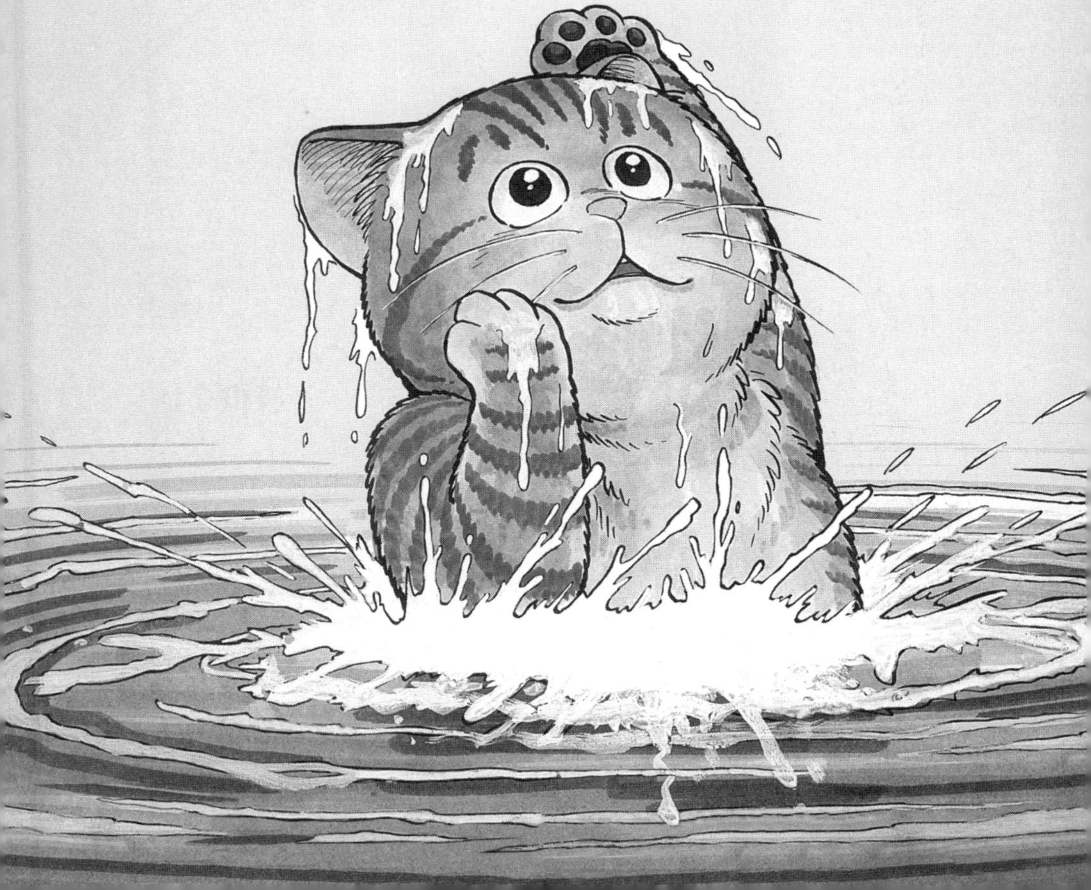

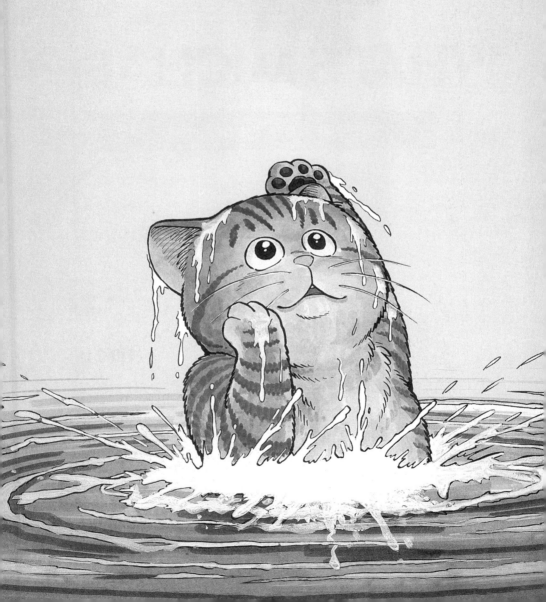

# WHAT'S MICHAEL?

## VOLUME 3: OFF THE DEEP END

*This section was translated by Dana Lewis, Jeanne Sather, and Toren Smith and lettered by L. Lois Buhalis.*

# MICHAEL'S DISASTER

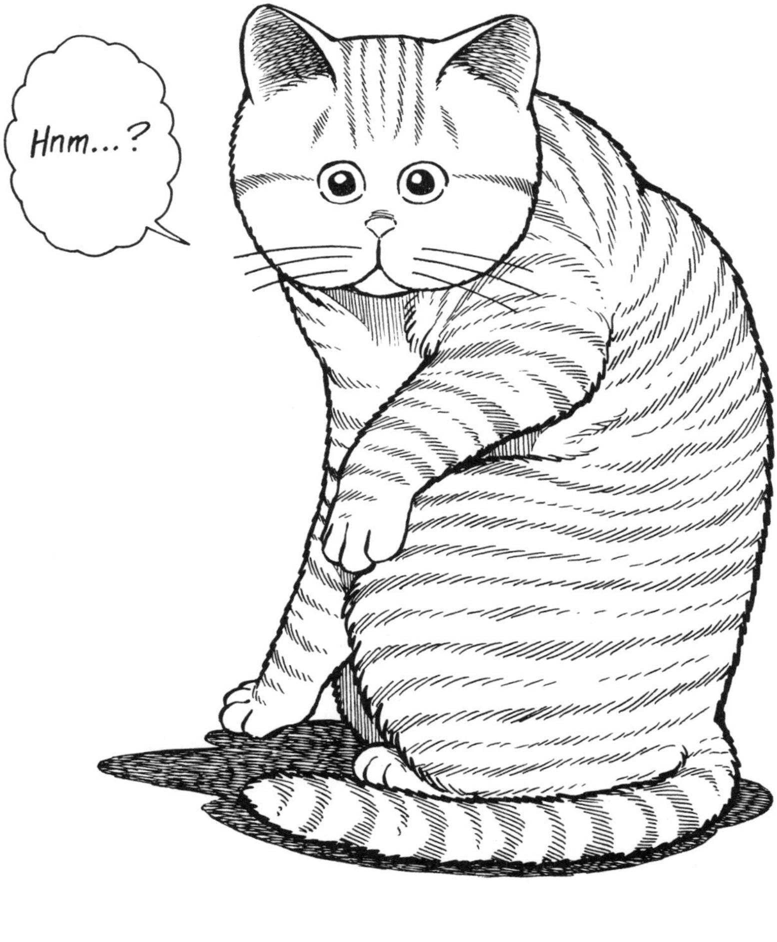
Hnm...?

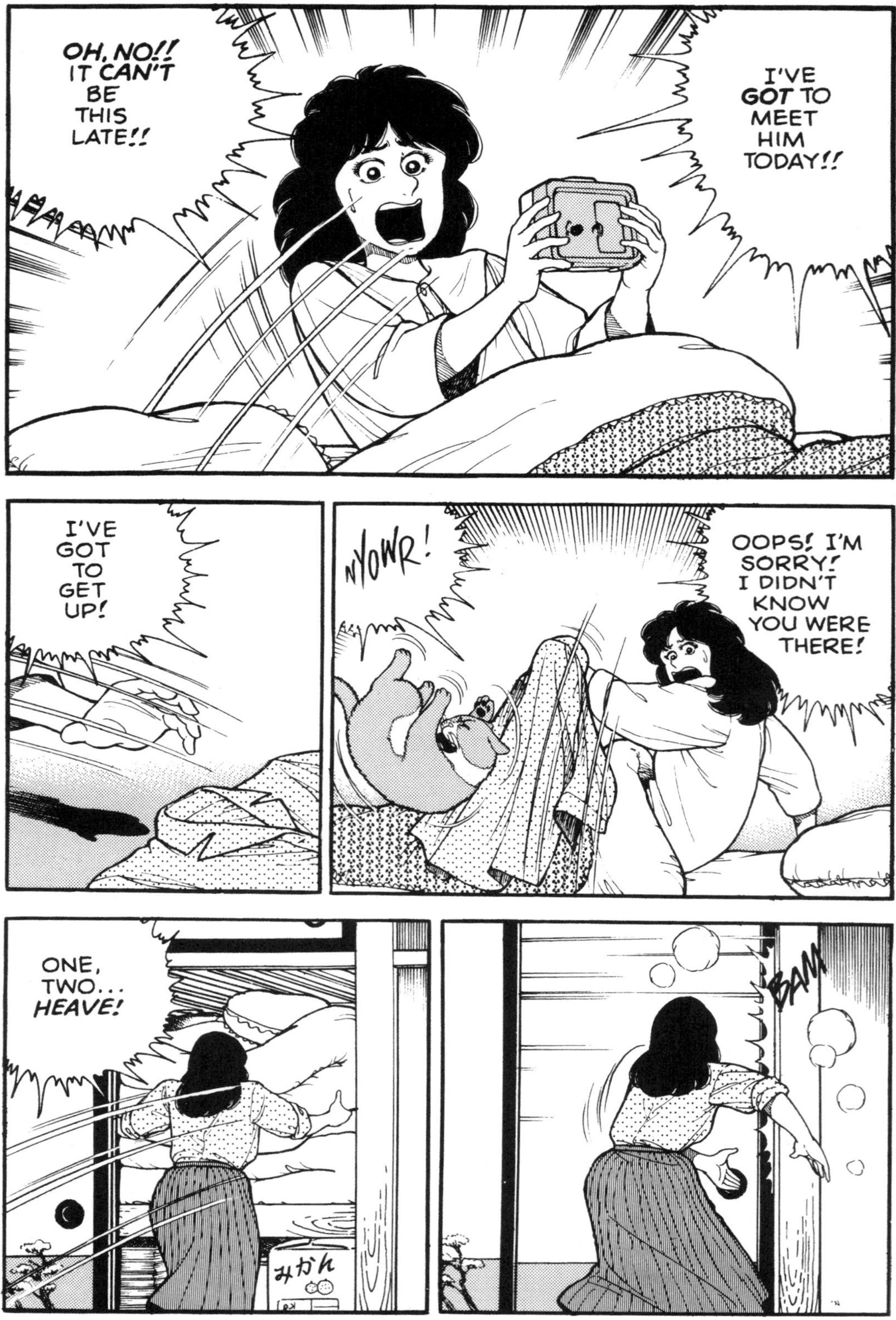

OH, NO!! IT CAN'T BE THIS LATE!!
I'VE GOT TO MEET HIM TODAY!!
I'VE GOT TO GET UP!
NYOWR!
OOPS! I'M SORRY! I DIDN'T KNOW YOU WERE THERE!
ONE, TWO... HEAVE!
みかん
BAM

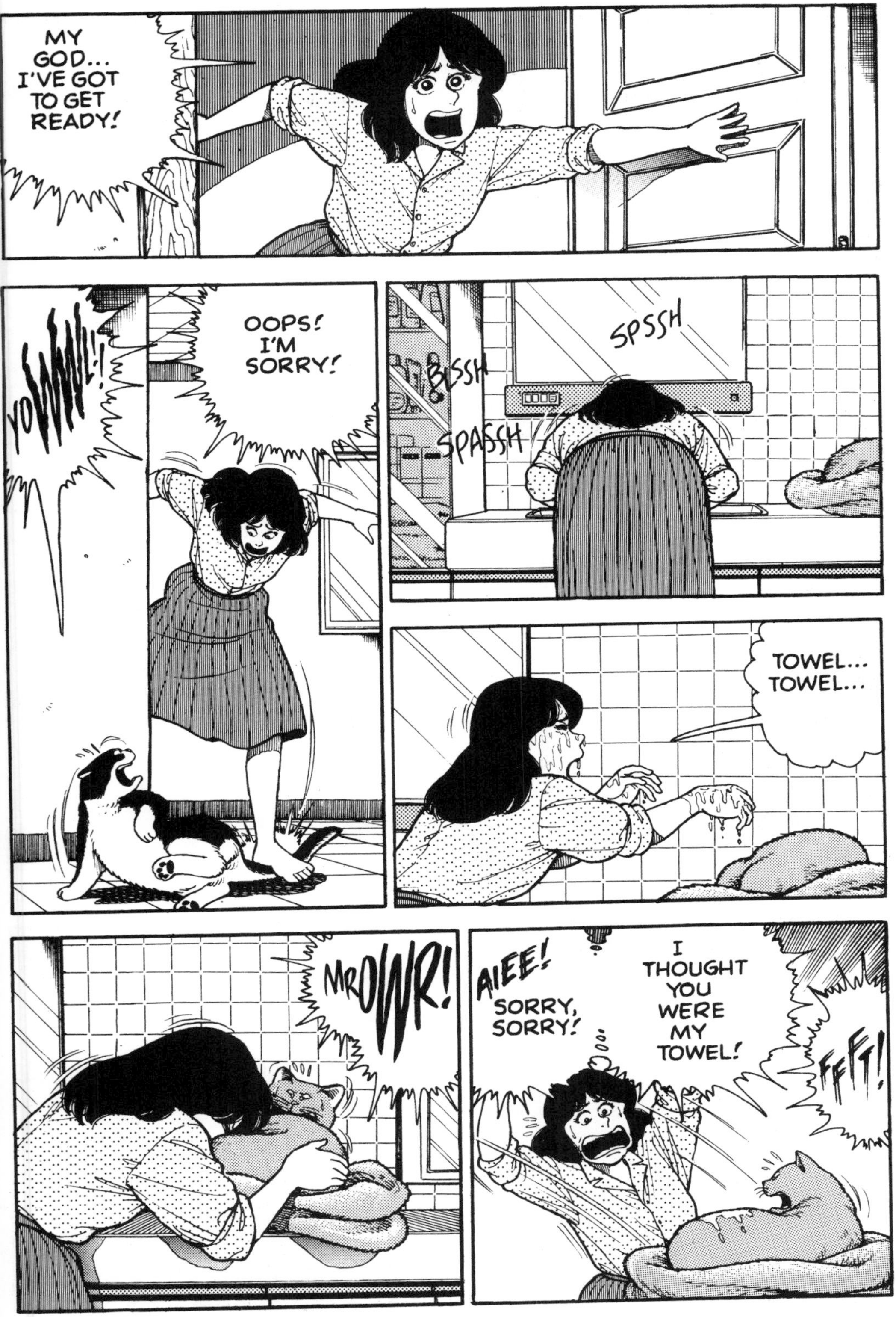
MY GOD... I'VE GOT TO GET READY!
YOWWL!!
OOPS! I'M SORRY!
SPSSH
BLSSH
SPASSH
TOWEL... TOWEL...
MROWR!
AIEE!
SORRY, SORRY!
I THOUGHT YOU WERE MY TOWEL!
FFFT!

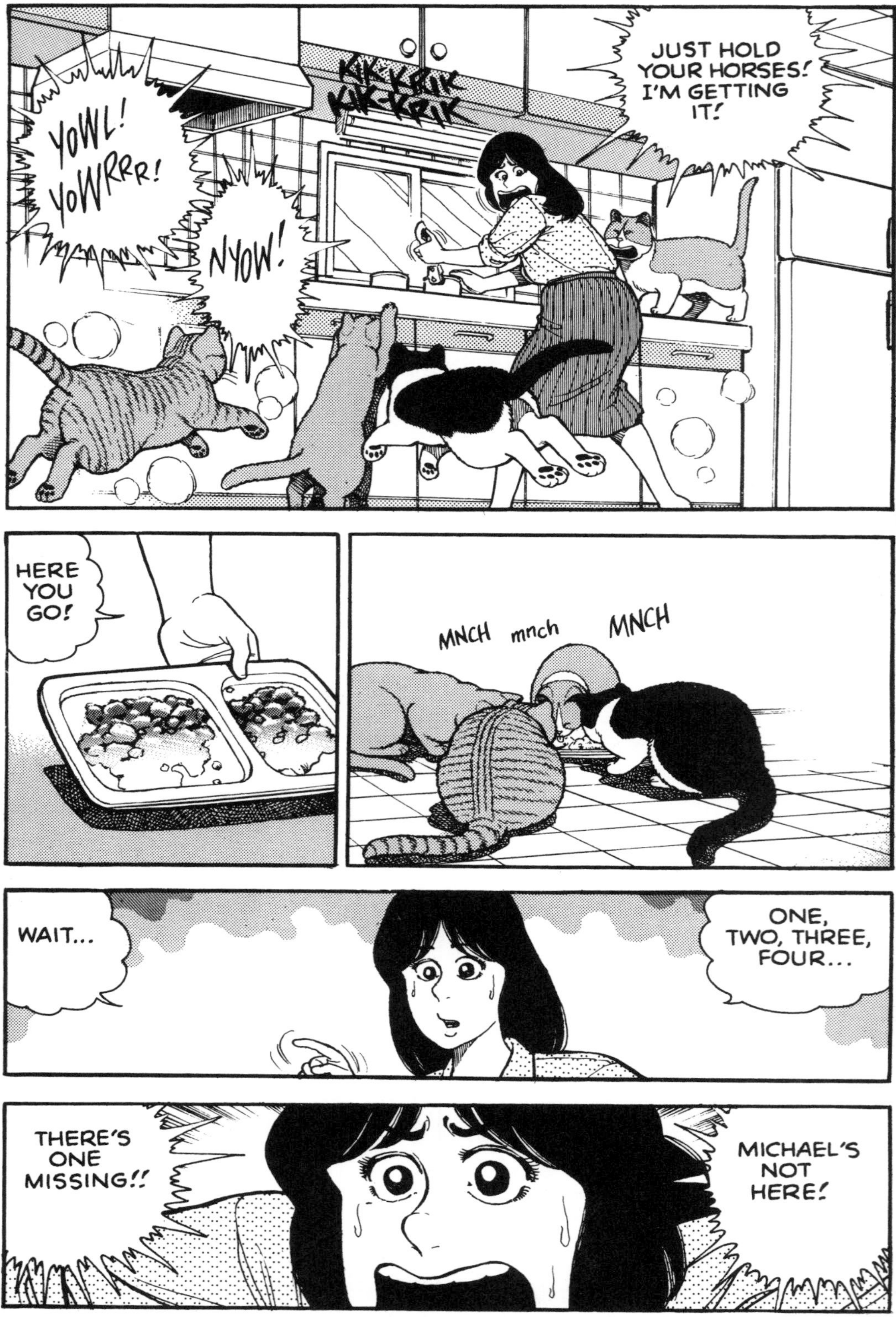

YOWL! YOWRRR!
KIK-KRIK KIK-KRIK
NYOW!
JUST HOLD YOUR HORSES! I'M GETTING IT!
HERE YOU GO!
MNCH mnch MNCH
WAIT...
ONE, TWO, THREE, FOUR...
THERE'S ONE MISSING!!
MICHAEL'S NOT HERE!

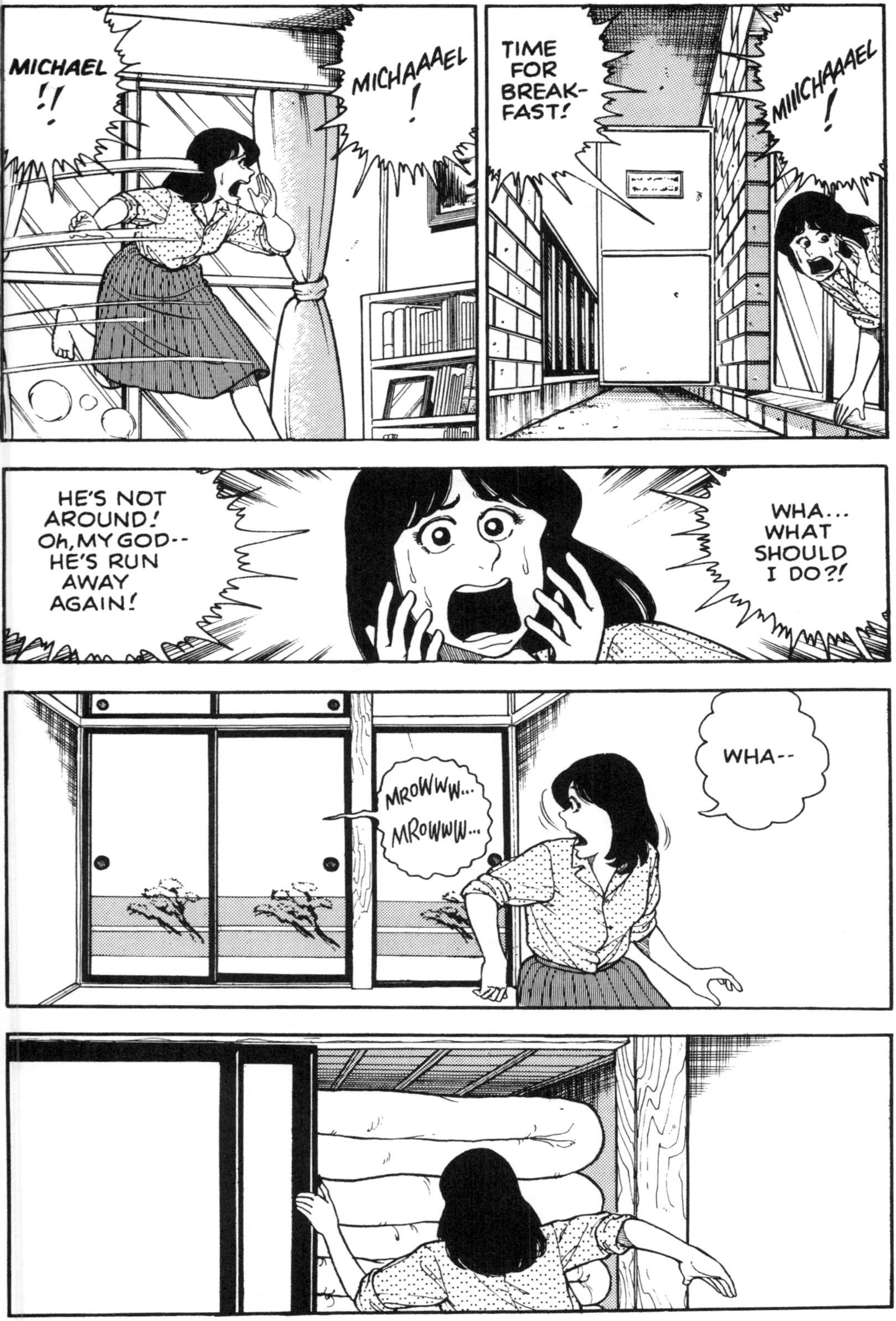

MICHAEL !!
MICHAAAEL !
TIME FOR BREAK-FAST!
MIIICHAAAEL !
HE'S NOT AROUND! Oh, MY GOD-- HE'S RUN AWAY AGAIN!
WHA... WHAT SHOULD I DO?!
MROWWW... MROWWW...
WHA--

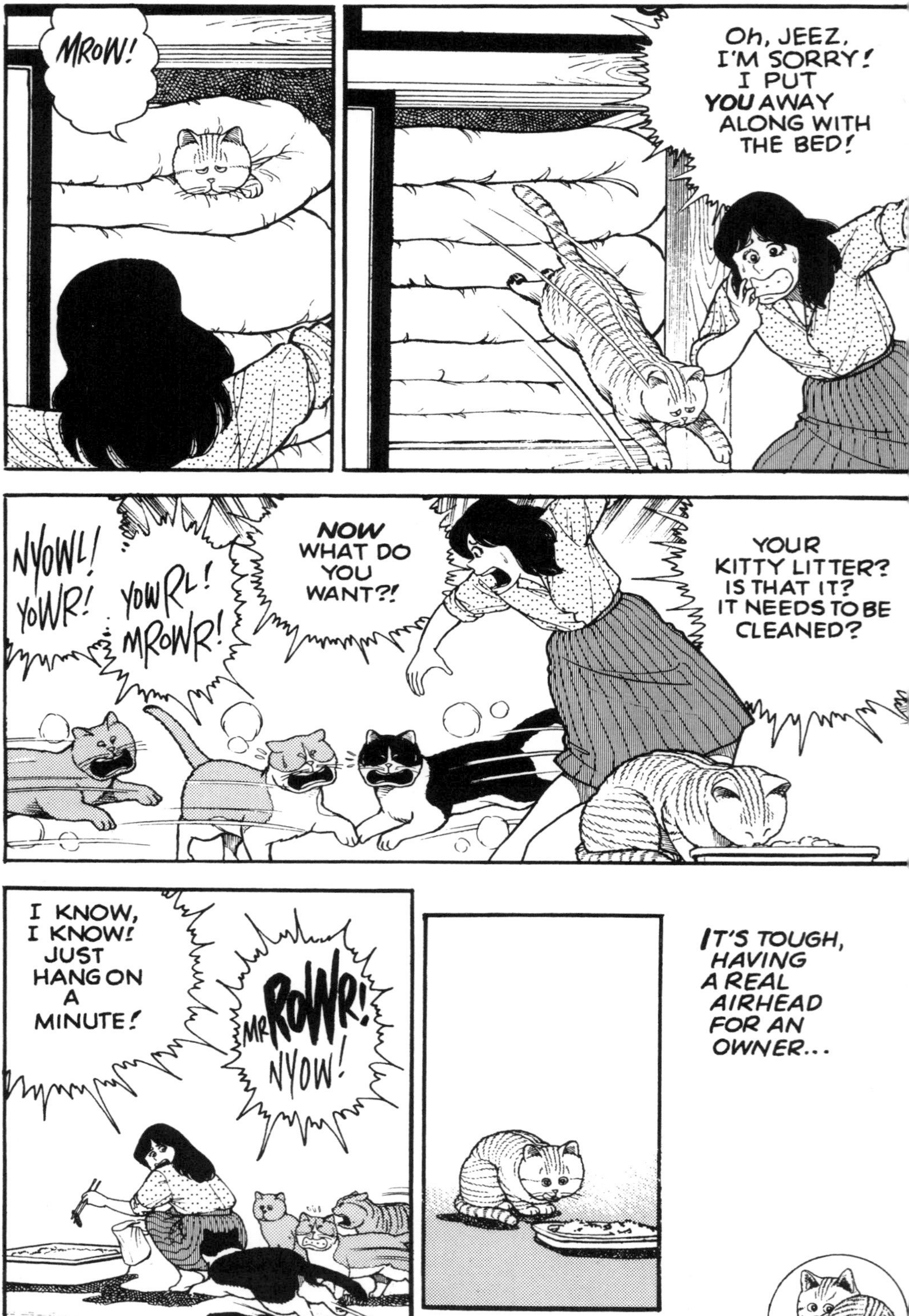
MROW!
Oh, JEEZ. I'M SORRY! I PUT YOU AWAY ALONG WITH THE BED!
NYOWL! YOWR!
YOWRL! MROWR!
NOW WHAT DO YOU WANT?!
YOUR KITTY LITTER? IS THAT IT? IT NEEDS TO BE CLEANED?
I KNOW, I KNOW! JUST HANG ON A MINUTE!
MRROWR! NYOW!
IT'S TOUGH, HAVING A REAL AIRHEAD FOR AN OWNER...
FIN.

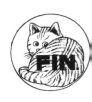

# DANCING MICHAEL!!

## PART ONE

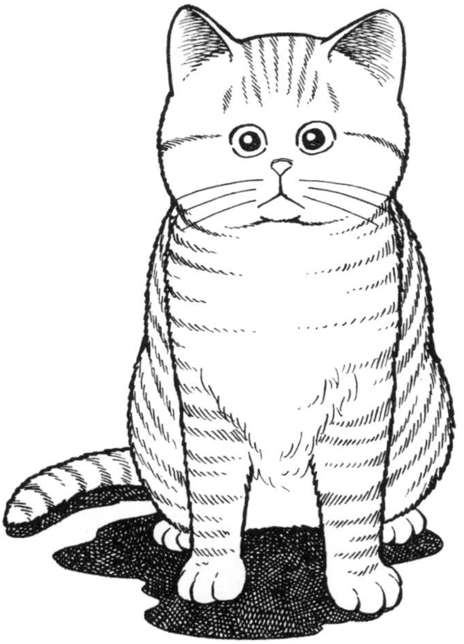

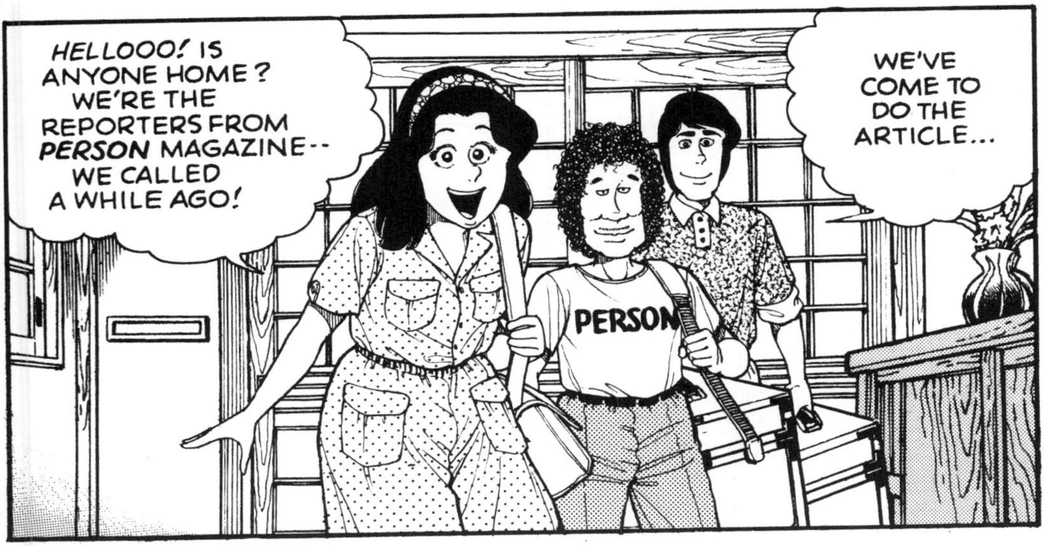
HELLOOO! IS ANYONE HOME? WE'RE THE REPORTERS FROM *PERSON* MAGAZINE-- WE CALLED A WHILE AGO!
PERSON
WE'VE COME TO DO THE ARTICLE...

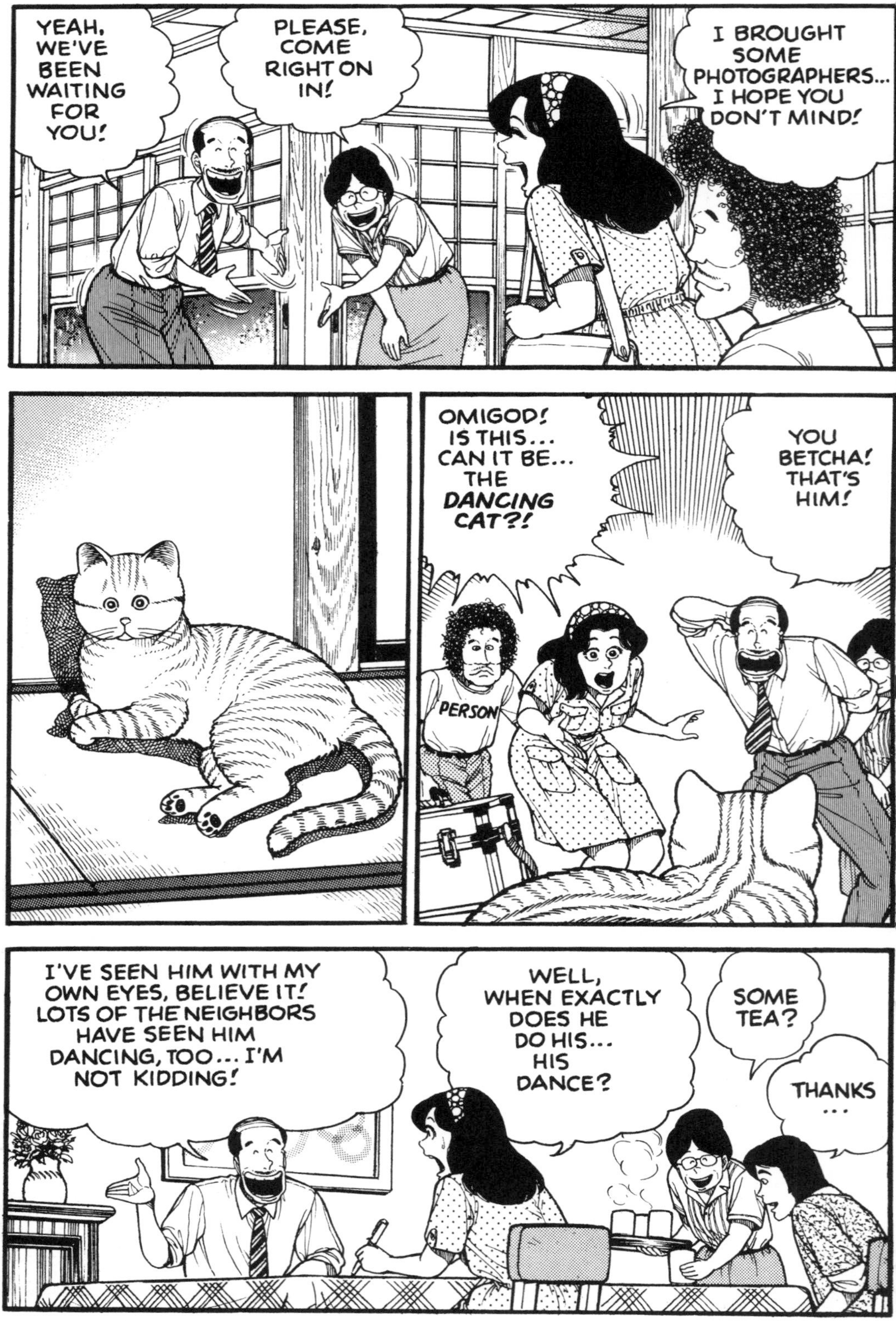
YEAH, WE'VE BEEN WAITING FOR YOU!
PLEASE, COME RIGHT ON IN!
I BROUGHT SOME PHOTOGRAPHERS... I HOPE YOU DON'T MIND!
OMIGOD! IS THIS... CAN IT BE... THE *DANCING CAT?!*
YOU BETCHA! THAT'S HIM!
PERSON
I'VE SEEN HIM WITH MY OWN EYES, BELIEVE IT! LOTS OF THE NEIGHBORS HAVE SEEN HIM DANCING, TOO... I'M NOT KIDDING!
WELL, WHEN EXACTLY DOES HE DO HIS... HIS DANCE?
SOME TEA?
THANKS...

THE FIRST TIME I SAW IT...   ...MICHAEL WAS CHASING A FLY.

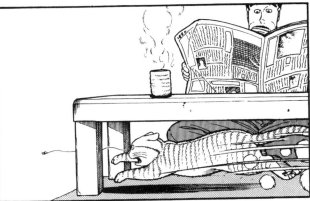

"WHEN THE FLY CAME OUT FROM UNDER THE TABLE, IT FLEW UP...

AND THEN *IT* HAPPENED!"

*BZZZzz*

*KONK*

. . . . .

. . . . .

. . . . !

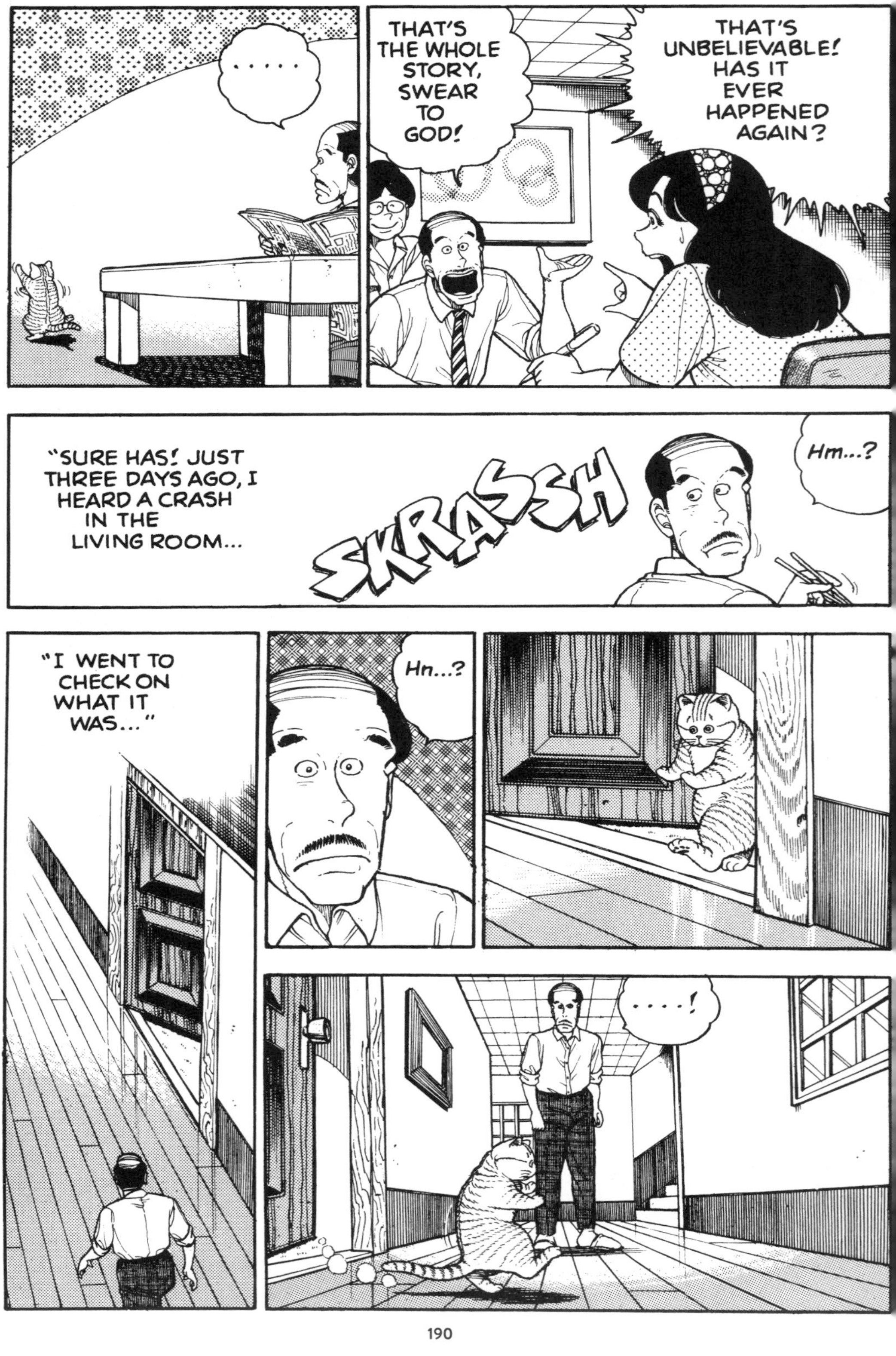
. . . . .
THAT'S THE WHOLE STORY, SWEAR TO GOD!
THAT'S UNBELIEVABLE! HAS IT EVER HAPPENED AGAIN?
"SURE HAS! JUST THREE DAYS AGO, I HEARD A CRASH IN THE LIVING ROOM...
SKRASSH
Hm...?
"I WENT TO CHECK ON WHAT IT WAS..."
Hn...?
. . . . !

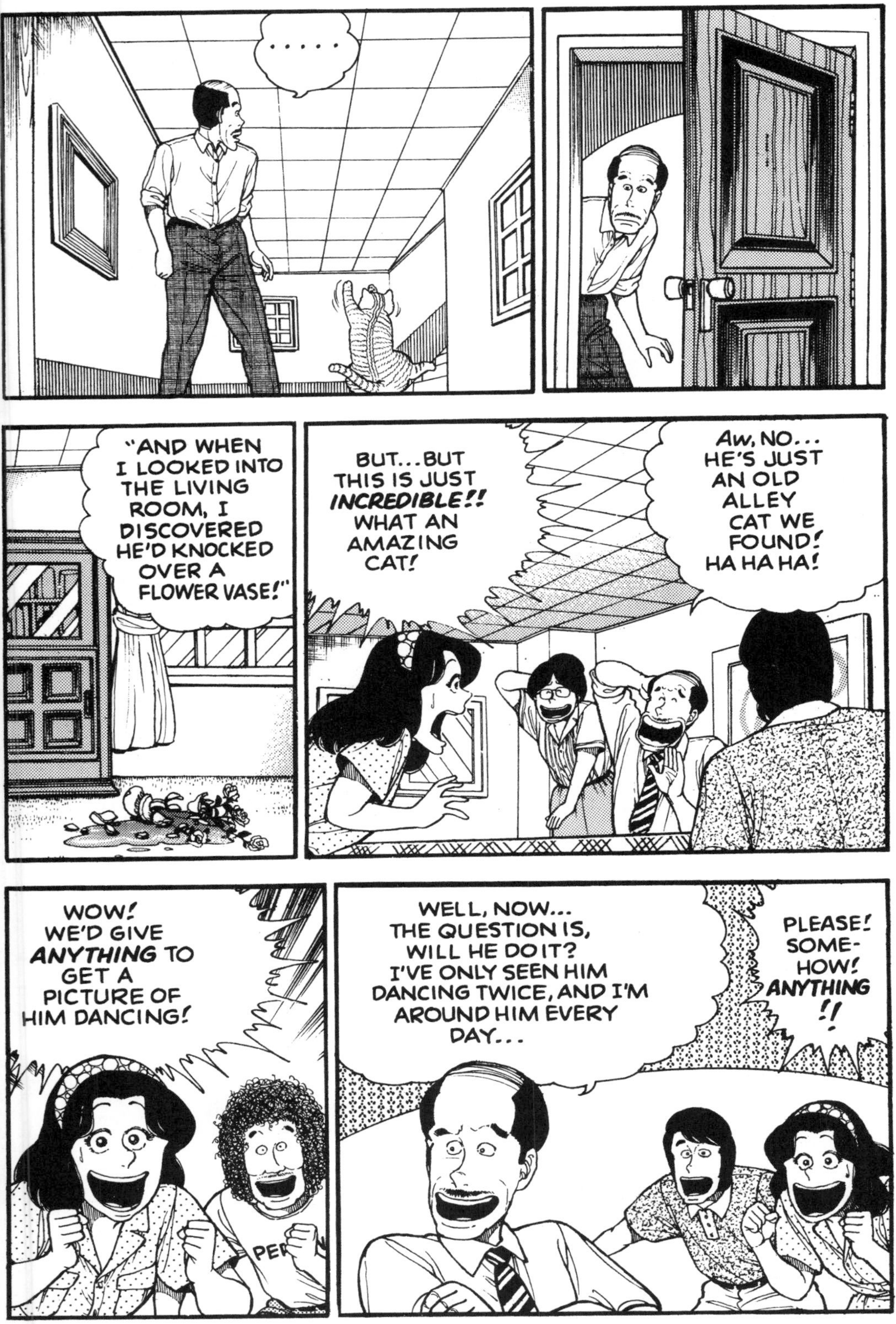
.....
"AND WHEN I LOOKED INTO THE LIVING ROOM, I DISCOVERED HE'D KNOCKED OVER A FLOWER VASE!"
BUT... BUT THIS IS JUST *INCREDIBLE!!* WHAT AN AMAZING CAT!
AW, NO... HE'S JUST AN OLD ALLEY CAT WE FOUND! HA HA HA!
WOW! WE'D GIVE *ANYTHING* TO GET A PICTURE OF HIM DANCING!
WELL, NOW... THE QUESTION IS, WILL HE DO IT? I'VE ONLY SEEN HIM DANCING TWICE, AND I'M AROUND HIM EVERY DAY...
PLEASE! SOME-HOW! *ANYTHING* !!

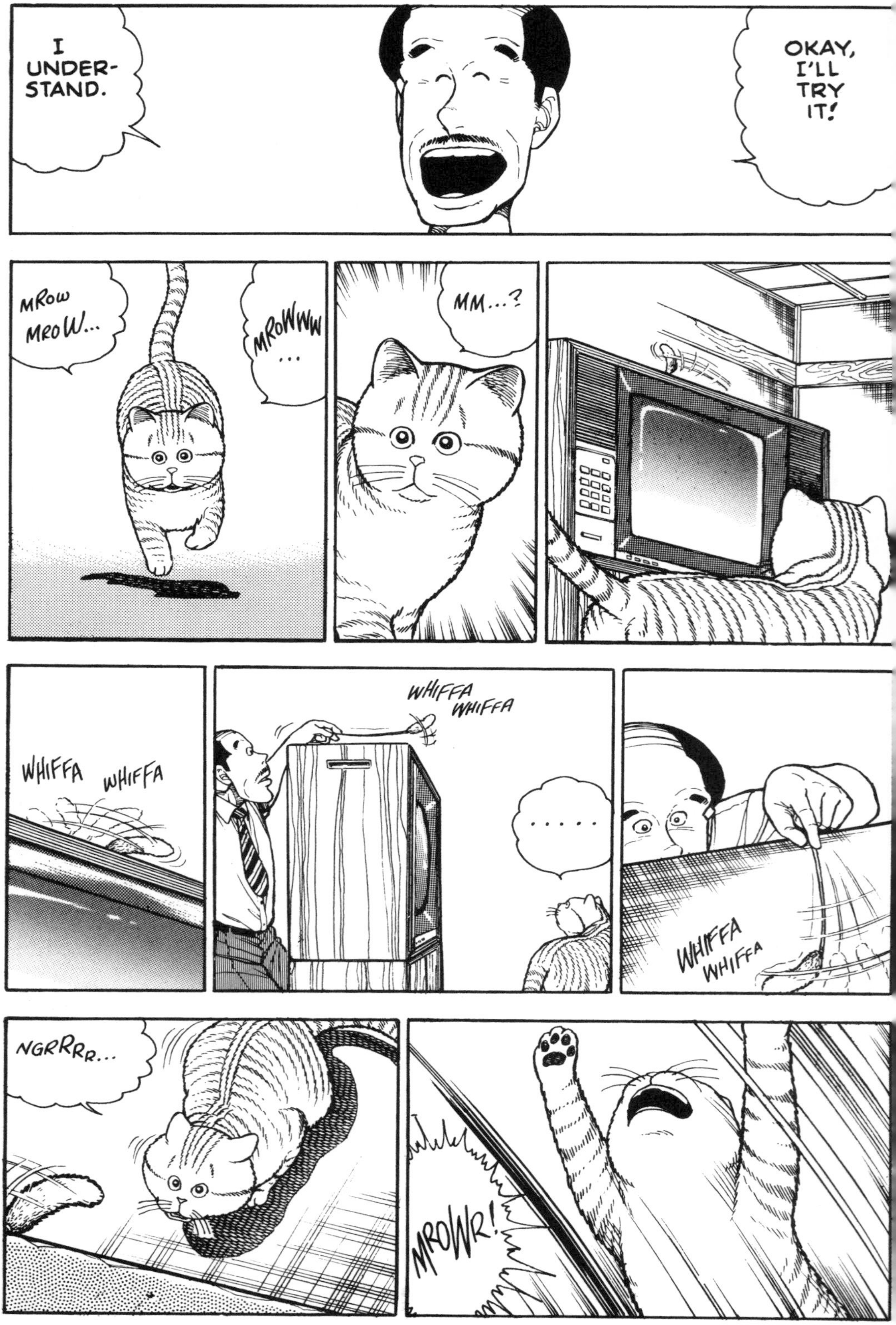
I UNDER-STAND.
OKAY, I'LL TRY IT!
MROW MROW...
MROWWW...
MM...?
WHIFFA WHIFFA
WHIFFA WHIFFA
......
WHIFFA WHIFFA
NGRRRR...
MROWR!

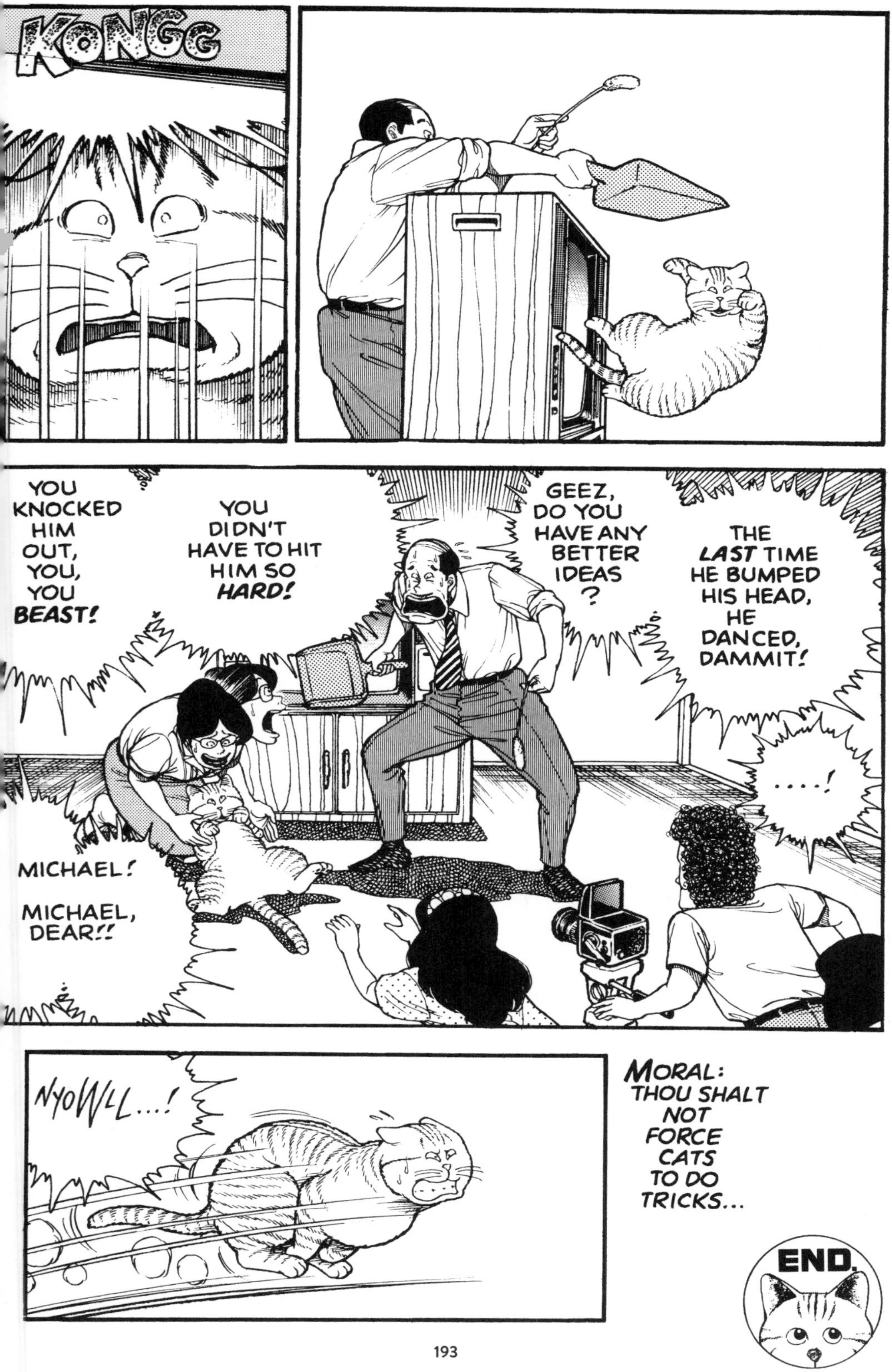
KONGG
YOU KNOCKED HIM OUT, YOU, YOU BEAST!
YOU DIDN'T HAVE TO HIT HIM SO HARD!
GEEZ, DO YOU HAVE ANY BETTER IDEAS?
THE LAST TIME HE BUMPED HIS HEAD, HE DANCED, DAMMIT!
....!
MICHAEL!
MICHAEL, DEAR!!
NYOWLL...!
MORAL: THOU SHALT NOT FORCE CATS TO DO TRICKS...
END.

# DANCING MICHAEL!!

## PART TWO

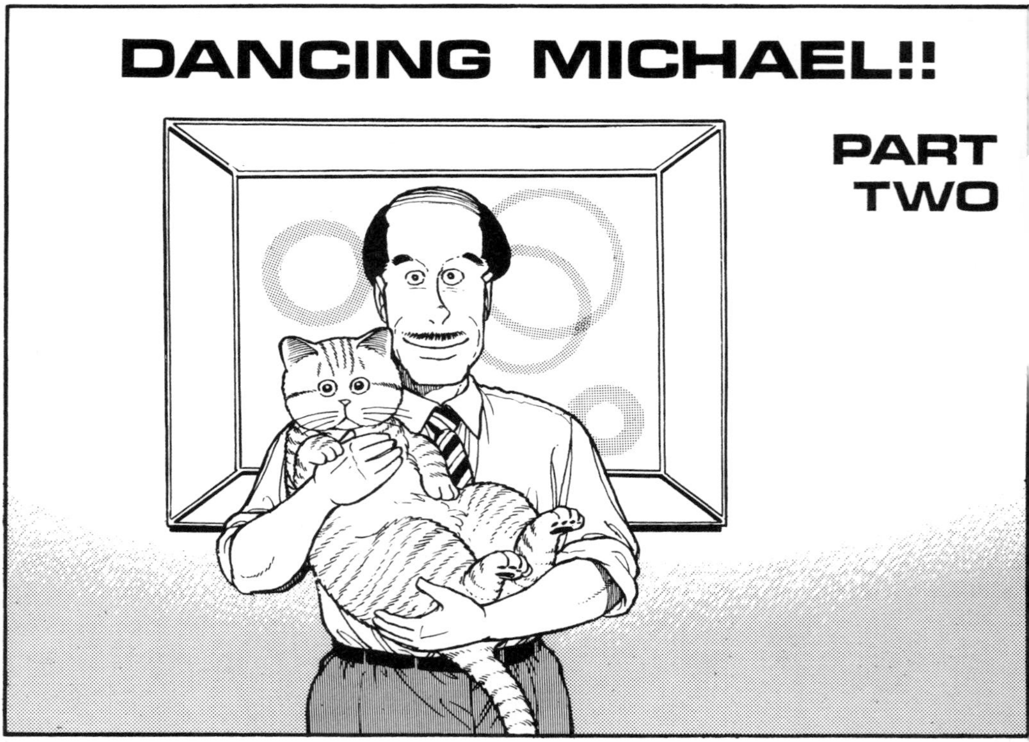

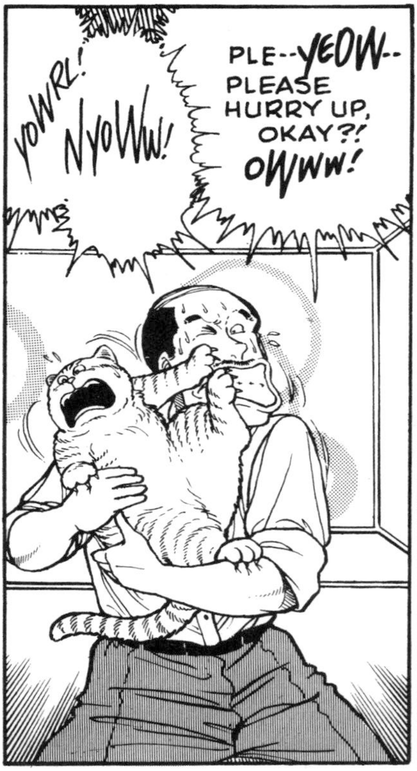
YOWRL!
NYOWW!
PLE--YEOW--
PLEASE HURRY UP, OKAY?!
OWWW!

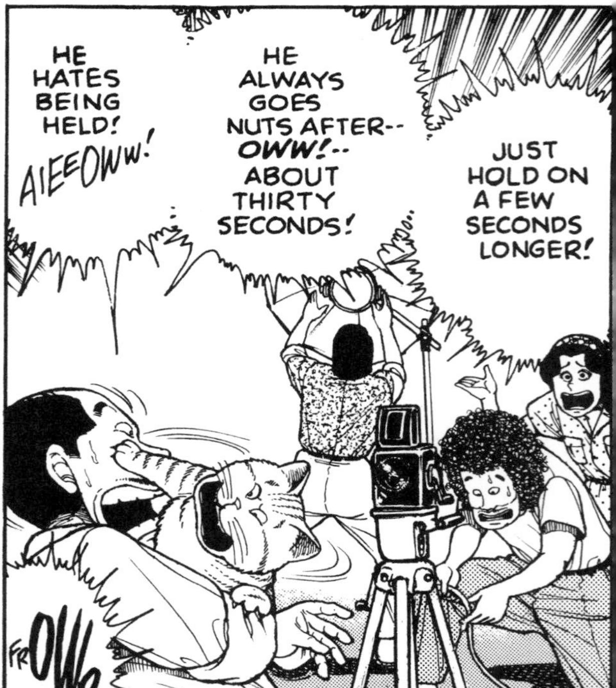
HE HATES BEING HELD!
AIEEOWW!
HE ALWAYS GOES NUTS AFTER--
OWW!--
ABOUT THIRTY SECONDS!
JUST HOLD ON A FEW SECONDS LONGER!
FROWR!

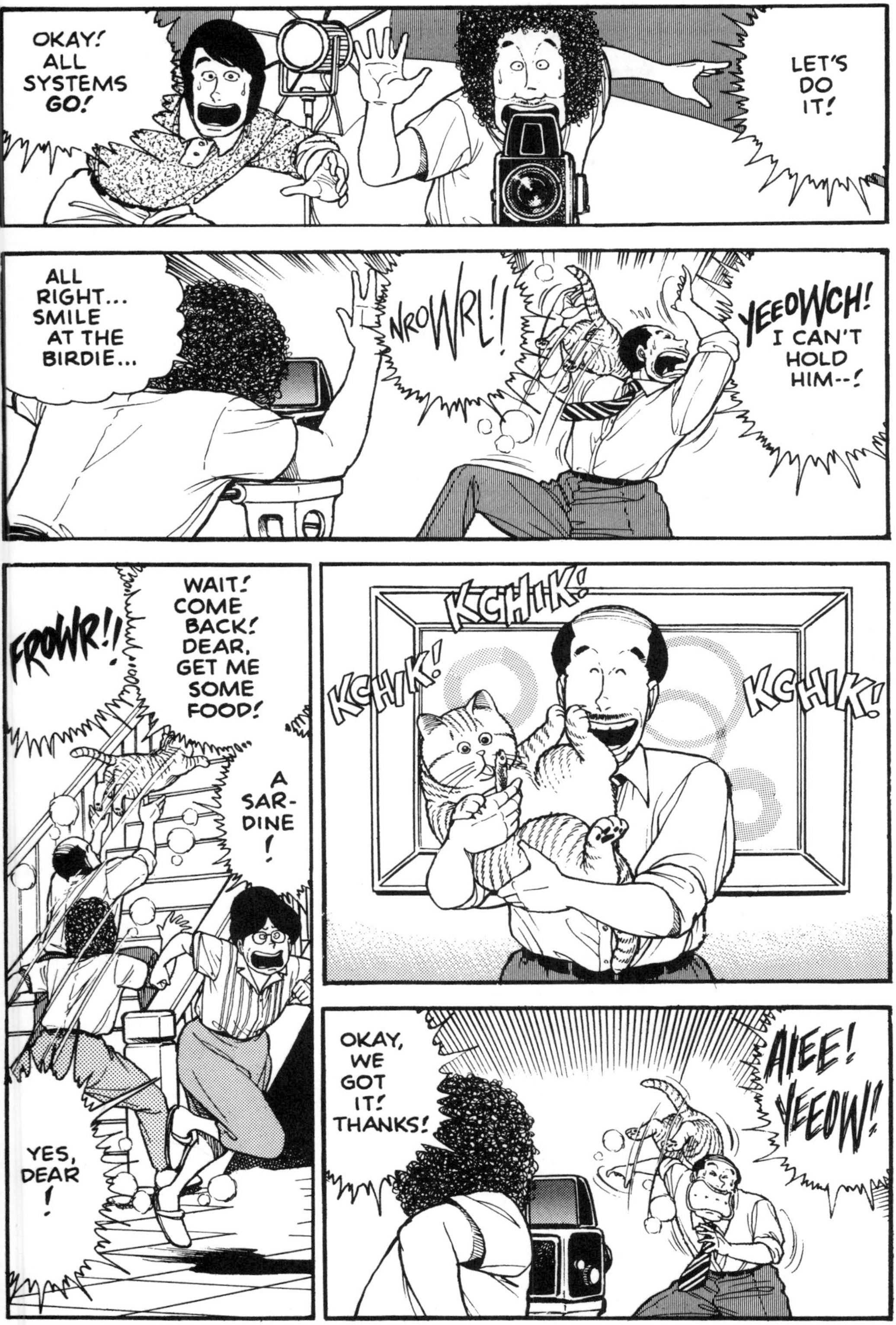
OKAY! ALL SYSTEMS GO!
LET'S DO IT!
ALL RIGHT... SMILE AT THE BIRDIE...
NROWRL!!
YEEOWCH! I CAN'T HOLD HIM--!
FROWR!!
WAIT! COME BACK! DEAR, GET ME SOME FOOD!
A SARDINE!
YES, DEAR!
KCHIK!
KCHIK!
KCHIK!
OKAY, WE GOT IT! THANKS!
AIEE! YEEOW!

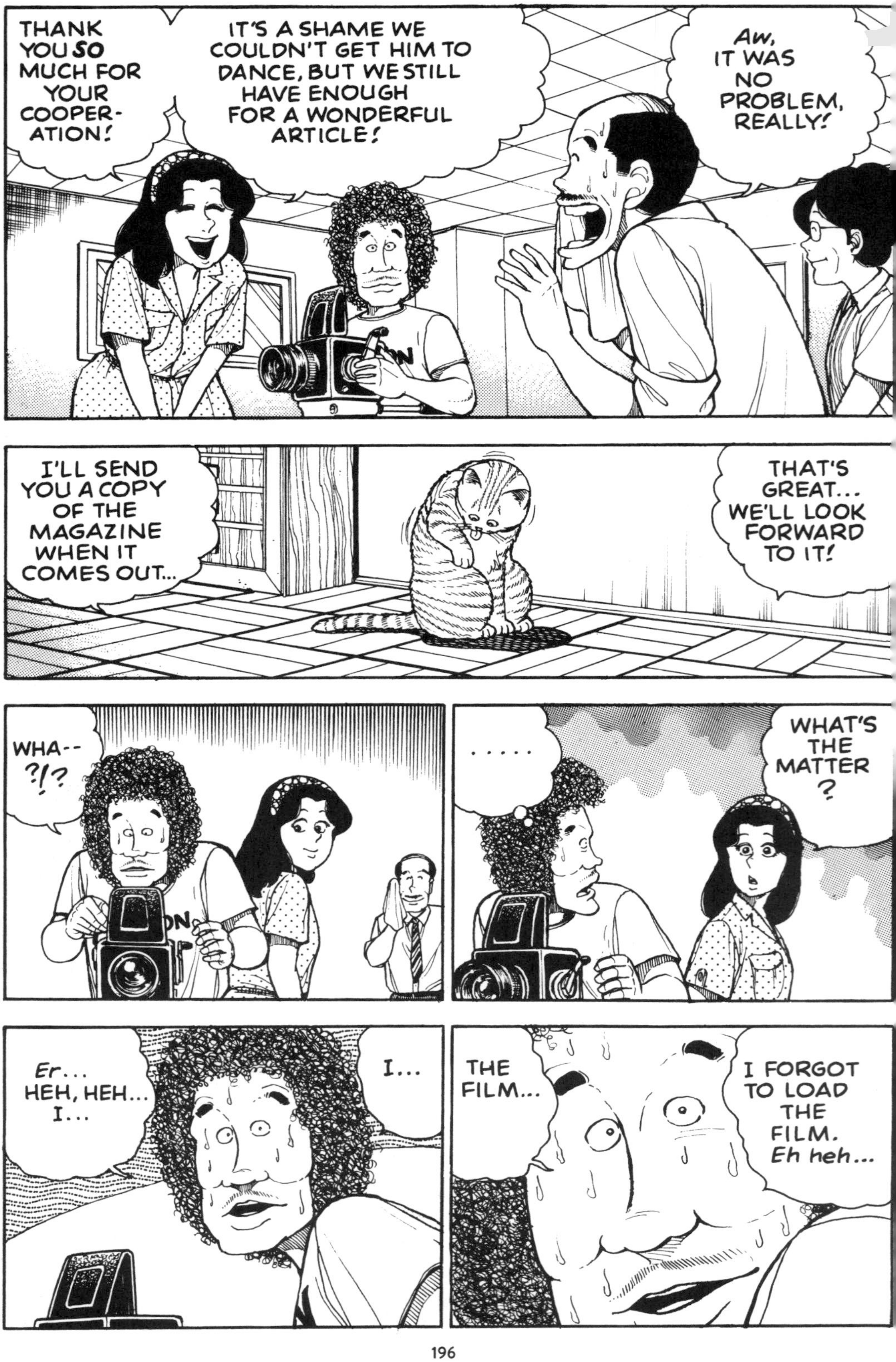
THANK YOU **SO** MUCH FOR YOUR COOPER-ATION!
IT'S A SHAME WE COULDN'T GET HIM TO DANCE, BUT WE STILL HAVE ENOUGH FOR A WONDERFUL ARTICLE!
*Aw,* IT WAS NO PROBLEM, REALLY!
I'LL SEND YOU A COPY OF THE MAGAZINE WHEN IT COMES OUT...
THAT'S GREAT... WE'LL LOOK FORWARD TO IT!
WHA-- ?!?
.....
WHAT'S THE MATTER ?
*Er...* HEH, HEH... I...
I...
THE FILM...
I FORGOT TO LOAD THE FILM. *Eh heh...*

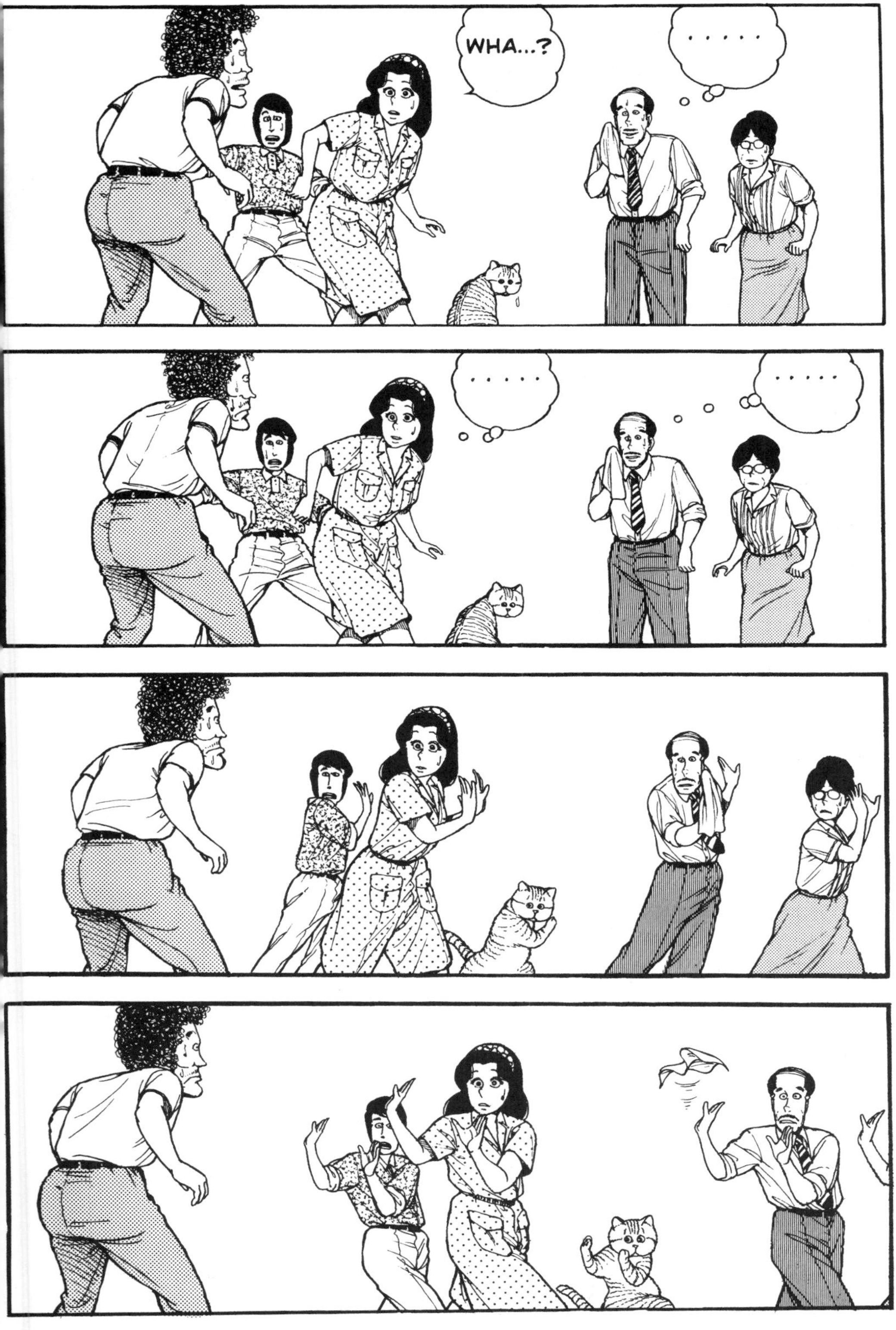
WHA...?
. . . . .
. . . . .
. . . . .

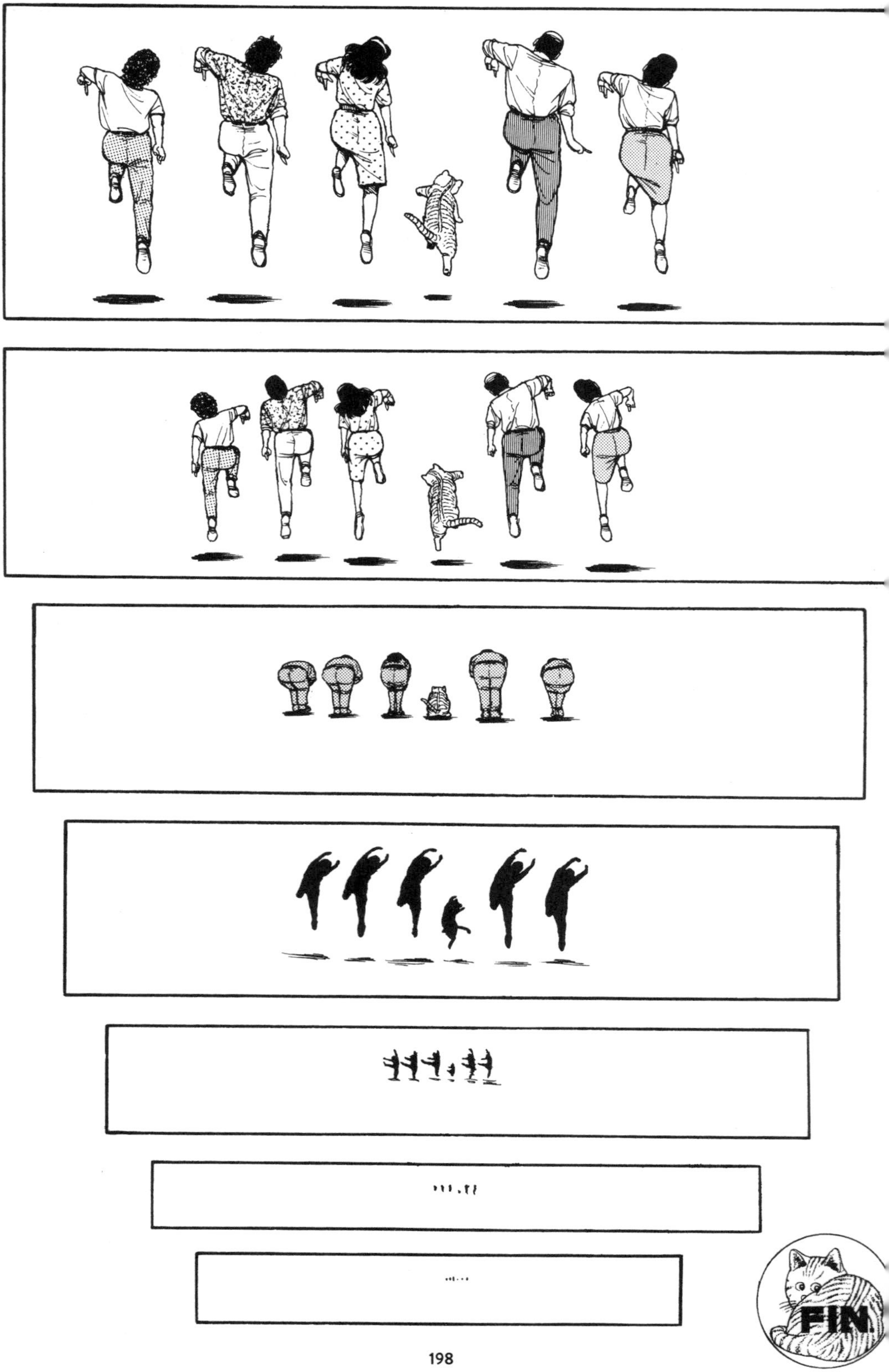
FIN

# WELCOME TO THE CATHOUSE

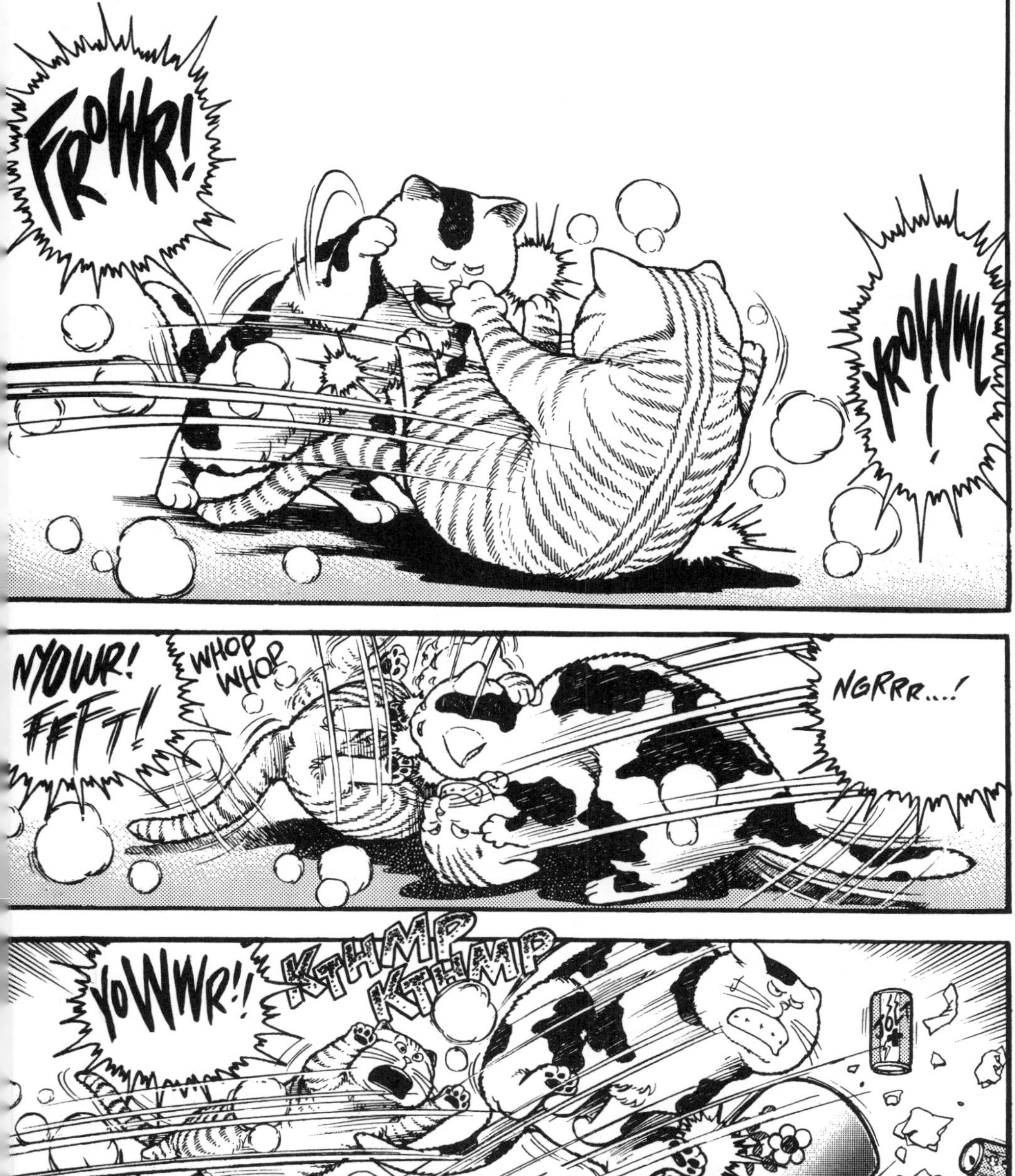
FROWR!
YROWWL!
NYOWR!
FFFT!
WHOP WHOP
NGRRR...!
YOWWR!!
KTHMP KTHMP
SHRANGG

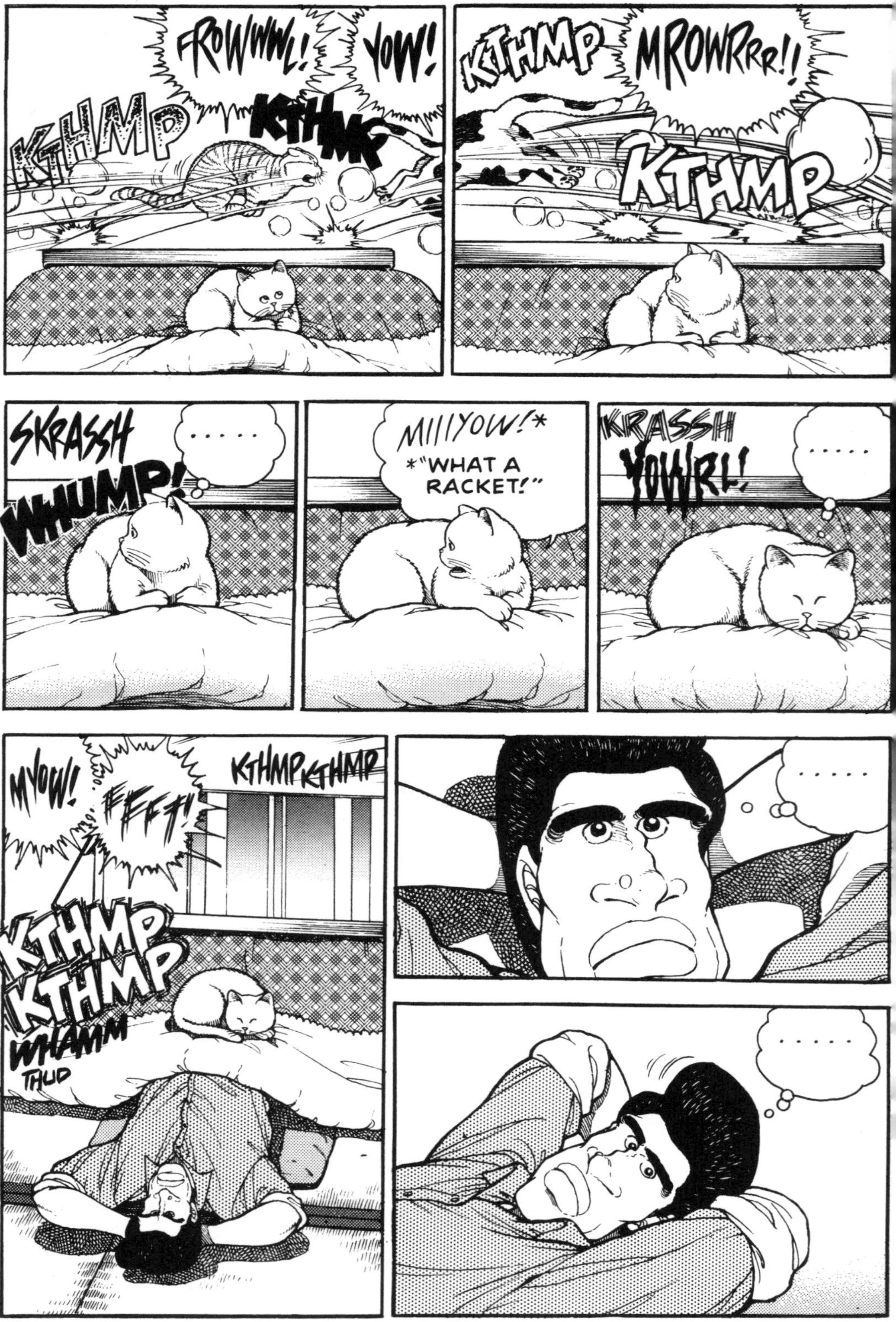
FROWWWL!
YOW!
KTHMP
KTHMP
KTHMP
MROWRRR!!
KTHMP
SKRASSH
.....
WHUMP!
MIIIYOW!*
*"WHAT A RACKET!"
KRASSH
YOWRL!
.....
MYOW!
FFFT!
KTHMP KTHMP
KTHMP
KTHMP
WHAMM
THUD
.....
.....

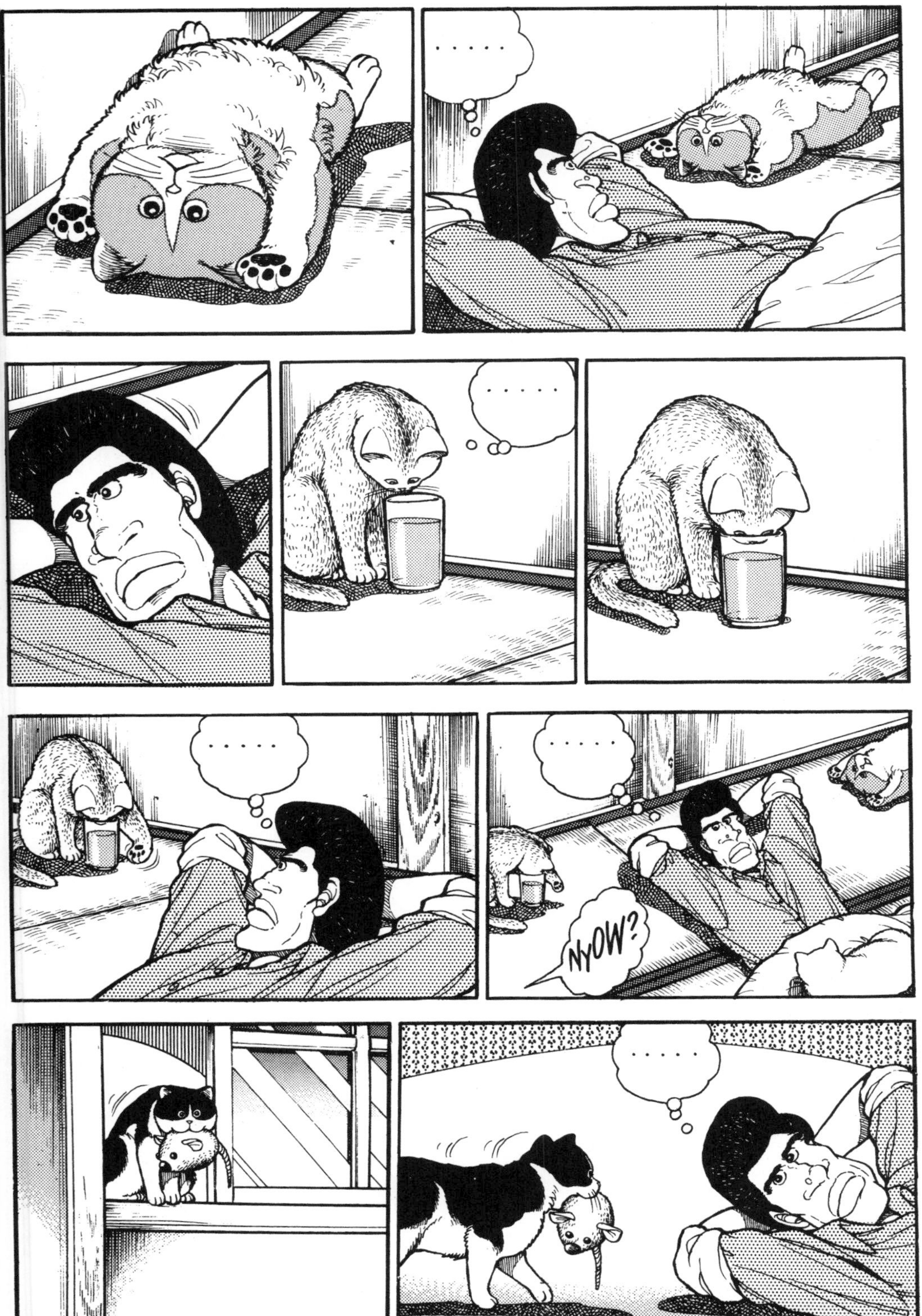
. . . . .
. . . . .
. . . . .
. . . . .
NYOW?
. . . . .

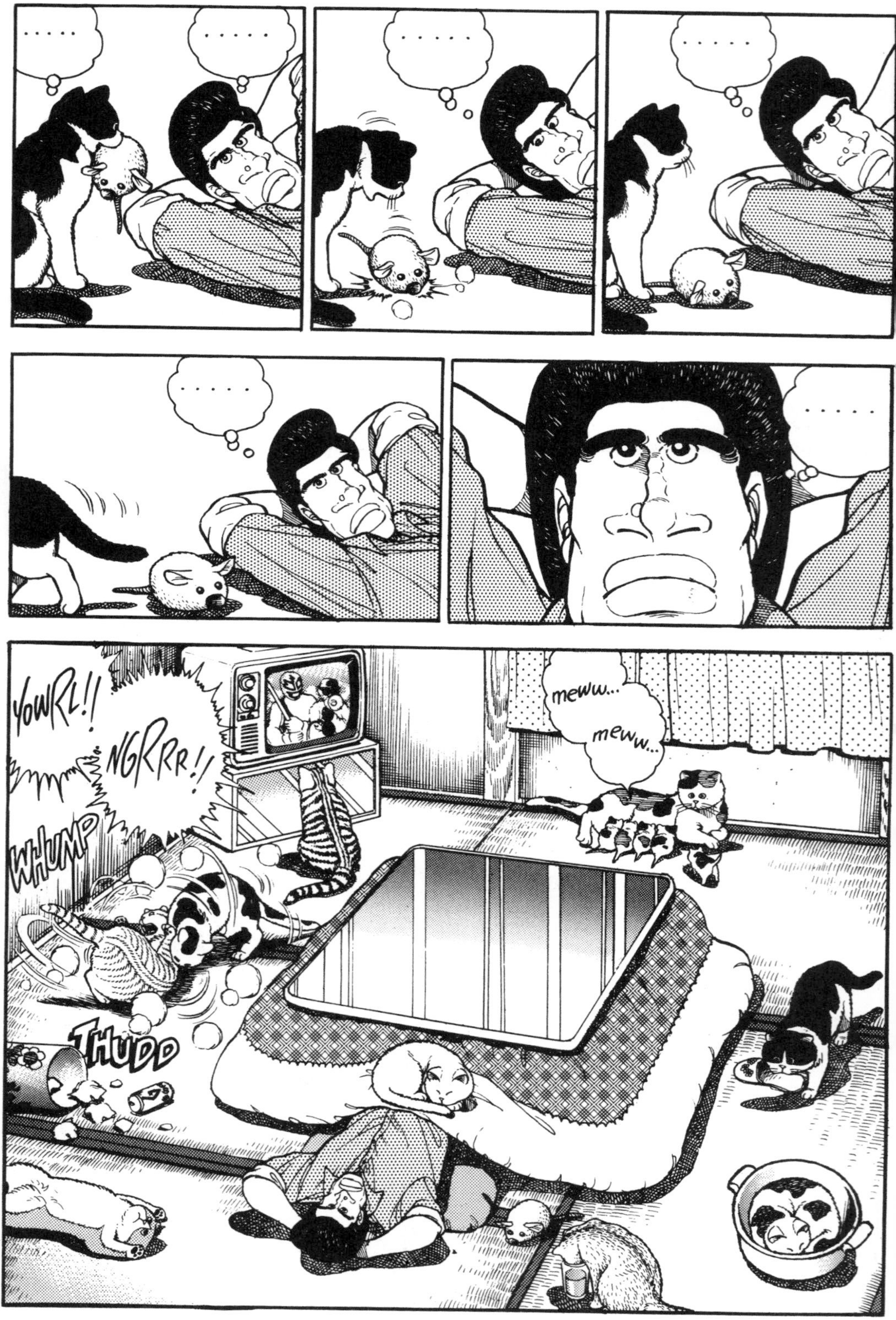
......
......
......
......
......
......
YOWRL!!
NGRRR!!
WHUMP
THUDD
meww...
meww...

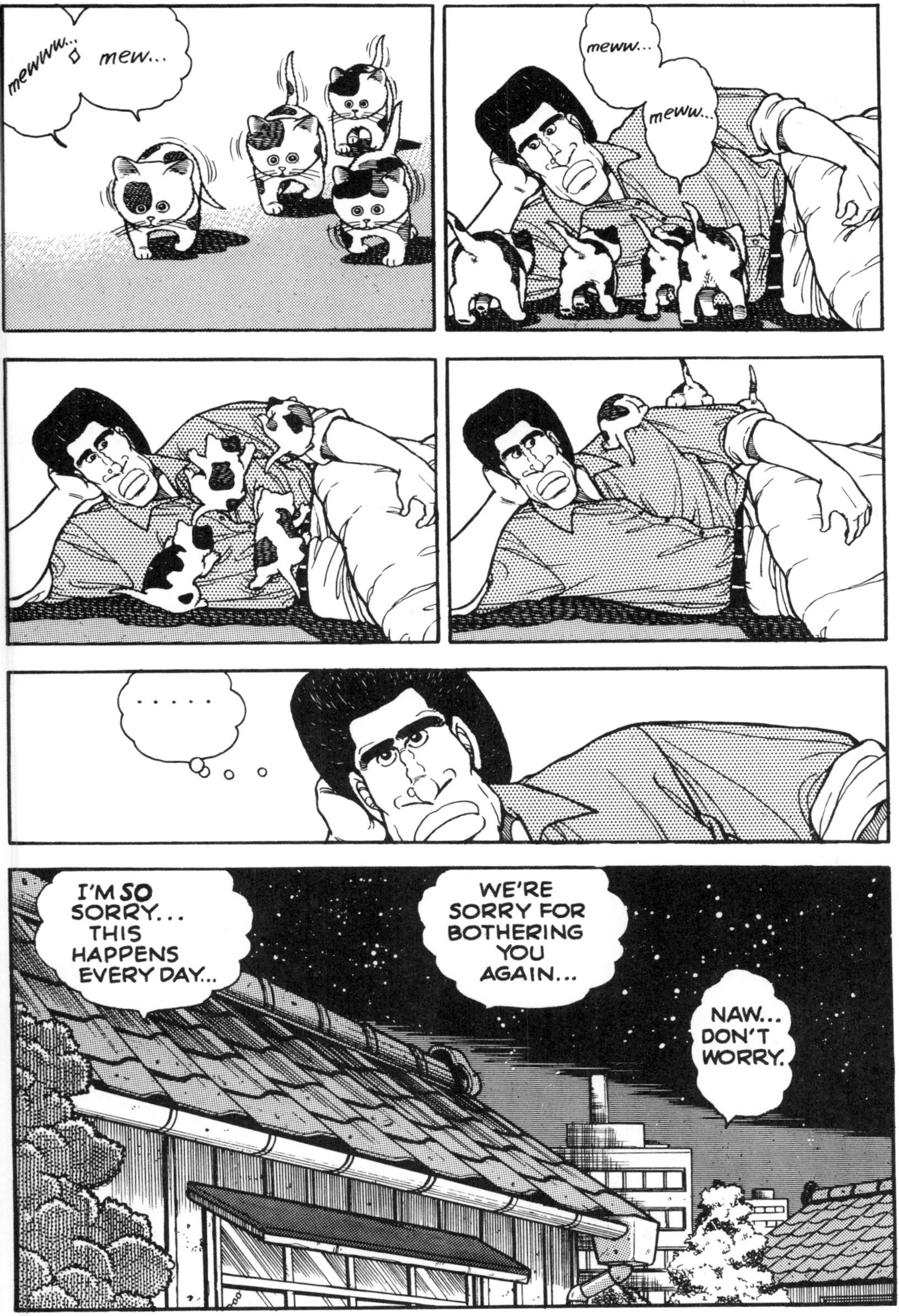
mewww...
mew...
meww...
meww...
. . . . .
I'M **SO** SORRY... THIS HAPPENS EVERY DAY...
WE'RE SORRY FOR BOTHERING YOU AGAIN...
NAW... DON'T WORRY.

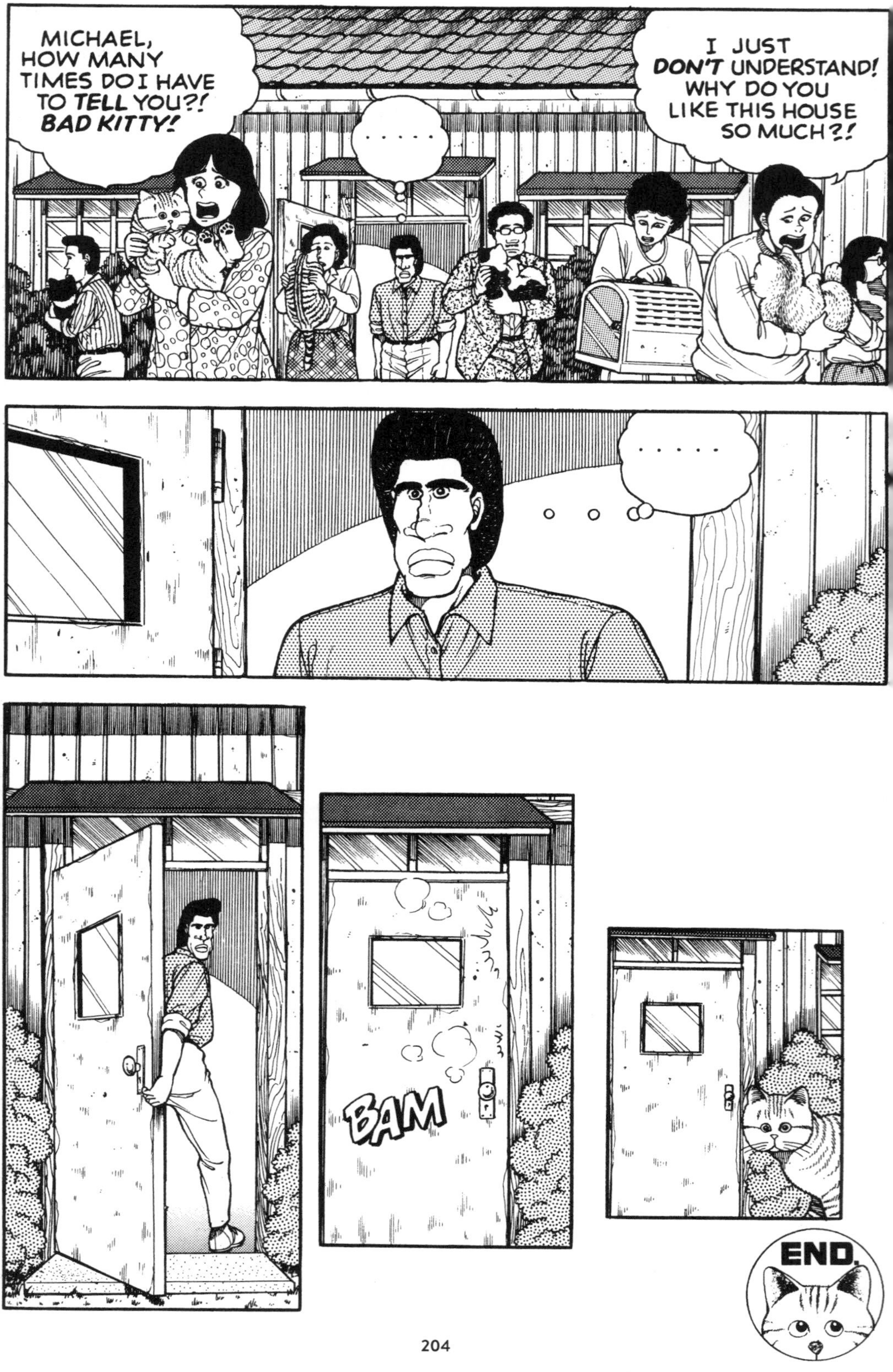

MICHAEL, HOW MANY TIMES DO I HAVE TO **TELL** YOU?! ***BAD KITTY!***
. . . . .
I JUST ***DON'T*** UNDERSTAND! WHY DO YOU LIKE THIS HOUSE SO MUCH?!
. . . . .
BAM
END.

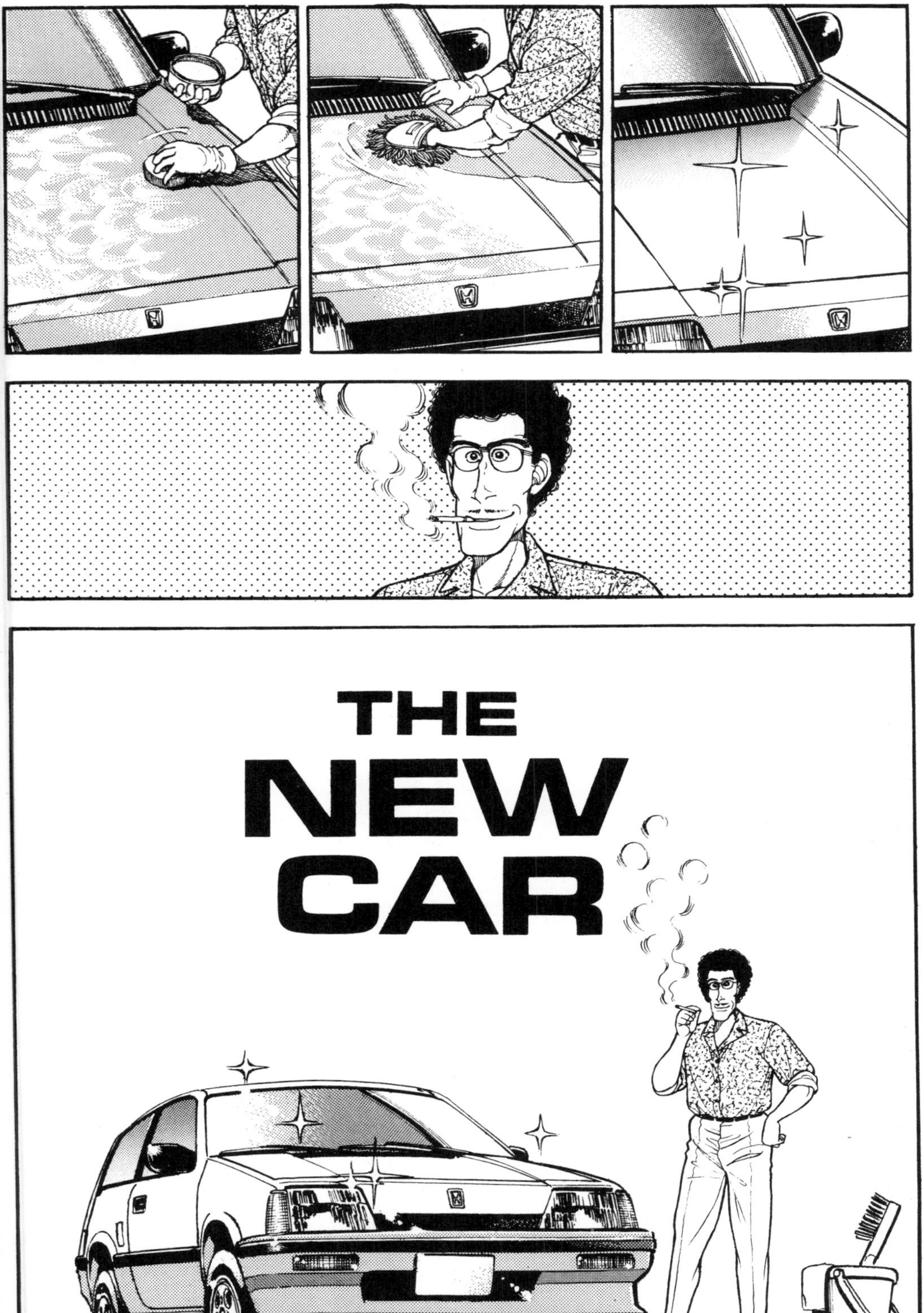
THE NEW CAR

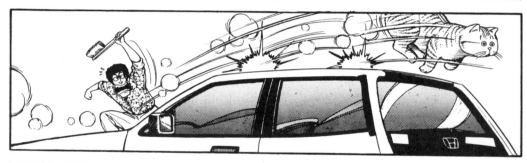

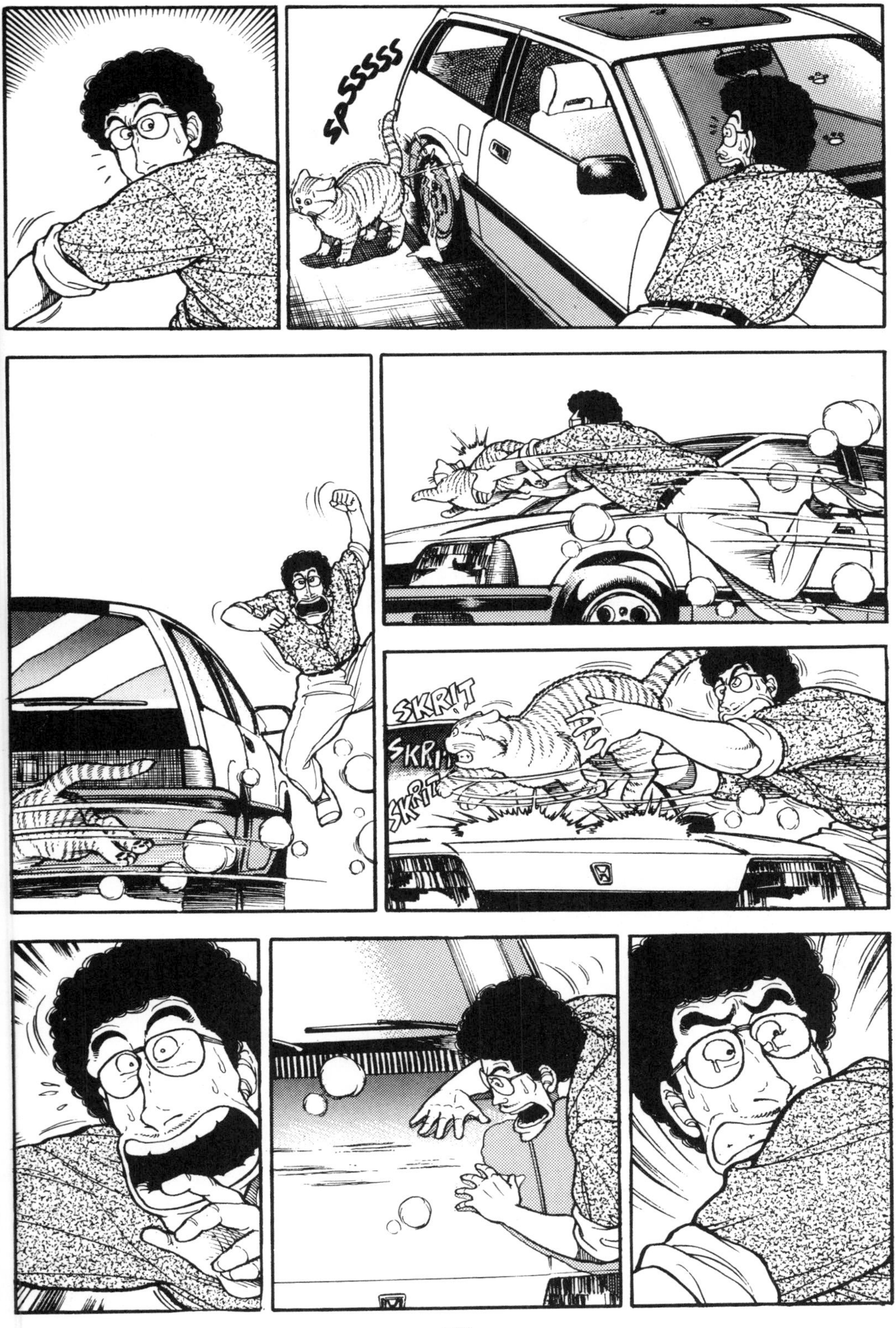
SPSSSS
SKRIT
SKRIT
SKRIT

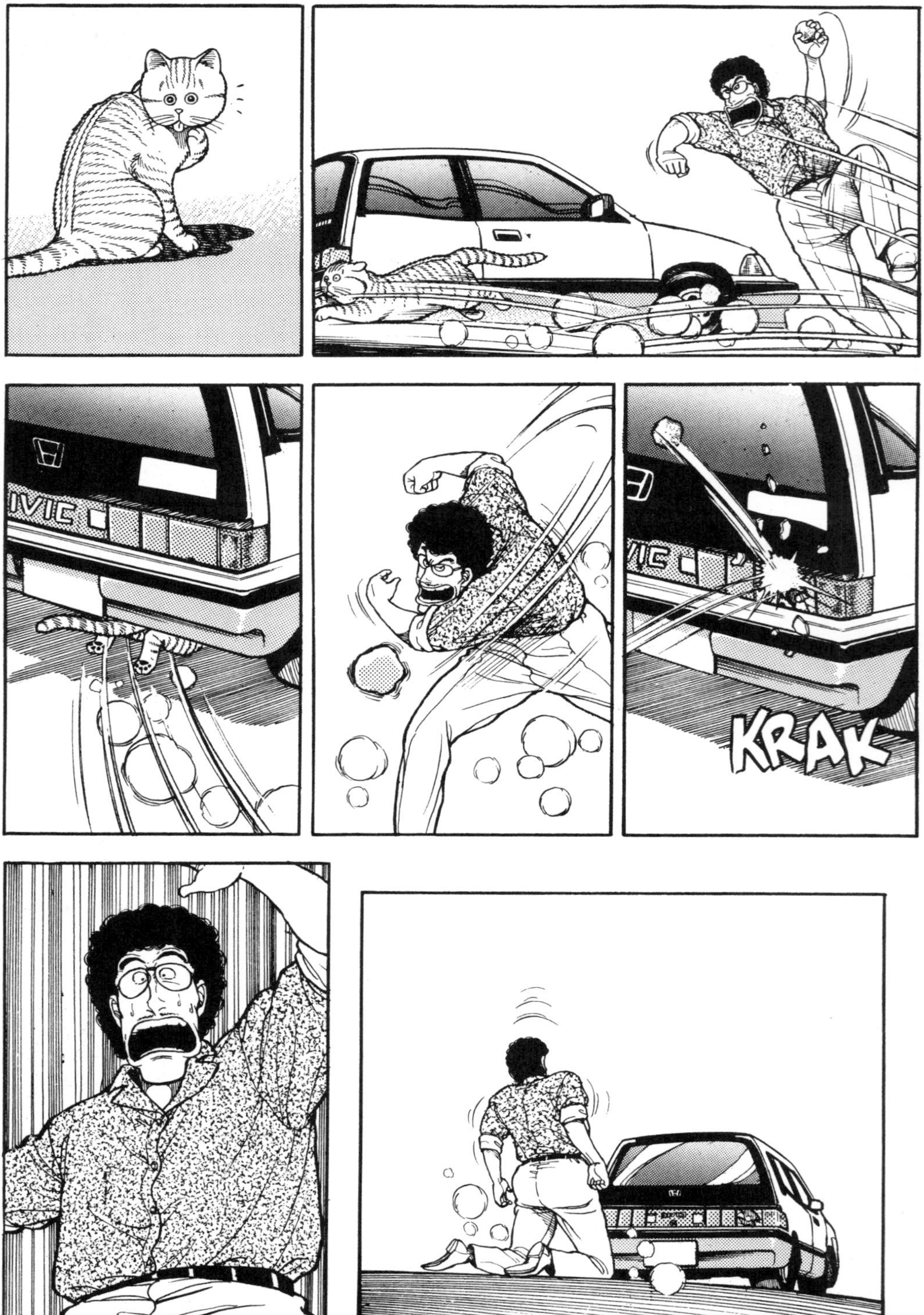
IVIC
IVIC
KRAK

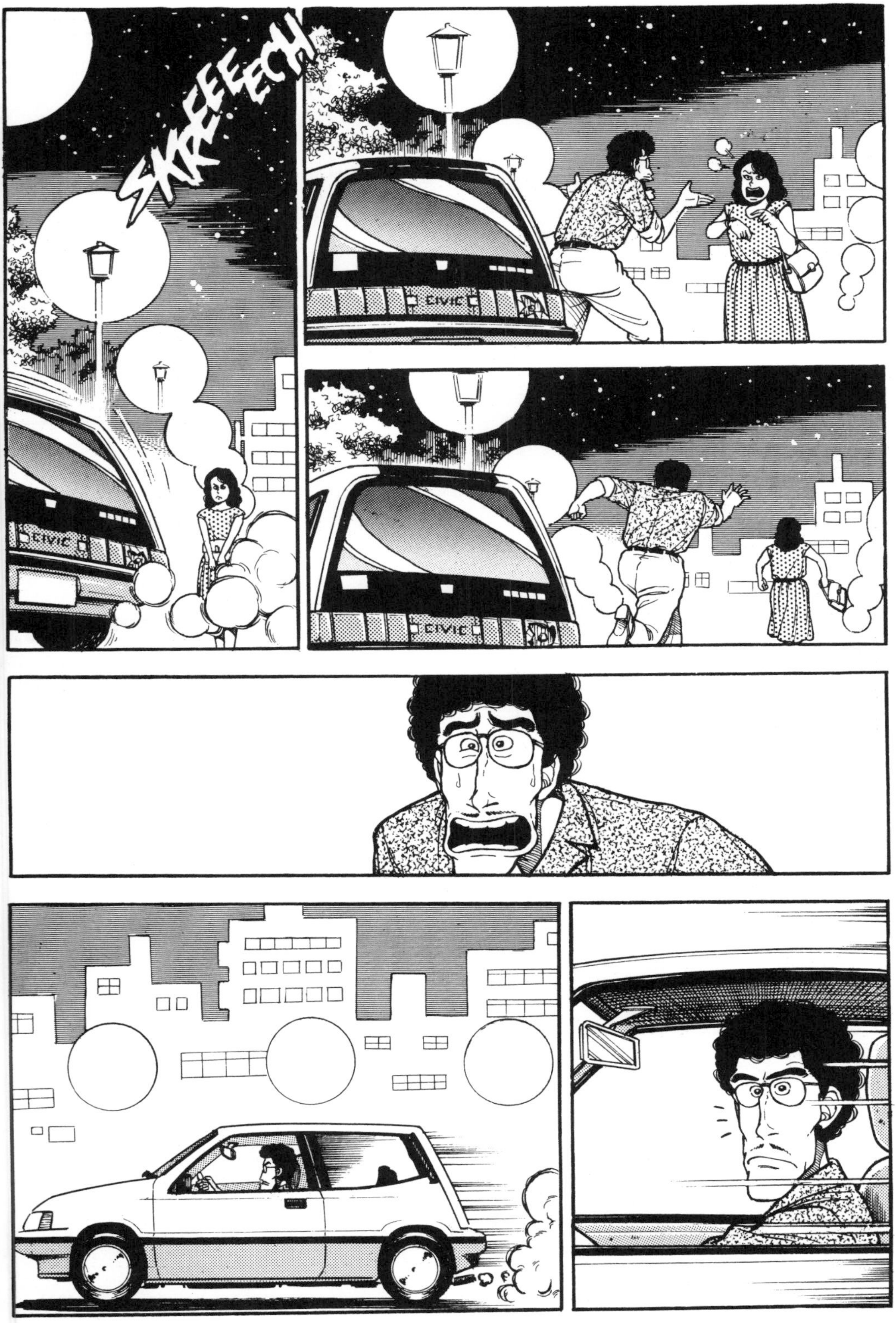
SKREEECH
CIVIC
CIVIC
CIVIC

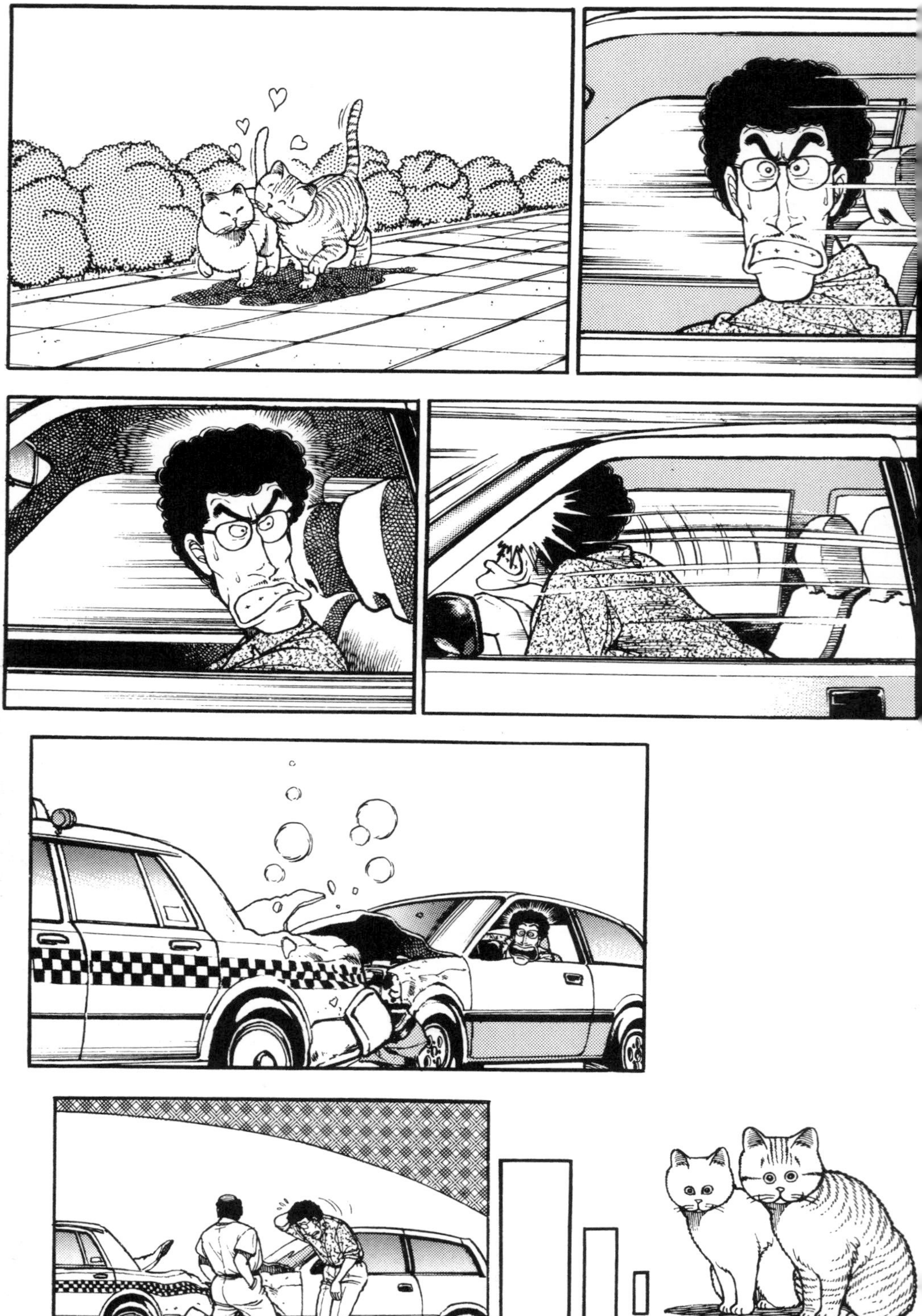

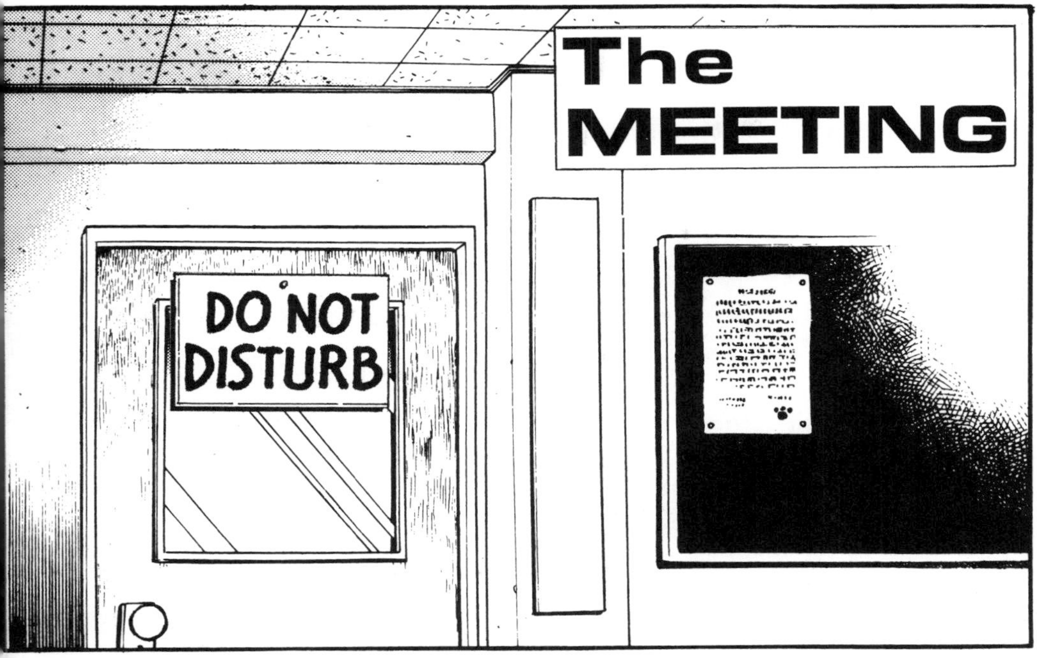
The MEETING
DO NOT DISTURB

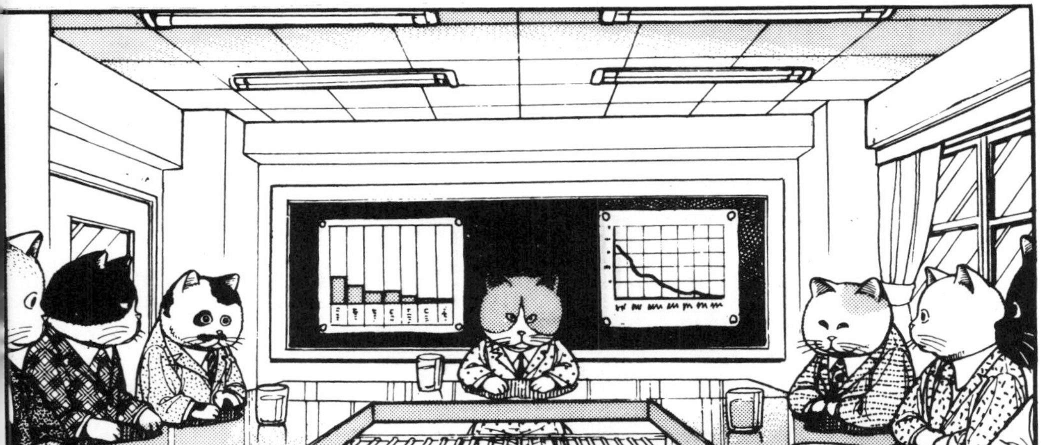

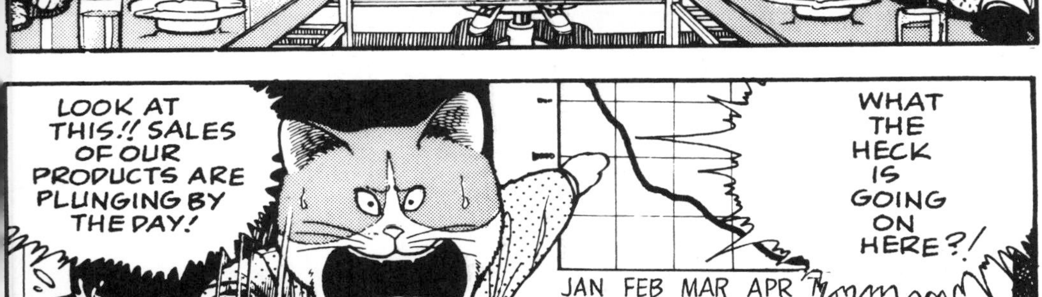
LOOK AT THIS!! SALES OF OUR PRODUCTS ARE PLUNGING BY THE DAY!
JAN FEB MAR APR
WHAT THE HECK IS GOING ON HERE?!

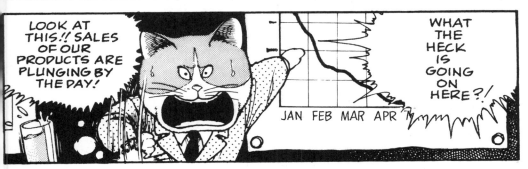

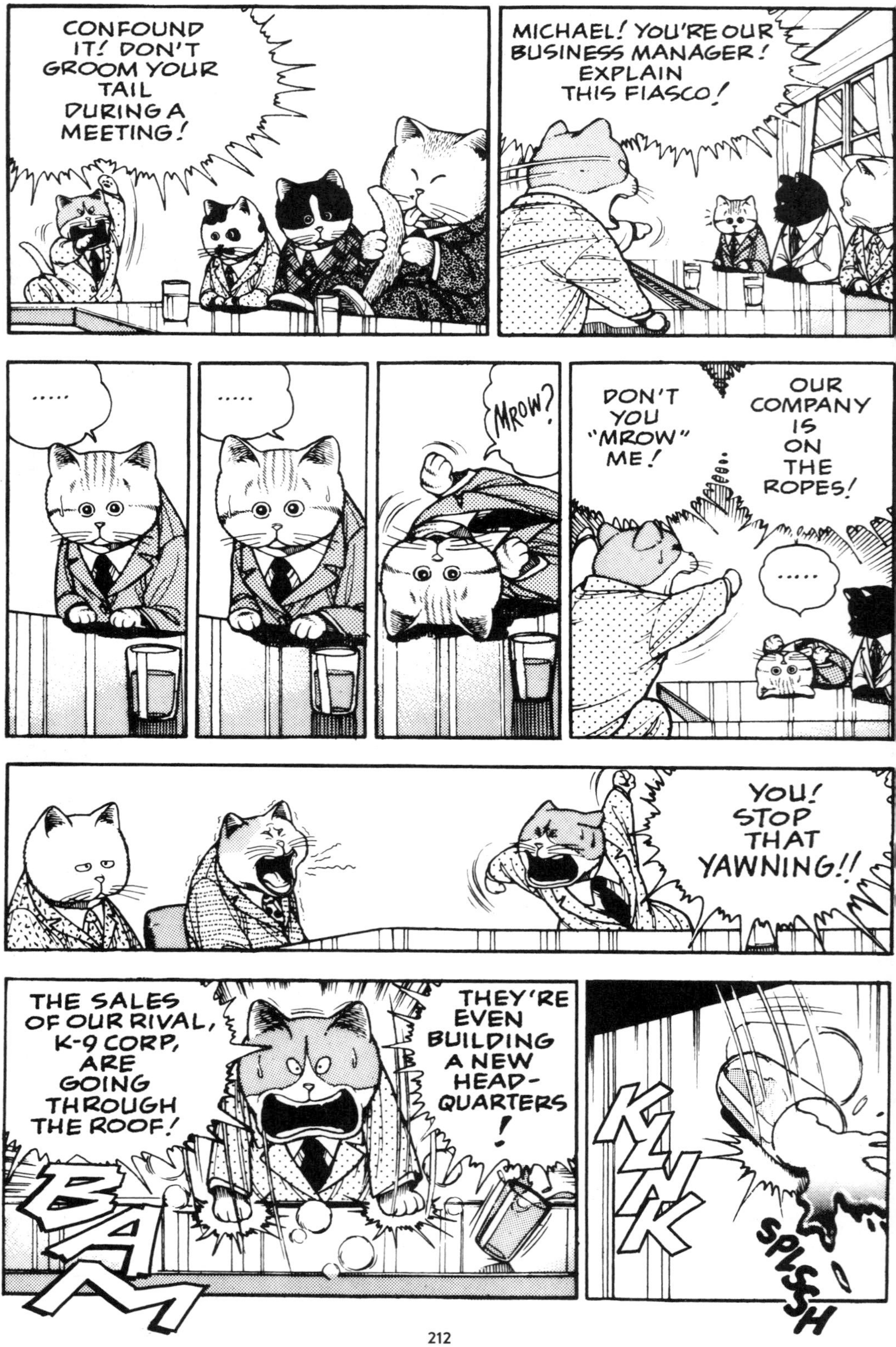
CONFOUND IT! DON'T GROOM YOUR TAIL DURING A MEETING!
MICHAEL! YOU'RE OUR BUSINESS MANAGER! EXPLAIN THIS FIASCO!
.....
.....
MROW?
DON'T YOU "MROW" ME!
OUR COMPANY IS ON THE ROPES!
.....
YOU! STOP THAT YAWNING!!
THE SALES OF OUR RIVAL, K-9 CORP, ARE GOING THROUGH THE ROOF!
THEY'RE EVEN BUILDING A NEW HEAD-QUARTERS!
BAM
KLINK
SPLSSH

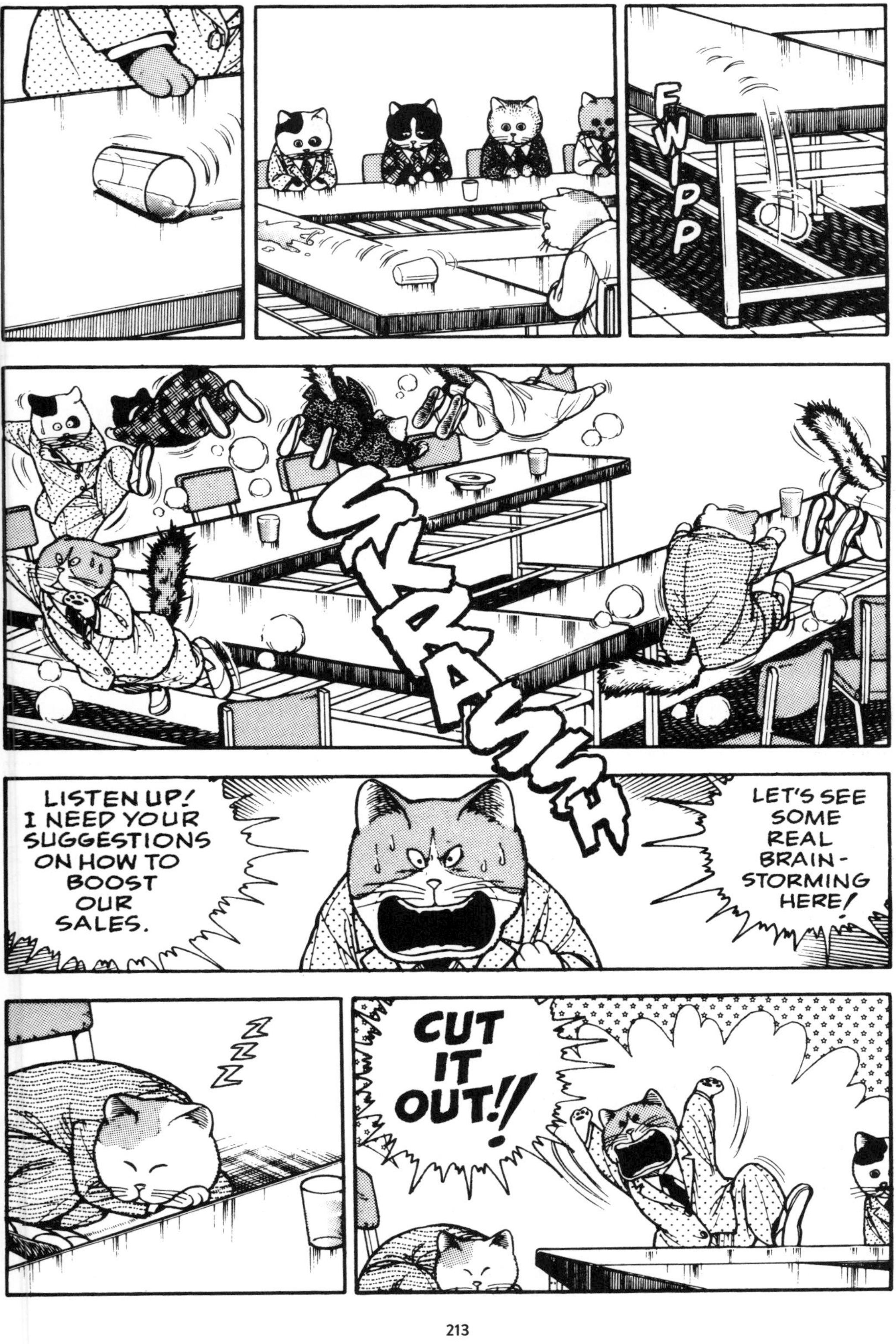
FWIPP
SKRASHH
LISTEN UP! I NEED YOUR SUGGESTIONS ON HOW TO BOOST OUR SALES.
LET'S SEE SOME REAL BRAIN-STORMING HERE!
Z Z Z
CUT IT OUT!!

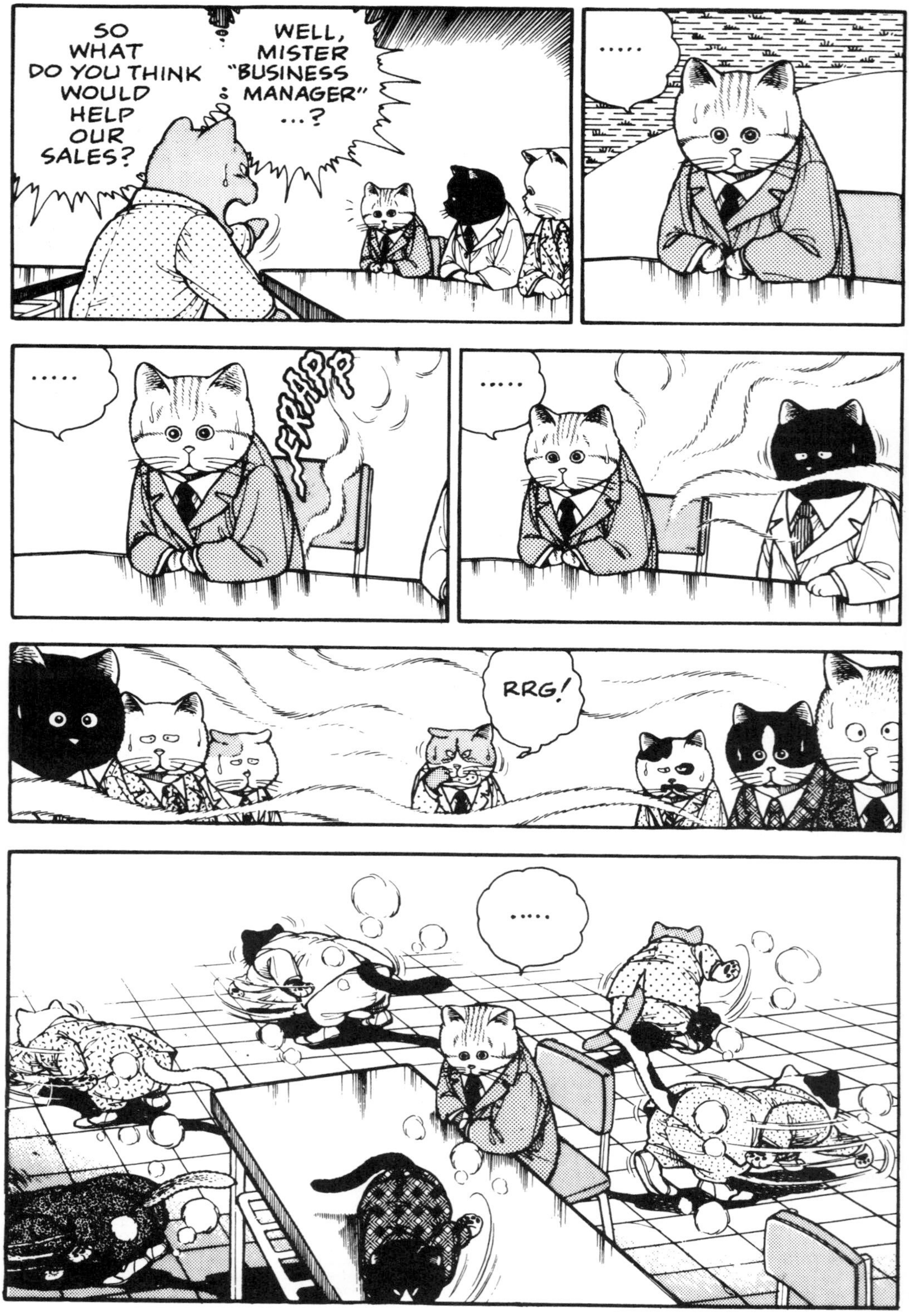
SO WHAT DO YOU THINK WOULD HELP OUR SALES?
WELL, MISTER "BUSINESS MANAGER" ...?
.....
.....
FRAPP
.....
RRG!
.....

THE BOTTOM LINE IS THAT WE'RE ALL GOING TO HAVE TO WORK TOGETHER TO PULL US OUT OF THIS CRISIS!

RIGHT?!

JAN FEB MAR APR

THEREFORE, I WILL BE FORMING AN EXECUTIVE "TIGER TEAM" TO--

ZZZ

MRR...

NROWW!

ZZZ

....!

YOU IDIOTS!!

LISTEN TO ME!

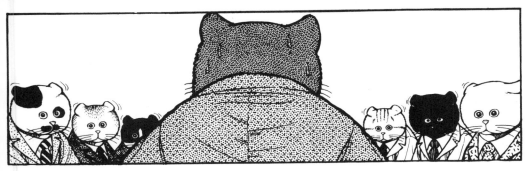

215

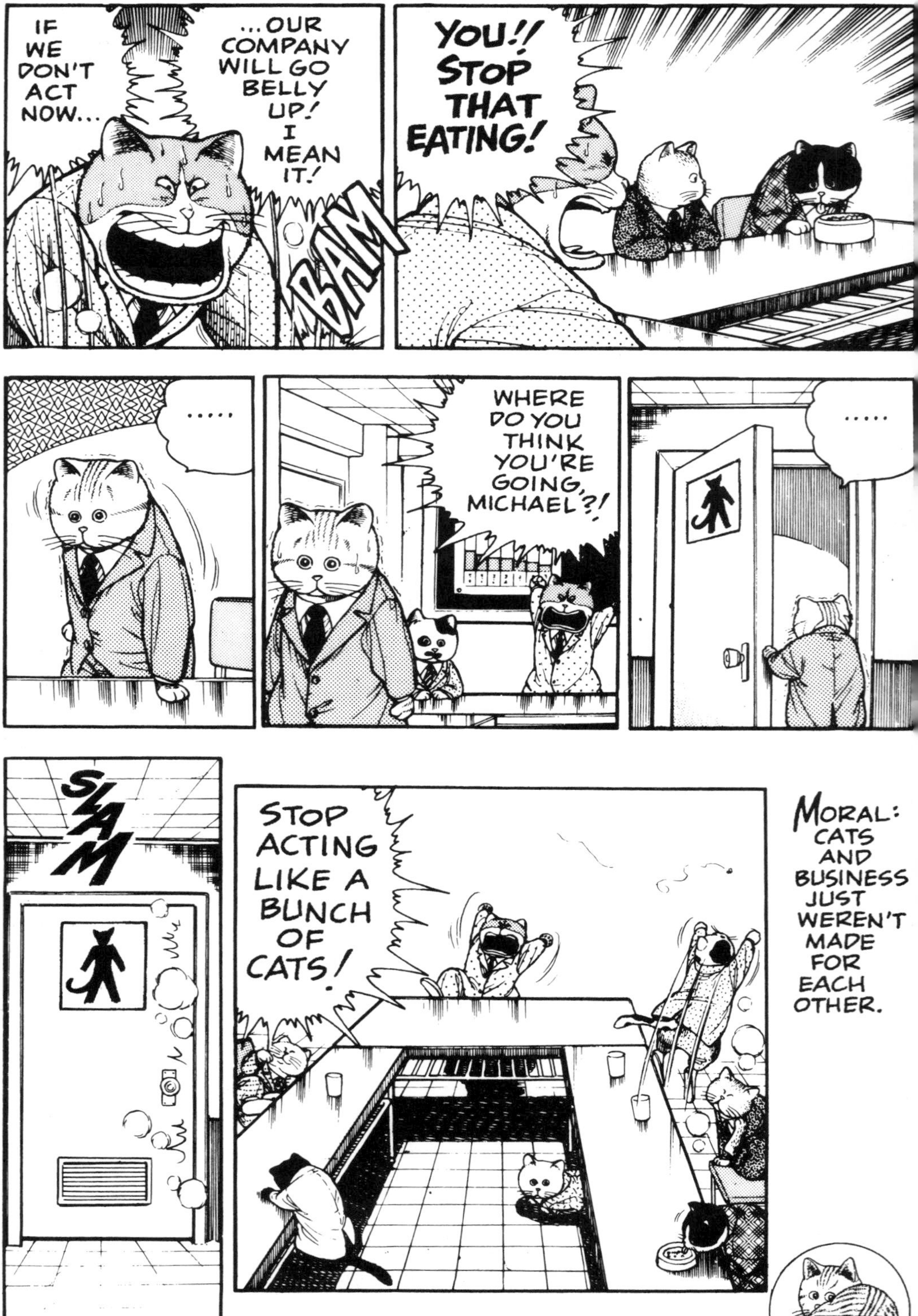

IF WE DON'T ACT NOW...
...OUR COMPANY WILL GO BELLY UP! I MEAN IT!
BAM
YOU!! STOP THAT EATING!
.....
WHERE DO YOU THINK YOU'RE GOING, MICHAEL?!
.....
SLAM
STOP ACTING LIKE A BUNCH OF CATS!
MORAL: CATS AND BUSINESS JUST WEREN'T MADE FOR EACH OTHER.
FIN

# HAIL AND FAREWELL

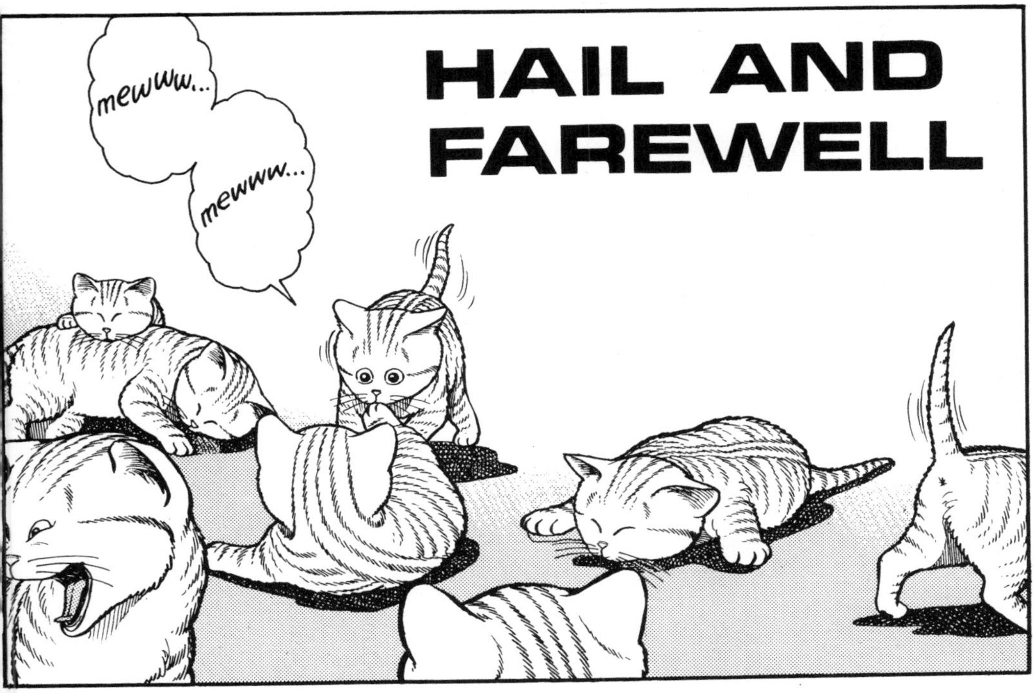
mewww...
mewww...

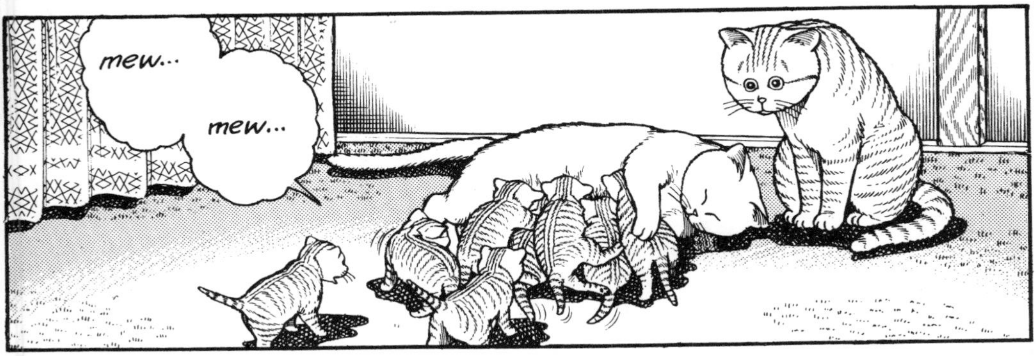
mew...
mew...

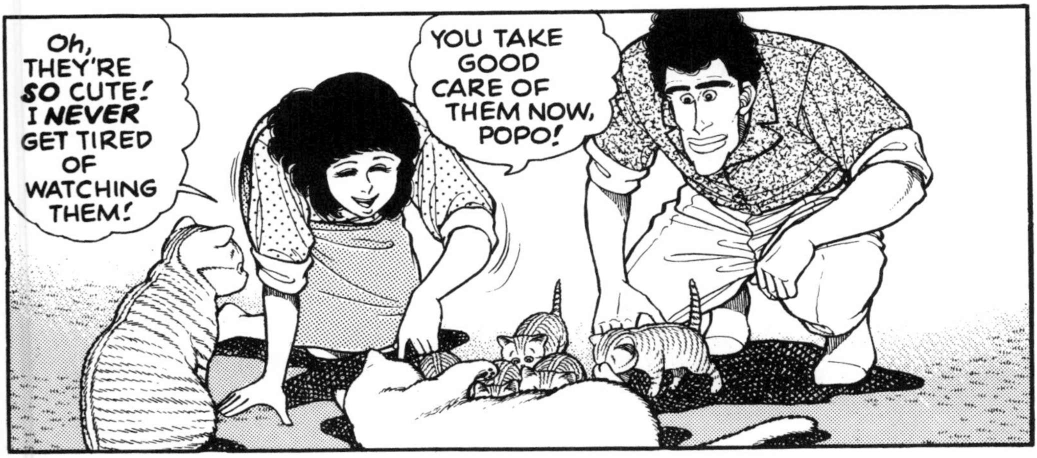
Oh, THEY'RE SO CUTE! I NEVER GET TIRED OF WATCHING THEM!
YOU TAKE GOOD CARE OF THEM NOW, POPO!

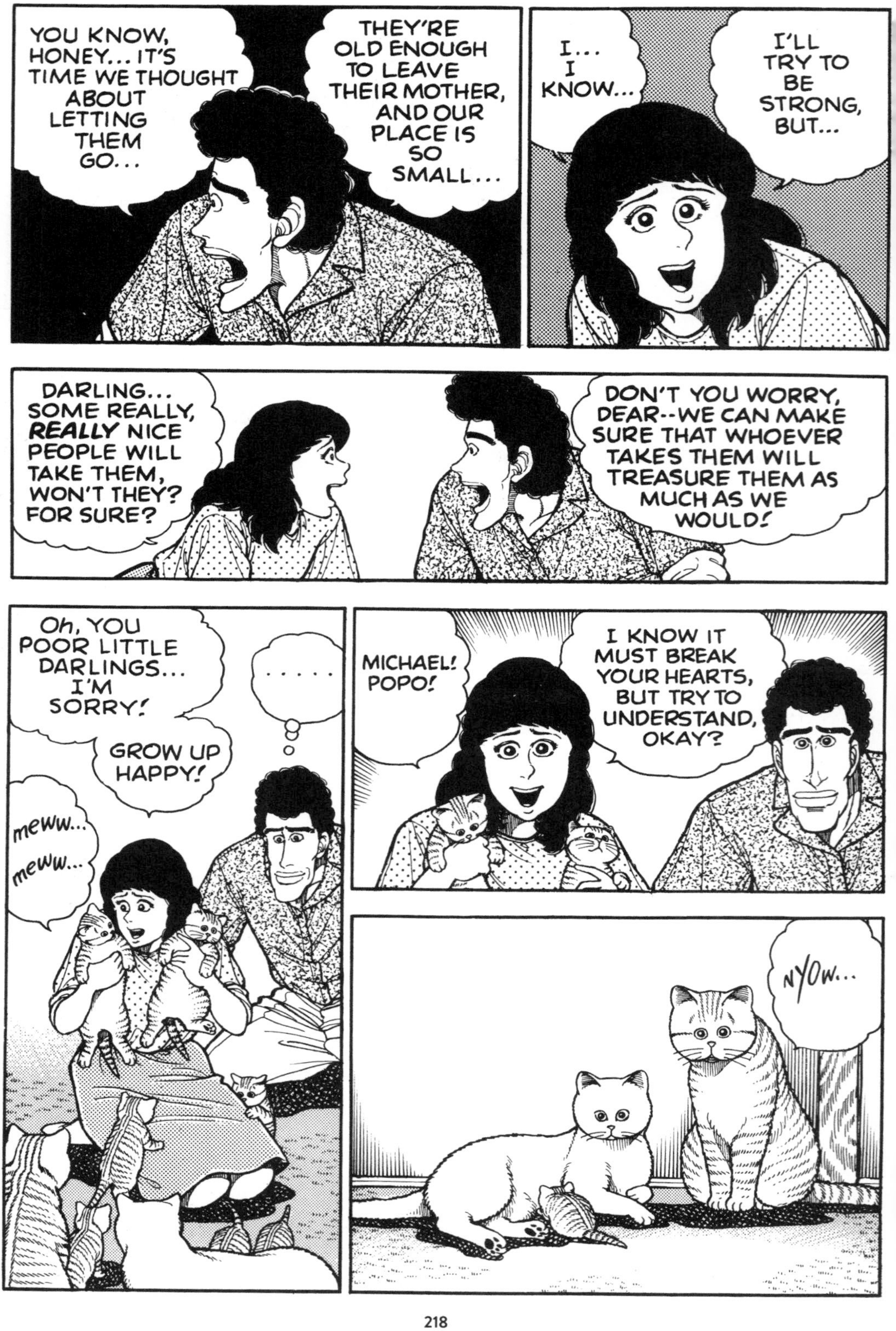
YOU KNOW, HONEY... IT'S TIME WE THOUGHT ABOUT LETTING THEM GO...
THEY'RE OLD ENOUGH TO LEAVE THEIR MOTHER, AND OUR PLACE IS SO SMALL...
I... I KNOW...
I'LL TRY TO BE STRONG, BUT...
DARLING... SOME REALLY, **REALLY** NICE PEOPLE WILL TAKE THEM, WON'T THEY? FOR SURE?
DON'T YOU WORRY, DEAR--WE CAN MAKE SURE THAT WHOEVER TAKES THEM WILL TREASURE THEM AS MUCH AS WE WOULD!
Oh, YOU POOR LITTLE DARLINGS... I'M SORRY!
......
GROW UP HAPPY!
meww...
meww...
MICHAEL! POPO!
I KNOW IT MUST BREAK YOUR HEARTS, BUT TRY TO UNDERSTAND, OKAY?
NYOW...

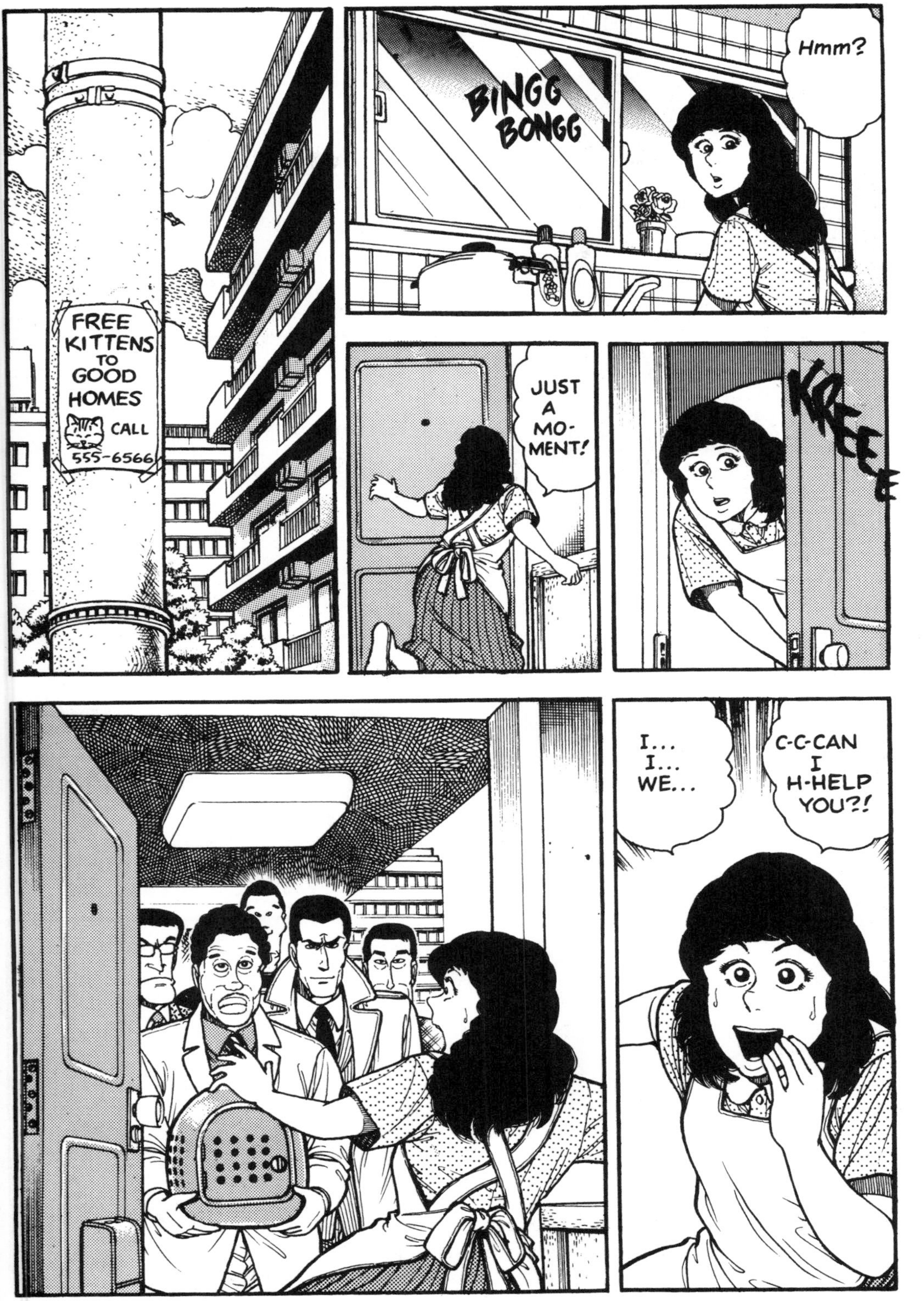
FREE KITTENS TO GOOD HOMES CALL 555-6566
BINGG BONGG
Hmm?
JUST A MO-MENT!
KREEEE
C-C-CAN I H-HELP YOU?!
I... I... WE...

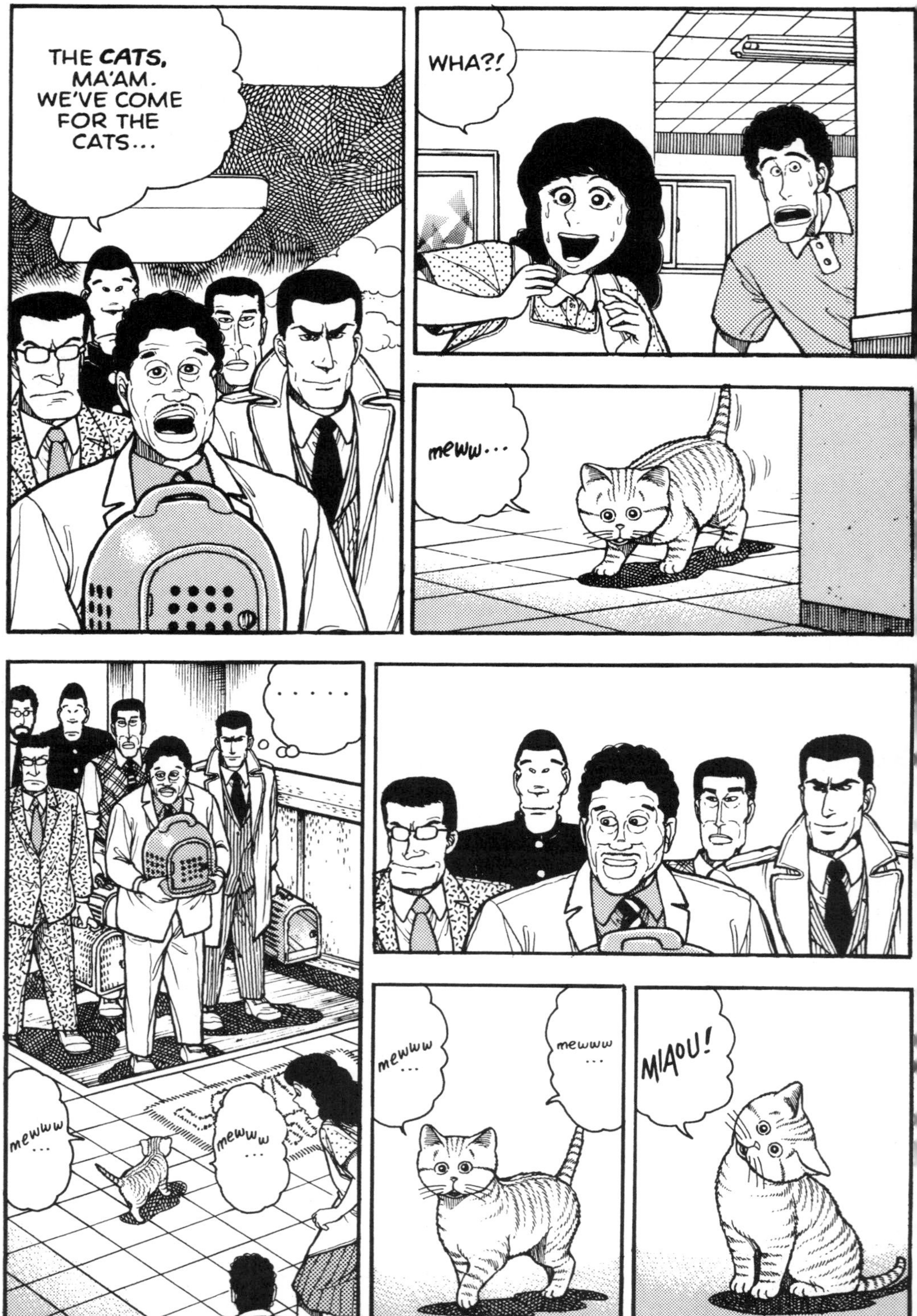
THE **CATS,** MA'AM. WE'VE COME FOR THE CATS...
WHA?!
mewww...
. . . . .
mewww ...
mewww ...
mewww ...
mewww ...
MIAOU!

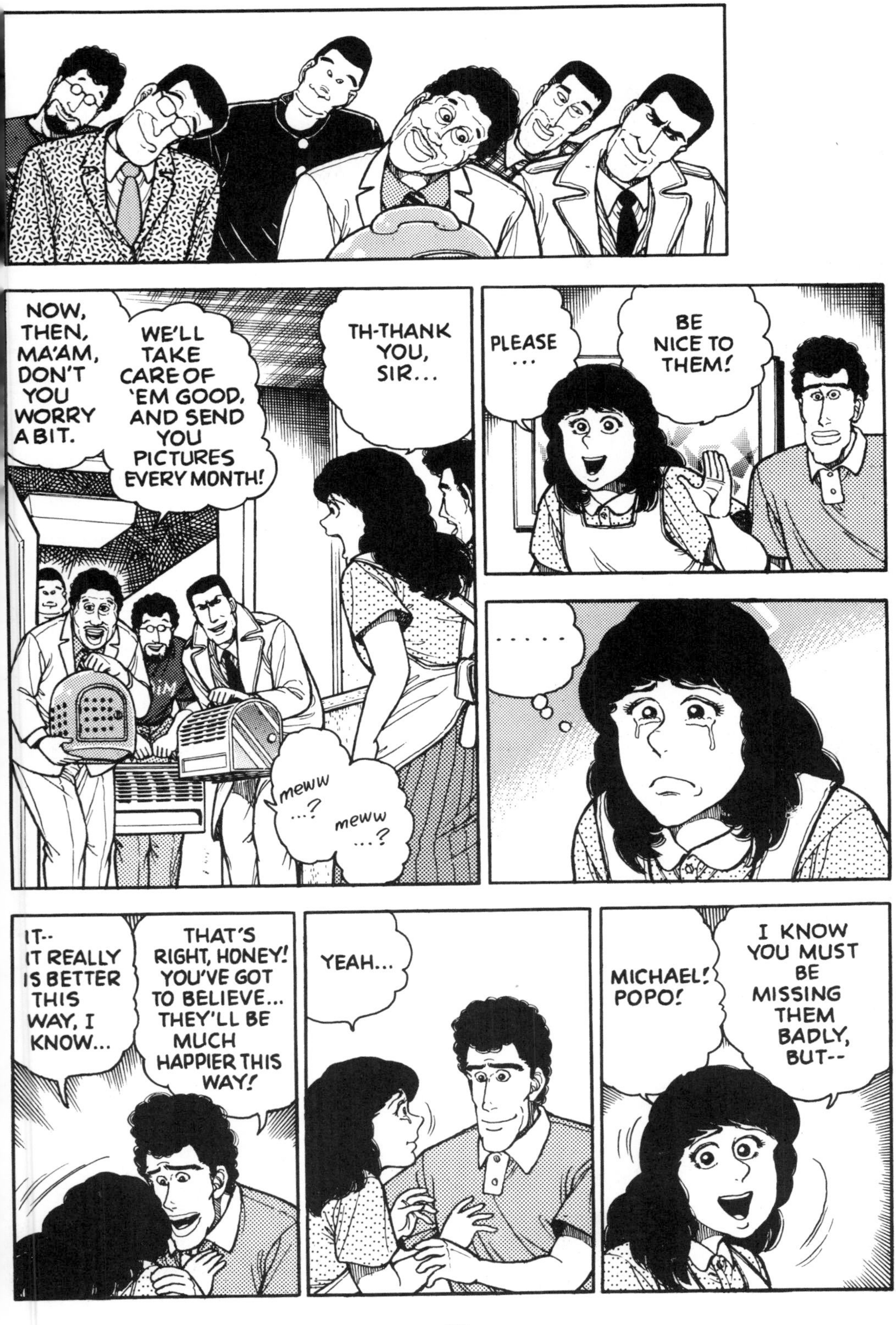

NOW, THEN, MA'AM, DON'T YOU WORRY A BIT.
WE'LL TAKE CARE OF 'EM GOOD, AND SEND YOU PICTURES EVERY MONTH!
TH-THANK YOU, SIR...
meww ...?
meww ...?
PLEASE ...
BE NICE TO THEM!
. . . . .
IT-- IT REALLY IS BETTER THIS WAY, I KNOW...
THAT'S RIGHT, HONEY! YOU'VE GOT TO BELIEVE... THEY'LL BE MUCH HAPPIER THIS WAY!
YEAH...
MICHAEL! POPO!
I KNOW YOU MUST BE MISSING THEM BADLY, BUT--

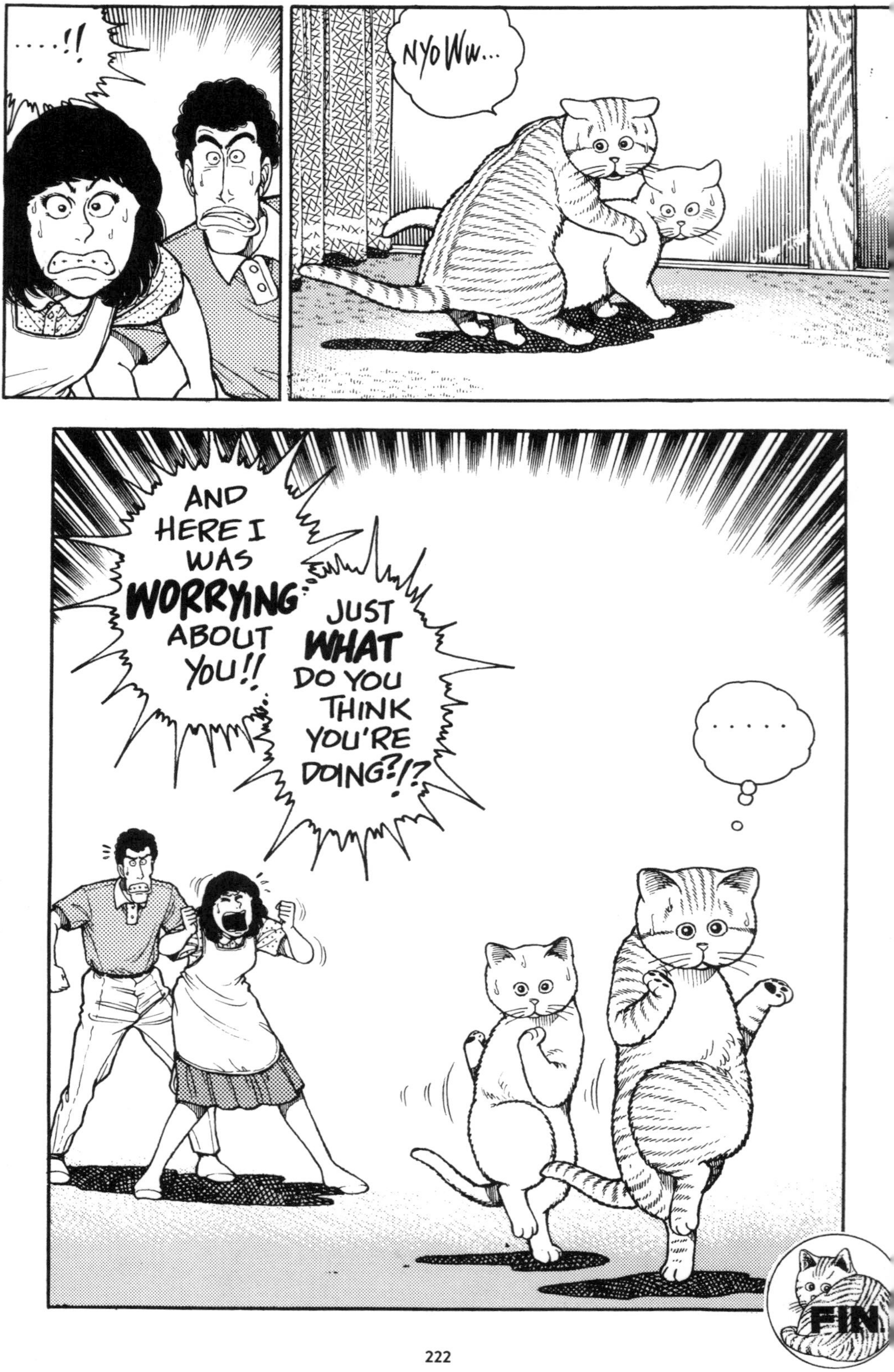

....!!
NYOWW...
AND HERE I WAS WORRYING ABOUT YOU!!
JUST WHAT DO YOU THINK YOU'RE DOING?!?
......
FIN

# A MOVEABLE FEAST

MROWR ?

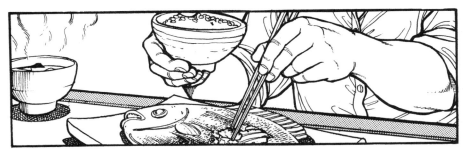

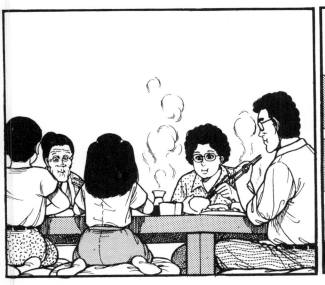

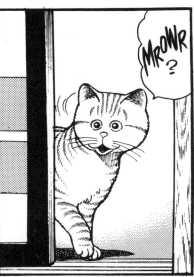

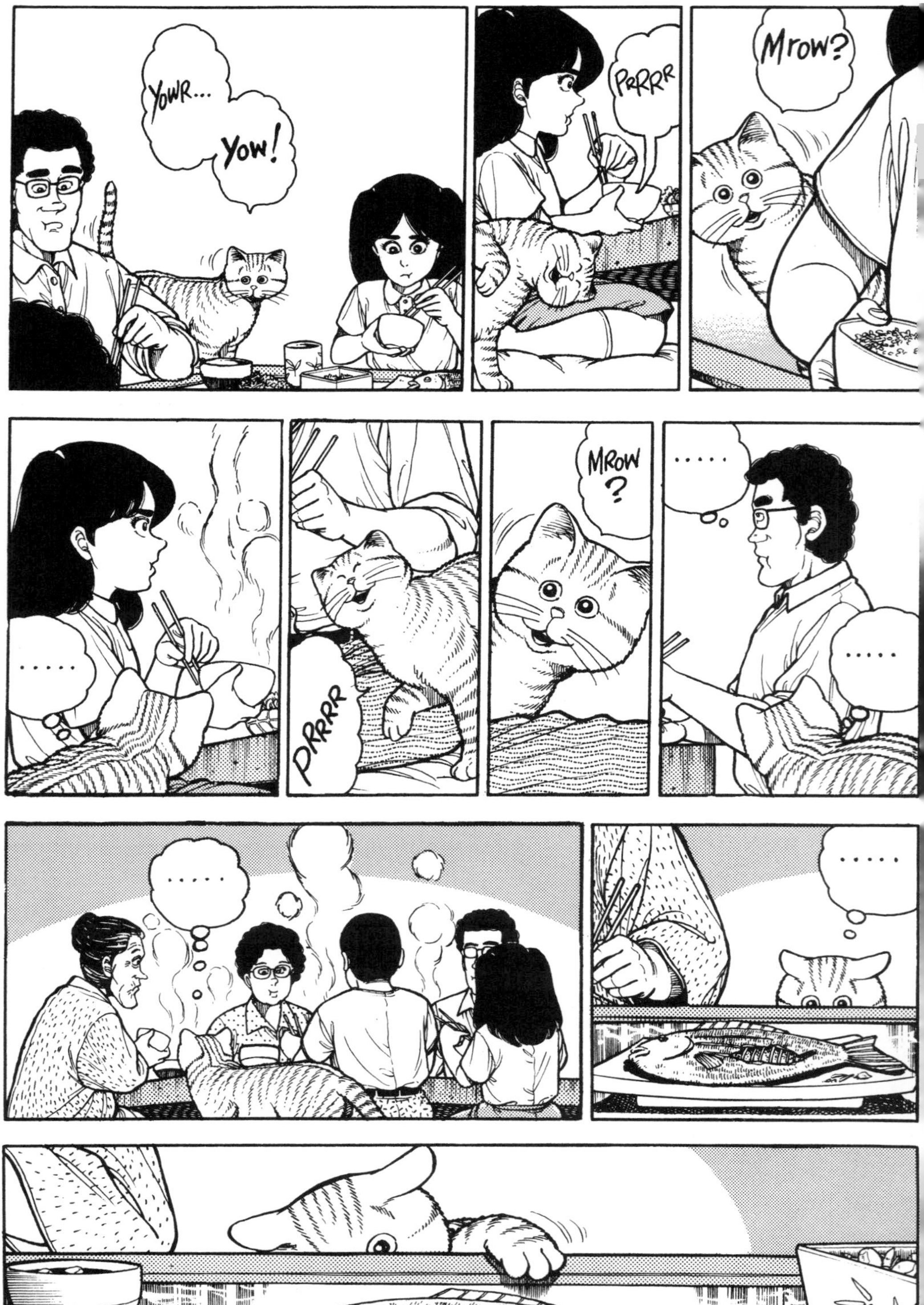

YOWR...
YOW!
PRRRR
Mrow?
.....
PRRRR
MROW ?
.....
.....
.....
.....

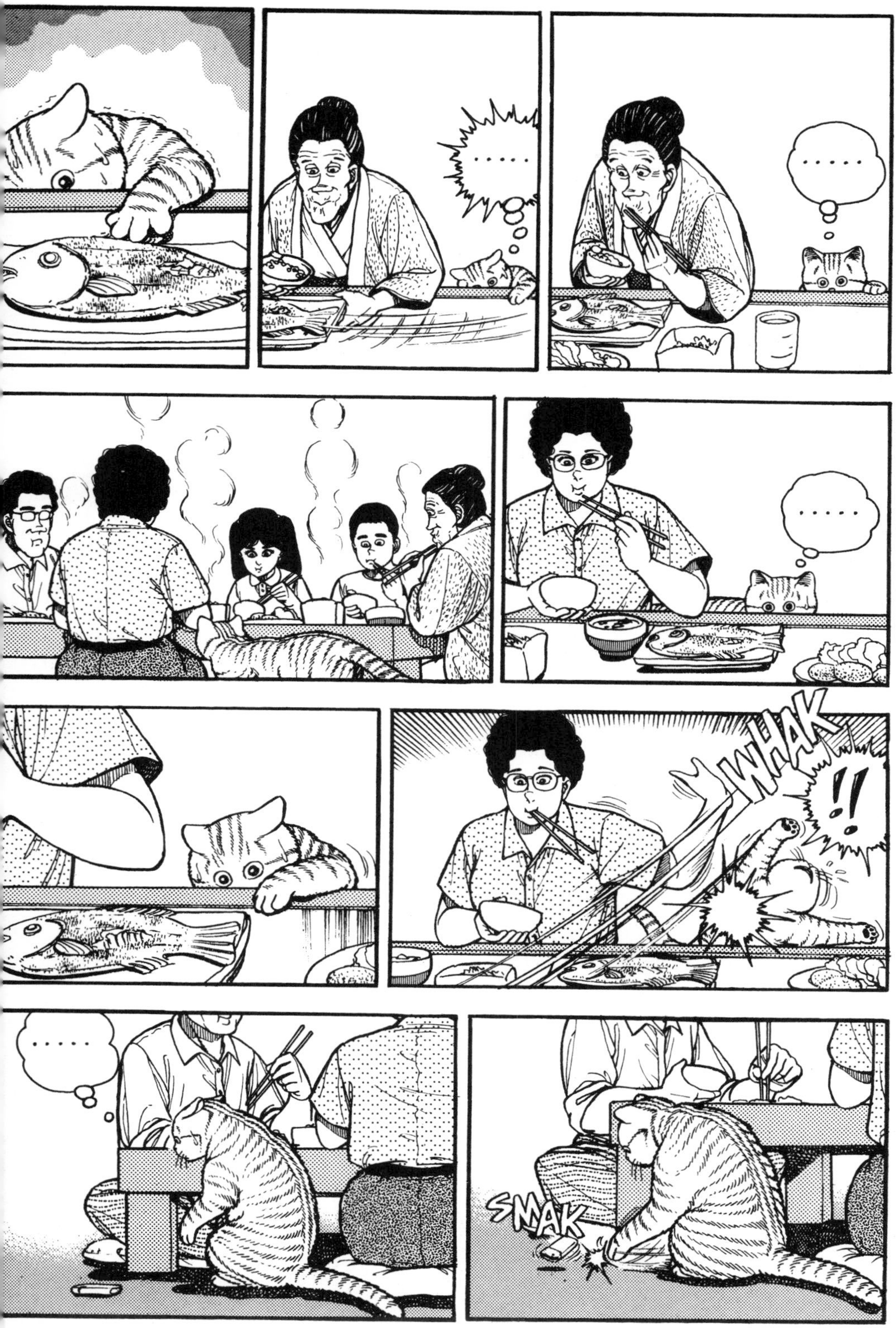
.....
.....
.....
WHAK
!!
.....
SMAK

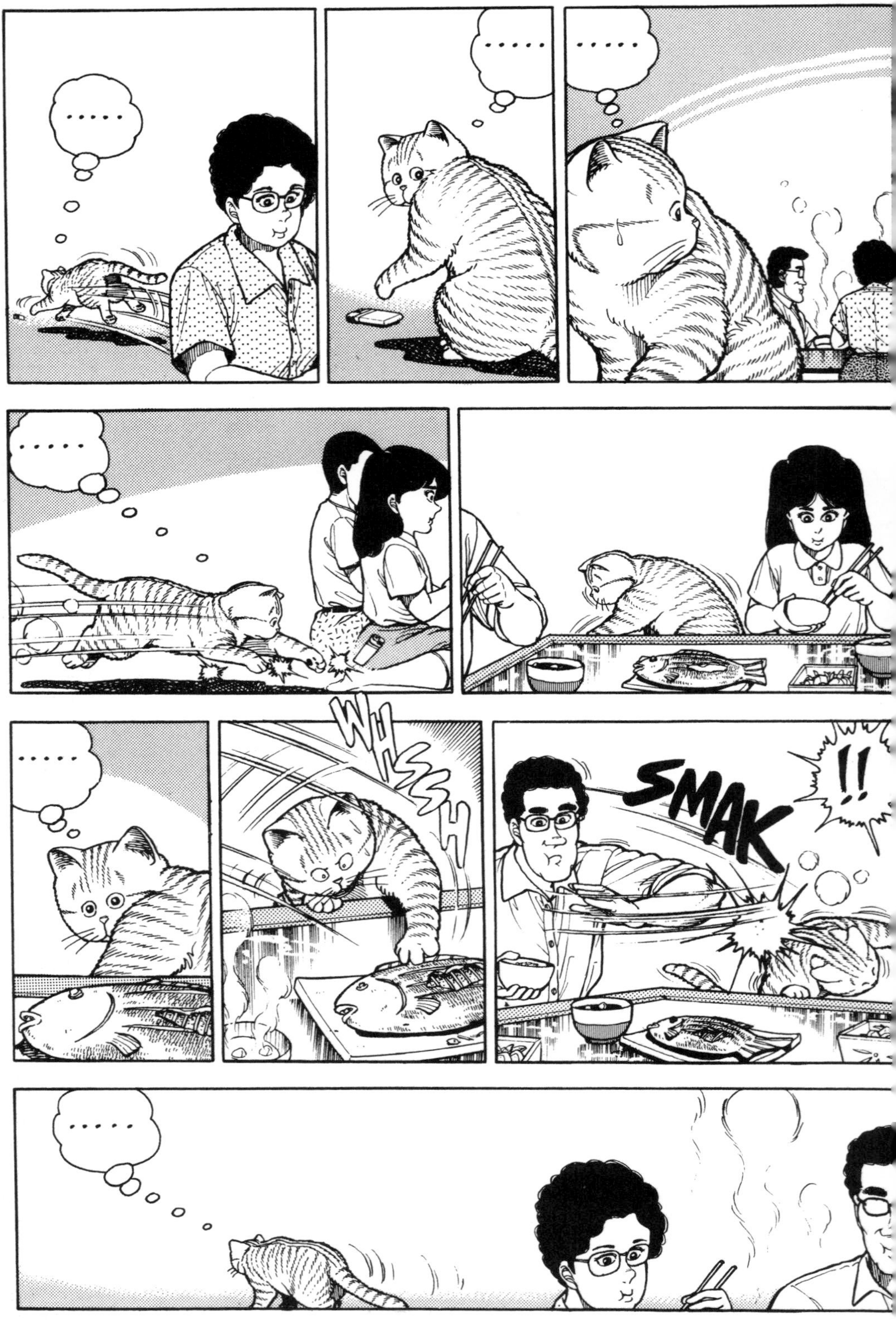
.....
.....
.....
.....
.....
WHSSH
SMAK
!!
.....

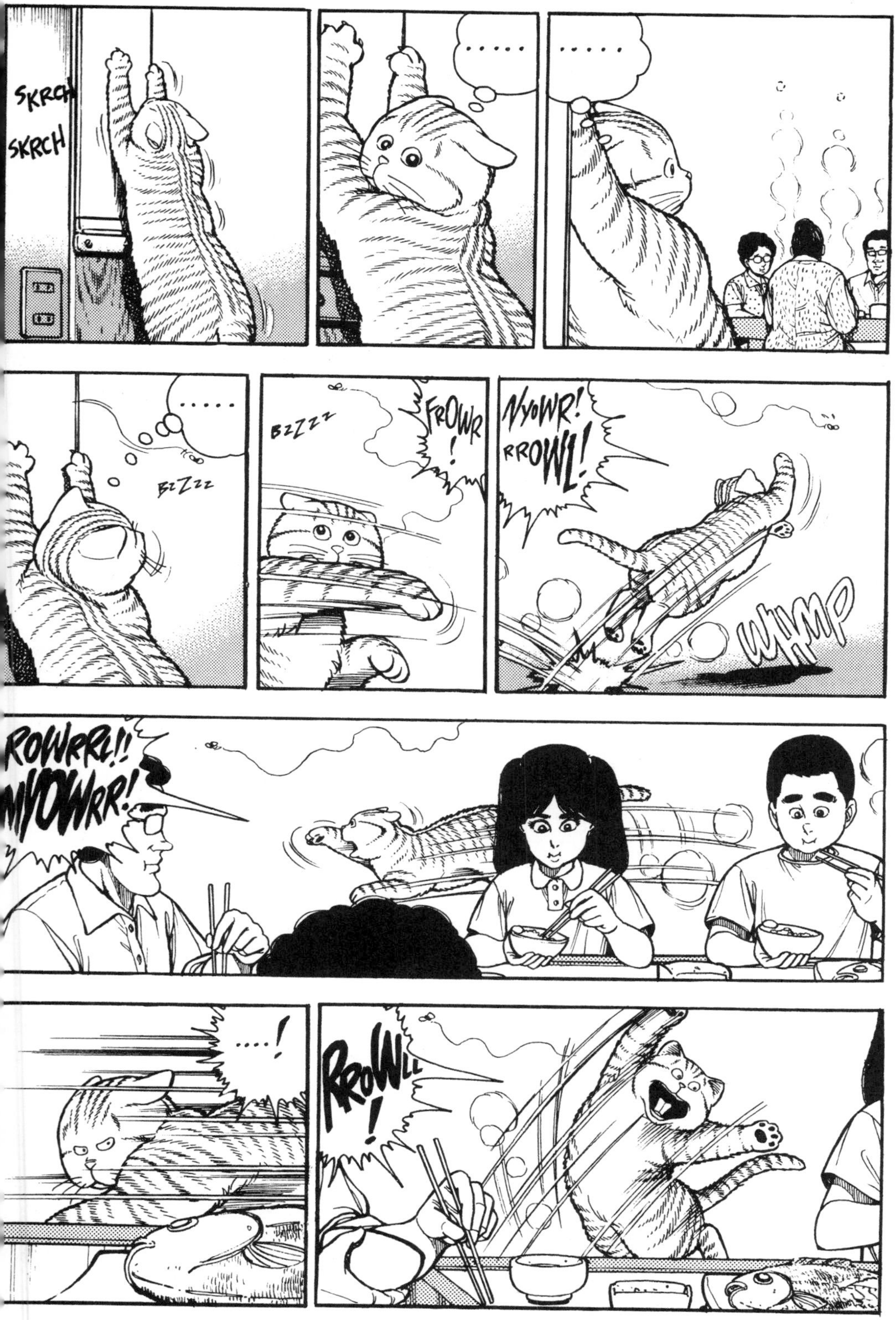

SKRCH
SKRCH
......
......
.....
BZZZZ
BZZZZ
FROWR!
NYOWR!
RROWL!
WHMP
ROWRRL!!
NYOWRR!
....!
RROWLL!

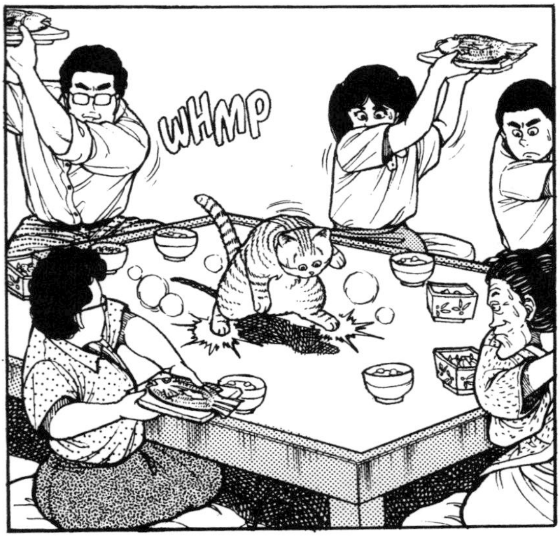
WHMP

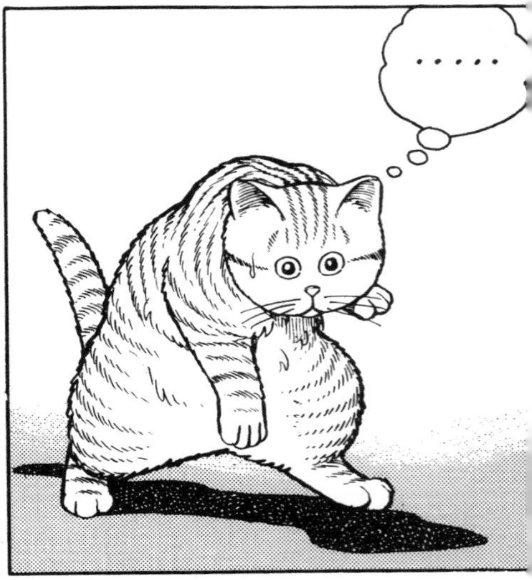
......

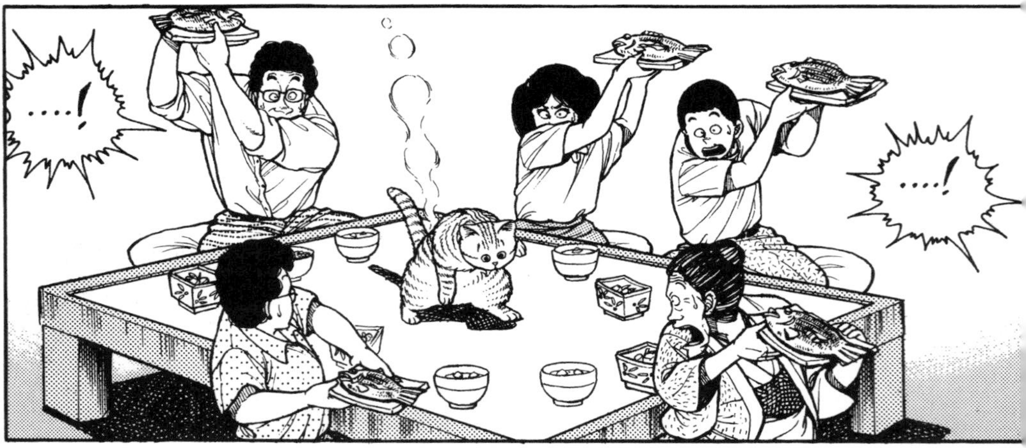
....!
....!

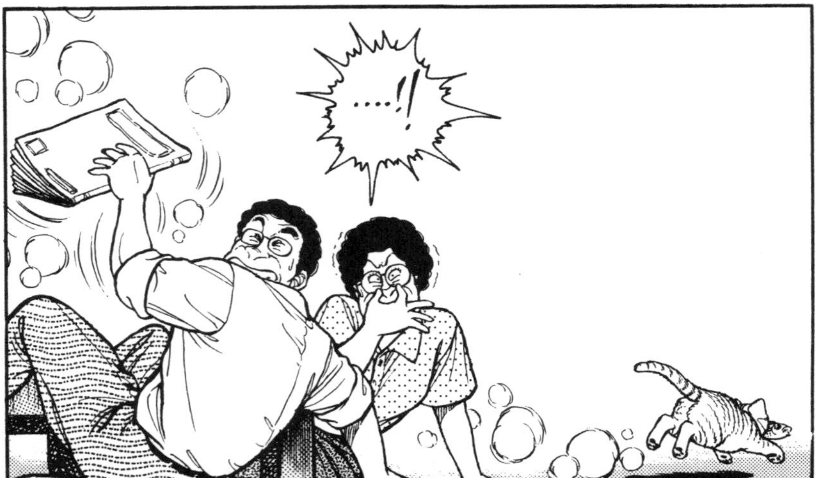
....!!

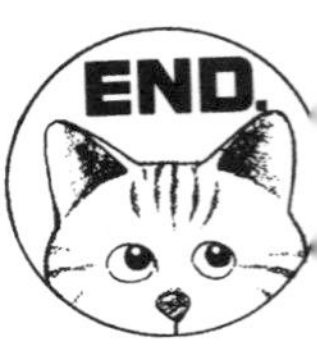
END.

# MICHAEL LENDS A PAW

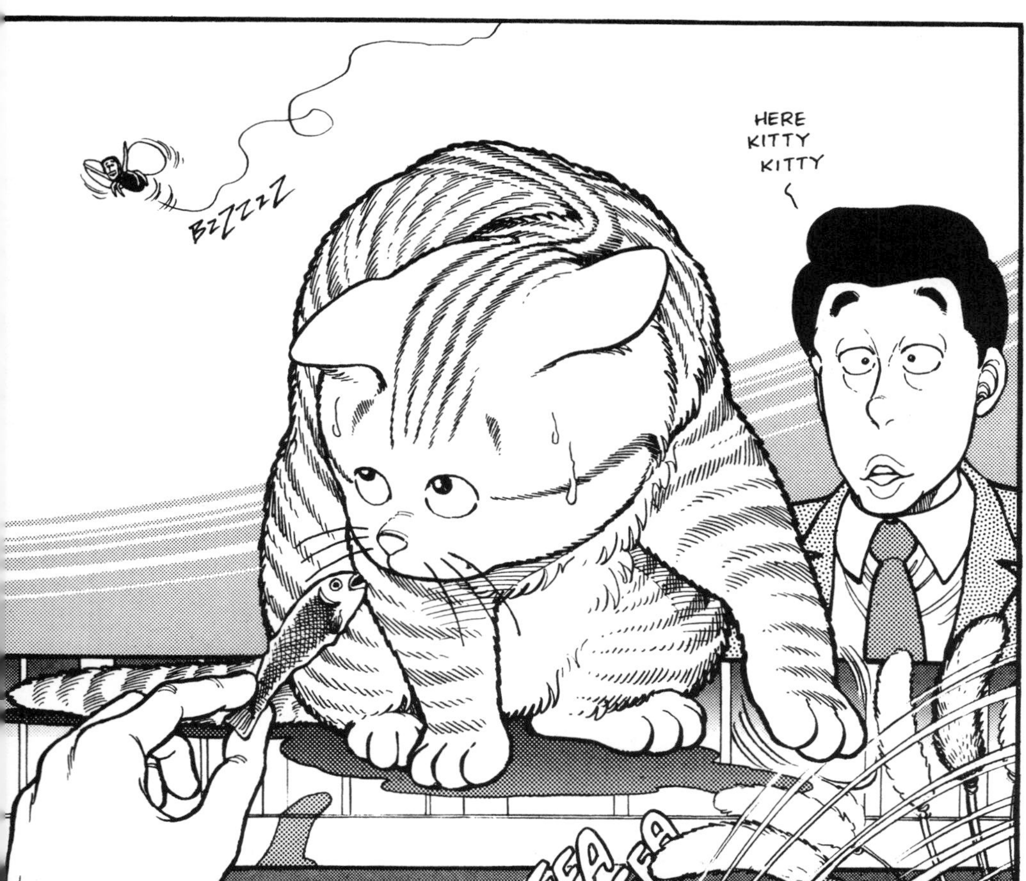
BZZZZZ
HERE KITTY KITTY
WHIFFA WHIFFA

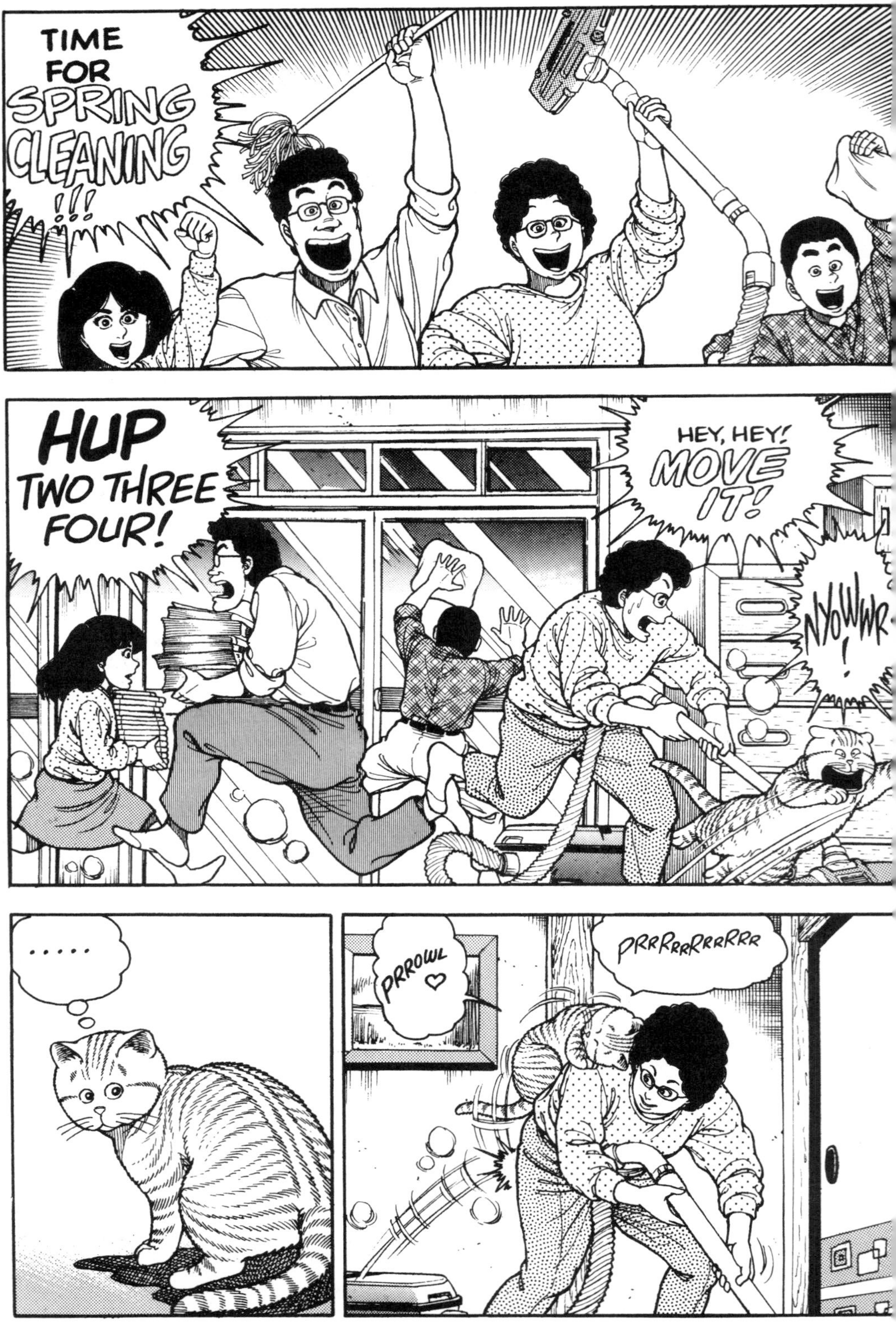
TIME FOR SPRING CLEANING !!!
HUP TWO THREE FOUR!
HEY, HEY! MOVE IT!
NYOWWR!
.....
PRROWL ♡
PRRRRRRRRRRR

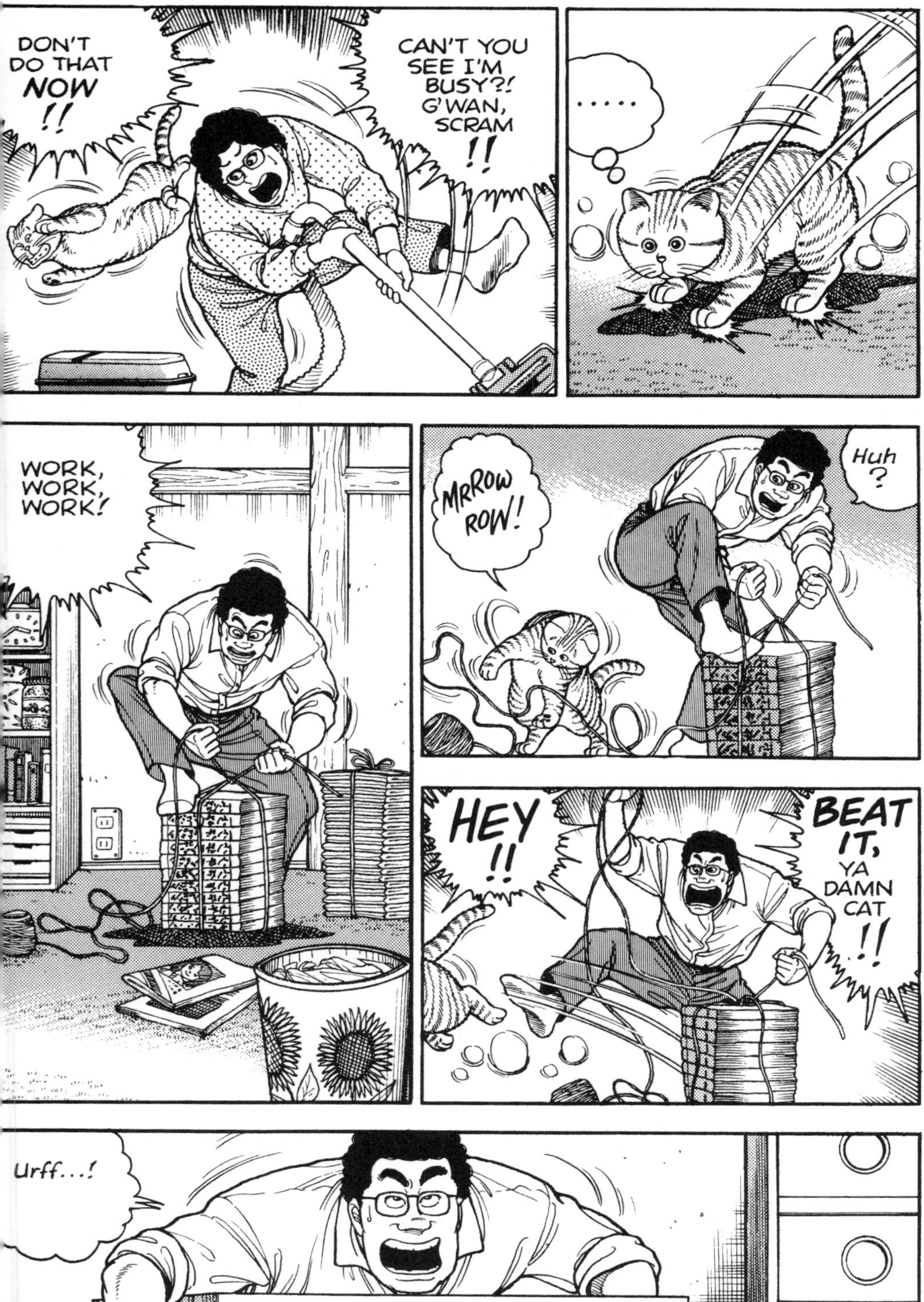
DON'T DO THAT NOW !!
CAN'T YOU SEE I'M BUSY?! G'WAN, SCRAM !!
. . . . .
WORK, WORK, WORK!
MRROW ROW!
Huh ?
HEY !!
BEAT IT, YA DAMN CAT !!
Urff...!

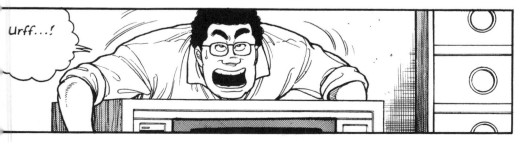

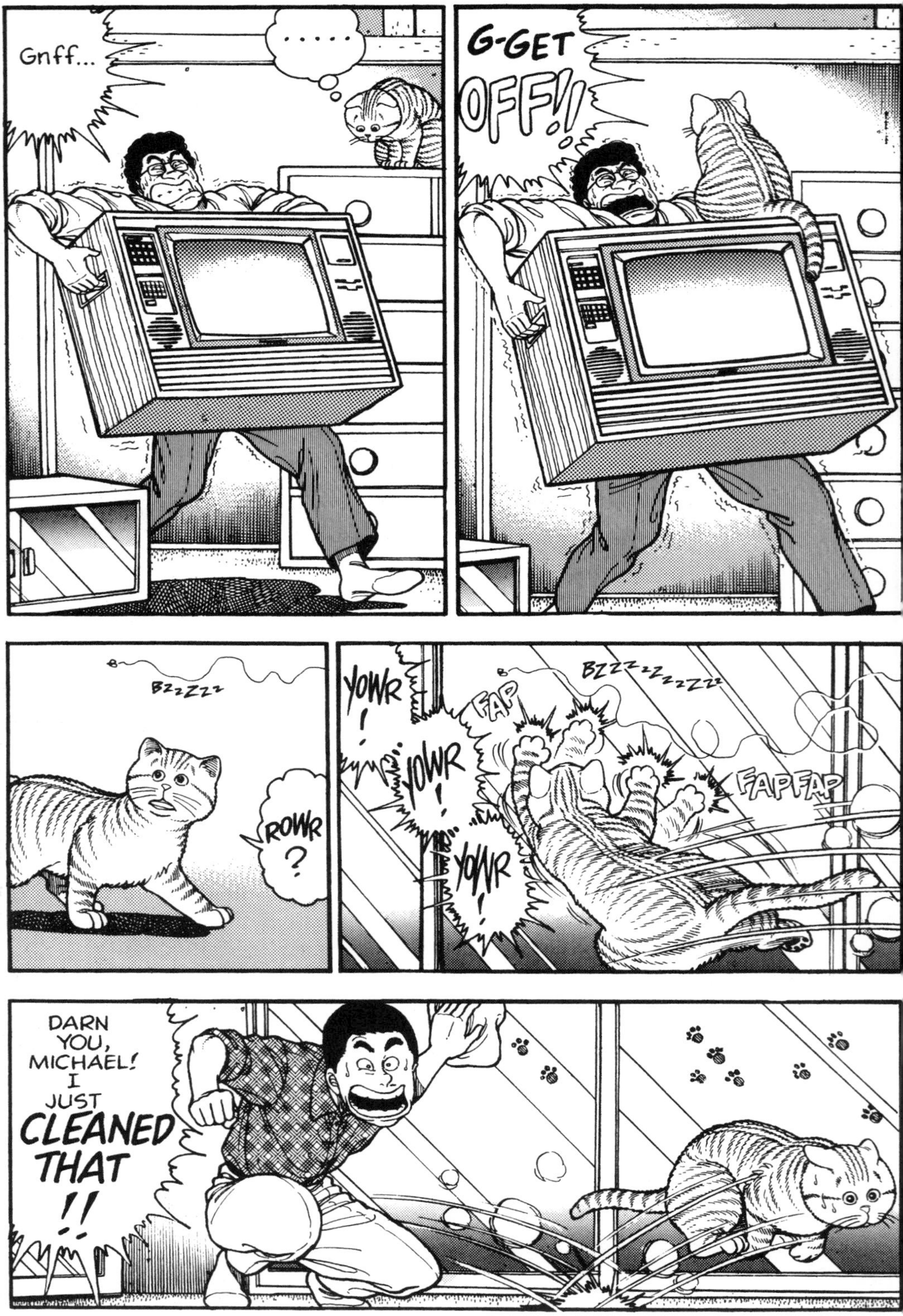
Gnff...
......
G-GET OFF!!
BZzZZZ
ROWR?
YOWR!
YOWR!
YOWR!
FAP
BZZZzzZzzZZZ
FAPFAP
DARN YOU, MICHAEL! I JUST CLEANED THAT!!

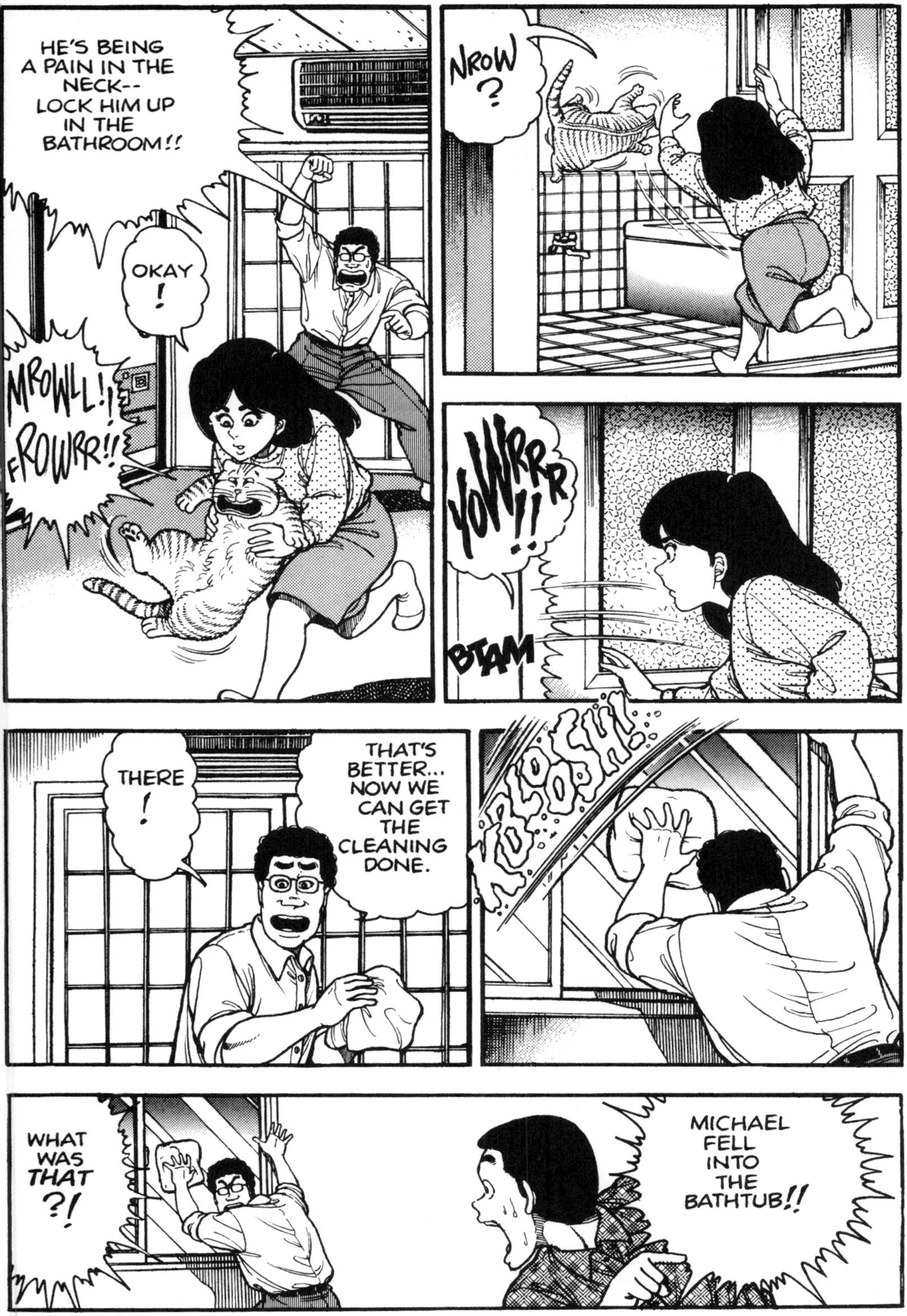
HE'S BEING A PAIN IN THE NECK-- LOCK HIM UP IN THE BATHROOM!!
OKAY!
MROWLL!!
FROWRR!!
NROW?
YOWRRR!!
BTAM
THERE!
THAT'S BETTER... NOW WE CAN GET THE CLEANING DONE.
SPLOOSH!
WHAT WAS THAT?!
MICHAEL FELL INTO THE BATHTUB!!

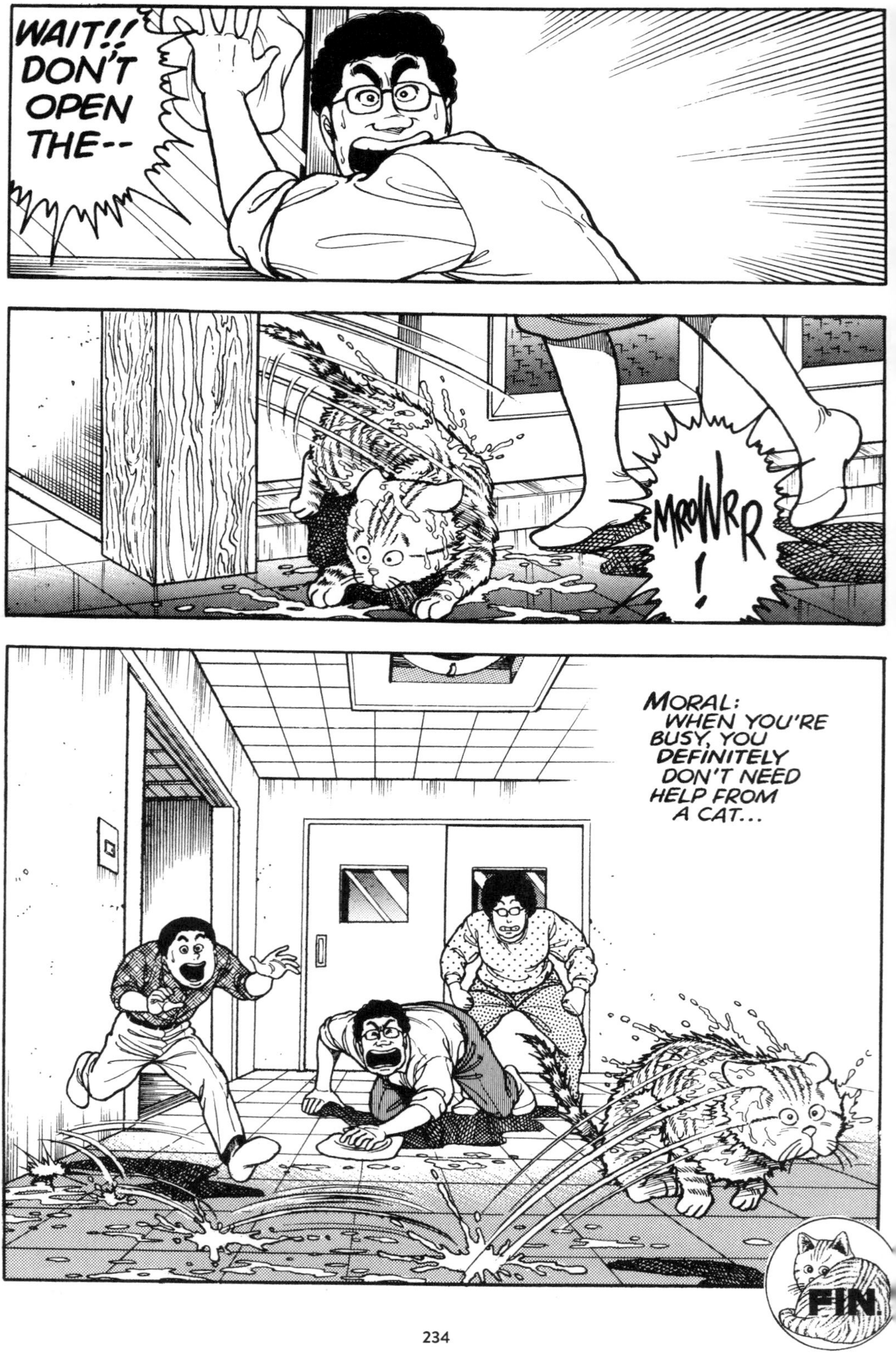
WAIT!! DON'T OPEN THE--
MROWRR !
MORAL: WHEN YOU'RE BUSY, YOU DEFINITELY DON'T NEED HELP FROM A CAT...
FIN.

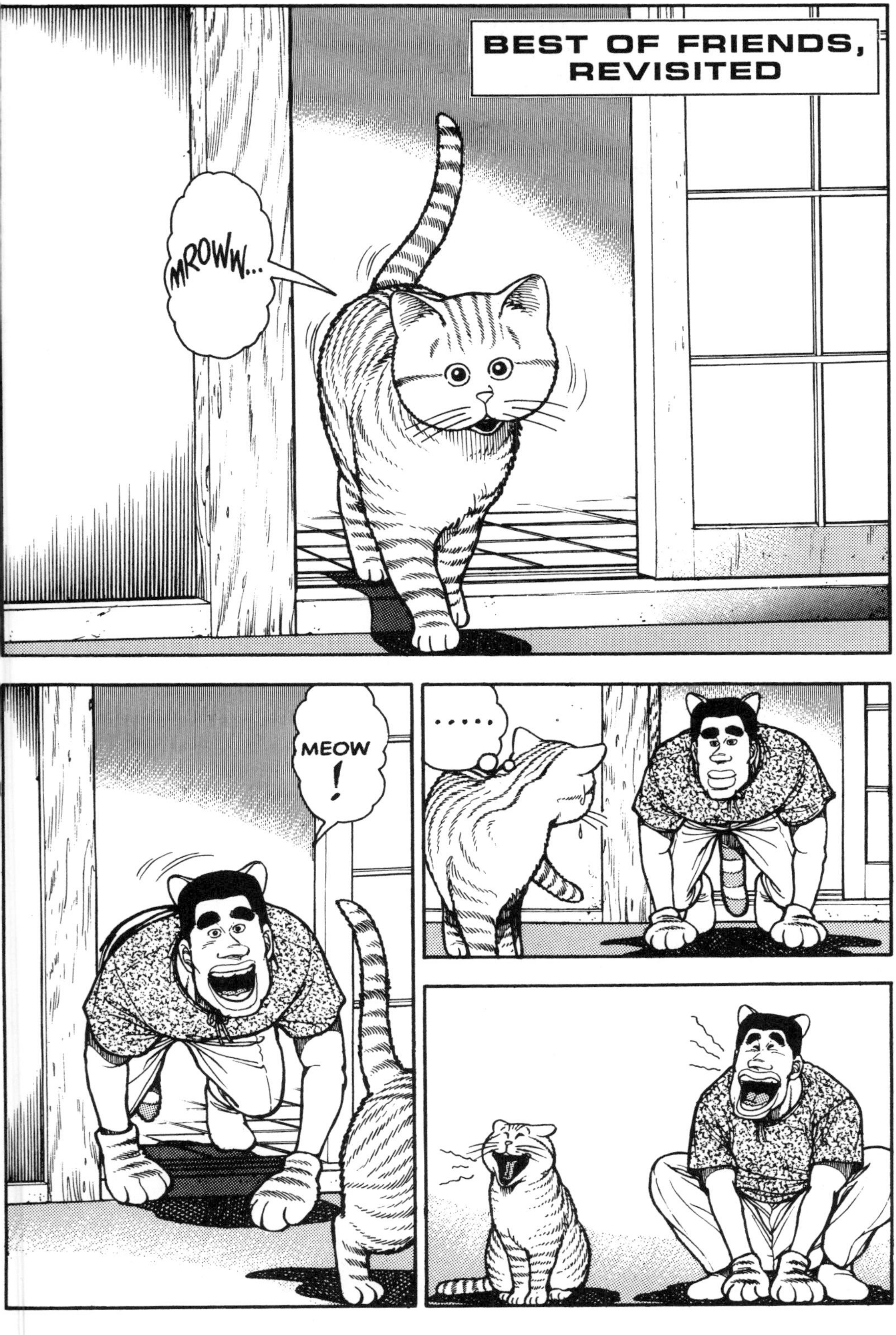
BEST OF FRIENDS, REVISITED
MROWW...
MEOW
!
.....

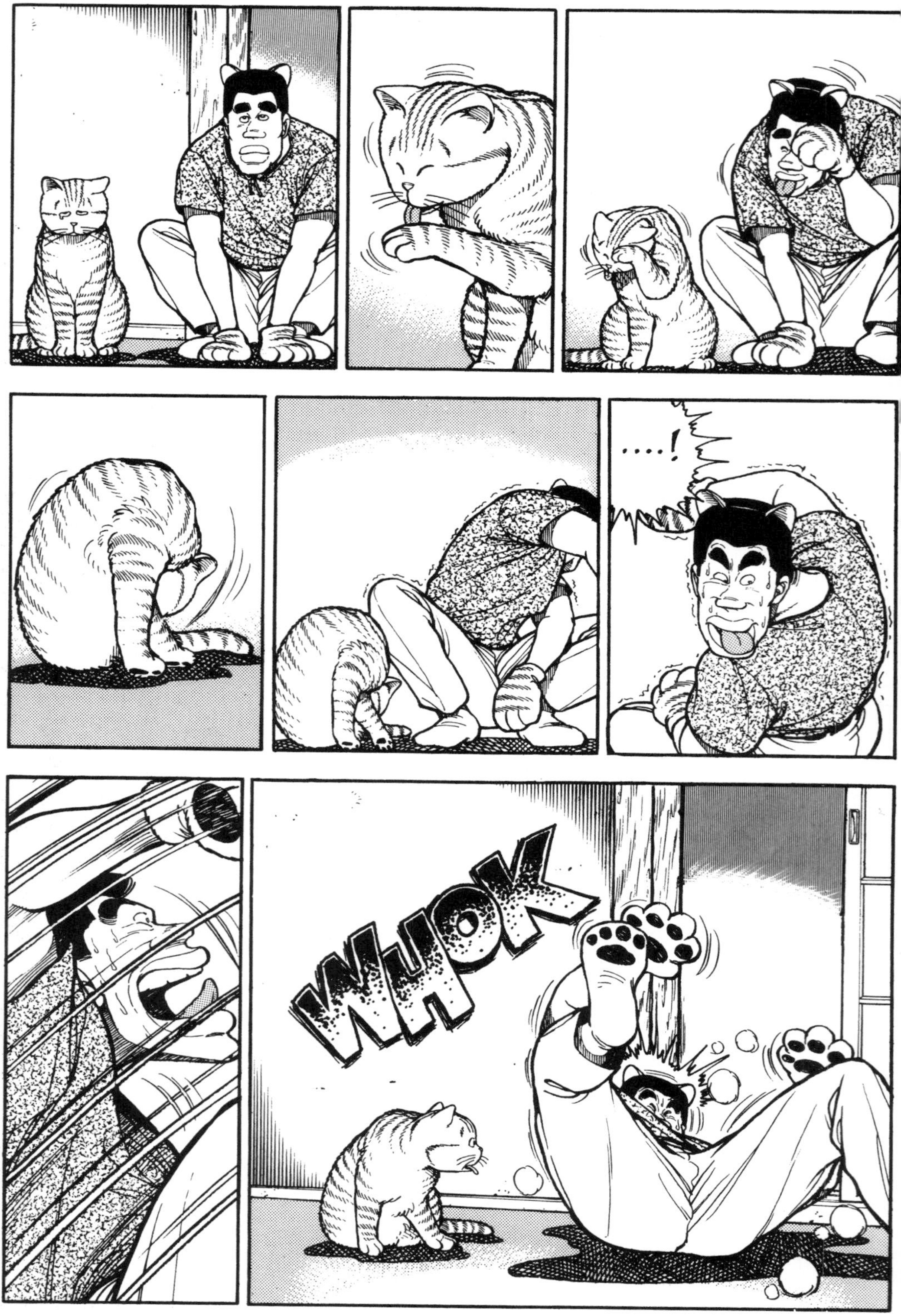
....!
WHOK

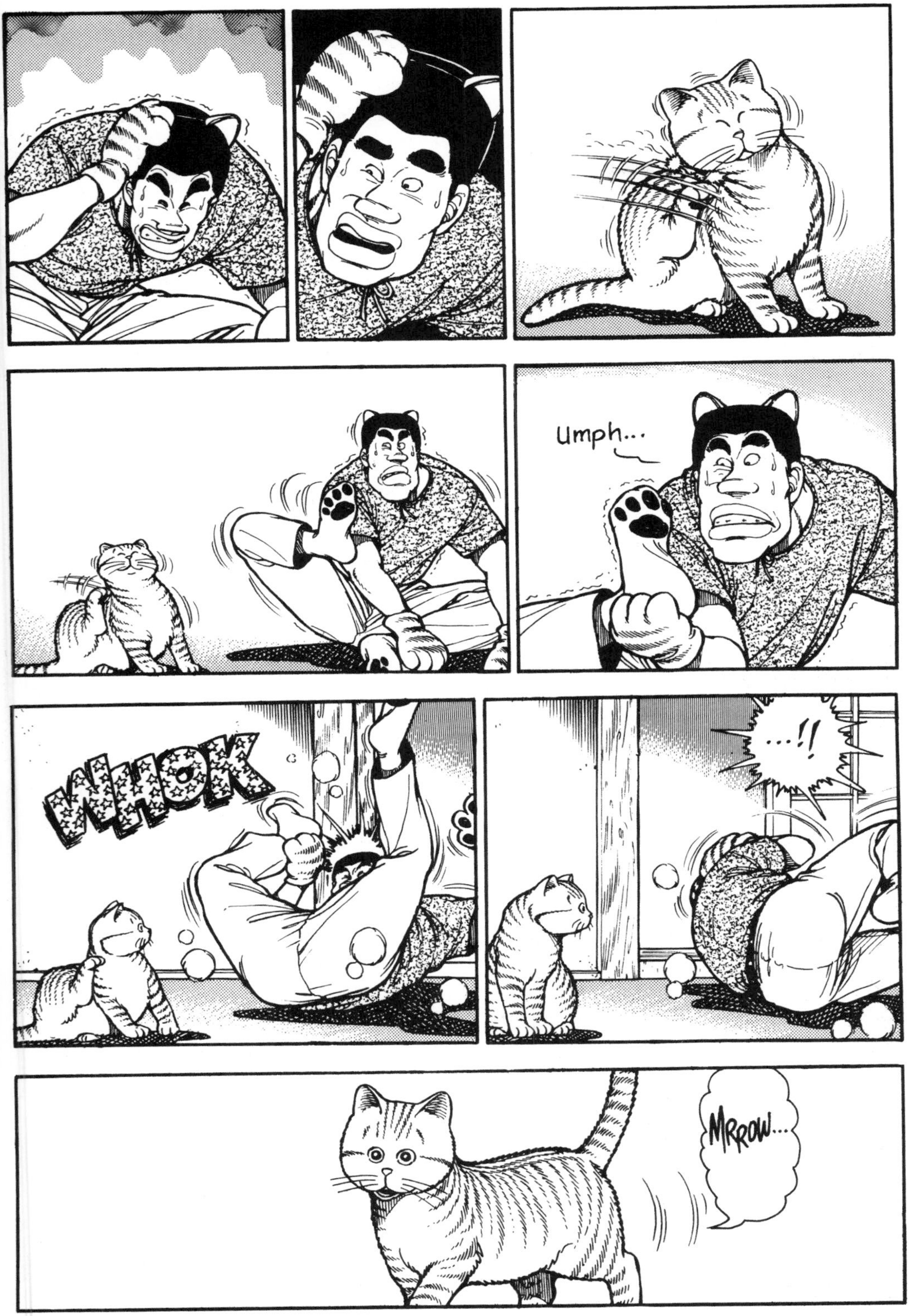
Umph...
WHOK
...!!
MRROW...

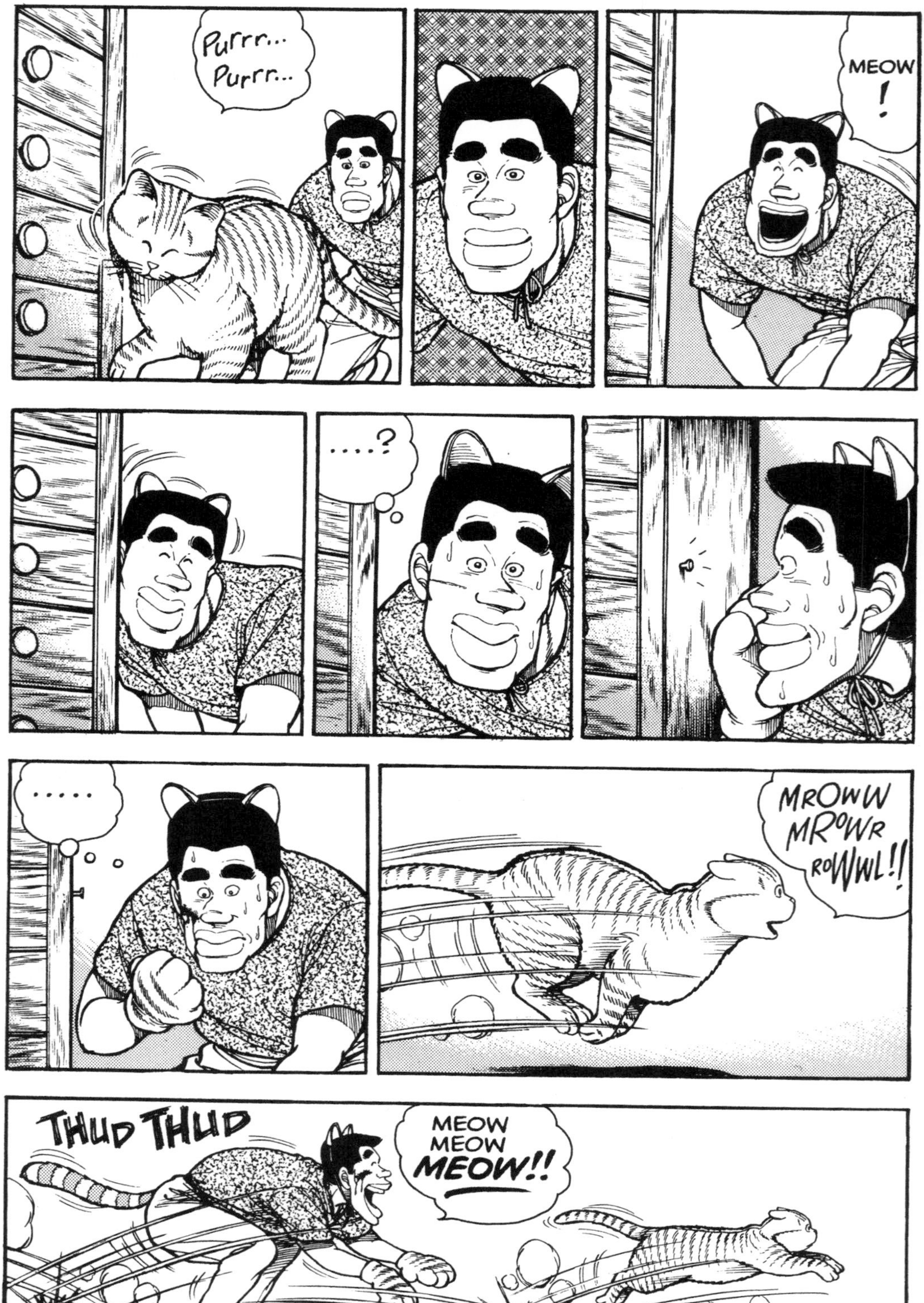
Purrr...
Purrr...
MEOW !
....?
.....
MROWW MROWR ROWWL!!
THUD THUD
MEOW MEOW MEOW!!

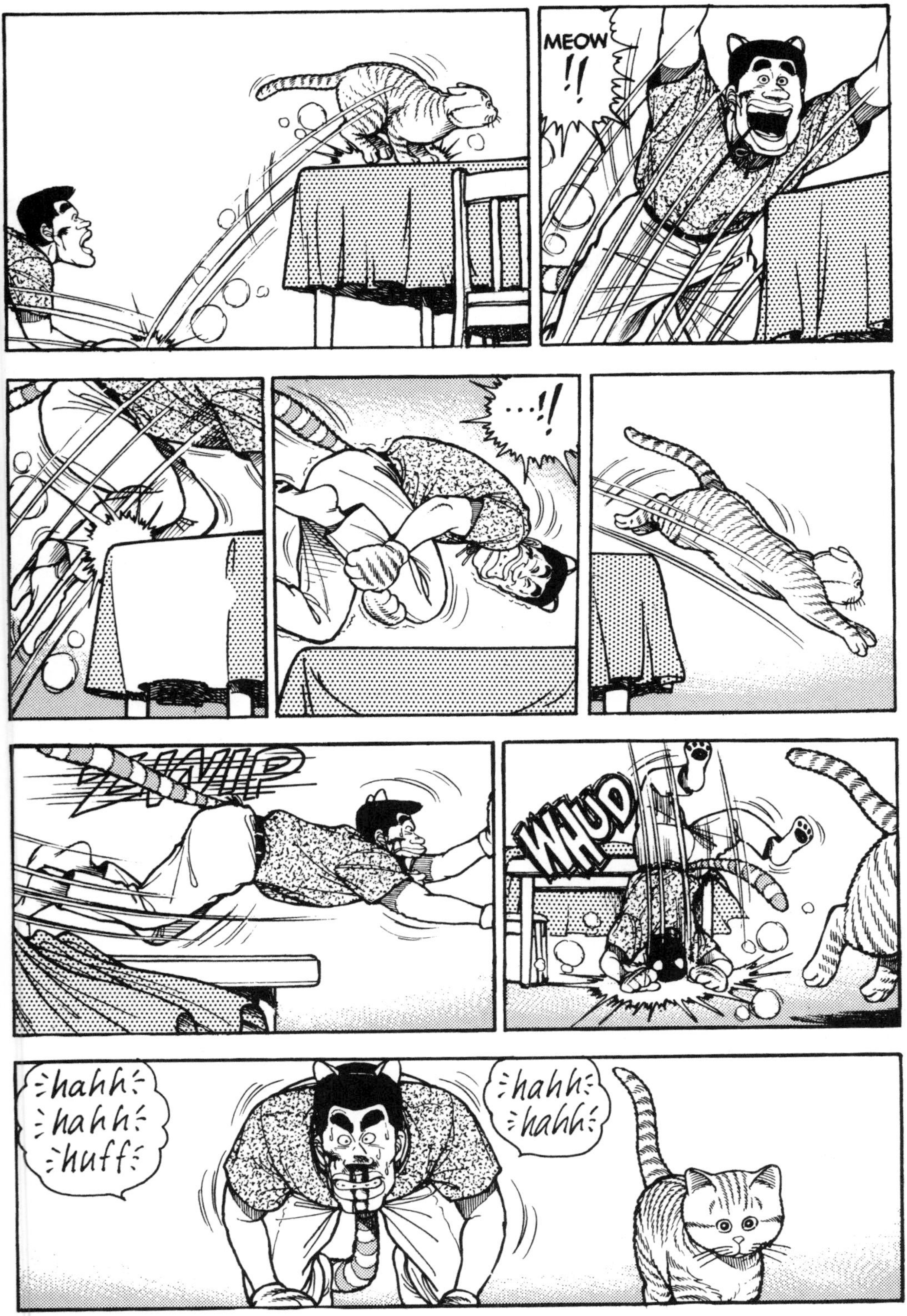
MEOW !!
...!!
WHIP
WHUD
hahh hahh huff
hahh hahh

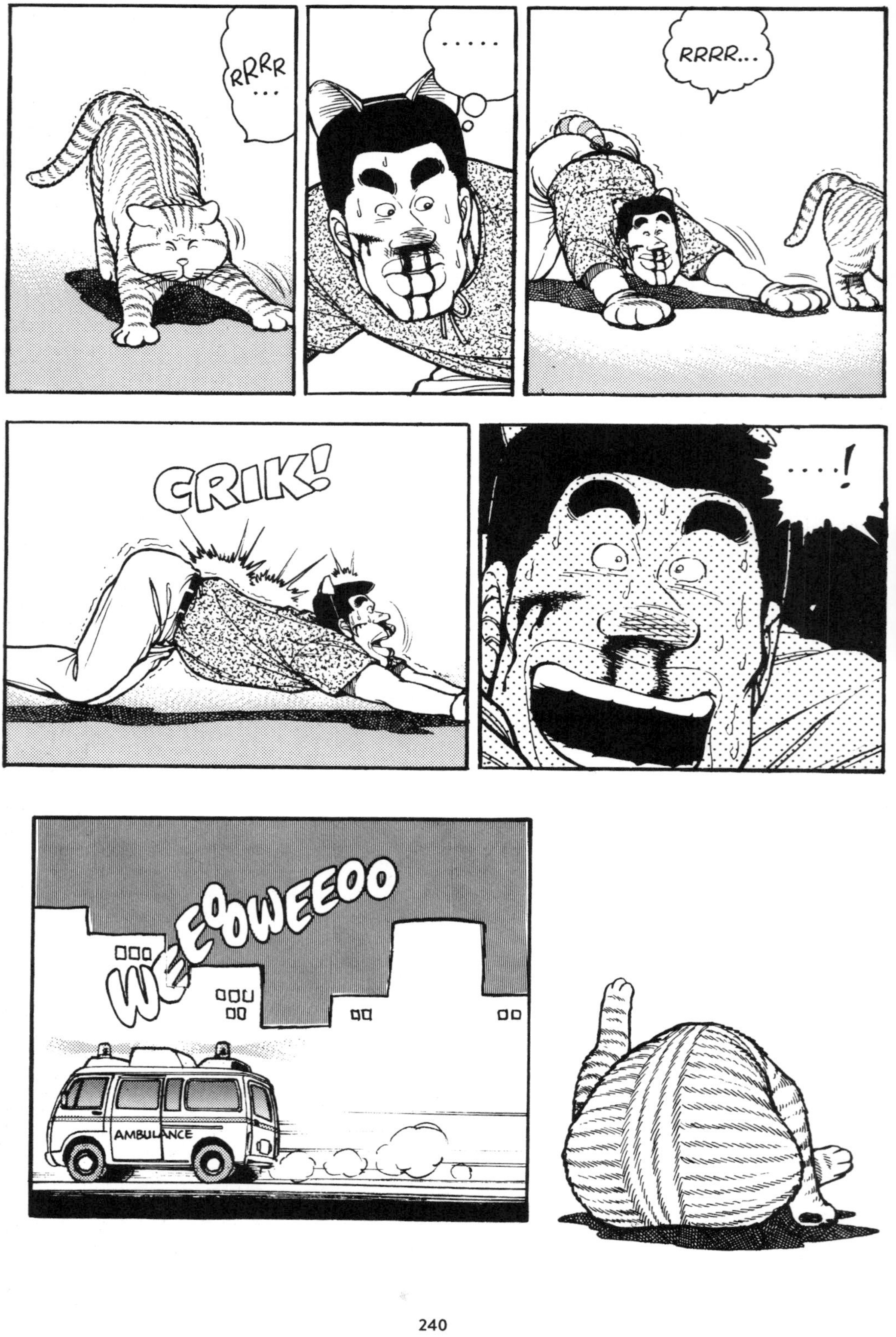
RRRR
...
......
RRRR...
CRIK!
....!
WEEOOWEEOO
AMBULANCE

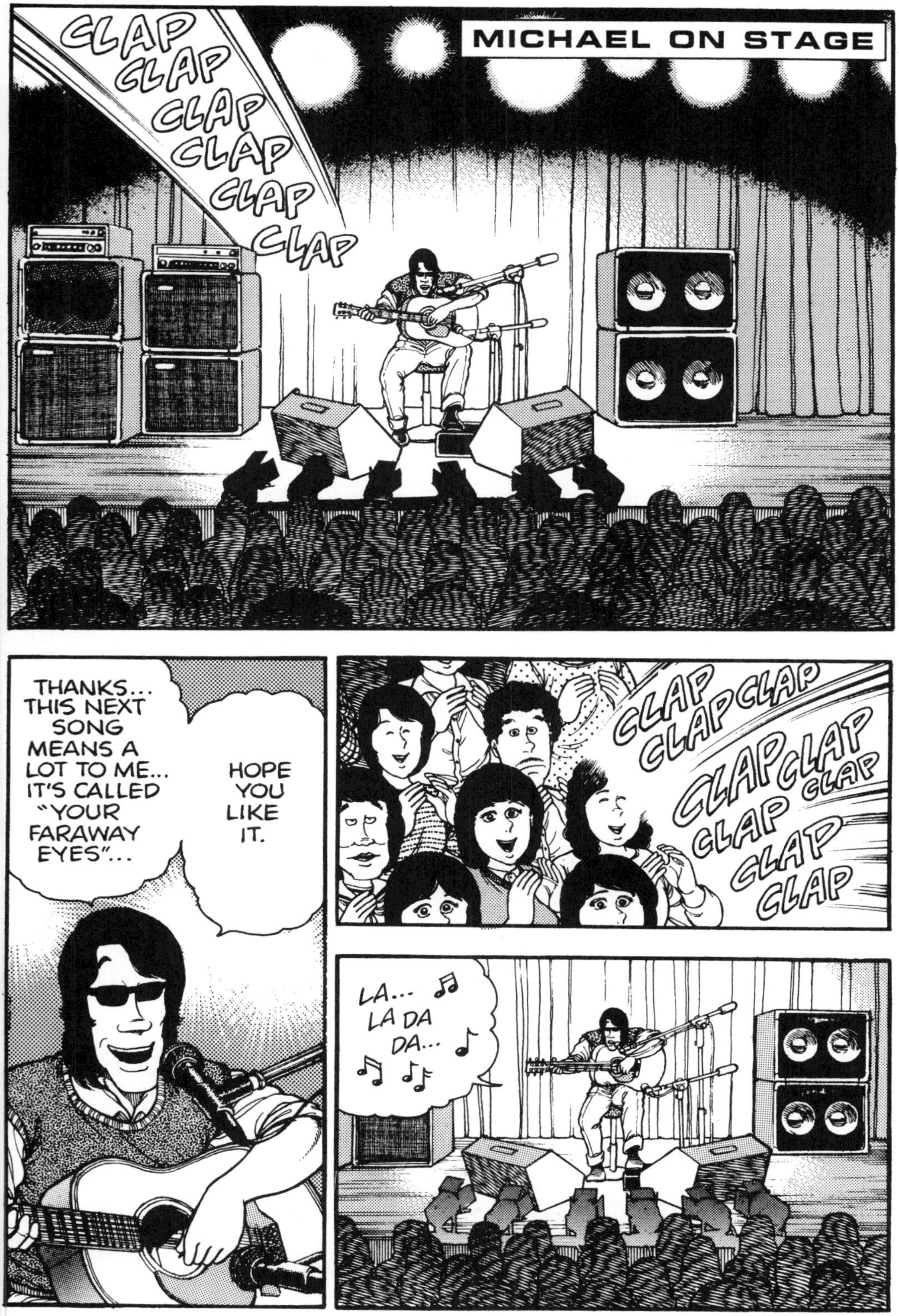
MICHAEL ON STAGE
CLAP CLAP CLAP CLAP CLAP CLAP
THANKS... THIS NEXT SONG MEANS A LOT TO ME... IT'S CALLED "YOUR FARAWAY EYES"...
HOPE YOU LIKE IT.
CLAP CLAP CLAP CLAP CLAP CLAP CLAP CLAP CLAP
LA... LA DA DA...

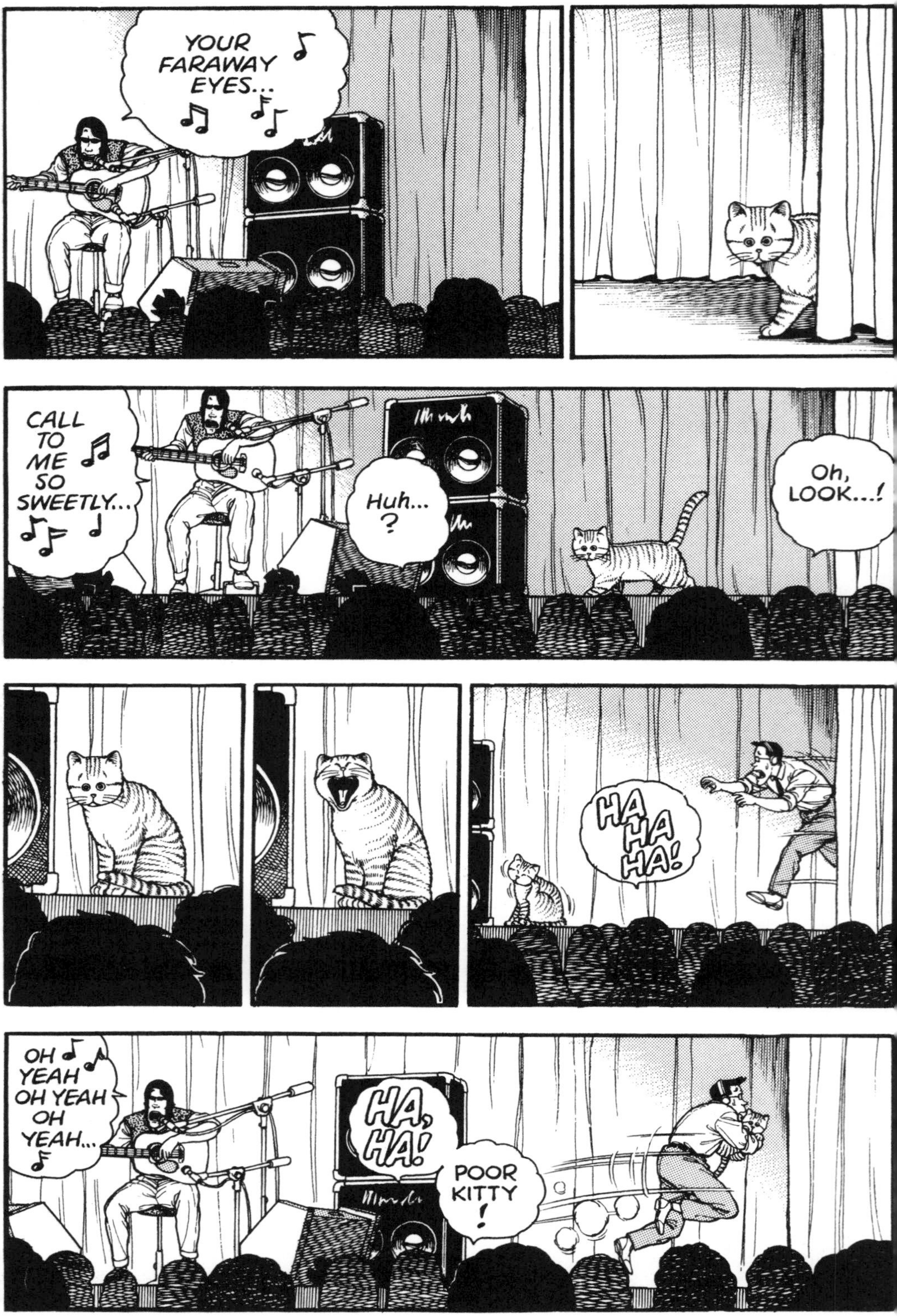
YOUR FARAWAY EYES...
CALL TO ME SO SWEETLY...
Huh...?
Oh, LOOK...!
HA HA HA!
OH YEAH OH YEAH OH YEAH...
HA, HA!
POOR KITTY!

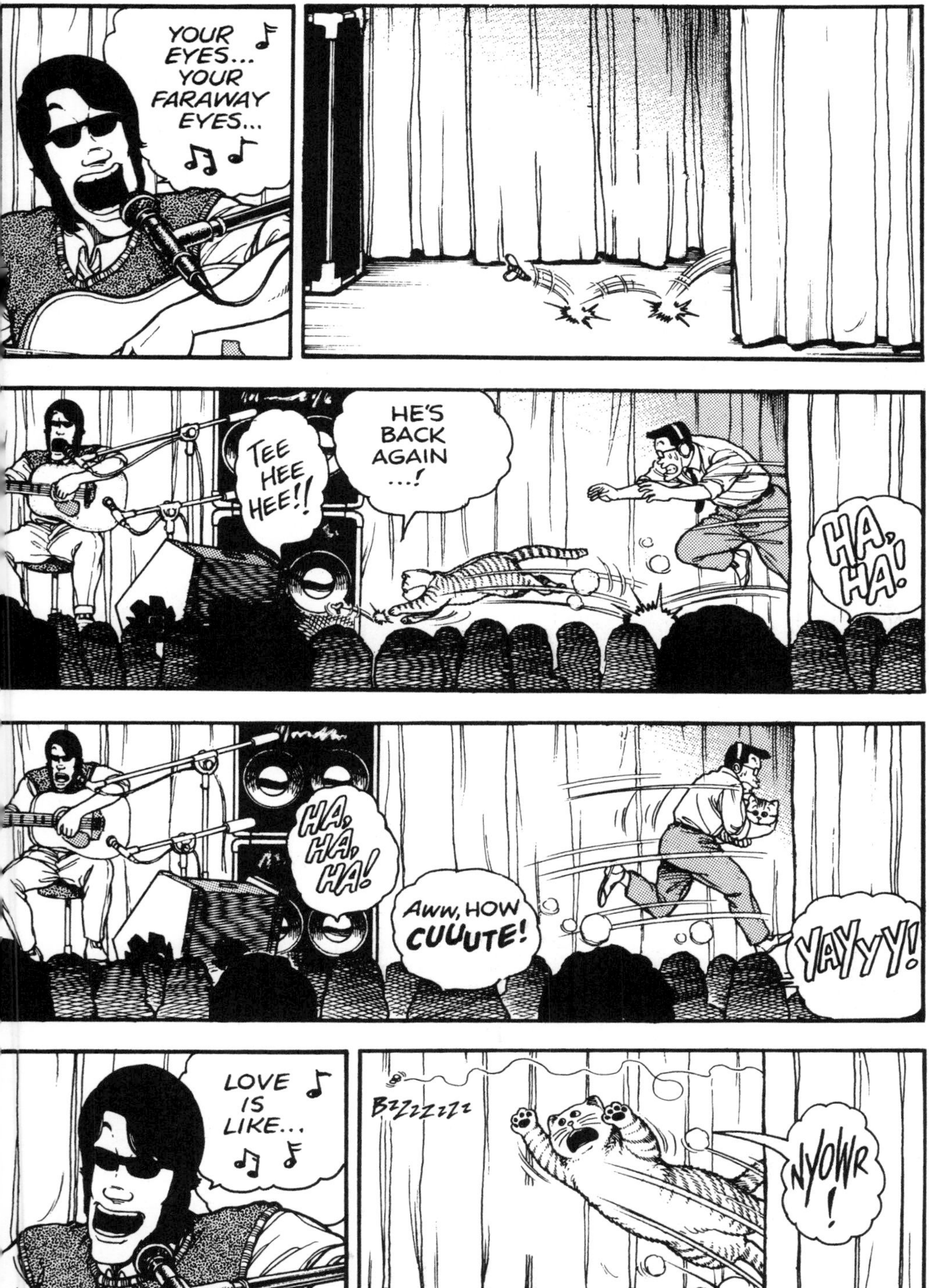
YOUR EYES... YOUR FARAWAY EYES...
TEE HEE HEE!!
HE'S BACK AGAIN ...!
HA, HA!
HA, HA, HA!
AWW, HOW CUUUTE!
YAYYY!
LOVE IS LIKE...
BZZZZZZZ
NYOWR!

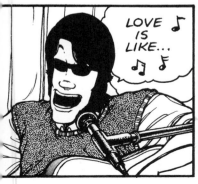

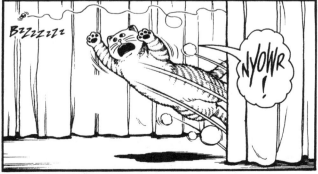

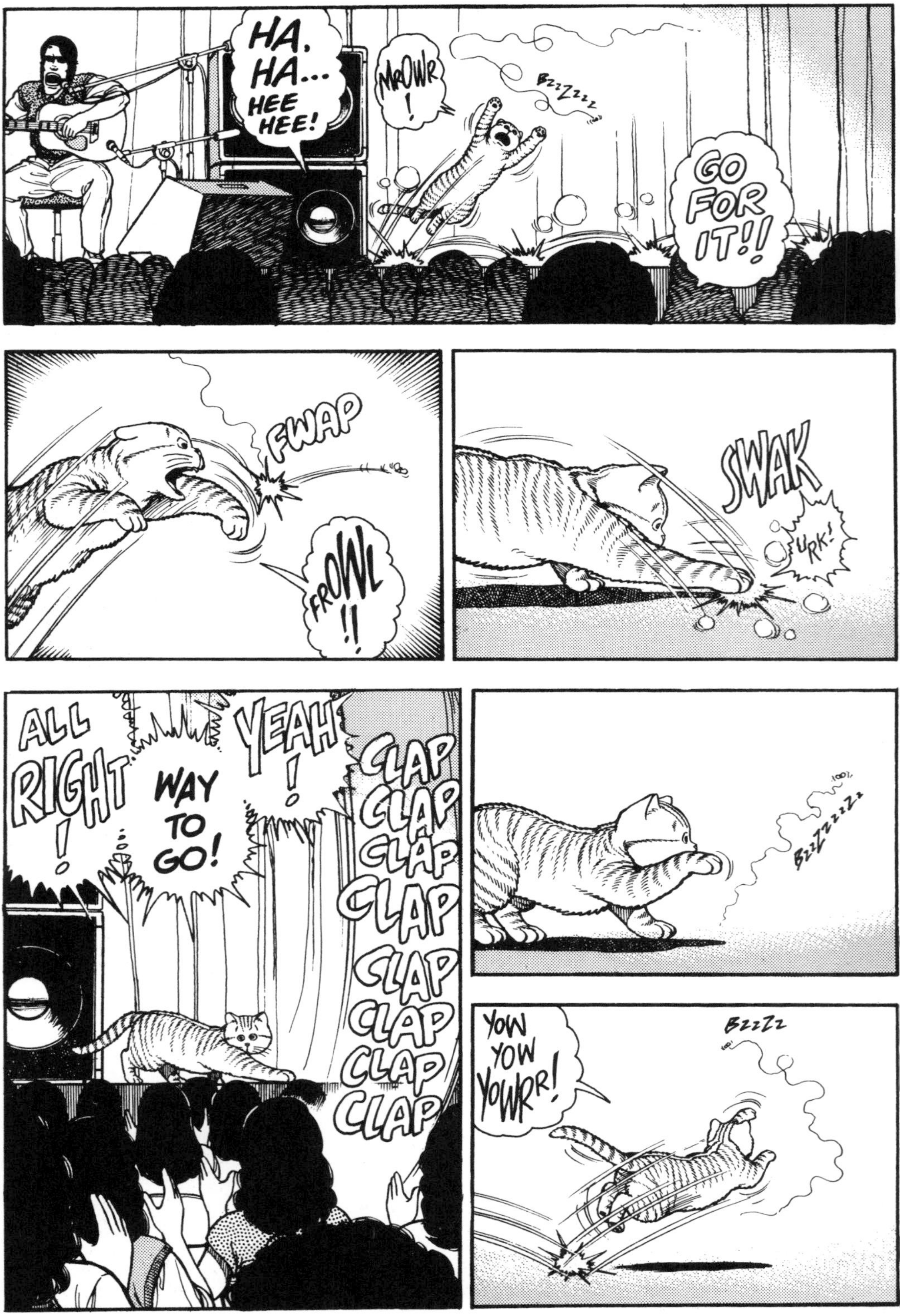
HA, HA... HEE HEE!
MROWR!
BZZZZZZ
GO FOR IT!!
FWAP
FROWL!!
SWAK
URK!
ALL RIGHT!
WAY TO GO!
YEAH!
CLAP CLAP CLAP CLAP CLAP CLAP CLAP CLAP
BZZZZZZZZ
YOW YOW YOWRR!
BZZZZ

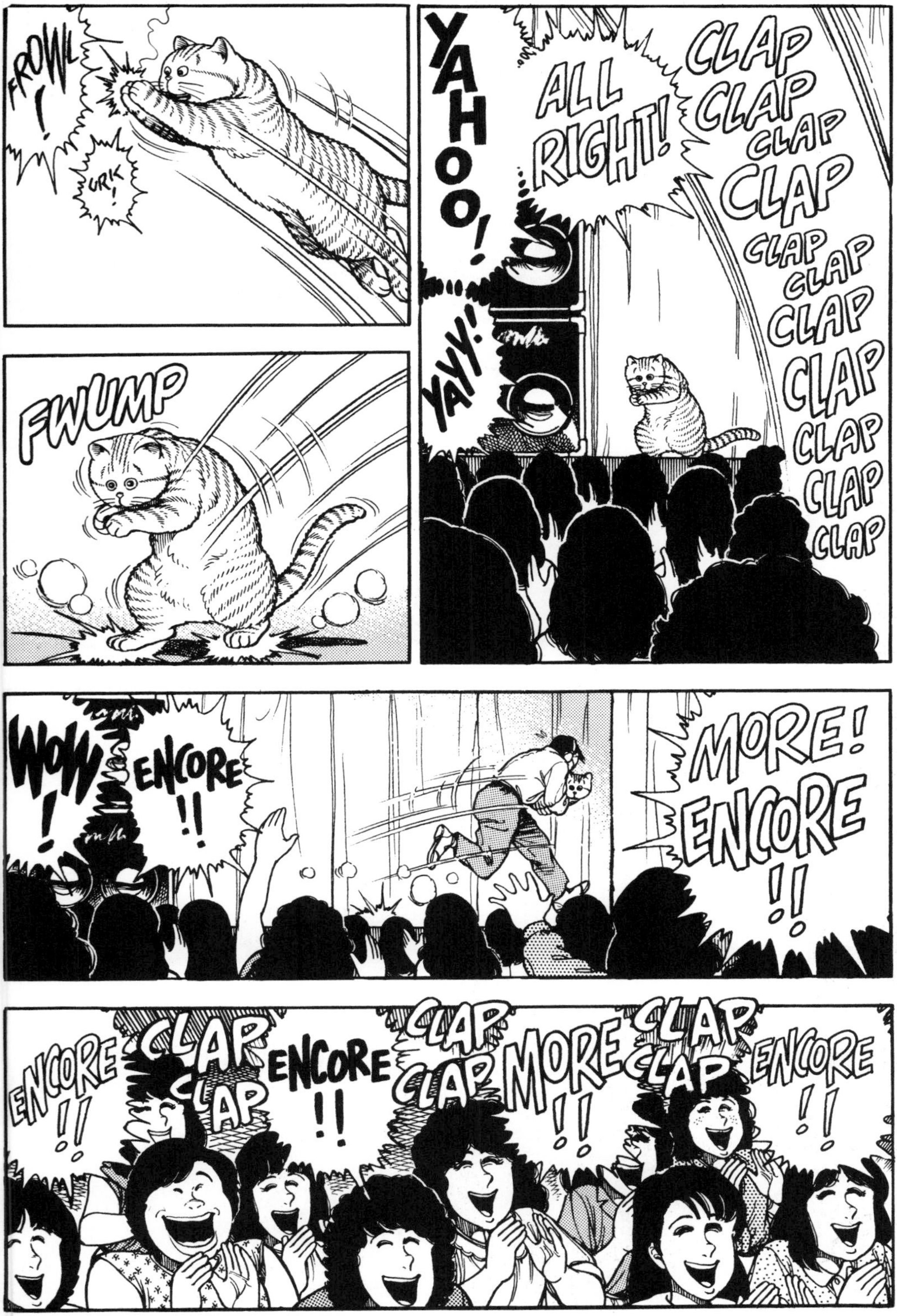

FROWL!
URK!
YAHOO!
ALL RIGHT!
CLAP CLAP CLAP CLAP CLAP CLAP CLAP CLAP CLAP CLAP CLAP
YAYY!
FWUMP
WOW!
ENCORE!!
MORE! ENCORE!!
ENCORE!!
CLAP CLAP
ENCORE!!
CLAP CLAP
MORE!!
CLAP CLAP
ENCORE!!

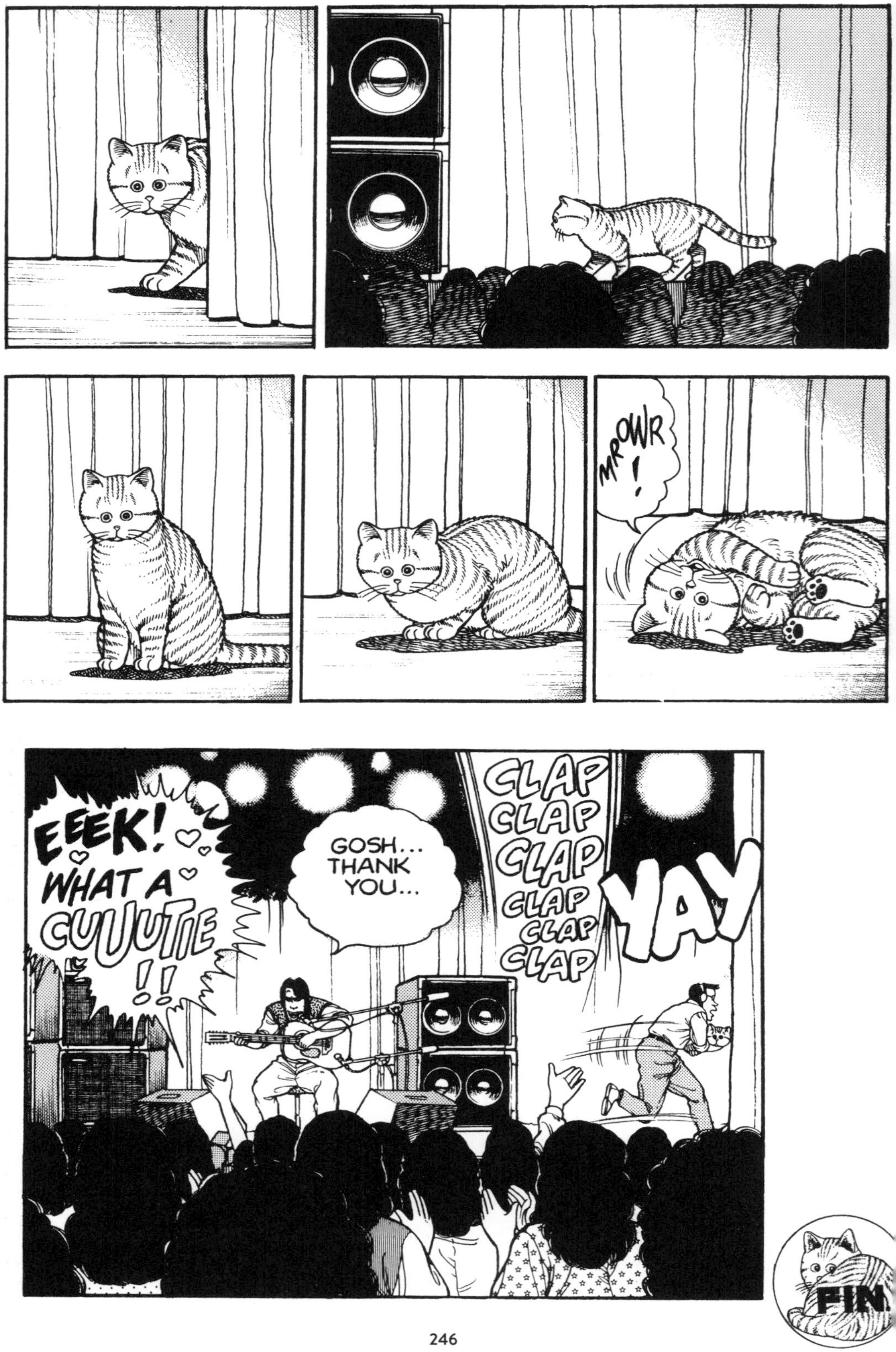
MROWR !
EEEK! WHAT A CUUUTIE !!
GOSH... THANK YOU...
CLAP CLAP CLAP CLAP CLAP CLAP
YAY
FIN

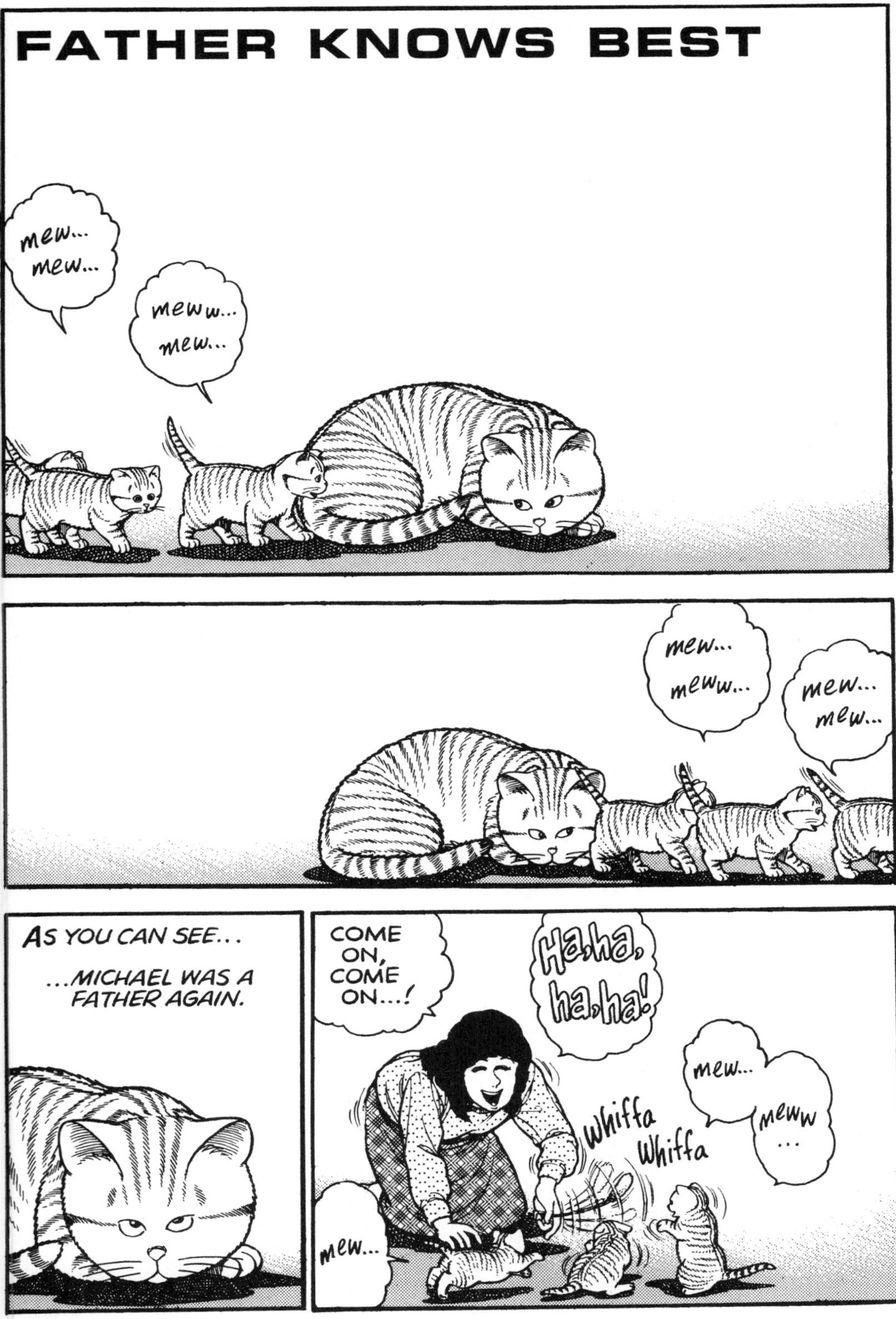
FATHER KNOWS BEST
mew... mew...
meww... mew...
mew... meww...
mew... mew...
AS YOU CAN SEE...
...MICHAEL WAS A FATHER AGAIN.
COME ON, COME ON...!
Ha, ha, ha, ha!
mew...
meww ...
whiffa Whiffa
mew...

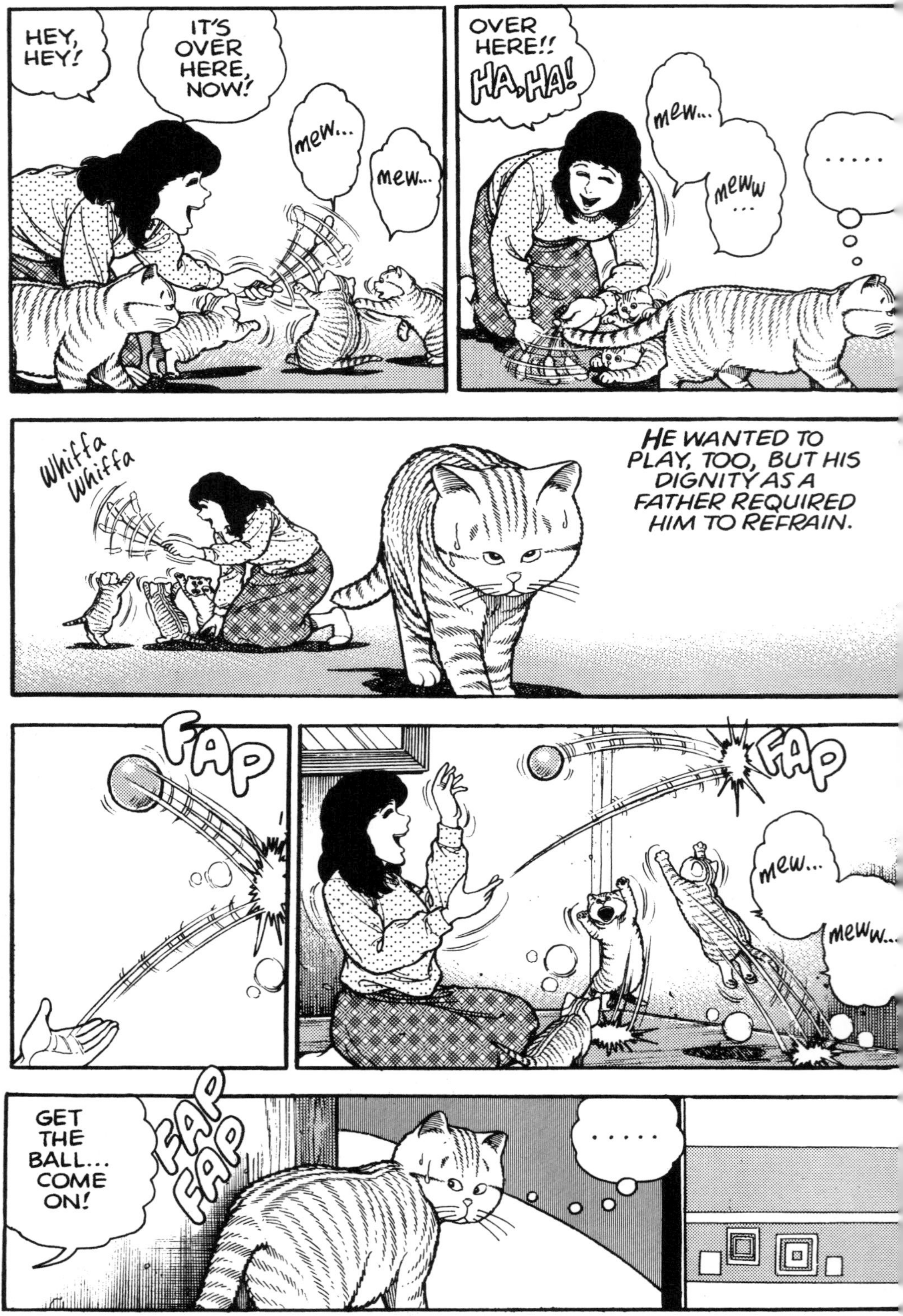

HEY, HEY!
IT'S OVER HERE, NOW!
mew...
mew...
OVER HERE!!
HA, HA!
mew...
meww ...
.....
Whiffa Whiffa
HE WANTED TO PLAY, TOO, BUT HIS DIGNITY AS A FATHER REQUIRED HIM TO REFRAIN.
FAP
FAP
mew...
meww...
GET THE BALL... COME ON!
FAP FAP
.....

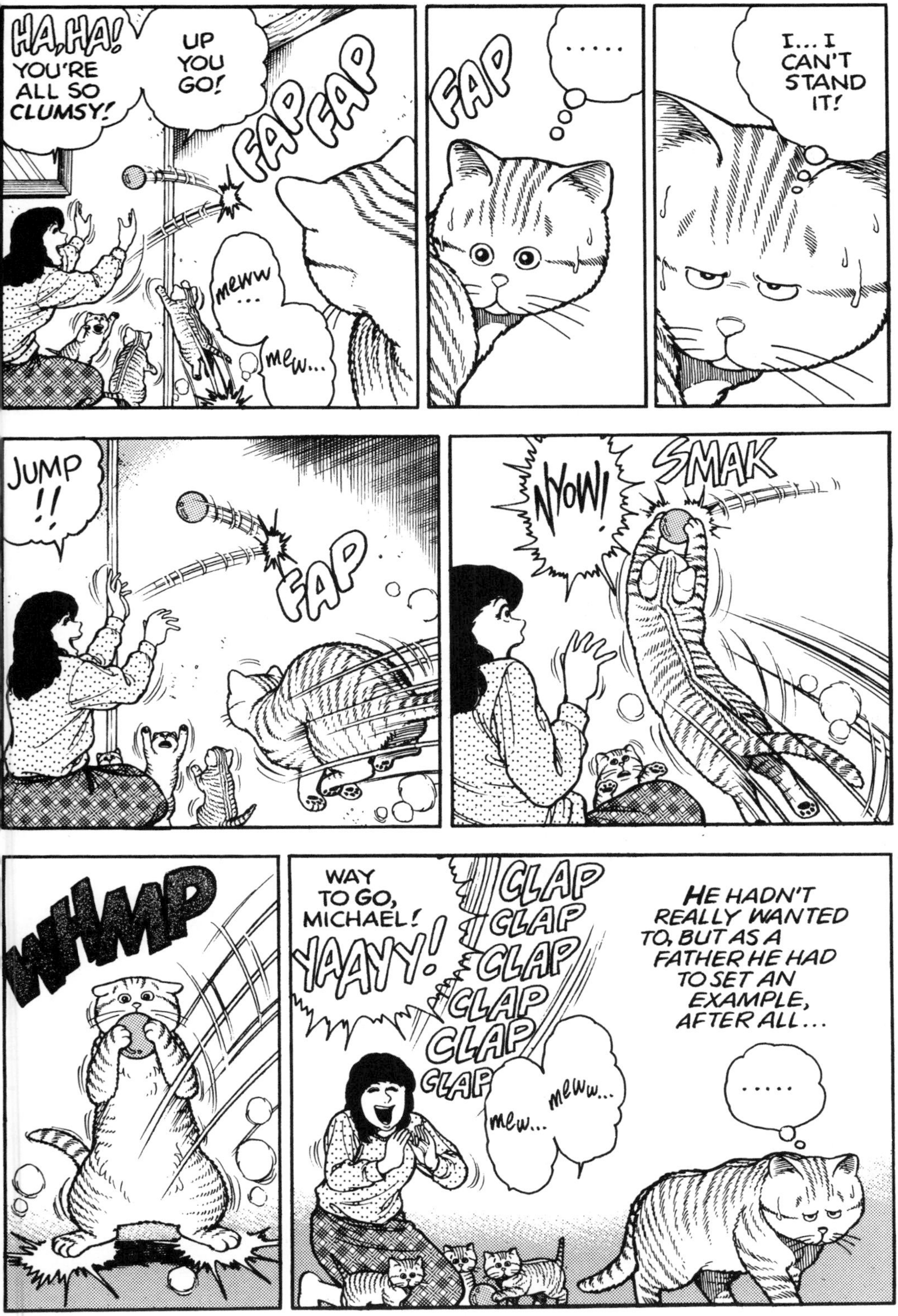
HA, HA! YOU'RE ALL SO CLUMSY!
UP YOU GO!
FAP FAP
meww ...
mew...
FAP
.....
I... I CAN'T STAND IT!
JUMP !!
FAP
NYOW!
SMAK
WHMP
WAY TO GO, MICHAEL!
YAAYY!
CLAP CLAP CLAP CLAP CLAP CLAP
mew... meww...
HE HADN'T REALLY WANTED TO, BUT AS A FATHER HE HAD TO SET AN EXAMPLE, AFTER ALL...
.....

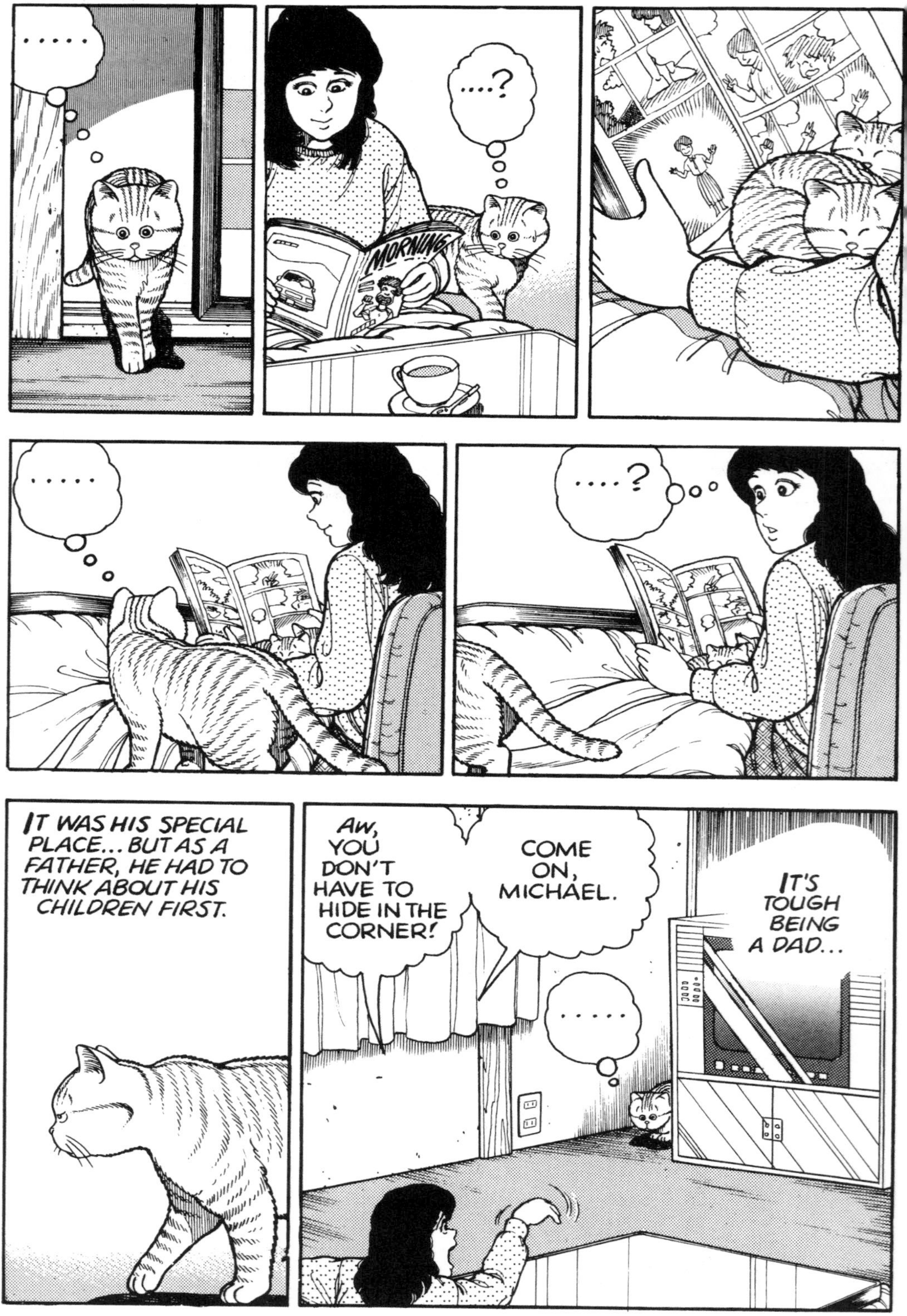
.....
....?
MORNING
.....
....?
IT WAS HIS SPECIAL PLACE... BUT AS A FATHER, HE HAD TO THINK ABOUT HIS CHILDREN FIRST.
AW, YOU DON'T HAVE TO HIDE IN THE CORNER!
COME ON, MICHAEL.
IT'S TOUGH BEING A DAD...
.....

ZZZZZ

ZZZZZ

FINALLY...
THEY'RE
ZONKED
OUT.

OKAY,
THEN
...

BTAM

Oh,
MICHAEL
... ♪

TIME
TO
PLAY
!!

HERE
WE
GO...

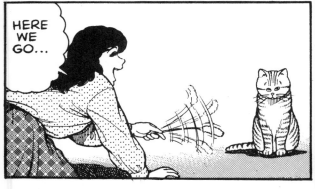

COME
ON...
YOU
CAN'T
FOOL
ME!

HEY,
HEY!

.....

Whiffa

Whiffa
Whiffa

.....

251

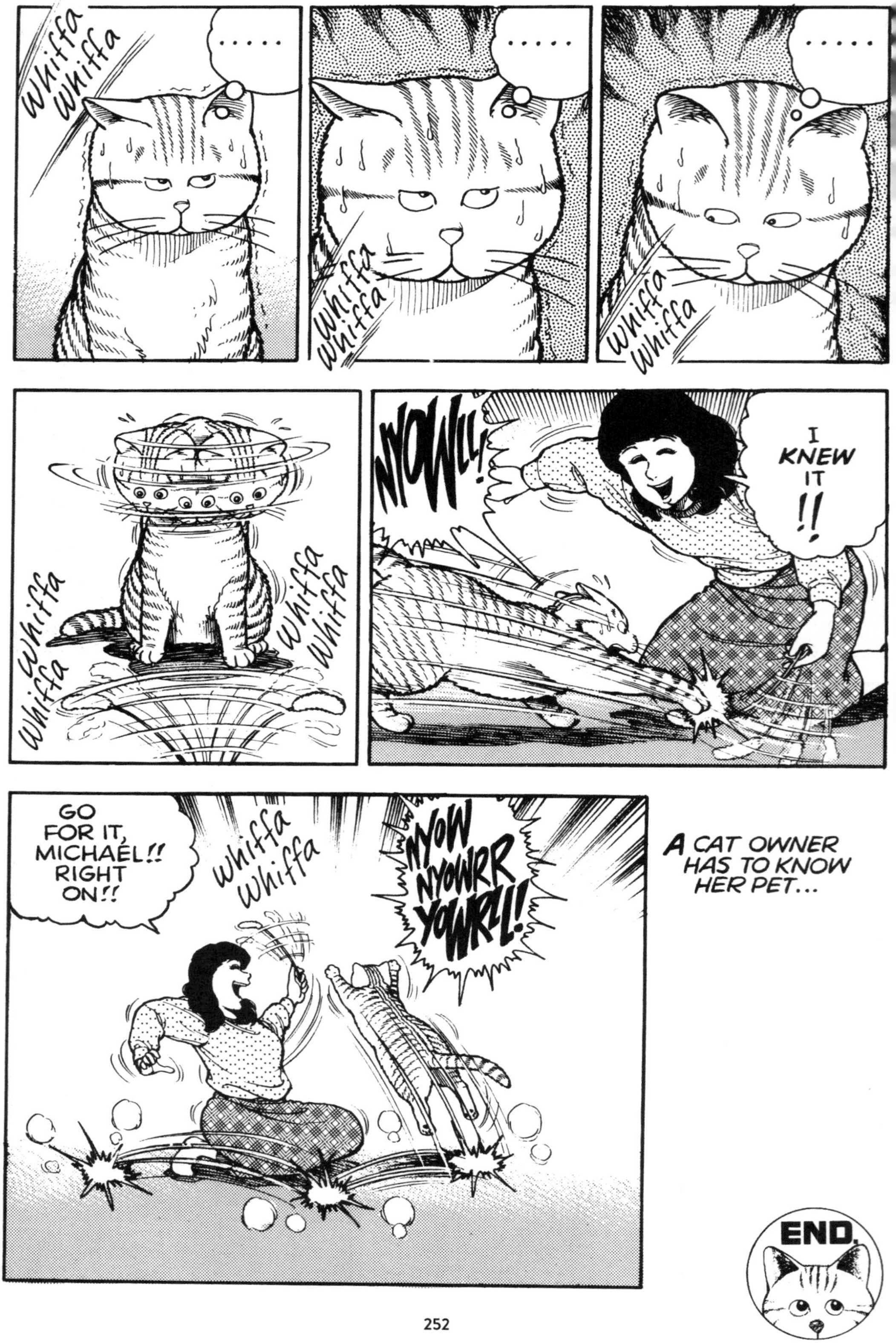
Whiffa Whiffa
......
......
Whiffa Whiffa
......
Whiffa Whiffa
Whiffa Whiffa
Whiffa Whiffa
NYOWLL!!
I KNEW IT !!
GO FOR IT, MICHAEL!! RIGHT ON!!
whiffa whiffa
NYOW NYOWRR YOWRLL!
A CAT OWNER HAS TO KNOW HER PET...
END.

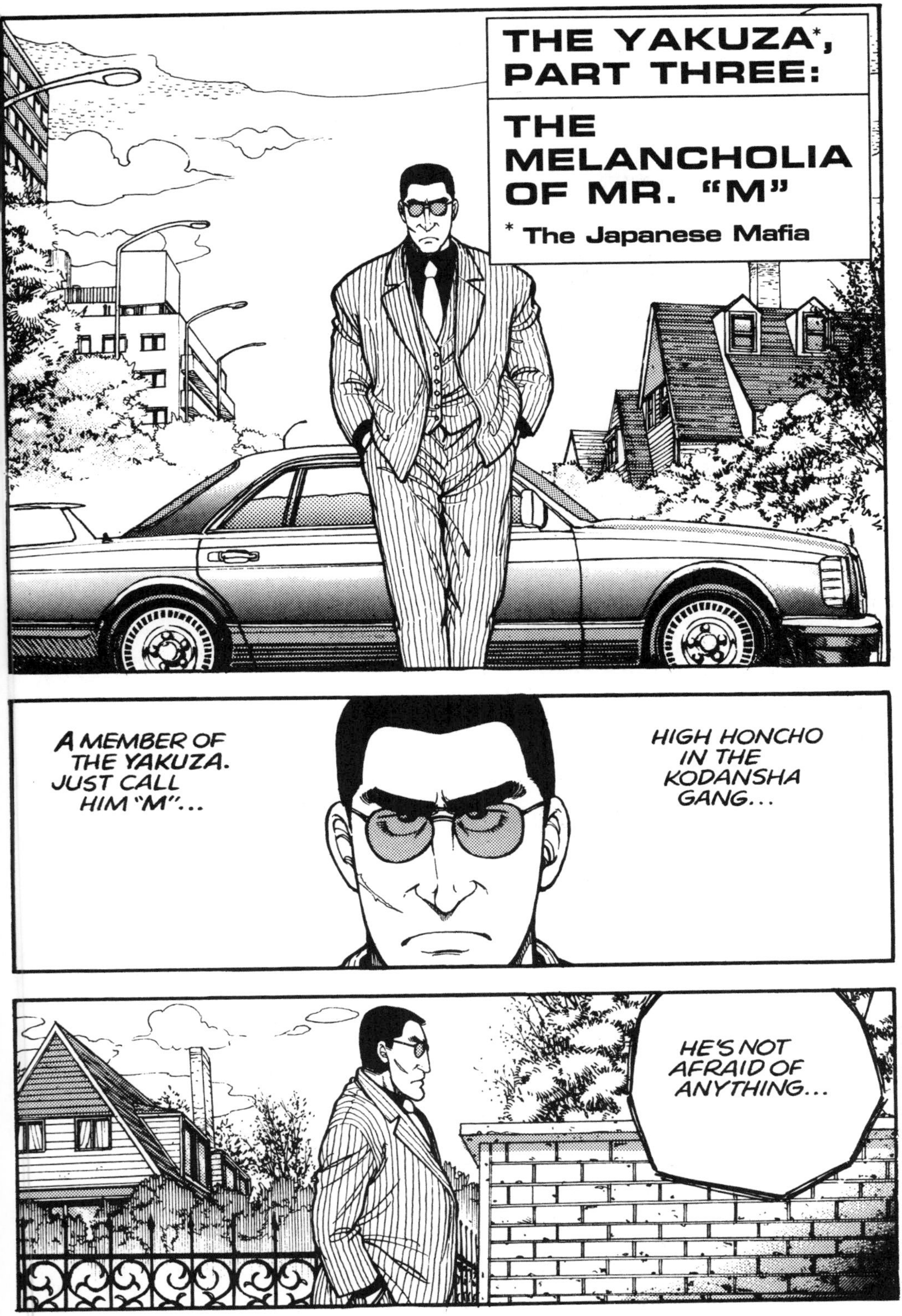
THE YAKUZA*, PART THREE:
THE MELANCHOLIA OF MR. "M"
* The Japanese Mafia
A MEMBER OF THE YAKUZA. JUST CALL HIM "M"...
HIGH HONCHO IN THE KODANSHA GANG...
HE'S NOT AFRAID OF ANYTHING...

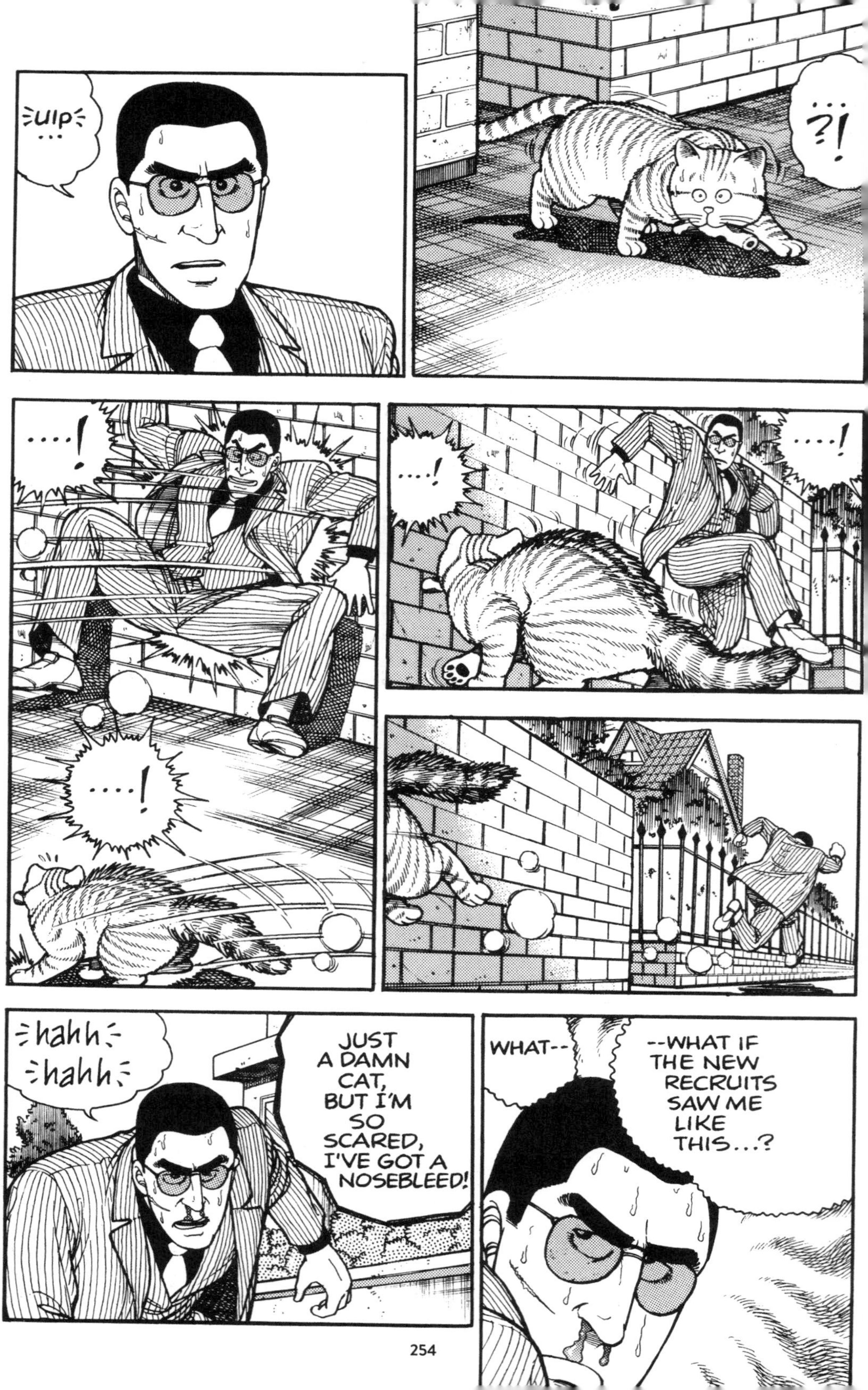
ulp
...
...
?!
....!
....!
....!
....!
hahh
hahh
JUST A DAMN CAT, BUT I'M SO SCARED, I'VE GOT A NOSEBLEED!
WHAT--
--WHAT IF THE NEW RECRUITS SAW ME LIKE THIS...?

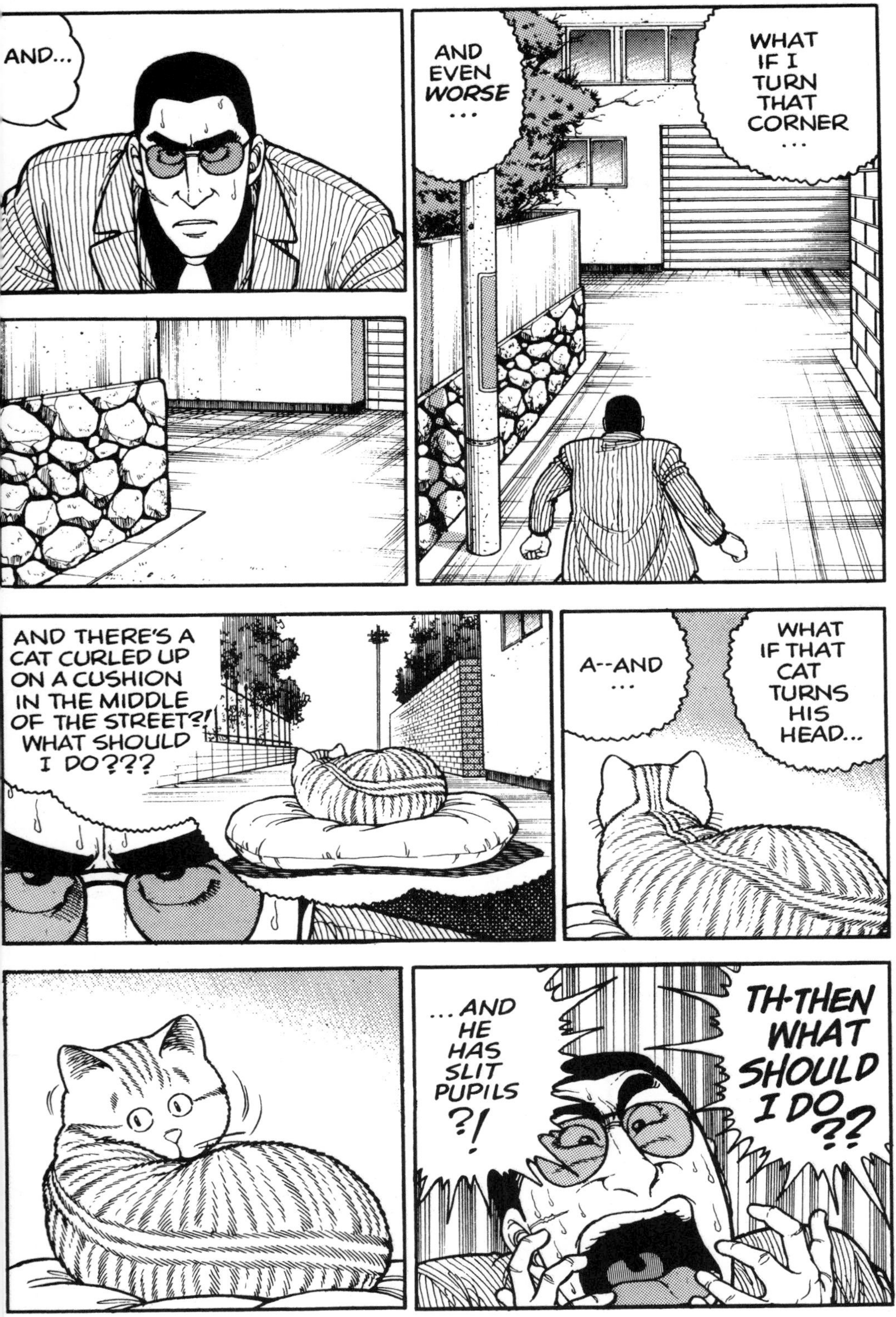
AND...
AND EVEN WORSE ...
WHAT IF I TURN THAT CORNER ...
AND THERE'S A CAT CURLED UP ON A CUSHION IN THE MIDDLE OF THE STREET?! WHAT SHOULD I DO???
A--AND ...
WHAT IF THAT CAT TURNS HIS HEAD...
... AND HE HAS SLIT PUPILS ?!
TH-THEN WHAT SHOULD I DO ??

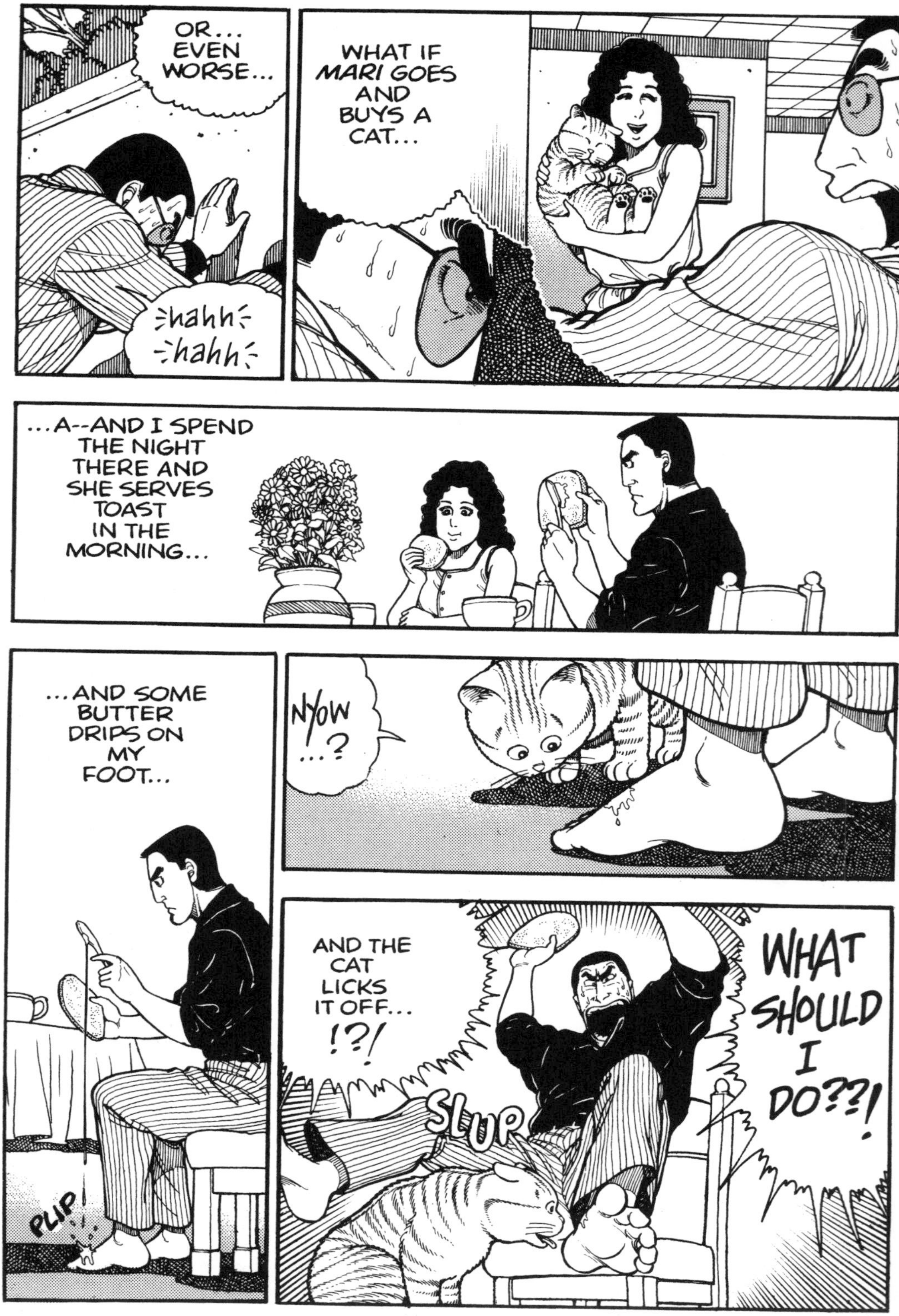
OR... EVEN WORSE...
hahh hahh
WHAT IF MARI GOES AND BUYS A CAT...
...A--AND I SPEND THE NIGHT THERE AND SHE SERVES TOAST IN THE MORNING...
...AND SOME BUTTER DRIPS ON MY FOOT...
PLIP
NYOW ...?
AND THE CAT LICKS IT OFF... !?!
SLUP
WHAT SHOULD I DO??!

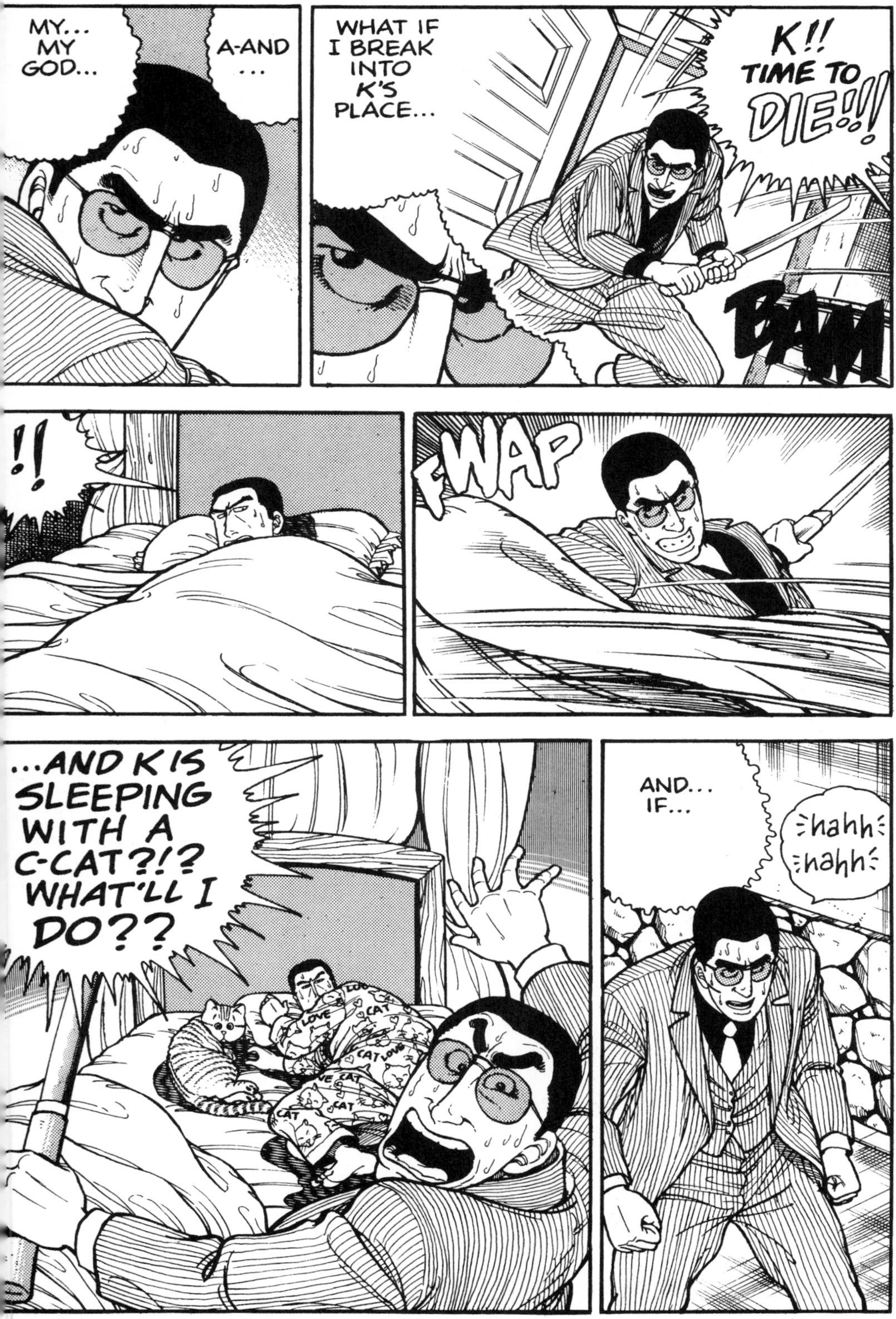
MY... MY GOD...
A-AND ...
WHAT IF I BREAK INTO K'S PLACE...
K!! TIME TO DIE!!!
BAM
!!
FWAP
...AND K IS SLEEPING WITH A C-CAT?!? WHAT'LL I DO??
LOVE
CAT
AND... IF...
hahh hahh

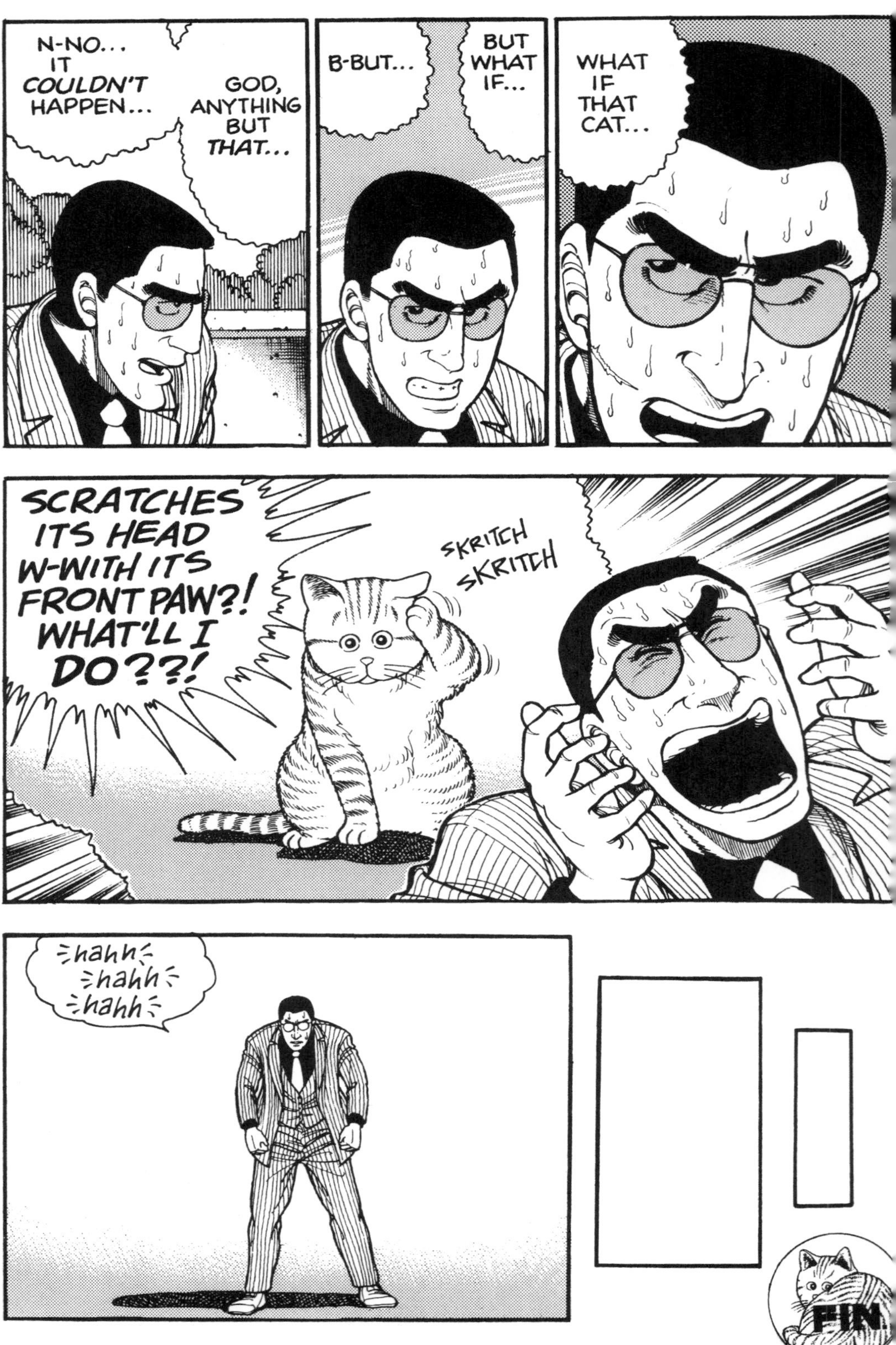

N-NO... IT COULDN'T HAPPEN...
GOD, ANYTHING BUT THAT...
B-BUT...
BUT WHAT IF...
WHAT IF THAT CAT...
SCRATCHES ITS HEAD W-WITH ITS FRONT PAW?! WHAT'LL I DO???!
SKRITCH SKRITCH
hahh hahh hahh
FIN

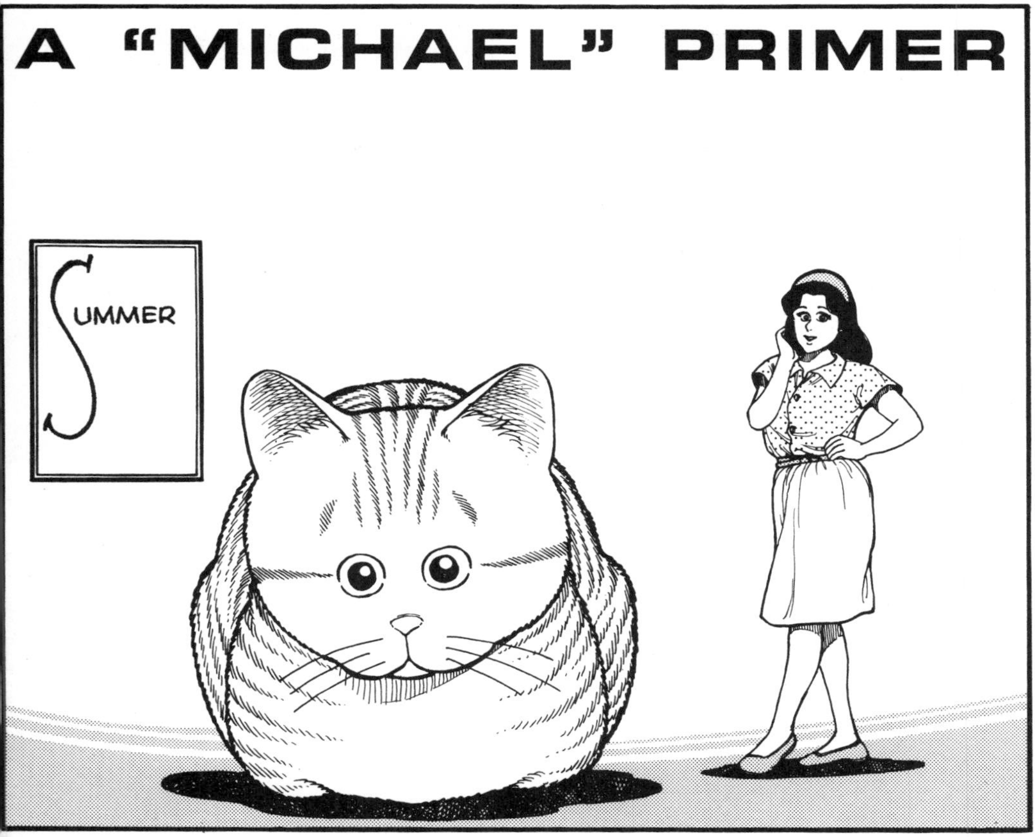
A "MICHAEL" PRIMER
SUMMER
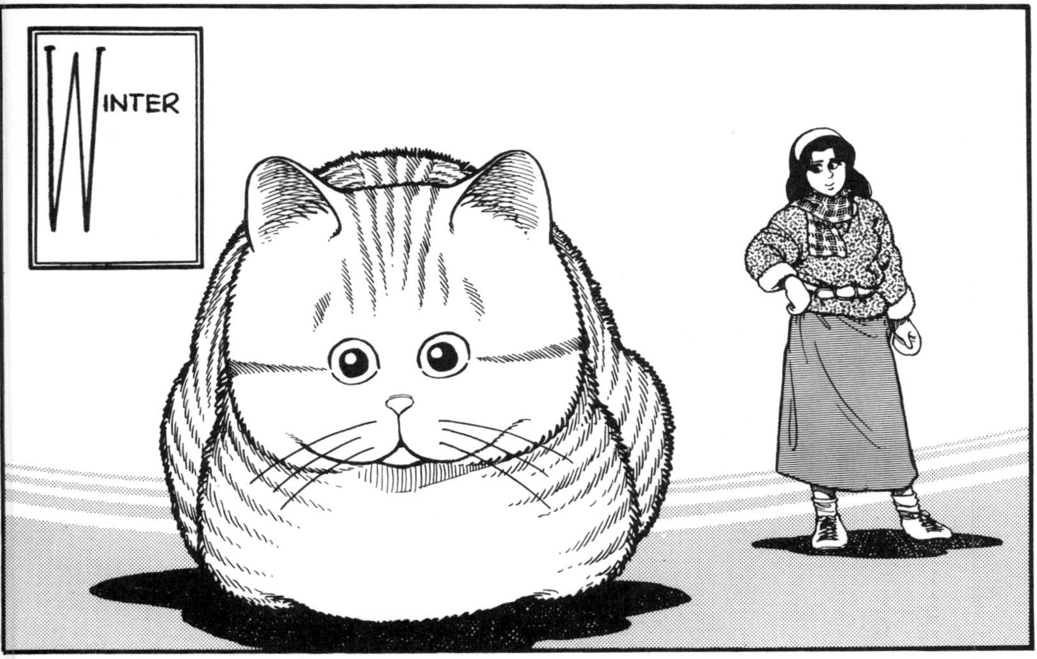
WINTER

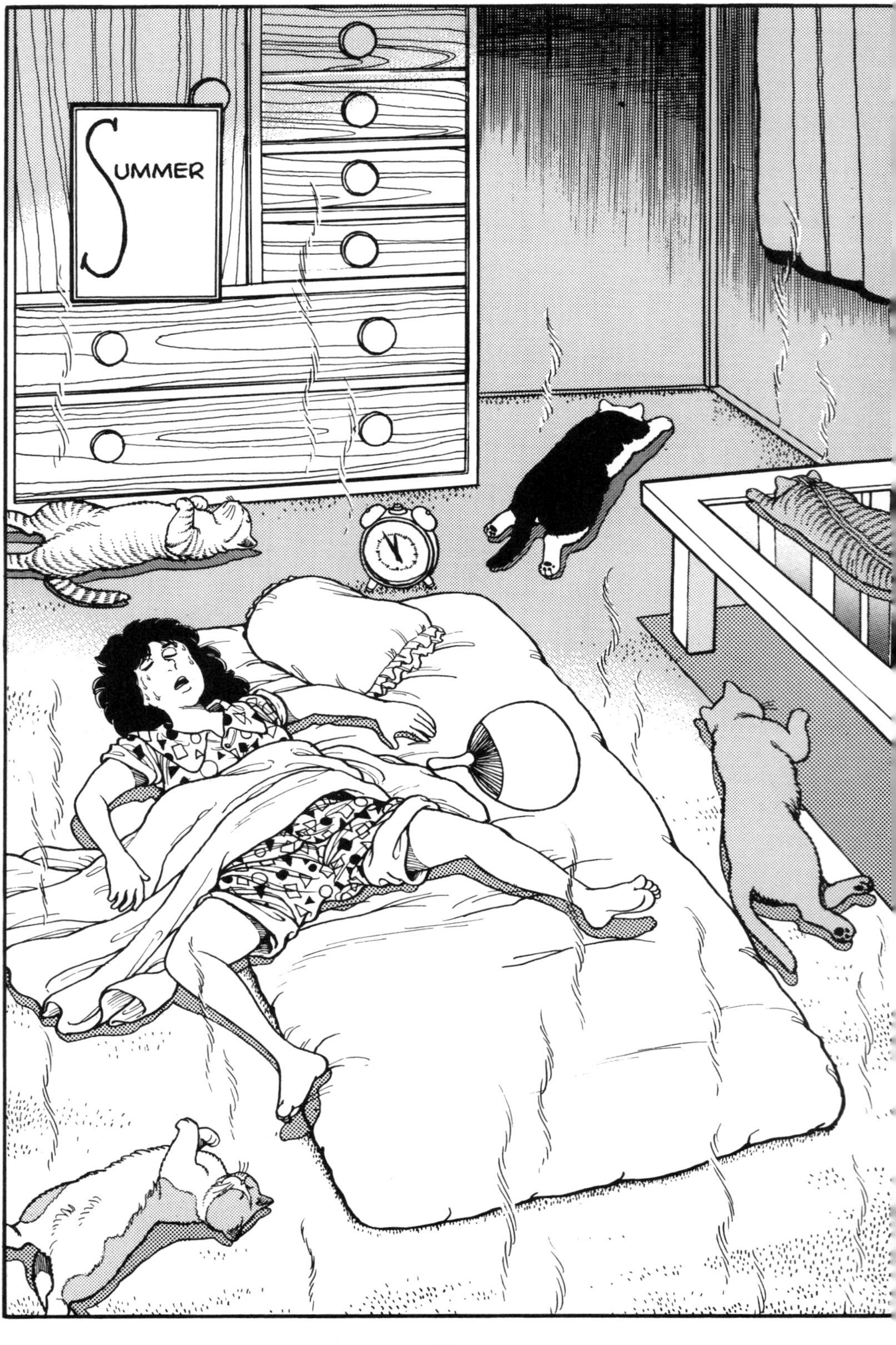
SUMMER

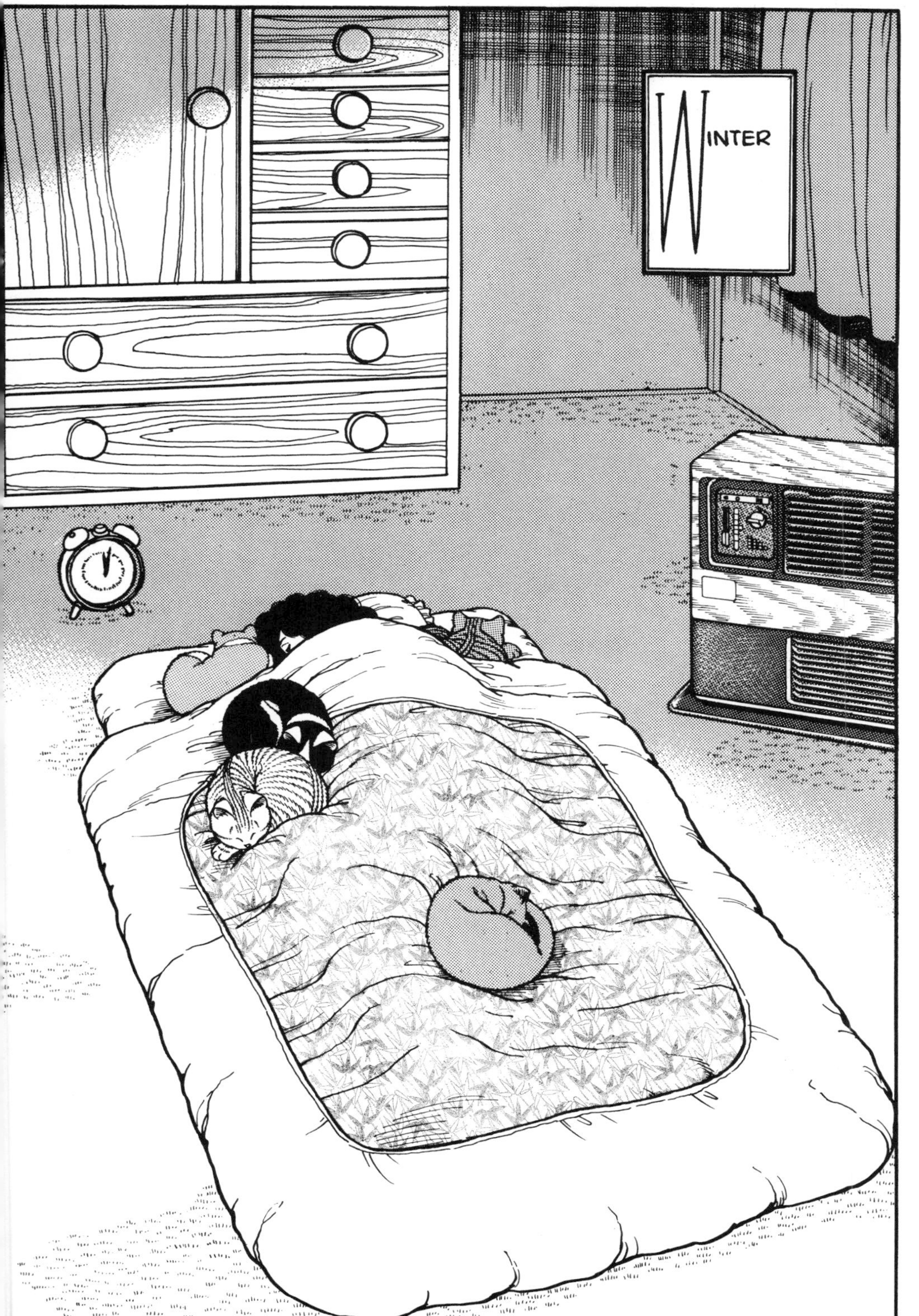
WINTER

DAY

NIGHT

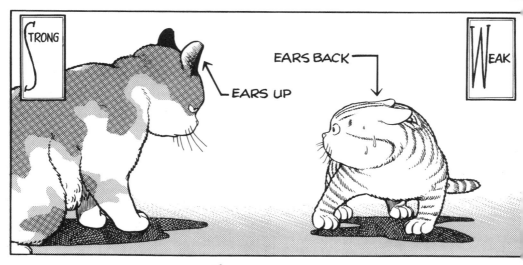

STRONG

WEAK

EARS UP

EARS BACK

WHEN HE'S ANGRY

FSSST

WHEN HE'S HAPPY

Prrr ♡ Prrr

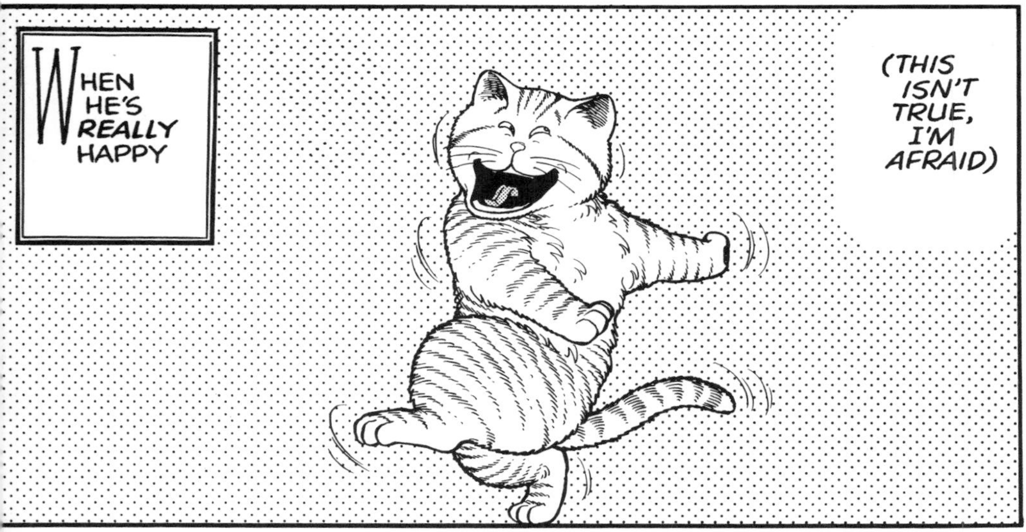
WHEN HE'S REALLY HAPPY
(THIS ISN'T TRUE, I'M AFRAID)

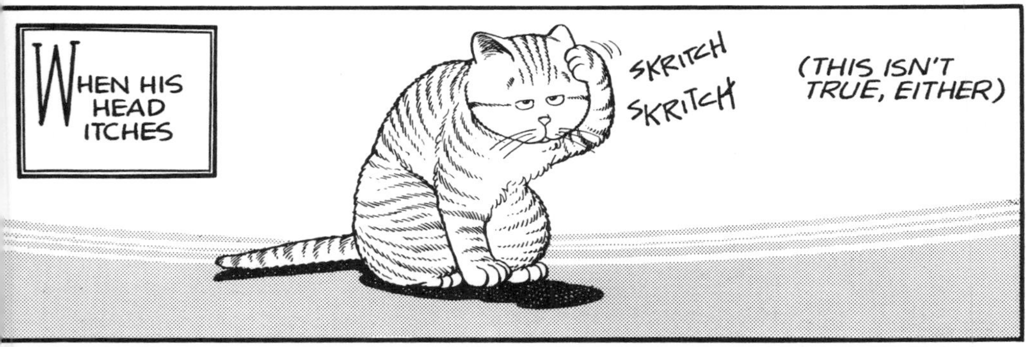
WHEN HIS HEAD ITCHES
SKRITCH
SKRITCH
(THIS ISN'T TRUE, EITHER)

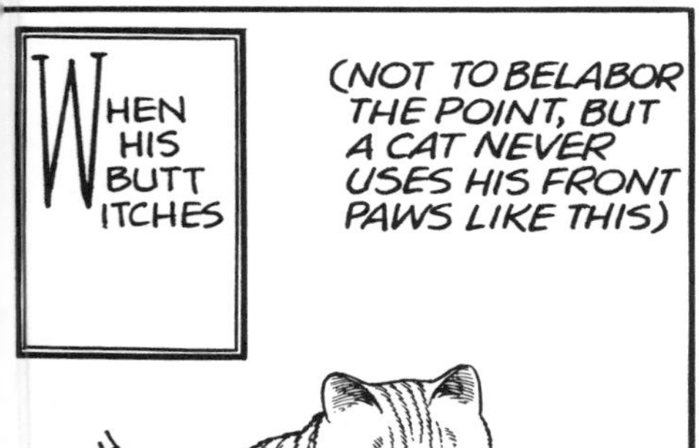
WHEN HIS BUTT ITCHES
(NOT TO BELABOR THE POINT, BUT A CAT NEVER USES HIS FRONT PAWS LIKE THIS)
SKRITCH
SKRITCH

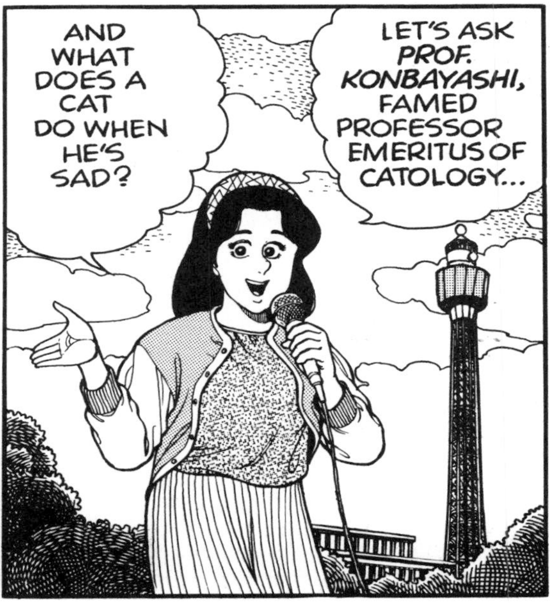
AND WHAT DOES A CAT DO WHEN HE'S SAD?
LET'S ASK PROF. KONBAYASHI, FAMED PROFESSOR EMERITUS OF CATOLOGY...

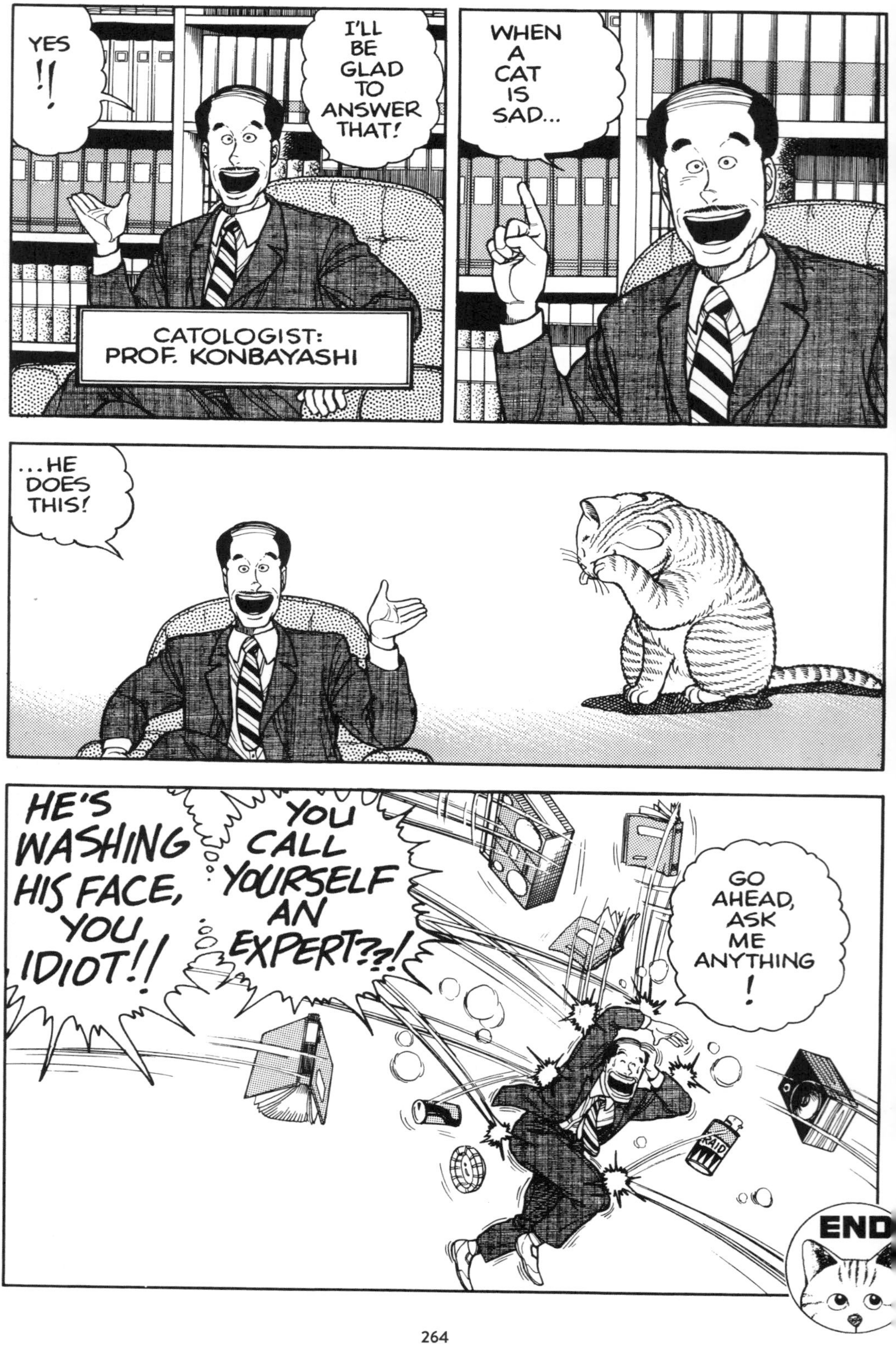
YES !!
I'LL BE GLAD TO ANSWER THAT!
CATOLOGIST: PROF. KONBAYASHI
WHEN A CAT IS SAD...
...HE DOES THIS!
HE'S WASHING HIS FACE, YOU IDIOT!!
YOU CALL YOURSELF AN EXPERT??!
GO AHEAD, ASK ME ANYTHING !
RAID
END

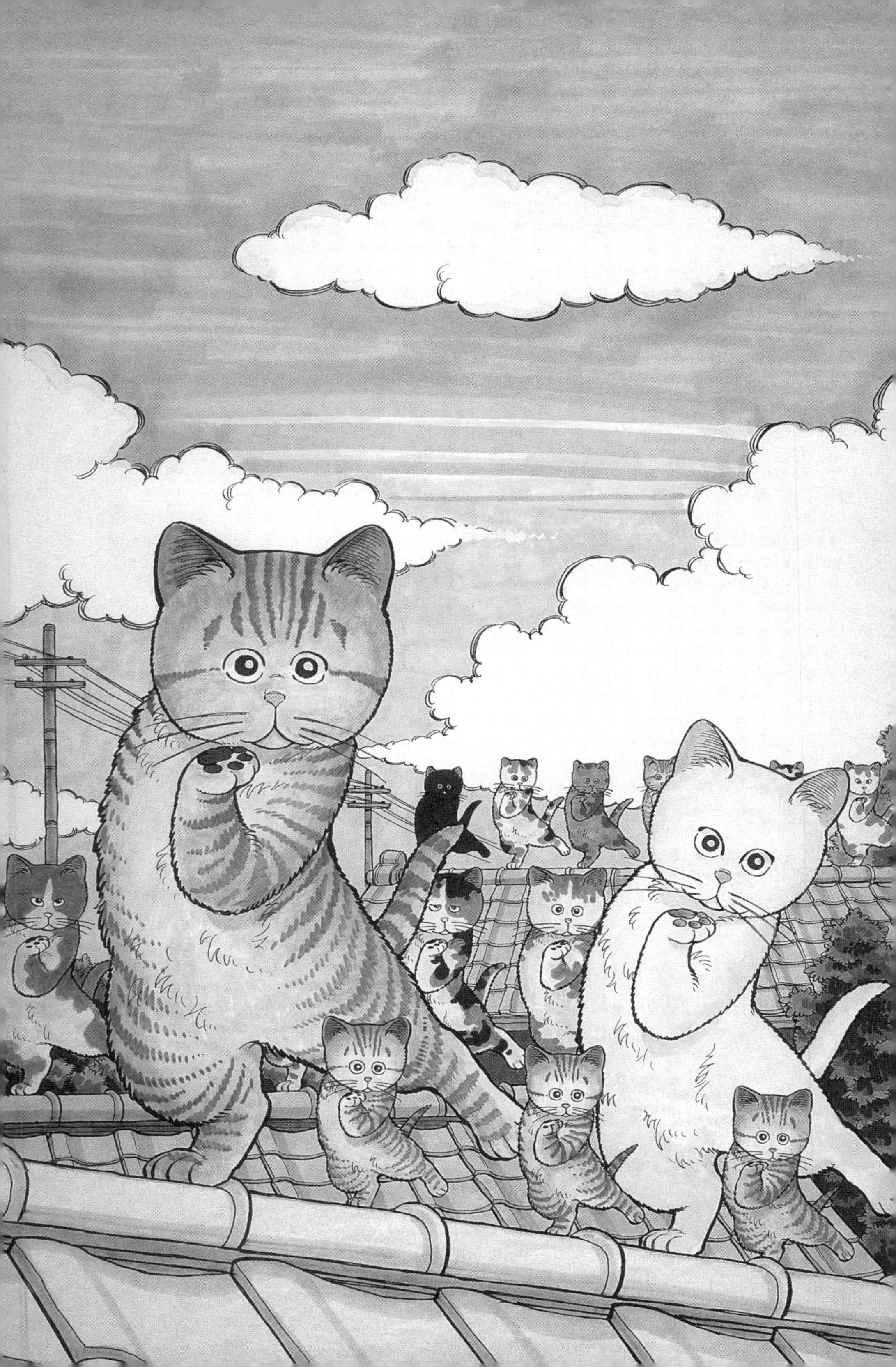

# WHAT'S MICHAEL?

## VOLUME 4: MICHAEL'S MAMBO

*This section was translated by Dana Lewis, Jeanne Sather,
and Toren Smith and lettered by L. Lois Buhalis.*

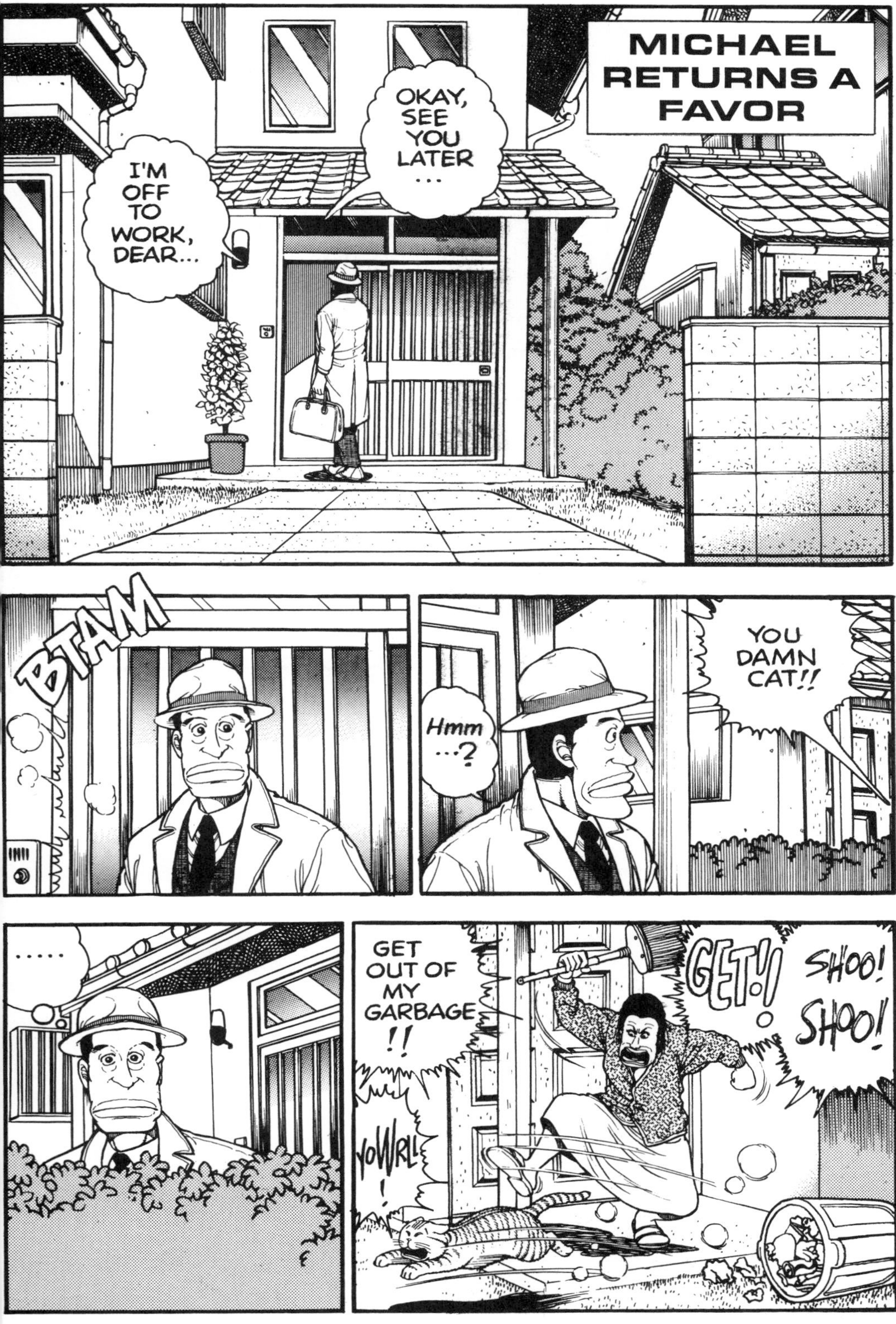
MICHAEL RETURNS A FAVOR
I'M OFF TO WORK, DEAR...
OKAY, SEE YOU LATER ...
BTAM
Hmm ...?
YOU DAMN CAT!!
.....
GET OUT OF MY GARBAGE !!
GET!!
SHOO! SHOO!
YOWRL!!

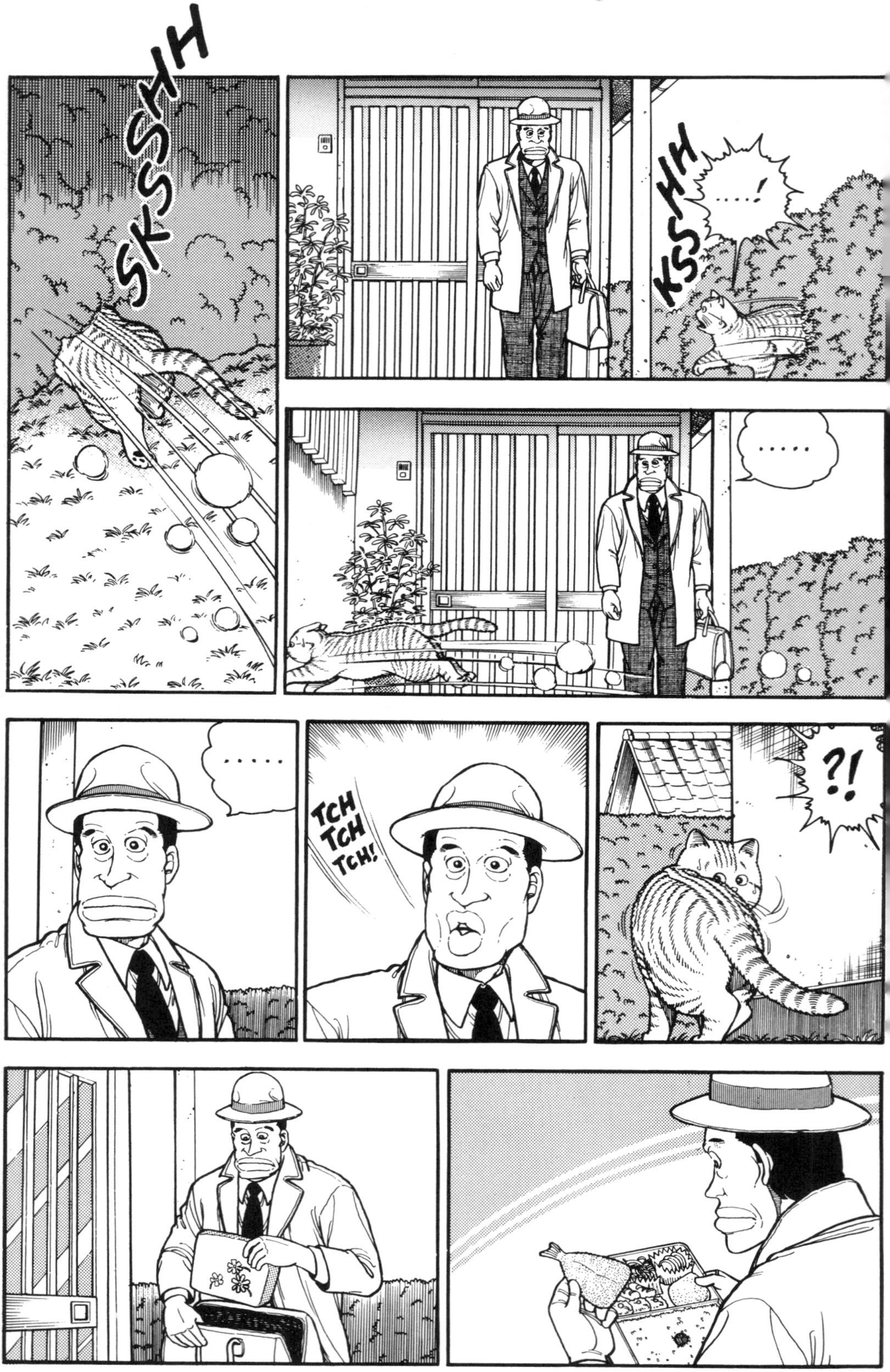
SKSSHH
KSSHH
.....!
.....
.....
TCH TCH TCH!
?!

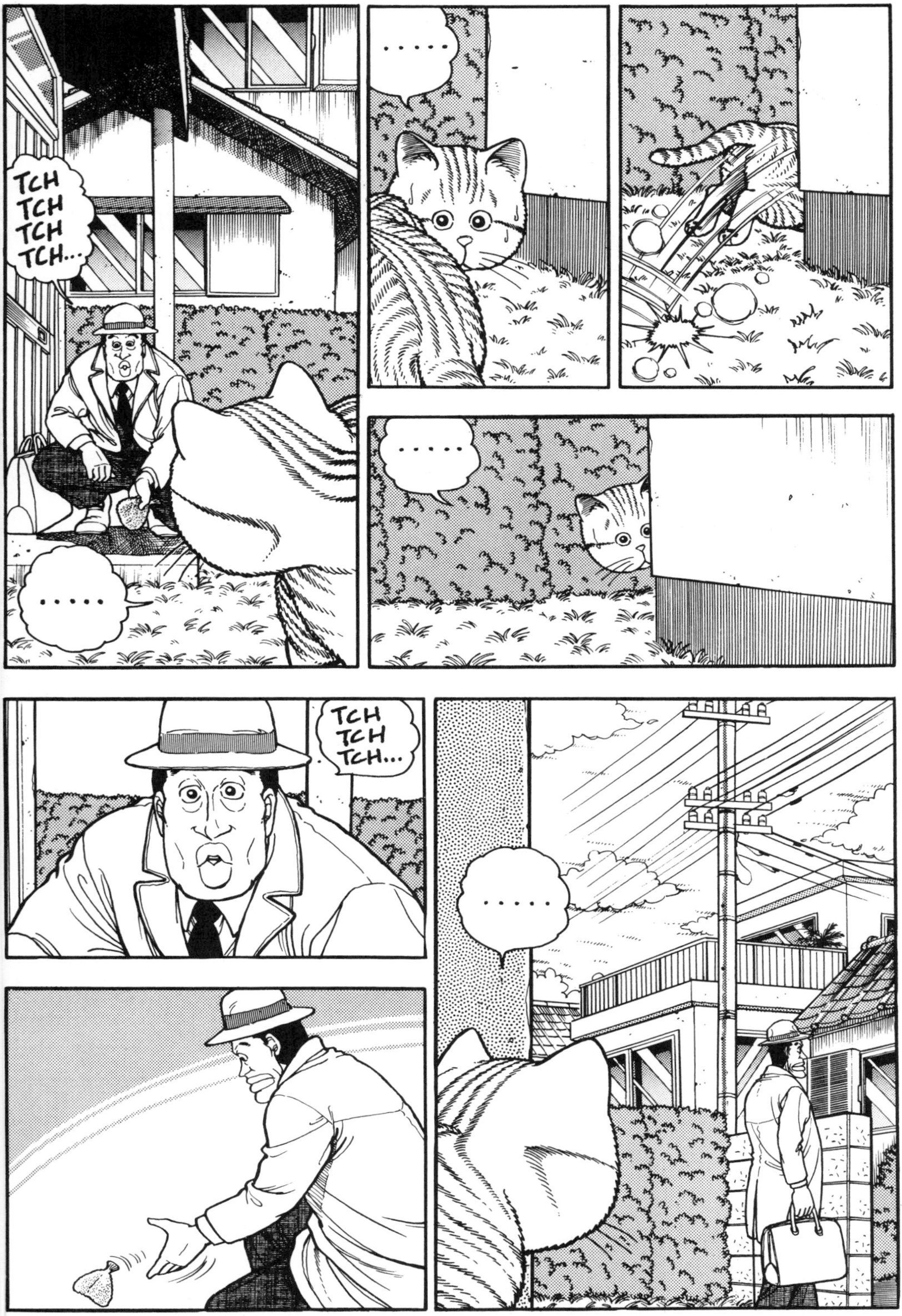
TCH TCH TCH TCH...
.....
.....
.....
TCH TCH TCH...
.....

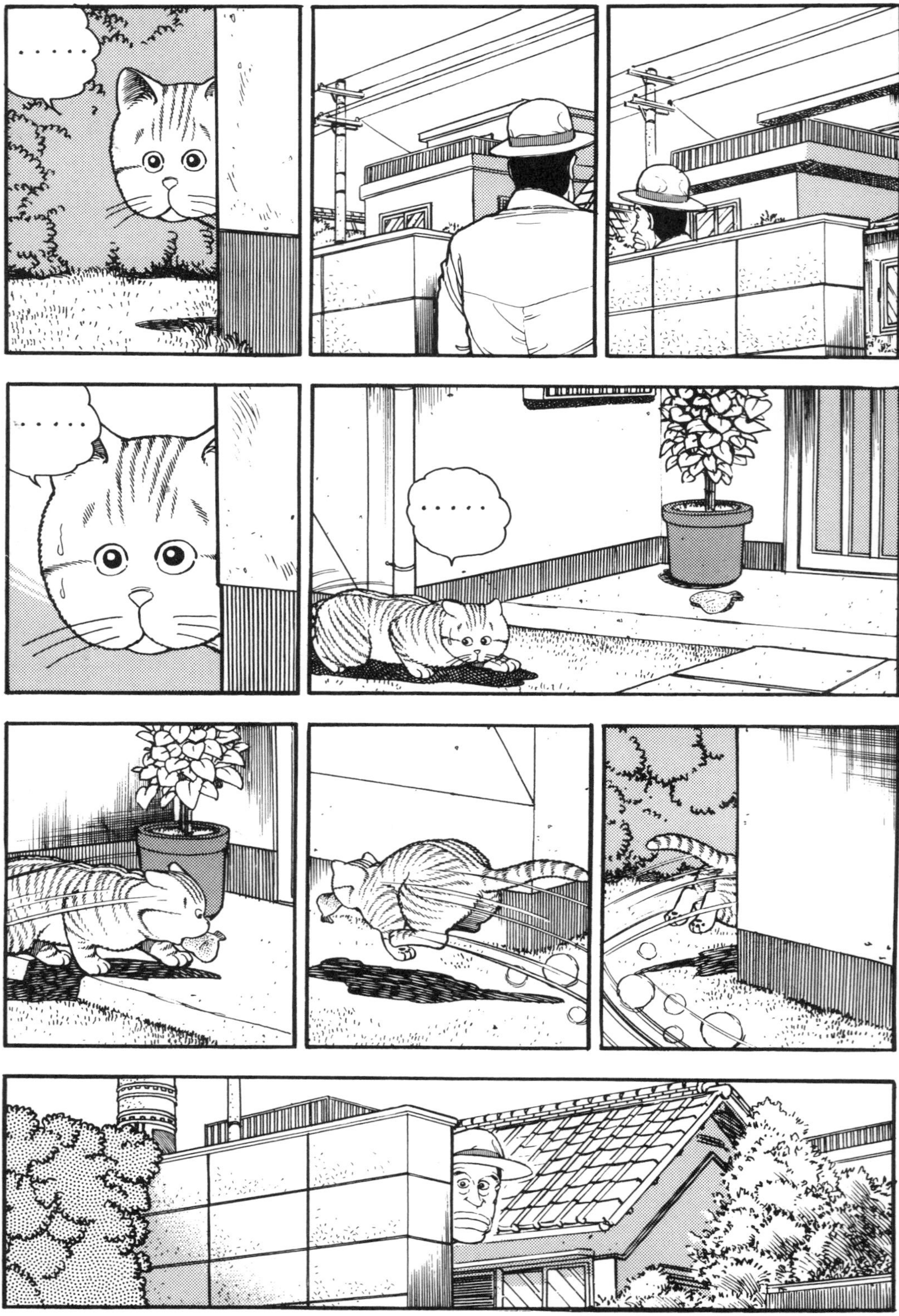

......
......
......

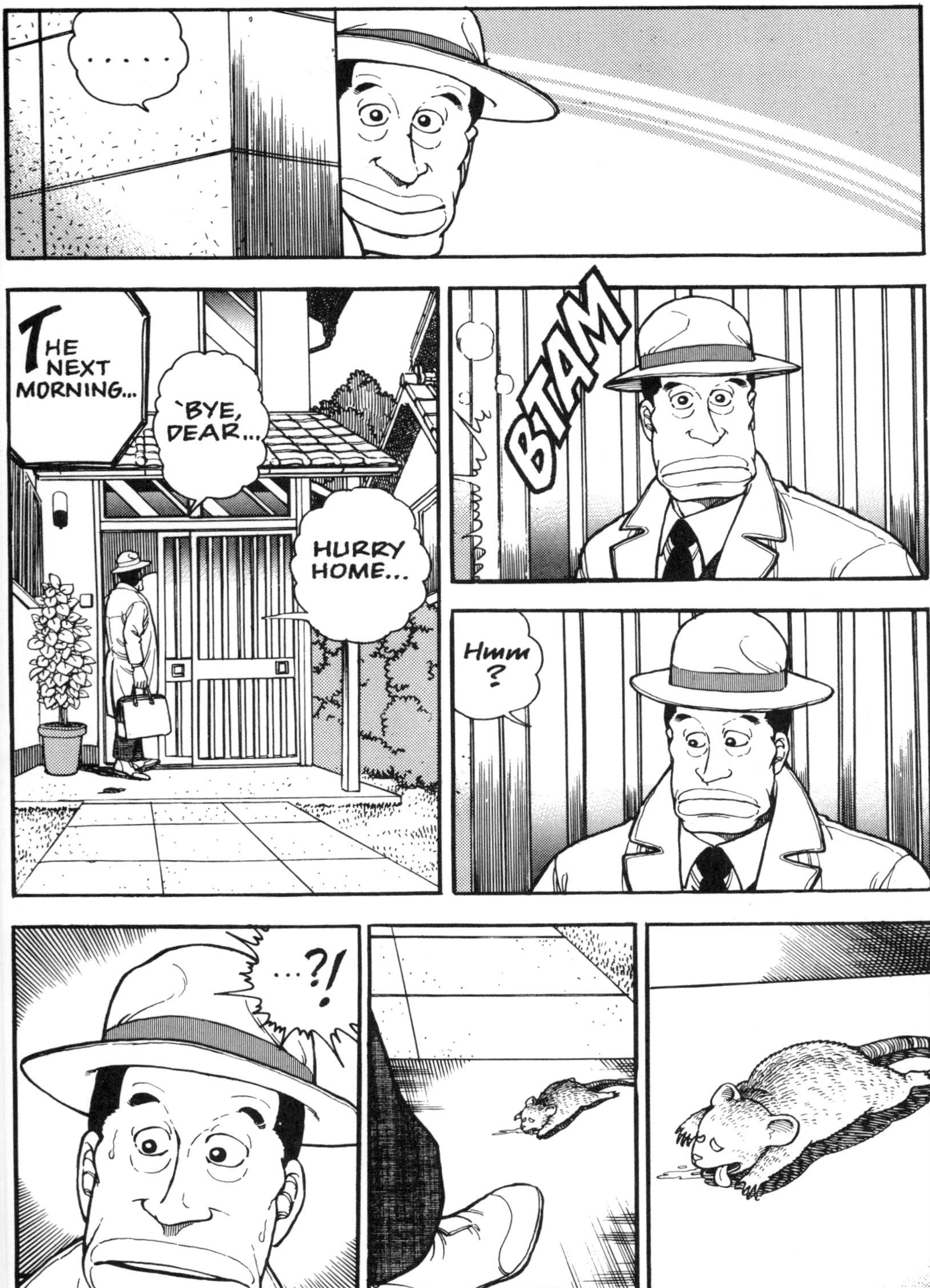

......
THE NEXT MORNING...
`BYE, DEAR...
HURRY HOME...
BTAM
Hmm ?
...?!

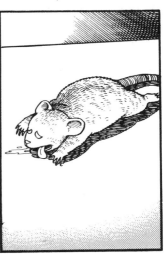

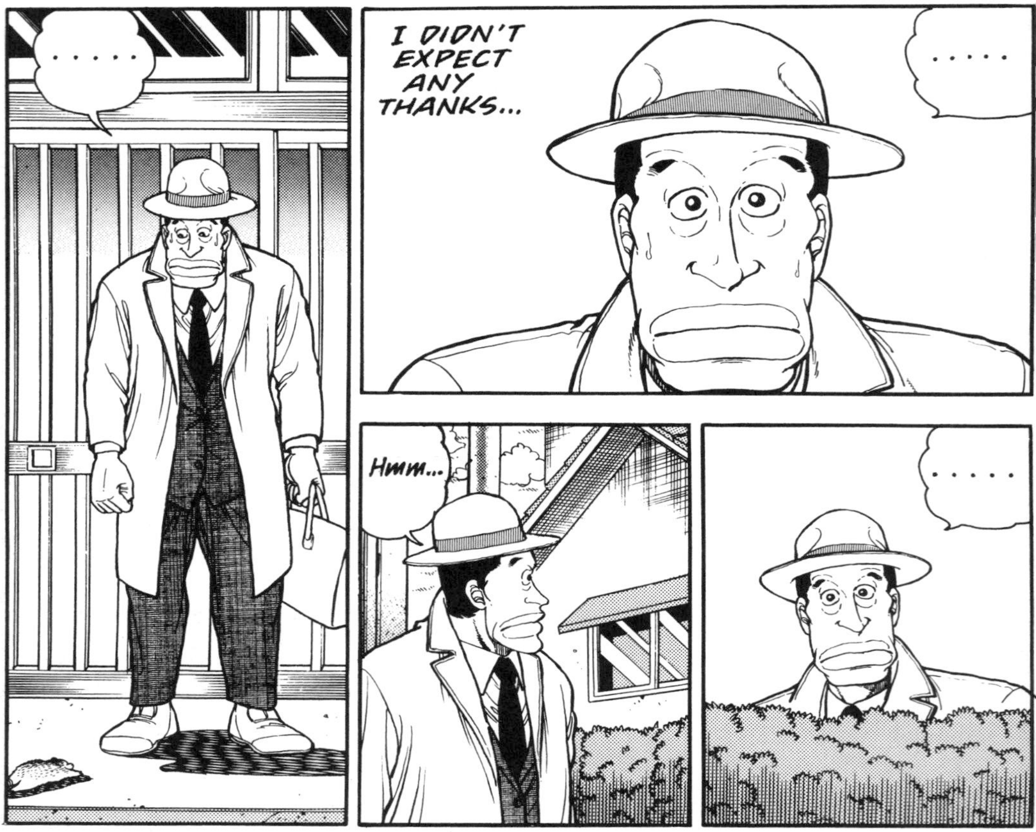
.....
I DIDN'T EXPECT ANY THANKS...
.....
Hmm...
.....

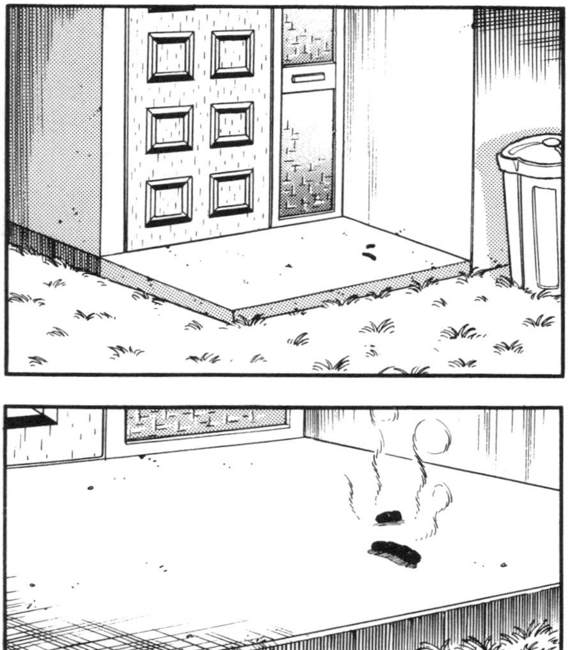

MORAL: CATS DON'T FORGET THOSE WHO HELP THEM. OR THOSE WHO HURT THEM...

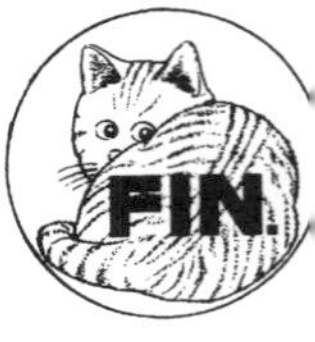
FIN

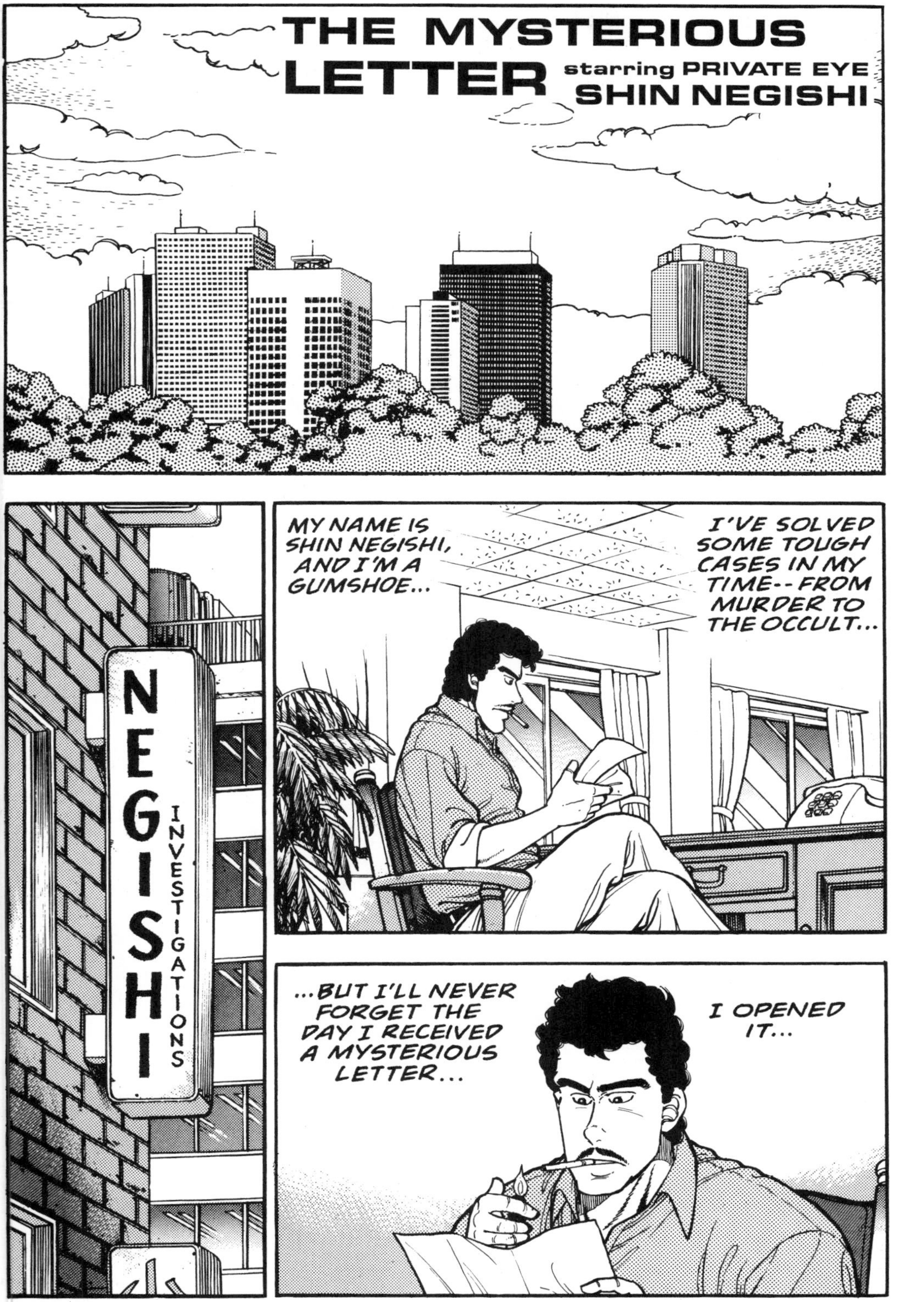
THE MYSTERIOUS LETTER
starring PRIVATE EYE SHIN NEGISHI
NEGISHI INVESTIGATIONS
MY NAME IS SHIN NEGISHI, AND I'M A GUMSHOE...
I'VE SOLVED SOME TOUGH CASES IN MY TIME--FROM MURDER TO THE OCCULT...
...BUT I'LL NEVER FORGET THE DAY I RECEIVED A MYSTERIOUS LETTER...
I OPENED IT...

"Hello, my name is Reiko Tachibana. I'm 22 and I work at a securities firm...

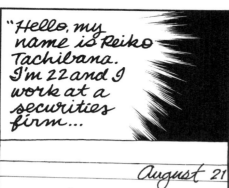

"It all began about a year ago... I was on my way home from work -- I think it was sometime between 7 and 8. I was walking through the park...

"When all of a sudden..."

Meww...! Meww...!

Meww...! Meww...!

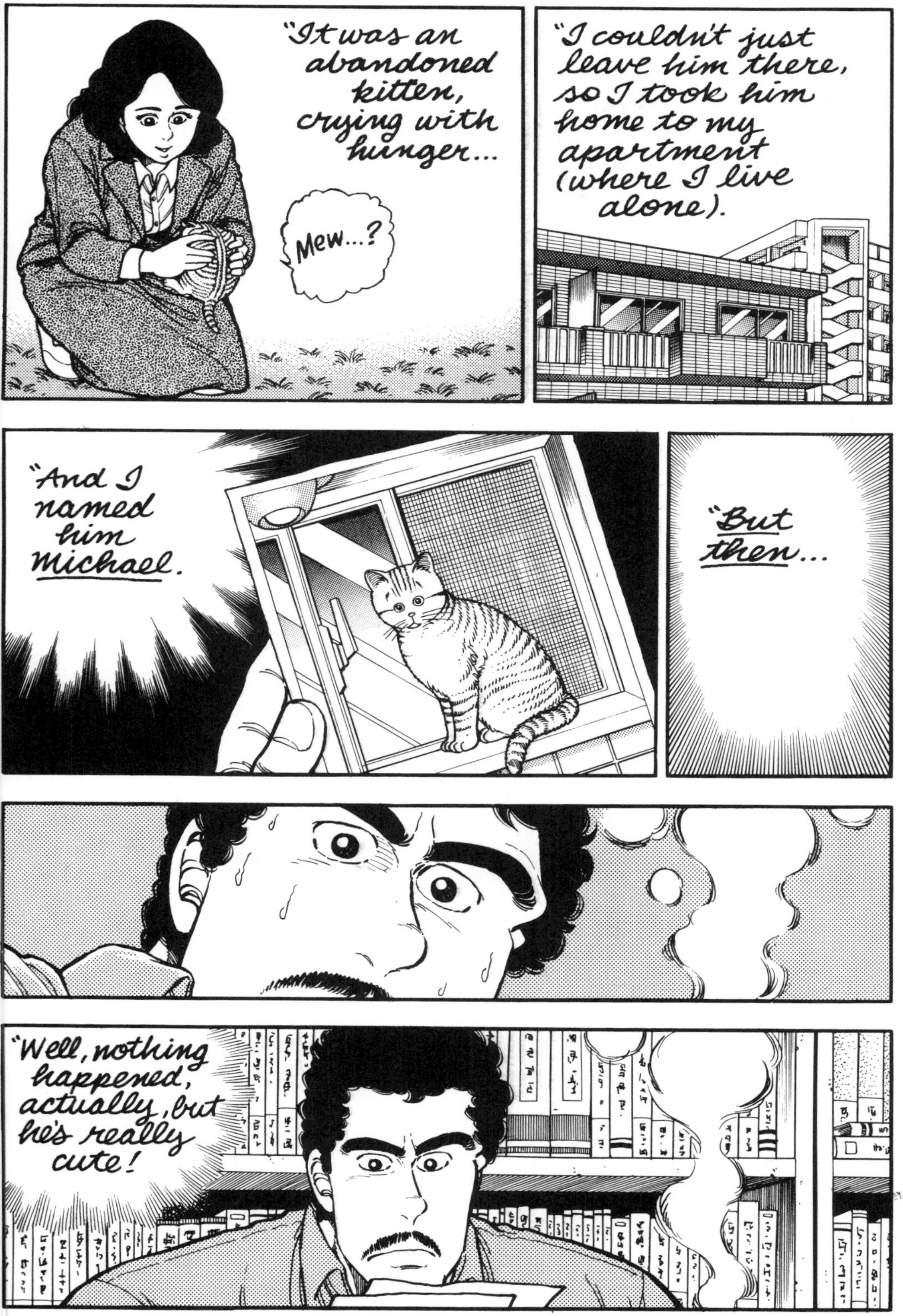
"It was an abandoned kitten, crying with hunger...
Mew...?
"I couldn't just leave him there, so I took him home to my apartment (where I live alone).
"And I named him Michael.
"But then...
"Well, nothing happened, actually, but he's really cute!

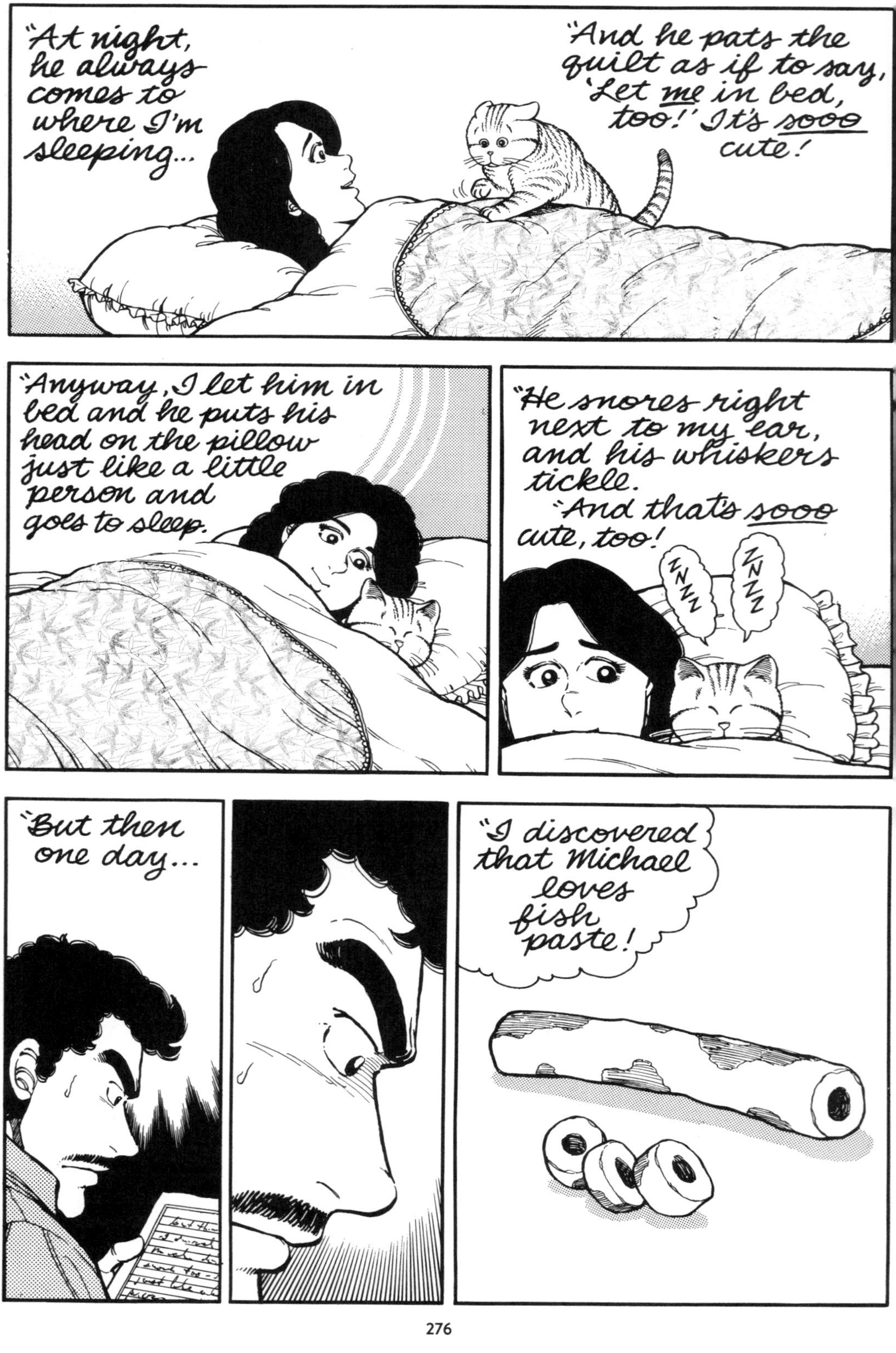
"At night, he always comes to where I'm sleeping...
"And he pats the quilt as if to say, 'Let me in bed, too!' It's sooo cute!
"Anyway, I let him in bed and he puts his head on the pillow just like a little person and goes to sleep.
"He snores right next to my ear, and his whiskers tickle.
"And that's sooo cute, too!
ZNZZ
ZNZZ
"But then one day...
"I discovered that Michael loves fish paste!

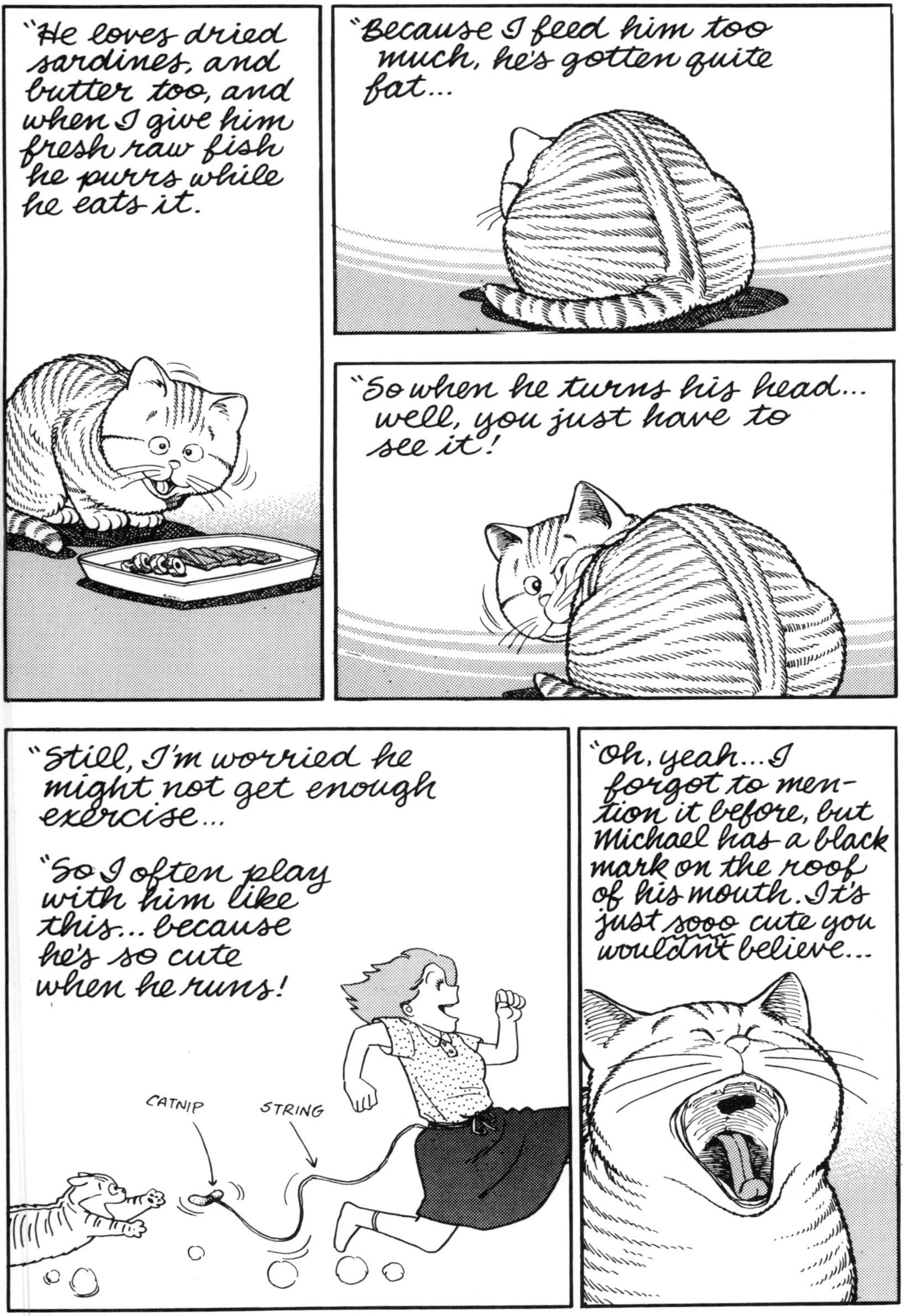
"He loves dried sardines, and butter too, and when I give him fresh raw fish he purrs while he eats it.
"Because I feed him too much, he's gotten quite fat...
"So when he turns his head... well, you just have to see it!
"Still, I'm worried he might not get enough exercise...
"So I often play with him like this... because he's so cute when he runs!
CATNIP
STRING
"Oh, yeah... I forgot to mention it before, but Michael has a black mark on the roof of his mouth. It's just sooo cute you wouldn't believe...

"Anyway, I can't imagine life without Michael. I hope he lives forever and ever!! ♡

"Well, bye for now! I'll write again soon!'"

. . . . .

. . . . .

. . . . .

Cat Lover's Magazine
ATTN: Readers' Forum
Nishi-Gotanda,
Shinagawa Ward,
Tokyo, Japan 141

. . . . .

AS I SAID... MY NAME IS SHIN NEGISHI... AND I'M A GUMSHOE...

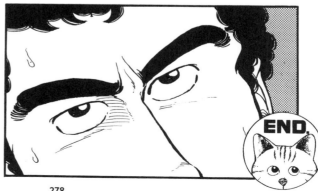

END.

278

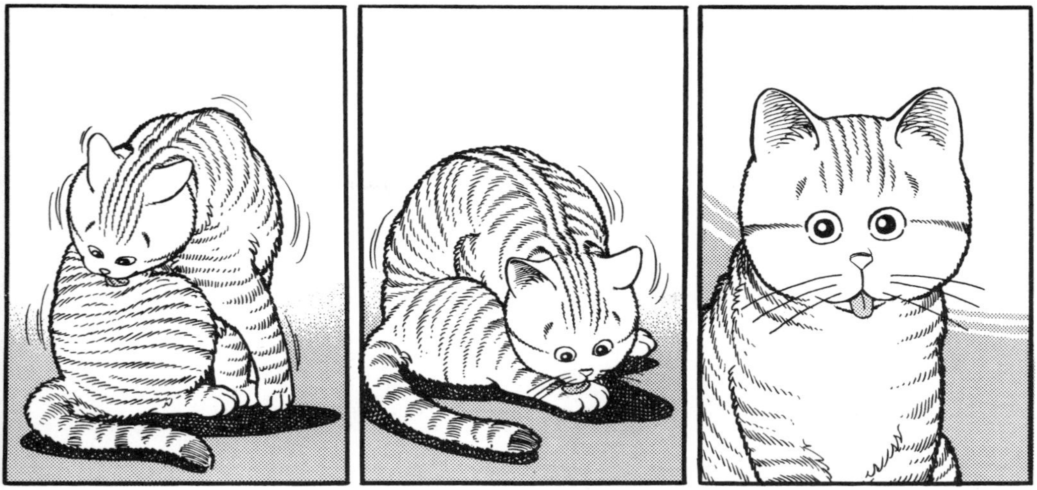

# MICHAEL'S BAD HABIT

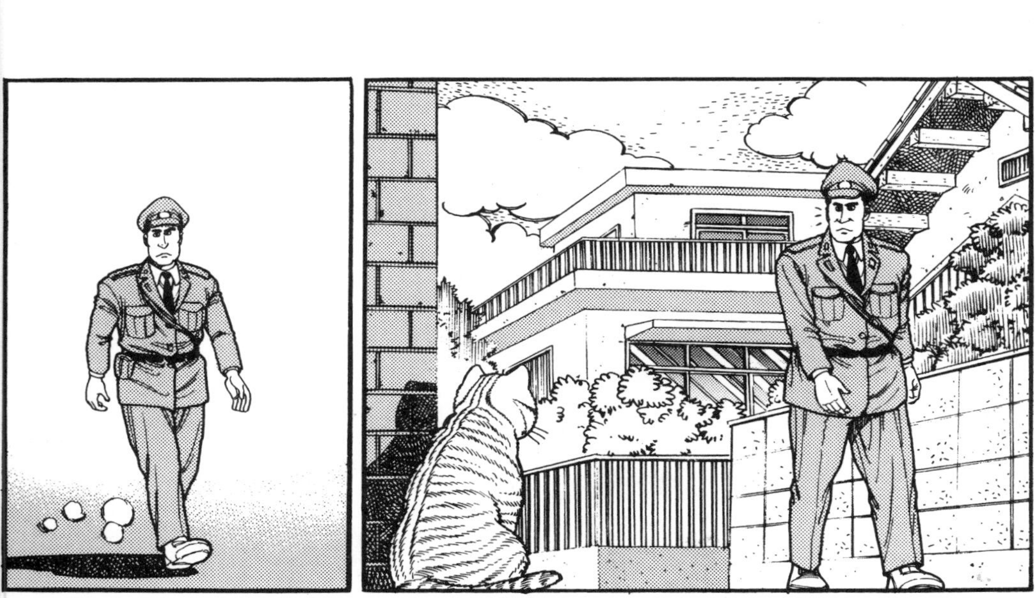

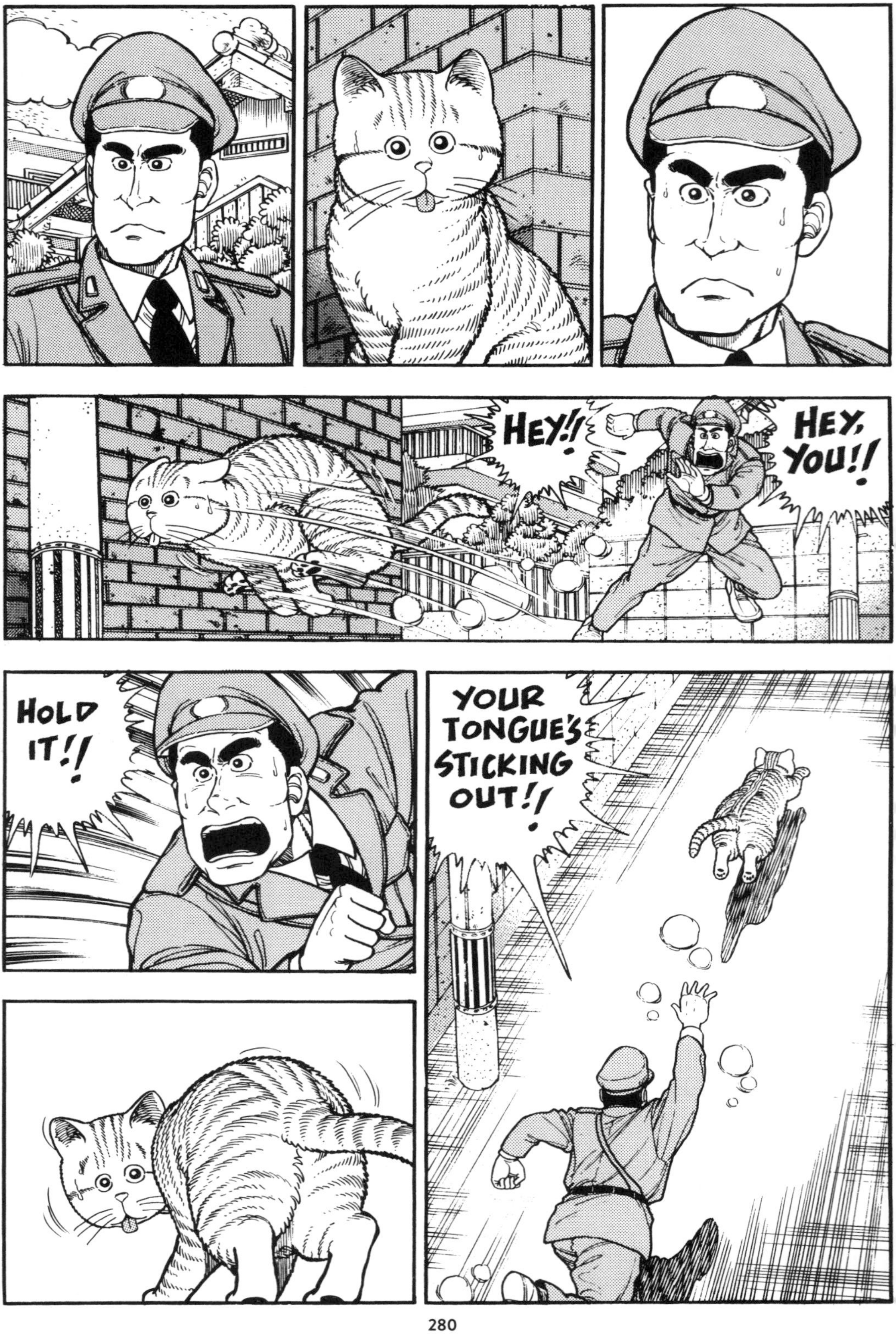
HEY!!
HEY, YOU!!
HOLD IT!!
YOUR TONGUE'S STICKING OUT!!

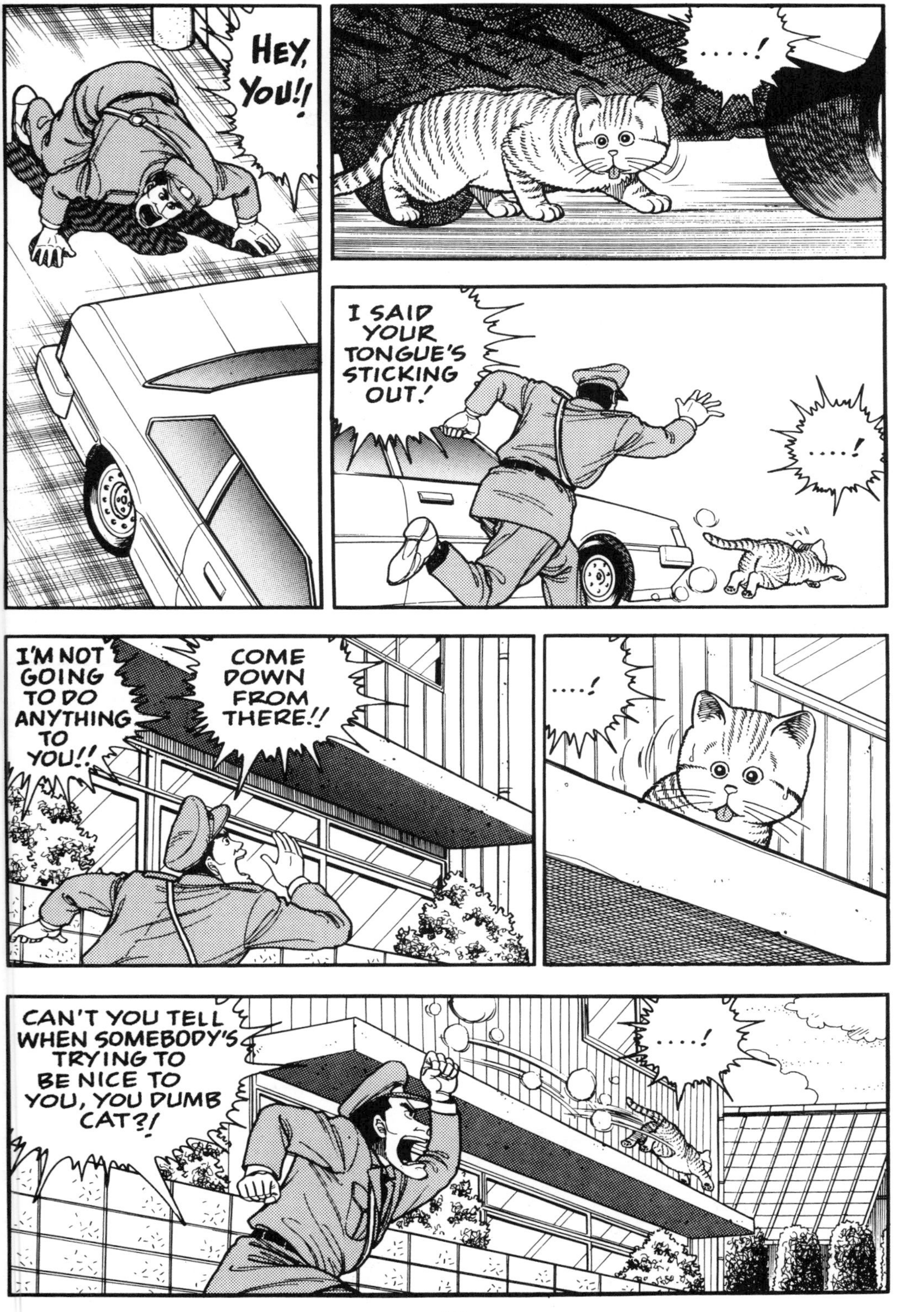
HEY, YOU!!
....!
I SAID YOUR TONGUE'S STICKING OUT!
....!
I'M NOT GOING TO DO ANYTHING TO YOU!!
COME DOWN FROM THERE!!
....!
CAN'T YOU TELL WHEN SOMEBODY'S TRYING TO BE NICE TO YOU, YOU DUMB CAT?!
....!

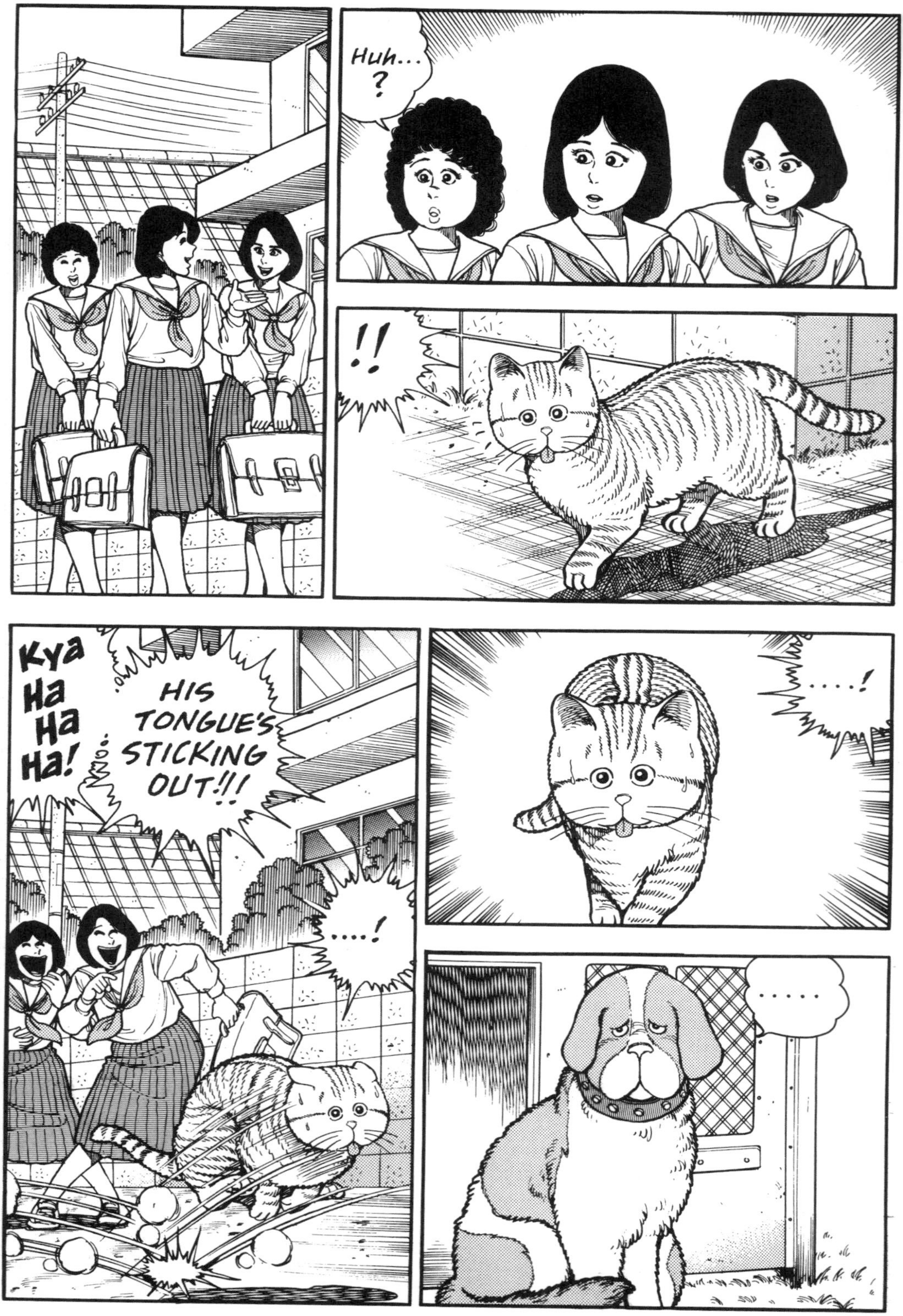
Huh...
?
!!
Kya
Ha
Ha
Ha!
HIS TONGUE'S STICKING OUT!!!
....!
....!
.....

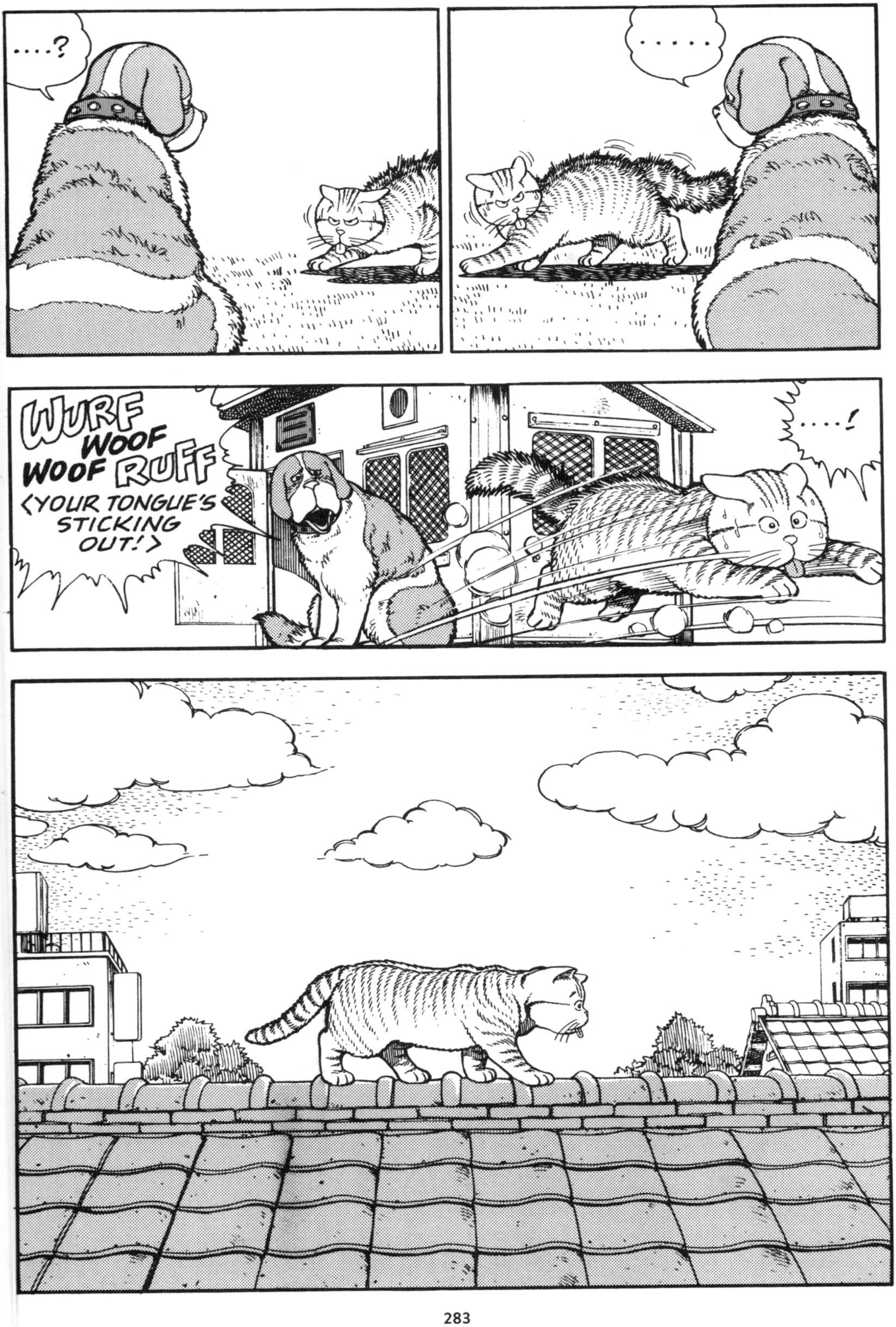

....?
......
WURF WOOF WOOF RUFF
⟨YOUR TONGUE'S STICKING OUT!⟩
....!

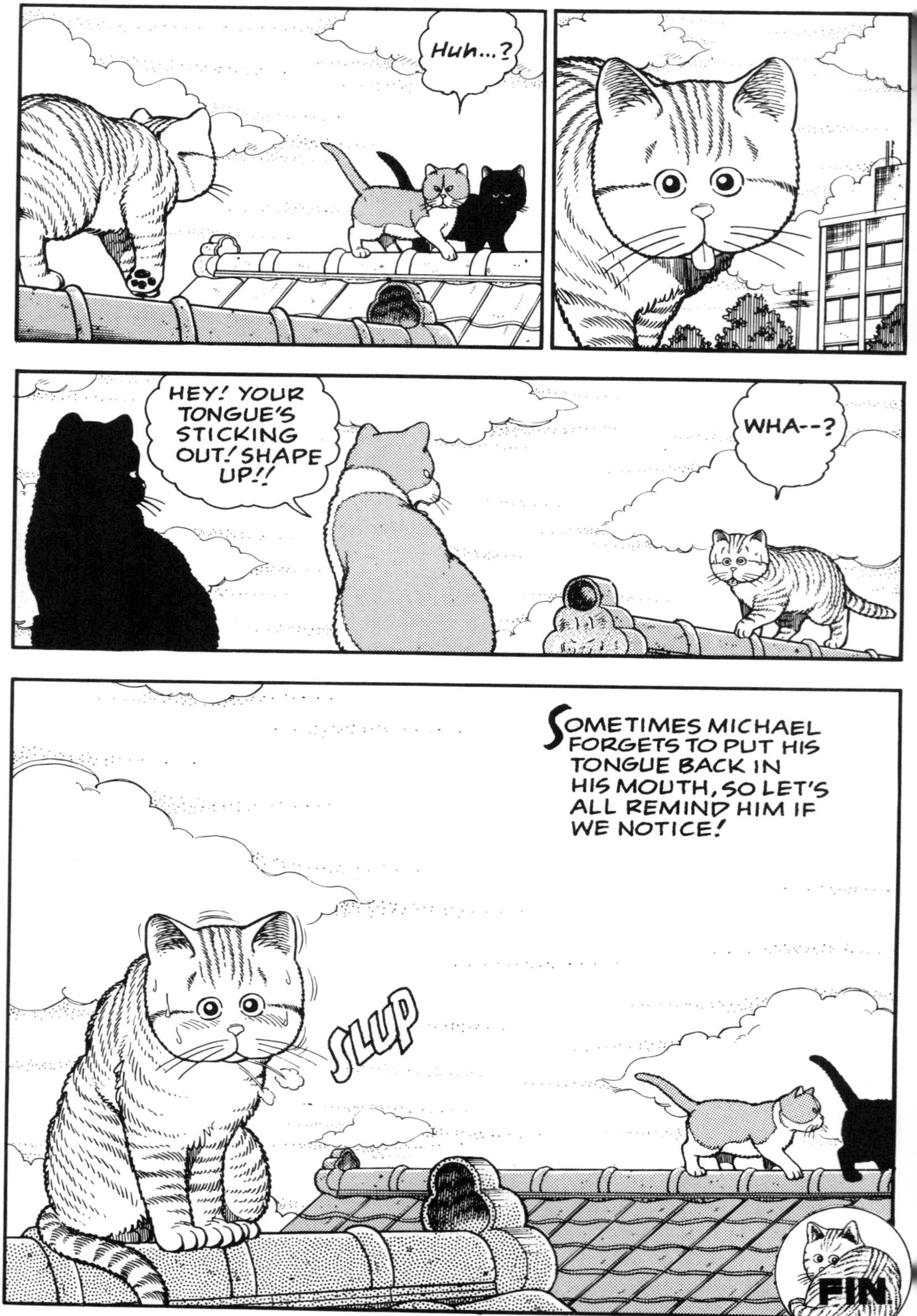
Huh...?
HEY! YOUR TONGUE'S STICKING OUT! SHAPE UP!!
WHA--?
SOMETIMES MICHAEL FORGETS TO PUT HIS TONGUE BACK IN HIS MOUTH, SO LET'S ALL REMIND HIM IF WE NOTICE!
SLUP
FIN.

# the CAT BURGLAR

starring
Detective YAMAMURA

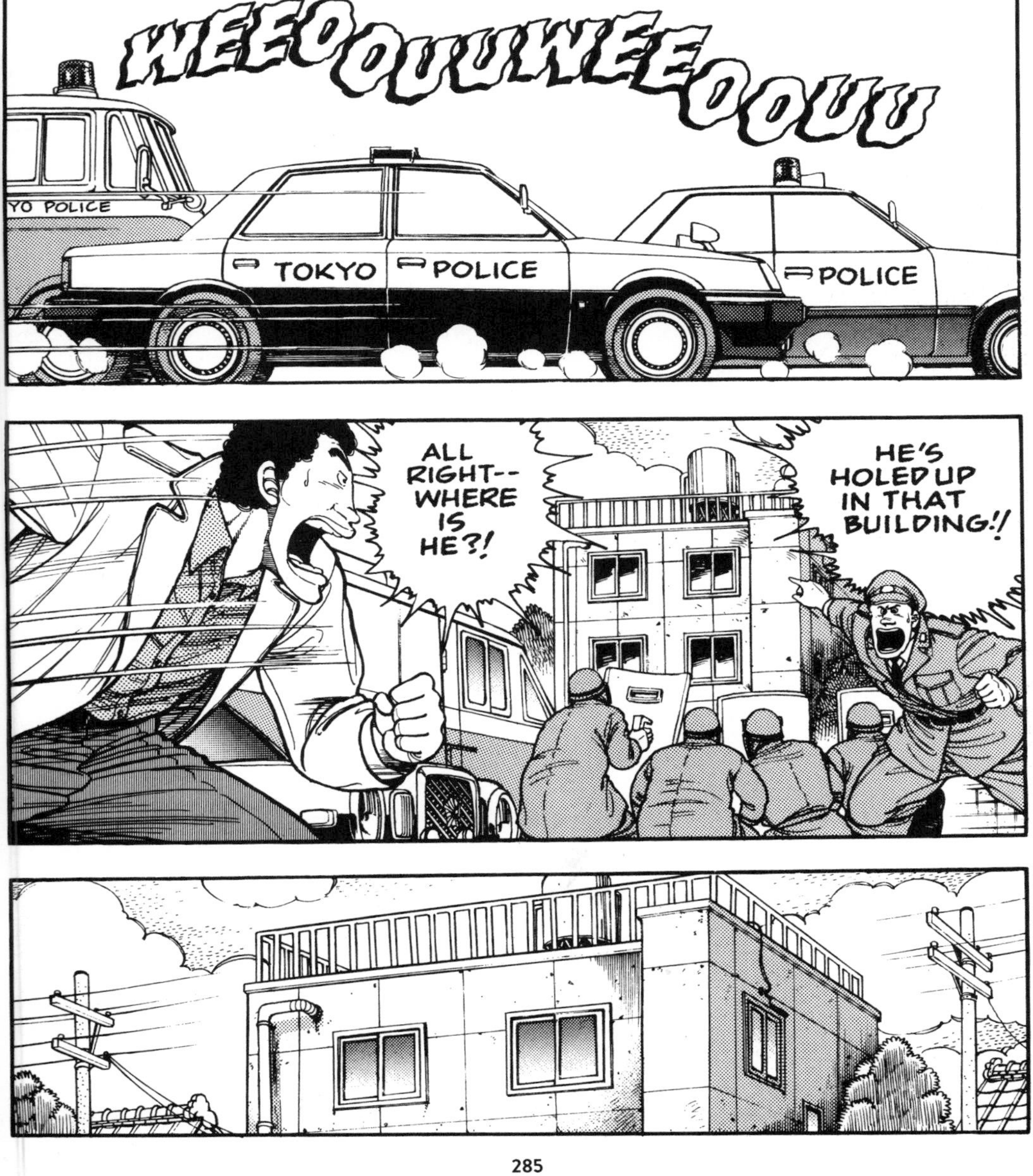
WEEOOUUWEEOOUU
YO POLICE
TOKYO POLICE
POLICE
ALL RIGHT-- WHERE IS HE?!
HE'S HOLED UP IN THAT BUILDING!!

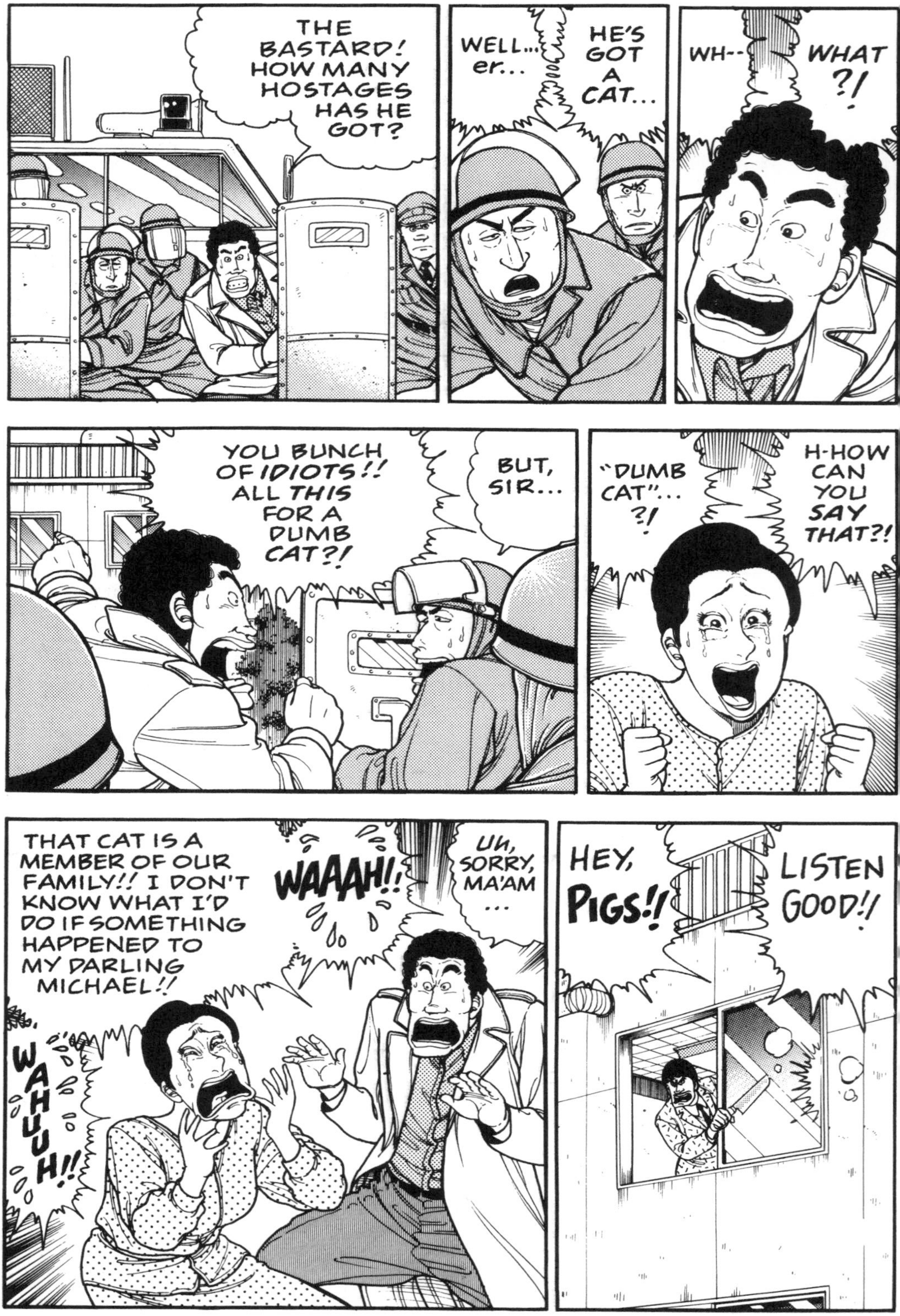
THE BASTARD! HOW MANY HOSTAGES HAS HE GOT?
WELL... er...
HE'S GOT A CAT...
WH--
WHAT ?!
YOU BUNCH OF IDIOTS!! ALL THIS FOR A DUMB CAT?!
BUT, SIR...
"DUMB CAT"... ?!
H-HOW CAN YOU SAY THAT?!
THAT CAT IS A MEMBER OF OUR FAMILY!! I DON'T KNOW WHAT I'D DO IF SOMETHING HAPPENED TO MY DARLING MICHAEL!!
WAAAH!!
WAHUUH!!
Uh, SORRY, MA'AM ...
HEY, PIGS!!
LISTEN GOOD!!

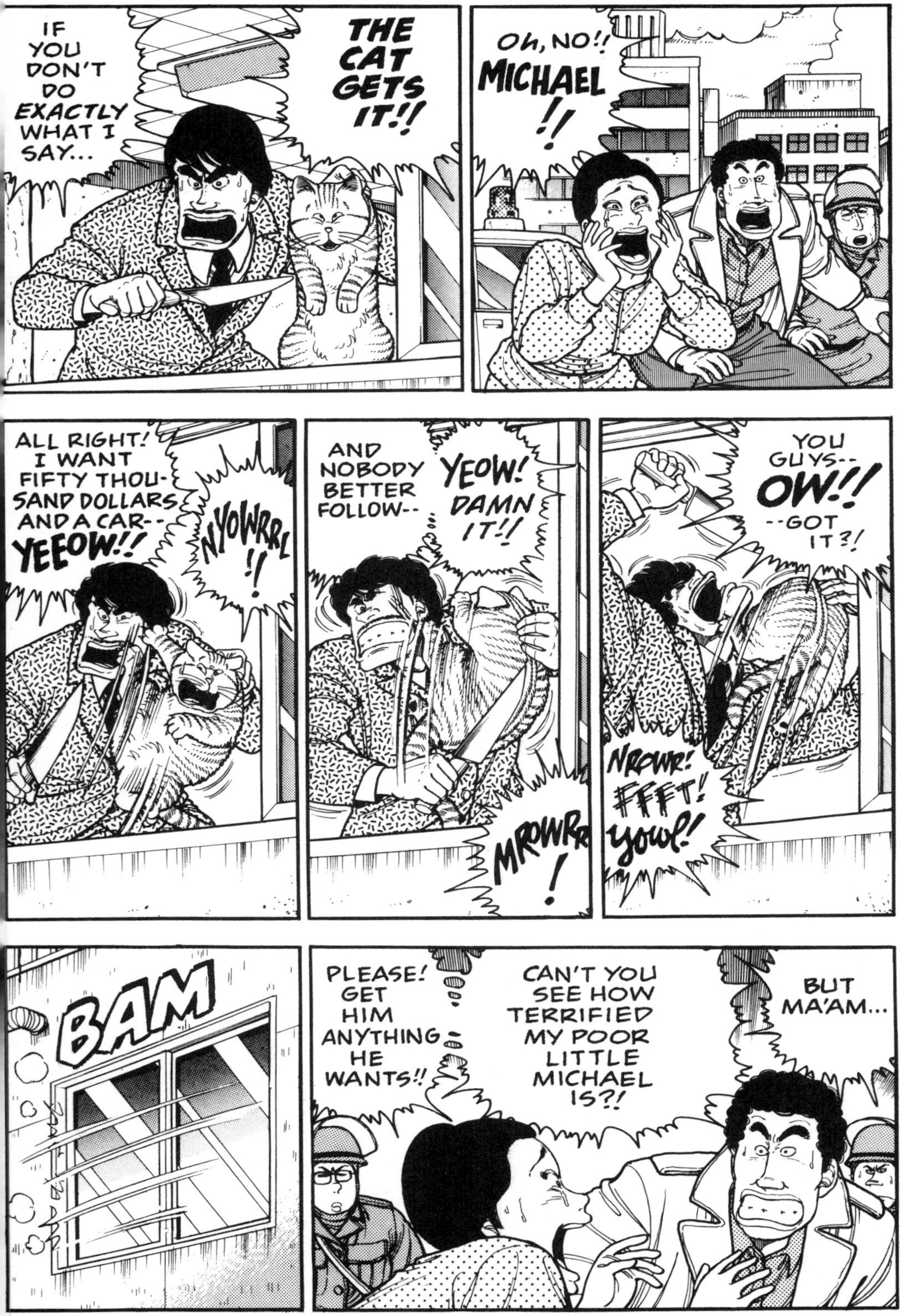
IF YOU DON'T DO EXACTLY WHAT I SAY...
THE CAT GETS IT!!
Oh, NO!! MICHAEL!!
ALL RIGHT! I WANT FIFTY THOU-SAND DOLLARS AND A CAR--YEEOW!!
NYOWRRL!!
AND NOBODY BETTER FOLLOW--
YEOW! DAMN IT!!
MROWRR!
YOU GUYS--OW!! --GOT IT?!
NROWR! FFFT! YOWL!
BAM
PLEASE! GET HIM ANYTHING HE WANTS!!
CAN'T YOU SEE HOW TERRIFIED MY POOR LITTLE MICHAEL IS?!
BUT MA'AM...

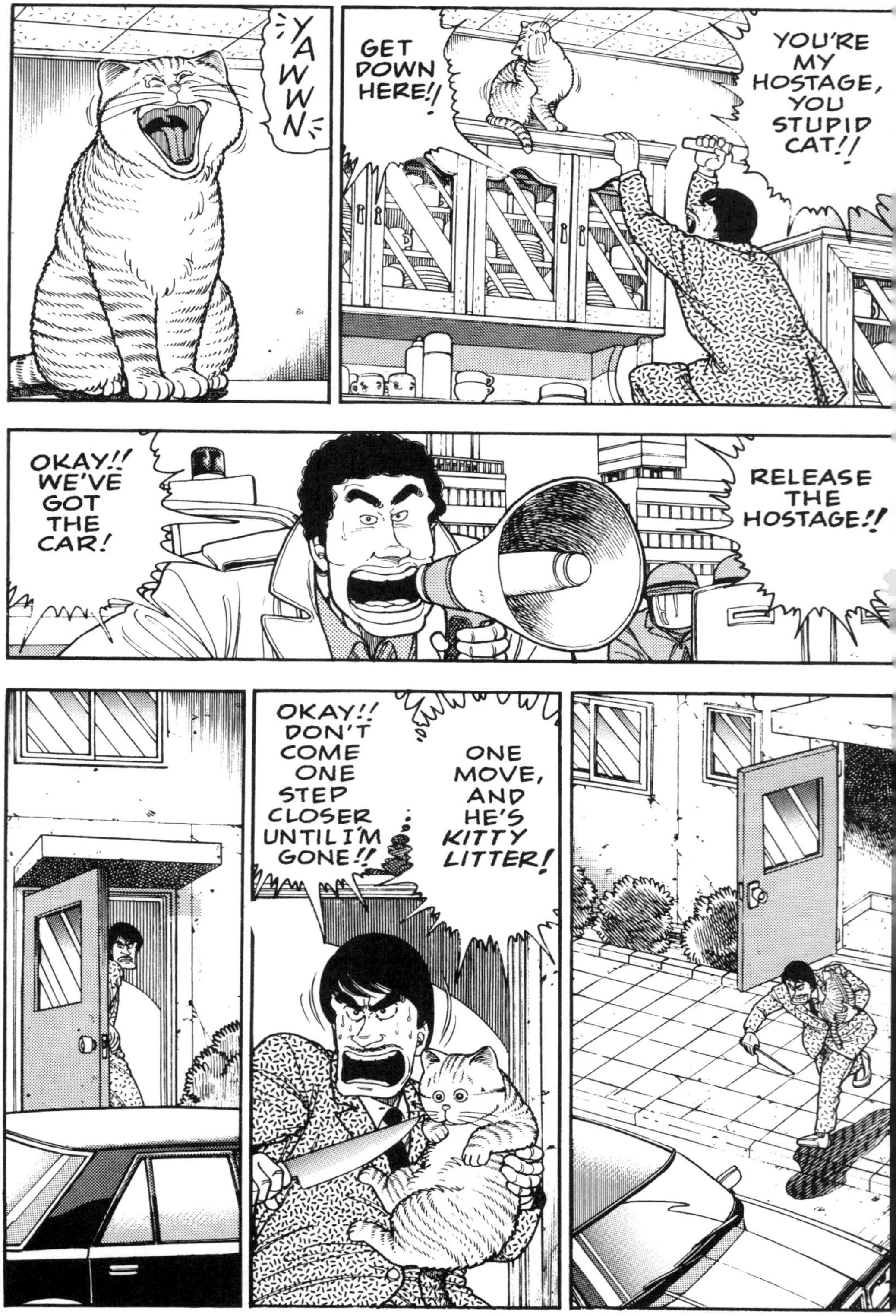
YAWWN
GET DOWN HERE!!
YOU'RE MY HOSTAGE, YOU STUPID CAT!!
OKAY!! WE'VE GOT THE CAR!
RELEASE THE HOSTAGE!!
OKAY!! DON'T COME ONE STEP CLOSER UNTIL I'M GONE!!
ONE MOVE, AND HE'S *KITTY LITTER!*

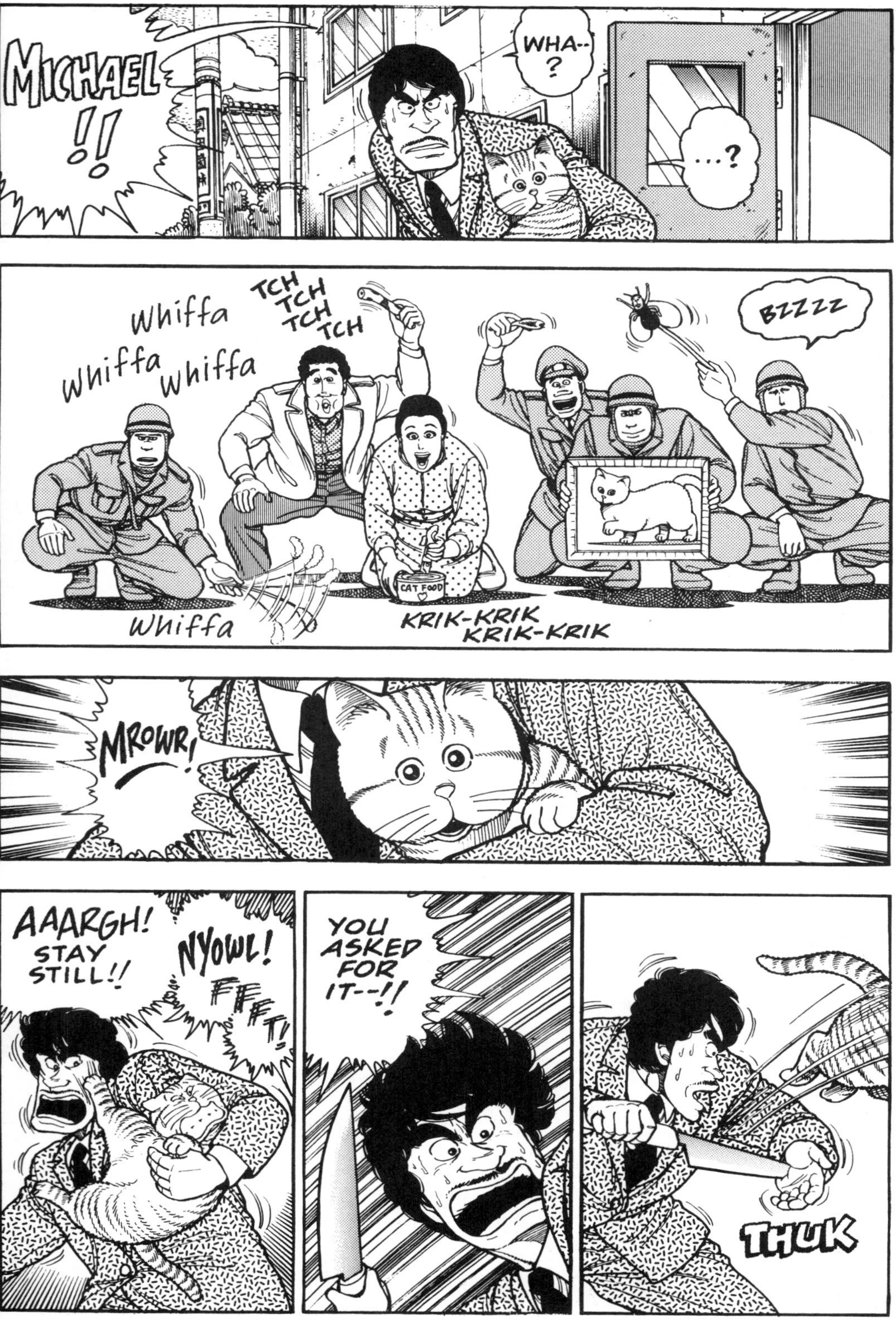
MICHAEL !!
WHA-- ?
...?
whiffa whiffa whiffa
TCH TCH TCH TCH
BZZZZ
CAT FOOD
whiffa
KRIK-KRIK KRIK-KRIK
MROWR!
AAARGH! STAY STILL!!
NYOWL!
FFFT!
YOU ASKED FOR IT--!!
THUK

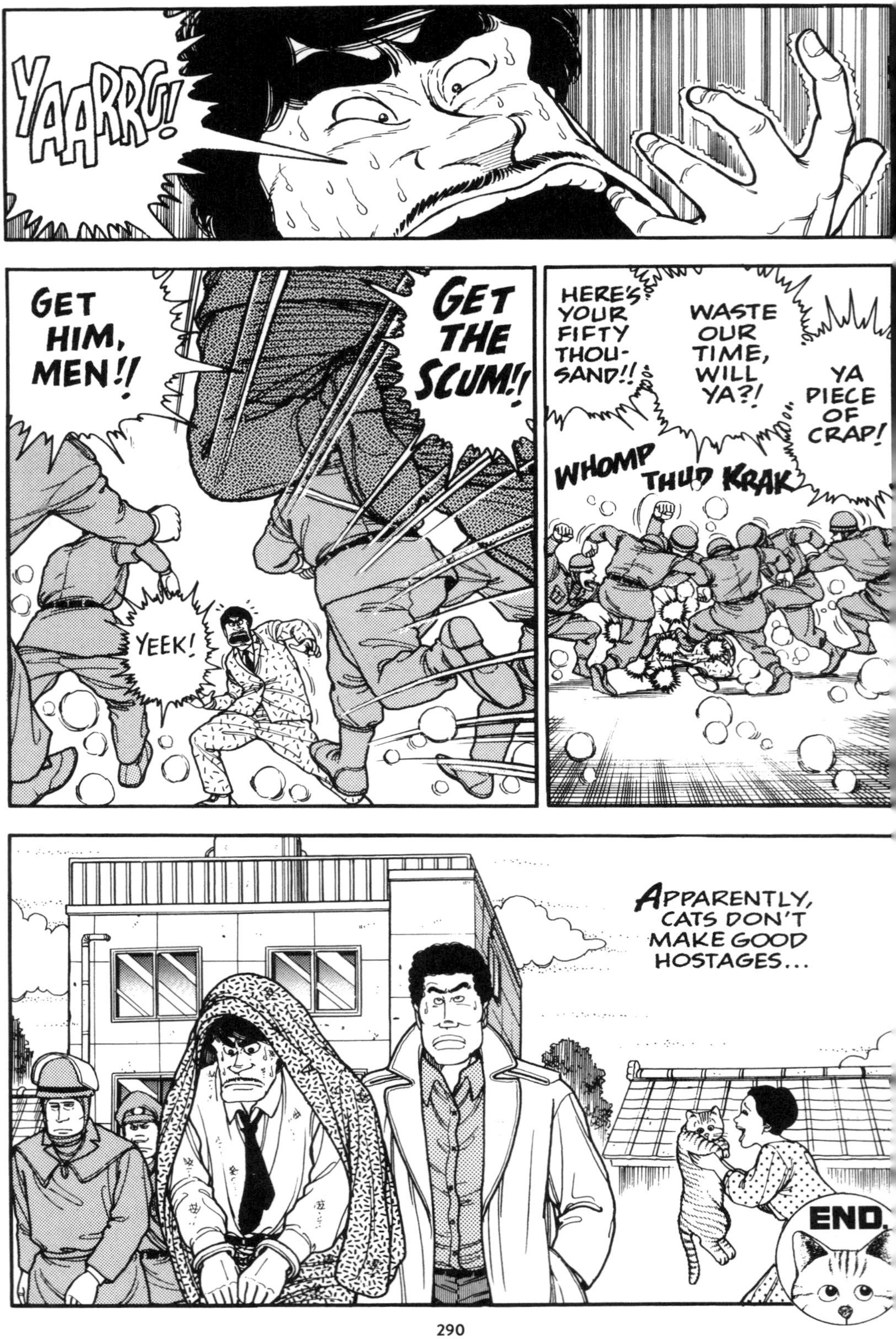
YAARRG!
GET HIM, MEN!!
GET THE SCUM!!
YEEK!
HERE'S YOUR FIFTY THOU-SAND!!
WASTE OUR TIME, WILL YA?!
YA PIECE OF CRAP!
WHOMP
THUD KRAK
APPARENTLY, CATS DON'T MAKE GOOD HOSTAGES...
END.

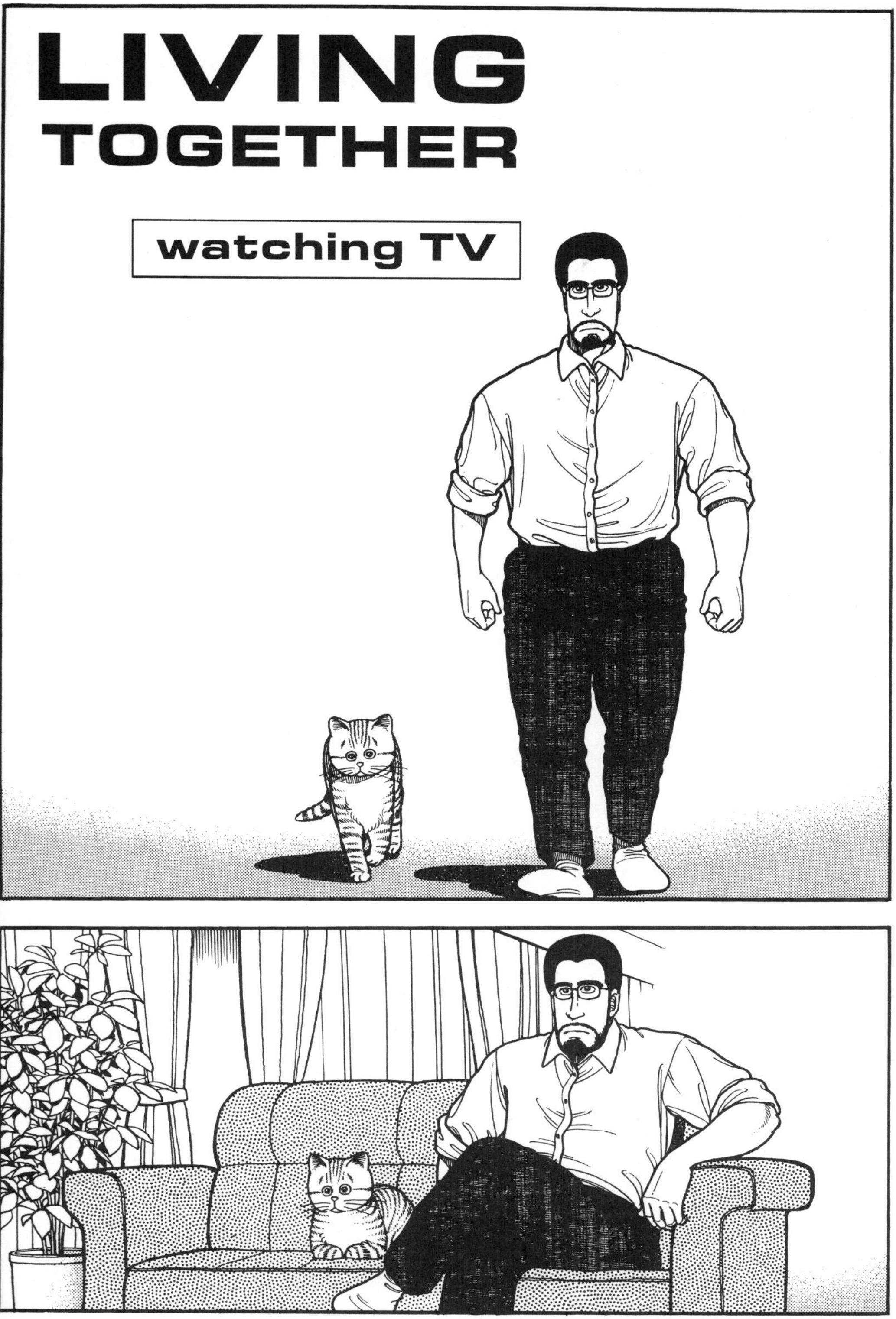
LIVING TOGETHER
watching TV

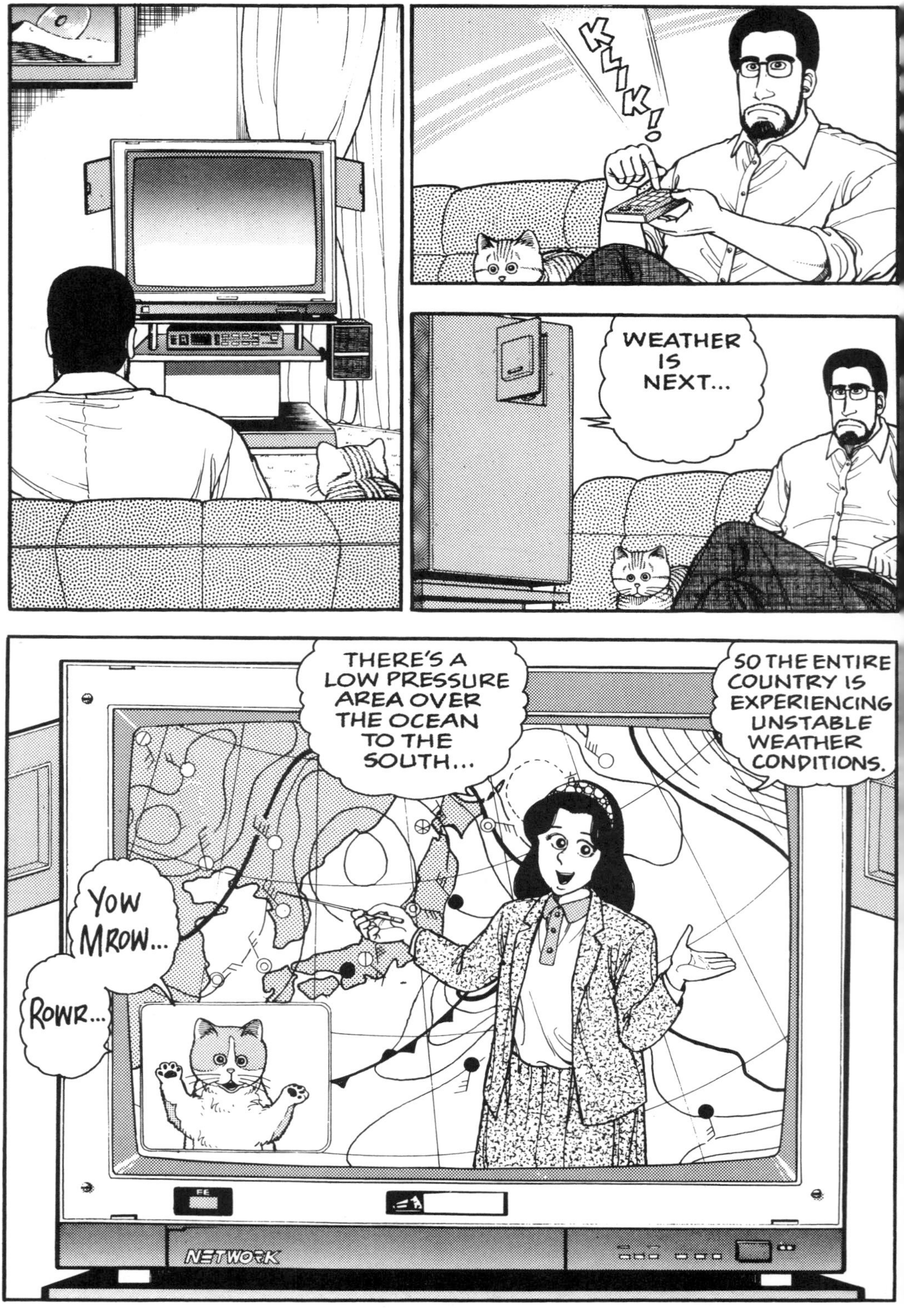

KLIK!
WEATHER IS NEXT...
THERE'S A LOW PRESSURE AREA OVER THE OCEAN TO THE SOUTH...
SO THE ENTIRE COUNTRY IS EXPERIENCING UNSTABLE WEATHER CONDITIONS.
YOW MROW...
ROWR...
NETWORK

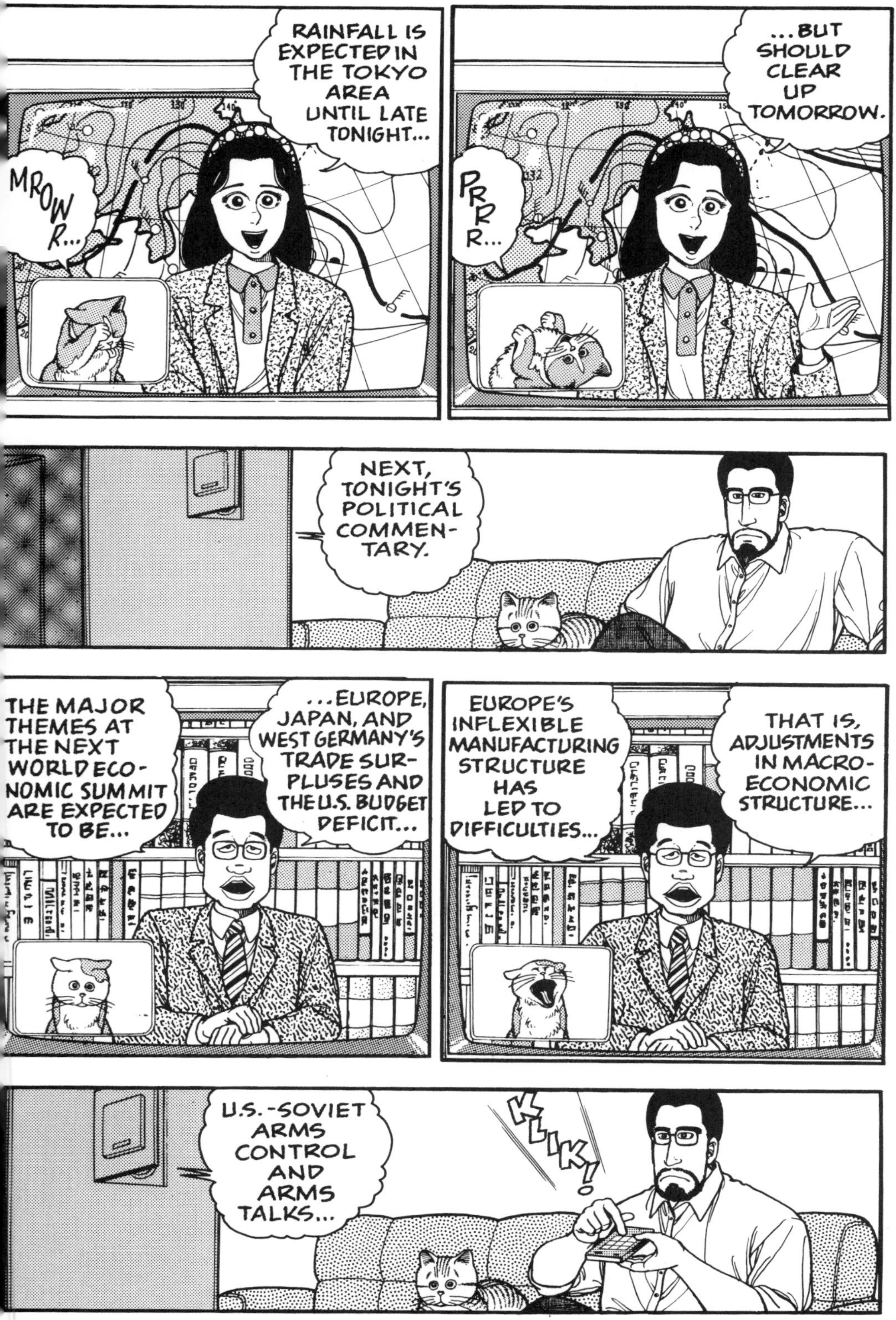
RAINFALL IS EXPECTED IN THE TOKYO AREA UNTIL LATE TONIGHT...
MROWR...
...BUT SHOULD CLEAR UP TOMORROW.
PRRR...
NEXT, TONIGHT'S POLITICAL COMMENTARY.
THE MAJOR THEMES AT THE NEXT WORLD ECONOMIC SUMMIT ARE EXPECTED TO BE...
...EUROPE, JAPAN, AND WEST GERMANY'S TRADE SURPLUSES AND THE U.S. BUDGET DEFICIT...
EUROPE'S INFLEXIBLE MANUFACTURING STRUCTURE HAS LED TO DIFFICULTIES...
THAT IS, ADJUSTMENTS IN MACROECONOMIC STRUCTURE...
U.S.-SOVIET ARMS CONTROL AND ARMS TALKS...
KLIK!

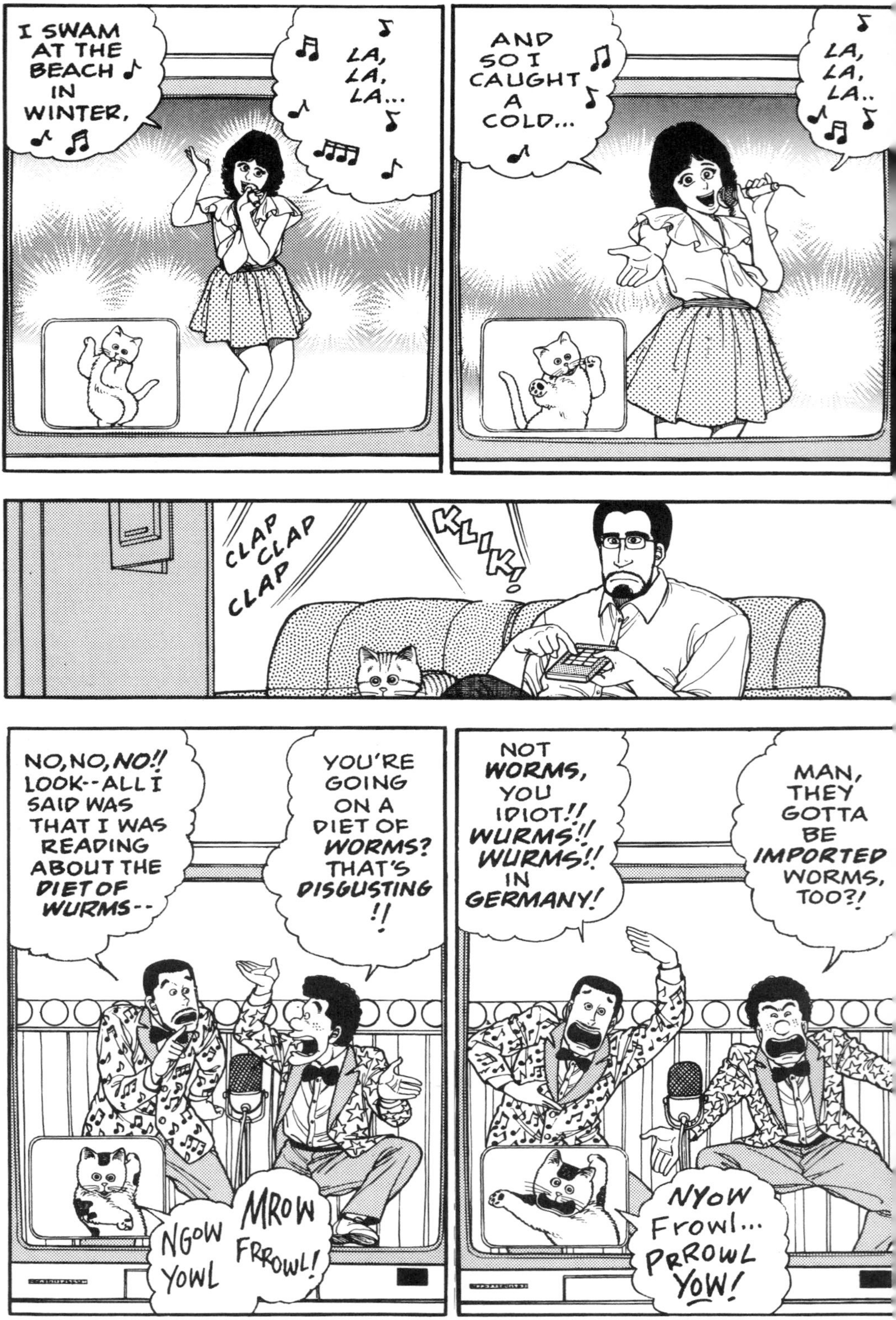
I SWAM AT THE BEACH IN WINTER,
LA, LA, LA...
AND SO I CAUGHT A COLD...
LA, LA, LA..
CLAP CLAP CLAP
KLIK!
NO, NO, NO!! LOOK--ALL I SAID WAS THAT I WAS READING ABOUT THE DIET OF WURMS--
YOU'RE GOING ON A DIET OF WORMS? THAT'S DISGUSTING!!
NGOW YOWL
MROW FRROWL!
NOT WORMS, YOU IDIOT!! WURMS!! WURMS!! IN GERMANY!
MAN, THEY GOTTA BE IMPORTED WORMS, TOO?!
NYOW Frowl... PRROWL YOW!

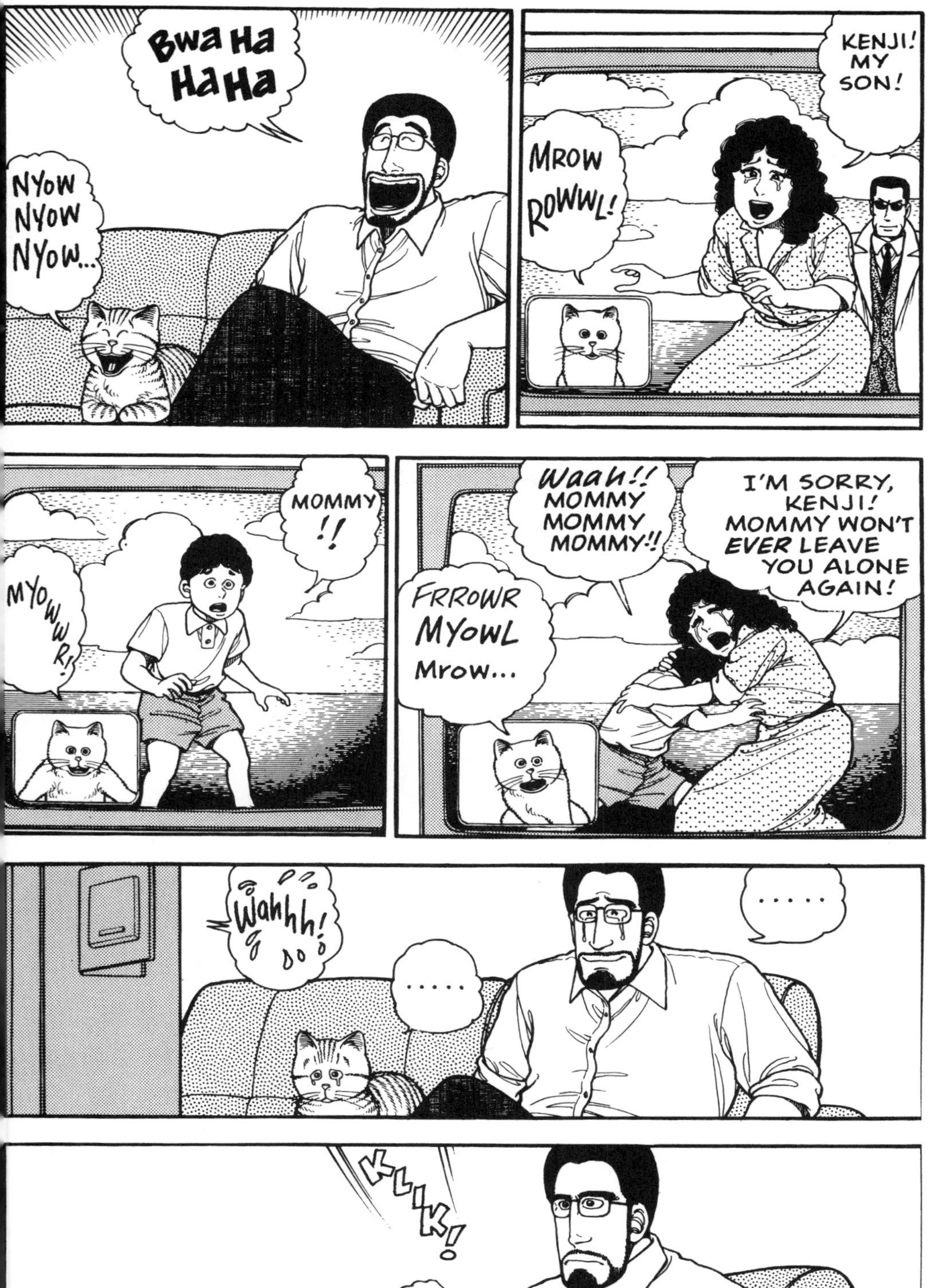

BWA HA HA HA
NYOW NYOW NYOW...
KENJI! MY SON!
MROW ROWWL!
MOMMY!!
MYOWWR!
WAAH!! MOMMY MOMMY MOMMY!!
I'M SORRY, KENJI! MOMMY WON'T *EVER* LEAVE YOU ALONE AGAIN!
FRROWR MYOWL Mrow...
Wahhh!
......
......
KLIK!

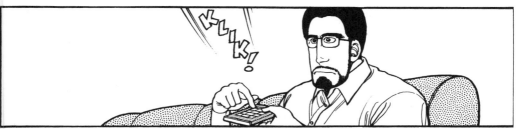

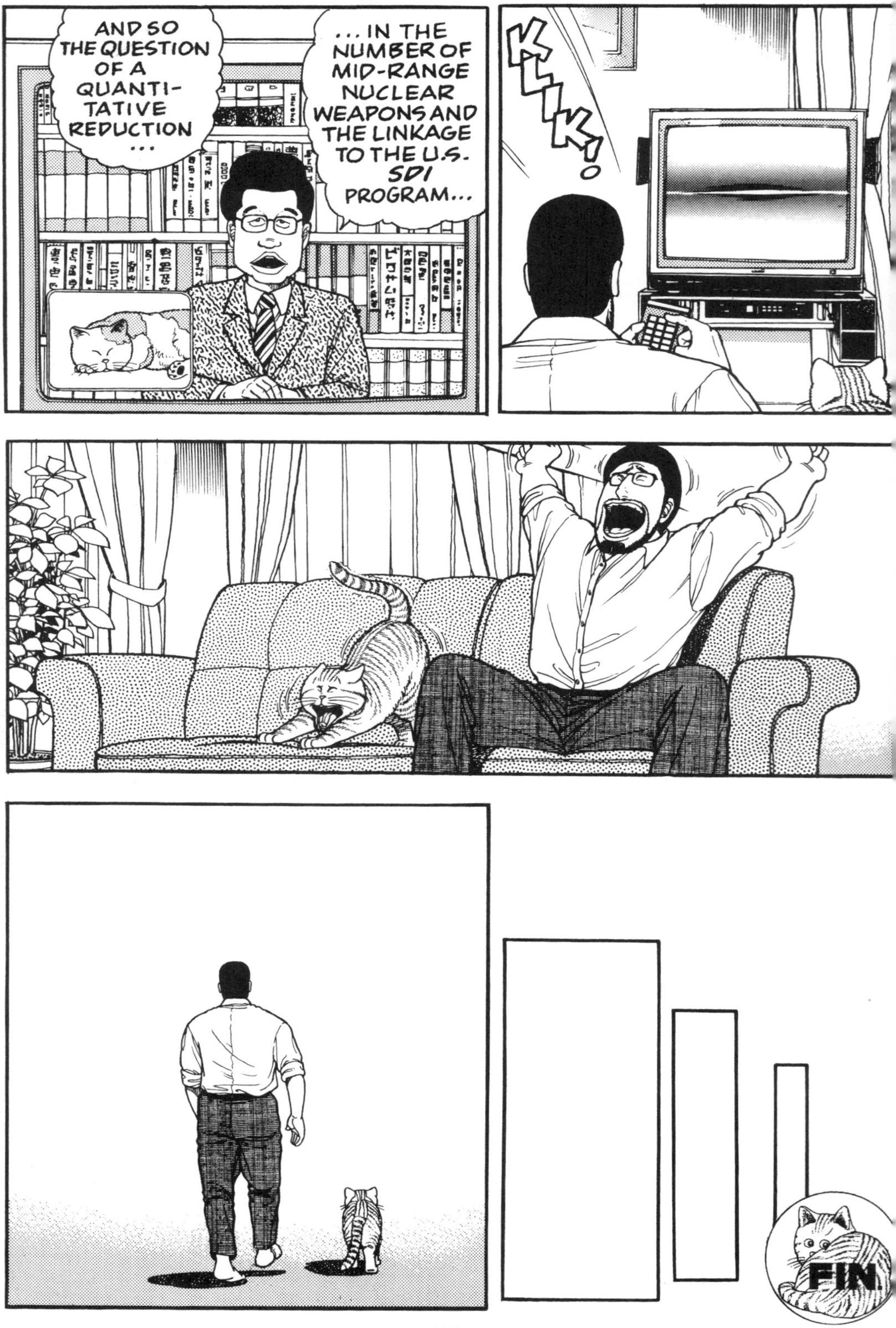
AND SO THE QUESTION OF A QUANTI- TATIVE REDUCTION ...
... IN THE NUMBER OF MID-RANGE NUCLEAR WEAPONS AND THE LINKAGE TO THE U.S. SDI PROGRAM...
KLIK!
FIN.

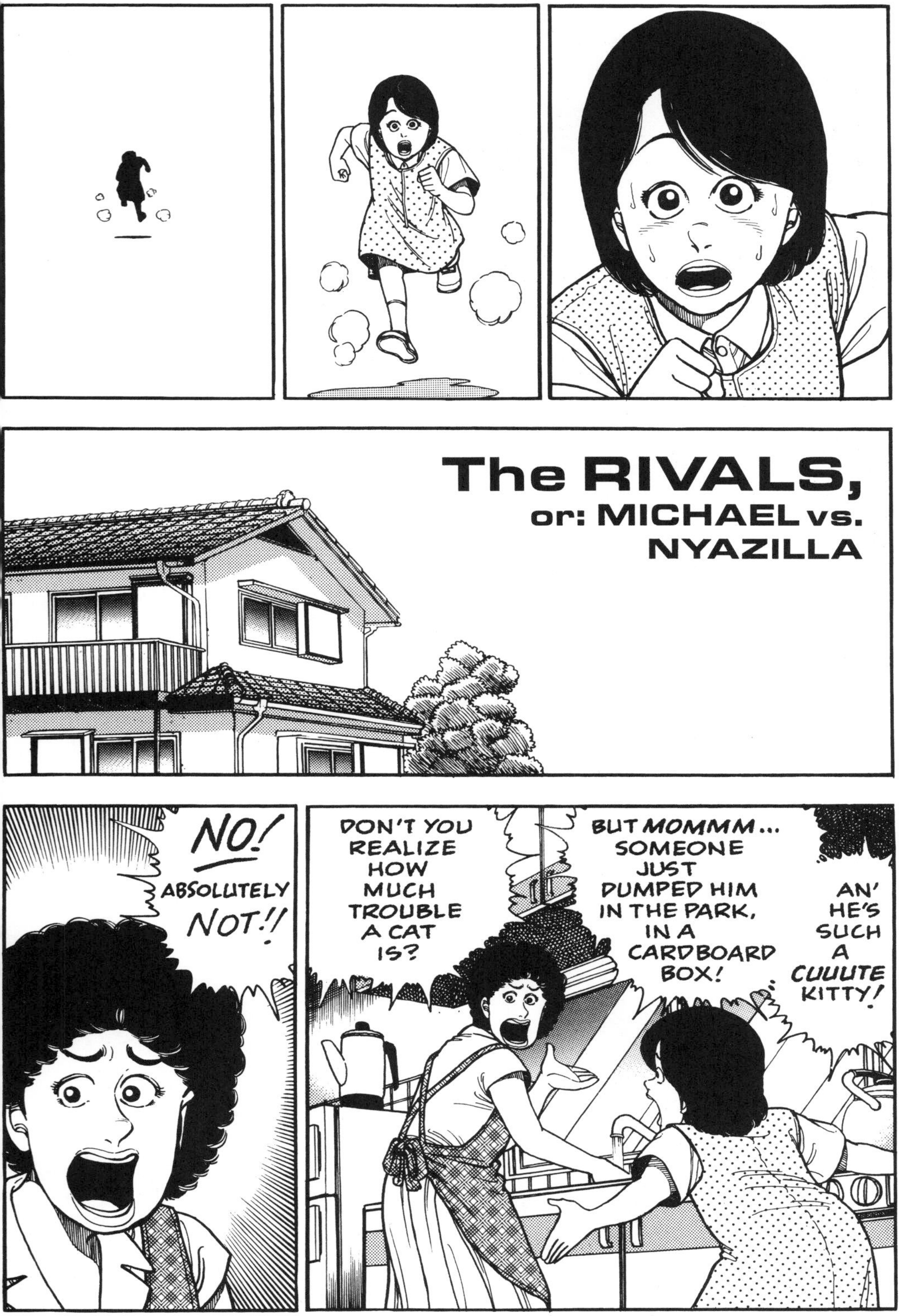

The RIVALS,
or: MICHAEL vs. NYAZILLA
NO! ABSOLUTELY NOT!!
DON'T YOU REALIZE HOW MUCH TROUBLE A CAT IS?
BUT MOMMM... SOMEONE JUST DUMPED HIM IN THE PARK, IN A CARDBOARD BOX!
AN' HE'S SUCH A CUUUTE KITTY!

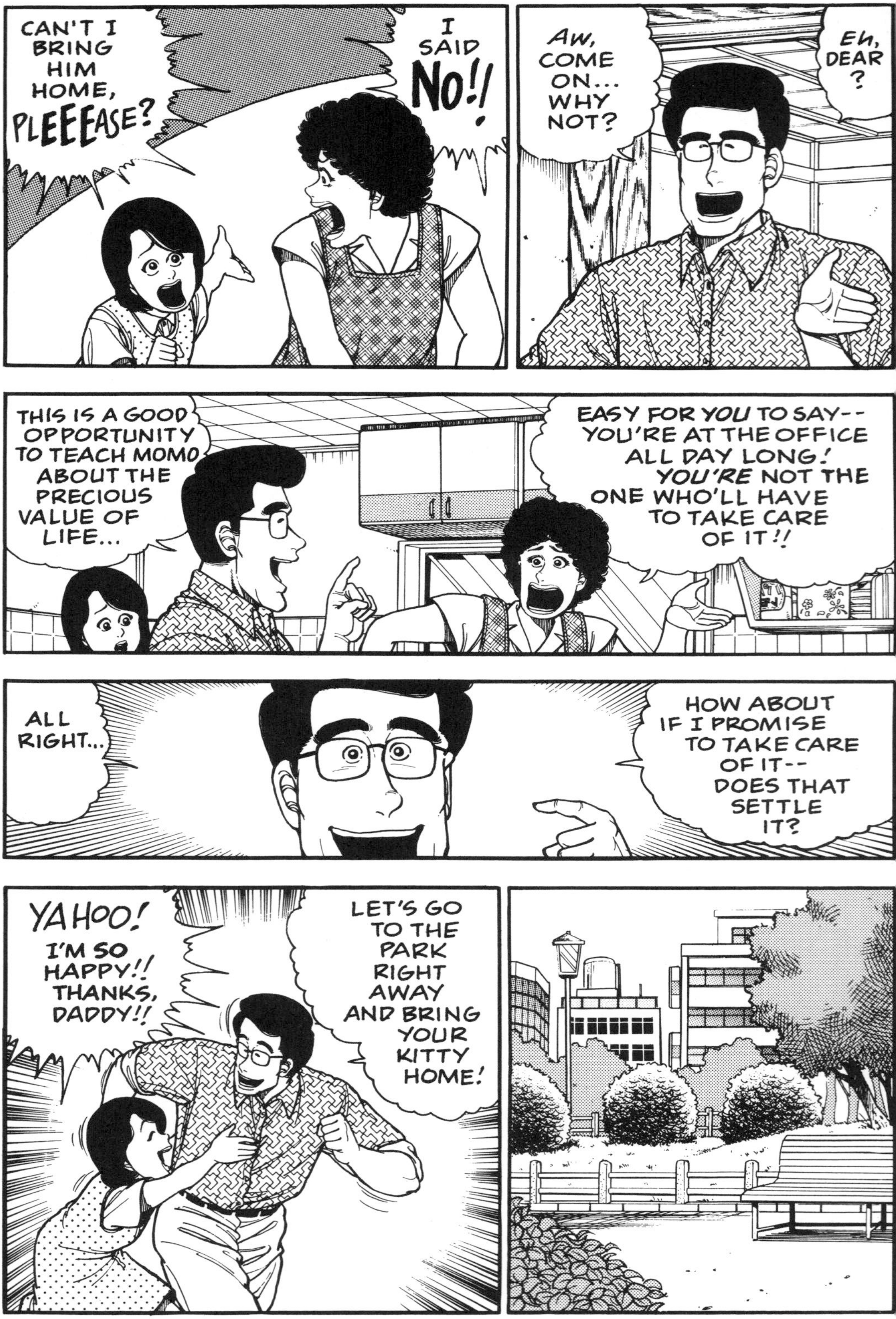
CAN'T I BRING HIM HOME, PLEEEASE?
I SAID NO!!
AW, COME ON... WHY NOT?
EH, DEAR?
THIS IS A GOOD OPPORTUNITY TO TEACH MOMO ABOUT THE PRECIOUS VALUE OF LIFE...
EASY FOR YOU TO SAY-- YOU'RE AT THE OFFICE ALL DAY LONG! YOU'RE NOT THE ONE WHO'LL HAVE TO TAKE CARE OF IT!!
ALL RIGHT...
HOW ABOUT IF I PROMISE TO TAKE CARE OF IT-- DOES THAT SETTLE IT?
YAHOO! I'M SO HAPPY!! THANKS, DADDY!!
LET'S GO TO THE PARK RIGHT AWAY AND BRING YOUR KITTY HOME!

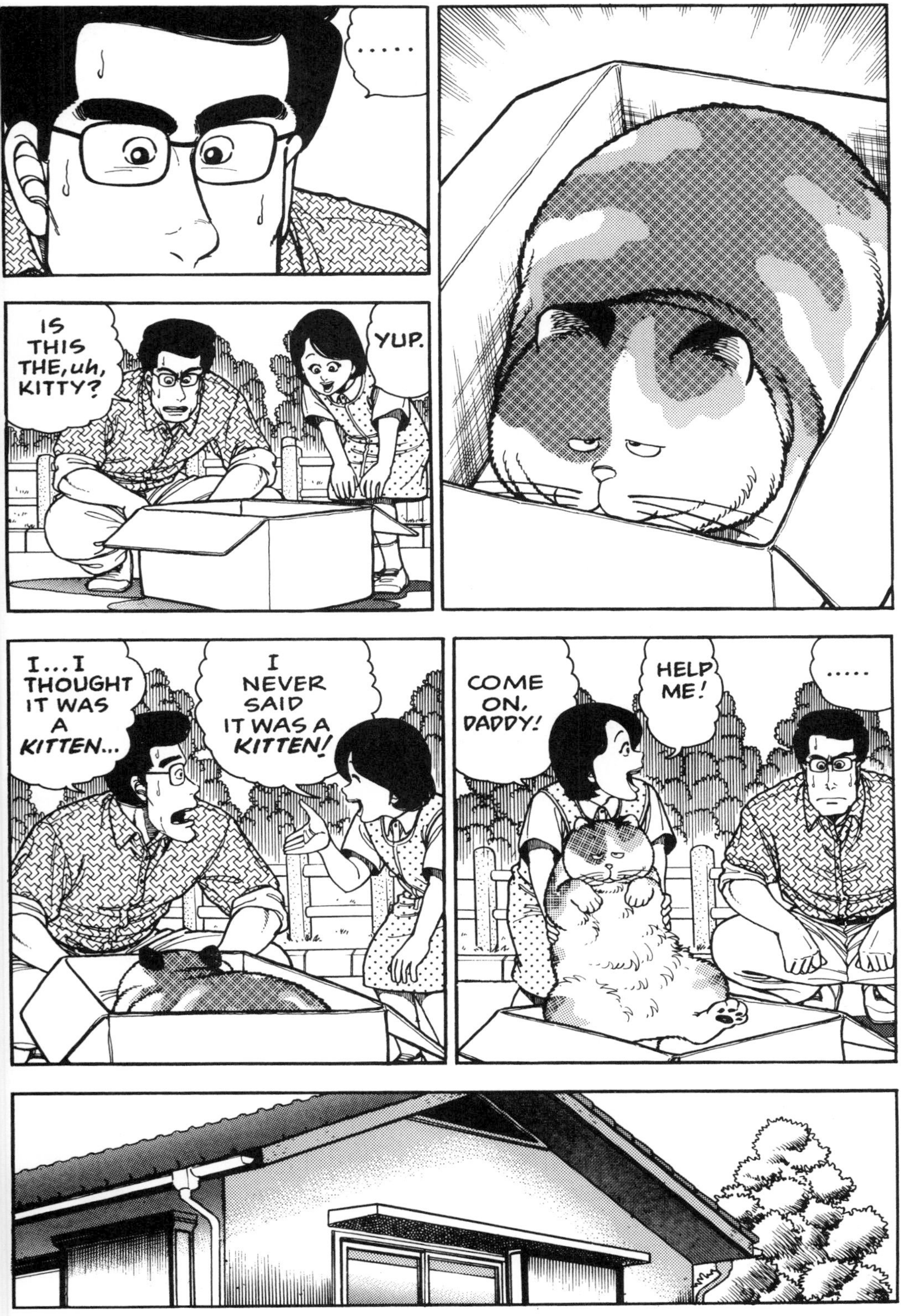
......
IS THIS THE, uh, KITTY?
YUP.
I... I THOUGHT IT WAS A KITTEN...
I NEVER SAID IT WAS A KITTEN!
COME ON, DADDY!
HELP ME!
.....

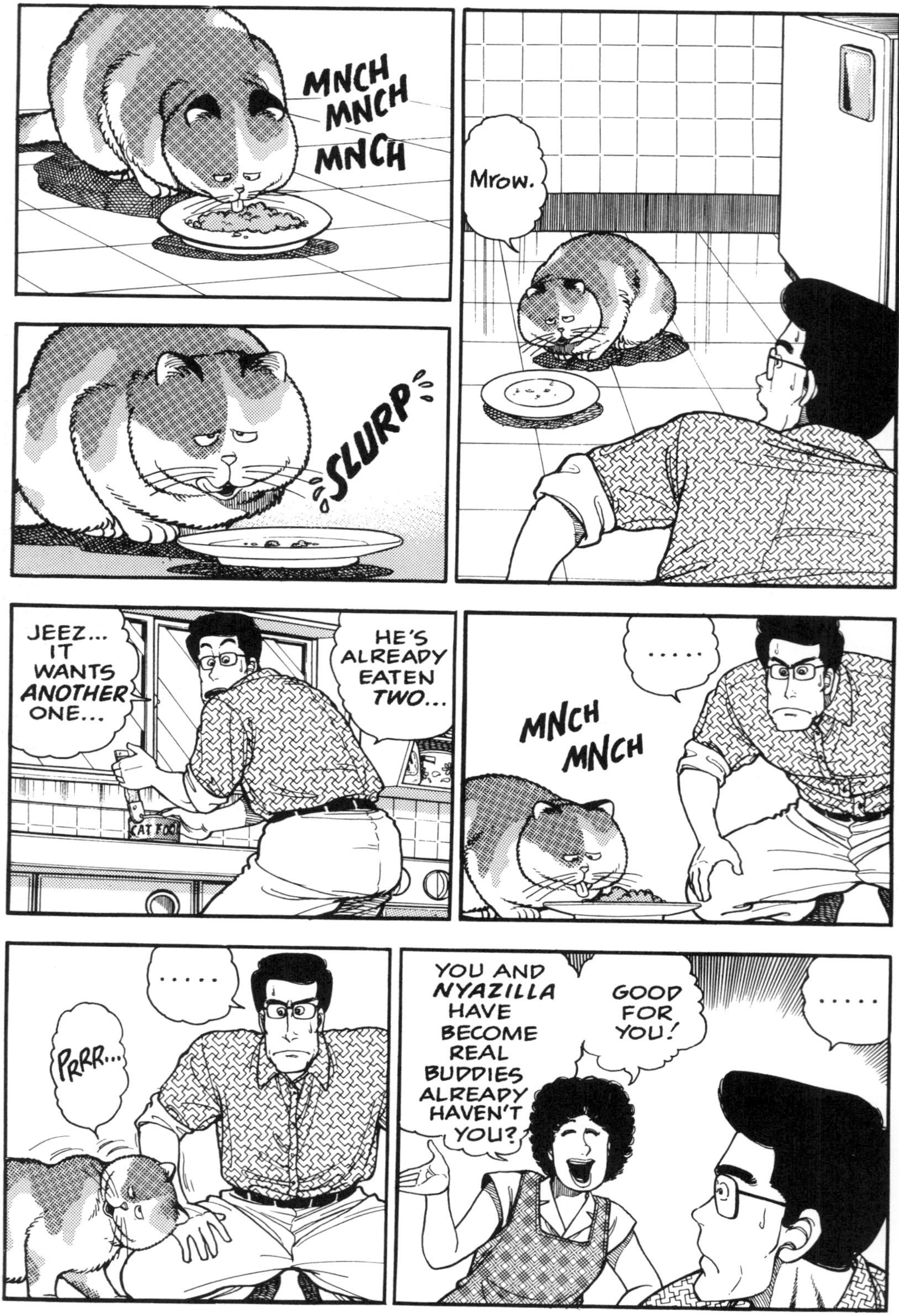
MNCH MNCH MNCH
SLURP
Mrow.
JEEZ... IT WANTS ANOTHER ONE...
CAT FOOD
HE'S ALREADY EATEN TWO...
.....
MNCH MNCH
.....
PRRR...
YOU AND NYAZILLA HAVE BECOME REAL BUDDIES ALREADY HAVEN'T YOU?
GOOD FOR YOU!
.....

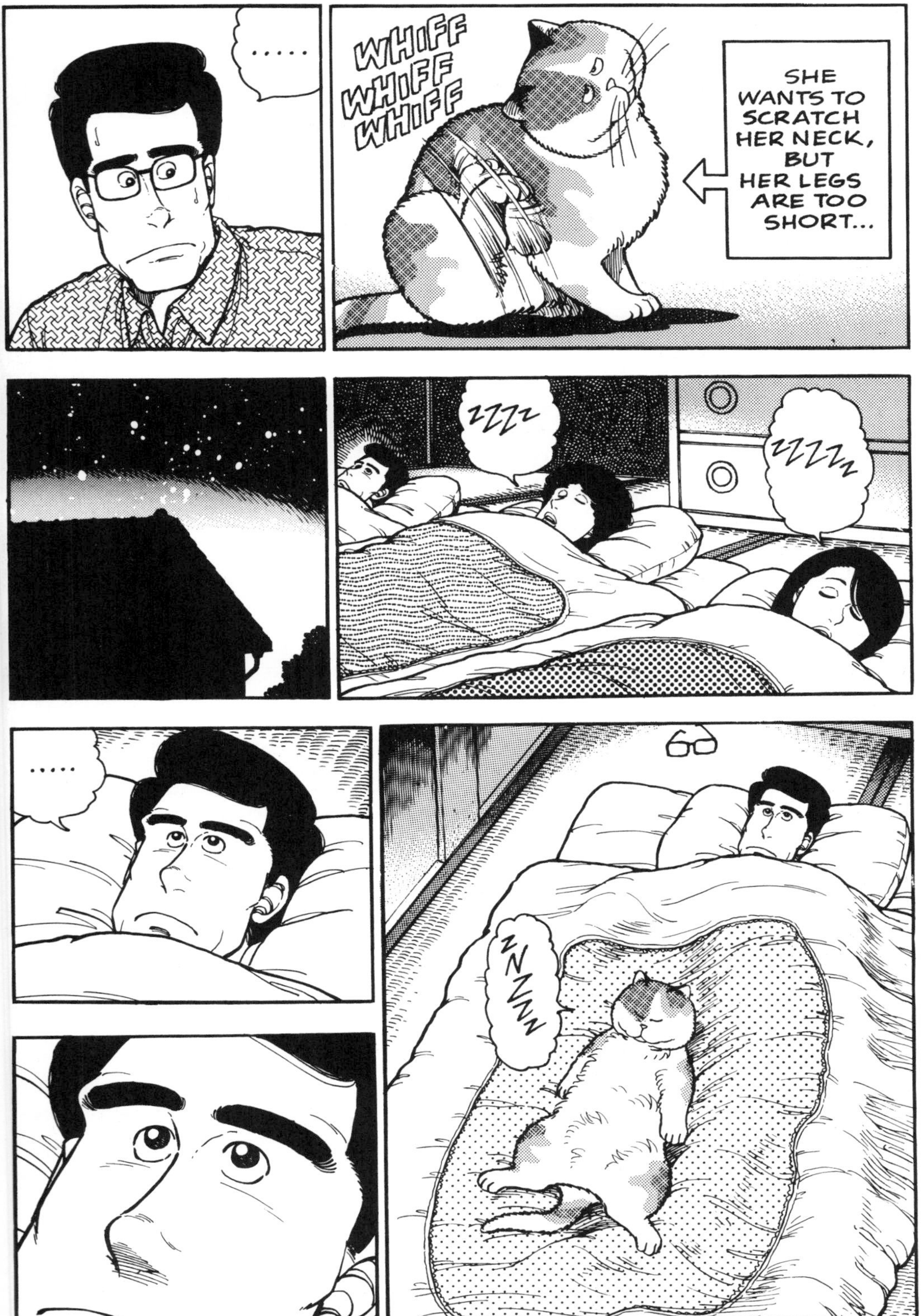
.....
WHIFF WHIFF WHIFF
SHE WANTS TO SCRATCH HER NECK, BUT HER LEGS ARE TOO SHORT...
ZZZZ
ZZZZZ
.....
ZZZZZ

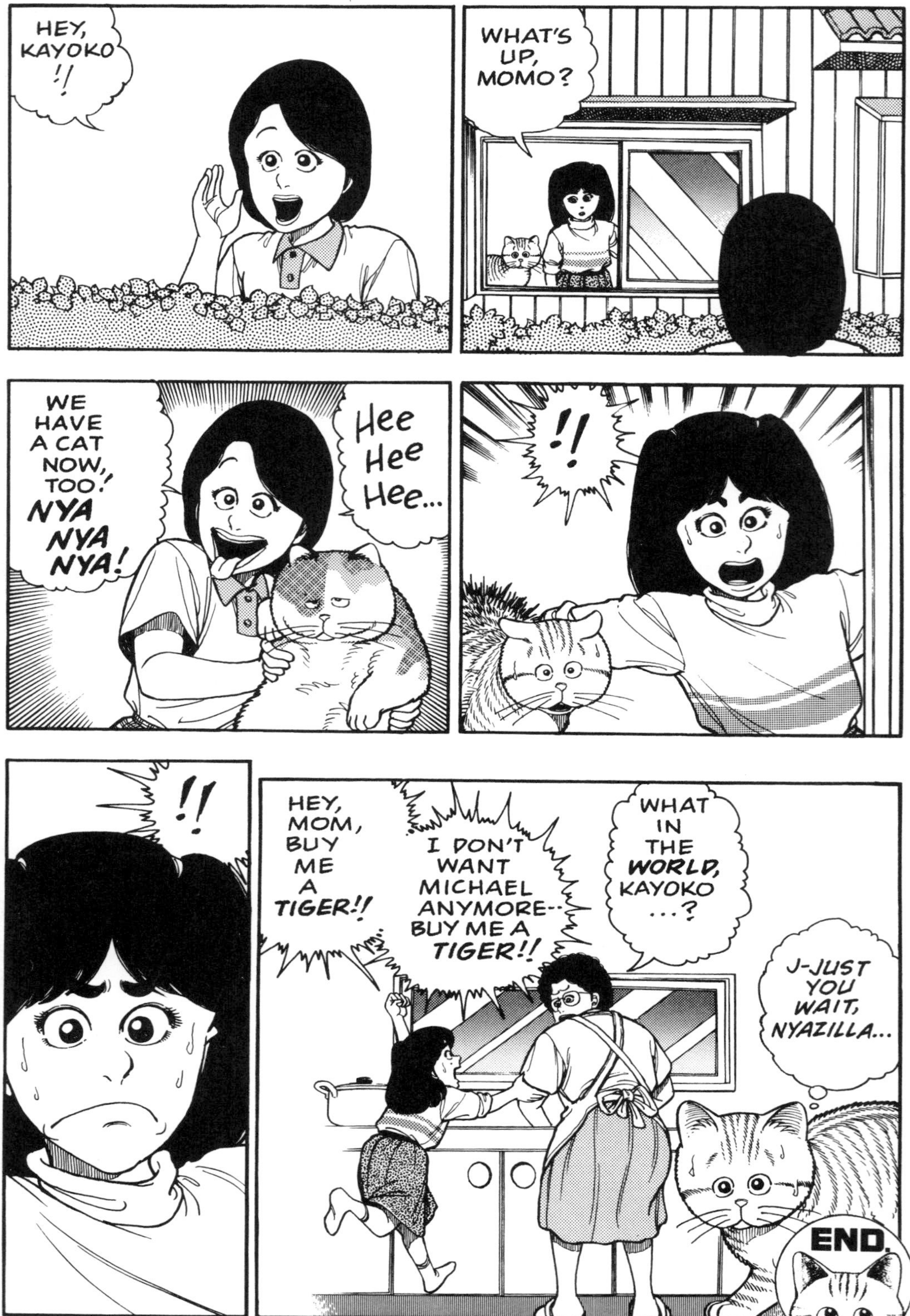
HEY, KAYOKO !!
WHAT'S UP, MOMO?
WE HAVE A CAT NOW, TOO! NYA NYA NYA!
Hee Hee Hee...
!!
!!
HEY, MOM, BUY ME A TIGER!!
I DON'T WANT MICHAEL ANYMORE-- BUY ME A TIGER!!
WHAT IN THE WORLD, KAYOKO ...?
J-JUST YOU WAIT, NYAZILLA...
END.

# The MICHAEL FAMILY on SAFARI

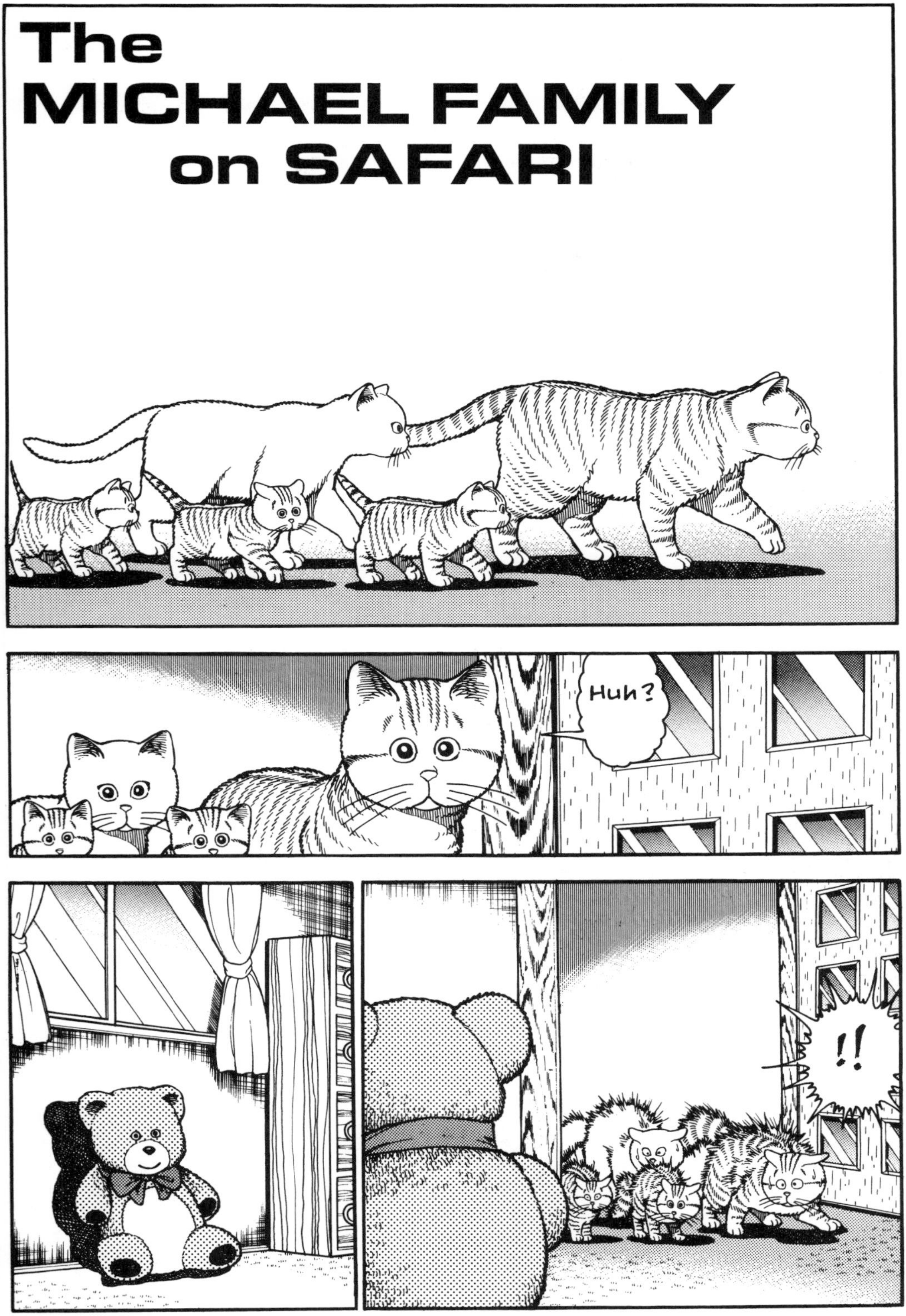
Huh?
!!

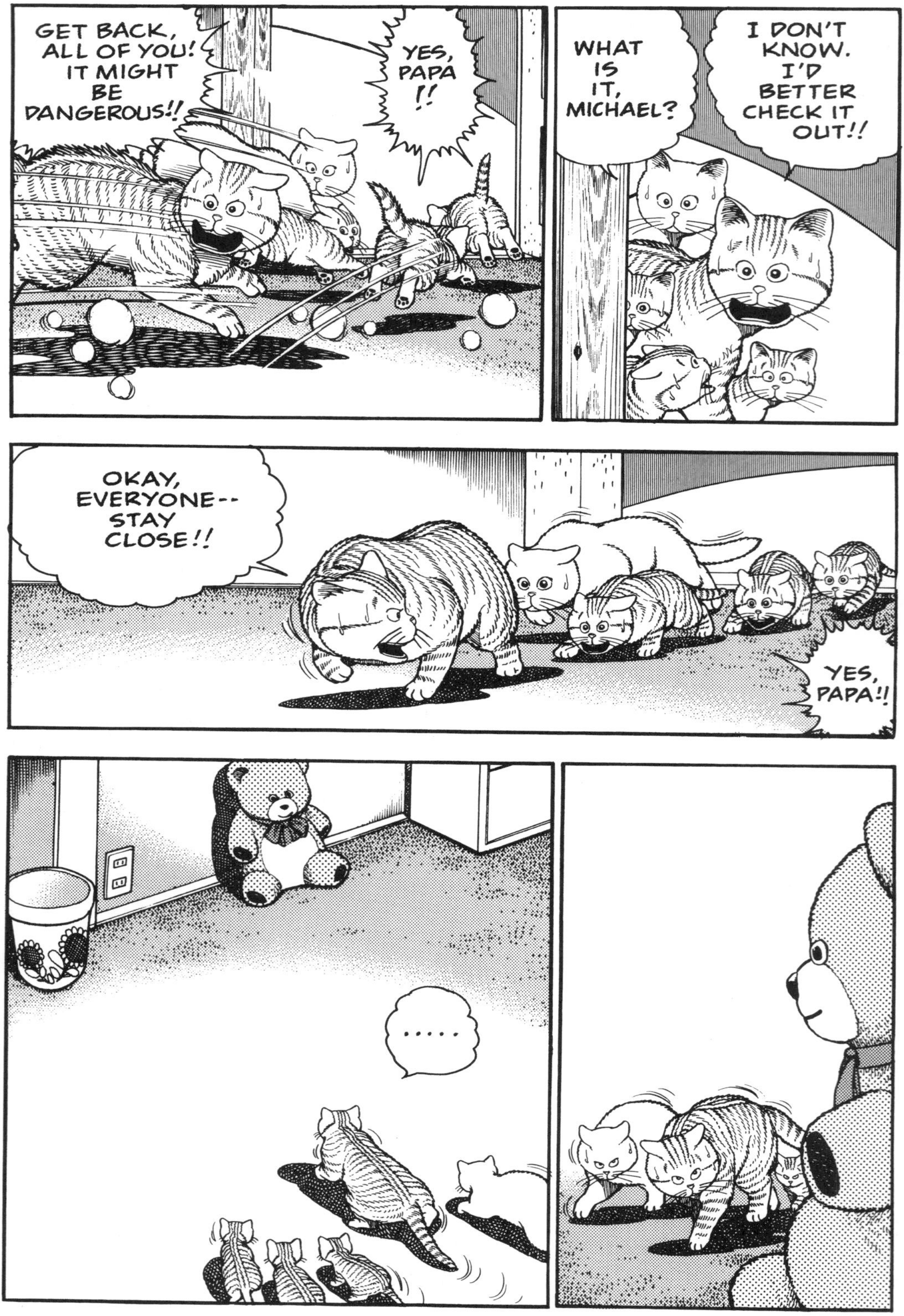
GET BACK, ALL OF YOU! IT MIGHT BE DANGEROUS!!
YES, PAPA!!
WHAT IS IT, MICHAEL?
I DON'T KNOW. I'D BETTER CHECK IT OUT!!
OKAY, EVERYONE-- STAY CLOSE!!
YES, PAPA!!
.....

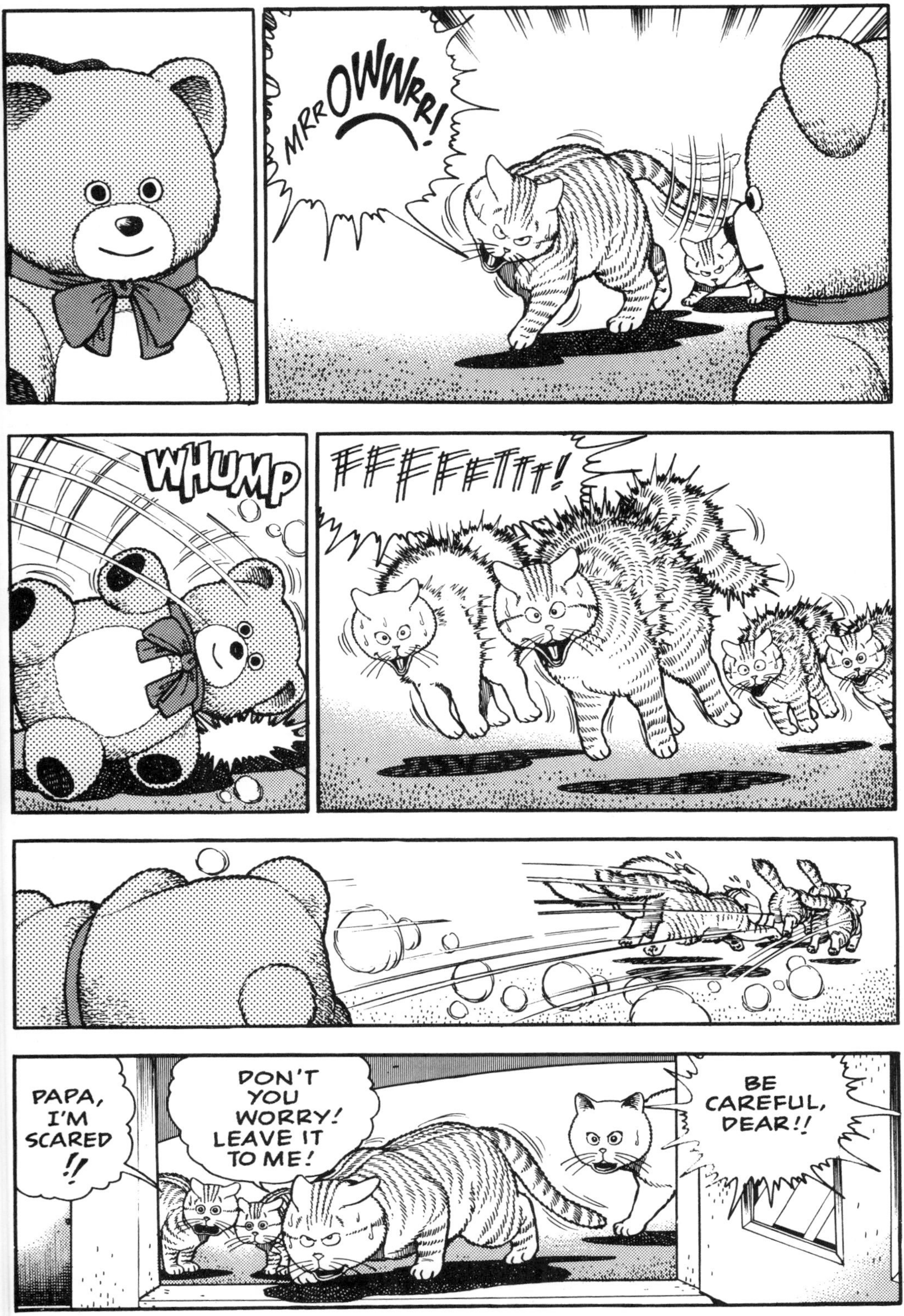
MRROWWRR!
WHUMP
FFFFFTTTT!
PAPA, I'M SCARED!!
DON'T YOU WORRY! LEAVE IT TO ME!
BE CAREFUL, DEAR!!

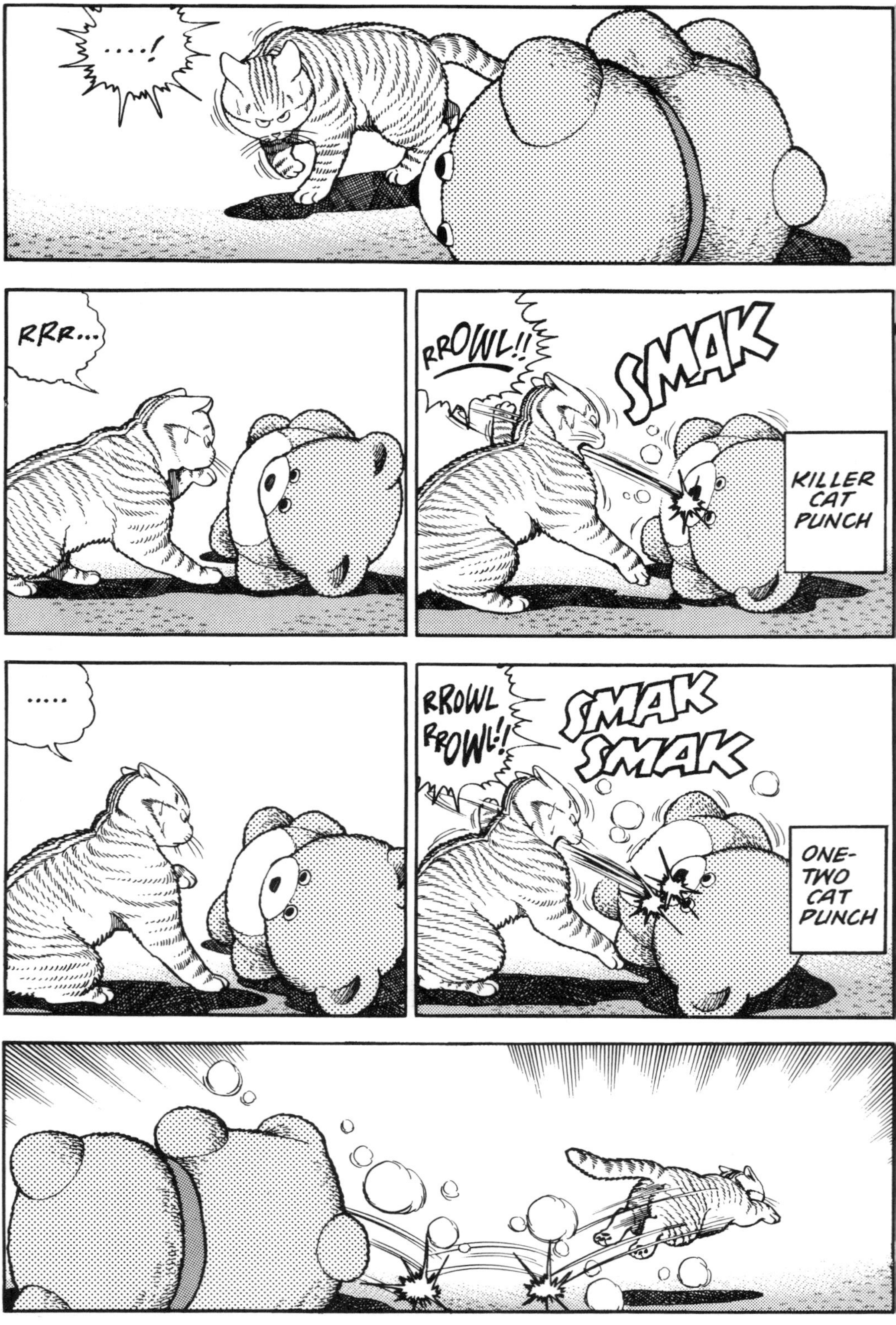
....!
RRR...
RROWL!!
SMAK
KILLER CAT PUNCH
.....
RROWL
RROWL!!
SMAK
SMAK
ONE-TWO CAT PUNCH

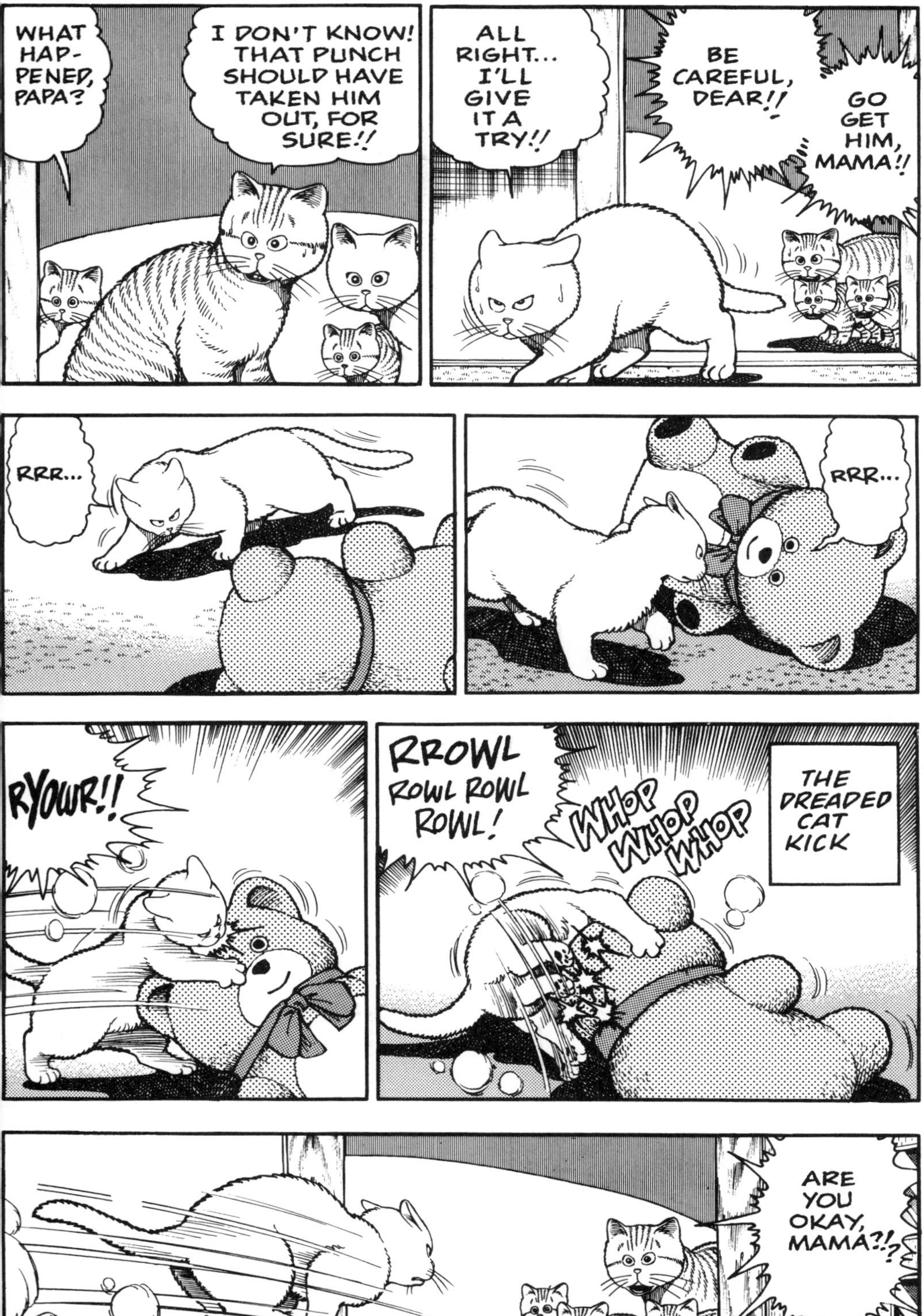

WHAT HAP-PENED, PAPA?
I DON'T KNOW! THAT PUNCH SHOULD HAVE TAKEN HIM OUT, FOR SURE!!
ALL RIGHT... I'LL GIVE IT A TRY!!
BE CAREFUL, DEAR!!
GO GET HIM, MAMA!!
RRR...
RRR...
RYOWR!!
RROWL ROWL ROWL ROWL!
WHOP WHOP WHOP
THE DREADED CAT KICK
ARE YOU OKAY, MAMA?!?

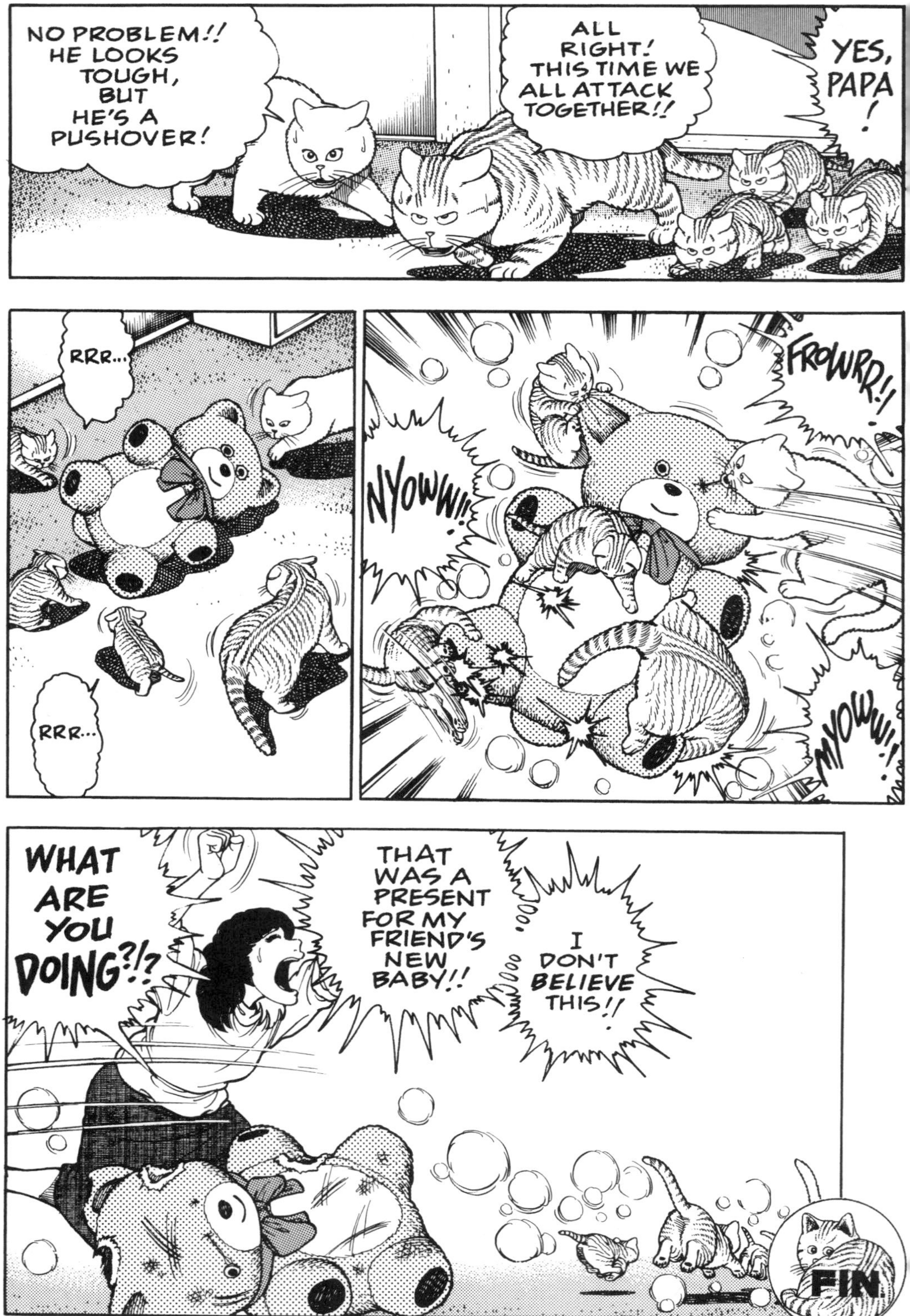
NO PROBLEM!! HE LOOKS TOUGH, BUT HE'S A PUSHOVER!
ALL RIGHT! THIS TIME WE ALL ATTACK TOGETHER!!
YES, PAPA!
RRR...
RRR...
FROWRR!!
NYOWW!!
MYOWW!!
WHAT ARE YOU DOING?!?
THAT WAS A PRESENT FOR MY FRIEND'S NEW BABY!!
I DON'T BELIEVE THIS!!
FIN

# WHAT'S NYAZILLA?

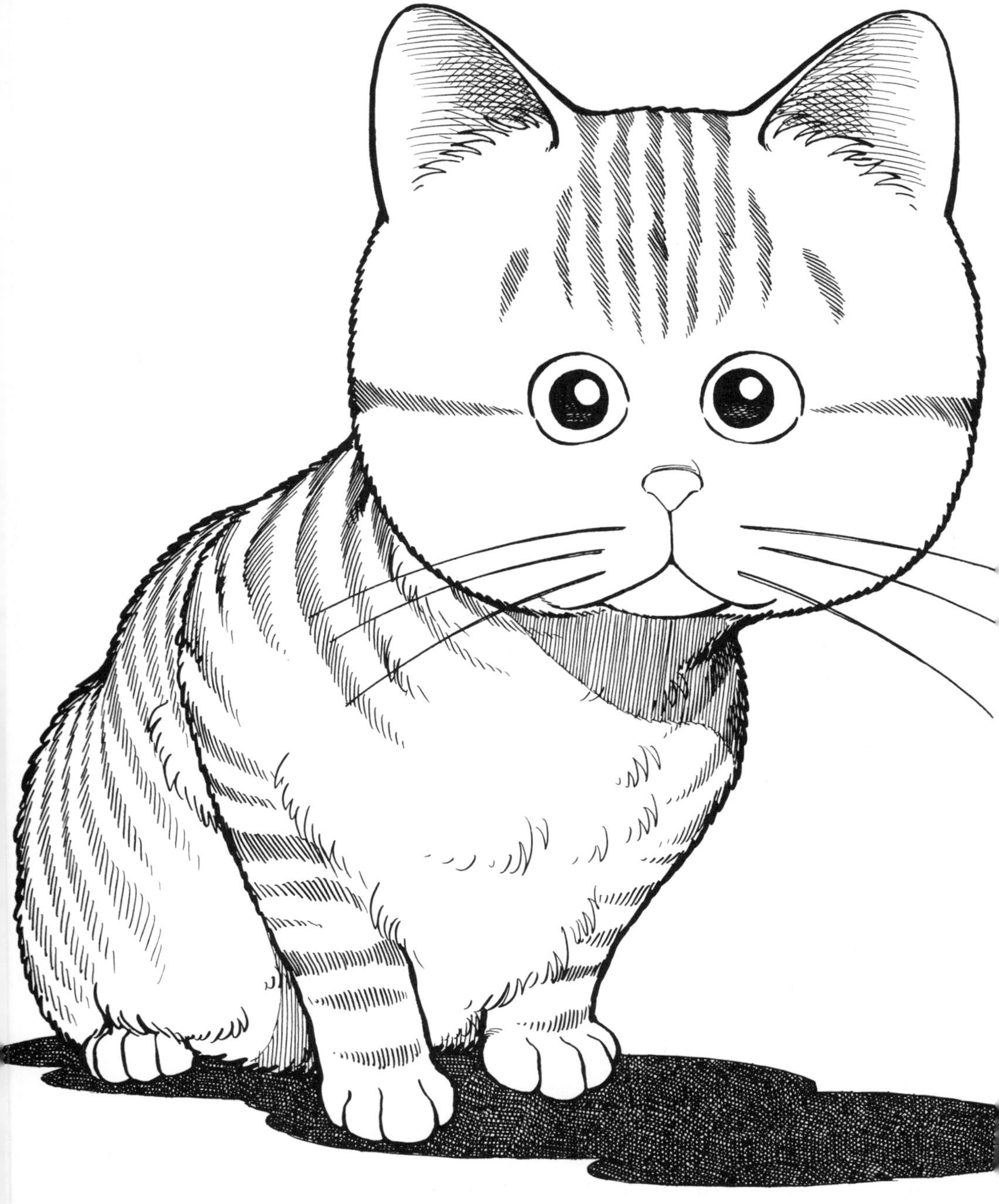

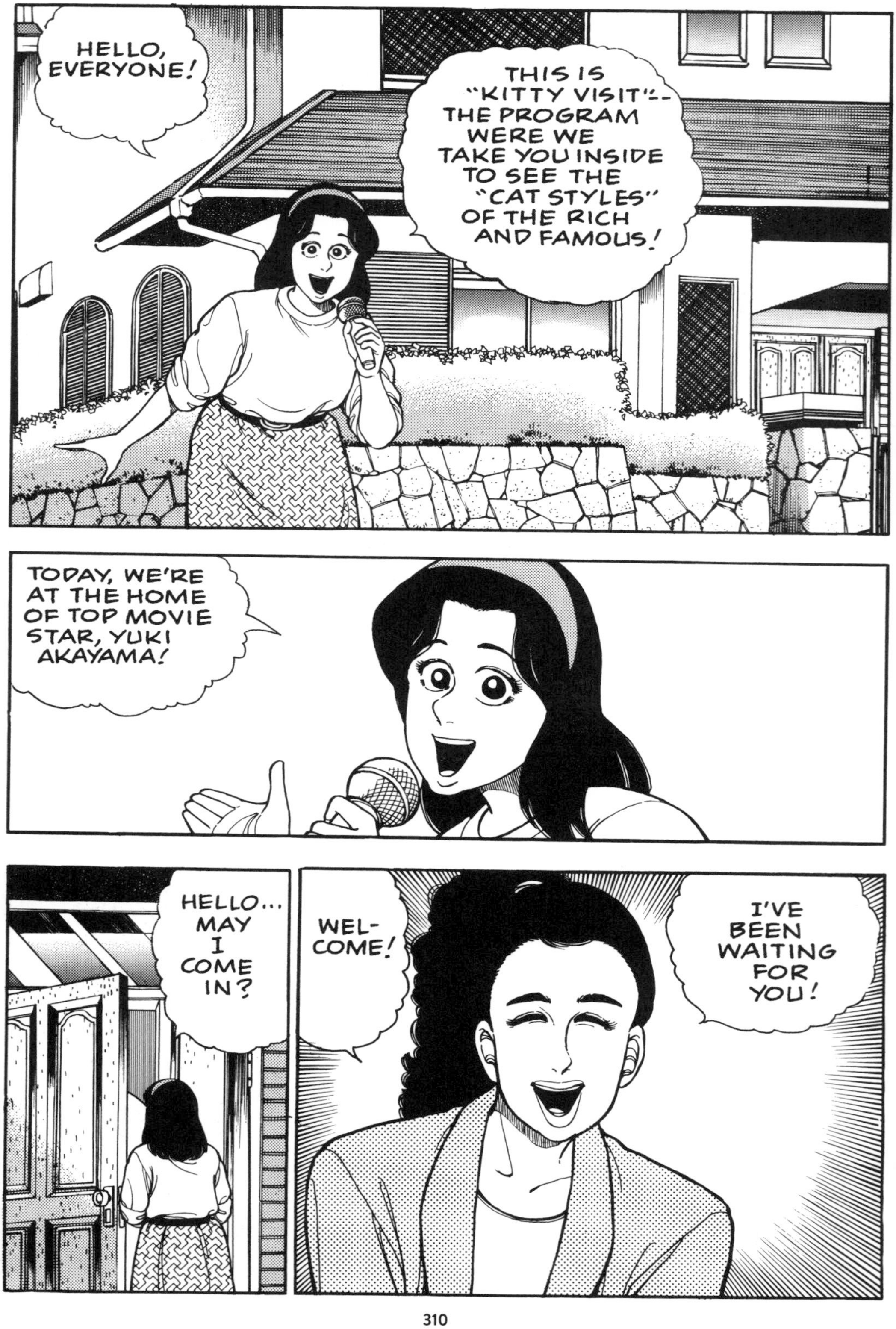
HELLO, EVERYONE!
THIS IS "KITTY VISIT"-- THE PROGRAM WERE WE TAKE YOU INSIDE TO SEE THE "CAT STYLES" OF THE RICH AND FAMOUS!
TODAY, WE'RE AT THE HOME OF TOP MOVIE STAR, YUKI AKAYAMA!
HELLO... MAY I COME IN?
WEL-COME!
I'VE BEEN WAITING FOR YOU!

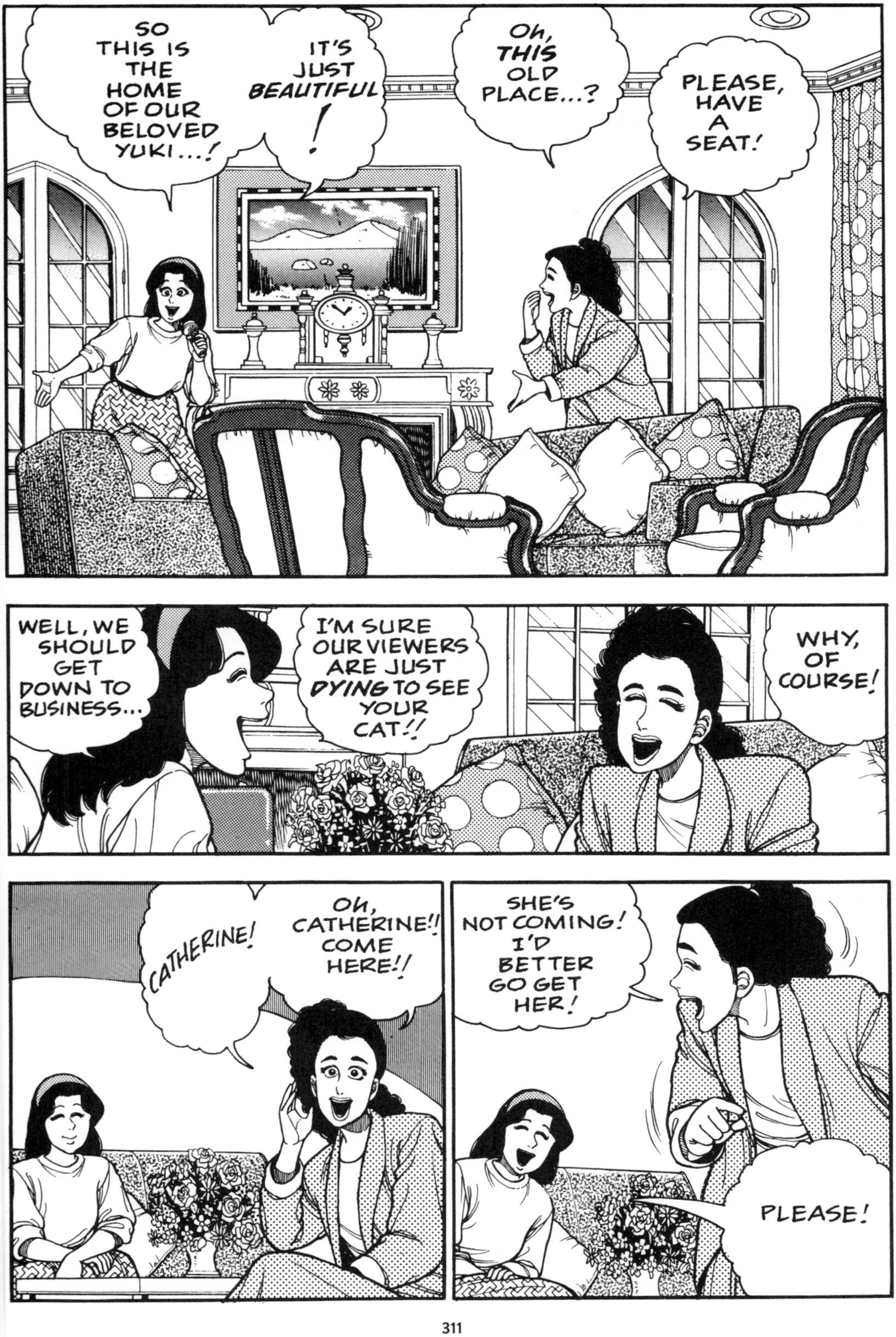
SO THIS IS THE HOME OF OUR BELOVED YUKI...!
IT'S JUST BEAUTIFUL!
Oh, THIS OLD PLACE...?
PLEASE, HAVE A SEAT!
WELL, WE SHOULD GET DOWN TO BUSINESS...
I'M SURE OUR VIEWERS ARE JUST DYING TO SEE YOUR CAT!!
WHY, OF COURSE!
CATHERINE!
Oh, CATHERINE!! COME HERE!!
SHE'S NOT COMING! I'D BETTER GO GET HER!
PLEASE!

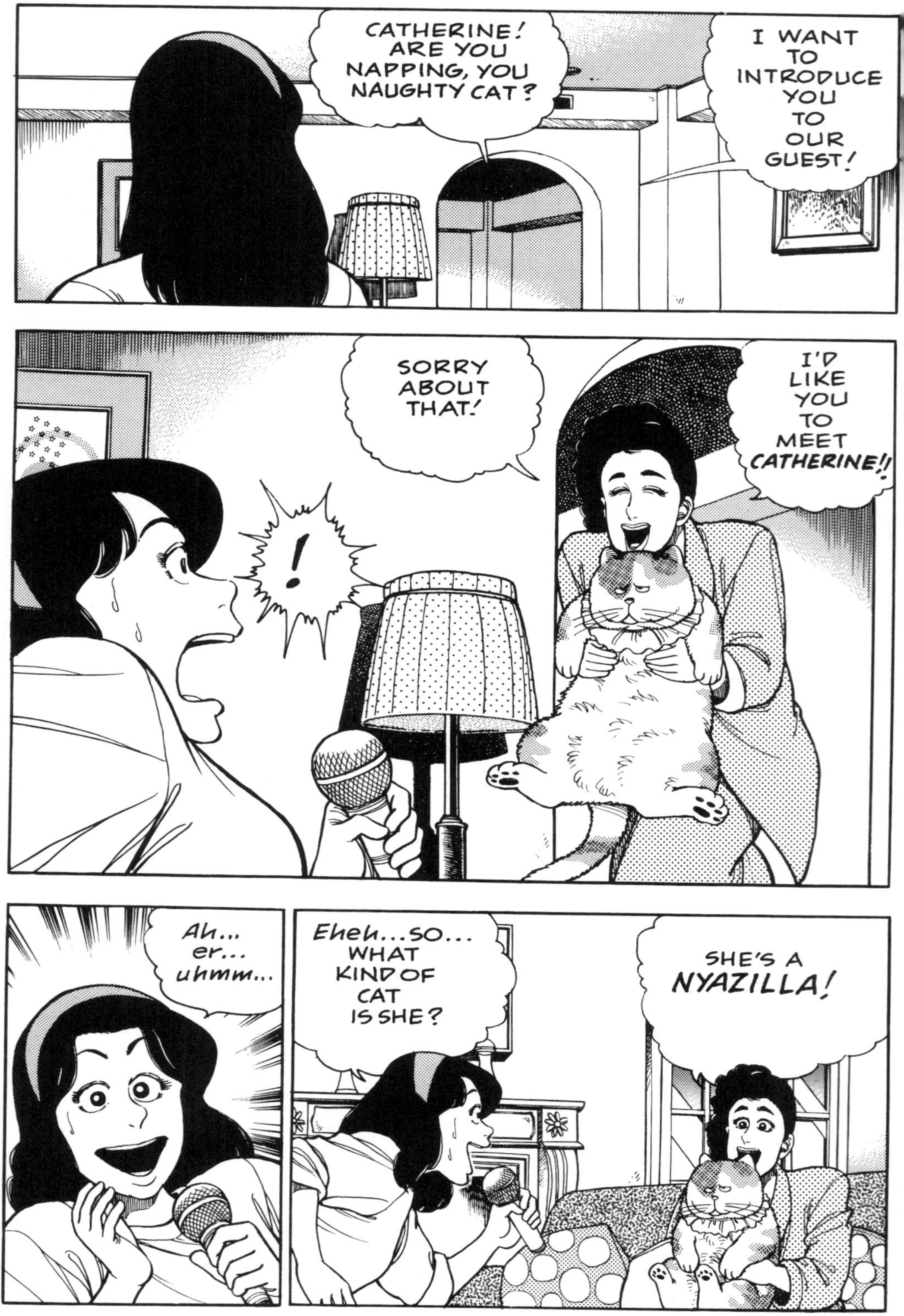
CATHERINE! ARE YOU NAPPING, YOU NAUGHTY CAT?
I WANT TO INTRODUCE YOU TO OUR GUEST!
SORRY ABOUT THAT!
I'D LIKE YOU TO MEET CATHERINE!!
!
Ah... er... uhmm...
Eheh...SO... WHAT KIND OF CAT IS SHE?
SHE'S A NYAZILLA!

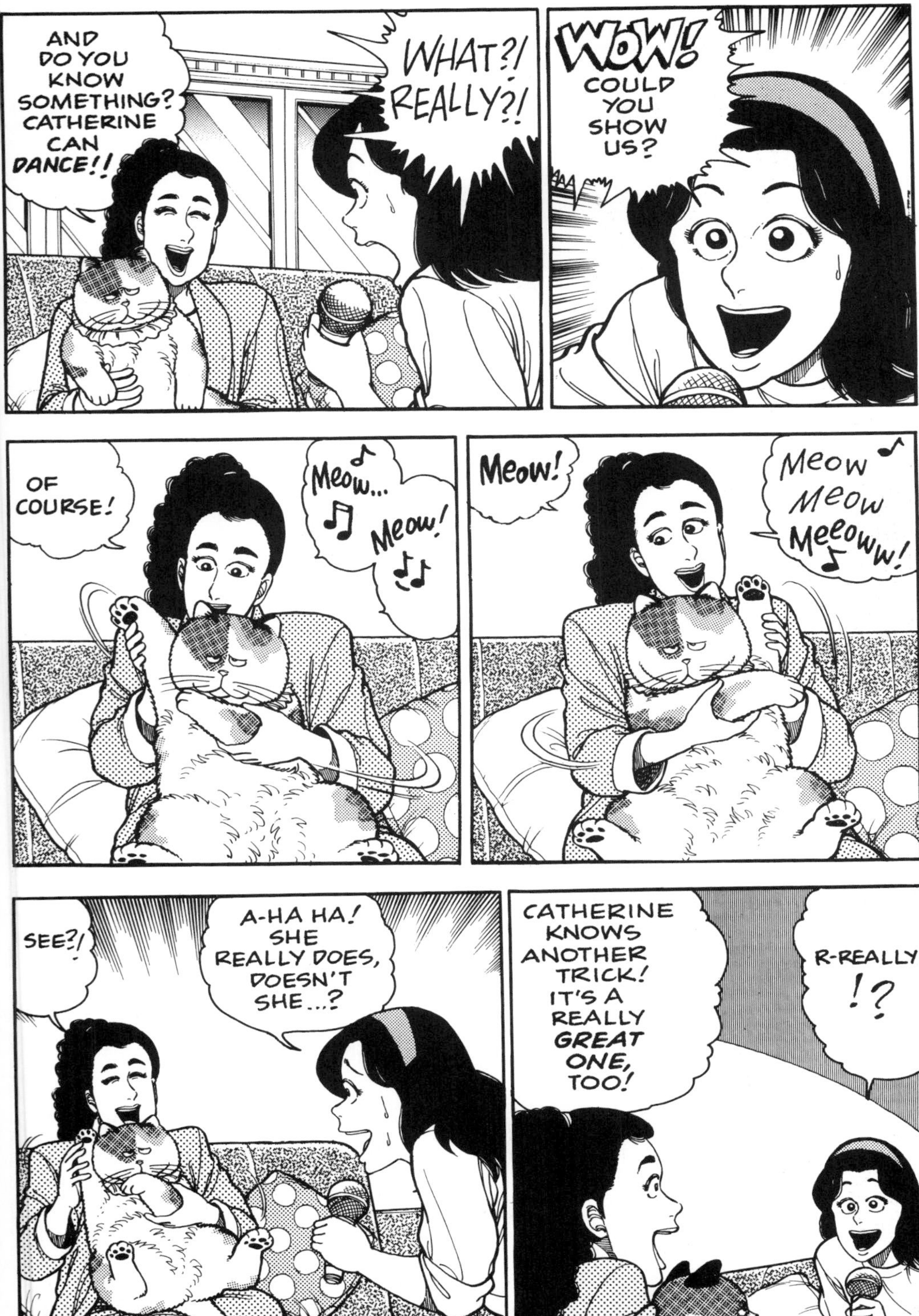
AND DO YOU KNOW SOMETHING? CATHERINE CAN DANCE!!
WHAT?! REALLY?!
WOW! COULD YOU SHOW US?
OF COURSE!
Meow... Meow!
Meow!
Meow Meow Meeoww!
SEE?!
A-HA HA! SHE REALLY DOES, DOESN'T SHE...?
CATHERINE KNOWS ANOTHER TRICK! IT'S A REALLY GREAT ONE, TOO!
R-REALLY !?

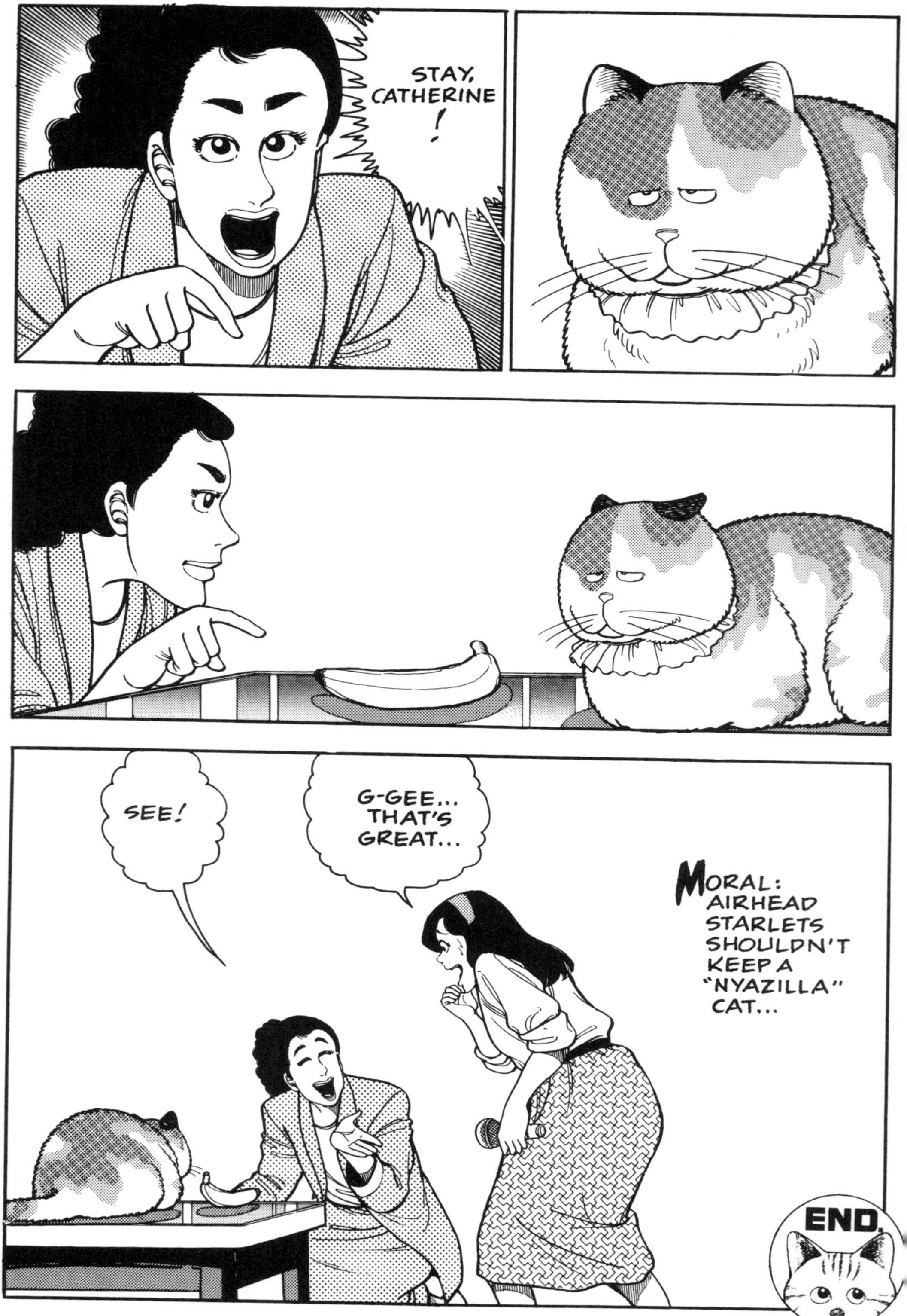
STAY, CATHERINE!
SEE!
G-GEE... THAT'S GREAT...
MORAL: AIRHEAD STARLETS SHOULDN'T KEEP A "NYAZILLA" CAT...
END.

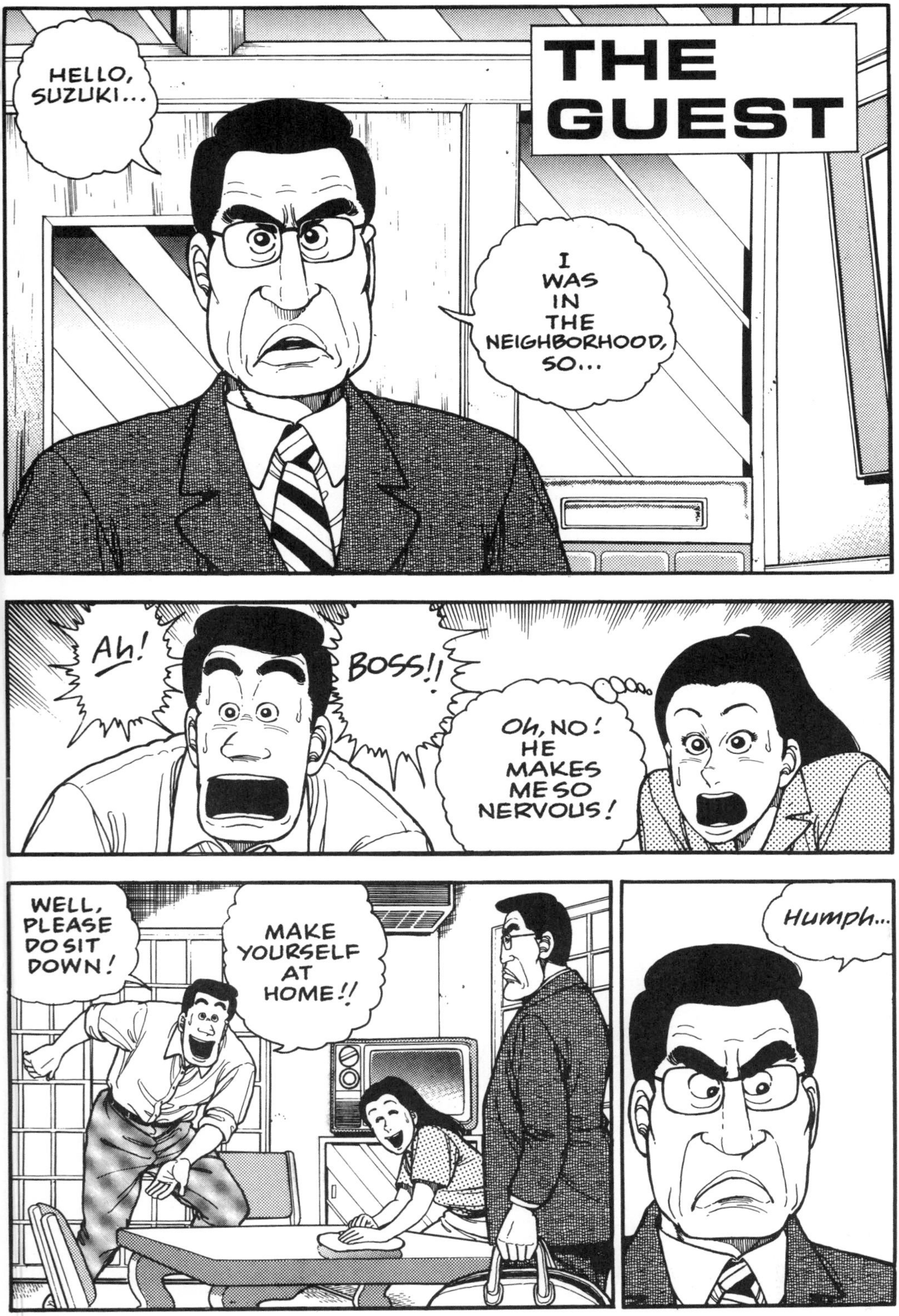
THE GUEST
HELLO, SUZUKI...
I WAS IN THE NEIGHBORHOOD, SO...
Ah!
BOSS!!
Oh, NO! HE MAKES ME SO NERVOUS!
WELL, PLEASE DO SIT DOWN!
MAKE YOURSELF AT HOME!!
Humph...

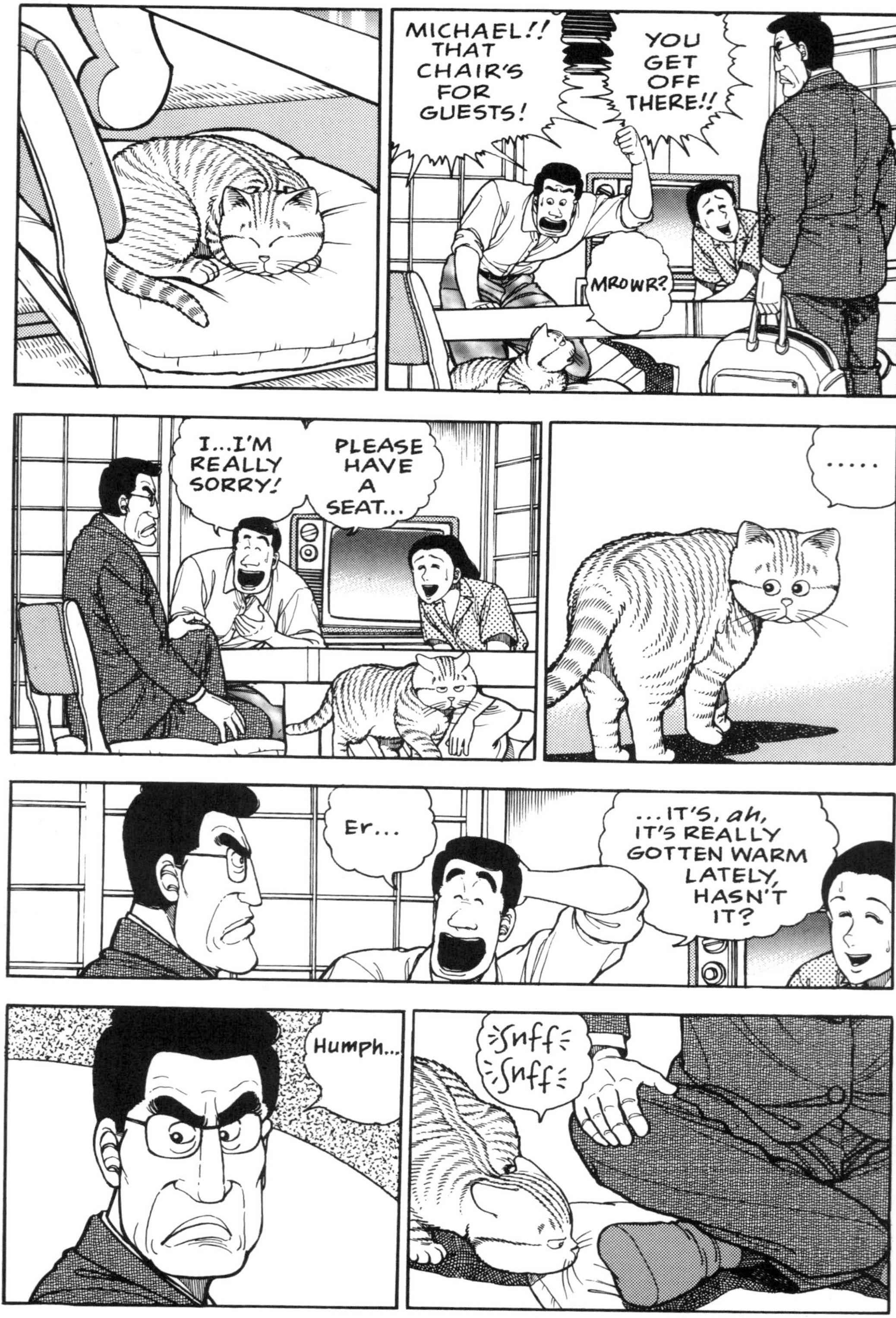
MICHAEL!! THAT CHAIR'S FOR GUESTS!
YOU GET OFF THERE!!
MROWR?
I...I'M REALLY SORRY!
PLEASE HAVE A SEAT...
.....
Er...
...IT'S, *ah*, IT'S REALLY GOTTEN WARM LATELY, HASN'T IT?
Humph...
Snff Snff

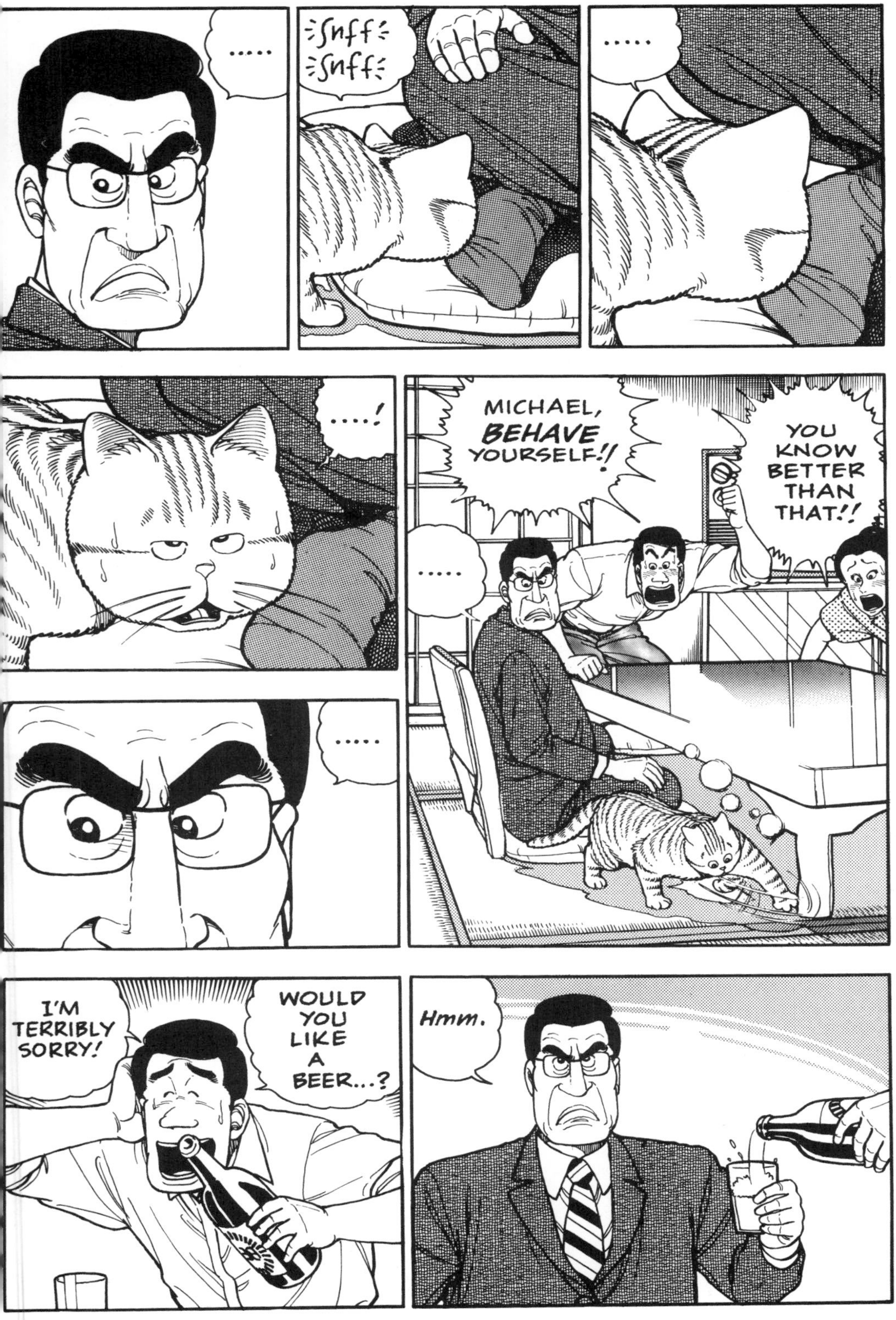

.....
SNFF SNFF
.....
....!
MICHAEL, BEHAVE YOURSELF!!
YOU KNOW BETTER THAN THAT!!
.....
.....
I'M TERRIBLY SORRY!
WOULD YOU LIKE A BEER...?
Hmm.

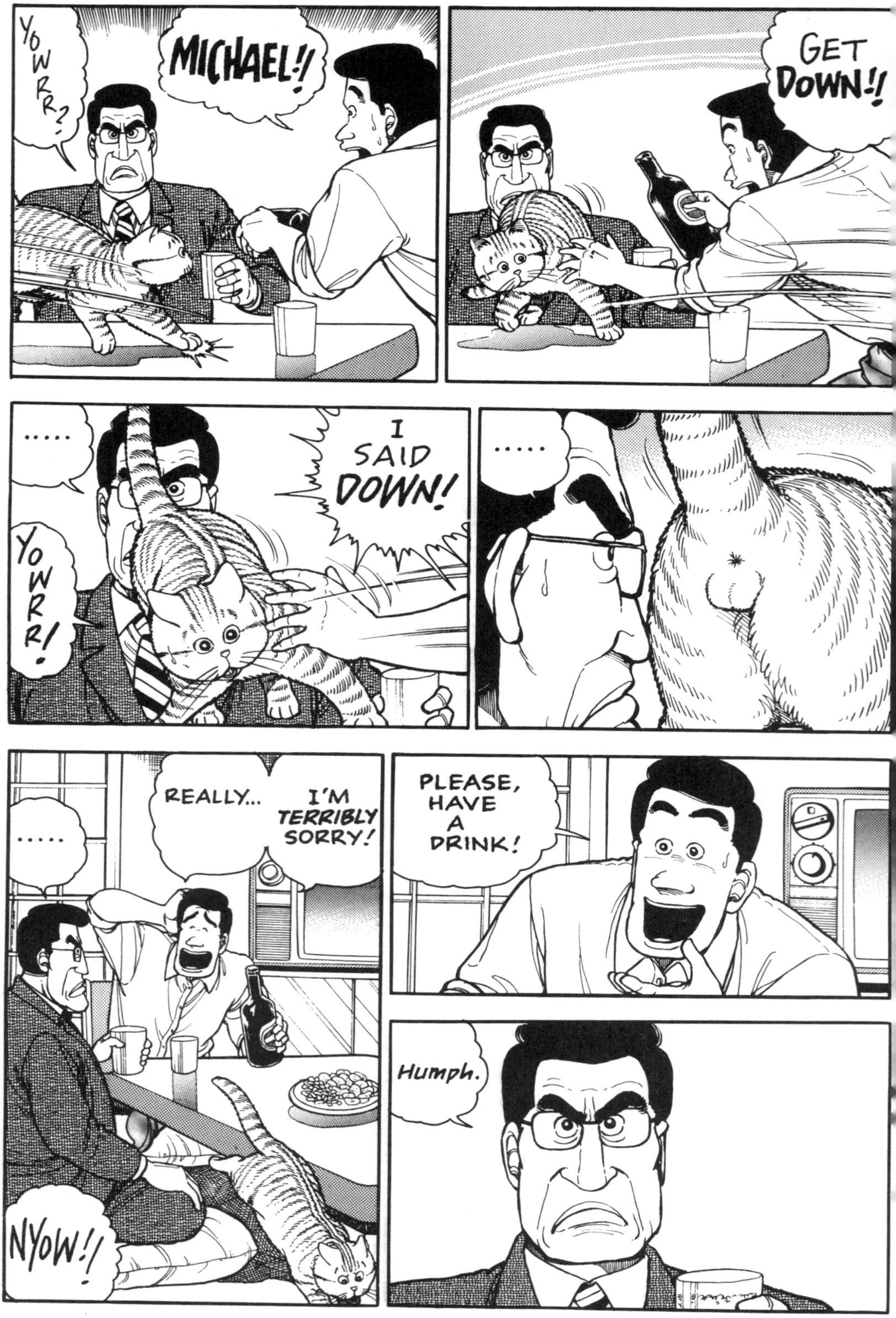
YOWRR?
MICHAEL!!
GET DOWN!!
.....
I SAID DOWN!
YOWRR!
.....
.....
REALLY...
I'M TERRIBLY SORRY!
NYOW!!
PLEASE, HAVE A DRINK!
Humph.

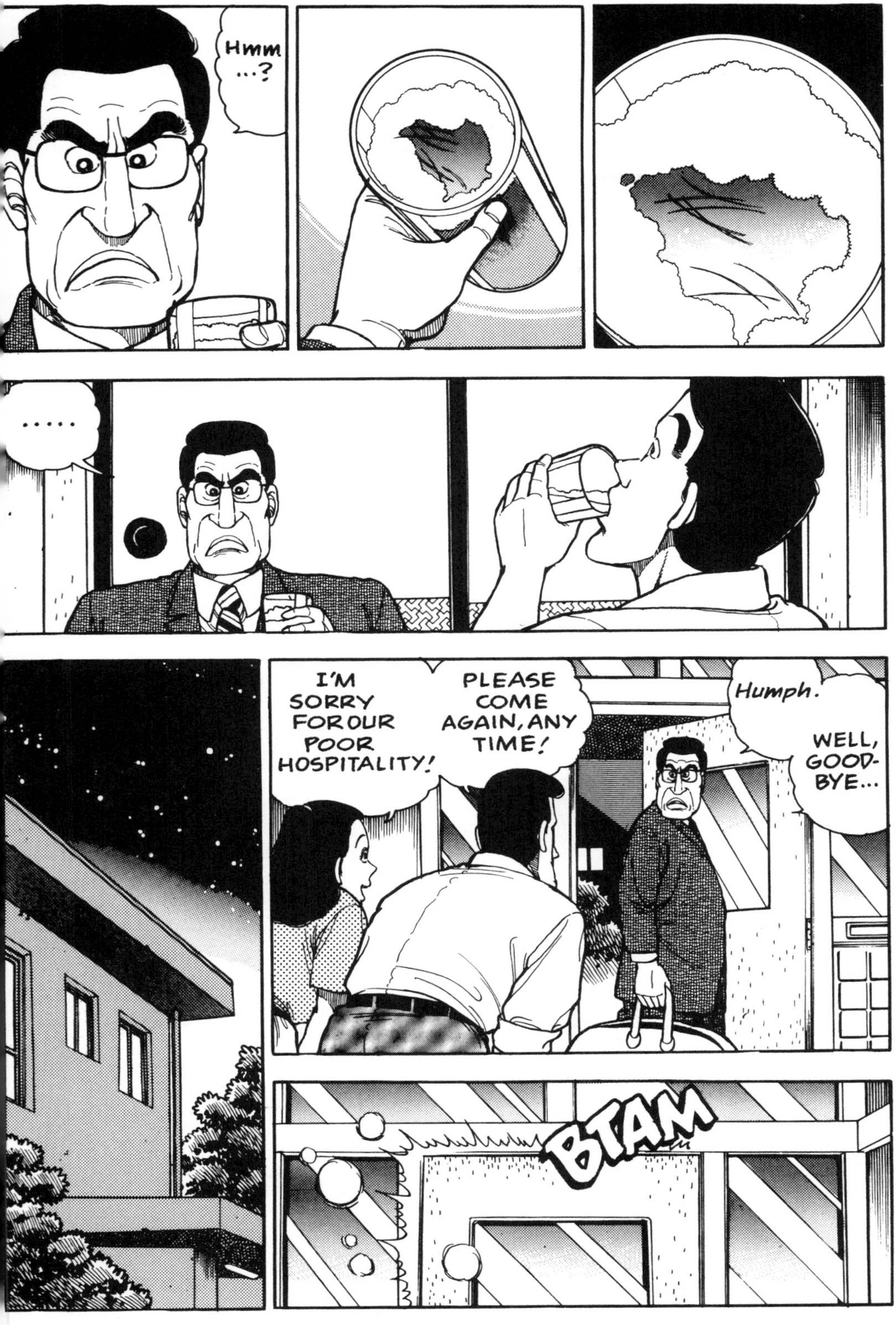

Hmm ...?
......
I'M SORRY FOROUR POOR HOSPITALITY!
PLEASE COME AGAIN, ANY TIME!
Humph.
WELL, GOOD-BYE...
BTAM

*Wheww!*

THAT WAS EXHAUSTING!!

SKREEK

WHA--

YOU... WHA...

.....

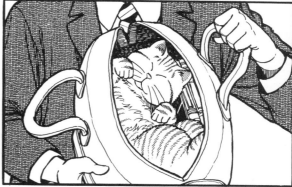

I-I'M SO SORRY!!

BTAM

FIN

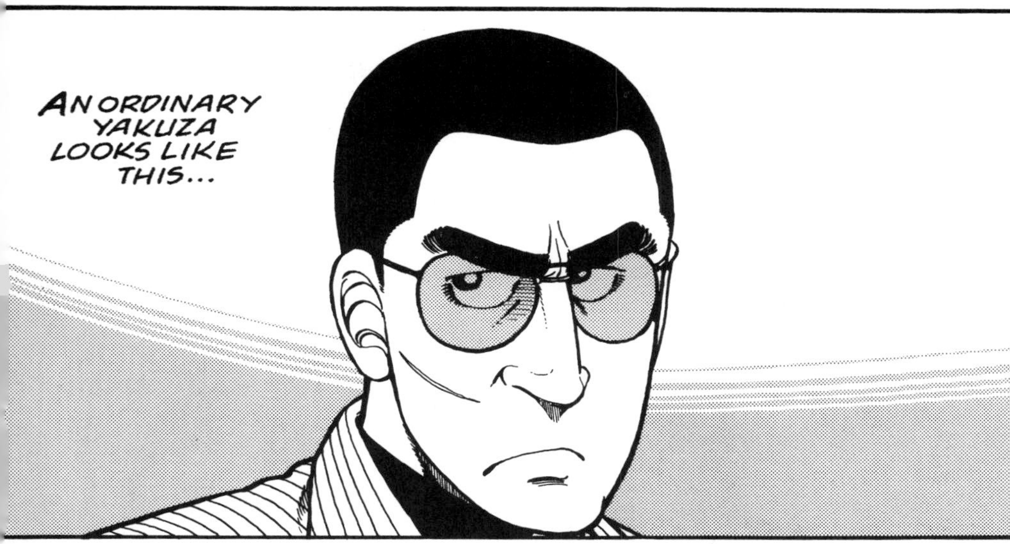
AN ORDINARY YAKUZA LOOKS LIKE THIS...

# MACHISMO!

## YAKUZA K vs. YAKUZA M!!

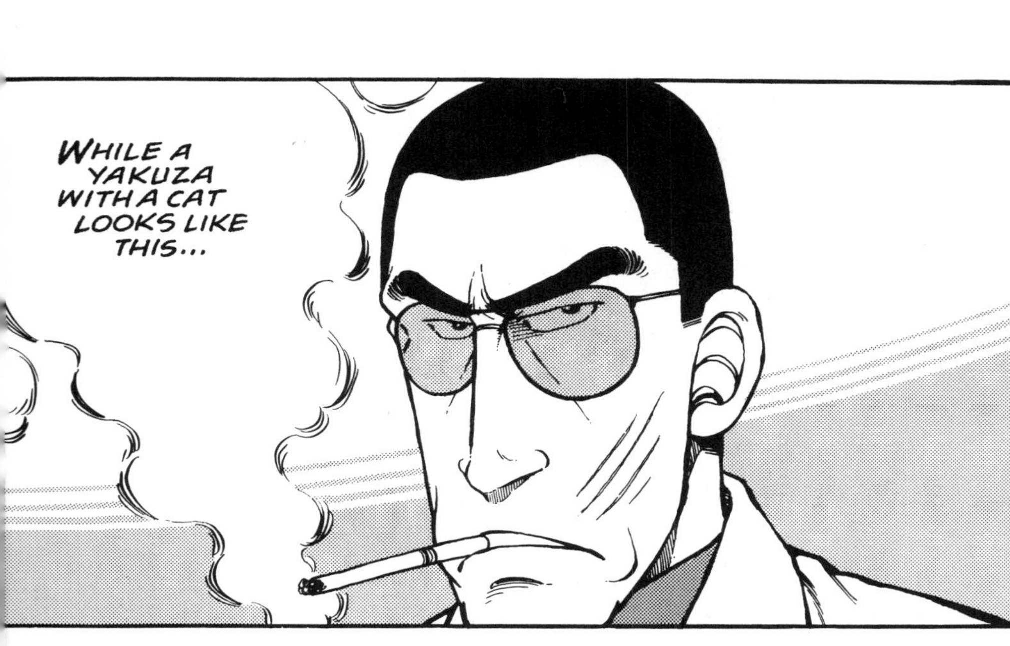
WHILE A YAKUZA WITH A CAT LOOKS LIKE THIS...

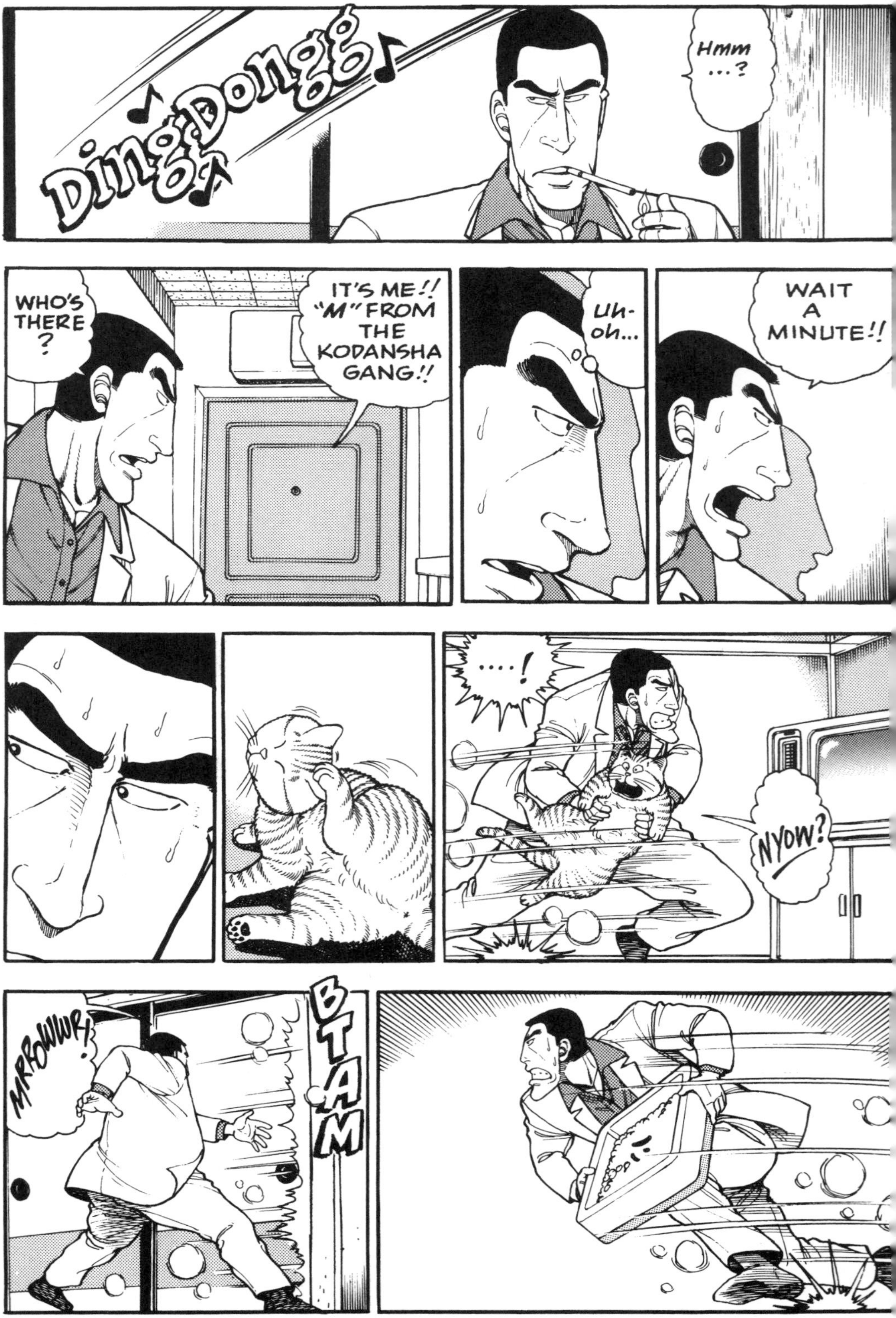

Ding-Dongg
Hmm ...?
WHO'S THERE?
IT'S ME!! "M" FROM THE KODANSHA GANG!!
Uh-oh...
WAIT A MINUTE!!
....!
NYOW?
MRROWWR!
BTAM

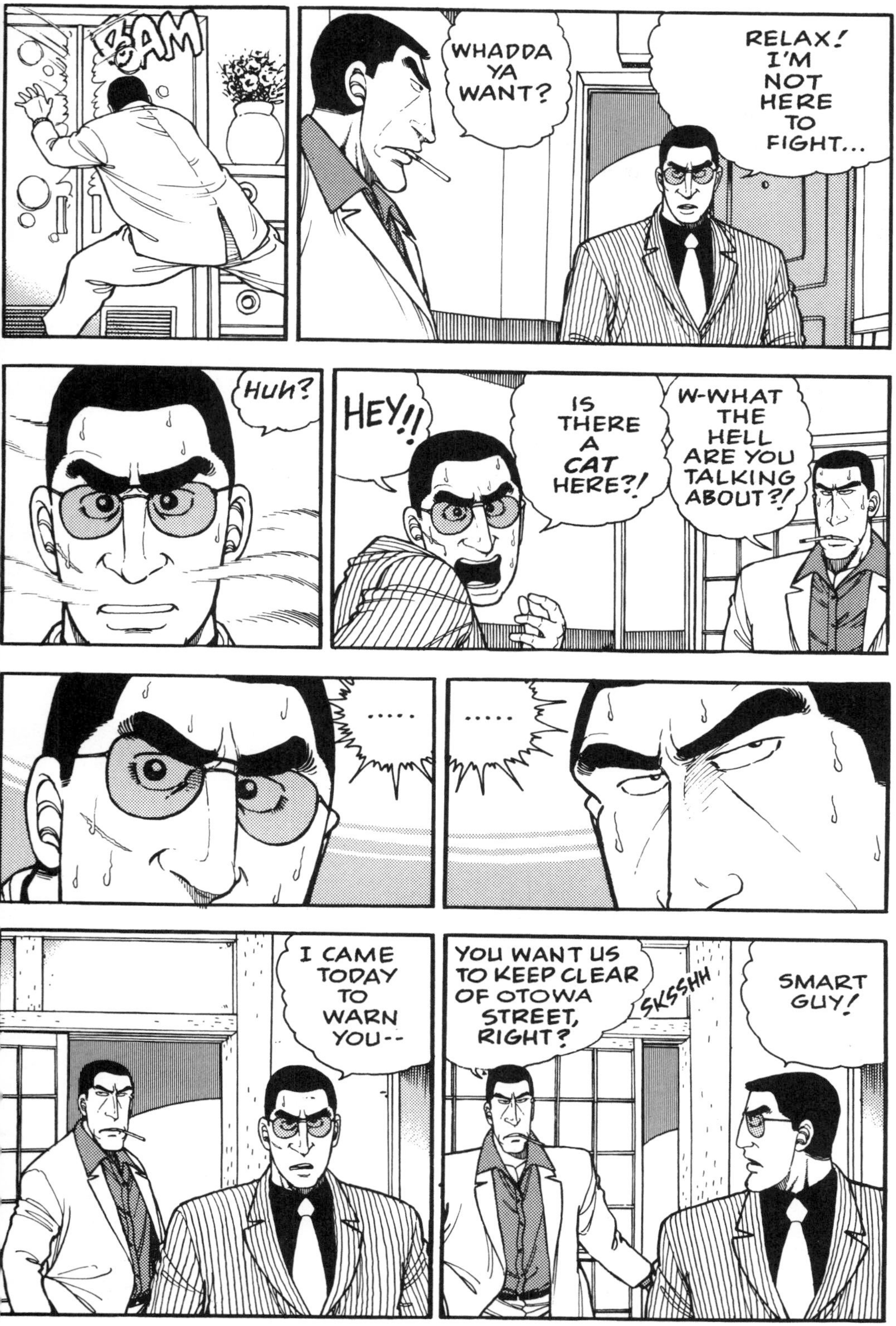
BAM
WHADDA YA WANT?
RELAX! I'M NOT HERE TO FIGHT...
HUH?
HEY!!
IS THERE A CAT HERE?!
W-WHAT THE HELL ARE YOU TALKING ABOUT?!
.....
.....
I CAME TODAY TO WARN YOU--
YOU WANT US TO KEEP CLEAR OF OTOWA STREET, RIGHT?
SKSSHH
SMART GUY!

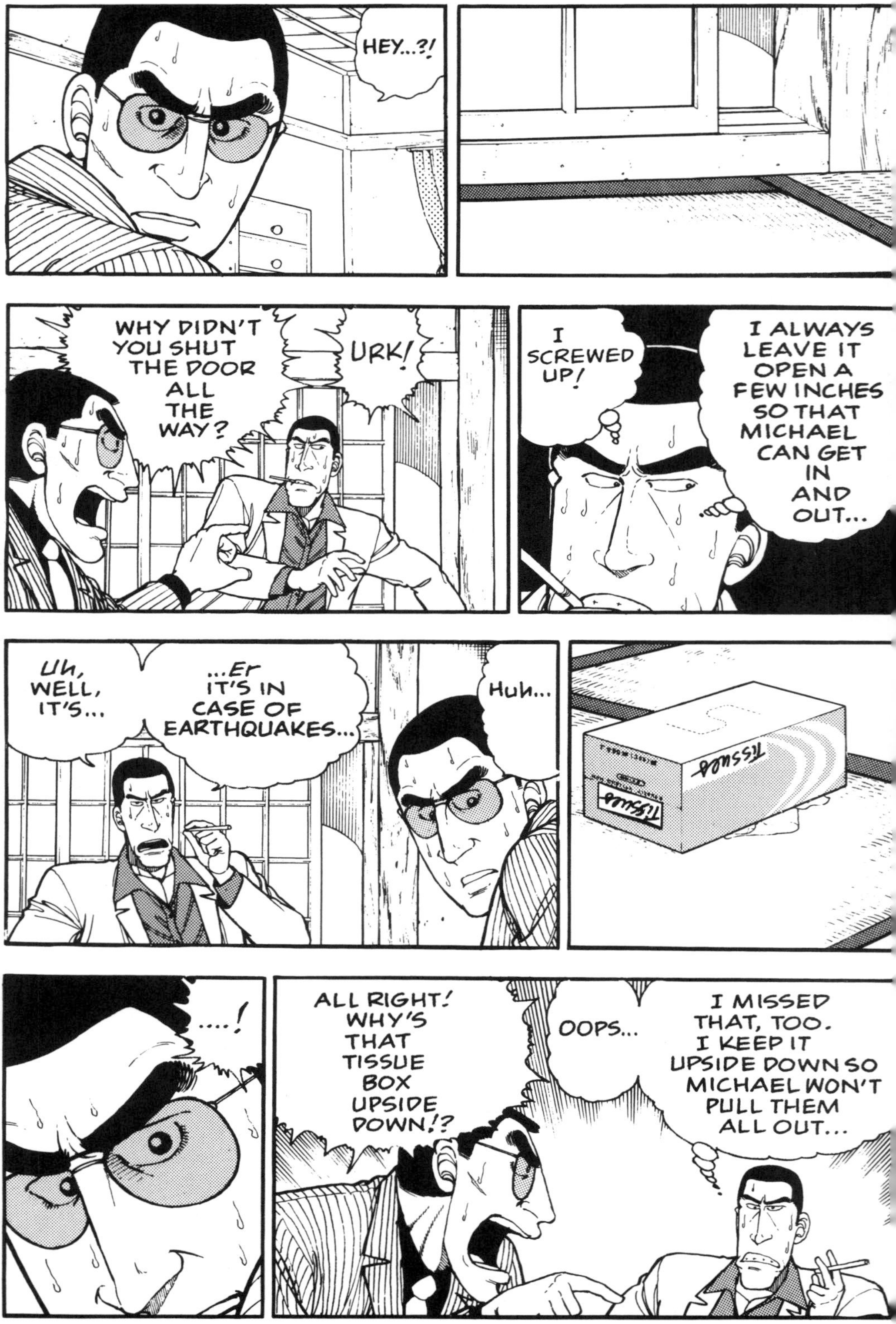
HEY...?!
WHY DIDN'T YOU SHUT THE DOOR ALL THE WAY?
URK!
I SCREWED UP!
I ALWAYS LEAVE IT OPEN A FEW INCHES SO THAT MICHAEL CAN GET IN AND OUT...
Uh, WELL, IT'S...
...Er IT'S IN CASE OF EARTHQUAKES...
Huh...
Tissue
....!
ALL RIGHT! WHY'S THAT TISSUE BOX UPSIDE DOWN!?
OOPS...
I MISSED THAT, TOO. I KEEP IT UPSIDE DOWN SO MICHAEL WON'T PULL THEM ALL OUT...

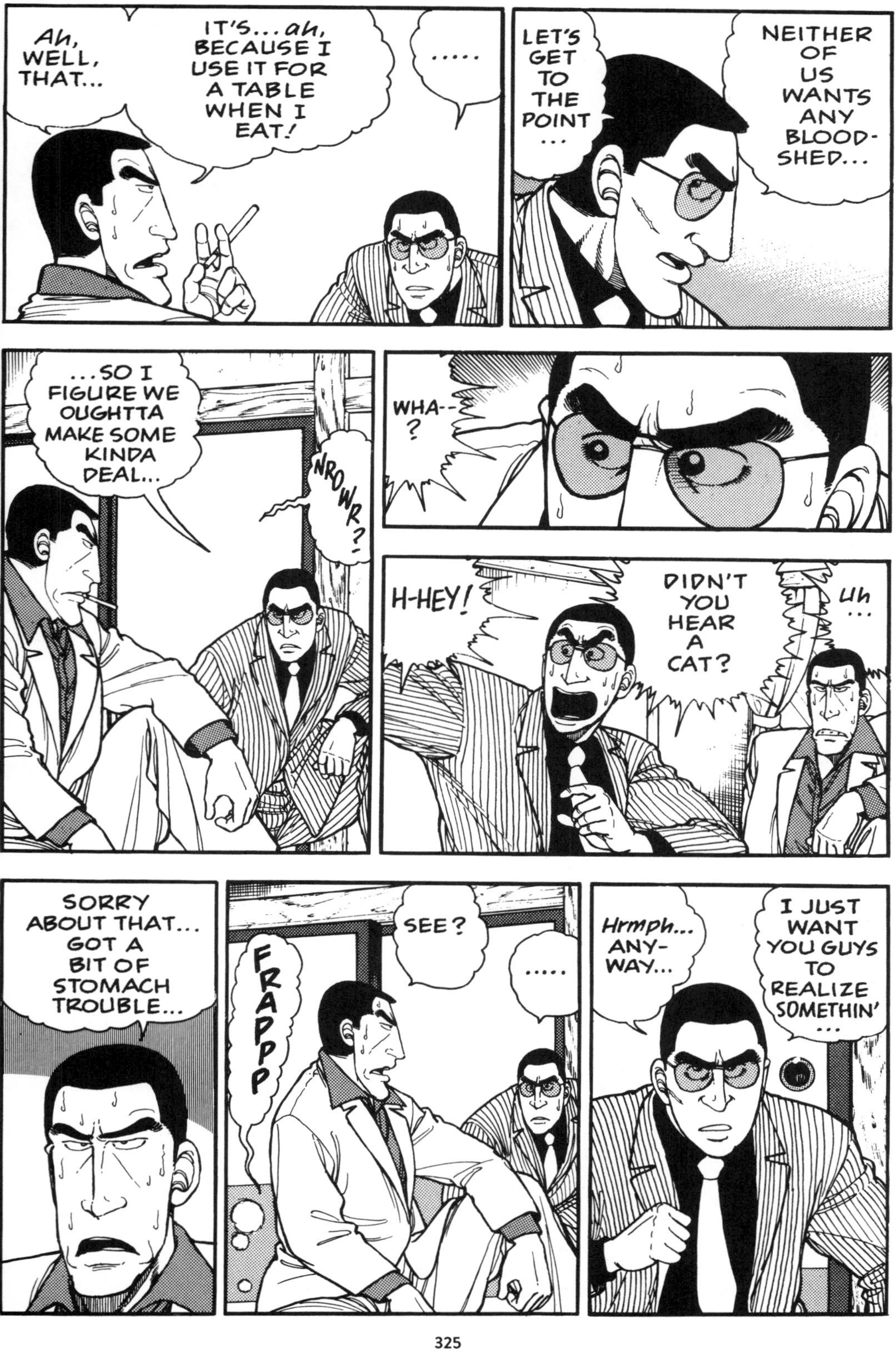
Ah, WELL, THAT...
IT'S...ah, BECAUSE I USE IT FOR A TABLE WHEN I EAT!
.....
LET'S GET TO THE POINT ...
NEITHER OF US WANTS ANY BLOOD-SHED...
...SO I FIGURE WE OUGHTTA MAKE SOME KINDA DEAL...
NROWR?
WHA-- ?
H-HEY!
DIDN'T YOU HEAR A CAT?
Uh ...
SORRY ABOUT THAT... GOT A BIT OF STOMACH TROUBLE...
SEE?
FRAPPP
.....
Hrmph... ANY-WAY...
I JUST WANT YOU GUYS TO REALIZE SOMETHIN' ...

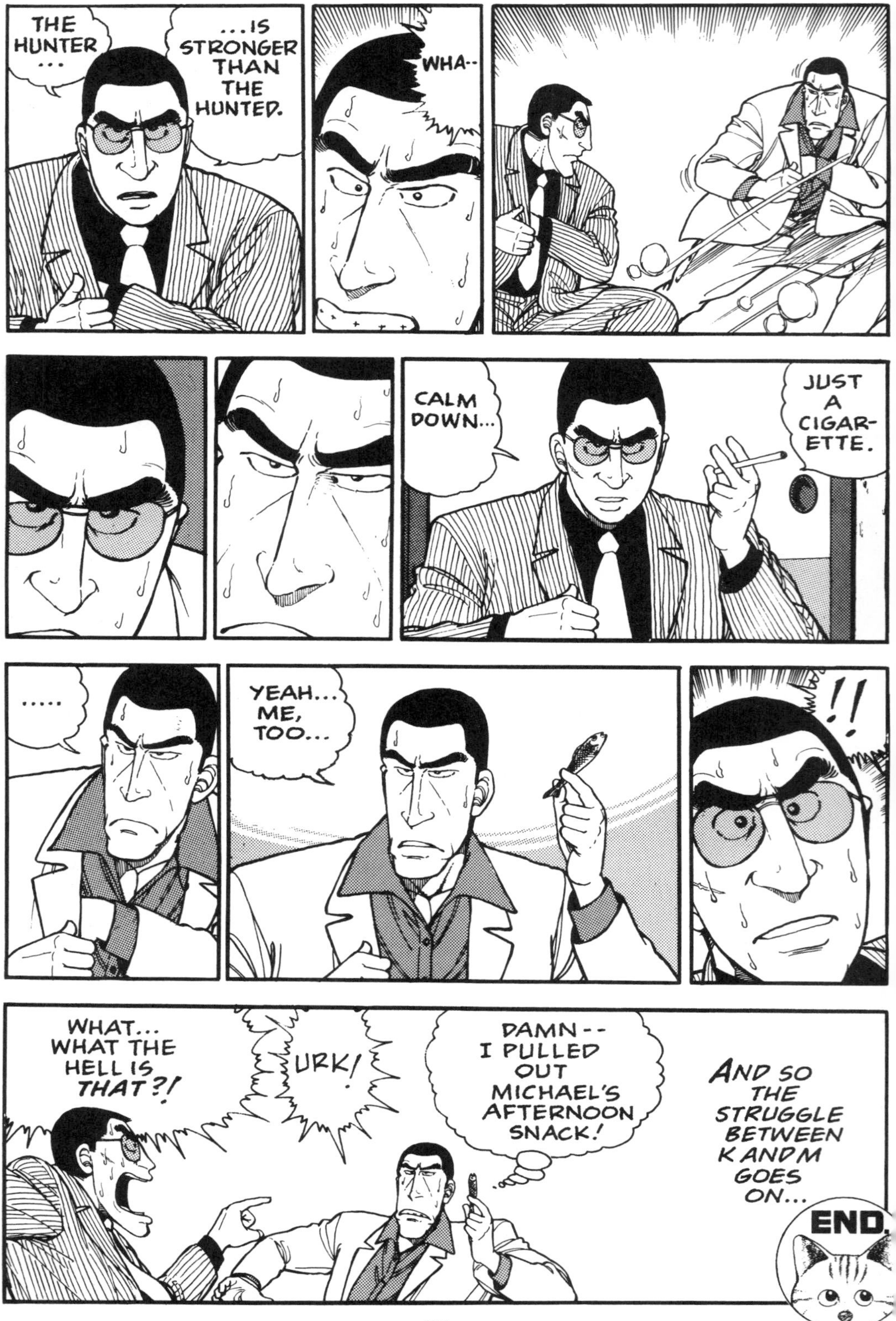
THE HUNTER...
...IS STRONGER THAN THE HUNTED.
WHA--
CALM DOWN...
JUST A CIGARETTE.
.....
YEAH... ME, TOO...
!!
WHAT... WHAT THE HELL IS THAT?!
URK!
DAMN-- I PULLED OUT MICHAEL'S AFTERNOON SNACK!
AND SO THE STRUGGLE BETWEEN K AND M GOES ON...
END.

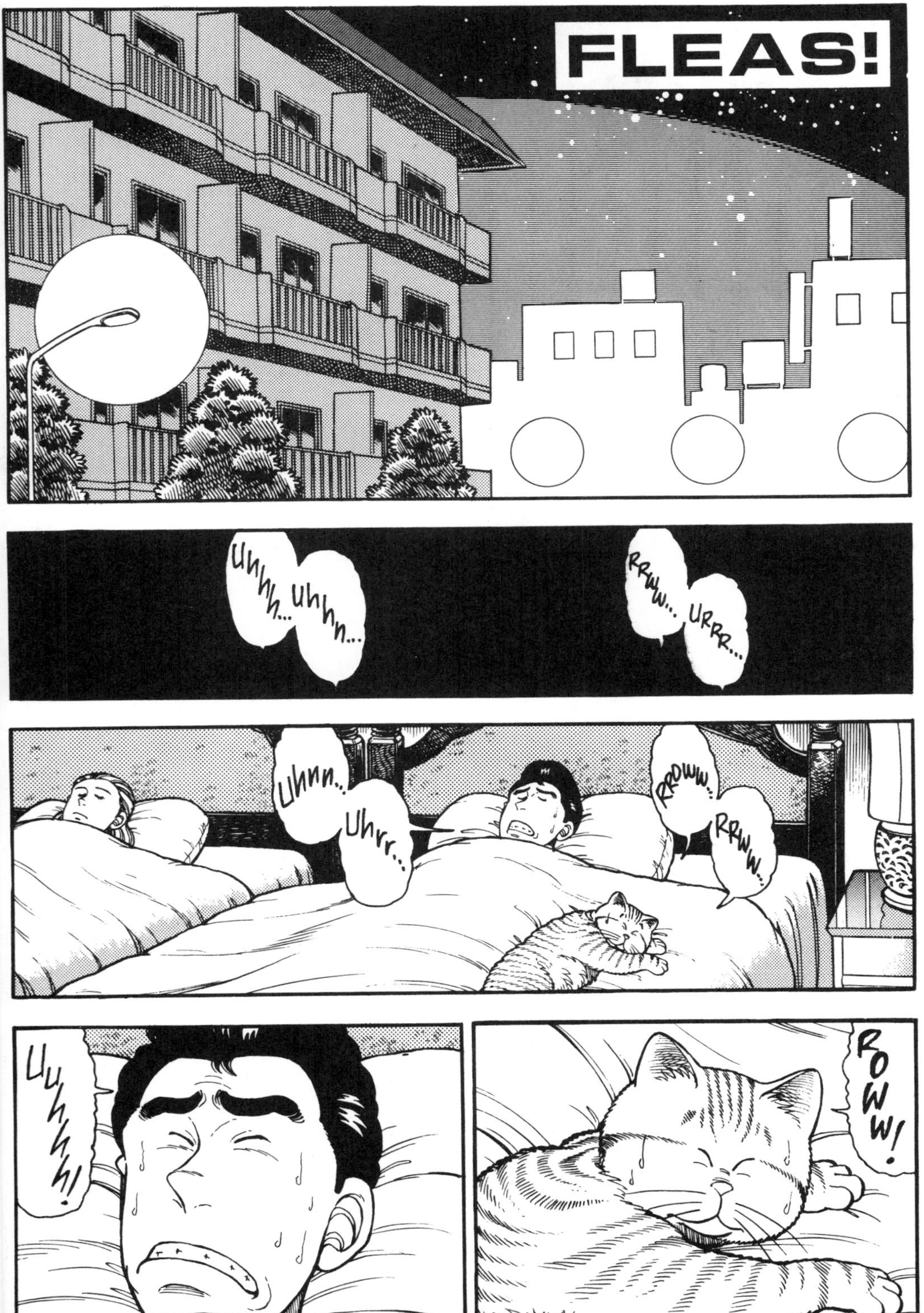
FLEAS!
Uhhh...
Uhhn...
Rrww...
Urrr...
Uhnn...
Uhrr...
Rroww...
Rrww...
Uuhhh!
Roww!

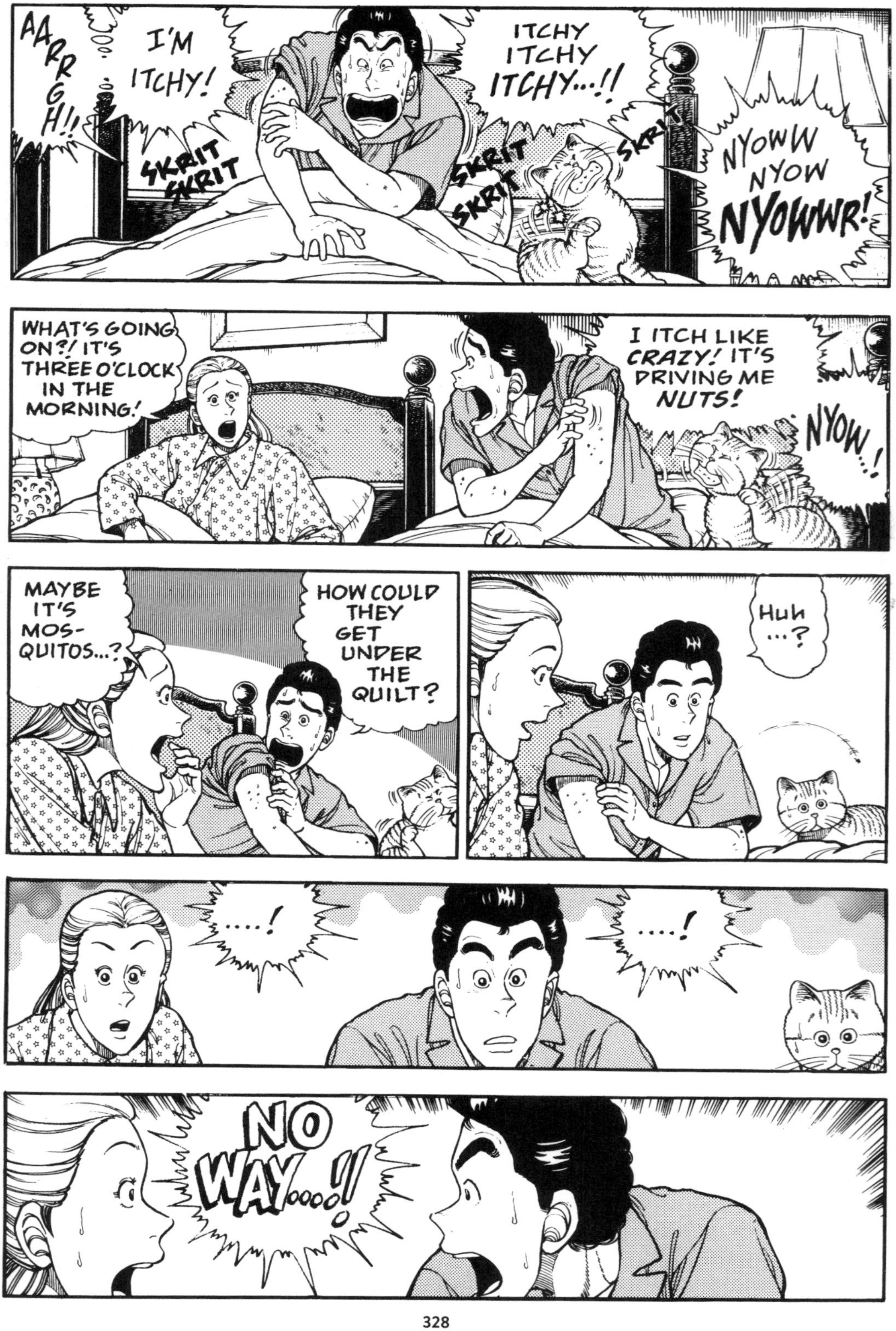
AARRGH!!
I'M ITCHY!
ITCHY ITCHY ITCHY...!!
SKRIT SKRIT
SKRIT SKRIT
SKRIT
NYOWW NYOW NYOWWR!
WHAT'S GOING ON?! IT'S THREE O'CLOCK IN THE MORNING!
I ITCH LIKE CRAZY! IT'S DRIVING ME NUTS!
NYOW...!
MAYBE IT'S MOS-QUITOS...?
HOW COULD THEY GET UNDER THE QUILT?
Huh ...?
....!
....!
NO WAYoooo!!

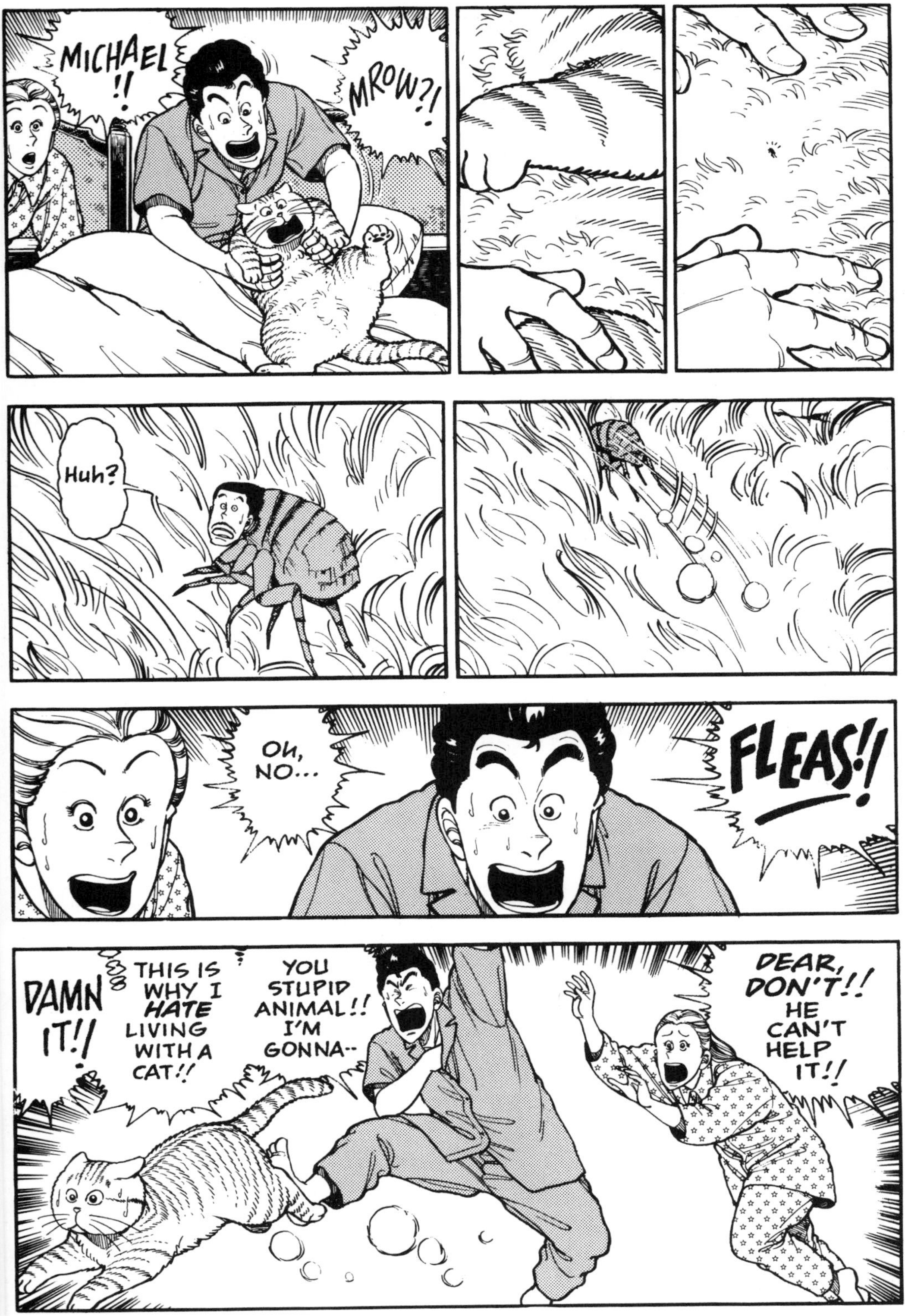
MICHAEL!!
MROW?!
Huh?
OH, NO...
FLEAS!!
DAMN IT!!
THIS IS WHY I HATE LIVING WITH A CAT!!
YOU STUPID ANIMAL!! I'M GONNA--
DEAR, DON'T!! HE CAN'T HELP IT!!

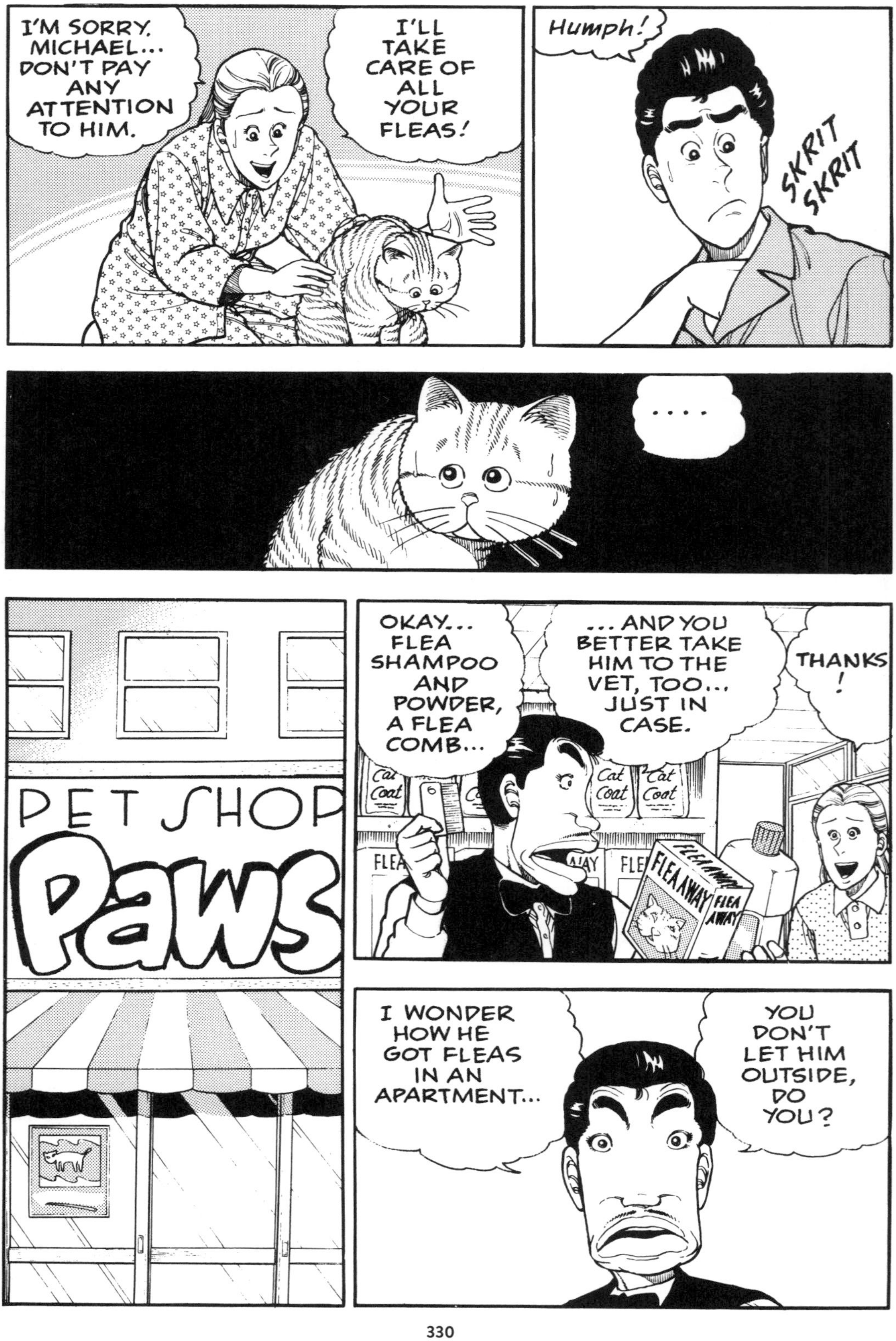
I'M SORRY, MICHAEL... DON'T PAY ANY ATTENTION TO HIM.
I'LL TAKE CARE OF ALL YOUR FLEAS!
Humph!
SKRIT SKRIT
....
PET SHOP
Paws
OKAY... FLEA SHAMPOO AND POWDER, A FLEA COMB...
...AND YOU BETTER TAKE HIM TO THE VET, TOO... JUST IN CASE.
THANKS!
Cat Coat
FLEA AWAY
I WONDER HOW HE GOT FLEAS IN AN APARTMENT...
YOU DON'T LET HIM OUTSIDE, DO YOU?

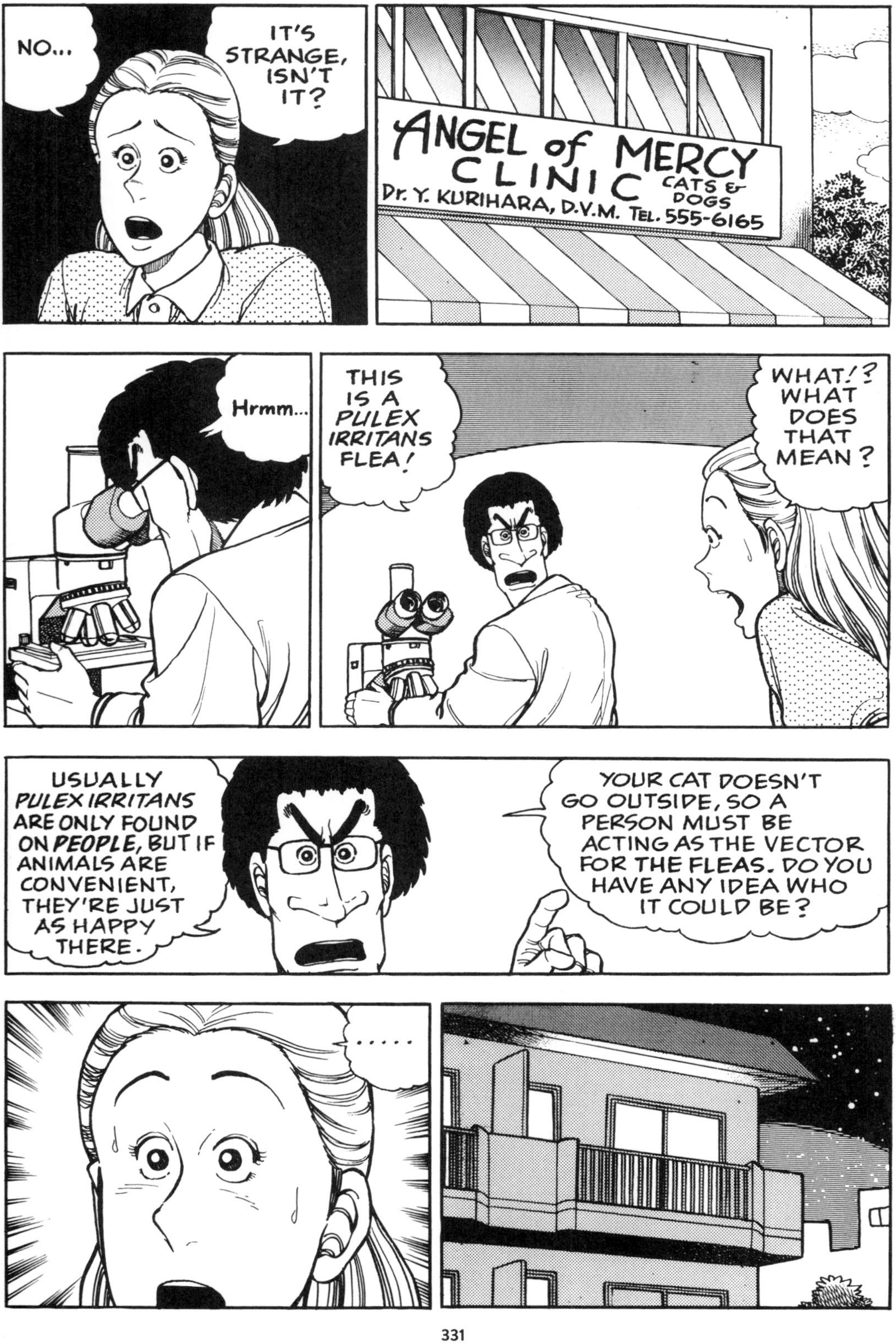

NO...
IT'S STRANGE, ISN'T IT?
ANGEL of MERCY CLINIC CATS & DOGS
Dr. Y. KURIHARA, D.V.M. TEL. 555-6165
Hrmm...
THIS IS A *PULEX IRRITANS* FLEA!
WHAT!? WHAT DOES THAT MEAN?
USUALLY *PULEX IRRITANS* ARE ONLY FOUND ON *PEOPLE*, BUT IF ANIMALS ARE CONVENIENT, THEY'RE JUST AS HAPPY THERE.
YOUR CAT DOESN'T GO OUTSIDE, SO A PERSON MUST BE ACTING AS THE VECTOR FOR THE FLEAS. DO YOU HAVE ANY IDEA WHO IT COULD BE?
.....

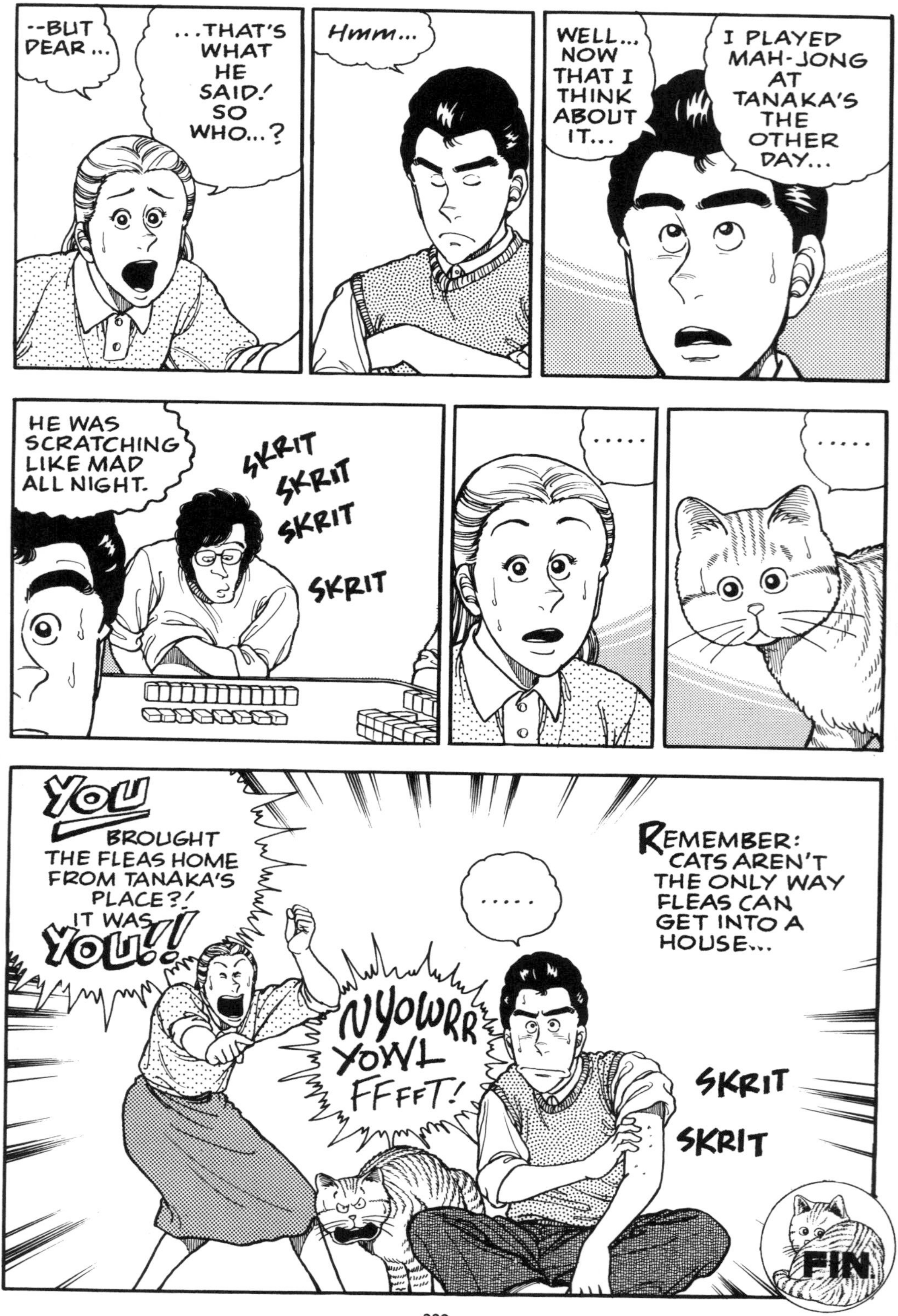

--BUT DEAR...
...THAT'S WHAT HE SAID! SO WHO...?
Hmm...
WELL... NOW THAT I THINK ABOUT IT...
I PLAYED MAH-JONG AT TANAKA'S THE OTHER DAY...
HE WAS SCRATCHING LIKE MAD ALL NIGHT.
SKRIT
SKRIT
SKRIT
SKRIT
.....
.....
YOU BROUGHT THE FLEAS HOME FROM TANAKA'S PLACE?! IT WAS YOU!!
.....
NYOWRR YOWL FFFFT!
REMEMBER: CATS AREN'T THE ONLY WAY FLEAS CAN GET INTO A HOUSE...
SKRIT
SKRIT
FIN

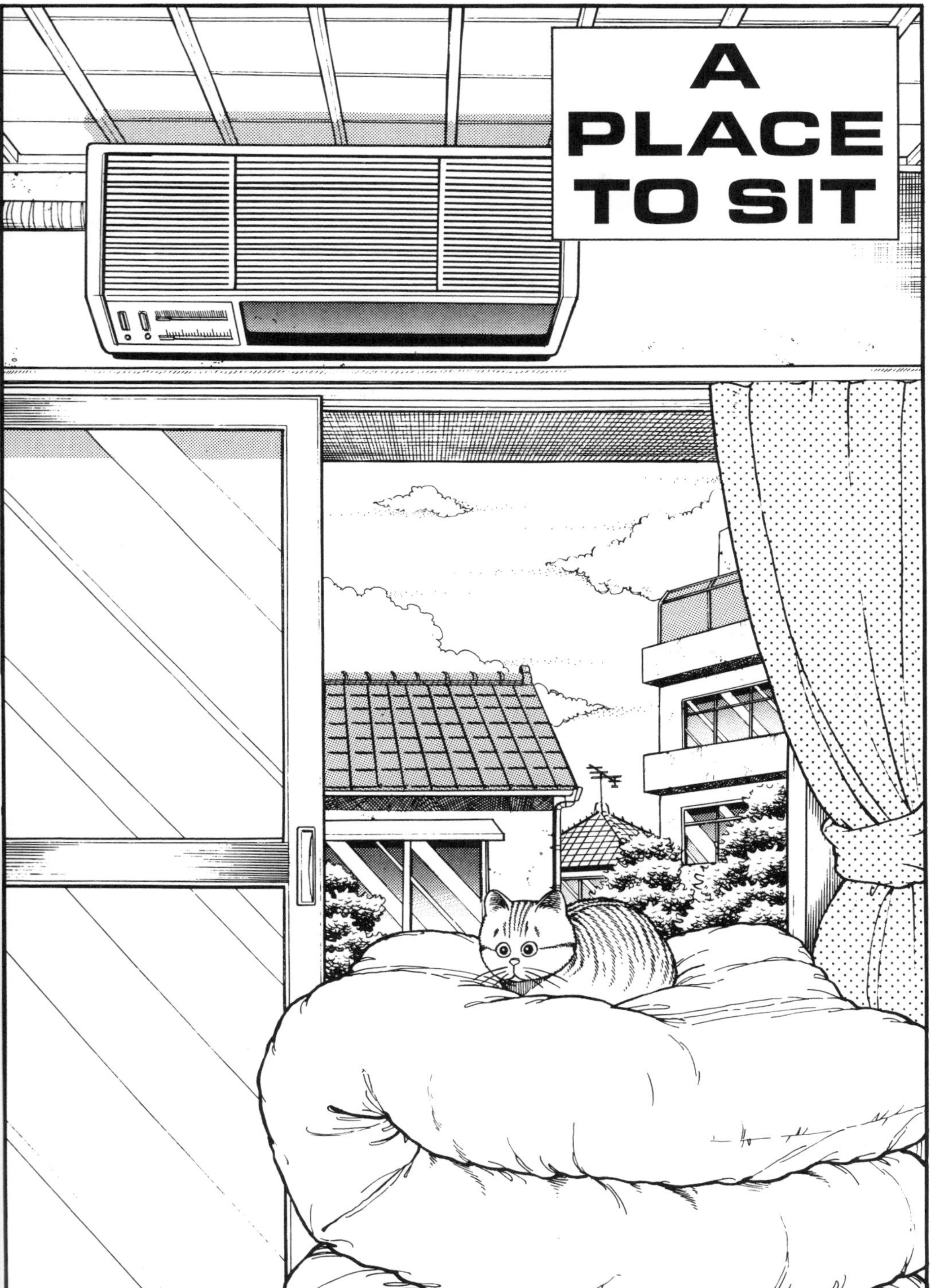
A PLACE TO SIT

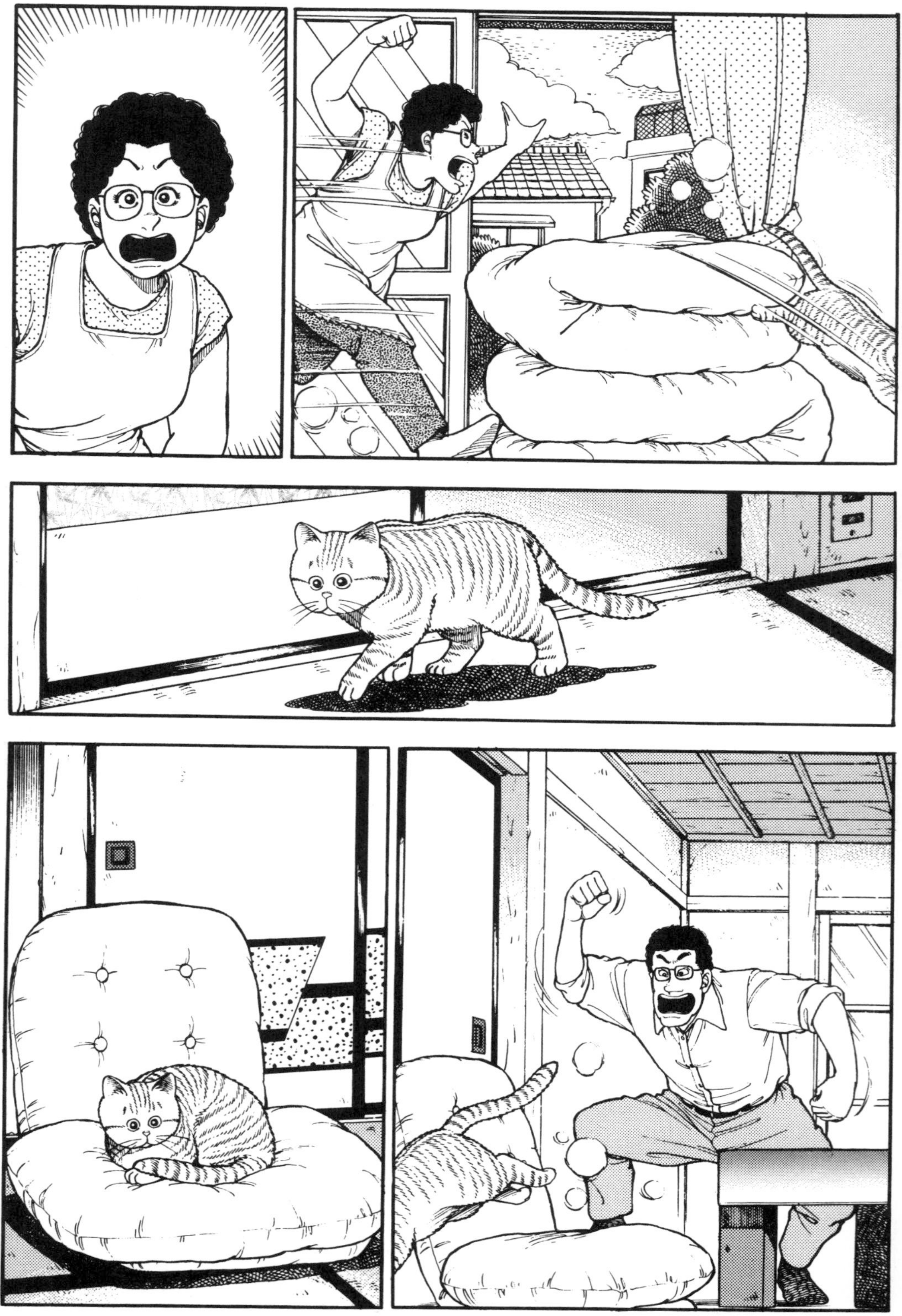

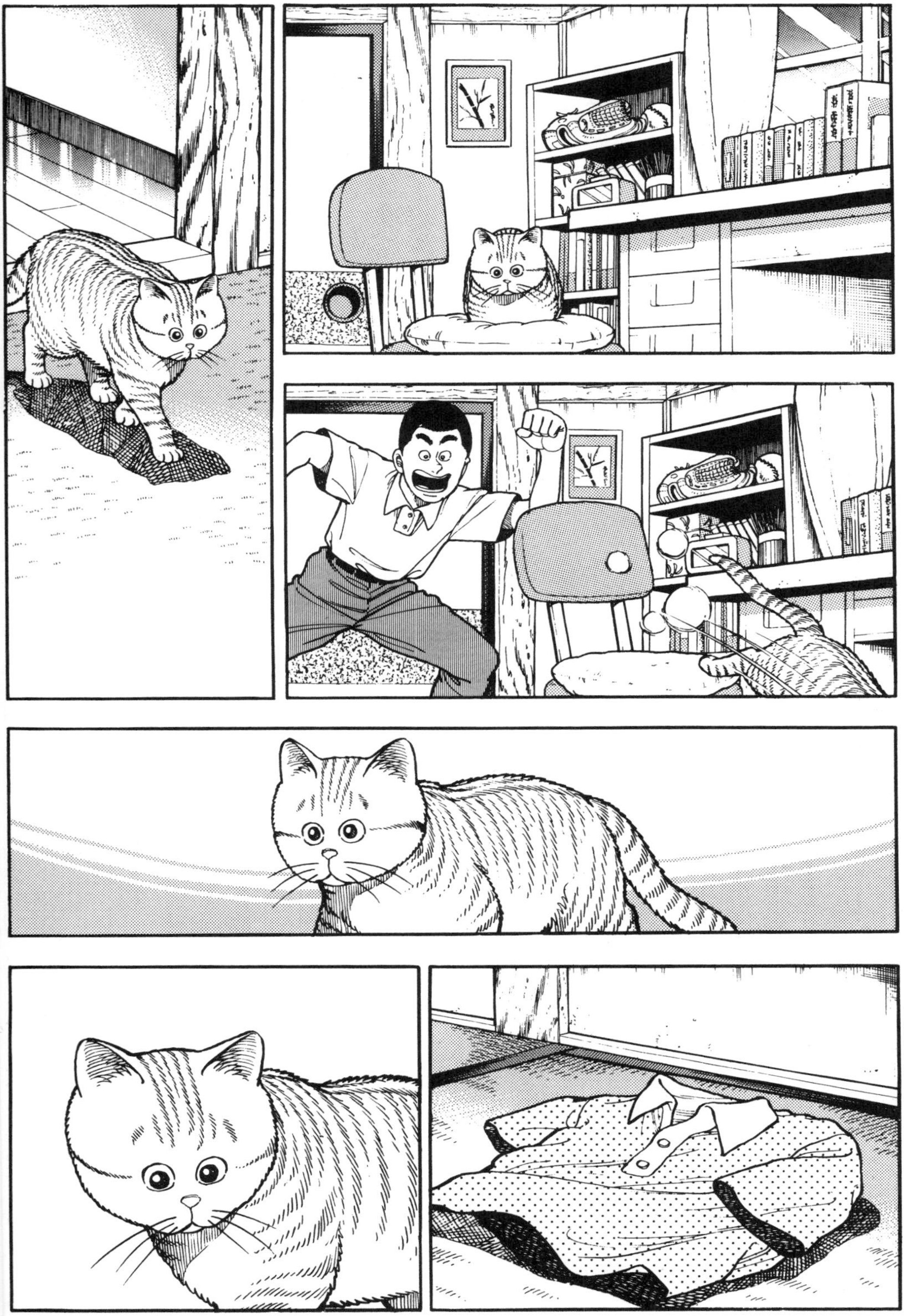

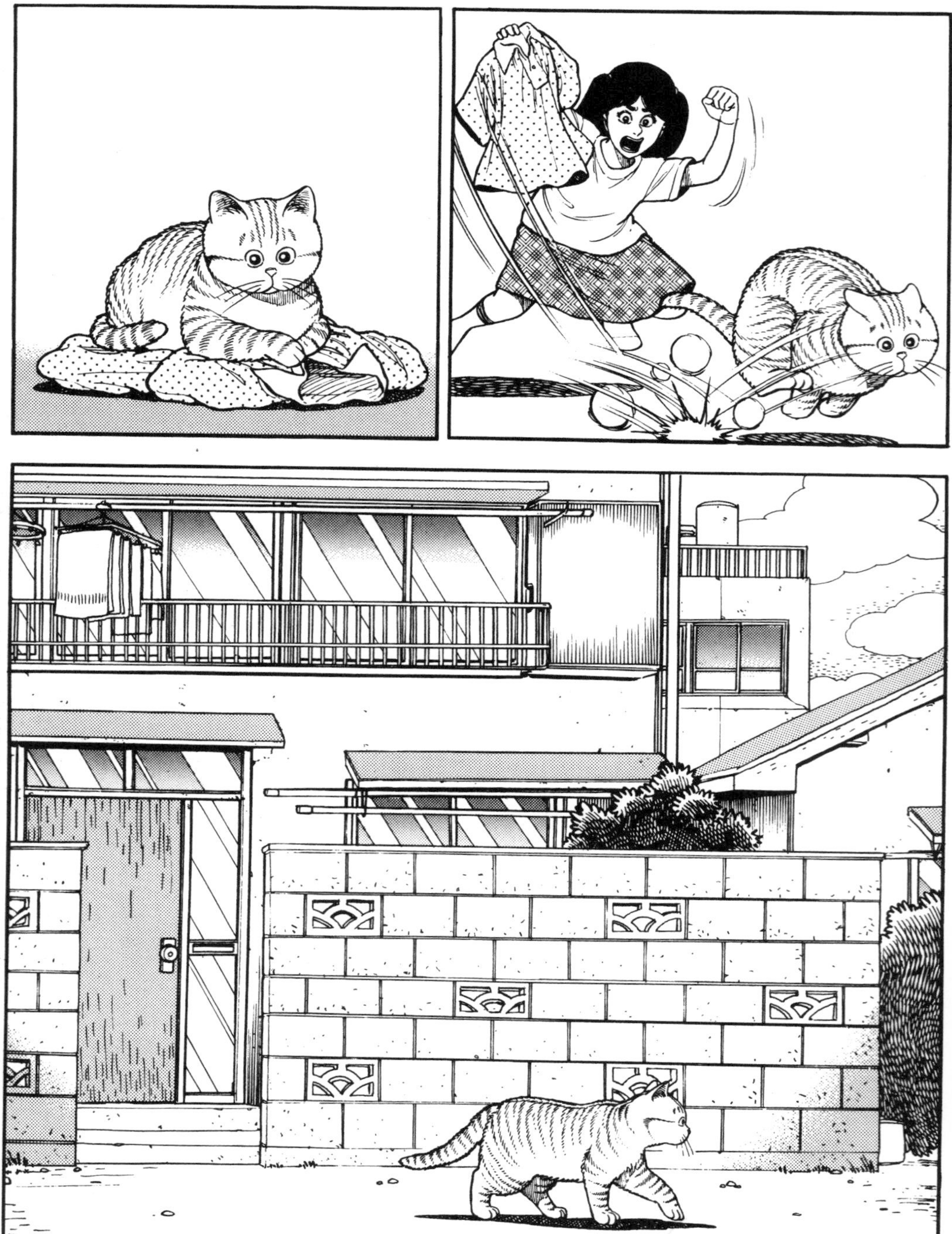

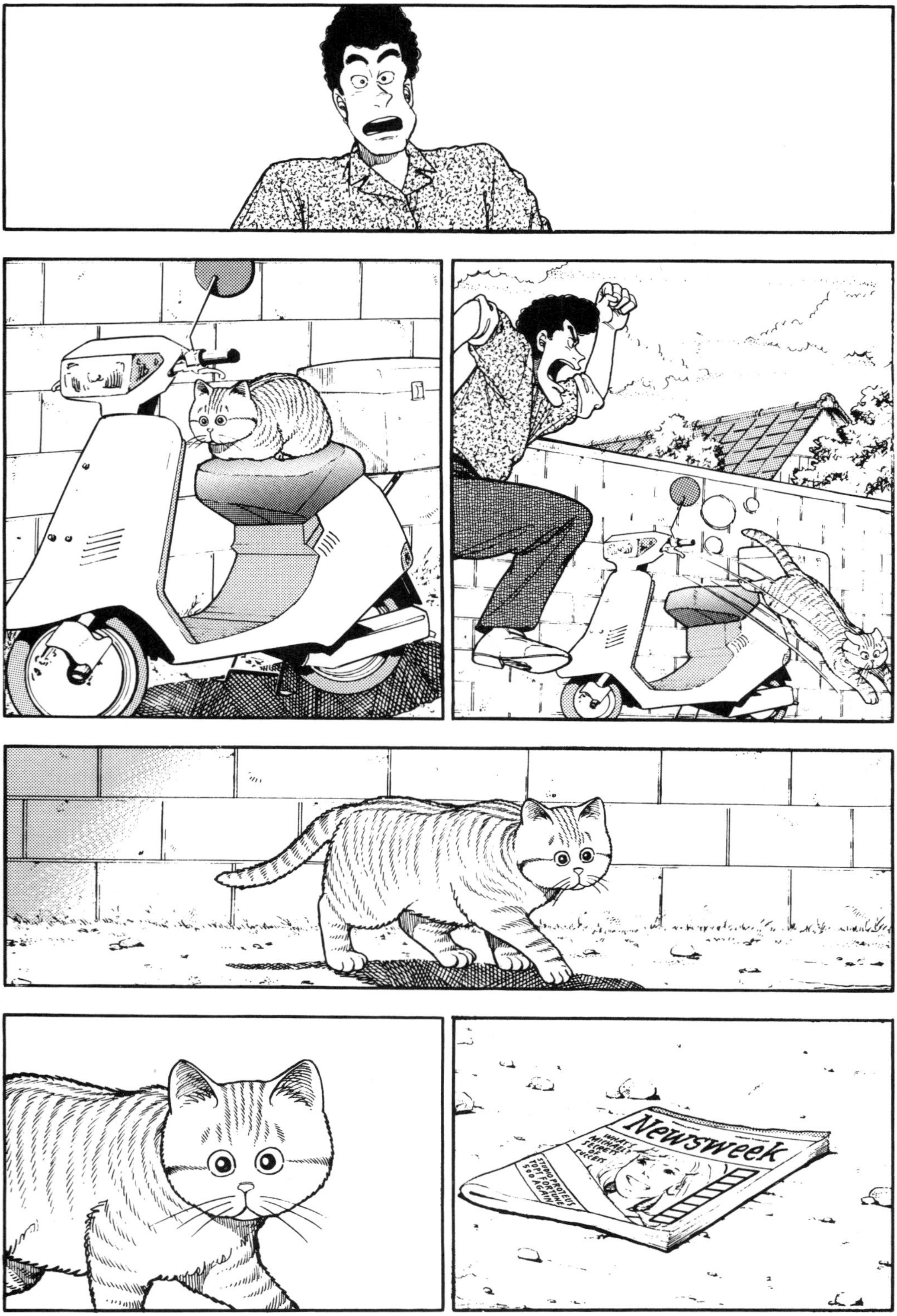
Newsweek
WHAT'S MICHAEL'S SECRETS OF SUCCESS
STUDIO PROTEUS TOPT FORTUNE 500 AGAIN

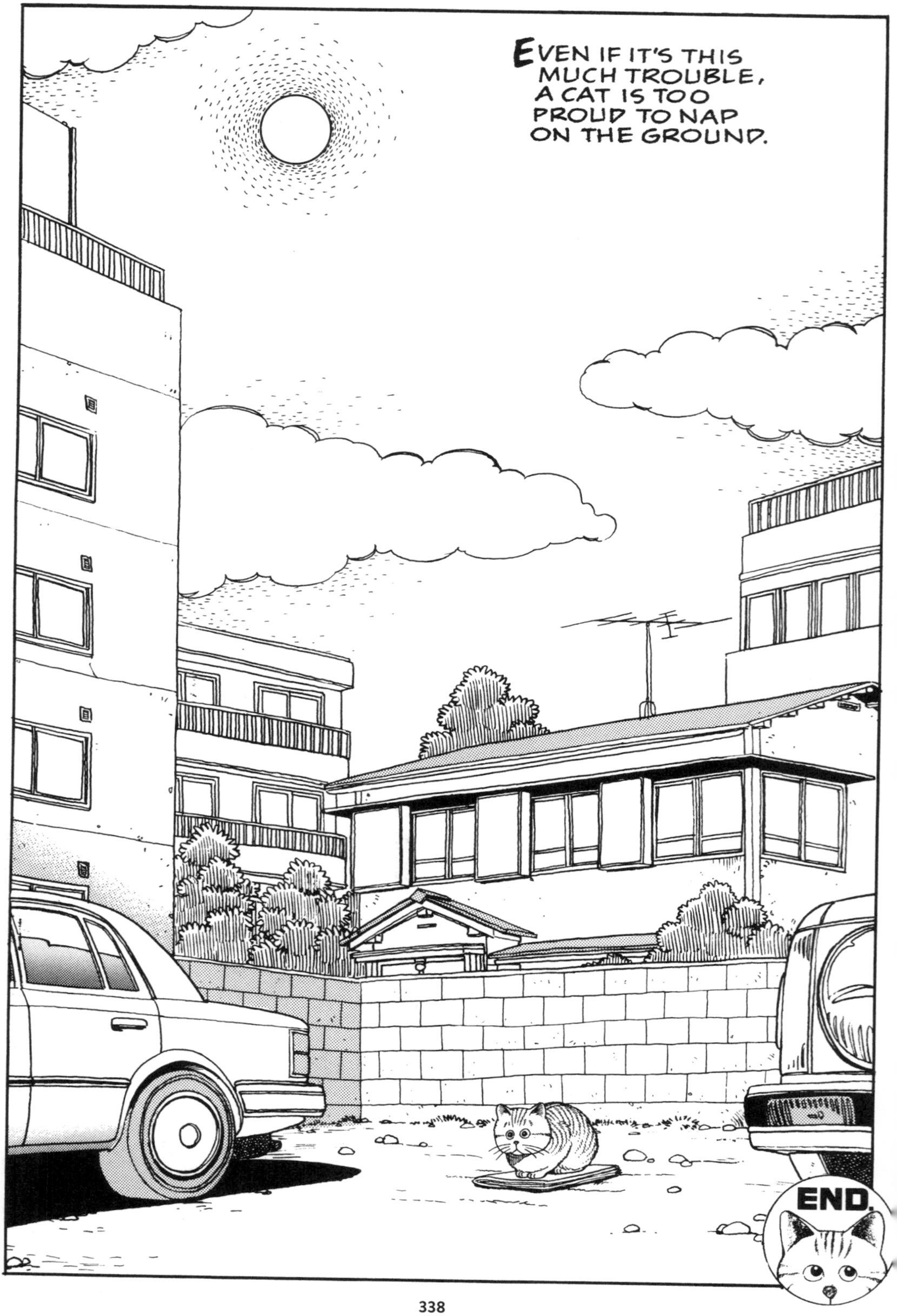
EVEN IF IT'S THIS MUCH TROUBLE, A CAT IS TOO PROUD TO NAP ON THE GROUND.
END.

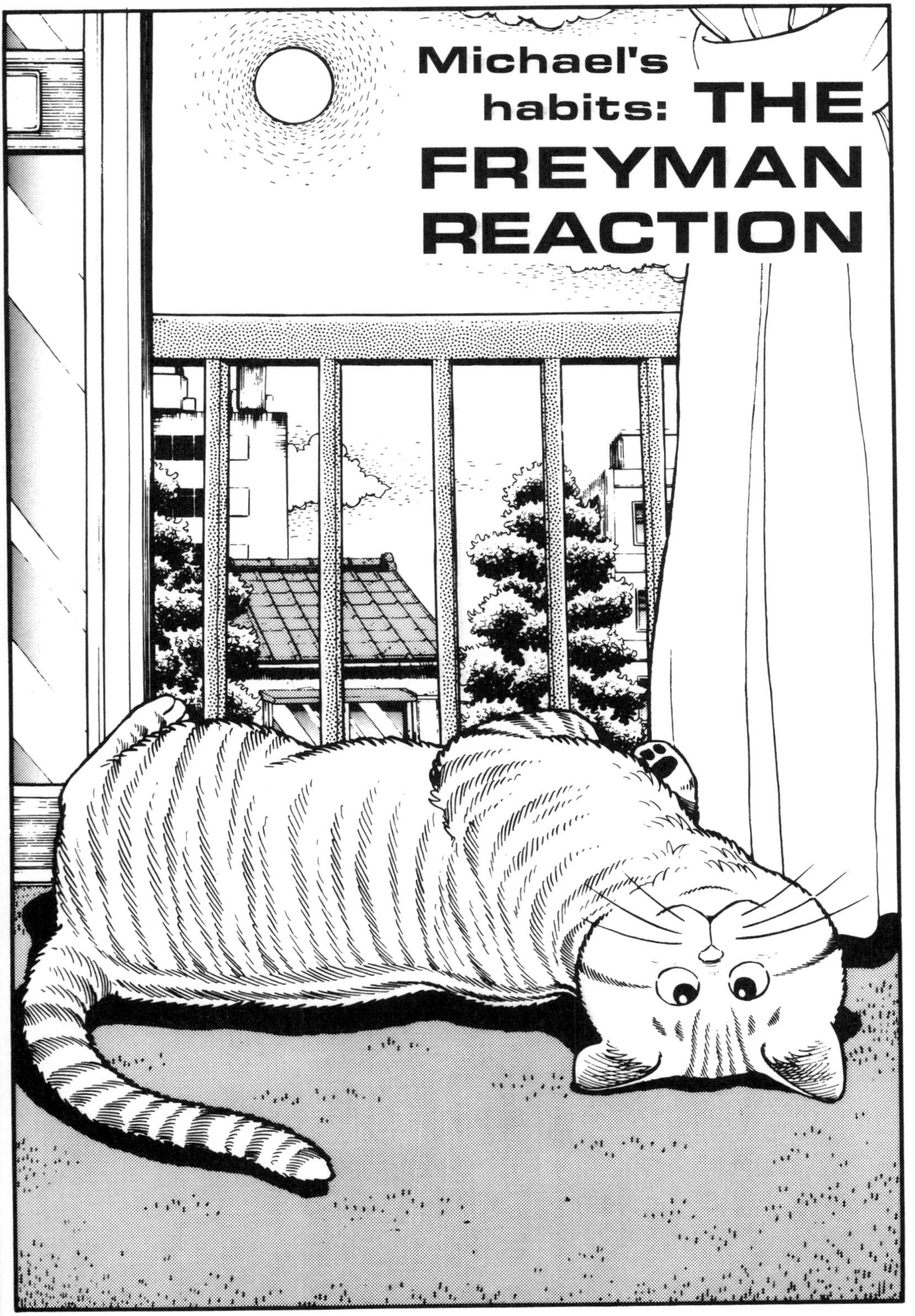
Michael's habits: THE FREYMAN REACTION

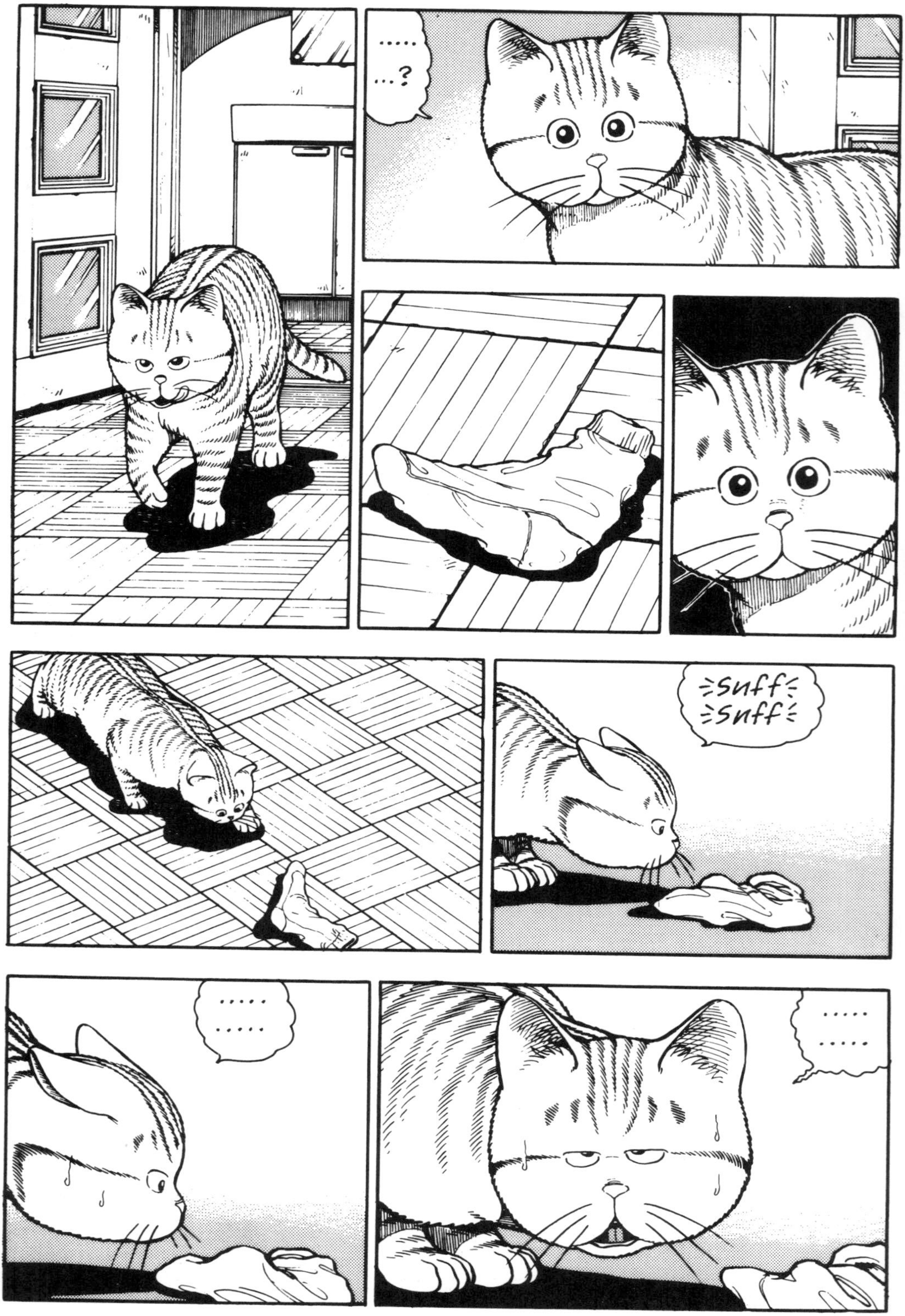
.....
...?
snff
snff
.....
.....
.....
.....

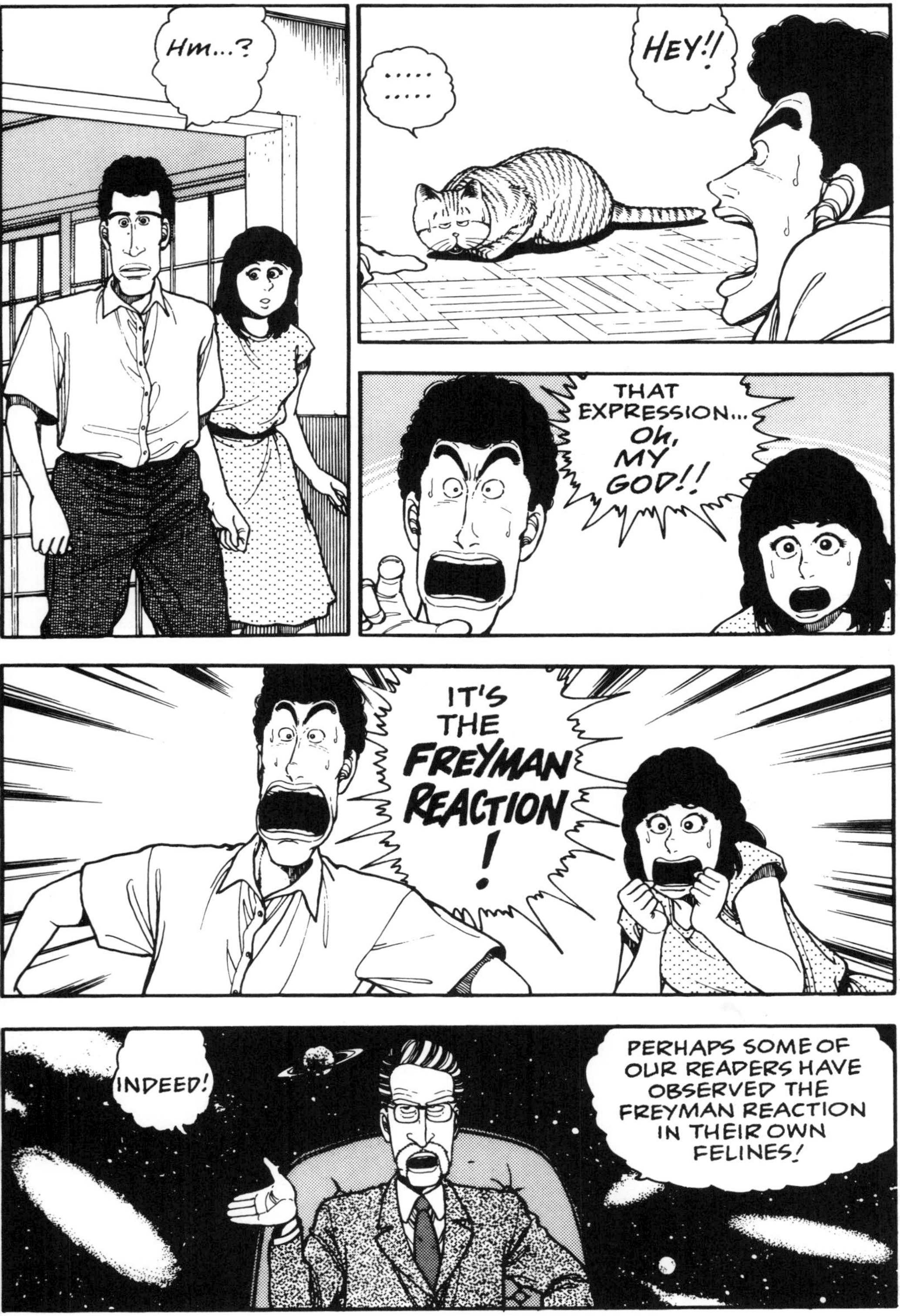
Hm...?
......
......
HEY!!
THAT EXPRESSION... Oh, MY GOD!!
IT'S THE FREYMAN REACTION!
INDEED!
PERHAPS SOME OF OUR READERS HAVE OBSERVED THE FREYMAN REACTION IN THEIR OWN FELINES!

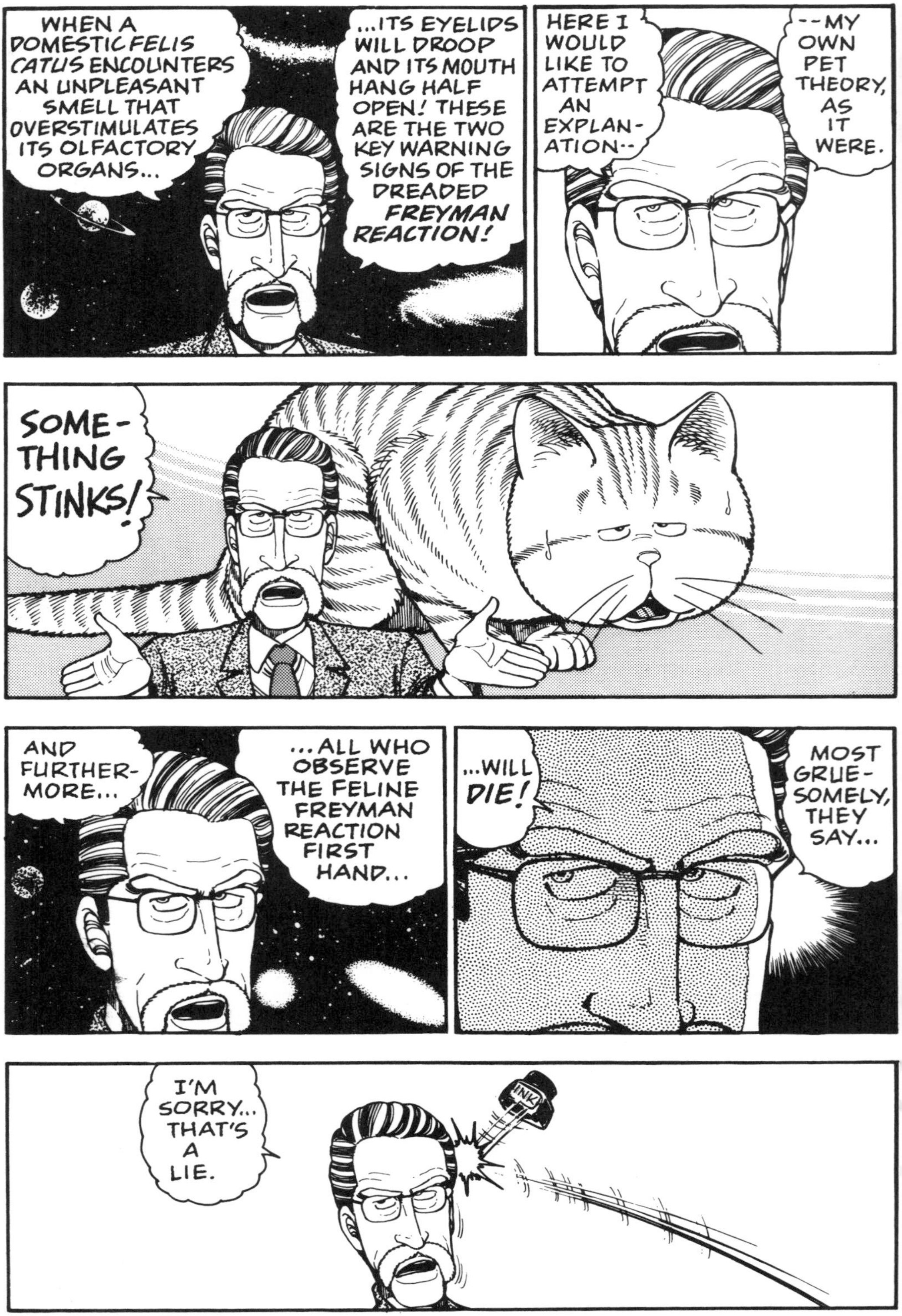
WHEN A DOMESTIC FELIS CATUS ENCOUNTERS AN UNPLEASANT SMELL THAT OVERSTIMULATES ITS OLFACTORY ORGANS...
...ITS EYELIDS WILL DROOP AND ITS MOUTH HANG HALF OPEN! THESE ARE THE TWO KEY WARNING SIGNS OF THE DREADED FREYMAN REACTION!
HERE I WOULD LIKE TO ATTEMPT AN EXPLANATION--
--MY OWN PET THEORY, AS IT WERE.
SOMETHING STINKS!
AND FURTHERMORE...
...ALL WHO OBSERVE THE FELINE FREYMAN REACTION FIRST HAND...
...WILL DIE!
MOST GRUESOMELY, THEY SAY...
I'M SORRY... THAT'S A LIE.
INK

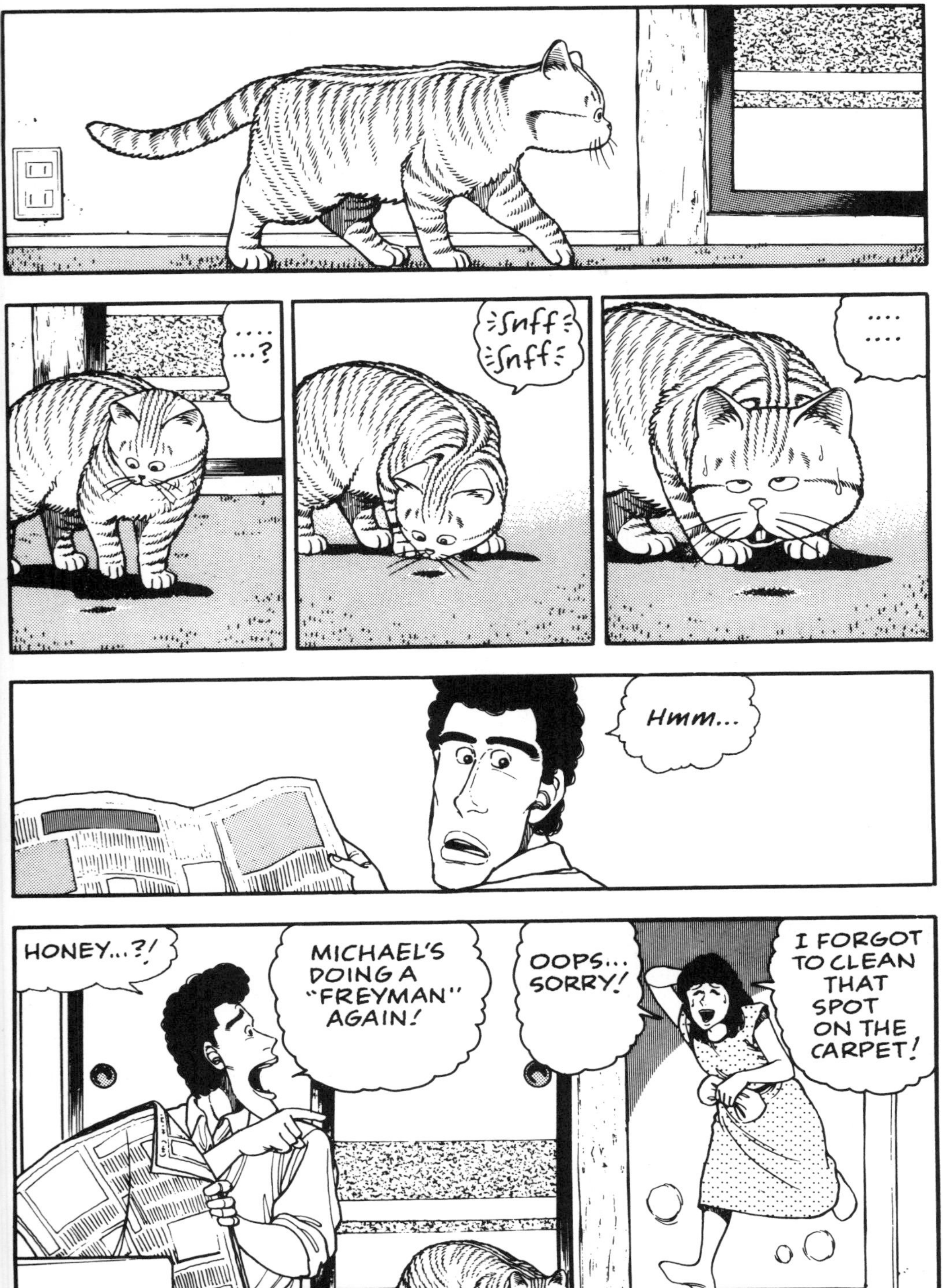
....
...?
Snff
Snff
....
....
Hmm...
HONEY...?!
MICHAEL'S DOING A "FREYMAN" AGAIN!
OOPS... SORRY!
I FORGOT TO CLEAN THAT SPOT ON THE CARPET!

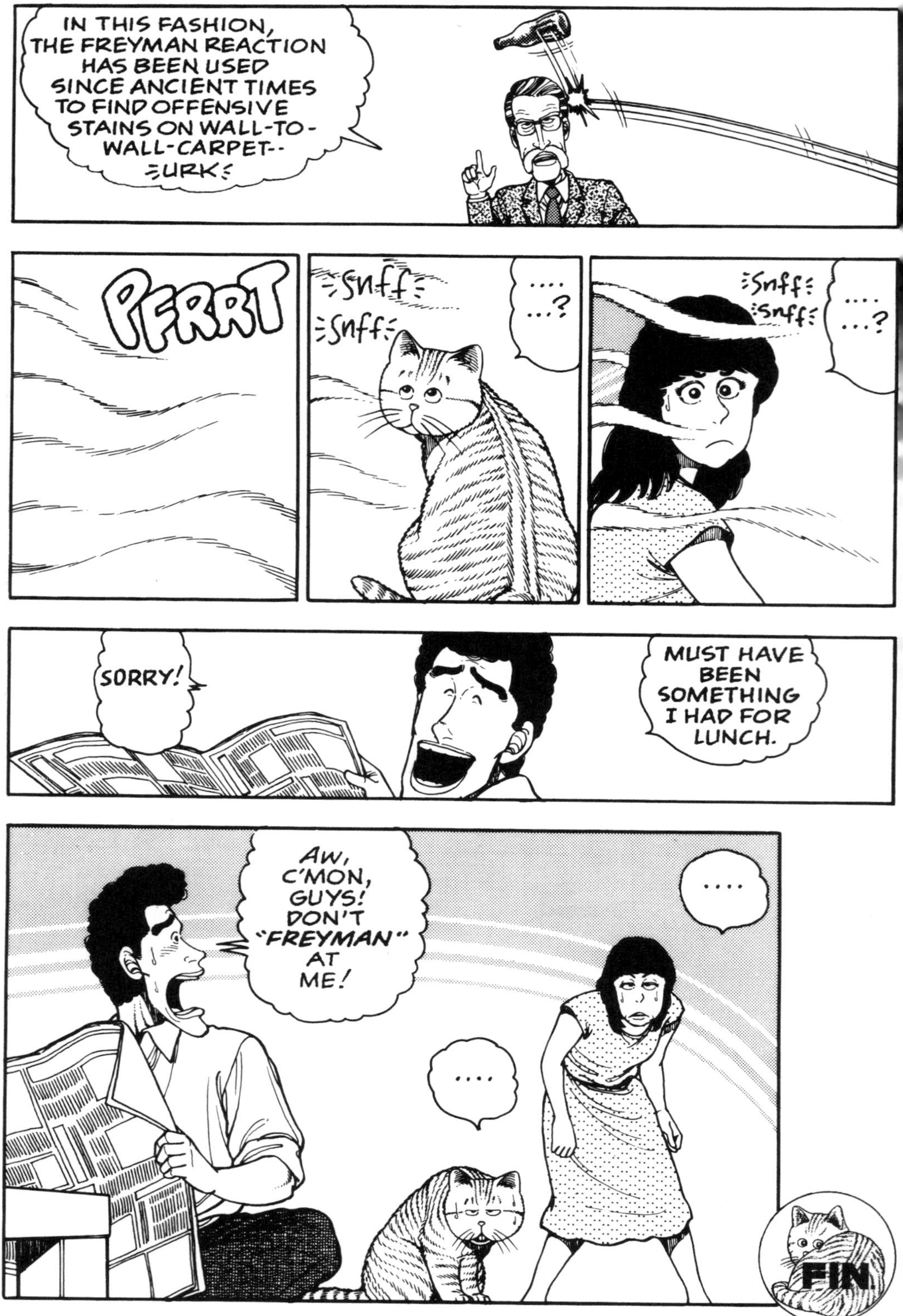
IN THIS FASHION, THE FREYMAN REACTION HAS BEEN USED SINCE ANCIENT TIMES TO FIND OFFENSIVE STAINS ON WALL-TO-WALL-CARPET-- URK
PFRRT
Snff
Snff
....
...?
Snff
Snff
....
...?
SORRY!
MUST HAVE BEEN SOMETHING I HAD FOR LUNCH.
AW, C'MON, GUYS! DON'T "FREYMAN" AT ME!
....
....
FIN

WHUD
Kitty Kleen
CAT SHAMPOO
FWHMP
Thmp
ZZZZZZIP
ALL RIGHT!
GO FOR IT!
Michael

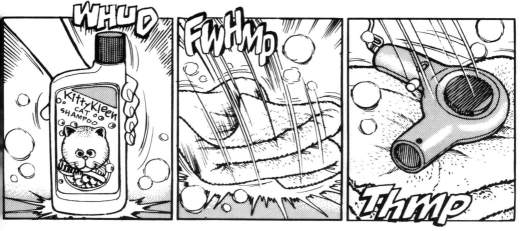

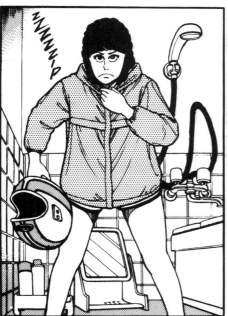

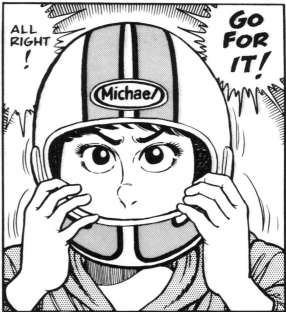

# The MICHAEL FAMILY'S DAY OF TERROR!

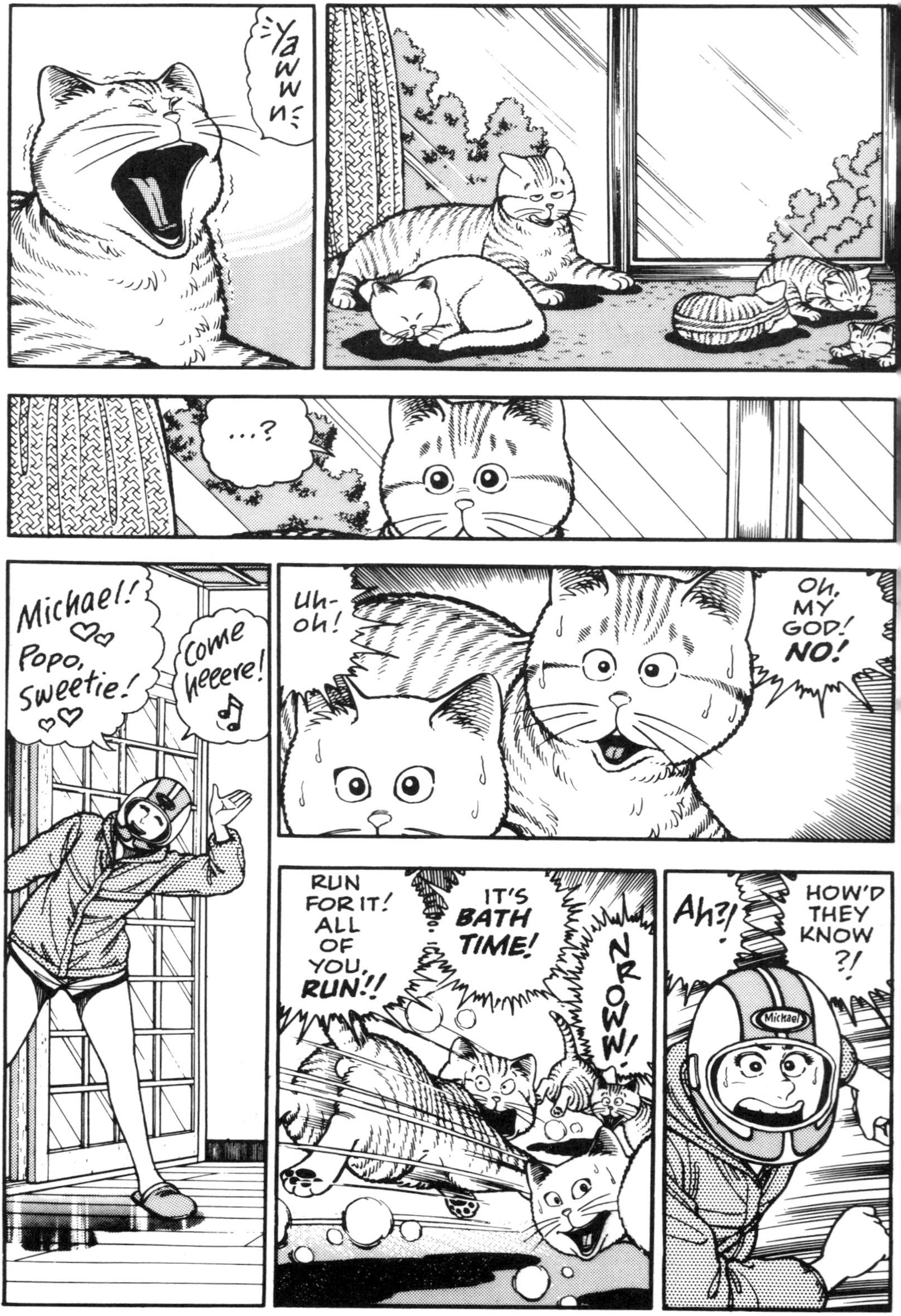
Yawwn
...?
Michael! Popo, Sweetie!
Come heeere!
Uh-oh!
Oh, MY GOD! NO!
RUN FOR IT! ALL OF YOU, RUN!!
IT'S BATH TIME!
NROWW!
Ah?!
HOW'D THEY KNOW?!
Michael

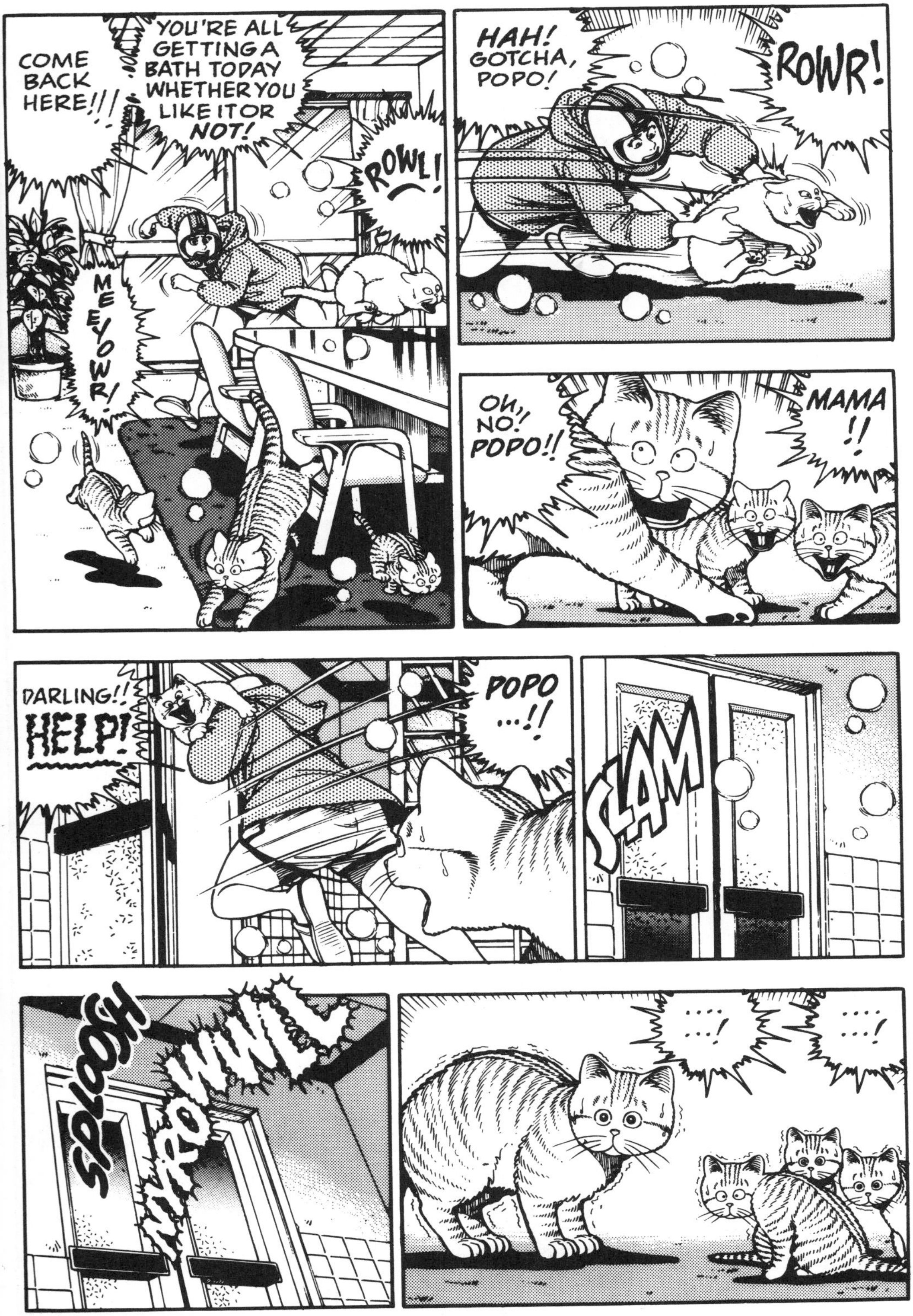

COME BACK HERE!!!
YOU'RE ALL GETTING A BATH TODAY WHETHER YOU LIKE IT OR NOT!
ROWL!
MEEYOWR!
HAH! GOTCHA, POPO!
ROWR!
OH, NO! POPO!!
MAMA !!
DARLING!! HELP!
POPO ...!!
SLAM
SPLOOSH
MROWWL
....
...!
....
...!

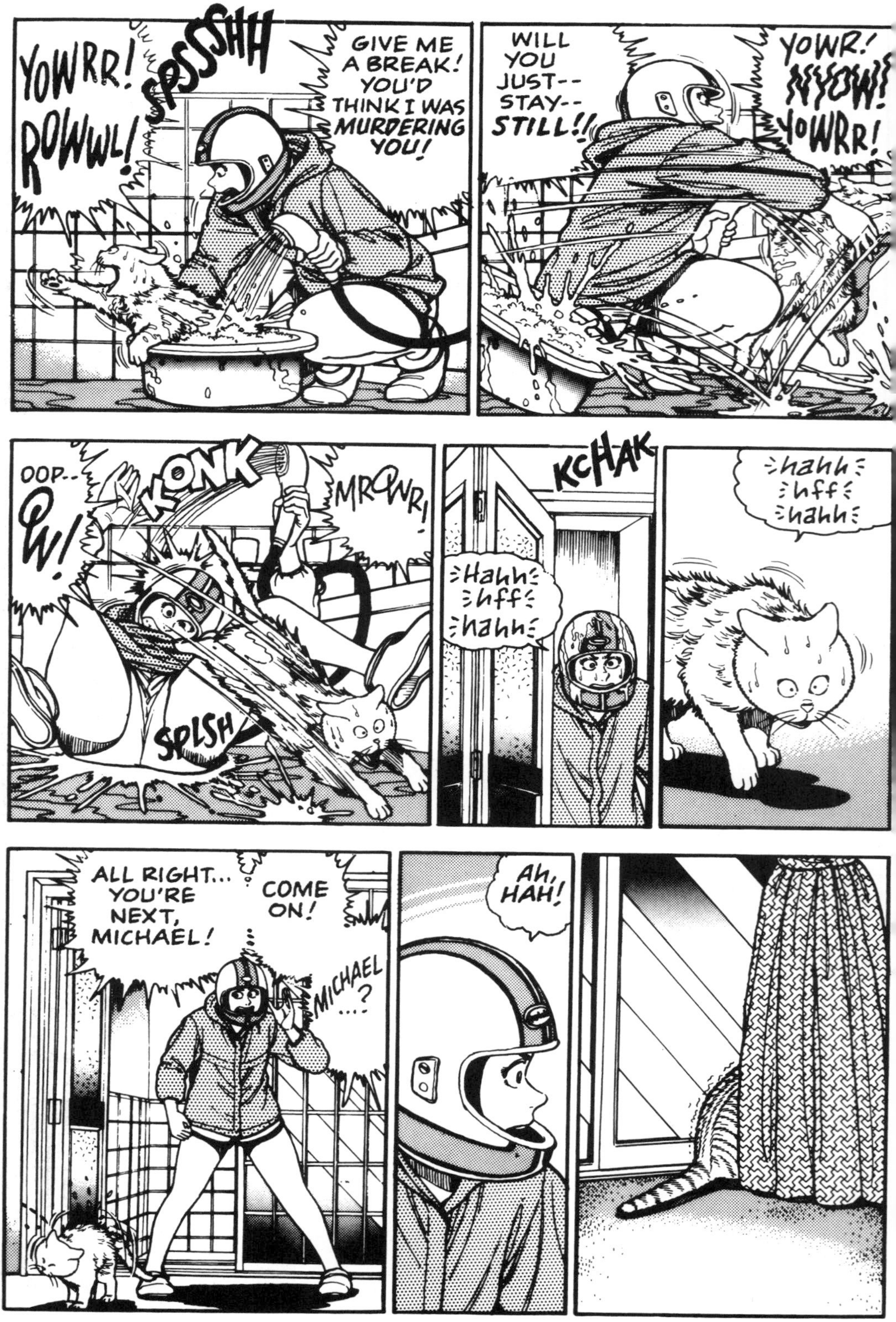
YOWRR!
ROWWL!
SPSSSHH
GIVE ME A BREAK! YOU'D THINK I WAS MURDERING YOU!
WILL YOU JUST-- STAY-- STILL!!
YOWR! NYOW! YOWRR!
OOP--
OW!
KONK
MROWR!
KCHAK
Hahh hff hahh
hahh hff hahh
SPLSH
ALL RIGHT... YOU'RE NEXT, MICHAEL!
COME ON!
MICHAEL ...?
Ah, HAH!

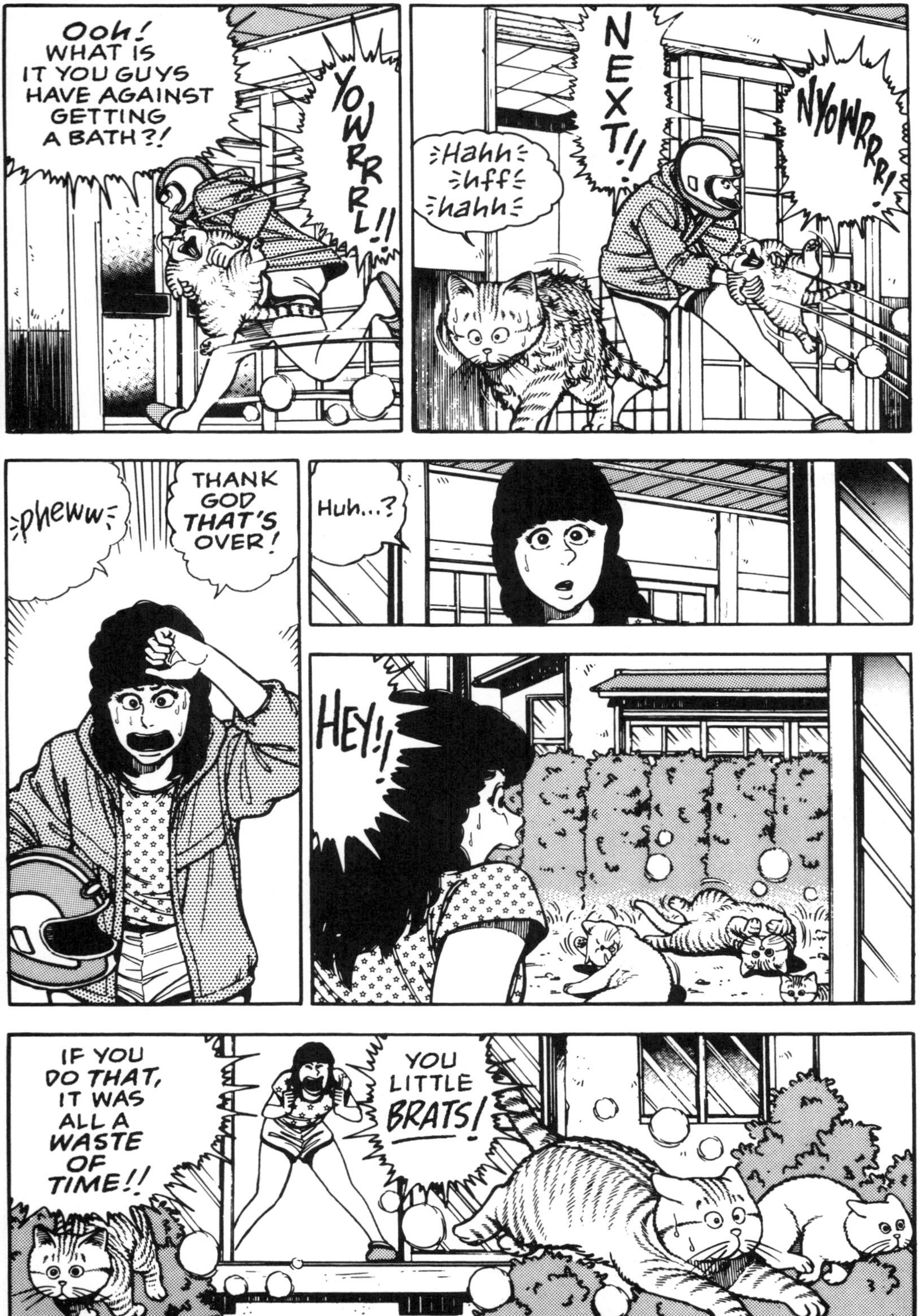

Ooh! WHAT IS IT YOU GUYS HAVE AGAINST GETTING A BATH?!
YOWRRRL!!
Hahh huff hahh
NEXT!!
NYOWRRR!
phewww
THANK GOD THAT'S OVER!
Huh...?
HEY!!
IF YOU DO THAT, IT WAS ALL A WASTE OF TIME!!
YOU LITTLE BRATS!

SO... DID ALL OF YOU SURVIVE UNSCATHED?

YES, DEAR. ANOTHER DAY OF TERROR BEHIND US.

GOOD. THEN IT'S TIME WE ALL SLEEP AND PREPARE FOR TOMORROW.

YES, PAPA!

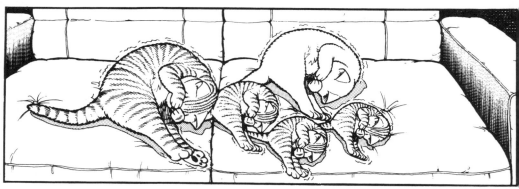

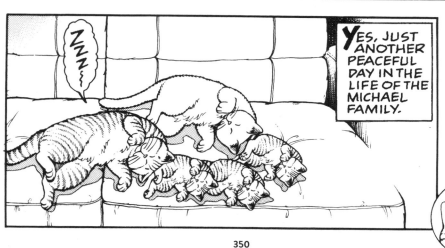

ZZZ

YES, JUST ANOTHER PEACEFUL DAY IN THE LIFE OF THE MICHAEL FAMILY.

END.

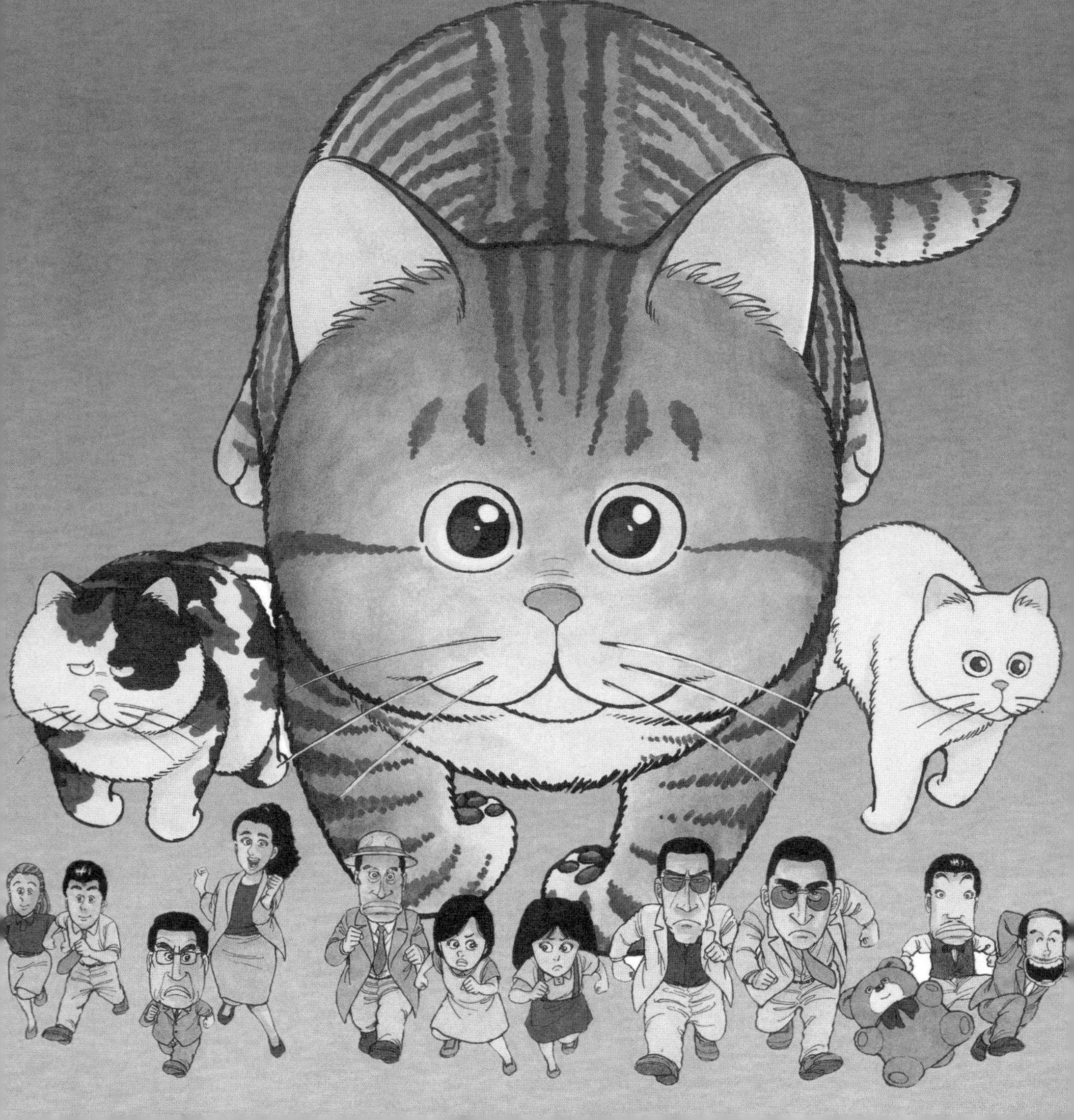

# WHAT'S MICHAEL?

## VOLUME 5: MICHAEL'S FAVORITE SPOT

*This section was translated by and lettered by Alan Gleason,*
*Dana Lewis, Hisashi Kotobuki, Lea Seidman, Toren Smith, and*
*Elin Winkler and lettered by Amador Cisneros, Pat Duke &*
*Radio Comix, Tom Orzechowski, and Amy Stella.*

## MICHAEL VS. CATZILLA: MICHAEL STEPS INTO THE RING

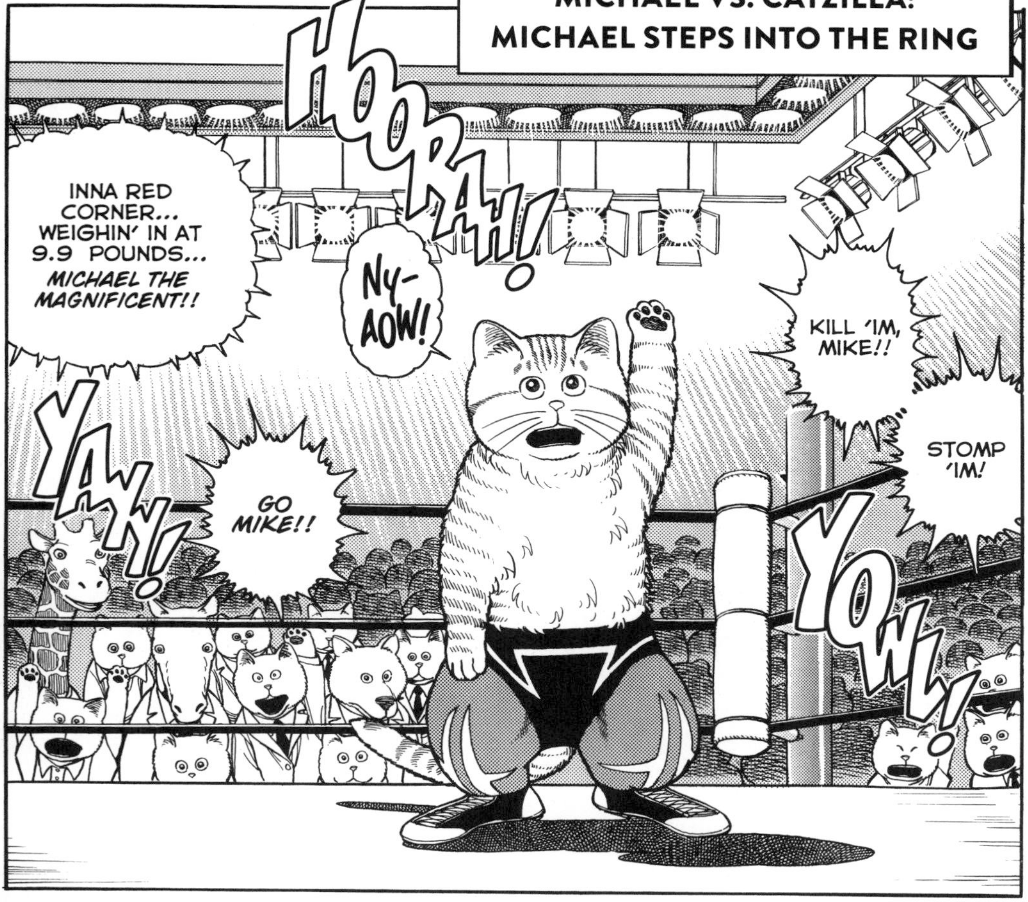
HOORAH!
INNA RED CORNER... WEIGHIN' IN AT 9.9 POUNDS... *MICHAEL THE MAGNIFICENT!!*
NY-AOW!
KILL 'IM, MIKE!!
YAWY!
GO MIKE!!
STOMP 'IM!
YOWL!

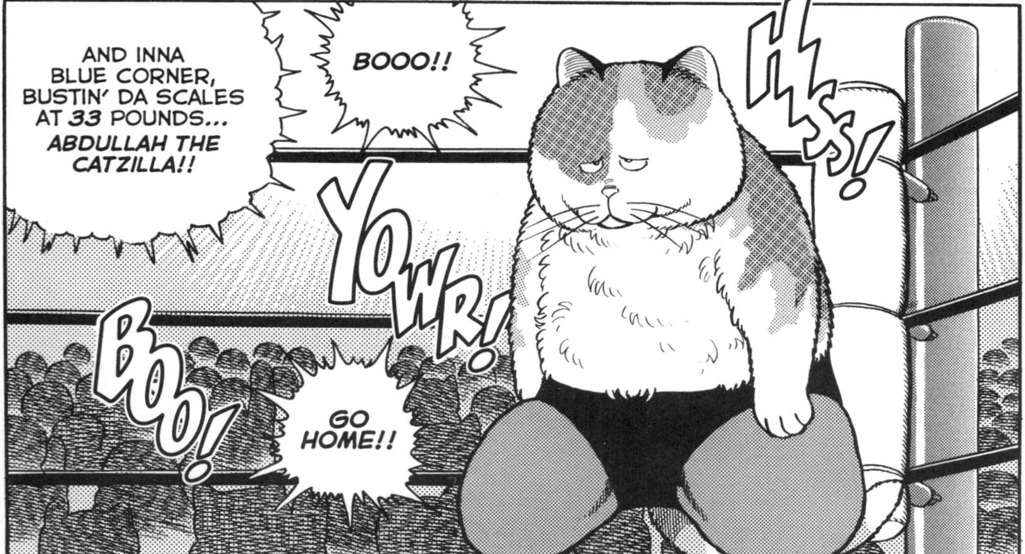
AND INNA BLUE CORNER, BUSTIN' DA SCALES AT *33* POUNDS... *ABDULLAH THE CATZILLA!!*
*BOOO!!*
HISS!
YOWR!
BOO!
GO HOME!!

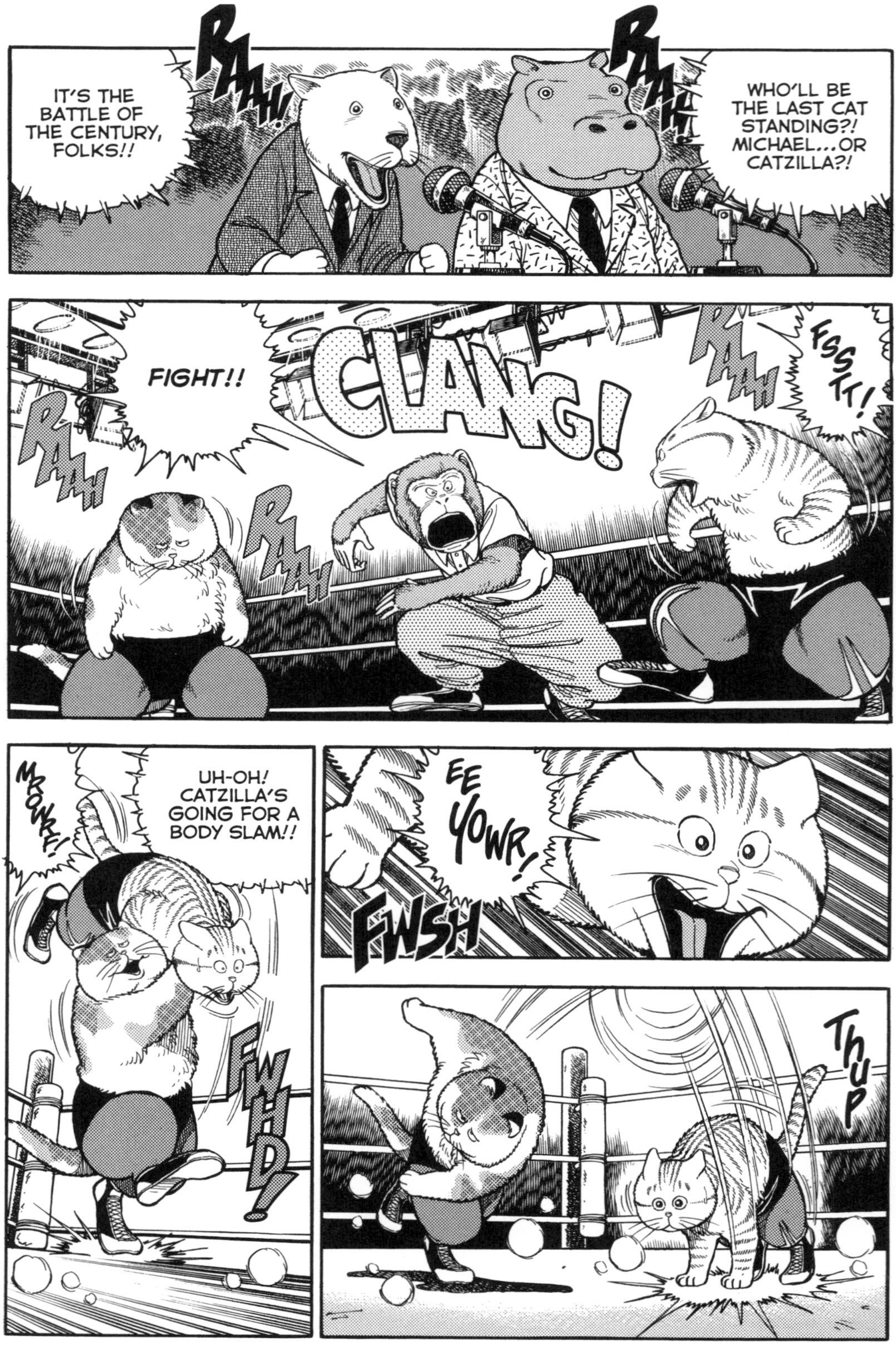

RAAH!
IT'S THE BATTLE OF THE CENTURY, FOLKS!!
RAAH!
WHO'LL BE THE LAST CAT STANDING?! MICHAEL...OR CATZILLA?!
RAAH
FIGHT!!
RAAH
CLANG!
RAAH
FSSTT!
MROWRF!
UH-OH! CATZILLA'S GOING FOR A BODY SLAM!!
FWHD!
EE YOWR!
FWSH
THUP

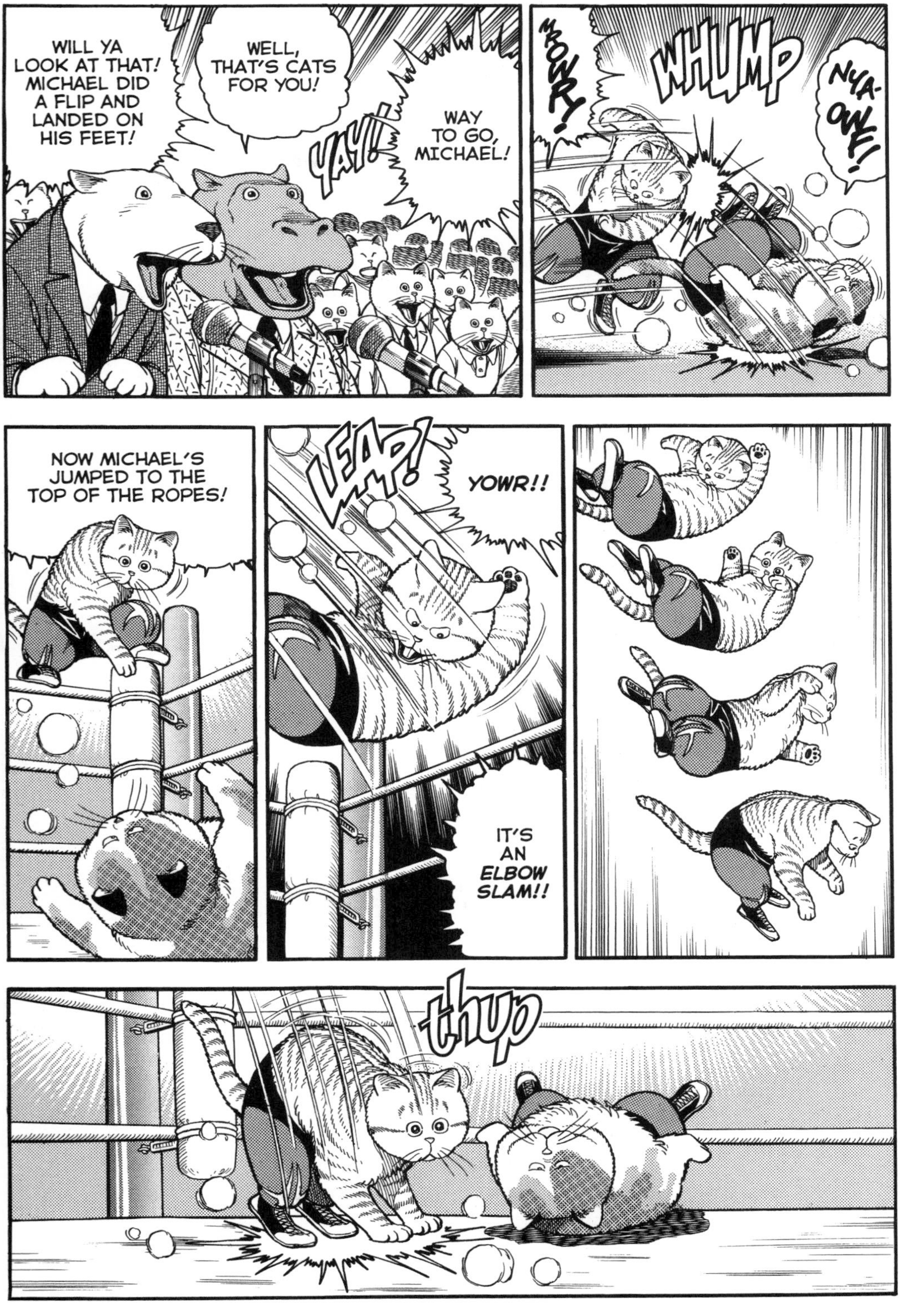
WILL YA LOOK AT THAT! MICHAEL DID A FLIP AND LANDED ON HIS FEET!
WELL, THAT'S CATS FOR YOU!
YAY!
WAY TO GO, MICHAEL!
MOWR!
WHUMP
NYA-OWK!!
NOW MICHAEL'S JUMPED TO THE TOP OF THE ROPES!
LEAP!
YOWR!!
IT'S AN ELBOW SLAM!!
thup

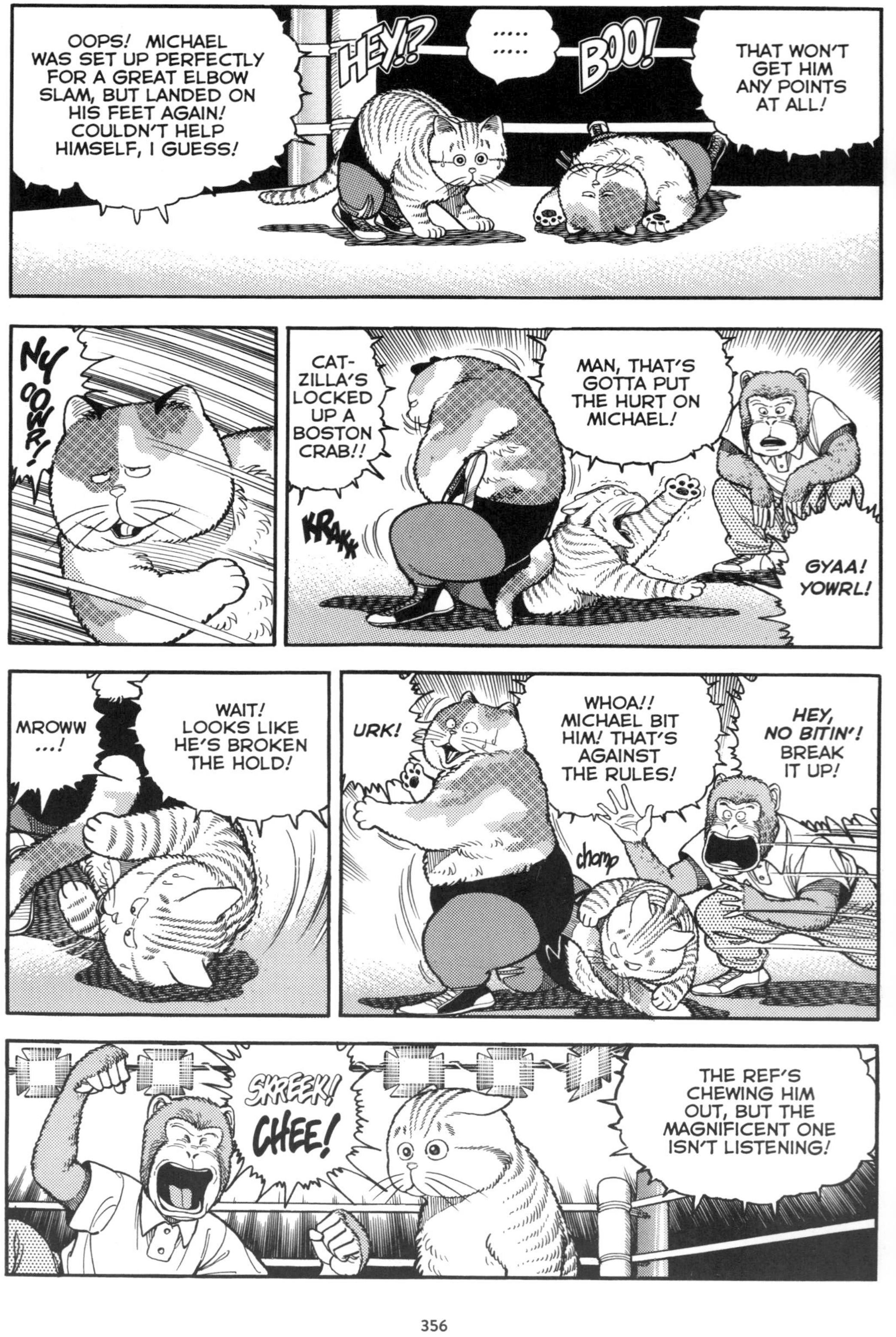

OOPS! MICHAEL WAS SET UP PERFECTLY FOR A GREAT ELBOW SLAM, BUT LANDED ON HIS FEET AGAIN! COULDN'T HELP HIMSELF, I GUESS!
HEY!?
.....
.....
BOO!
THAT WON'T GET HIM ANY POINTS AT ALL!
NYOOWR!
CAT-ZILLA'S LOCKED UP A BOSTON CRAB!!
MAN, THAT'S GOTTA PUT THE HURT ON MICHAEL!
KRAKK
GYAA! YOWRL!
MROWW ...!
WAIT! LOOKS LIKE HE'S BROKEN THE HOLD!
URK!
WHOA!! MICHAEL BIT HIM! THAT'S AGAINST THE RULES!
HEY, NO BITIN'! BREAK IT UP!
champ
SKREEK!
CHEE!
THE REF'S CHEWING HIM OUT, BUT THE MAGNIFICENT ONE ISN'T LISTENING!

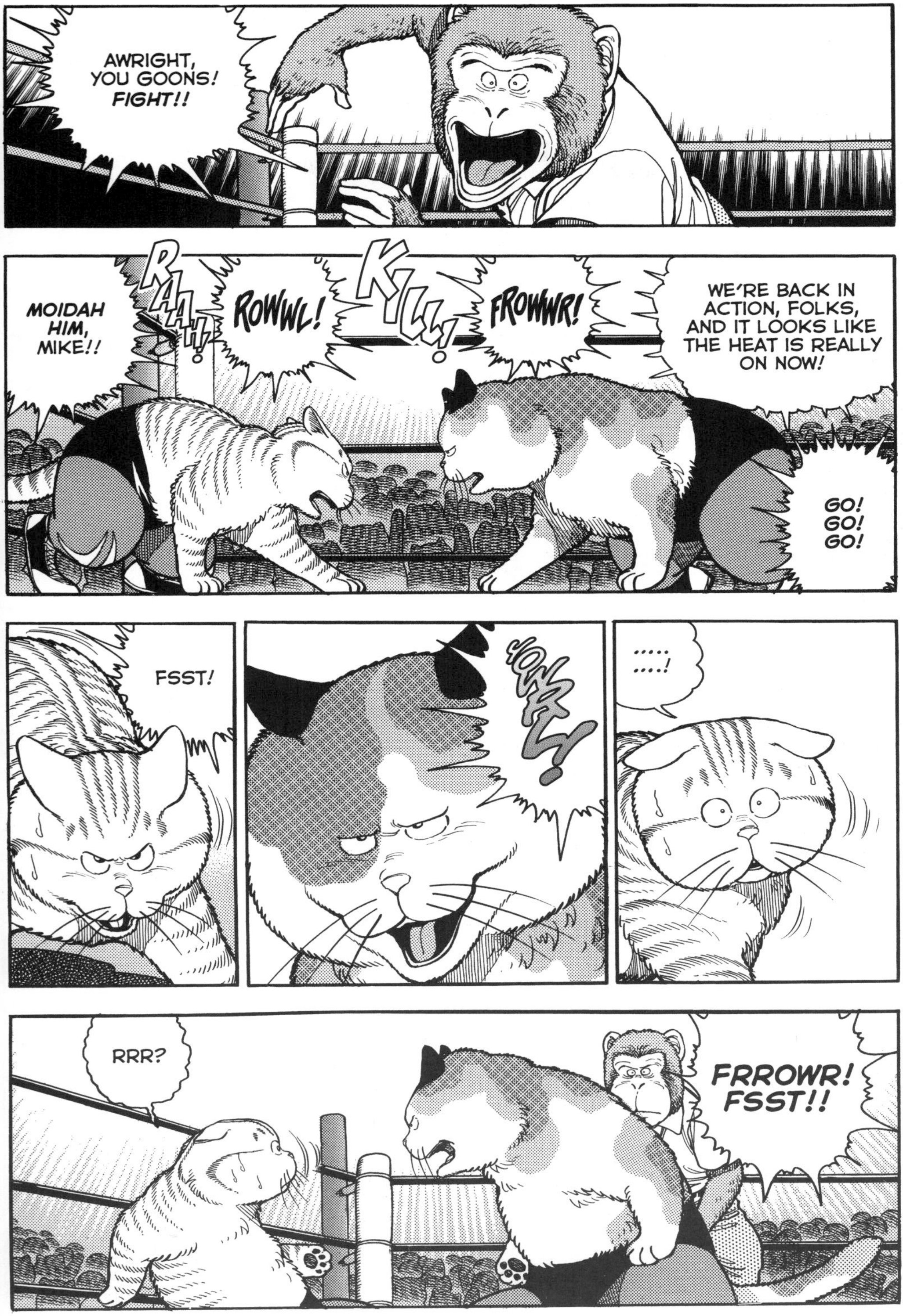
AWRIGHT, YOU GOONS! FIGHT!!
MOIDAH HIM, MIKE!!
RAAAH!
ROWWL!
KYLL!
FROWWR!
WE'RE BACK IN ACTION, FOLKS, AND IT LOOKS LIKE THE HEAT IS REALLY ON NOW!
GO! GO! GO!
FSST!
.....!
RRR?
FRROWR! FSST!!

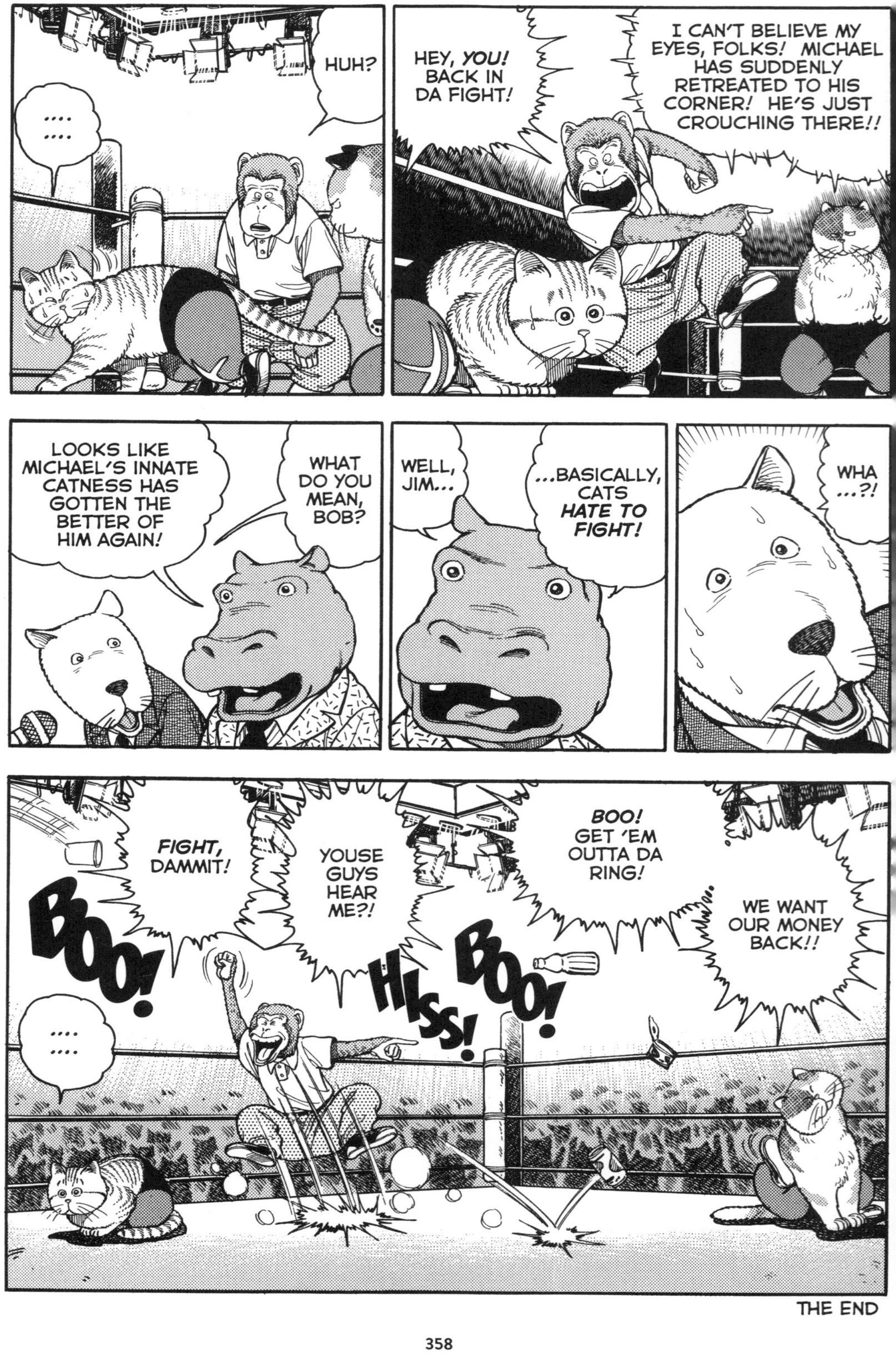
....
....
HUH?
HEY, YOU! BACK IN DA FIGHT!
I CAN'T BELIEVE MY EYES, FOLKS! MICHAEL HAS SUDDENLY RETREATED TO HIS CORNER! HE'S JUST CROUCHING THERE!!
LOOKS LIKE MICHAEL'S INNATE CATNESS HAS GOTTEN THE BETTER OF HIM AGAIN!
WHAT DO YOU MEAN, BOB?
WELL, JIM...
...BASICALLY, CATS HATE TO FIGHT!
WHA ...?!
FIGHT, DAMMIT!
YOUSE GUYS HEAR ME?!
BOO! GET 'EM OUTTA DA RING!
WE WANT OUR MONEY BACK!!
BOO!
HISS!
BOO!
....
....

THE END

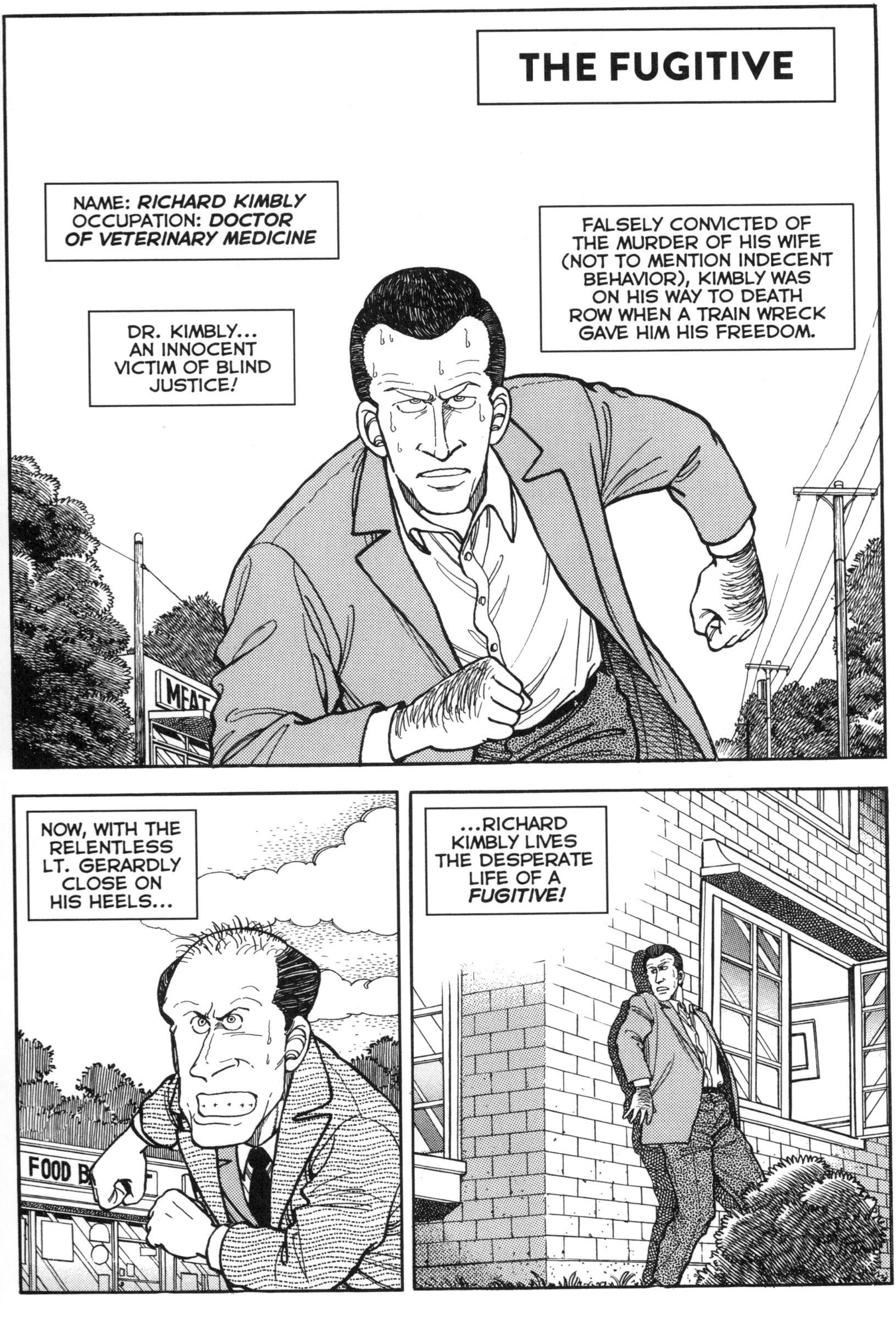
THE FUGITIVE
NAME: *RICHARD KIMBLY*
OCCUPATION: *DOCTOR OF VETERINARY MEDICINE*
DR. KIMBLY... AN INNOCENT VICTIM OF BLIND JUSTICE!
FALSELY CONVICTED OF THE MURDER OF HIS WIFE (NOT TO MENTION INDECENT BEHAVIOR), KIMBLY WAS ON HIS WAY TO DEATH ROW WHEN A TRAIN WRECK GAVE HIM HIS FREEDOM.
MEAT
NOW, WITH THE RELENTLESS LT. GERARDLY CLOSE ON HIS HEELS...
...RICHARD KIMBLY LIVES THE DESPERATE LIFE OF A *FUGITIVE!*

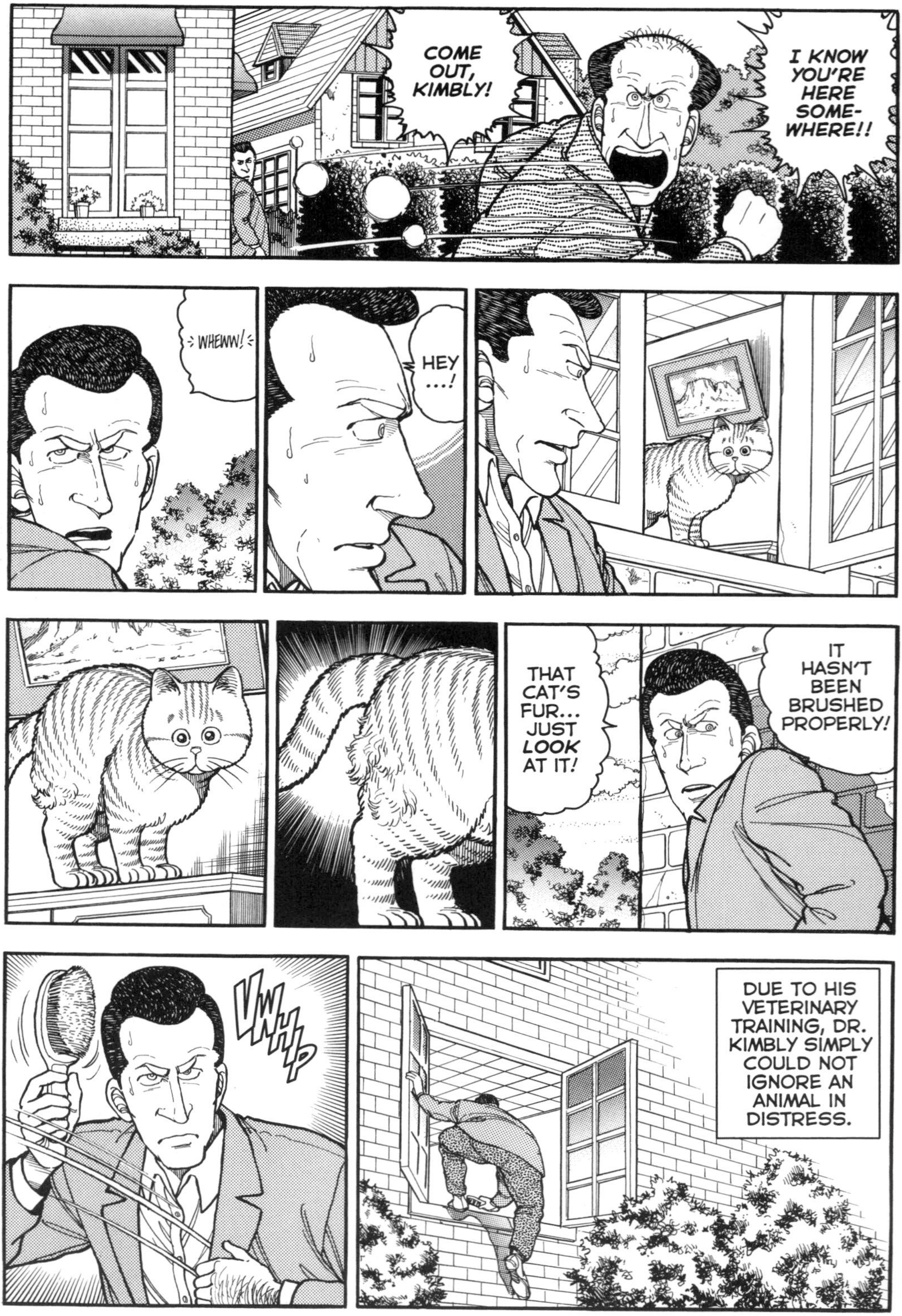

COME OUT, KIMBLY!
I KNOW YOU'RE HERE SOMEWHERE!!
WHEWW!
HEY ...!
THAT CAT'S FUR... JUST *LOOK* AT IT!
IT HASN'T BEEN BRUSHED PROPERLY!
VWHIP
DUE TO HIS VETERINARY TRAINING, DR. KIMBLY SIMPLY COULD NOT IGNORE AN ANIMAL IN DISTRESS.

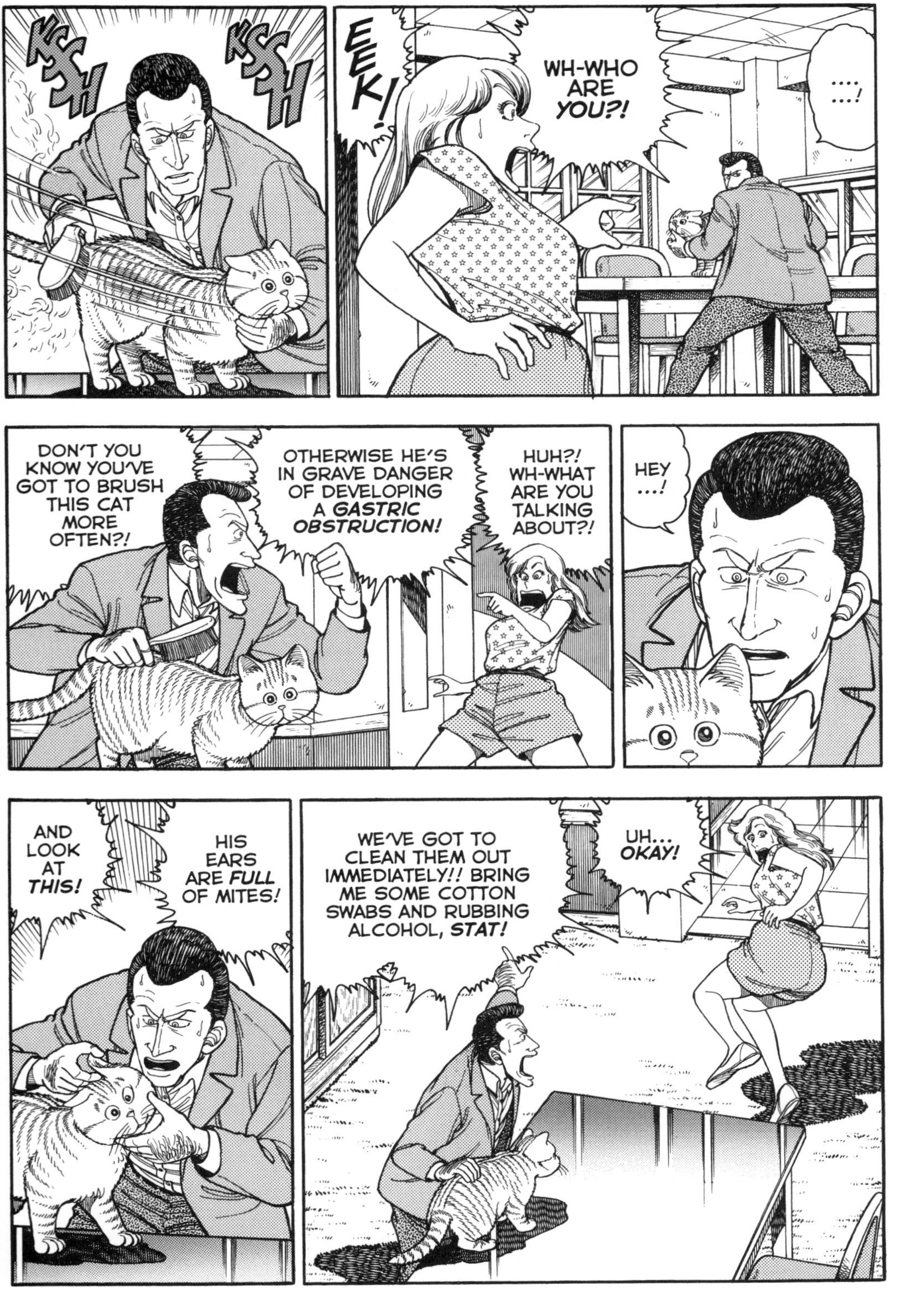
KSH KSH
EEK!
WH-WHO ARE YOU?!
...,
...!
DON'T YOU KNOW YOU'VE GOT TO BRUSH THIS CAT MORE OFTEN?!
OTHERWISE HE'S IN GRAVE DANGER OF DEVELOPING A GASTRIC OBSTRUCTION!
HUH?! WH-WHAT ARE YOU TALKING ABOUT?!
HEY ...!
AND LOOK AT THIS!
HIS EARS ARE FULL OF MITES!
WE'VE GOT TO CLEAN THEM OUT IMMEDIATELY!! BRING ME SOME COTTON SWABS AND RUBBING ALCOHOL, STAT!
UH... OKAY!

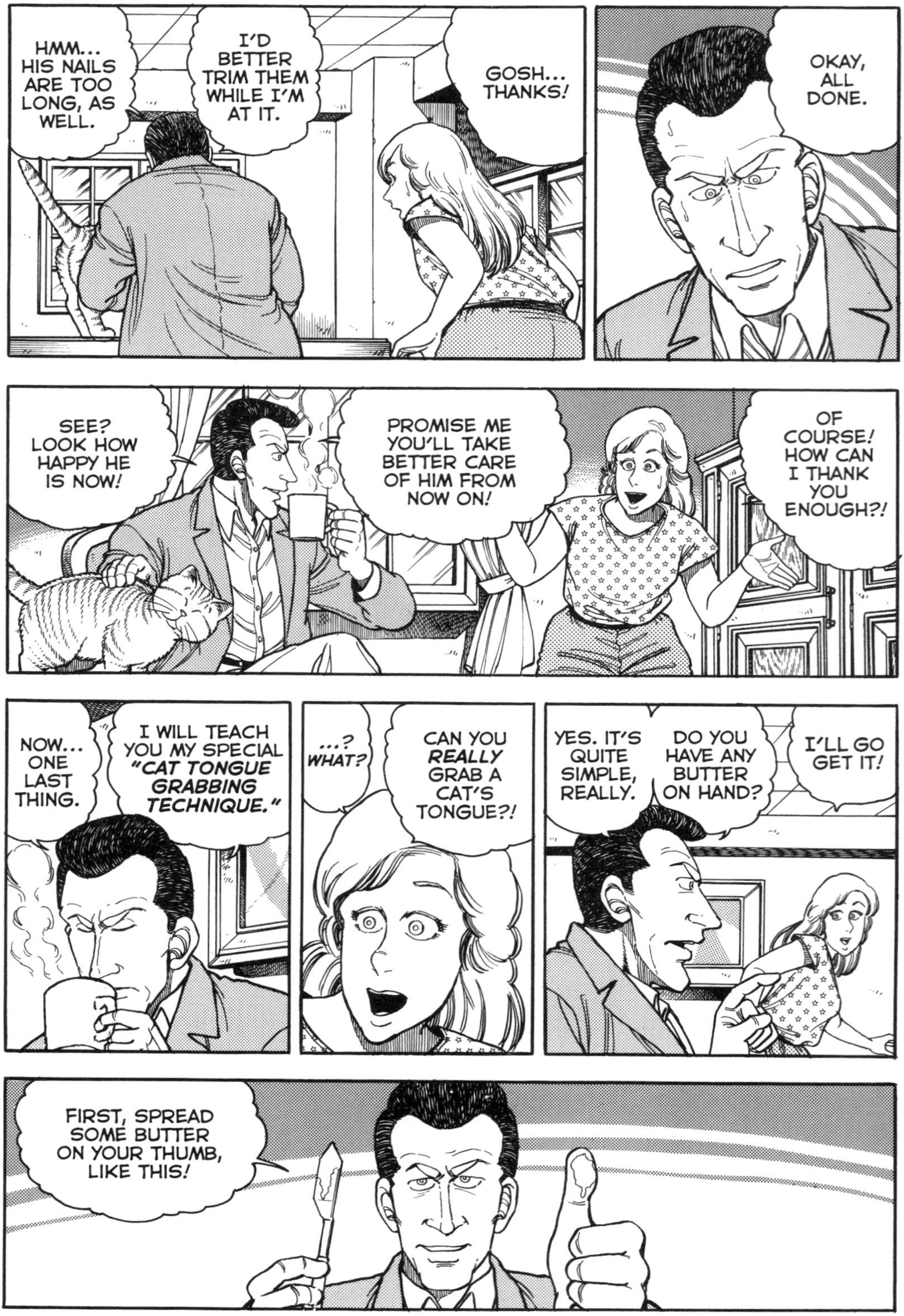
HMM... HIS NAILS ARE TOO LONG, AS WELL.
I'D BETTER TRIM THEM WHILE I'M AT IT.
GOSH... THANKS!
OKAY, ALL DONE.
SEE? LOOK HOW HAPPY HE IS NOW!
PROMISE ME YOU'LL TAKE BETTER CARE OF HIM FROM NOW ON!
OF COURSE! HOW CAN I THANK YOU ENOUGH?!
NOW... ONE LAST THING.
I WILL TEACH YOU MY SPECIAL ***"CAT TONGUE GRABBING TECHNIQUE."***
...? ***WHAT?***
CAN YOU ***REALLY*** GRAB A CAT'S TONGUE?!
YES. IT'S QUITE SIMPLE, REALLY.
DO YOU HAVE ANY BUTTER ON HAND?
I'LL GO GET IT!
FIRST, SPREAD SOME BUTTER ON YOUR THUMB, LIKE THIS!

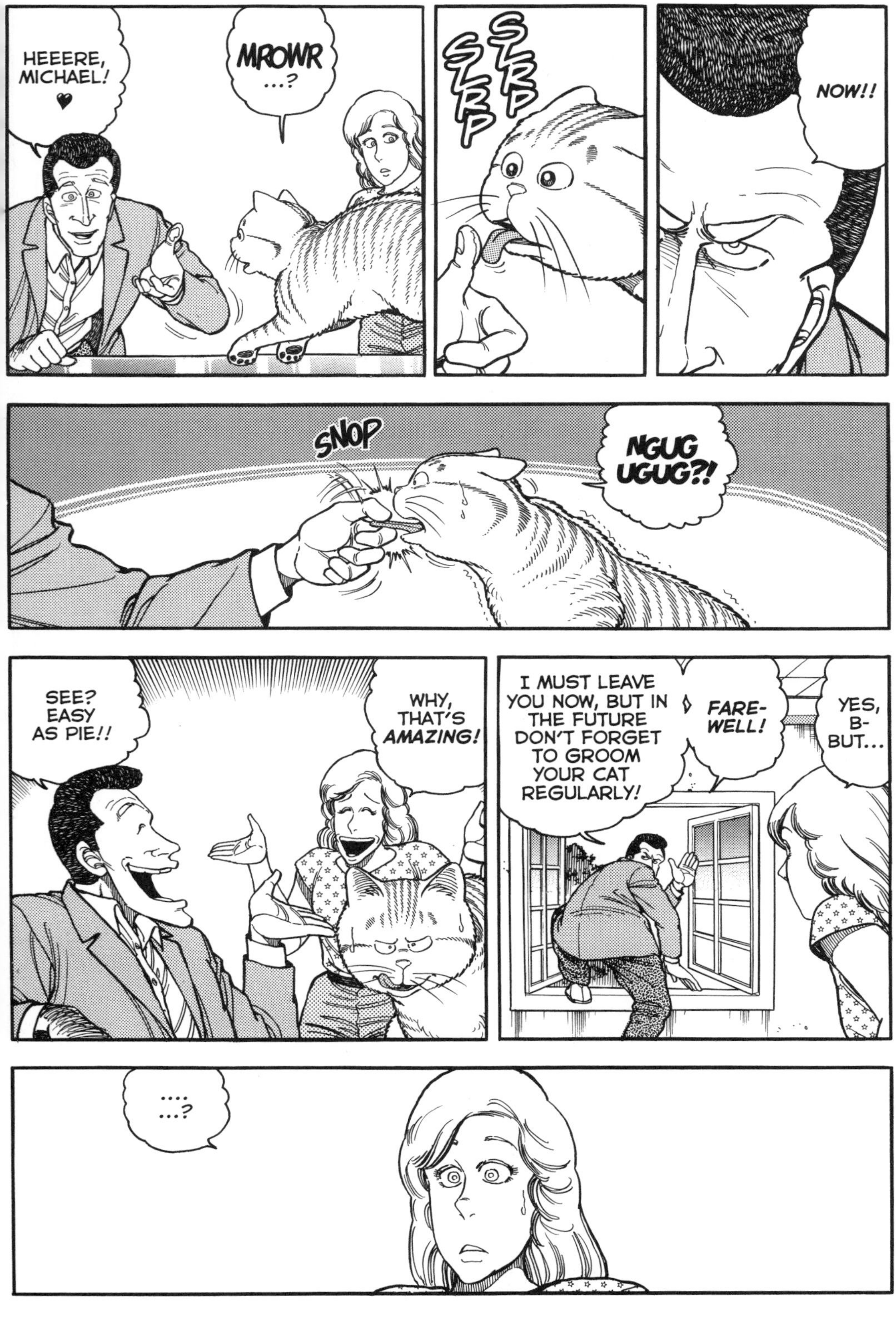
HEEERE, MICHAEL! ♥
MROWR ...?
SLRP SLRP
NOW!!
SNOP
NGUG UGUG?!
SEE? EASY AS PIE!!
WHY, THAT'S *AMAZING!*
I MUST LEAVE YOU NOW, BUT IN THE FUTURE DON'T FORGET TO GROOM YOUR CAT REGULARLY!
*FARE-WELL!*
YES, B-BUT...
.... ...?

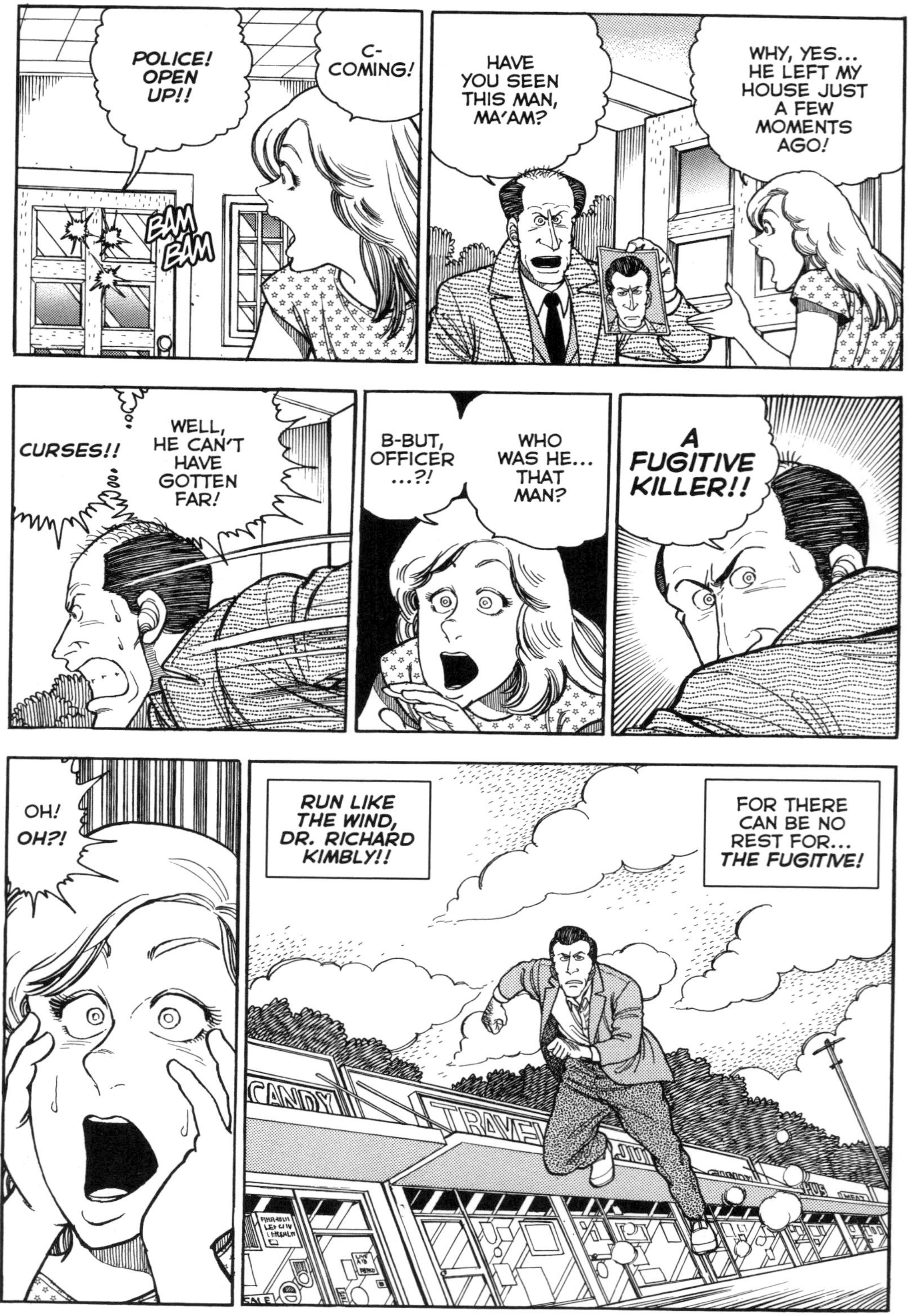
POLICE! OPEN UP!!
C-COMING!
BAM BAM
HAVE YOU SEEN THIS MAN, MA'AM?
WHY, YES... HE LEFT MY HOUSE JUST A FEW MOMENTS AGO!
CURSES!!
WELL, HE CAN'T HAVE GOTTEN FAR!
B-BUT, OFFICER ...?!
WHO WAS HE... THAT MAN?
A FUGITIVE KILLER!!
OH!
OH?!
RUN LIKE THE WIND, DR. RICHARD KIMBLY!!
FOR THERE CAN BE NO REST FOR... THE FUGITIVE!
CANDY

THE END

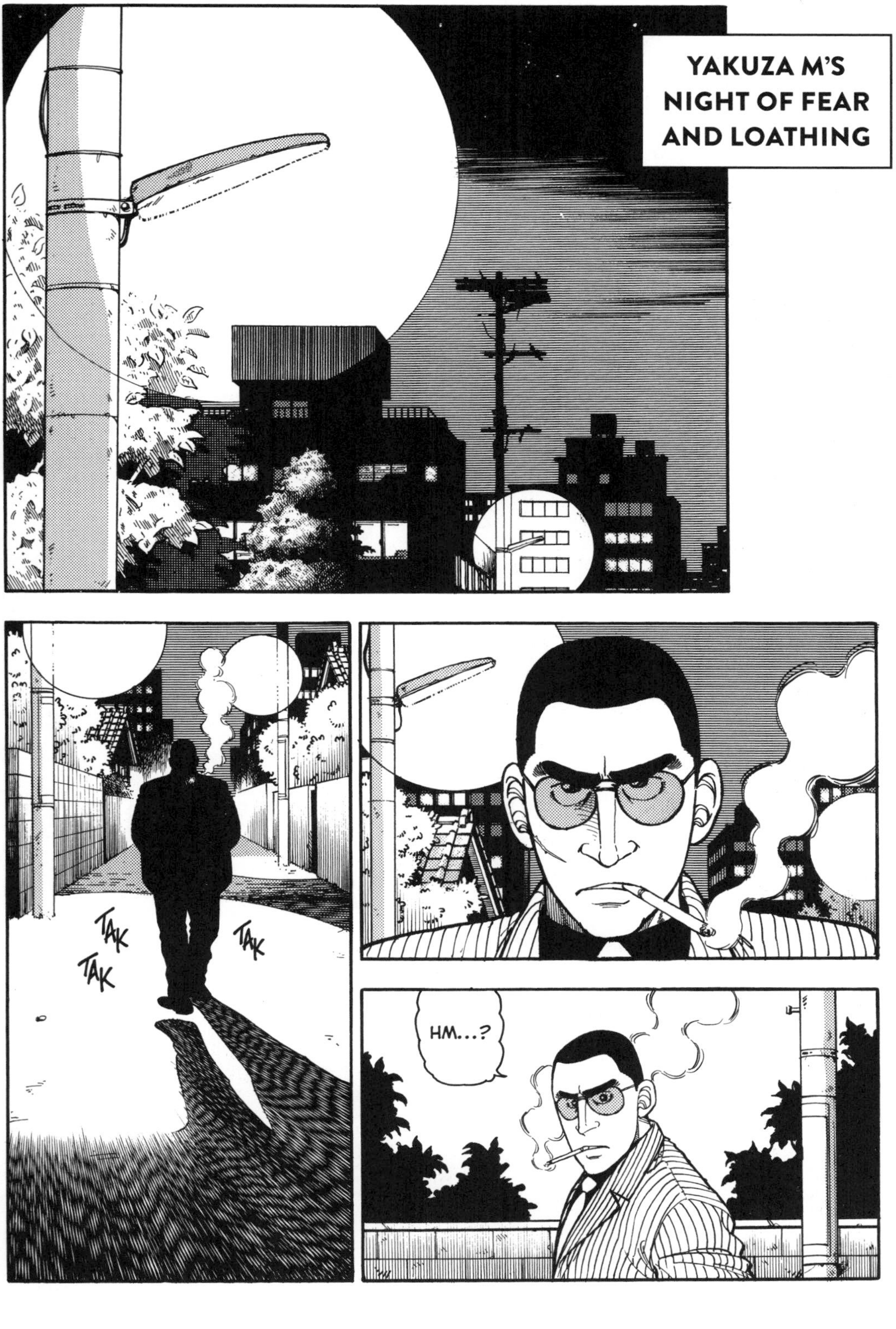
YAKUZA M'S
NIGHT OF FEAR
AND LOATHING
TAK
TAK
TAK
HM...?

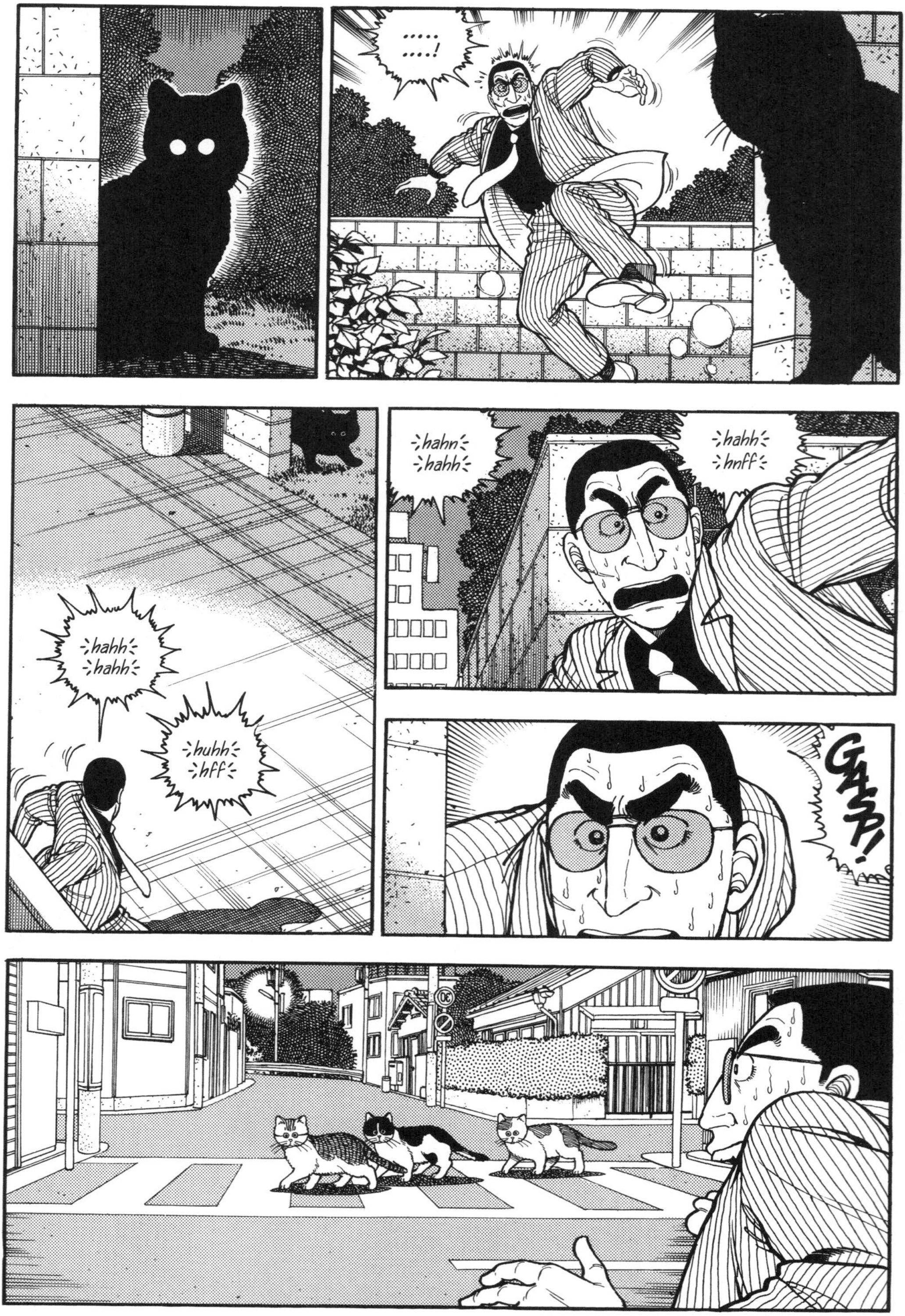
.....
.....!
hahh
hahh
huhh
hff
hahn
hahh
hahh
hnff
GASP!

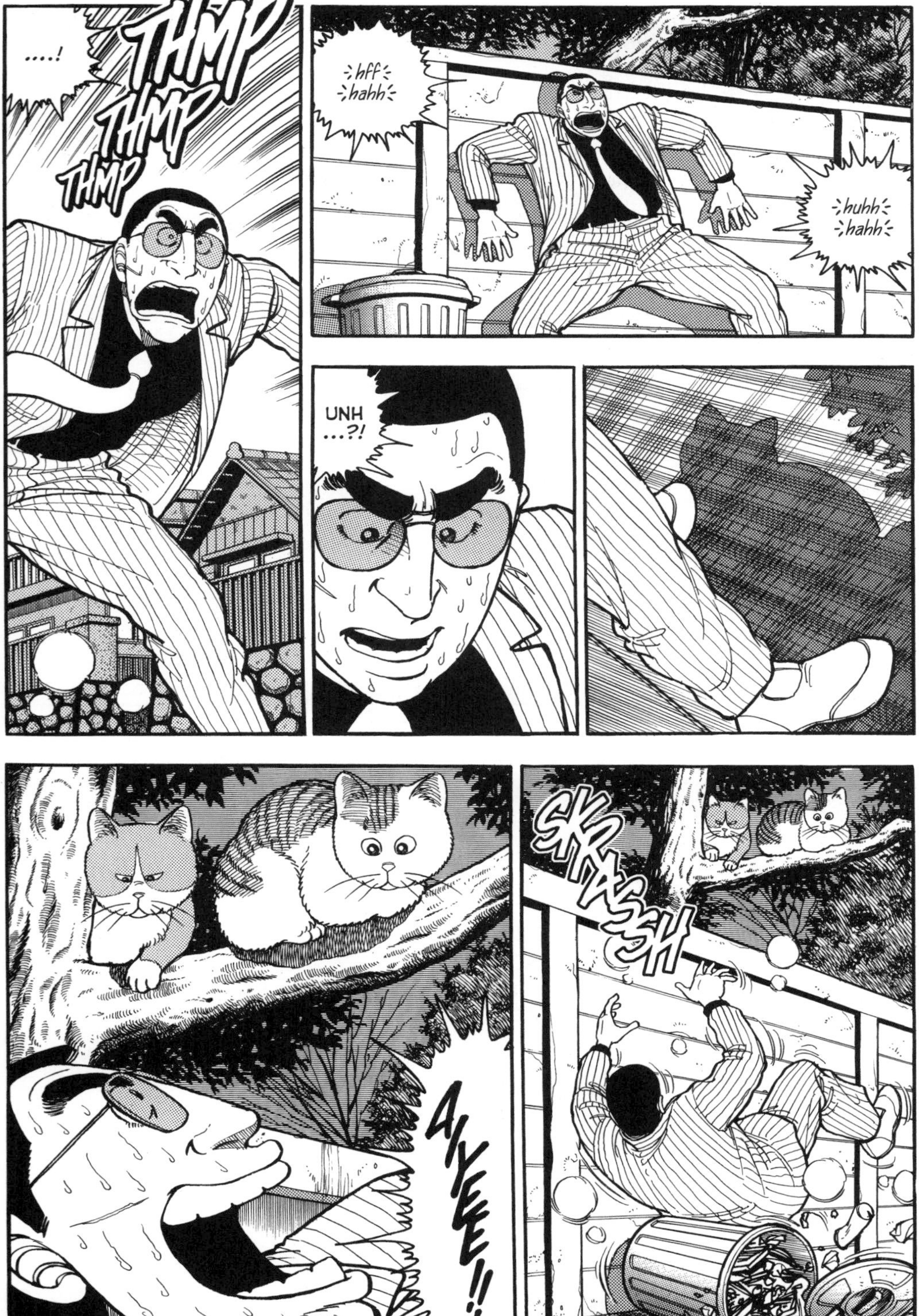

....!
THMP THMP THMP
hff hahh
huhh hahh
UNH ...?!
SKRASSH
AIYEEE!!

THUD
....!
HAIEEE!

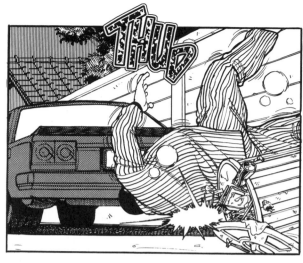

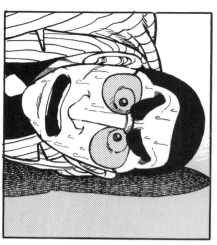

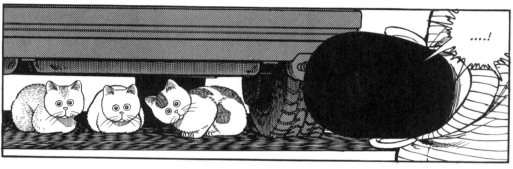

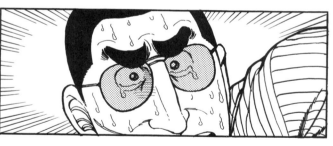

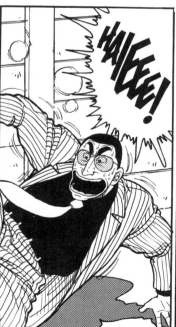

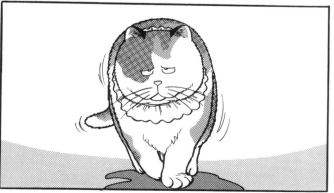

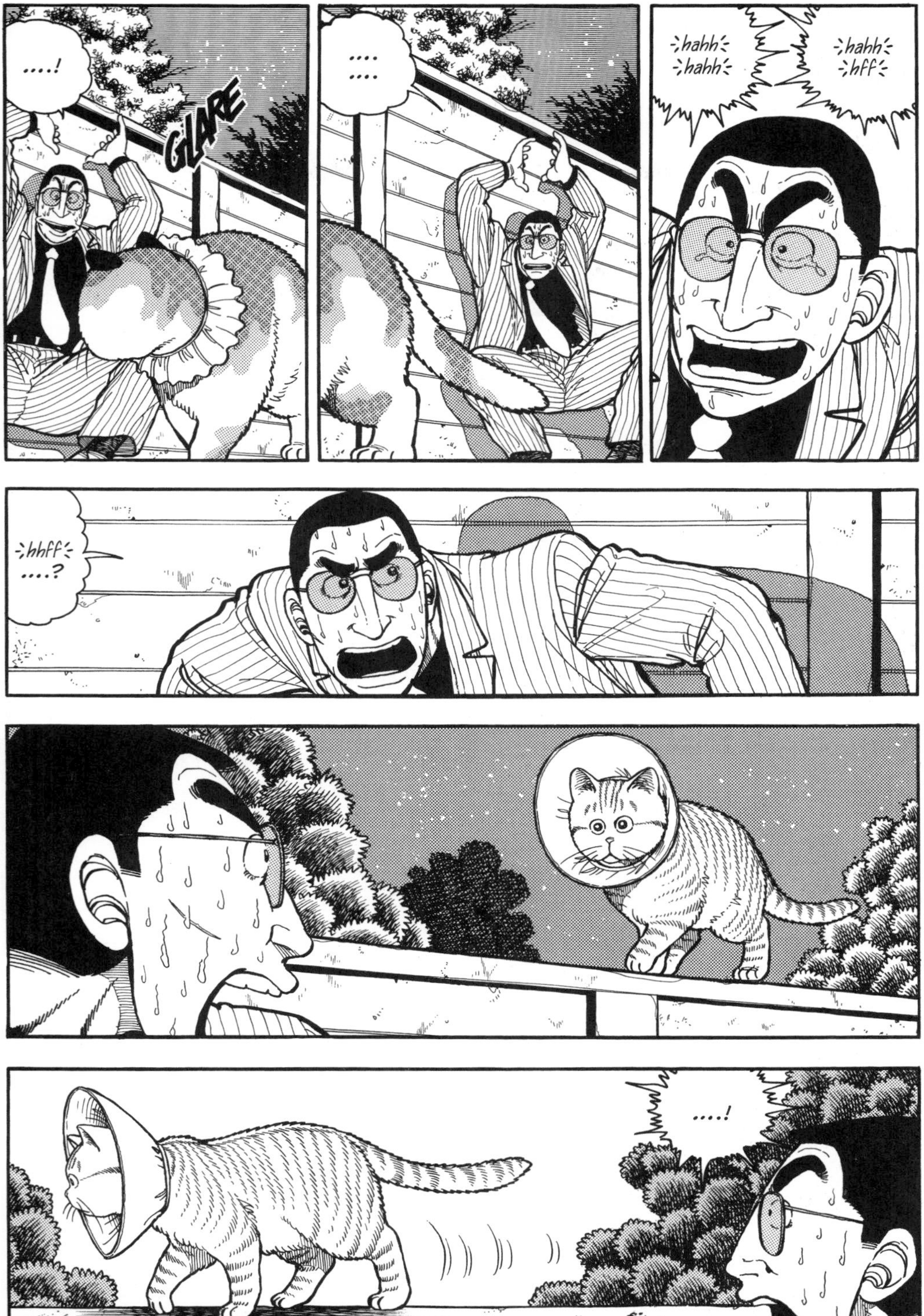

....!
GLARE
....
....
hahh
hahh
hahh
hff
hhff
....?
....!

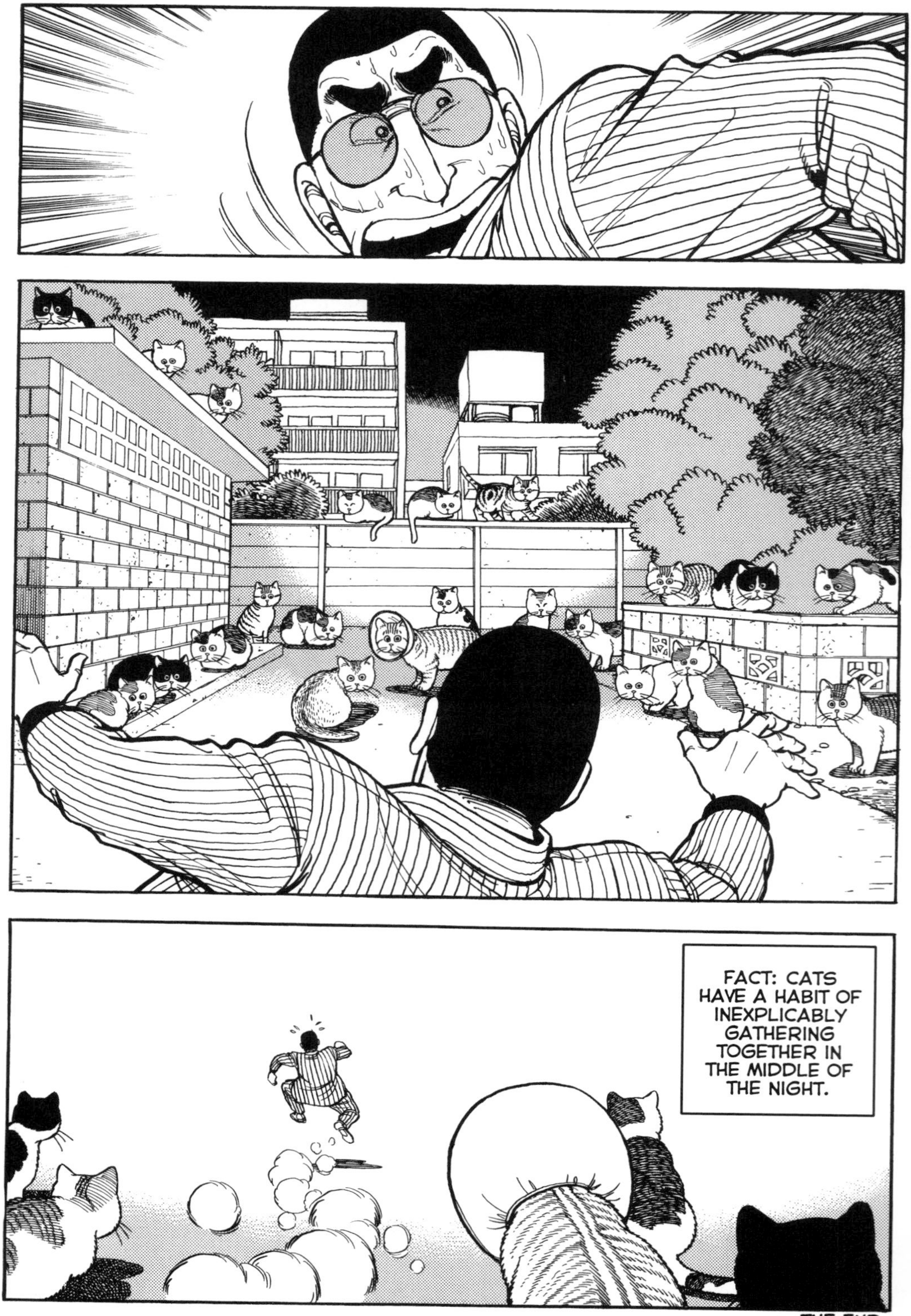
FACT: CATS HAVE A HABIT OF INEXPLICABLY GATHERING TOGETHER IN THE MIDDLE OF THE NIGHT.

THE END

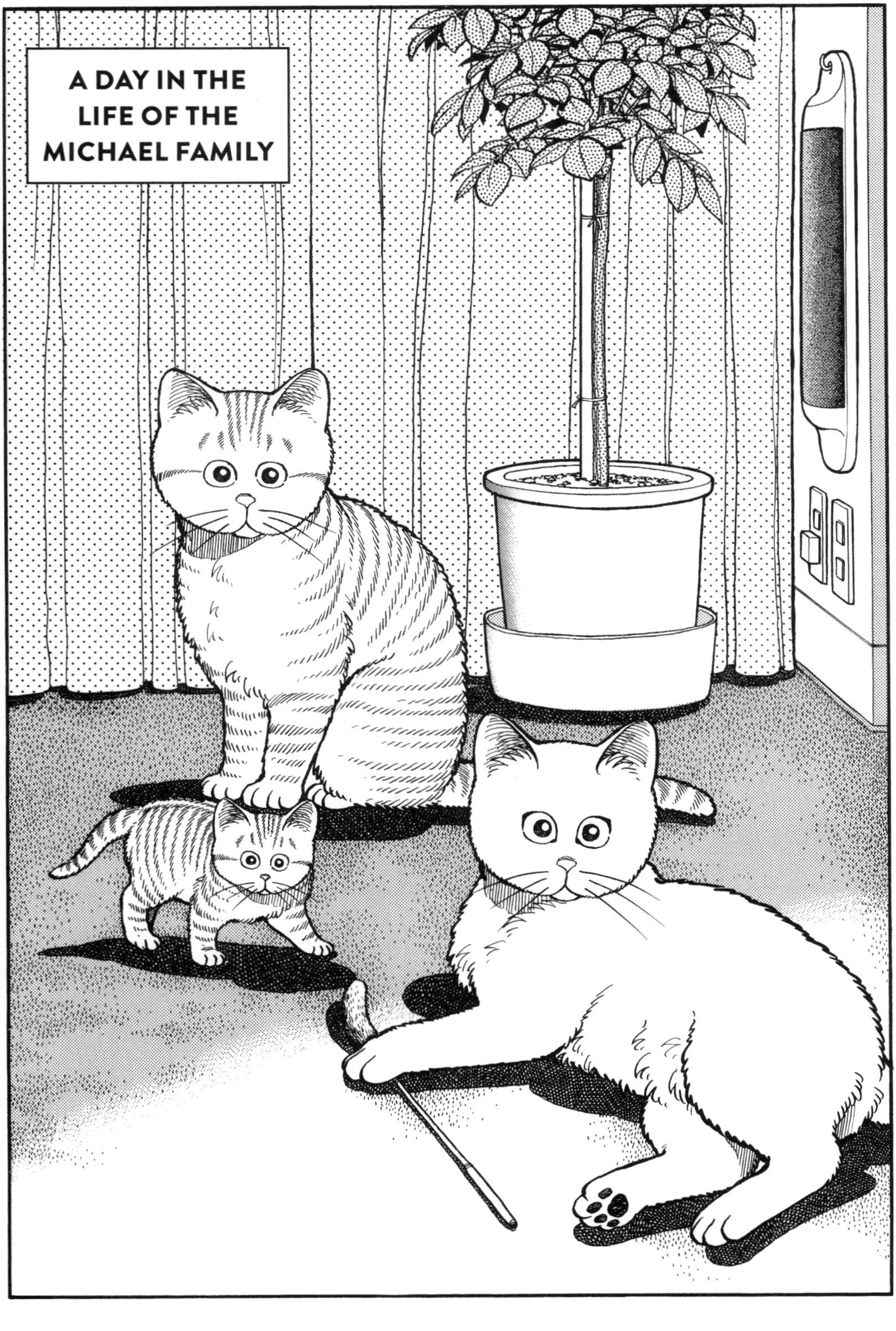
A DAY IN THE LIFE OF THE MICHAEL FAMILY

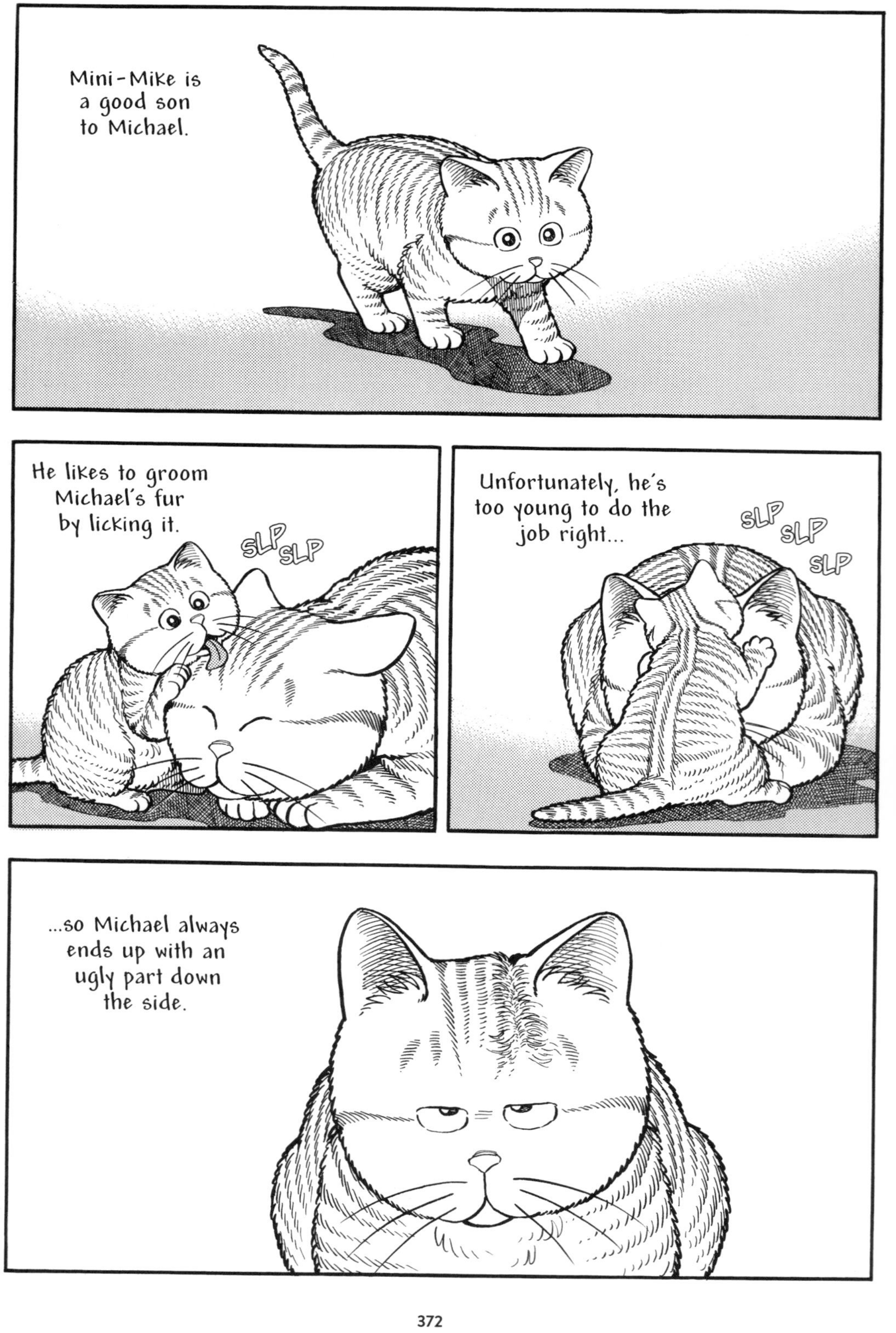
Mini-Mike is a good son to Michael.
He likes to groom Michael's fur by licking it.
SLP SLP
Unfortunately, he's too young to do the job right...
SLP SLP SLP
...so Michael always ends up with an ugly part down the side.

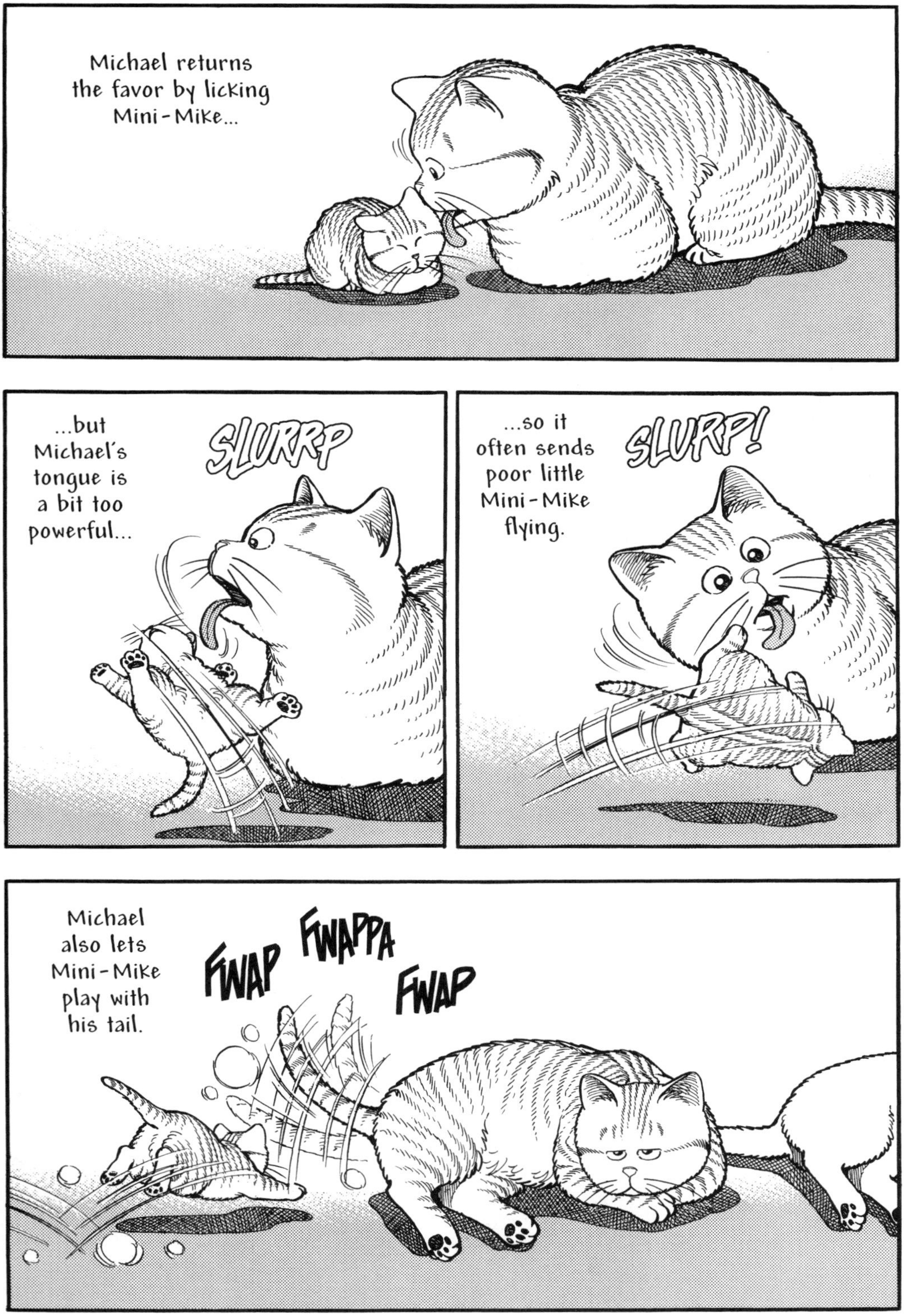
Michael returns the favor by licking Mini-Mike...
...but Michael's tongue is a bit too powerful...
SLURRP
...so it often sends poor little Mini-Mike flying.
SLURP!
Michael also lets Mini-Mike play with his tail.
FWAP
FWAPPA
FWAP

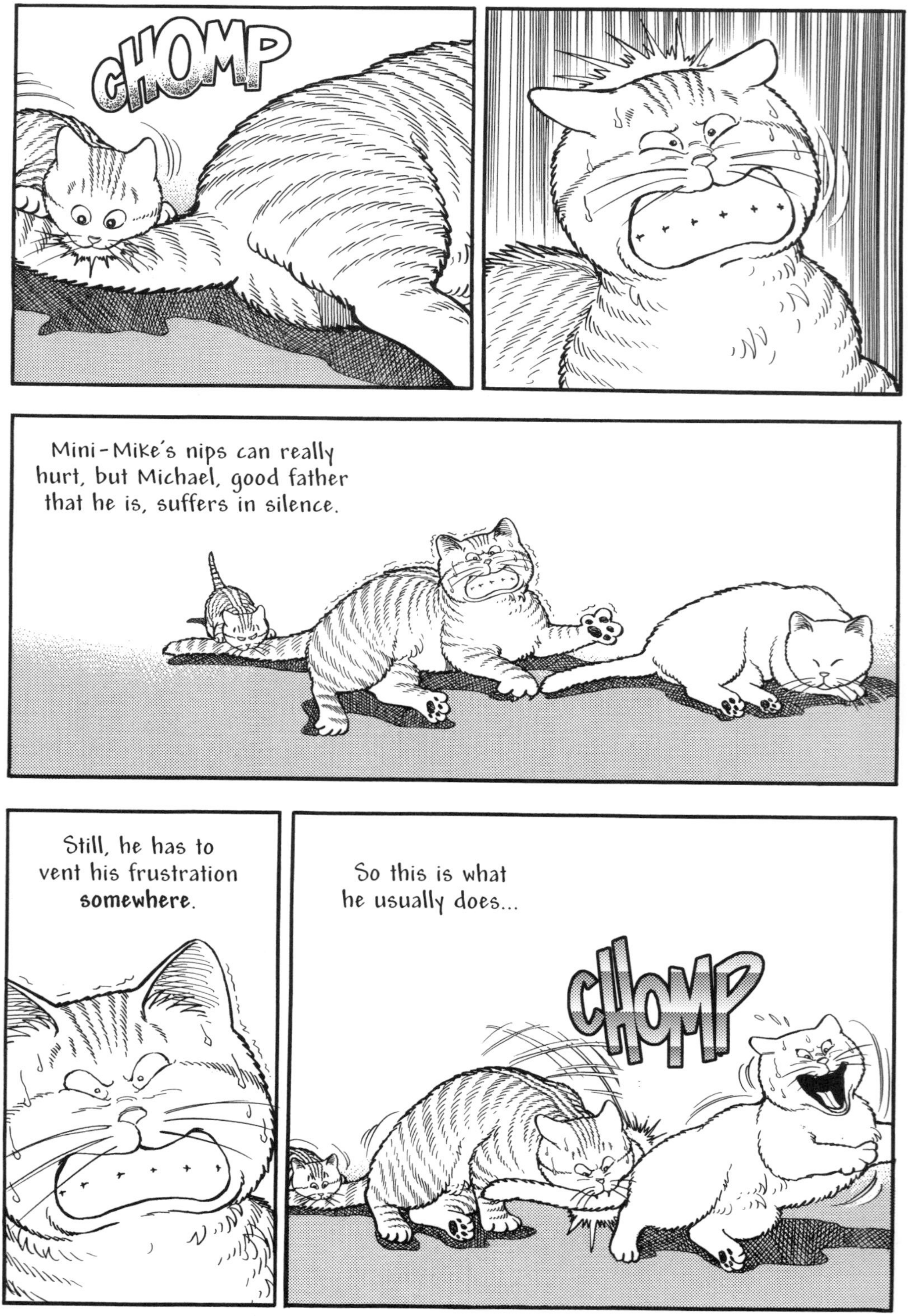
CHOMP
Mini-Mike's nips can really hurt, but Michael, good father that he is, suffers in silence.
Still, he has to vent his frustration **somewhere**.
So this is what he usually does...
CHOMP

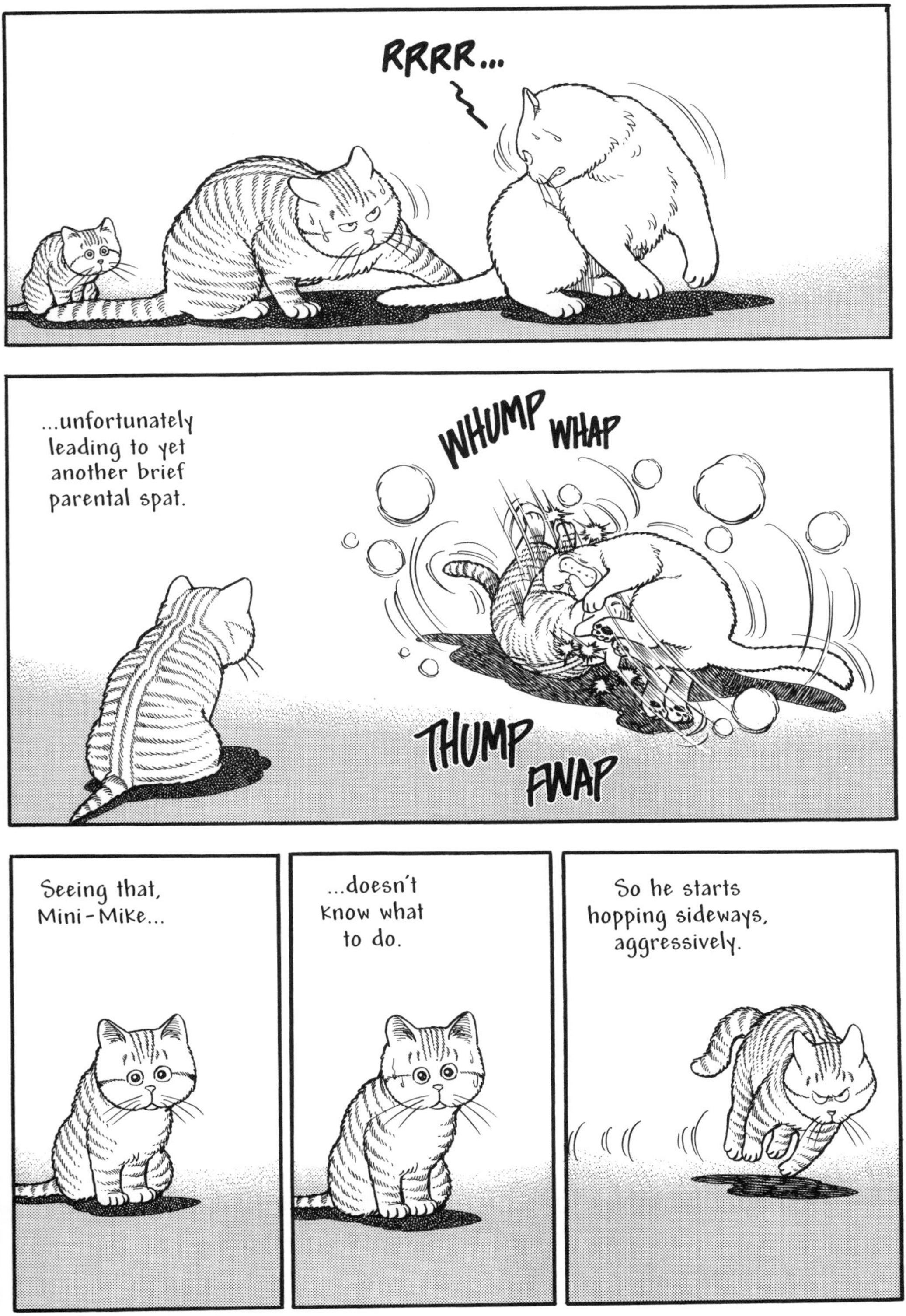
RRRR...
...unfortunately leading to yet another brief parental spat.
WHUMP
WHAP
THUMP
FWAP
Seeing that, Mini-Mike...
...doesn't know what to do.
So he starts hopping sideways, aggressively.

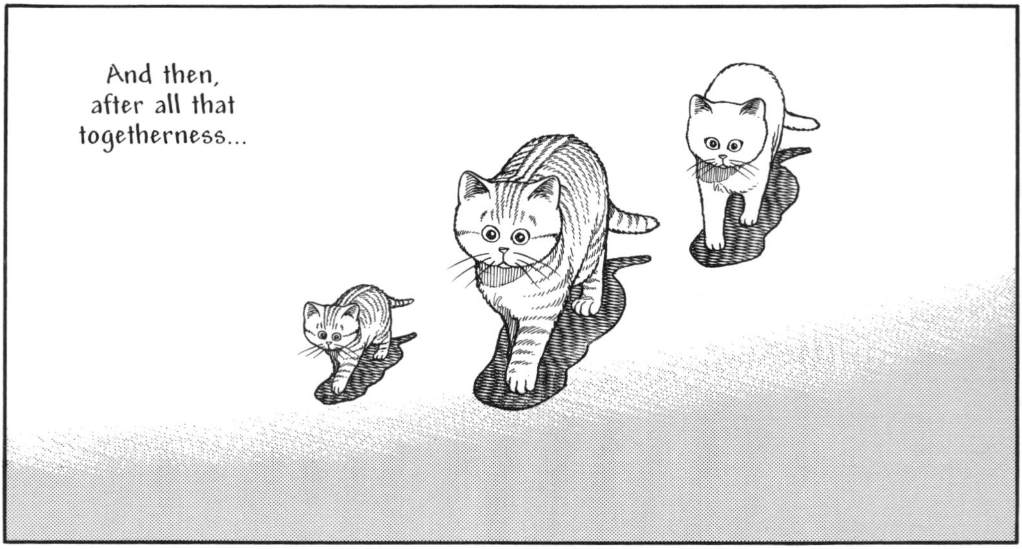
And then, after all that togetherness...

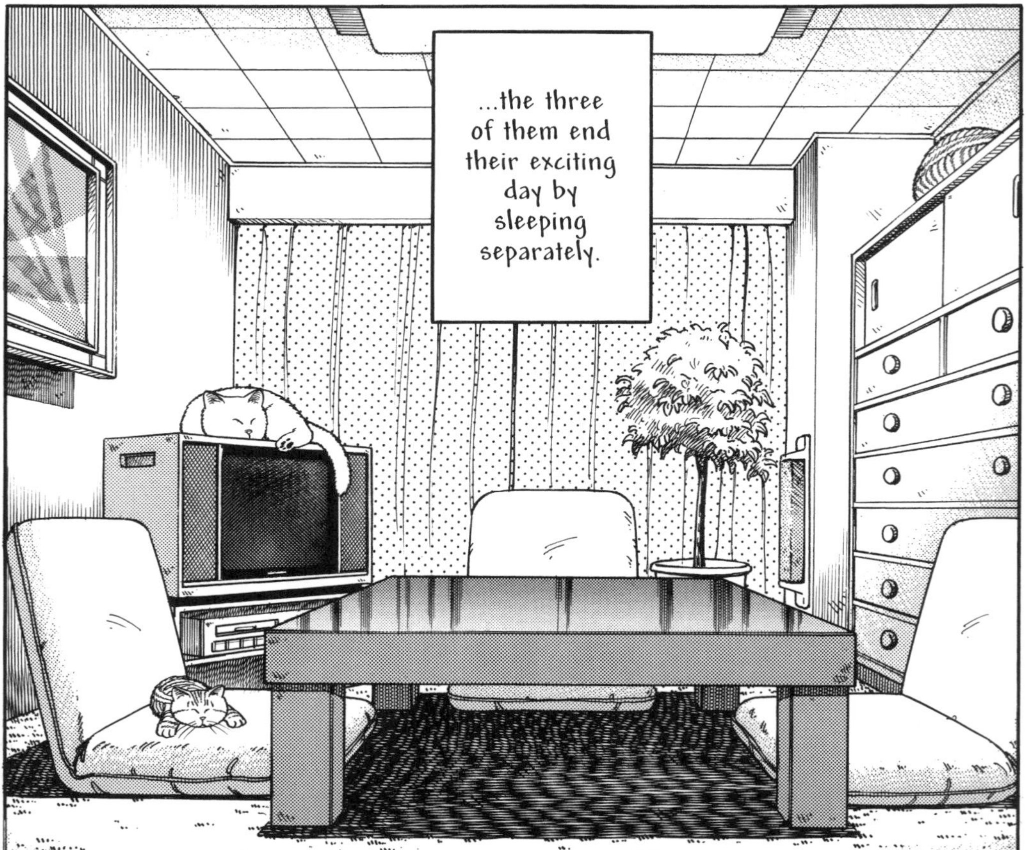
...the three of them end their exciting day by sleeping separately.

THE END

# THE OLD MAN AND THE CAT

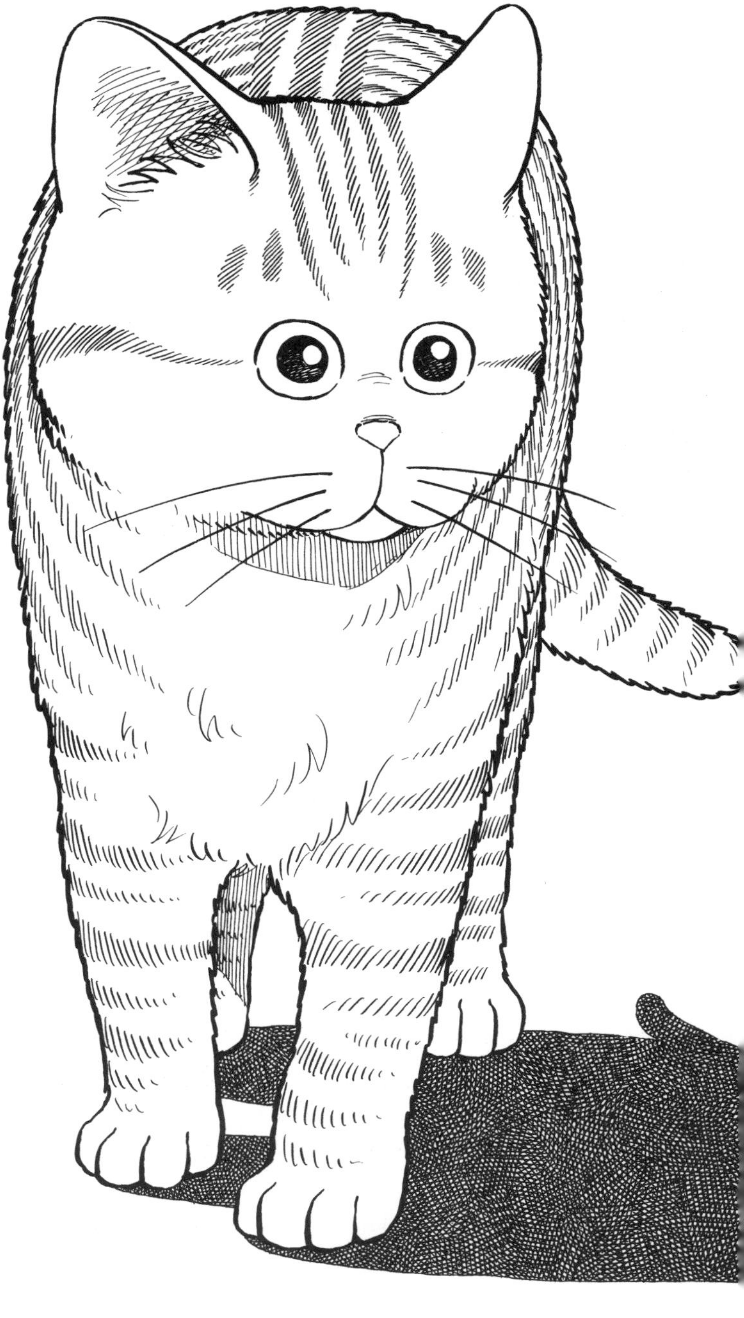

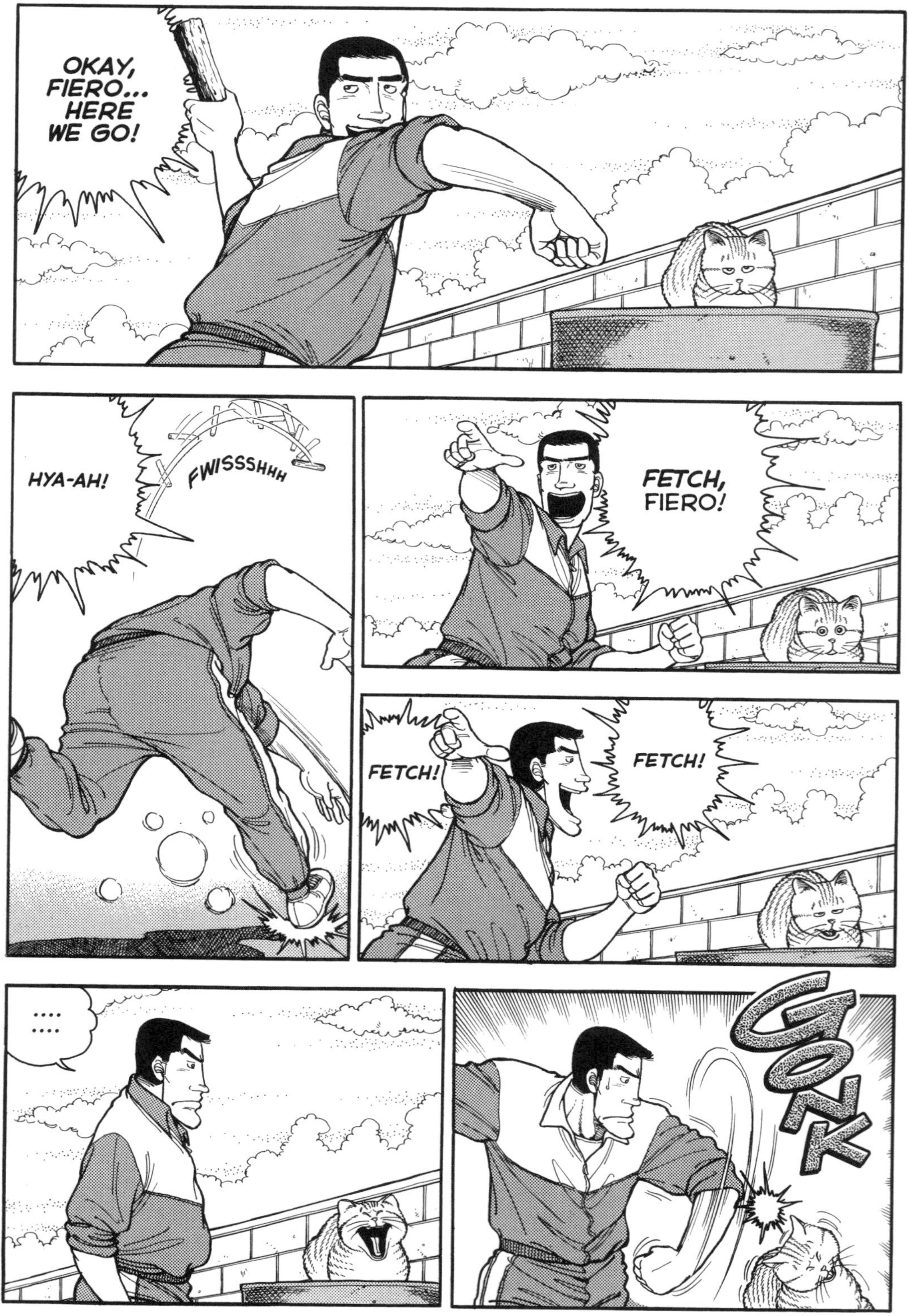

OKAY, FIERO... HERE WE GO!
HYA-AH!
FWISSSHHH
FETCH, FIERO!
FETCH!
FETCH!
....
....
GONK

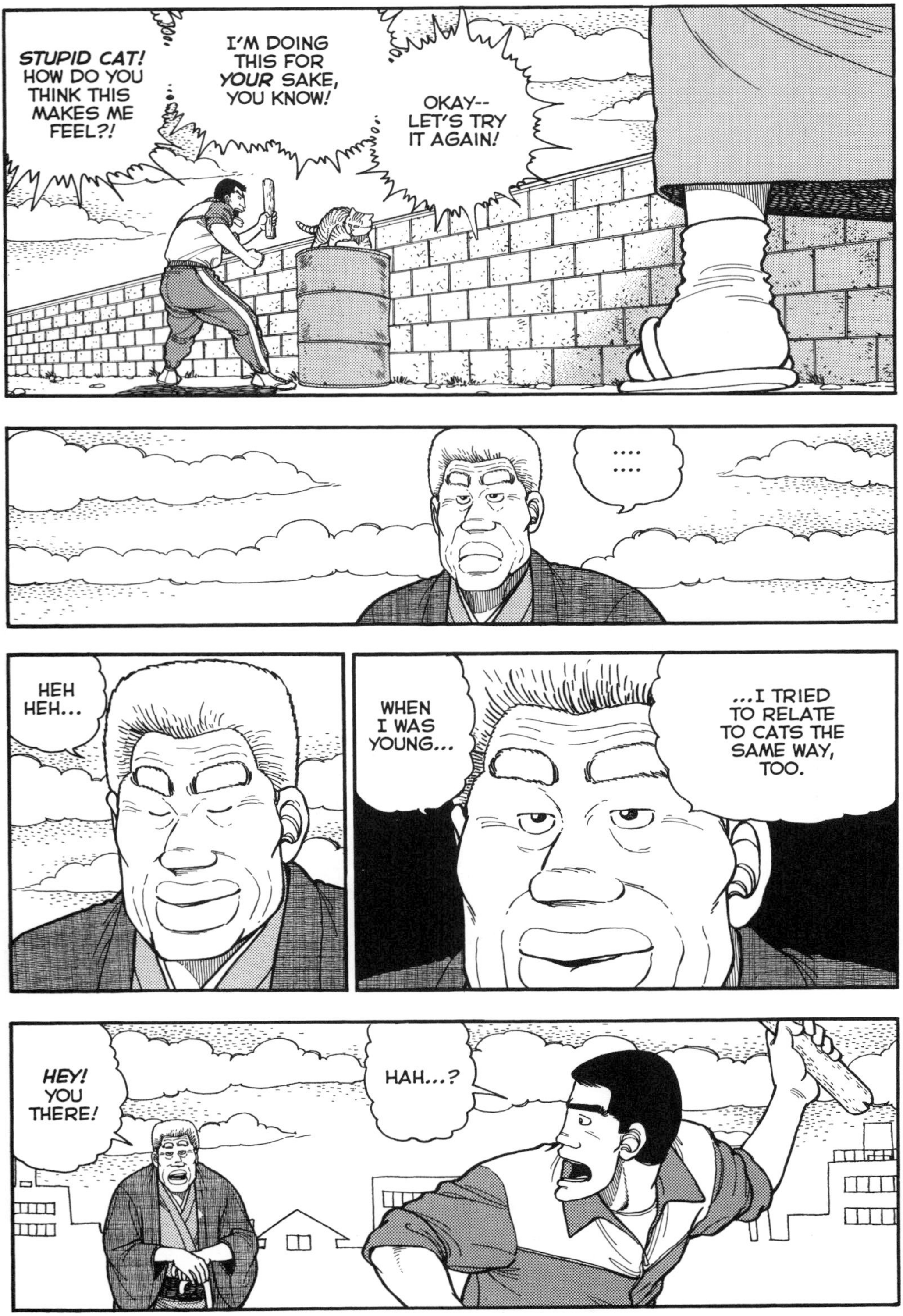
STUPID CAT! HOW DO YOU THINK THIS MAKES ME FEEL?!
I'M DOING THIS FOR YOUR SAKE, YOU KNOW!
OKAY-- LET'S TRY IT AGAIN!
....
....
HEH HEH...
WHEN I WAS YOUNG...
...I TRIED TO RELATE TO CATS THE SAME WAY, TOO.
HEY! YOU THERE!
HAH...?

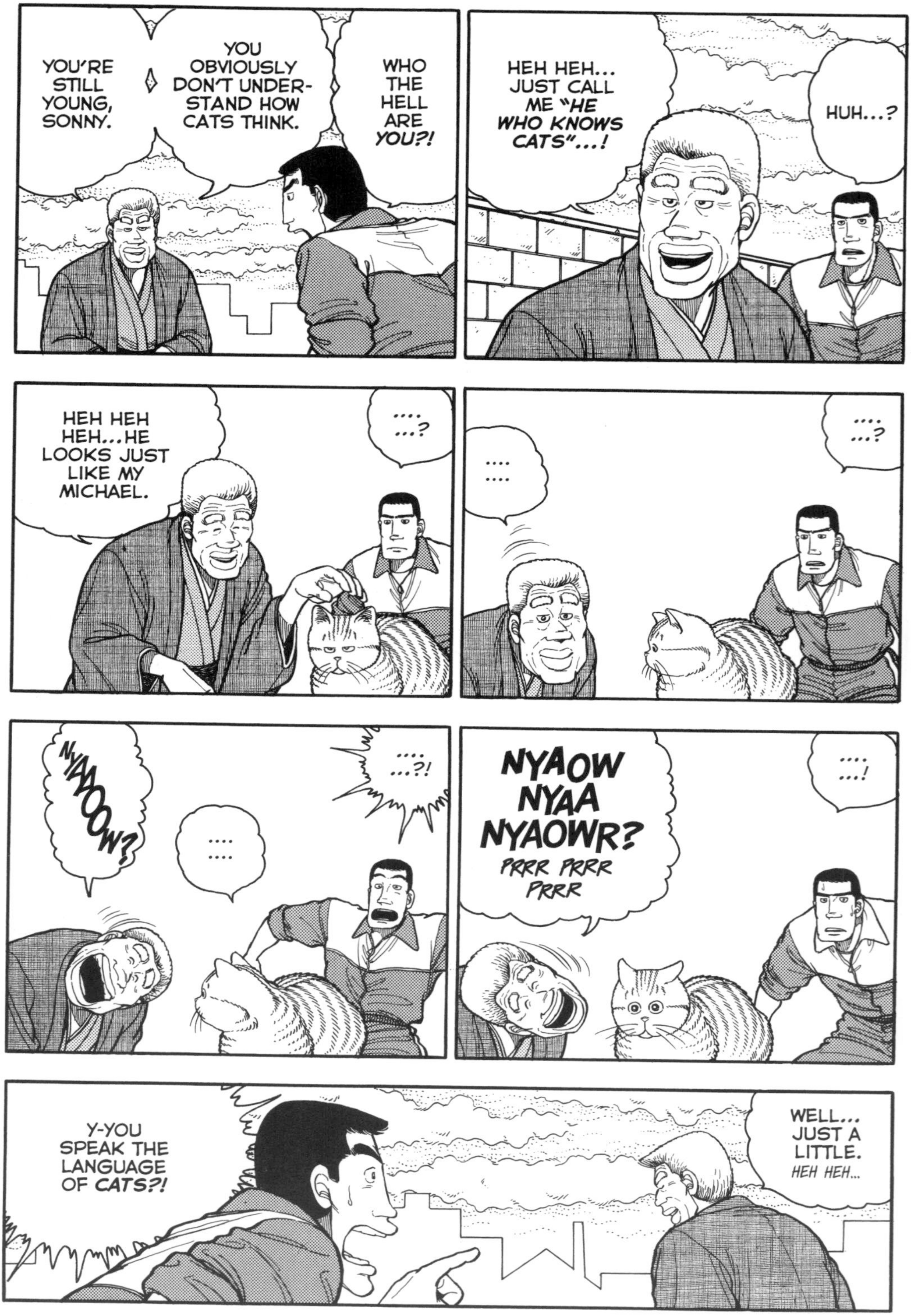
YOU'RE STILL YOUNG, SONNY.
YOU OBVIOUSLY DON'T UNDER-STAND HOW CATS THINK.
WHO THE HELL ARE YOU?!
HEH HEH... JUST CALL ME "HE WHO KNOWS CATS"...!
HUH...?
HEH HEH HEH...HE LOOKS JUST LIKE MY MICHAEL.
....
...?
....
....
....
...?
NYAAOOW?
....
....
....
...?!
NYAOW NYAA NYAOWR?
PRRR PRRR PRRR
....
...!
Y-YOU SPEAK THE LANGUAGE OF CATS?!
WELL... JUST A LITTLE. HEH HEH...

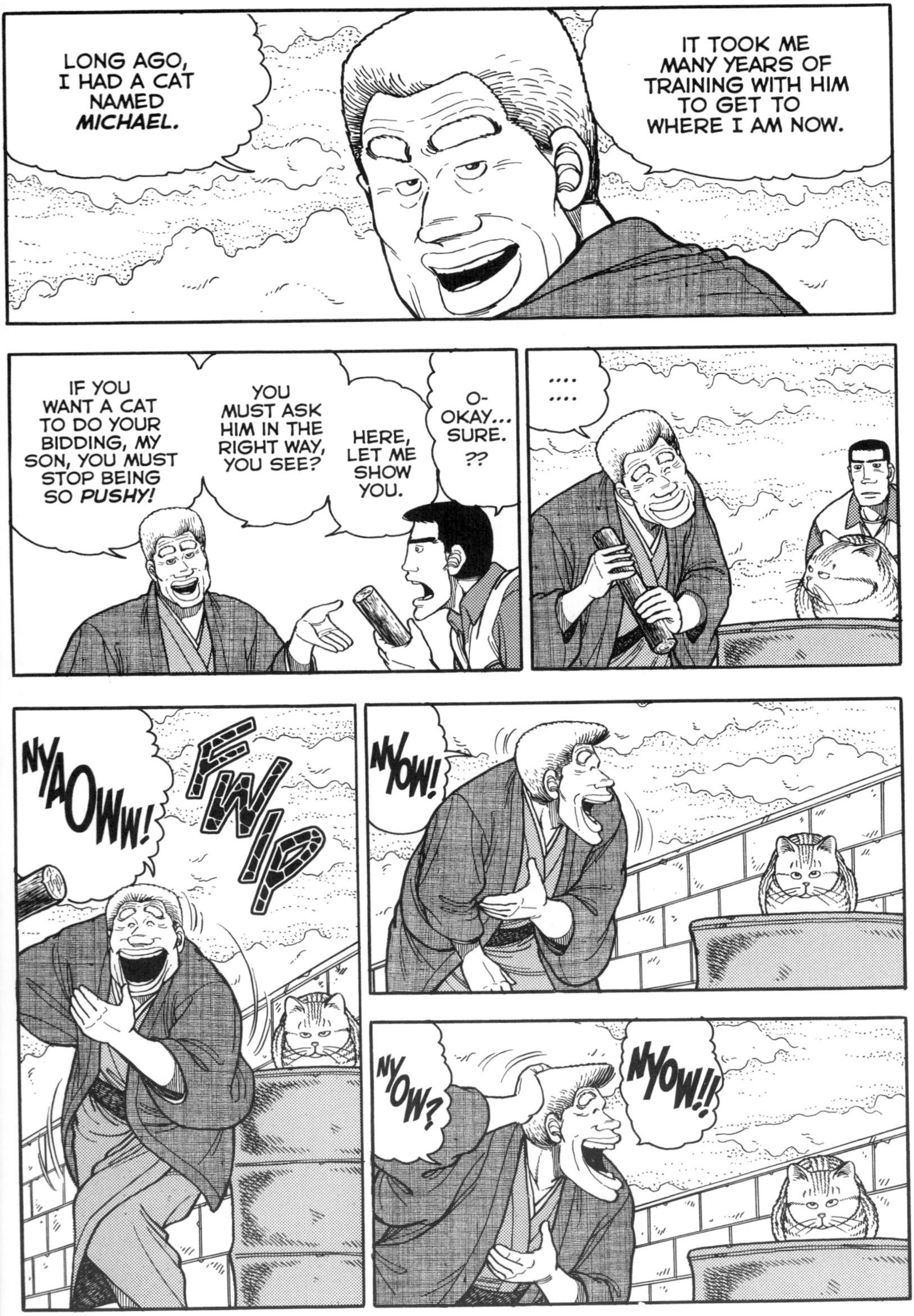
LONG AGO, I HAD A CAT NAMED MICHAEL.
IT TOOK ME MANY YEARS OF TRAINING WITH HIM TO GET TO WHERE I AM NOW.
IF YOU WANT A CAT TO DO YOUR BIDDING, MY SON, YOU MUST STOP BEING SO PUSHY!
YOU MUST ASK HIM IN THE RIGHT WAY, YOU SEE?
HERE, LET ME SHOW YOU.
O-OKAY... SURE.
??
....
....
NYAOWW!
FWIP
NYOW!
NYOW?
NYOW!!

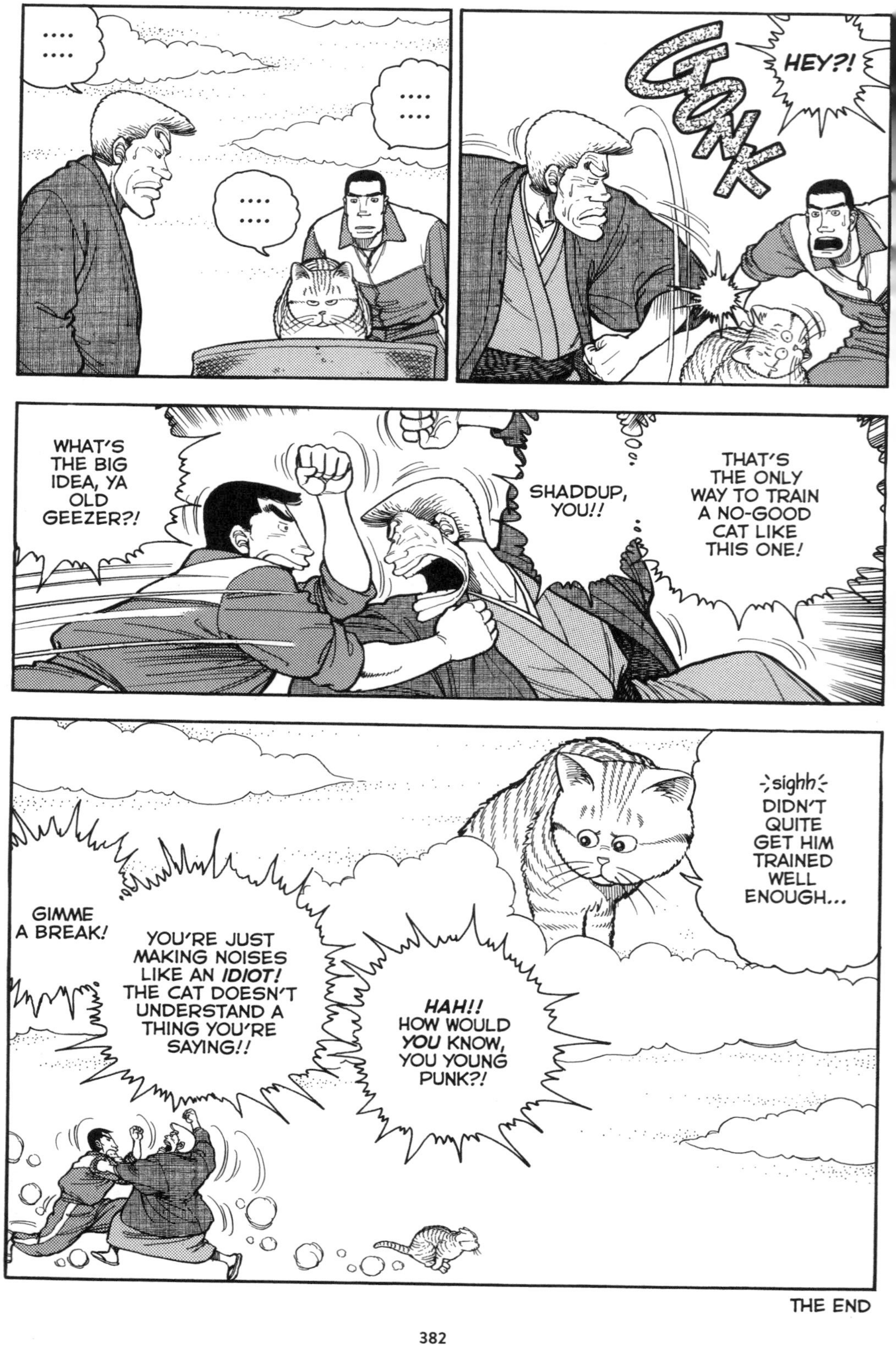

....
....
....
....
....
....
GONK
HEY?!
WHAT'S THE BIG IDEA, YA OLD GEEZER?!
SHADDUP, YOU!!
THAT'S THE ONLY WAY TO TRAIN A NO-GOOD CAT LIKE THIS ONE!
GIMME A BREAK!
YOU'RE JUST MAKING NOISES LIKE AN *IDIOT!* THE CAT DOESN'T UNDERSTAND A THING YOU'RE SAYING!!
*HAH!!* HOW WOULD *YOU* KNOW, YOU YOUNG PUNK?!
sighh DIDN'T QUITE GET HIM TRAINED WELL ENOUGH...

THE END

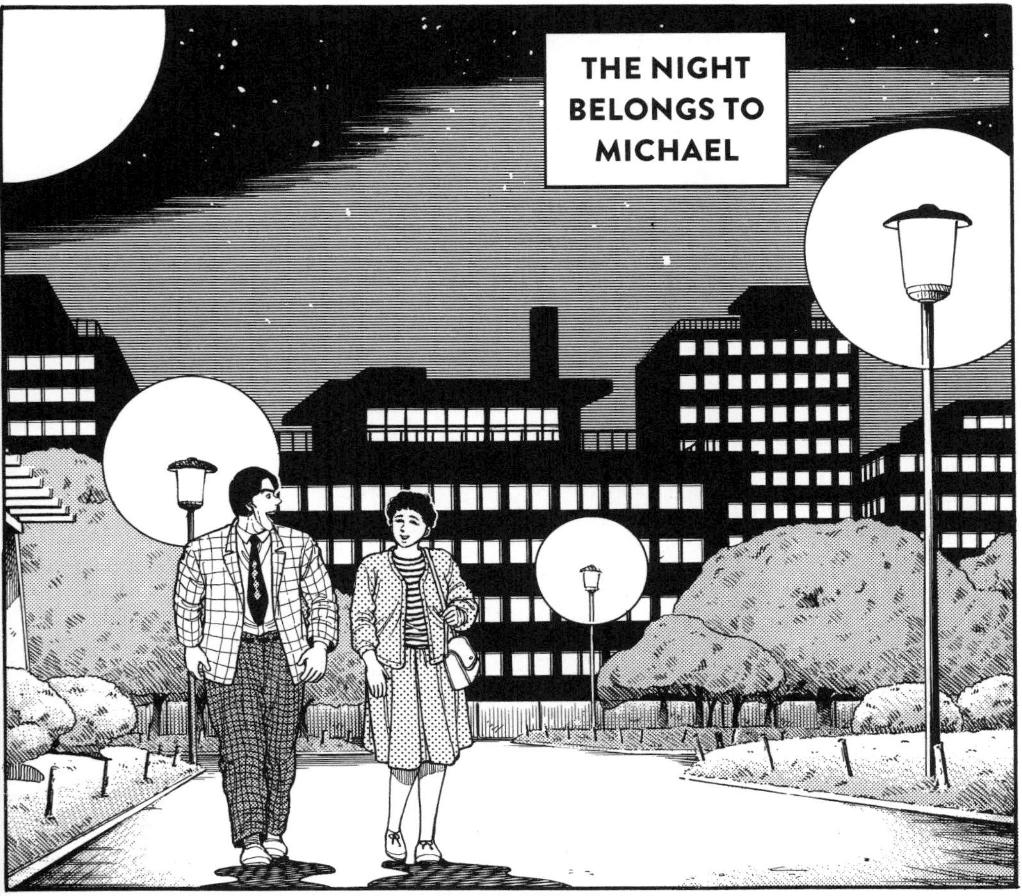
THE NIGHT BELONGS TO MICHAEL

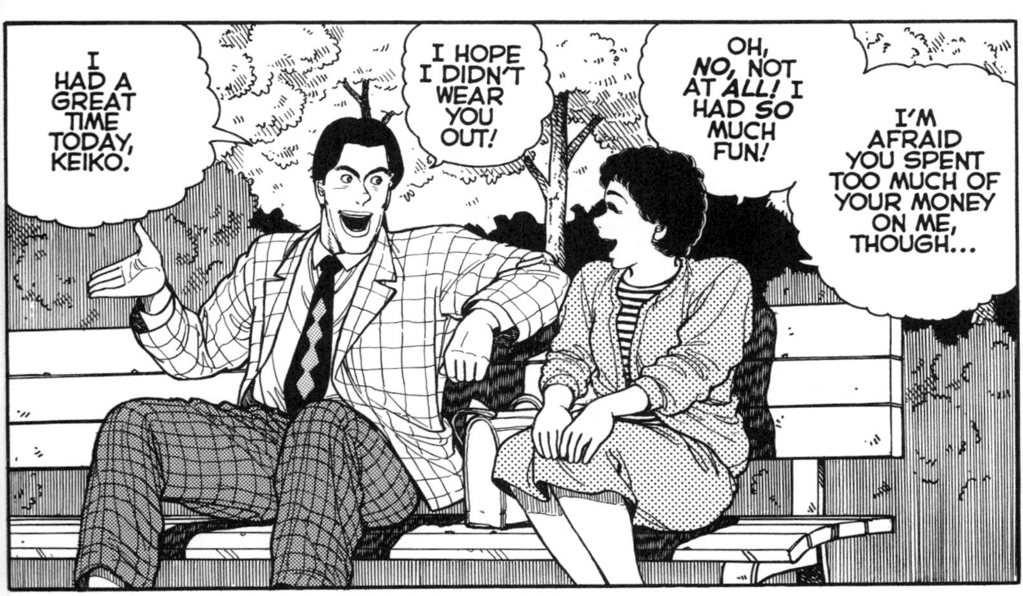
I HAD A GREAT TIME TODAY, KEIKO.
I HOPE I DIDN'T WEAR YOU OUT!
OH, NO, NOT AT ALL! I HAD SO MUCH FUN!
I'M AFRAID YOU SPENT TOO MUCH OF YOUR MONEY ON ME, THOUGH...

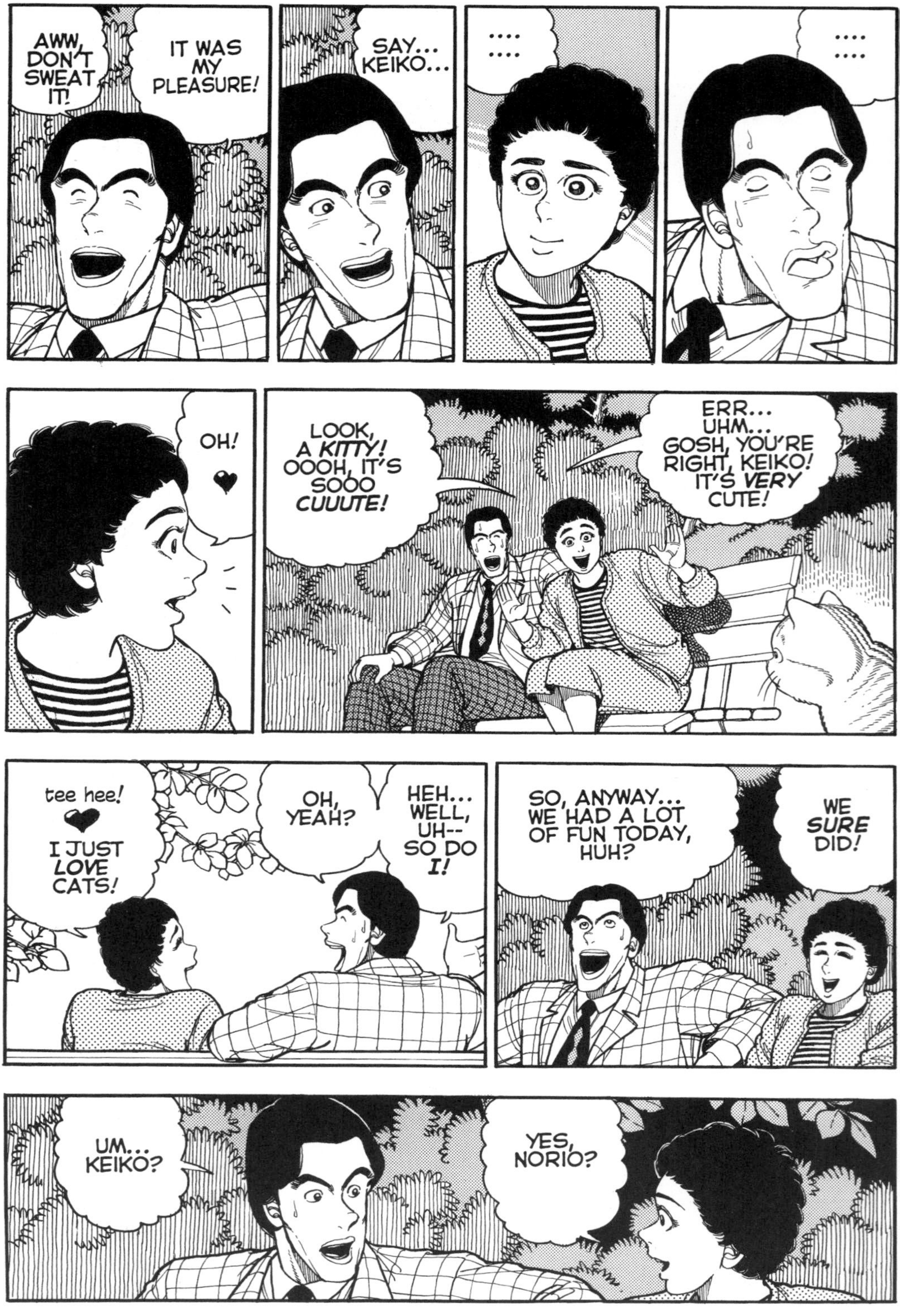

AWW, DON'T SWEAT IT!
IT WAS MY PLEASURE!
SAY... KEIKO...
........
........
OH! ❤
LOOK, A KITTY! OOOH, IT'S SOOO CUUUTE!
ERR... UHM... GOSH, YOU'RE RIGHT, KEIKO! IT'S VERY CUTE!
tee hee! ❤ I JUST LOVE CATS!
OH, YEAH?
HEH... WELL, UH-- SO DO I!
SO, ANYWAY... WE HAD A LOT OF FUN TODAY, HUH?
WE SURE DID!
UM... KEIKO?
YES, NORIO?

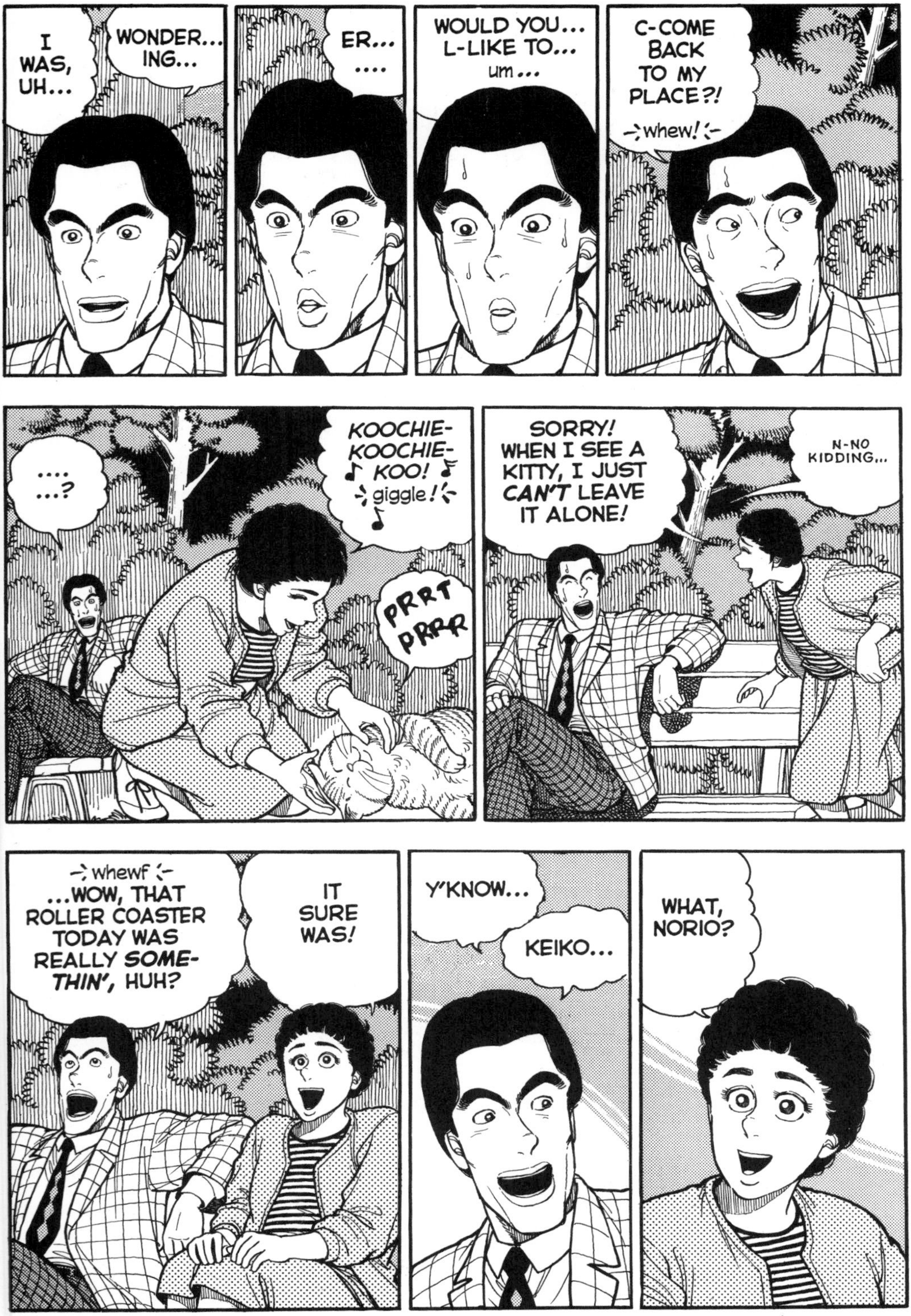
I WAS, UH...
WONDER... ING...
ER... ....
WOULD YOU... L-LIKE TO... um...
C-COME BACK TO MY PLACE?!
whew!
.... ...?
KOOCHIE-KOOCHIE-KOO!
giggle!
PRRT PRRR
SORRY! WHEN I SEE A KITTY, I JUST CAN'T LEAVE IT ALONE!
N-NO KIDDING...
whewf
...WOW, THAT ROLLER COASTER TODAY WAS REALLY SOMETHIN', HUH?
IT SURE WAS!
Y'KNOW...
KEIKO...
WHAT, NORIO?

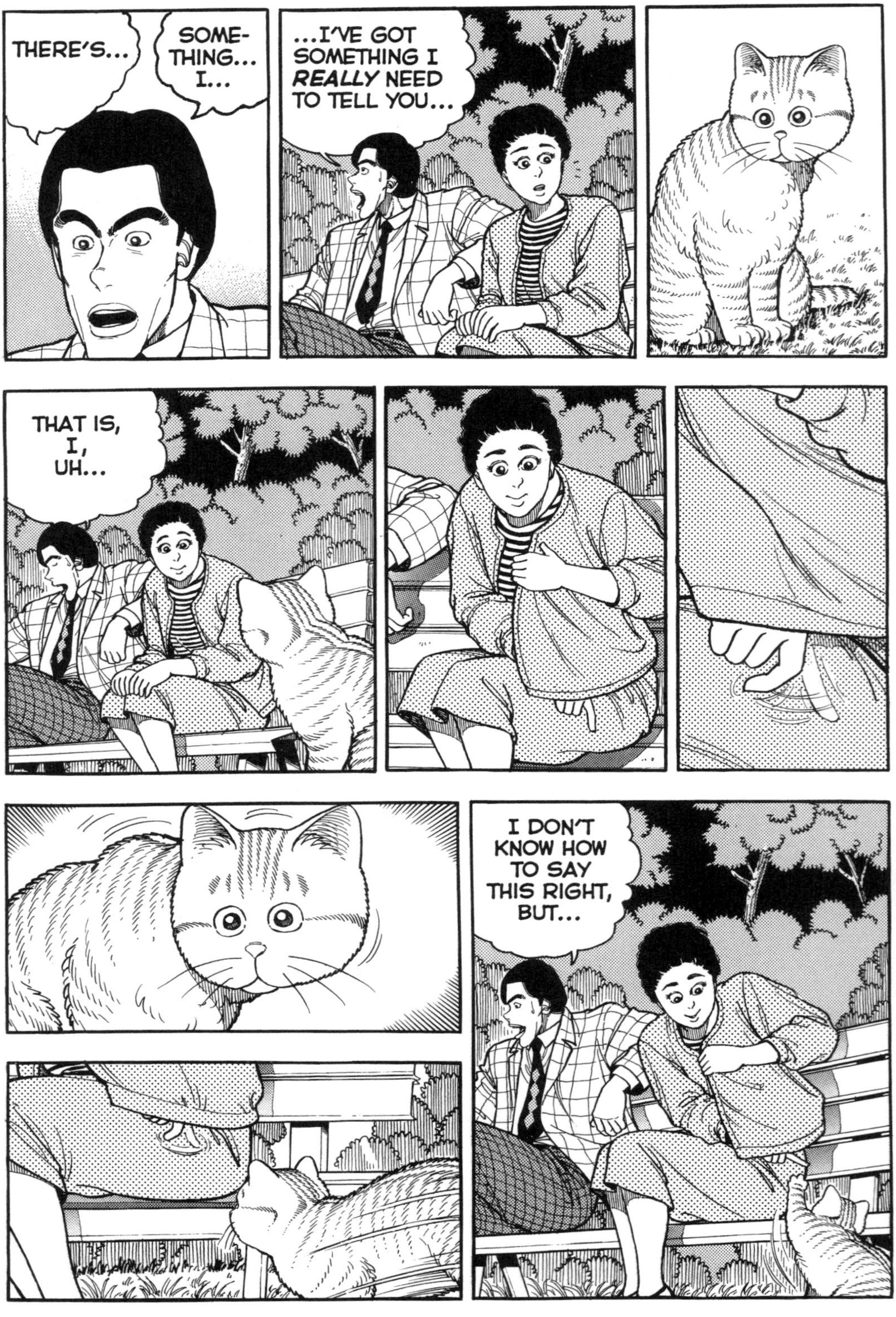
THERE'S...
SOME-THING... I...
...I'VE GOT SOMETHING I *REALLY* NEED TO TELL YOU...
THAT IS, I, UH...
I DON'T KNOW HOW TO SAY THIS RIGHT, BUT...

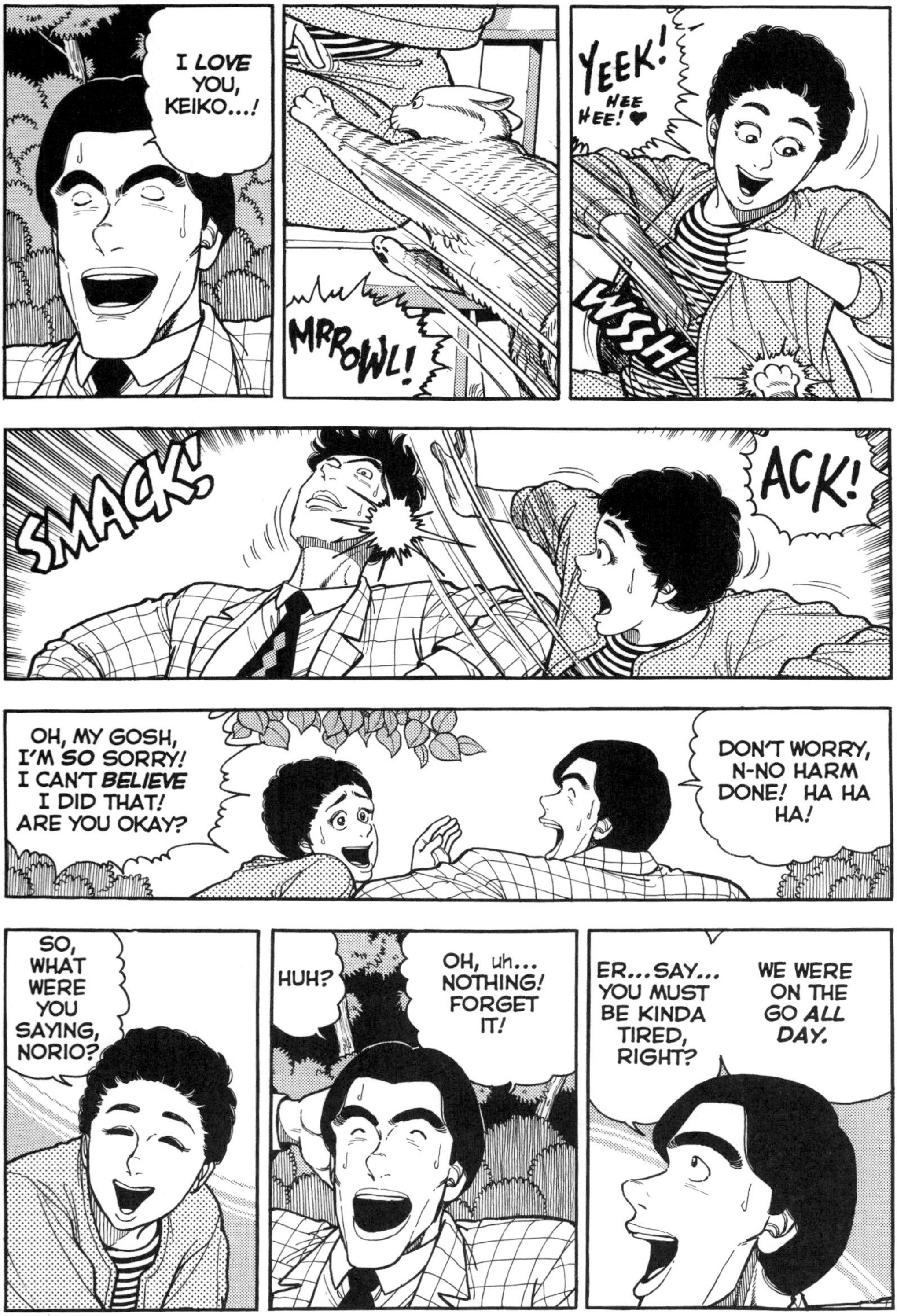
I LOVE YOU, KEIKO...!
MRROWL!
YEEK!
HEE HEE! ♥
WSSH
SMACK!
ACK!
OH, MY GOSH, I'M SO SORRY! I CAN'T BELIEVE I DID THAT! ARE YOU OKAY?
DON'T WORRY, N-NO HARM DONE! HA HA HA!
SO, WHAT WERE YOU SAYING, NORIO?
HUH?
OH, uh... NOTHING! FORGET IT!
ER...SAY... YOU MUST BE KINDA TIRED, RIGHT?
WE WERE ON THE GO ALL DAY.

SO, UH...WHY DON'T YOU JUST CRASH OUT AT MY PLACE INSTEAD OF, Y'KNOW...GOING ALL THE WAY BACK TO--
.....
.....
TEE HEE HEE!
LOOK AT THIS KITTY!
HE'S JUST SOOO FRIENDLY!
UH... GOSH... HE SURE IS!
klik

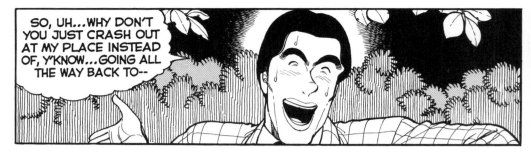

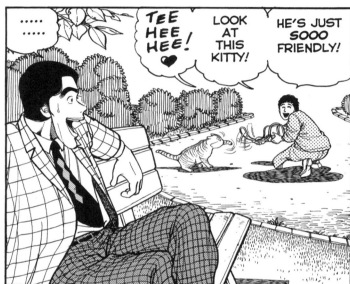

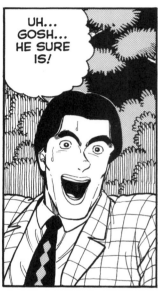

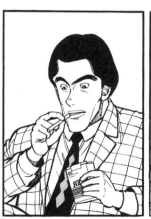

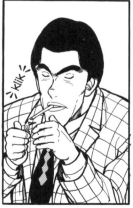

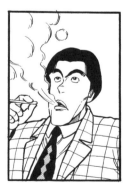

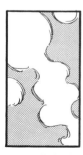

THE END

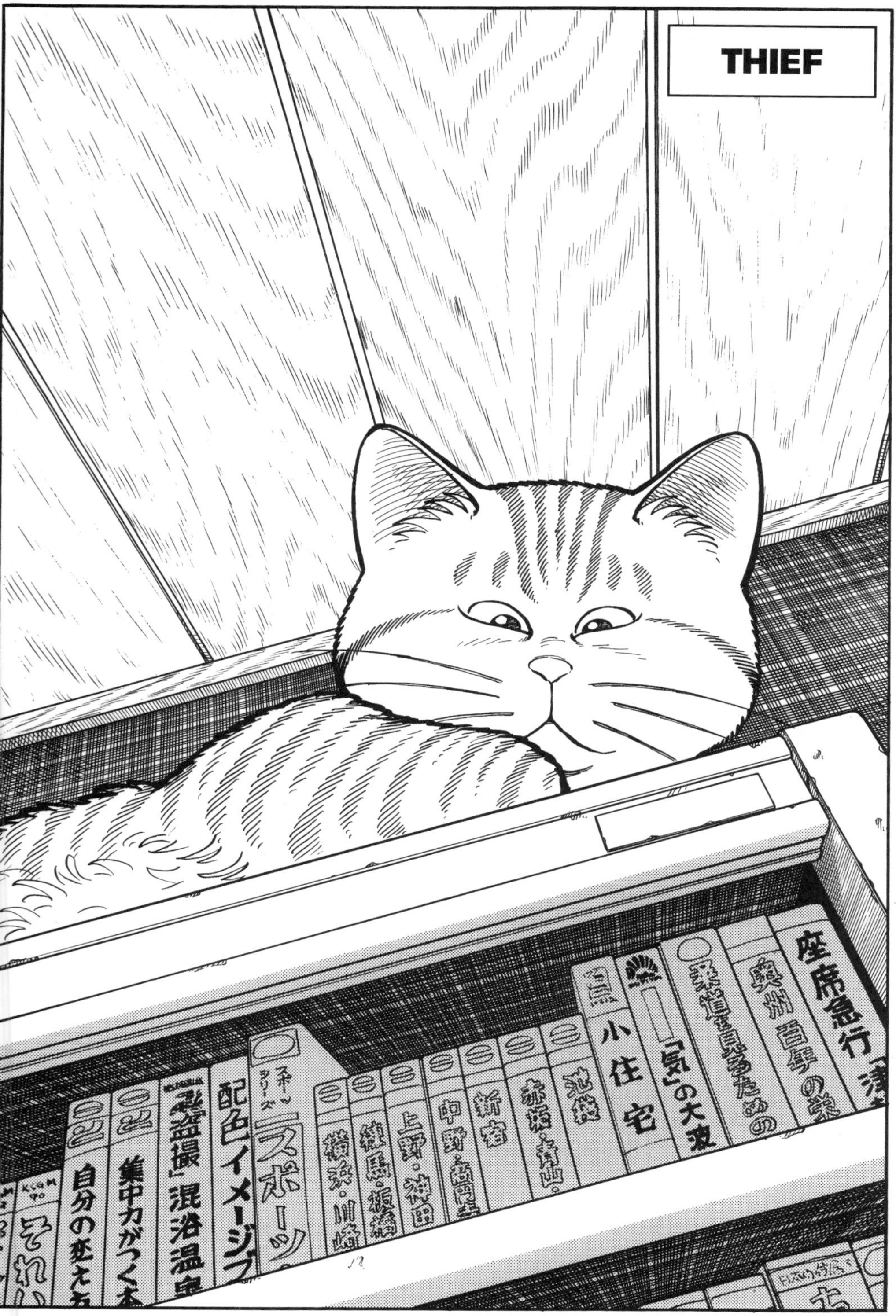
THIEF

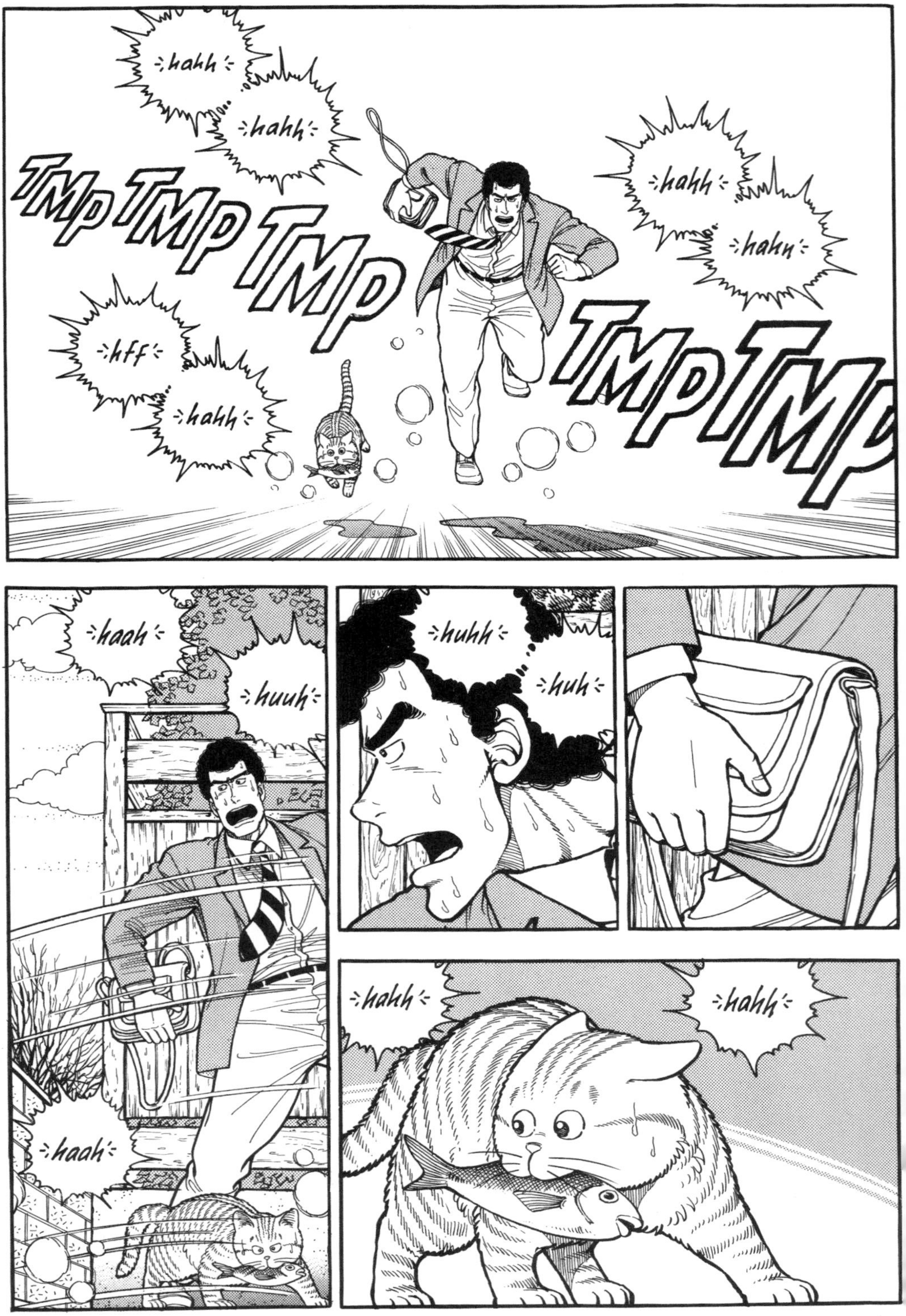
hahh
hahh
TMP TMP TMP
hahh
hahh
hff
hahh
TMP TMP
haah
huuh
haah
huhh
huh
hahh
hahh

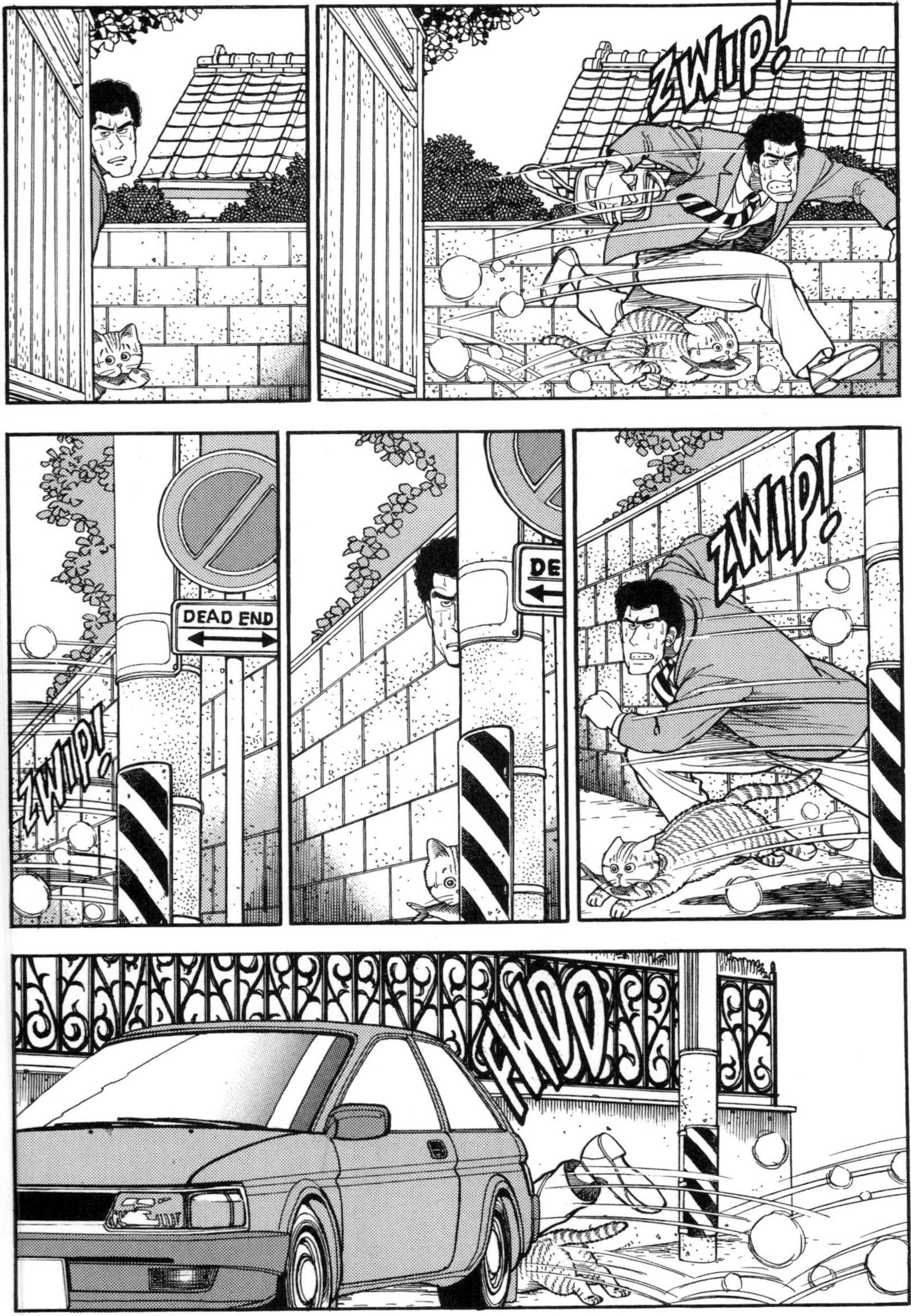
ZWIP!
DEAD END
ZWIP!
DE
ZWIP!
FWOO

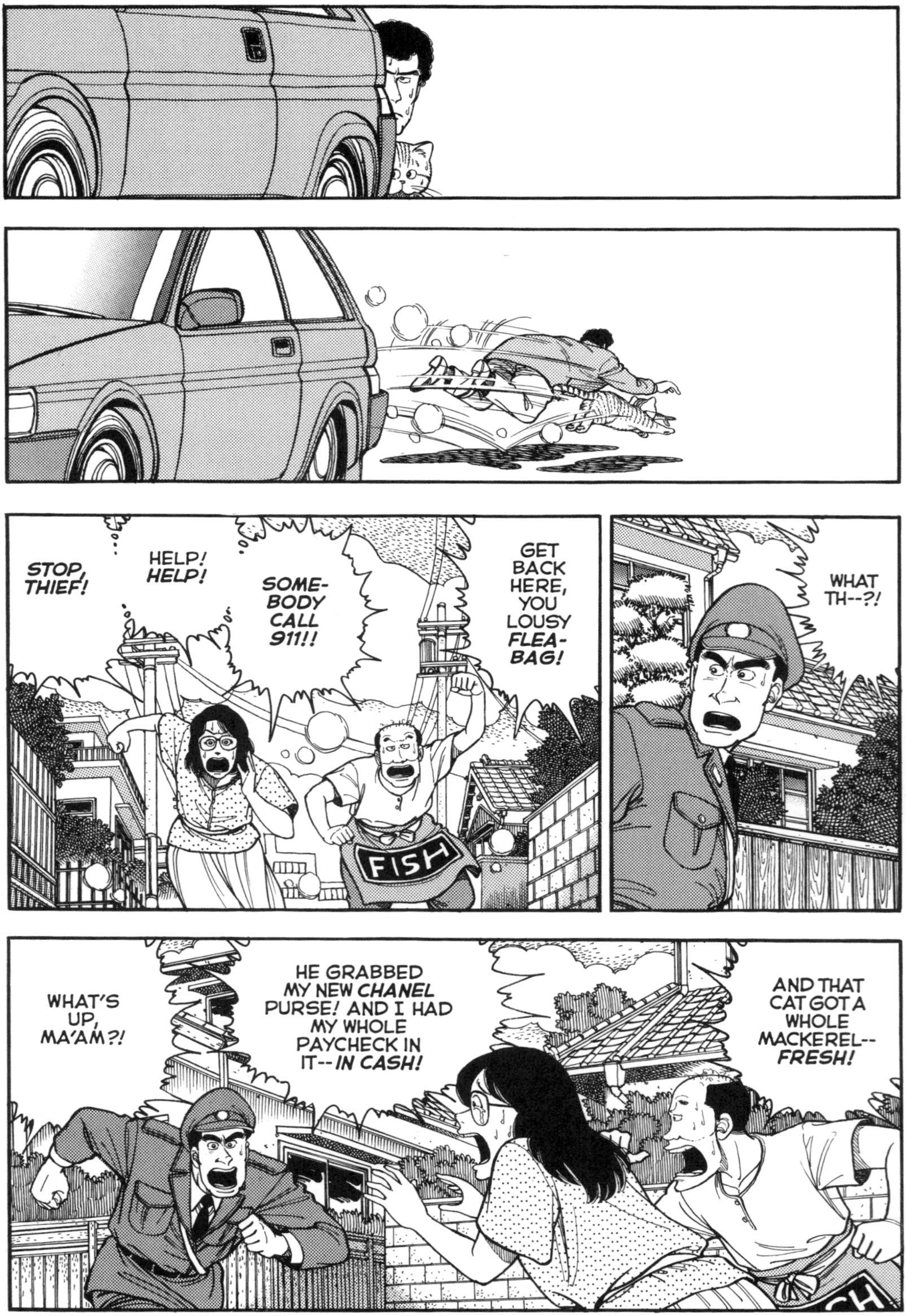
STOP, THIEF!
HELP! HELP!
SOME-BODY CALL 911!!
FISH
GET BACK HERE, YOU LOUSY FLEA-BAG!
WHAT TH--?!
WHAT'S UP, MA'AM?!
HE GRABBED MY NEW CHANEL PURSE! AND I HAD MY WHOLE PAYCHECK IN IT--IN CASH!
AND THAT CAT GOT A WHOLE MACKEREL--FRESH!

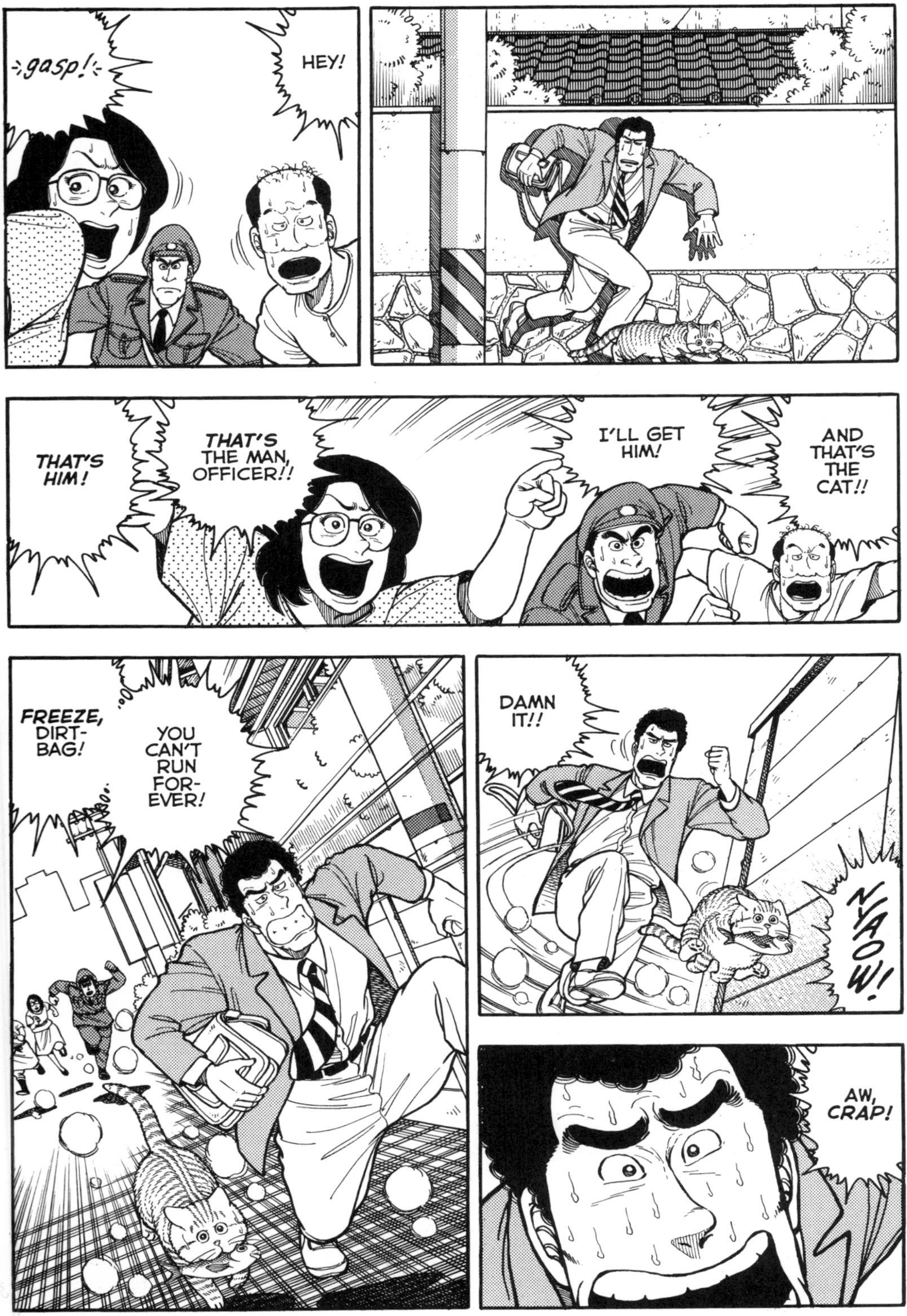
gasp!
HEY!
THAT'S HIM!
THAT'S THE MAN, OFFICER!!
I'LL GET HIM!
AND THAT'S THE CAT!!
FREEZE, DIRT-BAG!
YOU CAN'T RUN FOR-EVER!
DAMN IT!!
NYAOW!
AW, CRAP!

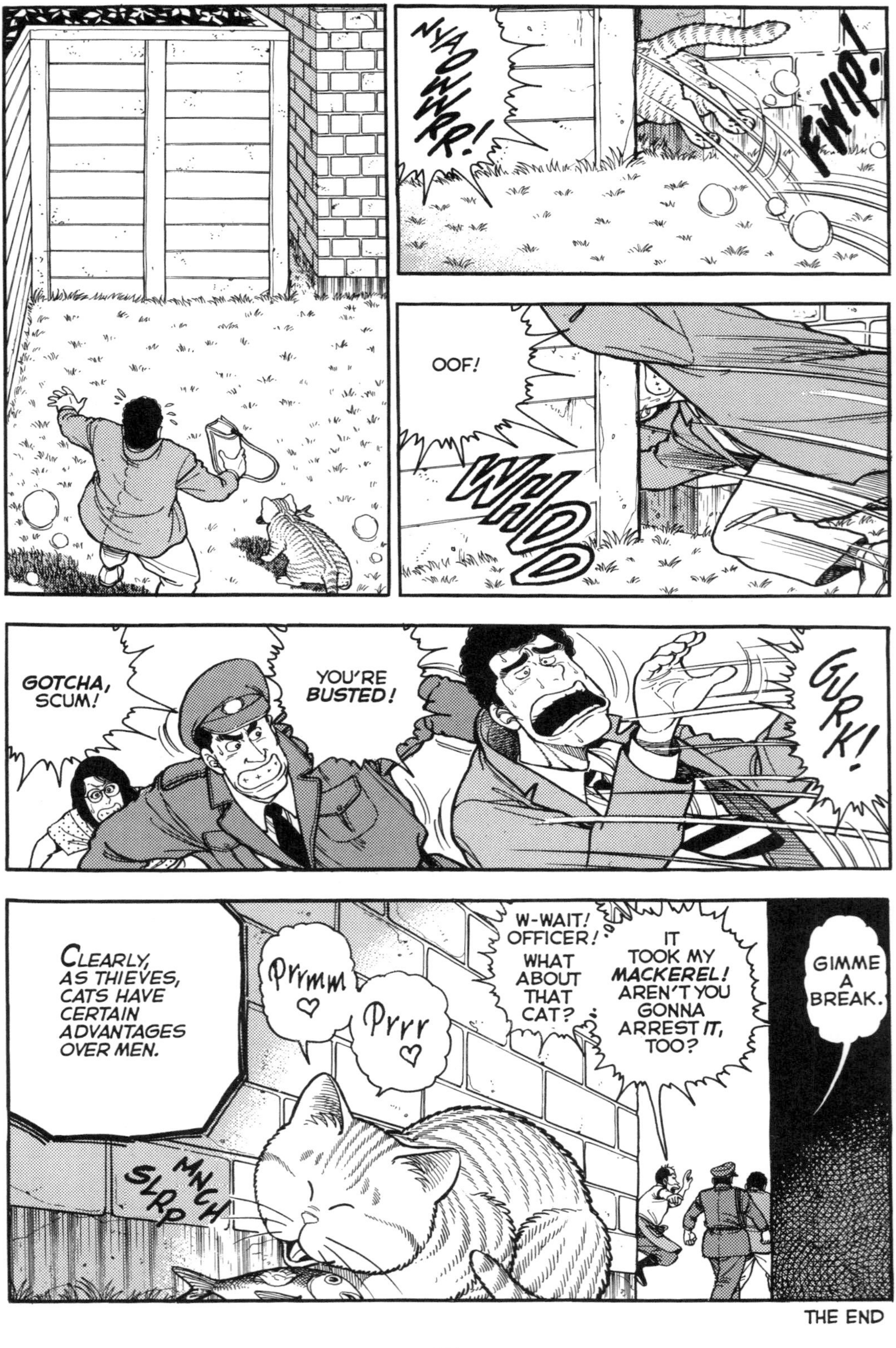
NYAOWWRR!
FWIP!
OOF!
WHOOO
GOTCHA, SCUM!
YOU'RE BUSTED!
GURK!
CLEARLY, AS THIEVES, CATS HAVE CERTAIN ADVANTAGES OVER MEN.
Prrmm ♡
Prrr ♡
W-WAIT! OFFICER! WHAT ABOUT THAT CAT?
IT TOOK MY MACKEREL! AREN'T YOU GONNA ARREST IT, TOO?
GIMME A BREAK.
MNCH SLRP
THE END

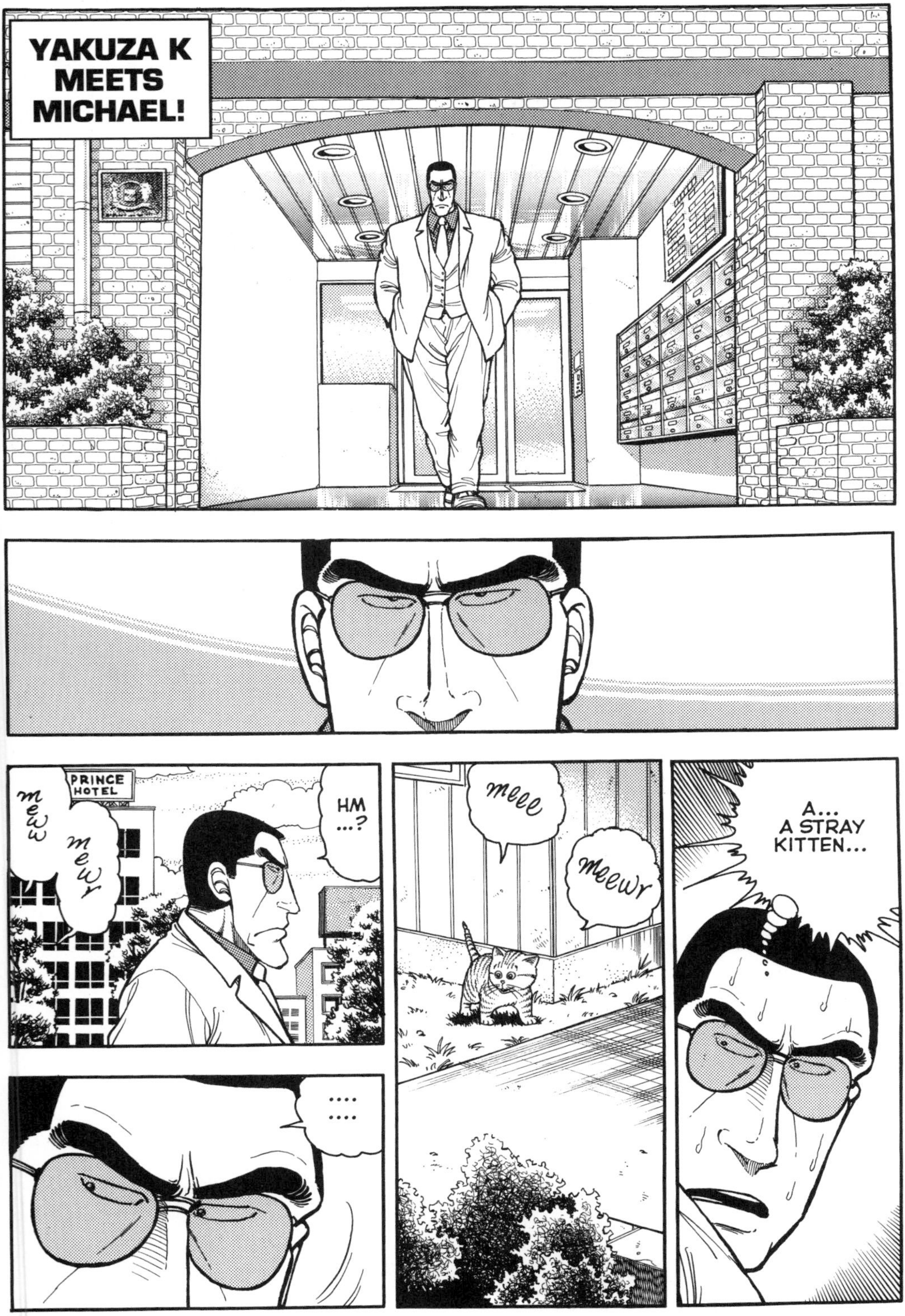
YAKUZA K MEETS MICHAEL!
mewww
mewr
HM ...?
meee
meewr
A... A STRAY KITTEN...
....
....

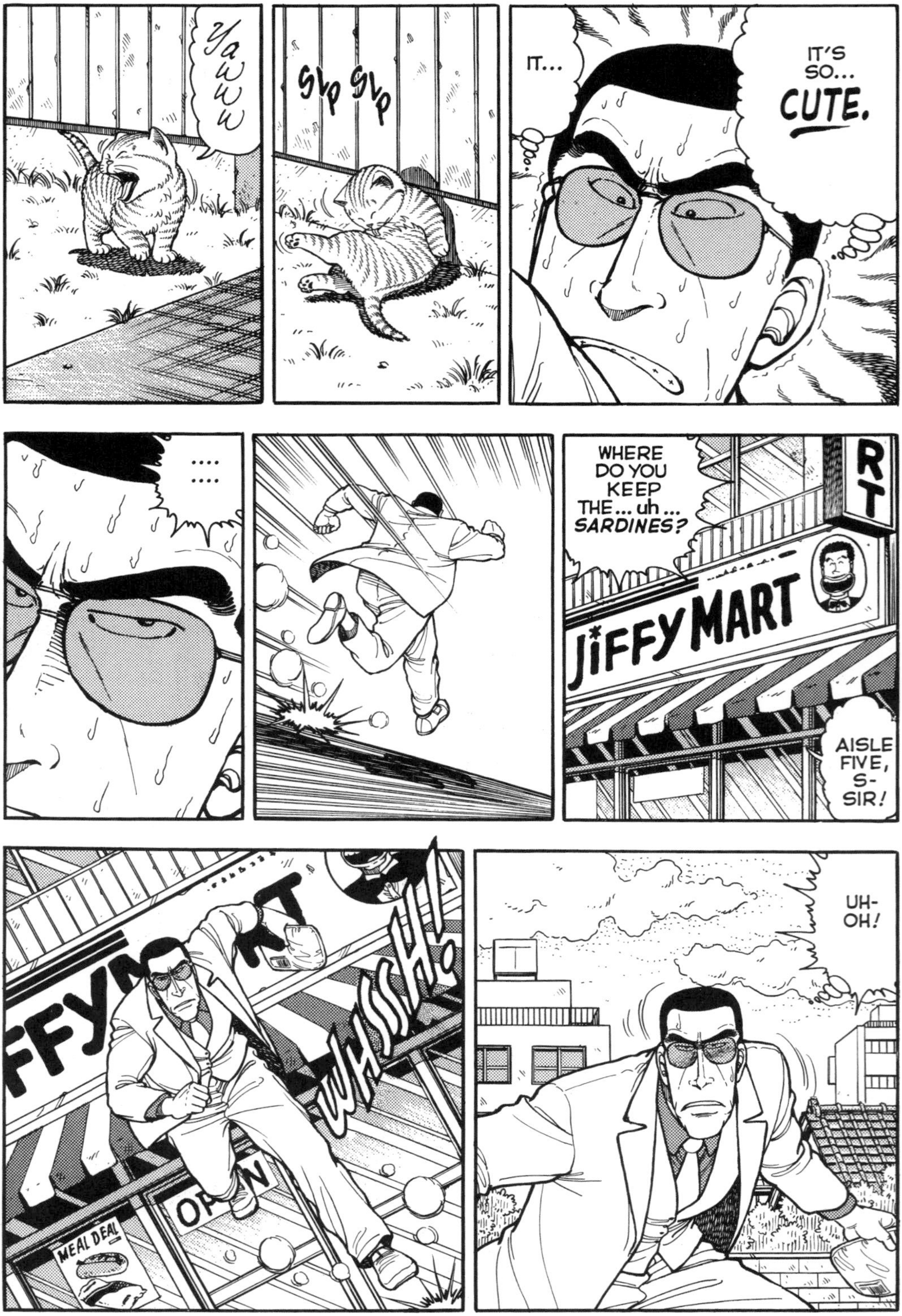

YAWWW
SLP SLP
IT...
IT'S SO... CUTE.
....
....
WHERE DO YOU KEEP THE... uh... SARDINES?
JIFFY MART
AISLE FIVE, S-SIR!
FFYM RT
WHSSH!
OPEN
MEAL DEAL
UH-OH!

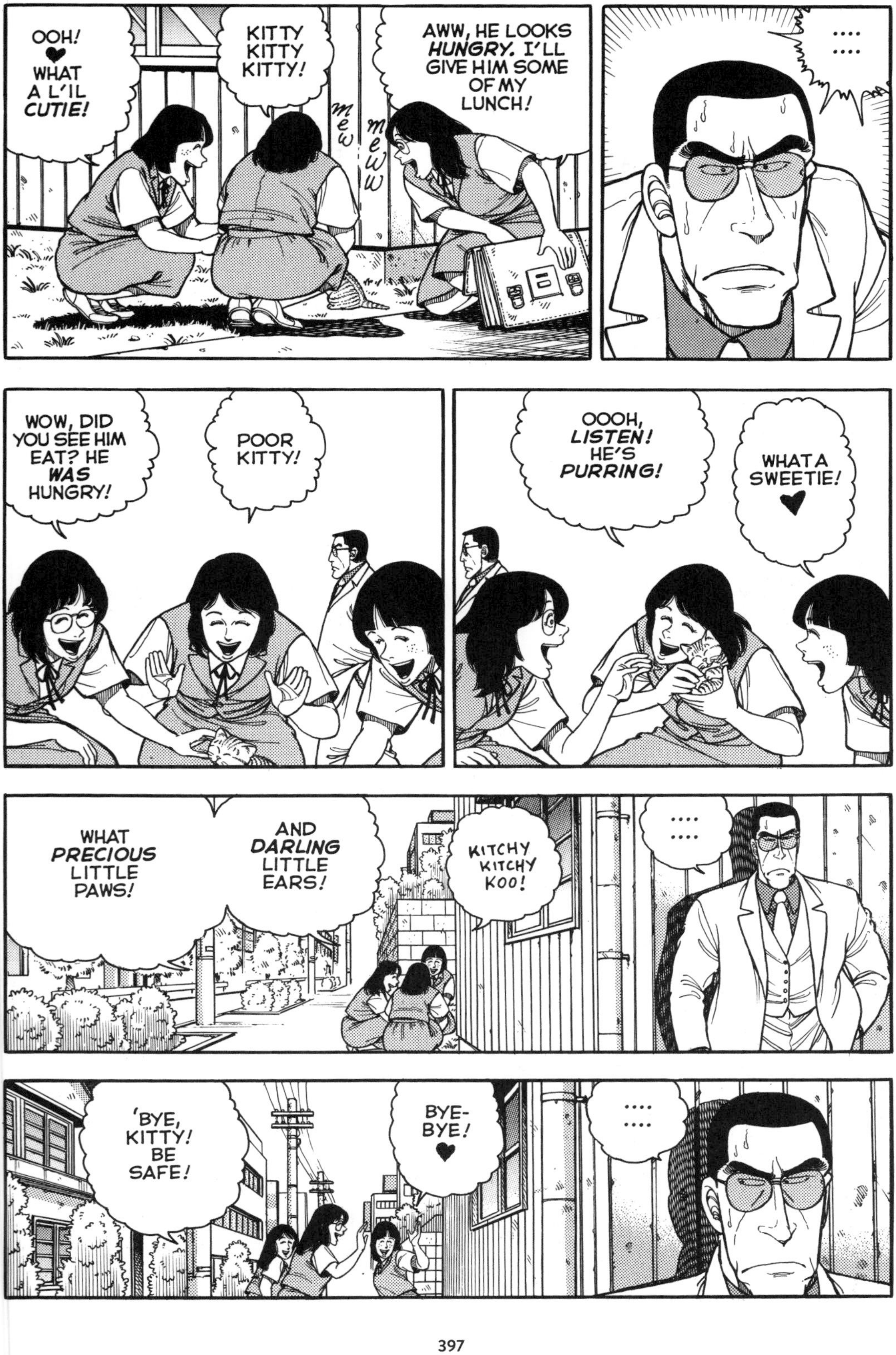
OOH! ♥ WHAT A L'IL CUTIE!
KITTY KITTY KITTY!
mew mew
AWW, HE LOOKS HUNGRY. I'LL GIVE HIM SOME OF MY LUNCH!
....
....
WOW, DID YOU SEE HIM EAT? HE WAS HUNGRY!
POOR KITTY!
OOOH, LISTEN! HE'S PURRING!
WHAT A SWEETIE! ♥
WHAT PRECIOUS LITTLE PAWS!
AND DARLING LITTLE EARS!
KITCHY KITCHY KOO!
....
....
'BYE, KITTY! BE SAFE!
BYE-BYE! ♥
....
....

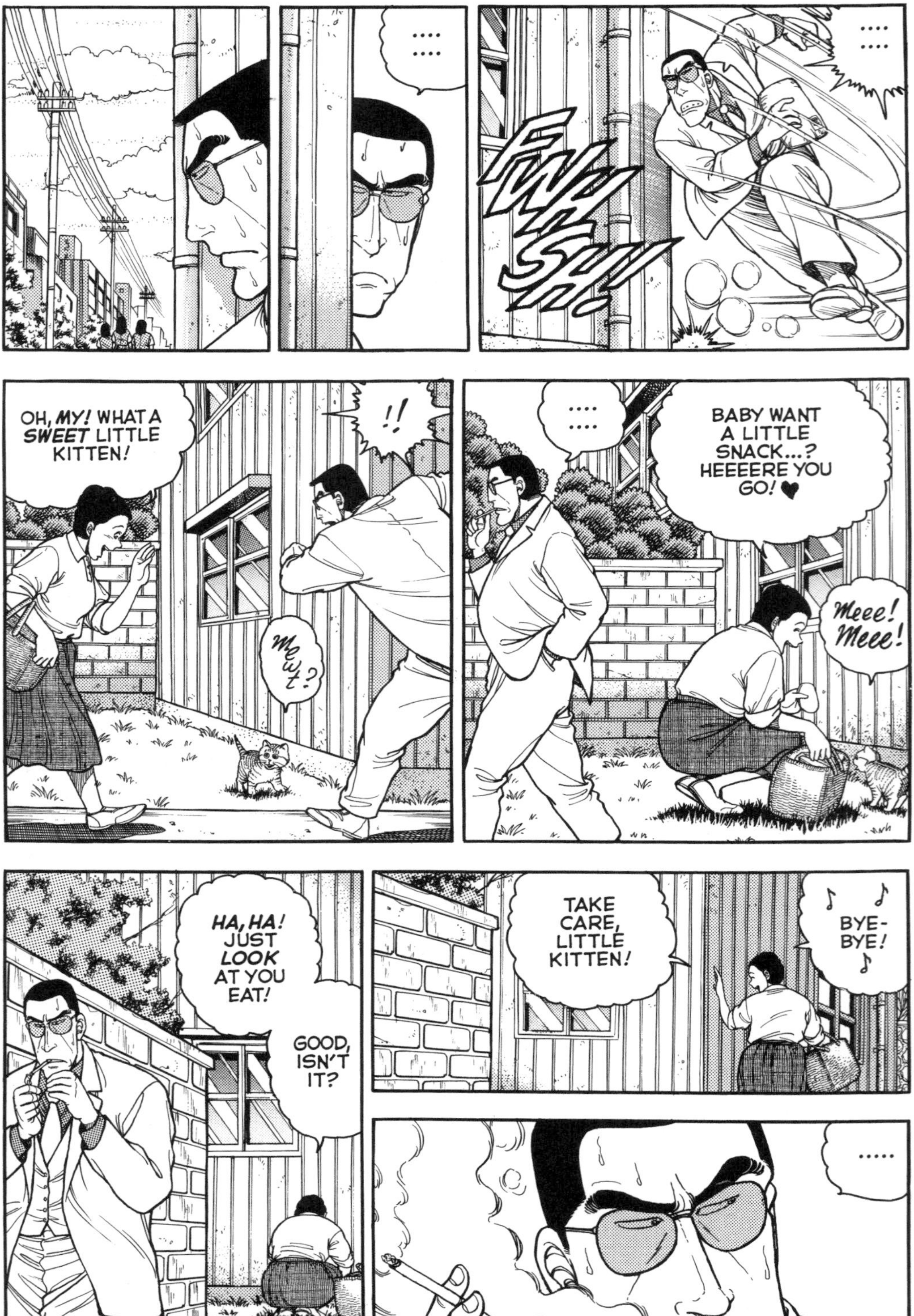
....
....
....
....
FWSHH!
OH, MY! WHAT A SWEET LITTLE KITTEN!
!!
Mewt?
....
....
BABY WANT A LITTLE SNACK...? HEEEERE YOU GO! ♥
Meee! Meee!
HA, HA! JUST LOOK AT YOU EAT!
GOOD, ISN'T IT?
TAKE CARE, LITTLE KITTEN!
♪ ♪ BYE-BYE! ♪
.....

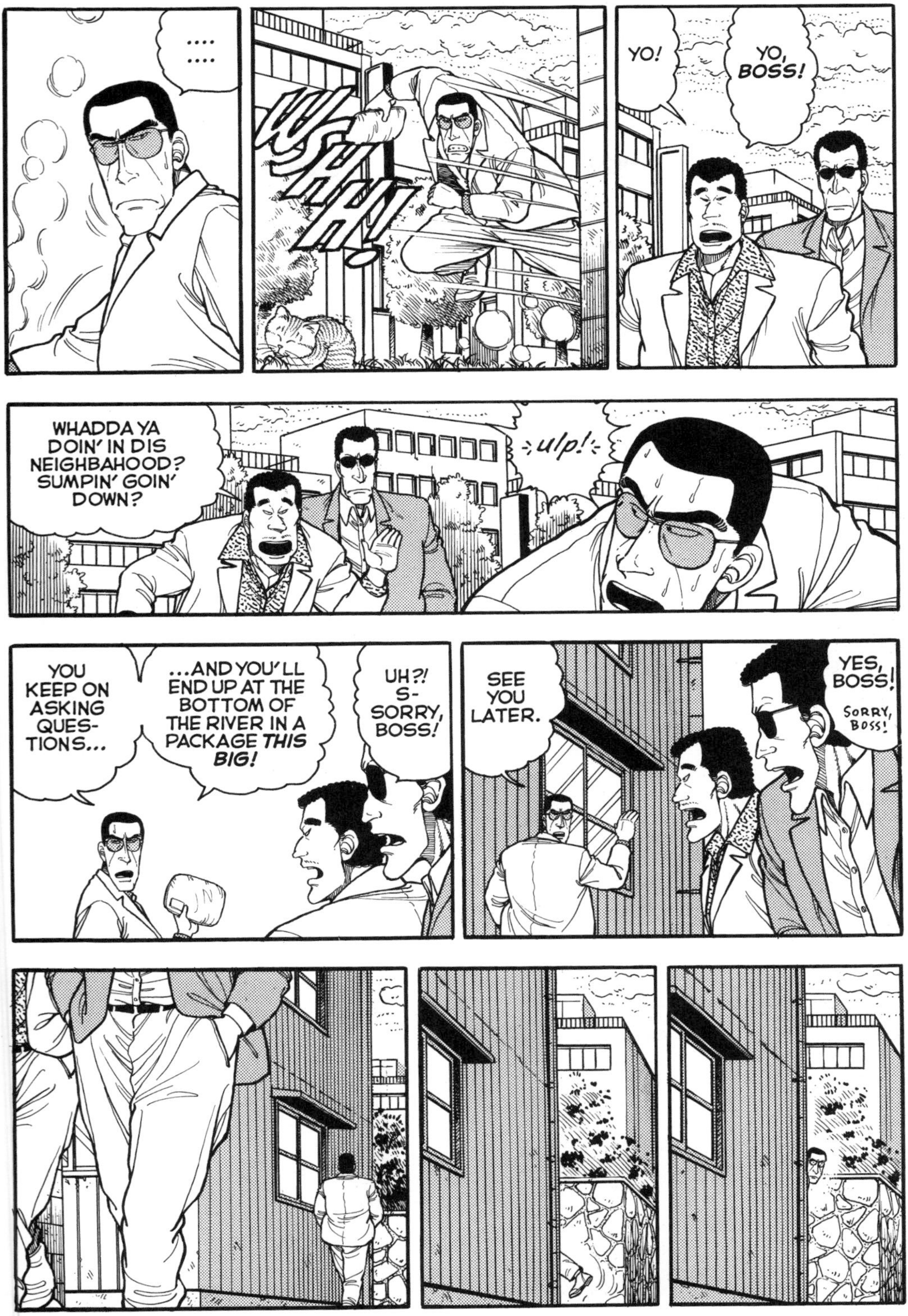
....
....
WUSHHH!
YO!
YO, BOSS!
WHADDA YA DOIN' IN DIS NEIGHBAHOOD? SUMPIN' GOIN' DOWN?
ulp!
YOU KEEP ON ASKING QUES- TIONS...
...AND YOU'LL END UP AT THE BOTTOM OF THE RIVER IN A PACKAGE THIS BIG!
UH?! S- SORRY, BOSS!
SEE YOU LATER.
YES, BOSS!
SORRY, BOSS!

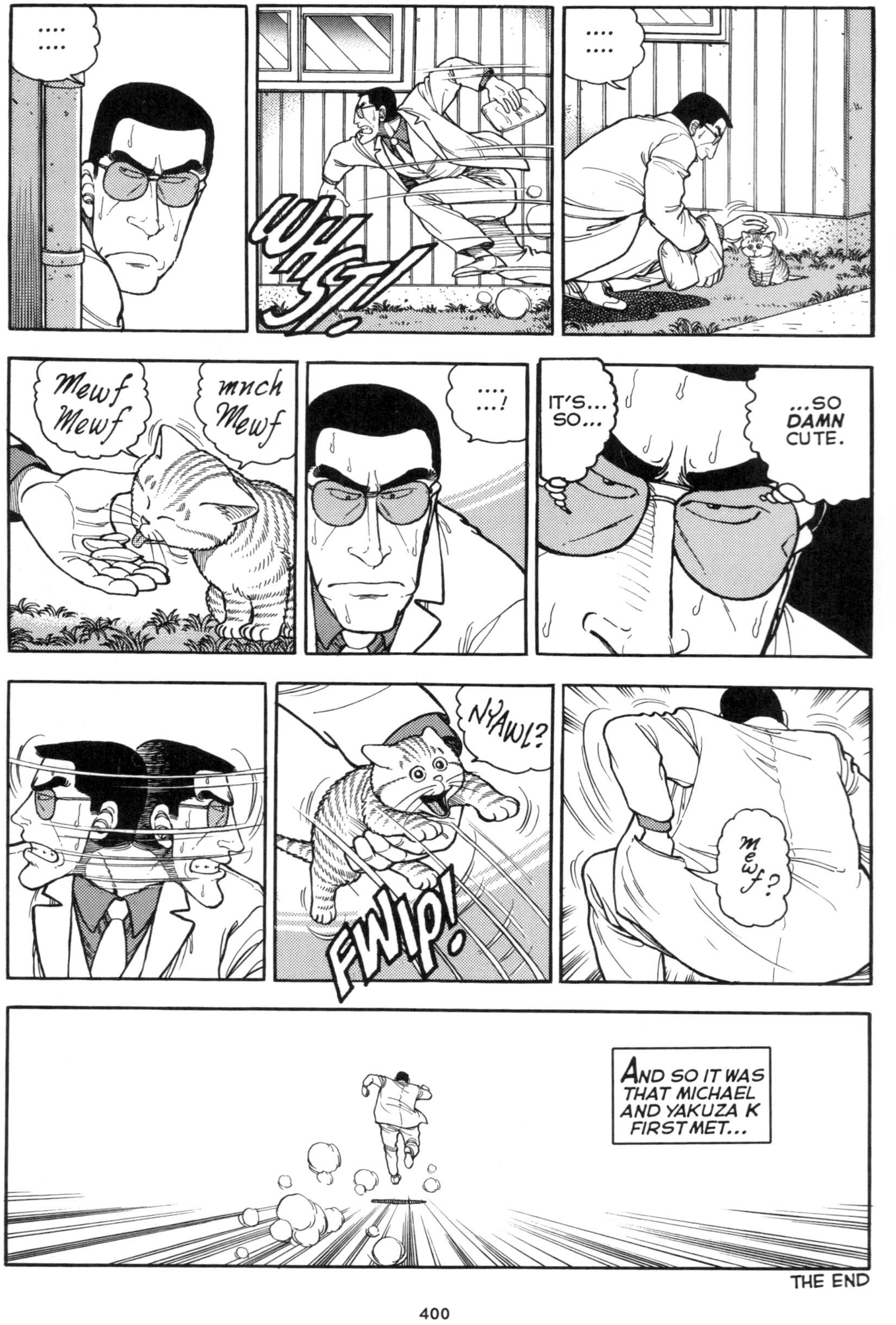
....
....
WHSH!
....
....
Mewf Mewf
mnch Mewf
....,
...!
IT'S... SO...
...SO DAMN CUTE.
NYAWL?
FWIP!
mewf?
AND SO IT WAS THAT MICHAEL AND YAKUZA K FIRST MET...

THE END

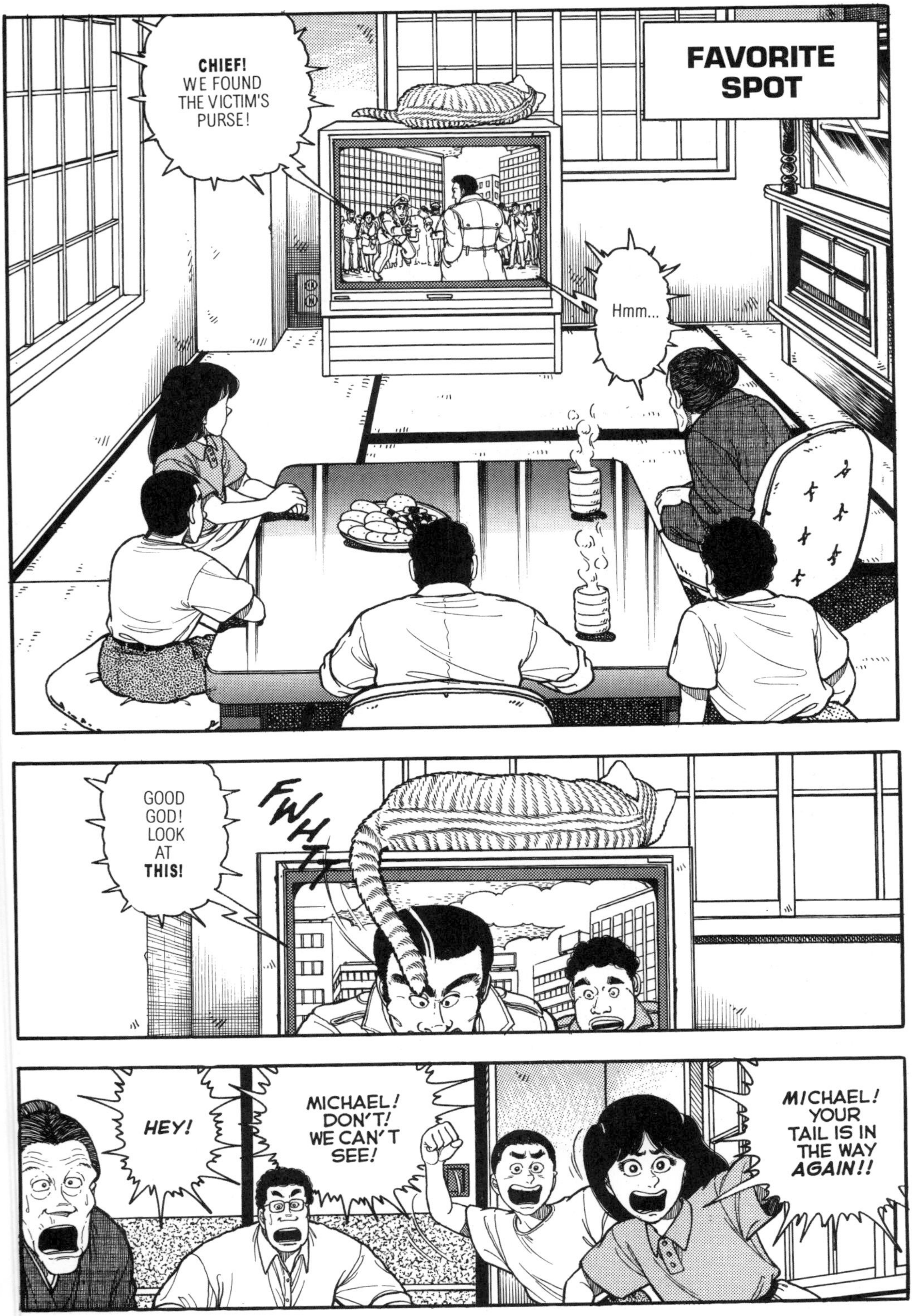
CHIEF! WE FOUND THE VICTIM'S PURSE!
FAVORITE SPOT
Hmm...
GOOD GOD! LOOK AT THIS!
FWHT
HEY!
MICHAEL! DON'T! WE CAN'T SEE!
MICHAEL! YOUR TAIL IS IN THE WAY AGAIN!!

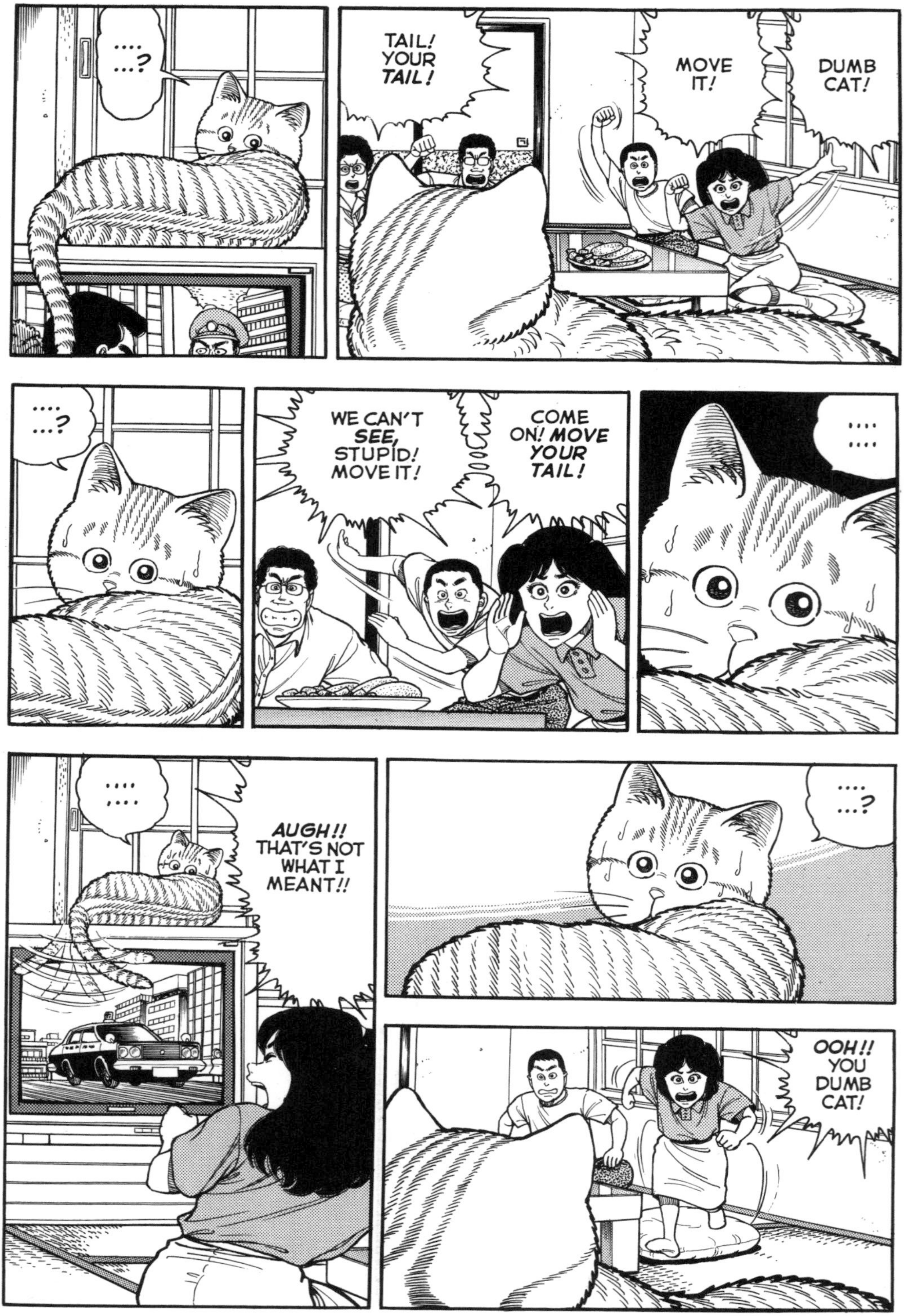
....
...?
TAIL! YOUR TAIL!
MOVE IT!
DUMB CAT!
....
...?
WE CAN'T SEE, STUPID! MOVE IT!
COME ON! MOVE YOUR TAIL!
....
....
....
....
AUGH!! THAT'S NOT WHAT I MEANT!!
....
...?
OOH!! YOU DUMB CAT!

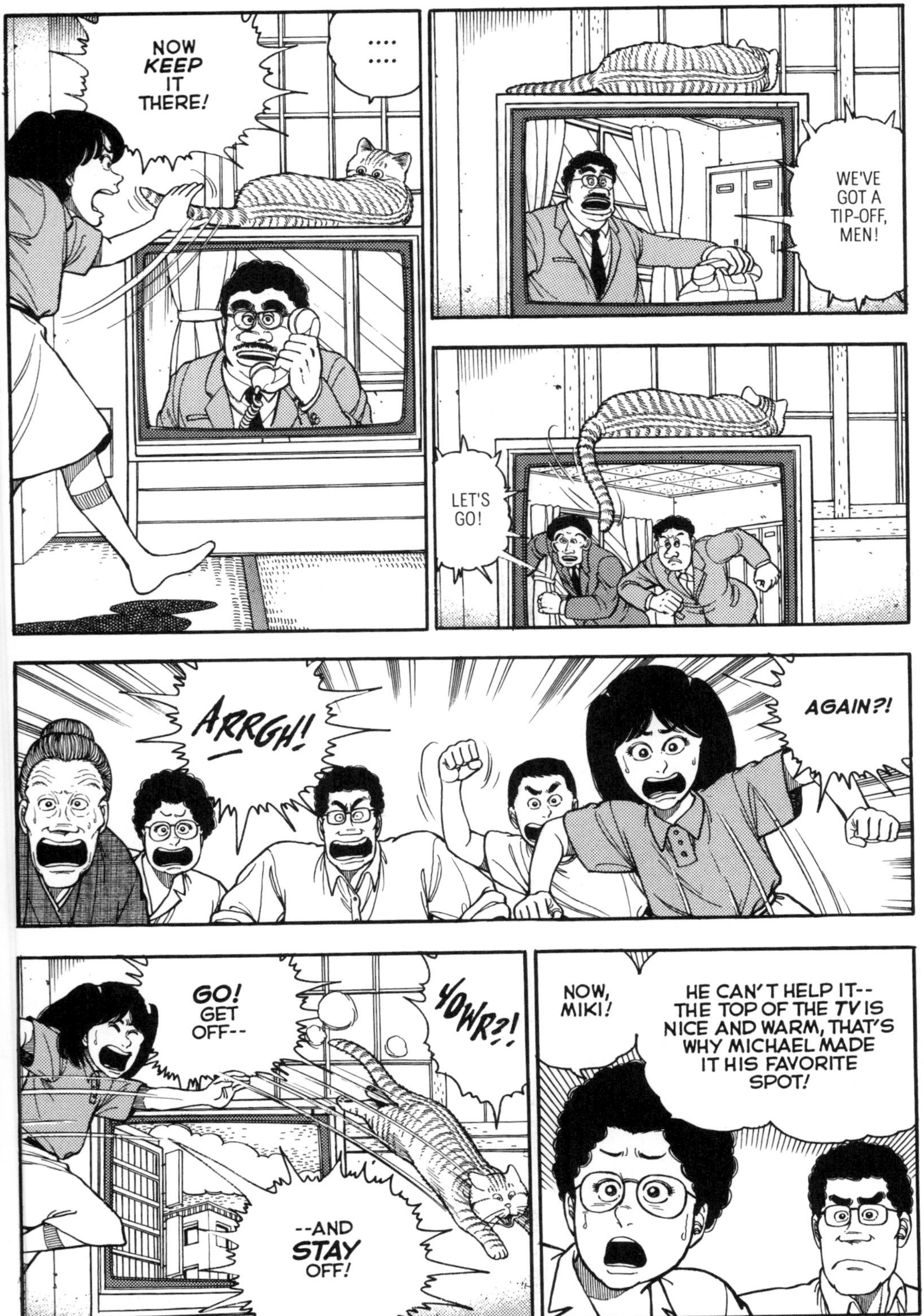
NOW KEEP IT THERE!
....
....
WE'VE GOT A TIP-OFF, MEN!
LET'S GO!
ARRGH!
AGAIN?!
GO! GET OFF--
YOWR?!
--AND STAY OFF!
NOW, MIKI!
HE CAN'T HELP IT-- THE TOP OF THE TV IS NICE AND WARM, THAT'S WHY MICHAEL MADE IT HIS FAVORITE SPOT!

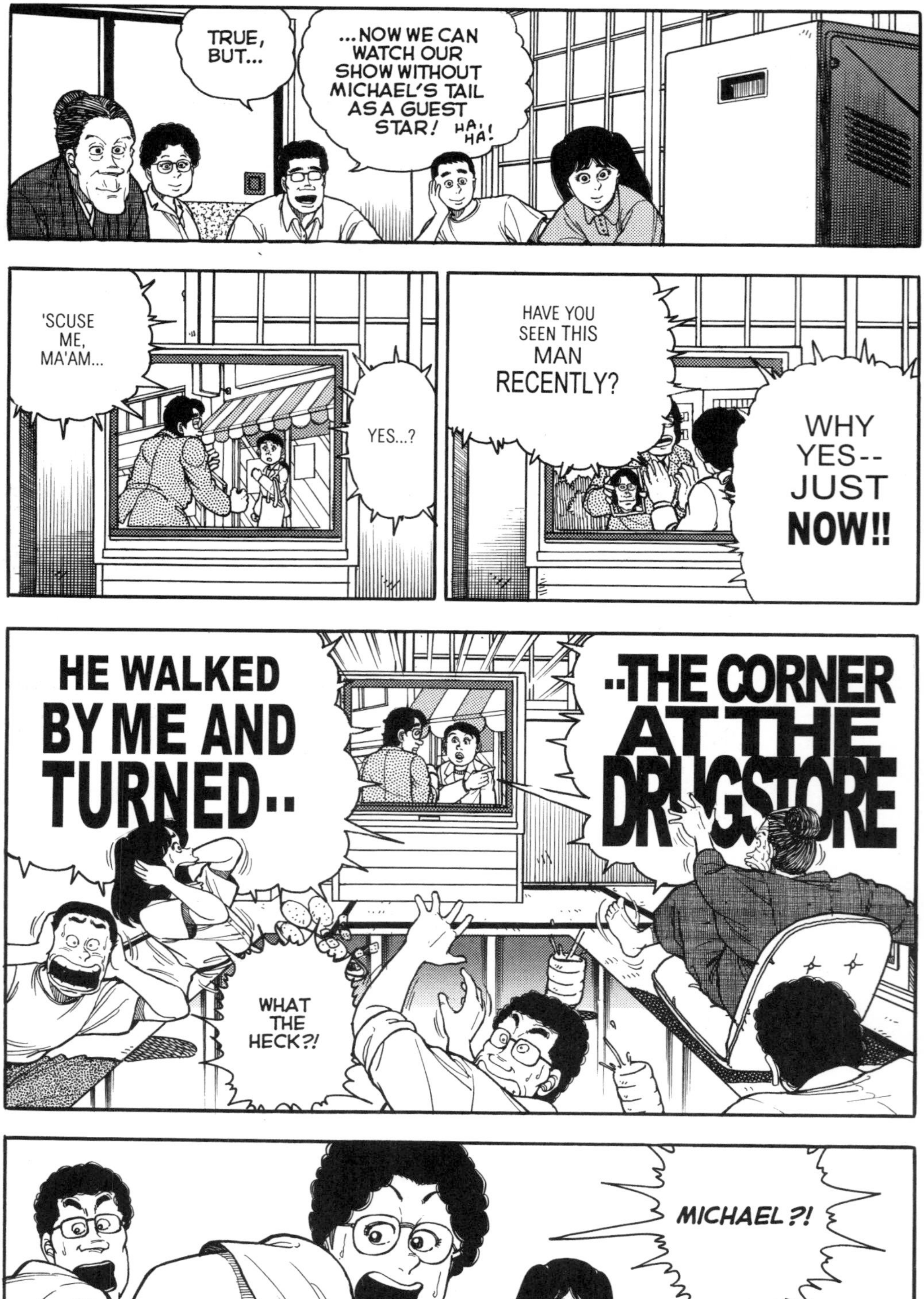
TRUE, BUT...
...NOW WE CAN WATCH OUR SHOW WITHOUT MICHAEL'S TAIL AS A GUEST STAR! HA, HA!
'SCUSE ME, MA'AM...
YES...?
HAVE YOU SEEN THIS MAN RECENTLY?
WHY YES-- JUST NOW!!
HE WALKED BY ME AND TURNED..
..THE CORNER AT THE DRUGSTORE
WHAT THE HECK?!
MICHAEL?!

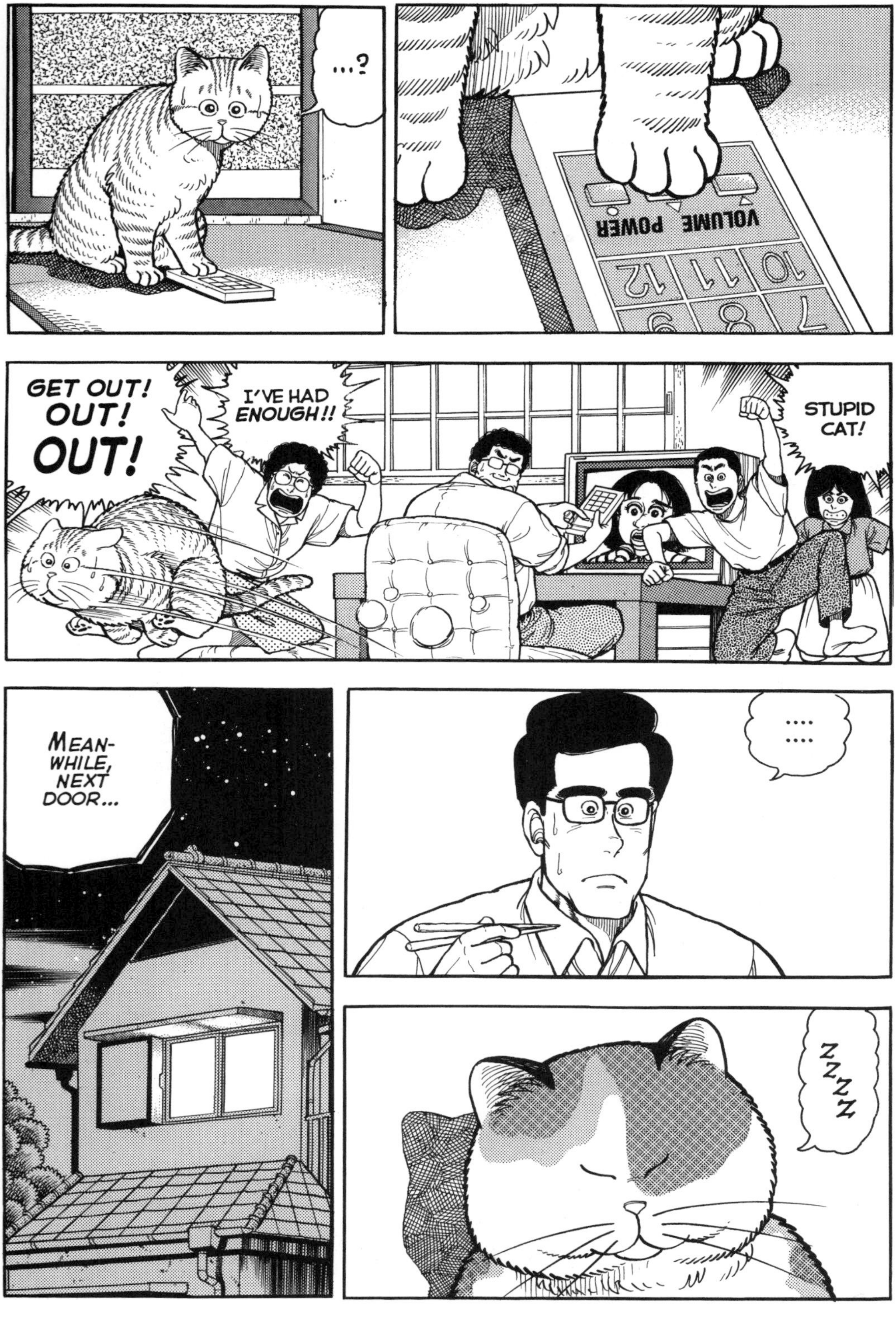
...?
VOLUME
POWER
GET OUT! OUT! OUT!
I'VE HAD ENOUGH!!
STUPID CAT!
MEAN-WHILE, NEXT DOOR...
.... ....
ZZZZ

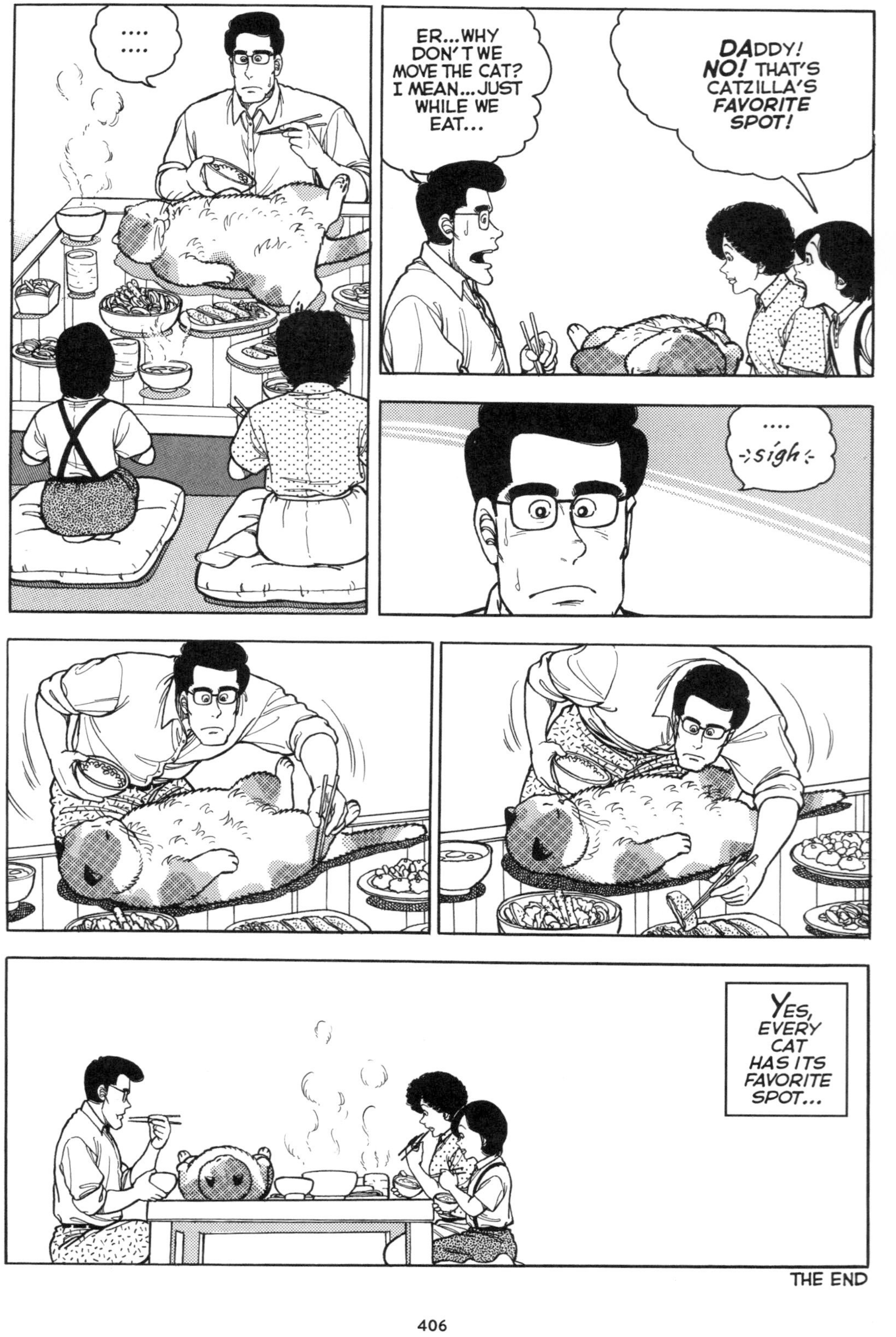
....
....
ER...WHY DON'T WE MOVE THE CAT? I MEAN...JUST WHILE WE EAT...
DADDY! NO! THAT'S CATZILLA'S FAVORITE SPOT!
....
-sigh-
YES, EVERY CAT HAS ITS FAVORITE SPOT...

THE END

# THE AUDIOPHILE

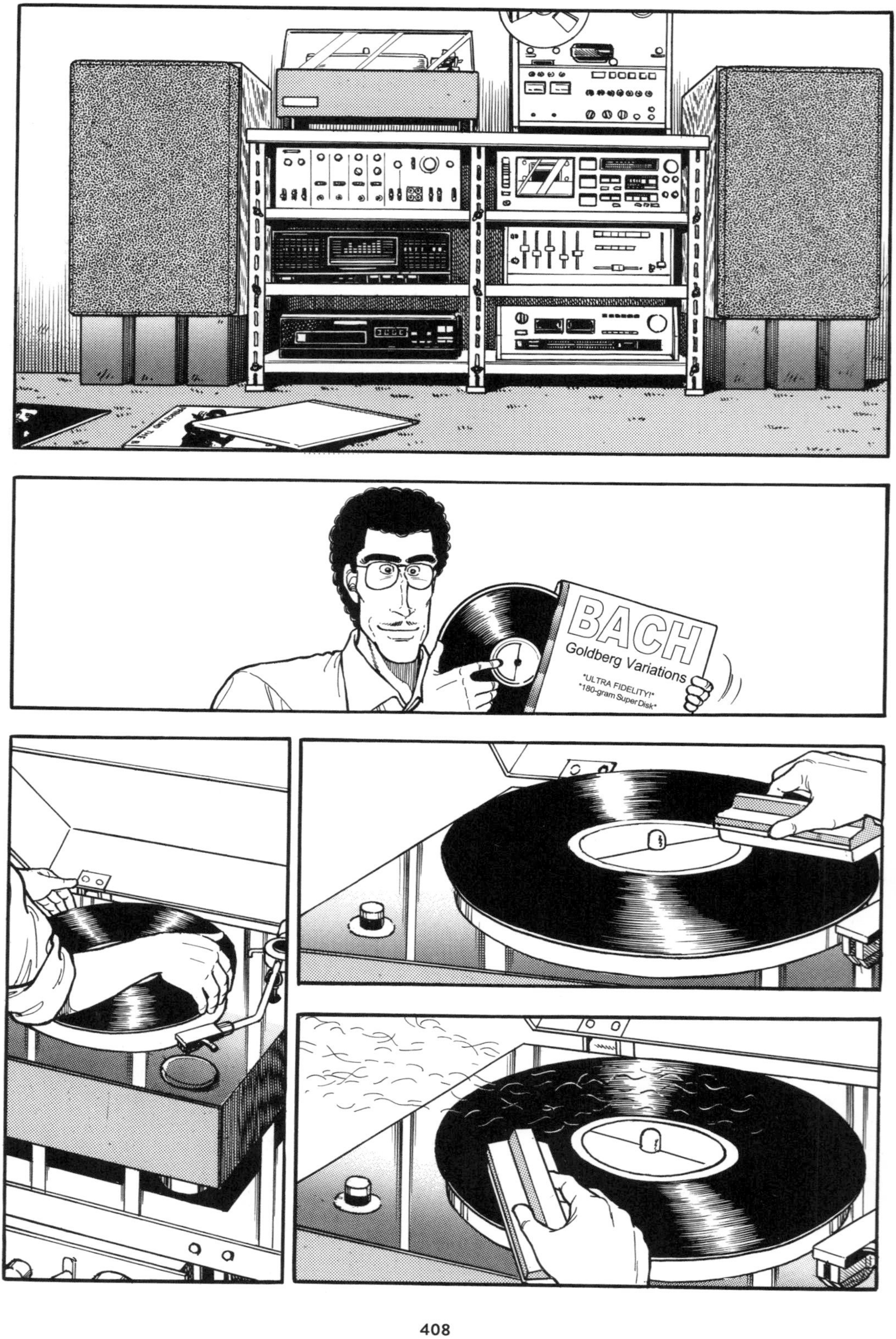
BACH
Goldberg Variations
*ULTRA FIDELITY!*
*180-gram SuperDisk*

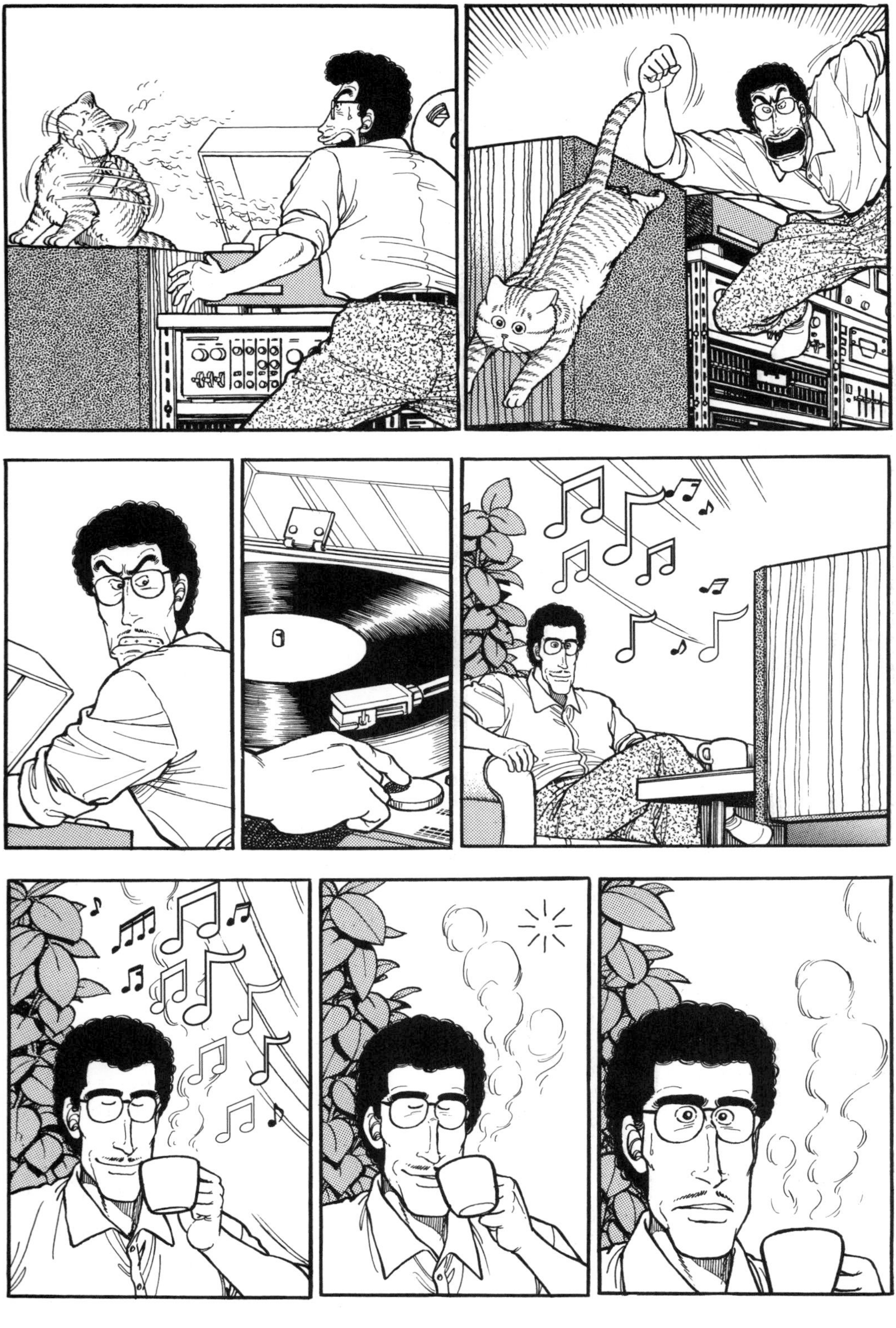

...?
SKRAWWK

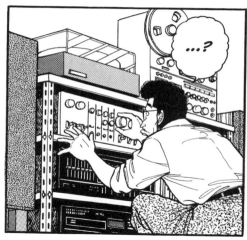

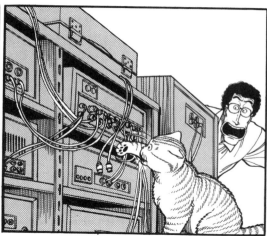

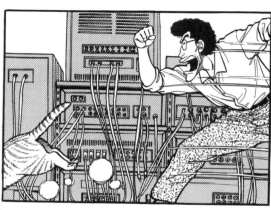

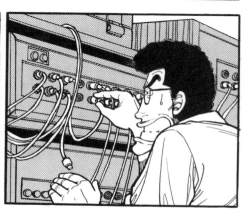

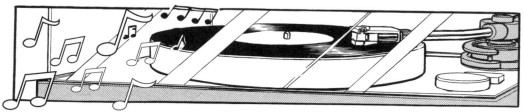

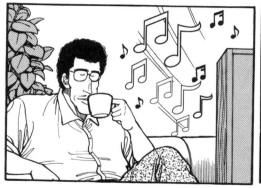

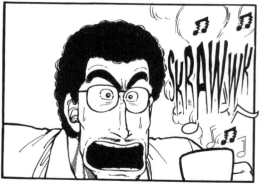

FWHDD

SHRIKK

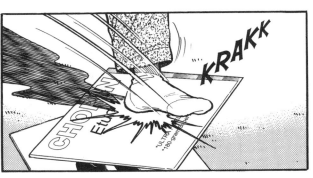

KRAKK

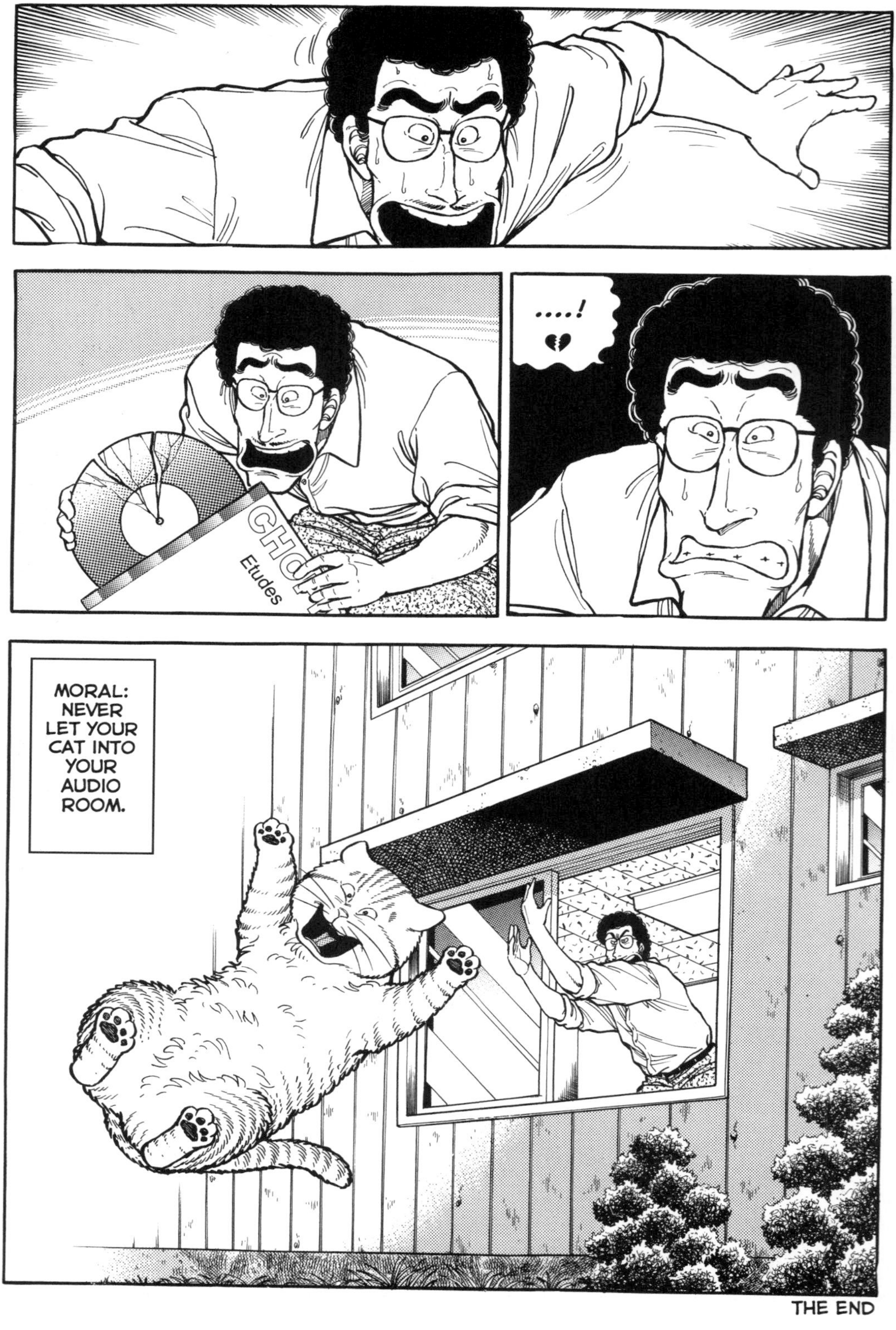
CHO
Etudes
....!
MORAL: NEVER LET YOUR CAT INTO YOUR AUDIO ROOM.

THE END

# CANINE VERSUS FELINE: MICHAEL'S MAH JONG LIFE

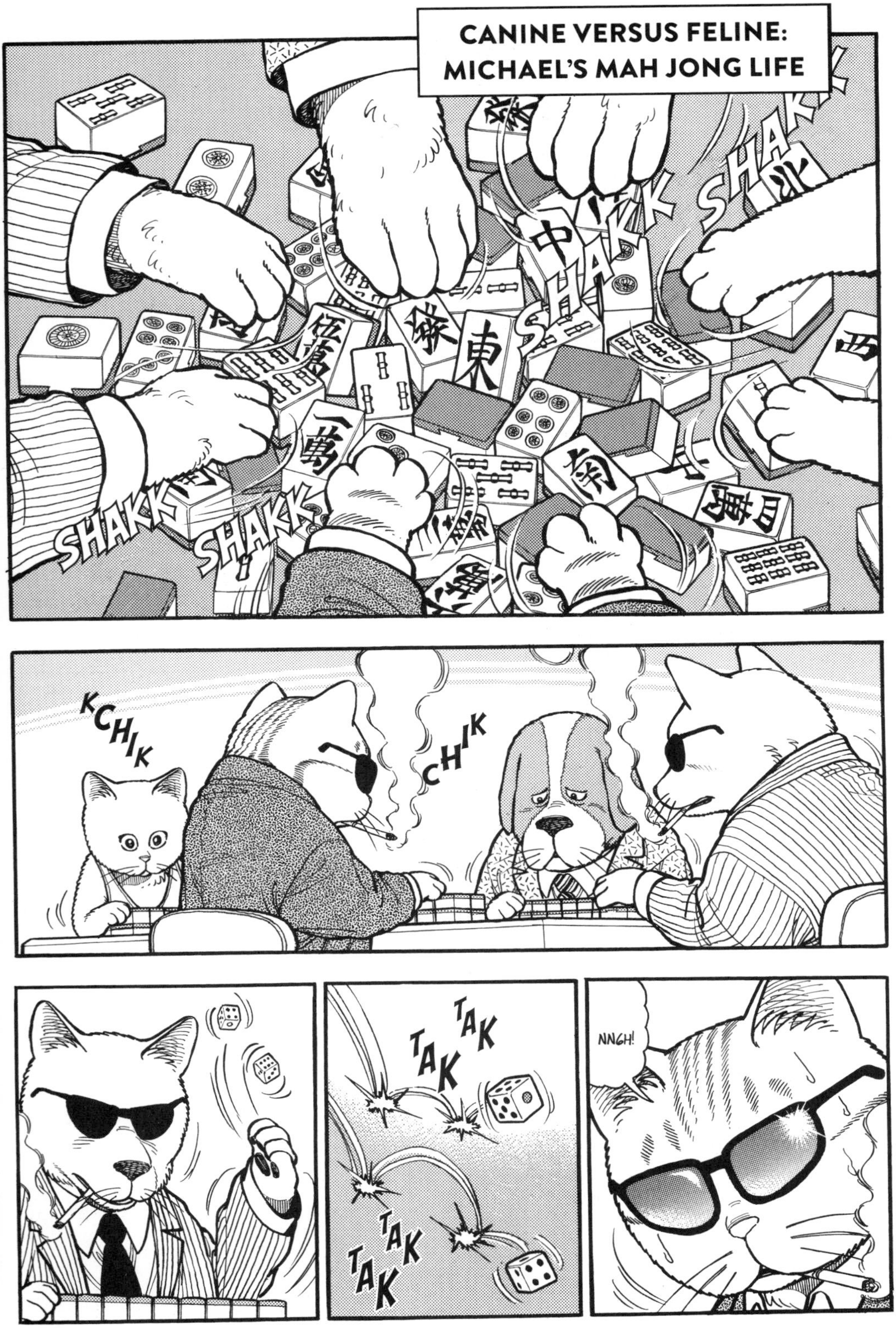
SHAKK
SHAKK
SHAKK
SHAKK
SHAKK
KCHIK
CHIK
TAK
TAK
TAK
TAK
NNGH!

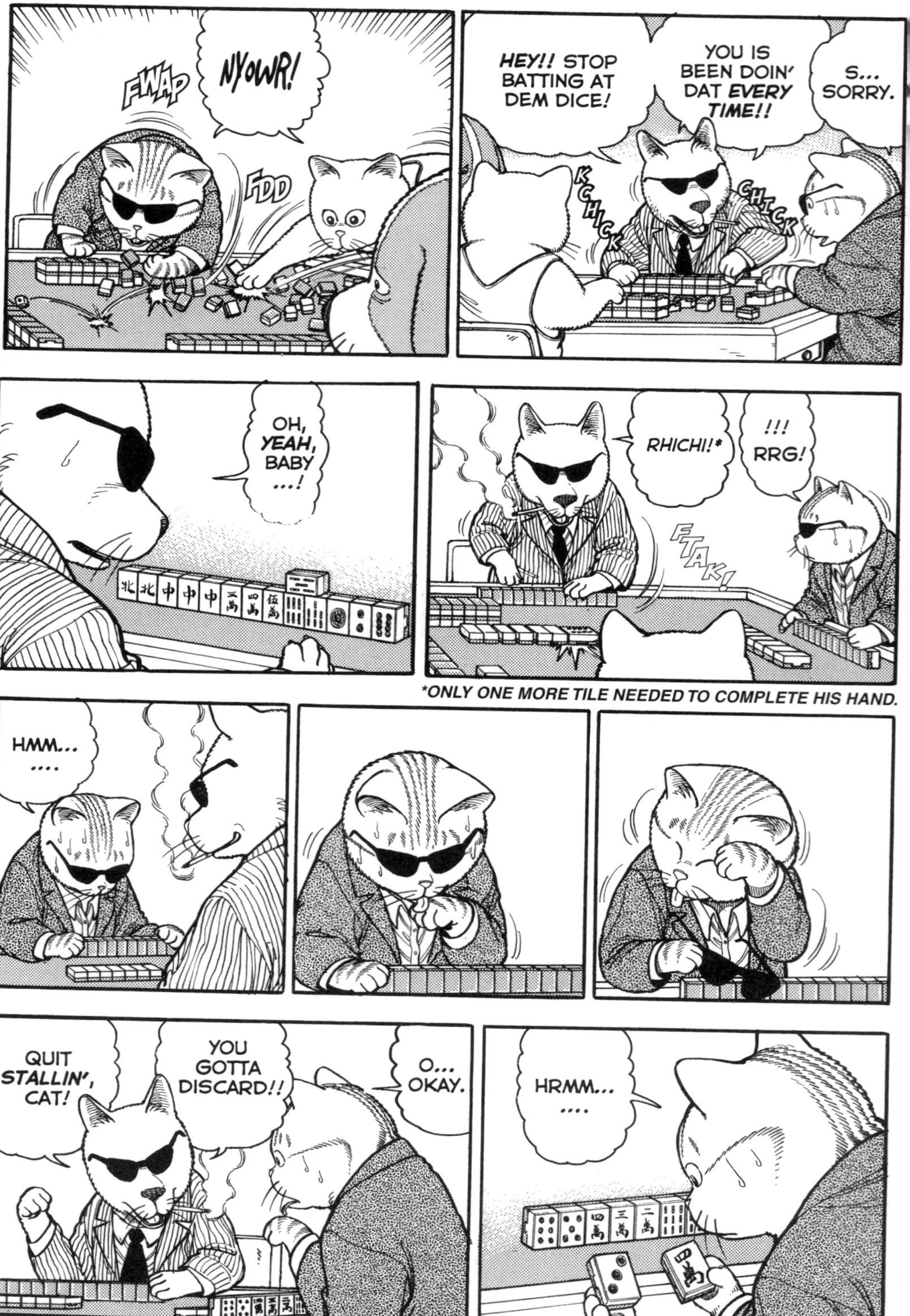
FWAP
NYOWR!
FDD
HEY!! STOP BATTING AT DEM DICE!
YOU IS BEEN DOIN' DAT EVERY TIME!!
S... SORRY.
KCHICK
CHICK
OH, YEAH, BABY ...!
RHICHI!*
!!! RRG!
FTAK!
*ONLY ONE MORE TILE NEEDED TO COMPLETE HIS HAND.
HMM... ....
QUIT STALLIN', CAT!
YOU GOTTA DISCARD!!
O... OKAY.
HRMM... ....

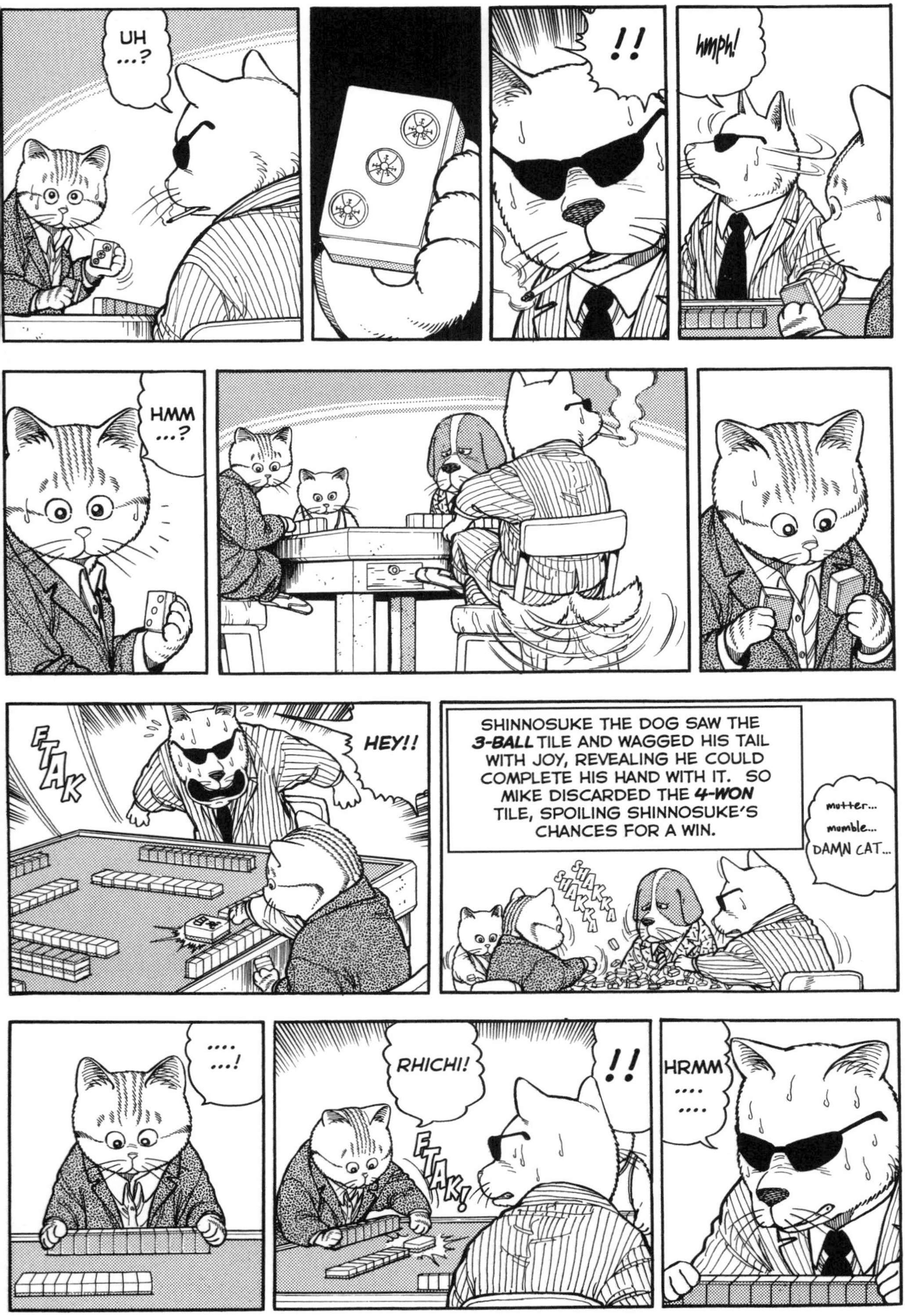
UH ...?
!!
hmph!
HMM ...?
FTAK
HEY!!
SHINNOSUKE THE DOG SAW THE 3-BALL TILE AND WAGGED HIS TAIL WITH JOY, REVEALING HE COULD COMPLETE HIS HAND WITH IT. SO MIKE DISCARDED THE 4-WON TILE, SPOILING SHINNOSUKE'S CHANCES FOR A WIN.
SHAKKA SHAKKA
mutter... mumble... DAMN CAT...
.... ...!
RHICHI!
!!
FTAK!
HRMM .... ....

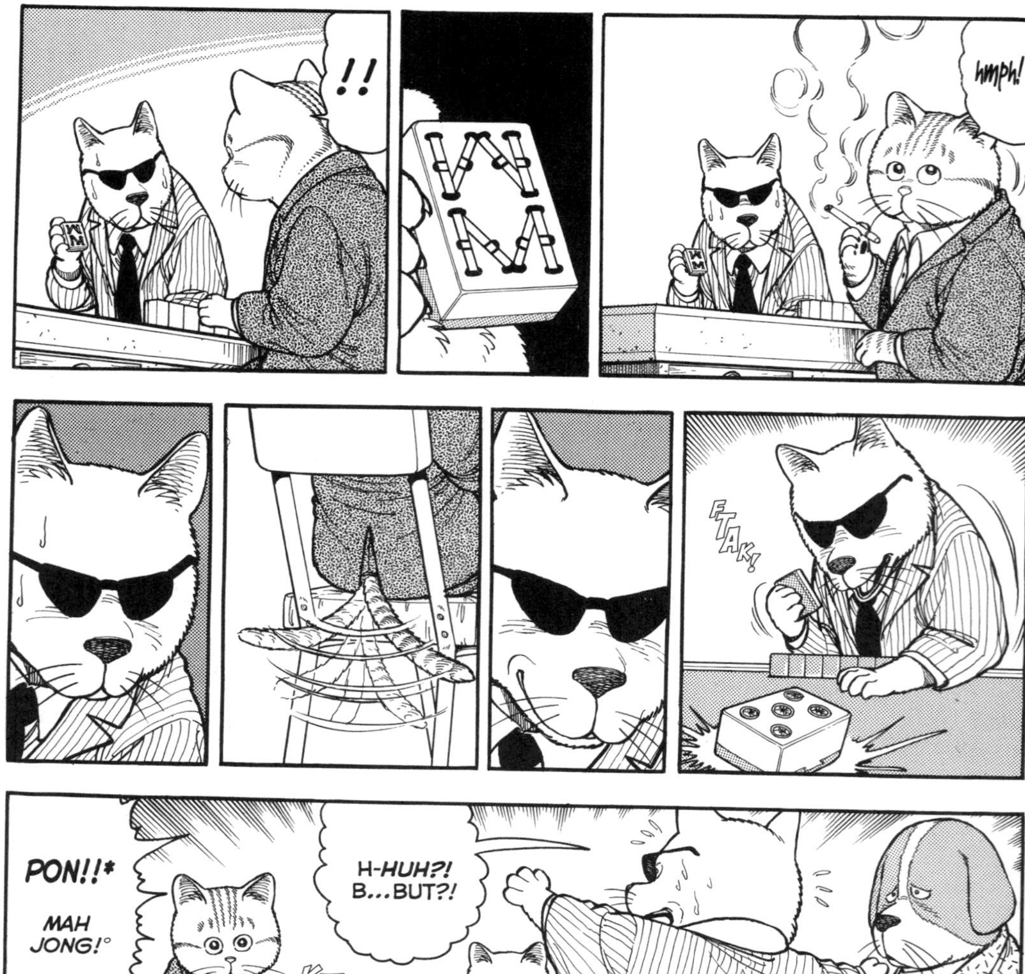
!!
hmph!
FTAK!
PON!!*
MAH JONG!°
KTAK
H-HUH?! B...BUT?!

*: THREE OF A KIND °: COMPLETED WINNING HAND

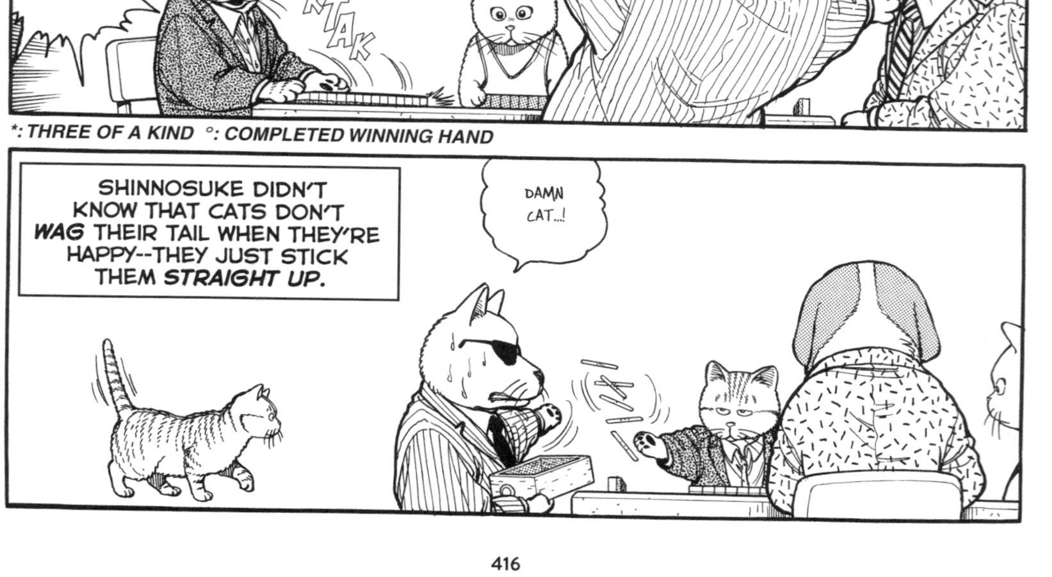
SHINNOSUKE DIDN'T KNOW THAT CATS DON'T *WAG* THEIR TAIL WHEN THEY'RE HAPPY--THEY JUST STICK THEM ***STRAIGHT UP.***
DAMN CAT...!

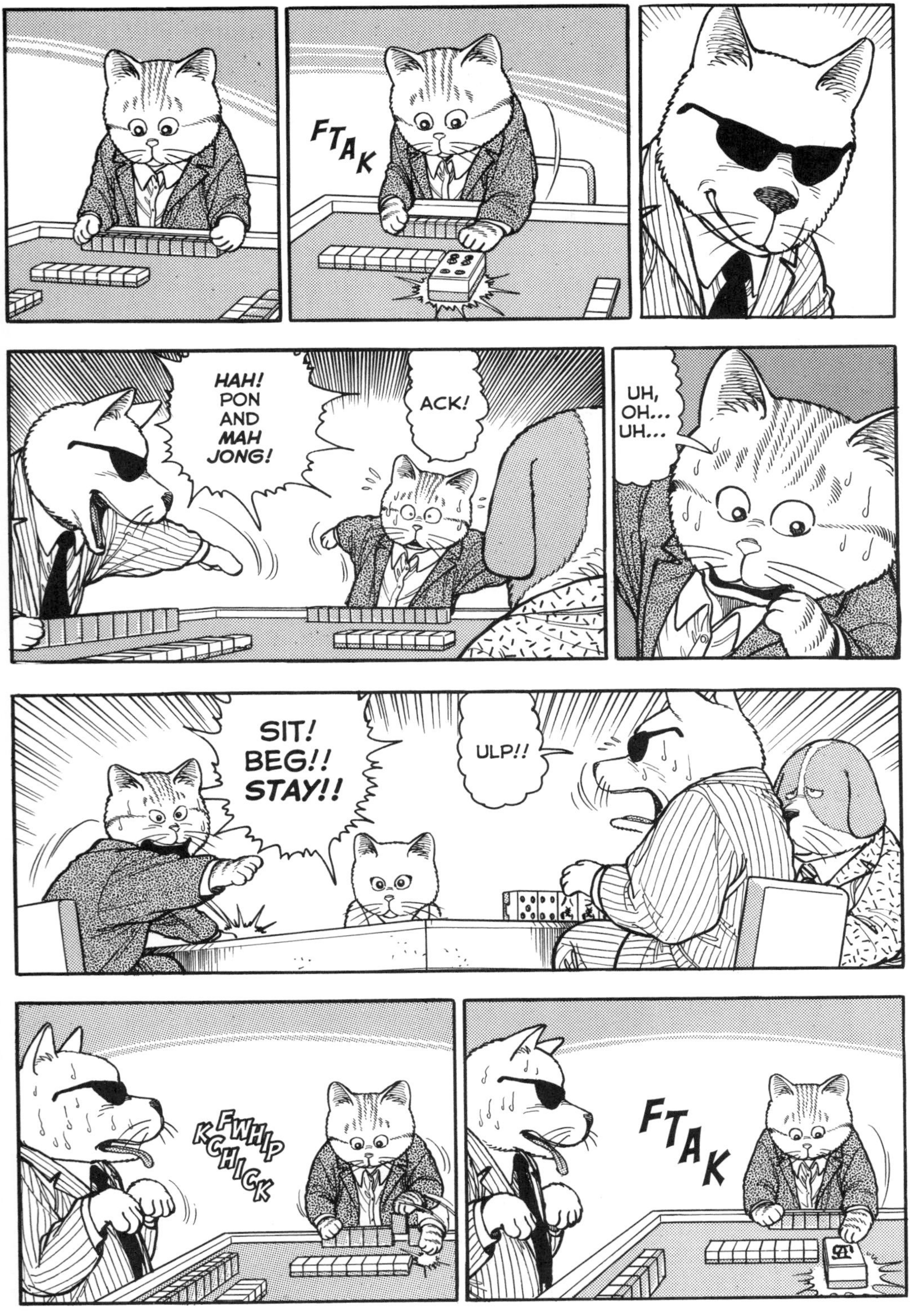

FTAK
HAH! PON AND MAH JONG!
ACK!
UH, OH... UH...
SIT! BEG!! STAY!!
ULP!!
FWHIP KCHICK
FTAK

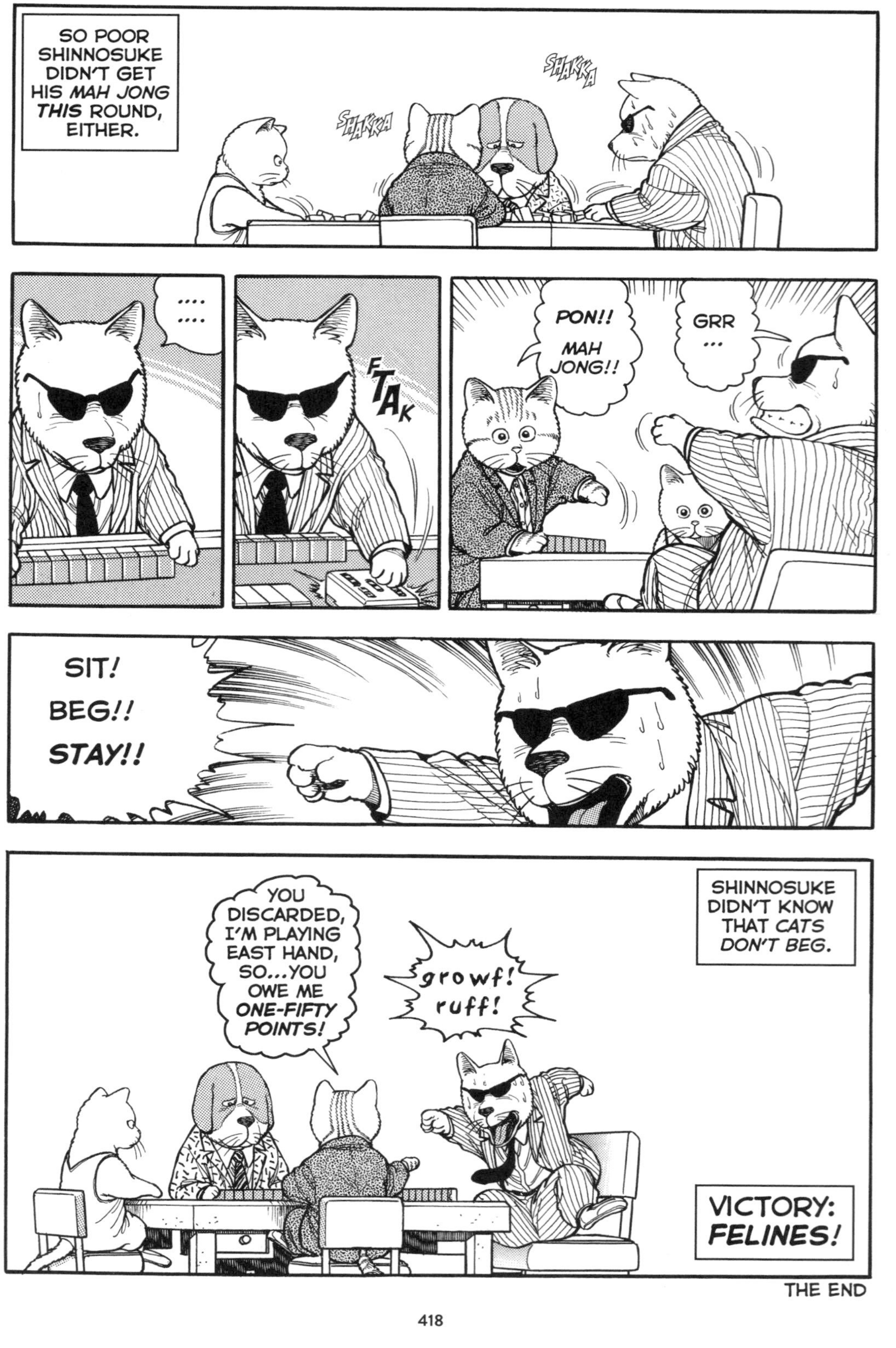
SO POOR SHINNOSUKE DIDN'T GET HIS *MAH JONG THIS* ROUND, EITHER.
SHAKKA
SHAKKA
....
....
FTAK
PON!! MAH JONG!!
GRR ...
SIT! BEG!! STAY!!
YOU DISCARDED, I'M PLAYING EAST HAND, SO...YOU OWE ME *ONE-FIFTY POINTS!*
growf! ruff!
SHINNOSUKE DIDN'T KNOW THAT *CATS DON'T BEG.*
VICTORY: *FELINES!*

THE END

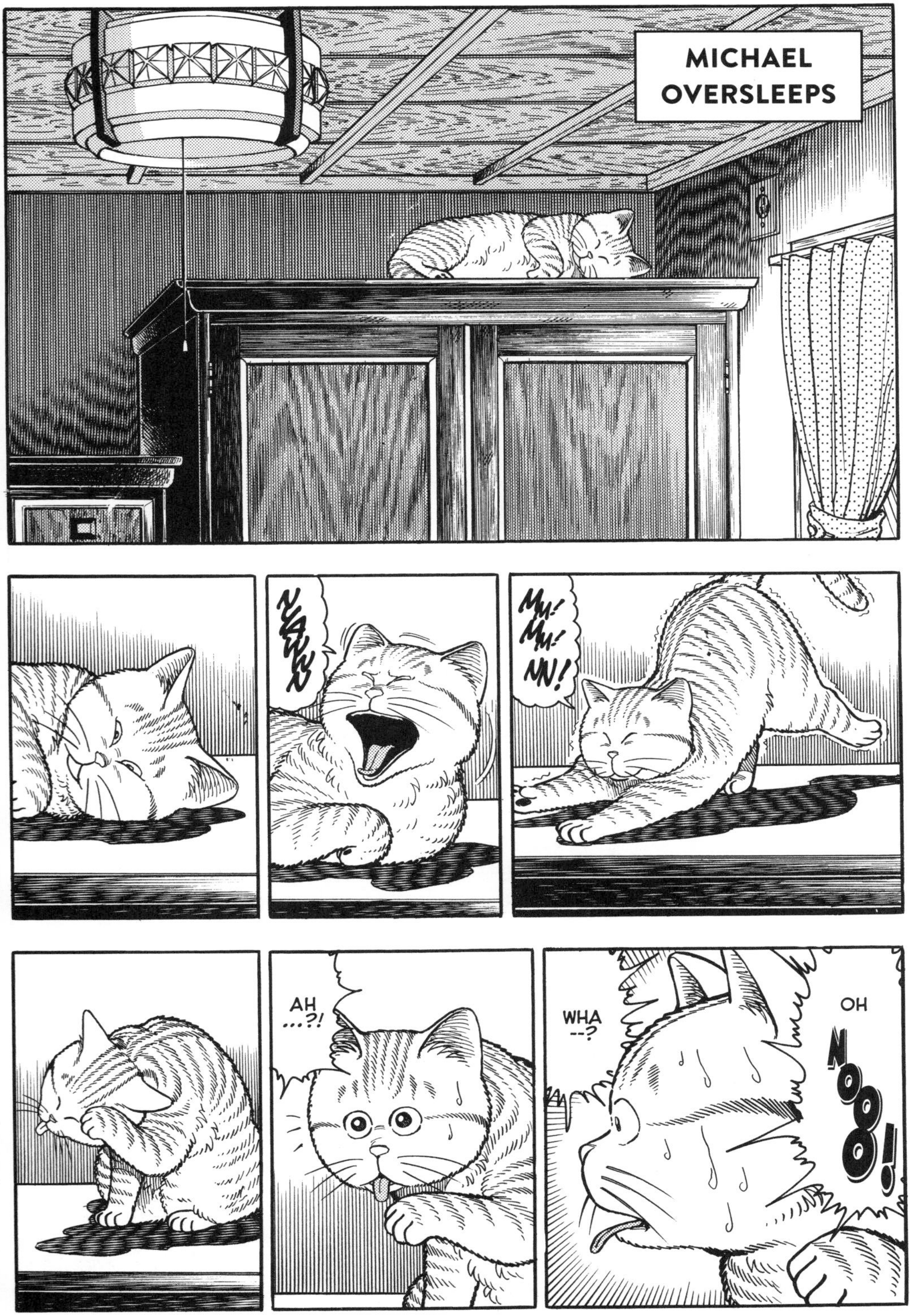
MICHAEL OVERSLEEPS
NYAWN
MM! MM! NN!
AH ...?!
WHA --?
OH
NOOO!!

AGH!

.....!

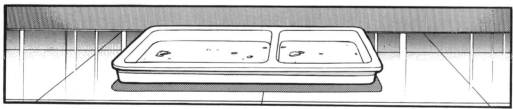

....
....

ONE MORNING,
MICHAEL OVERSLEPT
AND WAS LATE FOR
BREAKFAST. BY THE
TIME HE GOT THERE,
POPO AND MINI-MIKE
HAD GOBBLED THE
DISH CLEAN!

SLRRP

THERE WAS
HARDLY EVEN
A *TASTE* LEFT
FOR POOR
MICHAEL...

HE DID HIS BEST BEGGING TO GET MORE, BUT...

PRRP!

MROWW!

WHAT? YOU *CAN'T* BE *HUNGRY!*

I JUST FED YOU GUYS, YOU SILLY CAT!

SADLY, SHE WAS IMMUNE TO HIS CHARMS.

SO MICHAEL DECIDED TO SAVE HIS ENERGY AND WAIT UNTIL DINNER TIME.

MYOW! NOW!

BZZT

MEWW!

.....
.....

DIN-NER TIME

MICHAELLLL!

♪ POP *OOOH!* ♪
MINI-MIIKE!

COME AND GET IT! ♪

MRRGEE—

YOWWW!

SPYOINGG!!!

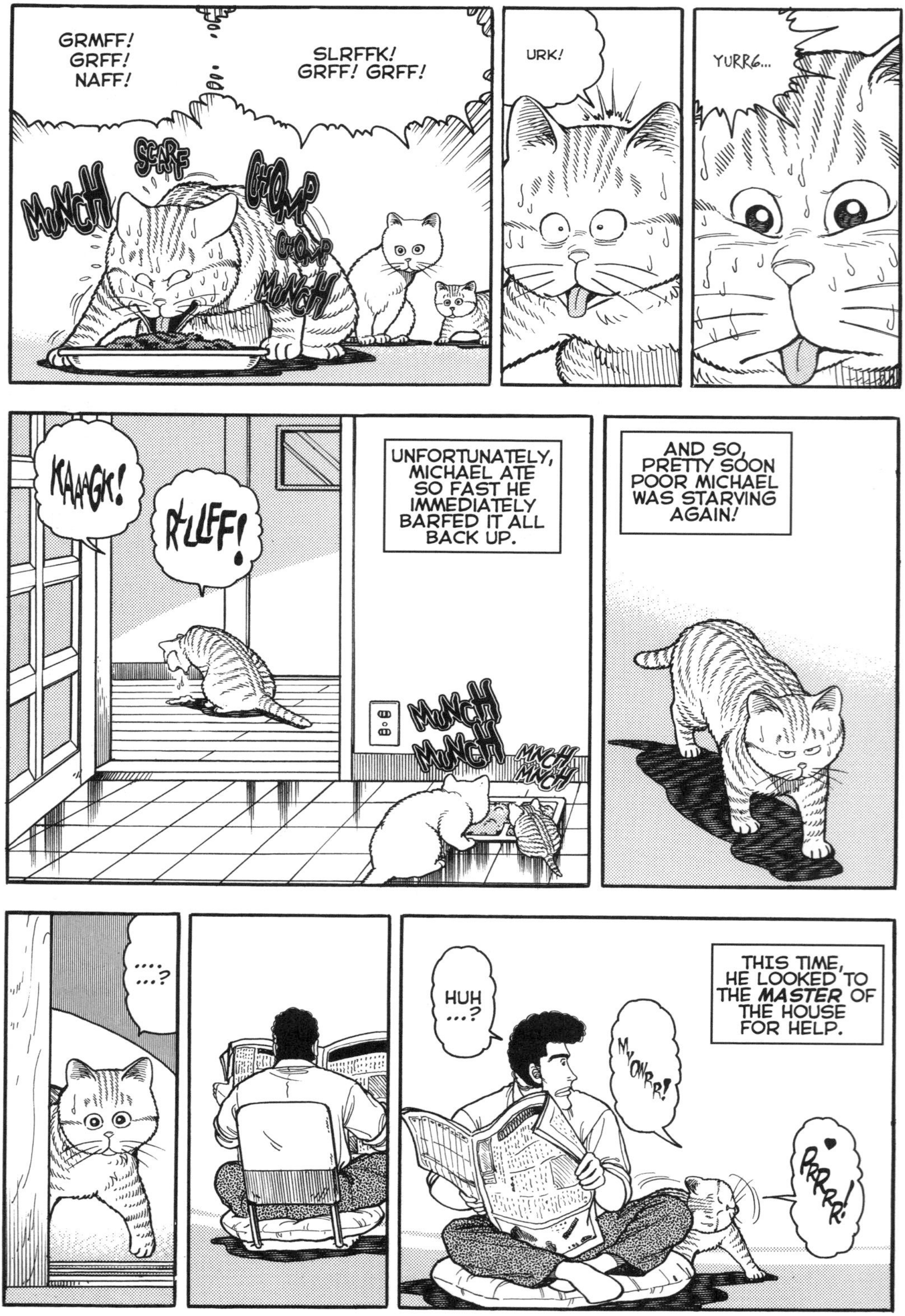
GRMFF! GRFF! NAFF!
SLRFFK! GRFF! GRFF!
MUNCH
SCARF
CHOMP
CHOMP
MUNCH
URK!
YURRG...
KAAAGK!
R'LLFF!
UNFORTUNATELY, MICHAEL ATE SO FAST HE IMMEDIATELY BARFED IT ALL BACK UP.
MUNCH
MUNCH
MNCH MNCH
AND SO, PRETTY SOON POOR MICHAEL WAS STARVING AGAIN!
...? ...?
HUH ...?
THIS TIME, HE LOOKED TO THE ***MASTER*** OF THE HOUSE FOR HELP.
MYOWRR!
PRRRR!

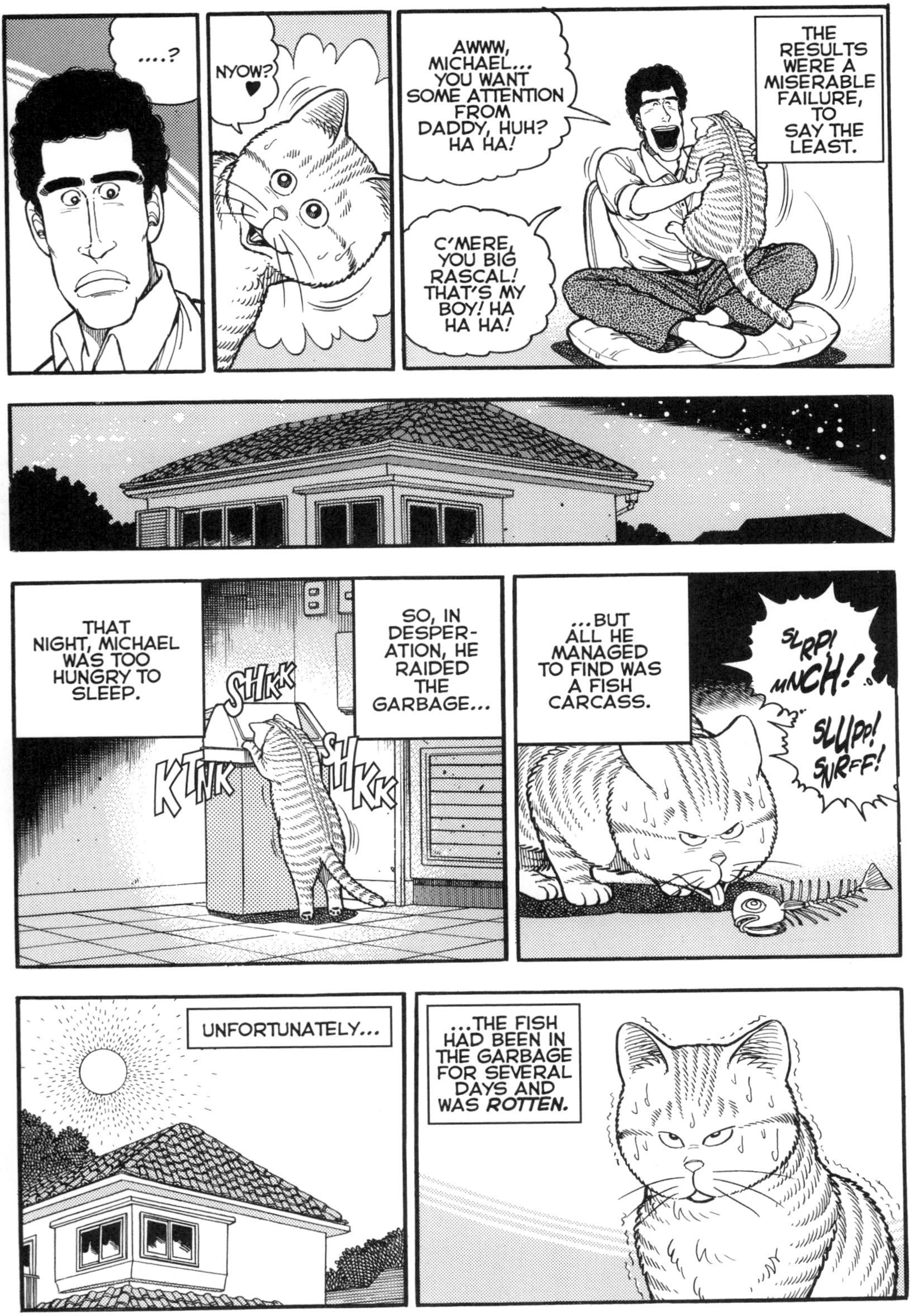
....?
NYOW? ♥
AWWW, MICHAEL... YOU WANT SOME ATTENTION FROM DADDY, HUH? HA HA!
C'MERE, YOU BIG RASCAL! THAT'S MY BOY! HA HA HA!
THE RESULTS WERE A MISERABLE FAILURE, TO SAY THE LEAST.
THAT NIGHT, MICHAEL WAS TOO HUNGRY TO SLEEP.
SHKK
KTNK
SHKK
SO, IN DESPERATION, HE RAIDED THE GARBAGE...
...BUT ALL HE MANAGED TO FIND WAS A FISH CARCASS.
SLRP! MNCH!
SLUPP! SNRFF!
UNFORTUNATELY...
...THE FISH HAD BEEN IN THE GARBAGE FOR SEVERAL DAYS AND WAS *ROTTEN.*

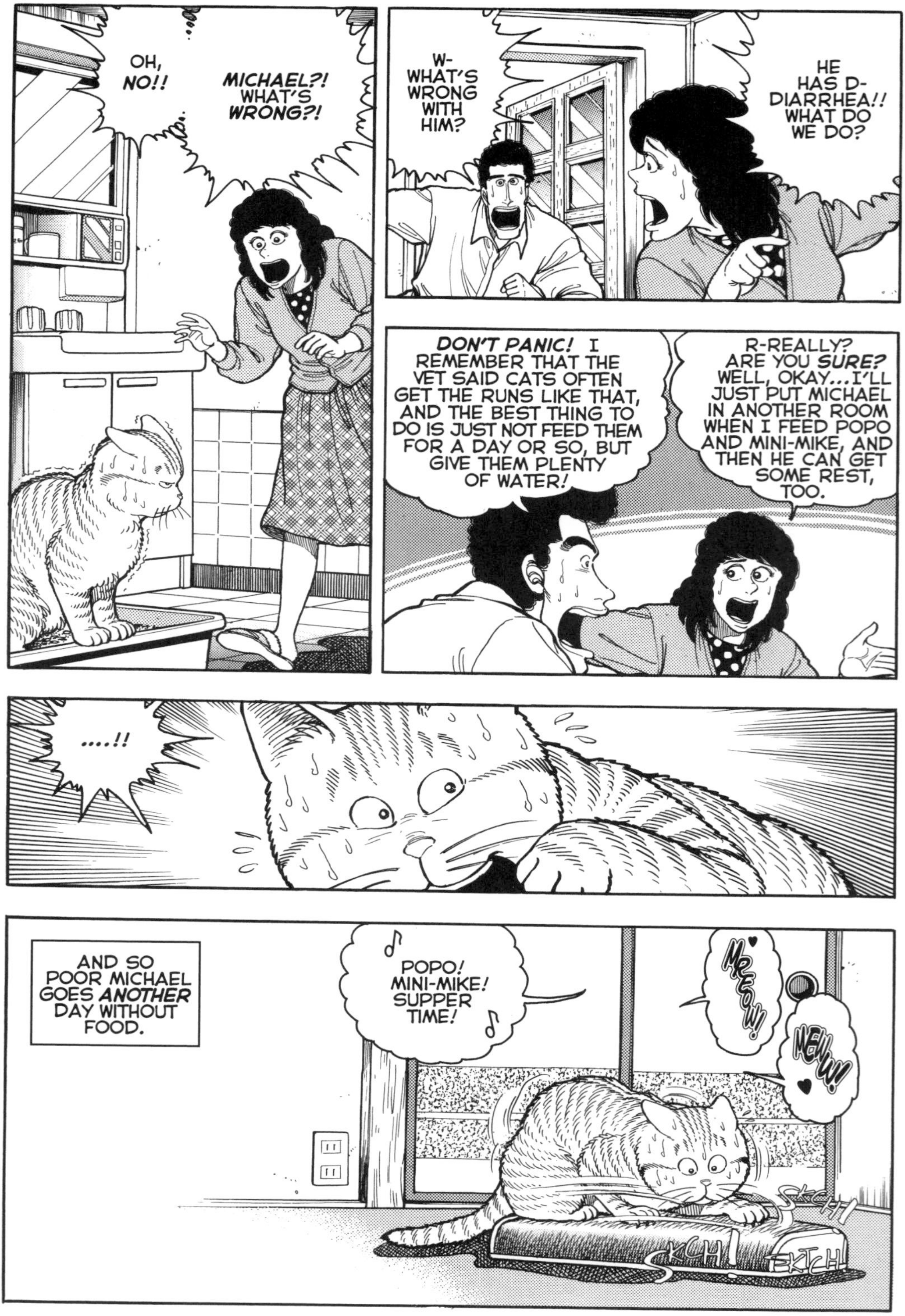

OH, *NO!!*
*MICHAEL?!* WHAT'S *WRONG?!*
W-WHAT'S WRONG WITH HIM?
HE HAS D-DIARRHEA!! WHAT DO WE DO?
*DON'T PANIC!* I REMEMBER THAT THE VET SAID CATS OFTEN GET THE RUNS LIKE THAT, AND THE BEST THING TO DO IS JUST NOT FEED THEM FOR A DAY OR SO, BUT GIVE THEM PLENTY OF WATER!
R-REALLY? ARE YOU *SURE?* WELL, OKAY...I'LL JUST PUT MICHAEL IN ANOTHER ROOM WHEN I FEED POPO AND MINI-MIKE, AND THEN HE CAN GET SOME REST, TOO.
....!!
AND SO POOR MICHAEL GOES *ANOTHER* DAY WITHOUT FOOD.
POPO! MINI-MIKE! SUPPER TIME!
MREOW!
MEW!
SKCH!
SKCH!
SKCH!


THE END

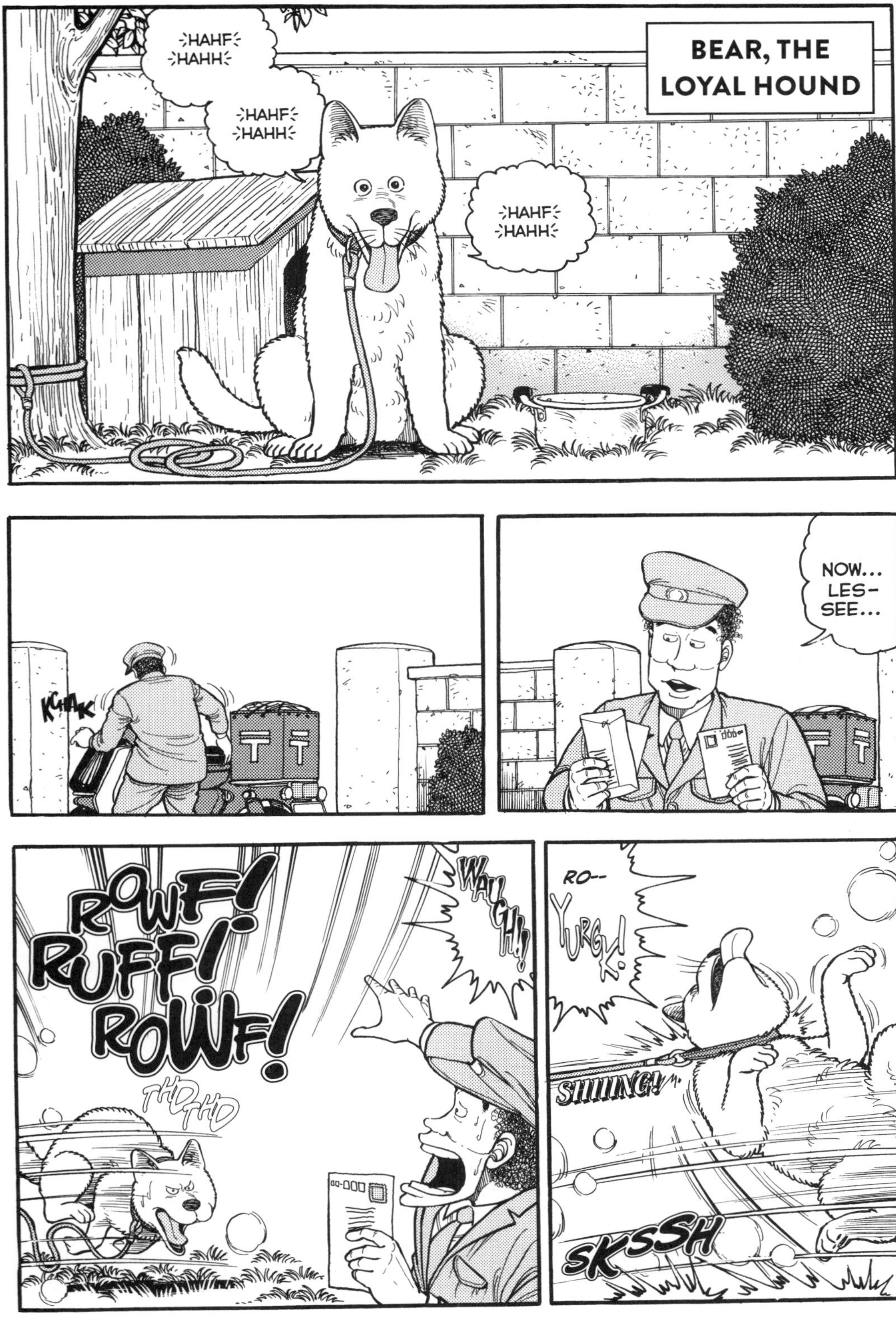

BEAR, THE LOYAL HOUND
HAHF HAHH
HAHF HAHH
HAHF HAHH
KCHAK
NOW... LES-SEE...
ROWF! RUFF! ROWF!
WAUGH!!
THD THD
RO--
YURGK!
SHIIING!
SKSSH

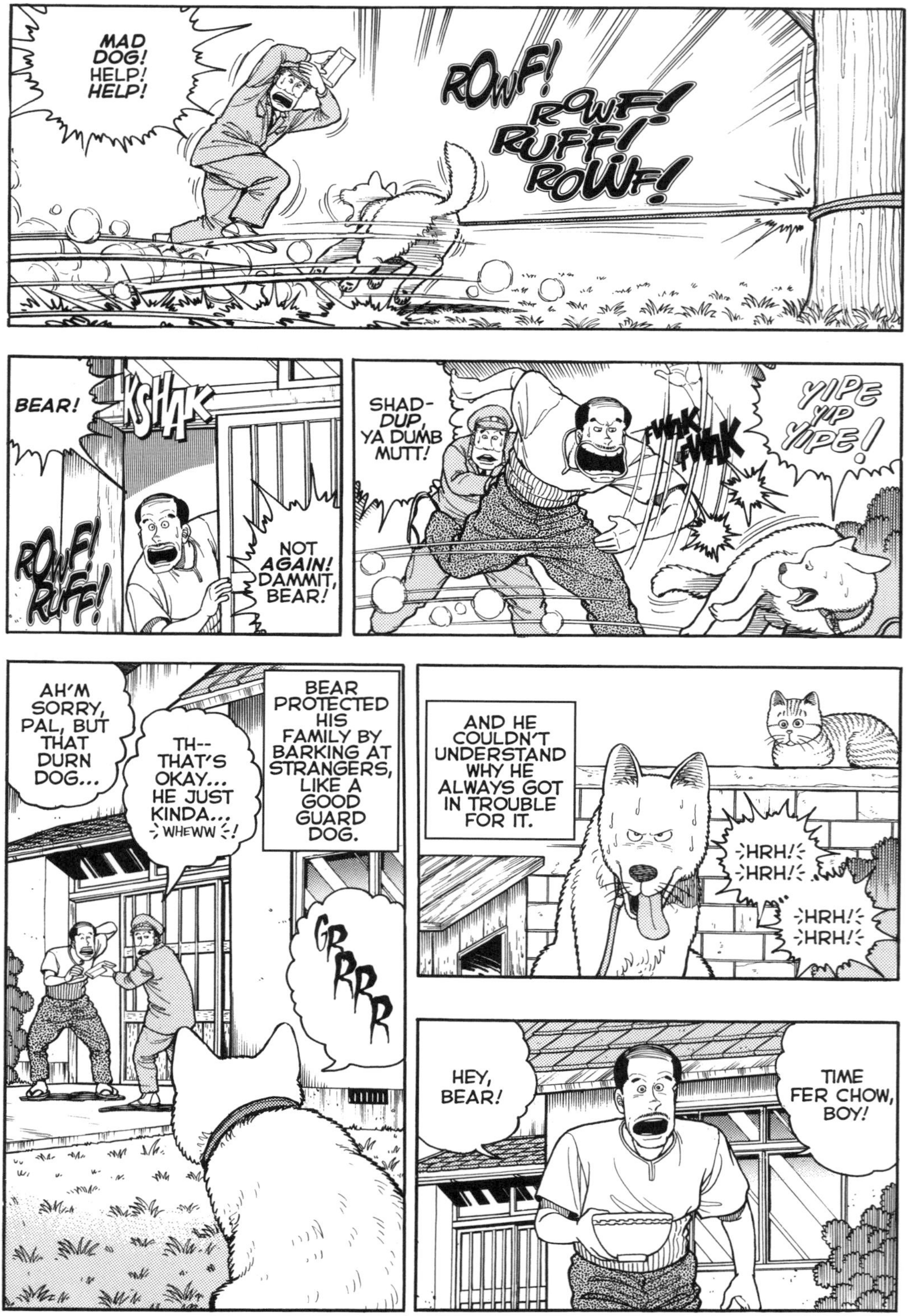
MAD DOG! HELP! HELP!
ROWF! ROWF! RUFF! ROWF!
BEAR!
KSHAK
ROWF! RUFF!
NOT AGAIN! DAMMIT, BEAR!
SHAD-DUP, YA DUMB MUTT!
FWAK FWAK
YIPE YIP YIPE!
AH'M SORRY, PAL, BUT THAT DURN DOG...
TH-- THAT'S OKAY... HE JUST KINDA... WHEWW !
BEAR PROTECTED HIS FAMILY BY BARKING AT STRANGERS, LIKE A GOOD GUARD DOG.
GRRRR
AND HE COULDN'T UNDERSTAND WHY HE ALWAYS GOT IN TROUBLE FOR IT.
HRH! HRH!
HRH! HRH!
HEY, BEAR!
TIME FER CHOW, BOY!

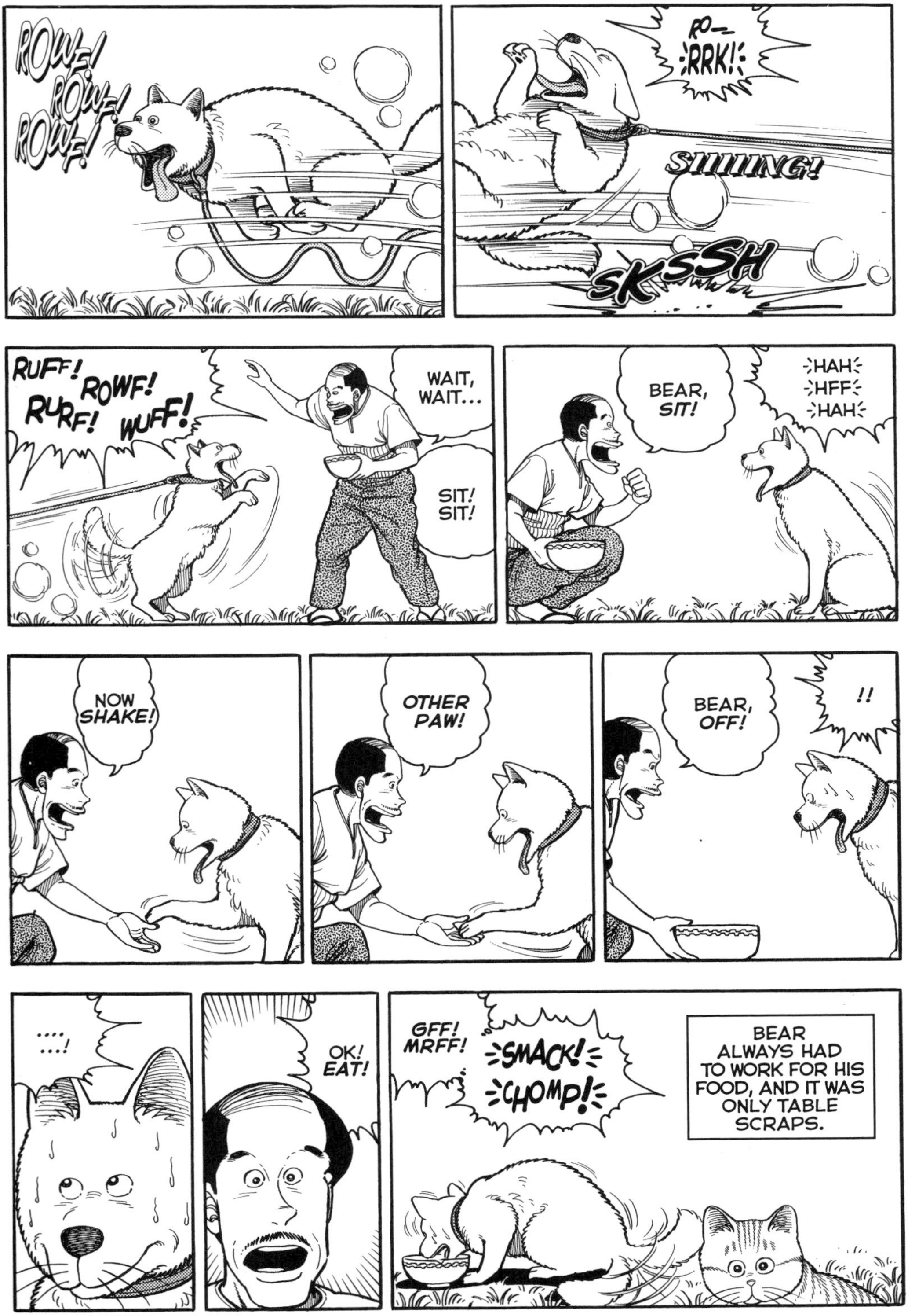
ROWF! ROWF! ROWF!
RO— RRK!
SHIIIING!
SKSSH
RUFF! ROWF! RURF! WUFF!
WAIT, WAIT...
SIT! SIT!
BEAR, SIT!
HAH HFF HAH
NOW SHAKE!
OTHER PAW!
BEAR, OFF!
!!
....
...!
OK! EAT!
GFF! MRFF!
SMACK!
CHOMP!
BEAR ALWAYS HAD TO WORK FOR HIS FOOD, AND IT WAS ONLY TABLE SCRAPS.

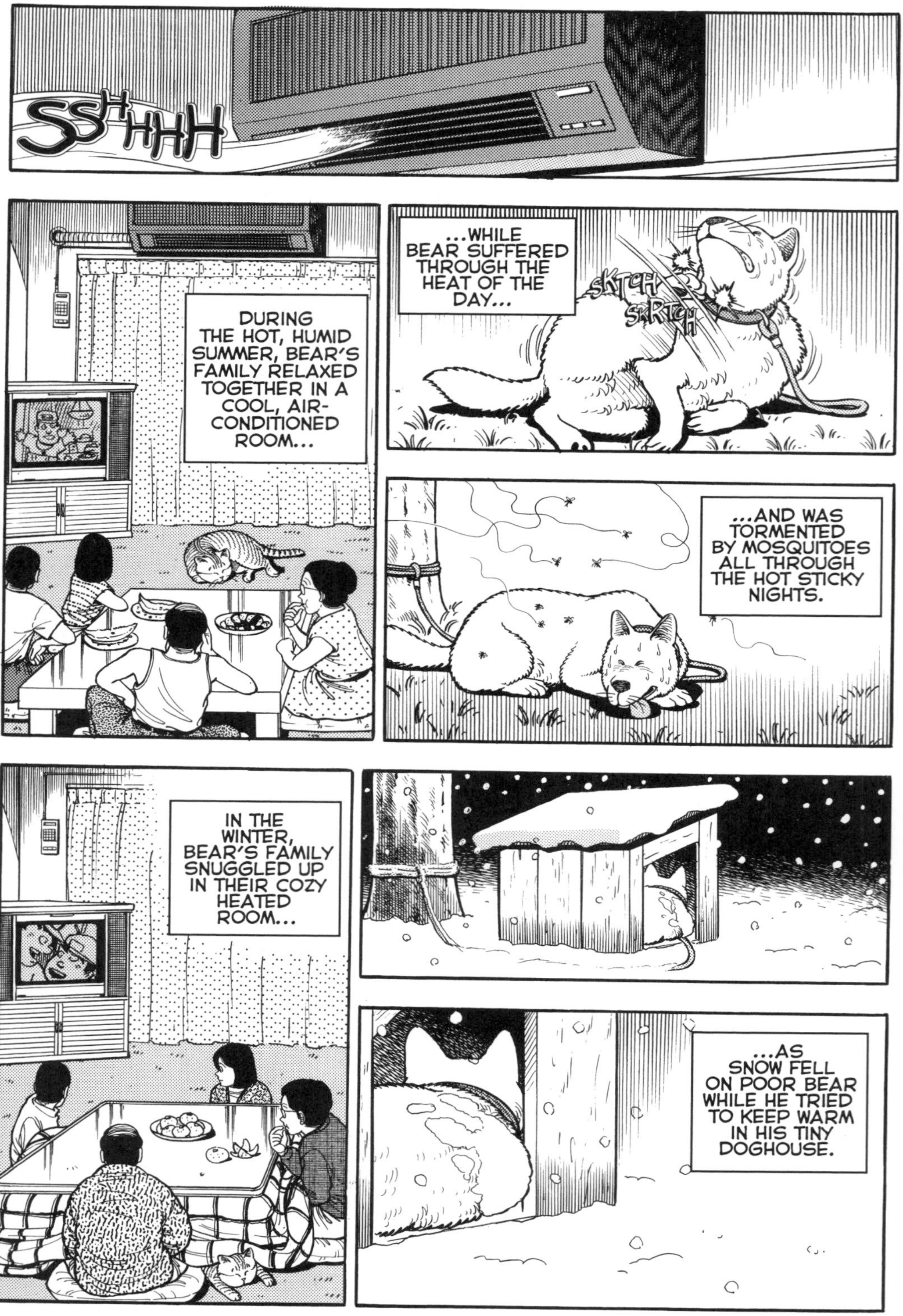
SSHHHH
DURING THE HOT, HUMID SUMMER, BEAR'S FAMILY RELAXED TOGETHER IN A COOL, AIR-CONDITIONED ROOM...
...WHILE BEAR SUFFERED THROUGH THE HEAT OF THE DAY...
SKTCH
SKRTCH
...AND WAS TORMENTED BY MOSQUITOES ALL THROUGH THE HOT STICKY NIGHTS.
IN THE WINTER, BEAR'S FAMILY SNUGGLED UP IN THEIR COZY HEATED ROOM...
...AS SNOW FELL ON POOR BEAR WHILE HE TRIED TO KEEP WARM IN HIS TINY DOGHOUSE.

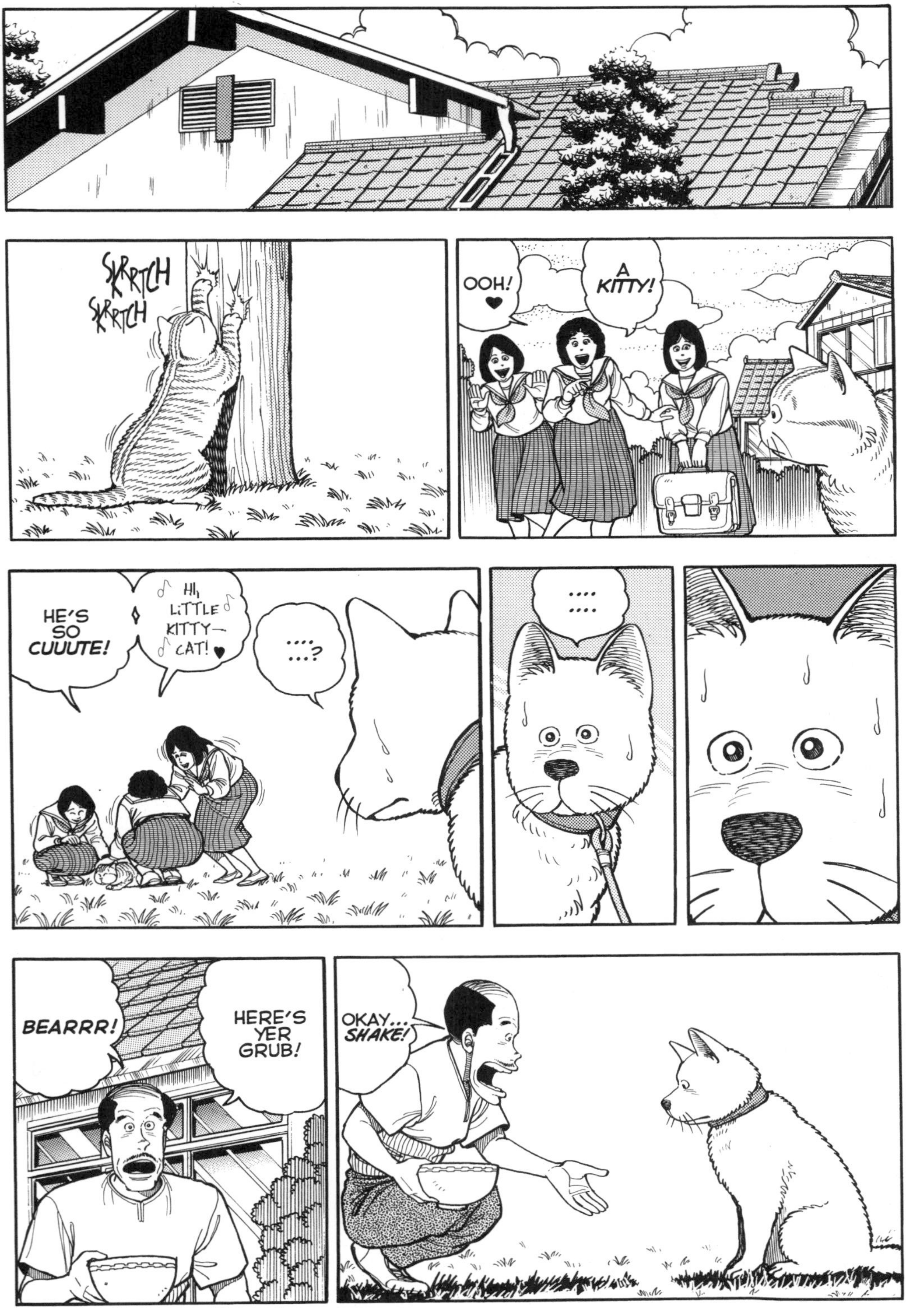
SKRRTCH
SKRRTCH
OOH! ♥
A KITTY!
HE'S SO CUUUTE!
HI, LITTLE KITTY-CAT! ♥
....
...?
....
....
BEARRR!
HERE'S YER GRUB!
OKAY... SHAKE!

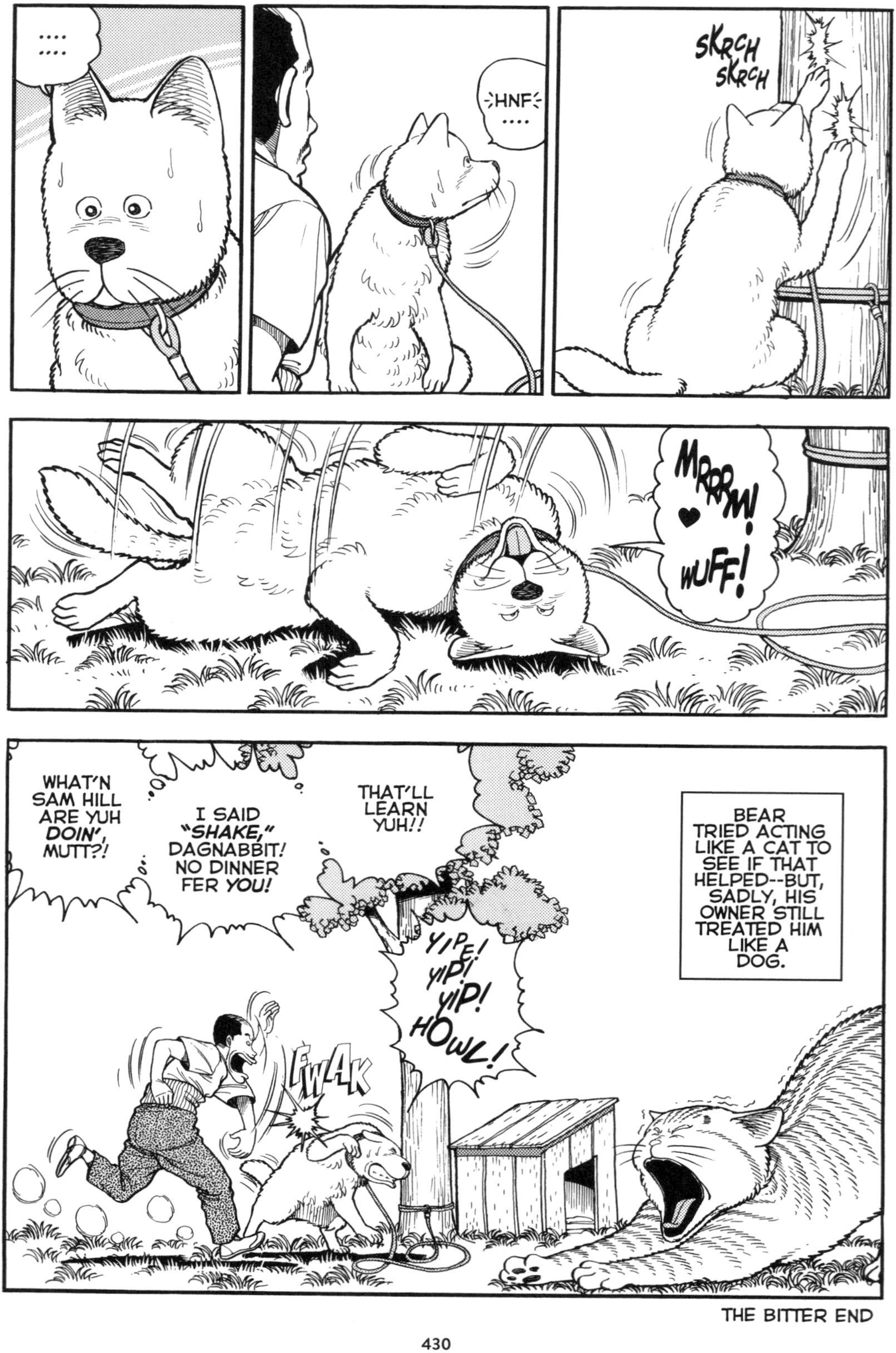

....
....
HNF
....
SKRCH
SKRCH
MRRRAW!
♥
WUFF!
WHAT'N SAM HILL ARE YUH DOIN', MUTT?!
I SAID "SHAKE," DAGNABBIT! NO DINNER FER YOU!
THAT'LL LEARN YUH!!
BEAR TRIED ACTING LIKE A CAT TO SEE IF THAT HELPED--BUT, SADLY, HIS OWNER STILL TREATED HIM LIKE A DOG.
YIPE! YIP! YIP! HOWL!
FWAK


THE BITTER END

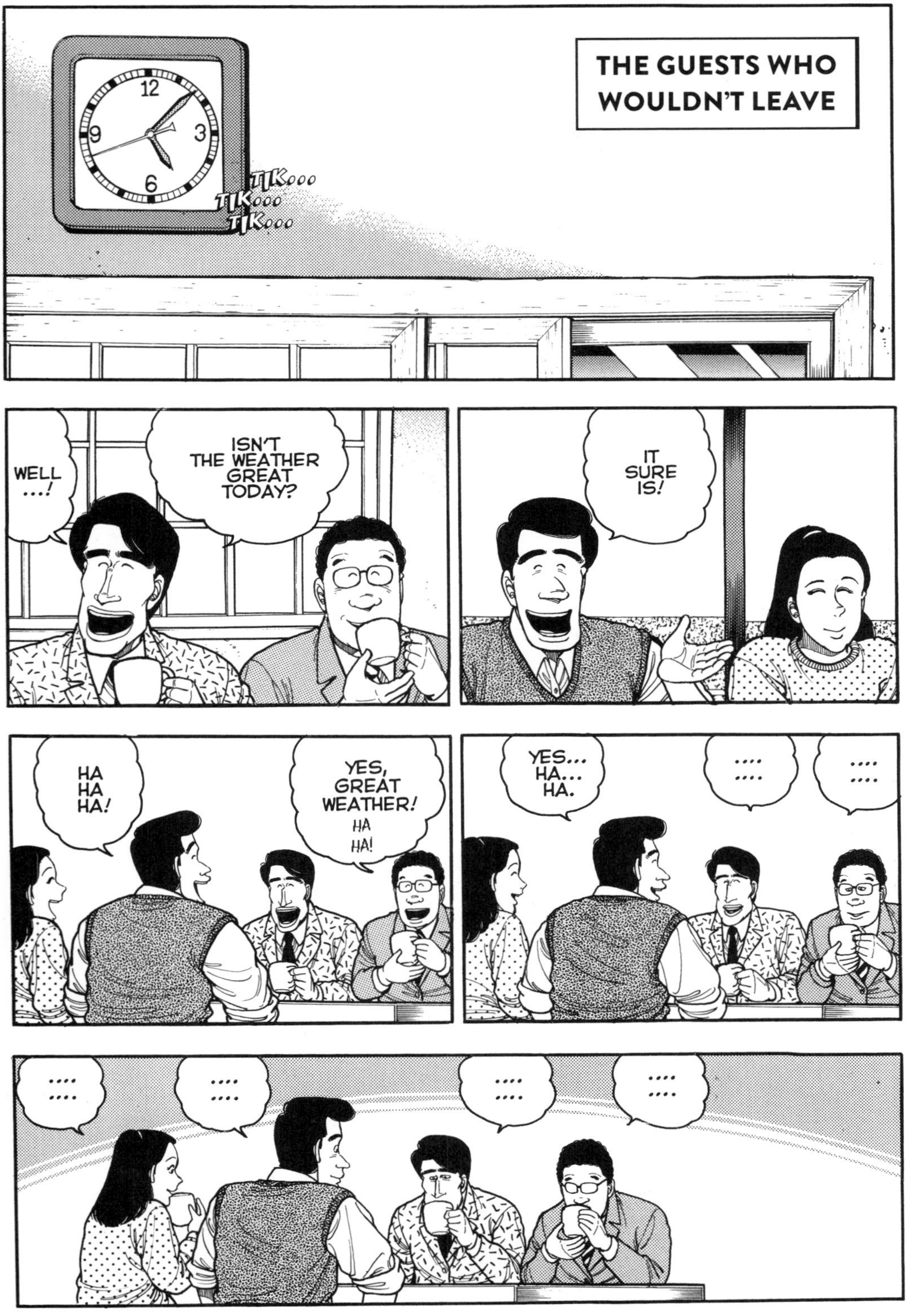
THE GUESTS WHO WOULDN'T LEAVE
TIKooo
TIKooo
TIKooo
WELL ...!
ISN'T THE WEATHER GREAT TODAY?
IT SURE IS!
HA HA HA!
YES, GREAT WEATHER!
HA HA!
YES... HA... HA.
.... ....
.... ....
.... ....
.... ....
.... ....
.... ....

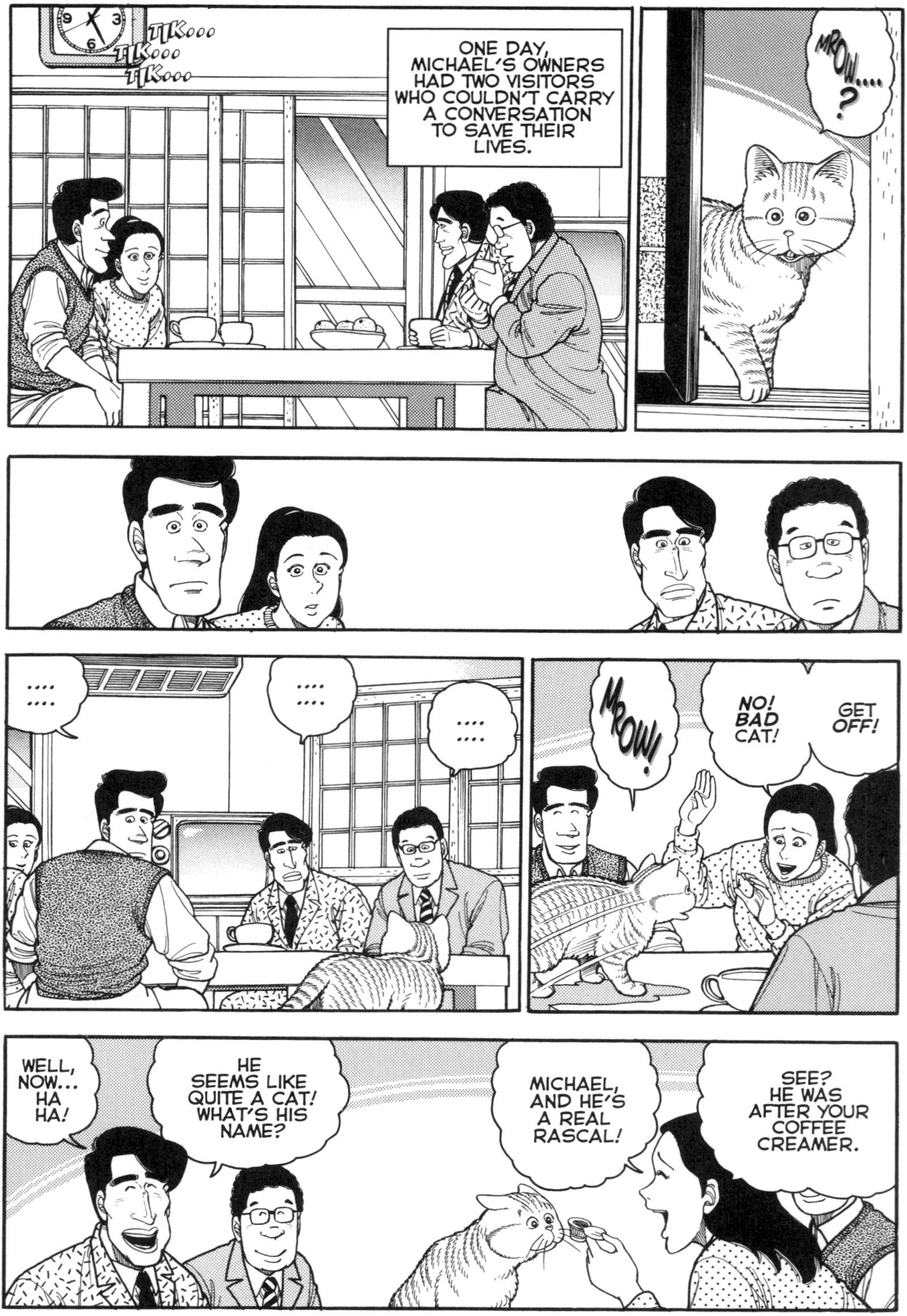
TIK...
TIK...
TIK...
ONE DAY, MICHAEL'S OWNERS HAD TWO VISITORS WHO COULDN'T CARRY A CONVERSATION TO SAVE THEIR LIVES.
MROW....?
........
........
........
MROW!
NO! BAD CAT!
GET OFF!
WELL, NOW... HA HA!
HE SEEMS LIKE QUITE A CAT! WHAT'S HIS NAME?
MICHAEL, AND HE'S A REAL RASCAL!
SEE? HE WAS AFTER YOUR COFFEE CREAMER.

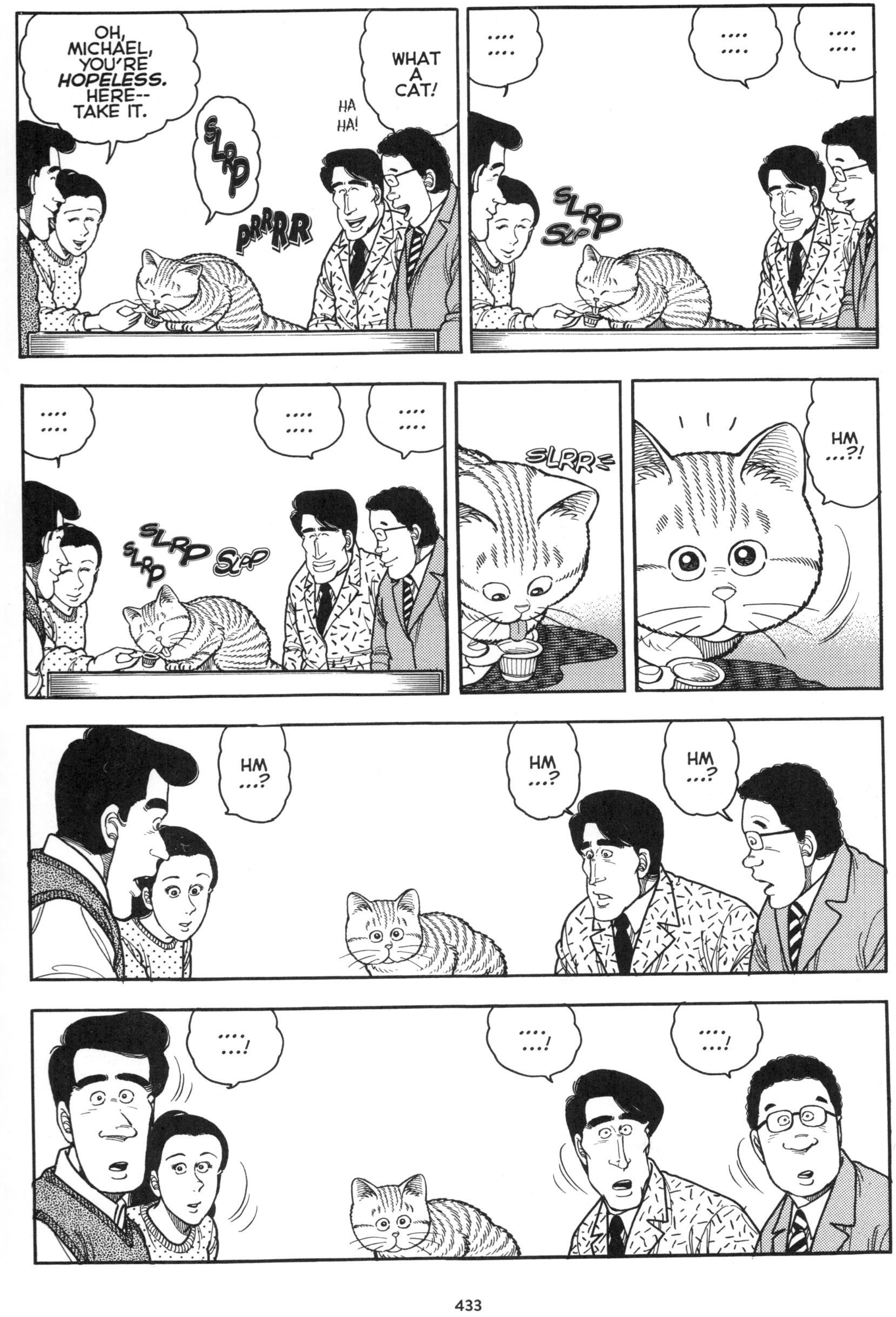
OH, MICHAEL, YOU'RE **HOPELESS.** HERE-- TAKE IT.
SLRP
PRRRRR
HA HA!
WHAT A CAT!
.... ....
.... ....
.... ....
SLRP SLRP
.... ....
.... ....
.... ....
SLRP SLRP SLRP
SLRR
HM ...?!
HM ...?
HM ...?
HM ...?
...., ...!
...., ...!
...., ...!

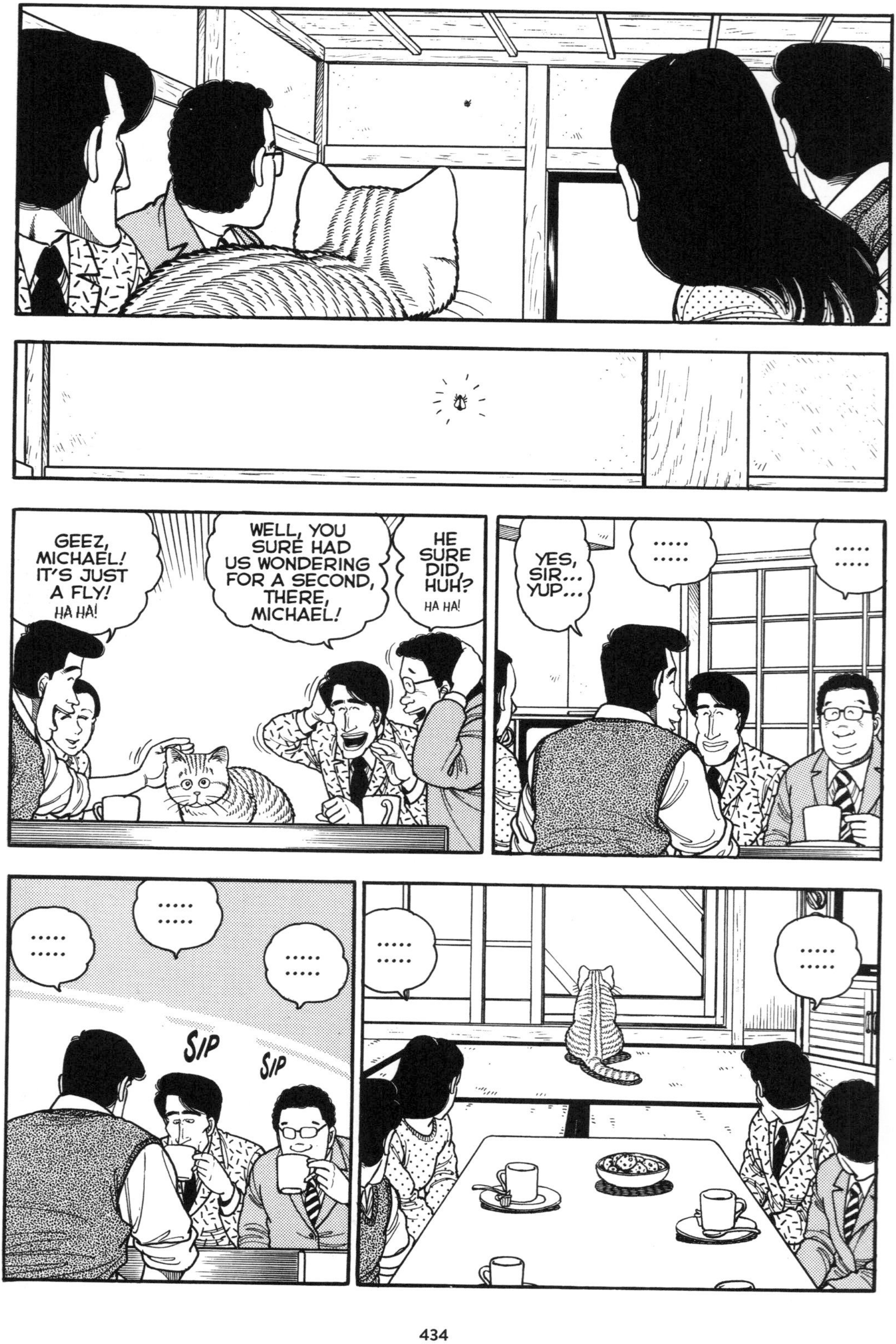
GEEZ, MICHAEL! IT'S JUST A FLY!
HA HA!
WELL, YOU SURE HAD US WONDERING FOR A SECOND, THERE, MICHAEL!
HE SURE DID, HUH?
HA HA!
YES, SIR... YUP...
.....
.....
.....
.....
.....
.....
.....
.....
.....
.....
SIP
SIP
.....
.....
.....
.....

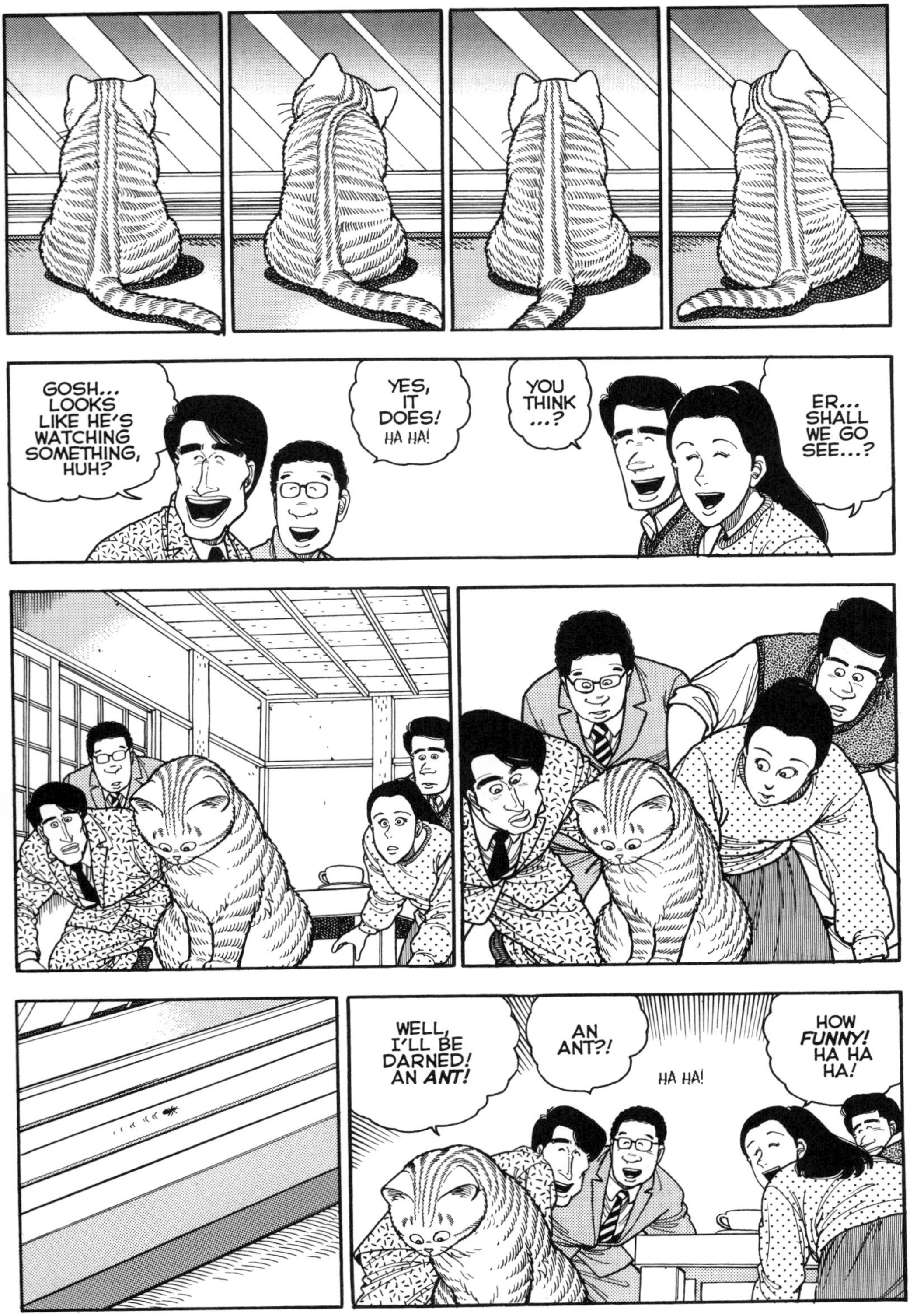
GOSH... LOOKS LIKE HE'S WATCHING SOMETHING, HUH?
YES, IT DOES!
HA HA!
YOU THINK ...?
ER... SHALL WE GO SEE...?
WELL, I'LL BE DARNED! AN *ANT*!
AN ANT?!
HA HA!
HOW *FUNNY*! HA HA HA!

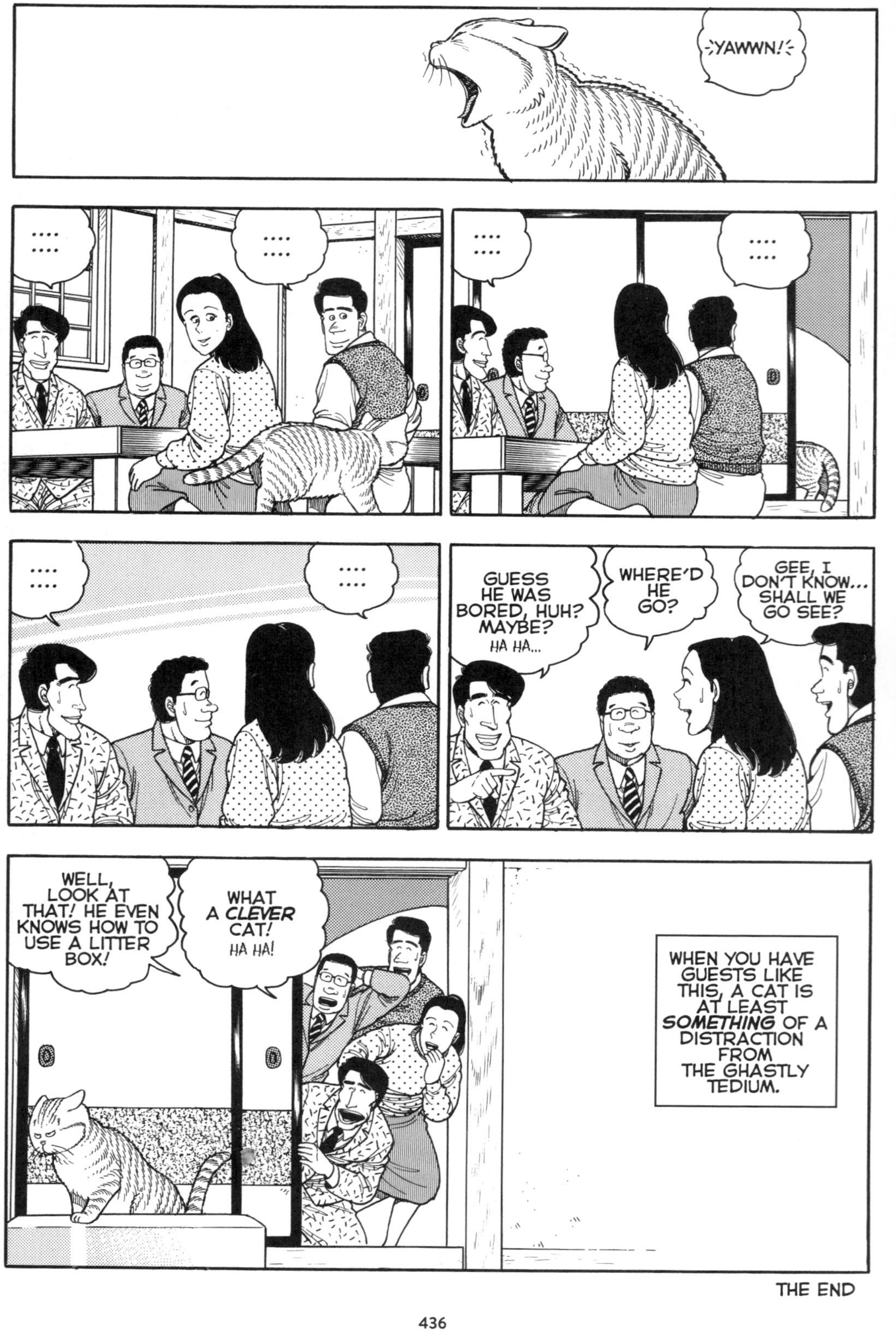
YAWWN!
.... ....
.... ....
.... ....
.... ....
.... ....
.... ....
GUESS HE WAS BORED, HUH? MAYBE? HA HA...
WHERE'D HE GO?
GEE, I DON'T KNOW... SHALL WE GO SEE?
WELL, LOOK AT THAT! HE EVEN KNOWS HOW TO USE A LITTER BOX!
WHAT A *CLEVER* CAT! HA HA!
WHEN YOU HAVE GUESTS LIKE THIS, A CAT IS AT LEAST *SOMETHING* OF A DISTRACTION FROM THE GHASTLY TEDIUM.

THE END

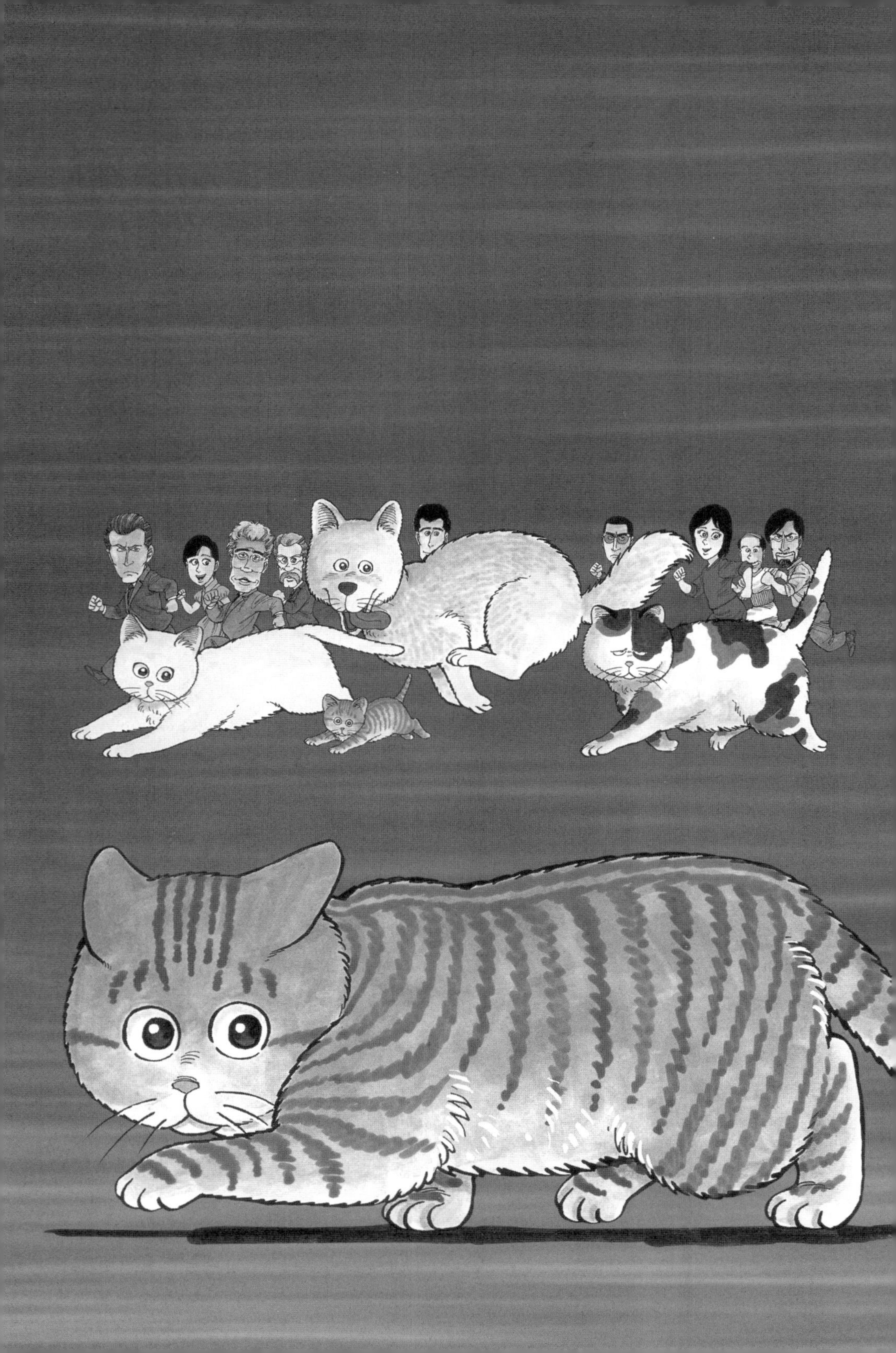

# WHAT'S MICHAEL?

## VOLUME 6: A HARD DAY'S LIFE

This section was translated by Dana Lewis and
Lea Seidman and lettered by Amador Cisneros.

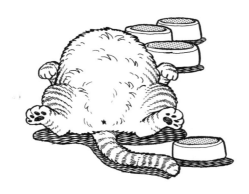

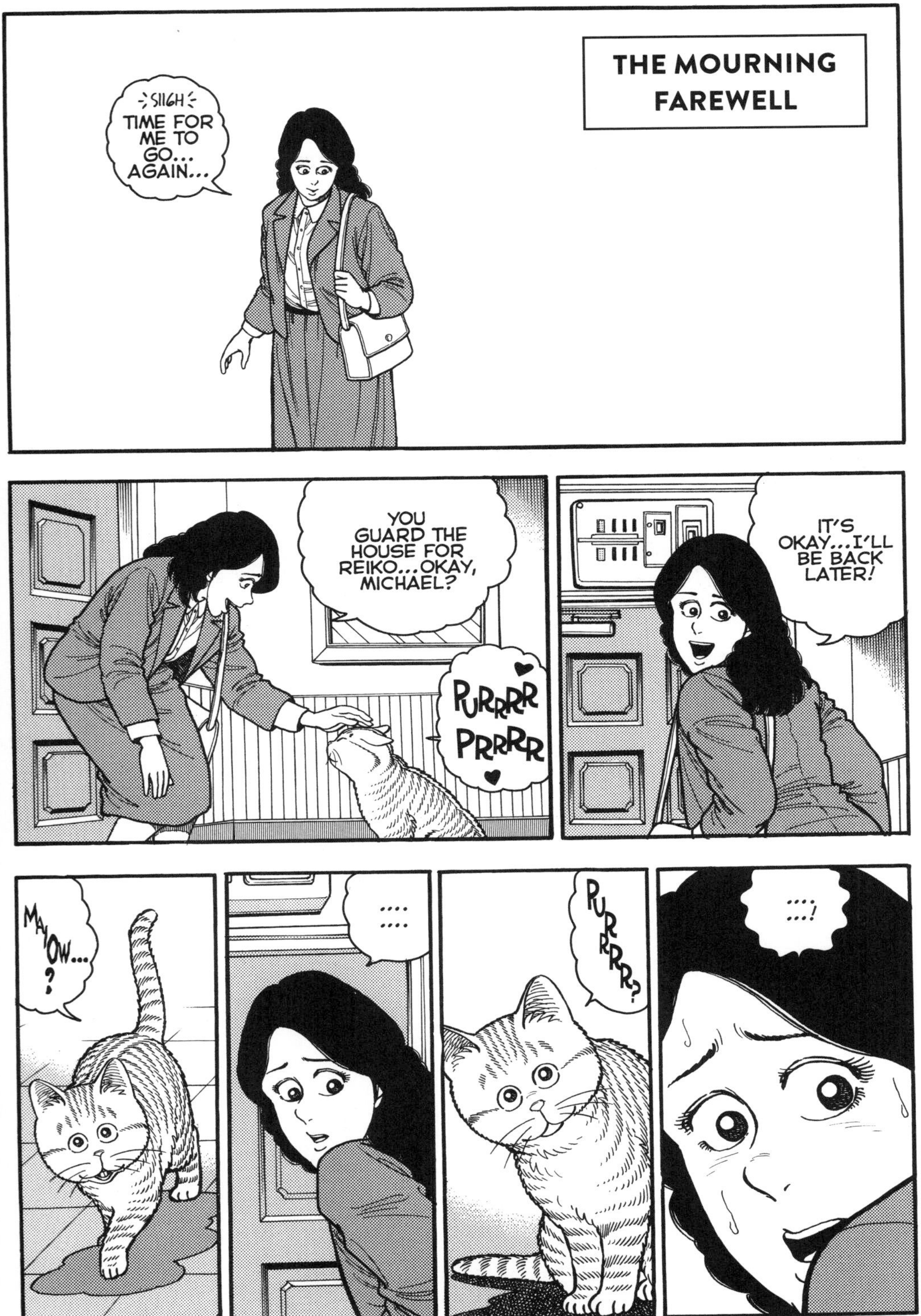
THE MOURNING FAREWELL
SIIGH
TIME FOR ME TO GO... AGAIN...
YOU GUARD THE HOUSE FOR REIKO...OKAY, MICHAEL?
PURRRR PRRRR
IT'S OKAY...I'LL BE BACK LATER!
MAIOW...?
PURRRR?

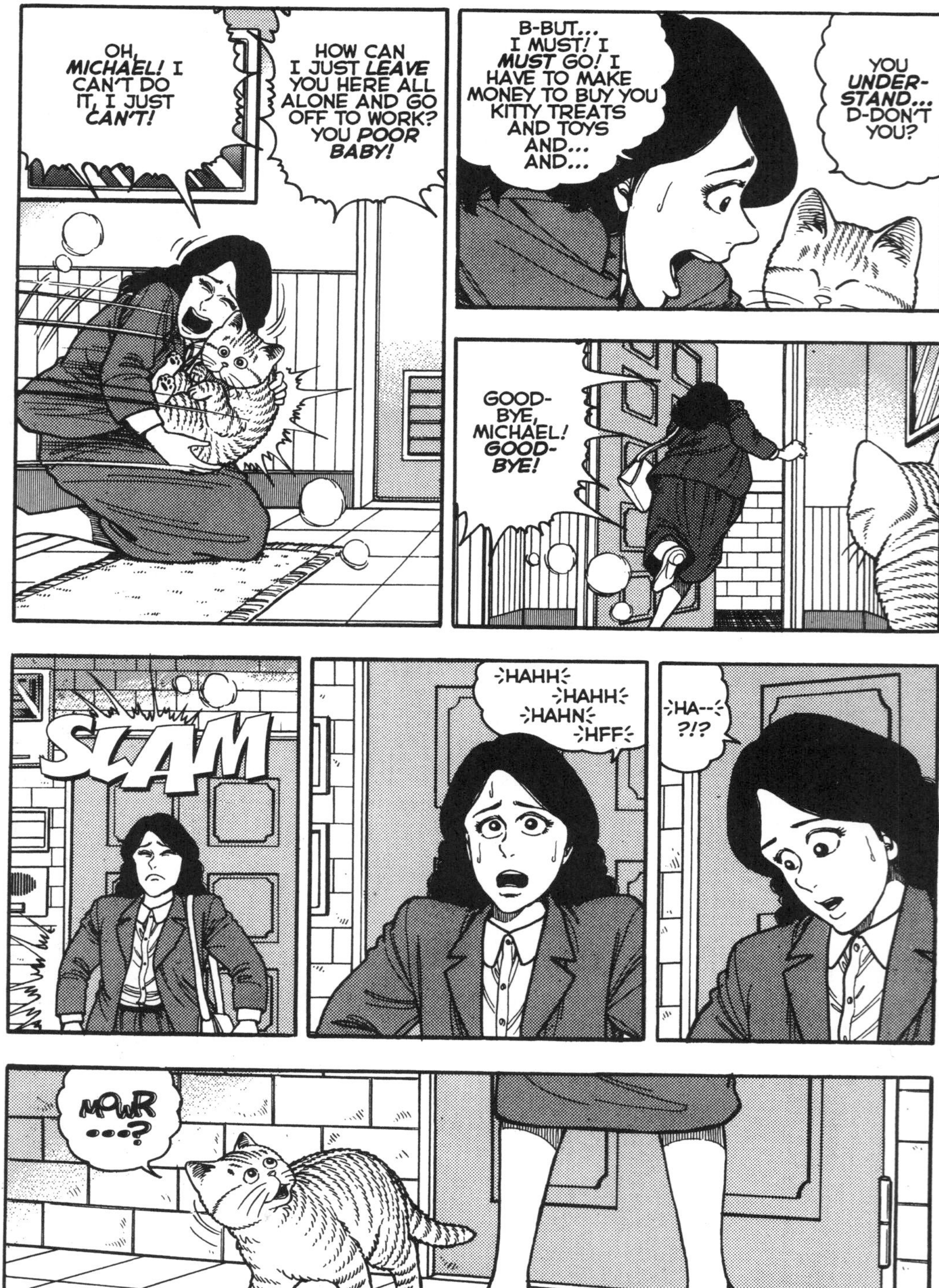
OH, MICHAEL! I CAN'T DO IT, I JUST CAN'T!
HOW CAN I JUST LEAVE YOU HERE ALL ALONE AND GO OFF TO WORK? YOU POOR BABY!
B-BUT... I MUST! I MUST GO! I HAVE TO MAKE MONEY TO BUY YOU KITTY TREATS AND TOYS AND... AND...
YOU UNDERSTAND... D-DON'T YOU?
GOOD-BYE, MICHAEL! GOOD-BYE!
SLAM
HAHH HAHH HAHN HFF
HA-- ?!?
MOWR ...?

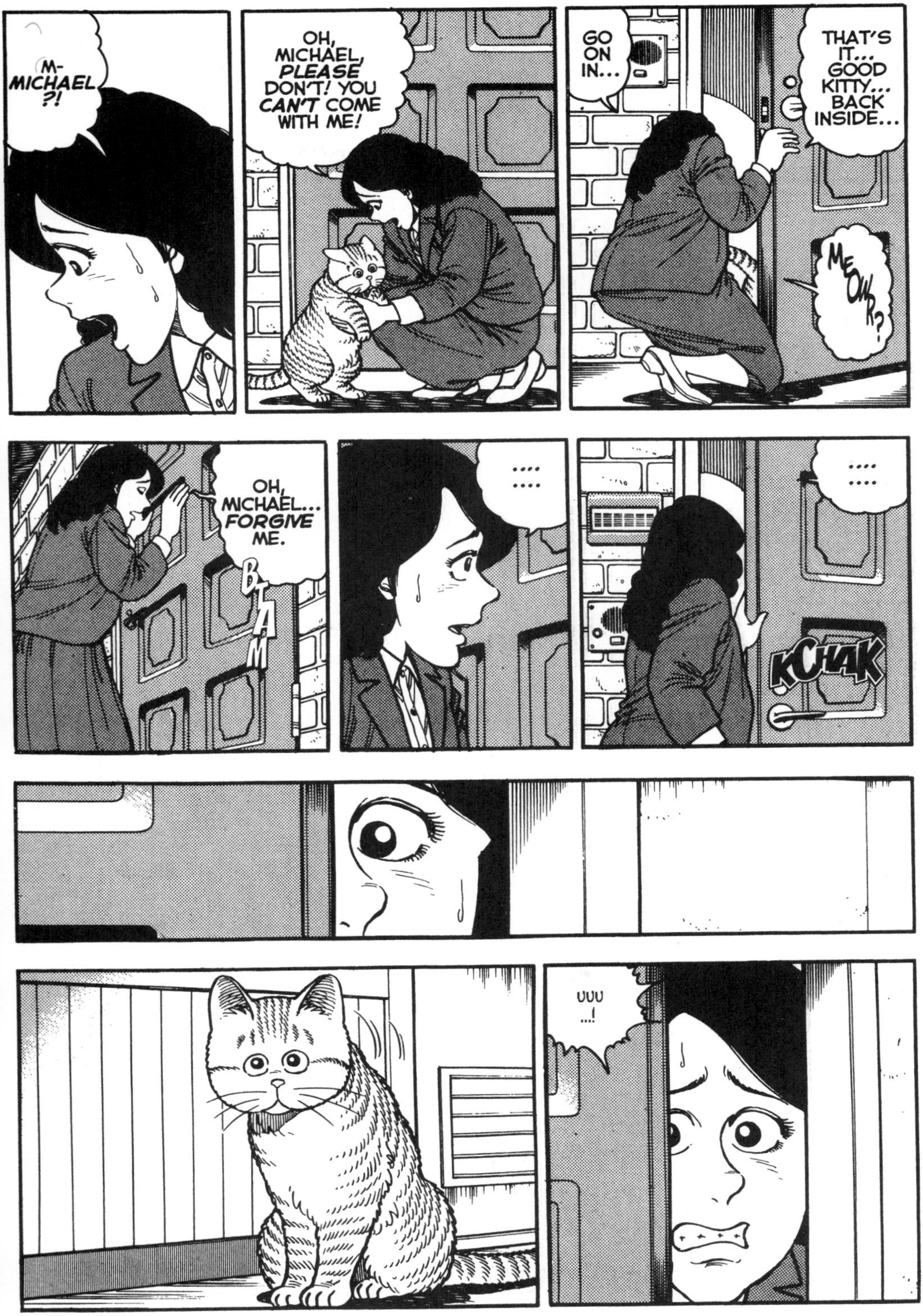
M-MICHAEL?!
OH, MICHAEL, PLEASE DON'T! YOU CAN'T COME WITH ME!
GO ON IN...
THAT'S IT... GOOD KITTY... BACK INSIDE...
MEOWR?
OH, MICHAEL... FORGIVE ME.
BLAM
....
....
....
....
KCHAK
UUU
...!

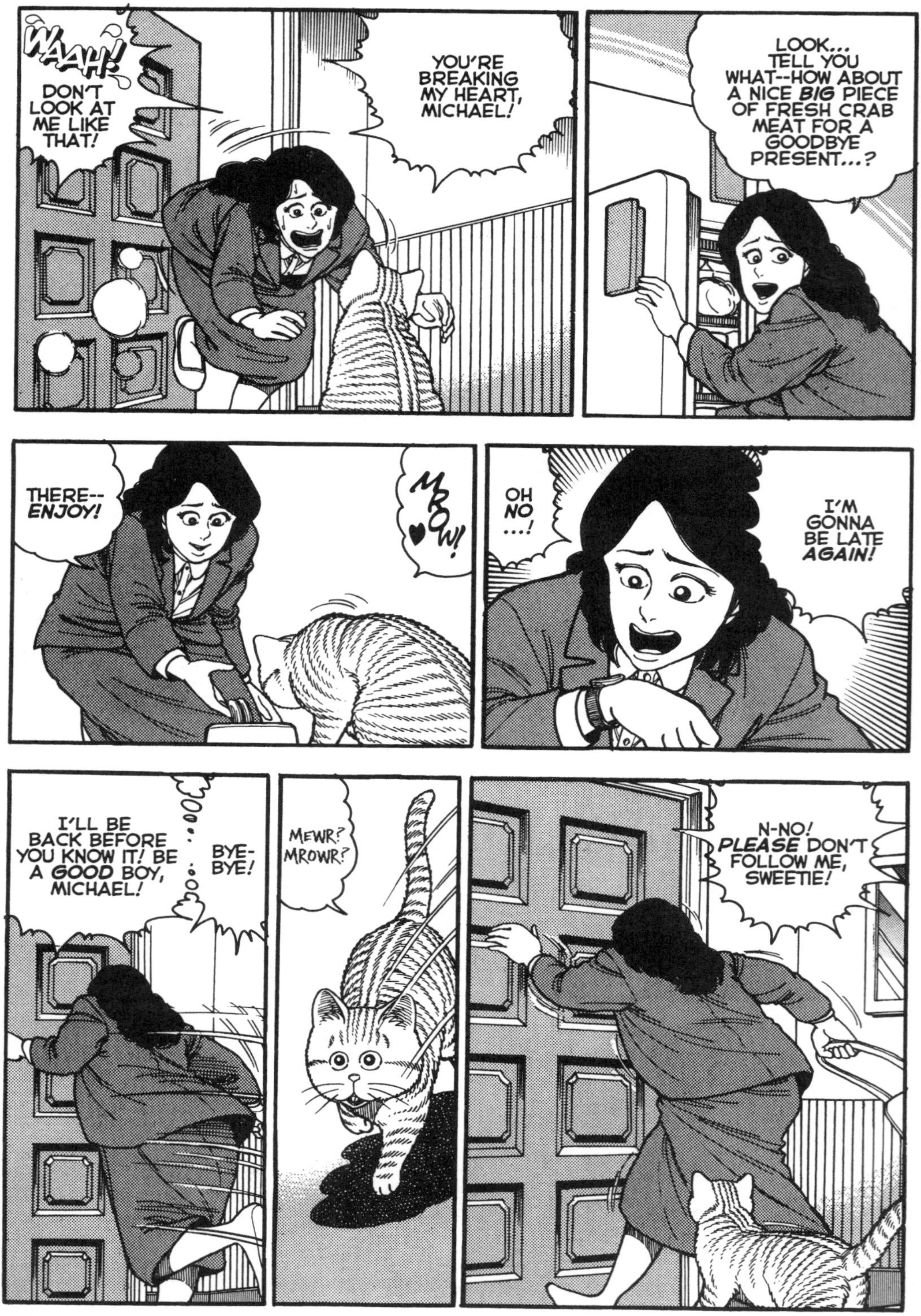

WAAH!
DON'T LOOK AT ME LIKE THAT!
YOU'RE BREAKING MY HEART, MICHAEL!
LOOK... TELL YOU WHAT--HOW ABOUT A NICE BIG PIECE OF FRESH CRAB MEAT FOR A GOODBYE PRESENT...?
THERE-- ENJOY!
MROW!
OH NO ...!
I'M GONNA BE LATE AGAIN!
I'LL BE BACK BEFORE YOU KNOW IT! BE A GOOD BOY, MICHAEL!
BYE-BYE!
MEWR? MROWR?
N-NO! PLEASE DON'T FOLLOW ME, SWEETIE!

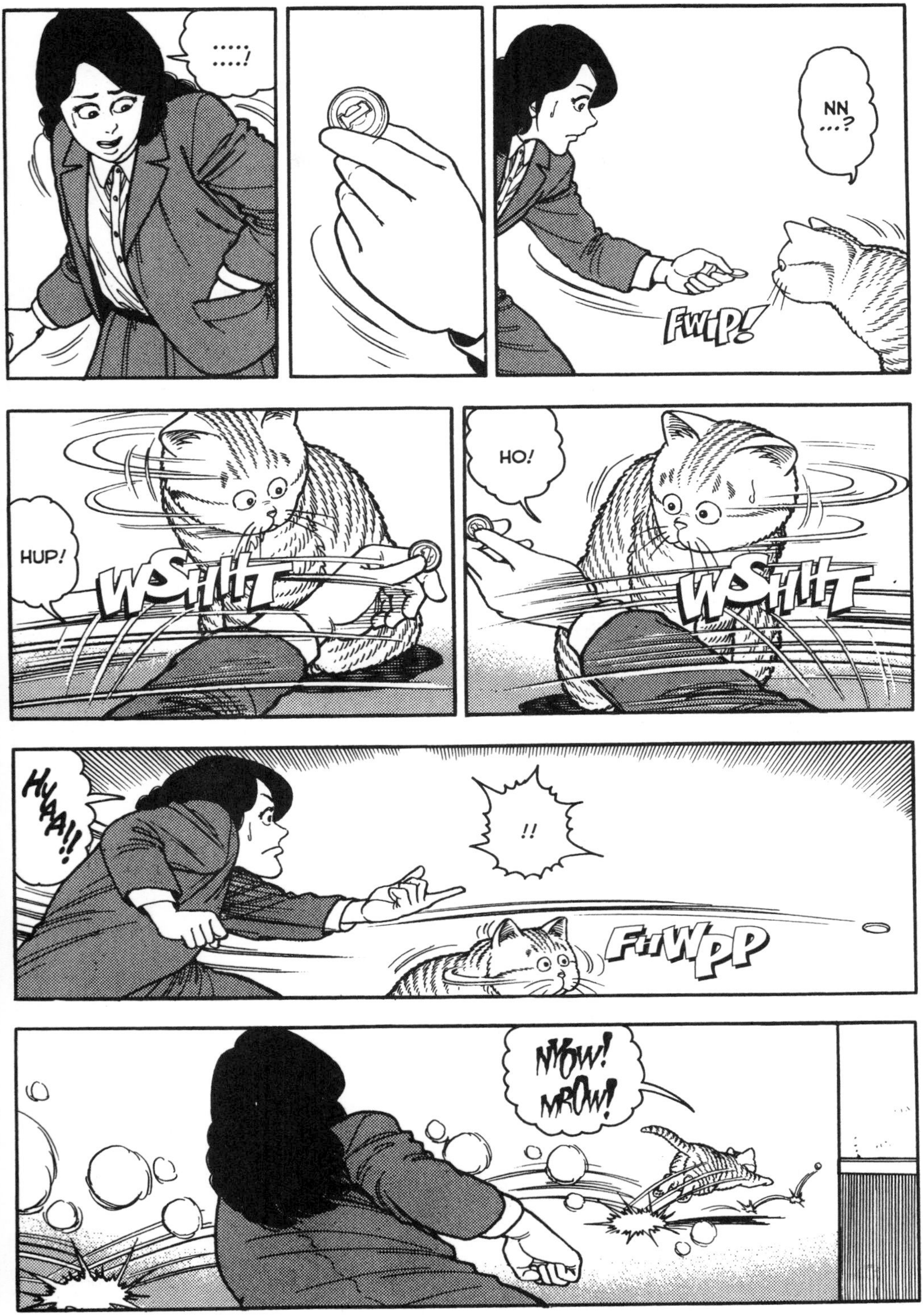
.....
.....!
NN
...?
FWIP!
HUP!
WSHHT
HO!
WSHHT
HYAA!!
!!
FHWPP
NYOW!
MROW!

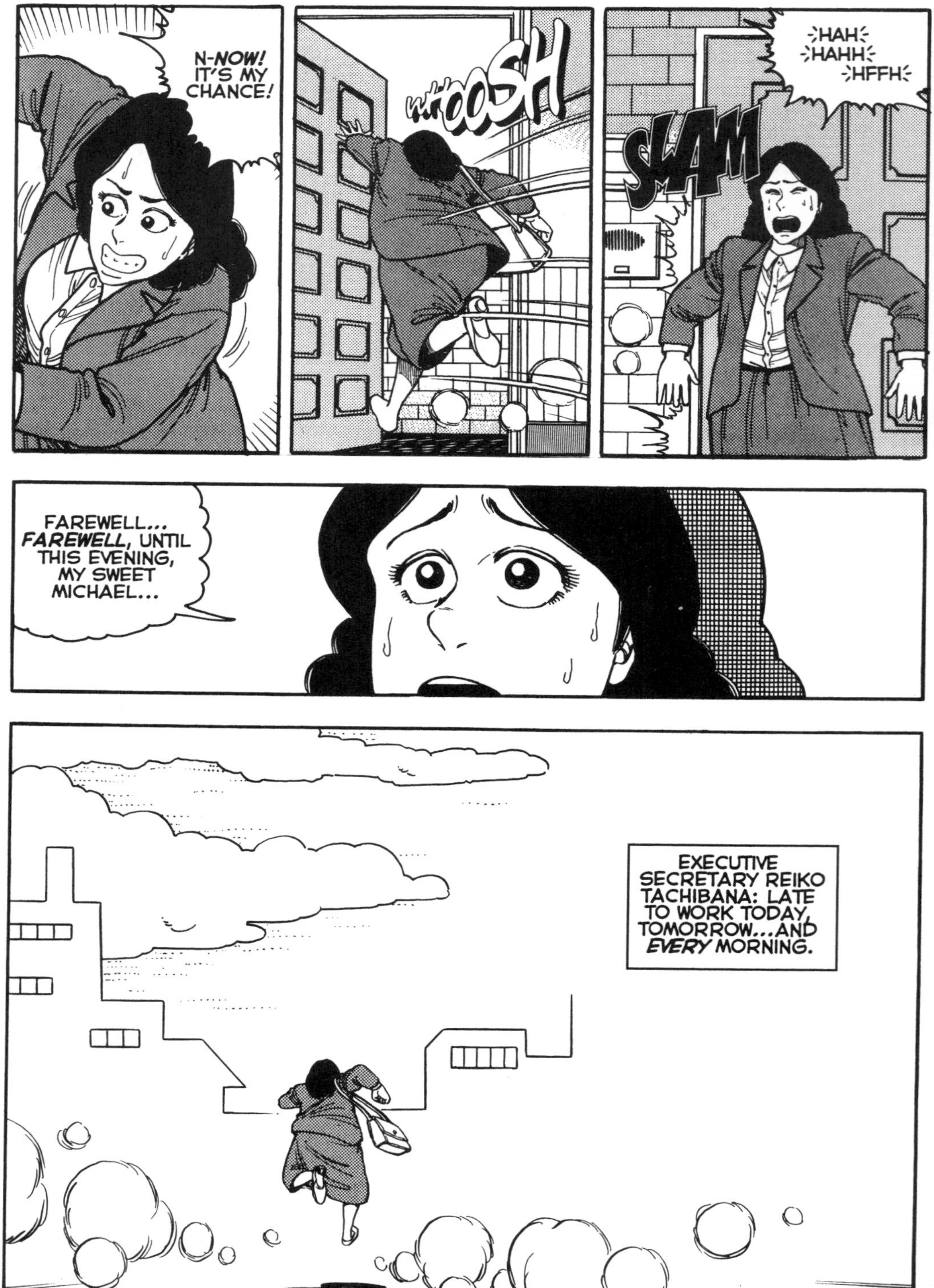
N-NOW! IT'S MY CHANCE!
WHOOSH
SLAM
HAH HAHH HFFH
FAREWELL... FAREWELL, UNTIL THIS EVENING, MY SWEET MICHAEL...
EXECUTIVE SECRETARY REIKO TACHIBANA: LATE TO WORK TODAY, TOMORROW...AND EVERY MORNING.

THE END

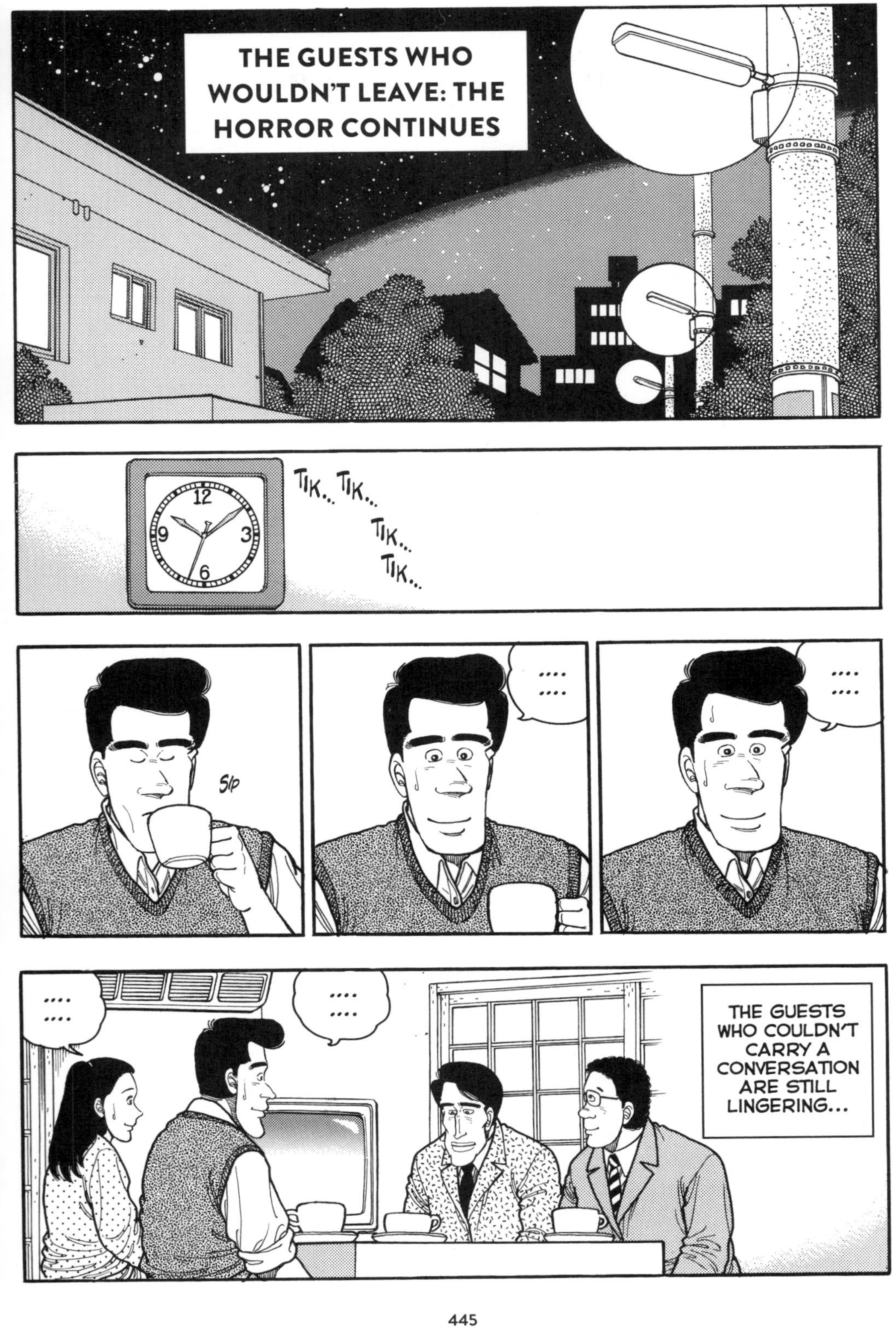

THE GUESTS WHO WOULDN'T LEAVE: THE HORROR CONTINUES
12
9
3
6
TIK... TIK...
TIK...
TIK...
SIP
.... ....
.... ....
.... ....
.... ....
THE GUESTS WHO COULDN'T CARRY A CONVERSATION ARE STILL LINGERING...

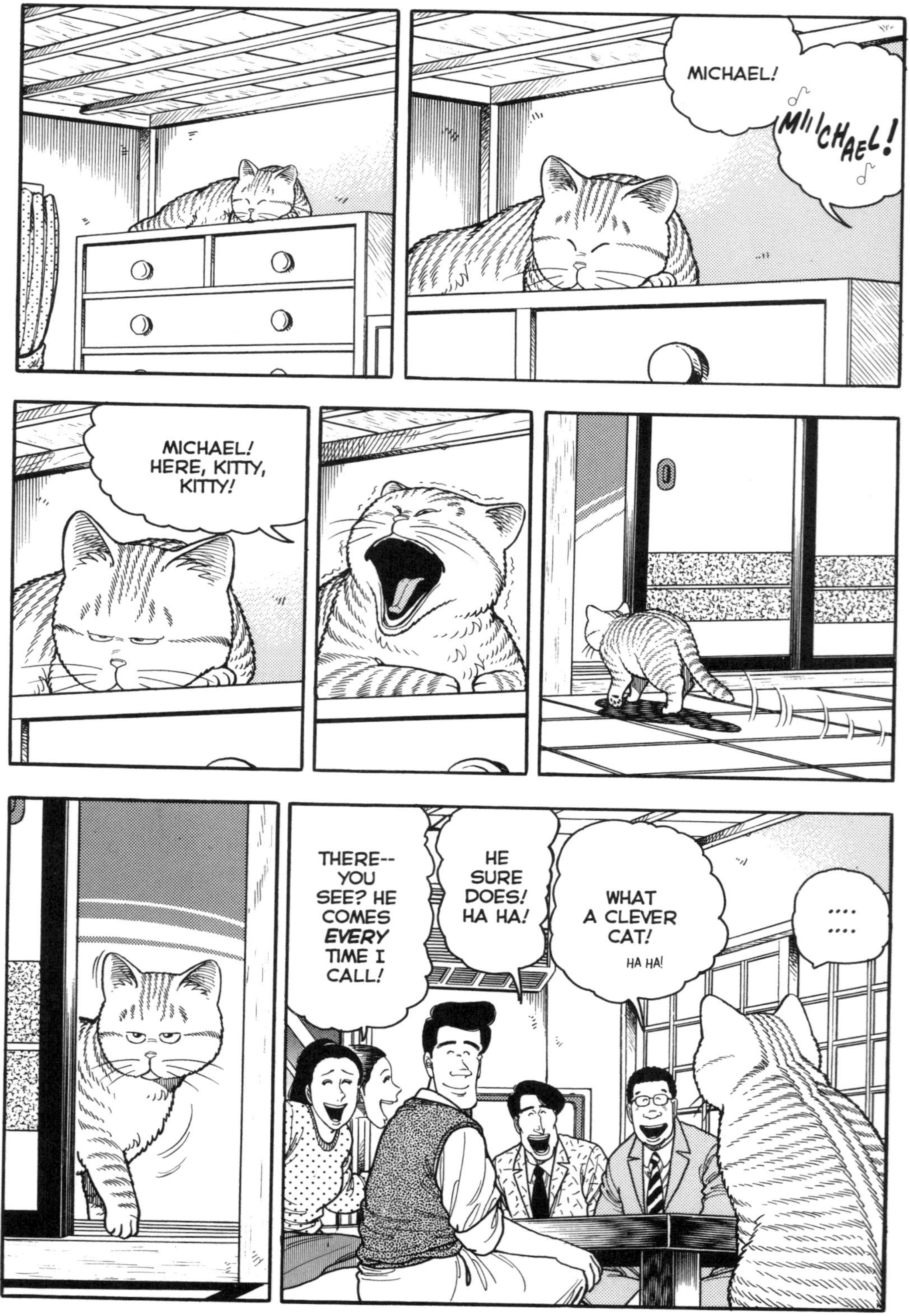
MICHAEL!
MIIICHAEL!
MICHAEL! HERE, KITTY, KITTY!
THERE-- YOU SEE? HE COMES *EVERY* TIME I CALL!
HE SURE DOES! HA HA!
WHAT A CLEVER CAT!
HA HA!
....
....

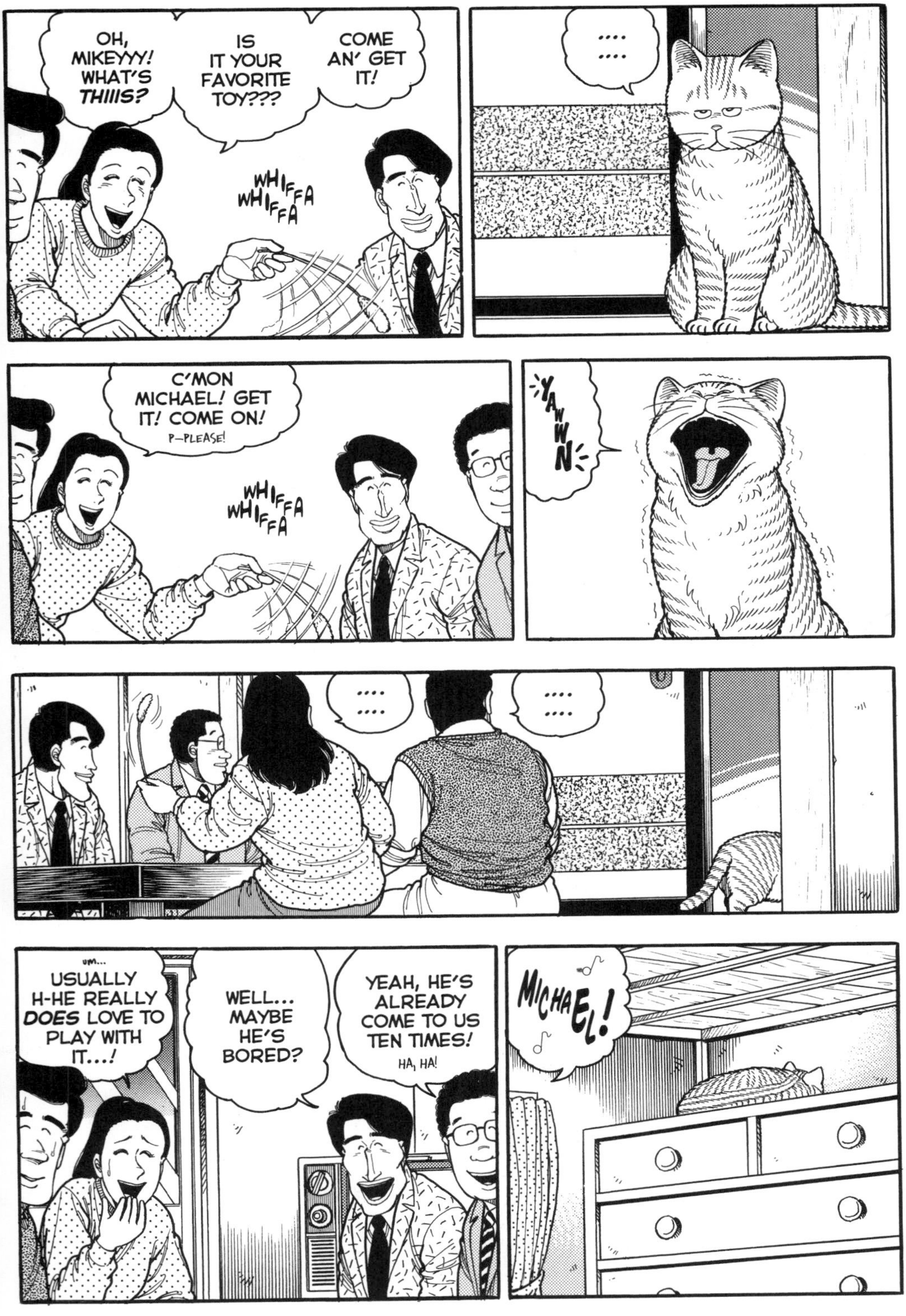
OH, MIKEYYY! WHAT'S THIIIS?
IS IT YOUR FAVORITE TOY???
COME AN' GET IT!
WHIFFA WHIFFA
....
....
C'MON MICHAEL! GET IT! COME ON!
P—PLEASE!
WHIFFA WHIFFA
YAWWN
....
....
....
....
um...
USUALLY H-HE REALLY DOES LOVE TO PLAY WITH IT...!
WELL... MAYBE HE'S BORED?
YEAH, HE'S ALREADY COME TO US TEN TIMES!
HA, HA!
MICHAEL!

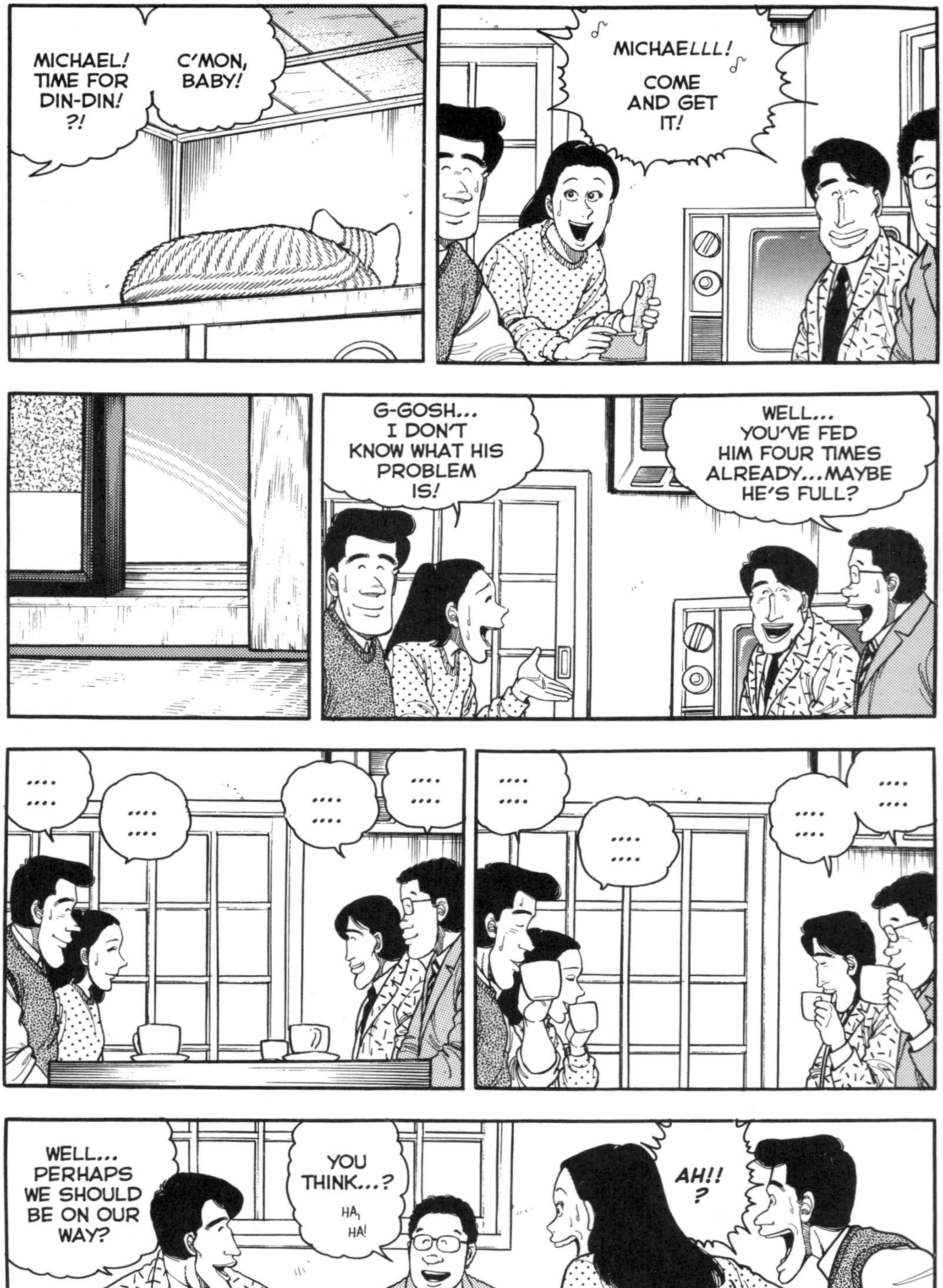
MICHAEL! TIME FOR DIN-DIN! ?!
C'MON, BABY!
MICHAELLL! COME AND GET IT!
G-GOSH... I DON'T KNOW WHAT HIS PROBLEM IS!
WELL... YOU'VE FED HIM FOUR TIMES ALREADY...MAYBE HE'S FULL?
....
....
....
....
....
....
....
....
....
....
....
....
....
....
....
....
WELL... PERHAPS WE SHOULD BE ON OUR WAY?
YOU THINK...?
HA, HA!
AH!! ?

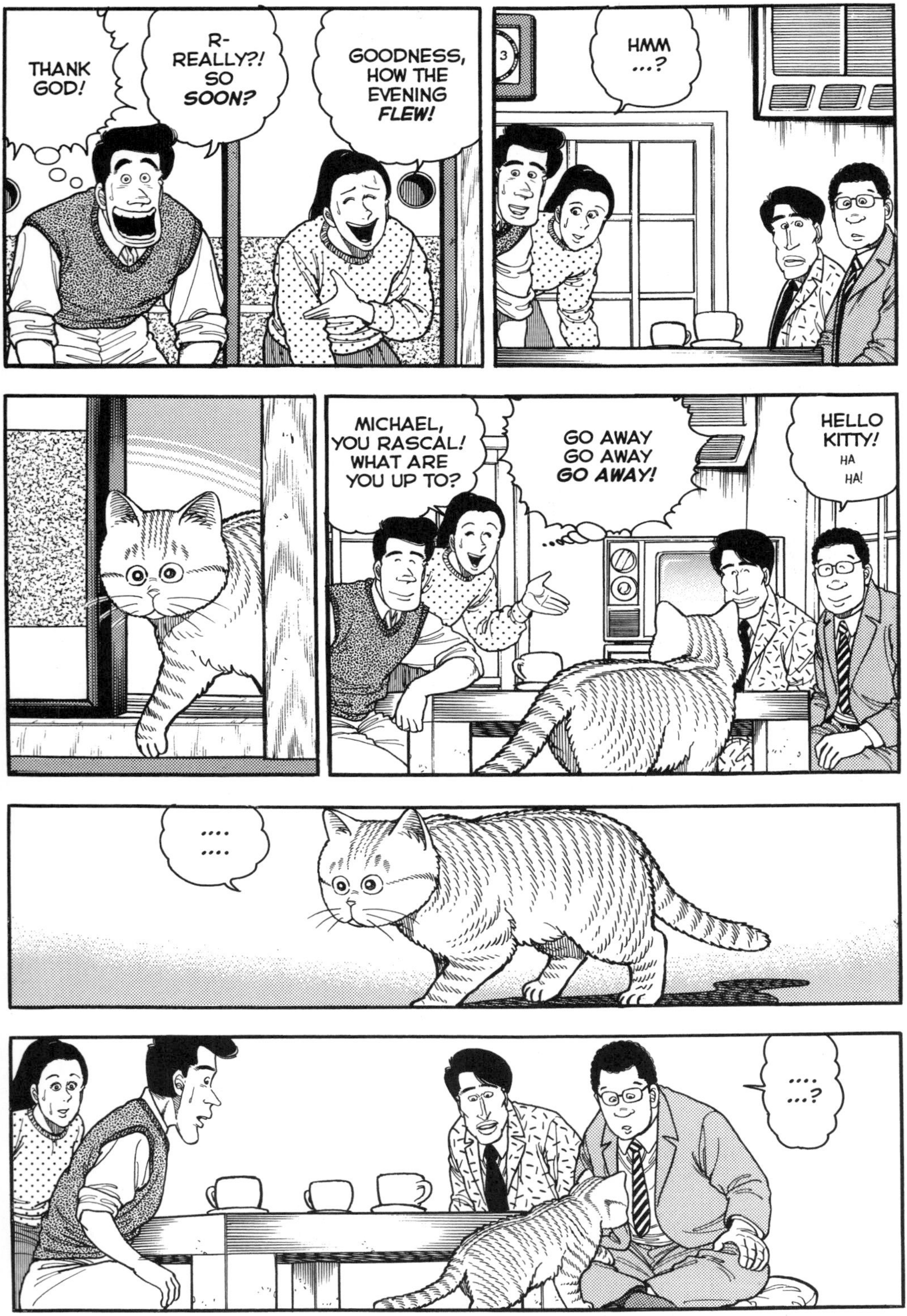
THANK GOD!
R- REALLY?! SO SOON?
GOODNESS, HOW THE EVENING FLEW!
HMM ...?
MICHAEL, YOU RASCAL! WHAT ARE YOU UP TO?
GO AWAY GO AWAY GO AWAY!
HELLO KITTY! HA HA!
.... ....
.... ...?

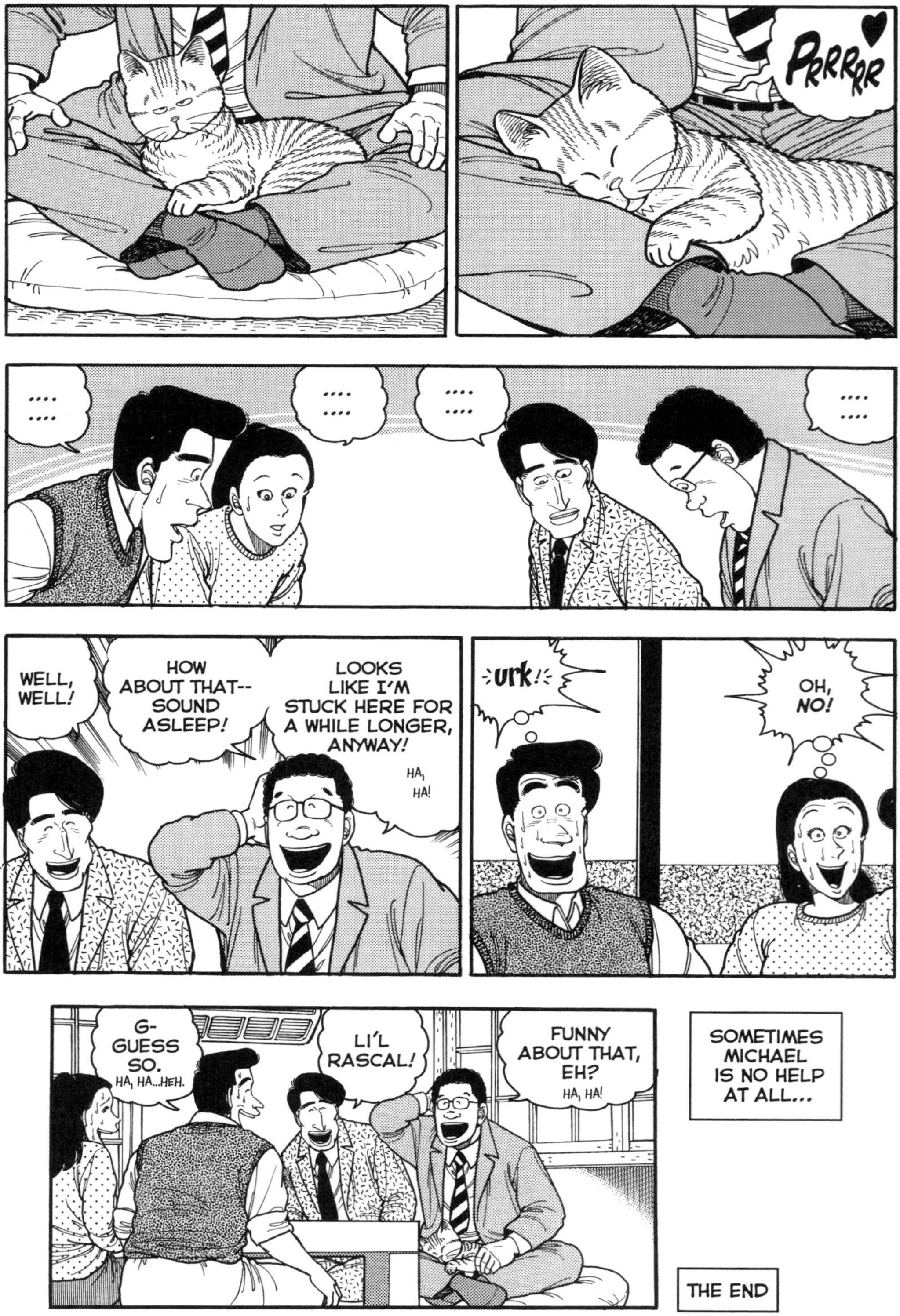
PRRRRR
....
....
....
....
....
....
....
....
WELL, WELL!
HOW ABOUT THAT-- SOUND ASLEEP!
LOOKS LIKE I'M STUCK HERE FOR A WHILE LONGER, ANYWAY!
HA, HA!
urk!
OH, NO!
G-GUESS SO.
HA, HA...HEH.
LI'L RASCAL!
FUNNY ABOUT THAT, EH?
HA, HA!
SOMETIMES MICHAEL IS NO HELP AT ALL...
THE END

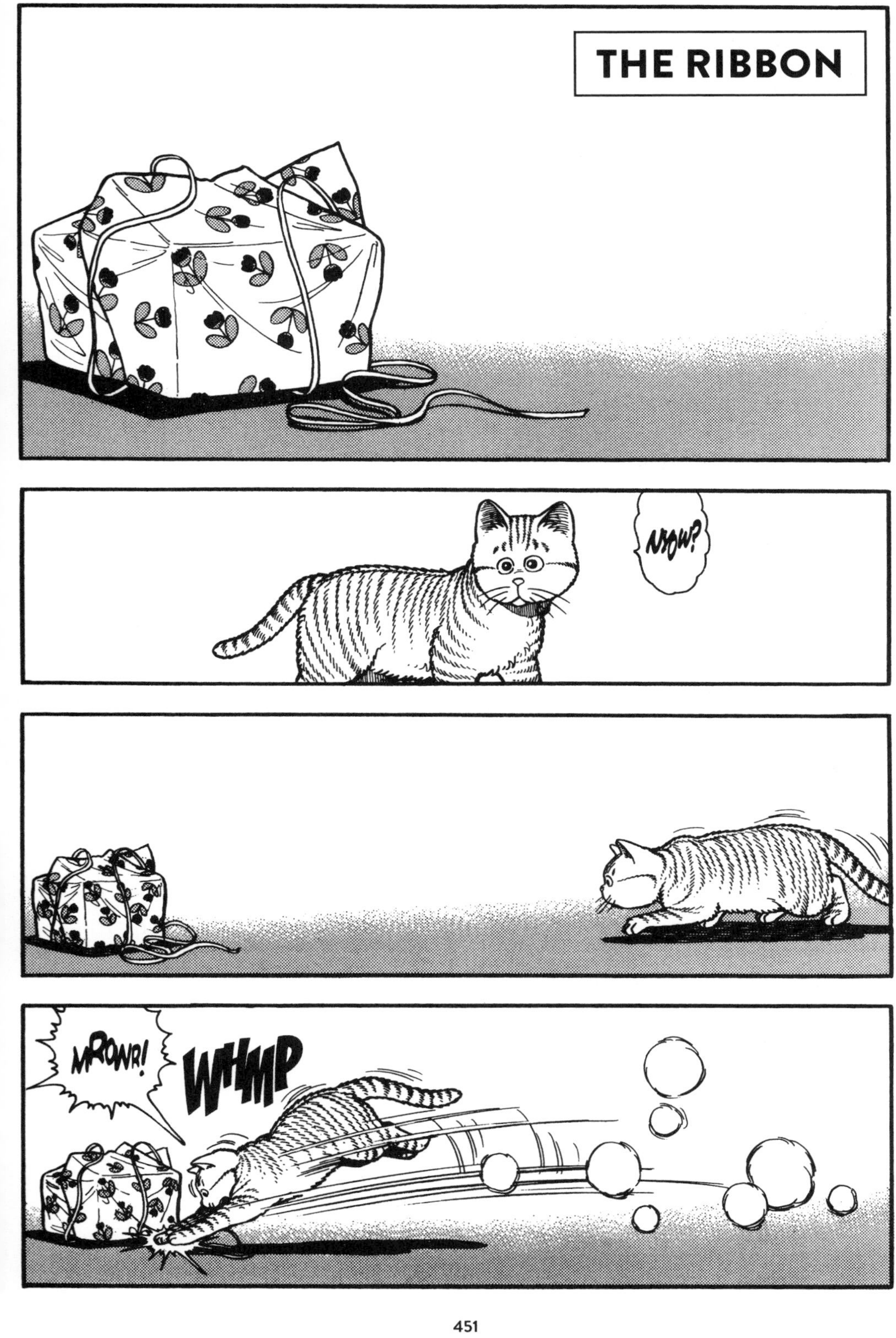
THE RIBBON
NYOW?
MROWR!
WHMP

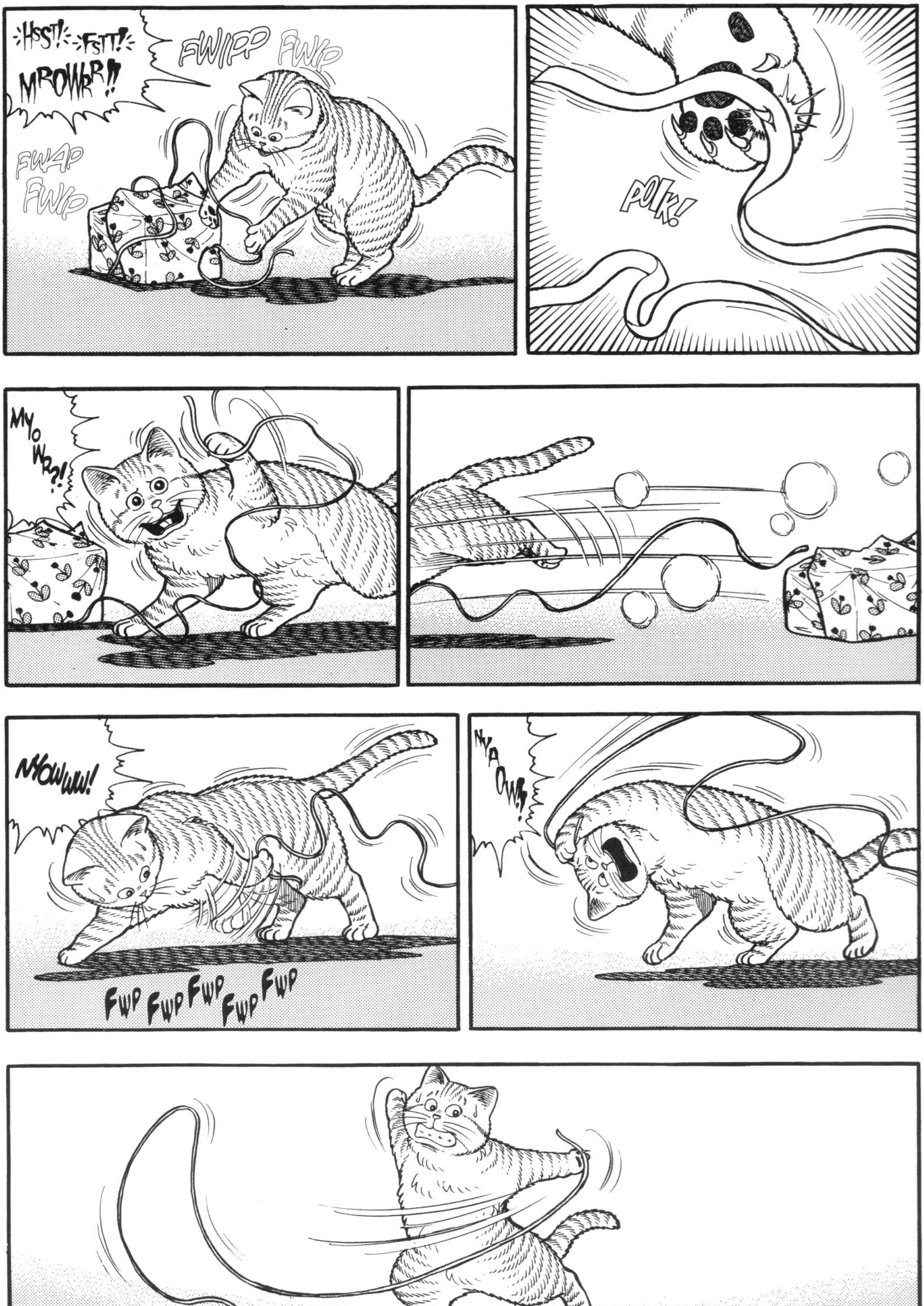
HSST! FSTT!
MROWRR!!
FWIPP FWIP
FWAP
FWIP
POIK!
MYOWR?!
NYOWWW!
FWP FWP FWP FWP FWP
NYAOW!

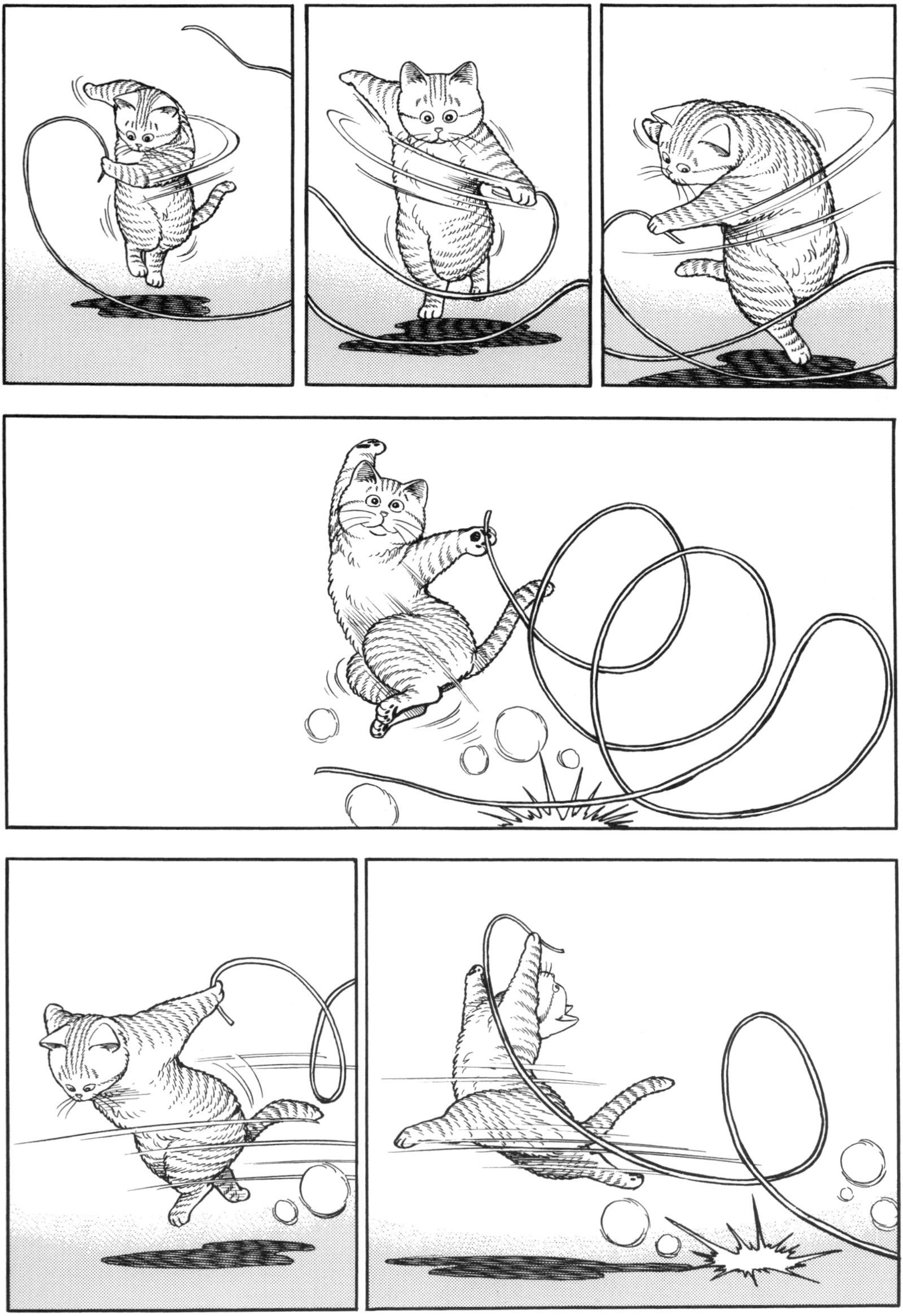

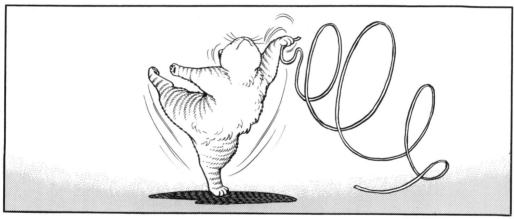

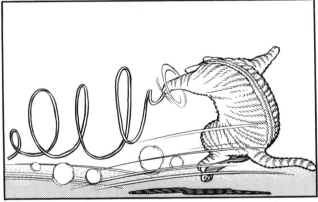

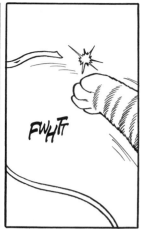

FWHTT

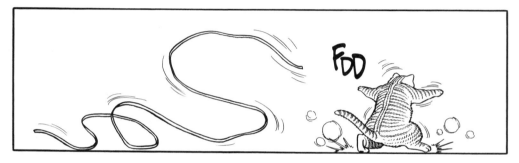

FDD

SLRP

THE END

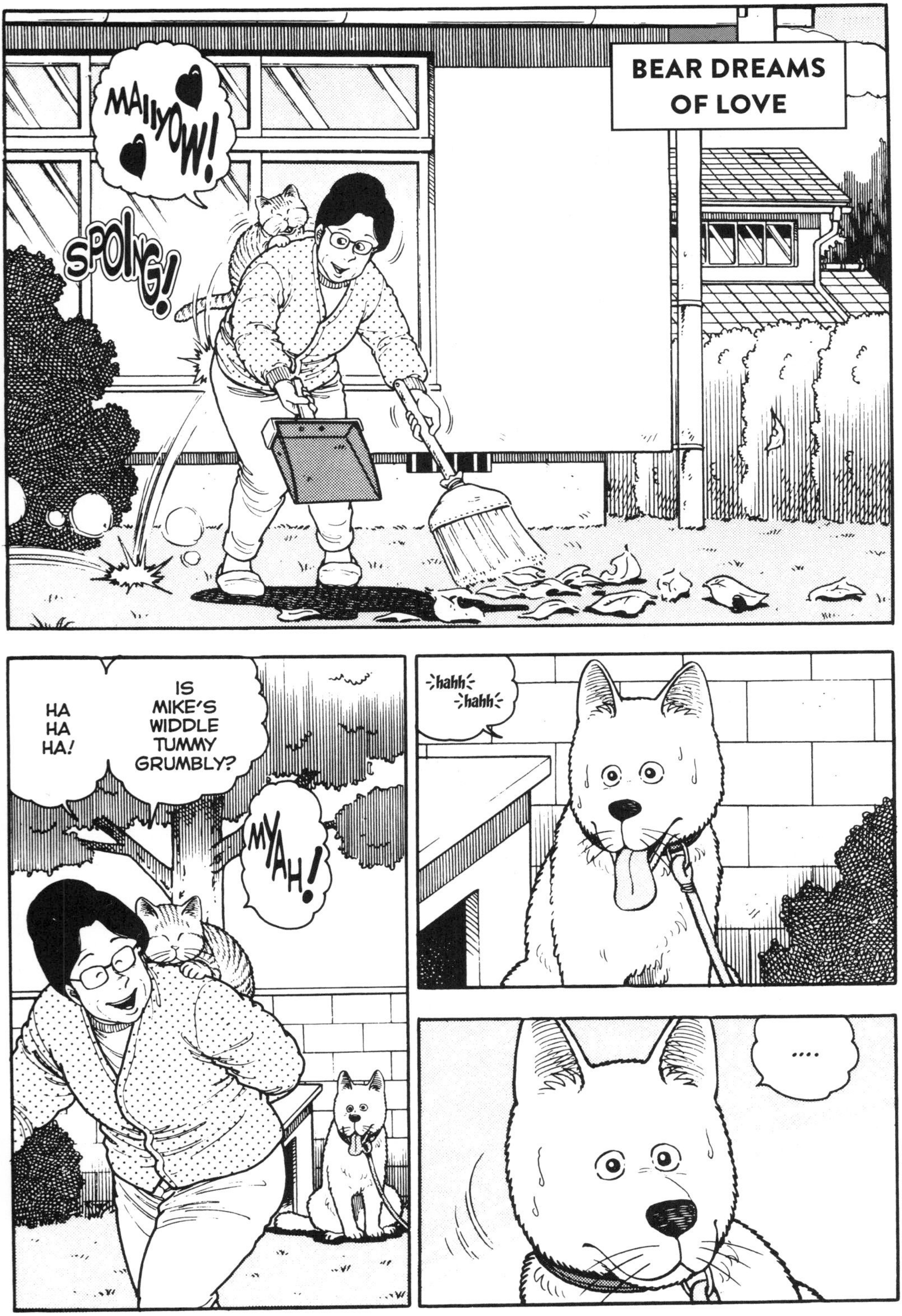

BEAR DREAMS OF LOVE
MAIIYOW!
SPOING!
HA HA HA!
IS MIKE'S WIDDLE TUMMY GRUMBLY?
MYAH!
hahh hahh
....

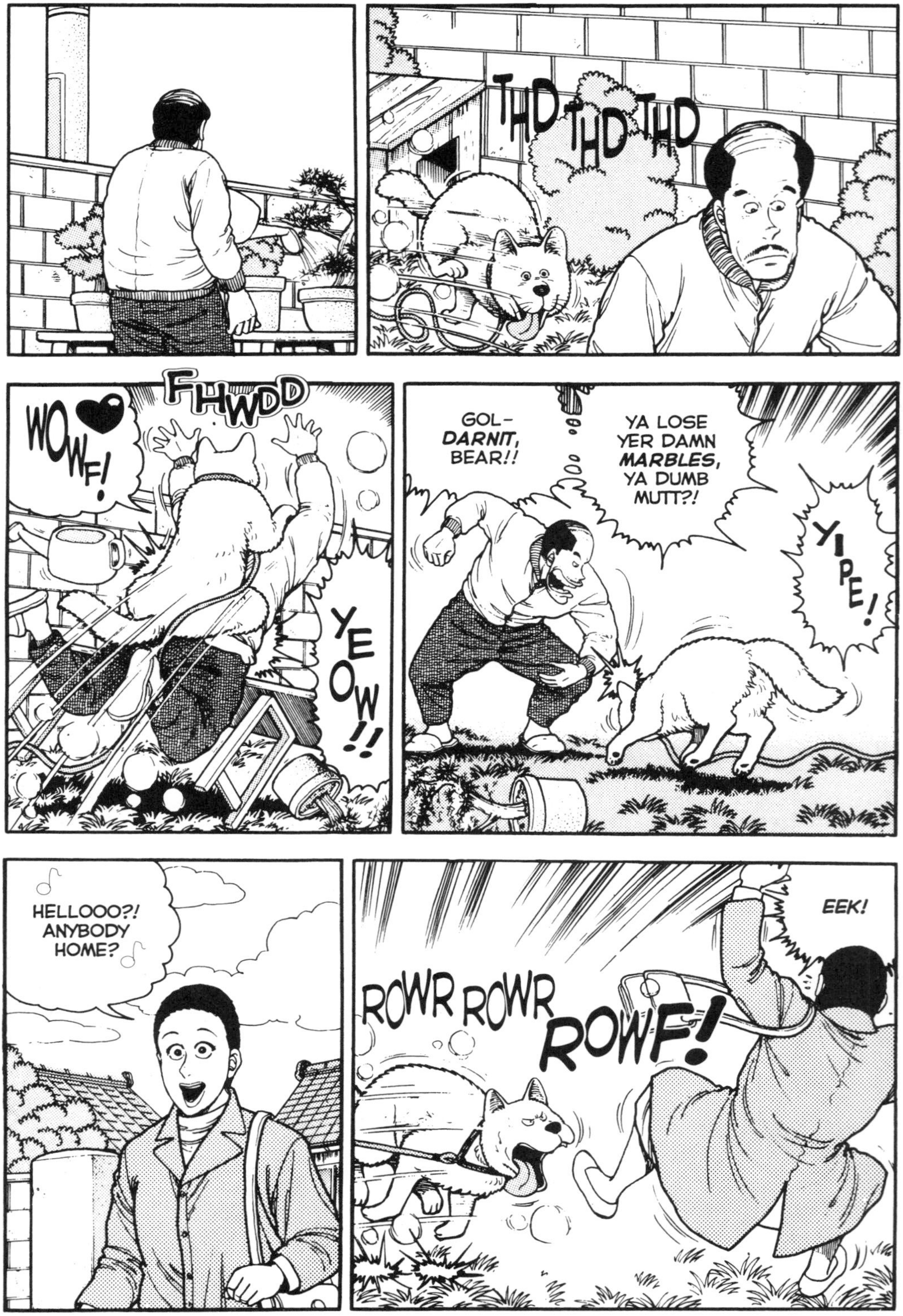
THD THD THD
WOWF!
FHWDD
YEOW!!
GOL-DARNIT, BEAR!!
YA LOSE YER DAMN MARBLES, YA DUMB MUTT?!
YIPE!
HELLOOO?! ANYBODY HOME?
EEK!
ROWR ROWR ROWF!

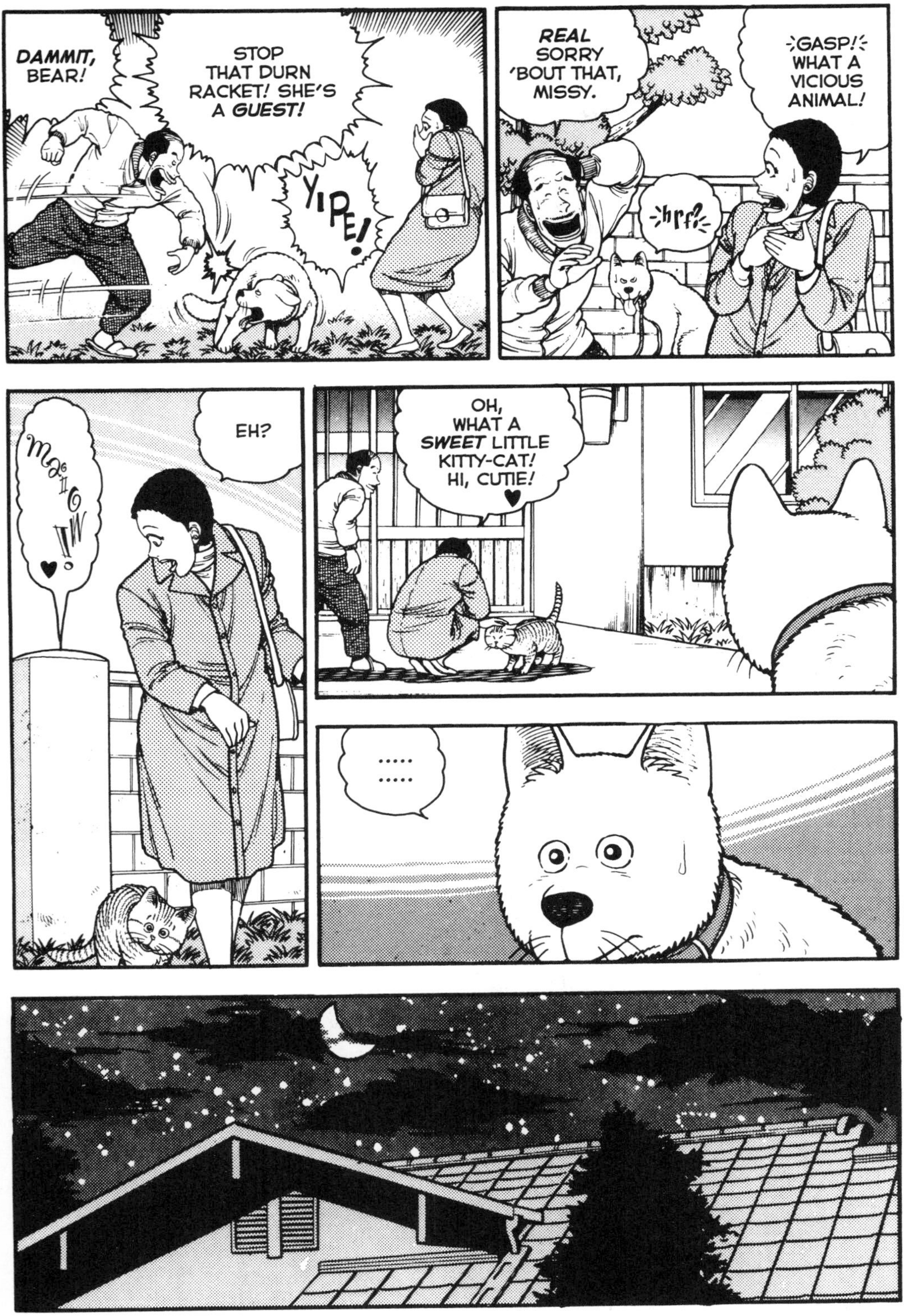
DAMMIT, BEAR!
STOP THAT DURN RACKET! SHE'S A GUEST!
YIPE!
REAL SORRY 'BOUT THAT, MISSY.
GASP! WHAT A VICIOUS ANIMAL!
hrf?
EH?
OH, WHAT A SWEET LITTLE KITTY-CAT! HI, CUTIE! ♥
.....
.....

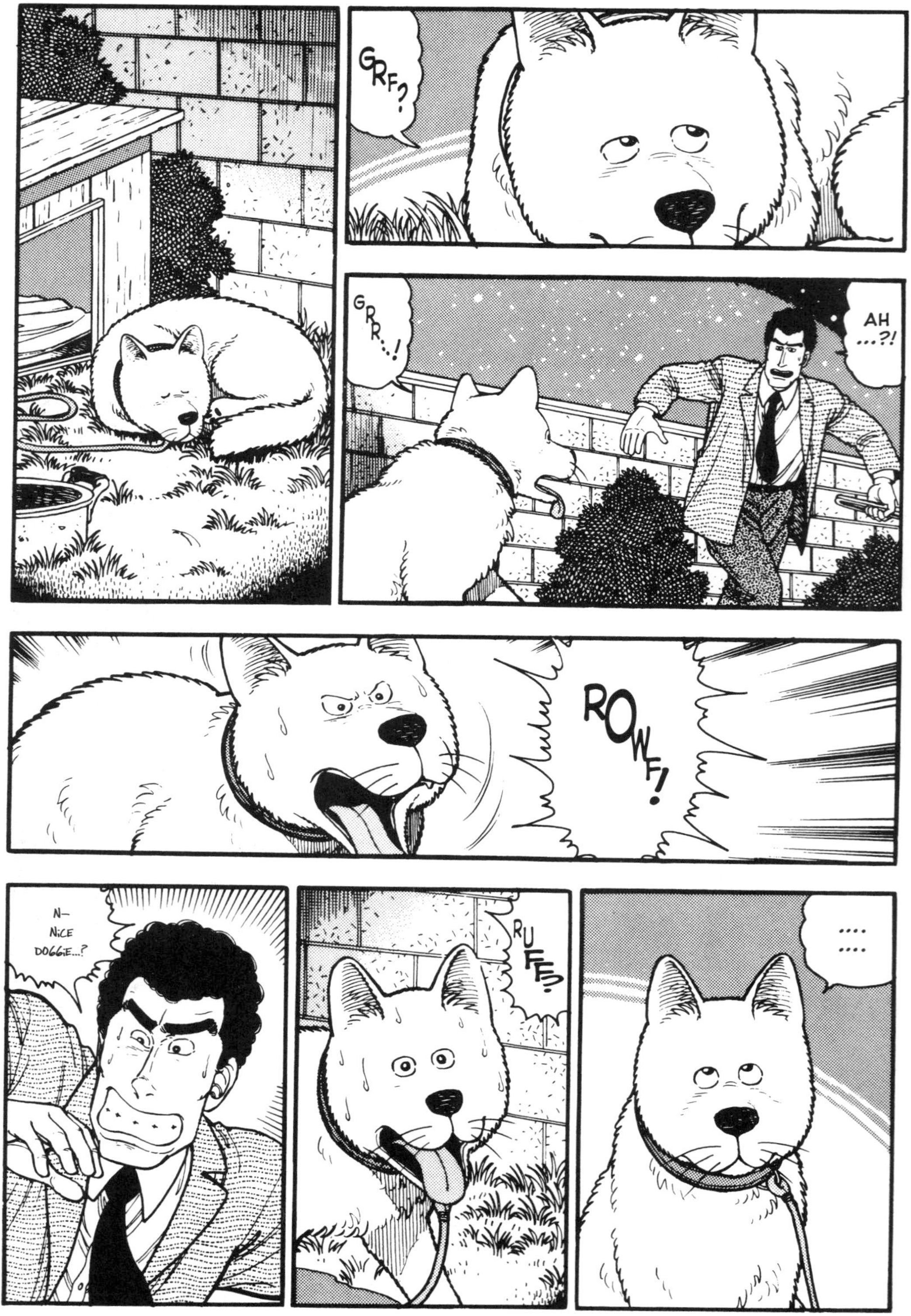

GRF?
GRR..!
AH ...?!
ROWF!
N-NICE DOGGIE...?
RUFF?
....
....

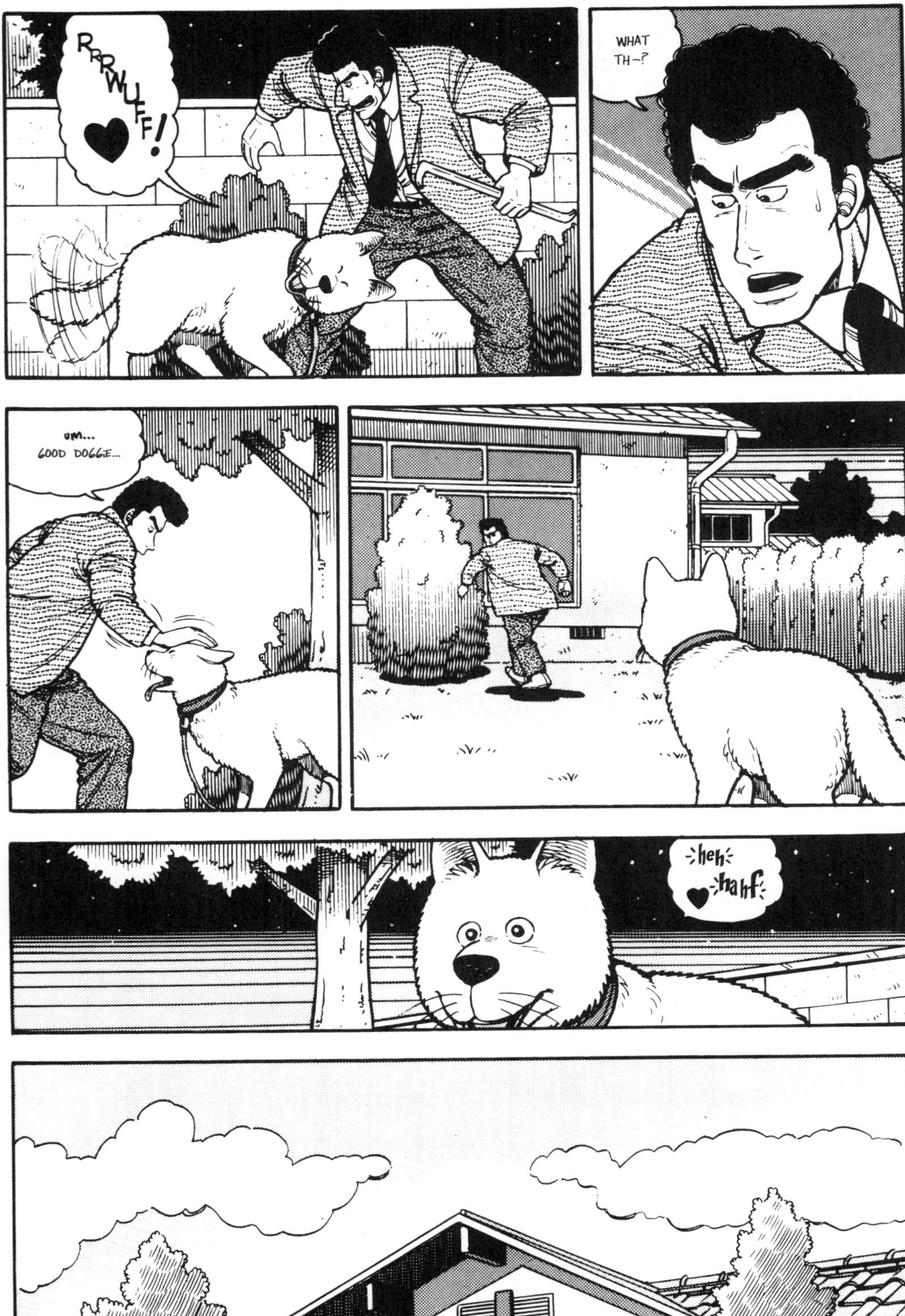
RRRWUFF!
WHAT TH--?
um...
GOOD DOGGiE...
heh
hahf

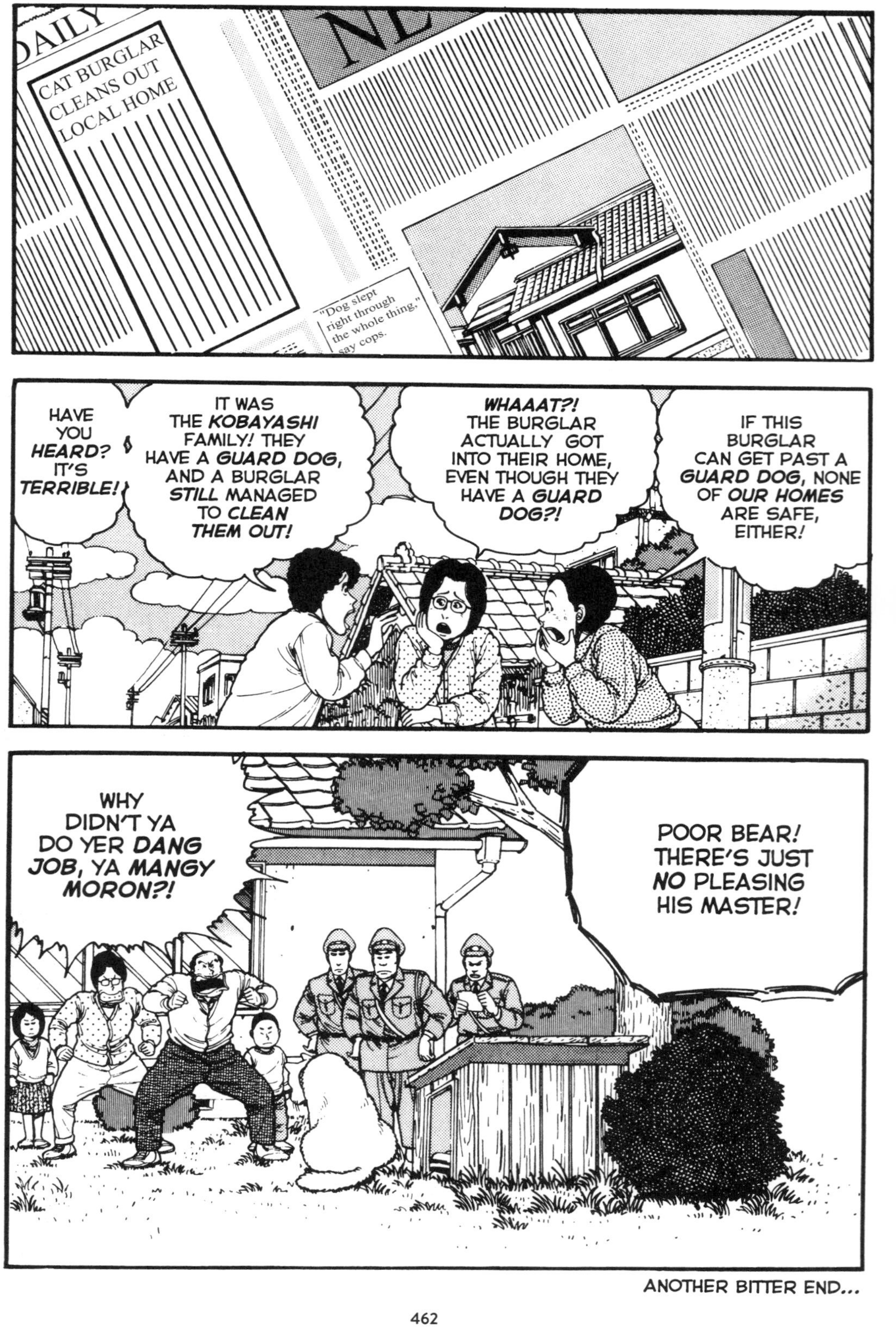
DAILY
NE
CAT BURGLAR CLEANS OUT LOCAL HOME
"Dog slept right through the whole thing," say cops.
HAVE YOU HEARD? IT'S TERRIBLE!
IT WAS THE KOBAYASHI FAMILY! THEY HAVE A GUARD DOG, AND A BURGLAR STILL MANAGED TO CLEAN THEM OUT!
WHAAAT?! THE BURGLAR ACTUALLY GOT INTO THEIR HOME, EVEN THOUGH THEY HAVE A GUARD DOG?!
IF THIS BURGLAR CAN GET PAST A GUARD DOG, NONE OF OUR HOMES ARE SAFE, EITHER!
WHY DIDN'T YA DO YER DANG JOB, YA MANGY MORON?!
POOR BEAR! THERE'S JUST NO PLEASING HIS MASTER!

ANOTHER BITTER END...

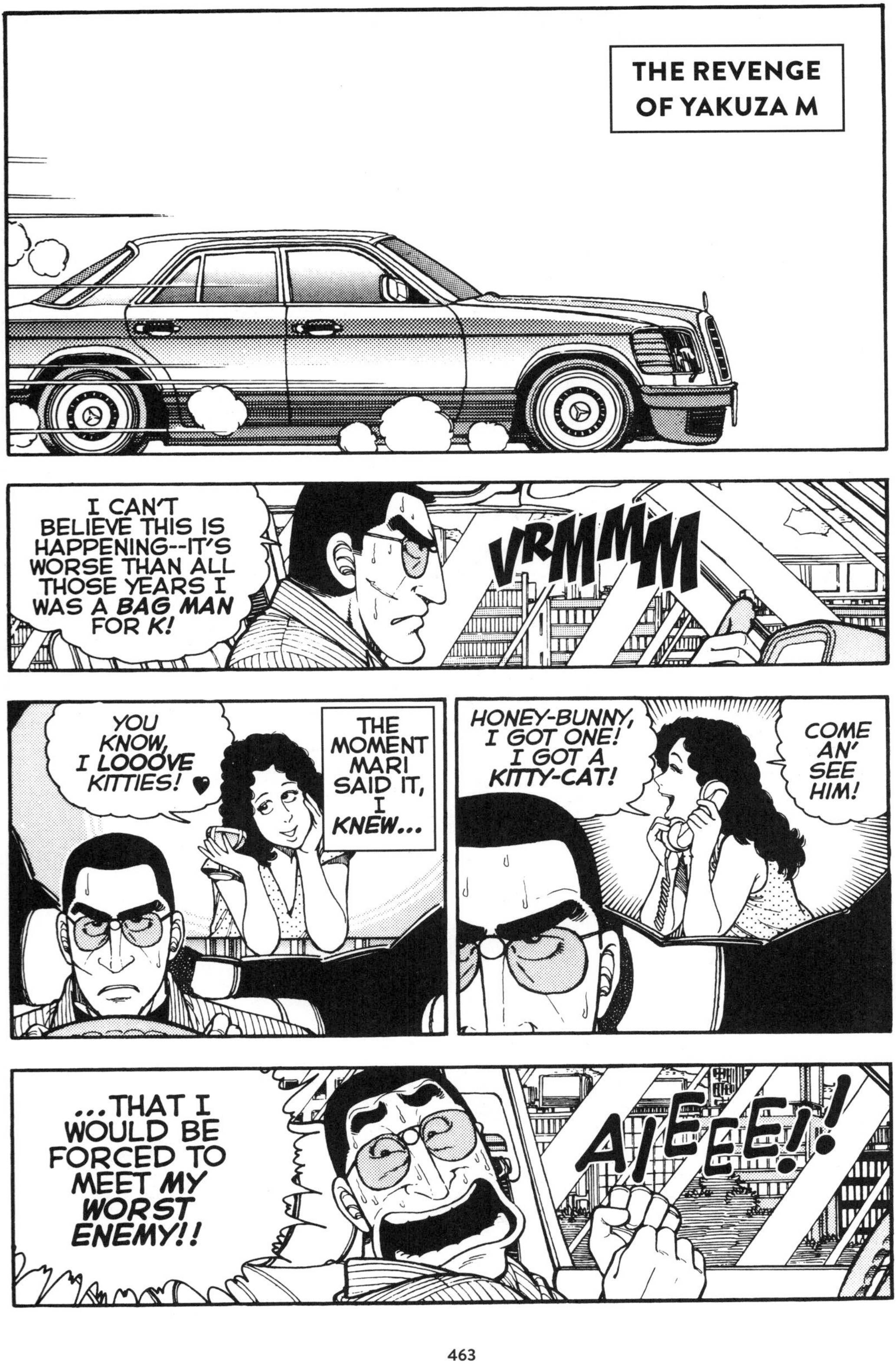
THE REVENGE OF YAKUZA M
I CAN'T BELIEVE THIS IS HAPPENING--IT'S WORSE THAN ALL THOSE YEARS I WAS A BAG MAN FOR K!
VRMMMM
YOU KNOW, I LOOOVE KITTIES! ♥
THE MOMENT MARI SAID IT, I KNEW...
HONEY-BUNNY, I GOT ONE! I GOT A KITTY-CAT!
COME AN' SEE HIM!
...THAT I WOULD BE FORCED TO MEET MY WORST ENEMY!!
AIEEE!!

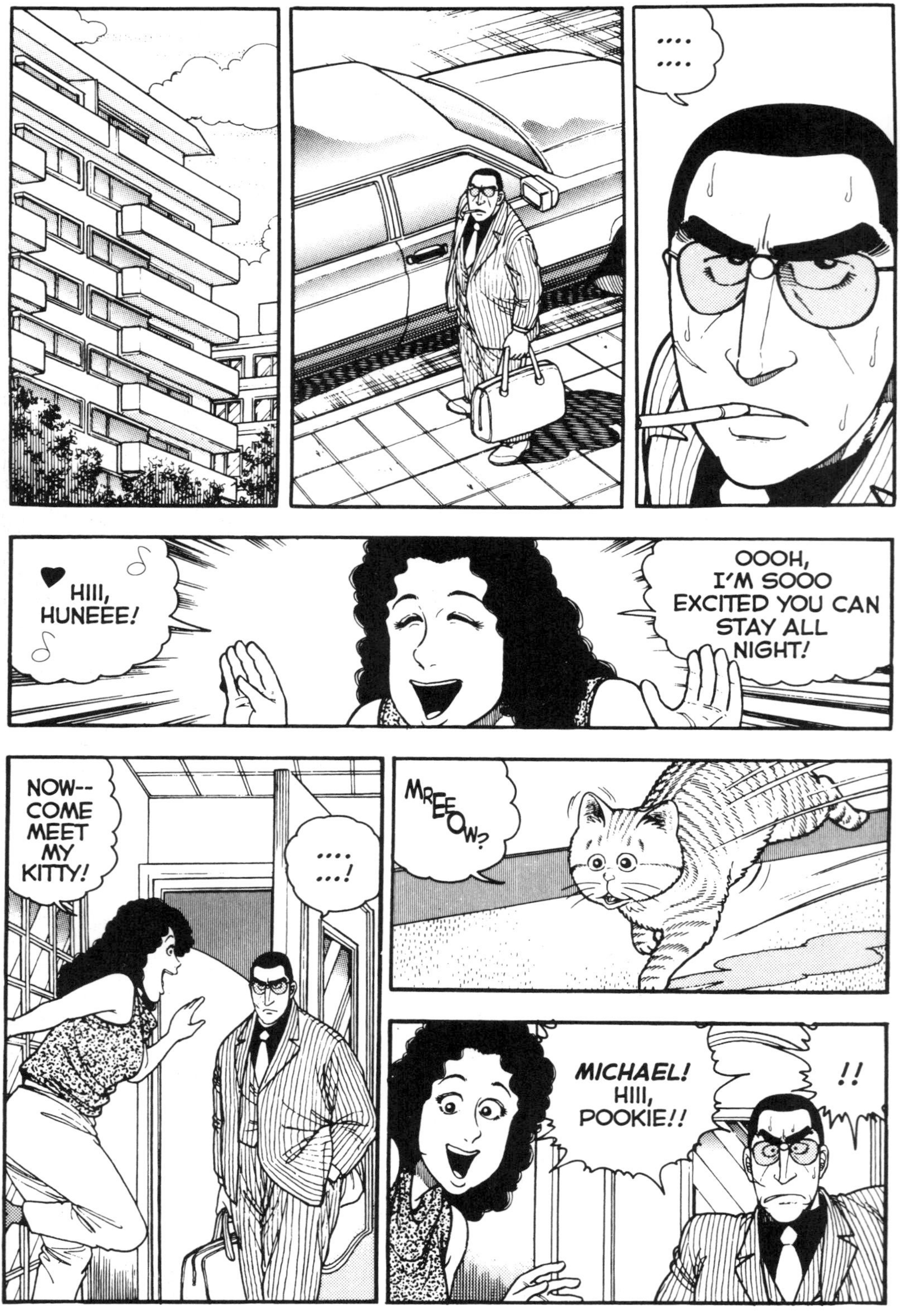
....
....
HIII, HUNEEE!
OOOH, I'M SOOO EXCITED YOU CAN STAY ALL NIGHT!
NOW-- COME MEET MY KITTY!
...., ...!
MREEOW?
MICHAEL! HIII, POOKIE!!
!!

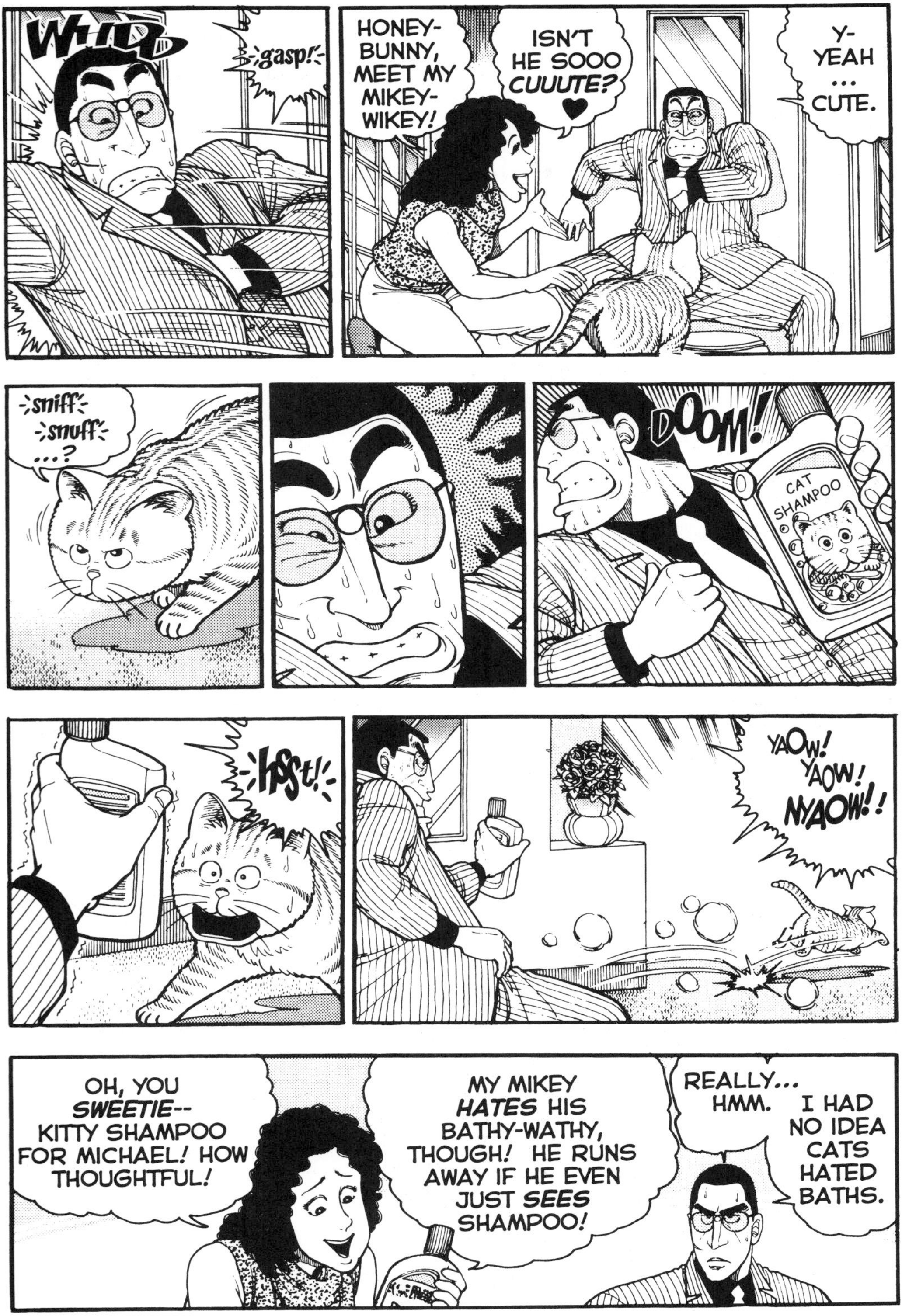
WHIP
-gasp!-
HONEY-BUNNY, MEET MY MIKEY-WIKEY!
ISN'T HE SOOO CUUUTE?
Y-YEAH ... CUTE.
-sniff- -snuff- ...?
DOOM!
CAT SHAMPOO
-hsst!-
YAOW! YAOW! NYAOW!!
OH, YOU SWEETIE-- KITTY SHAMPOO FOR MICHAEL! HOW THOUGHTFUL!
MY MIKEY HATES HIS BATHY-WATHY, THOUGH! HE RUNS AWAY IF HE EVEN JUST SEES SHAMPOO!
REALLY... HMM.
I HAD NO IDEA CATS HATED BATHS.

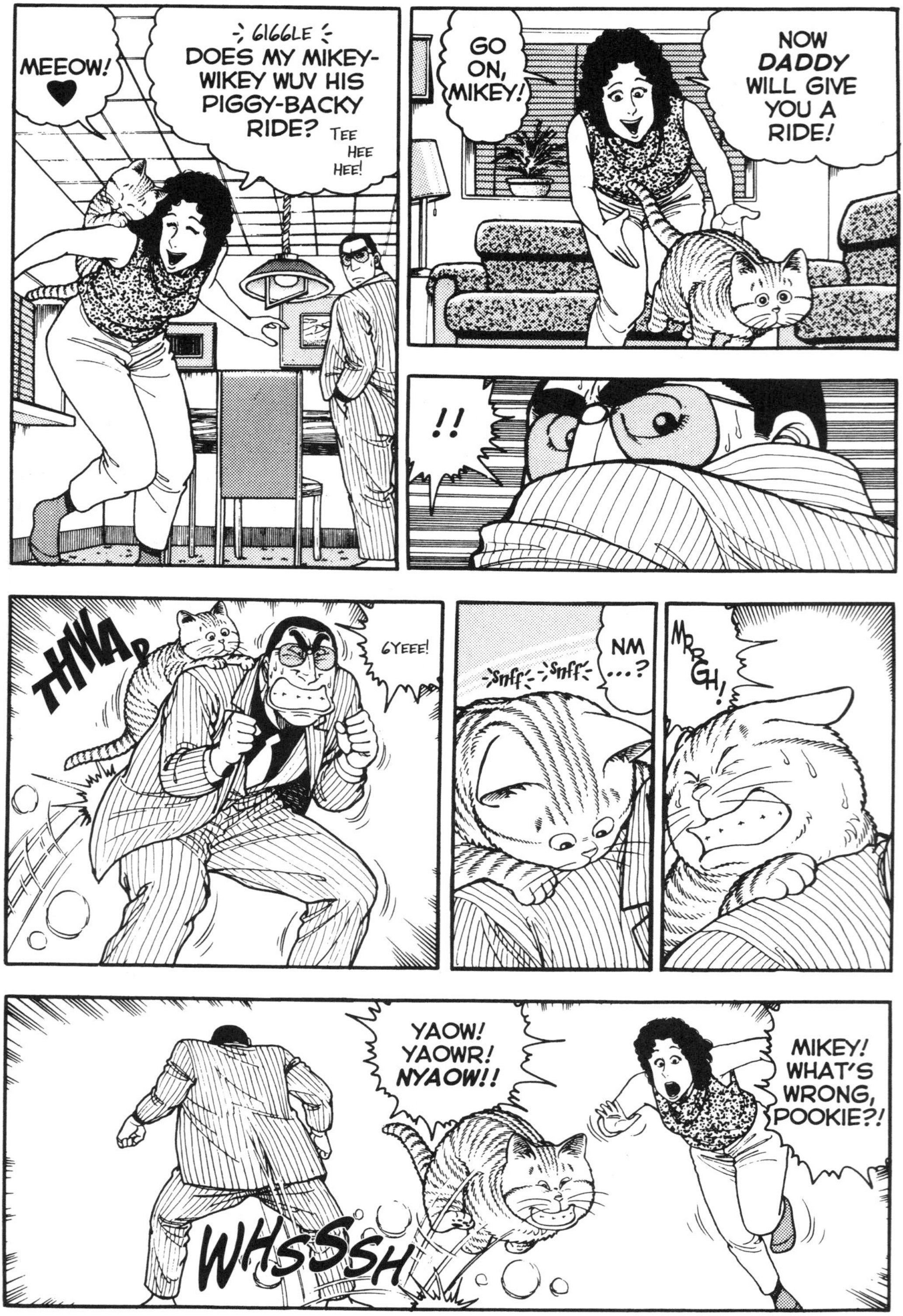
MEEOW! ♥
GIGGLE
DOES MY MIKEY-WIKEY WUV HIS PIGGY-BACKY RIDE?
TEE HEE HEE!
GO ON, MIKEY!
NOW DADDY WILL GIVE YOU A RIDE!
!!
THWAP
GYEEE!
-snff- -snff-
NM ...?
MRRGH!
YAOW! YAOWR! NYAOW!!
MIKEY! WHAT'S WRONG, POOKIE?!
WHSSSH

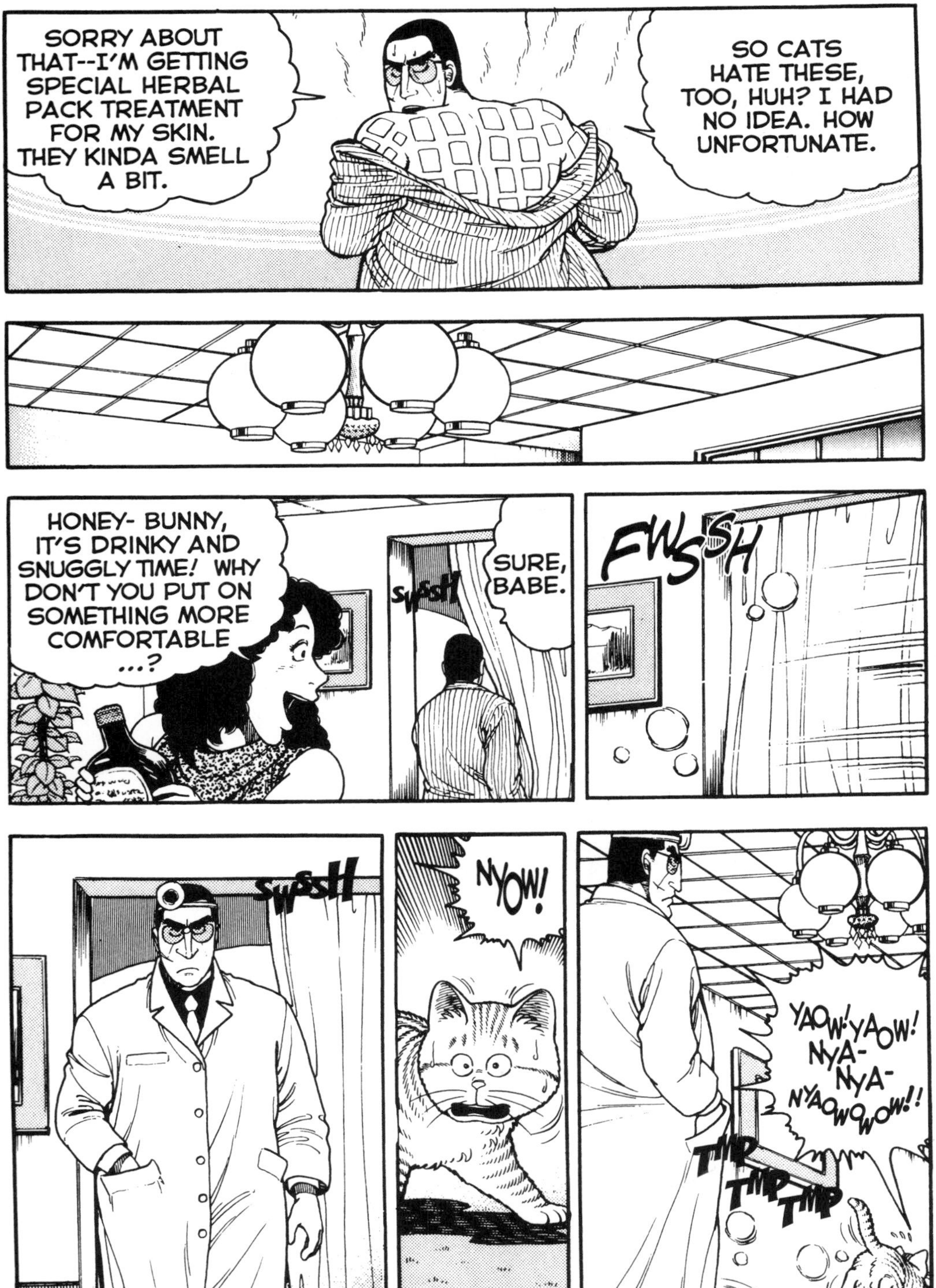
SORRY ABOUT THAT--I'M GETTING SPECIAL HERBAL PACK TREATMENT FOR MY SKIN. THEY KINDA SMELL A BIT.
SO CATS HATE THESE, TOO, HUH? I HAD NO IDEA. HOW UNFORTUNATE.
HONEY- BUNNY, IT'S DRINKY AND SNUGGLY TIME! WHY DON'T YOU PUT ON SOMETHING MORE COMFORTABLE ...?
SWSSH
SURE, BABE.
FWSSH
SWSSH
NYOW!
YAOW! YAOW! NYA- NYA- NYAOWOWOW!!
TMP TMP TMP TMP

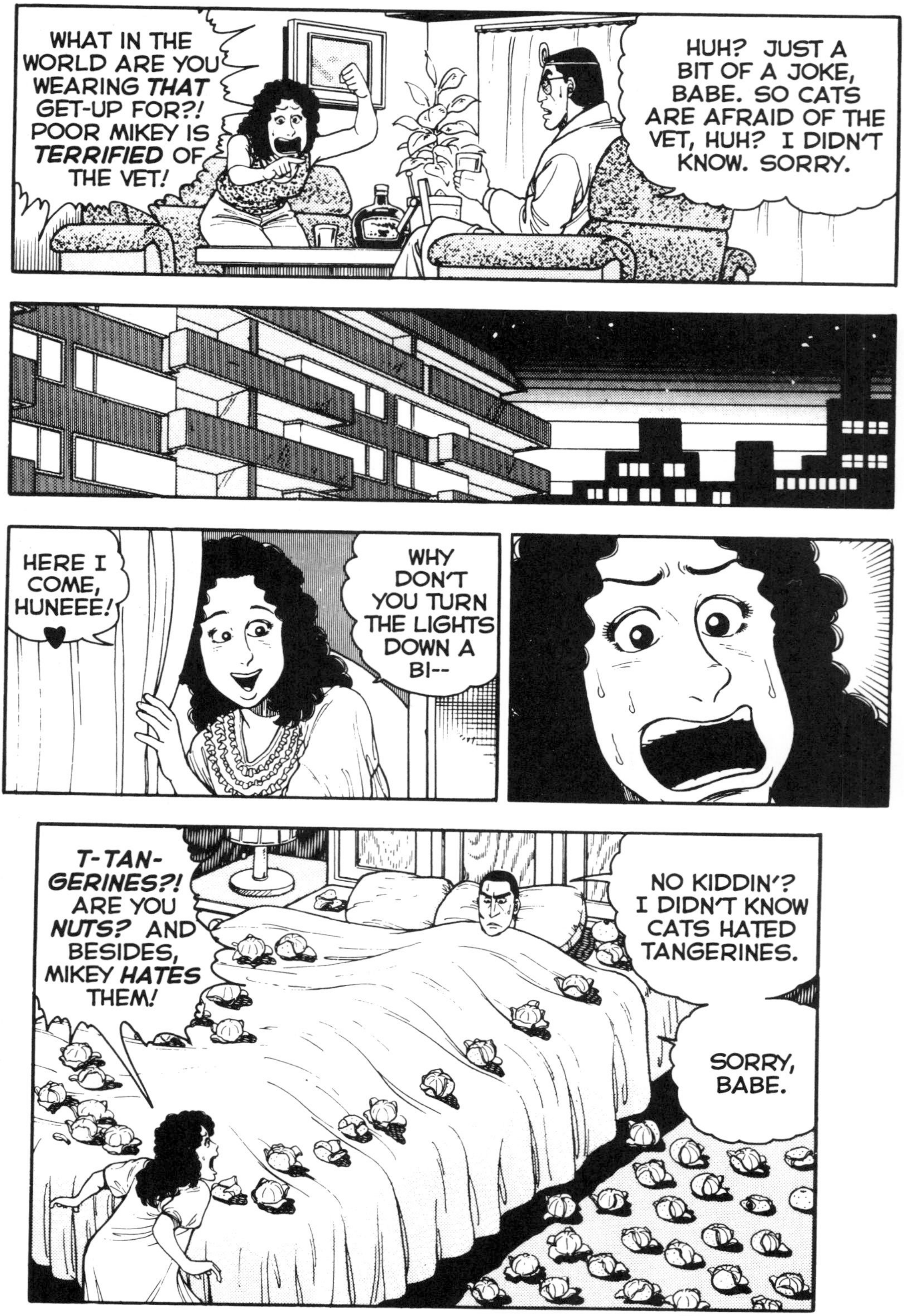
WHAT IN THE WORLD ARE YOU WEARING *THAT* GET-UP FOR?! POOR MIKEY IS *TERRIFIED* OF THE VET!
HUH? JUST A BIT OF A JOKE, BABE. SO CATS ARE AFRAID OF THE VET, HUH? I DIDN'T KNOW. SORRY.
HERE I COME, HUNEEE!
WHY DON'T YOU TURN THE LIGHTS DOWN A BI--
*T-TANGERINES?!* ARE YOU *NUTS?* AND BESIDES, MIKEY *HATES* THEM!
NO KIDDIN'? I DIDN'T KNOW CATS HATED TANGERINES.
SORRY, BABE.

THE END

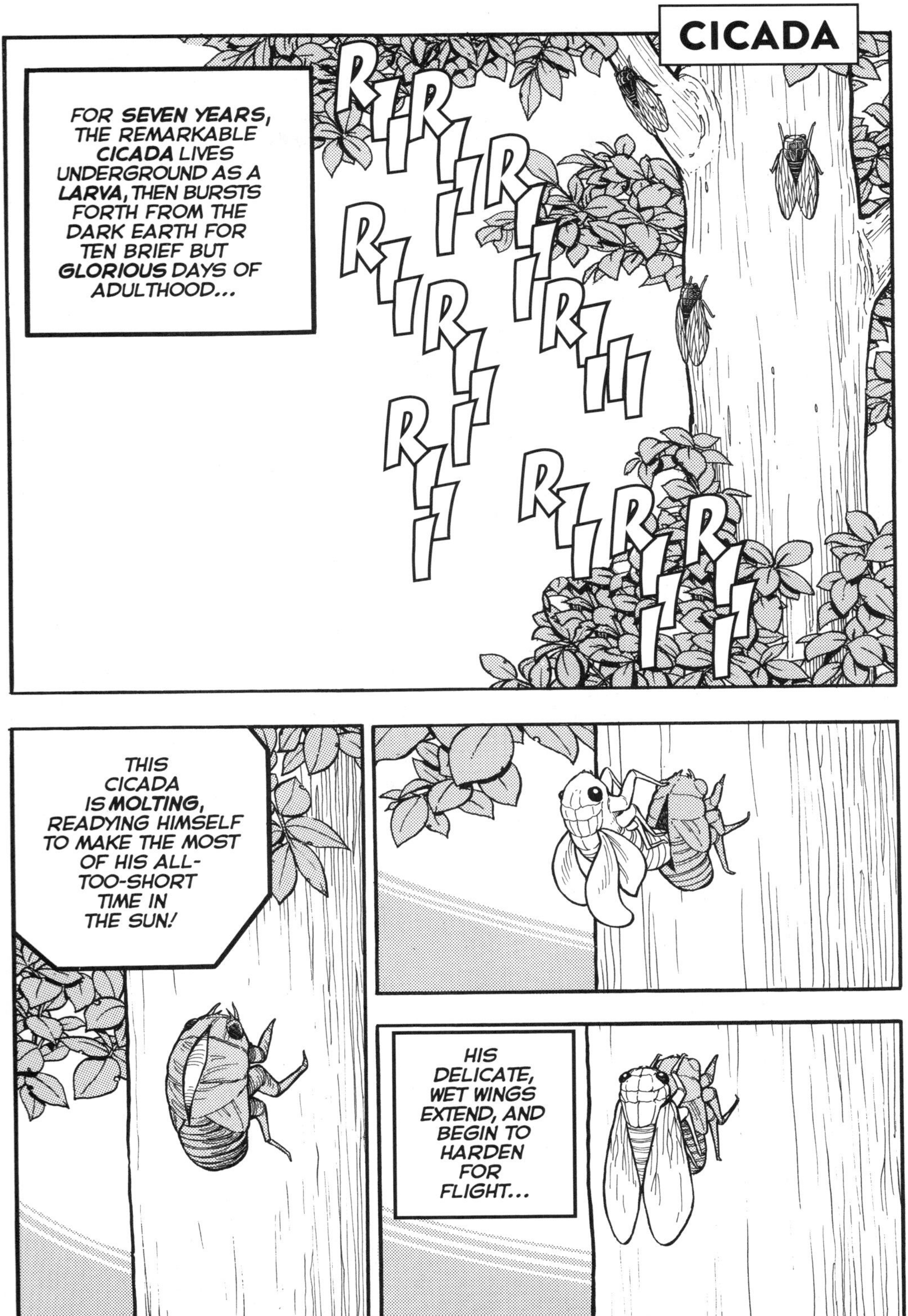
CICADA
FOR SEVEN YEARS, THE REMARKABLE CICADA LIVES UNDERGROUND AS A LARVA, THEN BURSTS FORTH FROM THE DARK EARTH FOR TEN BRIEF BUT GLORIOUS DAYS OF ADULTHOOD...
RIRIIII
RIIII
RIRIIII
RIIII
RIRIIII
RIIII
RIRIRIIII
THIS CICADA IS MOLTING, READYING HIMSELF TO MAKE THE MOST OF HIS ALL-TOO-SHORT TIME IN THE SUN!
HIS DELICATE, WET WINGS EXTEND, AND BEGIN TO HARDEN FOR FLIGHT...

OKAY...
READY!

SMAK!

R-
~GURK!

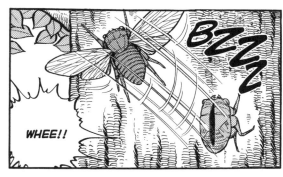

WHEE!!

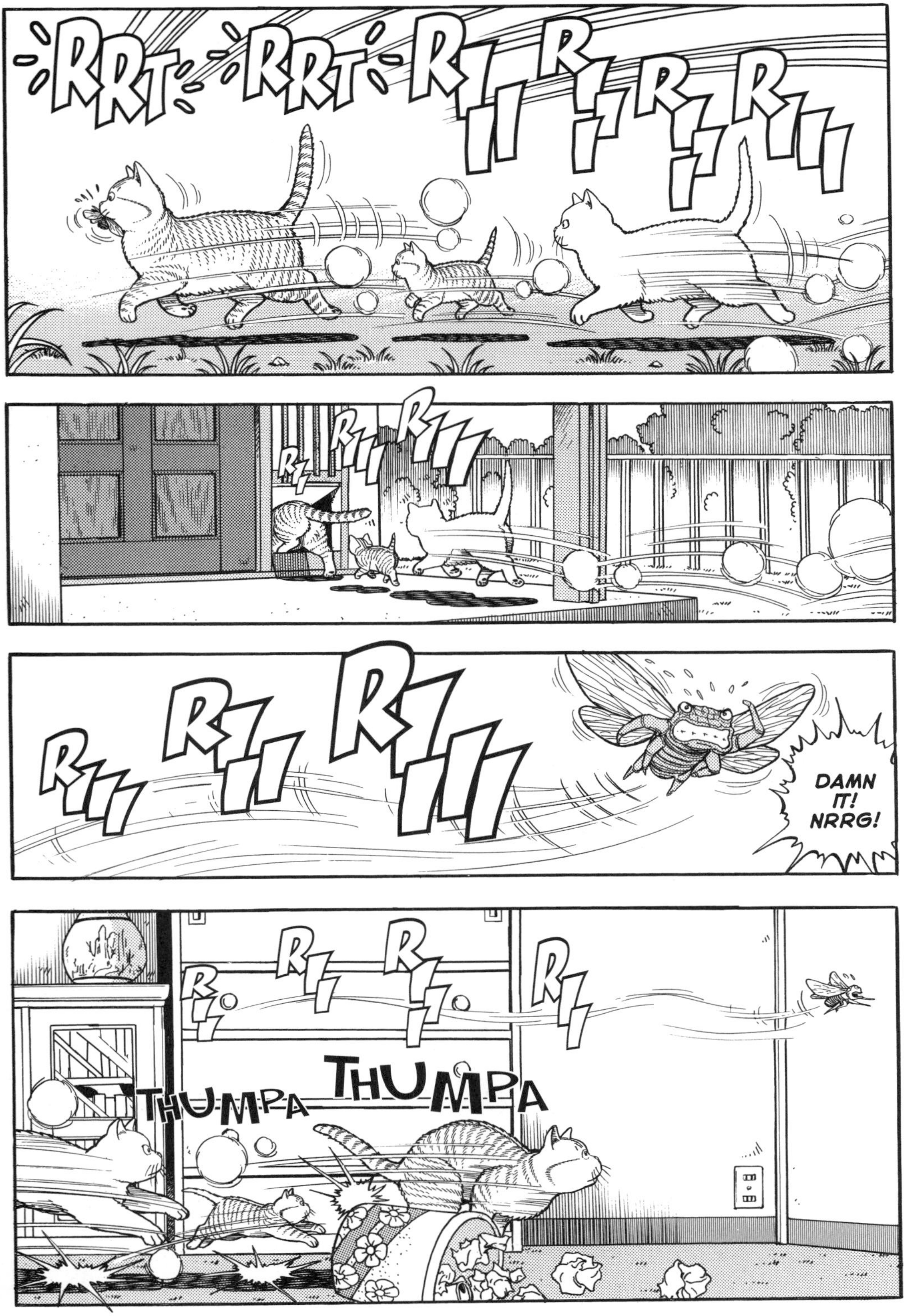
RRT
RRT
RII
RII
RII
RII
RII
RII
RII
RII
RII
RII
DAMN IT! NRRG!
RI
RI
RI
RI
THUMPA
THUMPA

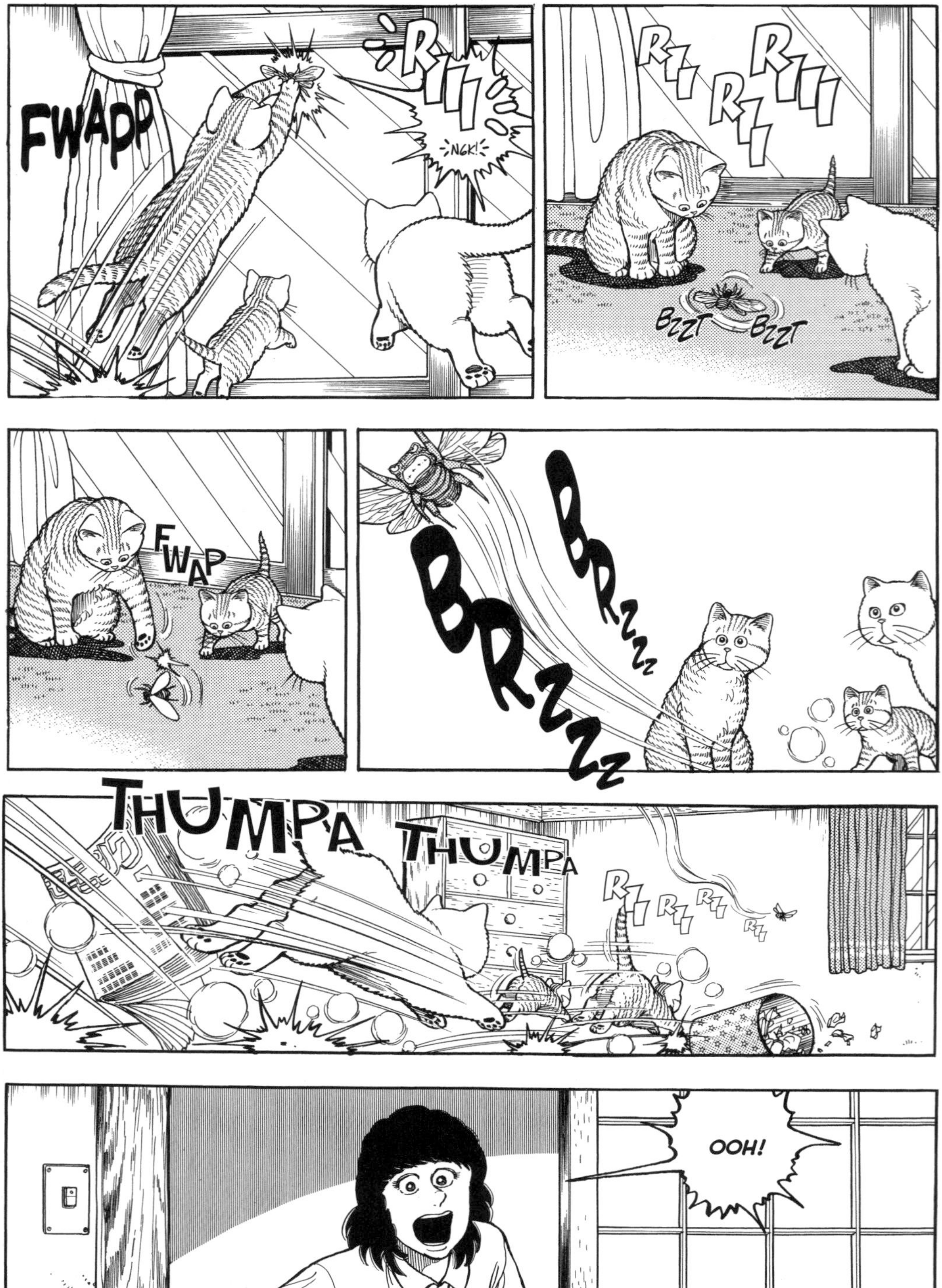
FWAPP
RIII
NGK!
RII
RII
RIII
BZZT
BZZT
FWAP
BRZZZZ
BRZZZ
THUMPA
THUMPA
RII
RII
RII
RII
OOH!

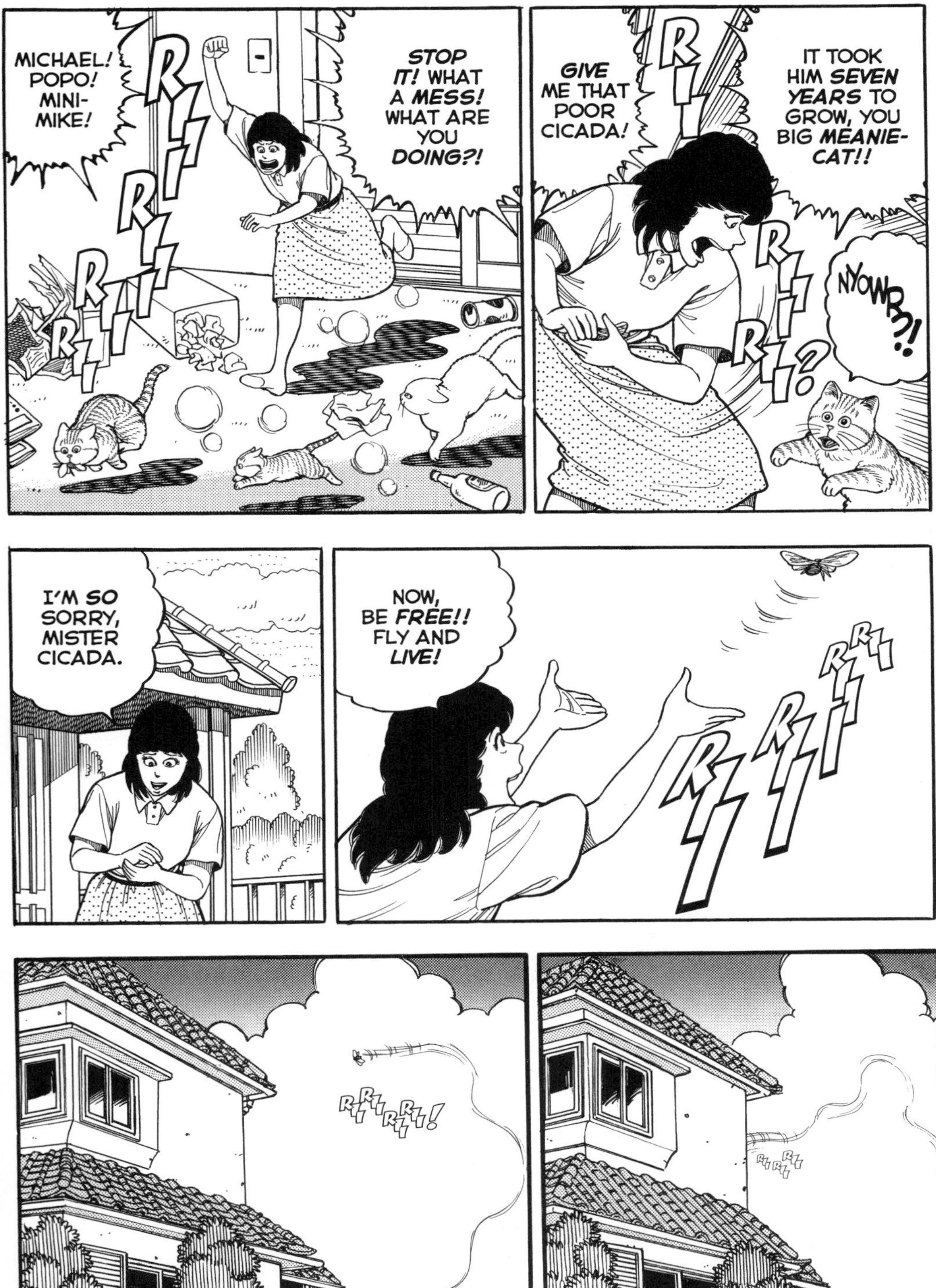
MICHAEL! POPO! MINI-MIKE!
RII RII RII RII
STOP IT! WHAT A MESS! WHAT ARE YOU DOING?!
GIVE ME THAT POOR CICADA!
RII
IT TOOK HIM SEVEN YEARS TO GROW, YOU BIG MEANIE-CAT!!
RII RII?
NYOWR?!
I'M SO SORRY, MISTER CICADA.
NOW, BE FREE!! FLY AND LIVE!
RII RII RII
RII RII RII RII!
RII RII RII

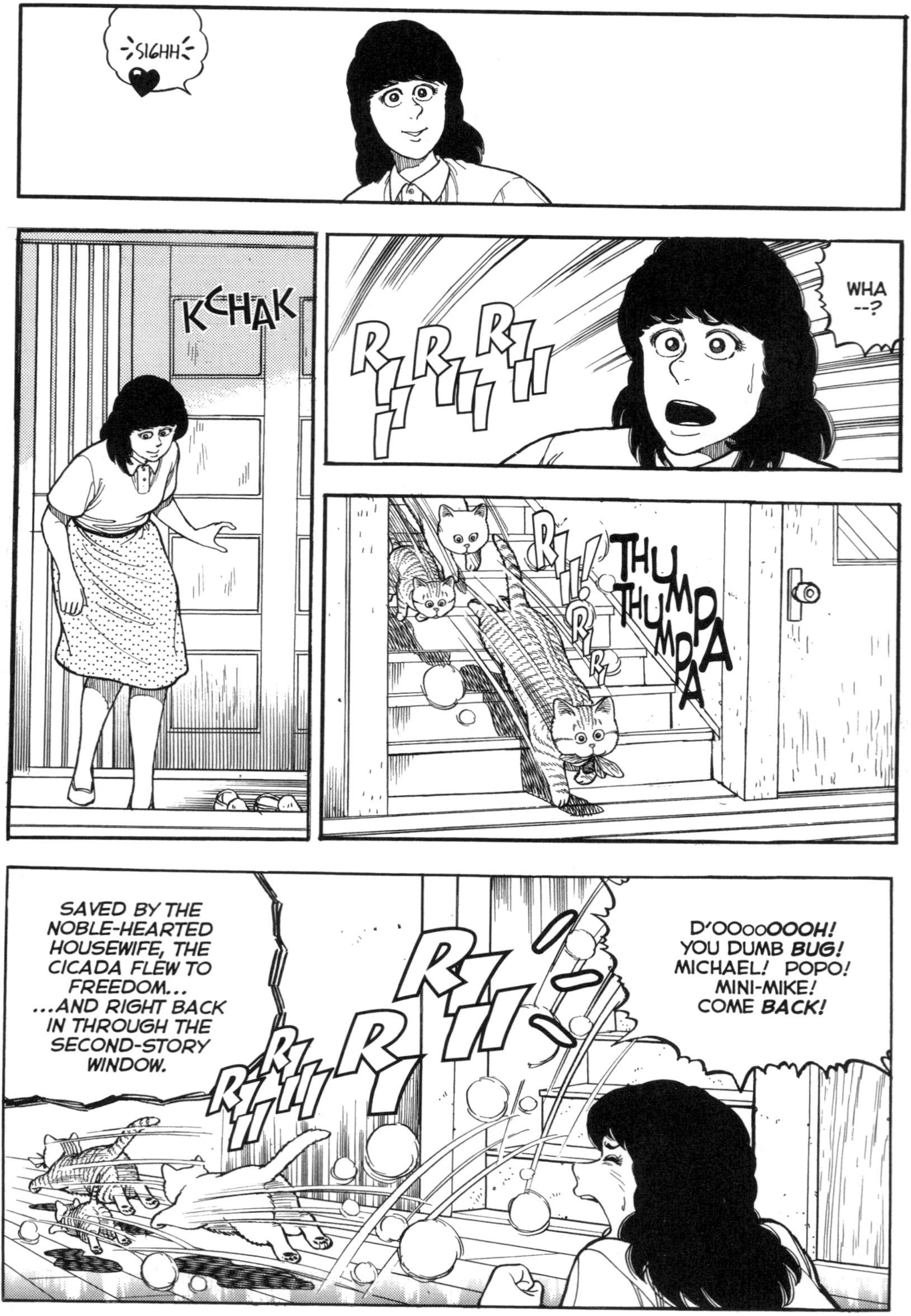
SIGHH
KCHAK
WHA --?
THUMPA THUMPA
SAVED BY THE NOBLE-HEARTED HOUSEWIFE, THE CICADA FLEW TO FREEDOM... ...AND RIGHT BACK IN THROUGH THE SECOND-STORY WINDOW.
D'OOooOOOH! YOU DUMB BUG! MICHAEL! POPO! MINI-MIKE! COME BACK!
THE END

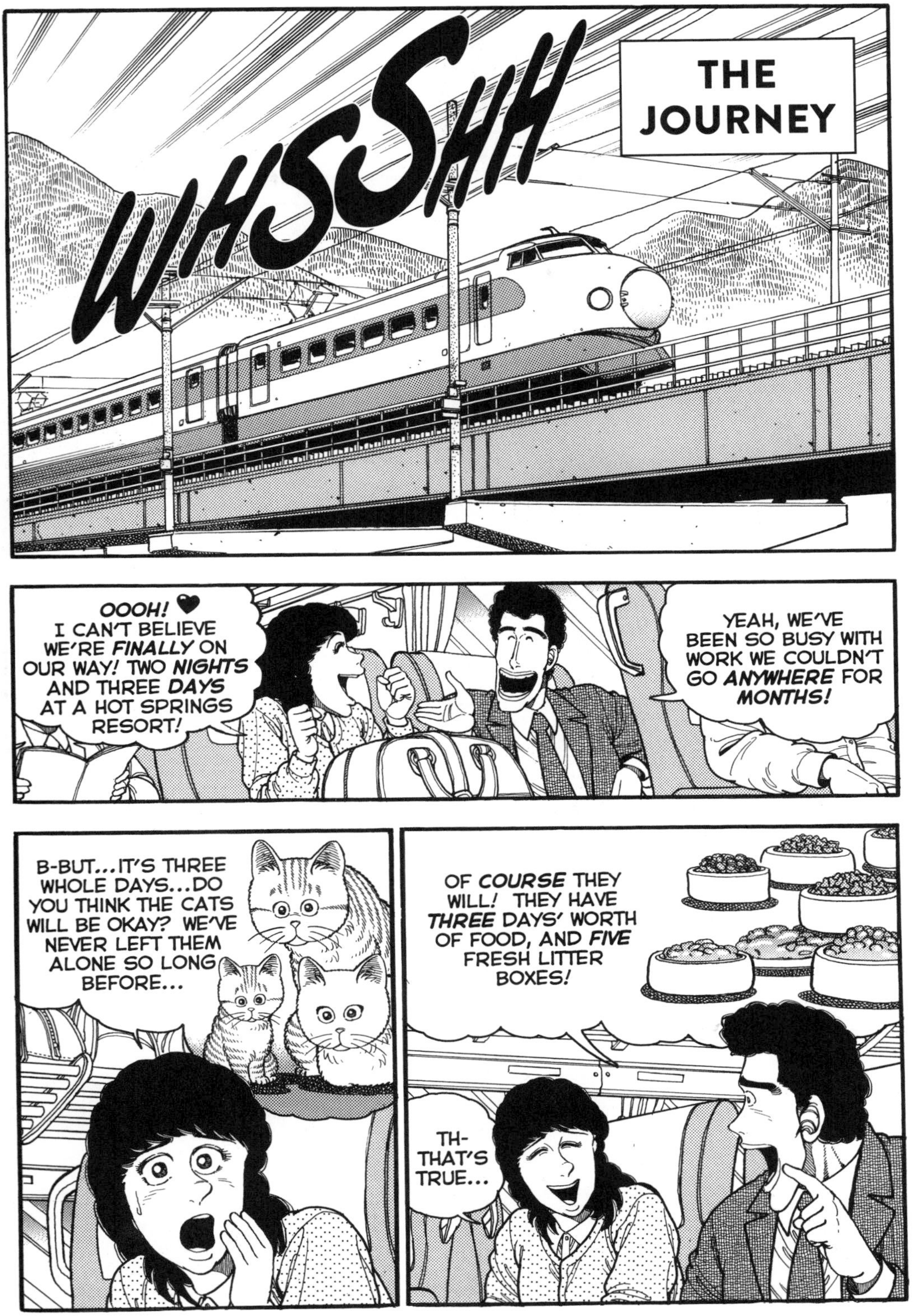
WHSSHH
THE JOURNEY
OOOH! ♥ I CAN'T BELIEVE WE'RE FINALLY ON OUR WAY! TWO NIGHTS AND THREE DAYS AT A HOT SPRINGS RESORT!
YEAH, WE'VE BEEN SO BUSY WITH WORK WE COULDN'T GO ANYWHERE FOR MONTHS!
B-BUT...IT'S THREE WHOLE DAYS...DO YOU THINK THE CATS WILL BE OKAY? WE'VE NEVER LEFT THEM ALONE SO LONG BEFORE...
OF COURSE THEY WILL! THEY HAVE THREE DAYS' WORTH OF FOOD, AND FIVE FRESH LITTER BOXES!
TH-THAT'S TRUE...

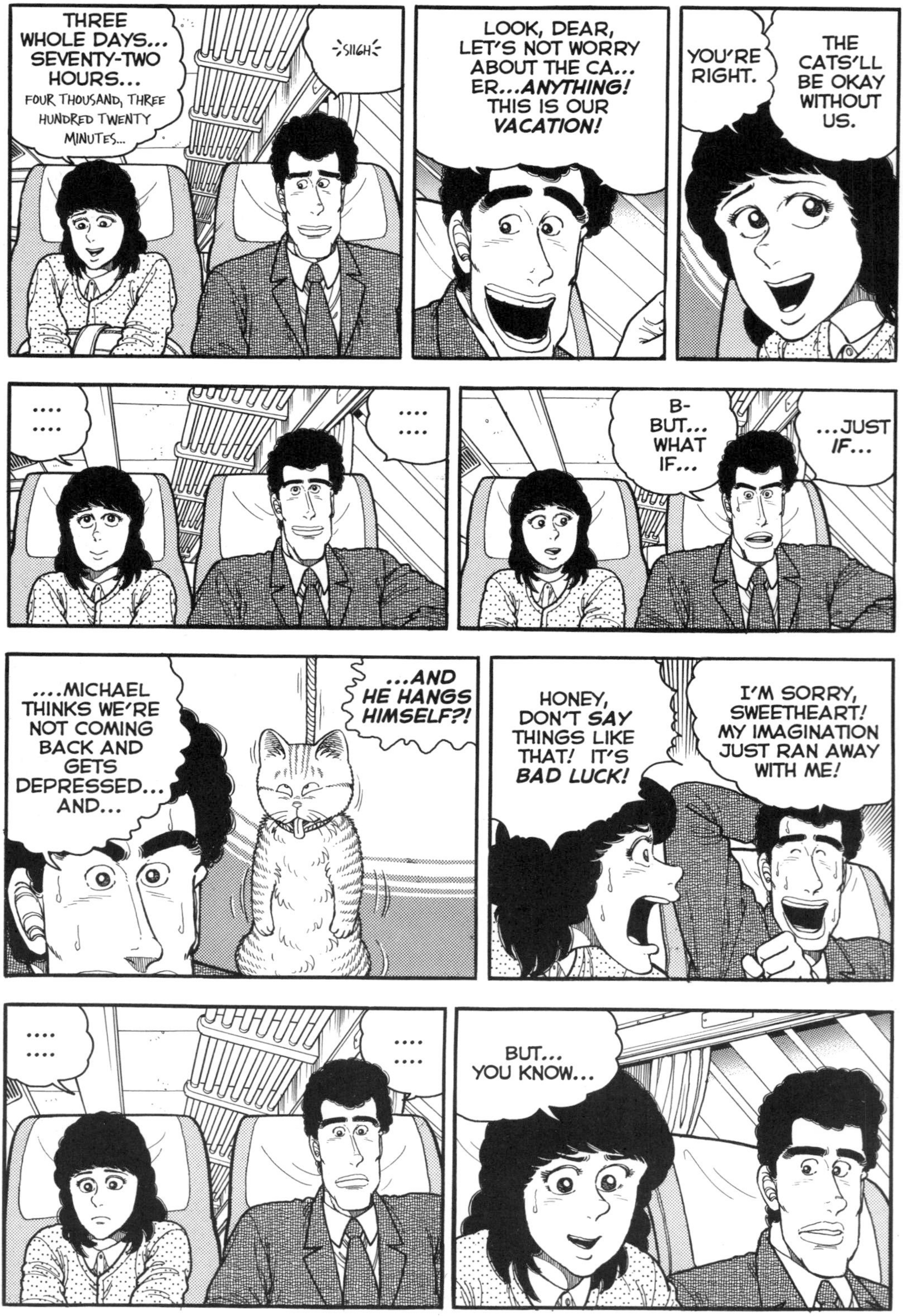
THREE WHOLE DAYS... SEVENTY-TWO HOURS... FOUR THOUSAND, THREE HUNDRED TWENTY MINUTES...
SIIGH
LOOK, DEAR, LET'S NOT WORRY ABOUT THE CA... ER...ANYTHING! THIS IS OUR VACATION!
YOU'RE RIGHT.
THE CATS'LL BE OKAY WITHOUT US.
....
....
....
....
B-BUT... WHAT IF...
...JUST IF...
....MICHAEL THINKS WE'RE NOT COMING BACK AND GETS DEPRESSED... AND...
...AND HE HANGS HIMSELF?!
HONEY, DON'T SAY THINGS LIKE THAT! IT'S BAD LUCK!
I'M SORRY, SWEETHEART! MY IMAGINATION JUST RAN AWAY WITH ME!
....
....
....
....
BUT... YOU KNOW...

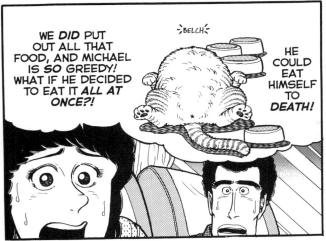

WE *DID* PUT OUT ALL THAT FOOD, AND MICHAEL IS *SO* GREEDY! WHAT IF HE DECIDED TO EAT IT *ALL AT ONCE?!*

-BELCH-

HE COULD EAT HIMSELF TO *DEATH!*

NOW *YOU'RE* GOING OFF THE DEEP END! MICHAEL WON'T GET DEPRESSED *OR* OVEREAT!

Y-YEAH... OF COURSE!

HMM. ....

HMM. ....

BUT... Y'KNOW...

...WHAT IF THEY LOOK FOR US ALL THREE DAYS, AND CRY AND *CRY?*

NYOWHR!

MAAAIOW!

MAIOW!

MEW MEW!

...A-AFTER *THREE SOLID DAYS* OF CRYING THEY MIGHT CRACK THEIR THROATS AND COULD NEVER MEOW AGAIN, *EVER!*

-KROAK-

-KEFF-

-GAKK-

.... ....!

477

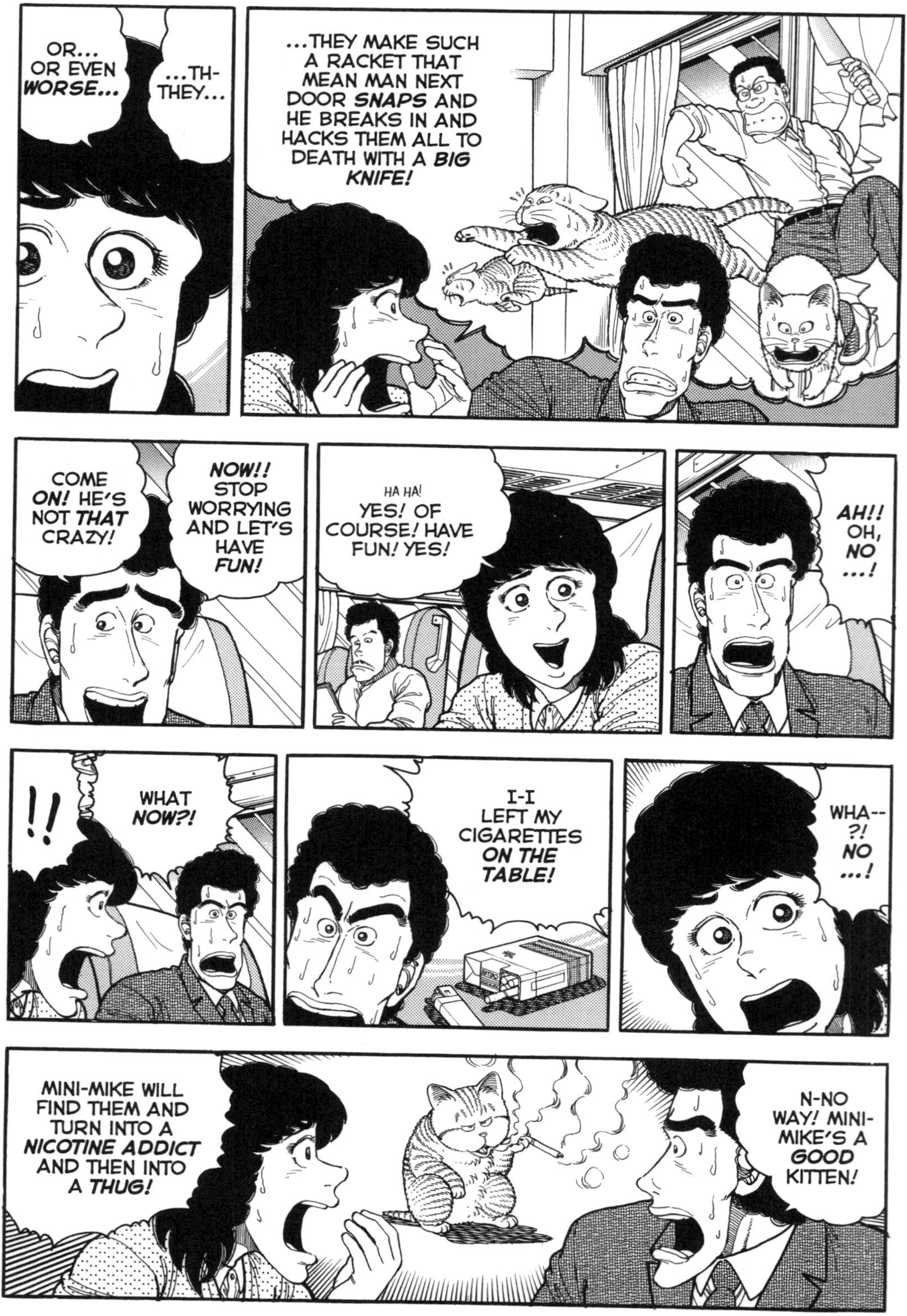
OR... OR EVEN WORSE...
...TH- THEY...
...THEY MAKE SUCH A RACKET THAT MEAN MAN NEXT DOOR SNAPS AND HE BREAKS IN AND HACKS THEM ALL TO DEATH WITH A BIG KNIFE!
COME ON! HE'S NOT THAT CRAZY!
NOW!! STOP WORRYING AND LET'S HAVE FUN!
HA HA!
YES! OF COURSE! HAVE FUN! YES!
AH!! OH, NO ...!
!!
WHAT NOW?!
I-I LEFT MY CIGARETTES ON THE TABLE!
WHA-- ?! NO ...!
MINI-MIKE WILL FIND THEM AND TURN INTO A NICOTINE ADDICT AND THEN INTO A THUG!
N-NO WAY! MINI-MIKE'S A GOOD KITTEN!

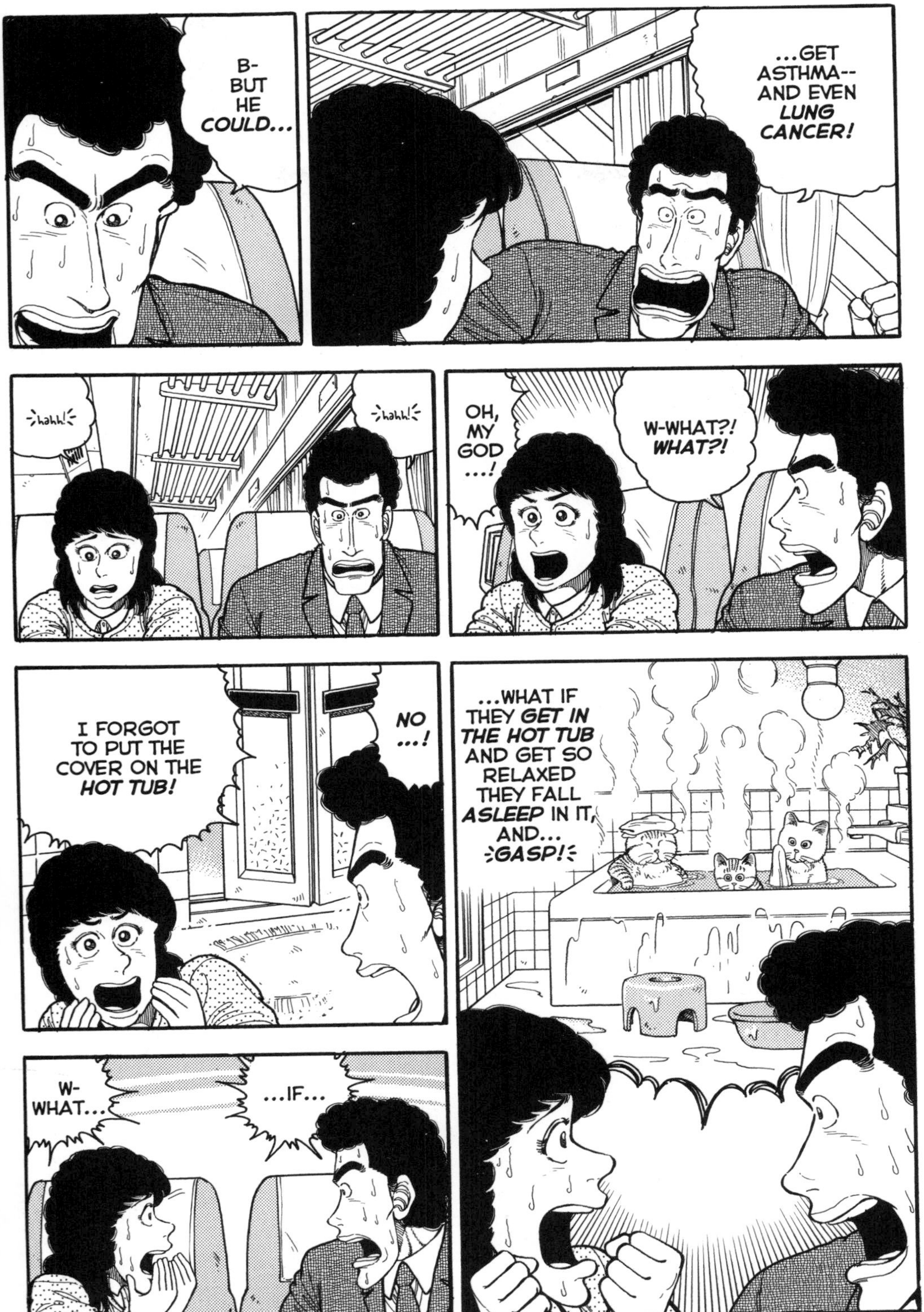

B- BUT HE *COULD...*
...GET ASTHMA-- AND EVEN *LUNG CANCER!*
hahh!
hahh!
OH, MY GOD ...!
W-WHAT?! *WHAT?!*
I FORGOT TO PUT THE COVER ON THE *HOT TUB!*
*NO ...!*
W- WHAT...
...IF...
...WHAT IF THEY *GET IN THE HOT TUB* AND GET SO RELAXED THEY FALL *ASLEEP* IN IT, AND...
*GASP!*

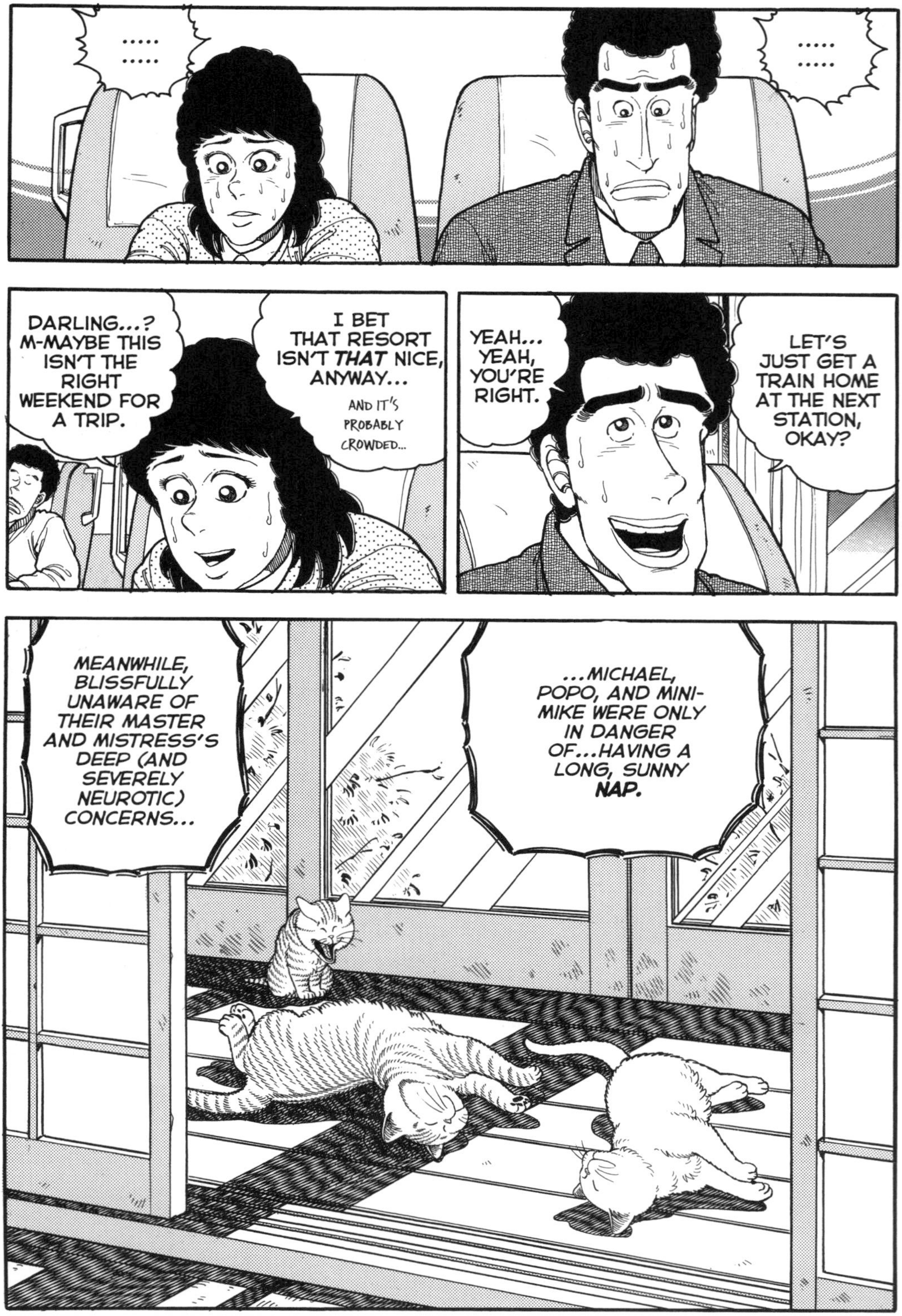
.....
.....
.....
.....
DARLING...? M-MAYBE THIS ISN'T THE RIGHT WEEKEND FOR A TRIP.
I BET THAT RESORT ISN'T ***THAT*** NICE, ANYWAY...
AND IT'S PROBABLY CROWDED...
YEAH... YEAH, YOU'RE RIGHT.
LET'S JUST GET A TRAIN HOME AT THE NEXT STATION, OKAY?
*MEANWHILE, BLISSFULLY UNAWARE OF THEIR MASTER AND MISTRESS'S DEEP (AND SEVERELY NEUROTIC) CONCERNS...*
*...MICHAEL, POPO, AND MINI-MIKE WERE ONLY IN DANGER OF...HAVING A LONG, SUNNY* ***NAP.***


THE END

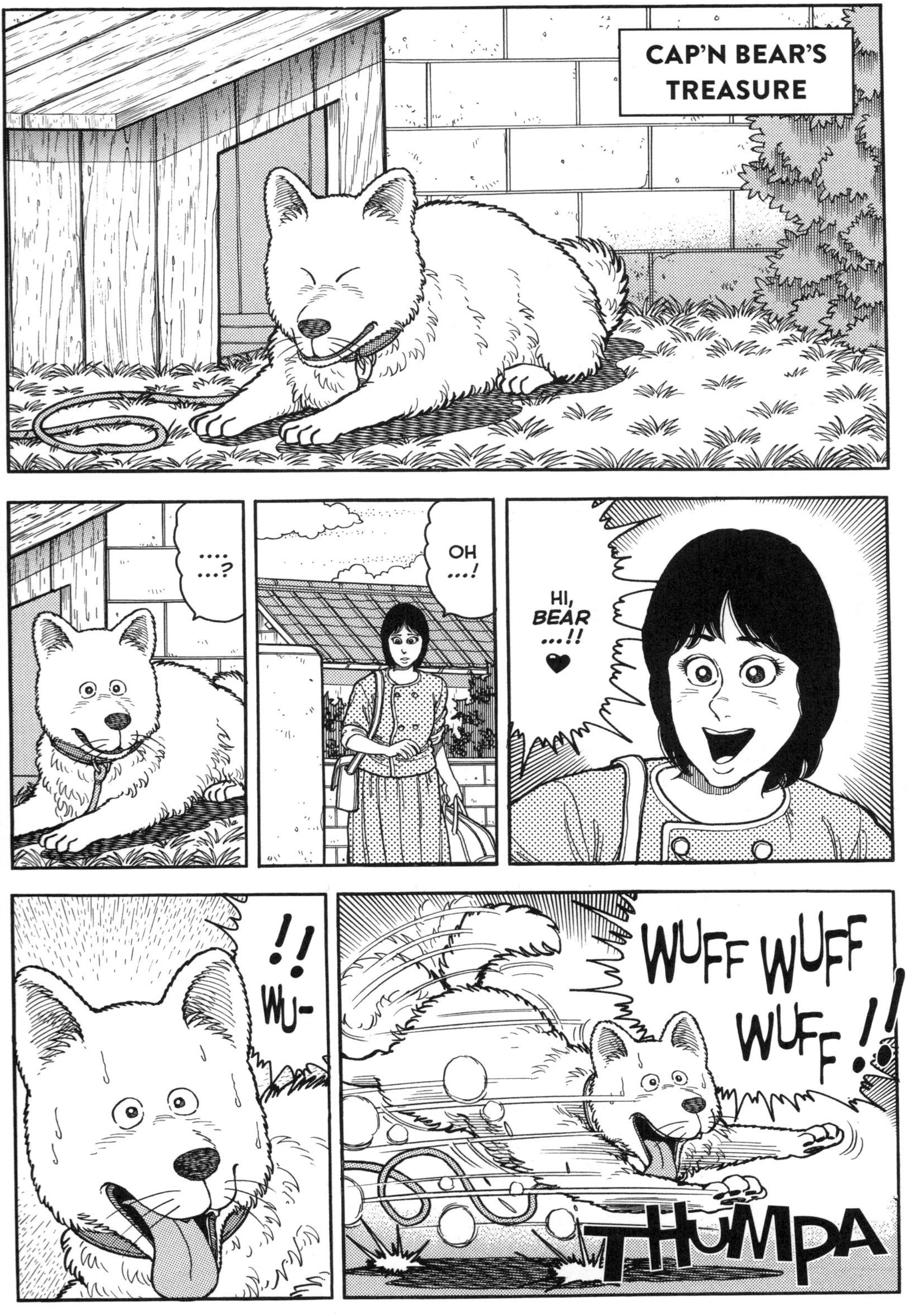
CAP'N BEAR'S
TREASURE
....
...?
OH
...!
HI,
BEAR
...!!
!!
WU-
WUFF WUFF
WUFF !!
THUMPA

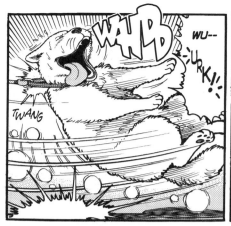

WAHB

WU--

--URK!!

TWANG

OH, BEAR! I'VE *MISSED* YOU SO *MUCH!*

HAVE YOU BEEN A *GOOD* DOGGIE FOR MOM AND DAD?

WUFF WUFF WOOF WURF!

AWW... THEY'RE STILL FEEDING YOU THE SAME OLD *LEFTOVERS*, AREN'T THEY?

POOR BEAR ...!

*I'LL* TALK TO *DADDY* AND MAKE HIM TREAT YOU *BETTER*, OKAY?!

WURF WUFF WOOF WAUF!

HUH? YER TALKIN' *NONSENSE*, GIRL!

DOGS EAT *LEFTOVERS!* BEEN THAT WAY SINCE TH' OLD DAYS!

THESE *AREN'T* THE OLD DAYS, DADDY! BEAR'S A PART OF OUR *FAMILY!*

YOU AT LEAST *WALK HIM* EVERY DAY... DON'T YOU?

HUH? ME?

HEY! YOU BEEN WALKIN' THE DAMN *DAWG?*

HMM ...?!

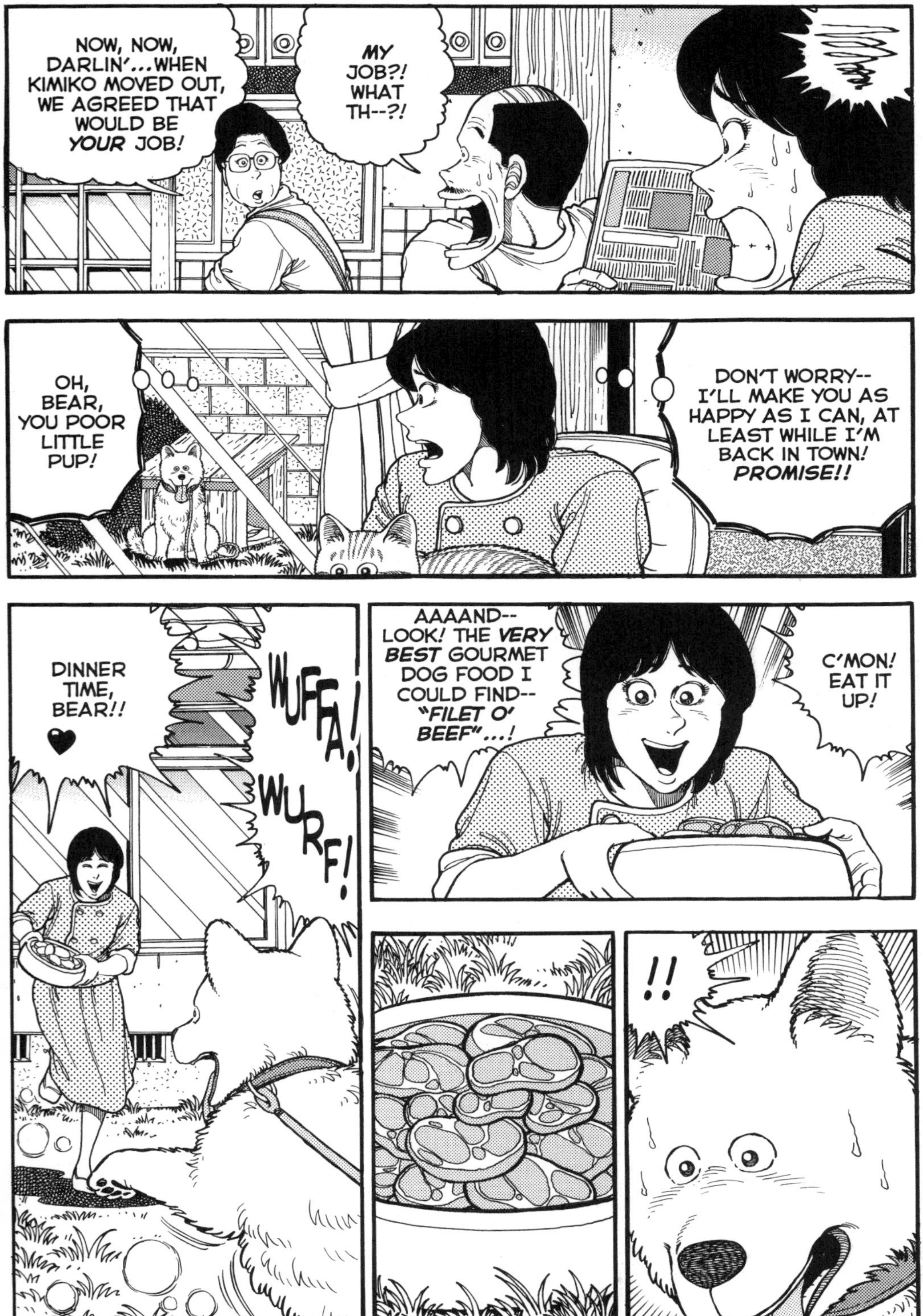

NOW, NOW, DARLIN'...WHEN KIMIKO MOVED OUT, WE AGREED THAT WOULD BE YOUR JOB!
MY JOB?! WHAT TH--?!
OH, BEAR, YOU POOR LITTLE PUP!
DON'T WORRY-- I'LL MAKE YOU AS HAPPY AS I CAN, AT LEAST WHILE I'M BACK IN TOWN! PROMISE!!
DINNER TIME, BEAR!! ♥
WUFFA! WURF!
AAAAND-- LOOK! THE VERY BEST GOURMET DOG FOOD I COULD FIND-- "FILET O' BEEF"...!
C'MON! EAT IT UP!
!!

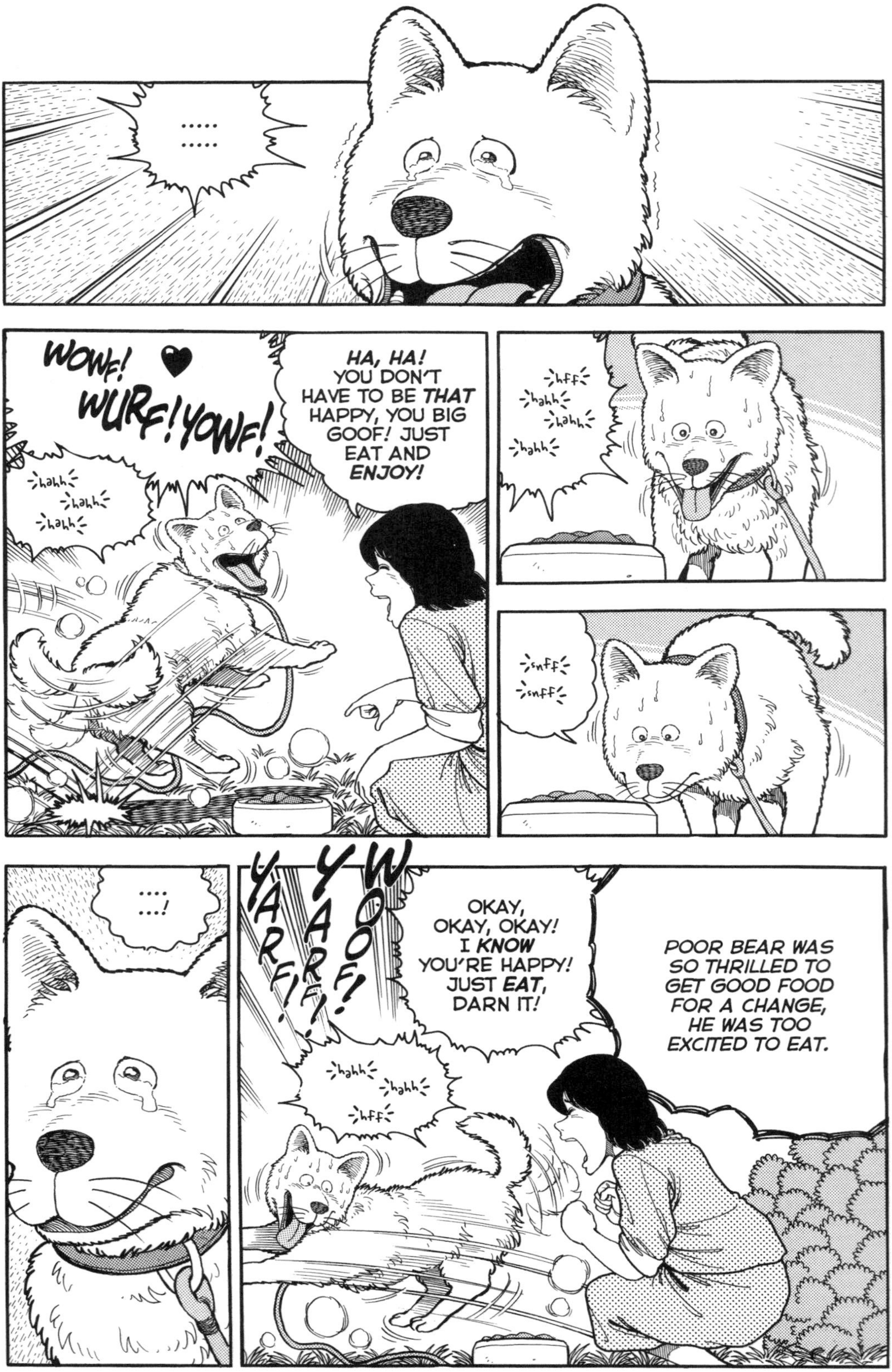

......
......
WOWF! ♥
WURF! YOWF!
hahh hahh hahh
HA, HA! YOU DON'T HAVE TO BE *THAT* HAPPY, YOU BIG GOOF! JUST EAT AND *ENJOY!*
hff hahh hahh hahh
snff snff
....
...!
YARF!!
YAARF!!
WOOF!!
OKAY, OKAY, OKAY! I *KNOW* YOU'RE HAPPY! JUST *EAT*, DARN IT!
hahh hahh hff
POOR BEAR WAS SO THRILLED TO GET GOOD FOOD FOR A CHANGE, HE WAS TOO EXCITED TO EAT.

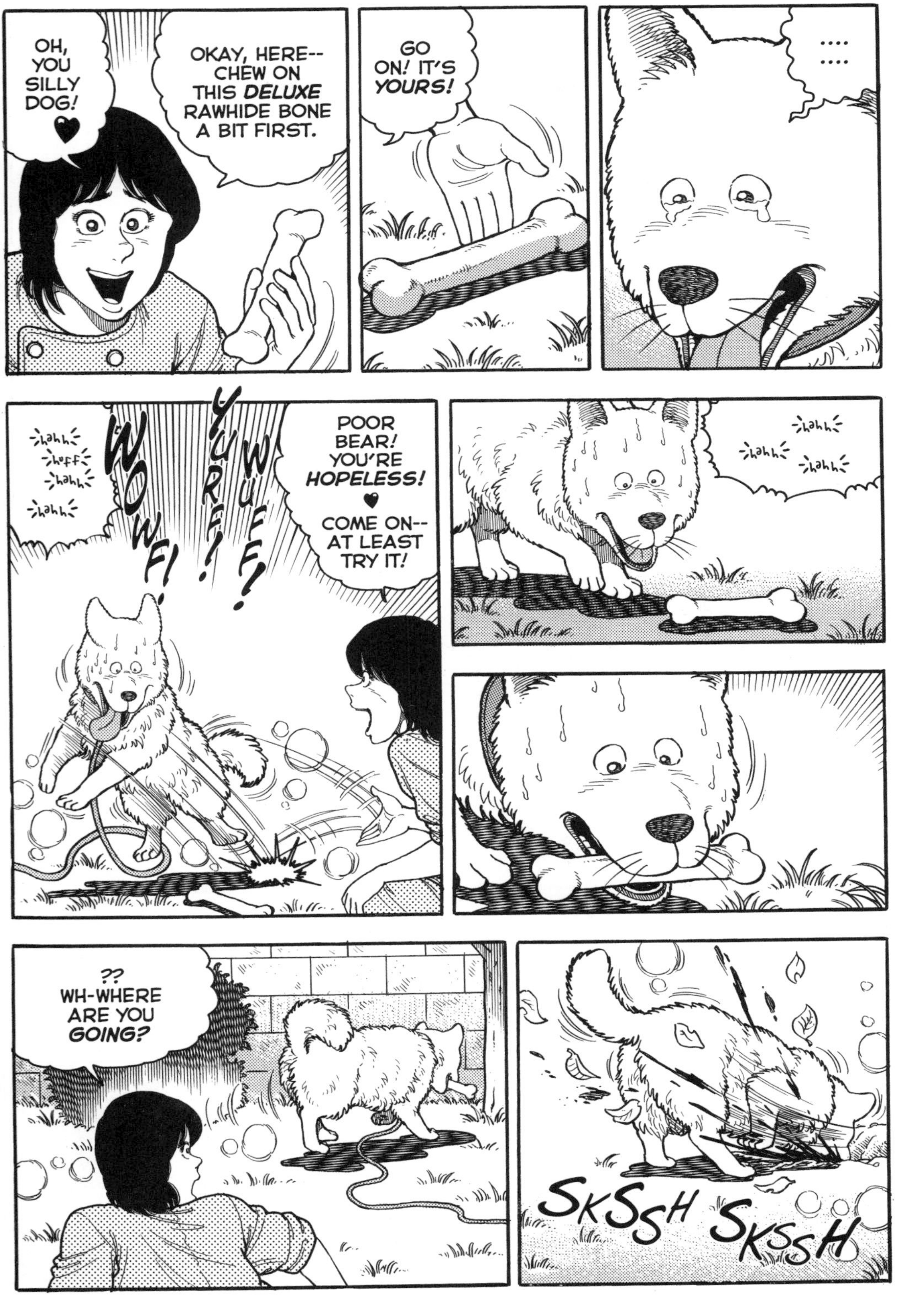
OH, YOU SILLY DOG! ♥
OKAY, HERE-- CHEW ON THIS *DELUXE* RAWHIDE BONE A BIT FIRST.
GO ON! IT'S *YOURS!*
....
....
hahh
hoff
hahh
hahh
WOWF!
YURF!
WUFF!
POOR BEAR! YOU'RE *HOPELESS!* ♥ COME ON-- AT LEAST TRY IT!
hahh
hahh
hahh
?? WH-WHERE ARE YOU *GOING?*
SKSSH SKSSH

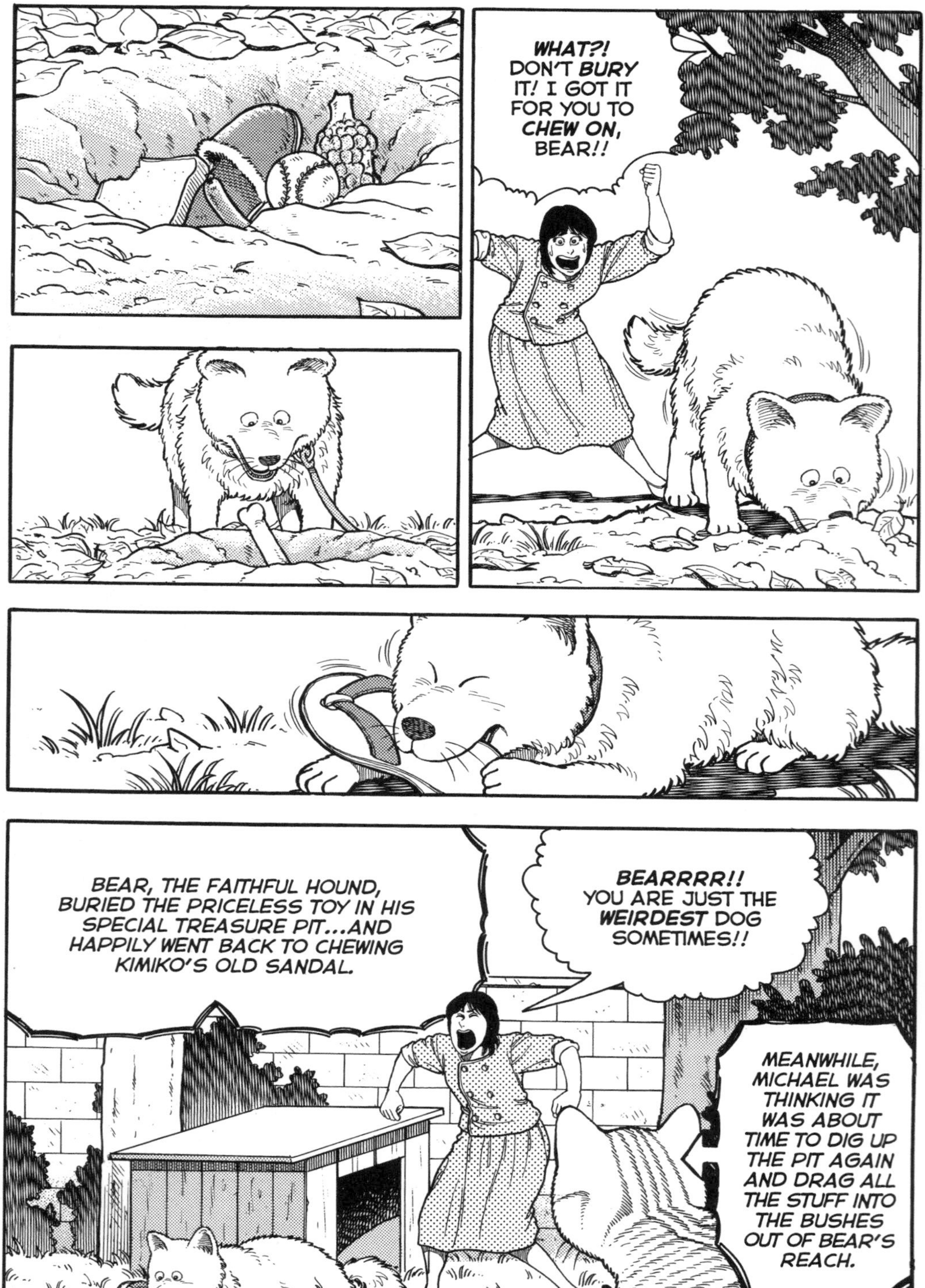
WHAT?! DON'T BURY IT! I GOT IT FOR YOU TO CHEW ON, BEAR!!
BEAR, THE FAITHFUL HOUND, BURIED THE PRICELESS TOY IN HIS SPECIAL TREASURE PIT...AND HAPPILY WENT BACK TO CHEWING KIMIKO'S OLD SANDAL.
BEARRRR!! YOU ARE JUST THE WEIRDEST DOG SOMETIMES!!
MEANWHILE, MICHAEL WAS THINKING IT WAS ABOUT TIME TO DIG UP THE PIT AGAIN AND DRAG ALL THE STUFF INTO THE BUSHES OUT OF BEAR'S REACH.

THE BITTERSWEET END

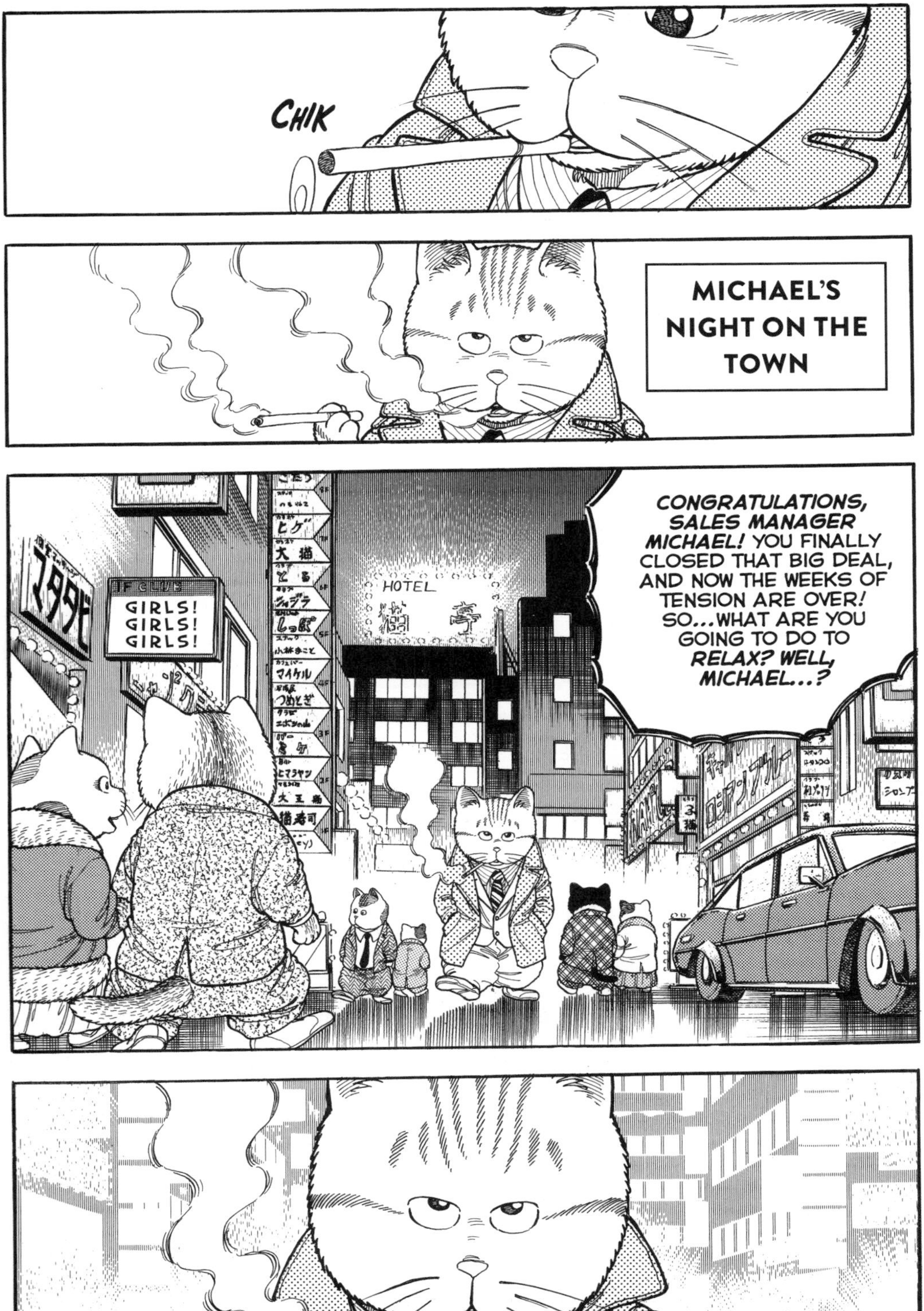
CHIK
MICHAEL'S NIGHT ON THE TOWN
GIRLS! GIRLS! GIRLS!
HOTEL
CONGRATULATIONS, SALES MANAGER MICHAEL! YOU FINALLY CLOSED THAT BIG DEAL, AND NOW THE WEEKS OF TENSION ARE OVER! SO...WHAT ARE YOU GOING TO DO TO RELAX? WELL, MICHAEL...?

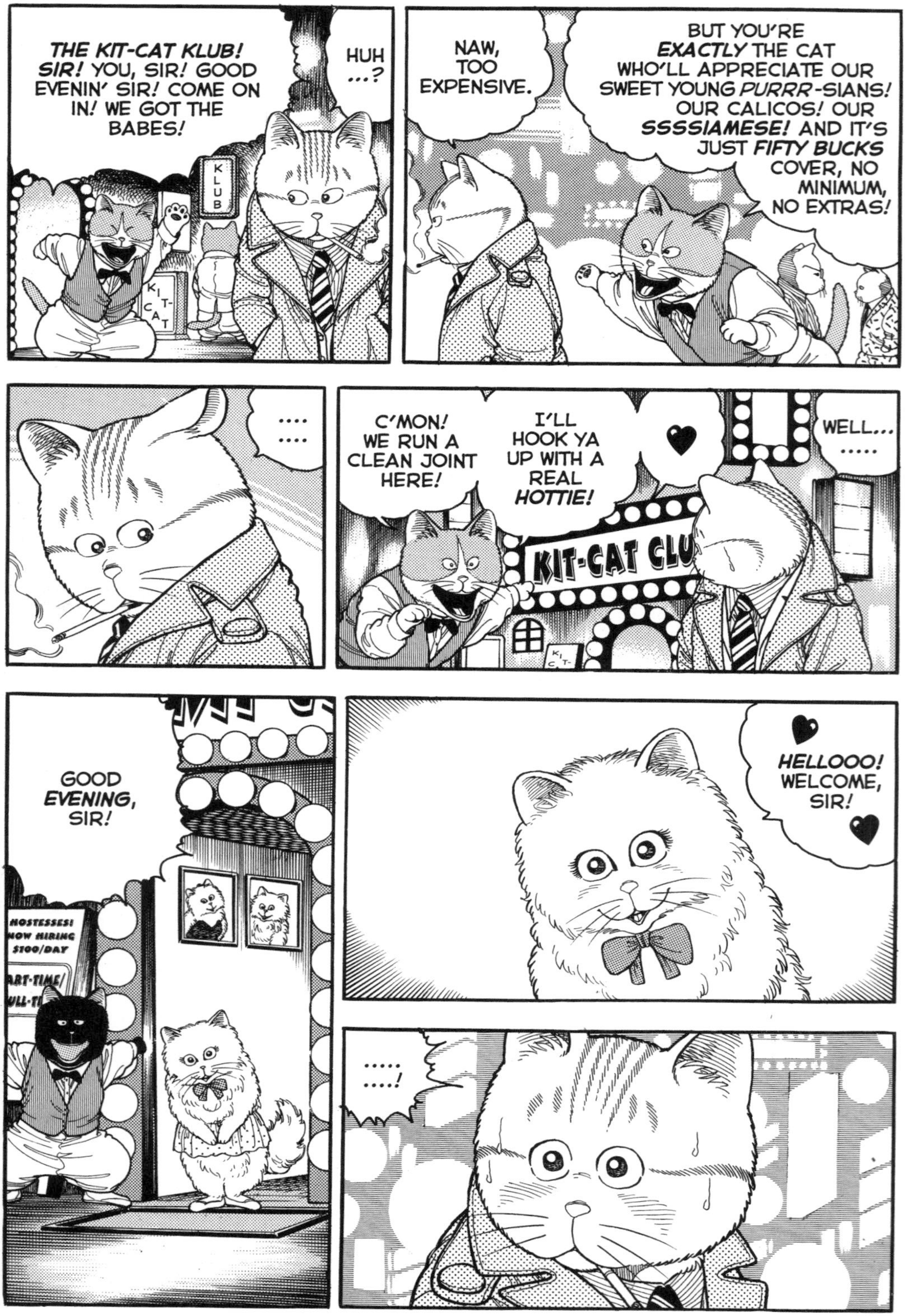
THE KIT-CAT KLUB! SIR! YOU, SIR! GOOD EVENIN' SIR! COME ON IN! WE GOT THE BABES!
HUH ...?
KLUB
KIT-CAT
NAW, TOO EXPENSIVE.
BUT YOU'RE EXACTLY THE CAT WHO'LL APPRECIATE OUR SWEET YOUNG PURRR-SIANS! OUR CALICOS! OUR SSSSIAMESE! AND IT'S JUST FIFTY BUCKS COVER, NO MINIMUM, NO EXTRAS!
.... ....
C'MON! WE RUN A CLEAN JOINT HERE!
I'LL HOOK YA UP WITH A REAL HOTTIE!
WELL... .....
KIT-CAT CLU
GOOD EVENING, SIR!
HOSTESSES! NOW HIRING $100/DAY
HELLOOO! WELCOME, SIR!
....., ....!

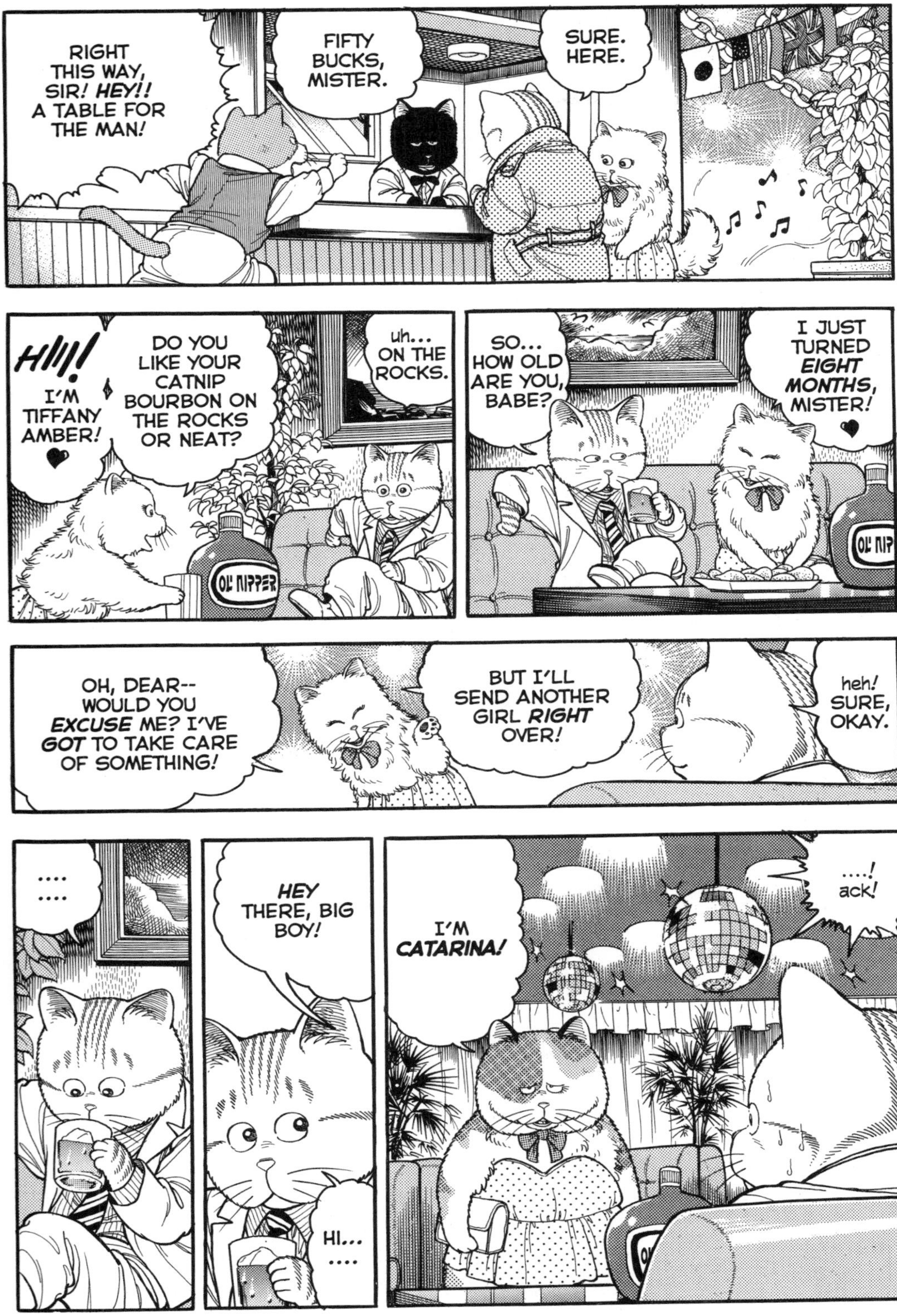
RIGHT THIS WAY, SIR! HEY!! A TABLE FOR THE MAN!
FIFTY BUCKS, MISTER.
SURE. HERE.
HI!
I'M TIFFANY AMBER!
DO YOU LIKE YOUR CATNIP BOURBON ON THE ROCKS OR NEAT?
uh... ON THE ROCKS.
OL' NIPPER
SO... HOW OLD ARE YOU, BABE?
I JUST TURNED EIGHT MONTHS, MISTER!
OL' NIP
OH, DEAR-- WOULD YOU EXCUSE ME? I'VE GOT TO TAKE CARE OF SOMETHING!
BUT I'LL SEND ANOTHER GIRL RIGHT OVER!
heh! SURE, OKAY.
.... ....
HEY THERE, BIG BOY!
HI... ....
I'M CATARINA!
....! ack!

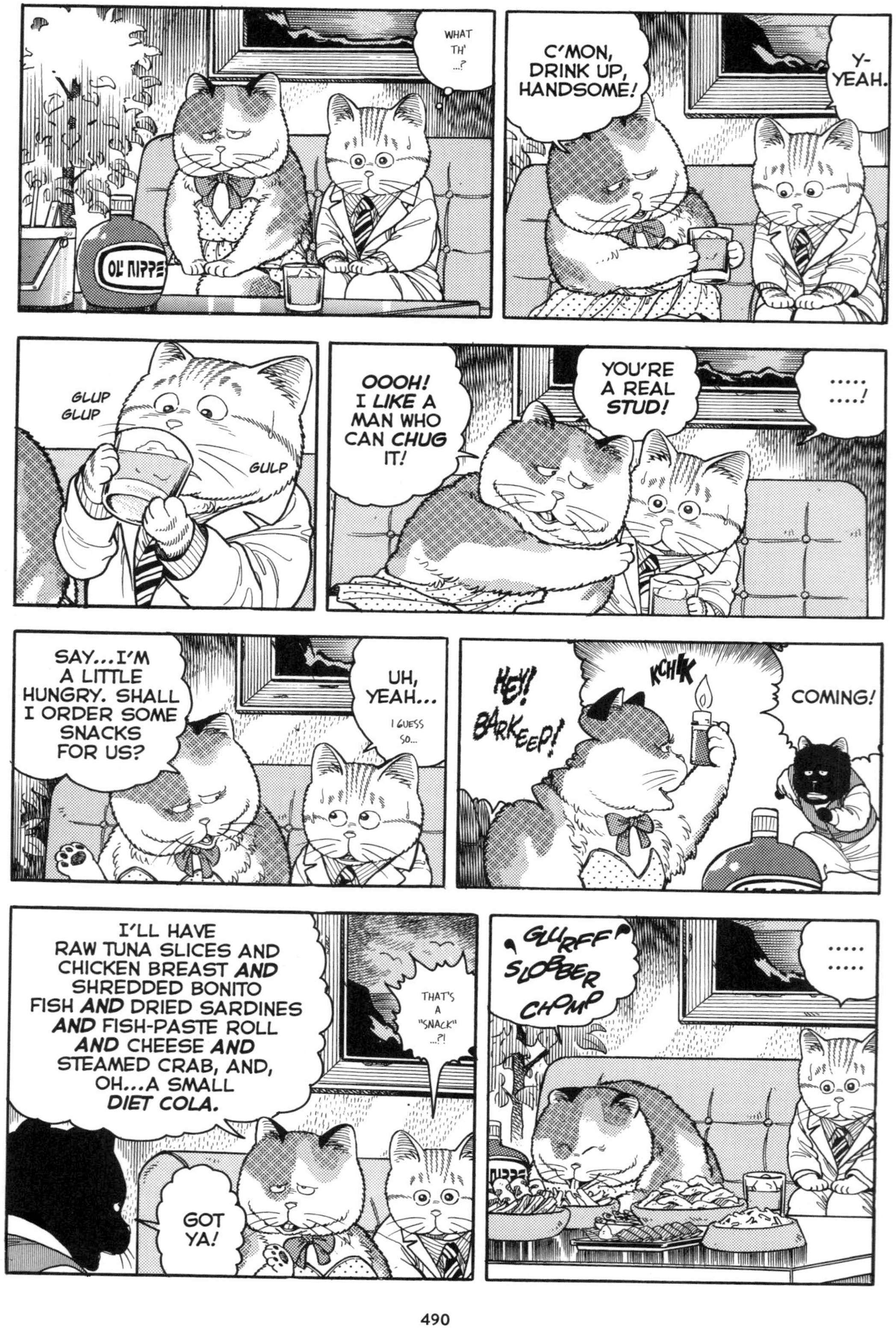
OL' NIPPE
WHAT TH' ...?
C'MON, DRINK UP, HANDSOME!
Y-YEAH.
GLUP GLUP
GULP
OOOH! I LIKE A MAN WHO CAN CHUG IT!
YOU'RE A REAL STUD!
.....
.....!
SAY...I'M A LITTLE HUNGRY. SHALL I ORDER SOME SNACKS FOR US?
UH, YEAH...
I GUESS SO...
HEY! BARKEEP!
KCHIK
COMING!
I'LL HAVE RAW TUNA SLICES AND CHICKEN BREAST AND SHREDDED BONITO FISH AND DRIED SARDINES AND FISH-PASTE ROLL AND CHEESE AND STEAMED CRAB, AND, OH...A SMALL DIET COLA.
THAT'S A "SNACK" ...?!
GOT YA!
GLURFF SLOBBER CHOMP
.....
.....

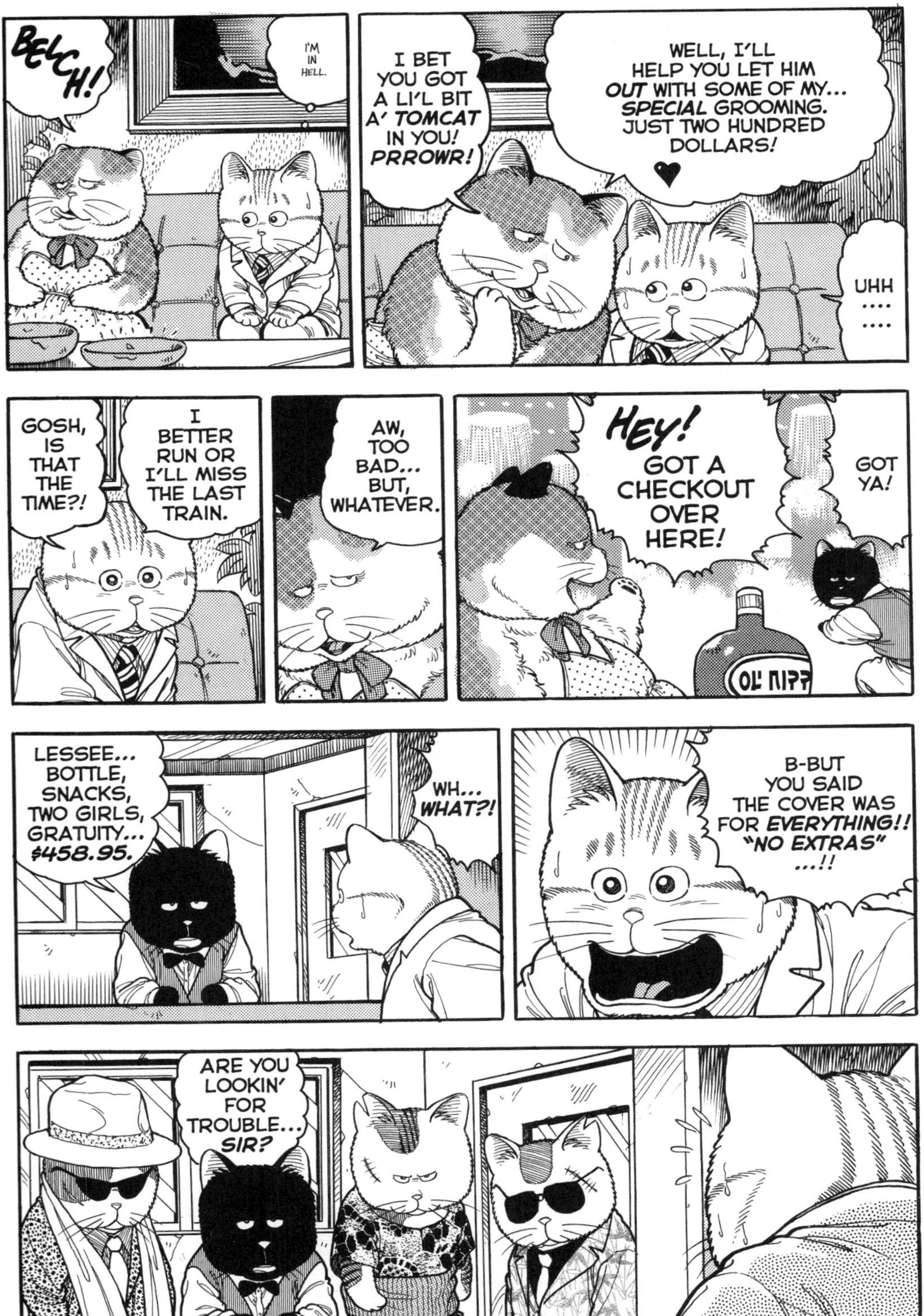
BELCH!
I'M IN HELL.
I BET YOU GOT A LI'L BIT A' TOMCAT IN YOU! PRROWR!
WELL, I'LL HELP YOU LET HIM OUT WITH SOME OF MY... SPECIAL GROOMING. JUST TWO HUNDRED DOLLARS! ♥
UHH........
GOSH, IS THAT THE TIME?!
I BETTER RUN OR I'LL MISS THE LAST TRAIN.
AW, TOO BAD... BUT, WHATEVER.
HEY! GOT A CHECKOUT OVER HERE!
GOT YA!
LESSEE... BOTTLE, SNACKS, TWO GIRLS, GRATUITY... $458.95.
WH... WHAT?!
B-BUT YOU SAID THE COVER WAS FOR EVERYTHING!! "NO EXTRAS" ...!!
ARE YOU LOOKIN' FOR TROUBLE... SIR?

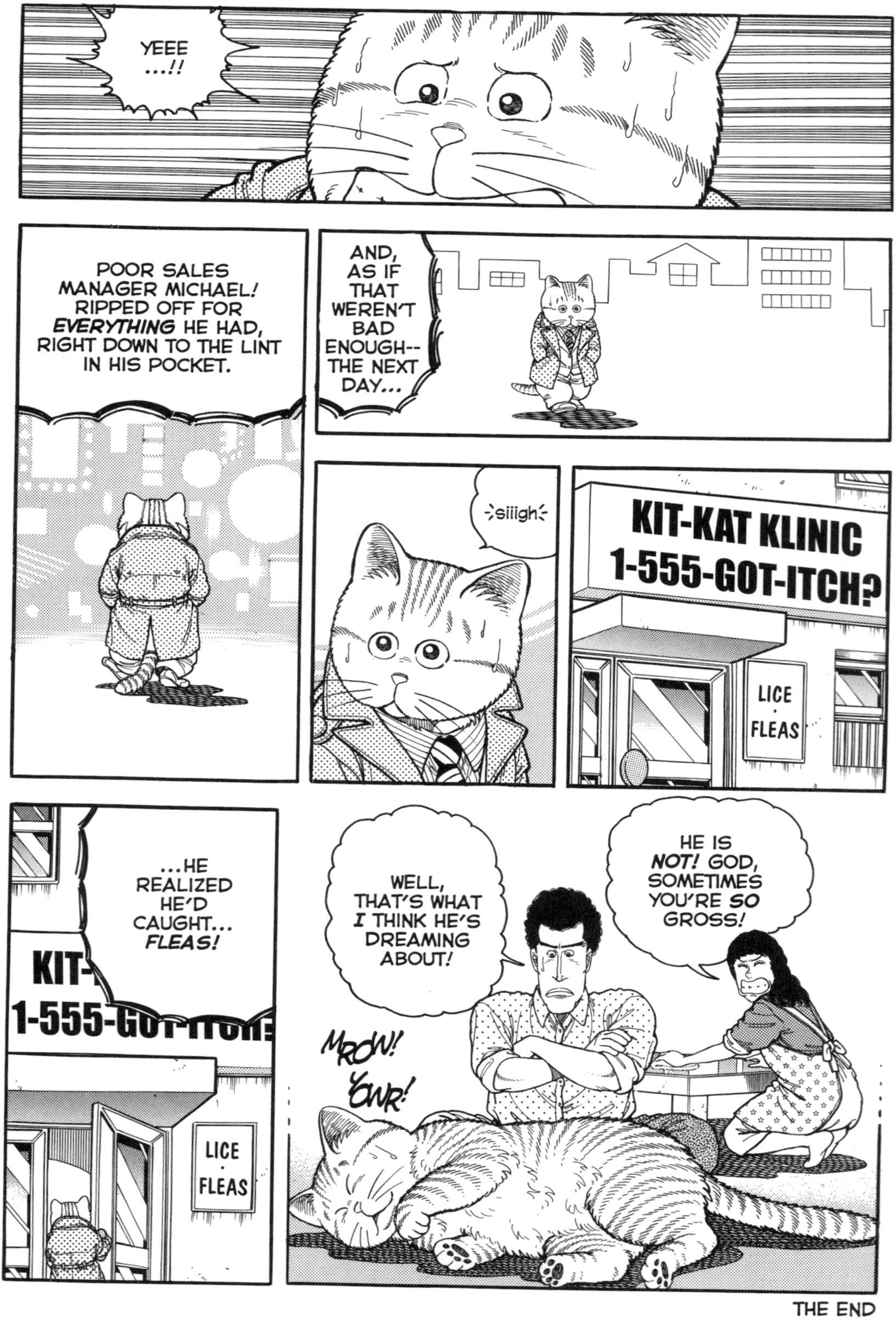
YEEE ...!!
POOR SALES MANAGER MICHAEL! RIPPED OFF FOR EVERYTHING HE HAD, RIGHT DOWN TO THE LINT IN HIS POCKET.
AND, AS IF THAT WEREN'T BAD ENOUGH-- THE NEXT DAY...
siiigh
KIT-KAT KLINIC
1-555-GOT-ITCH?
LICE · FLEAS
...HE REALIZED HE'D CAUGHT... FLEAS!
LICE · FLEAS
WELL, THAT'S WHAT I THINK HE'S DREAMING ABOUT!
HE IS NOT! GOD, SOMETIMES YOU'RE SO GROSS!
MROW! YOWR!

THE END

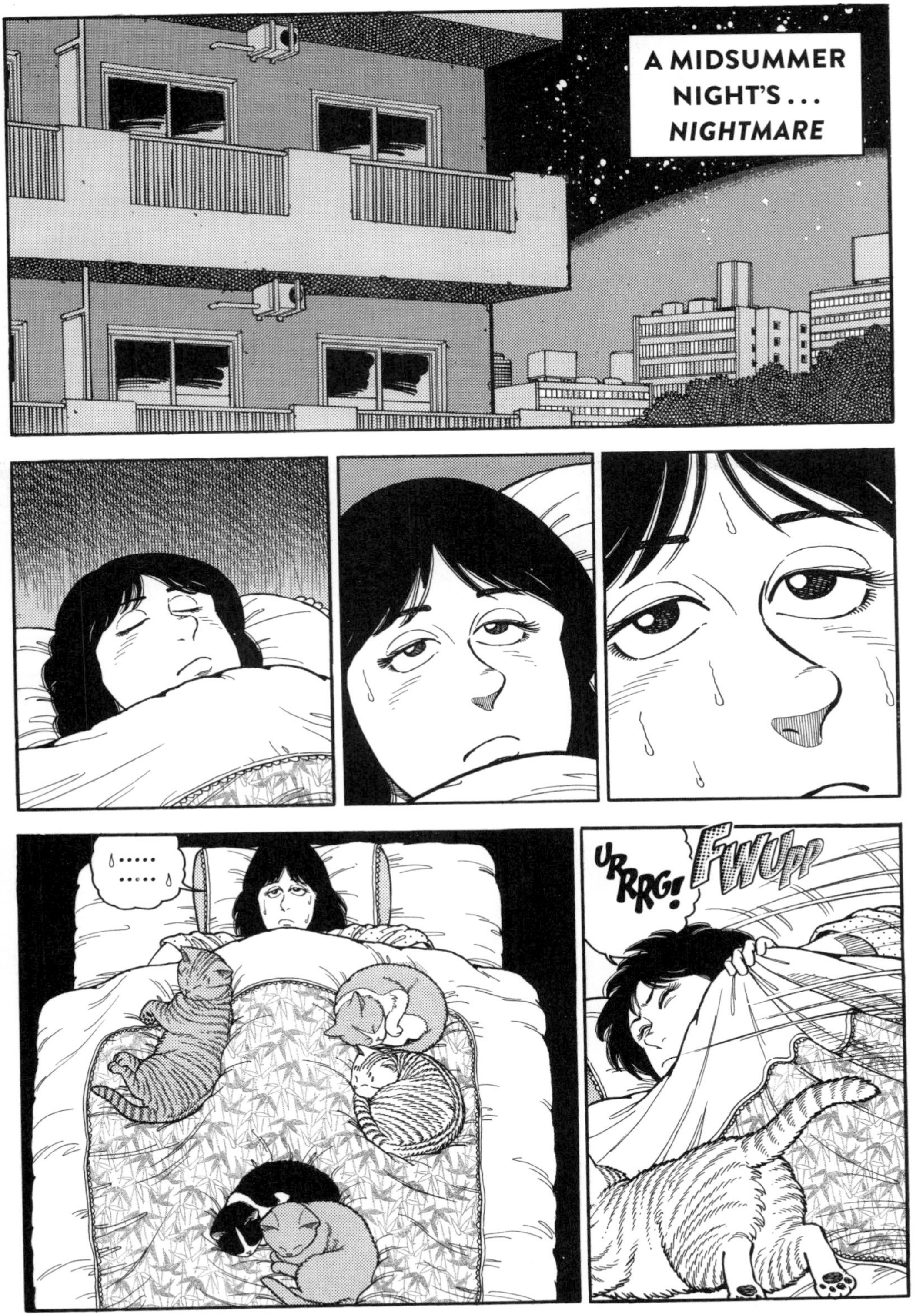
A MIDSUMMER NIGHT'S . . . *NIGHTMARE*
......
......
URRRG!
FWUPP

NNFFH!!
FWAPP
hrrf hrrf haahn hahn

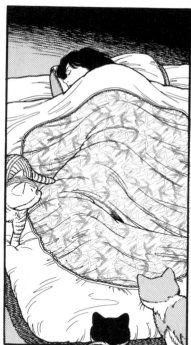

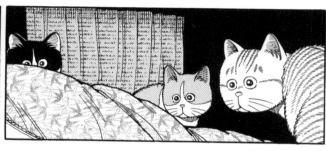

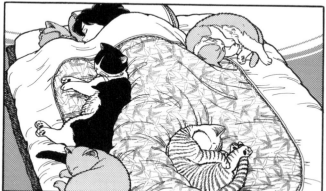

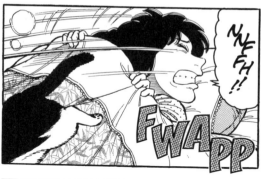

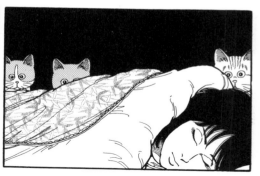

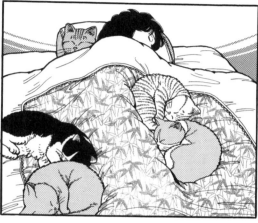

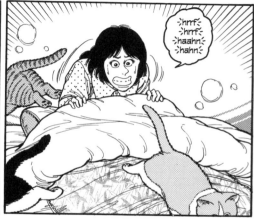

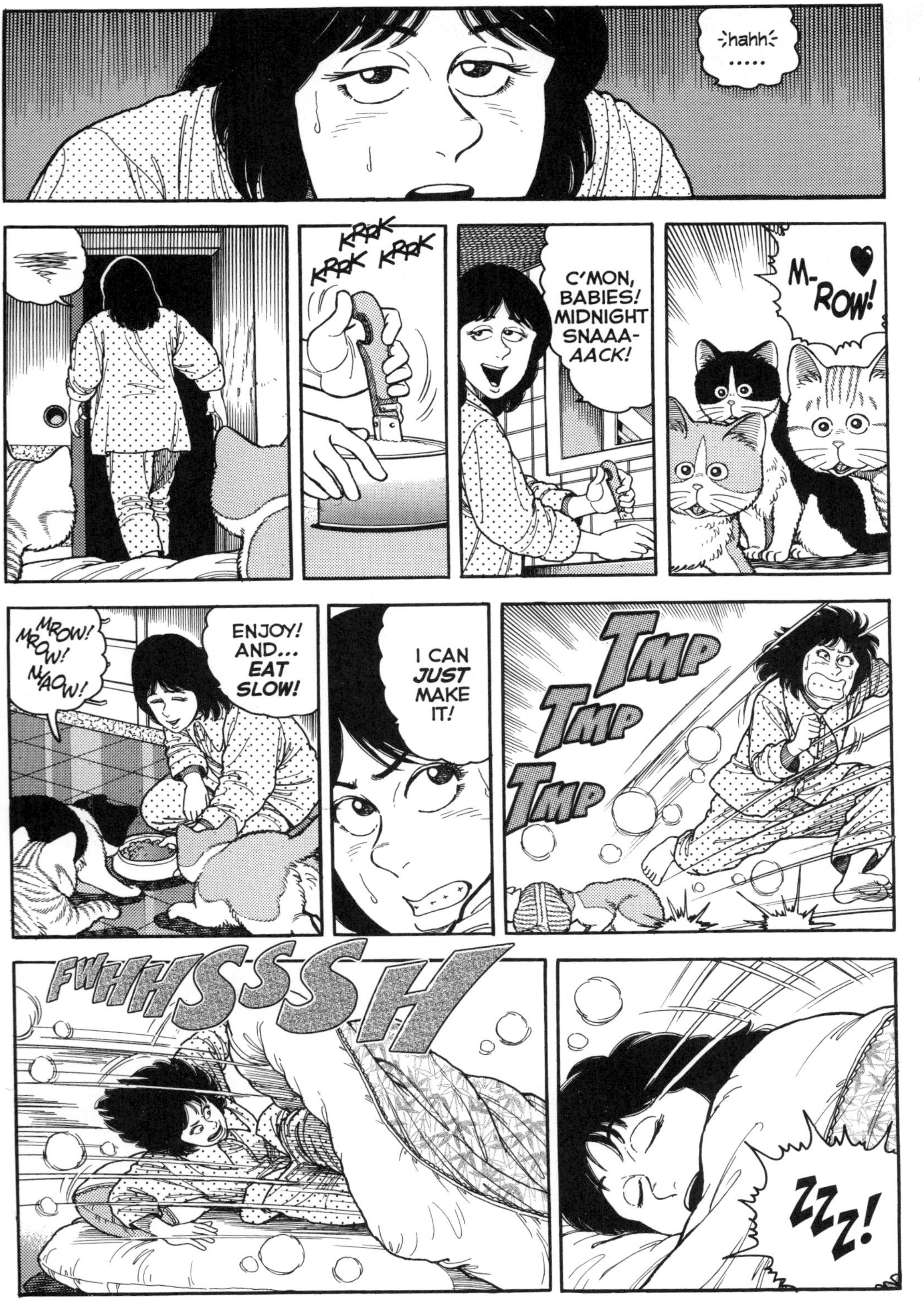
hahh
.....
KRRK KRRK KRRK
C'MON, BABIES! MIDNIGHT SNAAAA-AACK!
M-ROW!
MROW! MROW! NYAOW!
ENJOY! AND... EAT SLOW!
I CAN JUST MAKE IT!
TMP TMP TMP
FWHHSSSSH
ZZZ!

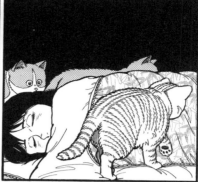

VVVHPP!

WHIFFA

WHIFFA

FWNNG

ktak

MEE-
YOW!

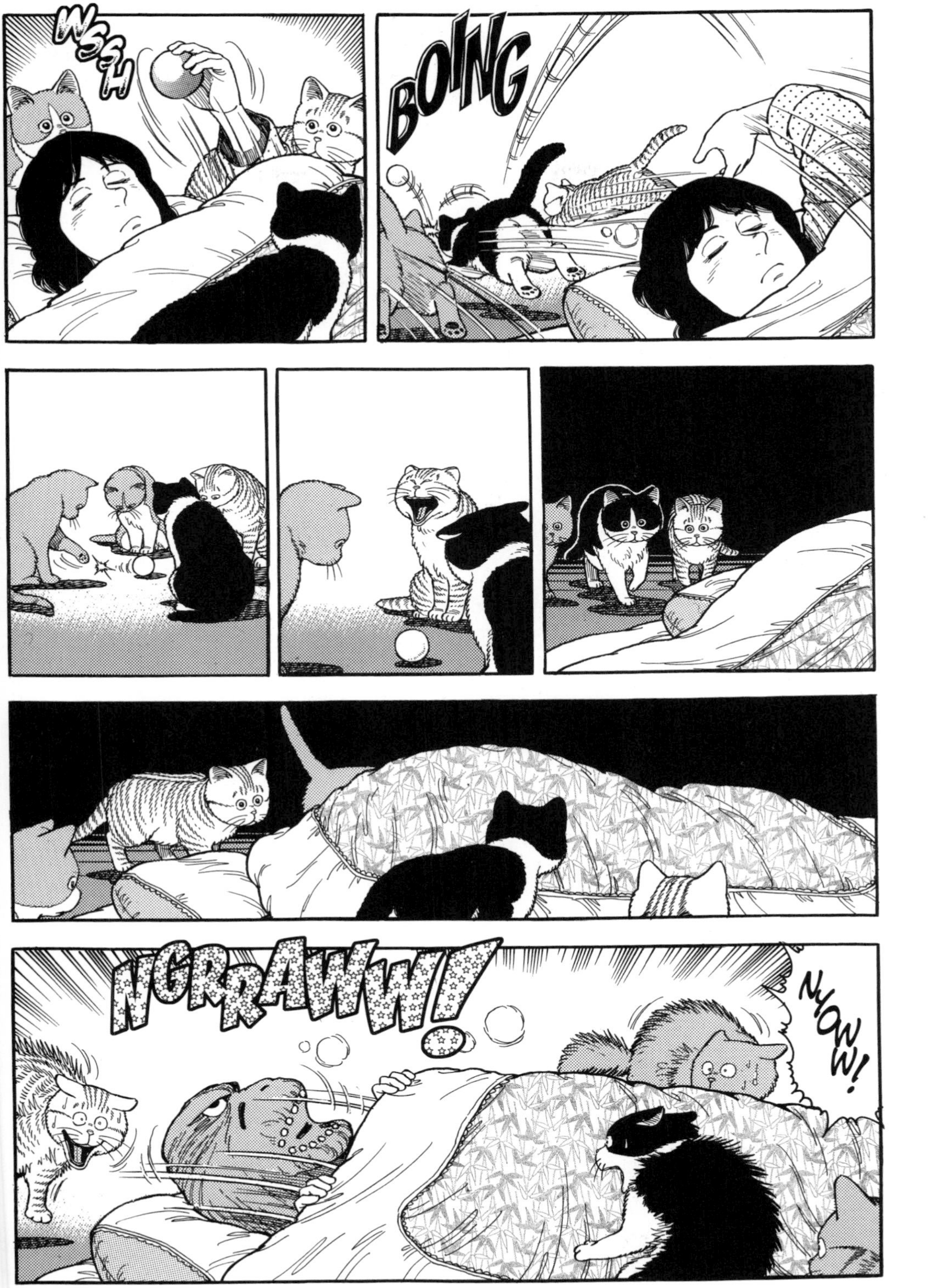

WSSH
BOING
NGRRAWWW!
MYOWW!

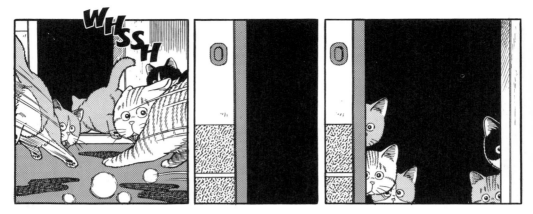

WHSSSH

~hnf~

FWAP

GASP!

~HUFF~
~HAHH~

AWWW, GUYSSS!

ANOTHER *LONG, HOT* SUMMER NIGHT AT HOME...TO BE FOLLOWED BY ANOTHER *ENDLESS* SLEEP-DEPRIVED DAY AT WORK...

THE END

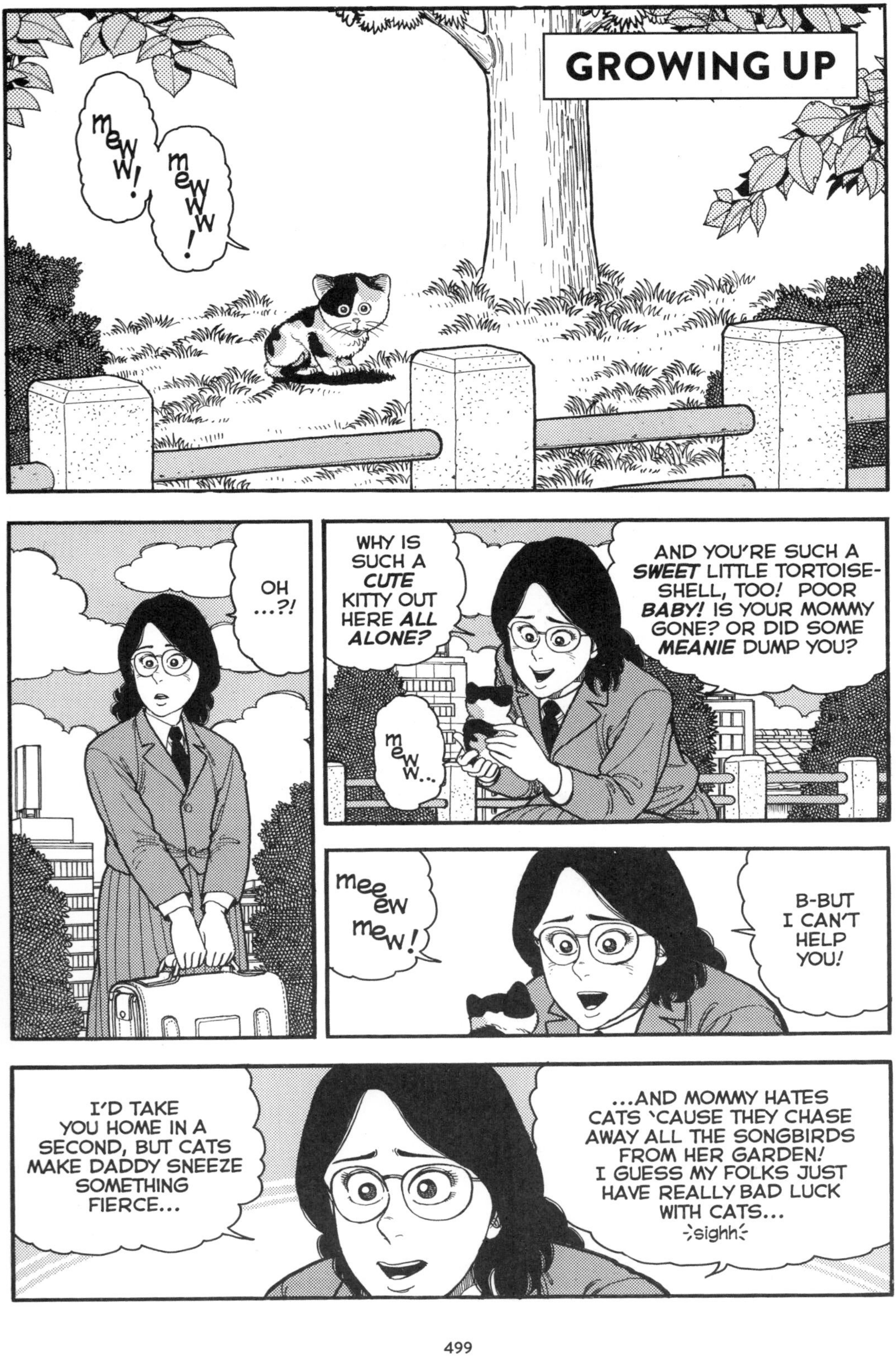
GROWING UP
mew!
meww!
OH ...?!
WHY IS SUCH A CUTE KITTY OUT HERE ALL ALONE?
AND YOU'RE SUCH A SWEET LITTLE TORTOISE-SHELL, TOO! POOR BABY! IS YOUR MOMMY GONE? OR DID SOME MEANIE DUMP YOU?
mew...
meeew mew!
B-BUT I CAN'T HELP YOU!
I'D TAKE YOU HOME IN A SECOND, BUT CATS MAKE DADDY SNEEZE SOMETHING FIERCE...
...AND MOMMY HATES CATS 'CAUSE THEY CHASE AWAY ALL THE SONGBIRDS FROM HER GARDEN! I GUESS MY FOLKS JUST HAVE REALLY BAD LUCK WITH CATS...
sighh

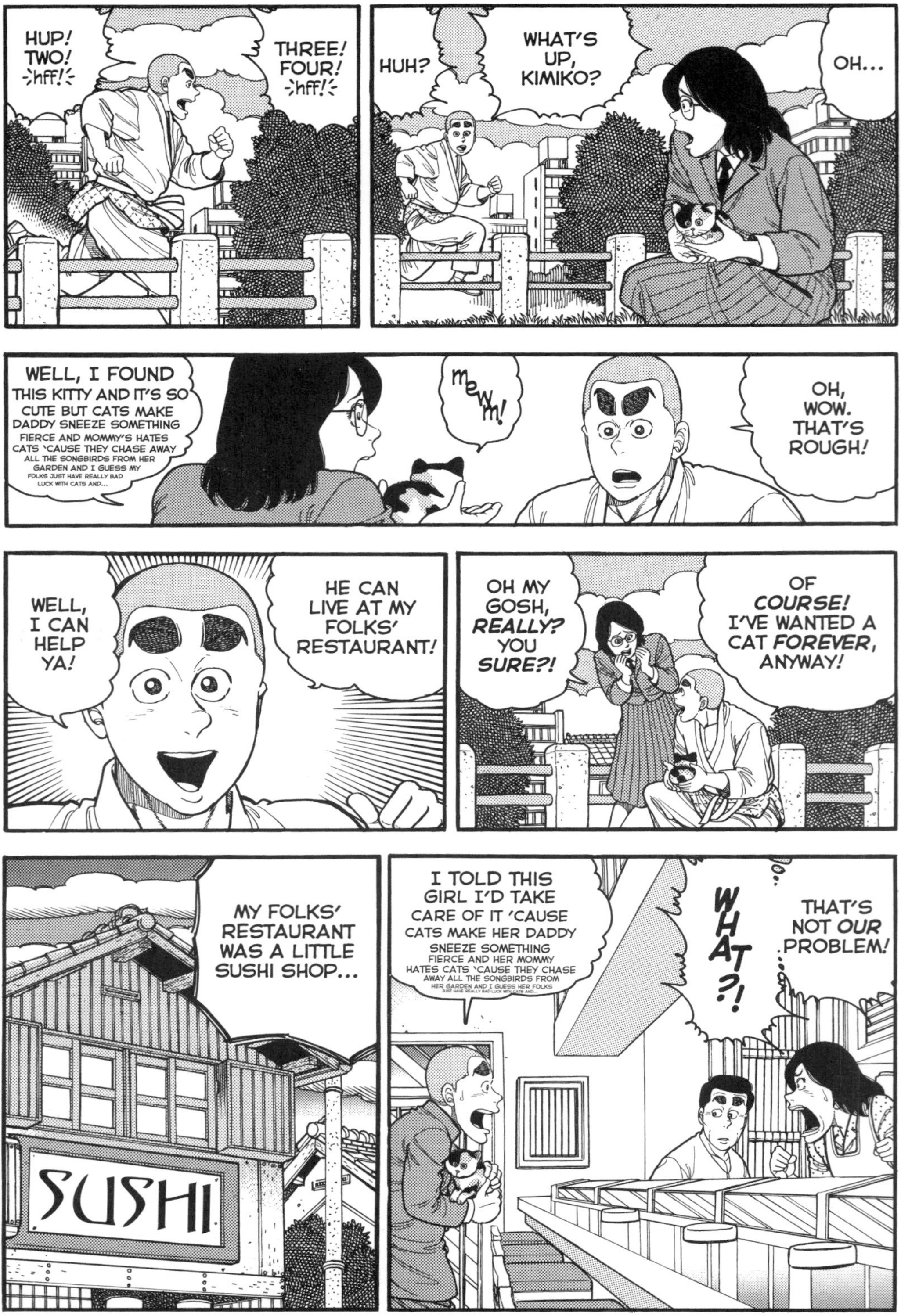
HUP! TWO! hff!
THREE! FOUR! hff!
HUH?
WHAT'S UP, KIMIKO?
OH...
WELL, I FOUND THIS KITTY AND IT'S SO CUTE BUT CATS MAKE DADDY SNEEZE SOMETHING FIERCE AND MOMMY'S HATES CATS 'CAUSE THEY CHASE AWAY ALL THE SONGBIRDS FROM HER GARDEN AND I GUESS MY FOLKS JUST HAVE REALLY BAD LUCK WITH CATS AND...
mewm!
OH, WOW. THAT'S ROUGH!
WELL, I CAN HELP YA!
HE CAN LIVE AT MY FOLKS' RESTAURANT!
OH MY GOSH, REALLY? YOU SURE?!
OF COURSE! I'VE WANTED A CAT FOREVER, ANYWAY!
MY FOLKS' RESTAURANT WAS A LITTLE SUSHI SHOP...
SUSHI
I TOLD THIS GIRL I'D TAKE CARE OF IT 'CAUSE CATS MAKE HER DADDY SNEEZE SOMETHING FIERCE AND HER MOMMY HATES CATS 'CAUSE THEY CHASE AWAY ALL THE SONGBIRDS FROM HER GARDEN AND I GUESS HER FOLKS JUST HAVE REALLY BAD LUCK WITH CATS AND...
WHAT?!
THAT'S NOT OUR PROBLEM!

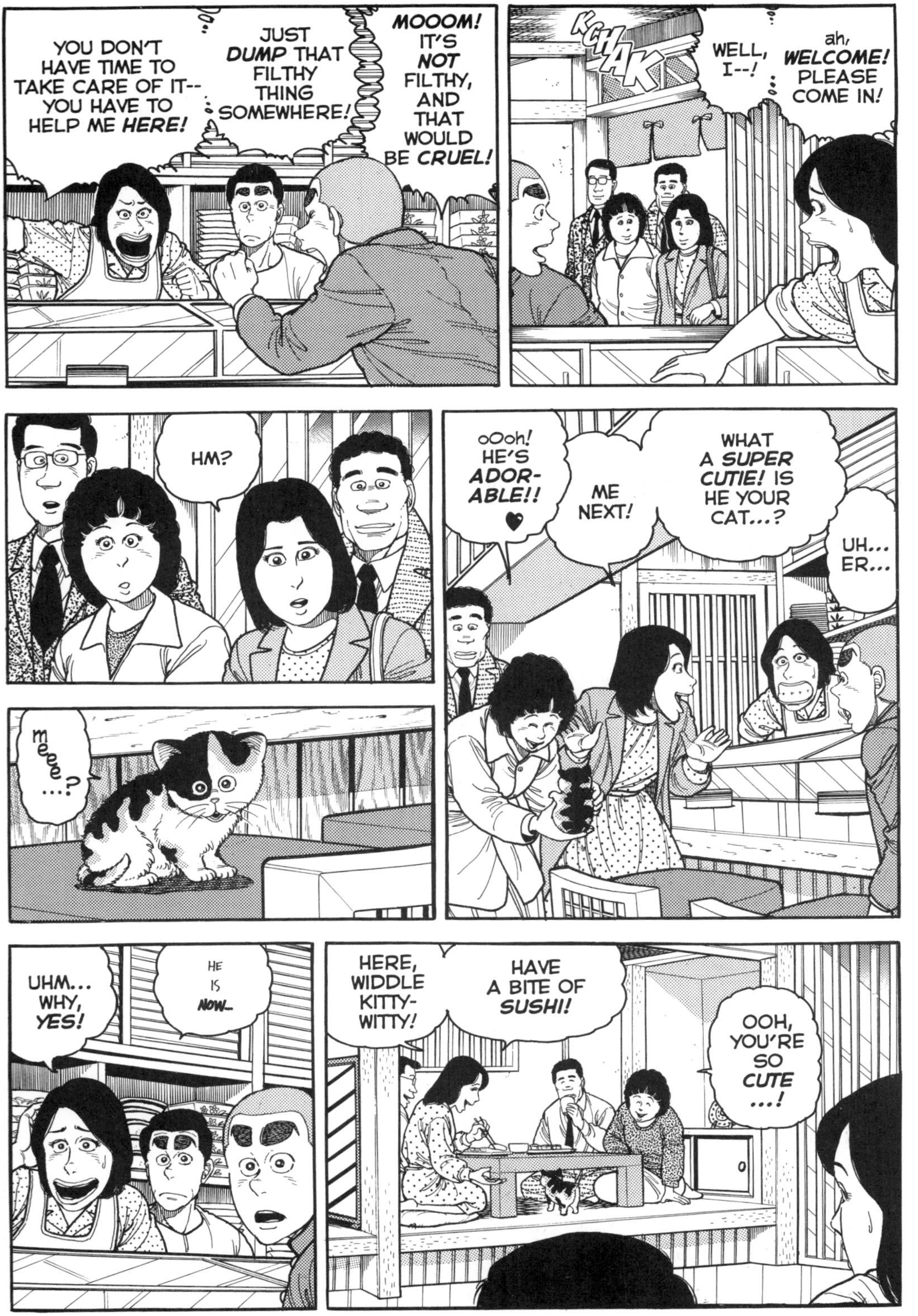
YOU DON'T HAVE TIME TO TAKE CARE OF IT-- YOU HAVE TO HELP ME HERE!
JUST DUMP THAT FILTHY THING SOMEWHERE!
MOOOM! IT'S NOT FILTHY, AND THAT WOULD BE CRUEL!
KCHAK
WELL, I--!
ah, WELCOME! PLEASE COME IN!
HM?
meee...?
oOoh! HE'S ADORABLE!!
ME NEXT!
WHAT A SUPER CUTIE! IS HE YOUR CAT...?
UH... ER...
UHM... WHY, YES!
HE IS NOW...
HERE, WIDDLE KITTY-WITTY!
HAVE A BITE OF SUSHI!
OOH, YOU'RE SO CUTE...!

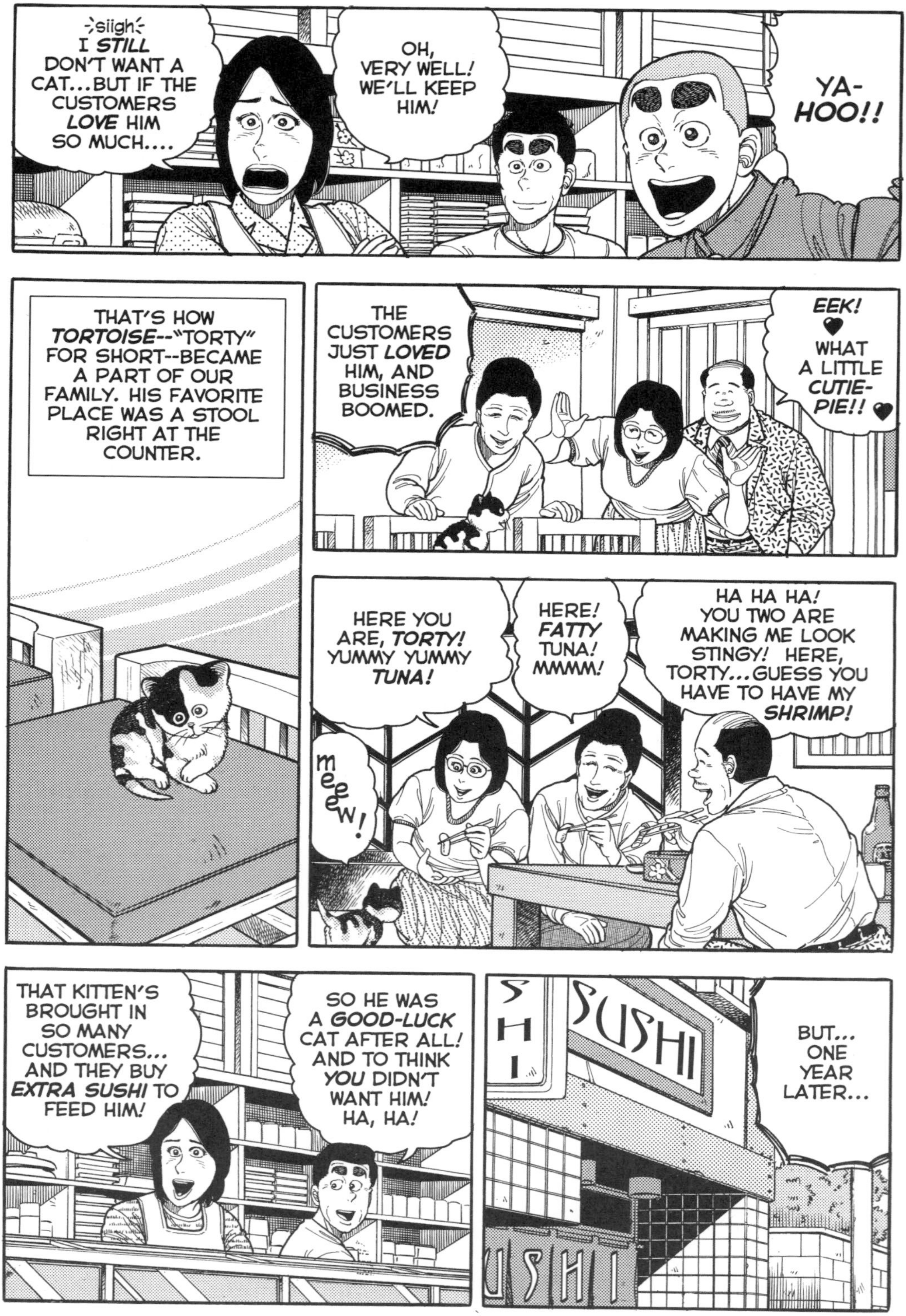

siigh
I STILL DON'T WANT A CAT...BUT IF THE CUSTOMERS LOVE HIM SO MUCH....
OH, VERY WELL! WE'LL KEEP HIM!
YA-HOO!!
THAT'S HOW TORTOISE--"TORTY" FOR SHORT--BECAME A PART OF OUR FAMILY. HIS FAVORITE PLACE WAS A STOOL RIGHT AT THE COUNTER.
THE CUSTOMERS JUST LOVED HIM, AND BUSINESS BOOMED.
EEK! ♥ WHAT A LITTLE CUTIE-PIE!! ♥
HERE YOU ARE, TORTY! YUMMY YUMMY TUNA!
HERE! FATTY TUNA! MMMM!
HA HA HA! YOU TWO ARE MAKING ME LOOK STINGY! HERE, TORTY...GUESS YOU HAVE TO HAVE MY SHRIMP!
meeew!
THAT KITTEN'S BROUGHT IN SO MANY CUSTOMERS... AND THEY BUY EXTRA SUSHI TO FEED HIM!
SO HE WAS A GOOD-LUCK CAT AFTER ALL! AND TO THINK YOU DIDN'T WANT HIM! HA, HA!
SUSHI
SHI
BUT... ONE YEAR LATER...
SUSHI

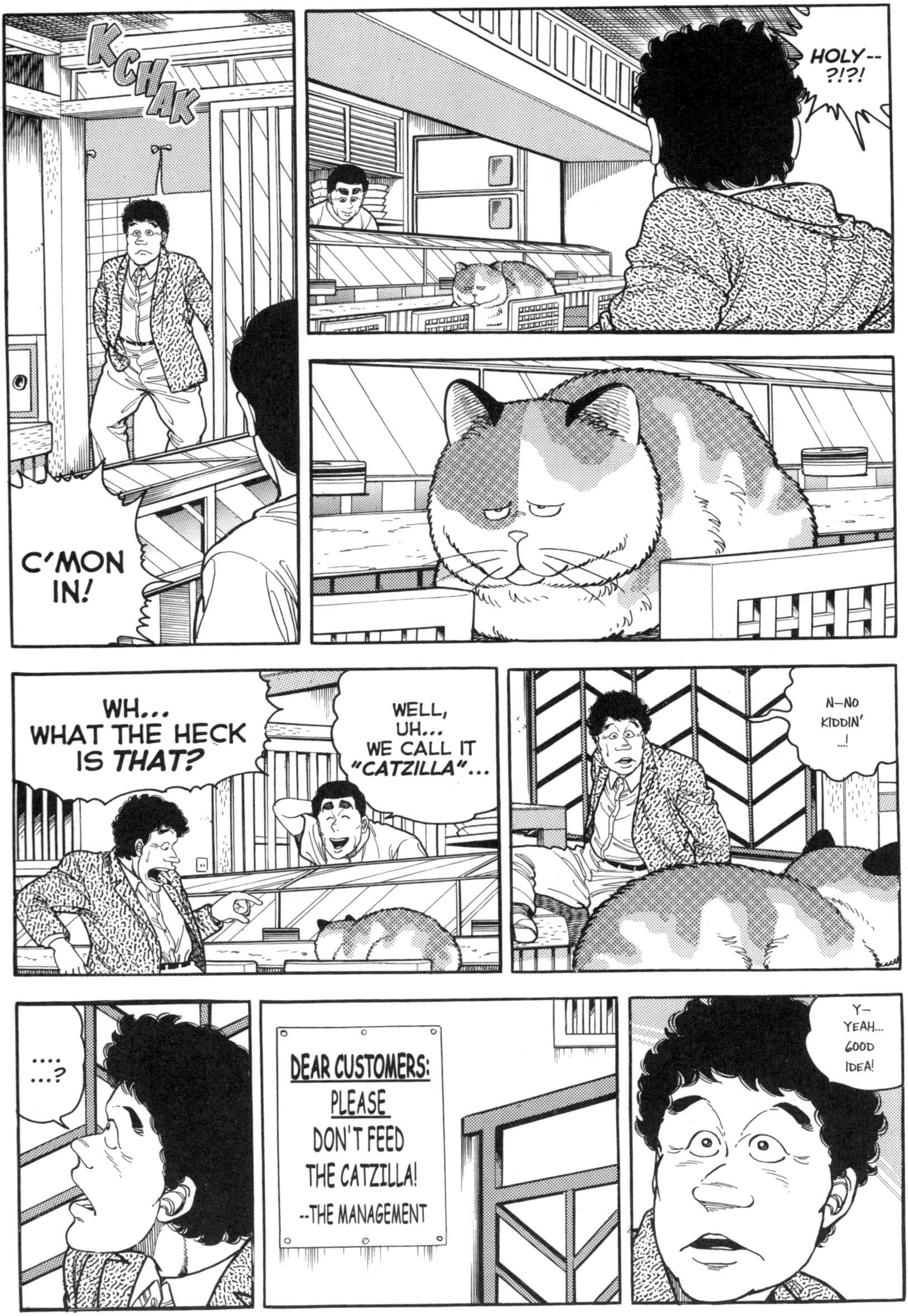
KCHAK
C'MON IN!
HOLY-- ?!?!
WH... WHAT THE HECK IS THAT?
WELL, UH... WE CALL IT "CATZILLA"...
N-NO KIDDIN' ...!
.... ...?
DEAR CUSTOMERS: PLEASE DON'T FEED THE CATZILLA! --THE MANAGEMENT
Y-YEAH... GOOD IDEA!

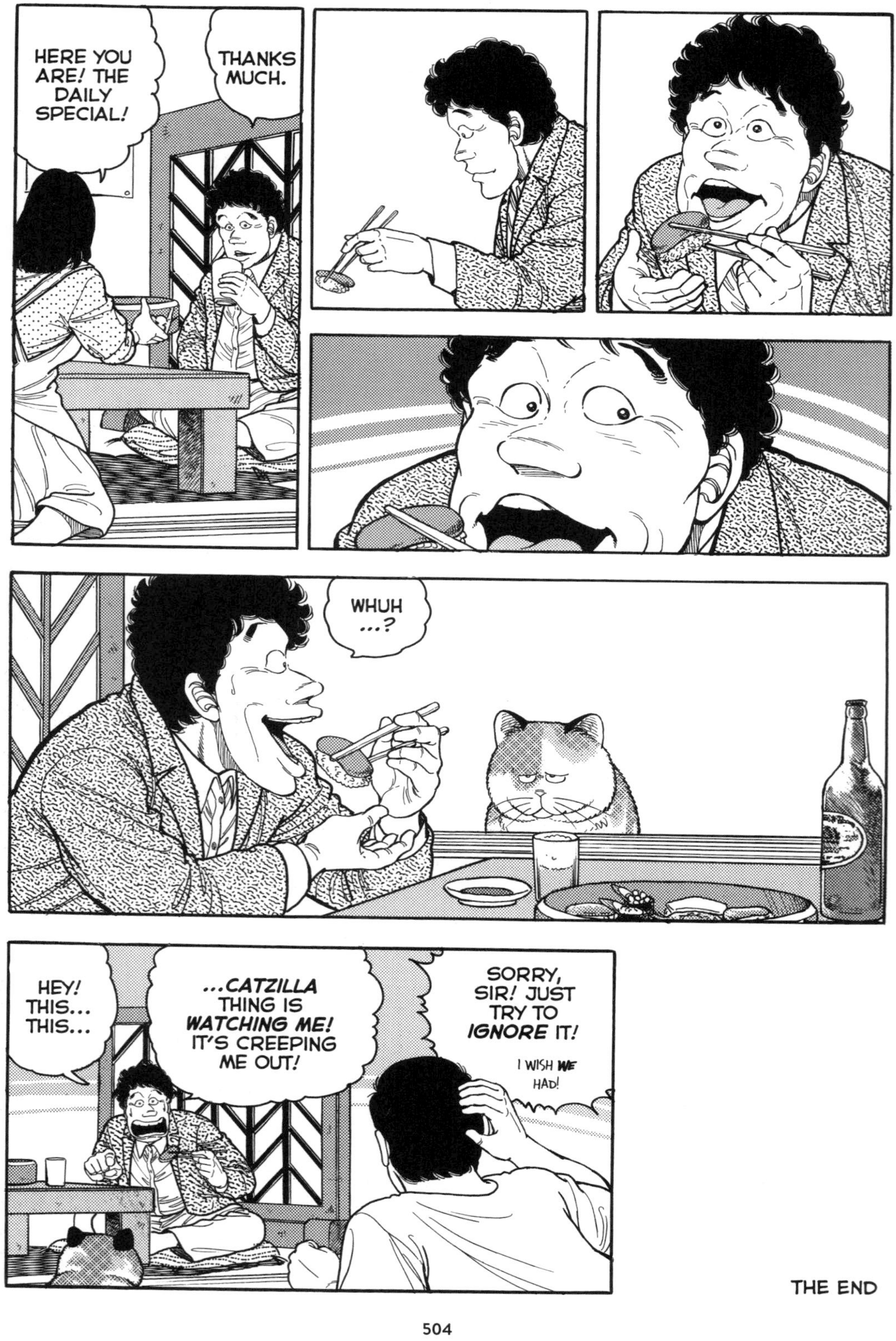
HERE YOU ARE! THE DAILY SPECIAL!
THANKS MUCH.
WHUH ...?
HEY! THIS... THIS...
...CATZILLA THING IS WATCHING ME! IT'S CREEPING ME OUT!
SORRY, SIR! JUST TRY TO IGNORE IT!
I WISH WE HAD!

THE END

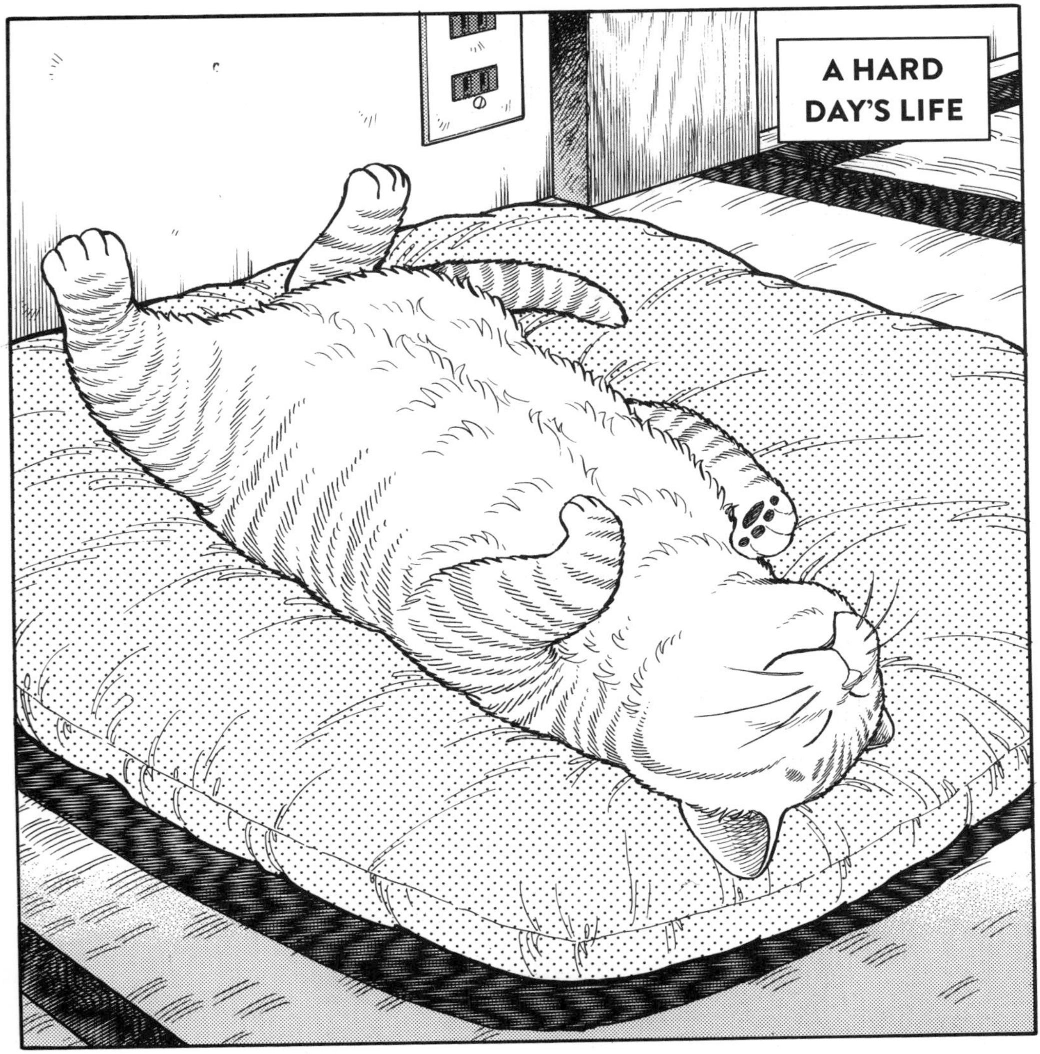
A HARD DAY'S LIFE

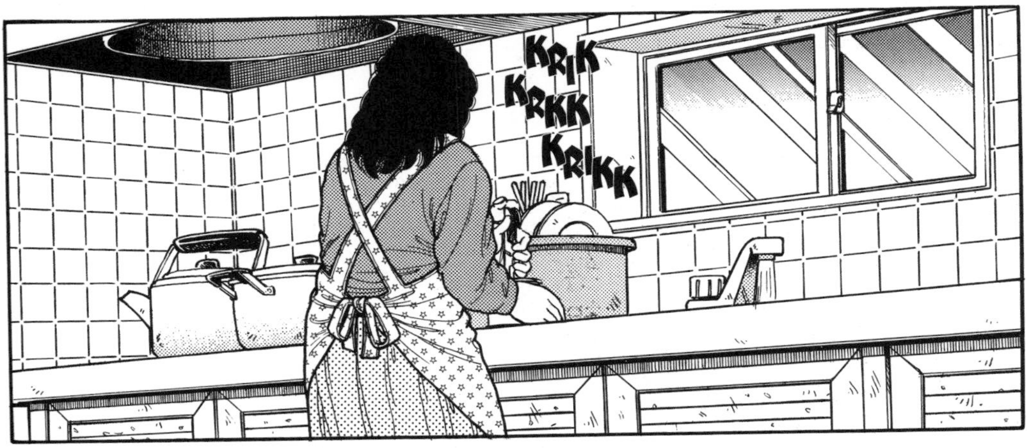
KRIK
KRKK
KRIKK

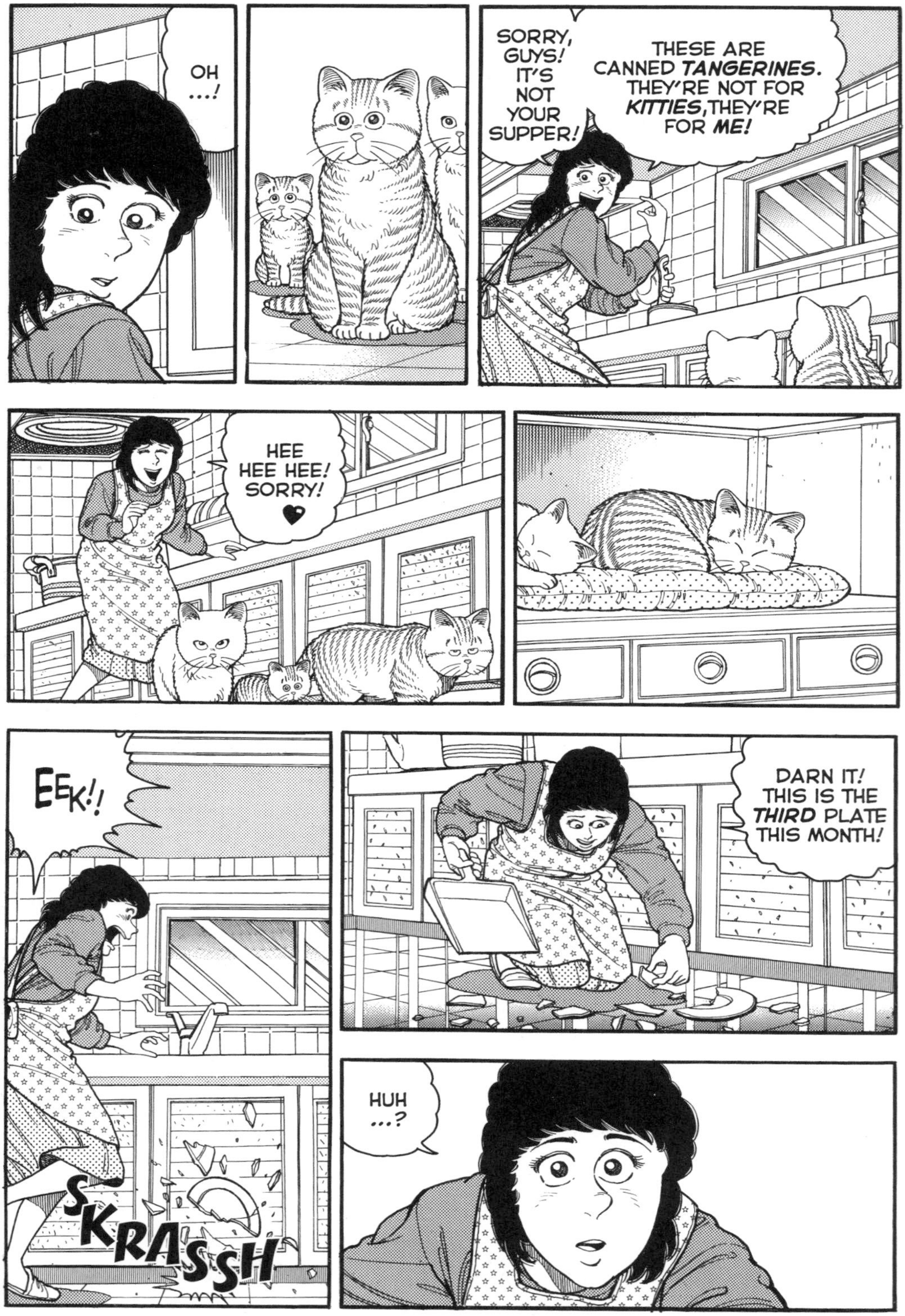
OH ...!
SORRY, GUYS! IT'S NOT YOUR SUPPER!
THESE ARE CANNED *TANGERINES.* THEY'RE NOT FOR *KITTIES*, THEY'RE FOR *ME!*
HEE HEE HEE! SORRY!
EEK!!
SKRASSH
DARN IT! THIS IS THE *THIRD* PLATE THIS MONTH!
HUH ...?

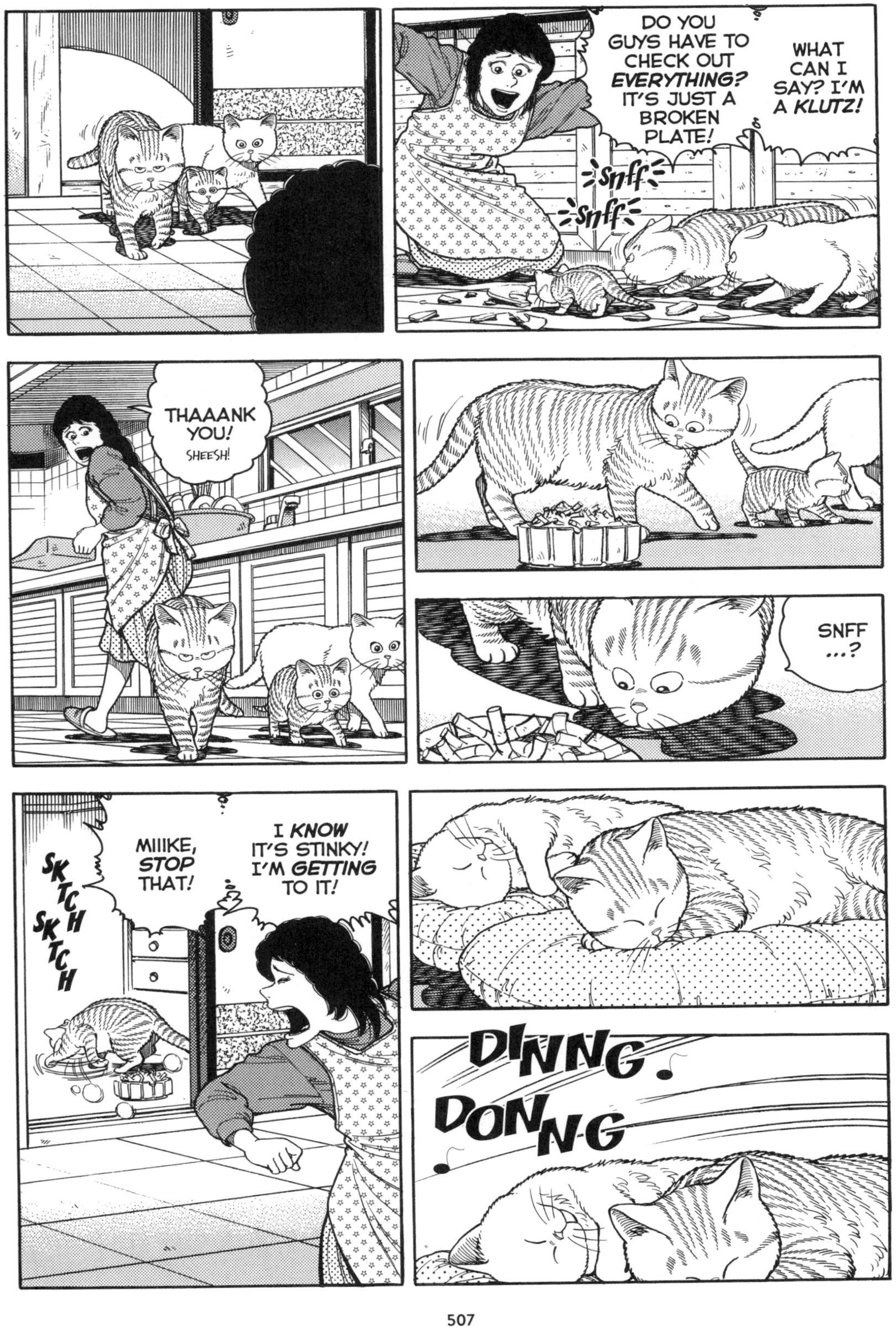
DO YOU GUYS HAVE TO CHECK OUT EVERYTHING? IT'S JUST A BROKEN PLATE!
WHAT CAN I SAY? I'M A KLUTZ!
SNFF
SNFF
THAAANK YOU!
SHEESH!
SNFF ...?
SKTCH SKTCH
MIIIKE, STOP THAT!
I KNOW IT'S STINKY! I'M GETTING TO IT!
DINNG.
DONNG

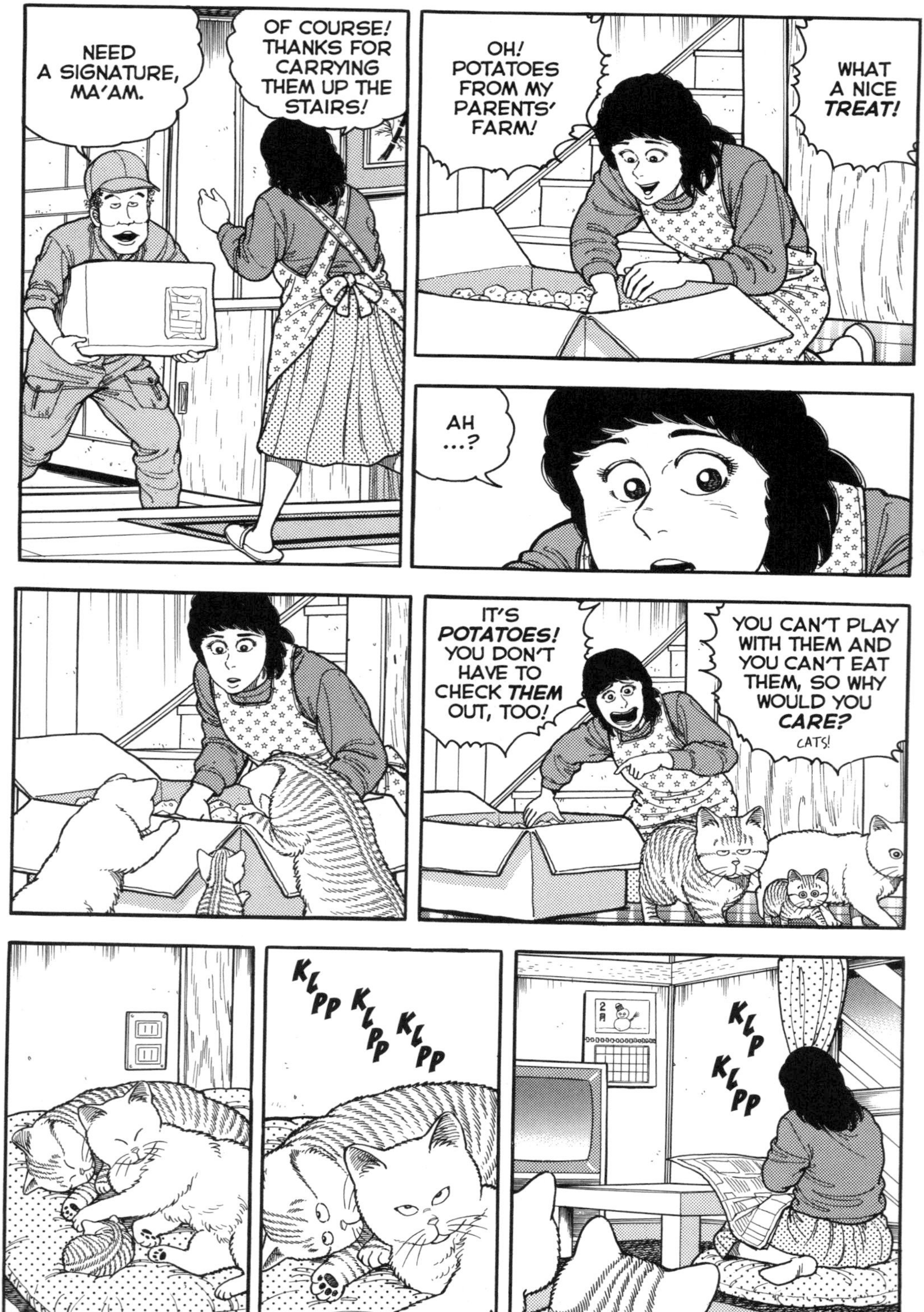
NEED A SIGNATURE, MA'AM.
OF COURSE! THANKS FOR CARRYING THEM UP THE STAIRS!
OH! POTATOES FROM MY PARENTS' FARM!
WHAT A NICE TREAT!
AH ...?
IT'S POTATOES! YOU DON'T HAVE TO CHECK THEM OUT, TOO!
YOU CAN'T PLAY WITH THEM AND YOU CAN'T EAT THEM, SO WHY WOULD YOU CARE?
CATS!
KLPP KLPP KLPP
2月
KLP KLPP

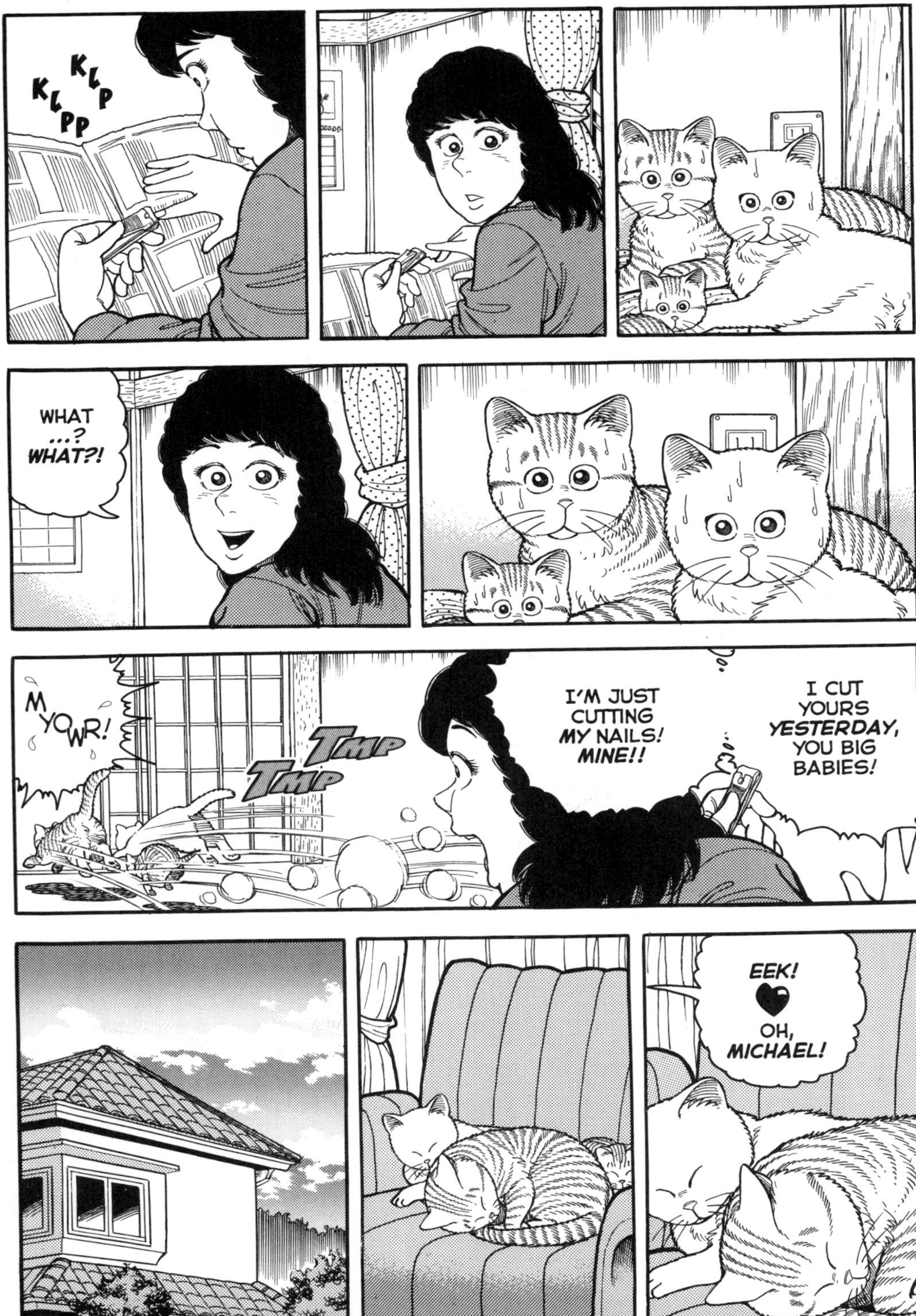
KLPP KLP
WHAT ...? WHAT?!
MYOWR!
TMP TMP
I'M JUST CUTTING MY NAILS! MINE!!
I CUT YOURS YESTERDAY, YOU BIG BABIES!
EEK! ♥ OH, MICHAEL!

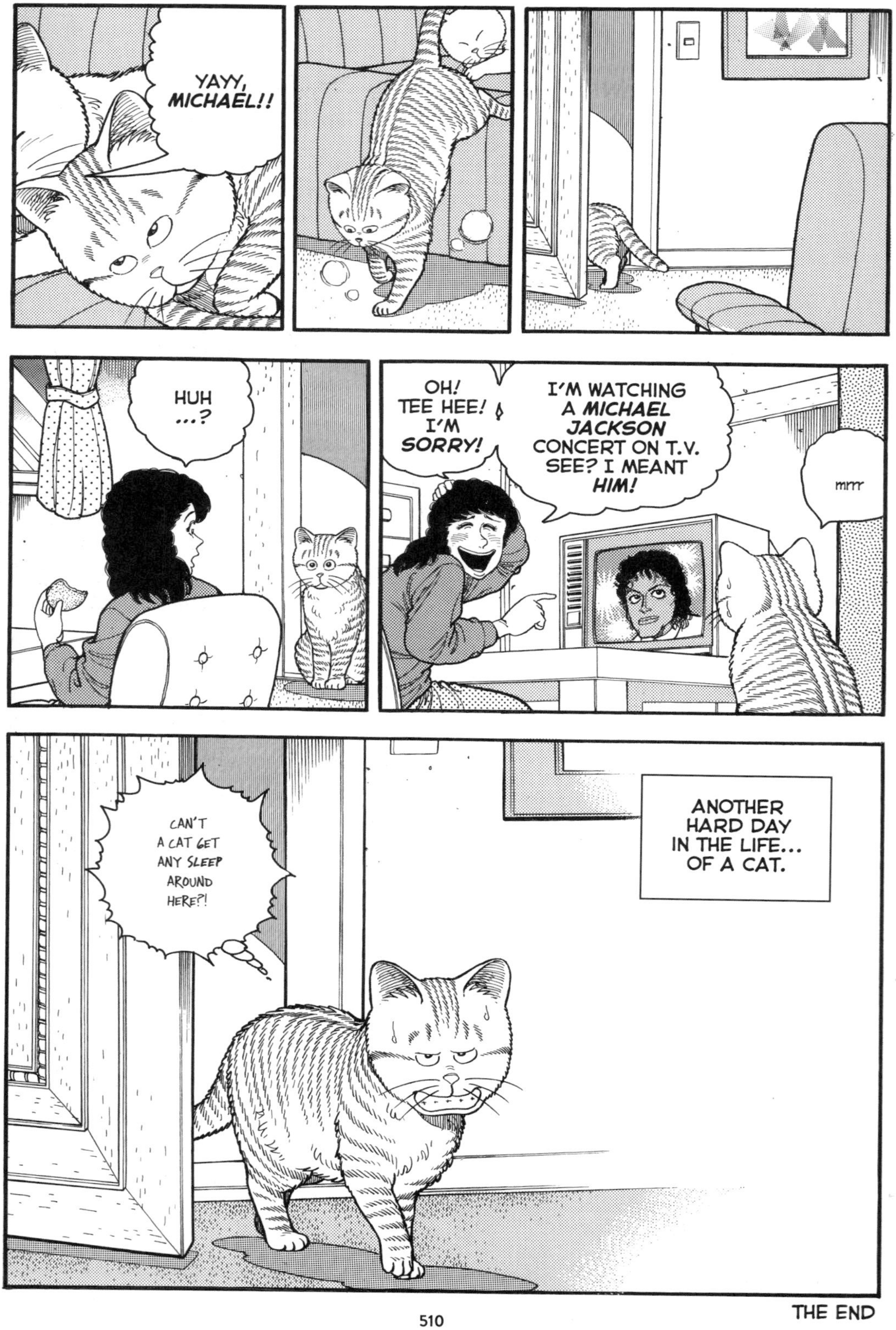
YAYY, MICHAEL!!
HUH ...?
OH! TEE HEE! I'M SORRY!
I'M WATCHING A MICHAEL JACKSON CONCERT ON T.V. SEE? I MEANT HIM!
mrrr
CAN'T A CAT GET ANY SLEEP AROUND HERE?!
ANOTHER HARD DAY IN THE LIFE... OF A CAT.

THE END

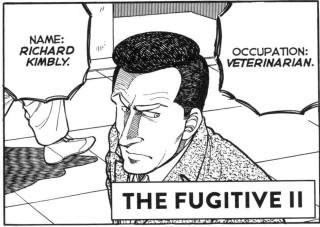

NAME: *RICHARD KIMBLY.*

OCCUPATION: *VETERINARIAN.*

# THE FUGITIVE II

SENTENCED TO *DEATH* FOR THE MURDER OF HIS *WIFE*...AND FOR *CAT-WRAPPING*--CRIMES HE DID *NOT COMMIT!*

EN ROUTE TO *DEATH ROW*, THE DOCTOR WAS FREED BY A CHANCE *TRAIN WRECK!*

NOW HE LIVES ON THE RUN-- CONSTANTLY CHANGING HIS NAME, HIS JOB, HIS *DEODORANT!*

THE RELENTLESS *LT. GERARDLY* ALWAYS MERE MOMENTS BEHIND HIM!

AND SO... RICHARD KIMBLY'S LIFE OF DESPERATION *CONTINUES!*

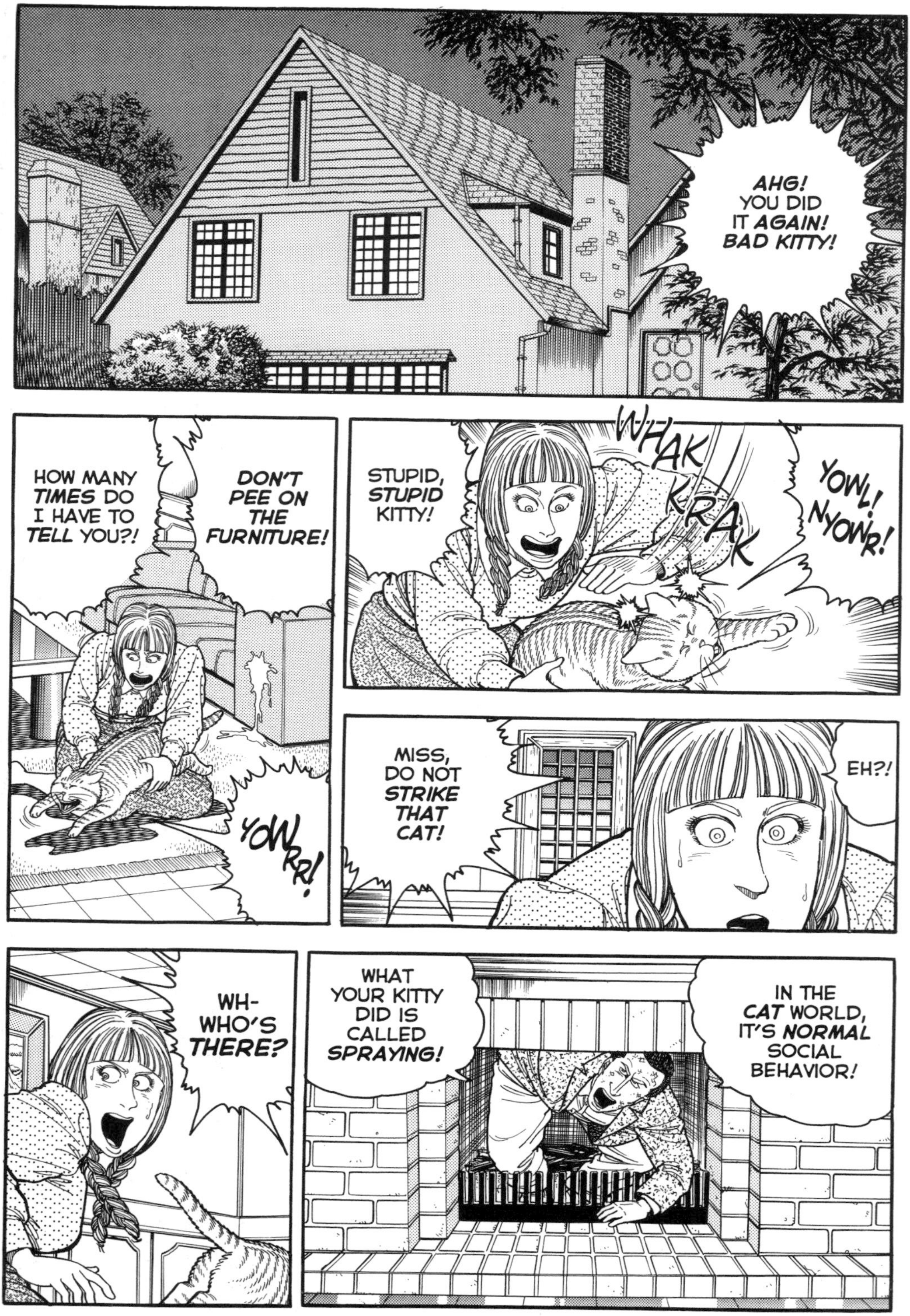
AHG! YOU DID IT AGAIN! BAD KITTY!
HOW MANY TIMES DO I HAVE TO TELL YOU?!
DON'T PEE ON THE FURNITURE!
YOWRR!
STUPID, STUPID KITTY!
WHAK
KRAK
YOWL! NYOWR!
MISS, DO NOT STRIKE THAT CAT!
EH?!
WH- WHO'S THERE?
WHAT YOUR KITTY DID IS CALLED SPRAYING!
IN THE CAT WORLD, IT'S NORMAL SOCIAL BEHAVIOR!

**EEK!!**

WHO ARE *YOU*?!

JUST A PASSING FUGIT...ER, I MEAN *STRANGER*, WHO HEARD A KITTY IN DISTRESS!

YOU DO *KNOW*, MA'AM, THAT *FIXING* A CAT WILL OFTEN CURE SPRAYING--

--BUT IT CAN *STILL* BE TRIGGERED BY... *STRESS!*

YOU MUST BE *ABUSING* YOUR CAT IN SOME WAY.

*EXCUSE ME?!*

-*SNIFF!*-

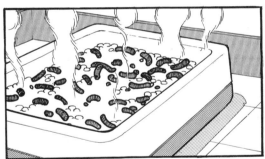

*URK...!*

TH-THE *LITTER BOX!* IT'S *FILTHY!*

DON'T YOU KNOW THE *FIRST* THING ABOUT CATS? YOU HAVE TO SCOOP THE FECES OUT OF THE BOX AND ADD FRESH LITTER OFTEN!

*YOU'RE* TO BLAME FOR THE SPRAYING!

OH!! I'M SO *SORRY!!*

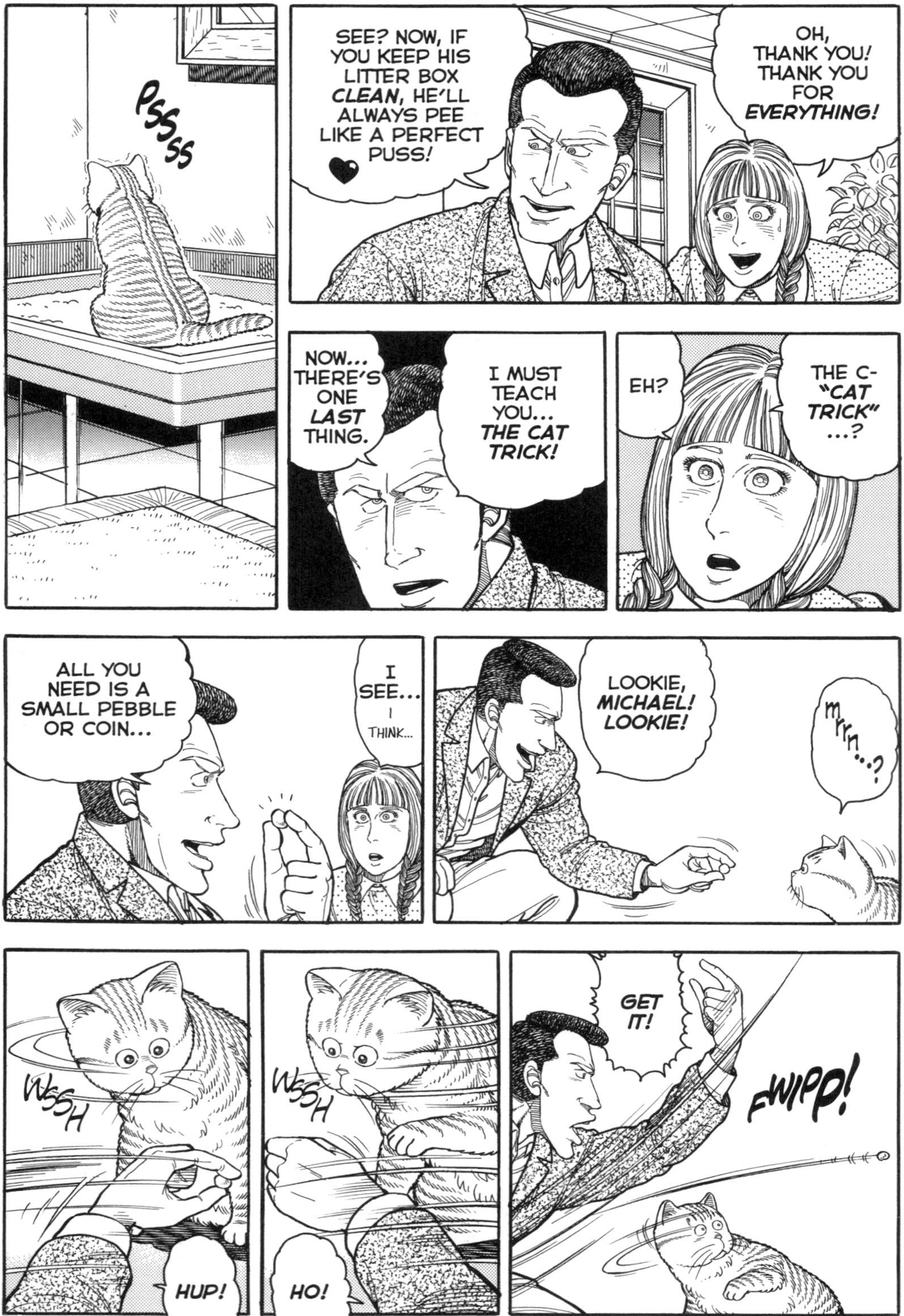
PSSSSS
SEE? NOW, IF YOU KEEP HIS LITTER BOX CLEAN, HE'LL ALWAYS PEE LIKE A PERFECT PUSS! ♥
OH, THANK YOU! THANK YOU FOR EVERYTHING!
NOW... THERE'S ONE LAST THING.
I MUST TEACH YOU... THE CAT TRICK!
EH?
THE C- "CAT TRICK" ...?
ALL YOU NEED IS A SMALL PEBBLE OR COIN...
I SEE... I THINK...
LOOKIE, MICHAEL! LOOKIE!
mrrn...?
WSSH
HUP!
WSSH
HO!
GET IT!
FWIPP!

FWD FOO FOO FOO

HUH?! BIG DEAL!! EVERYBODY KNOWS ABOUT *THAT!*

HEH HEH HEH... BUT WATCH *THIS!!*

LOOKIE, MICHAEL! LET'S PLAY AGAIN!

HUP!

HO!

THERE IT GOES!

NYOW!

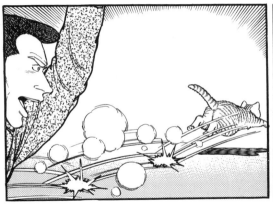

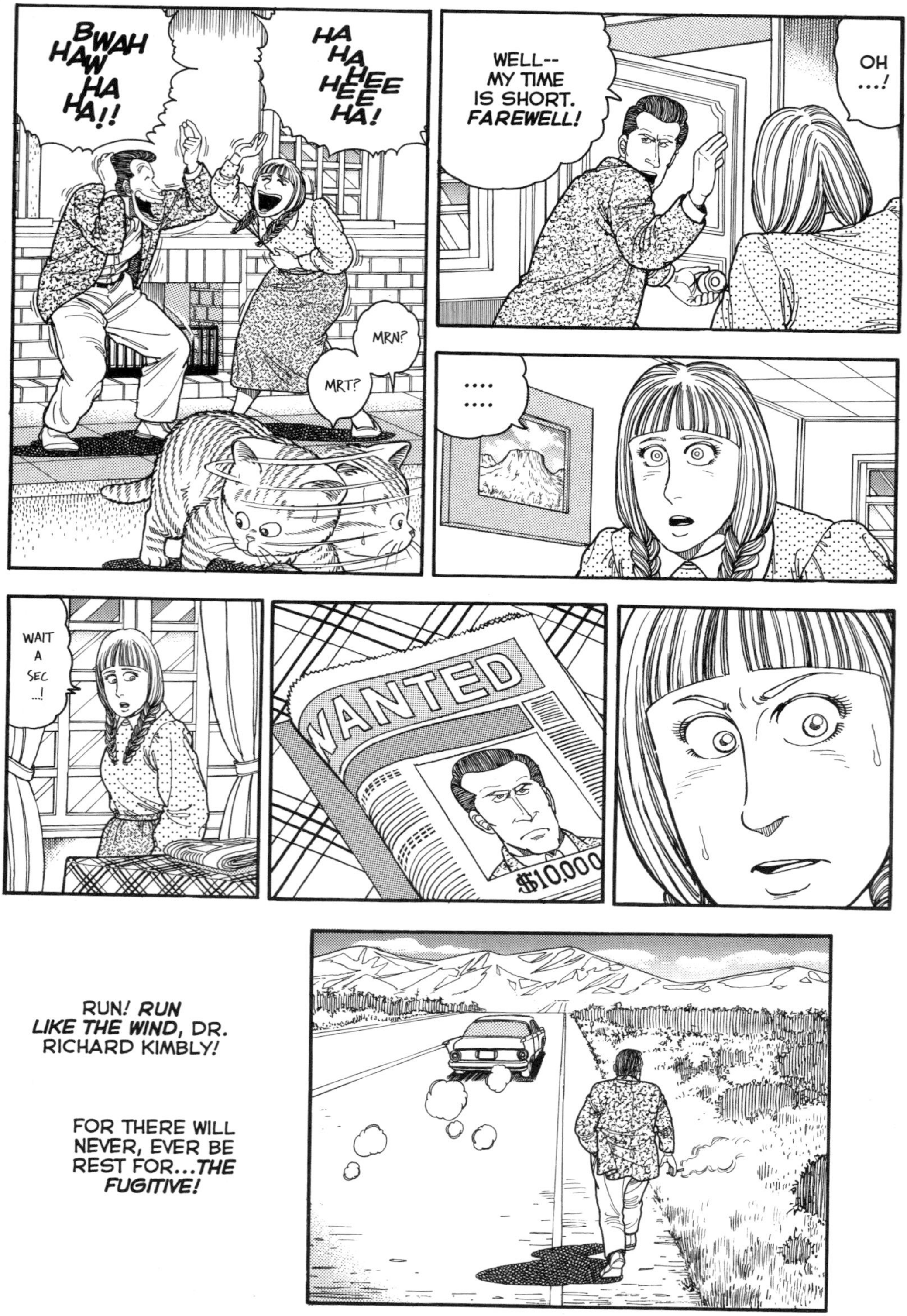
BWAH HAW HAW HA HA!!
HA HA HA HEE HEE HA!
MRN?
MRT?
WELL-- MY TIME IS SHORT. FAREWELL!
OH ...!
....
....
WAIT A SEC ...!
WANTED
$10,000
RUN! RUN LIKE THE WIND, DR. RICHARD KIMBLY!
FOR THERE WILL NEVER, EVER BE REST FOR...THE FUGITIVE!

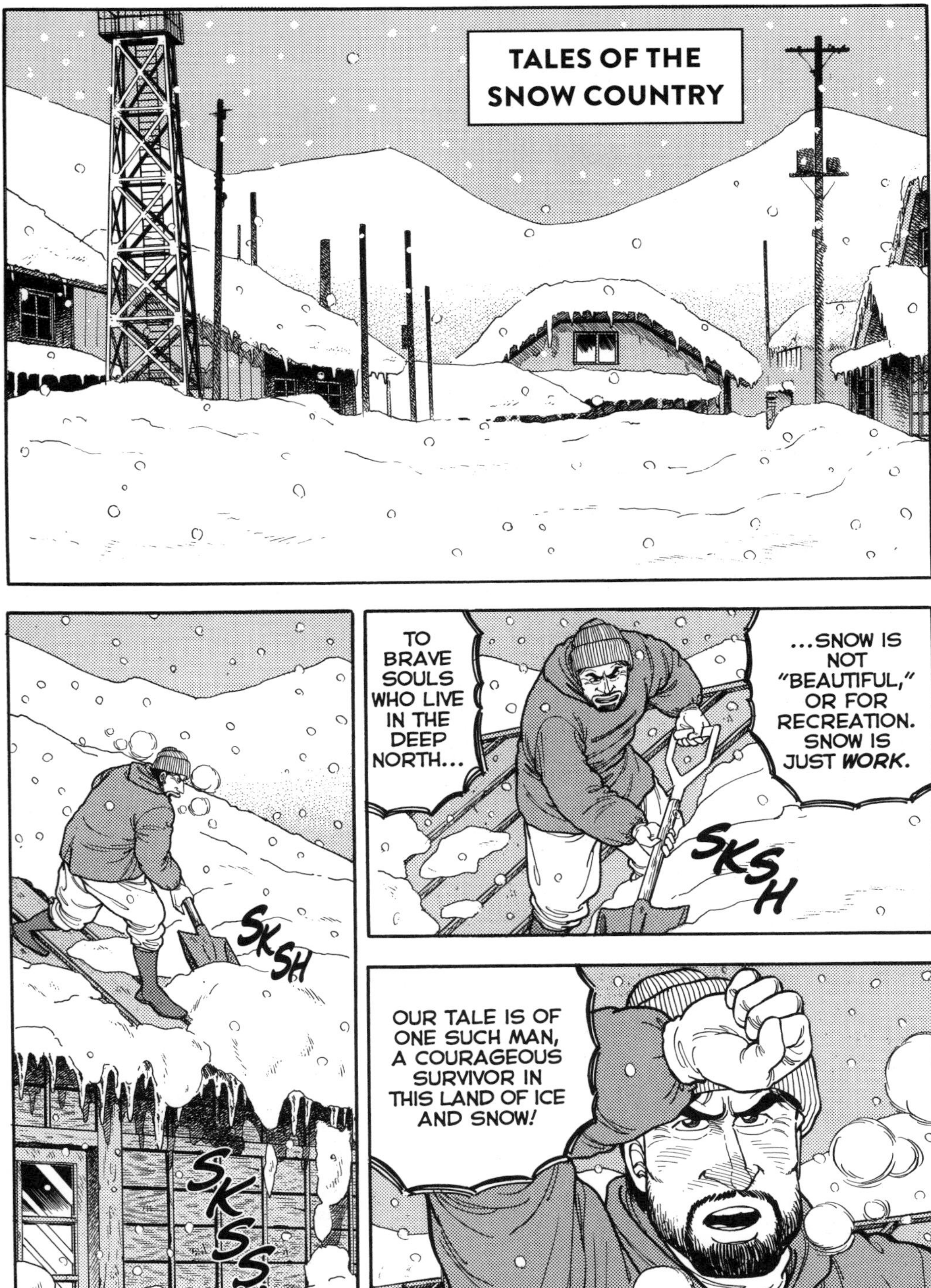
TALES OF THE SNOW COUNTRY
SKSH
SKSSH
TO BRAVE SOULS WHO LIVE IN THE DEEP NORTH...
...SNOW IS NOT "BEAUTIFUL," OR FOR RECREATION. SNOW IS JUST WORK.
SKSH
OUR TALE IS OF ONE SUCH MAN, A COURAGEOUS SURVIVOR IN THIS LAND OF ICE AND SNOW!

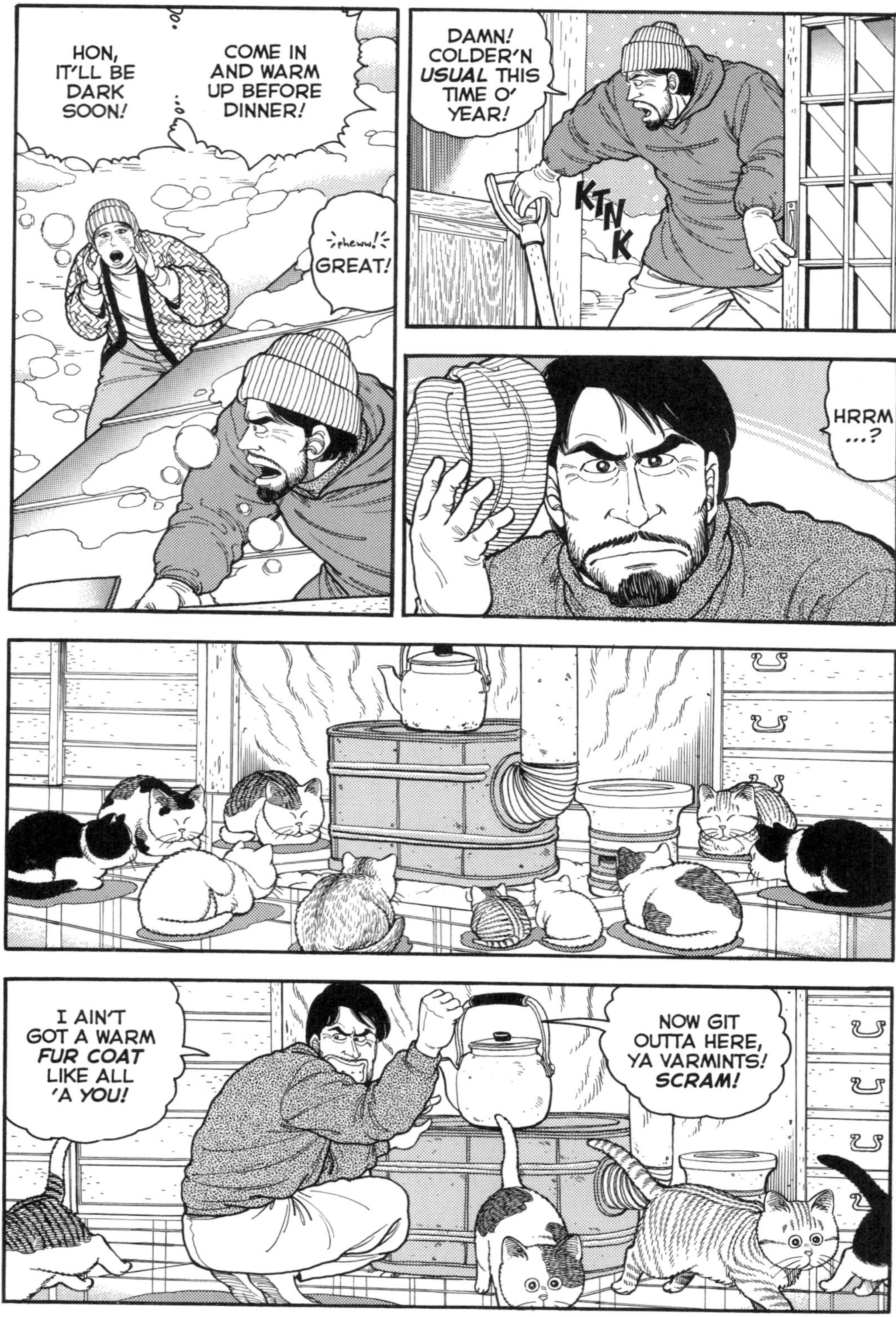
HON, IT'LL BE DARK SOON!
COME IN AND WARM UP BEFORE DINNER!
pheww!
GREAT!
DAMN! COLDER'N USUAL THIS TIME O' YEAR!
KTNK
HRRM ...?
I AIN'T GOT A WARM FUR COAT LIKE ALL 'A YOU!
NOW GIT OUTTA HERE, YA VARMINTS! SCRAM!

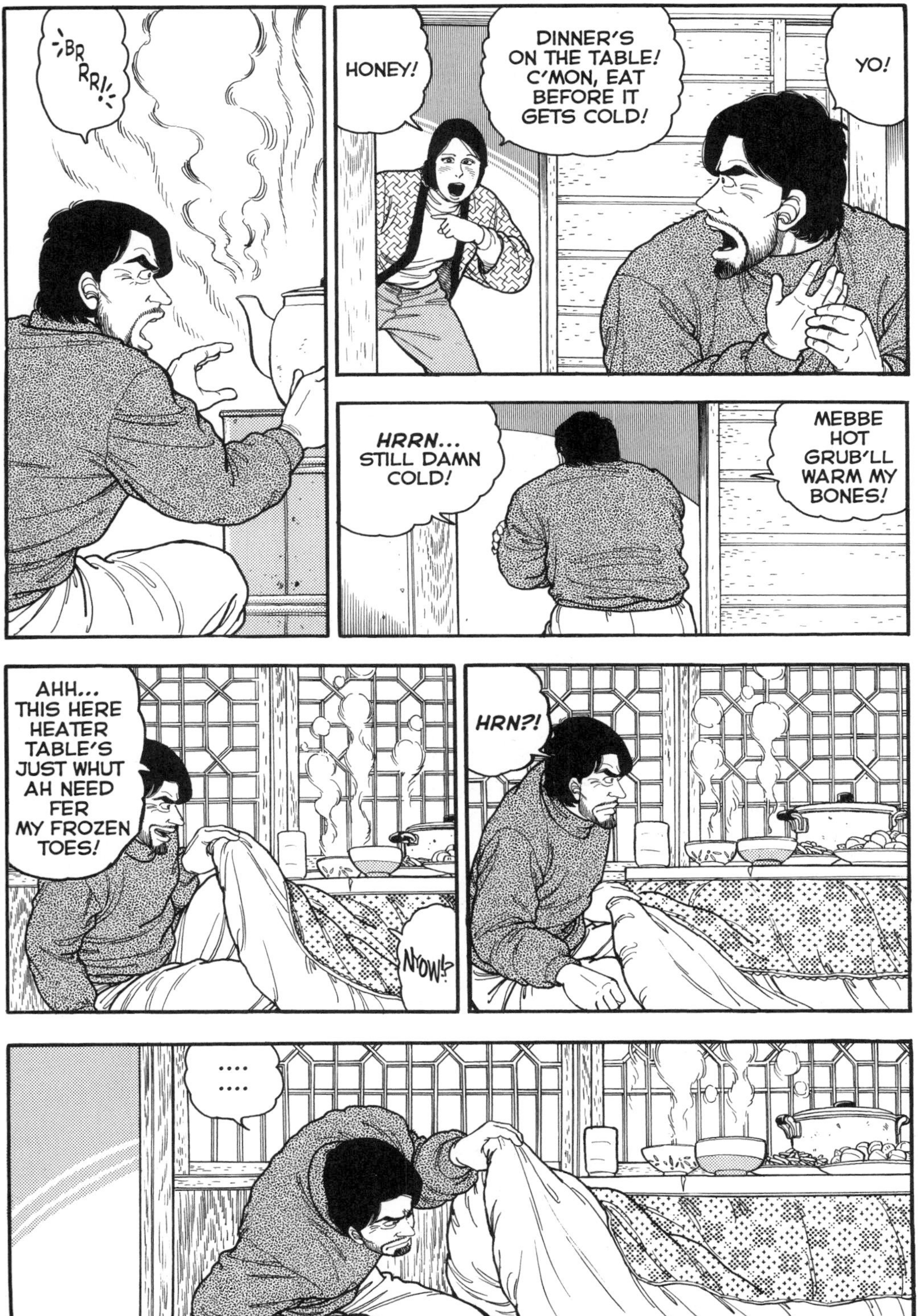
BRRRR!
HONEY!
DINNER'S ON THE TABLE! C'MON, EAT BEFORE IT GETS COLD!
YO!
HRRN... STILL DAMN COLD!
MEBBE HOT GRUB'LL WARM MY BONES!
AHH... THIS HERE HEATER TABLE'S JUST WHUT AH NEED FER MY FROZEN TOES!
NYOW!?
HRN?!
....
....

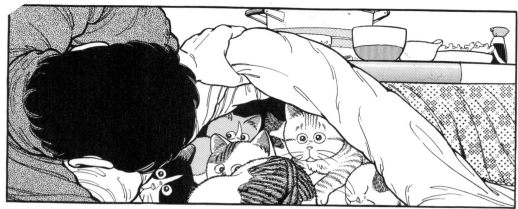

YUH DADGUM CATS!

THAT'S WHERE *MAH* PAWS GO!

GIT! GIT!!

DANGED CATS...

YOUR BATH'S READY, HON-- NICE AND *HOT!* ♥

MNPH!

YEAH... A *SOAK,* AND THEN TH' *SACK!*

♪ HMM HMMM HRMM HMM ♪

KCH AK

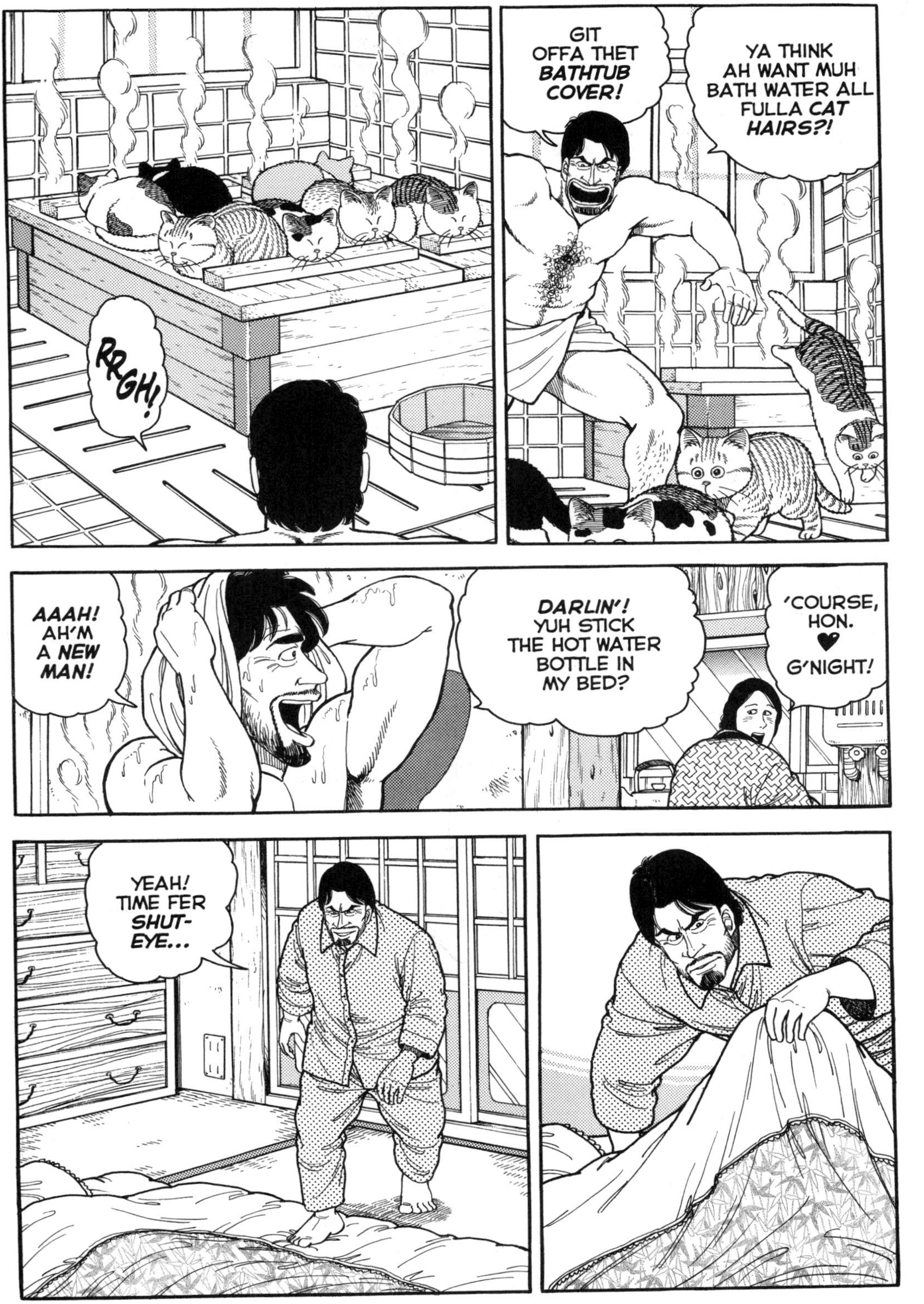
RRGH!
GIT OFFA THET BATHTUB COVER!
YA THINK AH WANT MUH BATH WATER ALL FULLA CAT HAIRS?!
AAAH! AH'M A NEW MAN!
DARLIN'! YUH STICK THE HOT WATER BOTTLE IN MY BED?
'COURSE, HON. ♥ G'NIGHT!
YEAH! TIME FER SHUT-EYE...

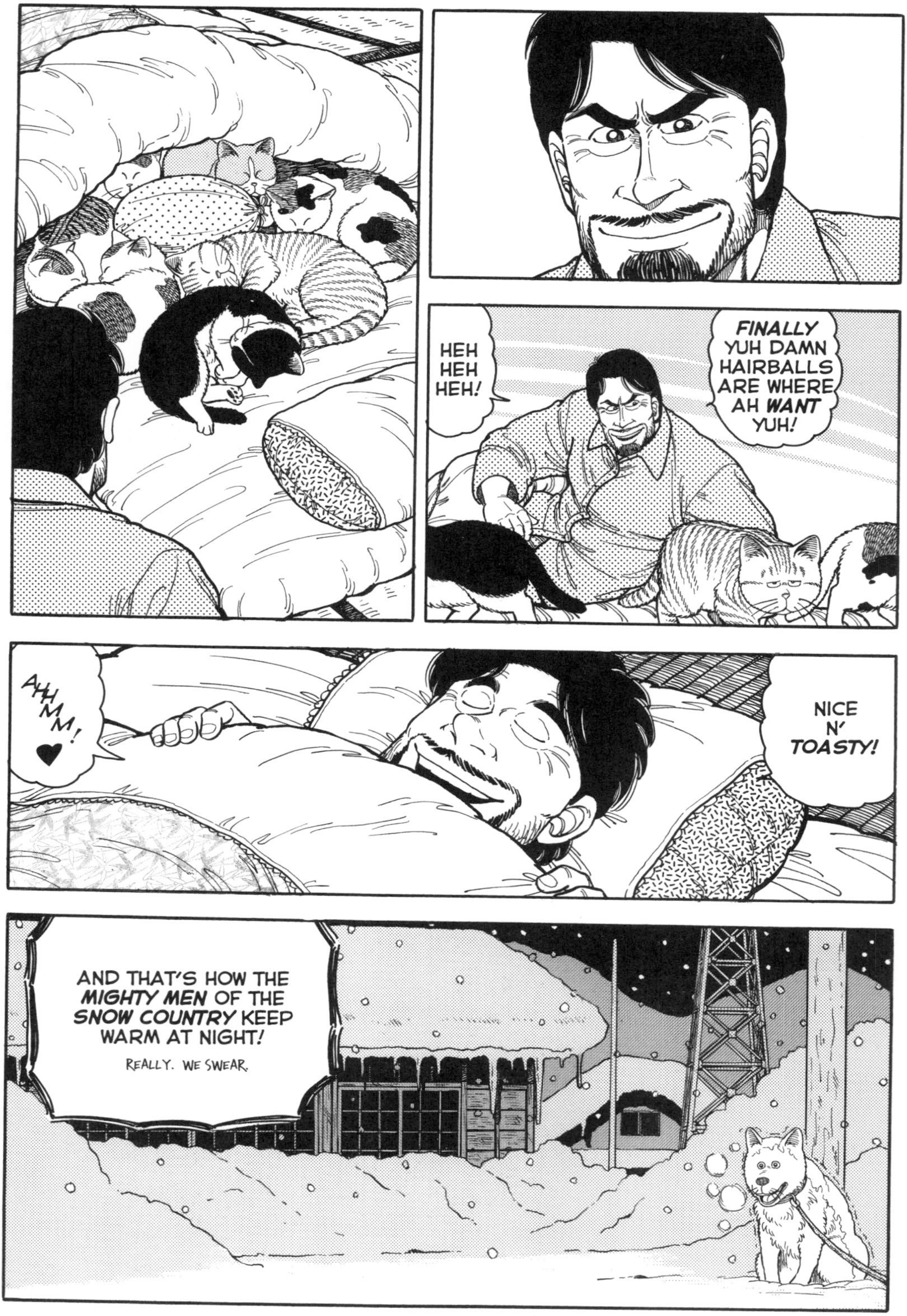
HEH HEH HEH!
FINALLY YUH DAMN HAIRBALLS ARE WHERE AH WANT YUH!
AHHMM! ♥
NICE N' TOASTY!
AND THAT'S HOW THE MIGHTY MEN OF THE SNOW COUNTRY KEEP WARM AT NIGHT!
REALLY. WE SWEAR.

THE END

# WHAT'S MICHAEL?

BONUS PINUPS BY MAKOTO KOBAYASHI

"MICHAEL ROLLING"

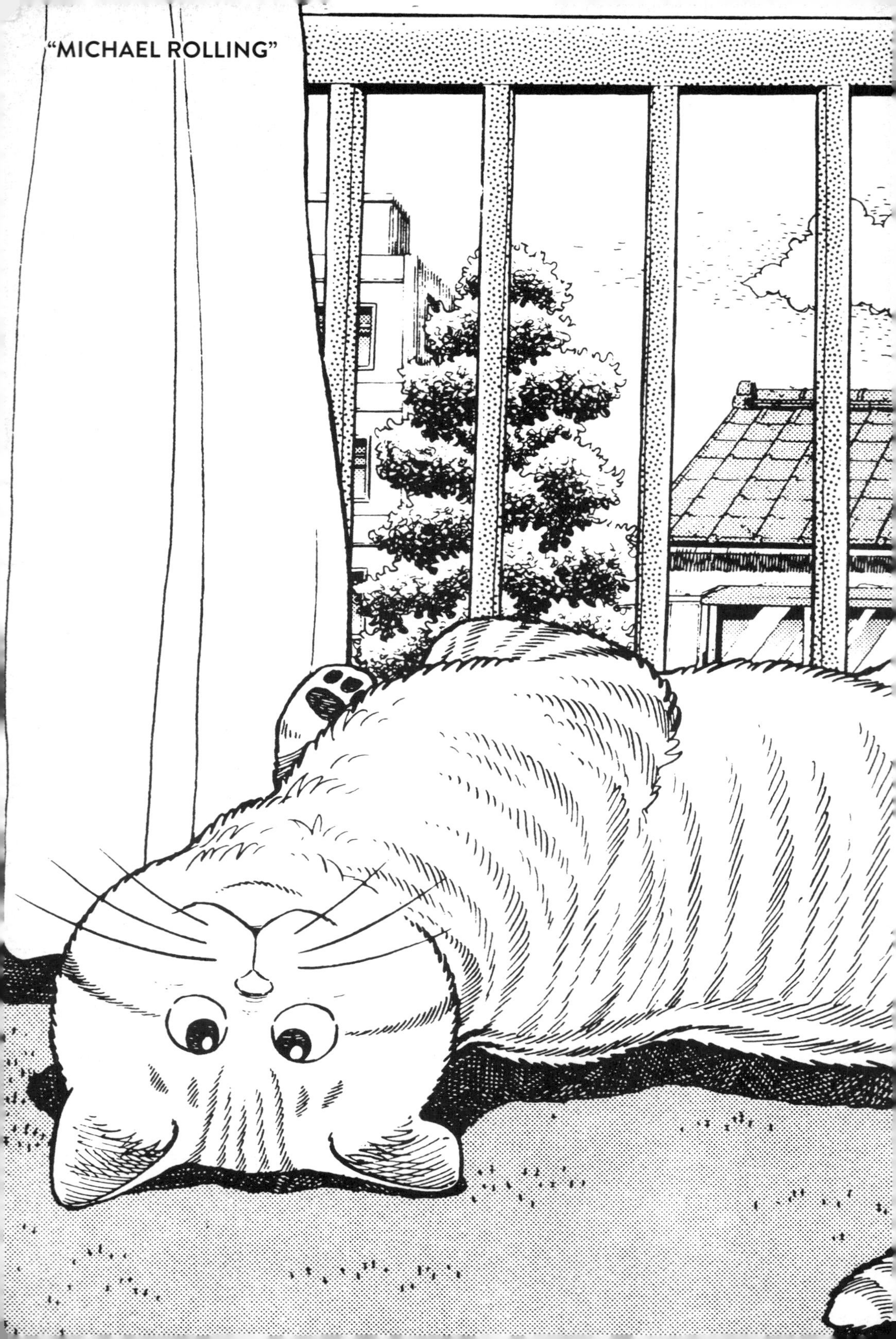

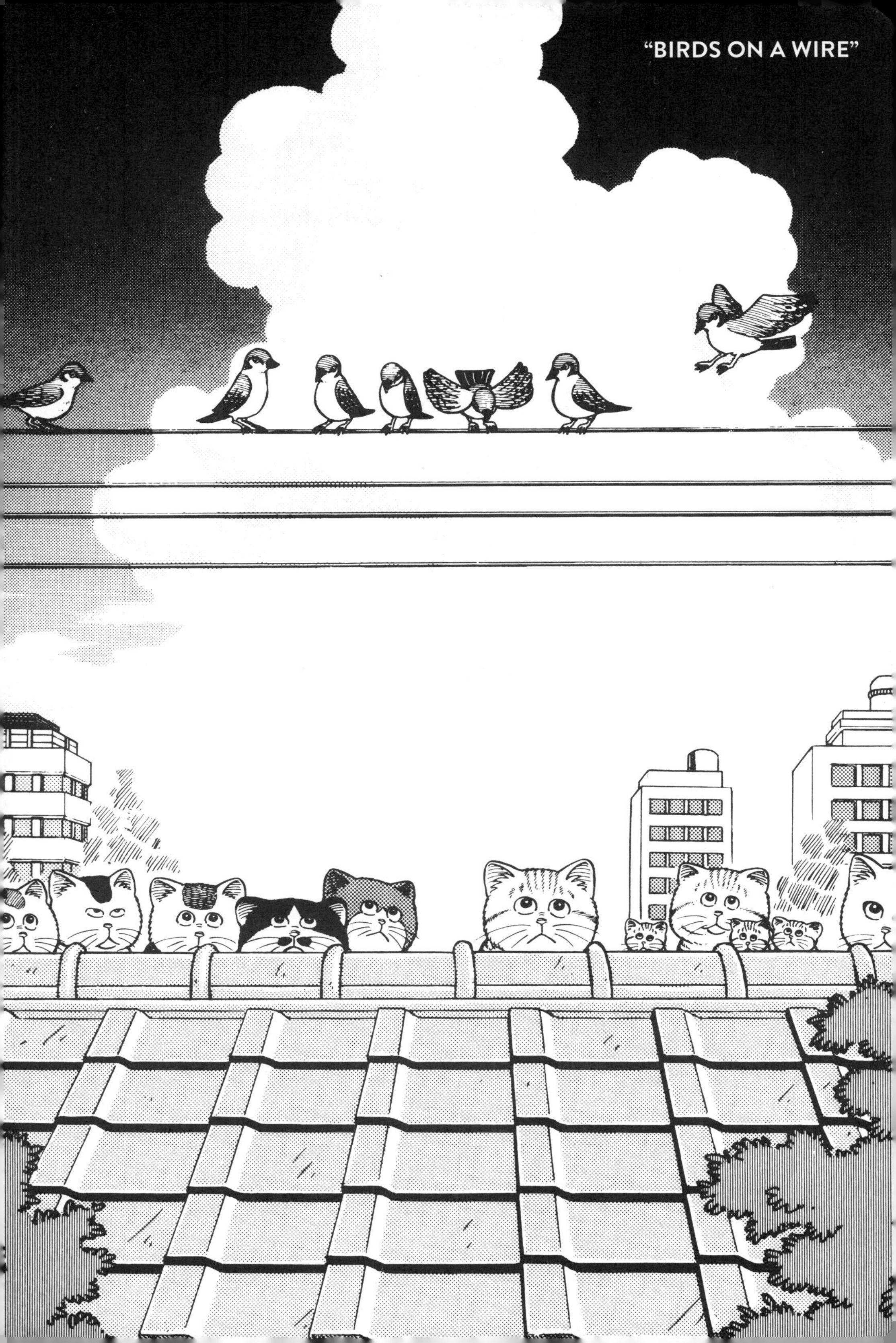
"BIRDS ON A WIRE"

"MICHAEL AT THE SHRINE"

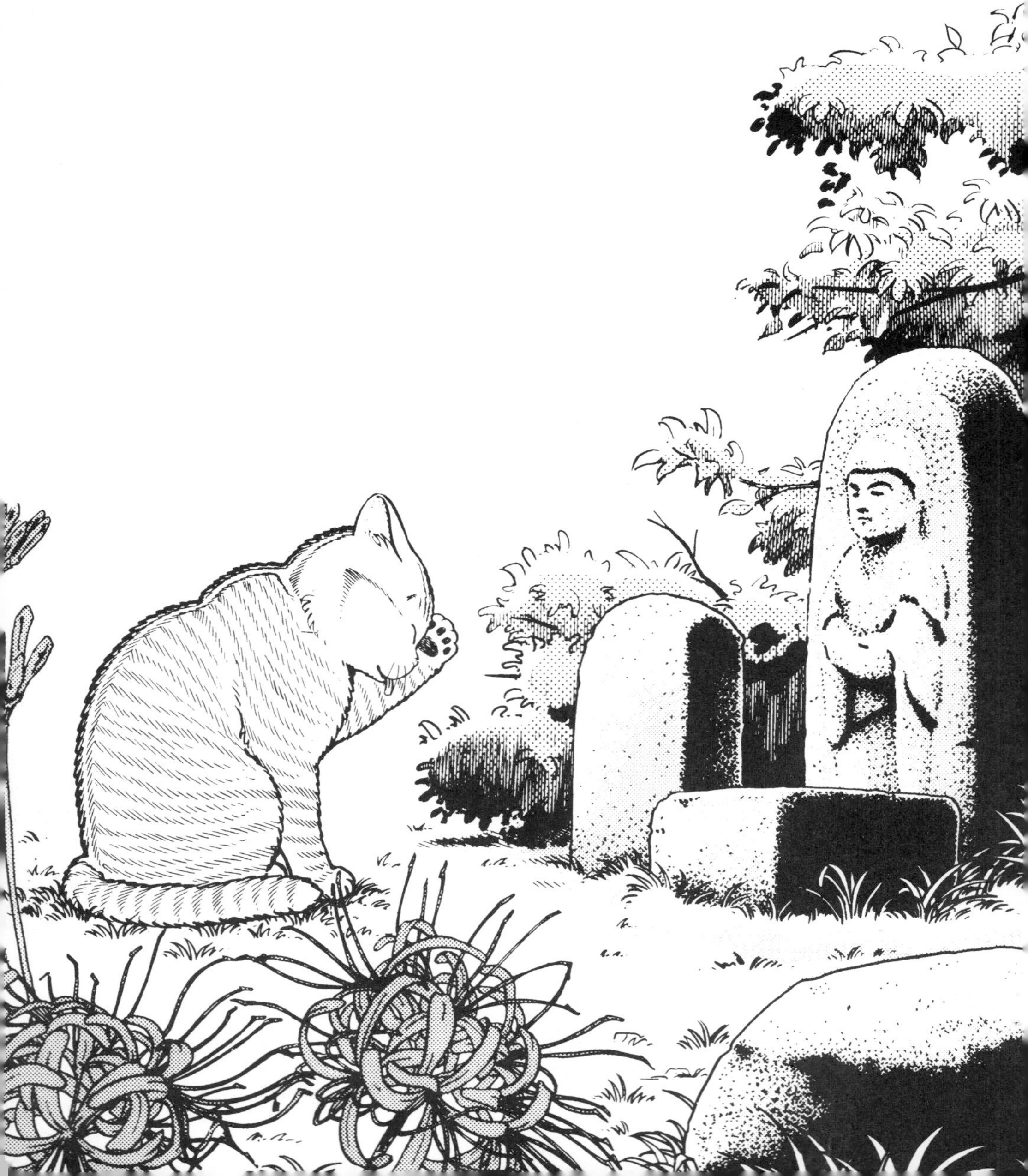